NINETY-NINTH EDITION
SINCE 1912

WHO'S WHO IN BASEBALL 2014

Official Lifetime Records Of Major League Players

Editor
Pete Palmer

Associate Editor
Stuart Shea

Managing Editor
Rory S. Slifkin

Cover Photo: ICON Sports Media

EDITOR'S NOTE: *Denotes League Leader throughout the publication.

WHO'S WHO IN BASEBALL is published annually by Who's Who in Baseball Magazine Co., Inc., 1115 Broadway, New York, New York 10010. Single copy price: $9.95. Submissions of manuscripts, illustrations and/or photographs must be accompanied by a stamped, self-addressed envelope. The publisher assumes no responsibility for unsolicited material.

BATTERS

ABREU, ETANISLAO TONI (TONY)

Born, Puerta Plato, Dominican Republic, November 13, 1984.
Bats Both. Throws Right. Height, 5 feet, 11 inches. Weight, 200 pounds.

Year	Club	Lea	Pos	G	AB	R	H	2B	3B	HR	RBI	SB	Avg
2003	Dodgers	Gulf Coast	2B-SS	44	163	30	48	7	5	0	20	9	.294
2003	Vero Beach	Fla.St.	2B	3	10	0	0	0	0	0	0	0	.000
2004	Columbus	So.Atl.	2B-SS	104	358	50	108	21	8	8	54	16	.302
2004	Vero Beach	Fla.St.	SS	11	43	8	18	3	1	0	3	4	.419
2005	Vero Beach	Fla.St.	2B-SS	96	394	54	129	23	7	4	43	14	.327
2005	Jacksonville	Southern	2B-SS	24	96	10	24	3	2	0	9	0	.250
2006	Jacksonville	Southern	2B-SS	118	457	66	131	24	3	6	55	8	.287
2007	Las Vegas	P.C.	2B-SS-3B	54	234	48	83	22	5	2	18	5	.355
2007	Los Angeles	N.L.	3B-2B-SS	59	166	19	45	14	1	2	17	0	.271
2008	Los Angeles a	N.L.					INJURED—Did Not Play						
2009	Chattanooga	Southern	2B-SS	23	89	11	26	4	1	0	5	0	.292
2009	Los Angeles	N.L.	2B-3B	6	8	0	2	0	0	0	1	0	.250
2009	Albuquerque b	P.C.	2B-3B-SS	54	218	36	77	18	3	11	48	3	.353
2010	Reno	P.C.	SS-2B-3B	24	94	17	33	7	1	2	21	2	.351
2010	Arizona c	N.L.	3B-SS-2B	81	193	16	45	11	1	1	13	2	.233
2011	Reno d	P.C.	2B-SS-3B	120	483	83	141	26	5	10	72	12	.292
2012	Omaha	P.C.	SS-2B	103	429	60	138	36	5	9	73	7	.322
2012	Kansas City	A.L.	2B-3B-SS	22	70	5	18	2	1	1	15	0	.257
2013	Fresno	P.C.	2B-3B	22	65	9	22	9	0	1	9	1	.338
2013	San Francisco e-f	N.L.	2B-3B-SS	53	138	21	37	12	3	2	14	0	.268
Major League Totals			5 Yrs.	221	575	61	147	39	6	6	60	2	.256

a On minor league disabled list from March 30 to September 28, 2008.
b Sent to Arizona Diamondbacks as player to be named later for pitcher Jon Garland, October 9, 2009.
c On disabled list from May 24 to June 15, 2010.
d Filed for free agency, November 2, 2011. Signed with Kansas City Royals organization, December 1, 2011.
e Claimed on waivers by San Francisco Giants, February 4, 2013.
f On disabled list from March 22 to June 8 and July 29 to September 1, 2013.

ACKLEY, DUSTIN MICHAEL

Born, Winston-Salem, North Carolina, February 26, 1988.
Bats Left. Throws Right. Height, 6 feet, 1 inch. Weight, 185 pounds.

Year	Club	Lea	Pos	G	AB	R	H	2B	3B	HR	RBI	SB	Avg
2010	Tacoma	P.C.	2B	52	212	37	58	12	4	5	23	2	.274
2010	West Tenn	Southern	2B	82	289	42	76	21	4	2	28	8	.263
2011	Tacoma	P.C.	2B	66	271	57	82	17	3	9	35	7	.303
2011	Seattle	A.L.	2B-1B	90	333	39	91	16	7	6	36	6	.273
2012	Seattle	A.L.	2B-1B	153	607	84	137	22	2	12	50	13	.226
2013	Tacoma	P.C.	OF-2B	25	104	21	38	8	0	2	14	0	.365
2013	Seattle	A.L.	OF-2B-1B	113	384	40	97	18	2	4	31	2	.253
Major League Totals			3 Yrs.	356	1324	163	325	56	11	22	117	21	.245

ADAMS, MATTHEW JAMES (MATT)

Born, Phillipsburg, Pennsylvania, August 31, 1988.
Bats Left. Throws Right. Height, 6 feet, 3 inches. Weight, 260 pounds.

Year	Club	Lea	Pos	G	AB	R	H	2B	3B	HR	RBI	SB	Avg
2009	Johnson City	Appal.	1B	32	115	15	42	6	0	6	25	0	.365
2009	Batavia	N.Y.-Penn.	1B	31	130	16	45	11	0	4	27	0	.346
2010	Quad Cities	Midwest	1B	121	464	71	144	41	0	22	88	5	.310
2011	Springfield	Texas	1B	115	463	80	139	23	2	32	101	0	.300
2012	St. Louis	N.L.	1B	27	86	8	21	6	0	2	13	0	.244
2012	Memphis	P.C.	1B	67	258	41	85	22	0	18	50	3	.329
2013	Springfield	Texas	1B	3	12	1	3	1	0	0	2	0	.250
2013	St. Louis a	N.L.	1B	108	296	46	84	14	0	17	51	0	.284
Major League Totals			2 Yrs.	135	382	54	105	20	0	19	64	0	.275
	Division Series												
2013	St. Louis	N.L.	1B	5	19	3	6	1	0	1	2	0	.316

Year	Club	Lea	Pos	G	AB	R	H	2B	3B	HR	RBI	SB	Avg
	Championship Series												
2013	St. Louis	N.L.	1B	6	22	2	5	1	0	0	2	0	.227
	World Series Record												
2013	St. Louis	N.L.	1B	6	22	0	3	1	0	0	0	0	.136

a On disabled list from April 22 to May 7, 2013.

ALONSO, YONDER

Born, Havana, Cuba, April 8, 1987.
Bats Left. Throws Right. Height, 6 feet, 2 inches. Weight, 240 pounds.

Year	Club	Lea	Pos	G	AB	R	H	2B	3B	HR	RBI	SB	Avg
2008	Sarasota	Fla.St.	1B	6	19	1	6	1	0	0	2	0	.316
2009	Reds	Gulf Coast	1B	6	15	0	2	0	0	0	0	0	.133
2009	Sarasota	Fla.St.	1B	49	175	21	53	13	0	7	38	0	.303
2009	Carolina	Southern	1B	29	105	12	31	11	0	2	14	1	.295
2010	Carolina	Southern	1B-OF	31	101	19	27	5	0	3	13	4	.267
2010	Louisville	Int.	1B-OF	101	406	50	120	31	2	12	56	9	.296
2010	Cincinnati	N.L.	1B	22	29	2	6	2	0	0	3	0	.207
2011	Louisville	Int.	OF-1B	91	358	46	106	24	4	12	56	6	.296
2011	Cincinnati a	N.L.	OF-1B-3B	47	88	9	29	4	0	5	15	0	.330
2012	San Diego	N.L.	1B	155	549	47	150	39	0	9	62	3	.273
2013	Tucson	P.C.	1B	4	14	1	8	0	0	0	2	0	.571
2013	San Diego b	N.L.	1B-2B-3B-OF	97	334	34	94	11	0	6	45	6	.281
Major League Totals			4 Yrs.	321	1000	92	279	56	0	20	125	9	.279

a Traded to San Diego Padres with pitcher Edinson Volquez, pitcher Brad Boxberger and catcher Yasmani Grandal for pitcher Mat Latos, December 17, 2011.
b On disabled list from June 1 to July 12, 2013.

ALTUVE, JOSE CARLOS

Born, Maracay, Venezuela, May 6, 1990.
Bats Right. Throws Right. Height, 5 feet, 7 inches. Weight, 170 pounds.

Year	Club	Lea	Pos	G	AB	R	H	2B	3B	HR	RBI	SB	Avg
2008	Greeneville	Appal.	2B-3B	40	141	26	40	9	3	2	21	8	.284
2009	Greeneville	Appal.	2B	45	179	45	58	20	2	3	18	21	.324
2009	Tri-City	N.Y.-Penn.	2B	21	76	13	19	5	0	0	7	7	.250
2010	Lexington	So.Atl.	2B-3B	94	393	75	121	15	3	11	45	39	.308
2010	Lancaster	Calif.	2B-3B	31	116	18	32	5	2	4	22	3	.276
2011	Lancaster	Calif.	2B	52	213	38	87	13	7	5	34	19	.408
2011	Corpus Christi	Texas	2B-3B	35	144	21	52	9	3	5	25	5	.361
2011	Houston	N.L.	2B	57	221	26	61	10	1	2	12	7	.276
2012	Houston	N.L.	2B	147	576	80	167	34	4	7	37	33	.290
2013	Houston	A.L.	2B	152	626	64	177	31	2	5	52	35	.283
Major League Totals			3 Yrs.	356	1423	170	405	75	7	14	101	75	.285

ALVAREZ, PEDRO MANUEL

Born, New York, New York, February 6, 1987.
Bats Left. Throws Right. Height, 6 feet, 3 inches. Weight, 225 pounds.

Year	Club	Lea	Pos	G	AB	R	H	2B	3B	HR	RBI	SB	Avg
2009	Lynchburg	Carolina	3B	66	243	38	60	14	1	14	55	1	.247
2009	Altoona	Eastern	3B	60	222	42	74	18	0	13	40	1	.333
2010	Indianapolis	Int.	3B	66	242	42	67	15	4	13	53	4	.277
2010	Pittsburgh	N.L.	3B	95	347	42	89	21	1	16	64	0	.256
2011	Pirates	Gulf Coast	3B	1	1	0	0	0	0	0	0	0	.000
2011	Bradenton	Fla.St.	3B	6	16	2	3	0	0	1	2	0	.188
2011	Indianapolis	Int.	3B	35	125	16	32	5	1	5	19	0	.256
2011	Pittsburgh a	N.L.	3B	74	235	18	45	9	1	4	19	1	.191
2012	Pittsburgh	N.L.	3B	149	525	64	128	25	1	30	85	1	.244
2013	Pittsburgh	N.L.	3B	152	558	70	130	22	2	*36	100	2	.233
Major League Totals			4 Yrs.	470	1665	194	392	77	5	86	268	4	.235
	Wild Card Playoff												
2013	Pittsburgh	N.L.	3B	1	3	0	0	0	0	0	1	0	.000
	Division Series												
2013	Pittsburgh	N.L.	3B	5	17	4	6	1	0	3	6	0	.353

a On disabled list from May 20 to July 9, 2011.

AMARISTA (AZOCAR), ALEXI JOSE

Born, Barcelona, Venezuela, April 6, 1989.
Bats Left. Throws Right. Height, 5 feet, 8 inches. Weight, 150 pounds.

Year	Club	Lea	Pos	G	AB	R	H	2B	3B	HR	RBI	SB	Avg
2008	Angels	Arizona	OF-2B	51	202	46	67	6	4	2	21	22	.332
2008	Cedar Rapids	Midwest	SS-OF	1	2	0	0	0	0	0	0	0	.000
2009	Cedar Rapids	Midwest	2B	125	477	84	152	39	10	4	49	38	.319
2010	Rancho Cucamonga	Calif.	2B	72	297	39	90	19	6	4	39	17	.303
2010	Salt Lake	P.C.	2B-SS	15	65	13	26	6	3	0	9	4	.400
2010	Arkansas	Texas	2B	48	191	25	55	2	1	1	20	4	.288
2011	Salt Lake	P.C.	2B-OF-SS	86	363	49	106	24	5	4	50	15	.292
2011	Los Angeles	A.L.	2B-OF-SS	23	52	2	8	3	1	0	5	0	.154
2012	Tucson	P.C.	2B-SS-3B	11	49	6	14	1	0	1	6	3	.286
2012	Salt Lake	P.C.	2B-3B-SS-OF	18	77	11	21	6	2	0	12	1	.273
2012	Los Angeles	A.L.	DH	1	0	1	0	0	0	0	0	0	.000
2012	San Diego a	N.L.	2B-OF-SS-3B	105	275	35	66	15	5	5	32	8	.240
2013	San Diego	N.L.	OF-2B-SS-3B	146	368	35	87	14	4	5	32	4	.236
Major League Totals			3 Yrs.	275	695	73	161	32	10	10	69	12	.232

a Traded to San Diego Padres with pitcher Donn Roach for pitcher Ernesto Frieri, May 3, 2012.

ANDRUS (TORRES), ELVIS AUGUSTO

Born, Maracay, Venezuela, August 26, 1988.
Bats Right. Throws Right. Height, 6 feet. Weight, 185 pounds.

Year	Club	Lea	Pos	G	AB	R	H	2B	3B	HR	RBI	SB	Avg
2005	Danville	Appal.	SS	6	18	3	5	1	0	0	1	1	.278
2005	Braves	Gulf Coast	SS-2B	46	166	26	49	6	1	3	20	7	.295
2006	Rome	So.Atl.	SS	111	437	67	116	25	4	3	50	23	.265
2007	Bakersfield	Calif.	SS	27	110	19	33	2	0	2	12	15	.300
2007	Myrtle Beach a	Carolina	SS	99	385	59	94	20	3	3	37	25	.244
2008	Frisco	Texas	SS	118	482	82	142	19	2	4	65	54	.295
2009	Texas	A.L.	SS	145	480	72	128	17	8	6	40	33	.267
2010	Texas	A.L.	SS	148	588	88	156	15	3	0	35	32	.265
2011	Texas	A.L.	SS	150	587	96	164	27	3	5	60	37	.279
2012	Texas	A.L.	SS	158	629	85	180	31	9	3	62	21	.286
2013	Texas	A.L.	SS	156	620	91	168	17	4	4	67	42	.271
Major League Totals			5 Yrs.	757	2904	432	796	107	27	18	264	165	.274
	Wild Card Playoff												
2012	Texas	A.L.	SS	1	4	0	2	0	0	0	0	0	.500
	Division Series												
2010	Texas	A.L.	SS	5	24	2	8	1	0	0	1	3	.333
2011	Texas	A.L.	SS	4	14	1	2	0	0	0	0	0	.143
Division Series Totals				9	38	3	10	1	0	0	1	3	.263
	Championship Series												
2010	Texas	A.L.	SS	6	27	4	9	2	0	0	2	4	.333
2011	Texas	A.L.	SS	6	25	4	6	0	0	0	1	1	.240
Championship Series Totals				12	52	8	15	2	0	0	3	5	.288
	World Series Record												
2010	Texas	A.L.	SS	5	17	2	3	0	0	0	1	1	.176
2011	Texas	A.L.	SS	7	29	5	8	1	0	0	0	0	.276
World Series Totals				12	46	7	11	1	0	0	1	1	.239

a Traded by Atlanta Braves to Texas Rangers with catcher Jarrod Saltalamacchia, pitcher Neftali Feliz, pitcher Matt Harrison and pitcher Beau James for infielder Mark Teixeira and pitcher Ron Mahay, July 31, 2007.

AOKI, NORICHIKA

Born, Hyuga City, Japan, January 5, 1982.
Bats Left. Throws Right. Height, 5 feet, 9 inches. Weight, 180 pounds.

Year	Club	Lea	Pos	G	AB	R	H	2B	3B	HR	RBI	SB	Avg
2004	Yakult	Japan Pac.	OF	10	15	1	3	0	0	0	0	1	.200
2005	Yakult	Japan Pac.	OF	144	588	100	202	26	4	3	28	29	.344
2006	Yakult	Japan Pac.	OF	146	599	112	192	26	3	13	62	41	.321
2007	Yakult	Japan Pac.	OF	143	557	114	193	26	2	20	58	17	.346
2008	Yakult	Japan Pac.	OF	112	444	85	154	29	5	14	64	31	.347
2009	Yakult	Japan Pac.	OF	142	531	87	161	23	2	16	66	18	.303
2010	Yakult	Japan Pac.	OF	144	583	92	209	44	1	14	63	19	.358
2011	Yakult	Japan Pac.	OF	144	583	73	170	18	5	4	44	8	.292
2012	Milwaukee a	N.L.	OF	151	520	81	150	37	4	10	50	30	.288

Year	Club	Lea	Pos	G	AB	R	H	2B	3B	HR	RBI	SB	Avg
2013	Milwaukee b..........	N.L.	OF	155	597	80	171	20	3	8	37	20	.286
Major League Totals	....	2 Yrs.		306	1117	161	321	57	7	18	87	50	.287

a Signed with Milwaukee Brewers, January 17, 2012.
b Traded to Kansas City Royals for pitcher Will Smith, December 5, 2013.

ARCIA, OSWALDO CELESTINO

Born, Anaco, Venezuela, May 9, 1991.
Bats Left. Throws Right. Height, 6 feet. Weight, 220 pounds.

Year	Club	Lea	Pos	G	AB	R	H	2B	3B	HR	RBI	SB	Avg
2009	Twins..........	Gulf Coast	OF	44	167	21	46	11	2	5	24	8	.275
2010	Elizabethton.........	Appal.	OF	64	259	47	97	21	7	14	51	4	.375
2011	Twins..........	Gulf Coast	OF	2	8	1	4	1	1	0	1	0	.500
2011	Beloit............	Midwest	DH	20	71	18	25	8	1	5	18	2	.352
2011	Fort Myers..........	Fla.St.	OF	59	213	27	56	14	2	8	32	1	.263
2012	Fort Myers..........	Fla.St.	OF	55	207	22	64	16	3	7	31	1	.309
2012	New Britain	Eastern	OF	69	262	54	86	20	5	10	67	3	.328
2013	Rochester.............	Int.	OF	38	128	25	40	6	0	10	30	2	.313
2013	Minnesota	A.L.	OF	97	351	34	88	17	2	14	43	1	.251

ARENADO, NOLAN JAMES

Born, Newport Beach, California, April 16, 1991.
Bats Right. Throws Right. Height, 6 feet, 1 inch. Weight, 205 pounds.

Year	Club	Lea	Pos	G	AB	R	H	2B	3B	HR	RBI	SB	Avg
2009	Casper............	Pioneer	3B	52	199	27	59	15	0	2	22	5	.296
2010	Asheville...........	So.Atl.	3B	92	373	45	115	41	1	12	65	1	.308
2011	Modesto............	Calif.	3B	134	517	82	154	32	3	20	122	2	.298
2012	Tulsa	Texas	3B	134	516	55	147	36	1	12	56	0	.285
2013	Colorado Springs.......	P.C.	3B	18	66	14	24	11	0	3	21	0	.364
2013	Colorado	N.L.	3B	133	486	49	130	29	4	10	52	2	.267

ARENCIBIA, JONATHAN PAUL (J.P.)

Born, Miami, Florida, January 5, 1986.
Bats Right. Throws Right. Height, 6 feet, 1 inch. Weight, 210 pounds.

Year	Club	Lea	Pos	G	AB	R	H	2B	3B	HR	RBI	SB	Avg
2007	Auburn.........	N.Y.-Penn.	C	63	228	31	58	17	1	3	25	0	.254
2008	Dunedin............	Fla.St.	C	59	248	38	78	22	0	13	62	0	.315
2008	New Hampshire.....	Eastern	C	67	262	32	74	14	0	14	43	0	.282
2009	Las Vegas.............	P.C.	C	116	466	67	110	32	1	21	75	0	.236
2010	Las Vegas.............	P.C.	C	104	412	76	124	36	1	32	85	0	.301
2010	Toronto	A.L.	C	11	35	3	5	1	0	2	4	0	.143
2011	Toronto	A.L.	C	129	443	47	97	20	4	23	78	1	.219
2012	Dunedin............	Fla.St.	DH	1	5	0	1	1	0	0	0	0	.200
2012	Toronto a............	A.L.	C	102	347	45	81	16	0	18	56	1	.233
2013	Toronto b............	A.L.	C	138	474	45	92	18	0	21	55	0	.194
Major League Totals	....	4 Yrs.		380	1299	140	275	55	4	64	193	2	.212

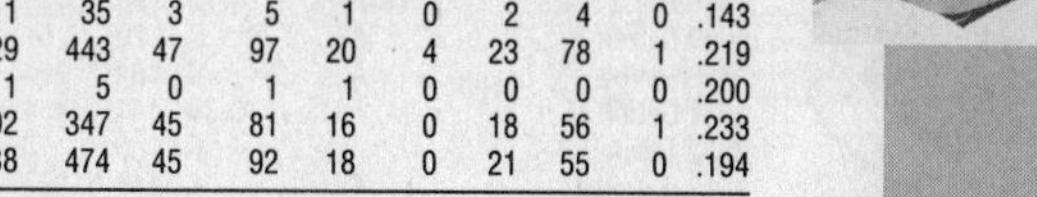

a On disabled list from July 26 to September 7, 2012.
b Not offered contract, December 2, 2013. Signed with Texas Rangers organization, December 10, 2013.

ARIAS, JOAQUIN

Born, Santo Domingo, Dominican Republic, September 21, 1984.
Bats Right. Throws Right. Height, 6 feet, 1 inch. Weight, 170 pounds.

Year	Club	Lea	Pos	G	AB	R	H	2B	3B	HR	RBI	SB	Avg
2002	Yankees.....	Gulf Coast	2B-SS-3B	57	203	29	61	7	6	0	21	2	.300
2003	Battle Creek ...	Midwest	SS	130	481	60	128	12	8	3	48	12	.266
2004	Stockton a	Calif.	SS	123	500	77	150	20	8	4	62	30	.300
2005	Frisco..........	Texas	SS	120	499	65	157	23	8	5	56	20	.315
2006	Oklahoma.........	P.C.	SS	124	493	56	132	14	10	4	49	26	.268
2006	Texas............	A.L.	SS-3B	6	11	4	6	1	0	0	1	0	.545
2007	Rangers.......	Arizona	SS	2	7	1	2	1	0	0	1	0	.286
2007	Oklahoma b	P.C.	SS	3	11	3	2	0	0	0	1	1	.182
2008	Oklahoma.........	P.C.	SS-2B	104	432	59	128	15	9	7	49	23	.296
2008	Texas............	A.L.	2B	32	110	15	32	7	3	0	9	4	.291
2009	Texas............	A.L.	2B-3B	3	8	0	0	0	0	0	0	0	.000
2009	Oklahoma.........	P.C.	SS	118	504	63	134	14	3	5	52	24	.266

Year	Club	Lea	Pos	G	AB	R	H	2B	3B	HR	RBI	SB	Avg
2010	Frisco..........	Texas	1B-SS-2B-3B	8	31	4	6	0	0	0	1	0	.194
2010	Texas	A.L.	2B-1B-SS	50	98	18	27	5	1	0	9	1	.276
2010	New York c-d-e	N.L.	2B-SS-OF	22	30	5	6	1	0	0	4	0	.200
2011	Omaha f...........	P.C.	3B-1B-SS-2B	69	241	37	56	12	4	3	25	7	.232
2012	Fresno	P.C.	SS	18	70	14	28	5	0	2	17	0	.400
2012	San Francisco	N.L.	3B-SS-2B	112	319	30	86	13	5	5	34	5	.270
2013	Fresno	P.C.	SS	2	8	0	2	0	0	0	0	0	.250
2013	San Francisco g	N.L.	3B-SS-2B-1B	102	225	17	61	9	2	1	19	1	.271
Major League Totals			6 Yrs.	327	801	89	218	36	11	6	76	11	.272
	Division Series												
2012	San Francisco	N.L.	SS-3B	4	6	3	3	2	0	0	0	0	.500
	Championship Series												
2012	San Francisco	N.L.	3B-SS	4	2	0	0	0	0	0	0	0	.000
	World Series Record												
2012	San Francisco	N.L.	3B	4	0	0	0	0	0	0	0	0	.000

a Sent to Texas Rangers as player to be named later for infielder Alex Rodriguez, March 23, 2004.
b On disabled list from March 23 to October 15, 2007.
c On disabled list from April 30 to May 16 and July 31 to August 16, 2010.
d Traded to New York Mets for outfielder Jeff Francoeur, September 1, 2010.
e Claimed on waivers by Kansas City Royals, November 4, 2010.
f Filed for free agency, November 2, 2011. Signed with San Francisco Giants organization, December 25, 2011.
g On disabled list from July 8 to July 26, 2013.

ASCHE, CODY JAMES

Born, St.Charles, Missouri, June 30, 1990.
Bats Left. Throws Right. Height, 6 feet, 1 inch. Weight, 180 pounds.

Year	Club	Lea	Pos	G	AB	R	H	2B	3B	HR	RBI	SB	Avg
2011	Williamsport.....	N.Y.-Penn.	2B	68	239	14	46	11	0	2	19	0	.192
2012	Clearwater	Fla.St.	3B	62	255	31	89	13	3	2	25	10	.349
2012	Reading	Eastern	3B	68	263	42	79	20	3	10	47	1	.300
2013	Lehigh Valley	Int.	3B	104	404	52	119	24	4	15	68	11	.295
2013	Philadelphia	N.L.	3B	50	162	18	38	8	1	5	22	1	.235

AVILA, ALEXANDER THOMAS (ALEX)

Born, Hialeah, Florida, January 29, 1987.
Bats Left. Throws Right. Height, 5 feet, 11 inches. Weight, 210 pounds.

Year	Club	Lea	Pos	G	AB	R	H	2B	3B	HR	RBI	SB	Avg
2008	West Michigan.....	Midwest	C	58	213	21	65	14	0	1	22	0	.305
2009	Erie..............	Eastern	C-1B	93	329	52	87	23	1	12	55	2	.264
2009	Detroit	A.L.	C	29	61	9	17	4	0	5	14	0	.279
2010	Detroit	A.L.	C	104	294	28	67	12	0	7	31	2	.228
2011	Detroit	A.L.	C-3B	141	464	63	137	33	4	19	82	3	.295
2012	Toledo	Int.	C	3	7	0	3	0	0	0	1	0	.429
2012	Detroit a............	A.L.	C	116	367	42	89	21	2	9	48	2	.243
2013	Toledo	Int.	C	12	44	5	11	3	0	1	5	0	.250
2013	Detroit b............	A.L.	C	102	330	39	75	14	1	11	47	0	.227
Major League Totals			5 Yrs.	492	1516	181	385	84	7	51	222	7	.254
	Division Series												
2011	Detroit	A.L.	C	5	16	0	1	0	0	0	1	0	.063
2012	Detroit	A.L.	C	4	12	2	3	1	0	1	1	0	.250
2013	Detroit	A.L.	C	5	15	1	2	0	0	0	1	0	.133
Division Series Totals				14	43	3	6	1	0	1	3	0	.140
	Championship Series												
2011	Detroit	A.L.	C	6	25	1	2	0	0	1	1	0	.080
2012	Detroit	A.L.	C	3	10	0	2	0	0	0	0	0	.200
2013	Detroit	A.L.	C	6	16	2	3	0	0	1	3	0	.188
Championship Series Totals				15	51	3	7	0	0	2	4	0	.137
	World Series Record												
2012	Detroit	A.L.	C	2	7	0	1	0	0	0	0	0	.143

a On disabled list from June 6 to June 21, 2012.
b On disabled list from June 17 to July 2 and August 11 to August 27, 2013.

AVILES, MICHAEL ANTHONY (MIKE)

Born, New York, New York, March 13, 1981.
Bats Right. Throws Right. Height, 5 feet, 9 inches. Weight, 195 pounds.

Year	Club	Lea	Pos	G	AB	R	H	2B	3B	HR	RBI	SB	Avg
2003	Royals 1	Arizona	SS	52	212	51	77	19	5	6	39	11	.363
2004	Wilmington	Carolina	SS	126	463	66	139	40	4	6	68	2	.300
2005	Wichita	Texas	SS-3B-2B	133	521	79	146	33	6	14	80	11	.280
2006	Omaha	P.C.	3B-SS-2B	129	469	52	124	21	3	8	47	14	.264
2007	Omaha	P.C.	SS-3B-2B	133	538	78	159	27	6	17	77	5	.296
2008	Omaha	P.C.	2B-SS	51	214	42	72	21	6	10	42	3	.336
2008	Kansas City	A.L.	SS-2B-3B	102	419	68	136	27	4	10	51	8	.325
2009	Kansas City a	A.L.	SS-3B	36	120	10	22	3	1	1	8	1	.183
2010	Omaha	P.C.	SS-2B	17	70	8	19	3	1	1	8	0	.271
2010	Kansas City	A.L.	2B-SS-3B	110	424	63	129	16	3	8	32	14	.304
2011	Omaha	P.C.	SS-2B	35	140	21	43	8	2	9	25	6	.307
2011	Kansas City-Boston b	A.L.	3B-2B-SS-OF	91	286	31	73	17	3	7	39	14	.255
2012	Boston c-d	A.L.	SS-2B-3B	136	512	57	128	28	0	13	60	14	.250
2013	Cleveland	A.L.	3B-SS-2B-OF	124	361	54	91	15	0	9	46	8	.252
Major League Totals			6 Yrs.	599	2122	283	579	106	11	48	236	59	.273

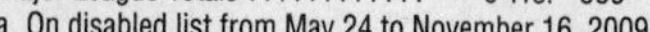

a On disabled list from May 24 to November 16, 2009.
b Traded to Boston Red Sox for infielder Yamaico Navarro and pitcher Kendal Volz, July 30, 2011.
c Traded to Toronto Blue Jays for manager John Farrell and pitcher David Carpenter, October 21, 2012.
d Traded to Cleveland Indians with catcher Yan Gomes for pitcher Esmil Rogers, November 3, 2012.

AYBAR, ERICK JOHAN

Born, Bani, Dominican Republic, January 14, 1984.
Bats Both. Throws Right. Height, 5 feet, 10 inches. Weight, 170 pounds.

Year	Club	Lea	Pos	G	AB	R	H	2B	3B	HR	RBI	SB	Avg
2002	Provo	Pioneer	SS	67	273	64	89	15	6	4	29	15	.326
2003	Cedar Rapids	Midwest	SS	125	496	83	153	30	10	6	57	32	.308
2004	Rancho Cucamonga	Calif.	SS-2B	136	573	102	189	25	11	14	65	51	.330
2005	Arkansas	Texas	SS	134	535	101	162	29	10	9	54	49	.303
2006	Salt Lake	P.C.	SS	81	339	63	96	20	3	6	45	32	.283
2006	Los Angeles	A.L.	SS-2B	34	40	5	10	1	1	0	2	1	.250
2007	Rancho Cucamonga	Calif.	SS	2	5	3	2	0	0	0	0	3	.400
2007	Salt Lake	P.C.	SS-2B	3	12	2	4	0	0	0	2	2	.333
2007	Los Angeles a	A.L.	2B-SS-OF-3B	79	194	18	46	5	1	1	19	4	.237
2008	Rancho Cucamonga	Calif.	SS	3	10	2	4	1	0	0	3	2	.400
2008	Los Angeles b	A.L.	SS-2B	98	346	53	96	18	5	3	39	7	.277
2009	Los Angeles	A.L.	SS	137	504	70	157	23	9	5	58	14	.312
2010	Los Angeles	A.L.	SS	138	534	69	135	18	4	5	29	22	.253
2011	Salt Lake	P.C.	SS	1	4	1	1	0	0	0	0	0	.250
2011	Los Angeles c	A.L.	SS	143	556	71	155	33	8	10	59	30	.279
2012	Los Angeles d	A.L.	SS	141	517	67	150	31	5	8	45	20	.290
2013	Salt Lake	P.C.	SS	1	5	1	2	1	0	1	2	0	.400
2013	Los Angeles e	A.L.	SS	138	550	68	149	33	5	6	54	12	.271
Major League Totals			8 Yrs.	908	3241	421	898	162	38	38	305	110	.277
	Division Series												
2007	Los Angeles	A.L.	OF	1	1	0	0	0	0	0	0	0	.000
2008	Los Angeles	A.L.	SS	4	18	0	2	0	0	0	1	0	.111
2009	Los Angeles	A.L.	SS	3	11	2	4	1	1	0	2	0	.364
Division Series Totals				8	30	2	6	1	1	0	3	0	.200
	Championship Series												
2009	Los Angeles	A.L.	SS	6	20	2	5	1	0	0	1	3	.250

a On disabled list from July 2 to August 6 and August 20 to September 5, 2007.
b On disabled list from May 21 to June 18, 2008.
c On disabled list from April 3 to April 20, 2011.
d On disabled list from July 22 to August 6, 2012.
e On disabled list from April 10 to April 30, 2013.

BAKER, JEFFREY GLEN (JEFF)

Born, Bad Kissingen, West Germany, June 21, 1981.
Bats Right. Throws Right. Height, 6 feet, 2 inches. Weight, 210 pounds.

Year	Club	Lea	Pos	G	AB	R	H	2B	3B	HR	RBI	SB	Avg
2003	Asheville	So.Atl.	3B	70	263	44	76	17	0	11	44	4	.289
2004	Visalia	Calif.	3B-SS	73	271	60	88	23	1	11	64	1	.325
2004	Tulsa	Texas	3B	24	91	10	27	5	1	4	20	1	.297
2005	Colorado	N.L.	3B	12	38	6	8	4	0	1	4	0	.211

Year	Club	Lea	Pos	G	AB	R	H	2B	3B	HR	RBI	SB	Avg
2005	Colorado Springs	P.C.	3B	61	228	40	69	16	1	10	41	3	.303
2006	Colorado Springs	P.C.	OF-3B	128	482	71	147	30	4	20	108	7	.305
2006	Colorado	N.L.	OF-1B	18	57	13	21	7	2	5	21	2	.368
2007	Colorado Springs	P.C.	1B-OF	7	26	3	6	1	0	1	2	0	.231
2007	Colorado a	N.L.	1B-OF-3B	85	144	17	32	2	2	4	12	0	.222
2008	Colorado	N.L.	2B-1B-3B-OF	104	299	55	80	22	1	12	48	4	.268
2009	Modesto	Calif.	2B-3B	2	5	1	2	1	0	0	1	0	.400
2009	Colorado Springs	P.C.	2B-3B	7	23	3	5	2	0	1	1	0	.217
2009	Colorado-Chicago b-c	N.L.	2B-3B-1B	81	226	27	65	15	2	4	24	1	.288
2010	Chicago	N.L.	3B-2B-1B-OF	79	206	29	56	13	2	4	21	1	.272
2011	Iowa	P.C.	1B-2B-OF	3	10	1	3	1	1	0	1	0	.300
2011	Chicago d	N.L.	1B-2B-3B-OF	81	201	20	54	12	1	3	23	0	.269
2012	Detroit	A.L.	OF-3B	15	35	1	7	2	0	0	4	0	.200
2012	Chicago-Atlanta e-f-g	N.L.	1B-OF-2B	68	153	17	38	10	1	4	21	4	.248
2013	Frisco	Texas	1B-OF	3	11	0	2	0	0	0	0	0	.182
2013	Texas h-i	A.L.	OF-1B-3B	74	154	21	43	8	0	11	21	1	.279
Major League Totals			9 Yrs.	617	1513	206	404	95	11	48	199	13	.267
	Division Series												
2007	Colorado	N.L.	PH	1	1	0	1	0	0	0	1	0	1.000
	Championship Series												
2007	Colorado	N.L.	PH	2	2	0	1	0	0	0	0	0	.500
	World Series Record												
2007	Colorado	N.L.	PH	1	1	0	0	0	0	0	0	0	.000

a On disabled list from August 12 to September 1, 2007.
b Traded to Chicago Cubs for pitcher Al Alburquerque, July 2, 2009.
c On disabled list from April 27 to July 2, 2009.
d On disabled list from May 30 to June 13, 2011.
e Traded to Detroit Tigers for player to be named later and cash, August 5, 2012. Chicago Cubs received pitcher Marcelo Carreno to complete trade, October 16, 2012.
f Traded to Atlanta Braves for player to be named later, August 31, 2012. Detroit Tigers received pitcher Greg Ross to complete trade, September 25, 2012.
g Filed for free agency, November 3, 2012. Signed with Texas Rangers organization, January 26, 2013.
h On disabled list from June 13 to July 18, 2013.
i Filed for free agency, October 14, 2013.

BARMES, CLINT HAROLD

Born, Vincennes, Indiana, March 6, 1979.
Bats Right. Throws Right. Height, 6 feet. Weight, 210 pounds.

Year	Club	Lea	Pos	G	AB	R	H	2B	3B	HR	RBI	SB	Avg
2000	Portland	Northwest	SS-OF	45	181	37	51	6	4	2	16	12	.282
2000	Asheville	So.Atl.	2B-SS-3B-OF	19	81	11	14	4	0	0	4	4	.173
2001	Salem	Carolina	SS	38	121	17	30	3	3	0	9	4	.248
2001	Asheville	So.Atl.	SS	74	285	40	74	14	1	5	24	21	.260
2002	Carolina	Southern	SS	103	438	62	119	23	2	15	60	15	.272
2003	Colorado Springs	P.C.	SS-2B	136	493	63	136	35	1	7	54	12	.276
2003	Colorado	N.L.	SS	12	25	2	8	2	0	0	2	0	.320
2004	Colorado Springs	P.C.	SS-2B	125	533	104	175	42	2	16	51	20	.328
2004	Colorado	N.L.	2B-SS	20	71	14	20	3	1	2	10	0	.282
2005	Tulsa	Texas	SS	8	34	6	11	1	0	0	0	1	.324
2005	Colorado a	N.L.	SS	81	350	55	101	19	1	10	46	6	.289
2006	Colorado	N.L.	SS-2B	131	478	57	105	26	4	7	56	5	.220
2007	Colorado Springs	P.C.	SS-OF-2B-3B	108	428	68	128	20	6	11	44	8	.299
2007	Colorado	N.L.	SS-2B-OF-3B	27	37	5	8	3	0	0	1	0	.216
2008	Colorado Springs	P.C.	2B-SS	5	18	2	5	0	0	0	3	0	.278
2008	Colorado b	N.L.	2B-SS-3B-OF	107	393	47	114	25	6	11	44	13	.290
2009	Colorado	N.L.	2B-SS	154	550	69	135	32	3	23	76	12	.245
2010	Colorado c	N.L.	2B-SS-3B	133	387	43	91	21	0	8	50	3	.235
2011	Corpus Christi	Texas	SS	2	9	2	4	0	0	0	2	0	.444
2011	Oklahoma	P.C.	SS	2	6	2	2	1	0	0	1	0	.333
2011	Houston d-e	N.L.	SS	123	446	47	109	27	0	12	39	3	.244
2012	Pittsburgh	N.L.	SS-1B	144	455	34	104	16	1	8	45	0	.229
2013	Pittsburgh f	N.L.	SS	108	304	22	64	15	0	5	23	0	.211
Major League Totals			11 Yrs.	1040	3496	395	859	189	16	86	392	42	.246
	Wild Card Playoff												
2013	Pittsburgh	N.L.	SS	1	4	0	1	0	0	0	0	0	.250
	Division Series												
2009	Colorado	N.L.	2B	4	14	0	0	0	0	0	0	0	.000
2013	Pittsburgh	N.L.	SS	5	7	0	2	0	0	0	0	0	.286
Division Series Totals				9	21	0	2	0	0	0	0	0	.095

a On disabled list from June 6 to September 2, 2005.
b On disabled list from May 24 to June 23, 2008.
c Traded to Houston Astros for pitcher Felipe Paulino, November 18, 2010.
d On disabled list from March 26 to April 29, 2011.
e Filed for free agency, October 30, 2011. Signed with Pittsburgh Pirates, November 21, 2011.
f Filed for free agency, October 31, 2013, re-signed with Pittsburgh Pirates, December 13, 2013.

BARNES, BRANDON MICHAEL

Born, Orange, California, May 15, 1986.
Bats Right. Throws Right. Height, 6 feet, 2 inches. Weight, 205 pounds.

Year	Club	Lea	Pos	G	AB	R	H	2B	3B	HR	RBI	SB	Avg
2005	Greeneville	Appal.	OF	39	145	21	29	5	2	2	13	3	.200
2006	Greeneville	Appal.	OF	52	173	19	38	11	1	2	14	5	.220
2007	Tri-City	N.Y.-Penn.	OF	63	231	34	58	16	1	10	41	5	.251
2008	Lexington	So.Atl.	OF	87	311	27	75	19	1	2	19	7	.241
2009	Lexington	So.Atl.	OF	57	197	23	52	11	3	5	25	3	.264
2009	Lancaster	Calif.	OF	68	266	51	78	19	3	12	52	1	.293
2009	Corpus Christi	Texas	OF	7	21	2	2	0	0	1	1	0	.095
2010	Lancaster	Calif.	OF	126	491	81	132	31	5	27	80	14	.269
2010	Round Rock	P.C.	OF	6	21	2	6	1	0	1	1	1	.286
2011	Corpus Christi	Texas	OF-2B	54	203	25	58	13	0	7	27	6	.286
2011	Oklahoma	P.C.	OF	71	229	34	45	13	5	8	27	5	.197
2012	Corpus Christi	Texas	OF	44	164	30	52	20	0	7	31	7	.317
2012	Oklahoma	P.C.	OF	62	235	51	76	19	1	5	38	14	.323
2012	Houston	N.L.	OF	43	98	8	20	3	0	1	7	1	.204
2013	Houston a	A.L.	OF	136	408	46	98	17	1	8	41	11	.240
Major League Totals			2 Yrs.	179	506	54	118	20	1	9	48	12	.233

a Traded to Colorado Rockies with pitcher Jordan Lyles for outfielder Dexter Fowler and player to be named later, December 3, 2013.

BARNEY, DARWIN JAMES KUNANE

Born, Portland, Oregon, November 8, 1985.
Bats Right. Throws Right. Height, 5 feet, 10 inches. Weight, 180 pounds.

Year	Club	Lea	Pos	G	AB	R	H	2B	3B	HR	RBI	SB	Avg
2007	Cubs	Arizona	SS	5	18	6	8	3	0	0	2	0	.444
2007	Peoria	Midwest	SS	44	176	27	48	9	3	2	21	5	.273
2008	Daytona	Fla.St.	SS	123	409	46	107	22	4	3	51	8	.262
2009	Tennessee	Southern	SS-2B-3B	74	252	30	80	12	0	3	32	5	.317
2009	Iowa	P.C.	SS-2B	63	212	25	56	12	1	0	17	4	.264
2010	Iowa	P.C.	SS-2B	114	479	72	143	24	4	2	49	11	.299
2010	Chicago	N.L.	SS-2B-3B	30	79	12	19	4	0	0	2	0	.241
2011	Iowa	P.C.	2B	4	14	3	5	1	0	1	3	1	.357
2011	Chicago a	N.L.	2B-SS	143	529	66	146	23	6	2	43	9	.276
2012	Chicago	N.L.	2B-SS	156	548	73	139	26	4	7	44	6	.254
2013	Iowa	P.C.	2B	3	10	4	5	1	0	0	0	1	.500
2013	Chicago b	N.L.	2B	141	501	49	104	25	1	7	41	4	.208
Major League Totals			4 Yrs.	470	1657	200	408	78	11	16	130	19	.246

a On disabled list from June 15 to June 29, 2011.
b On disabled list from March 31 to April 15, 2013.

BAUTISTA, JOSE ANTONIO

Born, Santo Domingo, Dominican Republic, October 19, 1980.
Bats Right. Throws Right. Height, 6 feet. Weight, 190 pounds.

Year	Club	Lea	Pos	G	AB	R	H	2B	3B	HR	RBI	SB	Avg
2001	Williamsport	N.Y.-Penn.	3B-OF	62	220	43	63	10	3	5	30	8	.286
2002	Hickory	So.Atl.	3B-SS	129	438	72	132	26	3	14	57	3	.301
2003	Lynchburg	Carolina	3B-2B	51	165	28	40	14	2	4	20	1	.242
2003	Pirates a	Gulf Coast	3B	7	23	5	8	1	0	1	3	0	.348
2004	Pittsburgh	N.L.	OF	23	40	1	8	2	0	0	0	0	.200
2004	Baltimore-T.B.-K.C. b-c-d-e	A.L.	3B-OF	41	48	5	10	1	0	0	2	0	.208
2005	Altoona	Eastern	3B	117	445	63	126	27	1	23	90	7	.283
2005	Indianapolis	Int.	3B	13	51	6	13	3	0	1	4	1	.255
2005	Pittsburgh	N.L.	3B	11	28	3	4	1	0	0	1	1	.143
2006	Indianapolis	Int.	3B-OF-2B	29	101	12	28	9	0	2	9	2	.277
2006	Pittsburgh	N.L.	OF-3B-2B	117	400	58	94	20	3	16	51	2	.235
2007	Pirates	Gulf Coast	3B	2	8	1	3	2	0	0	1	0	.375
2007	Pittsburgh f	N.L.	3B-OF	142	532	75	135	36	2	15	63	6	.254
2008	Indianapolis	Int.	OF-2B	5	20	6	6	2	0	2	8	1	.300

Year	Club	Lea	Pos	G	AB	R	H	2B	3B	HR	RBI	SB	Avg
2008	Pittsburgh	N.L.	3B	107	314	38	76	15	0	12	44	1	.242
2008	Toronto g	A.L.	3B-1B-2B	21	56	7	12	2	0	3	10	0	.214
2009	Toronto	A.L.	OF-3B	113	336	54	79	13	3	13	40	4	.235
2010	Toronto	A.L.	OF-3B-1B	161	569	109	148	35	3	*54	124	9	.260
2011	Toronto	A.L.	OF-3B	149	513	105	155	24	2	*43	103	9	.302
2012	Blue Jays	Gulf Coast	DH	1	3	0	0	0	0	0	0	0	.000
2012	New Hampshire	Eastern	OF	1	4	2	2	0	0	2	5	0	.500
2012	Toronto h	A.L.	OF-1B-3B	92	332	64	80	14	0	27	65	5	.241
2013	Toronto i	A.L.	OF-3B-1B	118	452	82	117	24	0	28	73	7	.259
Major League Totals			10 Yrs.	1095	3620	601	918	187	13	211	576	44	.254

a Selected by Baltimore Orioles from Pittsburgh in Rule V draft, December 15, 2003.
b Claimed on waivers by Tampa Bay Devil Rays, June 3, 2004.
c Sold to Kansas City Royals, June 28, 2004.
d Traded to New York Mets for catcher Justin Huber, July 30, 2004.
e Traded to Pittsburgh Pirates with infielder Ty Wigginton and pitcher Matt Peterson for pitcher Kris Benson and infielder Jeff Keppinger, July 30, 2004.
f On disabled list from July 15 to August 1, 2007.
g Traded to Toronto Blue Jays for player to be named later, August 21, 2008. Pittsburgh Pirates received infielder Robinzon Diaz to complete trade, August 25, 2008.
h On disabled list from July 17 to August 24 and August 26 to October 4, 2012.
i On disabled list from August 21 to October 1, 2013.

BAXTER, MICHAEL JOSEPH (MIKE)

Born, Queens, New York, December 7, 1984.
Bats Left. Throws Right. Height, 6 feet. Weight, 195 pounds.

Year	Club	Lea	Pos	G	AB	R	H	2B	3B	HR	RBI	SB	Avg
2005	Fort Wayne	Midwest	1B	45	183	11	40	12	1	1	17	4	.219
2006	Fort Wayne	Midwest	OF-1B-2B	117	476	67	122	28	7	3	40	13	.256
2007	Lake Elsinore	Calif.	OF	111	417	74	115	21	6	7	44	12	.276
2007	Portland	P.C.	OF	10	29	1	6	2	1	0	7	1	.207
2008	Lake Elsinore	Calif.	OF-1B	24	92	13	22	4	1	1	17	3	.239
2008	San Antonio	Texas	OF-1B	100	324	41	88	18	4	8	48	2	.272
2009	Portland	P.C.	OF-1B	82	303	38	84	17	4	5	34	9	.277
2009	San Antonio	Texas	OF-1B	51	202	38	76	23	1	4	45	5	.376
2010	Portland	P.C.	OF-1B-3B	136	482	89	145	30	10	18	72	22	.301
2010	San Diego	N.L.	1B	9	8	0	1	0	0	0	1	0	.125
2011	Lake Elsinore	Calif.	OF-1B	11	36	5	10	1	0	0	2	0	.278
2011	St. Lucie	Fla.St.	OF	4	16	2	7	2	0	0	4	0	.438
2011	Buffalo	Int.	OF-1B	18	64	4	12	0	2	1	7	1	.188
2011	New York a-b-c	N.L.	OF	22	34	6	8	2	1	1	4	0	.235
2012	St. Lucie	Fla.St.	DH	4	15	1	4	3	0	0	4	0	.267
2012	Binghamton	Eastern	OF	3	10	1	3	0	0	0	1	0	.300
2012	Buffalo	Int.	OF	6	24	2	9	1	0	0	3	0	.375
2012	New York d	N.L.	OF	89	179	26	47	14	2	3	17	5	.263
2013	Las Vegas	P.C.	OF	53	187	38	54	12	5	7	22	4	.289
2013	New York e	N.L.	OF	74	132	14	25	6	1	0	4	5	.189
Major League Totals			4 Yrs.	194	353	46	81	22	4	4	26	10	.229

a On disabled list from March 28 to July 22, 2011.
b Claimed on waivers by New York Mets, July 22, 2011.
c Not offered contract, December 12, 2011, re-signed with New York Mets organization, January 3, 2012.
d On disabled list from June 2 to July 30, 2012.
e Claimed on waivers by Los Angeles Dodgers, October 17, 2013.

BECKHAM, JAMES GORDON (GORDON)

Born, Atlanta, Georgia, September 16, 1986.
Bats Right. Throws Right. Height, 6 feet. Weight, 190 pounds.

Year	Club	Lea	Pos	G	AB	R	H	2B	3B	HR	RBI	SB	Avg
2008	Kannapolis	So.Atl.	SS	14	58	11	18	2	0	3	8	0	.310
2009	Birmingham	Southern	SS-2B-3B	38	147	23	44	17	0	4	22	1	.299
2009	Charlotte	Int.	3B-SS	7	28	6	13	6	0	0	3	1	.464
2009	Chicago	A.L.	3B	103	378	58	102	28	1	14	63	7	.270
2010	Chicago	A.L.	2B	131	444	58	112	25	2	9	49	4	.252
2011	Chicago	A.L.	2B	150	499	60	115	23	0	10	44	5	.230
2012	Chicago	A.L.	2B	151	525	62	123	24	0	16	60	5	.234
2013	Charlotte	Int.	2B-SS	8	36	7	12	2	0	0	5	0	.333
2013	Chicago a	A.L.	2B-SS	103	371	46	99	22	1	5	24	5	.267
Major League Totals			5 Yrs.	638	2217	284	551	122	4	54	240	26	.249

a On disabled list from April 10 to June 3, 2013.

BECKHAM, TIMOTHY LAMAR (TIM)

Born, Griffin, Georgia, January 27, 1990.
Bats Right. Throws Right. Height, 6 feet. Weight, 190 pounds.

Year Club	Lea	Pos	G	AB	R	H	2B	3B	HR	RBI	SB	Avg
2008 Princeton	Appal.	SS	46	177	30	43	12	0	2	14	5	.243
2008 Hudson Valley	N.Y.-Penn.	SS	2	6	5	2	1	0	0	0	1	.333
2009 Bowling Green	So.Atl.	SS	125	491	58	135	33	4	5	63	13	.275
2010 Charlotte	Fla.St.	SS	123	465	68	119	23	5	5	57	22	.256
2011 Montgomery	Southern	SS	107	418	82	115	25	2	7	57	15	.275
2011 Durham	Int.	SS	24	106	12	27	3	2	5	13	2	.255
2012 Durham	Int.	SS-2B	72	285	40	73	10	1	6	28	6	.256
2013 Durham	Int.	SS-2B	122	460	71	127	25	7	4	51	17	.276
2013 Tampa Bay a	A.L.	2B-SS	5	7	1	3	0	0	0	1	0	.429

a Suspended for 50 games for performance-enhancing drug use, May 2012.

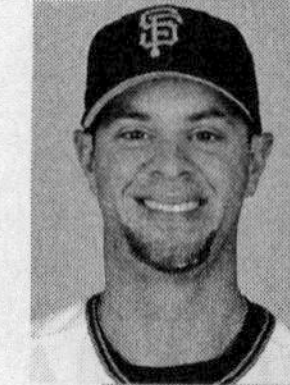

BELT, BRANDON KYLE

Born, Nacogdoches, Texas, April 20, 1988.
Bats Left. Throws Left. Height, 6 feet, 5 inches. Weight, 220 pounds.

Year Club	Lea	Pos	G	AB	R	H	2B	3B	HR	RBI	SB	Avg
2010 San Jose	Calif.	1B	77	269	62	103	28	4	10	62	18	.383
2010 Richmond	Eastern	1B-OF	46	175	26	59	11	6	9	40	2	.337
2010 Fresno	P.C.	OF-1B	13	48	11	11	4	0	4	10	2	.229
2011 San Jose	Calif.	1B	4	13	3	6	1	0	0	4	1	.462
2011 Fresno	P.C.	OF-1B	49	165	32	51	12	0	8	32	4	.309
2011 San Francisco a	N.L.	OF-1B	63	187	21	42	6	1	9	18	3	.225
2012 San Francisco	N.L.	1B-OF	145	411	47	113	27	6	7	56	12	.275
2013 San Francisco	N.L.	1B	150	509	76	147	39	4	17	67	5	.289
Major League Totals		3 Yrs.	358	1107	144	302	72	11	33	141	20	.273
Division Series												
2012 San Francisco	N.L.	1B	5	13	0	1	0	0	0	0	0	.077
Championship Series												
2012 San Francisco	N.L.	1B	6	23	6	7	1	1	1	2	1	.304
World Series Record												
2012 San Francisco	N.L.	1B	4	13	1	1	0	1	0	1	0	.077

a On disabled list from June 1 to July 7, 2011.

BELTRAN, CARLOS IVAN

Born, Manati, Puerto Rico, April 24, 1977.
Bats Both. Throws Right. Height, 6 feet. Weight, 200 pounds.

Year Club	Lea	Pos	G	AB	R	H	2B	3B	HR	RBI	SB	Avg
1995 Royals	Gulf Coast	OF	52	180	29	50	9	0	0	23	5	.278
1996 Lansing	Midwest	OF	11	42	3	6	2	0	0	0	1	.143
1996 Spokane	Northwest	OF	59	215	29	58	8	3	7	29	10	.270
1997 Wilmington	Carolina	OF	120	419	57	96	15	4	11	46	17	.229
1998 Wilmington	Carolina	OF	52	192	32	53	14	0	5	32	11	.276
1998 Wichita	Texas	OF	47	182	50	64	13	3	14	44	7	.352
1998 Kansas City	A.L.	OF	14	58	12	16	5	3	0	7	3	.276
1999 Kansas City a	A.L.	OF	156	663	112	194	27	7	22	108	27	.293
2000 GC Royals	Gulf Coast	PH	1	4	3	2	1	0	1	1	0	.500
2000 Wilmington	Carolina	OF	3	13	2	4	0	1	2	6	0	.308
2000 Omaha	P.C.	OF	5	18	4	6	1	0	2	2	1	.333
2000 Kansas City b	A.L.	OF	98	372	49	92	15	4	7	44	13	.247
2001 Kansas City	A.L.	OF	155	617	106	189	32	12	24	101	31	.306
2002 Kansas City	A.L.	OF	*162	637	114	174	44	7	29	105	35	.273
2003 Wichita	Texas	OF	3	9	3	3	2	0	0	1	1	.333
2003 Kansas City c	A.L.	OF	141	521	102	160	14	10	26	100	41	.307
2004 Kansas City	A.L.	OF	69	266	51	74	19	2	15	51	14	.278
2004 Houston d-e	N.L.	OF	90	333	70	86	17	7	23	53	28	.258
2005 New York	N.L.	OF	151	582	83	155	34	2	16	78	17	.266
2006 New York	N.L.	OF	140	510	127	140	38	1	41	116	18	.275
2007 New York f	N.L.	OF	144	554	93	153	33	3	33	112	23	.276
2008 New York	N.L.	OF	161	606	116	172	40	5	27	112	25	.284
2009 Brooklyn	N.Y.-Penn.	OF	5	18	1	3	0	0	0	2	0	.167
2009 New York g	N.L.	OF	81	308	50	100	22	1	10	48	11	.325
2010 St. Lucie	Fla.St.	OF	14	49	5	18	5	0	0	5	0	.367
2010 New York h	N.L.	OF	64	220	21	56	11	3	7	27	3	.255
2011 New York-San Fran. i-j-k	N.L.	OF	142	520	78	156	39	6	22	84	4	.300
2012 St. Louis	N.L.	OF	151	547	83	147	26	1	32	97	13	.269
2013 St. Louis l	N.L.	OF	145	554	79	164	30	3	24	84	2	.296
Major League Totals		16 Yrs.	2064	7868	1346	2228	446	77	358	1327	308	.283

Year	Club	Lea	Pos	G	AB	R	H	2B	3B	HR	RBI	SB	Avg
	Wild Card Playoff												
2012	St. Louis	N.L.	OF	1	4	1	1	0	0	0	0	0	.250
	Division Series												
2004	Houston	N.L.	OF	5	22	9	10	2	0	4	9	2	.455
2006	New York	N.L.	OF	3	9	2	2	0	0	0	1	1	.222
2012	St. Louis	N.L.	OF	5	18	5	8	3	0	2	4	1	.444
2013	St. Louis	N.L.	OF	5	18	3	4	1	0	2	6	0	.222
Division Series Totals				18	67	19	24	6	0	8	20	4	.358
	Championship Series												
2004	Houston	N.L.	OF	7	24	12	10	1	0	4	5	4	.417
2006	New York	N.L.	OF	7	27	8	8	1	0	3	4	1	.296
2012	St. Louis	N.L.	OF	6	20	2	6	3	0	1	2	2	.300
2013	St. Louis	N.L.	OF	6	21	2	6	2	1	0	6	0	.286
Championship Series Totals				26	92	24	30	7	1	8	17	7	.326
	World Series Record												
2013	St. Louis	N.L.	OF	6	17	1	5	0	0	0	3	0	.294

a Selected Rookie of the Year in American League for 1999.
b On disabled list from July 4 to September 3, 2000.
c On disabled list from March 21 to April 18, 2003.
d Traded to Houston Astros for pitcher Octavio Dotel and catcher John Buck, June 24, 2004.
e Filed for free agency, October 28, 2004. Signed with New York Mets, January 11, 2005.
f On disabled list from July 25 to August 10, 2007.
g On disabled list from June 22 to September 8, 2009.
h On disabled list from March 26 to July 15, 2010.
i Traded to San Francisco Giants for pitcher Zack Wheeler, July 28, 2011.
j On disabled list from August 8 to August 23, 2011.
k Filed for free agency, October 30, 2011. Signed with St. Louis Cardinals, December 23, 2011.
l Filed for free agency, October 31, 2013. Signed with New York Yankees, December 19, 2013.

BELTRE, ADRIAN

Born, Santo Domingo, Dominican Republic, April 7, 1979.
Bats Right. Throws Right. Height, 5 feet, 11 inches. Weight, 220 pounds.

Year	Club	Lea	Pos	G	AB	R	H	2B	3B	HR	RBI	SB	Avg
1995	LA-S.Domingo	Dominican	3B	62	218	56	67	15	3	8	40	2	.307
1996	Savannah	So.Atl.	3B-2B	68	244	48	75	14	3	16	59	4	.307
1996	San Berndno a	California	3B	63	238	40	62	13	1	10	40	3	.261
1997	Vero Beach	Fla.St.	3B-OF	123	435	95	138	24	2	26	104	25	.317
1998	San Antonio	Texas	3B	64	246	49	79	21	2	13	56	20	.321
1998	Los Angeles	N.L.	3B-SS	77	195	18	42	9	0	7	22	3	.215
1999	Los Angeles	N.L.	3B	152	538	84	148	27	5	15	67	18	.275
2000	Los Angeles b	N.L.	3B-SS	138	510	71	148	30	2	20	85	12	.290
2001	Vero Beach	Fla.St.	3B	3	9	0	4	1	0	0	1	0	.444
2001	Las Vegas	P.C.	3B	2	5	2	3	1	0	1	2	0	.600
2001	Los Angeles c	N.L.	3B-SS	126	475	59	126	22	4	13	60	13	.265
2002	Los Angeles	N.L.	3B	159	587	70	151	26	5	21	75	7	.257
2003	Los Angeles	N.L.	3B-SS	158	559	50	134	30	2	23	80	2	.240
2004	Los Angeles d	N.L.	3B-SS	156	598	104	200	32	0	*48	121	7	.334
2005	Seattle	A.L.	3B	156	603	69	154	36	1	19	87	3	.255
2006	Seattle	A.L.	3B-2B	156	620	88	166	39	4	25	89	11	.268
2007	Seattle	A.L.	3B	149	595	87	164	41	2	26	99	14	.276
2008	Seattle	A.L.	3B	143	556	74	148	29	1	25	77	8	.266
2009	Seattle e-f	A.L.	3B	111	449	54	119	27	0	8	44	13	.265
2010	Boston g	A.L.	3B	154	589	84	189	*49	2	28	102	2	.321
2011	Round Rock	P.C.	3B	2	8	1	2	0	0	0	0	0	.250
2011	Texas h	A.L.	3B	124	487	82	144	33	0	32	105	1	.296
2012	Texas	A.L.	3B	156	604	95	194	33	2	36	102	1	.321
2013	Texas	A.L.	3B	161	631	88	*199	32	0	30	92	1	.315
Major League Totals			16 Yrs.	2276	8596	1177	2426	495	30	376	1307	116	.282
	Wild Card Playoff												
2012	Texas	A.L.	3B	1	4	0	0	0	0	0	0	0	.000
	Division Series												
2004	Los Angeles	N.L.	3B	4	15	1	4	0	0	0	1	0	.267
2011	Texas	A.L.	3B	4	15	5	4	0	0	3	4	0	.267
Division Series Totals				8	30	6	8	0	0	3	5	0	.267
	Championship Series												
2011	Texas	A.L.	3B	6	27	4	6	3	0	0	2	0	.222
	World Series Record												
2011	Texas	A.L.	3B	7	30	5	9	2	0	2	3	0	.300

a On disabled list from June 25 to July 2, 1996.
b On disabled list from May 28 to June 16, 2000.
c On disabled list from March 23 to May 12, 2001.
d Filed for free agency, October 29, 2004. Signed with Seattle Mariners, December 17, 2004.
e On disabled list from June 29 to August 4 and August 13 to September 1, 2009.
f Filed for free agency, November 5, 2009. Signed with Boston Red Sox, January 7, 2010.
g Filed for free agency, November 2, 2010. Signed with Texas Rangers, January 5, 2011.
h On disabled list from July 23 to September 1, 2011.

BERKMAN, WILLIAM LANCE (LANCE)

Born, Waco, Texas, February 10, 1976.
Bats Both. Throws Left. Height, 6 feet, 1 inch. Weight, 220 pounds.

Year Club	Lea	Pos	G	AB	R	H	2B	3B	HR	RBI	SB	Avg
1997 Kissimmee..........	Fla.St.	OF	53	184	31	54	10	0	12	35	2	.293
1998 Jackson............	Texas	OF	122	425	82	130	34	0	24	89	6	.306
1998 New Orleans...........	P.C.	OF	17	59	14	16	4	0	6	13	0	.271
1999 New Orleans...........	P.C.	OF	64	226	42	73	20	0	8	49	7	.323
1999 Houston a	N.L.	OF-1B	34	93	10	22	2	0	4	15	5	.237
2000 New Orleans...........	P.C.	OF	31	112	18	37	4	2	6	27	4	.330
2000 Houston.............	N.L.	OF-1B	114	353	76	105	28	1	21	67	6	.297
2001 Houston.............	N.L.	OF	156	577	110	191	*55	5	34	126	7	.331
2002 Houston.............	N.L.	OF	158	578	106	169	35	2	42	*128	8	.292
2003 Houston.............	N.L.	OF	153	538	110	155	35	6	25	93	5	.288
2004 Houston.............	N.L.	OF-1B	160	544	104	172	40	3	30	106	9	.316
2005 Round Rock...........	P.C.	OF	4	14	2	4	1	0	0	1	0	.286
2005 Houston b	N.L.	1B-OF	132	468	76	137	34	1	24	82	4	.293
2006 Houston.............	N.L.	1B-OF	152	536	95	169	29	0	45	136	3	.315
2007 Houston.............	N.L.	1B-OF	153	561	95	156	24	2	34	102	7	.278
2008 Houston.............	N.L.	1B	159	554	114	173	*46	4	29	106	18	.312
2009 Houston c	N.L.	1B	136	460	73	126	31	1	25	80	7	.274
2010 Trenton............	Eastern	DH	2	8	1	2	0	0	0	0	0	.250
2010 Round Rock...........	P.C.	1B	2	6	3	3	2	0	1	3	0	.500
2010 Houston.............	N.L.	1B	85	298	39	73	16	1	13	49	3	.245
2010 New York d-e-f-g	A.L.	DH-1B	37	106	9	27	7	0	1	9	0	.255
2011 St. Louis.............	N.L.	OF-1B	145	488	90	147	23	2	31	94	2	.301
2012 Memphis	P.C.	1B	6	17	1	4	1	0	0	1	0	.235
2012 St. Louis h-i..........	N.L.	1B	32	81	12	21	7	1	2	7	2	.259
2013 Frisco.............	Texas	DH	2	4	2	1	0	0	0	1	0	.250
2013 Round Rock...........	P.C.	DH	2	7	1	3	0	0	1	2	0	.429
2013 Texas j-k............	A.L.	DH-1B	73	256	27	62	10	1	6	34	0	.242
Major League Totals		15 Yrs.	1879	6491	1146	1905	422	30	366	1234	86	.293
Division Series												
2001 Houston.............	N.L.	OF	3	12	0	2	0	0	0	0	0	.167
2004 Houston.............	N.L.	OF	5	22	5	9	1	0	1	3	0	.409
2005 Houston.............	N.L.	1B-OF	4	14	4	5	1	0	1	5	0	.357
2010 New York............	A.L.	DH	1	4	2	2	1	0	1	2	0	.500
2011 St. Louis.............	N.L.	OF	5	18	4	3	1	0	1	4	1	.167
Division Series Totals			18	70	15	21	4	0	4	14	1	.300
Championship Series												
2004 Houston.............	N.L.	OF	7	24	7	7	2	0	3	9	1	.292
2005 Houston.............	N.L.	1B-OF	6	21	2	6	2	0	1	3	0	.286
2010 New York............	A.L.	1B-DH	4	12	1	3	0	1	0	2	0	.250
2011 St. Louis.............	N.L.	OF	6	20	4	6	0	0	0	2	1	.300
Championship Series Totals			23	77	14	22	4	1	4	16	2	.286
World Series Record												
2005 Houston.............	N.L.	OF-1B	4	13	0	5	2	0	0	6	1	.385
2011 St. Louis.............	N.L.	OF-DH	7	26	9	11	1	0	1	7	0	.423
World Series Totals.............			11	39	9	16	3	0	1	13	1	.410

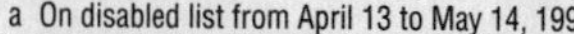

a On disabled list from April 13 to May 14, 1999.
b On disabled list from March 25 to May 6, 2005.
c On disabled list from July 23 to August 12, 2009.
d On disabled list from March 26 to April 20, 2010.
e Traded to New York Yankees with cash for pitcher Mark Melancon and infielder Jimmy Paredes, July 31, 2010.
f On disabled list from August 16 to September 1, 2010.
g Filed for free agency, November 1, 2010. Signed with St. Louis Cardinals, December 4, 2010.
h On disabled list from April 19 to May 13 and May 20 to July 14 and August 3 to September 1, 2012.
i Filed for free agency, November 3, 2012. Signed with Texas Rangers, January 7, 2013.
j On disabled list from July 7 to September 1, 2013.
k Filed for free agency, October 31, 2013.

BERNADINA, ROGEARVIN ARGELO (ROGER)

Born, Willemstad, Curacao, Netherlands Antilles, June 12, 1984.
Bats Left. Throws Left. Height, 6 feet, 1 inch. Weight, 200 pounds.

Year Club	Lea	Pos	G	AB	R	H	2B	3B	HR	RBI	SB	Avg
2002 Expos	Gulf Coast	OF	57	196	22	54	7	0	3	18	1	.276
2003 Savannah	So.Atl.	OF	77	278	36	66	12	3	4	39	11	.237
2004 Savannah	So.Atl.	OF	129	450	67	107	24	7	7	66	24	.238
2005 Savannah	So.Atl.	OF	122	417	64	97	15	3	12	54	35	.233
2006 Potomac	Carolina	OF	123	434	60	117	19	3	6	42	28	.270
2007 Harrisburg	Eastern	OF	97	371	58	100	15	2	6	36	40	.270
2007 Columbus	Int.	OF	13	42	6	7	3	0	0	1	0	.167
2008 Harrisburg	Eastern	OF	73	266	47	86	11	7	5	38	26	.323
2008 Columbus	Int.	OF	47	191	33	67	13	3	4	16	15	.351
2008 Washington	N.L.	OF	26	76	10	16	1	1	0	2	4	.211
2009 Syracuse	Int.	OF	5	18	1	3	0	0	0	0	1	.167
2009 Washington	N.L.	OF	3	4	1	1	1	0	0	0	1	.250
2009 Nationals a	Gulf Coast	OF	2	4	0	1	0	0	0	0	0	.250
2010 Syracuse	Int.	OF	14	61	8	23	2	1	2	8	7	.377
2010 Washington	N.L.	OF	134	414	52	102	18	3	11	47	16	.246
2011 Syracuse	Int.	OF	46	164	26	41	9	0	6	14	14	.250
2011 Washington	N.L.	OF	91	309	40	75	12	2	7	27	17	.243
2012 Washington	N.L.	OF	129	227	25	66	11	0	5	25	15	.291
2013 Wash.-Phil. b	N.L.	OF	112	227	26	41	10	2	4	11	4	.181
Major League Totals		6 Yrs.	495	1257	154	301	53	8	27	112	57	.239
Division Series												
2012 Washington	N.L.	PH	4	2	0	0	0	0	0	0	0	.000

a On disabled list from April 19 to November 8, 2009.
b Released by Washington Nationals, August 19, 2013. Signed with Philadelphia Phillies, August 21, 2013.

BETANCOURT (PEREZ), YUNIESKY

Born, Santa Clara, Cuba, January 31, 1982.
Bats Right. Throws Right. Height, 5 feet, 10 inches. Weight, 205 pounds.

Year Club	Lea	Pos	G	AB	R	H	2B	3B	HR	RBI	SB	Avg
2005 San Antonio a	Texas	SS-2B	52	227	25	62	10	3	5	20	12	.273
2005 Tacoma	P.C.	SS-2B	49	183	13	54	9	6	2	30	7	.295
2005 Seattle	A.L.	SS-2B	60	211	24	54	11	5	1	15	1	.256
2006 Seattle	A.L.	SS	157	558	68	161	28	6	8	47	11	.289
2007 Seattle	A.L.	SS	155	536	72	155	38	2	9	67	5	.289
2008 Seattle	A.L.	SS	153	559	66	156	36	3	7	51	4	.279
2009 Tacoma	P.C.	2B	1	2	0	1	1	0	0	1	0	.500
2009 NW Arkansas	Texas	SS	3	13	2	2	0	0	1	1	0	.154
2009 Seattle-KC b-c	A.L.	SS	134	470	40	115	20	6	6	49	3	.245
2010 Kansas City d	A.L.	SS	151	556	60	144	29	2	16	78	2	.259
2011 Milwaukee e	N.L.	SS	152	556	51	140	27	3	13	68	4	.252
2012 NW Arkansas	Texas	2B	4	15	1	5	1	0	1	4	0	.333
2012 Omaha	P.C.	2B	2	8	1	5	0	0	1	2	0	.625
2012 Kansas City f-g	A.L.	2B-3B-SS	57	215	21	49	14	1	7	36	0	.228
2013 Milwaukee h-i-j	N.L.	1B-3B-2B-SS	137	391	35	83	15	1	13	46	0	.212
Major League Totals		9 Yrs.	1156	4052	437	1057	218	29	80	457	30	.261
Division Series												
2011 Milwaukee	N.L.	SS	5	18	5	5	1	1	0	1	0	.278
Championship Series												
2011 Milwaukee	N.L.	SS	6	24	2	8	2	0	1	5	0	.333

a Played in Cuba 2000-2004. Signed with Seattle Mariners, January 26, 2005.
b On disabled list from June 25 to July 16, 2009.
c Traded to Kansas City Royals with cash for pitcher Dan Cortes and pitcher Derrick Saito, July 10, 2009.
d Traded to Milwaukee Brewers with pitcher Zack Greinke for outfielder Lorenzo Cain, infielder Alcides Escobar, pitcher Jeremy Jeffress and pitcher Jake Odorizzi, December 19, 2010.
e Filed for free agency, October 30, 2011. Signed with Kansas City Royals, December 20, 2011.
f On disabled list from May 2 to June 1, 2012.
g Released by Kansas City Royals, August 14, 2012.
h Signed with Philadelphia Phillies organization, January 28, 2013.
i Released by Philadelphia Phillies, March 24, 2013. Signed with Milwaukee Brewers, March 27, 2013.
j Filed for free agency, October 31, 2013.

BIANCHI, JEFFREY THOMAS (JEFF)

Born, Lancaster, Pennsylvania, October 5, 1986.
Bats Right. Throws Right. Height, 5 feet, 11 inches. Weight, 180 pounds.

Year	Club	Lea	Pos	G	AB	R	H	2B	3B	HR	RBI	SB	Avg
2005	Royals	Arizona	SS	28	98	29	40	7	4	6	30	5	.408
2006	Royals	Arizona	SS	12	42	13	18	4	0	2	6	1	.429
2007	Burlington	Midwest	SS-2B	99	368	43	91	19	0	2	36	15	.247
2008	Wilmington	Carolina	2B-SS	104	396	57	101	34	5	10	61	13	.255
2009	Wilmington	Carolina	SS	60	220	32	66	12	2	4	28	12	.300
2009	NW Arkansas	Texas	SS-2B	68	270	42	85	17	1	5	42	10	.315
2010 a			INJURED—Did Not Play										
2011	NW Arkansas b	Texas	2B-SS	119	444	63	115	23	2	2	48	20	.259
2012	Huntsville	Southern	SS	19	77	11	27	4	0	0	6	3	.351
2012	Nashville	P.C.	SS	73	249	33	79	13	1	5	19	11	.317
2012	Milwaukee c	N.L.	SS-3B-2B	33	69	8	13	2	0	3	9	0	.188
2013	Huntsville	Southern	2B-SS-3B	5	15	0	4	0	0	0	1	0	.267
2013	Nashville	P.C.	3B-SS-2B-OF	10	41	6	10	1	1	1	6	0	.244
2013	Milwaukee d	N.L.	3B-SS-2B-OF	100	236	22	56	8	1	1	25	4	.237
Major League Totals			2 Yrs.	133	305	30	69	10	1	4	34	4	.226

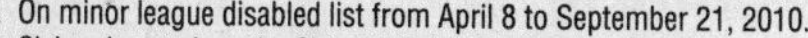

a On minor league disabled list from April 8 to September 21, 2010.
b Claimed on waivers by Chicago Cubs, December 9, 2011.
c Claimed on waivers by Milwaukee Brewers, January 11, 2012.
d On disabled list from March 22 to May 2, 2013.

BLACKMON, CHARLES COBB (CHARLIE)

Born, Dallas, Texas, July 1, 1986.
Bats Left. Throws Left. Height, 6 feet, 3 inches. Weight, 210 pounds.

Year	Club	Lea	Pos	G	AB	R	H	2B	3B	HR	RBI	SB	Avg
2008	Tri-City	Northwest	OF	68	290	42	98	21	5	2	33	13	.338
2009	Modesto	Calif.	OF	133	550	87	169	34	7	7	69	30	.307
2010	Tulsa	Texas	OF	86	337	53	100	22	4	11	55	19	.297
2011	Colorado Springs	P.C.	OF	58	243	49	82	19	4	10	49	12	.337
2011	Colorado a	N.L.	OF	27	98	9	25	1	0	1	8	5	.255
2012	Tri-City	Northwest	OF	17	59	8	14	5	0	1	3	3	.237
2012	Colorado Springs	P.C.	OF	59	228	55	69	18	4	5	34	10	.303
2012	Colorado b	N.L.	OF	42	113	15	32	8	0	2	9	1	.283
2013	Colorado Springs	P.C.	OF	68	257	56	74	15	6	3	40	7	.288
2013	Colorado	N.L.	OF	82	246	35	76	17	2	6	22	7	.309
Major League Totals			3 Yrs.	151	457	59	133	26	2	9	39	13	.291

a On disabled list from July 8 to October 31, 2011.
b On disabled list from March 26 to April 14, 2012.

BLANCO (PEDRAZA), GREGOR MIGUEL

Born, Caracas, Venezuela, December 24, 1983.
Bats Left. Throws Left. Height, 5 feet, 11 inches. Weight, 185 pounds.

Year	Club	Lea	Pos	G	AB	R	H	2B	3B	HR	RBI	SB	Avg
2002	Macon	So.Atl.	OF	132	468	87	127	14	9	7	36	40	.271
2003	Myrtle Beach	Carolina	OF	126	461	66	125	19	7	5	36	34	.271
2004	Myrtle Beach	Carolina	OF	119	435	73	117	17	9	8	41	25	.269
2005	Mississippi	Southern	OF	123	401	64	101	11	12	6	37	28	.252
2006	Richmond	Int.	OF	73	269	43	79	12	1	0	19	14	.294
2006	Mississippi	Southern	OF	66	251	45	72	16	3	0	9	17	.287
2007	Richmond	Int.	OF	124	464	81	131	18	5	3	35	23	.282
2008	Atlanta	N.L.	OF	144	430	52	108	14	4	1	38	13	.251
2009	Atlanta	N.L.	OF	24	43	5	8	0	1	0	1	2	.186
2009	Gwinnett	Int.	OF	90	333	54	76	9	1	2	30	10	.228
2010	Atlanta	N.L.	OF	36	58	9	18	1	1	0	3	1	.310
2010	Gwinnett	Int.	OF	44	154	26	44	8	0	1	11	9	.286
2010	Kansas City a	A.L.	OF	49	179	22	49	8	3	1	11	10	.274
2011	Syracuse	Int.	OF	51	143	28	29	7	2	3	10	15	.203
2011	Omaha b-c	P.C.	OF	23	56	13	11	5	0	0	4	9	.196
2012	San Francisco	N.L.	OF	141	393	56	96	14	5	5	34	26	.244
2013	San Francisco	N.L.	OF	141	452	50	120	17	6	3	41	14	.265
Major League Totals			5 Yrs.	535	1555	194	399	54	20	10	128	66	.257
	Division Series												
2012	San Francisco	N.L.	OF	5	14	3	4	1	0	1	2	0	.286
	Championship Series												
2012	San Francisco	N.L.	OF	7	22	6	4	1	1	0	2	0	.182

Year	Club	Lea	Pos	G	AB	R	H	2B	3B	HR	RBI	SB	Avg
	World Series Record												
2012	San Francisco	N.L.	OF	4	15	1	4	0	1	0	1	0	.267

a Traded to Kansas City Royals with pitcher Jesse Chavez and pitcher Tim Collins for outfielder Rick Ankiel, pitcher Kyle Farnsworth and cash, July 31, 2010.
b Sold to Washington Nationals, May 8, 2011.
c Filed for free agency, November 2, 2011. Signed with San Francisco Giants organization, November 16, 2011.

BLOOMQUIST, WILLIAM PAUL (WILLIE)

Born, Bremerton, Washington, November 27, 1977.
Bats Right. Throws Right. Height, 5 feet, 11 inches. Weight, 195 pounds.

Year	Club	Lea	Pos	G	AB	R	H	2B	3B	HR	RBI	SB	Avg
1999	Everett	Northwest	2B	41	178	35	51	10	3	2	27	17	.287
2000	Lancaster....	California	2B-SS	64	256	63	97	19	6	2	51	22	.379
2000	Tacoma a	P.C.	2B	51	191	17	43	5	1	1	23	5	.225
2001	San Antonio	Texas	SS-2B	123	491	59	125	23	2	0	28	34	.255
2002	Tacoma	P.C.	OF-2B-3B-SS	104	337	47	91	14	3	6	47	20	.270
2002	Seattle b..........	A.L.	OF-2B	12	33	11	15	4	0	0	7	3	.455
2003	Seattle	A.L.	3B-SS-OF	89	196	30	49	7	2	1	14	4	.250
2004	Tacoma	P.C.	SS-OF	3	12	2	5	0	0	1	3	1	.417
2004	Seattle c..........	A.L.	3B-SS-1B-OF	93	188	27	46	10	0	2	18	13	.245
2005	Seattle d..........	A.L.	2B-SS-OF-3B	82	249	27	64	15	2	0	22	14	.257
2006	Seattle	A.L.	OF-SS-2B-3B	102	251	36	62	6	2	1	15	16	.247
2007	Seattle	A.L.	OF-2B-3B-SS	91	173	28	48	3	0	2	13	7	.277
2008	Seattle e-f.........	A.L.	OF-SS-2B-3B	71	165	32	46	1	0	0	9	14	.279
2009	Kansas City	A.L.	OF-SS-2B-1B	125	434	52	115	11	8	4	29	25	.265
2010	Kansas City	A.L.	OF-3B-2B	72	170	31	45	10	1	3	17	8	.265
2010	Cincinnati g-h......	N.L.	OF-2B	11	17	0	5	0	0	0	0	0	.294
2011	Arizona i-j.........	N.L.	SS-OF-2B	97	350	44	93	10	2	4	26	20	.266
2012	D-Backs	Arizona	SS	4	9	3	3	1	1	0	4	0	.333
2012	Arizona k	N.L.	SS-3B-OF-2B	80	324	47	98	21	5	0	23	7	.302
2013	D-Backs	Arizona	SS	4	12	4	6	1	0	0	1	0	.500
2013	Reno	P.C.	2B-SS	6	21	5	9	0	1	0	9	0	.429
2013	Arizona l-m	N.L.	2B-SS-OF	48	139	16	44	5	1	0	14	0	.317
Major League Totals			12 Yrs.	973	2689	381	730	103	23	17	207	131	.271
	Division Series												
2011	Arizona...........	N.L.	SS	5	22	3	7	0	0	0	1	3	.318

a On disabled list from August 6 to September 29, 2000.
b On disabled list from April 22 to May 3 and June 6 to 18, 2002.
c On disabled list from May 2 to May 21, 2004.
d On disabled list from August 30 to October 31, 2005.
e On disabled list from August 10 to September 29, 2008.
f Filed for free agency, October 30, 2008. Signed with Kansas City Royals, January 9, 2009.
g Sold to Cincinnati Reds, September 13, 2010.
h Filed for free agency, November 1, 2010. Signed with Arizona Diamondbacks, January 18, 2011.
i On disabled list from April 22 to May 18, 2011.
j Filed for free agency, October 31, 2011, re-signed with Arizona Diamondbacks, November 9, 2011.
k On disabled list from August 9 to September 1, 2012.
l On disabled list from March 27 to May 31 and June 28 to August 28, 2013.
m Filed for free agency, October 31, 2013. Signed with Seattle Mariners, December 5, 2013.

BOGAERTS, XANDER JAN

Born, Oranjestad, Aruba, October 1, 1992.
Bats Right. Throws Right. Height, 6 feet, 3 inches. Weight, 185 pounds.

Year	Club	Lea	Pos	G	AB	R	H	2B	3B	HR	RBI	SB	Avg
2011	Greenville..........	So.Atl.	SS	72	265	38	69	14	2	16	45	1	.260
2012	Salem............	Carolina	SS	104	384	59	116	27	3	15	64	4	.302
2012	Portland...........	Eastern	SS	23	92	12	30	10	0	5	17	1	.326
2013	Portland...........	Eastern	SS	56	219	40	68	12	6	6	35	5	.311
2013	Pawtucket	Int.	SS-3B	60	225	32	64	11	0	9	32	2	.284
2013	Boston..............	A.L.	3B-SS	18	44	7	11	2	0	1	5	1	.250
	Division Series												
2013	Boston..............	A.L.	3B-SS	2	0	3	0	0	0	0	0	0	.000
	Championship Series												
2013	Boston..............	A.L.	3B	4	6	4	3	3	0	0	0	0	.500
	World Series Record												
2013	Boston..............	A.L.	3B-SS	6	21	2	5	0	1	0	2	0	.238

BOGUSEVIC, BRIAN THOMAS

Born, Palos Heights, Illinois, February 18, 1984.
Bats Left. Throws Left. Height, 6 feet, 3 inches. Weight, 220 pounds.

Year	Club	Lea	Pos	G	AB	R	H	2B	3B	HR	RBI	SB	Avg
2007	Corpus Christi a	Texas	PH	2	2	0	1	0	0	0	0	0	.500
2008	Salem	Carolina	OF	8	23	4	5	2	0	1	6	1	.217
2008	Corpus Christi	Texas	OF	42	124	21	46	10	2	3	20	8	.371
2009	Round Rock	P.C.	OF	138	520	68	141	25	3	6	53	22	.271
2010	Round Rock	P.C.	OF-1B	131	502	91	139	26	2	13	57	23	.277
2010	Houston	N.L.	OF	19	28	5	5	3	0	0	3	1	.179
2011	Oklahoma	P.C.	OF-1B	58	218	27	57	11	5	3	35	20	.261
2011	Houston	N.L.	OF	87	164	22	47	14	1	4	15	4	.287
2012	Houston b	N.L.	OF-P	146	355	39	72	9	2	7	28	15	.203
2013	Cubs	Arizona	OF	7	25	7	10	4	1	0	5	3	.400
2013	Iowa	P.C.	OF-1B	79	265	50	84	14	3	10	32	16	.317
2013	Chicago c-d	N.L.	OF	47	143	18	39	7	1	6	16	2	.273
Major League Totals			4 Yrs.	299	690	84	163	33	4	17	62	22	.236

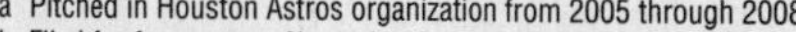

a Pitched in Houston Astros organization from 2005 through 2008.
b Filed for free agency, November 3, 2012. Signed with Chicago Cubs organization, November 14, 2012.
c On disabled list from July 15 to August 19, 2013.
d Traded to Miami Marlins for outfielder Justin Ruggiano, December 12, 2013.

BONIFACIO, EMILIO JOSE

Born, Santo Domingo, Dominican Republic, April 23, 1985.
Bats Both. Throws Right. Height, 5 feet, 11 inches. Weight, 195 pounds.

Year	Club	Lea	Pos	G	AB	R	H	2B	3B	HR	RBI	SB	Avg
2003	Missoula	Pioneer	2B	54	146	20	29	1	1	0	16	15	.199
2004	South Bend	Midwest	2B	120	411	59	107	9	6	1	37	40	.260
2005	South Bend	Midwest	2B	127	522	81	141	14	7	1	44	55	.270
2006	Lancaster	Calif.	2B	130	546	117	175	35	7	7	50	61	.321
2007	Mobile	Southern	2B-SS	132	551	84	157	21	5	2	40	41	.285
2007	Arizona	N.L.	2B	11	23	2	5	1	0	0	2	0	.217
2008	Tucson	P.C.	2B-OF-SS	85	367	49	111	18	5	1	29	17	.302
2008	Columbus	Int.	2B	8	31	9	14	2	0	0	3	4	.452
2008	Arizona-Washington a-b	N.L.	2B-OF	49	169	29	41	6	5	0	14	7	.243
2009	Florida	N.L.	3B-SS-OF-2B	127	461	72	116	11	6	1	27	21	.252
2010	New Orleans	P.C.	OF-2B-SS	40	164	19	45	8	3	0	11	8	.274
2010	Florida	N.L.	OF-SS-3B-2B	73	180	30	47	6	3	0	10	12	.261
2011	Florida	N.L.	SS-OF-3B-2B	152	565	78	167	26	7	5	36	40	.296
2012	Jupiter	Fla.St.	OF	9	30	6	5	1	0	0	4	3	.167
2012	Miami c-d	N.L.	OF-2B	64	244	30	63	3	4	1	11	30	.258
2013	Toronto-KC e	A.L.	2B-OF-3B-SS	136	420	54	102	22	3	3	31	28	.243
Major League Totals			7 Yrs.	612	2062	295	541	75	28	10	131	138	.262

a Traded to Washington Nationals for pitcher Jon Rauch, July 22, 2008.
b Traded to Florida Marlins with pitcher P.J. Dean and infielder Jake Smolinski for pitcher Scott Olsen and outfielder Josh Willingham, November 11, 2008.
c On disabled list from May 19 to July 13 and August 4 to August 19 and August 22 to October 31, 2012.
d Traded to Toronto Blue Jays with catcher John Buck, pitcher Mark Buehrle, pitcher Josh Johnson and infielder Jose Reyes for pitcher Henderson Alvarez, infielder Yunel Escobar, infielder Adeiny Hechavarria, catcher Jeff Mathis, pitcher Anthony De Sclafani, outfielder Jake Marisnick and pitcher Justin Nicolino, November 19, 2012.
e Sold to Kansas City Royals, August 14, 2013.

BOURJOS, PETER CHRISTOPHER

Born, Park Ridge, Illinois, March 31, 1987.
Bats Right. Throws Right. Height, 6 feet, 1 inch. Weight, 180 pounds.

Year	Club	Lea	Pos	G	AB	R	H	2B	3B	HR	RBI	SB	Avg
2006	Orem	Pioneer	OF	65	250	42	73	16	7	5	28	13	.292
2007	Angels	Arizona	OF	4	16	3	5	0	1	0	2	0	.313
2007	Cedar Rapids	Midwest	OF	63	237	37	65	9	6	5	29	19	.274
2008	Rancho Cucamonga	Calif.	OF	121	509	83	150	29	10	9	51	50	.295
2009	Arkansas	Texas	OF	110	437	72	123	16	14	6	51	32	.281
2010	Salt Lake	P.C.	OF	102	414	85	130	13	12	13	52	27	.314
2010	Los Angeles	A.L.	OF	51	181	19	37	6	4	6	15	10	.204
2011	Los Angeles a	A.L.	OF	147	502	72	136	26	*11	12	43	22	.271
2012	Salt Lake	P.C.	OF	7	29	4	9	1	3	0	3	0	.310
2012	Los Angeles b	A.L.	OF	101	168	27	37	7	0	3	19	3	.220
2013	Inland Empire	Calif.	OF	3	11	3	3	0	1	1	2	0	.273
2013	Salt Lake	P.C.	OF	12	48	13	10	4	0	2	7	0	.208

Year	Club	Lea	Pos	G	AB	R	H	2B	3B	HR	RBI	SB	Avg
2013	Los Angeles c-d	A.L.	OF	55	175	26	48	3	3	3	12	6	.274
Major League Totals			4 Yrs.	354	1026	144	258	42	18	24	89	41	.251

a On disabled list from July 8 to July 23, 2011.
b On disabled list from August 19 to September 3, 2012.
c On disabled list from April 30 to June 10 and June 30 to August 16 and September 16 to November 4, 2013.
d Traded to St. Louis Cardinals with infielder Randal Grichuk for infielder David Freese and pitcher Fernando Salas, November 22, 2013.

BOURN, MICHAEL RAY

Born, Houston, Texas, December 27, 1982.
Bats Left. Throws Right. Height, 5 feet, 11 inches. Weight, 180 pounds.

Year	Club	Lea	Pos	G	AB	R	H	2B	3B	HR	RBI	SB	Avg
2003	Batavia	N.Y.-Penn.	OF	35	125	12	35	0	1	0	4	23	.280
2004	Lakewood	So.Atl.	OF	109	413	92	130	20	14	5	53	58	.315
2005	Reading	Eastern	OF	135	544	80	146	18	8	6	44	38	.268
2006	Reading	Eastern	OF	80	318	62	87	5	6	4	26	30	.274
2006	Scranton-WB	Int.	OF	38	152	34	43	5	7	1	15	15	.283
2006	Philadelphia	N.L.	OF	17	8	2	1	0	0	0	0	1	.125
2007	Philadelphia a-b	N.L.	OF	105	119	29	33	3	3	1	6	18	.277
2008	Houston	N.L.	OF	138	467	57	107	10	4	5	29	41	.229
2009	Houston	N.L.	OF	157	606	97	173	27	12	3	35	*61	.285
2010	Houston	N.L.	OF	141	535	84	142	25	6	2	38	*52	.265
2011	Houston-Atlanta c	N.L.	OF	158	656	94	193	34	10	2	50	*61	.294
2012	Atlanta d	N.L.	OF	155	624	96	171	26	10	9	57	42	.274
2013	Columbus	Int.	OF	2	7	0	1	0	0	0	0	1	.143
2013	Cleveland e	A.L.	OF	130	525	75	138	21	6	6	50	23	.263
Major League Totals			8 Yrs.	1001	3540	534	958	146	51	28	265	299	.271
	Wild Card Playoff												
2012	Atlanta	N.L.	OF	1	5	0	1	0	0	0	1	0	.200
2013	Cleveland	A.L.	OF	1	4	0	0	0	0	0	0	0	.000
Wild Card Totals				2	9	0	1	0	0	0	1	0	.111
	Division Series												
2007	Philadelphia	N.L.	PH	2	1	0	0	0	0	0	0	0	.000

a On disabled list from July 31 to September 10, 2007.
b Traded to Houston Astros with pitcher Geoff Geary and infielder Mike Costanzo for infielder Eric Bruntlett and pitcher Brad Lidge, November 12, 2007.
c Traded to Atlanta Braves with cash for outfielder Jordan Schafer, pitcher Juan Abreu, pitcher Paul Clemens and pitcher Brett Oberholtzer, July 31, 2011.
d Filed for free agency, November 3, 2012. Signed with Cleveland Indians, February 15, 2013.
e On disabled list from April 15 to May 10, 2013.

BRADLEY, JACKIE JR.

Born, Richmond, Virginia, April 19, 1990.
Bats Left. Throws Right. Height, 5 feet, 10 inches. Weight, 195 pounds.

Year	Club	Lea	Pos	G	AB	R	H	2B	3B	HR	RBI	SB	Avg
2011	Lowell	N.Y.-Penn.	OF	6	21	5	4	0	0	0	0	0	.190
2011	Greenville	So.Atl.	OF	4	15	2	5	1	0	1	3	0	.333
2012	Salem	Carolina	OF	67	234	53	84	26	2	3	34	16	.359
2012	Portland	Eastern	OF	61	229	37	62	16	2	6	29	8	.271
2013	Pawtucket	Int.	OF	80	320	57	88	26	3	10	35	7	.275
2013	Boston	A.L.	OF	37	95	18	18	5	0	3	10	2	.189

BRANTLEY, MICHAEL CHARLES JR.

Born, Bellevue, Washington, May 15, 1987.
Bats Left. Throws Left. Height, 6 feet, 2 inches. Weight, 200 pounds.

Year	Club	Lea	Pos	G	AB	R	H	2B	3B	HR	RBI	SB	Avg
2005	Brewers	Arizona	OF	44	173	34	60	3	1	0	19	14	.347
2005	Helena	Pioneer	OF	10	34	8	11	2	0	0	3	2	.324
2006	West Virginia	So.Atl.	OF	108	360	47	108	10	2	0	42	24	.300
2007	West Virginia	So.Atl.	1B-OF	56	218	41	73	15	1	2	32	18	.335
2007	Huntsville	Southern	OF-1B	59	187	28	47	6	1	0	21	17	.251
2008	Huntsville a	Southern	OF-1B	106	420	80	134	17	2	4	40	28	.319
2009	Columbus	Int.	OF	116	457	80	122	21	2	6	37	46	.267
2009	Cleveland	A.L.	OF	28	112	10	35	4	0	0	11	4	.313
2010	Columbus	Int.	OF	67	273	54	87	13	2	4	29	13	.319
2010	Cleveland	A.L.	OF	72	297	38	73	9	3	3	22	10	.246

Year	Club	Lea	Pos	G	AB	R	H	2B	3B	HR	RBI	SB	Avg
2011	Cleveland b	A.L.	OF	114	451	63	120	24	4	7	46	13	.266
2012	Cleveland	A.L.	OF	149	552	63	159	37	4	6	60	12	.288
2013	Cleveland	A.L.	OF	151	556	66	158	26	3	10	73	17	.284
Major League Totals			5 Yrs.	514	1968	240	545	100	14	26	212	56	.277
	Wild Card Playoff												
2013	Cleveland	A.L.	OF	1	4	0	1	0	0	0	0	0	.250

a Sent by Milwaukee Brewers to Cleveland Indians as player to be named later for pitcher C.C. Sabathia, October 3, 2008.
b On disabled list from August 23 to November 2, 2011.

BRAUN, RYAN JOSEPH

Born, Mission Hills, California, November 17, 1983.
Bats Right. Throws Right. Height, 6 feet, 2 inches. Weight, 200 pounds.

Year	Club	Lea	Pos	G	AB	R	H	2B	3B	HR	RBI	SB	Avg
2005	Helena	Pioneer	3B	10	41	6	14	2	1	2	10	2	.341
2005	West Virginia	So.Atl.	3B	37	152	21	54	16	2	8	35	2	.355
2006	Brevard County	Fla.St.	3B	59	226	34	62	12	2	7	37	14	.274
2006	Huntsville	Southern	3B	59	231	42	70	19	1	15	40	12	.303
2007	Nashville	P.C.	3B	34	117	28	40	12	0	10	22	4	.342
2007	Milwaukee a	N.L.	3B	113	451	91	146	26	6	34	97	15	.324
2008	Milwaukee	N.L.	OF	151	611	92	174	39	7	37	106	14	.285
2009	Milwaukee	N.L.	OF	158	635	113	*203	39	6	32	114	20	.320
2010	Milwaukee	N.L.	OF	157	619	101	188	45	1	25	103	14	.304
2011	Milwaukee b	N.L.	OF	150	563	109	187	38	6	33	111	33	.332
2012	Milwaukee	N.L.	OF	154	*598	108	191	36	3	*41	112	30	.319
2013	Milwaukee c	N.L.	OF	61	225	30	67	14	2	9	38	4	.298
Major League Totals			7 Yrs.	944	3702	644	1156	237	31	211	681	130	.312
	Division Series												
2008	Milwaukee	N.L.	OF	4	16	0	5	2	0	0	2	0	.313
2011	Milwaukee	N.L.	OF	5	18	5	9	4	0	1	4	1	.500
Division Series Totals				9	34	5	14	6	0	1	6	1	.412
	Championship Series												
2011	Milwaukee	N.L.	OF	6	24	2	8	3	0	1	6	0	.333

a Selected Rookie of the Year in National League for 2007.
b Selected Most Valuable Player in National League for 2011.
c Suspended for 65 games for performance-enhancing drug use, August 5, 2013.

BROWN, DOMONIC LARUN

Born, Lithonia, Georgia, September 3, 1987.
Bats Left. Throws Left. Height, 6 feet, 5 inches. Weight, 200 pounds.

Year	Club	Lea	Pos	G	AB	R	H	2B	3B	HR	RBI	SB	Avg
2006	Phillies	Gulf Coast	OF	34	117	13	25	3	0	1	7	13	.214
2007	Clearwater	Fla.St.	OF	3	9	2	4	1	0	1	7	0	.444
2007	Williamsport	N.Y.-Penn.	OF	74	285	43	84	11	5	3	32	14	.295
2008	Lakewood	So.Atl.	OF	114	444	77	129	23	3	9	54	22	.291
2009	Reading	Eastern	OF	37	147	20	41	9	4	3	20	8	.279
2009	Clearwater	Fla.St.	OF	66	238	41	72	12	3	11	44	15	.303
2009	Phillies	Gulf Coast	OF	3	10	4	5	0	2	0	0	0	.500
2010	Reading	Eastern	OF	65	236	50	75	16	3	15	47	12	.318
2010	Lehigh Valley	Int.	OF	28	107	15	37	6	1	5	21	5	.346
2010	Philadelphia	N.L.	OF	35	62	8	13	3	0	2	13	2	.210
2011	Clearwater	Fla.St.	OF	5	19	4	7	1	0	2	4	0	.368
2011	Lehigh Valley	Int.	OF	41	138	22	36	6	0	3	15	12	.261
2011	Philadelphia a	N.L.	OF	56	184	28	45	10	1	5	19	3	.245
2012	Phillies	Gulf Coast	OF	5	19	4	11	7	0	0	4	1	.579
2012	Lehigh Valley	Int.	OF	60	220	33	63	13	2	5	28	4	.286
2012	Philadelphia	N.L.	OF	56	187	21	44	11	2	5	26	0	.235
2013	Lakewood	So.Atl.	OF	1	5	2	3	0	0	1	2	0	.600
2013	Philadelphia b	N.L.	OF	139	496	65	135	21	4	27	83	8	.272
Major League Totals			4 Yrs.	286	929	122	237	45	7	39	141	13	.255
	Division Series												
2010	Philadelphia	N.L.	PH	1	1	1	0	0	0	0	0	0	.000
	Championship Series												
2010	Philadelphia	N.L.	PH	2	2	0	0	0	0	0	0	0	.000

a On disabled list from March 22 to May 2, 2011.
b On disabled list from July 24 to August 6, 2013.

BRUCE, JAY ALLEN

Born, Beaumont, Texas, April 3, 1987.

Bats Left. Throws Left. Height, 6 feet, 3 inches. Weight, 205 pounds.

Year	Club	Lea	Pos	G	AB	R	H	2B	3B	HR	RBI	SB	Avg
2005	Reds	Gulf Coast	OF	37	122	29	33	9	2	5	25	4	.270
2005	Billings	Pioneer	OF	17	70	16	18	2	0	4	13	2	.257
2006	Dayton	Midwest	OF	117	444	69	129	42	5	16	81	19	.291
2007	Sarasota	Fla.St.	OF	67	268	49	87	27	5	11	49	4	.325
2007	Louisville	Int.	OF	50	187	28	57	12	2	11	25	2	.305
2007	Chattanooga	Southern	OF	16	66	10	22	7	1	4	15	2	.333
2008	Louisville	Int.	OF	49	184	34	67	9	5	10	37	8	.364
2008	Cincinnati	N.L.	OF	108	413	63	105	17	1	21	52	4	.254
2009	Louisville	Int.	OF	5	18	3	5	0	0	0	0	2	.278
2009	Cincinnati a	N.L.	OF	101	345	47	77	15	2	22	58	3	.223
2010	Cincinnati	N.L.	OF	148	509	80	143	23	5	25	70	5	.281
2011	Cincinnati	N.L.	OF	157	585	84	150	27	2	32	97	8	.256
2012	Cincinnati	N.L.	OF	155	560	89	141	35	5	34	99	9	.252
2013	Cincinnati	N.L.	OF	160	626	89	164	43	1	30	109	7	.262
Major League Totals			6 Yrs.	829	3038	452	780	160	16	164	485	36	.257
	Wild Card Playoff												
2013	Cincinnati	N.L.	OF	1	4	0	1	0	0	0	1	0	.250
	Division Series												
2010	Cincinnati	N.L.	OF	3	8	1	2	0	0	1	1	0	.250
2012	Cincinnati	N.L.	OF	5	19	2	5	2	0	1	4	0	.263
Division Series Totals				8	27	3	7	2	0	2	5	0	.259

a On disabled list from July 12 to September 14, 2009.

BUCK, JOHNATHAN RICHARD (JOHN)

Born, Kemmerer, Wyoming, July 7, 1980.

Bats Right. Throws Right. Height, 6 feet, 3 inches. Weight, 220 pounds.

Year	Club	Lea	Pos	G	AB	R	H	2B	3B	HR	RBI	SB	Avg
1998	Astros	Gulf Coast	C	36	126	24	36	9	0	3	15	2	.286
1999	Auburn	N.Y.-Penn.	C	63	233	36	57	17	0	3	29	7	.245
1999	Michigan	Midwest	C	4	10	1	1	1	0	0	0	0	.100
2000	Michigan	Midwest	C	109	390	57	110	33	0	10	71	2	.282
2001	Lexington	So.Atl.	C	122	443	72	122	24	1	22	73	4	.275
2002	Round Rock	Texas	C	120	448	48	118	29	3	12	89	2	.263
2003	New Orleans	P.C.	C	78	274	32	70	18	2	2	39	1	.255
2004	New Orleans	P.C.	C	65	227	31	68	11	0	12	35	0	.300
2004	Kansas City a	A.L.	C	71	238	36	56	9	0	12	30	1	.235
2005	Kansas City	A.L.	C	118	401	40	97	21	1	12	47	2	.242
2006	Kansas City	A.L.	C	114	371	37	91	21	1	11	50	0	.245
2007	Kansas City	A.L.	C	113	347	41	77	18	0	18	48	0	.222
2008	Kansas City	A.L.	C	109	370	48	83	23	1	9	48	0	.224
2009	Omaha	P.C.	C	7	27	3	7	1	0	2	4	0	.259
2009	Kansas City b-c	A.L.	C	59	186	16	46	12	4	8	36	1	.247
2010	New Hampshire	Eastern	C	3	11	2	3	0	0	2	6	0	.273
2010	Toronto d-e	A.L.	C	118	409	53	115	25	0	20	66	0	.281
2011	Florida	N.L.	C	140	466	41	106	15	1	16	57	0	.227
2012	Miami f-g	N.L.	C	106	343	29	66	15	1	12	41	0	.192
2013	NY-Pittsburgh h-i	N.L.	C	110	392	39	87	11	0	15	62	2	.222
Major League Totals			10 Yrs.	1058	3523	380	824	170	9	133	485	6	.234
	Division Series												
2013	Pittsburgh	N.L.	C	1	0	0	0	0	0	0	0	0	.000

a Traded by Houston Astros to Kansas City Royals with pitcher Octavio Dotel for outfielder Carlos Beltran, June 24, 2004.

b On disabled list from May 31 to July 6, 2009.

c Not offered contract, December 12, 2009. Signed with Toronto Blue Jays, December 16, 2009.

d On disabled list from August 5 to August 20, 2010.

e Filed for free agency, November 1, 2010. Signed with Florida Marlins, November 16, 2010.

f Traded to Toronto Blue Jays with outfielder Emilio Bonifacio, pitcher Mark Buehrle, pitcher Josh Johnson and infielder Jose Reyes for pitcher Henderson Alvarez, infielder Yunel Escobar, infielder Adeiny Hechavarria, catcher Jeff Mathis, pitcher Anthony De Sclafani, outfielder Jake Marisnick and pitcher Justin Nicolino, November 19, 2012.

g Traded to New York Mets with pitcher Noah Syndergaard, catcher Travis D'Arnaud and outfielder Wuilmer Becerra for catcher Josh Thole, catcher Mike Nickeas and pitcher R.A. Dickey, December 17, 2012.

h Traded to Pittsburgh Pirates with outfielder Marlon Byrd and cash for infielder Dilson Herrera and player to be named later, August 28, 2013. New York Mets received pitcher Vic Black to complete trade, August 29, 2013.

i Filed for free agency, October 31, 2013. Signed with Seattle Mariners, January 16, 2014.

BUTLER, BILLY RAY

Born, Orange Park, Florida, April 18, 1986.
Bats Right. Throws Right. Height, 6 feet, 1 inch. Weight, 240 pounds.

Year	Club	Lea	Pos	G	AB	R	H	2B	3B	HR	RBI	SB	Avg
2004	Idaho Falls	Pioneer	3B	72	260	74	97	22	3	10	68	5	.373
2005	High Desert	Calif.	3B-OF	92	379	70	132	30	2	25	91	0	.348
2005	Wichita	Texas	OF	29	112	14	35	9	0	5	19	0	.313
2006	Wichita	Texas	OF	119	477	82	158	33	1	15	96	1	.331
2007	Omaha	P.C.	OF-1B	57	203	40	59	10	1	13	46	1	.291
2007	Kansas City	A.L.	DH-1B-OF	92	329	38	96	23	2	8	52	0	.292
2008	Omaha	P.C.	1B	26	101	18	34	6	1	5	13	0	.337
2008	Kansas City	A.L.	DH-1B	124	443	44	122	22	0	11	55	0	.275
2009	Kansas City	A.L.	1B	159	608	78	183	51	1	21	93	1	.301
2010	Kansas City	A.L.	1B	158	595	77	189	45	0	15	78	0	.318
2011	Kansas City	A.L.	DH-1B	159	597	74	174	44	0	19	95	2	.291
2012	Kansas City	A.L.	DH-1B	161	614	72	192	32	1	29	107	2	.313
2013	Kansas City	A.L.	DH-1B	*162	582	62	168	27	0	15	82	0	.289
Major League Totals			7 Yrs.	1015	3768	445	1124	244	4	118	562	5	.298

BYRD, MARLON JERRARD

Born, Boynton Beach, Florida, August 30, 1977.
Bats Right. Throws Right. Height, 6 feet. Weight, 215 pounds.

Year	Club	Lea	Pos	G	AB	R	H	2B	3B	HR	RBI	SB	Avg
1999	Batavia	N.Y.-Penn.	OF	65	243	40	72	7	6	13	50	8	.296
2000	Piedmont	So.Atl.	OF	133	515	104	159	29	13	17	93	41	.309
2001	Reading	Eastern	OF	137	510	108	161	22	8	28	89	32	.316
2002	Scranton/WB	Int.	OF	136	538	103	160	37	7	15	63	15	.297
2002	Philadelphia	N.L.	OF	10	35	2	8	2	0	1	1	0	.229
2003	Scranton/WB	Int.	OF	1	4	1	3	1	0	0	0	0	.750
2003	Reading	Eastern	OF	3	16	3	5	0	0	1	3	0	.313
2003	Philadelphia a	N.L.	OF	135	495	86	150	28	4	7	45	11	.303
2004	Scranton/WB	Int.	OF	37	152	13	40	11	1	2	17	2	.263
2004	Philadelphia	N.L.	OF	106	346	48	79	13	2	5	33	2	.228
2005	Scranton/WB	Int.	OF	5	19	4	7	1	0	3	5	0	.368
2005	New Orleans	P.C.	OF	21	81	19	33	6	0	5	11	4	.407
2005	Philadelphia-Wash. b-c	N.L.	OF	79	229	20	61	15	2	2	26	5	.266
2006	Washington	N.L.	OF	78	197	28	44	8	1	5	18	3	.223
2006	New Orleans d	P.C.	OF	46	155	20	42	9	0	7	29	3	.271
2007	Oklahoma	P.C.	OF	44	176	29	63	15	2	6	32	3	.358
2007	Texas	A.L.	OF	109	414	60	127	17	8	10	70	5	.307
2008	Oklahoma	P.C.	OF	4	16	3	5	2	0	0	3	0	.313
2008	Texas e	A.L.	OF	122	403	70	120	28	4	10	53	7	.298
2009	Texas f	A.L.	OF	146	547	66	155	43	2	20	89	8	.283
2010	Chicago	N.L.	OF	152	580	84	170	39	2	12	66	5	.293
2011	Iowa	P.C.	OF	4	15	4	4	1	0	1	3	1	.267
2011	Chicago g	N.L.	OF	119	446	51	123	22	2	9	35	3	.276
2012	Chicago	N.L.	OF	13	43	1	3	0	0	0	2	0	.070
2012	Boston h-i-j	A.L.	OF	34	100	9	27	2	0	1	7	0	.270
2013	NY-Pittsburgh k-l-m	N.L.	OF	147	532	75	155	35	5	24	88	2	.291
Major League Totals			12 Yrs.	1250	4367	600	1222	252	32	106	533	51	.280
Wild Card Playoff													
2013	Pittsburgh	N.L.	OF	1	4	1	2	0	0	1	2	0	.500
Division Series													
2013	Pittsburgh	N.L.	OF	5	18	3	6	2	0	0	3	0	.333

a On disabled list from April 14 to April 29, 2003.
b On disabled list from March 29 to May 3, 2005.
c Traded to Washington Nationals for outfielder Endy Chavez, May 14, 2005.
d Filed for free agency, October 2, 2006. Signed with Texas Rangers, December 8, 2006.
e On disabled list from April 17 to May 14, 2008.
f Filed for free agency, November 5, 2009. Signed with Chicago Cubs, December 31, 2009.
g On disabled list from May 22 to July 2, 2011.
h Traded to Boston Red Sox with cash for pitcher Michael Bowden and player to be named later, April 21, 2012. Chicago Cubs Sox received pitcher Hunter Cervenka to complete trade, May 15, 2012.
i Released by Boston Red Sox, June 12, 2012.
j Suspended for 50 games for performance-enhancing drug use, June 25, 2012.
k Signed with New York Mets organization, February 1, 2013.
l Traded to Pittsburgh Pirates with catcher John Buck and cash for infielder Dilson Herrera and player to be named later, August 28, 2013. New York Mets received pitcher Vic Black to complete trade, August 29, 2013.
m Filed for free agency, October 31, 2013. Signed with Philadelphia Phillies, November 12, 2013.

CABRERA, ASDRUBAL JOSE

Born, Puerto La Cruz, Venezuela, November 13, 1985.
Bats Both. Throws Right. Height, 6 feet. Weight, 170 pounds.

Year	Club	Lea	Pos	G	AB	R	H	2B	3B	HR	RBI	SB	Avg
2004	Everett	Northwest	SS-2B-3B	63	239	44	65	16	3	5	41	7	.272
2005	Inland Empire	Calif.	SS	55	225	31	64	15	6	1	26	3	.284
2005	Wisconsin	Midwest	2B-SS-3B	51	192	26	61	12	3	4	30	2	.318
2005	Tacoma	P.C.	SS	6	23	4	5	0	1	0	3	0	.217
2006	Buffalo	Int.	SS	52	190	26	50	11	0	1	14	5	.263
2006	Tacoma a	P.C.	SS	60	203	27	48	12	2	3	22	7	.236
2007	Akron	Eastern	SS-2B	96	368	78	114	23	3	8	54	23	.310
2007	Buffalo	Int.	SS-2B	9	38	6	12	3	0	0	3	2	.316
2007	Cleveland	A.L.	2B-SS-3B	45	159	30	45	9	2	3	22	0	.283
2008	Buffalo	Int.	SS-2B	34	141	25	46	7	1	4	13	2	.326
2008	Cleveland	A.L.	2B-SS	114	352	48	91	20	0	6	47	4	.259
2009	Akron	Eastern	SS	4	16	5	4	1	0	0	0	2	.250
2009	Cleveland b	A.L.	SS-2B	131	523	81	161	42	4	6	68	17	.308
2010	Mahoning Valley	N.Y.-Penn.	SS	2	6	0	2	1	0	0	2	0	.333
2010	Akron	Eastern	SS	4	14	4	5	2	0	1	1	2	.357
2010	Cleveland c	A.L.	SS	97	381	39	105	16	1	3	29	6	.276
2011	Cleveland	A.L.	SS	151	604	87	165	32	3	25	92	17	.273
2012	Cleveland	A.L.	SS	143	555	70	150	35	1	16	68	9	.270
2013	Cleveland d	A.L.	SS	136	508	66	123	35	2	14	64	9	.242
Major League Totals			7 Yrs.	817	3082	421	840	189	13	73	390	62	.273
	Wild Card Playoff												
2013	Cleveland	A.L.	SS	1	4	0	0	0	0	0	0	0	.000
	Division Series												
2007	Cleveland	A.L.	2B	4	17	3	3	0	0	1	2	0	.176
	Championship Series												
2007	Cleveland	A.L.	2B	7	29	2	7	0	0	0	4	0	.241

a Traded to Cleveland Indians by Seattle Mariners for outfielder Eduardo Perez, June 30, 2006.
b On disabled list from June 3 to June 28, 2009.
c On disabled list from May 18 to July 20, 2010.
d On disabled list from June 4 to June 26, 2013.

CABRERA, EVERTH

Born, Nandaime, Nicaragua, November 17, 1986.
Bats Both. Throws Right. Height, 5 feet, 10 inches. Weight, 175 pounds.

Year	Club	Lea	Pos	G	AB	R	H	2B	3B	HR	RBI	SB	Avg
2006	Casper	Pioneer	2B	54	185	30	47	4	2	0	14	18	.254
2007	Modesto	Calif.	2B	4	15	3	4	0	1	0	2	1	.267
2007	Tri-City	Northwest	2B-SS	42	150	29	45	8	3	1	23	12	.300
2008	Asheville a	So.Atl.	2B-SS	121	479	80	136	25	6	6	38	73	.284
2009	Lake Elsinore	Calif.	SS-2B	7	23	7	9	1	1	0	4	4	.391
2009	Portland	P.C.	SS	7	27	5	9	2	0	0	0	1	.333
2009	San Diego b	N.L.	SS	103	377	59	96	18	8	2	31	25	.255
2010	Lake Elsinore	Calif.	SS	3	10	1	3	0	0	0	1	1	.300
2010	Portland	P.C.	SS	8	31	7	8	1	0	0	3	3	.258
2010	San Diego c	N.L.	SS-2B	76	212	22	44	6	3	1	22	10	.208
2011	San Diego	N.L.	SS	2	8	1	1	0	0	0	0	2	.125
2011	Tucson	P.C.	SS	58	246	52	73	12	4	2	15	29	.297
2012	Tucson	P.C.	SS-3B-OF-2B	34	144	27	48	9	1	0	15	15	.333
2012	San Diego	N.L.	SS-2B-3B	115	398	49	98	19	3	2	24	*44	.246
2013	Fort Wayne	Midwest	SS	2	7	1	0	0	0	0	0	0	.000
2013	San Diego d-e	N.L.	SS	95	381	54	108	15	5	4	31	37	.283
Major League Totals			5 Yrs.	391	1376	185	347	58	19	9	108	118	.252

a Selected by San Diego Padres from Colorado Rockies in Rule V draft, December 11, 2008.
b On disabled list from April 20 to June 19, 2009.
c On disabled list from April 27 to May 14 and May 24 to June 25, 2010.
d On disabled list from June 17 to July 5, 2013.
e Suspended for 50 games for performance-enhancing drug use, August 5, 2013.

CABRERA, JOSE MIGUEL (MIGUEL)

Born, Maracay, Venezuela, April 18, 1983.
Bats Right. Throws Right. Height, 6 feet, 2 inches. Weight, 240 pounds.

Year	Club	Lea	Pos	G	AB	R	H	2B	3B	HR	RBI	SB	Avg
2000	Marlins	Gulf Coast	SS	57	219	38	57	10	2	2	22	1	.260
2000	Utica	N.Y.-Penn	SS	8	32	3	8	2	0	0	6	0	.250

Year Club	Lea	Pos	G	AB	R	H	2B	3B	HR	RBI	SB	Avg
2001 Kane County	Midwest	SS	110	422	61	134	19	4	7	66	3	.318
2002 Jupiter	Fla.St.	3B	124	478	77	134	43	1	9	75	10	.274
2003 Carolina	Southern	3B-OF	69	266	46	97	29	3	10	59	9	.365
2003 Florida	N.L.	OF-3B	87	314	39	84	21	3	12	62	0	.268
2004 Florida	N.L.	OF	160	603	101	177	31	1	33	112	5	.294
2005 Florida	N.L.	OF-3B	158	613	106	198	43	2	33	116	1	.323
2006 Florida	N.L.	3B	158	576	112	195	50	2	26	114	9	.339
2007 Florida a	N.L.	3B	157	588	91	188	38	2	34	119	2	.320
2008 Detroit	A.L.	1B-3B	160	616	85	180	36	2	*37	127	1	.292
2009 Detroit	A.L.	1B	160	611	96	198	34	0	34	103	6	.324
2010 Detroit	A.L.	1B	150	548	111	180	45	1	38	*126	3	.328
2011 Detroit	A.L.	1B	*161	572	111	197	*48	0	30	105	2	*.344
2012 Detroit b	A.L.	3B-1B	161	622	109	205	40	0	*44	*139	4	*.330
2013 Detroit c	A.L.	3B	148	555	103	193	26	1	44	137	3	*.348
Major League Totals		11 Yrs.	1660	6218	1064	1995	412	14	365	1260	36	.321
Division Series												
2003 Florida	N.L.	3B	4	14	1	4	2	0	0	3	0	.286
2011 Detroit	A.L.	1B	5	15	2	3	0	0	1	3	1	.200
2012 Detroit	A.L.	3B	5	20	1	5	2	0	0	1	0	.250
2013 Detroit	A.L.	3B	5	20	1	5	0	0	1	3	0	.250
Division Series Totals			19	69	5	17	4	0	2	10	1	.246
Championship Series												
2003 Florida	N.L.	OF-3B-SS	7	30	9	10	0	0	3	6	0	.333
2011 Detroit	A.L.	1B	6	20	5	8	4	0	3	7	1	.400
2012 Detroit	A.L.	3B	4	16	3	5	1	0	1	4	0	.313
2013 Detroit	A.L.	3B	6	22	3	6	0	0	1	4	1	.273
Championship Series Totals			23	88	20	29	5	0	8	21	2	.330
World Series Record												
2003 Florida	N.L.	OF	6	24	1	4	0	0	1	3	0	.167
2012 Detroit	A.L.	3B	4	13	1	3	0	0	1	3	0	.231
World Series Totals			10	37	2	7	0	0	2	6	0	.189

a Traded to Detroit Tigers with pitcher Dontrelle Willis for pitcher Burke Badenhop, pitcher Eulogio De La Cruz, pitcher Andrew Miller, catcher Mike Rabelo and outfielder Cameron Maybin, December 5, 2007.

b Selected Most Valuable Player in American League for 2012.

c Selected Most Valuable Player in American League for 2013.

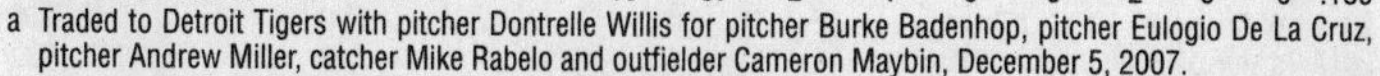

CABRERA, MELKY

Born, Santo Domingo, Dominican Republic, August 11, 1984.
Bats Both. Throws Left. Height, 5 feet, 11 inches. Weight, 200 pounds.

Year Club	Lea	Pos	G	AB	R	H	2B	3B	HR	RBI	SB	Avg
2003 Staten Island	N.Y.-Penn.	OF	67	279	34	79	10	2	2	31	13	.283
2004 Tampa	Fla.St.	OF	85	333	48	96	20	3	8	51	3	.288
2004 Battle Creek	Midwest	OF	42	171	35	57	16	3	0	16	7	.333
2005 New York	A.L.	OF	6	19	1	4	0	0	0	0	0	.211
2005 Columbus	Int.	OF	26	101	15	25	3	0	3	17	2	.248
2005 Trenton	Eastern	OF	106	426	57	117	22	3	10	60	11	.275
2006 Columbus	Int.	OF	31	122	19	47	6	2	4	24	3	.385
2006 New York	A.L.	OF	130	460	75	129	26	2	7	50	12	.280
2007 New York	A.L.	OF	150	545	66	149	24	8	8	73	13	.273
2008 Scranton-WB	Int.	OF	15	57	8	19	2	0	0	5	1	.333
2008 New York	A.L.	OF	129	414	42	103	12	1	8	37	9	.249
2009 New York a	A.L.	OF	154	485	66	133	28	1	13	68	10	.274
2010 Atlanta b	N.L.	OF	147	458	50	117	27	3	4	42	7	.255
2011 Kansas City c	A.L.	OF	155	658	102	201	44	5	18	87	20	.305
2012 San Francisco d-e	N.L.	OF	113	459	84	159	25	10	11	60	13	.346
2013 Dunedin	Fla.St.	OF	2	6	0	1	0	0	0	0	0	.167
2013 New Hampshire	Eastern	OF	3	11	1	4	0	0	1	2	1	.364
2013 Buffalo	Int.	OF	2	5	1	3	0	0	0	1	0	.600
2013 Toronto f	A.L.	OF	88	344	39	96	15	2	3	30	2	.279
Major League Totals		9 Yrs.	1072	3842	525	1091	201	32	72	447	86	.284
Division Series												
2006 New York	A.L.	OF	2	3	0	0	0	0	0	0	0	.000
2007 New York	A.L.	OF	4	16	2	3	0	0	1	2	0	.188
2009 New York	A.L.	OF	3	12	1	2	0	0	0	0	0	.167
2010 Atlanta	N.L.	OF	3	8	1	0	0	0	0	1	0	.000
Division Series Totals			12	39	4	5	0	0	1	3	0	.128

Year	Club	Lea	Pos	G	AB	R	H	2B	3B	HR	RBI	SB	Avg
	Championship Series												
2009	New York	A.L.	OF	6	23	3	9	2	0	0	4	0	.391
	World Series Record												
2009	New York	A.L.	OF	4	13	1	2	0	0	0	0	0	.154

a Traded to Atlanta Braves with pitcher Arodys Vizcaino, pitcher Michael Dunn and cash for pitcher Javier Vazquez and pitcher Boone Logan, December 22, 2009.
b Released by Atlanta Braves, October 18, 2010. Signed with Kansas City Royals, December 10, 2010.
c Traded to San Francisco Giants for pitcher Jonathan Sanchez and pitcher Ryan Verdugo, November 7, 2011.
d Suspended for 50 games for performance-enhancing drug use, August 15, 2012.
e Filed for free agency, November 3, 2012. Signed with Toronto Blue Jays, November 19, 2012.
f On disabled list from June 28 to July 21 and August 2 to October 31, 2013.

CAIN, LORENZO LAMAR

Born, Valdosta, Georgia, April 13, 1986.
Bats Right. Throws Right. Height, 6 feet, 2 inches. Weight, 200 pounds.

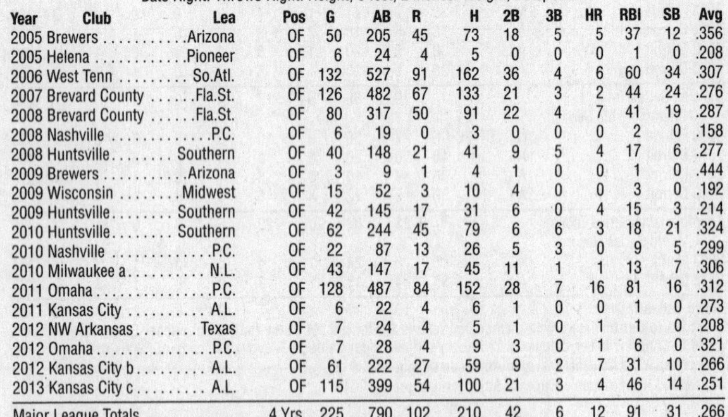

Year	Club	Lea	Pos	G	AB	R	H	2B	3B	HR	RBI	SB	Avg
2005	Brewers	Arizona	OF	50	205	45	73	18	5	5	37	12	.356
2005	Helena	Pioneer	OF	6	24	4	5	0	0	0	1	0	.208
2006	West Tenn	So.Atl.	OF	132	527	91	162	36	4	6	60	34	.307
2007	Brevard County	Fla.St.	OF	126	482	67	133	21	3	2	44	24	.276
2008	Brevard County	Fla.St.	OF	80	317	50	91	22	4	7	41	19	.287
2008	Nashville	P.C.	OF	6	19	0	3	0	0	0	2	0	.158
2008	Huntsville	Southern	OF	40	148	21	41	9	5	4	17	6	.277
2009	Brewers	Arizona	OF	3	9	1	4	1	0	0	1	0	.444
2009	Wisconsin	Midwest	OF	15	52	3	10	4	0	0	3	0	.192
2009	Huntsville	Southern	OF	42	145	17	31	6	0	4	15	3	.214
2010	Huntsville	Southern	OF	62	244	45	79	6	6	3	18	21	.324
2010	Nashville	P.C.	OF	22	87	13	26	5	3	0	9	5	.299
2010	Milwaukee a	N.L.	OF	43	147	17	45	11	1	1	13	7	.306
2011	Omaha	P.C.	OF	128	487	84	152	28	7	16	81	16	.312
2011	Kansas City	A.L.	OF	6	22	4	6	1	0	0	1	0	.273
2012	NW Arkansas	Texas	OF	7	24	4	5	1	0	1	1	0	.208
2012	Omaha	P.C.	OF	7	28	4	9	3	0	1	6	0	.321
2012	Kansas City b	A.L.	OF	61	222	27	59	9	2	7	31	10	.266
2013	Kansas City c	A.L.	OF	115	399	54	100	21	3	4	46	14	.251
Major League Totals			4 Yrs.	225	790	102	210	42	6	12	91	31	.266

a Traded to Kansas City Royals with infielder Alcides Escobar, pitcher Jeremy Jeffress and pitcher Jake Odorizzi for outfielder Yuniesky Betancourt and pitcher Zack Greinke, December 19, 2010.
b On disabled list from April 11 to July 9, 2012.
c On disabled list from August 9 to September 4, 2013.

CALHOUN, KOLE ALAN

Born, Buckeye, Arizona, October 14, 1987.
Bats Left. Throws Left. Height, 5 feet, 10 inches. Weight, 190 pounds.

Year	Club	Lea	Pos	G	AB	R	H	2B	3B	HR	RBI	SB	Avg
2010	Orem	Pioneer	OF	56	202	43	59	14	4	7	42	3	.292
2011	Inland Empire	Calif.	OF-1B	133	512	94	166	36	6	22	99	20	.324
2012	Salt Lake	P.C.	OF-1B	105	410	79	122	30	7	14	73	12	.298
2012	Los Angeles	A.L.	OF	21	23	2	4	1	0	0	1	1	.174
2013	Salt Lake	P.C.	OF	59	240	48	85	15	6	12	49	10	.354
2013	Los Angeles	A.L.	OF-1B	58	195	29	55	7	2	8	32	2	.282
Major League Totals			2 Yrs.	79	218	31	59	8	2	8	33	3	.271

CALLASPO, ALBERTO JOSE

Born, Maracay, Venezuela, April 19, 1983.
Bats Both. Throws Right. Height, 5 feet, 10 inches. Weight, 180 pounds.

Year	Club	Lea	Pos	G	AB	R	H	2B	3B	HR	RBI	SB	Avg
2002	Provo	Pioneer	2B-SS	70	299	70	101	16	10	3	60	13	.338
2003	Cedar Rapids	Midwest	2B-SS	133	514	86	168	38	4	2	67	20	.327
2004	Arkansas	Texas	SS-2B	136	550	76	156	29	2	6	48	15	.284
2005	Salt Lake	P.C.	2B	50	212	28	67	21	2	1	31	2	.316
2005	Arkansas	Texas	2B	89	350	53	104	8	0	10	49	9	.297
2006	Tucson	P.C.	2B-SS-3B-OF	114	490	93	165	24	12	7	68	8	.337
2006	Arizona a	N.L.	SS-2B-3B	23	42	2	10	1	1	0	6	0	.238
2007	Tucson	P.C.	SS-2B-3B	59	226	48	77	15	2	5	30	1	.341

Year	Club	Lea	Pos	G	AB	R	H	2B	3B	HR	RBI	SB	Avg
2007	Arizona b	N.L.	3B-2B-OF-SS	56	144	10	31	8	0	0	7	1	.215
2008	Omaha	P.C.	2B	4	16	5	3	0	0	0	0	0	.188
2008	Kansas City c	A.L.	2B-SS-OF-3B	74	213	21	65	8	3	0	16	2	.305
2009	Kansas City	A.L.	2B-3B-SS	155	576	79	173	41	8	11	73	2	.300
2010	Kansas City-LA d	A.L.	3B-2B-OF	146	562	61	149	27	2	10	56	5	.265
2011	Los Angeles	A.L.	3B	141	475	54	137	23	0	6	46	8	.288
2012	Los Angeles	A.L.	3B	138	457	55	115	20	0	10	53	4	.252
2013	Inland Empire	Calif.	3B	3	7	1	2	0	0	1	3	0	.286
2013	LA-Oakland e-f	A.L.	3B-2B	136	453	52	117	20	0	10	58	0	.258
Major League Totals			8 Yrs.	869	2922	334	797	148	14	47	315	22	.273
	Division Series												
2013	Oakland	A.L.	2B	4	6	0	1	1	0	0	0	0	.167
	Championship Series												
2007	Arizona	N.L.	PH	2	2	0	0	0	0	0	0	0	.000

a Traded by Los Angeles Angels to Arizona Diamondbacks for pitcher Jason Bulger, February 28, 2006.
b Traded to Kansas City Royals for pitcher Billy Buckner, December 14, 2007.
c On disabled list from June 28 to August 23, 2008.
d Traded to Anaheim Angels for pitcher Sean O'Sullivan and pitcher Will Smith, July 22, 2010.
e On disabled list from April 12 to May 3, 2013.
f Traded to Oakland Athletics for infielder Grant Green, July 31, 2013.

CANO (MERCEDES), ROBINSON JOSE

Born, San Pedro de Macoris, Dominican Republic, October 22, 1982.
Bats Left. Throws Right. Height, 6 feet. Weight, 200 pounds.

Year	Club	Lea	Pos	G	AB	R	H	2B	3B	HR	RBI	SB	Avg
2001	Yankees	Gulf Coast	2B-SS-3B	57	200	37	46	14	2	3	34	11	.230
2001	Staten Island	N.Y.-Penn.	3B-SS	2	8	0	2	0	0	0	2	0	.250
2002	Staten Island	N.Y.-Penn.	2B-SS	22	87	11	24	5	1	1	15	6	.276
2002	Greensboro	So.Atl.	SS-2B	113	474	67	131	20	9	14	66	2	.276
2003	Trenton	Eastern	2B-SS-C	46	164	21	46	9	1	1	13	0	.280
2003	Tampa	Fla.St.	2B	90	366	50	101	16	3	5	50	1	.276
2004	Trenton	Eastern	2B-3B	74	292	43	88	20	8	7	44	2	.301
2004	Columbus	Int.	2B	61	216	22	56	9	2	6	30	0	.259
2005	Columbus	Int.	2B-3B	24	108	19	36	8	3	4	24	0	.333
2005	New York	A.L.	2B	132	522	78	155	34	4	14	62	1	.297
2006	Yankees	Gulf Coast	DH	1	5	0	2	0	0	0	1	0	.400
2006	Trenton	Eastern	2B	3	10	1	5	2	0	0	2	0	.500
2006	New York a	A.L.	2B	122	482	62	165	41	1	15	78	5	.342
2007	New York	A.L.	2B	160	617	93	189	41	7	19	97	4	.306
2008	New York	A.L.	2B	159	597	70	162	35	3	14	72	2	.271
2009	New York	A.L.	2B	*161	637	103	204	48	2	25	85	5	.320
2010	New York	A.L.	2B	160	626	103	200	41	3	29	109	3	.319
2011	New York	A.L.	2B	159	623	104	188	46	7	28	118	8	.302
2012	New York	A.L.	2B	161	627	105	196	48	1	33	94	3	.313
2013	New York b	A.L.	2B-SS	160	605	81	190	41	0	27	107	7	.314
Major League Totals			9 Yrs.	1374	5336	799	1649	375	28	204	822	38	.309
	Division Series												
2005	New York	A.L.	2B	5	19	3	5	3	0	0	5	0	.263
2006	New York	A.L.	2B	4	15	0	2	0	0	0	0	0	.133
2007	New York	A.L.	2B	4	15	3	5	1	0	2	3	0	.333
2009	New York	A.L.	2B	3	12	1	2	0	0	0	1	0	.167
2010	New York	A.L.	2B	3	12	3	4	0	1	0	1	0	.333
2011	New York	A.L.	2B	5	22	2	7	2	0	2	9	0	.318
2012	New York	A.L.	2B	5	22	1	2	2	0	0	4	0	.091
Division Series Totals				29	117	13	27	8	1	4	23	0	.231
	Championship Series												
2009	New York	A.L.	2B	6	23	4	6	1	2	0	4	0	.261
2010	New York	A.L.	2B	6	23	5	8	1	0	4	5	0	.348
2012	New York	A.L.	2B	4	18	0	1	0	0	0	0	0	.056
Championship Series Totals				16	64	9	15	2	2	4	9	0	.234
	World Series Record												
2009	New York	A.L.	2B	6	22	0	3	0	0	0	1	0	.136

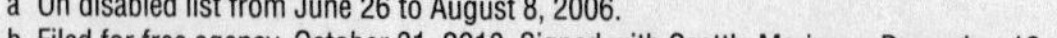

a On disabled list from June 26 to August 8, 2006.
b Filed for free agency, October 31, 2013. Signed with Seattle Mariners, December 12, 2013.

CARP, CHRISTOPHER MICHAEL (MIKE)

Born, Long Beach, California, June 30, 1986.
Bats Left. Throws Right. Height, 6 feet, 2 inches. Weight, 210 pounds.

Year	Club	Lea	Pos	G	AB	R	H	2B	3B	HR	RBI	SB	Avg
2004	Mets	Gulf Coast	1B-3B-OF	57	191	30	51	12	0	4	26	2	.267
2005	Hagerstown	So.Atl.	1B-3B	89	313	49	78	12	1	19	63	2	.249
2006	St. Lucie	Fla.St.	1B	137	491	69	141	27	1	17	88	2	.287
2007	St. Lucie	Fla.St.	1B	1	4	0	1	0	0	0	0	0	.250
2007	Binghamton	Eastern	1B	97	359	55	90	16	0	11	48	2	.251
2008	Binghamton a	Eastern	1B-OF	134	478	67	143	29	1	17	72	1	.299
2009	Tacoma	P.C.	1B-OF	110	413	66	112	25	1	15	64	0	.271
2009	Seattle	A.L.	1B	21	54	7	17	3	1	1	5	0	.315
2010	Tacoma	P.C.	1B-OF	110	409	67	105	17	1	29	76	1	.257
2010	Seattle	A.L.	1B-OF	14	37	1	7	2	0	0	0	0	.189
2011	Tacoma	P.C.	OF-1B	66	251	55	86	14	0	21	64	6	.343
2011	Seattle	A.L.	1B-OF	79	290	27	80	17	1	12	46	0	.276
2012	High Desert	Calif.	DH	2	9	2	6	1	0	1	4	1	.667
2012	Tacoma	P.C.	1B-OF	35	139	13	31	8	0	2	17	1	.223
2012	Seattle b	A.L.	OF-1B	59	164	17	35	6	0	5	20	1	.213
2013	Boston c	A.L.	OF-1B	86	216	34	64	18	2	9	43	1	.296
Major League Totals			5 Yrs.	259	761	86	203	46	4	27	114	2	.267
	Division Series												
2013	Boston	A.L.	PH	1	1	0	0	0	0	0	0	0	.000
	Championship Series												
2013	Boston	A.L.	1B	3	5	0	0	0	0	0	0	0	.000
	World Series Record												
2013	Boston	A.L.	PH	2	2	0	0	0	0	0	1	0	.000

a Traded by New York Mets to Seattle Mariners with pitcher Aaron Heilman, outfielder Endy Chavez, pitcher Jason Vargas, outfielder Ezequiel Carrera, pitcher Maikel Cleto and pitcher Joe Smith for pitcher J.J. Putz, pitcher Sean Green and outfielder Jeremy Reed, December 10, 2008.

b On disabled list from March 29 to May 1 and June 11 to July 24 and August 13 to September 4, 2012.

c Sold to Boston Red Sox, February 20, 2013.

CARPENTER, MATT MARTIN

Born, Sugar Land, Texas, November 26, 1985.
Bats Left. Throws Right. Height, 6 feet, 3 inches. Weight, 200 pounds.

Year	Club	Lea	Pos	G	AB	R	H	2B	3B	HR	RBI	SB	Avg
2009	Palm Beach	Fla.St.	3B	32	114	13	25	6	1	2	9	1	.219
2009	Quad Cities	Midwest	3B	29	105	11	31	6	2	0	10	2	.295
2009	Batavia	N.Y.-Penn.	3B-1B	9	32	9	15	3	0	0	3	0	.469
2010	Palm Beach	Fla.St.	3B	28	99	17	28	5	2	1	16	0	.283
2010	Springfield	Texas	3B	105	396	76	125	26	3	12	53	11	.316
2011	Memphis	P.C.	3B	130	434	61	130	29	3	12	70	5	.300
2011	St. Louis	N.L.	3B	7	15	0	1	1	0	0	0	0	.067
2012	Springfield	Texas	1B-OF	3	10	3	3	0	0	1	3	0	.300
2012	Memphis	P.C.	OF-3B	3	7	1	1	0	0	0	0	0	.143
2012	St. Louis a	N.L.	1B-3B-OF-2B	114	296	44	87	22	5	6	46	1	.294
2013	St. Louis	N.L.	2B-3B-1B-OF	157	626	*126	*199	*55	7	11	78	3	.318
Major League Totals			3 Yrs.	278	937	170	287	78	12	17	124	4	.306
	Wild Card Playoff												
2012	St. Louis	N.L.	3B	1	1	0	1	0	0	0	1	0	1.000
	Division Series												
2012	St. Louis	N.L.	3B	5	4	0	0	0	0	0	0	0	.000
2013	St. Louis	N.L.	2B	5	19	1	1	0	0	0	0	0	.053
Division Series Totals				10	23	1	1	0	0	0	0	0	.043
	Championship Series												
2012	St. Louis	N.L.	1B-OF	3	9	3	3	1	0	1	2	0	.333
2013	St. Louis	N.L.	2B-3B	6	23	4	6	2	1	0	2	1	.261
Championship Series Totals				9	32	7	9	3	1	1	4	1	.281
	World Series Record												
2013	St. Louis	N.L.	2B-3B	6	27	3	8	1	0	0	2	0	.296

a On disabled list from May 23 to June 22, 2012.

CARROLL, JAMEY BLAKE

Born, Evansville, Indiana, February 18, 1974.
Bats Right. Throws Right. Height, 5 feet, 9 inches. Weight, 170 pounds.

Year	Club	Lea	Pos	G	AB	R	H	2B	3B	HR	RBI	SB	Avg
1996	Vermont	N.Y.-Penn.	SS-2B-3B	54	203	40	56	6	1	0	17	16	.276
1997	Wst Plm Bch	Fla.St.	SS-2B-3B	121	407	56	99	19	1	0	38	17	.243
1998	Jupiter	Fla.St.	2B-SS	55	222	40	58	5	0	0	14	11	.261
1998	Harrisburg	Eastern	2B-SS	75	261	43	66	11	3	0	20	11	.253
1999	Harrisburg	Eastern	2B	141	561	78	164	34	5	5	63	21	.292
2000	Harrisburg	Eastern	3B-SS-2B	45	169	23	49	5	3	0	18	8	.290
2000	Ottawa	Int.	2B-3B-SS	91	349	53	97	17	2	2	23	6	.278
2001	Ottawa	Int.	2B-SS-3B	83	267	26	64	8	2	0	16	5	.240
2002	Harrisburg	Eastern	2B	3	9	1	4	0	0	0	1	0	.444
2002	Ottawa	Int.	3B-2B-SS	117	421	57	118	19	2	8	49	6	.280
2002	Montreal	N.L.	3B-SS-2B	16	71	16	22	5	3	1	6	1	.310
2003	Montreal	N.L.	3B-SS-2B	105	227	31	59	10	1	1	10	5	.260
2004	Montreal	N.L.	2B-3B-SS-OF	102	218	36	63	14	2	0	16	5	.289
2005	Washington	N.L.	2B-SS-3B	113	303	44	76	8	1	0	22	3	.251
2006	Colorado a	N.L.	2B-SS-3B	136	463	84	139	23	5	5	36	10	.300
2007	Colorado b	N.L.	2B-3B-SS-OF	108	227	45	51	9	1	2	22	6	.225
2008	Cleveland	A.L.	2B-3B-OF	113	347	60	96	13	4	1	36	7	.277
2009	Columbus	Int.	2B-3B	3	11	2	3	1	0	0	0	0	.273
2009	Cleveland c-d	A.L.	2B-3B-OF	93	315	53	87	10	2	2	26	4	.276
2010	Los Angeles	N.L.	SS-2B-3B-OF	133	351	48	102	15	1	0	23	12	.291
2011	Los Angeles e	N.L.	2B-SS	146	452	52	131	14	6	0	17	10	.290
2012	Minnesota	A.L.	2B-3B-SS	138	470	65	126	18	1	1	40	9	.268
2013	Minnesota-KC f-g	A.L.	3B-2B-SS-P	73	227	26	48	9	0	0	11	2	.211
Major League Totals			12 Yrs.	1276	3671	560	1000	148	27	13	265	74	.272
	Division Series												
2007	Colorado	N.L.	2B	1	0	0	0	0	0	0	0	0	.000
	Championship Series												
2007	Colorado	N.L.	3B	2	1	0	0	0	0	0	0	0	.000
	World Series Record												
2007	Colorado	N.L.	2B	1	1	0	0	0	0	0	0	0	.000

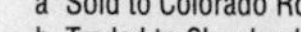

a Sold to Colorado Rockies, February 11, 2006.
b Traded to Cleveland Indians for player to be named later, December 8, 2007. Colorado Rockies received pitcher Sean Smith to complete trade, April 22, 2008
c On disabled list from April 5 to May 12, 2009.
d Filed for free agency, November 5, 2009. Signed with Los Angeles Dodgers, December 16, 2009.
e Filed for free agency, October 30, 2011. Signed with Minnesota Twins, November 16, 2011.
f Sold to Kansas City Royals, August 12, 2013.
g Filed for free agency, October 11, 2013. Signed with Washington Nationals organization, January 9, 2014.

CARTER, VERNON CHRISTOPHER (CHRIS)

Born, Redwood City, California, December 18, 1986.
Bats Right. Throws Right. Height, 6 feet, 5 inches. Weight, 245 pounds.

Year	Club	Lea	Pos	G	AB	R	H	2B	3B	HR	RBI	SB	Avg
2005	Bristol	Appal.	3B-1B-SS	65	233	33	66	17	0	10	37	2	.283
2006	Great Falls	Pioneer	1B	69	251	37	75	21	1	15	59	4	.299
2006	Kannapolis	So.Atl.	1B	13	46	4	6	3	0	1	5	0	.130
2007	Kannapolis a-b	So.Atl.	1B	126	467	84	136	27	3	25	93	3	.291
2008	Stockton	Calif.	1B-3B-OF	137	506	101	131	32	4	39	104	4	.259
2009	Sacramento	P.C.	1B-OF	13	54	7	14	2	0	4	14	0	.259
2009	Midland	Texas	1B-OF-3B	125	490	108	165	41	2	24	101	13	.337
2010	Sacramento	P.C.	1B-OF	125	465	92	120	29	2	31	94	1	.258
2010	Oakland	A.L.	OF	24	70	8	13	1	0	3	7	1	.186
2011	Stockton	Calif.	1B	6	24	3	8	0	0	3	7	0	.333
2011	Sacramento	P.C.	1B-OF-3B	75	296	55	81	18	2	18	72	5	.274
2011	Oakland	A.L.	1B	15	44	2	6	0	0	0	0	0	.136
2012	Sacramento	P.C.	1B	72	276	48	77	19	1	12	53	5	.279
2012	Oakland	A.L.	1B	67	218	38	52	12	0	16	39	0	.239
2013	Houston c	A.L.	1B-OF	148	506	64	113	24	2	29	82	2	.223
Major League Totals			4 Yrs.	254	838	112	184	37	2	48	128	3	.220

a Traded by Chicago White Sox to Arizona Diamondbacks for outfielder Carlos Quentin, December 3, 2007.
b Traded to Oakland Athletics with pitcher Brett Anderson, pitcher Dana Eveland, pitcher Greg Smith, outfielder Aaron Cunningham and outfielder Carlos Gonzalez for pitcher Danny Haren and pitcher Connor Robertson, December 14, 2007.
c Traded to Houston Astros with pitcher Brad Peacock and catcher Max Stassi for infielder Jed Lowrie and pitcher Franklin Rodriguez, February 4, 2013.

CASILLA (LORA), ALEXI

Born, San Cristobal, Dominican Republic, July 20, 1984.
Bats Both. Throws Right. Height, 5 feet, 9 inches. Weight, 180 pounds.

Year	Club	Lea	Pos	G	AB	R	H	2B	3B	HR	RBI	SB	Avg
2004	Angels	Arizona	2B-SS	45	163	29	42	1	4	0	10	24	.258
2004	Cedar Rapids	Midwest	2B	9	29	6	9	2	1	0	1	1	.310
2004	Provo	Pioneer	2B-3B	4	12	4	4	1	1	0	1	1	.333
2005	Cedar Rapids	Midwest	SS-2B	78	308	62	100	11	3	3	17	47	.325
2005	Salt Lake	P.C.	2B-SS	13	39	3	10	0	0	0	1	1	.256
2005	Arkansas a	Texas	SS-2B	7	19	4	4	0	0	0	4	1	.211
2006	Fort Myers	Fla.St.	2B-SS	78	323	56	107	12	6	0	33	31	.331
2006	New Britain	Eastern	SS	45	170	28	50	10	1	1	13	19	.294
2006	Minnesota	A.L.	2B-SS	9	4	1	1	0	0	0	0	0	.250
2007	Rochester	Int.	2B-SS	84	320	53	86	13	1	3	20	24	.269
2007	Minnesota	A.L.	2B-SS	56	189	15	42	5	1	0	9	11	.222
2008	Beloit	Midwest	2B	2	7	2	4	0	0	0	1	0	.571
2008	Rochester	Int.	SS-2B	32	96	11	21	3	0	0	2	4	.219
2008	Minnesota b	A.L.	2B-SS	98	385	58	108	15	0	7	50	7	.281
2009	Rochester	Int.	2B	40	156	21	53	3	4	2	17	9	.340
2009	Minnesota	A.L.	2B-SS	80	228	25	46	7	3	0	17	11	.202
2010	Twins	Gulf Coast	2B	5	14	1	2	1	0	0	0	0	.143
2010	Fort Myers	Fla.St.	2B-SS	3	12	0	2	0	0	0	1	1	.167
2010	New Britain	Eastern	2B-3B-SS	6	20	1	7	0	0	0	0	1	.350
2010	Minnesota c	A.L.	SS-2B-3B-OF	69	152	26	42	7	4	1	20	6	.276
2011	Fort Myers	Fla.St.	2B	1	2	0	0	0	0	0	0	0	.000
2011	Minnesota d	A.L.	2B-SS	97	323	52	84	21	4	2	21	15	.260
2012	Minnesota e	A.L.	2B-3B	106	299	33	72	17	2	1	30	21	.241
2013	Baltimore f	A.L.	2B-SS	62	112	15	24	4	1	1	10	9	.214
Major League Totals			8 Yrs.	577	1692	225	419	76	15	12	157	80	.248

a Traded to Minnesota Twins for pitcher J.C. Romero, December 9, 2005.
b On disabled list from July 29 to August 21, 2008.
c On disabled list from June 1 to July 22, 2010.
d On disabled list from July 28 to August 12 and August 13 to October 14, 2011.
e Claimed on waivers by Baltimore Orioles, November 2, 2012.
f Filed for free agency, November 5, 2013, re-signed with Baltimore Orioles organization, January 10, 2014.

CASTELLANOS, NICHOLAS A. (NICK)

Born, Davie, Florida, March 4, 1992.
Bats Right. Throws Right. Height, 6 feet, 4 inches. Weight, 210 pounds.

Year	Club	Lea	Pos	G	AB	R	H	2B	3B	HR	RBI	SB	Avg
2010	Tigers	Gulf Coast	3B	7	24	5	8	2	0	0	3	0	.333
2011	West Michigan	Midwest	3B	135	507	65	158	36	3	7	76	3	.312
2012	Lakeland	Fla.St.	3B	55	215	37	87	17	3	3	32	3	.405
2012	Erie	Eastern	OF-3B	79	322	35	85	15	1	7	25	5	.264
2013	Toledo	Int.	OF	134	533	81	147	37	1	18	76	4	.276
2013	Detroit	A.L.	OF	11	18	1	5	0	0	0	0	0	.278

CASTILLO, WELINGTON ANDRES

Born, San Isidro, Dominican Republic, April 24, 1987.
Bats Right. Throws Right. Height, 5 feet, 10 inches. Weight, 210 pounds.

Year	Club	Lea	Pos	G	AB	R	H	2B	3B	HR	RBI	SB	Avg
2006	Cubs	Arizona	C-1B	7	26	4	5	0	0	0	0	0	.192
2006	Boise	Northwest	C	3	6	1	1	0	0	0	0	0	.167
2007	Peoria	Midwest	C	98	317	41	86	11	2	11	44	1	.271
2008	Daytona	Fla.St.	C	33	121	15	33	8	0	0	12	1	.273
2008	Iowa	P.C.	C	1	5	0	1	0	0	0	1	0	.200
2008	Tennessee	Southern	C	57	198	25	59	11	0	4	24	0	.298
2009	Tennessee	Southern	C	95	319	27	74	16	0	11	39	1	.232
2010	Iowa	P.C.	C	69	239	35	61	17	1	13	59	0	.255
2010	Chicago	N.L.	C	7	20	3	6	4	0	1	5	0	.300
2011	Daytona	Fla.St.	C	12	42	6	10	3	0	1	7	0	.238
2011	Chicago	N.L.	C	4	13	0	2	0	0	0	0	0	.154
2011	Cubs	Arizona	C	2	6	2	4	3	0	0	0	0	.667
2011	Iowa	P.C.	C	61	227	38	65	9	0	15	35	0	.286
2012	Tennessee	Southern	C-1B	5	11	3	4	0	0	2	6	0	.364
2012	Iowa	P.C.	C	44	146	22	38	6	0	6	22	0	.260
2012	Chicago a	N.L.	C-1B	52	170	16	45	11	0	5	22	0	.265
2013	Chicago b	N.L.	C	113	380	41	104	23	0	8	32	2	.274
Major League Totals			4 Yrs.	176	583	60	157	38	0	14	59	2	.269

a On disabled list from May 19 to June 14, 2012.
b On disabled list from September 20 to October 1, 2013.

CASTRO, JASON MICHAEL

Born, Castro Valley, California, June 18, 1987.
Bats Left. Throws Right. Height, 6 feet, 3 inches. Weight, 215 pounds.

Year	Club	Lea	Pos	G	AB	R	H	2B	3B	HR	RBI	SB	Avg
2008	Tri-City	N.Y.-Penn.	C	39	138	10	38	9	0	2	12	0	.275
2009	Lancaster	Calif.	C	56	207	27	64	20	1	7	44	1	.309
2009	Corpus Christi	Texas	C	63	239	38	70	11	1	3	29	2	.293
2010	Round Rock	P.C.	C	57	211	31	56	7	0	4	26	1	.265
2010	Houston	N.L.	C	67	195	26	40	8	1	2	8	0	.205
2011	Houston a	N.L.	INJURED—Did Not Play										
2012	Corpus Christi	Texas	C	3	5	1	4	2	0	0	0	0	.800
2012	Oklahoma	P.C.	C	4	13	1	6	1	0	1	2	0	.462
2012	Houston b	N.L.	C	87	257	29	66	15	2	6	29	0	.257
2013	Houston c	A.L.	C	120	435	63	120	35	1	18	56	2	.276
Major League Totals			3 Yrs.	274	887	118	226	58	4	26	93	2	.255

a On disabled list from March 22 to October 31, 2011.
b On disabled list from July 8 to August 13, 2012.
c On disabled list from September 17 to October 1, 2013.

CASTRO, STARLIN DE JESUS

Born, Monte Cristi, Dominican Republic, March 24, 1990.
Bats Right. Throws Right. Height, 6 feet. Weight, 190 pounds.

Year	Club	Lea	Pos	G	AB	R	H	2B	3B	HR	RBI	SB	Avg
2008	Cubs	Arizona	SS-2B-3B-OF	51	196	33	61	11	5	3	22	6	.311
2009	Daytona	Fla.St.	SS	96	358	45	108	17	3	3	35	22	.302
2009	Tennessee	Southern	SS	31	111	11	32	6	3	0	14	6	.288
2010	Tennessee	Southern	SS	26	109	20	41	8	5	1	20	4	.376
2010	Chicago	N.L.	SS	125	463	53	139	31	5	3	41	10	.300
2011	Chicago	N.L.	SS	158	*674	91	*207	36	9	10	66	22	.307
2012	Chicago	N.L.	SS	*162	*646	78	183	29	12	14	78	25	.283
2013	Chicago	N.L.	SS	161	*666	59	163	34	2	10	44	9	.245
Major League Totals			4 Yrs.	606	2449	281	692	130	28	37	229	66	.283

CEDENO, RONNY ALEXANDER

Born, Puerto Cabello, Venezuela, February 2, 1983.
Bats Right. Throws Right. Height, 6 feet. Weight, 180 pounds.

Year	Club	Lea	Pos	G	AB	R	H	2B	3B	HR	RBI	SB	Avg
2001	Cubs	Arizona	SS-2B-OF	52	206	36	72	13	4	1	17	17	.350
2001	Lansing	Midwest	2B-SS-3B	17	56	9	11	4	1	1	2	0	.196
2002	Lansing	Midwest	SS-2B	98	376	44	80	17	4	2	31	14	.213
2002	Boise	Northwest	SS-2B	29	110	17	24	5	2	0	6	8	.218
2003	Daytona	Fla.St.	SS-2B	107	380	43	80	18	1	4	36	19	.211
2004	West Tenn	Southern	SS	116	384	39	107	19	5	6	48	10	.279
2005	Iowa	P.C.	SS	65	245	42	87	14	1	8	36	11	.355
2005	Chicago	N.L.	SS-2B	41	80	13	24	3	0	1	6	1	.300
2006	Chicago	N.L.	SS-2B	151	534	51	131	18	7	6	41	8	.245
2007	Iowa	P.C.	SS	75	287	52	103	15	3	10	37	6	.359
2007	Chicago	N.L.	SS-2B-3B	38	74	6	15	2	0	4	13	2	.203
2008	Chicago	N.L.	2B-SS-3B-OF	99	216	36	58	12	0	2	28	4	.269
2009	Seattle	A.L.	SS-2B-OF-3B	59	186	15	31	4	2	5	17	3	.167
2009	Pittsburgh a-b	N.L.	SS	46	155	17	40	4	1	5	21	2	.258
2010	Pittsburgh	N.L.	SS	139	468	42	120	29	3	8	38	12	.256
2011	Indianapolis	Int.	SS	4	15	2	4	1	1	0	1	0	.267
2011	Pittsburgh c-d	N.L.	SS-2B	128	413	43	103	25	3	2	32	2	.249
2012	St. Lucie	Fla.St.	SS	1	4	0	0	0	0	0	0	0	.000
2012	Buffalo	Int.	SS-2B	7	29	2	5	0	0	0	1	0	.172
2012	New York e-f	N.L.	2B-SS-3B	78	166	18	43	11	1	4	22	0	.259
2013	Houston g	A.L.	SS-1B	51	141	12	31	6	1	1	12	2	.220
2013	Lake Elsinore	Calif.	SS	2	8	1	1	1	0	0	0	0	.125
2013	San Diego h-i	N.L.	SS-3B	38	123	12	33	2	2	2	9	3	.268
Major League Totals			9 Yrs.	868	2556	265	629	116	20	40	239	39	.246
Division Series													
2007	Chicago	N.L.	PH	2	0	0	0	0	0	0	0	0	.000
2008	Chicago	N.L.	PH	1	0	0	0	0	0	0	0	1	.000
Division Series Totals				3	0	0	0	0	0	0	0	1	.000

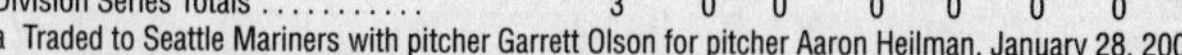

a Traded to Seattle Mariners with pitcher Garrett Olson for pitcher Aaron Heilman, January 28, 2009.
b Traded to Pittsburgh Pirates with infielder Jeff Clement, pitcher Aaron Pribanic, pitcher Brett Lorin and pitcher Nathan Adcock for infielder Jack Wilson and pitcher Ian Snell, July 29, 2009.

c On disabled list from July 2 to July 22, 2011.
d Filed for free agency, October 31, 2011. Signed with New York Mets, January 10, 2012.
e On disabled list from April 21 to May 11 and May 27 to June 22, 2012.
f Filed for free agency, November 3, 2012. Signed with St. Louis Cardinals, January 28, 2013.
g Filed for free agency, March 19, 2013. Signed with Houston Astros, March 24, 2013.
h Released by Houston Astros, July 28, 2013. Signed with San Diego Padres organization, August 3, 2013.
i Filed for free agency, October 31, 2013. Signed with Philadelphia Phillies organization, January 13, 2014.

CERVELLI, FRANCISCO

Born, Valencia, Venezuela, March 6, 1986.
Bats Right. Throws Right. Height, 6 feet, 1 inch. Weight, 205 pounds.

Year Club	Lea	Pos	G	AB	R	H	2B	3B	HR	RBI	SB	Avg
2005 Yankees	Gulf Coast	C-OF	24	58	10	11	2	0	1	9	1	.190
2006 Staten Island	N.Y.-Penn.	C	42	136	21	42	10	0	2	16	0	.309
2007 Tampa	Fla.St.	C	89	290	34	81	24	2	2	32	4	.279
2008 Tampa	Fla.St.	C	3	10	2	3	0	0	0	1	0	.300
2008 Yankees	Gulf Coast	C	3	8	0	2	1	0	0	0	0	.250
2008 Trenton............	Eastern	C	21	73	8	23	5	0	0	8	0	.315
2008 New York	A.L.	C	3	5	0	0	0	0	0	0	0	.000
2009 Trenton............	Eastern	C	16	58	8	11	1	0	2	7	0	.190
2009 Yankees	Gulf Coast	C	2	6	1	1	0	0	0	0	0	.167
2009 Scranton/WB	Int.	C	21	69	7	19	5	0	1	7	0	.275
2009 New York	A.L.	C	42	94	13	28	4	0	1	11	0	.298
2010 New York	A.L.	C-3B	93	266	27	72	11	3	0	38	1	.271
2011 Tampa	Fla.St.	C	3	10	0	3	0	0	0	1	0	.300
2011 Scranton/WB	Int.	C	3	13	2	2	0	0	0	1	0	.154
2011 New York a...........	A.L.	C-3B-2B	43	124	17	33	4	0	4	22	4	.266
2012 Scranton/WB	Int.	C	99	354	43	87	15	2	2	39	6	.246
2012 New York	A.L.	C	3	1	1	0	0	0	0	0	0	.000
2013 New York b-c..........	A.L.	C-2B	17	52	12	14	3	0	3	8	0	.269
Major League Totals		6 Yrs.	201	542	70	147	22	3	8	79	5	.271
Division Series												
2009 New York	A.L.	C	1	0	0	0	0	0	0	0	0	.000
Championship Series												
2009 New York	A.L.	PH	1	1	0	0	0	0	0	0	0	.000
2010 New York	A.L.	C	1	2	0	0	0	0	0	0	0	.000
Championship Series Totals			2	3	0	0	0	0	0	0	0	.000

a On disabled list from March 22 to April 29 and September 13 to October 11, 2011.
b Suspended for 50 games for performance-enhancing drug use, August 5, 2013.
c On disabled list from April 27 to November 4, 2013.

CESPEDES (MILANES), YOENIS

Born, Granma, Cuba, October 18, 1985.
Bats Right. Throws Right. Height, 5 feet, 10 inches. Weight, 210 pounds.

Year Club	Lea	Pos	G	AB	R	H	2B	3B	HR	RBI	SB	Avg
2012 Sacramento	P.C.	OF	3	9	1	3	0	0	0	0	0	.333
2012 Oakland a-b-c..........	A.L.	OF	129	487	70	142	25	5	23	82	16	.292
2013 Sacramento	P.C.	OF	3	9	5	3	0	0	1	4	1	.333
2013 Oakland d............	A.L.	OF	135	529	74	127	21	4	26	80	7	.240
Major League Totals		2 Yrs.	264	1016	144	269	46	9	49	162	23	.265
Division Series												
2012 Oakland	A.L.	OF	5	19	1	6	1	0	0	2	2	.316
2013 Oakland	A.L.	OF	5	21	3	8	1	1	1	4	0	.381
Division Series Totals			10	40	4	14	2	1	1	6	2	.350

a Played in Cuba 2003-2011.
b Signed with Oakland Athletics, March 3, 2012.
c On disabled list from May 7 to June 1, 2012.
d On disabled list from April 13 to April 28, 2013.

CHAVEZ, ENDY DE JESUS

Born, Valencia, Venezuela, February 7, 1978.
Bats Left. Throws Left. Height, 6 feet. Weight, 170 pounds.

Year Club	Lea	Pos	G	AB	R	H	2B	3B	HR	RBI	SB	Avg
1997 Mets...........	Gulf Coast	OF	33	119	26	33	6	3	0	15	1	.277
1997 Kingsport...........	Appal.	OF	19	73	16	22	4	0	0	4	5	.301
1998 Kingsport...........	Appal.	OF	33	114	26	33	8	4	0	16	10	.289

Year Club	Lea	Pos	G	AB	R	H	2B	3B	HR	RBI	SB	Avg
1999 St. Lucie	Fla.St.	OF	45	183	33	57	8	3	2	18	9	.311
1999 Columbia	So.Atl.	OF	73	253	40	64	8	1	0	15	20	.253
2000 St. Lucie a	Fla.St.	OF	111	433	84	129	20	2	1	43	38	.298
2001 Wichita	Texas	OF	43	168	27	50	6	1	1	13	11	.298
2001 Kansas City	A.L.	OF	29	77	4	16	2	0	0	5	0	.208
2001 Omaha b-c	P.C.	OF	23	104	18	35	6	0	0	4	4	.337
2002 Ottawa	Int.	OF	103	405	67	139	28	5	4	41	21	.343
2002 Montreal d-e	N.L.	OF	36	125	20	37	8	5	1	9	3	.296
2003 Montreal	N.L.	OF	141	483	66	121	25	5	5	47	18	.251
2004 Edmonton	P.C.	OF	14	61	9	21	3	2	0	7	5	.344
2004 Montreal	N.L.	OF	132	502	65	139	20	6	5	34	32	.277
2005 New Orleans	P.C.	OF	23	87	11	22	4	0	1	4	6	.253
2005 Washington-Philadelphia f-g	N.L.	OF	98	116	19	25	4	3	0	11	2	.216
2006 New York	N.L.	OF	133	353	48	108	22	5	4	42	12	.306
2007 Mets	Gulf Goast	OF	2	8	2	5	0	0	0	4	0	.625
2007 St. Lucie	Fla.St.	OF	4	16	3	8	1	0	0	2	0	.500
2007 Binghamton	Eastern	OF	1	3	0	0	0	0	0	0	0	.000
2007 New York h	N.L.	OF	71	150	20	43	7	2	1	17	5	.287
2008 New York i	N.L.	OF	133	270	30	72	10	2	1	12	6	.267
2009 Seattle j	A.L.	OF	54	161	17	44	3	1	2	13	9	.273
2010 Rangers	Arizona	OF	3	11	3	6	0	0	0	1	3	.545
2010 Oklahoma	P.C.	OF	1	5	2	1	1	0	0	0	0	.200
2010 Frisco k	Texas	OF	4	15	3	5	0	0	0	1	2	.333
2011 Round Rock	P.C.	OF	30	128	16	39	8	2	2	17	6	.305
2011 Texas l	A.L.	OF	83	256	37	77	11	3	5	27	10	.301
2012 Orioles	Gulf Coast	OF	1	4	0	0	0	0	0	0	0	.000
2012 Delmarva	So.Atl.	OF	3	9	2	1	0	0	0	1	0	.111
2012 Bowie	Eastern	OF	3	10	3	2	0	0	0	0	0	.200
2012 Norfolk	Int.	OF	15	47	2	7	3	0	0	4	0	.149
2012 Baltimore m-n	A.L.	OF	64	158	15	32	6	0	2	12	3	.203
2013 Tacoma o	P.C.	OF	6	28	8	12	1	0	0	1	0	.429
2013 Seattle p	A.L.	OF	97	266	22	71	10	0	2	14	1	.267
Major League Totals		12 Yrs.	1071	2917	363	785	128	32	28	243	101	.269
Wild Card Playoff												
2012 Baltimore	A.L.	OF	1	0	0	0	0	0	0	0	0	.000
Division Series												
2006 New York	N.L.	OF	3	8	1	3	0	0	0	0	0	.375
2012 Baltimore	A.L.	OF	3	1	0	0	0	0	0	0	0	.000
Division Series Totals			6	9	1	3	0	0	0	0	0	.333
Championship Series												
2006 New York	N.L.	OF	7	27	1	5	2	0	0	0	0	.185
2011 Texas	A.L.	OF	2	4	0	0	0	0	0	0	0	.000
Championship Series Totals			9	31	1	5	2	0	0	0	0	.161
World Series Record												
2011 Texas	A.L.	OF	3	1	0	0	0	0	0	0	0	.000

a Selected by Kansas City Royals from New York Mets in Rule V draft, December 11, 2000.

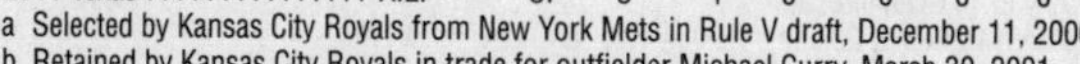

b Retained by Kansas City Royals in trade for outfielder Michael Curry, March 30, 2001.

c Claimed on waivers by Detroit Tigers, December 20, 2001.

d Claimed on waivers by New York Mets, February 1, 2002.

e Claimed on waivers by Montreal Expos, February 22, 2002.

f Traded to Philadelphia Phillies for outfielder Marlon Byrd, May 14, 2005.

g Not offered contract, December 21, 2005. Signed with New York Mets, December 23, 2005.

h On disabled list from June 7 to August 28, 2007.

i Traded to Seattle Mariners with pitcher Aaron Heilman, pitcher Jason Vargas, infielder Mike Carp, outfielder Ezequiel Carrera, pitcher Maikel Cleto and pitcher Joe Smith for pitcher J.J. Putz, pitcher Sean Green and outfielder Jeremy Reed, December 10, 2008.

j On disabled list from June 20 to November 6, 2009.

k Filed for free agency, November 6, 2009. Signed with Texas Rangers organization, February 15, 2010.

l Filed for free agency, October 30, 2011. Signed with Baltimore Orioles, December 20, 2011.

m On disabled list from May 10 to May 29 and June 13 to July 13, 2012.

n Filed for free agency, November 3, 2012. Signed with Kansas City Royals organization, December 31, 2012.

o Released by Kansas City Royals, March 22, 2013. Signed with Seattle Mariners organization, March 24, 2013.

p Filed for free agency, October 31, 2013.

CHAVEZ, ERIC CESAR

Born, Los Angeles, California, December 7, 1977.
Bats Left. Throws Right. Height, 6 feet. Weight, 215 pounds.

Year	Club	Lea	Pos	G	AB	R	H	2B	3B	HR	RBI	SB	Avg
1997	Visalia	Calif.	3B	134	520	67	141	30	3	18	100	13	.271
1998	Huntsville	Southern	3B	88	335	66	110	27	1	22	86	12	.328
1998	Edmonton	P.C.	3B	47	194	38	63	18	0	11	40	2	.325
1998	Oakland	A.L.	3B	16	45	6	14	4	1	0	6	1	.311
1999	Oakland a	A.L.	3B-SS	115	356	47	88	21	2	13	50	1	.247
2000	Oakland	A.L.	3B-SS	153	501	89	139	23	4	26	86	2	.277
2001	Oakland	A.L.	3B-1B-SS	151	552	91	159	43	0	32	114	8	.288
2002	Oakland	A.L.	3B-OF	153	585	87	161	31	3	34	109	8	.275
2003	Oakland	A.L.	3B	156	588	94	166	39	5	29	101	8	.282
2004	Sacramento	P.C.	3B	3	13	2	4	1	0	0	0	0	.308
2004	Oakland b	A.L.	3B-OF	125	475	87	131	20	0	29	77	6	.276
2005	Oakland	A.L.	3B	160	625	92	168	40	1	27	101	6	.269
2006	Oakland	A.L.	3B	137	485	74	117	24	2	22	72	3	.241
2007	Oakland c	A.L.	3B	90	341	43	82	21	2	15	46	4	.240
2008	Sacramento	P.C.	3B	9	30	7	11	3	0	2	3	0	.367
2008	Oakland d	A.L.	3B	23	89	10	22	7	0	2	14	0	.247
2009	Oakland e	A.L.	3B	8	30	0	3	1	0	0	1	0	.100
2010	Athletics	Arizona	DH	1	3	0	1	0	0	0	0	0	.333
2010	Oakland f	A.L.	DH-1B	33	111	10	26	8	0	1	10	0	.234
2011	Tampa	Fla.St.	3B	6	21	4	7	2	0	1	3	0	.333
2011	New York g-h-i	A.L.	3B-1B	58	160	16	42	7	1	2	26	0	.262
2012	New York j-k	A.L.	3B-1B	113	278	36	78	12	0	16	37	0	.281
2013	D-Backs	Arizona	3B	3	7	1	1	0	0	1	2	0	.143
2013	Reno	P.C.	3B	3	8	0	2	0	0	0	0	0	.250
2013	Arizona l-m	N.L.	3B-1B	80	228	28	64	14	2	9	44	1	.281
Major League Totals			16 Yrs.	1571	5449	810	1460	315	23	257	894	48	.268
	Division Series												
2000	Oakland	A.L.	3B	5	21	4	7	3	0	0	4	0	.333
2001	Oakland	A.L.	3B	5	21	0	3	1	0	0	0	0	.143
2002	Oakland	A.L.	3B	5	21	3	8	0	0	1	5	0	.381
2003	Oakland	A.L.	3B	5	22	1	1	1	0	0	0	1	.045
2006	Oakland	A.L.	3B	3	10	2	2	1	0	1	1	0	.200
2011	New York	A.L.	PH	1	1	0	0	0	0	0	0	0	.000
2012	New York	A.L.	3B	3	8	0	0	0	0	0	0	0	.000
Division Series Totals				27	104	10	21	6	0	2	10	1	.202
	Championship Series												
2006	Oakland	A.L.	3B	4	13	1	3	1	0	1	2	0	.231
2012	New York	A.L.	3B	3	8	0	0	0	0	0	0	0	.000
Championship Series Totals				7	21	1	3	1	0	1	2	0	.143

a On disabled list from August 21 to September 19, 1999.
b On disabled list from June 2 to July 9, 2004.
c On disabled list from July 27 to October 8, 2007.
d On disabled list from March 19 to May 29 and from July 2 to November 14, 2008.
e On disabled list from April 25 to November 6, 2009.
f On disabled list from May 21 to November 2, 2010.
g Filed for free agency, November 3, 2010. Signed with New York Yankees organization, February 11, 2011.
h On disabled list from May 6 to July 26, 2011.
i Filed for free agency, October 30, 2011, re-signed with New York Yankees, February 27, 2012.
j On disabled list from May 3 to May 11, 2012.
k Filed for free agency, November 3, 2012. Signed with Arizona Diamondbacks, December 8, 2012.
l On disabled list from May 31 to June 28 and August 10 to August 26, 2013.
m Filed for free agency, October 3, 2013, re-signed with Arizona Diamondbacks, December 20, 2013.

CHISENHALL, LONNIE DAVID

Born, Morehead City, North Carolina, October 4, 1988.
Bats Left. Throws Right. Height, 6 feet, 1 inch. Weight, 200 pounds.

Year	Club	Lea	Pos	G	AB	R	H	2B	3B	HR	RBI	SB	Avg
2008	Mahoning Valley	N.Y.-Penn.	SS	68	276	38	80	20	3	5	45	7	.290
2009	Kinston	Carolina	3B	99	388	59	107	26	2	18	79	2	.276
2009	Akron	Eastern	3B	24	93	13	17	5	1	4	13	1	.183
2010	Akron	Eastern	3B	117	460	81	128	22	3	17	84	3	.278
2011	Columbus	Int.	3B	66	255	45	68	15	3	7	45	0	.267
2011	Cleveland	A.L.	3B-OF	66	212	27	54	13	0	7	22	1	.255
2012	Columbus	Int.	3B	30	118	16	37	12	0	4	17	0	.314
2012	Cleveland a	A.L.	3B	43	142	16	38	6	1	5	16	2	.268

Year Club	Lea	Pos	G	AB	R	H	2B	3B	HR	RBI	SB	Avg
2013 Columbus.............	Int.	3B	27	105	21	41	8	2	6	26	2	.390
2013 Cleveland............	A.L.	3B	94	289	30	65	17	0	11	36	1	.225
Major League Totals............		3 Yrs.	203	643	73	157	36	1	23	74	4	.244
Wild Card Playoff												
2013 Cleveland............	A.L.	3B	1	4	0	3	0	0	0	0	0	.750

a On disabled list from June 30 to September 9, 2012.

CHOO, SHIN-SOO

Born, Pusan, South Korea, July 13, 1982.
Bats Left. Throws Left. Height, 5 feet, 11 inches. Weight, 200 pounds.

Year Club	Lea	Pos	G	AB	R	H	2B	3B	HR	RBI	SB	Avg
2001 Mariners...........	Arizona	OF	51	199	51	60	10	10	4	35	12	.302
2001 Wisconsin	Midwest	OF	3	13	1	6	0	0	0	3	2	.462
2002 San Bernardino	Calif.	OF	11	39	14	12	5	1	1	9	3	.308
2002 Wisconsin	Midwest	OF	119	420	69	127	24	8	6	48	34	.302
2003 Inland Empire.........	Calif.	OF	110	412	62	118	18	13	9	55	18	.286
2004 San Antonio	Texas	OF	132	517	89	163	17	7	15	84	40	.315
2005 Tacoma	P.C.	OF	115	429	73	121	21	5	11	54	20	.282
2005 Seattle	A.L.	OF	10	18	1	1	0	0	0	1	0	.056
2006 Tacoma	P.C.	OF	94	375	71	121	21	3	13	48	26	.323
2006 Seattle-Cleveland a.....	A.L.	OF	49	157	23	44	12	3	3	22	5	.280
2007 Cleveland	A.L.	OF	6	17	5	5	0	0	0	5	0	.294
2007 Indians.........	Gulf Coast	OF	2	5	0	1	1	0	0	2	0	.200
2007 Buffalo	Int.	OF	59	208	34	54	11	2	3	26	10	.260
2008 Buffalo	Int.	OF	12	42	1	11	2	0	1	3	1	.262
2008 Cleveland b	A.L.	OF	94	317	68	98	28	3	14	66	4	.309
2009 Cleveland	A.L.	OF	156	583	87	175	38	6	20	86	21	.300
2010 Akron	Eastern	OF	3	11	1	1	0	0	0	0	1	.091
2010 Cleveland c...........	A.L.	OF	144	550	81	165	31	2	22	90	22	.300
2011 Lake County......	Midwest.	OF	3	8	0	0	0	0	0	1	0	.000
2011 Cleveland d	A.L.	OF	85	313	37	81	11	3	8	36	12	.259
2012 Cleveland e...........	A.L.	OF	155	598	88	169	43	2	16	67	21	.283
2013 Cincinnati f...........	N.L.	OF	154	569	107	162	34	2	21	54	20	.285
Major League Totals............		9 Yrs.	853	3122	497	900	197	21	104	427	105	.288
Wild Card Playoff												
2013 Cincinnati............	N.L.	OF	1	3	2	1	0	0	1	1	0	.333

a Traded to Cleveland Indians with player to be named later for infielder Ben Broussard and cash, July 27, 2006. Cleveland Indians received pitcher Shawn Nottingham to complete trade, August 24, 2006.

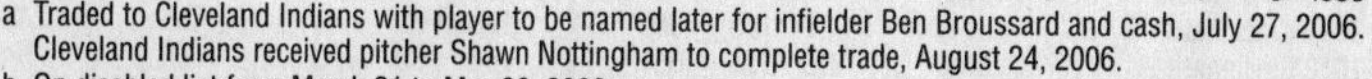

b On disabled list from March 21 to May 30, 2008.
c On disabled list from July 3 to July 23, 2010.
d On disabled list from June 25 to August 12 and September 1 to September 15 and September 16 to November 2, 2011.
e Traded to Cincinnati Reds with infielder Jason Donald for infielder Didi Gregorius and outfielder Drew Stubbs, December 11, 2012.
f Filed for free agency, October 31, 2013. Signed with Texas Rangers, December 27, 2013.

CONGER, HYUN CHOI (HANK)

Born, Federal Way, Washington, January 29, 1988.
Bats Both. Throws Right. Height, 6 feet, 1 inch. Weight, 220 pounds.

Year Club	Lea	Pos	G	AB	R	H	2B	3B	HR	RBI	SB	Avg
2006 Angels	Arizona	C	19	69	11	22	3	4	1	11	1	.319
2007 Angels	Arizona	C	3	15	2	4	1	0	0	3	0	.267
2007 Cedar Rapids	Midwest	C	84	290	33	84	20	0	11	48	9	.290
2008 Rancho Cucamonga....	Calif.	C	73	294	47	89	20	2	13	75	2	.303
2009 Arkansas	Texas	C	123	458	61	135	20	3	11	68	4	.295
2010 Salt Lake	P.C.	C	108	387	56	116	26	2	11	49	0	.300
2010 Los Angeles..........	A.L.	C	13	29	2	5	1	1	0	5	0	.172
2011 Salt Lake	P.C.	C	27	100	14	30	4	0	5	26	0	.300
2011 Los Angeles..........	A.L.	C	59	177	14	37	8	0	6	19	0	.209
2012 Salt Lake	P.C.	C	67	264	48	78	17	0	10	42	2	.295
2012 Los Angeles..........	A.L.	C	7	18	0	3	0	0	0	1	0	.167
2013 Los Angeles..........	A.L.	C	92	233	23	58	13	1	7	21	0	.249
Major League Totals............		4 Yrs.	171	457	39	103	22	2	13	46	0	.225

CORPORAN, CARLOS FERNANDO

Born, Hato Rey, Puerto Rico, January 7, 1984.
Bats Both. Throws Right. Height, 6 feet, 2 inches. Weight, 230 pounds.

Year Club	Lea	Pos	G	AB	R	H	2B	3B	HR	RBI	SB	Avg
2003 Brewers	Arizona	C-1B	34	120	13	30	6	0	2	9	0	.250
2003 Helena	Pioneer	C	10	27	4	6	1	0	0	4	0	.222
2004 Beloit	Midwest	1B-C	63	197	20	45	7	2	1	16	1	.228
2005 West Virginia	So.Atl.	C-1B	99	343	46	82	15	2	9	38	0	.239
2006 Brevard County	Fla.St.	C-1B	86	282	29	76	14	0	3	38	0	.270
2006 Huntsville	Southern	C-1B	3	9	2	3	0	0	0	1	0	.333
2007 Brevard County	Fla.St.	C-1B	23	80	11	29	8	0	3	19	0	.363
2007 Huntsville	Southern	C-1B	56	179	18	36	14	0	2	24	1	.201
2008 Huntsville	Southern	C	34	113	14	30	8	0	3	15	1	.265
2008 Nashville	P.C.	C-1B	26	87	8	20	6	1	3	12	1	.230
2009 Milwaukee	N.L.	C	1	1	1	1	0	0	0	0	0	1.000
2009 Brevard County	Fla.St.	C	14	46	1	12	1	0	0	6	0	.261
2009 Nashville a	P.C.	C	57	179	9	36	9	1	1	18	0	.201
2010 Reno b	P.C.	C	87	286	38	83	20	4	12	50	3	.290
2011 Oklahoma	P.C.	C	22	80	9	20	4	0	3	12	0	.250
2011 Houston c	N.L.	C	52	154	9	29	8	1	0	11	0	.188
2012 Oklahoma	P.C.	C	68	206	35	59	15	0	6	31	2	.286
2012 Houston	N.L.	C	27	78	5	21	2	0	4	13	0	.269
2013 Houston d	A.L.	C-1B	64	191	16	43	5	0	7	20	0	.225
Major League Totals		4 Yrs.	144	424	31	94	15	1	11	44	0	.222

a Filed for free agency, November 9, 2009. Signed with Arizona Diamondbacks organization, November 27, 2009.
b Filed for free agency, November 6, 2010. Signed with Houston Astros organization, November 15, 2010.
c Filed for free agency, November 18, 2011, re-signed with Houston Astros organization, November 29, 2011.
d On disabled list from August 20 to September 9, 2013.

COZART, ZACHARY WARREN (ZACK)

Born, Memphis, Tennessee, August 12, 1985.
Bats Right. Throws Right. Height, 6 feet. Weight, 195 pounds.

Year Club	Lea	Pos	G	AB	R	H	2B	3B	HR	RBI	SB	Avg
2007 Dayton	Midwest	SS-2B	53	184	28	44	7	2	2	18	3	.239
2008 Dayton	Midwest	SS-2B	109	418	57	117	20	6	14	49	3	.280
2009 Carolina	Southern	SS	131	462	72	121	29	2	10	59	10	.262
2010 Louisville	Int.	SS	136	553	91	141	30	4	17	67	30	.255
2011 Louisville	Int.	SS	77	323	57	100	26	2	7	32	9	.310
2011 Cincinnati a	N.L.	SS	11	37	6	12	0	0	2	3	0	.324
2012 Cincinnati	N.L.	SS	138	561	72	138	33	4	15	35	4	.246
2013 Cincinnati	N.L.	SS	151	567	74	144	30	3	12	63	0	.254
Major League Totals		3 Yrs.	300	1165	152	294	63	7	29	101	4	.252
Wild Card Playoff												
2013 Cincinnati	N.L.	SS	1	3	0	0	0	0	0	0	0	.000
Division Series												
2012 Cincinnati	N.L.	SS	5	21	2	5	0	0	0	0	0	.238

a On disabled list from July 24 to November 2, 2011.

CRAIG, ALLEN THOMAS

Born, Mission Viejo, California, July 18, 1984.
Bats Right. Throws Right. Height, 6 feet, 2 inches. Weight, 210 pounds.

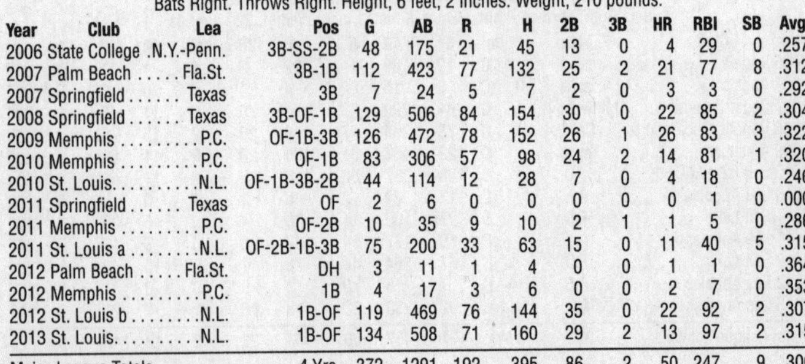

Year Club	Lea	Pos	G	AB	R	H	2B	3B	HR	RBI	SB	Avg
2006 State College	N.Y.-Penn.	3B-SS-2B	48	175	21	45	13	0	4	29	0	.257
2007 Palm Beach	Fla.St.	3B-1B	112	423	77	132	25	2	21	77	8	.312
2007 Springfield	Texas	3B	7	24	5	7	2	0	3	3	0	.292
2008 Springfield	Texas	3B-OF-1B	129	506	84	154	30	0	22	85	2	.304
2009 Memphis	P.C.	OF-1B-3B	126	472	78	152	26	1	26	83	3	.322
2010 Memphis	P.C.	OF-1B	83	306	57	98	24	2	14	81	1	.320
2010 St. Louis	N.L.	OF-1B-3B-2B	44	114	12	28	7	0	4	18	0	.246
2011 Springfield	Texas	OF	2	6	0	0	0	0	0	1	0	.000
2011 Memphis	P.C.	OF-2B	10	35	9	10	2	1	1	5	0	.286
2011 St. Louis a	N.L.	OF-2B-1B-3B	75	200	33	63	15	0	11	40	5	.315
2012 Palm Beach	Fla.St.	DH	3	11	1	4	0	0	1	1	0	.364
2012 Memphis	P.C.	1B	4	17	3	6	0	0	2	7	0	.353
2012 St. Louis b	N.L.	1B-OF	119	469	76	144	35	0	22	92	2	.307
2013 St. Louis	N.L.	1B-OF	134	508	71	160	29	2	13	97	2	.315
Major League Totals		4 Yrs.	372	1291	192	395	86	2	50	247	9	.306

Year	Club	Lea	Pos	G	AB	R	H	2B	3B	HR	RBI	SB	Avg
	Wild Card Playoff												
2012	St. Louis	N.L.	1B	1	4	1	2	1	0	0	1	0	.500
	Division Series												
2011	St. Louis	N.L.	OF	3	10	3	1	0	1	0	0	0	.100
2012	St. Louis	N.L.	1B	5	19	2	6	2	0	1	3	0	.316
Division Series Totals				8	29	5	7	2	1	1	3	0	.241
	Championship Series												
2011	St. Louis	N.L.	OF	5	8	1	3	0	0	1	3	0	.375
2012	St. Louis	N.L.	1B-OF	7	24	1	3	1	0	0	2	0	.125
Championship Series Totals				12	32	2	6	1	0	1	5	0	.188
	World Series Record												
2011	St. Louis	N.L.	OF	7	19	5	5	0	0	3	5	0	.263
2013	St. Louis	N.L.	DH-1B	6	16	1	6	1	0	0	0	0	.375
World Series Totals				13	35	6	11	1	0	3	5	0	.314

a On disabled list from April 17 to May 2 and June 8 to August 10, 2011.
b On disabled list from March 26 to May 1 and May 17 to June 1, 2012.

CRAWFORD, BRANDON MICHAEL

Born, Mountain View, California, January 21, 1987.
Bats Left. Throws Right. Height, 6 feet, 2 inches. Weight, 215 pounds.

Year	Club	Lea	Pos	G	AB	R	H	2B	3B	HR	RBI	SB	Avg
2008	Giants	Arizona	SS	4	14	3	6	1	1	0	3	0	.429
2008	Salem-Keizer	Northwest	SS	1	2	0	0	0	0	0	0	0	.000
2009	San Jose	Calif.	SS	25	105	21	39	2	2	6	17	2	.371
2009	Connecticut	Eastern	SS	108	392	38	101	26	2	4	31	11	.258
2010	San Jose	Calif.	3B-SS	5	18	4	3	1	0	0	1	0	.167
2010	Richmond	Eastern	SS	79	291	43	70	12	3	7	22	4	.241
2011	San Jose	Calif.	SS	14	59	14	19	5	1	3	15	0	.322
2011	Fresno	P.C.	SS	29	107	13	25	5	1	1	9	5	.234
2011	San Francisco	N.L.	SS	66	196	22	40	5	2	3	21	1	.204
2012	San Francisco	N.L.	SS	143	435	44	108	26	3	4	45	1	.248
2013	San Francisco	N.L.	SS	149	499	52	124	24	3	9	43	1	.248
Major League Totals			3 Yrs.	358	1130	118	272	55	8	16	109	3	.241
	Division Series												
2012	San Francisco	N.L.	SS	5	11	1	2	0	1	0	1	0	.182
	Championship Series												
2012	San Francisco	N.L.	SS	7	23	2	5	1	0	0	5	0	.217
	World Series Record												
2012	San Francisco	N.L.	SS	4	12	0	3	0	0	0	1	1	.250

CRAWFORD, CARL DEMONTE

Born, Houston, Texas, August 5, 1981.
Bats Left. Throws Left. Height, 6 feet, 2 inches. Weight, 220 pounds.

Year	Club	Lea	Pos	G	AB	R	H	2B	3B	HR	RBI	SB	Avg
1999	Princeton	Appal.	OF	60	260	62	83	14	4	0	25	17	.319
2000	Charleston-SC	So.Atl.	OF	135	564	99	170	21	11	6	57	55	.301
2001	Orlando	Southern	OF	132	537	64	147	24	3	4	51	36	.274
2002	Durham	Int.	OF	85	353	59	105	17	9	7	52	26	.297
2002	Tampa Bay	A.L.	OF	63	259	23	67	11	6	2	30	9	.259
2003	Tampa Bay	A.L.	OF	151	630	80	177	18	9	5	54	*55	.281
2004	Tampa Bay	A.L.	OF	152	626	104	185	26	*19	11	55	*59	.296
2005	Tampa Bay	A.L.	OF	156	644	101	194	33	*15	15	81	46	.301
2006	Tampa Bay	A.L.	OF	151	600	89	183	20	*16	18	77	*58	.305
2007	Tampa Bay	A.L.	OF	143	584	93	184	37	9	11	80	*50	.315
2008	Tampa Bay a	A.L.	OF	109	443	69	121	12	10	8	57	25	.273
2009	Tampa Bay	A.L.	OF	156	606	96	185	28	8	15	68	60	.305
2010	Tampa Bay b	A.L.	OF	154	600	110	184	30	*13	19	90	47	.307
2011	Pawtucket	Int.	OF	2	5	1	1	0	0	0	1	0	.200
2011	Boston c	A.L.	OF	130	506	65	129	29	7	11	56	18	.255
2012	Red Sox	Gulf Coast	OF	5	14	2	3	1	0	0	0	0	.214
2012	Portland	Eastern	OF	3	10	2	4	0	1	0	1	1	.400
2012	Pawtucket	Int.	OF	3	12	2	4	0	0	0	1	1	.333
2012	Boston d-e	A.L.	OF	31	117	23	33	10	2	3	19	5	.282
2013	Rancho Cucamonga	Calif.	OF	4	13	2	5	1	0	0	3	1	.385
2013	Los Angeles f	N.L.	OF	116	435	62	123	30	3	6	31	15	.283
Major League Totals			12 Yrs.	1512	6050	915	1765	284	117	124	698	447	.292

Year Club	Lea	Pos	G	AB	R	H	2B	3B	HR	RBI	SB	Avg
Division Series												
2008 Tampa Bay	A.L.	OF	4	14	2	3	0	0	0	2	3	.214
2010 Tampa Bay	A.L.	OF	5	21	1	3	0	0	1	1	1	.143
2013 Los Angeles	N.L.	OF	4	17	6	6	0	0	3	5	1	.353
Division Series Totals			13	52	9	12	0	0	4	8	5	.231
Championship Series												
2008 Tampa Bay	A.L.	OF	7	29	3	10	2	1	0	4	3	.345
2013 Los Angeles	N.L.	OF	6	25	2	7	1	0	1	1	0	.280
Championship Series Totals			13	54	5	17	3	1	1	5	3	.315
World Series Record												
2008 Tampa Bay	A.L.	OF	5	19	4	5	1	0	2	2	1	.263

a On disabled list from August 10 to September 26, 2008.
b Filed for free agency, November 1, 2010. Signed with Boston Red Sox, December 11, 2010.
c On disabled list from June 18 to July 18, 2011.
d On disabled list from March 26 to July 16 and August 20 to October 29, 2012.
e Traded to Los Angeles Dodgers with infielder Adrian Gonzalez, pitcher Josh Beckett, infielder Nick Punto and cash for infielder James Loney, infielder Ivan DeJesus, pitcher Allen Webster and player to be named later, August 25, 2012. Boston Red Sox received pitcher Rubby De La Rosa to complete trade, October 4, 2012.
f On disabled list from June 2 to July 5, 2013.

CRISP, COVELLI LOYCE (COCO)

Born, Los Angeles, California, November 1, 1979.
Bats Both. Throws Right. Height, 6 feet. Weight, 180 pounds.

Year Club	Lea	Pos	G	AB	R	H	2B	3B	HR	RBI	SB	Avg
1999 Johnson City	Appal.	2B	65	229	55	59	5	4	3	22	27	.258
2000 New Jersey	N.Y.-Penn.	OF-2B	36	134	18	32	5	0	0	14	25	.239
2000 Peoria............	Midwest	OF	27	98	14	27	9	0	0	7	7	.276
2001 Potomac..........	Carolina	OF	139	530	80	162	23	3	11	47	39	.306
2002 New Haven.........	Eastern	OF	89	355	61	107	16	1	9	47	26	.301
2002 Akron.............	Eastern	OF	7	32	9	13	1	0	1	4	4	.406
2002 Buffalo	Int.	OF	4	21	3	5	1	0	0	2	1	.238
2002 Cleveland a...........	A.L.	OF	32	127	16	33	9	2	1	9	4	.260
2003 Buffalo	Int.	OF	56	225	42	81	19	6	1	24	20	.360
2003 Cleveland	A.L.	OF	99	414	55	110	15	6	3	27	15	.266
2004 Cleveland	A.L.	OF	139	491	78	146	24	2	15	71	20	.297
2005 Cleveland b	A.L.	OF	145	594	86	178	42	4	16	69	15	.300
2006 Pawtucket	Int.	OF	1	3	0	1	0	0	0	2	0	.333
2006 Boston c-d...........	A.L.	OF	105	413	58	109	22	2	8	36	22	.264
2007 Boston	A.L.	OF	145	526	85	141	28	7	6	60	28	.268
2008 Boston e..............	A.L.	OF	118	361	55	102	18	3	7	41	20	.283
2009 Kansas City f-g........	A.L.	OF	49	180	30	41	8	5	3	14	13	.228
2010 Stockton.............	Calif.	OF	2	6	2	5	0	1	1	3	0	.833
2010 Sacramento	P.C.	OF	6	22	7	13	2	1	0	5	2	.591
2010 Oakland h............	A.L.	OF	75	290	51	81	14	4	8	38	32	.279
2011 Oakland i	A.L.	OF	136	531	69	140	27	5	8	54	*49	.264
2012 Oakland j	A.L.	OF	120	455	68	118	25	7	11	46	39	.259
2013 Oakland k............	A.L.	OF	131	513	93	134	22	3	22	66	21	.261
Major League Totals		12 Yrs.	1294	4895	744	1333	254	50	108	531	278	.272
Division Series												
2007 Boston	A.L.	OF	3	10	0	2	0	0	0	2	1	.200
2008 Boston	A.L.	OF	2	4	2	1	0	0	0	0	1	.250
2012 Oakland	A.L.	OF	5	22	3	4	0	0	1	2	0	.182
2013 Oakland	A.L.	OF	5	18	4	7	2	1	0	2	1	.389
Division Series Totals			15	54	9	14	2	1	1	6	3	.259
Championship Series												
2007 Boston	A.L.	OF	7	21	2	3	1	0	0	0	1	.143
2008 Boston	A.L.	OF	5	20	2	9	2	0	0	1	0	.450
Championship Series Totals			12	41	4	12	3	0	0	1	1	.293
World Series Record												
2007 Boston	A.L.	OF	3	2	1	1	0	0	0	0	0	.500

a Sent by St. Louis Cardinals to Cleveland Indians as player to be named later for pitcher Chuck Finley, August 6, 2002.
b On disabled list from May 18 to June 2, 2005.
c Traded to Boston Red Sox with pitcher David Riske and catcher Josh Bard for infielder Andy Marte, catcher Kelly Shoppach and pitcher Guillermo Mota, January 27, 2006.
d On disabled list from April 9 to May 28, 2006.
e Traded to Kansas City Royals for pitcher Ramon Ramirez, November 19, 2008.
f On disabled list from June 13 to November 9, 2009.

g Filed for free agency, November 9, 2009. Signed with Oakland Athletics, December 23, 2009.
h On disabled list from April 3 to May 21 and May 26 to June 22, 2010.
i Filed for free agency, October 30, 2011, re-signed with Oakland Athletics, January 5, 2012.
j On disabled list from May 3 to May 21, 2012.
k On disabled list from April 30 to May 15, 2013.

CRUZ, NELSON RAMON

Born, Monte Cristi, Dominican Republic, July 1, 1980.
Bats Right. Throws Right. Height, 6 feet, 3 inches. Weight, 230 pounds.

Year	Club	Lea	Pos	G	AB	R	H	2B	3B	HR	RBI	SB	Avg
2001	Athletics a	Arizona	OF	23	88	11	22	3	1	3	16	6	.250
2002	Vancouver	Northwest	OF	63	214	23	59	14	0	4	25	12	.276
2003	Kane County	Midwest	OF	119	470	65	112	26	2	20	85	10	.238
2004	Modesto	Calif.	OF	66	261	54	90	27	1	11	52	8	.345
2004	Sacramento	P.C.	OF	4	13	4	3	1	0	1	2	0	.231
2004	Midland b	Texas	OF	67	262	51	82	14	2	14	46	8	.313
2005	Huntsville	Southern	OF	68	248	45	76	19	0	16	54	10	.306
2005	Nashville	P.C.	OF	60	208	33	56	13	0	11	27	9	.269
2005	Milwaukee	N.L.	OF	8	5	1	1	1	0	0	0	0	.200
2006	Nashville	P.C.	OF	104	371	68	112	22	1	20	73	17	.302
2006	Texas c	A.L.	OF	41	130	15	29	3	0	6	22	1	.223
2007	Oklahoma	P.C.	OF	44	162	32	57	9	1	15	45	1	.352
2007	Texas	A.L.	OF	96	307	35	72	15	2	9	34	2	.235
2008	Rangers	Arizona	OF	1	4	1	1	1	0	0	1	0	.250
2008	Oklahoma	P.C.	OF	103	383	93	131	18	3	37	99	24	.342
2008	Texas	A.L.	OF	31	115	19	38	9	1	7	26	3	.330
2009	Oklahoma	P.C.	OF	3	10	0	0	0	0	0	0	1	.000
2009	Texas d	A.L.	OF	128	462	75	120	21	1	33	76	20	.260
2010	Frisco	Texas	OF	3	11	1	4	1	0	0	1	1	.364
2010	Oklahoma	P.C.	OF	5	19	1	4	1	0	0	4	0	.211
2010	Texas e	A.L.	OF	108	399	60	127	31	3	22	78	17	.318
2011	Frisco	Texas	OF	3	11	1	2	1	0	0	1	0	.182
2011	Round Rock	P.C.	OF	3	11	3	5	0	0	3	4	0	.455
2011	Texas f	A.L.	OF	124	475	64	125	28	1	29	87	9	.263
2012	Texas	A.L.	OF	159	585	86	152	45	0	24	90	8	.260
2013	Texas g-h	A.L.	OF	109	413	49	110	18	0	27	76	5	.266
Major League Totals			9 Yrs.	804	2891	404	774	171	8	157	489	65	.268
	Wild Card Playoff												
2012	Texas	A.L.	OF	1	4	0	2	0	0	0	0	0	.500
	Division Series												
2010	Texas	A.L.	OF	5	20	5	8	2	0	3	3	1	.400
2011	Texas	A.L.	OF	4	15	1	1	0	0	0	0	0	.067
Division Series Totals				9	35	6	9	2	0	3	3	1	.257
	Championship Series												
2010	Texas	A.L.	OF	6	20	6	7	3	0	2	5	0	.350
2011	Texas	A.L.	OF	6	22	7	8	2	0	6	13	0	.364
Championship Series Totals				12	42	13	15	5	0	8	18	0	.357
	World Series Record												
2010	Texas	A.L.	OF	5	20	2	4	2	0	1	3	0	.200
2011	Texas	A.L.	OF	7	25	5	5	0	0	2	3	0	.200
World Series Totals				12	45	7	9	2	0	3	6	0	.200

a Traded by New York Mets to Oakland Athletics for infielder Jorge Velandia, August 30, 2000.
b Traded to Milwaukee Brewers with pitcher Justin Lehr for infielder Keith Ginter, December 15, 2004.
c Traded to Texas Rangers with outfielder Carlos Lee for pitcher Francisco Cordero, outfielder Kevin Mench, outfielder Laynce Nix and pitcher Julian Cordero, July 28, 2006.

d On disabled list from August 4 to August 20, 2009.
e On disabled list from April 27 to May 14 and May 29 to June 22 and August 15 to August 30, 2010.
f On disabled list from May 4 to May 23 and August 29 to September 13, 2011.
g Suspended for 50 games for performance-enhancing drug use, August 5, 2013.
h Filed for free agency, October 31, 2013.

CUDDYER, MICHAEL BRENT

Born, Norfolk, Virginia, March 27, 1979.
Bats Right. Throws Right. Height, 6 feet, 2 inches. Weight, 220 pounds.

Year	Club	Lea	Pos	G	AB	R	H	2B	3B	HR	RBI	SB	Avg
1998	Fort Wayne	Midwest	SS-2B	129	497	82	137	37	7	12	81	16	.276
1999	Fort Myers	Fla.St.	3B	130	466	87	139	24	4	16	82	14	.298
2000	New Britain	Eastern	3B	138	490	72	129	30	8	6	61	5	.263

Year	Club	Lea	Pos	G	AB	R	H	2B	3B	HR	RBI	SB	Avg
2001	New Britain	Eastern	3B-1B-OF	141	509	95	153	36	3	30	87	5	.301
2001	Minnesota	A.L.	1B-3B	8	18	1	4	2	0	0	1	1	.222
2002	Edmonton	P.C.	OF-1B-3B	86	330	70	102	16	9	20	53	12	.309
2002	Minnesota	A.L.	OF-3B-1B	41	112	12	29	7	0	4	13	2	.259
2003	Twins	Gulf Coast	OF	2	5	1	4	0	0	1	3	0	.800
2003	Rochester	Int.	OF-2B-3B-1B	53	186	25	57	17	0	3	34	5	.306
2003	Minnesota	A.L.	OF-3B-1B-2B	35	102	14	25	1	3	4	8	1	.245
2004	Minnesota	A.L.	2B-3B-OF-1B	115	339	49	89	22	1	12	45	5	.263
2005	Rochester	Int.	3B-1B	3	9	1	1	0	0	0	0	2	.111
2005	Minnesota a	A.L.	3B-OF-2B-1B	126	422	55	111	25	3	12	42	3	.263
2006	Minnesota	A.L.	OF-1B	150	557	102	158	41	5	24	109	6	.284
2007	Minnesota b	A.L.	OF-1B	144	547	87	151	28	5	16	81	5	.276
2008	Rochester	Int.	OF	4	10	3	3	2	0	0	1	0	.300
2008	Minnesota c	A.L.	OF-1B	71	249	30	62	13	4	3	36	5	.249
2009	Minnesota	A.L.	OF-1B-2B	153	588	93	162	34	7	32	94	6	.276
2010	Minnesota	A.L.	1B-OF-3B-2B	157	609	93	165	37	5	14	81	7	.271
2011	Minnesota d	A.L.	OF-1B-2B-P	139	529	70	150	29	2	20	70	11	.284
2012	Colorado Springs	P.C.	1B-OF	2	9	4	6	1	0	1	3	0	.667
2012	Colorado e	N.L.	OF-1B	101	358	53	93	30	2	16	58	8	.260
2013	Colorado f	N.L.	OF-1B	130	489	74	162	31	3	20	84	10	*.331
Major League Totals			13 Yrs.	1370	4919	733	1361	300	40	177	722	70	.277
	Division Series												
2002	Minnesota	A.L.	OF	5	13	1	5	1	0	0	1	0	.385
2003	Minnesota	A.L.	DH	1	4	0	1	0	0	0	1	0	.250
2004	Minnesota	A.L.	2B-1B	4	15	1	7	0	0	0	2	0	.467
2006	Minnesota	A.L.	OF	3	12	2	3	0	1	1	1	0	.250
2009	Minnesota	A.L.	1B	3	14	0	6	0	0	0	1	0	.429
2010	Minnesota	A.L.	1B	3	11	1	2	1	0	1	2	0	.182
Division Series Totals				19	69	5	24	2	1	2	8	0	.348
	Championship Series												
2002	Minnesota	A.L.	OF	3	5	0	1	0	0	0	0	0	.200

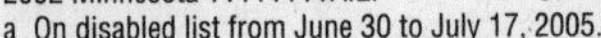

a On disabled list from June 30 to July 17, 2005.
b On disabled list from July 19 to August 3, 2007.
c On disabled list from April 5 to April 25 and June 28 to September 13, 2008.
d Filed for free agency, October 30, 2011. Signed with Colorado Rockies, December 20, 2011.
e On disabled list from August 1 to August 16 and August 19 to October 5, 2012.
f On disabled list from May 9 to May 24, 2013.

DANKS, JORDAN COOPER

Born, Austin, Texas, August 7, 1986.
Bats Left. Throws Right. Height, 6 feet, 4 inches. Weight, 210 pounds.

Year	Club	Lea	Pos	G	AB	R	H	2B	3B	HR	RBI	SB	Avg
2008	Kannapolis	So.Atl.	OF	10	40	10	13	4	1	2	7	1	.325
2009	Winston-Salem	Carolina	OF	30	118	25	38	11	2	3	21	5	.322
2009	Birmingham	Southern	OF	73	284	50	69	12	1	6	20	7	.243
2010	Charlotte	Int.	OF-2B	119	445	62	109	27	3	8	42	15	.245
2011	Charlotte	Int.	OF	133	463	65	119	24	6	14	65	18	.257
2012	Charlotte	Int.	OF	64	218	37	69	17	1	8	30	6	.317
2012	Chicago	A.L.	OF	50	67	12	15	1	0	1	4	3	.224
2013	Charlotte	Int.	OF	54	208	35	58	9	2	6	28	3	.279
2013	Chicago	A.L.	OF	79	160	15	37	7	0	5	12	7	.231
Major League Totals			2 Yrs.	129	227	27	52	8	0	6	16	10	.229

D'ARNAUD, TRAVIS E.

Born, Long Beach, California, February 10, 1989.
Bats Right. Throws Right. Height, 6 feet, 2 inches. Weight, 195 pounds.

Year	Club	Lea	Pos	G	AB	R	H	2B	3B	HR	RBI	SB	Avg
2007	Phillies	Gulf Coast	C	41	141	18	34	3	0	4	20	4	.241
2008	Williamsport	N.Y.-Penn.	C	48	175	21	54	13	1	4	25	1	.309
2008	Lakewood	So.Atl.	C	16	64	12	19	5	0	2	5	0	.297
2009	Lakewood a	So.Atl.	C	126	482	71	123	38	1	13	71	8	.255
2010	Dunedin	Fla.St.	C	71	263	36	68	20	1	6	38	3	.259
2011	New Hampshire	Eastern	C	114	424	72	132	33	1	21	78	4	.311
2012	Las Vegas b	P.C.	C-1B	67	279	45	93	21	2	16	52	1	.333
2013	Mets	Gulf Coast	C	6	22	4	7	3	0	0	5	0	.318
2013	Binghamton	Eastern	C	7	27	2	6	2	1	1	3	0	.222
2013	Las Vegas	P.C.	C	19	56	19	17	8	0	2	12	0	.304

Year	Club	Lea	Pos	G	AB	R	H	2B	3B	HR	RBI	SB	Avg
2013	New York	N.L.	C	31	99	4	20	3	0	1	5	0	.202

a Traded by Philadelphia Phillies to Toronto Blue Jays with pitcher Kyle Drabek and pitcher Michael Taylor for pitcher Roy Halladay, December 16, 2009.

b Traded to New York Mets with catcher John Buck, pitcher Noah Syndergaard and outfielder Wuilmer Becerra for catcher Josh Thole, catcher Mike Nickeas and pitcher R.A. Dickey, December 17, 2012.

DAVIS, CHRISTOPHER LYN (CHRIS)

Born, Longview, Texas, March 17, 1986.
Bats Left. Throws Right. Height, 6 feet, 4 inches. Weight, 230 pounds.

Year	Club	Lea	Pos	G	AB	R	H	2B	3B	HR	RBI	SB	Avg
2006	Spokane	Northwest	OF-1B	69	253	38	70	18	1	15	42	2	.277
2007	Bakersfield	Calif.	3B	99	386	69	115	28	3	24	93	3	.298
2007	Frisco	Texas	3B	30	109	21	32	7	0	12	25	0	.294
2008	Frisco	Texas	1B	46	186	43	62	14	0	13	42	5	.333
2008	Oklahoma	P.C.	1B	31	111	25	37	7	1	10	31	2	.333
2008	Texas	A.L.	1B-3B	80	295	51	84	23	2	17	55	1	.285
2009	Oklahoma	P.C.	3B-1B	44	165	27	54	12	1	6	30	0	.327
2009	Texas	A.L.	1B-3B	113	391	48	93	15	1	21	59	0	.238
2010	Oklahoma	P.C.	3B-1B-OF	103	398	67	130	31	2	14	80	3	.327
2010	Texas	A.L.	1B-3B	45	120	7	23	9	0	1	4	3	.192
2011	Bowie	Eastern	1B-3B	2	6	2	3	1	0	0	0	0	.500
2011	Round Rock	P.C.	3B-OF	48	193	39	71	14	1	24	66	1	.368
2011	Texas-Baltimore a-b	A.L.	1B-3B	59	199	25	53	12	0	5	19	1	.266
2012	Baltimore	A.L.	DH-OF-1B-P	139	515	75	139	20	0	33	85	2	.270
2013	Baltimore	A.L.	1B	160	584	103	167	42	1	*53	*138	4	.286
Major League Totals			6 Yrs.	596	2104	309	559	121	4	130	360	11	.266
	Wild Card Playoff												
2012	Baltimore	A.L.	OF	1	4	0	1	0	0	0	0	0	.250
	Division Series												
2012	Baltimore	A.L.	OF	5	20	1	4	0	0	0	2	0	.200

a Traded to Baltimore Orioles with pitcher Tommy Hunter for pitcher Koji Uehara and cash, July 30, 2011.

b On disabled list from August 15 to September 6, 2011.

DAVIS, ISAAC BENJAMIN (IKE)

Born, Edina, Minnesota, March 22, 1987.
Bats Left. Throws Left. Height, 6 feet, 4 inches. Weight, 215 pounds.

Year	Club	Lea	Pos	G	AB	R	H	2B	3B	HR	RBI	SB	Avg
2008	Brooklyn	N.Y.-Penn.	1B	58	215	17	55	15	0	0	17	0	.256
2009	Binghamton	Eastern	1B-OF	55	207	30	64	14	0	13	43	0	.309
2009	St. Lucie	Fla.St.	1B	59	222	28	64	17	3	7	28	0	.288
2010	Buffalo	Int.	1B	10	33	8	12	3	0	2	4	0	.364
2010	New York	N.L.	1B	147	523	73	138	33	1	19	71	3	.264
2011	New York a	N.L.	1B	36	129	20	39	8	1	7	25	0	.302
2012	New York	N.L.	1B	156	519	66	118	26	0	32	90	0	.227
2013	Las Vegas	P.C.	1B	21	75	21	22	7	0	7	13	0	.293
2013	New York b	N.L.	1B	103	317	37	65	14	0	9	33	4	.205
Major League Totals			4 Yrs.	442	1488	196	360	81	2	67	219	7	.242

a On disabled list from May 11 to October 24, 2011.

b On disabled list from September 9 to October 31, 2013.

DAVIS, KHRISTOPHER ADRIAN (KHRIS)

Born, Lakewood, California, December 21, 1987.
Bats Right. Throws Right. Height, 5 feet, 11 inches. Weight, 200 pounds.

Year	Club	Lea	Pos	G	AB	R	H	2B	3B	HR	RBI	SB	Avg
2009	Brewers	Arizona	OF	10	37	7	9	0	2	2	8	4	.243
2009	Helena	Pioneer	DH	1	1	0	0	0	0	0	0	0	.000
2010	Wisconsin	Midwest	OF	128	457	86	128	26	4	22	72	17	.280
2011	Brevard County	Fla.St.	OF	90	304	50	94	21	1	15	68	10	.309
2011	Huntsville	Southern	OF	35	124	10	26	7	1	2	16	0	.210
2012	Brewers	Arizona	OF	6	19	7	7	0	0	3	5	1	.368
2012	Huntsville	Southern	OF	44	128	23	49	9	0	8	23	2	.383
2012	Nashville	P.C.	OF	32	113	23	35	12	0	4	24	1	.310
2013	Nashville	P.C.	OF	69	243	35	62	12	1	13	37	6	.255
2013	Milwaukee	N.L.	OF	56	136	27	38	10	0	11	27	3	.279

DAVIS, RAJAI LAVAE

Born, Norwich, Connecticut, October 19, 1980.
Bats Right. Throws Right. Height, 5 feet, 11 inches. Weight, 195 pounds.

Year	Club	Lea	Pos	G	AB	R	H	2B	3B	HR	RBI	SB	Avg
2001	Pirates	Gulf Coast	OF	26	84	19	22	1	0	0	4	11	.262
2001	Williamsport	N.Y.-Penn.	OF-2B	6	12	1	1	0	0	0	0	0	.083
2002	Pirates	Gulf Coast	OF	58	224	38	86	16	5	4	35	24	.384
2002	Williamsport	N.Y.-Penn.	OF	1	4	0	0	0	0	0	0	0	.000
2002	Hickory	So.Atl.	OF	6	14	4	6	0	0	0	3	2	.429
2003	Hickory	So.Atl.	OF	125	478	84	146	21	7	6	54	40	.305
2004	Lynchburg	Carolina	OF	127	509	91	160	27	7	5	38	57	.314
2005	Altoona	Eastern	OF	123	499	82	140	22	5	4	34	45	.281
2006	Indianapolis	Int.	OF	100	385	53	109	17	1	2	21	45	.283
2006	Pittsburgh	N.L.	OF	20	14	1	2	1	0	0	0	1	.143
2007	Indianapolis	Int.	OF	53	211	31	67	12	4	4	30	27	.318
2007	Pittsburgh-San Francisco a	N.L.	OF	75	190	32	53	11	2	1	9	22	.279
2008	San Francisco	N.L.	OF	12	18	2	1	0	0	0	0	4	.056
2008	Oakland b	A.L.	OF-2B	101	196	28	51	5	4	3	19	25	.260
2009	Oakland	A.L.	OF	125	390	65	119	27	5	3	48	41	.305
2010	Oakland c	A.L.	OF	143	525	66	149	28	3	5	52	50	.284
2011	Dunedin	Fla.St.	OF	2	5	1	2	0	0	1	1	0	.400
2011	New Hampshire	Eastern	OF	4	10	1	3	1	0	0	0	0	.300
2011	Toronto d	A.L.	OF	95	320	44	76	21	6	1	29	34	.237
2012	Toronto e	A.L.	OF	142	447	64	115	24	3	8	43	46	.257
2013	Dunedin	Fla.St.	OF	3	10	2	3	0	1	0	0	0	.300
2013	Toronto f-g	A.L.	OF	108	331	49	86	16	2	6	24	45	.260
Major League Totals			8 Yrs.	821	2431	351	652	133	25	27	224	268	.268

a Traded to San Francisco Giants with player to be named later for pitcher Matt Morris, July 31, 2007. San Francisco Giants received pitcher Steve MacFarland to complete trade, August 27, 2007.
b Claimed on waivers by Oakland Athletics, April 23, 2008.
c Traded to Toronto Blue Jays for pitcher Daniel Farquhar and pitcher Trystan Magnuson, November 17, 2010.
d On disabled list from April 11 to April 29 and August 14 to November 1, 2011.
e Filed for free agency, October 31, 2012, re-signed with Toronto Blue Jays, October 31, 2012.
f On disabled list from May 11 to June 4, 2013.
g Filed for free agency, October 31, 2013. Signed with Detroit Tigers, December 12, 2013.

DE AZA (CEDA), ALEJANDRO ALBERTO

Born, Guaymate, Dominican Republic, April 11, 1984.
Bats Left. Throws Left. Height, 6 feet. Weight, 190 pounds.

Year	Club	Lea	Pos	G	AB	R	H	2B	3B	HR	RBI	SB	Avg
2002	Dodgers	Gulf Coast	OF-C	39	128	27	29	6	1	1	14	16	.227
2003	Ogden	Pioneer	OF	55	208	36	48	11	1	2	24	15	.231
2004	Columbus a	So.Atl.	OF-1B	102	341	63	87	17	2	4	45	24	.255
2005	Jupiter	Fla.St.	OF	123	472	75	135	24	9	3	37	34	.286
2006	Jupiter	Fla.St.	OF	2	7	1	1	0	1	0	0	0	.143
2006	Marlins	Gulf Coast	OF	7	24	7	11	1	0	0	4	3	.458
2006	Carolina	Southern	OF	69	230	40	64	12	2	2	16	27	.278
2007	Marlins	Gulf Coast	OF	4	9	2	6	2	0	0	1	2	.667
2007	Jupiter	Fla.St.	OF	2	8	1	4	1	1	0	0	0	.500
2007	Carolina	Southern	OF	5	20	7	7	2	0	2	3	0	.350
2007	Florida	N.L.	OF	45	144	14	33	8	2	0	8	2	.229
2008	Florida b	N.L.				INJURED—Did Not Play							
2009	Florida	N.L.	OF	22	20	6	5	1	0	0	3	0	.250
2009	New Orleans c	P.C.	OF	87	267	45	80	21	5	8	34	11	.300
2010	Charlotte	Int.	OF	79	318	53	96	21	4	5	49	16	.302
2010	Chicago	A.L.	OF	19	30	7	9	3	0	0	2	2	.300
2011	Charlotte	Int.	OF	99	385	64	124	29	5	9	37	22	.322
2011	Chicago	A.L.	OF	54	152	29	50	11	3	4	23	12	.329
2012	Charlotte	Int.	OF	5	20	3	5	1	0	1	2	0	.250
2012	Chicago d	A.L.	OF	131	524	81	147	29	6	9	50	26	.281
2013	Chicago	A.L.	OF	153	607	84	160	27	4	17	62	20	.264
Major League Totals			6 Yrs.	424	1477	221	404	79	15	30	148	62	.274

a Selected Florida Marlins from Los Angeles Dodgers in Rule V draft, December 13, 2004.
b On disabled list from March 30 to October 1, 2008.
c Claimed on waivers by Chicago White Sox, October 21, 2009.
d On disabled list from August 18 to September 2, 2012.

DE JESUS, DAVID CHRISTOPHER

Born, Brooklyn, New York, December 20, 1979.
Bats Left. Throws Left. Height, 6 feet. Weight, 190 pounds.

Year Club	Lea	Pos	G	AB	R	H	2B	3B	HR	RBI	SB	Avg
2001 a		INJURED—Did Not Play										
2002 Wilmington	Carolina	OF	87	334	69	99	22	6	4	41	15	.296
2002 Wichita	Texas	OF	25	79	7	20	5	2	2	15	3	.253
2003 Wichita	Texas	OF	17	71	14	24	4	0	2	10	1	.338
2003 Omaha	P.C.	OF	59	215	49	64	16	3	5	23	8	.298
2003 Kansas City	A.L.	OF	12	7	0	2	0	1	0	0	0	.286
2004 Omaha	P.C.	OF	50	197	38	62	14	4	6	16	7	.315
2004 Kansas City	A.L.	OF	96	363	58	104	15	3	7	39	8	.287
2005 Kansas City	A.L.	OF	122	461	69	135	31	6	9	56	5	.293
2006 Omaha	P.C.	OF	3	13	0	5	0	0	0	2	0	.385
2006 Kansas City b	A.L.	OF	119	491	83	145	36	7	8	56	6	.295
2007 Kansas City	A.L.	OF	157	605	101	157	29	9	7	58	10	.260
2008 Kansas City	A.L.	OF	135	518	70	159	25	7	12	73	11	.307
2009 Kansas City	A.L.	OF	144	558	74	157	28	9	13	71	4	.281
2010 Kansas City c-d	A.L.	OF	91	352	46	112	23	3	5	37	3	.318
2011 Oakland e	A.L.	OF	131	442	60	106	20	5	10	46	4	.240
2012 Chicago	N.L.	OF	148	506	76	133	28	8	9	50	7	.263
2013 Cubs	Arizona	OF	4	12	4	4	2	0	0	0	1	.333
2013 Chicago-Washington f-g	N.L.	OF	87	287	39	71	19	3	6	27	3	.247
2013 Tampa Bay h	A.L.	OF	35	104	13	27	10	0	2	11	2	.260
Major League Totals		11 Yrs.	1277	4694	689	1308	264	61	88	524	63	.279
Wild Card Playoff												
2013 Tampa Bay	A.L.	OF	1	4	0	0	0	0	0	0	0	.000
Division Series												
2013 Tampa Bay	A.L.	OF	4	9	2	3	1	0	0	1	0	.333

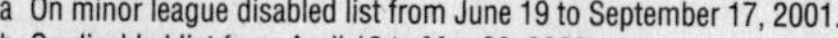

a On minor league disabled list from June 19 to September 17, 2001.
b On disabled list from April 19 to May 29, 2006.
c On disabled list from July 23 to November 10, 2010.
d Traded to Oakland Athletics for pitcher Vin Mazzaro and pitcher Justin Marks, November 10, 2010.
e Filed for free agency, October 30, 2011. Signed with Chicago Cubs, November 30, 2011.
f On disabled list from June 15 to July 24, 2013.
g Sold to Washington Nationals, August 19, 2013.
h Traded to Tampa Bay Rays for player to be named later, August 23, 2013. Washington Nationals received pitcher Matthew Spann to complete trade, September 19, 2013.

DENORFIA, CHRISTOPHER ANTHONY (CHRIS)

Born, Bristol, Connecticut, July 15, 1980.
Bats Right. Throws Right. Height, 6 feet, 1 inch. Weight, 205 pounds.

Year Club	Lea	Pos	G	AB	R	H	2B	3B	HR	RBI	SB	Avg
2002 Reds	Gulf Coast	OF	57	200	38	68	9	2	0	19	18	.340
2002 Dayton	Midwest	OF	3	10	2	0	0	0	0	0	0	.000
2002 Chattanooga	Southern	OF	3	7	0	3	2	1	0	0	0	.429
2003 Potomac	Carolina	OF	128	470	60	111	10	5	4	39	20	.236
2004 Potomac	Carolina	OF	75	269	52	84	18	4	11	51	10	.312
2004 Chattanooga	Southern	OF	61	221	30	55	10	2	6	27	5	.249
2005 Chattanooga	Southern	OF	46	188	40	62	17	3	7	26	4	.330
2005 Louisville	Int.	OF	91	323	50	100	12	6	13	61	8	.310
2005 Cincinnati	N.L.	OF	18	38	8	10	3	0	1	2	1	.263
2006 Louisville	Int.	OF	83	312	46	109	19	1	7	45	15	.349
2006 Cincinnati	N.L.	OF	49	106	14	30	6	0	1	7	1	.283
2007 Cincinnati	N.L.	INJURED—Did Not Play										
2007 Oakland a-b	A.L.	INJURED—Did Not Play										
2008 Stockton	Calif.	OF	2	9	1	3	0	0	0	0	0	.333
2008 Sacramento	P.C.	OF	45	189	34	57	13	1	2	20	5	.302
2008 Oakland c	A.L.	OF	29	62	10	18	3	0	1	9	2	.290
2009 Oakland	A.L.	OF	4	2	1	0	0	0	0	1	0	.000
2009 Sacramento d	P.C.	OF	107	432	62	117	18	5	9	49	15	.271
2010 Portland	P.C.	OF	34	121	17	37	10	4	2	12	7	.306
2010 San Diego	N.L.	OF	99	284	41	77	15	2	9	36	8	.271
2011 Lake Elsinore	Calif.	OF	2	6	1	4	1	0	0	2	0	.667
2011 Tucson	P.C.	OF	7	17	0	2	1	0	0	0	0	.118
2011 San Diego e	N.L.	OF	111	307	38	85	13	2	5	19	11	.277
2012 San Diego	N.L.	OF	130	348	56	102	19	6	8	36	13	.293
2013 San Diego	N.L.	OF	144	473	67	132	21	2	10	47	11	.279
Major League Totals		8 Yrs.	584	1620	235	454	80	12	35	157	47	.280

a On disabled list from March 24 to October 15, 2007.
b Traded to Oakland Athletics for pitcher Marcus McBeth and player to be named later, April 27, 2007. Cincinnati Reds received pitcher Ben Jukich to complete trade, June 12, 2007.
c On disabled list from May 7 to July 19, 2008.
d Filed for free agency, November 9, 2009. Signed with San Diego Padres organization, December 17, 2009.
e On disabled list from August 4 to September 5, 2011.

DESCALSO, DANIEL WILLIAM

Born, Redwood City, California, October 19, 1986.
Bats Left. Throws Right. Height, 5 feet, 10 inches. Weight, 190 pounds.

Year Club Lea	Pos	G	AB	R	H	2B	3B	HR	RBI	SB	Avg
2007 Batavia......N.Y.-Penn.	3B-2B	66	250	29	67	7	5	0	31	12	.268
2008 Palm Beach ..... Fla.St.	2B-SS-3B	115	403	57	98	24	2	8	50	7	.243
2008 Springfield ...... Texas	2B	9	37	6	13	1	1	0	4	1	.351
2009 Memphis .... P.C.	2B-1B	46	150	23	38	4	0	2	17	3	.253
2009 Springfield ...... Texas	2B	73	288	46	93	26	5	8	51	0	.323
2010 Memphis .... P.C.	2B-1B	116	468	86	132	32	3	9	71	8	.282
2010 St. Louis..........N.L.	3B-SS	11	34	6	9	2	0	0	4	1	.265
2011 St. Louis..........N.L.	3B-2B-SS	148	326	35	86	20	3	1	28	2	.264
2012 St. Louis..........N.L.	2B-SS-3B-1B	143	374	41	85	10	7	4	26	6	.227
2013 St. Louis..........N.L.	SS-2B-3B	123	328	43	78	25	1	5	43	6	.238
Major League Totals	4 Yrs.	425	1062	125	258	57	11	10	101	15	.243
Wild Card Playoff											
2012 St. Louis..........N.L.	2B	1	3	0	0	0	0	0	0	0	.000
Division Series											
2011 St. Louis..........N.L.	3B	4	3	0	0	0	0	0	0	0	.000
2012 St. Louis..........N.L.	2B	5	19	7	6	1	0	2	6	1	.316
2013 St. Louis..........N.L.	3B-SS	5	9	0	1	0	0	0	0	0	.111
Division Series Totals		14	31	7	7	1	0	2	6	1	.226
Championship Series											
2011 St. Louis..........N.L.	3B-2B	4	3	1	1	0	0	0	0	0	.333
2012 St. Louis..........N.L.	2B	7	25	2	5	1	0	0	0	1	.200
2013 St. Louis..........N.L.	3B-SS	5	7	2	2	0	0	0	0	0	.286
Championship Series Totals		16	35	5	8	1	0	0	0	1	.229
World Series Record											
2011 St. Louis..........N.L.	3B-SS	5	3	2	2	0	0	0	0	0	.667
2013 St. Louis..........N.L.	SS-3B	4	10	2	1	0	0	0	0	0	.100
World Series Totals.............		9	13	4	3	0	0	0	0	0	.231

DESMOND, IAN M.

Born, Sarasota, Florida, September 20, 1985.
Bats Right. Throws Right. Height, 6 feet, 2 inches. Weight, 210 pounds.

Year Club Lea	Pos	G	AB	R	H	2B	3B	HR	RBI	SB	Avg
2004 Expos.......Gulf Coast	SS	55	216	28	49	11	0	1	27	13	.227
2004 Vermont.....N.Y.-Penn.	SS	4	12	2	3	0	0	1	1	0	.250
2005 Potomac...... Carolina	SS	55	219	37	56	13	3	3	15	13	.256
2005 Savannah........So.Atl.	SS	73	296	37	73	10	2	4	23	20	.247
2006 Potomac...... Carolina	SS	92	365	50	89	20	2	9	45	14	.244
2006 Harrisburg ..... Eastern	SS	37	121	8	22	4	1	0	3	4	.182
2007 Potomac...... Carolina	SS	129	458	69	121	30	4	13	45	27	.264
2008 Harrisburg ..... Eastern	SS	93	323	42	81	14	0	12	44	12	.251
2008 Nationals ....Gulf Coast	SS	3	13	1	5	1	0	0	2	3	.385
2009 Harrisburg ..... Eastern	SS	42	170	29	52	12	1	6	18	13	.306
2009 Syracuse .... Int.	SS-OF	55	178	25	63	12	2	1	14	8	.354
2009 Washington ........N.L.	SS-2B-OF	21	82	9	23	7	2	4	12	1	.280
2010 Washington ........N.L.	SS-OF	154	525	59	141	27	4	10	65	17	.269
2011 Washington ........N.L.	SS	154	584	65	148	27	5	8	49	25	.253
2012 Washington a.......N.L.	SS	130	513	72	150	33	2	25	73	21	.292
2013 Washington ........N.L.	SS	158	600	77	168	38	3	20	80	21	.280
Major League Totals	5 Yrs.	617	2304	282	630	132	16	67	279	85	.273
Division Series											
2012 Washington ........N.L.	SS	5	19	2	7	1	0	0	0	0	.368

a On disabled list from July 22 to August 17, 2012.

DICKERSON, MC KENZIE COREY (COREY)

Born, McComb, Mississippi, May 22, 1989.
Bats Left. Throws Right. Height, 6 feet, 1 inch. Weight, 205 pounds.

Year Club	Lea	Pos	G	AB	R	H	2B	3B	HR	RBI	SB	Avg
2010 Casper	Pioneer	OF	69	276	54	96	22	9	13	61	12	.348
2011 Asheville	So.Atl.	OF	106	383	78	108	27	5	32	87	9	.282
2012 Modesto	Calif.	OF	60	240	43	81	24	4	9	43	9	.338
2012 Tulsa	Texas	OF	67	266	40	73	16	3	13	38	7	.274
2013 Colorado Springs	P.C.	OF	75	315	61	117	21	14	11	50	6	.371
2013 Colorado	N.L.	OF	69	194	32	51	13	5	5	17	2	.263

DIRKS, ANDREW LEE (ANDY)

Born, Hutchinson, Kansas, January 24, 1986.
Bats Left. Throws Left. Height, 6 feet. Weight, 195 pounds.

Year Club	Lea	Pos	G	AB	R	H	2B	3B	HR	RBI	SB	Avg
2008 Tigers	Gulf Coast	OF	10	34	10	14	3	2	0	7	2	.412
2008 West Michigan	Midwest	OF	3	10	0	1	0	0	0	2	0	.100
2009 Erie	Eastern	OF	98	361	46	92	14	1	6	44	11	.255
2009 Lakeland	Fla.St.	OF	27	103	11	34	5	0	0	18	10	.330
2010 Erie	Eastern	OF	98	388	64	108	20	2	11	46	19	.278
2010 Toledo	Int.	OF	22	88	14	33	10	1	4	17	3	.375
2011 Toledo	Int.	OF	41	157	30	51	8	1	7	24	12	.325
2011 Detroit	A.L.	OF	78	219	34	55	13	0	7	28	5	.251
2012 Toledo	Int.	OF	10	37	4	8	1	0	2	5	2	.216
2012 Detroit a	A.L.	OF	88	314	56	101	18	5	8	35	1	.322
2013 Detroit	A.L.	OF	131	438	60	112	16	2	9	37	7	.256
Major League Totals		3 Yrs.	297	971	150	268	47	7	24	100	13	.276
Division Series												
2012 Detroit	A.L.	OF	5	17	0	5	1	0	0	0	1	.294
2013 Detroit	A.L.	OF	2	3	2	0	0	0	0	0	0	.000
Division Series Totals			7	20	2	5	1	0	0	0	1	.250
Championship Series												
2011 Detroit	A.L.	OF	2	5	1	1	0	0	0	0	1	.200
2012 Detroit	A.L.	OF	4	18	0	4	1	0	0	1	0	.222
2013 Detroit	A.L.	OF	1	2	0	0	0	0	0	0	0	.000
Championship Series Totals			7	25	1	5	1	0	0	1	1	.200
World Series Record												
2012 Detroit	A.L.	OF	4	9	0	1	0	0	0	0	0	.111

a On disabled list from May 31 to August 3, 2012.

DOBBS, GREGORY STUART (GREG)

Born, Los Angeles, California, July 2, 1978.
Bats Left. Throws Right. Height, 6 feet, 1 inch. Weight, 205 pounds.

Year Club	Lea	Pos	G	AB	R	H	2B	3B	HR	RBI	SB	Avg
2001 San Bernardino	Calif.	OF	3	13	2	5	1	0	1	3	0	.385
2001 Everett	Northwest	1B-OF-3B	65	249	37	80	17	2	6	41	5	.321
2002 Wisconsin	Midwest	3B	86	320	43	88	16	2	10	48	13	.275
2002 San Antonio	Texas	OF-1B	27	96	13	35	2	0	5	15	1	.365
2003 San Antonio	Texas	3B	2	6	0	2	2	0	0	0	0	.333
2004 San Antonio	Texas	3B	51	203	25	66	14	4	5	34	5	.325
2004 Tacoma	P.C.	3B	67	255	28	69	9	2	8	31	4	.271
2004 Seattle	A.L.	3B	18	53	4	12	1	0	1	9	0	.226
2005 Tacoma	P.C.	1B-3B-OF	50	190	27	61	9	0	3	22	5	.321
2005 Seattle	A.L.	DH-1B-OF-3B	59	142	8	35	7	1	1	20	1	.246
2006 Tacoma	P.C.	3B-1B-OF	99	379	60	119	19	3	9	55	14	.314
2006 Seattle	A.L.	1B-OF-3B	23	27	4	10	3	1	0	3	0	.370
2007 Philadelphia a	N.L.	3B-OF-1B-2B	142	324	45	88	20	4	10	55	3	.272
2008 Philadelphia	N.L.	3B-OF-1B	128	226	30	68	14	1	9	40	3	.301
2009 Philadelphia b	N.L.	3B-OF-1B	97	154	15	38	6	0	5	20	1	.247
2010 Lehigh Valley	Int.	OF-3B	16	62	10	13	3	1	2	9	2	.210
2010 Philadelphia c	N.L.	3B-1B-OF	88	163	13	32	7	0	5	15	1	.196
2011 Florida d	N.L.	3B-OF-1B	134	411	38	113	23	0	8	49	0	.275
2012 Miami	N.L.	OF-3B-1B	120	319	26	91	13	2	5	39	4	.285
2013 Miami	N.L.	1B-OF	114	237	21	54	11	0	2	22	1	.228
Major League Totals		10 Yrs.	923	2056	204	541	105	9	46	272	14	.263
Division Series												
2007 Philadelphia	N.L.	3B	3	3	0	0	0	0	0	0	0	.000

Year	Club	Lea	Pos	G	AB	R	H	2B	3B	HR	RBI	SB	Avg
2008	Philadelphia	N.L.	3B	3	5	0	3	0	0	0	0	0	.600
2009	Philadelphia	N.L.	PH	3	3	0	0	0	0	0	0	0	.000
Division Series Totals				9	11	0	3	0	0	0	0	0	.273
	Championship Series												
2008	Philadelphia	N.L.	3B	3	6	2	3	1	0	0	0	0	.500
2009	Philadelphia	N.L.	PH	2	1	0	0	0	0	0	0	0	.000
Championship Series Totals				5	7	2	3	1	0	0	0	0	.429
	World Series Record												
2008	Philadelphia	N.L.	DH	2	3	0	1	0	0	0	0	0	.333

a Claimed by Philadelphia Phillies on waivers, January 16, 2007.
b On disabled list from August 22 to September 16, 2009.
c Filed for free agency, October 28, 2010. Signed with Florida Marlins organization, January 31, 2011.
d Filed for free agency, October 30, 2011, re-signed with Florida Marlins, January 5, 2012.

DOMINGUEZ, MATTHEW SCOTT (MATT)

Born, Chatsworth, California, August 28, 1989.
Bats Right. Throws Right. Height, 6 feet, 1 inch. Weight, 215 pounds.

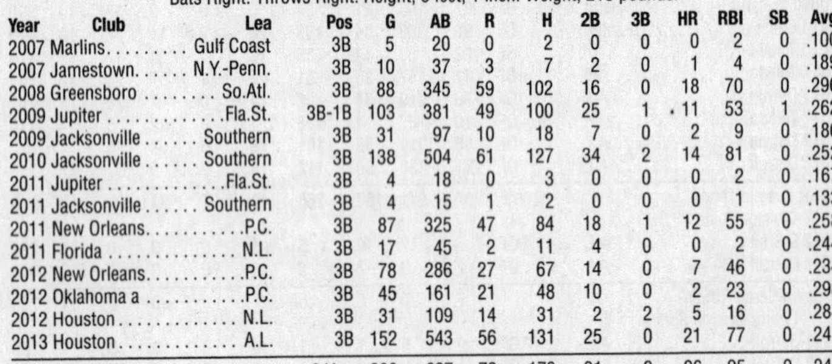

Year	Club	Lea	Pos	G	AB	R	H	2B	3B	HR	RBI	SB	Avg
2007	Marlins.........	Gulf Coast	3B	5	20	0	2	0	0	0	2	0	.100
2007	Jamestown......	N.Y.-Penn.	3B	10	37	3	7	2	0	1	4	0	.189
2008	Greensboro	So.Atl.	3B	88	345	59	102	16	0	18	70	0	.296
2009	Jupiter	Fla.St.	3B-1B	103	381	49	100	25	1	11	53	1	.262
2009	Jacksonville	Southern	3B	31	97	10	18	7	0	2	9	0	.186
2010	Jacksonville	Southern	3B	138	504	61	127	34	2	14	81	0	.252
2011	Jupiter	Fla.St.	3B	4	18	0	3	0	0	0	2	0	.167
2011	Jacksonville	Southern	3B	4	15	1	2	0	0	0	1	0	.133
2011	New Orleans...........	P.C.	3B	87	325	47	84	18	1	12	55	0	.258
2011	Florida	N.L.	3B	17	45	2	11	4	0	0	2	0	.244
2012	New Orleans...........	P.C.	3B	78	286	27	67	14	0	7	46	0	.234
2012	Oklahoma a	P.C.	3B	45	161	21	48	10	0	2	23	0	.298
2012	Houston.............	N.L.	3B	31	109	14	31	2	2	5	16	0	.284
2013	Houston.............	A.L.	3B	152	543	56	131	25	0	21	77	0	.241
Major League Totals			3 Yrs.	200	697	72	173	31	2	26	95	0	.248

a Traded to Houston Astros with pitcher Rob Rasmussen for outfielder Carlos Lee and cash, July 5, 2012.

DONALDSON, JOSHUA ADAM (JOSH)

Born, Pensacola, Florida, December 8, 1985.
Bats Right. Throws Right. Height, 6 feet. Weight, 220 pounds.

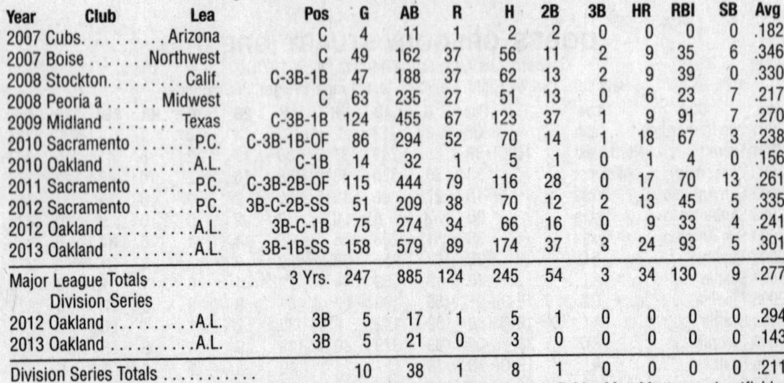

Year	Club	Lea	Pos	G	AB	R	H	2B	3B	HR	RBI	SB	Avg
2007	Cubs..........	Arizona	C	4	11	1	2	2	0	0	0	0	.182
2007	Boise	Northwest	C	49	162	37	56	11	2	9	35	6	.346
2008	Stockton.........	Calif.	C-3B-1B	47	188	37	62	13	2	9	39	0	.330
2008	Peoria a	Midwest	C	63	235	27	51	13	0	6	23	7	.217
2009	Midland	Texas	C-3B-1B	124	455	67	123	37	1	9	91	7	.270
2010	Sacramento	P.C.	C-3B-1B-OF	86	294	52	70	14	1	18	67	3	.238
2010	Oakland	A.L.	C-1B	14	32	1	5	1	0	1	4	0	.156
2011	Sacramento	P.C.	C-3B-2B-OF	115	444	79	116	28	0	17	70	13	.261
2012	Sacramento	P.C.	3B-C-2B-SS	51	209	38	70	12	2	13	45	5	.335
2012	Oakland	A.L.	3B-C-1B	75	274	34	66	16	0	9	33	4	.241
2013	Oakland	A.L.	3B-1B-SS	158	579	89	174	37	3	24	93	5	.301
Major League Totals			3 Yrs.	247	885	124	245	54	3	34	130	9	.277
	Division Series												
2012	Oakland	A.L.	3B	5	17	1	5	1	0	0	0	0	.294
2013	Oakland	A.L.	3B	5	21	0	3	0	0	0	0	0	.143
Division Series Totals				10	38	1	8	1	0	0	0	0	.211

a Traded by Chicago Cubs to Oakland Athletics with pitcher Sean Gallagher, outfielder Matt Murton and outfielder Eric Patterson for pitcher Rich Harden and pitcher Chad Gaudin, July 8, 2008.

DOUMIT, RYAN MATTHEW

Born, Moses Lake, Washington, April 3, 1981.
Bats Both. Throws Right. Height, 6 feet. Weight, 200 pounds.

Year	Club	Lea	Pos	G	AB	R	H	2B	3B	HR	RBI	SB	Avg
1999	Pirates	Gulf Coast	C	29	85	17	24	5	0	1	7	4	.282
2000	Williamsport.....	N.Y.-Penn.	C	66	246	25	77	15	5	2	40	2	.313
2001	Altoona............	Eastern	C	2	4	0	1	0	0	0	2	0	.250

Year	Club	Lea	Pos	G	AB	R	H	2B	3B	HR	RBI	SB	Avg
2001	Pirates	Gulf Coast	C	7	17	2	4	2	0	0	3	0	.235
2001	Hickory	So.Atl.	C	39	148	14	40	6	0	2	14	2	.270
2002	Hickory	So.Atl.	C	68	258	46	83	14	1	6	47	3	.322
2003	Lynchburg	Carolina	C	127	458	75	126	38	1	11	77	4	.275
2004	Altoona	Eastern	C	67	221	31	58	20	0	10	34	0	.262
2005	Indianapolis	Int.	C-OF	51	165	41	57	11	0	12	35	1	.345
2005	Pittsburgh	N.L.	C-OF	75	231	25	59	13	1	6	35	2	.255
2006	Pirates	Gulf Coast	C-1B	5	14	1	0	0	0	0	0	0	.000
2006	Altoona	Eastern	C-1B	4	15	4	5	3	0	0	4	0	.333
2006	Indianapolis	Int.	C	6	22	3	7	1	1	0	7	0	.318
2006	Pittsburgh a	N.L.	1B-C	61	149	15	31	9	0	6	17	0	.208
2007	Indianapolis	Int.	C	16	53	15	22	4	0	4	20	3	.415
2007	Pittsburgh b	N.L.	OF-C-1B	83	252	33	69	19	2	9	32	1	.274
2008	Altoona	Eastern	C	3	7	0	3	0	0	0	0	0	.429
2008	Pittsburgh c	N.L.	C-1B	116	431	71	137	34	0	15	69	2	.318
2009	Pirates	Gulf Coast	C	2	7	0	0	0	0	0	0	0	.000
2009	Indianapolis	Int.	C	5	17	1	2	0	0	0	0	0	.118
2009	Pittsburgh d	N.L.	C-OF	75	280	31	70	16	0	10	38	4	.250
2010	Indianapolis	Int.	OF-C	4	12	2	2	1	0	1	2	0	.167
2010	Pittsburgh e	N.L.	C-OF-1B	124	406	42	102	22	1	13	45	1	.251
2011	Bradenton	Fla.St.	C	5	14	1	2	0	0	0	1	0	.143
2011	Indianapolis	Int.	C	8	26	4	6	1	1	0	3	0	.231
2011	Pittsburgh f-g	N.L.	C	77	218	17	66	12	1	8	30	0	.303
2012	Minnesota	A.L.	C-OF-1B	134	484	56	133	34	1	18	75	0	.275
2013	Minnesota h-i	A.L.	DH-C-OF	135	485	49	120	28	1	14	55	1	.247
Major League Totals			9 Yrs.	880	2936	339	787	187	7	99	396	11	.268

a On disabled list from April 12 to May 3 and June 5 to August 23, 2006.
b On disabled list from August 13 to September 8 and September 9 to November 13, 2007.
c On disabled list from May 14 to June 6, 2008.
d On disabled list from April 20 to July 10, 2009.
e On disabled list from July 22 to August 7, 2010.
f On disabled list from May 30 to August 3, 2011.
g Filed for free agency, October 31, 2011. Signed with Minnesota Twins, November 23, 2011.
h On disabled list from August 8 to August 16, 2013.
i Traded to Atlanta Braves for pitcher Sean Gilmartin, December 18, 2013.

DOZIER, JAMES BRIAN (BRIAN)

Born, Tupelo, Mississippi, May 15, 1987.
Bats Right. Throws Right. Height, 5 feet, 11 inches. Weight, 190 pounds.

Year	Club	Lea	Pos	G	AB	R	H	2B	3B	HR	RBI	SB	Avg
2009	Twins	Gulf Coast	SS	5	14	1	4	0	0	0	0	0	.286
2009	Elizabethton	Appal.	SS	53	218	38	77	17	0	0	14	3	.353
2010	Beloit	Midwest	SS-2B-3B	39	151	24	42	7	1	0	17	6	.278
2010	Fort Myers	Fla.St.	SS-3B-2B	93	350	44	96	11	1	5	42	10	.274
2011	Fort Myers	Fla.St.	SS-2B-3B	49	180	32	58	11	5	2	22	13	.322
2011	New Britain	Eastern	SS-2B-3B	78	311	60	99	22	7	7	34	11	.318
2012	Minnesota	A.L.	SS	84	316	33	74	11	1	6	33	9	.234
2012	Rochester	Int.	SS-2B	48	181	15	42	11	1	2	17	3	.232
2013	Minnesota	A.L.	2B	147	558	72	136	33	4	18	66	14	.244
Major League Totals			2 Yrs.	231	874	105	210	44	5	24	99	23	.240

DREW, STEPHEN ORIS

Born, Hahira, Georgia, March 16, 1983.
Bats Left. Throws Right. Height, 6 feet, 1 inch. Weight, 185 pounds.

Year	Club	Lea	Pos	G	AB	R	H	2B	3B	HR	RBI	SB	Avg
2005	Tennessee	Southern	SS	27	101	11	22	5	0	4	13	2	.218
2006	Tucson	P.C.	SS	83	342	55	97	16	3	13	51	3	.284
2006	Arizona	N.L.	SS	59	209	27	66	13	7	5	23	2	.316
2007	Arizona	N.L.	SS	150	543	60	129	28	4	12	60	9	.238
2008	Arizona	N.L.	SS	152	611	91	178	44	11	21	67	3	.291
2009	Reno	P.C.	SS	2	9	0	3	0	1	0	1	0	.333
2009	Arizona a	N.L.	SS	135	533	71	139	29	12	12	65	5	.261
2010	Arizona	N.L.	SS	151	565	83	157	33	12	15	61	10	.278
2011	Arizona b	N.L.	SS	86	321	44	81	21	5	5	45	4	.252
2012	Mobile	Southern	SS	2	5	0	1	0	0	0	0	0	.200
2012	Reno	P.C.	SS	9	36	6	9	1	1	2	5	0	.250
2012	Arizona	N.L.	SS	40	135	17	26	8	1	2	12	0	.193
2012	Oakland c-d-e	A.L.	SS	39	152	21	38	5	0	5	16	1	.250

Year	Club	Lea	Pos	G	AB	R	H	2B	3B	HR	RBI	SB	Avg
2013	Portland	Eastern	SS	6	20	1	4	2	0	1	4	0	.200
2013	Boston f-g	A.L.	SS	124	442	57	112	29	8	13	67	6	.253
Major League Totals			8 Yrs.	936	3511	471	926	210	60	90	416	40	.264
	Division Series												
2007	Arizona	N.L.	SS	3	14	4	7	1	1	2	4	1	.500
2012	Oakland	A.L.	SS	5	19	0	4	2	0	0	1	0	.211
2013	Boston	A.L.	SS	4	15	1	2	0	1	0	2	0	.133
Division Series Totals				12	48	5	13	3	2	2	7	1	.271
	Championship Series												
2007	Arizona	N.L.	SS	4	17	2	5	0	0	0	0	0	.294
2013	Boston	A.L.	SS	6	20	0	1	0	0	0	0	0	.050
Championship Series Totals				10	37	2	6	0	0	0	0	0	.162
	World Series Record												
2013	Boston	A.L.	SS	6	19	3	3	0	0	1	2	0	.158

a On disabled list from April 25 to May 12, 2009.
b On disabled list from July 21 to October 31, 2011.
c On disabled list from March 26 to June 27, 2012.
d Traded to Oakland Athletics for infielder Sean Jamieson, August 21, 2012.
e Filed for free agency, November 3, 2012. Signed with Boston Red Sox, December 26, 2012.
f On disabled list from March 27 to April 10 and June 29 to July 20, 2013.
g Filed for free agency, October 31, 2013.

DUDA, LUCAS CHRISTOPHER

Born, Fontana, California, February 3, 1986.
Bats Left. Throws Right. Height, 6 feet, 5 inches. Weight, 255 pounds.

Year	Club	Lea	Pos	G	AB	R	H	2B	3B	HR	RBI	SB	Avg
2007	Brooklyn	N.Y.-Penn.	1B-OF	67	234	32	70	20	3	4	32	3	.299
2008	St. Lucie	Fla.St.	1B-OF	133	483	58	127	26	3	11	66	2	.263
2009	Binghamton	Eastern	1B-OF	110	395	49	111	29	1	9	53	2	.281
2010	Binghamton	Eastern	OF-1B	45	161	30	46	17	0	6	34	1	.286
2010	Buffalo	Int.	OF-1B	70	264	44	83	23	2	17	53	0	.314
2010	New York	N.L.	OF	29	84	11	17	6	0	4	13	0	.202
2011	Buffalo	Int.	OF-1B	38	129	22	39	8	0	10	24	0	.302
2011	New York	N.L.	OF-1B	100	301	38	88	21	3	10	50	1	.292
2012	Buffalo	Int.	OF-1B	25	96	12	25	4	0	3	8	0	.260
2012	New York	N.L.	OF-1B	121	401	43	96	15	0	15	57	1	.239
2013	Mets	Gulf Coast	OF	4	13	1	0	0	0	0	1	0	.000
2013	St. Lucie	Fla.St.	OF	7	28	4	7	2	0	1	5	0	.250
2013	Las Vegas	P.C.,	1B-OF	18	62	13	19	3	0	0	8	1	.306
2013	New York a	N.L.	OF-1B	100	318	42	71	16	0	15	33	0	.223
Major League Totals			4 Yrs.	350	1104	134	272	58	3	44	153	2	.246

a On disabled list from June 22 to August 7, 2013.

DUNN, ADAM TROY

Born, Houston, Texas, November 9, 1979.
Bats Left. Throws Right. Height, 6 feet, 6 inches. Weight, 275 pounds.

Year	Club	Lea	Pos	G	AB	R	H	2B	3B	HR	RBI	SB	Avg
1998	Billings	Pioneer	OF	34	125	26	36	3	1	4	13	4	.288
1999	Rockford	Midwest	OF	92	313	62	96	16	2	11	44	21	.307
2000	Dayton	Midwest	OF	122	420	101	118	29	1	16	79	24	.281
2001	Chattanooga	Southern	OF	39	140	30	48	9	0	12	31	6	.343
2001	Louisville	Int.	OF	55	210	44	69	13	0	20	53	5	.329
2001	Cincinnati	N.L.	OF	66	244	54	64	18	1	19	43	4	.262
2002	Cincinnati	N.L.	OF-1B	158	535	84	133	28	2	26	71	19	.249
2003	Cincinnati a	N.L.	OF-1B	116	381	70	82	12	1	27	57	8	.215
2004	Cincinnati	N.L.	OF-1B	161	568	105	151	34	0	46	102	6	.266
2005	Cincinnati	N.L.	OF-1B	160	543	107	134	35	2	40	101	4	.247
2006	Cincinnati	N.L.	OF-1B	160	561	99	131	24	0	40	92	7	.234
2007	Cincinnati	N.L.	OF	152	522	101	138	27	2	40	106	9	.264
2008	Cincinnati-Arizona b-c	N.L.	OF-1B	158	517	79	122	23	0	40	100	2	.236
2009	Washington	N.L.	OF-1B	159	546	81	146	29	0	38	105	0	.267
2010	Washington d	N.L.	1B	158	558	85	145	36	2	38	103	0	.260
2011	Chicago	A.L.	DH-1B-OF	122	415	36	66	16	0	11	42	0	.159
2012	Chicago	A.L.	DH-1B-OF	151	539	87	110	19	0	41	96	2	.204
2013	Chicago	A.L.	DH-1B-OF	149	525	60	115	15	0	34	86	1	.219
Major League Totals			13 Yrs.	1870	6454	1048	1537	316	10	440	1104	62	.238

a On disabled list from August 16 to October 2, 2003.
b Traded to Arizona Diamondbacks for pitcher Dallas Buck and two players to be named later, August 12, 2008. To complete trade, Cincinnati Reds received catcher Wilkin Castillo on August 14, 2008 and pitcher Micah Owings on September 10, 2008.
c Filed for free agency, November 1, 2008. Signed with Washington Nationals, February 11, 2009.
d Filed for free agency, November 1, 2010. Signed with Chicago White Sox, December 3, 2010.

DYSON, JARROD MARTEL

Born, McComb, Mississippi, August 15, 1984.
Bats Left. Throws Right. Height, 5 feet, 9 inches. Weight, 165 pounds.

Year	Club	Lea	Pos	G	AB	R	H	2B	3B	HR	RBI	SB	Avg
2006	Royals	Arizona	OF	51	161	40	44	4	6	0	19	19	.273
2007	Burlington	Midwest	OF	10	37	6	10	1	0	0	0	3	.270
2008	Wilmington	Carolina	OF	93	288	40	75	8	0	0	24	39	.260
2009	Burlington	Midwest	OF	17	67	14	23	2	1	0	5	9	.343
2009	NW Arkansas	Texas	OF	63	248	38	64	7	4	0	14	37	.258
2010	Royals	Arizona	OF	6	25	4	13	1	1	0	6	3	.520
2010	Wilmington	Carolina	OF	12	49	7	16	6	2	0	9	5	.327
2010	NW Arkansas	Texas	OF	7	25	6	6	0	0	0	6	3	.240
2010	Omaha	P.C.	OF	46	195	33	53	10	1	1	19	13	.272
2010	Kansas City	A.L.	OF	18	57	11	12	4	2	1	5	9	.211
2011	Omaha	P.C.	OF	83	319	69	89	10	3	3	26	38	.279
2011	Kansas City	A.L.	OF	26	44	8	9	1	0	0	3	11	.205
2012	Omaha	P.C.	OF	15	63	12	21	3	3	0	5	7	.333
2012	Kansas City	A.L.	OF	102	292	52	76	8	5	0	9	30	.260
2013	Omaha	P.C.	OF	15	52	8	8	2	0	0	1	5	.154
2013	Kansas City a	A.L.	OF	87	213	30	55	9	4	2	17	34	.258
Major League Totals		4 Yrs.		233	606	101	152	22	11	3	34	84	.251

a On disabled list from May 16 to June 22, 2013.

EATON, ADAM C.

Born, Springfield, Ohio, December 6, 1988.
Bats Left. Throws Left. Height, 5 feet, 8 inches. Weight, 185 pounds.

Year	Club	Lea	Pos	G	AB	R	H	2B	3B	HR	RBI	SB	Avg
2010	Missoula	Pioneer	OF	68	226	48	87	14	4	7	37	20	.385
2011	Visalia	Calif.	OF	65	244	54	81	15	3	6	39	24	.332
2011	Mobile	Southern	OF	56	212	31	64	7	4	4	28	10	.302
2012	Mobile	Southern	OF	11	40	11	12	1	0	0	3	6	.300
2012	Reno	P.C.	OF	119	488	119	186	46	5	7	45	38	.381
2012	Arizona	N.L.	OF	22	85	19	22	3	2	2	5	2	.259
2013	D-Backs	Arizona	DH	1	2	1	1	0	0	0	2	0	.500
2013	Visalia	Calif.	OF	15	53	12	17	3	0	1	6	8	.321
2013	Reno	P.C.	OF	10	35	5	5	2	0	1	5	0	.143
2013	Arizona a-b	N.L.	OF	66	250	40	63	10	4	3	22	5	.252
Major League Totals		2 Yrs.		88	335	59	85	13	6	5	27	7	.254

a On disabled list from March 22 to July 9, 2013.
b Traded to Chicago White Sox for pitcher Hector Santiago and player to be named later, December 10, 2013. Diamondbacks received outfielder Brandon Jacobs to complete trade, December 13, 2013.

ELLIS, ANDREW JAMES (A.J.)

Born, Cape Girardeau, Missouri, April 9, 1981.
Bats Right. Throws Right. Height, 6 feet, 3 inches. Weight, 225 pounds.

Year	Club	Lea	Pos	G	AB	R	H	2B	3B	HR	RBI	SB	Avg
2003	South Georgia	So.Atl.	C-1B	3	6	0	0	0	0	0	0	0	.000
2004	Vero Beach	Fla.St.	C-1B	40	114	15	25	4	0	2	22	1	.219
2005	Vero Beach	Fla.St.	C	57	176	27	45	8	0	3	22	1	.256
2006	Jacksonville	Southern	C	81	252	34	63	9	1	0	21	2	.250
2007	Jacksonville	Southern	C-1B-OF	109	357	59	96	22	2	8	57	1	.269
2008	Las Vegas	P.C.	C-1B	84	274	44	88	17	4	4	59	0	.321
2008	Los Angeles	N.L.	C	4	3	1	0	0	0	0	0	0	.000
2009	Albuquerque	P.C.	C	90	283	48	89	13	2	0	39	2	.314
2009	Los Angeles	N.L.	C	8	10	0	1	0	0	0	1	0	.100
2010	Albuquerque	P.C.	C	18	61	11	16	5	1	0	7	1	.262
2010	Los Angeles	N.L.	C	44	108	6	30	5	0	0	16	0	.278
2011	Albuquerque	P.C.	C-1B	59	184	36	56	15	0	2	28	0	.304
2011	Los Angeles	N.L.	C	31	85	8	23	1	1	2	11	0	.271
2012	Los Angeles	N.L.	C	133	423	44	114	20	1	13	52	0	.270
2013	Rancho Cucamonga	Calif.	DH	2	7	0	0	0	0	0	0	0	.000

Year	Club	Lea	Pos	G	AB	R	H	2B	3B	HR	RBI	SB	Avg
2013	Los Angeles a	N.L.	C	115	390	43	93	17	1	10	52	0	.238
Major League Totals			6 Yrs.	335	1019	102	261	43	3	25	132	0	.256
	Division Series												
2013	Los Angeles	N.L.	C	4	12	2	4	2	0	0	1	0	.333
	Championship Series												
2013	Los Angeles	N.L.	C	6	19	1	6	2	1	1	2	0	.316

a On disabled list from May 30 to June 14, 2013.

ELLIS, MARK WILLIAM

Born, Rapid City, South Dakota, June 6, 1977.

Bats Right. Throws Right. Height, 5 feet, 11 inches. Weight, 195 pounds.

Year	Club	Lea	Pos	G	AB	R	H	2B	3B	HR	RBI	SB	Avg
1999	Spokane	Northwest	SS	71	281	67	92	14	0	7	47	21	.327
2000	Wilmington	Carolina	SS-2B	132	484	83	146	27	4	6	62	25	.302
2000	Wichita	Texas	2B	7	22	4	7	1	0	0	4	1	.318
2001	Sacramento a	P.C.	SS	132	472	71	129	38	0	10	53	21	.273
2002	Sacramento	P.C.	SS	21	84	14	25	10	1	0	5	4	.298
2002	Oakland	A.L.	2B-SS-3B	98	345	58	94	16	4	6	35	4	.272
2003	Oakland	A.L.	2B	154	553	78	137	31	5	9	52	6	.248
2004	Oakland b	A.L.	INJURED—Did Not Play										
2005	Oakland	A.L.	2B-SS-1B	122	434	76	137	21	5	13	52	1	.316
2006	Sacramento	P.C.	2B	4	12	1	2	0	0	0	2	0	.167
2006	Oakland c	A.L.	2B-1B	124	441	64	110	25	1	11	52	4	.249
2007	Oakland	A.L.	2B	150	583	84	161	33	3	19	76	9	.276
2008	Oakland d	A.L.	2B	117	442	55	103	20	3	12	41	14	.233
2009	Stockton	Calif.	2B	2	4	0	0	0	0	0	0	0	.000
2009	Sacramento	P.C.	2B	8	33	2	6	1	0	0	3	0	.182
2009	Oakland e	A.L.	2B	105	377	52	99	23	0	10	61	10	.263
2010	Stockton	Calif.	2B	2	5	0	1	0	0	0	1	0	.200
2010	Sacramento	P.C.	2B	1	4	0	1	0	0	0	0	0	.250
2010	Oakland f	A.L.	2B	124	436	45	127	24	0	5	49	7	.291
2011	Sacramento	P.C.	2B	3	10	0	2	1	0	0	1	0	.200
2011	Oakland	A.L.	2B-1B	62	217	21	47	11	1	1	16	7	.217
2011	Colorado g-h-i	N.L.	2B	70	263	34	72	13	0	6	25	7	.274
2012	Rancho Cucamonga	Calif.	2B	4	14	3	4	0	0	0	3	0	.286
2012	Los Angeles j	N.L.	2B	110	415	62	107	21	1	7	31	5	.258
2013	Chattanooga	Southern	2B	2	4	1	0	0	0	0	0	0	.000
2013	Los Angeles k-l	N.L.	2B-3B	126	433	46	117	13	2	6	48	4	.270
Major League Totals			11 Yrs.	1362	4939	675	1311	251	25	105	538	78	.265
	Division Series												
2002	Oakland	A.L.	2B	5	19	1	7	2	0	1	4	0	.368
2003	Oakland	A.L.	2B	5	17	2	2	0	0	0	0	0	.118
2006	Oakland	A.L.	2B	2	7	0	2	0	0	0	0	0	.286
2013	Los Angeles	N.L.	2B	4	15	4	4	2	0	0	1	0	.267
Division Series Totals				16	58	7	15	4	0	1	5	0	.259
	Championship Series												
2013	Los Angeles	N.L.	2B	6	25	1	6	1	1	0	0	1	.240

a Traded to Oakland Athletics by Kansas City Royals with outfielder Johnny Damon and player to be named later for pitcher Roberto Hernandez, catcher A.J. Hinch, infielder Angel Berroa and cash, January 8, 2001.
b On disabled list from March 26 to October 20, 2004.
c On disabled list from June 1 to June 30, 2006.
d On disabled list from September 21 to November 14, 2008.
e On disabled list from April 29 to June 28, 2009.
f On disabled list from April 21 to May 22, 2010.
g On disabled list from June 7 to June 22, 2011.
h Traded to Colorado Rockies for pitcher Bruce Billings, cash and player to be named later, June 30, 2011. Oakland Athletics received outfielder Eliezer Mesa to complete trade, September 30, 2011.
i Filed for free agency, October 30, 2011. Signed with Los Angeles Dodgers, November 14, 2011.
j On disabled list from May 19 to July 4, 2012.
k On disabled list from April 27 to May 19, 2013.
l Filed for free agency, October 31, 2013. Signed with St. Louis Cardinals, December 16, 2013.

ELLSBURY, JACOBY McCABE

Born, Madras, Oregon, September 11, 1983.

Bats Left. Throws Left. Height, 6 feet, 1 inch. Weight, 185 pounds.

Year	Club	Lea	Pos	G	AB	R	H	2B	3B	HR	RBI	SB	Avg
2005	Lowell	N.Y.-Penn.	OF	35	139	28	44	3	5	1	19	23	.317
2006	Wilmington	Carolina	OF	61	244	35	73	7	5	4	32	25	.299

Year	Club	Lea	Pos	G	AB	R	H	2B	3B	HR	RBI	SB	Avg
2006	Portland	Eastern	OF	50	198	29	61	10	3	3	19	16	.308
2007	Portland	Eastern	OF	17	73	16	33	10	2	0	13	8	.452
2007	Pawtucket	Int.	OF	87	363	66	108	14	5	2	28	33	.298
2007	Boston	A.L.	OF	33	116	20	41	7	1	3	18	9	.353
2008	Boston	A.L.	OF	145	554	98	155	22	7	9	47	*50	.280
2009	Boston	A.L.	OF	153	624	94	188	27	*10	8	60	*70	.301
2010	Red Sox	Gulf Coast	OF	3	8	3	2	0	0	0	0	1	.250
2010	Portland	Eastern	OF	2	7	2	3	1	0	0	0	1	.429
2010	Pawtucket	Int.	OF	4	17	5	8	1	0	0	2	0	.471
2010	Boston a	A.L.	OF	18	78	10	15	4	0	0	5	7	.192
2011	Boston	A.L.	OF	158	660	119	212	46	5	32	105	39	.321
2012	Red Sox	Gulf Coast	OF	4	10	3	2	1	0	1	3	0	.200
2012	Portland	Eastern	OF	2	9	1	2	1	0	0	0	0	.222
2012	Pawtucket	Int.	OF	2	8	1	1	0	0	0	0	0	.125
2012	Boston b	A.L.	OF	74	303	43	82	18	0	4	26	14	.271
2013	Boston c	A.L.	OF	134	577	92	172	31	8	9	53	*52	.298
Major League Totals			7 Yrs.	715	2912	476	865	155	31	65	314	241	.297
	Division Series												
2007	Boston	A.L.	OF	2	1	1	0	0	0	0	0	0	.000
2008	Boston	A.L.	OF	4	18	2	6	3	0	0	6	3	.333
2009	Boston	A.L.	OF	3	12	2	3	0	1	0	0	0	.250
2013	Boston	A.L.	OF	4	18	7	9	2	0	0	2	4	.500
Division Series Totals				13	49	12	18	5	1	0	8	7	.367
	Championship Series												
2007	Boston	A.L.	OF	5	8	3	2	0	0	0	1	1	.250
2008	Boston	A.L.	OF	4	14	0	0	0	0	0	1	0	.000
2013	Boston	A.L.	OF	6	22	3	7	1	1	0	3	2	.318
Championship Series Totals				15	44	6	9	1	1	0	5	3	.205
	World Series Record												
2007	Boston	A.L.	OF	4	16	4	7	4	0	0	3	1	.438
2013	Boston	A.L.	OF	6	24	4	6	1	0	0	1	0	.250
World Series Totals				10	40	8	13	5	0	0	4	1	.325

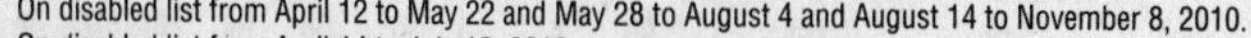

a On disabled list from April 12 to May 22 and May 28 to August 4 and August 14 to November 8, 2010.
b On disabled list from April 14 to July 13, 2012.
c Filed for free agency, October 31, 2013. Signed with New York Yankees, December 4, 2013.

ENCARNACION, EDWIN ELPIDIO

Born, La Romana, Dominican Republic, January 7, 1983.
Bats Right. Throws Right. Height, 6 feet, 1 inch. Weight, 215 pounds.

Year	Club	Lea	Pos	G	AB	R	H	2B	3B	HR	RBI	SB	Avg
2000	Rangers	Gulf Coast	3B	51	177	31	55	6	3	0	36	3	.311
2001	Dayton	Midwest	3B	9	37	2	6	2	0	1	6	0	.162
2001	Billings	Pioneer	3B	52	211	27	55	8	2	5	26	8	.261
2001	Savannah a	So.Atl.	3B	45	170	23	52	9	2	4	25	3	.306
2002	Dayton	Midwest	3B-SS	136	517	80	146	32	4	17	73	25	.282
2003	Potomac	Carolina	3B	58	215	40	69	15	1	6	29	7	.321
2003	Chattanooga	Southern	3B-SS	67	254	40	69	13	1	5	36	8	.272
2004	Chattanooga	Southern	3B	120	469	73	132	35	1	13	76	17	.281
2005	Louisville	Int.	3B	78	290	44	91	23	0	15	54	7	.314
2005	Cincinnati	N.L.	3B	69	211	25	49	16	0	9	31	3	.232
2006	Louisville	Int.	3B-1B	10	36	6	11	3	0	1	1	0	.306
2006	Cincinnati b	N.L.	3B-1B	117	406	60	112	33	1	15	72	6	.276
2007	Louisville	Int.	3B	11	46	12	19	3	0	3	7	1	.413
2007	Cincinnati	N.L.	3B	139	502	66	145	25	1	16	76	8	.289
2008	Cincinnati	N.L.	3B	146	506	75	127	29	1	26	68	1	.251
2009	Louisville	Int.	3B	11	37	5	10	1	0	2	8	0	.270
2009	Cincinnati	N.L.	3B	43	139	10	29	6	1	5	16	1	.209
2009	Toronto c-d-e	A.L.	3B	42	154	25	37	5	1	8	23	1	.240
2010	Dunedin	Fla.St.	3B	3	10	2	1	0	0	1	1	0	.100
2010	Las Vegas	P.C.	3B	7	32	9	14	2	0	3	13	0	.438
2010	Toronto f-g-h	A.L.	3B	96	332	47	81	16	0	21	51	1	.244
2011	Toronto	A.L.	DH-3B-1B	134	481	70	131	36	0	17	55	8	.272
2012	Toronto	A.L.	DH-1B-OF-3B	151	542	93	152	24	0	42	110	13	.280
2013	Toronto i	A.L.	1B-3B	142	530	90	144	29	1	36	104	7	.272
Major League Totals			9 Yrs.	1079	3803	561	1007	219	6	195	606	49	.265

a Traded by Texas Rangers to Cincinnati Reds with outfielder Ruben Mateo for pitcher Rob Bell, June 15, 2001.
b On disabled list from June 7 to July 6, 2006.
c On disabled list from April 28 to July 3, 2009.

d Traded to Toronto Blue Jays with pitcher Josh Roenicke and pitcher Zach Stewart for infielder Scott Rolen, July 31, 2009.
e On disabled list from August 21 to September 5, 2009.
f On disabled list from April 15 to May 18 and August 29 to September 13, 2010.
g Claimed on waivers by Oakland Athletics, November 12, 2010.
h Not offered contract, December 2, 2010. Signed with Toronto Blue Jays, December 16, 2010.
i On disabled list from September 16 to October 1, 2013.

ESCOBAR, ALCIDES

Born, Lasabana, Venezuela, December 16, 1986.
Bats Right. Throws Right. Height, 6 feet, 1 inch. Weight, 180 pounds.

Year	Club	Lea	Pos	G	AB	R	H	2B	3B	HR	RBI	SB	Avg
2004	Helena	Pioneer	SS	67	231	38	65	8	0	2	24	20	.281
2005	West Virginia	So.Atl.	SS	127	520	80	141	25	8	2	36	30	.271
2006	Brevard County	Fla.St.	SS	87	350	47	90	9	1	2	33	28	.257
2007	Brevard County	Fla.St.	SS	63	268	37	87	8	3	0	25	18	.325
2007	Huntsville	Southern	SS	62	226	27	64	5	4	1	28	4	.283
2008	Huntsville	Southern	SS	131	546	95	179	24	5	8	76	34	.328
2008	Milwaukee	N.L.	SS	9	4	2	2	0	0	0	0	0	.500
2009	Nashville	P.C.	SS-2B	109	430	76	128	24	6	4	34	42	.298
2009	Milwaukee	N.L.	SS	38	125	20	38	3	1	1	11	4	.304
2010	Milwaukee a	N.L.	SS-OF	145	506	57	119	14	10	4	41	10	.235
2011	Kansas City	A.L.	SS	158	548	69	139	21	8	4	46	26	.254
2012	Kansas City	A.L.	SS	155	605	68	177	30	7	5	52	35	.293
2013	Kansas City	A.L.	SS	158	607	57	142	20	4	4	52	22	.234
Major League Totals			6 Yrs.	663	2395	273	617	88	30	18	202	97	.258

a Traded to Kansas City Royals with outfielder Lorenzo Cain, pitcher Jeremy Jeffress and pitcher Jake Odorizzi for outfielder Yuniesky Betancourt and pitcher Zack Greinke, December 19, 2010.

ESCOBAR, EDUARDO JOSE

Born, Villa de Cura, Venezuela, January 5, 1989.
Bats Both. Throws Right. Height, 5 feet, 10 inches. Weight, 165 pounds.

Year	Club	Lea	Pos	G	AB	R	H	2B	3B	HR	RBI	SB	Avg
2008	Great Falls	Pioneer	SS	6	24	6	10	2	1	1	4	1	.417
2008	Kannapolis	So.Atl.	SS-2B	60	243	37	65	6	1	0	22	4	.267
2009	Kannapolis	So.Atl.	SS-2B	128	464	64	119	10	7	3	41	20	.256
2010	Winston-Salem	Carolina	SS	87	368	57	105	18	8	3	39	8	.285
2010	Birmingham	Southern	SS	49	202	22	53	8	3	3	22	3	.262
2011	Charlotte	Int.	SS-2B	137	489	55	130	23	4	4	49	13	.266
2011	Chicago	A.L.	SS-2B	9	7	0	2	0	0	0	0	0	.286
2012	Rochester	Int.	3B-SS-2B	35	138	19	30	3	3	1	9	3	.217
2012	Chicago-Minnesota a	A.L.	3B-2B-SS-OF	50	131	18	28	4	1	0	9	3	.214
2013	Rochester	Int.	SS-2B-3B	43	166	22	51	16	2	4	27	6	.307
2013	Minnesota	A.L.	SS-3B-2B-OF	66	165	23	39	5	2	3	10	0	.236
Major League Totals			3 Yrs.	125	303	41	69	9	3	3	19	3	.228

a Traded to Minnesota Twins with pitcher Pedro Hernandez for pitcher Francisco Liriano, July 29, 2012.

ESCOBAR, YUNEL

Born, Havana, Cuba, November 2, 1982.
Bats Right. Throws Right. Height, 6 feet, 2 inches. Weight, 200 pounds.

Year	Club	Lea	Pos	G	AB	R	H	2B	3B	HR	RBI	SB	Avg
2005	Danville	Appal.	SS	8	30	9	12	2	1	2	8	0	.400
2005	Rome	So.Atl.	SS	48	198	30	62	13	3	4	19	0	.313
2006	Mississippi	Southern	SS-3B-2B	121	428	55	113	21	4	2	45	7	.264
2007	Richmond	Int.	SS	46	180	20	60	10	3	2	29	7	.333
2007	Atlanta	N.L.	SS-3B-2B	94	319	54	104	25	0	5	28	5	.326
2008	Atlanta	N.L.	SS	136	514	71	148	24	2	10	60	2	.288
2009	Atlanta	N.L.	SS	141	528	89	158	26	2	14	76	5	.299
2010	Gwinnett	Int.	SS	1	3	1	2	0	0	0	0	0	.667
2010	Atlanta	N.L.	SS	75	261	28	62	12	0	0	19	5	.238
2010	Toronto a-b	A.L.	SS	60	236	32	65	7	0	4	16	1	.275
2011	Toronto c	A.L.	SS	133	513	77	149	24	3	11	48	3	.290
2012	Toronto d-e	A.L.	SS	145	558	58	141	22	1	9	51	5	.253
2013	Tampa Bay	A.L.	SS	153	508	61	130	27	1	9	56	4	.256
Major League Totals			7 Yrs.	937	3437	470	957	167	9	62	354	30	.278
	Wild Card Playoff												
2013	Tampa Bay	A.L.	SS	1	4	0	1	0	0	0	1	0	.250

Year	Club	Lea	Pos	G	AB	R	H	2B	3B	HR	RBI	SB	Avg
	Division Series												
2013	Tampa Bay	A.L.	SS	4	15	3	7	2	0	0	1	0	.467

a On disabled list from April 30 to May 15, 2010.
b Traded to Toronto Blue Jays with pitcher Jo-Jo Reyes for infielder Alex Gonzalez, pitcher Tim Collins and infielder Tyler Pastornicky, July 14, 2010.
c On disabled list from September 11 to September 29, 2011.
d Traded to Miami Marlins with pitcher Henderson Alvarez, infielder Adeiny Hechavarria, catcher Jeff Mathis, pitcher Anthony De Sclafani, outfielder Jake Marisnick and pitcher Justin Nicolino for outfielder Emilio Bonifacio, catcher John Buck, pitcher Mark Buehrle, pitcher Josh Johnson and infielder Jose Reyes, November 19, 2012.
e Traded to Tampa Bay Rays for infielder Derek Dietrich, December 4, 2012.

ETHIER, ANDRE EVERETT

Born, Phoenix, Arizona, April 10, 1982.
Bats Left. Throws Left. Height, 6 feet, 1 inch. Weight, 210 pounds.

Year	Club	Lea	Pos	G	AB	R	H	2B	3B	HR	RBI	SB	Avg
2003	Kane County	Midwest	OF	40	162	23	44	10	0	0	11	2	.272
2003	Vancouver	Northwest	OF	10	41	7	16	4	1	1	7	2	.390
2004	Modesto	Calif.	OF	99	419	72	131	23	5	7	53	2	.313
2005	Sacramento	P.C.	OF	4	15	0	4	1	0	0	2	0	.267
2005	Midland a	Texas	OF	131	505	104	161	30	3	18	80	1	.319
2006	Las Vegas	P.C.	OF	25	86	15	30	4	3	1	12	2	.349
2006	Los Angeles	N.L.	OF	126	396	50	122	20	7	11	55	5	.308
2007	Los Angeles	N.L.	OF	153	447	50	127	32	2	13	64	0	.284
2008	Los Angeles	N.L.	OF	141	525	90	160	38	5	20	77	6	.305
2009	Los Angeles	N.L.	OF	160	596	92	162	42	3	31	106	6	.272
2010	Albuquerque	P.C.	OF	2	5	4	3	0	0	0	2	0	.600
2010	Los Angeles b	N.L.	OF-1B	139	517	71	151	33	1	23	82	2	.292
2011	Los Angeles	N.L.	OF	135	487	67	142	30	0	11	62	0	.292
2012	Rancho Cucamonga	Calif.	OF	2	4	0	0	0	0	0	1	0	.000
2012	Los Angeles c	N.L.	OF	149	556	79	158	36	1	20	89	2	.284
2013	Los Angeles	N.L.	OF	142	482	54	131	33	2	12	52	4	.272
Major League Totals			8 Yrs.	1145	4006	553	1153	264	21	141	587	25	.288
	Division Series												
2006	Los Angeles	N.L.	OF	2	1	0	0	0	0	0	0	0	.000
2008	Los Angeles	N.L.	OF	3	10	2	1	0	0	0	0	0	.100
2009	Los Angeles	N.L.	OF	3	12	5	6	2	1	2	3	0	.500
2013	Los Angeles	N.L.	PH	4	3	0	0	0	0	0	0	0	.000
Division Series Totals				12	26	7	7	2	1	2	3	0	.269
	Championship Series												
2008	Los Angeles	N.L.	OF	5	22	4	5	1	0	0	0	0	.227
2009	Los Angeles	N.L.	OF	5	19	2	5	1	0	1	3	0	.263
2013	Los Angeles	N.L.	OF	6	20	1	3	0	0	0	0	0	.150
Championship Series Totals				16	61	7	13	2	0	1	3	0	.213

a Traded by Oakland Athletics to Los Angeles for outfielder Milton Bradley and infielder Antonio Perez, December 13, 2005.
b On disabled list from May 15 to May 31, 2010.
c On disabled list from June 28 to July 13, 2012.

FEDEROWICZ, TIMOTHY JOSEPH (TIM)

Born, Erie, Pennsylvania, August 5, 1987.
Bats Right. Throws Right. Height, 5 feet, 11 inches. Weight, 215 pounds.

Year	Club	Lea	Pos	G	AB	R	H	2B	3B	HR	RBI	SB	Avg
2008	Lowell	N.Y.-Penn.	C	36	127	14	31	6	0	1	15	10	.244
2009	Greenville	So.Atl.	C	55	226	34	78	19	0	10	34	1	.345
2009	Salem	Carolina	C	51	187	18	48	13	0	4	24	1	.257
2010	Salem	Carolina	C	109	407	47	103	34	1	4	61	1	.253
2011	Portland a	Eastern	C	90	339	46	94	20	0	8	52	1	.277
2011	Albuquerque	P.C.	C	25	83	17	27	7	0	6	17	0	.325
2011	Los Angeles	N.L.	C	7	13	0	2	0	0	0	1	0	.154
2012	Albuquerque	P.C.	C	115	412	71	121	34	1	11	76	0	.294
2012	Los Angeles	N.L.	C	3	3	0	1	0	0	0	0	0	.333
2013	Albuquerque	P.C.	C	21	79	20	33	8	1	8	25	0	.418
2013	Los Angeles	N.L.	C-1B	56	160	12	37	8	0	4	16	0	.231
Major League Totals			3 Yrs.	66	176	12	40	8	0	4	17	0	.227

a Traded by Boston Red Sox to Los Angeles Dodgers with pitcher Stephen Fife and pitcher Juan Rodriguez for outfielder Trayvon Robinson, July 31, 2011.

FIELDER, PRINCE SEMIEN

Born, Ontario, California, May 9, 1984.
Bats Left. Throws Right. Height, 6 feet. Weight, 260 pounds.

Year	Club	Lea	Pos	G	AB	R	H	2B	3B	HR	RBI	SB	Avg
2002	Beloit	Midwest	1B	32	112	15	27	7	0	3	11	0	.241
2002	Ogden	Pioneer	1B	41	146	35	57	12	0	10	40	3	.390
2003	Beloit	Midwest	1B	137	502	81	157	22	2	27	112	2	.313
2004	Huntsville	Southern	1B-OF	136	497	70	135	29	1	23	78	11	.272
2005	Nashville	P.C.	1B	103	378	68	110	21	0	28	86	8	.291
2005	Milwaukee	N.L.	1B	39	59	2	17	4	0	2	10	0	.288
2006	Milwaukee	N.L.	1B	157	569	82	154	35	1	28	81	7	.271
2007	Milwaukee	N.L.	1B	158	573	109	165	35	2	*50	119	2	.288
2008	Milwaukee	N.L.	1B	159	588	86	162	30	2	34	102	3	.276
2009	Milwaukee	N.L.	1B	*162	591	103	177	35	3	46	*141	2	.299
2010	Milwaukee	N.L.	1B	161	578	94	151	25	0	32	83	1	.261
2011	Milwaukee a	N.L.	1B	*162	569	95	170	36	1	38	120	1	.299
2012	Detroit	A.L.	1B	*162	581	83	182	33	1	30	108	1	.313
2013	Detroit b	A.L.	1B	*162	624	82	174	36	0	25	106	1	.279
Major League Totals			9 Yrs.	1322	4732	736	1352	269	10	285	870	18	.286
	Division Series												
2008	Milwaukee	N.L.	1B	4	14	1	1	0	0	1	2	0	.071
2011	Milwaukee	N.L.	1B	5	18	2	5	2	0	1	3	0	.278
2012	Detroit	A.L.	1B	5	21	1	4	0	0	1	2	0	.190
2013	Detroit	A.L.	1B	5	18	2	5	0	0	0	0	0	.278
Division Series Totals				19	71	6	15	2	0	3	7	0	.211
	Championship Series												
2011	Milwaukee	N.L.	1B	6	20	4	4	2	0	2	3	0	.200
2012	Detroit	A.L.	1B	4	17	1	4	0	0	0	1	0	.235
2013	Detroit	A.L.	1B	6	22	1	4	1	0	0	0	0	.182
Championship Series Totals				16	59	6	12	3	0	2	4	0	.203
	World Series Record												
2012	Detroit	A.L.	1B	4	14	0	1	0	0	0	0	0	.071

a Filed for free agency, October 30, 2011. Signed with Detroit Tigers, January 26, 2012.
b Traded to Texas Rangers with cash for infielder Ian Kinsler, November 20, 2013.

FLAHERTY, RYAN EDWARD

Born, Portland, Maine, July 27, 1986.
Bats Left. Throws Right. Height, 6 feet, 3 inches. Weight, 210 pounds.

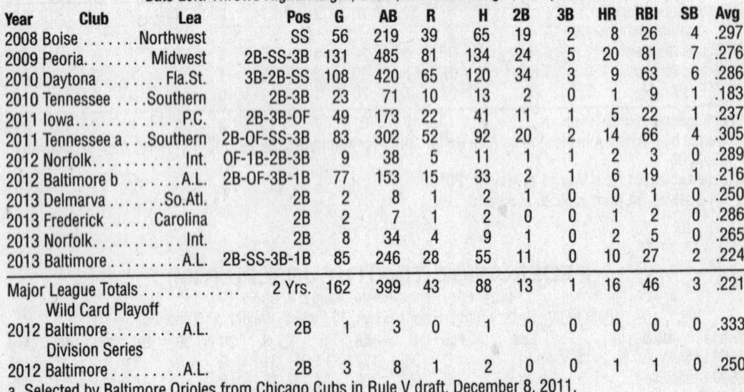

Year	Club	Lea	Pos	G	AB	R	H	2B	3B	HR	RBI	SB	Avg
2008	Boise	Northwest	SS	56	219	39	65	19	2	8	26	4	.297
2009	Peoria	Midwest	2B-SS-3B	131	485	81	134	24	5	20	81	7	.276
2010	Daytona	Fla.St.	3B-2B-SS	108	420	65	120	34	3	9	63	6	.286
2010	Tennessee	Southern	2B-3B	23	71	10	13	2	0	1	9	1	.183
2011	Iowa	P.C.	2B-3B-OF	49	173	22	41	11	1	5	22	1	.237
2011	Tennessee a	Southern	2B-OF-SS-3B	83	302	52	92	20	2	14	66	4	.305
2012	Norfolk	Int.	OF-1B-2B-3B	9	38	5	11	1	1	2	3	0	.289
2012	Baltimore b	A.L.	2B-OF-3B-1B	77	153	15	33	2	1	6	19	1	.216
2013	Delmarva	So.Atl.	2B	2	8	1	2	1	0	0	1	0	.250
2013	Frederick	Carolina	2B	2	7	1	2	0	0	1	2	0	.286
2013	Norfolk	Int.	2B	8	34	4	9	1	0	2	5	0	.265
2013	Baltimore	A.L.	2B-SS-3B-1B	85	246	28	55	11	0	10	27	2	.224
Major League Totals			2 Yrs.	162	399	43	88	13	1	16	46	3	.221
	Wild Card Playoff												
2012	Baltimore	A.L.	2B	1	3	0	1	0	0	0	0	0	.333
	Division Series												
2012	Baltimore	A.L.	2B	3	8	1	2	0	0	1	1	0	.250

a Selected by Baltimore Orioles from Chicago Cubs in Rule V draft, December 8, 2011.
b On disabled list from August 2 to August 24, 2012.

FLORIMON, PEDRO ALEXANDER

Born, LaRomana, Dominican Republic, December 10, 1986.
Bats Both. Throws Right. Height, 6 feet, 2 inches. Weight, 180 pounds.

Year	Club	Lea	Pos	G	AB	R	H	2B	3B	HR	RBI	SB	Avg
2006	Bluefield	Appal.	SS	33	120	23	40	6	1	1	8	7	.333
2006	Aberdeen	N.Y.-Penn.	SS	26	105	13	26	4	1	0	5	0	.248
2007	Delmarva	So.Atl.	SS	111	371	50	73	14	1	4	34	16	.197
2008	Delmarva	So.Atl.	SS-2B	81	269	28	60	18	1	0	19	13	.223
2009	Frederick	Carolina	SS	115	430	76	115	32	5	9	68	26	.267

Year	Club	Lea	Pos	G	AB	R	H	2B	3B	HR	RBI	SB	Avg
2009	Bowie	Eastern	SS	7	22	0	2	0	0	0	1	0	.091
2010	Frederick	Carolina	SS	62	222	32	64	10	4	4	33	8	.288
2010	Bowie	Eastern	SS	37	120	16	22	3	0	1	12	4	.183
2010	Aberdeen	N.Y.-Penn.	SS	5	19	1	3	0	0	0	0	0	.158
2011	Bowie	Eastern	SS-2B-OF	133	454	53	121	27	4	8	60	15	.267
2011	Baltimore a	A.L.	SS	4	8	1	1	1	0	0	2	0	.125
2012	New Britain	Eastern	SS	30	113	11	32	4	0	2	8	7	.283
2012	Rochester	Int.	SS	83	311	38	78	16	2	3	27	6	.251
2012	Minnesota	A.L.	SS	43	137	16	30	5	2	1	10	3	.219
2013	Minnesota	A.L.	SS	134	403	44	89	17	0	9	44	15	.221
Major League Totals			3 Yrs.	181	548	61	120	23	2	10	56	18	.219

a Claimed on waivers by Minnesota Twins, December 5, 2011.

FLOWERS, COLE TYLER (TYLER)

Born, Roswell, Georgia, January 24, 1986.
Bats Right. Throws Right. Height, 6 feet, 4 inches. Weight, 245 pounds.

Year	Club	Lea	Pos	G	AB	R	H	2B	3B	HR	RBI	SB	Avg
2006	Danville	Appal.	1B-C	34	129	24	36	9	0	5	16	0	.279
2007	Rome	So.Atl.	1B-C	106	389	65	116	34	2	12	70	3	.298
2008	Myrtle Beach a	Carolina	C-1B	122	413	72	119	32	1	17	88	8	.288
2009	Birmingham	Southern	C	77	248	54	75	18	2	13	43	3	.302
2009	Charlotte	Int.	C	31	105	13	30	10	0	2	13	0	.286
2009	Chicago	A.L.	C	10	16	3	3	1	0	0	0	0	.188
2010	Charlotte	Int.	C	100	346	43	76	22	2	16	53	2	.220
2010	Chicago	A.L.	C	8	11	2	1	0	0	0	0	0	.091
2011	Charlotte	Int.	C	65	222	36	58	8	0	15	32	2	.261
2011	Chicago	A.L.	C-1B	38	110	13	23	5	1	5	16	0	.209
2012	Chicago	A.L.	C-1B	52	136	19	29	6	0	7	13	2	.213
2013	Chicago b	A.L.	C	84	256	24	50	11	0	10	24	0	.195
Major League Totals			5 Yrs.	192	529	61	106	23	1	22	53	2	.200

a Traded by Atlanta Braves to Chicago White Sox with infielder Jonathan Gilmore, infielder Brent Lillibridge and pitcher Santos Rodriguez for pitcher Javier Vazquez and pitcher Boone Logan, December 4, 2008.
b On disabled list from September 2 to October 24, 2013.

FOWLER, WILLIAM DEXTER (DEXTER)

Born, Atlanta, Georgia, March 22, 1986.
Bats Both. Throws Right. Height, 6 feet, 4 inches. Weight, 185 pounds.

Year	Club	Lea	Pos	G	AB	R	H	2B	3B	HR	RBI	SB	Avg
2005	Casper	Pioneer	OF	62	220	43	60	10	4	4	23	18	.273
2006	Asheville	So.Atl.	OF	99	405	92	120	31	6	8	46	43	.296
2007	Modesto	Calif.	OF	65	245	43	67	7	5	2	23	20	.273
2008	Tulsa	Texas	OF	108	421	92	141	31	9	9	64	20	.335
2008	Colorado	N.L.	OF	13	26	3	4	0	0	0	0	0	.154
2009	Tulsa	Texas	OF	3	10	3	4	2	0	0	3	1	.400
2009	Colorado a	N.L.	OF	135	433	73	115	29	10	4	34	27	.266
2010	Colorado Springs	P.C.	OF	27	106	23	36	10	4	2	13	1	.340
2010	Colorado	N.L.	OF	132	439	73	114	20	*14	6	36	13	.260
2011	Colorado Springs	P.C.	OF	24	97	17	23	6	1	2	9	2	.237
2011	Colorado b	N.L.	OF	125	481	84	128	35	15	5	45	12	.266
2012	Colorado	N.L.	OF	143	454	72	136	18	11	13	53	12	.300
2013	Colorado Springs	P.C.	OF	2	6	0	0	0	0	0	0	1	.000
2013	Colorado c-d	N.L.	OF	119	415	71	109	18	3	12	42	19	.263
Major League Totals			6 Yrs.	667	2248	376	606	120	53	40	210	83	.270
Division Series													
2009	Colorado	N.L.	OF	4	14	1	3	0	0	0	2	0	.214

a On disabled list from August 25 to September 9, 2009.
b On disabled list from June 5 to June 20, 2011.
c On disabled list from June 26 to July 11, 2013.
d Traded to Houston Astros with player to be named later for pitcher Jordan Lyles and outfielder Brandon Barnes, December 3, 2013.

FRANCISCO (GONZALEZ), JUAN RAMON

Born, Bonao, Dominican Republic, June 24, 1987.
Bats Left. Throws Right. Height, 6 feet, 2 inches. Weight, 245 pounds.

Year	Club	Lea	Pos	G	AB	R	H	2B	3B	HR	RBI	SB	Avg
2006	Reds	Gulf Coast	3B	45	182	24	51	14	0	3	30	2	.280
2006	Billings	Pioneer	3B	9	36	6	12	3	0	0	2	2	.333

Year	Club	Lea	Pos	G	AB	R	H	2B	3B	HR	RBI	SB	Avg
2007	Dayton	Midwest	3B	135	534	69	143	21	4	25	90	12	.268
2008	Sarasota	Fla.St.	3B-OF	127	516	71	143	34	5	23	92	1	.277
2009	Carolina	Southern	3B	109	437	64	123	26	2	22	74	6	.281
2009	Louisville	Int.	3B-OF	22	92	17	33	5	1	5	19	0	.359
2009	Cincinnati	N.L.	3B	14	21	4	9	1	0	1	7	0	.429
2010	Louisville	Int.	3B-OF-1B	77	308	46	88	24	4	18	59	1	.286
2010	Cincinnati	N.L.	3B	36	55	3	15	3	0	1	7	0	.273
2011	Reds	Arizona	3B	5	18	3	9	3	0	1	3	0	.500
2011	Louisville	Int.	3B-OF	74	300	46	92	23	1	15	50	0	.307
2011	Cincinnati a	N.L.	3B	31	93	10	24	7	1	3	15	1	.258
2012	Atlanta b	N.L.	3B	93	192	17	45	11	0	9	32	1	.234
2013	Atlanta-Milwaukee c	N.L.	1B-3B	124	348	36	79	12	1	18	48	0	.227
Major League Totals			5 Yrs.	298	709	70	172	34	2	32	109	2	.243
	Division Series												
2010	Cincinnati	N.L.	PH	1	1	0	0	0	0	0	0	0	.000

a On disabled list from April 17 to May 17, 2011.
b Traded to Atlanta Braves for pitcher J.J Hoover, April 1, 2012.
c Traded to Milwaukee Brewers for pitcher Thomas Keeling, June 3, 2013.

FRANDSEN, KEVIN VINCENT

Born, San Jose, California, May 24, 1982.
Bats Right. Throws Right. Height, 6 feet. Weight, 185 pounds.

Year	Club	Lea	Pos	G	AB	R	H	2B	3B	HR	RBI	SB	Avg
2004	Salem-Keizer	Northwest	2B-SS	25	98	22	29	5	0	3	14	0	.296
2005	San Jose	Calif.	2B-SS	75	291	57	102	22	3	2	40	13	.351
2005	Norwich	Eastern	2B-SS-3B	33	129	22	37	8	0	2	20	7	.287
2005	Fresno	P.C.	2B	20	94	18	33	10	1	2	16	1	.351
2006	Fresno	P.C.	2B-3B-SS	71	293	46	89	25	3	3	30	7	.304
2006	San Jose	Calif.	SS	2	7	1	3	0	0	0	1	0	.429
2006	San Francisco a	N.L.	2B-SS	41	93	12	20	4	0	2	7	0	.215
2007	Fresno	P.C.	2B-SS-3B	19	67	13	27	5	0	1	7	4	.403
2007	San Francisco	N.L.	2B-SS-OF-3B	109	264	26	71	12	1	5	31	4	.269
2008	San Francisco b	N.L.	PH	1	1	0	0	0	0	0	0	0	.000
2009	Fresno	P.C.	SS-2B-1B-3B	110	427	67	126	18	2	13	55	3	.295
2009	San Francisco	N.L.	2B-SS	23	50	3	7	2	0	0	1	0	.140
2010	Pawtucket c	Int.	SS-2B-3B	17	62	9	16	3	0	2	4	2	.258
2010	Salt Lake	P.C.	3B-2B-SS-1B	36	137	25	38	9	1	1	12	2	.277
2010	Los Angeles d	A.L.	3B-1B-2B-OF	54	160	24	40	11	0	0	14	2	.250
2011	Reading	Eastern	2B	1	4	1	2	0	0	1	2	0	.500
2011	Clearwater	Fla.St.	SS-2B	3	10	1	4	2	0	0	1	0	.400
2011	Lehigh Valley e-f-g-h	Int.	2B-SS-3B-1B	77	284	32	86	13	3	4	40	10	.303
2012	Lehigh Valley	Int.	2B-1B-3B-SS	99	391	38	118	34	0	1	33	2	.302
2012	Philadelphia	N.L.	3B	55	195	24	66	10	3	2	14	0	.338
2013	Philadelphia	N.L.	1B-2B-3B	119	252	27	59	10	1	5	26	1	.234
Major League Totals			7 Yrs.	402	1015	116	263	49	5	14	93	7	.259

a On disabled list from August 18 to September 2, 2006.
b On disabled list from March 21 to September 27, 2008.
c Sold to Boston Red Sox, March 26, 2010.
d Claimed on waivers by Los Angeles Angels, April 29, 2010.
e Not offered contract, December 2, 2010. Signed with San Diego Padres organization, January 6, 2011.
f Released by San Diego Padres, March 25, 2011. Signed with Philadelphia Phillies organization, April 1, 2011.
g Suspended for 50 games for performance-enhancing drug use, May 11, 2011.
h Filed for free agency, November 2, 2011. Signed with Philadelphia Phillies organization, November 30, 2011.

FRANKLIN, NICHOLAS EDWARD (NICK)

Born, Sanford, Florida, March 2, 1991.
Bats Both. Throws Right. Height, 6 feet, 1 inch. Weight, 195 pounds.

Year	Club	Lea	Pos	G	AB	R	H	2B	3B	HR	RBI	SB	Avg
2009	Mariners	Arizona	SS-2B	10	43	6	13	2	0	1	4	0	.302
2009	Everett	Northwest	SS	6	20	4	8	2	1	0	2	1	.400
2010	Clinton	Midwest	SS-2B	129	513	89	144	22	7	23	65	25	.281
2010	West Tenn	Southern	2B-SS	1	3	3	2	0	0	0	0	0	.667
2011	Mariners	Arizona	SS	3	11	1	1	0	0	0	0	0	.091
2011	High Desert	Calif.	SS-2B	64	258	50	71	10	5	5	20	13	.275
2011	Jackson	Southern	SS-2B	21	83	13	27	3	2	2	6	5	.325
2012	Jackson	Southern	SS-2B	57	205	25	66	17	4	4	26	9	.322
2012	Tacoma	P.C.	2B-SS	64	267	39	65	15	5	7	29	3	.243
2013	Tacoma	P.C.	2B-SS	39	142	28	46	9	0	4	20	7	.324
2013	Seattle	A.L.	2B-SS	102	369	38	83	20	1	12	45	6	.225

FRAZIER, TODD B.

Born, Point Pleasant, New Jersey, February 12, 1986.
Bats Right. Throws Right. Height, 6 feet, 3 inches. Weight, 215 pounds.

Year	Club	Lea	Pos	G	AB	R	H	2B	3B	HR	RBI	SB	Avg
2007	Dayton	Midwest	SS	6	22	4	7	3	0	2	5	0	.318
2007	Billings	Pioneer	SS	41	160	29	51	6	5	5	25	3	.319
2008	Sarasota	Fla.St.	SS-1B-3B-OF	100	366	62	103	20	3	12	54	8	.281
2008	Dayton	Midwest	SS-1B-3B-OF	30	112	25	36	10	0	7	20	4	.321
2009	Louisville	Int.	2B-OF	16	63	9	19	5	0	2	9	2	.302
2009	Carolina	Southern	OF-2B-1B-3B	119	451	59	131	40	2	14	68	7	.290
2010	Louisville	Int.	OF-3B-1B	130	480	71	124	32	4	17	66	14	.258
2011	Louisville	Int.	3B-1B-OF-2B	90	315	47	82	18	1	15	46	17	.260
2011	Cincinnati	N.L.	3B-OF-2B-SS	41	112	17	26	5	0	6	15	1	.232
2012	Louisville	Int.	3B-OF	10	39	4	9	2	0	1	7	3	.231
2012	Cincinnati	N.L.	3B-1B-OF	128	422	55	115	26	6	19	67	3	.273
2013	Cincinnati	N.L.	3B-OF	150	531	63	124	29	3	19	73	6	.234
Major League Totals			3 Yrs.	319	1065	135	265	60	9	44	155	10	.249
	Wild Card Playoff												
2013	Cincinnati	N.L.	3B	1	4	0	1	1	0	0	0	0	.250
	Division Series												
2012	Cincinnati	N.L.	3B-1B	4	6	0	1	0	0	0	1	0	.167

FREEMAN, FREDERICK CHARLES (FREDDIE)

Born, Fountain Valley, California, September 12, 1989.
Bats Left. Throws Right. Height, 6 feet, 5 inches. Weight, 225 pounds.

Year	Club	Lea	Pos	G	AB	R	H	2B	3B	HR	RBI	SB	Avg
2007	Braves	Gulf Coast	1B-3B	59	224	24	60	7	0	6	30	1	.268
2008	Rome	So.Atl.	1B	130	491	70	155	33	7	18	95	5	.316
2009	Myrtle Beach	Carolina	1B	70	255	43	77	19	0	6	34	1	.302
2009	Mississippi	Southern	1B	41	149	15	37	8	0	2	24	0	.248
2010	Gwinnett	Int.	1B	124	461	73	147	35	2	18	87	6	.319
2010	Atlanta	N.L.	1B	20	24	3	4	1	0	1	1	0	.167
2011	Atlanta	N.L.	1B	157	571	67	161	32	0	21	76	4	.282
2012	Atlanta	N.L.	1B	147	540	91	140	33	2	23	94	2	.259
2013	Gwinnett	Int.	1B	3	10	3	5	2	0	0	2	0	.500
2013	Atlanta a	N.L.	1B	147	551	89	176	27	2	23	109	1	.319
Major League Totals			4 Yrs.	471	1686	250	481	93	4	68	280	7	.285
	Wild Card Playoff												
2012	Atlanta	N.L.	1B	1	4	0	3	1	0	0	0	0	.750
	Division Series												
2013	Atlanta	N.L.	1B	4	16	4	5	1	0	0	0	0	.313

a On disabled list from April 7 to April 22, 2013.

FREESE, DAVID RICHARD

Born, Corpus Christi, Texas, April 28, 1983.
Bats Right. Throws Right. Height, 6 feet, 2 inches. Weight, 220 pounds.

Year	Club	Lea	Pos	G	AB	R	H	2B	3B	HR	RBI	SB	Avg
2006	Fort Wayne	Midwest	3B	53	204	27	61	13	3	8	44	1	.299
2006	Eugene	Northwest	3B	18	58	19	22	8	0	5	26	0	.379
2007	Lake Elsinore a	Calif.	3B	128	503	104	152	31	6	17	96	6	.302
2008	Memphis	P.C.	3B	131	464	83	142	29	3	26	91	5	.306
2009	Cardinals	Gulf Coast	3B	4	11	2	5	2	0	1	6	0	.455
2009	Springfield	Texas	3B	4	16	3	6	1	0	1	5	0	.375
2009	Memphis	P.C.	3B-1B	56	200	34	60	15	0	10	37	1	.300
2009	St. Louis	N.L.	3B-1B-C	17	31	3	10	2	0	1	7	0	.323
2010	Springfield	Texas	DH	1	2	0	1	1	0	0	0	0	.500
2010	St. Louis b	N.L.	3B-1B	70	240	28	71	12	1	4	36	1	.296
2011	Memphis	P.C.	3B	4	13	1	3	1	0	0	1	0	.231
2011	St. Louis c	N.L.	3B-1B	97	333	41	99	16	1	10	55	1	.297
2012	St. Louis	N.L.	3B	144	501	70	147	25	1	20	79	3	.293
2013	Memphis	P.C.	3B	3	12	2	4	2	0	0	4	0	.333
2013	St. Louis d-e	N.L.	3B	138	462	53	121	26	1	9	60	1	.262
Major League Totals			5 Yrs.	466	1567	195	448	81	4	44	237	6	.286
	Wild Card Playoff												
2012	St. Louis	N.L.	3B	1	2	0	0	0	0	0	1	0	.000
	Division Series												
2011	St. Louis	N.L.	3B	5	18	1	5	2	0	1	5	0	.278
2012	St. Louis	N.L.	3B	5	19	3	8	3	0	0	1	0	.421

Year	Club	Lea	Pos	G	AB	R	H	2B	3B	HR	RBI	SB	Avg
2013	St. Louis	N.L.	3B	5	16	1	3	0	0	1	4	0	.188
Division Series Totals				15	53	5	16	5	0	2	10	0	.3021
	Championship Series												
2011	St. Louis	N.L.	3B	6	22	7	12	3	0	3	9	0	.545
2012	St. Louis	N.L.	3B	7	26	2	5	2	0	1	2	0	.192
2013	St. Louis	N.L.	3B	6	21	2	4	1	0	0	0	0	.190
Championship Series Totals				19	69	11	21	6	0	4	11	0	.304
	World Series Record												
2011	St. Louis	N.L.	3B	7	23	4	8	3	1	1	7	0	.348
2013	St. Louis	N.L.	3B	6	19	0	3	1	0	0	0	0	.158
World Series Totals				13	42	4	11	4	1	1	7	0	.262

a Traded by San Diego Padres to St. Louis Cardinals for outfielder Jim Edmonds, December 15, 2007.
b On disabled list from June 28 to November 2, 2010.
c On disabled list from May 2 to June 27, 2011.
d On disabled list from March 23 to April 8, 2013.
e Traded to Los Angeles Angels with pitcher Fernando Salas for outfielder Peter Bourjos and infielder Randal Grichuk, November 22, 2013.

FREIMAN, NATHAN SAMUEL (NATE)

Born, Washington, District of Columbia, December 31, 1986.
Bats Right. Throws Right. Height, 6 feet, 8 inches. Weight, 250 pounds.

Year	Club	Lea	Pos	G	AB	R	H	2B	3B	HR	RBI	SB	Avg
2009	Eugene	Northwest	1B	72	289	36	85	22	0	11	68	2	.294
2010	Fort Wayne	Midwest	1B	136	523	83	154	43	0	14	84	0	.294
2011	Lake Elsinore	Calif.	1B	138	548	81	158	35	4	22	111	6	.288
2012	San Antonio a-b	Texas	1B	137	516	80	154	31	1	24	105	0	.298
2013	Oakland	A.L.	1B	80	190	10	52	8	1	4	24	0	.274

a Selected by Houston Astros from San Diego Padres in Rule V draft, December 6, 2012.
b Claimed on waivers by Oakland Athletics, March 23, 2013.

FULD, SAMUEL BABSON (SAM)

Born, Durham, New Hampshire, November 20, 1981.
Bats Left. Throws Left. Height, 5 feet, 10 inches. Weight, 180 pounds.

Year	Club	Lea	Pos	G	AB	R	H	2B	3B	HR	RBI	SB	Avg
2005	Peoria	Midwest	OF	125	443	82	133	32	6	5	37	18	.300
2006	Daytona	Fla.St.	OF	89	353	63	106	19	6	4	40	22	.300
2007	Iowa	P.C.	OF	14	52	13	14	4	1	1	2	2	.269
2007	Tennessee	Southern	OF	90	335	56	97	23	2	2	27	10	.290
2007	Chicago	N.L.	OF	14	6	3	0	0	0	0	0	0	.000
2008	Iowa	P.C.	OF	20	63	11	14	3	0	1	4	3	.222
2008	Tennessee	Southern	OF	85	339	48	92	16	3	5	48	7	.271
2009	Iowa	P.C.	OF	84	328	62	93	17	10	2	33	23	.284
2009	Chicago	N.L.	OF	65	97	17	29	6	1	1	2	2	.299
2010	Iowa	P.C.	OF	112	368	69	100	15	9	4	27	21	.272
2010	Chicago	N.L.	OF	19	28	3	4	1	0	0	3	0	.143
2011	Tampa Bay a	A.L.	OF	105	308	41	74	18	5	3	27	20	.240
2012	Charlotte	Fla.St.	OF	5	13	0	2	0	0	0	0	0	.154
2012	Durham	Int.	OF	5	18	0	3	1	0	0	0	0	.167
2012	Tampa Bay b	A.L.	OF	44	98	14	25	3	2	0	5	7	.255
2013	Tampa Bay c	A.L.	OF-P	119	176	25	35	0	3	2	17	8	.199
Major League Totals			6 Yrs.	366	713	103	167	28	11	6	54	37	.234
	Wild Card Playoff												
2013	Tampa Bay	A.L.	OF	1	1	0	0	0	0	0	0	0	.000
	Division Series												
2011	Tampa Bay	A.L.	OF	3	3	0	0	0	0	0	0	0	.000
2013	Tampa Bay	A.L.	OF	1	0	1	0	0	0	0	0	0	.000
Division Series Totals				4	3	1	0	0	0	0	0	0	.000

a Traded to Tampa Bay Rays with infielder Hak-Ju Lee, outfielder Brandon Guyer, pitcher Chris Archer and catcher Robinson Chirinos for outfielder Fernando Perez, pitcher Matt Garza and pitcher Zachary Rosscup, January 8, 2011.
b On disabled list from April 4 to July 24, 2012.
c Not offered contract, December 2, 2013.

FURCAL, RAFAEL

Born, Loma de Cabrera, Dominican Republic, August 24, 1977.
Bats Both. Throws Right. Height, 5 feet, 8 inches. Weight, 195 pounds.

Year Club	Lea	Pos	G	AB	R	H	2B	3B	HR	RBI	SB	Avg
1997 Braves	Gulf Coast	2B-OF	50	190	31	49	5	4	1	9	15	.258
1998 Danville	Appal.	2B	66	268	56	88	15	4	0	23	60	.328
1999 Myrtle Beach	Carolina	SS	43	184	32	54	9	3	0	12	23	.293
1999 Macon	So.Atl.	SS	83	335	73	113	15	1	1	29	73	.337
2000 Greenville........	Southern	SS	3	10	1	2	0	0	1	3	0	.200
2000 Atlanta a-b	N.L.	SS-2B	131	455	87	134	20	4	4	37	40	.295
2001 Atlanta c.............	N.L.	SS	79	324	39	89	19	0	4	30	22	.275
2002 Atlanta	N.L.	SS-2B	154	636	95	175	31	8	8	47	27	.275
2003 Atlanta	N.L.	SS	156	664	130	194	35	*10	15	61	25	.292
2004 Atlanta	N.L.	SS-2B	143	563	103	157	24	5	14	59	29	.279
2005 Atlanta d.............	N.L.	SS	154	616	100	175	31	11	12	58	46	.284
2006 Los Angeles	N.L.	SS	159	654	113	196	32	9	15	63	37	.300
2007 Inland Empire.........	Calif.	SS	2	6	0	1	0	0	0	0	1	.167
2007 Los Angeles e.........	N.L.	SS	138	581	87	157	23	4	6	47	25	.270
2008 Las Vegas.............	P.C.	SS	1	3	0	1	1	0	0	1	0	.333
2008 Los Angeles f-g	N.L.	SS	36	143	34	51	12	2	5	16	8	.357
2009 Los Angeles	N.L.	SS	150	613	92	165	28	5	9	47	12	.269
2010 Inland Empire.........	Calif.	SS	2	4	0	0	0	0	0	0	0	.000
2010 Albuquerque...........	P.C.	SS	2	5	3	3	1	1	1	4	0	.600
2010 Los Angeles h	N.L.	SS	97	383	66	115	23	7	8	43	22	.300
2011 Rancho Cucamonga....	Calif.	SS	6	22	10	7	0	0	0	1	1	.318
2011 Albuquerque...........	P.C.	SS	4	13	2	5	1	0	1	6	0	.385
2011 Los Angeles-St. Louis i-j-k.	N.L.	SS	87	333	44	77	15	0	8	28	9	.231
2012 St. Louis l............	N.L.	SS	121	477	69	126	18	3	5	49	12	.264
2013 St. Louis m-n.........	N.L.	INJURED—Did Not Play										
Major League Totals		13 Yrs.	1605	6442	1059	1811	311	68	113	585	314	.281
Division Series												
2000 Atlanta	N.L.	SS	3	11	2	1	0	0	0	0	1	.091
2002 Atlanta	N.L.	SS	5	24	2	6	1	1	0	2	1	.250
2003 Atlanta	N.L.	SS	5	19	3	4	0	0	0	0	1	.211
2004 Atlanta	N.L.	SS	5	21	5	8	0	1	2	4	3	.381
2005 Atlanta	N.L.	SS	4	20	1	3	0	0	0	0	3	.150
2006 Los Angeles	N.L.	SS	3	11	1	2	0	0	0	1	2	.182
2008 Los Angeles	N.L.	SS	3	12	4	4	0	0	0	2	0	.333
2009 Los Angeles	N.L.	SS	3	12	2	6	0	1	0	2	0	.500
2011 St. Louis.............	N.L.	SS	5	22	2	5	0	2	0	1	1	.227
Division Series Totals			36	152	22	39	1	5	2	12	12	.257
Championship Series												
2008 Los Angeles	N.L.	SS	5	19	5	4	0	0	1	1	0	.211
2009 Los Angeles	N.L.	SS	5	21	0	3	1	0	0	1	1	.143
2011 St. Louis.............	N.L.	SS	6	27	5	5	2	0	1	1	0	.185
Championship Series Totals			16	67	10	12	3	0	2	3	1	.179
World Series Record												
2011 St. Louis.............	N.L.	SS	7	28	1	5	1	0	0	1	0	.179

a On disabled list from June 13 to June 28, 2000.
b Selected Rookie of the Year in National League for 2000.
c On disabled list from July 7 to November 6, 2001.
d Filed for free agency, October 31, 2005. Signed with Los Angeles Dodgers, December 7, 2005.
e On disabled list from March 23 to April 13, 2007.
f On disabled list from May 6 to September 24, 2008.
g Filed for free agency, November 3, 2008, re-signed with Los Angeles Dodgers, December 19, 2008.
h On disabled list from April 28 to May 25 and August 3 to September 3, 2010.
i On disabled list from April 12 to May 22 and June 4 to July 3, 2011.
j Traded to St. Louis Cardinals with cash for outfielder Alex Castellanos, July 31, 2011.
k Filed for free agency, October 31, 2011, re-signed with St. Louis Cardinals, December 10, 2011.
l On disabled list from August 31 to October 26, 2012.
m On disabled list from March 22 to October 31, 2013.
n Filed for free agency, October 31, 2013. Signed with Miami Marlins, December 6, 2013.

GALVIS, FREDDY JOSE

Born, Punto Fijo, Venezuela, November 14, 1989.
Bats Both. Throws Right. Height, 5 feet, 10 inches. Weight, 170 pounds.

Year Club	Lea	Pos	G	AB	R	H	2B	3B	HR	RBI	SB	Avg
2007 Williamsport.	.N.Y.-Penn.	SS	38	143	20	29	5	1	0	7	9	.203
2008 Lakewood.......	So.Atl.	SS	127	458	59	109	12	1	3	42	14	.238

Year	Club	Lea	Pos	G	AB	R	H	2B	3B	HR	RBI	SB	Avg
2009	Reading	Eastern	SS	16	61	6	12	0	0	1	5	0	.197
2009	Clearwater	Fla.St.	SS-3B	63	251	29	62	8	2	1	15	6	.247
2009	Phillies	Gulf Coast	SS	7	29	6	8	1	0	0	0	1	.276
2010	Reading	Eastern	SS	138	502	58	117	16	4	5	48	15	.233
2011	Reading	Eastern	SS	104	422	63	115	22	4	8	35	19	.273
2011	Lehigh Valley	Int.	SS	33	121	15	36	6	1	0	8	4	.298
2012	Philadelphia a-b	N.L.	2B-SS	58	190	14	43	15	1	3	24	0	.226
2013	Lehigh Valley	Int.	SS-2B-3B	62	241	26	59	14	2	3	25	3	.245
2013	Philadelphia	N.L.	2B-3B-SS-OF	70	205	13	48	5	4	6	19	1	.234
Major League Totals			2 Yrs.	128	395	27	91	20	5	9	43	1	.230

a On disabled list from June 6 to October 5, 2012.

b Suspended for 50 games for performance-enhancing drug use, June 19, 2012.

GARCIA, AVISAIL ANTONIO

Born, Anaco, Venezuela, June 12, 1991.

Bats Right. Throws Right. Height, 6 feet, 4 inches. Weight, 240 pounds.

Year	Club	Lea	Pos	G	AB	R	H	2B	3B	HR	RBI	SB	Avg
2009	West Michigan	Midwest	OF	81	299	36	79	11	2	1	31	8	.264
2009	Lakeland	Fla.St.	OF	3	8	1	2	0	0	0	0	0	.250
2010	West Michigan	Midwest	OF	125	494	58	139	17	4	4	63	20	.281
2011	Lakeland	Fla.St.	OF	129	488	53	129	16	6	11	56	14	.264
2012	Lakeland	Fla.St.	OF	67	266	47	77	8	5	8	36	14	.289
2012	Erie	Eastern	OF	55	215	31	67	9	3	6	22	9	.312
2012	Detroit	A.L.	OF	23	47	7	15	0	0	0	3	0	.319
2013	Lakeland	Fla.St.	OF	6	24	9	10	0	2	1	4	2	.417
2013	Toledo	Int.	OF	33	147	23	55	7	1	5	23	4	.374
2013	Charlotte	Int.	OF	8	27	6	10	0	1	1	9	0	.370
2013	Detroit-Chicago a-b-c	A.L.	OF	72	244	31	69	7	3	7	31	3	.283
Major League Totals			2 Yrs.	95	291	38	84	7	3	7	34	3	.289
	Division Series												
2012	Detroit	A.L.	OF	5	7	0	1	0	0	0	1	0	.143
	Championship Series												
2012	Detroit	A.L.	OF	4	11	0	5	1	0	0	3	1	.455
	World Series Record												
2012	Detroit	A.L.	OF	3	5	0	0	0	0	0	0	0	.000

a On disabled list from March 22 to April 30, 2013.

b Traded to Boston Red Sox with pitcher Brayan Villarreal for infielder Jose Iglesias, July 31, 2013.

c Traded to Chicago White Sox with pitcher Francelis Montas, infielder Cleuluis Rondon and pitcher Jeffrey Wendelken for pitcher Jake Peavy, July 31, 2013.

GARDNER, BRETT MICHAEL

Born, Holly Hill, South Carolina, August 24, 1983.

Bats Left. Throws Left. Height, 5 feet, 10 inches. Weight, 185 pounds.

Year	Club	Lea	Pos	G	AB	R	H	2B	3B	HR	RBI	SB	Avg
2005	Staten Island	N.Y.-Penn.	OF-3B	73	282	62	80	9	1	5	32	19	.284
2006	Trenton	Eastern	OF	55	217	41	59	4	3	0	13	28	.272
2006	Tampa	Fla.St.	OF	63	232	46	75	12	5	0	22	30	.323
2007	Trenton	Eastern	OF	54	203	43	61	14	5	0	17	18	.300
2007	Scranton/WB	Int.	OF	45	181	37	47	4	3	1	9	21	.260
2008	Scranton/WB	Int.	OF	94	341	68	101	12	11	3	32	37	.296
2008	New York	A.L.	OF	42	127	18	29	5	2	0	16	13	.228
2009	Scranton/WB	Int.	OF	4	11	3	1	0	0	0	0	3	.091
2009	New York a	A.L.	OF	108	248	48	67	6	6	3	23	26	.270
2010	New York	A.L.	OF	150	477	97	132	20	7	5	47	47	.277
2011	New York	A.L.	OF	159	510	87	132	19	8	7	36	*49	.259
2012	Charleston	So.Atl.	OF	1	3	1	1	0	0	0	0	1	.333
2012	Scranton-WB	Int.	OF	2	5	1	3	0	1	0	0	0	.600
2012	New York b	A.L.	OF	16	31	7	10	2	0	0	3	2	.323
2013	New York	A.L.	OF	145	539	81	147	33	*10	8	52	24	.273
Major League Totals			6 Yrs.	620	1932	338	517	85	33	23	177	161	.268
	Division Series												
2009	New York	A.L.	OF	3	0	0	0	0	0	0	0	1	.000
2010	New York	A.L.	OF	3	10	1	2	0	0	0	1	1	.200
2011	New York	A.L.	OF	5	17	3	7	1	0	0	5	0	.412
2012	New York	A.L.	OF	2	0	0	0	0	0	0	0	0	.000
Division Series Totals				13	27	4	9	1	0	0	6	2	.333

Year	Club	Lea	Pos	G	AB	R	H	2B	3B	HR	RBI	SB	Avg
	Championship Series												
2009	New York	A.L.	OF	6	3	2	2	0	0	0	0	0	.667
2010	New York	A.L.	OF	6	17	1	3	0	0	0	1	1	.176
2012	New York	A.L.	OF	3	8	0	0	0	0	0	0	2	.000
Championship Series Totals				15	28	3	5	0	0	0	1	3	.179
	World Series Record												
2009	New York	A.L.	OF	5	10	1	0	0	0	0	0	0	.000

a On disabled list from July 26 to September 7, 2009.
b On disabled list from April 18 to September 25, 2012.

GATTIS, JAMES EVAN (EVAN)

Born, Forney, Texas, August 18, 1986.
Bats Right. Throws Right. Height, 6 feet, 4 inches. Weight, 230 pounds.

Year	Club	Lea	Pos	G	AB	R	H	2B	3B	HR	RBI	SB	Avg
2010	Danville	Appal.	C	60	222	33	64	10	0	4	29	0	.288
2011	Rome	So.Atl.	C-1B	88	338	58	109	24	2	22	71	2	.322
2012	Braves	Gulf Coast	OF	4	12	2	6	0	0	0	1	0	.500
2012	Lynchburg	Carolina	C-OF	21	78	14	30	7	0	9	29	1	.385
2012	Mississippi	Southern	OF-C	49	182	24	47	13	4	9	37	1	.258
2013	Gwinnett	Int.	OF-C	5	21	1	7	4	0	1	1	0	.333
2013	Atlanta a	N.L.	OF-C-1B	105	354	44	86	21	0	21	65	0	.243
	Division Series												
2013	Atlanta	N.L.	OF	4	14	3	5	0	0	0	1	0	.357

a On disabled list from June 18 to July 14, 2013.

GENNETT, RYAN JOSEPH (SCOOTER)

Born, Cincinnati, Ohio, May 1, 1990.
Bats Left. Throws Right. Height, 5 feet, 10 inches. Weight, 180 pounds.

Year	Club	Lea	Pos	G	AB	R	H	2B	3B	HR	RBI	SB	Avg
2010	Wisconsin	Midwest	2B-SS	118	482	87	149	39	4	9	55	14	.309
2011	Brevard County	Fla.St.	2B	134	556	74	167	20	6	9	51	11	.300
2012	Huntsville	Southern	2B	133	533	66	156	30	2	5	44	11	.293
2013	Nashville	P.C.	2B	79	321	44	90	10	5	3	22	10	.280
2013	Milwaukee	N.L.	2B	69	213	29	69	11	2	6	21	2	.324

GENTRY, CRAIG ALAN

Born, Fort Smith, Arkansas, November 29, 1983.
Bats Right. Throws Right. Height, 6 feet, 2 inches. Weight, 190 pounds.

Year	Club	Lea	Pos	G	AB	R	H	2B	3B	HR	RBI	SB	Avg
2006	Spokane	Northwest	OF	56	221	27	62	15	4	0	13	20	.281
2007	Rangers	Arizona	OF	3	11	4	3	0	0	0	1	2	.273
2007	Clinton	Midwest	OF	55	223	40	61	15	0	3	12	24	.274
2007	Bakersfield	Calif.	OF	51	213	31	58	16	1	1	18	16	.272
2008	Frisco	Texas	OF	76	301	43	83	17	0	4	33	16	.276
2008	Oklahoma	P.C.	OF	18	59	6	12	1	0	0	1	1	.203
2009	Frisco	Texas	OF	127	512	100	155	21	7	8	53	49	.303
2009	Texas	A.L.	OF	11	17	4	2	1	0	0	1	0	.118
2010	Texas	A.L.	OF	20	33	4	7	0	0	0	3	1	.212
2010	Oklahoma a	P.C.	OF	69	259	43	80	7	4	4	35	12	.309
2011	Round Rock	P.C.	OF	30	110	21	27	5	1	1	10	5	.245
2011	Texas b	A.L.	OF	64	133	26	36	5	1	1	13	18	.271
2012	Texas	A.L.	OF-P	122	240	31	73	12	3	1	26	13	.304
2013	Frisco	Texas	OF	4	13	2	3	1	0	0	1	0	.231
2013	Texas c-d	A.L.	OF	106	246	39	69	12	4	2	22	24	.280
Major League Totals			5 Yrs.	323	669	104	187	30	8	4	65	56	.280
	Wild Card Playoff												
2012	Texas	A.L.	OF	1	2	0	0	0	0	0	0	0	.000
	Division Series												
2011	Texas	A.L.	OF	4	5	1	2	0	0	0	0	2	.400
	Championship Series												
2011	Texas	A.L.	OF	3	5	0	2	0	0	0	1	0	.400
	World Series Record												
2011	Texas	A.L.	OF	6	5	1	1	0	0	0	0	0	.200

a On disabled list from August 30 to November 5, 2010.
b On disabled list from July 28 to August 11, 2011.
c On disabled list from June 21 to July 18, 2013.
d Traded to Oakland Athletics with pitcher Josh Lindblom for outfielder Michael Choice and infielder Chris Bostick, December 3, 2013.

GIAMBI, JASON GILBERT

Born, West Covina, California, January 8, 1971.
Bats Left. Throws Right. Height, 6 feet, 3 inches. Weight, 230 pounds.

Year Club	Lea	Pos	G	AB	R	H	2B	3B	HR	RBI	SB	Avg
1992 South Oregon....	Northwest	3B	13	41	9	13	3	0	3	13	1	.317
1993 Modesto.........	California	3B	89	313	72	91	16	2	12	60	2	.291
1994 Huntsville........	Southern	3B-1B	56	193	31	43	9	0	6	30	0	.223
1994 Tacoma	P.C.	3B-1B-SS	52	176	28	56	20	0	4	38	1	.318
1995 Edmonton	P.C.	3B-1B	55	190	34	65	26	1	3	41	0	.342
1995 Oakland	A.L.	3B-1B	54	176	27	45	7	0	6	25	2	.256
1996 Oakland	A.L.	1B-OF-3B	140	536	84	156	40	1	20	79	0	.291
1997 Oakland	A.L.	OF-1B	142	519	66	152	41	2	20	81	0	.293
1998 Oakland	A.L.	1B	153	562	92	166	28	0	27	110	2	.295
1999 Oakland	A.L.	1B-3B	158	575	115	181	36	1	33	123	1	.315
2000 Oakland a............	A.L.	1B	152	510	108	170	29	1	43	137	2	.333
2001 Oakland b............	A.L.	1B	154	520	109	178	*47	2	38	120	2	.342
2002 New York............	A.L.	1B	155	560	120	176	34	1	41	122	2	.314
2003 New York............	A.L.	1B	156	535	97	134	25	0	41	107	2	.250
2004 Tampa	Fla.St.	1B	2	6	0	1	0	0	0	0	0	.167
2004 New York c..........	A.L.	1B	80	264	33	55	9	0	12	40	0	.208
2005 New York............	A.L.	1B	139	417	74	113	14	0	32	87	0	.271
2006 New York............	A.L.	DH-1B	139	446	92	113	25	0	37	113	2	.253
2007 Tampa	Fla.St.	DH	5	13	0	4	1	0	0	1	0	.308
2007 Scranton-WB	Int.	1B	4	9	1	1	0	0	1	1	0	.111
2007 New York d...........	A.L.	DH-1B	83	254	31	60	8	0	14	39	1	.236
2008 New York e...........	A.L.	1B	145	458	68	113	19	1	32	96	2	.247
2009 Colorado Springs.......	P.C.	1B	6	18	4	8	1	0	2	4	0	.444
2009 Oakland	A.L.	1B	83	269	39	52	13	0	11	40	0	.193
2009 Colorado f-g-h........	N.L.	1B	19	24	4	7	1	0	2	11	0	.292
2010 Colorado i	N.L.	1B	87	176	17	43	9	0	6	35	2	.244
2011 Colorado Springs.......	P.C.	1B	3	7	2	3	0	0	0	3	0	.429
2011 Colorado j	N.L.	1B	64	131	20	34	6	0	13	32	0	.260
2012 Tulsa	Texas	1B	3	7	1	3	0	0	0	1	0	.429
2012 Colorado Springs.......	P.C.	1B	2	6	0	2	1	0	0	0	0	.333
2012 Colorado k-l..........	N.L.	1B	60	89	7	20	4	0	1	8	0	.225
2013 Cleveland m-n	A.L.	DH	71	186	21	34	8	0	9	31	0	.183
Major League Totals		19 Yrs.	2234	7207	1224	2002	403	9	438	1436	20	.278
Division Series												
2000 Oakland	A.L.	1B	5	14	2	4	0	0	0	1	1	.286
2001 Oakland	A.L.	1B	5	17	2	6	0	0	1	4	0	.353
2002 New York............	A.L.	1B-DH	4	14	5	5	0	0	1	3	0	.357
2003 New York............	A.L.	DH	4	16	1	4	2	0	0	2	0	.250
2005 New York............	A.L.	1B-DH	5	19	1	8	3	0	0	2	0	.421
2006 New York............	A.L.	DH-1B	3	8	1	1	0	0	1	2	1	.125
2007 New York............	A.L.	1B	3	4	0	1	0	0	0	0	0	.250
2009 Colorado	N.L.	PH	3	3	1	1	0	0	0	1	0	.333
Division Series Totals			32	95	13	30	5	0	3	15	2	.316
Championship Series												
2003 New York............	A.L.	DH	7	26	4	6	0	0	3	3	0	.231
World Series Record												
2003 New York............	A.L.	1B	6	17	2	4	1	0	1	1	0	.235

a Selected Most Valuable Player in American League for 2000.
b Filed for free agency, November 5, 2001. Signed with New York Yankees, December 13, 2001.
c On disabled list from May 22 to June 6 and from July 26 to September 14, 2004.
d On disabled list from May 31 to August 7, 2007.
e Not offered contract, November 4, 2008. Signed with Oakland A's, January 7, 2009.
f On disabled list from July 20 to August 7, 2009.
g Released by Oakland Athletics, August 7, 2009. Signed with Colorado Rockies organization, August 24, 2009.
h Filed for free agency, November 5, 2009, re-signed with Colorado Rockies, January 28, 2010.
i Filed for free agency, November 1, 2010, re-signed with Colorado Rockies organization, January 17, 2011.
j On disabled list from July 26 to August 12, 2011.
k On disabled list from July 21 to September 1, 2012.
l Filed for free agency, November 3, 2012. Signed with Cleveland Indians organization, February 9, 2013.
m On disabled list from March 25 to April 12, 2013.
n Filed for free agency, October 31, 2013, re-signed with Cleveland Indians organization, October 31, 2013.

GILLASPIE, CONOR MICHAEL

Born, Omaha, Nebraska, July 18, 1987.
Bats Left. Throws Right. Height, 6 feet, 1 inch. Weight, 205 pounds.

Year	Club	Lea	Pos	G	AB	R	H	2B	3B	HR	RBI	SB	Avg
2008	Giants	Arizona	3B	6	22	2	6	3	0	0	7	0	.273
2008	Salem-Keizer	Northwest	3B	18	71	4	19	4	0	0	8	2	.268
2008	San Francisco	N.L.	3B	8	5	1	1	0	0	0	0	0	.200
2009	San Jose	Calif.	3B	126	469	62	134	31	2	4	67	2	.286
2010	Richmond	Eastern	3B	132	491	57	141	25	8	8	67	0	.287
2011	Fresno	P.C.	3B-1B-OF	124	428	63	127	22	6	11	61	9	.297
2011	San Francisco	N.L.	3B	15	19	2	5	0	0	1	2	0	.263
2012	San Francisco	N.L.	3B	6	20	2	3	1	0	0	2	0	.150
2012	Fresno	P.C.	3B-1B	108	413	60	116	18	3	14	49	0	.281
2013	Chicago a	A.L.	3B-1B	134	408	46	100	14	3	13	40	0	.245
Major League Totals			4 Yrs.	163	452	51	109	15	3	14	44	0	.241

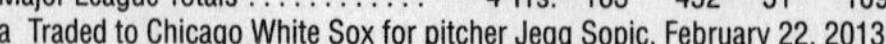

a Traded to Chicago White Sox for pitcher Jegg Sopic, February 22, 2013.

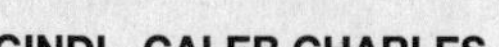

GINDL, CALEB CHARLES

Born, Pensacola, Florida, August 31, 1988.
Bats Left. Throws Left. Height, 5 feet, 7 inches. Weight, 205 pounds.

Year	Club	Lea	Pos	G	AB	R	H	2B	3B	HR	RBI	SB	Avg
2007	Helena	Pioneer	OF	55	207	40	77	22	3	5	42	4	.372
2008	West Virginia	So.Atl.	OF	137	508	86	156	38	4	13	81	14	.307
2009	Brevard County	Fla.St.	OF	112	394	61	109	15	3	17	71	18	.277
2010	Huntsville	Southern	OF	128	463	61	126	33	1	9	60	10	.272
2011	Nashville	P.C.	OF	126	472	84	145	23	5	15	60	6	.307
2012	Nashville	P.C.	OF	127	452	54	118	27	5	12	50	4	.261
2013	Nashville	P.C.	OF	83	312	33	92	21	3	11	51	1	.295
2013	Milwaukee	N.L.	OF	57	132	17	32	7	2	5	14	2	.242

GOLDSCHMIDT, PAUL EDWARD

Born, Wilmington, Delaware, September 10, 1987.
Bats Right. Throws Right. Height, 6 feet, 3 inches. Weight, 245 pounds.

Year	Club	Lea	Pos	G	AB	R	H	2B	3B	HR	RBI	SB	Avg
2009	Missoula	Pioneer	1B-OF	72	278	48	91	26	2	17	61	4	.327
2010	Visalia	Calif.	1B	138	525	102	165	42	3	35	108	5	.314
2011	Mobile	Southern	1B	103	366	84	112	21	3	30	94	9	.306
2011	Arizona	N.L.	1B	48	156	28	39	9	1	8	26	4	.250
2012	Arizona	N.L.	1B	145	514	82	147	43	1	20	82	18	.286
2013	Arizona	N.L.	1B	160	602	103	182	36	3	*36	*125	15	.302
Major League Totals			3 Yrs.	353	1272	213	368	88	5	64	233	37	.289
	Division Series												
2011	Arizona	N.L.	1B	4	16	4	7	0	0	2	6	1	.438

GOMES, JONNY JOHNSON

Born, Petaluma, California, November 22, 1980.
Bats Right. Throws Right. Height, 6 feet, 1 inch. Weight, 225 pounds.

Year	Club	Lea	Pos	G	AB	R	H	2B	3B	HR	RBI	SB	Avg
2001	Princeton	Appal.	OF	62	206	58	60	11	2	16	44	15	.291
2002	Bakersfield	California	OF	133	446	102	123	24	9	30	72	15	.276
2003	Orlando	Southern	OF	120	442	68	110	28	3	17	56	23	.249
2003	Durham	Int.	OF	5	19	2	6	2	1	0	1	0	.316
2003	Tampa Bay	A.L.	DH	8	15	1	2	1	0	0	0	0	.133
2004	Durham	Int.	OF	114	389	73	100	27	1	26	78	8	.257
2004	Tampa Bay	A.L.	DH	5	14	0	1	0	0	0	1	0	.071
2005	Durham	Int.	OF	45	162	34	52	13	0	14	46	7	.321
2005	Tampa Bay	A.L.	OF	101	348	61	98	13	6	21	54	9	.282
2006	Tampa Bay a	A.L.	DH-OF	117	385	53	83	21	1	20	59	1	.216
2007	Durham	Int.	OF	13	43	6	13	2	0	1	7	4	.302
2007	Tampa Bay	A.L.	OF	107	348	48	85	20	2	17	49	12	.244
2008	Durham	Int.	OF	26	107	19	27	11	0	2	14	0	.252
2008	Tampa Bay b	A.L.	DH-OF	77	154	23	28	5	1	8	21	8	.182
2009	Louisville	Int.	OF	37	131	18	37	10	1	9	27	4	.282
2009	Cincinnati c	N.L.	OF	98	281	39	75	17	0	20	51	3	.267
2010	Cincinnati	N.L.	OF	148	511	77	136	24	3	18	86	5	.266
2011	Cincinnati-Washington d-e	N.L.	OF	120	311	41	65	12	1	14	43	7	.209
2012	Oakland f	A.L.	DH-OF	99	279	46	73	10	0	18	47	3	.262

Year	Club	Lea	Pos	G	AB	R	H	2B	3B	HR	RBI	SB	Avg
2013	Boston	A.L.	OF	116	312	49	77	17	0	13	52	1	.247
Major League Totals			11 Yrs.	996	2958	438	723	140	14	149	463	49	.244
	Division Series												
2010	Cincinnati	N.L.	OF	2	6	0	0	0	0	0	0	0	.000
2012	Oakland	A.L.	PH	1	1	0	0	0	0	0	0	0	.000
2013	Boston	A.L.	OF	4	9	3	2	1	0	0	2	0	.222
Division Series Totals				7	16	3	2	1	0	0	2	0	.125
	Championship Series												
2013	Boston	A.L.	OF	5	16	3	3	1	0	0	0	0	.188
	World Series Record												
2013	Boston	A.L.	OF	6	17	2	2	0	0	1	3	0	.118

a On disabled list from August 22 to October 2, 2006.
b Not offered contract, December 12, 2008. Signed with Cincinnati Reds organization, January 19, 2009.
c Not offered contract, December 12, 2009, re-signed with Cincinnati Reds, February 22, 2010.
d Traded to Washington Nationals with cash for pitcher Chris Manno and outfielder Bill Rhinehart, July 26, 2011.
e Filed for free agency, October 30, 2011. Signed with Oakland Athletics, January 26, 2012.
f Filed for free agency, November 3, 2012. Signed with Boston Red Sox, November 22, 2012.

GOMES, YAN

Born, Sao Paolo, Brazil, July 19, 1987.
Bats Right. Throws Right. Height, 6 feet, 2 inches. Weight, 215 pounds.

Year	Club	Lea	Pos	G	AB	R	H	2B	3B	HR	RBI	SB	Avg
2009	Blue Jays	Gulf Coast	C	4	14	1	5	0	0	0	2	0	.357
2009	Auburn	N.Y.-Penn.	C	60	223	22	66	23	2	2	44	0	.296
2010	Lansing	Midwest	C	7	26	2	6	2	0	0	8	0	.231
2010	Dunedin	Fla.St.	C	68	233	37	64	21	1	9	40	0	.275
2011	New Hampshire	Eastern	C-1B	79	276	34	69	18	1	13	51	0	.250
2011	Las Vegas	P.C.	C	4	14	1	3	1	0	0	1	0	.214
2012	Las Vegas	P.C.	C-3B-1B-OF	79	305	44	100	29	1	13	59	4	.328
2012	Toronto a	A.L.	1B-C-3B-OF	43	98	9	20	4	0	4	13	0	.204
2013	Columbus	Int.	C	6	20	2	6	4	0	0	3	0	.300
2013	Cleveland	A.L.	C-1B	88	293	45	86	18	2	11	38	2	.294
Major League Totals			2 Yrs.	131	391	54	106	22	2	15	51	2	.271
	Wild Card Playoff												
2013	Cleveland	A.L.	C	1	4	0	2	1	0	0	0	0	.500

a Traded to Cleveland Indians with infielder Mike Aviles for pitcher Esmil Rogers, November 3, 2012.

GOMEZ (PENA), CARLOS ARGELIS

Born, Santiago, Dominican Republic, December 4, 1985.
Bats Right. Throws Right. Height, 6 feet, 4 inches. Weight, 195 pounds.

Year	Club	Lea	Pos	G	AB	R	H	2B	3B	HR	RBI	SB	Avg
2004	Kingsport	Appal.	OF	38	150	24	43	10	4	1	20	8	.287
2004	Mets	Gulf Coast	OF	19	71	10	19	7	0	0	11	9	.268
2005	Hagerstown	So.Atl.	OF	120	487	75	134	13	6	8	48	64	.275
2006	Binghamton	Eastern	OF	120	430	53	121	24	8	7	48	41	.281
2007	New Orleans	P.C.	OF	36	140	24	40	8	2	2	13	17	.286
2007	St. Lucie	Fla.St.	OF	5	13	1	2	0	0	0	0	2	.154
2007	New York a	N.L.	OF	58	125	14	29	3	0	2	12	12	.232
2008	Minnesota b	A.L.	OF	153	577	79	149	24	7	7	59	33	.258
2009	Minnesota c	A.L.	OF	137	315	51	72	15	5	3	28	14	.229
2010	Wisconsin	Midwest	OF	2	7	0	2	0	0	0	0	2	.286
2010	Nashville	P.C.	OF	8	28	7	8	0	0	0	2	2	.286
2010	Milwaukee d	N.L.	OF	97	291	38	72	11	3	5	24	18	.247
2011	Wisconsin	Midwest	OF	4	12	3	4	0	0	0	0	3	.333
2011	Milwaukee e	N.L.	OF	94	231	37	52	11	3	8	24	16	.225
2012	Wisconsin	Midwest	OF	4	13	2	2	0	0	1	3	0	.154
2012	Milwaukee f	N.L.	OF	137	415	72	108	19	4	19	51	37	.260
2013	Milwaukee	N.L.	OF	147	536	80	152	27	10	24	73	40	.284
Major League Totals			7 Yrs.	823	2490	371	634	110	32	68	271	170	.255
	Division Series												
2009	Minnesota	A.L.	OF	1	4	1	0	0	0	0	0	0	.000
2011	Milwaukee	N.L.	OF	3	4	2	3	0	0	1	2	2	.750
Division Series Totals				4	8	3	3	0	0	1	2	2	.375
	Championship Series												
2011	Milwaukee	N.L.	OF	5	10	1	2	0	0	0	0	0	.200

a On disabled list from July 5 to September 7, 2007.

b Traded to Minnesota Twins with pitcher Philip Humber, pitcher Kevin Mulvey and pitcher Deolis Garcia for pitcher Johan Santana, February 2, 2008.
c Traded to Milwaukee Brewers for infielder J.J. Hardy, November 6, 2009.
d On disabled list from May 6 to May 21 and August 3 to August 24, 2010.
e On disabled list from July 21 to September 1, 2011.
f On disabled list from May 5 to May 20, 2012.

GONZALEZ, ADRIAN

Born, San Diego, California, May 8, 1982.
Bats Left. Throws Left. Height, 6 feet, 2 inches. Weight, 220 pounds.

Year Club	Lea	Pos	G	AB	R	H	2B	3B	HR	RBI	SB	Avg
2000 Marlins.........	Gulf Coast	1B	53	193	24	57	10	1	0	30	0	.295
2000 Utica...........	N.Y.-Penn.	1B	8	29	7	9	3	0	0	3	0	.310
2001 Kane County.......	Midwest	1B	127	516	86	161	37	1	17	103	5	.312
2002 Portland...........	Eastern	1B	138	508	70	135	34	1	17	96	6	.266
2003 Albuquerque...........	P.C.	1B	39	139	17	30	5	1	1	18	1	.216
2003 Carolina..........	Southern	1B	36	137	15	42	9	1	1	16	1	.307
2003 Frisco a............	Texas	1B	45	173	16	49	6	2	3	17	0	.283
2004 Oklahoma.............	P.C.	1B	123	457	61	139	28	3	12	88	1	.304
2004 Texas...............	A.L.	1B	16	42	7	10	3	0	1	7	0	.238
2005 Oklahoma.............	P.C.	1B	84	328	61	111	17	1	18	65	0	.338
2005 Texas...............	A.L.	DH-1B-OF	43	150	17	34	7	1	6	17	0	.227
2006 San Diego b..........	N.L.	1B	156	570	83	173	38	1	24	82	0	.304
2007 San Diego...........	N.L.	1B	161	646	101	182	46	3	30	100	0	.282
2008 San Diego...........	N.L.	1B	*162	616	103	172	32	1	36	119	0	.279
2009 San Diego...........	N.L.	1B	160	552	90	153	27	2	40	99	1	.277
2010 San Diego c..........	N.L.	1B	160	591	87	176	33	0	31	101	0	.298
2011 Boston...............	A.L.	1B-OF	159	630	108	*213	45	3	27	117	1	.338
2012 Boston...............	A.L.	1B-OF	123	484	63	145	37	0	15	86	0	.300
2012 Los Angeles d........	N.L.	1B	36	145	12	43	10	1	3	22	2	.297
2013 Los Angeles..........	N.L.	1B	157	583	69	171	32	0	22	100	1	.293
Major League Totals............		10 Yrs.	1333	5009	740	1472	310	12	235	850	5	.294
Division Series												
2006 San Diego...........	N.L.	1B	4	14	2	5	0	0	0	0	0	.357
2013 Los Angeles..........	N.L.	1B	4	18	1	6	0	0	1	4	0	.333
Division Series Totals..........			8	32	3	11	0	0	1	4	0	.344
Championship Series												
2013 Los Angeles..........	N.L.	1B	6	20	6	6	2	0	2	3	0	.300

a Traded to Texas Rangers with pitcher Ryan Snare and outfielder Will Smith for pitcher Ugueth Urbina, July 11, 2003.
b Traded to San Diego Padres with pitcher Chris Young and outfielder Terrmel Sledge for pitcher Adam Eaton, pitcher Akinori Otsuka and catcher Billy Killian, January 4, 2006.
c Traded to Boston Red Sox for pitcher Casey Kelly, outfielder Reymond Fuentes, infielder Anthony Rizzo and player to be named later, December 5, 2010. San Diego Padres received outfielder Eric Patterson to complete trade, December 16, 2010.
d Traded to Los Angeles Dodgers with outfielder Carl Crawford, pitcher Josh Beckett, infielder Nick Punto and cash for infielder James Loney, infielder Ivan DeJesus, pitcher Allen Webster and player to be named later, August 25, 2012. Boston Red Sox received pitcher Rubby De La Rosa to complete trade, October 4, 2012.

GONZALEZ, CARLOS EDUARDO

Born, Maracaibo, Venezuela, October 17, 1985.
Bats Left. Throws Left. Height, 6 feet, 1 inch. Weight, 200 pounds.

Year Club	Lea	Pos	G	AB	R	H	2B	3B	HR	RBI	SB	Avg
2003 Missoula..........	Pioneer	OF	72	275	45	71	14	4	6	25	12	.258
2004 South Bend.......	Midwest	OF	12	42	3	11	4	0	1	6	0	.262
2004 Yakima.........	Northwest	OF	73	300	44	83	15	2	9	44	2	.277
2005 South Bend.......	Midwest	OF	129	515	91	158	28	6	18	92	7	.307
2006 Lancaster............	Calif.	OF	104	403	82	121	35	4	21	94	15	.300
2006 Tennessee.......	Southern	OF	18	61	11	13	6	0	2	5	1	.213
2007 Tucson..............	P.C.	OF	10	42	9	13	5	0	1	11	1	.310
2007 Mobile a.........	Southern	OF	120	458	63	131	33	3	16	75	9	.286
2008 Sacramento...........	P.C.	OF	46	173	23	49	9	1	4	28	1	.283
2008 Oakland b............	A.L.	OF	85	302	31	73	22	1	4	26	4	.242
2009 Colorado Springs.......	P.C.	OF	48	192	43	65	12	7	10	59	6	.339
2009 Colorado............	N.L.	OF	89	278	53	79	14	7	13	29	16	.284
2010 Colorado............	N.L.	OF	145	587	111	*197	34	9	34	117	26	*.336
2011 Colorado Springs.......	P.C.	OF	3	10	1	3	0	0	0	0	0	.300
2011 Colorado c............	N.L.	OF	127	481	92	142	27	3	26	92	20	.295
2012 Colorado............	N.L.	OF	135	518	89	157	31	5	22	85	20	.303
2013 Colorado Springs.......	P.C.	OF	2	6	0	1	0	0	0	0	0	.167

Year	Club	Lea	Pos	G	AB	R	H	2B	3B	HR	RBI	SB	Avg
2013	Colorado d	N.L.	OF	110	391	72	118	23	6	26	70	21	.302
Major League Totals			6 Yrs.	691	2557	448	766	151	31	125	419	107	.300
	Division Series												
2009	Colorado	N.L.	OF	4	17	5	10	2	0	1	1	2	.588

a Traded by Arizona Diamondbacks to Oakland Athletics with pitcher Brett Anderson, pitcher Dana Eveland, pitcher Greg Smith, infielder Chris Carter and outfielder Aaron Cunningham for pitcher Danny Haren and pitcher Connor Robertson, December 14, 2007.
b Traded to Colorado Rockies with pitcher Greg Smith and pitcher Huston Street for outfielder Matt Holliday, November 12, 2008.
c On disabled list from July 22 to August 6, 2011.
d On disabled list from August 5 to September 3, 2013.

GORDON, ALEX JONATHAN

Born, Lincoln, Nebraska, February 10, 1984.
Bats Left. Throws Right. Height, 6 feet, 1 inch. Weight, 220 pounds.

Year	Club	Lea	Pos	G	AB	R	H	2B	3B	HR	RBI	SB	Avg
2006	Wichita	Texas	3B-1B	130	486	111	158	39	1	29	101	22	.325
2007	Kansas City	A.L.	3B-1B-SS	151	543	60	134	36	4	15	60	14	.247
2008	Kansas City a	A.L.	3B	134	493	72	128	35	1	16	59	9	.260
2009	Azl Royals	Arizona	3B	4	7	1	2	0	0	1	3	0	.286
2009	NW Arkansas	Texas	3B	8	30	4	11	3	0	2	10	0	.367
2009	Omaha	P.C.	3B	18	67	17	21	4	1	2	10	0	.313
2009	Kansas City b	A.L.	3B	49	164	28	38	6	0	6	22	5	.232
2010	Wilmington	Carolina	3B	7	17	7	4	3	0	0	2	1	.235
2010	Omaha	P.C.	OF	68	260	59	82	20	3	14	44	7	.315
2010	Kansas City c	A.L.	OF-3B-1B	74	242	34	52	10	0	8	20	1	.215
2011	Kansas City	A.L.	OF-1B	151	611	101	185	45	4	23	87	17	.303
2012	Kansas City	A.L.	OF	161	642	93	189	*51	5	14	72	10	.294
2013	Kansas City	A.L.	OF	156	633	90	168	27	6	20	81	11	.265
Major League Totals			7 Yrs.	876	3328	478	894	210	20	102	401	67	.269

a On disabled list from August 22 to September 12, 2008.
b On disabled list from April 16 to July 16, 2009.
c On disabled list from March 26 to April 17, 2010.

GOSE, ANTHONY ROBERT

Born, Paramount, California, August 10, 1990.
Bats Left. Throws Left. Height, 6 feet, 1 inch. Weight, 195 pounds.

Year	Club	Lea	Pos	G	AB	R	H	2B	3B	HR	RBI	SB	Avg
2008	Phillies	Gulf Coast	OF	11	39	4	10	2	1	0	3	3	.256
2009	Lakewood	So.Atl.	OF	131	510	72	132	24	9	2	52	76	.259
2010	Clearwater	Fla.St.	OF	103	418	67	110	17	11	4	20	36	.263
2010	Dunedin a-b	Fla.St.	OF	27	94	21	24	3	2	3	6	9	.255
2011	New Hampshire	Eastern	OF	137	509	87	129	20	7	16	59	70	.253
2012	Las Vegas	P.C.	OF	102	420	87	120	21	10	5	43	34	.286
2012	Toronto	A.L.	OF	56	166	25	37	7	3	1	11	15	.223
2013	Buffalo	Int.	OF	106	393	64	94	17	6	3	27	22	.239
2013	Toronto	A.L.	OF	52	147	15	38	6	5	2	12	4	.259
Major League Totals			2 Yrs.	108	313	40	75	13	8	3	23	19	.240

a Traded by Philadelphia Phillies to Houston Astros with pitcher J.A.Happ and infielder Jonathan Villar for pitcher Roy Oswalt and cash, July 29, 2010.
b Traded to Toronto Blue Jays for infielder Brett Wallace, July 29, 2010.

GRANDERSON, CURTIS

Born, Blue Island, Illinois, March 16, 1981.
Bats Left. Throws Right. Height, 6 feet, 1 inch. Weight, 185 pounds.

Year	Club	Lea	Pos	G	AB	R	H	2B	3B	HR	RBI	SB	Avg
2002	Oneonta	N.Y.-Penn.	OF	52	212	45	73	15	4	3	34	9	.344
2003	Lakeland	Fla.St.	OF	127	476	71	136	29	10	11	51	10	.286
2004	Erie	Eastern	OF	123	462	89	139	19	8	21	94	14	.301
2004	Detroit	A.L.	OF	9	25	2	6	1	1	0	0	0	.240
2005	Toledo	Int.	OF	111	445	79	129	29	13	15	65	22	.290
2005	Detroit	A.L.	OF	47	162	18	44	6	3	8	20	1	.272
2006	Detroit	A.L.	OF	159	596	90	155	31	9	19	68	8	.260
2007	Detroit	A.L.	OF	158	612	122	185	38	*23	23	74	26	.302
2008	West Michigan	Midwest	OF	3	11	1	4	0	2	0	1	0	.364
2008	Toledo	Int.	OF	2	9	1	3	1	0	0	0	0	.333

Year Club	Lea	Pos	G	AB	R	H	2B	3B	HR	RBI	SB	Avg
2008 Detroit a	A.L.	OF	141	553	112	155	26	*13	22	66	12	.280
2009 Detroit b	A.L.	OF	160	631	91	157	23	8	30	71	20	.249
2010 Scranton/WB	Int.	OF	5	16	0	4	0	0	0	2	0	.250
2010 New York c	A.L.	OF	136	466	76	115	17	7	24	67	12	.247
2011 New York	A.L.	OF	156	583	*136	153	26	10	41	*119	25	.262
2012 New York	A.L.	OF	160	596	102	138	18	4	43	106	10	.232
2013 Tampa	Fla.St.	OF	4	13	2	2	0	0	0	1	0	.154
2013 Trenton	Eastern	OF	2	6	1	2	0	1	0	0	0	.333
2013 Scranton/WB	Int.	OF	5	20	2	8	0	0	1	3	0	.400
2013 New York d-e	A.L.	OF	61	214	31	49	13	2	7	15	8	.229
Major League Totals		10 Yrs.	1187	4438	780	1157	199	80	217	606	122	.261
Division Series												
2006 Detroit	A.L.	OF	4	17	3	5	0	1	2	5	1	.294
2010 New York	A.L.	OF	3	11	2	5	1	1	0	3	1	.455
2011 New York	A.L.	OF	5	20	4	5	1	1	1	3	0	.250
2012 New York	A.L.	OF	5	19	1	3	0	0	1	1	1	.158
Division Series Totals			17	67	10	18	2	3	4	12	3	.269
Championship Series												
2006 Detroit	A.L.	OF	4	15	4	5	2	0	1	2	1	.333
2010 New York	A.L.	OF	6	17	1	5	1	0	1	3	0	.294
2012 New York	A.L.	OF	4	11	0	0	0	0	0	0	1	.000
Championship Series Totals			14	43	5	10	3	0	2	5	2	.233
World Series Record												
2006 Detroit	A.L.	OF	5	21	1	2	1	0	0	0	0	.095

a On disabled list from March 23 to April 23, 2008.
b Traded to New York Yankees for outfielder Austin Jackson, pitcher Phil Coke and pitcher Ian Kennedy, December 9, 2009.
c On disabled list from May 2 to May 28, 2010.
d On disabled list from March 22 to May 14 and May 25 to August 2, 2013.
e Filed for free agency, October 31, 2013. Signed with New York Mets, December 9, 2013.

GREGORIUS, MARIEKSON JULIUS (DIDI)

Born, Amsterdam, Netherlands, February 18, 1990.
Bats Left. Throws Right. Height, 6 feet, 1 inch. Weight, 185 pounds.

Year Club	Lea	Pos	G	AB	R	H	2B	3B	HR	RBI	SB	Avg
2008 Reds	Gulf Coast	SS	31	97	6	15	0	0	0	9	2	.155
2009 Billings	Pioneer	SS-2B	50	204	28	64	10	1	1	16	8	.314
2009 Sarasota	Fla.St.	SS	22	71	8	18	4	0	0	2	0	.254
2010 Dayton	Midwest	SS	120	501	65	137	16	11	5	41	16	.273
2010 Lynchburg	Carolina	SS	7	25	4	6	0	0	0	0	0	.240
2011 Bakersfield	Calif.	SS	46	188	30	57	12	1	5	28	8	.303
2011 Carolina	Southern	SS	38	148	18	40	6	3	2	16	3	.270
2012 Pensacola	Southern	SS	81	316	45	88	11	8	1	31	3	.278
2012 Louisville	Int.	SS-2B	48	185	25	45	10	3	6	23	0	.243
2012 Cincinnati a-b	N.L.	SS	8	20	1	6	0	0	0	2	0	.300
2013 Reno	P.C.	SS	7	31	7	12	2	0	2	2	1	.387
2013 Arizona c	N.L.	SS	103	357	47	90	16	3	7	28	0	.252
Major League Totals		2 Yrs.	111	377	48	96	16	3	7	30	0	.255

a Traded to Cleveland Indians with outfielder Drew Stubbs for outfielder Shin-Soo Choo and infielder Jason Donald, December 11, 2012.
b Traded to Arizona Diamondbacks with infielder Lars Anderson and pitcher Tony Sipp for pitcher Matt Albers, pitcher Trevor Bauer and pitcher Bryan Shaw, December 11, 2012.
c On disabled list from March 31 to April 16 and April 27 to May 4, 2013.

GROSSMAN, ROBERT EDWARD (ROBBIE)

Born, San Diego, California, September 16, 1989.
Bats Both. Throws Left. Height, 6 feet. Weight, 205 pounds.

Year Club	Lea	Pos	G	AB	R	H	2B	3B	HR	RBI	SB	Avg
2008 Pirates	Gulf Coast	OF	5	16	3	3	1	0	0	1	1	.188
2009 West Virginia	So.Atl.	OF	116	451	83	120	21	2	5	42	35	.266
2010 Bradenton	Fla.St.	OF	125	470	84	115	29	3	4	50	15	.245
2011 Bradenton	Fla.St.	OF	134	490	127	144	34	2	13	56	24	.294
2012 Altoona	Eastern	OF	95	350	59	93	20	4	7	36	9	.266
2012 Corpus Christi a	Texas	OF	36	135	22	36	8	2	3	11	4	.267
2013 Oklahoma	P.C.	OF	70	253	42	71	11	2	2	20	15	.281
2013 Houston	A.L.	OF	63	257	29	69	14	0	4	21	6	.268

a Traded by Pittsburgh Pirates to Houston Astros with pitcher Rudy Owens and pitcher Colton Cain for pitcher Wandy Rodriguez and cash, July 25, 2012.

GUTIERREZ, FRANKLIN RAFAEL

Born, Caracas, Venezuela, February 21, 1983.
Bats Right. Throws Right. Height, 6 feet, 2 inches. Weight, 180 pounds.

Year	Club	Lea	Pos	G	AB	R	H	2B	3B	HR	RBI	SB	Avg
2001	Dodgers	Gulf Coast	OF	56	234	38	63	16	0	4	30	9	.269
2002	Las Vegas	P.C.	OF	2	10	2	3	2	0	0	2	0	.300
2002	South Bend	So.Atl.	OF	92	361	61	102	18	4	12	45	13	.283
2003	Vero Beach	Fla.St.	OF	110	425	65	120	28	5	20	68	17	.282
2003	Jacksonville	Southern	OF	18	67	12	21	3	2	4	12	3	.313
2004	Akron	Eastern	OF	70	262	38	79	24	2	5	35	6	.302
2004	Buffalo a	Int.	DH	7	27	4	4	1	0	1	3	0	.148
2005	Akron	Eastern	OF	95	383	70	100	25	2	11	42	14	.261
2005	Buffalo	Int.	OF	19	67	10	17	6	2	0	7	2	.254
2005	Cleveland	A.L.	OF	7	1	2	0	0	0	0	0	0	.000
2006	Buffalo	Int.	OF	90	349	63	97	27	0	9	38	13	.278
2006	Cleveland	A.L.	OF	43	136	21	37	9	0	1	8	0	.272
2007	Buffalo	Int.	OF	30	129	29	44	7	0	4	16	7	.341
2007	Cleveland b	A.L.	OF	100	271	41	72	13	2	13	36	8	.266
2008	Cleveland c	A.L.	OF	134	399	54	99	26	2	8	41	9	.248
2009	Seattle	A.L.	OF	153	565	85	160	24	1	18	70	16	.283
2010	Seattle	A.L.	OF	152	568	61	139	25	3	12	64	25	.245
2011	Tacoma	P.C.	OF	11	40	7	11	2	2	0	6	0	.275
2011	Seattle d	A.L.	OF	92	322	26	72	13	0	1	19	13	.224
2012	Tacoma	P.C.	OF	17	62	11	16	5	0	2	8	0	.258
2012	Seattle e	A.L.	OF	40	150	18	39	10	1	4	17	3	.260
2013	Tacoma	P.C.	OF	47	194	27	41	16	0	3	25	4	.211
2013	Seattle e-f	A.L.	OF	41	145	18	36	7	0	10	24	3	.248
Major League Totals			9 Yrs.	762	2557	326	654	127	9	67	279	77	.256
	Division Series												
2007	Cleveland	A.L.	OF	4	10	2	2	0	0	0	0	0	.200
	Championship Series												
2007	Cleveland	A.L.	OF	6	19	3	4	0	0	1	4	0	.211

a Traded to Cleveland Indians with player to be named later for outfielder Milton Bradley, April 4, 2004. Cleveland Indians received pitcher Andrew Brown to complete trade, May 19, 2004.
b On disabled list from March 23 to April 13, 2007.
c Traded to Seattle Mariners for infielder Luis Valbuena and pitcher Joe Smith, December 10, 2008.
d On disabled list from March 22 to May 18 and September 6 to October 31, 2011.
e On disabled list from March 24 to June 13 and June 29 to August 27, 2012.
e On disabled list from April 23 to June 22 and June 24 to August 26, 2013.
f Filed for free agency, November 1, 2013, re-signed with Seattle Mariners, December 18, 2013.

GUZMAN, JESUS ANTONIO

Born, Cumana, Venezuela, June 14, 1984.
Bats Right. Throws Right. Height, 6 feet, 1 inch. Weight, 215 pounds.

Year	Club	Lea	Pos	G	AB	R	H	2B	3B	HR	RBI	SB	Avg
2004	Inland Empire	Calif.	3B-SS	114	442	80	137	35	3	6	71	10	.310
2005	San Antonio	Texas	3B	119	453	61	117	18	8	9	53	6	.258
2006	San Antonio	Texas	3B-2B	115	408	57	105	18	3	9	55	7	.257
2007	High Desert a	Calif.	2B-3B-OF-1B	130	518	102	156	38	5	25	112	3	.301
2008	Sacramento	P.C.	3B	15	59	5	14	2	0	2	9	0	.237
2008	Athletics	Arizona	3B-SS-2B	5	15	2	7	3	0	1	3	1	.467
2008	Midland b	Texas	3B-2B	80	341	57	124	21	2	14	76	5	.364
2009	Fresno	P.C.	1B-3B	115	452	75	145	26	5	16	71	0	.321
2009	San Francisco	N.L.	1B	12	20	0	5	0	0	0	0	0	.250
2010	Fresno c	P.C.	3B-OF-1B	125	445	66	143	28	1	18	72	6	.321
2011	Tucson	P.C.	3B-OF-1B-2B	63	244	40	81	22	1	8	57	4	.332
2011	San Diego	N.L.	1B-OF	76	247	33	77	22	2	5	44	9	.312
2012	San Diego	N.L.	OF-1B-2B	120	287	32	71	18	2	9	48	3	.247
2013	San Diego d	N.L.	OF-1B-3B-2B	126	288	33	65	17	0	9	35	3	.226
Major League Totals			4 Yrs.	334	842	98	218	57	4	23	127	15	.259

a Filed for free agency from Seattle Mariners, October 29, 2007. Signed with Oakland Athletics organization, November 16, 2007.
b Filed for free agency, November 3, 2008. Signed with San Francisco Giants organization, November 18, 2008.
c Filed for free agency, November 6, 2010. Signed with San Diego Padres organization, November 29, 2010.
d Traded to Houston Astros for infielder Ryan Jackon, December 18, 2013.

GYORKO, JEDD LINDON

Born, Morgantown, West Virginia, September 23, 1988.
Bats Right. Throws Right. Height, 5 feet, 10 inches. Weight, 210 pounds.

Year	Club	Lea	Pos	G	AB	R	H	2B	3B	HR	RBI	SB	Avg
2010	Eugene	Northwest	3B	26	106	16	35	6	0	5	18	1	.330
2010	Fort Wayne	Midwest	3B-2B	42	162	19	46	11	0	2	23	1	.284
2011	Lake Elsinore	Calif.	3B	81	340	78	124	35	2	18	74	11	.365
2011	San Antonio	Texas	3B	59	236	41	68	12	0	7	40	1	.288
2012	San Antonio	Texas	2B-3B	34	130	18	34	4	0	6	17	1	.262
2012	Tucson	P.C.	3B-2B	92	369	62	121	24	0	24	83	4	.328
2013	Lake Elsinore	Calif.	2B	2	7	2	4	1	0	0	1	0	.571
2013	San Antonio	Texas	2B	1	1	0	1	0	0	0	0	0	1.000
2013	San Diego a	N.L.	2B-3B	125	486	62	121	26	0	23	63	1	.249

a On disabled list from June 10 to July 12, 2013.

HAFNER, TRAVIS LEE

Born, Jamestown, North Dakota, June 3, 1977.
Bats Left. Throws Right. Height, 6 feet, 3 inches. Weight, 240 pounds.

Year	Club	Lea	Pos	G	AB	R	H	2B	3B	HR	RBI	SB	Avg
1997	Rangers	Gulf Coast	1B-OF	55	189	38	54	14	0	5	24	7	.286
1998	Savannah	So.Atl.	1B-3B-OF	123	405	62	96	15	4	16	84	7	.237
1999	Savannah	So.Atl.	1B	134	480	94	140	30	4	28	111	5	.292
2000	Charlotte a	Fla.St.	1B-3B	122	436	90	151	34	1	22	109	0	.346
2001	Tulsa b	Texas	1B	88	323	59	91	25	0	20	74	3	.282
2002	Oklahoma	P.C.	1B	110	401	79	137	22	1	21	77	2	.342
2002	Texas c	A.L.	DH-1B	23	62	6	15	4	1	1	6	0	.242
2003	Buffalo	Int.	1B	29	100	15	27	4	0	2	10	2	.270
2003	Cleveland d	A.L.	DH-1B	91	291	35	74	19	3	14	40	2	.254
2004	Cleveland	A.L.	DH-1B	140	482	96	150	41	3	28	109	3	.311
2005	Akron	Eastern	DH	3	9	0	0	0	0	0	0	0	.000
2005	Cleveland e	A.L.	DH-1B	137	486	94	148	42	0	33	108	0	.305
2006	Cleveland	A.L.	DH-1B	129	454	100	140	31	1	42	117	0	.308
2007	Cleveland	A.L.	DH-1B	152	545	80	145	25	2	24	100	1	.266
2008	Buffalo	Int.	DH	7	22	4	7	3	0	0	4	0	.318
2008	Cleveland f	A.L.	DH	57	198	21	39	10	0	5	24	1	.197
2009	Columbus	Int.	DH	12	39	6	13	4	0	1	8	0	.333
2009	Cleveland g	A.L.	DH	94	338	46	92	19	0	16	49	0	.272
2010	Cleveland h	A.L.	DH	118	396	46	110	29	0	13	50	2	.278
2011	Akron	Eastern	DH	2	6	2	3	1	0	0	0	0	.500
2011	Cleveland i	A.L.	DH	94	325	41	91	16	0	13	57	0	.280
2012	Columbus	Int.	DH	3	10	0	1	0	0	0	1	0	.100
2012	Cleveland j-k	A.L.	DH	66	219	23	50	6	2	12	34	0	.228
2013	New York l-m	A.L.	DH	82	262	31	53	8	1	12	37	2	.202
Major League Totals			12 Yrs.	1183	4058	619	1107	250	13	213	731	11	.273
	Division Series												
2007	Cleveland	A.L.	DH	4	16	4	4	0	0	1	2	0	.250
	Championship Series												
2007	Cleveland	A.L.	DH	7	27	2	4	1	0	1	2	0	.148

a On disabled list from August 6 to 22, 2000.
b On disabled list from April 5 to May 11, 2001.
c Traded to Cleveland Indians with pitcher Aaron Myette for catcher Einar Diaz and pitcher Ryan Drese, December 6, 2002.
d On disabled list from May 10 to May 26, 2003.
e On disabled list from July 17 to August 4, 2005.
f On disabled list from May 26 to September 9, 2008.
g On disabled list from April 29 to June 5, 2009.
h On disabled list from July 29 to August 15, 2010.
i On disabled list from May 18 to June 17 and August 22 to September 11, 2011.
j On disabled list from May 24 to July 4 and August 6 to September 18, 2012.
k Filed for free agency, November 3, 2012. Signed with New York Yankees, February 1, 2013.
l On disabled list from July 27 to September 25, 2013.
m Filed for free agency, October 31, 2013.

HAIRSTON, SCOTT ALEXANDER

Born, Fort Worth, Texas, May 25, 1980.
Bats Right. Throws Right. Height, 6 feet. Weight, 190 pounds.

Year	Club	Lea	Pos	G	AB	R	H	2B	3B	HR	RBI	SB	Avg
2001	Missoula	Pioneer	2B	74	291	81	101	16	6	14	65	2	.347
2002	Lancaster	Calif.	2B-3B	18	79	20	32	11	1	6	26	1	.405

Year	Club	Lea	Pos	G	AB	R	H	2B	3B	HR	RBI	SB	Avg
2002	South Bend	Midwest	2B-3B	109	394	79	131	35	4	16	72	9	.332
2003	Tucson	P.C.	DH	1	0	0	0	0	0	0	1	0	.000
2003	El Paso	Texas	2B	88	337	53	93	21	7	10	47	6	.276
2004	Tucson	P.C.	2B-OF	28	115	29	36	8	3	5	20	0	.313
2004	Arizona	N.L.	2B-OF	101	339	39	84	15	6	13	29	3	.248
2005	Arizona	N.L.	OF	15	20	0	2	1	0	0	0	0	.100
2005	Tucson a	P.C.	OF-2B	58	209	45	65	8	3	16	40	3	.311
2006	Tucson	P.C.	OF	98	381	83	123	22	1	26	81	3	.323
2006	Arizona b	N.L.	OF	9	15	2	6	2	0	0	2	0	.400
2007	Arizona-San Diego c-d	N.L.	OF	107	263	37	64	18	2	11	36	2	.243
2008	San Diego e	N.L.	OF-2B	112	326	42	81	18	3	17	31	3	.248
2009	Lake Elsinore	Calif.	OF	3	10	1	1	0	0	0	0	0	.100
2009	San Diego	N.L.	OF	56	197	26	59	14	1	10	29	8	.299
2009	Oakland f-g-h	A.L.	OF	60	233	24	55	13	1	7	35	3	.236
2010	Lake Elsinore	Calif.	OF	3	7	1	4	1	0	0	1	0	.571
2010	San Diego i-j	N.L.	OF	104	295	34	62	10	0	10	36	6	.210
2011	New York k-l	N.L.	OF-2B	79	132	20	31	8	1	7	24	1	.235
2012	New York m	N.L.	OF	134	377	52	99	25	3	20	57	8	.263
2013	Chicago-Washington n	N.L.	OF	85	157	18	30	5	0	10	26	2	.191
Major League Totals			10 Yrs.	862	2354	294	573	129	17	105	305	36	.243

a On disabled list from September 2 to November 14, 2005.
b On disabled list from June 20 to July 29, 2006.
c Traded to San Diego Padres for pitcher Leo Rosales, July 27, 2007.
d On disabled list from August 10 to September 8, 2007.
e On disabled list from August 28 to October 2, 2008.
f On disabled list from June 3 to June 23, 2009.
g Traded to Oakland Athletics for pitcher Ryan Webb, pitcher Craig Italiano and player to be named later, July 5, 2009. San Diego Padres received pitcher Sean Gallagher to complete trade, July 28, 2009.
h Traded to San Diego Padres with outfielder Aaron Cunningham for third baseman Kevin Kouzmanoff and infielder Eric Sogard, January 16, 2010.
i On disabled list from May 16 to June 2, 2010.
j Not offered contract, December 2, 2010. Signed with New York Mets, January 20, 2011.
k On disabled list from August 24 to September 30, 2011.
l Filed for free agency, October 30, 2011, re-signed with New York Mets, January 6, 2012.
m Filed for free agency, November 3, 2012. Signed with Chicago Cubs, February 10, 2013.
n Traded to Washington Nationals with player to be named later for pitcher Ivan Pineyro, July 8, 2013.

HAMILTON, BILLY R.

Born, Collins, Mississippi, September 9, 1990.
Bats Both. Throws Right. Height, 6 feet. Weight, 160 pounds.

Year	Club	Lea	Pos	G	AB	R	H	2B	3B	HR	RBI	SB	Avg
2009	Reds	Gulf Coast	SS	43	166	19	34	6	3	0	11	14	.205
2010	Billings	Pioneer	2B-SS	69	283	61	90	13	10	2	24	48	.318
2011	Dayton	Midwest	SS	135	550	99	153	18	9	3	50	103	.278
2012	Bakersfield	Calif.	SS	82	337	79	109	18	9	1	30	104	.323
2012	Pensacola	Southern	SS	50	175	33	50	4	5	1	15	51	.286
2013	Louisville	Int.	OF-SS	123	504	75	129	18	4	6	41	75	.256
2013	Cincinnati	N.L.	OF	13	19	9	7	2	0	0	1	13	.368

HAMILTON, JOSHUA HOLT (JOSH)

Born, Raleigh, North Carolina, May 21, 1981.
Bats Left. Throws Left. Height, 6 feet, 4 inches. Weight, 235 pounds.

Year	Club	Lea	Pos	G	AB	R	H	2B	3B	HR	RBI	SB	Avg
1999	Princeton	Appal.	OF	56	236	49	82	20	4	10	48	17	.347
1999	Hudson Valley	N.Y.-Penn.	OF	16	72	7	14	3	0	0	7	1	.194
2000	Charleston-SC	So.Atl.	OF	96	391	62	118	23	3	13	61	14	.302
2001	Charleston-SC	So.Atl.	OF	4	11	3	4	1	0	1	2	0	.364
2001	Orlando	Southern	OF	23	89	5	16	5	0	0	4	2	.180
2002	Bakersfield	Calif.	OF	56	211	32	64	14	1	9	44	10	.303
2003-05			RESTRICTED—Did not play										
2006	Hudson Valley a	N.Y.-Penn.	OF	15	50	7	13	3	1	0	5	0	.260
2007	Louisville	Int.	OF	11	40	9	14	1	0	4	8	3	.350
2007	Cincinnati b-c	N.L.	OF	90	298	52	87	17	2	19	47	3	.292
2008	Texas	A.L.	OF	156	624	98	190	35	5	32	*130	9	.304
2009	Frisco	Texas	DH	1	4	1	1	0	0	0	1	1	.250
2009	Oklahoma	P.C.	OF	7	28	3	5	2	1	0	0	1	.179
2009	Texas d	A.L.	OF	89	336	43	90	19	2	10	54	8	.268
2010	Texas e	A.L.	OF	133	518	95	186	40	3	32	100	8	*.359

Year	Club	Lea	Pos	G	AB	R	H	2B	3B	HR	RBI	SB	Avg
2011	Frisco	Texas	DH	2	7	3	2	0	0	1	3	0	.286
2011	Round Rock	P.C.	DH	3	11	2	2	1	0	1	3	0	.182
2011	Texas f	A.L.	OF	121	487	80	145	31	5	25	94	8	.298
2012	Texas g	A.L.	OF	148	562	103	160	31	2	43	128	7	.285
2013	Los Angeles	A.L.	OF	151	576	73	144	32	5	21	79	4	.250
Major League Totals			7 Yrs.	888	3401	544	1002	205	24	182	632	47	.295
	Wild Card Playoff												
2012	Texas	A.L.	OF	1	4	0	0	0	0	0	0	0	.000
	Division Series												
2010	Texas	A.L.	OF	5	18	1	2	0	0	0	1	1	.111
2011	Texas	A.L.	OF	4	15	1	4	1	0	0	2	0	.267
Division Series Totals				9	33	2	6	1	0	0	3	1	.182
	Championship Series												
2010	Texas	A.L.	OF	6	20	6	7	1	0	4	7	3	.350
2011	Texas	A.L.	OF	6	26	4	8	4	0	0	5	0	.308
Championship Series Totals				12	46	10	15	5	0	4	12	3	.326
	World Series Record												
2010	Texas	A.L.	OF	5	20	2	2	0	0	1	1	0	.100
2011	Texas	A.L.	OF	7	29	4	7	2	0	1	6	0	.241
World Series Totals				12	49	6	9	2	0	2	7	0	.184

a Selected by Chicago Cubs from Tampa Bay Devil Rays in Rule V draft, December 7, 2006. Sold to Cincinnati Reds, December 7, 2006.
b On disabled list from May 19 to June 4 and July 8 to August 12, 2007.
c Traded to Texas Rangers for pitcher Edinson Volquez and pitcher Danny Herrera, December 21, 2007.
d On disabled list from April 27 to May 12 and June 1 to July 6, 2009.
e Selected Most Valuable Player in American League for 2010.
f On disabled list from April 13 to May 23, 2011.
g Filed for free agency, November 3, 2012. Signed with Los Angeles Angels, December 15, 2012.

HANIGAN, RYAN M.

Born, Washington, District of Columbia, August 16, 1980.
Bats Right. Throws Right. Height, 6 feet. Weight, 195 pounds.

Year	Club	Lea	Pos	G	AB	R	H	2B	3B	HR	RBI	SB	Avg
2002	Dayton	Midwest	C	6	11	1	3	1	0	0	0	0	.273
2003	Louisville	Int.	C	1	3	1	1	0	0	0	0	0	.333
2003	Dayton	Midwest	C	92	311	43	86	12	0	1	31	3	.277
2004	Potomac	Carolina	C	119	429	58	127	21	0	5	56	6	.296
2005	Chattanooga	Southern	1B-C	100	333	45	107	14	1	4	29	4	.321
2006	Louisville	Int.	C-1B	8	13	2	2	0	0	0	1	0	.154
2006	Chattanooga	Southern	C-1B-OF	56	126	17	31	2	0	0	14	0	.246
2007	Chattanooga	Southern	C-1B	60	197	30	59	14	1	3	27	0	.299
2007	Louisville	Int.	C-1B	41	127	16	32	5	0	1	9	0	.252
2007	Cincinnati	N.L.	C	5	10	3	3	1	0	0	2	0	.300
2008	Louisville	Int.	C-1B	75	272	37	88	14	0	4	35	1	.324
2008	Cincinnati	N.L.	C	31	85	9	23	2	0	2	9	0	.271
2009	Louisville	Int.	C	5	18	4	7	2	0	0	2	0	.389
2009	Cincinnati a	N.L.	C	90	251	22	66	6	1	3	11	0	.263
2010	Louisville	Int.	C	13	46	6	11	3	0	0	2	0	.239
2010	Cincinnati b	N.L.	C	70	203	25	61	11	0	5	40	0	.300
2011	Cincinnati	N.L.	C	91	266	27	71	6	0	6	31	0	.267
2012	Cincinnati	N.L.	C	112	317	25	87	14	0	2	24	0	.274
2013	Louisville	Int.	C	3	8	2	3	0	0	0	2	0	.375
2013	Cincinnati c-d	N.L.	C	75	222	17	44	8	0	2	21	0	.198
Major League Totals			7 Yrs.	474	1354	128	355	48	1	20	138	0	.262
	Wild Card Playoff												
2013	Cincinnati	N.L.	C	1	3	0	0	0	0	0	0	0	.000
	Division Series												
2010	Cincinnati	N.L.	C	2	4	0	0	0	0	0	0	0	.000
2012	Cincinnati	N.L.	C	4	15	3	3	0	0	0	3	0	.200
Division Series Totals				6	19	3	3	0	0	0	3	0	.158

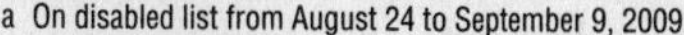

a On disabled list from August 24 to September 9, 2009.
b On disabled list from May 29 to July 9, 2010.
c On disabled list from April 20 to May 10 and July 10 to August 9, 2013.
d Traded to Tampa Bay Rays for pitcher David Holmberg, December 3, 2013.

HANNAHAN, JOHN JOSEPH (JACK)

Born, St.Paul, Minnesota, March 4, 1980.

Bats Left. Throws Right. Height, 6 feet, 2 inches. Weight, 210 pounds.

Year	Club	Lea	Pos	G	AB	R	H	2B	3B	HR	RBI	SB	Avg
2001	Oneonta	N.Y.-Penn.	3B	14	55	11	16	4	1	0	8	2	.291
2001	West Michigan	Midwest	3B	46	170	24	54	11	0	1	27	4	.318
2002	Lakeland	Fla.St.	3B	66	246	28	67	11	1	6	42	9	.272
2002	Erie	Eastern	3B	65	226	17	54	12	1	3	20	2	.239
2003	Erie	Eastern	3B	135	471	64	121	18	0	9	45	2	.257
2004	Erie	Eastern	3B-SS	108	374	48	102	21	1	8	39	7	.273
2005	Erie	Eastern	3B	7	22	1	3	0	0	0	1	0	.136
2005	Toledo	Int.	3B-1B-2B	68	238	31	64	15	0	4	28	6	.269
2006	Detroit	A.L.	1B	3	9	0	0	0	0	0	0	0	.000
2006	Toledo	Int.	2B-3B-1B	119	415	59	117	27	0	9	62	9	.282
2007	Toledo	Int.	2B-3B-1B	101	336	56	99	20	1	13	63	5	.295
2007	Oakland a	A.L.	3B	41	144	16	40	12	0	3	24	1	.278
2008	Oakland	A.L.	3B-1B	143	436	48	95	27	0	9	47	2	.218
2009	Sacramento	P.C.	3B-2B	21	81	8	18	7	0	2	11	0	.222
2009	Oakland-Seattle b	A.L.	3B-1B-SS-2B	103	267	27	57	14	2	4	19	1	.213
2010	Pawtucket	Int.	3B-2B-1B	33	110	15	28	8	0	4	12	2	.255
2010	Tacoma c	P.C.	2B-3B-SS	63	224	32	51	9	1	5	33	1	.228
2011	Cleveland	A.L.	3B-1B	110	320	38	80	16	2	8	40	2	.250
2012	Lake County	Midwest	3B	2	8	0	1	0	0	0	1	0	.125
2012	Columbus	Int.	DH	1	4	0	0	0	0	0	0	0	.000
2012	Cleveland d-e	A.L.	3B-SS-1B	105	287	23	70	16	0	4	29	0	.244
2013	Cincinnati	N.L.	3B-1B-2B	83	139	12	30	5	1	1	14	0	.216
Major League Totals			7 Yrs.	588	1602	164	372	90	5	29	173	6	.232

a Traded by Detroit Tigers to Oakland Athletics for outfielder Jason Perry, August 13, 2007.

b Traded to Seattle Mariners for pitcher Justin Souza, July 11, 2009.

c On disabled list from March 26 to April 30, 2010.

d On disabled list from May 27 to June 14, 2012.

e Not offered contract, November 30, 2012. Signed with Cincinnati Reds, December 13, 2012.

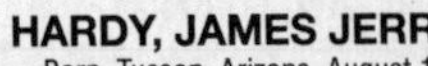

HARDY, JAMES JERRY (J.J.)

Born, Tucson, Arizona, August 19, 1982.

Bats Right. Throws Right. Height, 6 feet, 2 inches. Weight, 190 pounds.

Year	Club	Lea	Pos	G	AB	R	H	2B	3B	HR	RBI	SB	Avg
2001	Brewers	Arizona	SS	5	20	6	5	2	1	0	1	0	.250
2001	Ogden	Pioneer	SS	35	125	20	31	5	0	2	15	1	.248
2002	High Desert	California	SS	84	335	53	98	19	1	6	48	9	.293
2002	Huntsville	Southern	SS	38	145	14	33	7	0	1	13	1	.228
2003	Huntsville	Southern	SS	114	416	67	116	26	0	12	62	6	.279
2004	Indianapolis	Int.	SS	26	101	17	28	10	0	4	20	0	.277
2005	Milwaukee	N.L.	SS	124	372	46	92	22	1	9	50	0	.247
2006	Milwaukee a	N.L.	SS	35	128	13	31	5	0	5	14	1	.242
2007	Milwaukee	N.L.	SS	151	592	89	164	30	1	26	80	2	.277
2008	Milwaukee	N.L.	SS	146	569	78	161	31	4	24	74	2	.283
2009	Nashville	P.C.	SS	18	71	7	18	2	0	4	12	0	.254
2009	Milwaukee b	N.L.	SS	115	414	53	95	16	2	11	47	0	.229
2010	Beloit	Midwest	SS	3	10	0	2	0	0	0	0	0	.200
2010	Minnesota c-d	A.L.	SS	101	340	44	91	19	3	6	38	1	.268
2011	Norfolk	Int.	SS	3	9	2	2	0	0	0	0	0	.222
2011	Baltimore e	A.L.	SS	129	527	76	142	27	0	30	80	0	.269
2012	Baltimore	A.L.	SS	158	663	85	158	30	2	22	68	0	.238
2013	Baltimore	A.L.	SS	159	601	66	158	27	0	25	76	2	.263
Major League Totals			9 Yrs.	1118	4206	550	1092	207	13	158	527	8	.260
	Wild Card Playoff												
2012	Baltimore	A.L.	SS	1	5	1	2	0	0	0	1	0	.400
	Division Series												
2008	Milwaukee	N.L.	SS	4	14	2	6	1	0	0	2	0	.429
2010	Minnesota	A.L.	SS	3	10	0	1	1	0	0	0	0	.100
2012	Baltimore	A.L.	SS	5	22	0	3	2	0	0	1	0	.136
Division Series Totals				12	46	2	10	4	0	0	3	0	.217

a On disabled list from May 17 to October 31, 2006.

b Traded to Minnesota Twins for outfielder Carlos Gomez, November 6, 2009.

c On disabled list from May 5 to May 25 and June 7 to July 3, 2010.

d Traded to Baltimore Orioles with infielder Brendan Harris and cash for pitcher Jim Hoey and pitcher Brett Jacobson, December 9, 2010.

e On disabled list from April 10 to May 10, 2011.

HARPER, BRYCE ARON MAX (BRYCE)

Born, Las Vegas, Nevada, October 16, 1992.
Bats Left. Throws Right. Height, 6 feet, 3 inches. Weight, 215 pounds.

Year	Club	Lea	Pos	G	AB	R	H	2B	3B	HR	RBI	SB	Avg
2011	Hagerstown	So.Atl.	OF	72	258	49	82	17	1	14	46	19	.318
2011	Harrisburg	Eastern	OF	37	129	14	33	7	1	3	12	7	.256
2012	Syracuse	Int.	OF	21	74	8	18	4	1	1	3	1	.243
2012	Washington a	N.L.	OF	139	533	98	144	26	9	22	59	18	.270
2013	Potomac	Carolina	OF	2	4	2	2	1	0	1	1	0	.500
2013	Harrisburg	Eastern	OF	2	7	3	2	0	1	0	2	0	.286
2013	Washington b	N.L.	OF	118	424	71	116	24	3	20	58	11	.274
Major League Totals			2 Yrs.	257	957	169	260	50	12	42	117	29	.272
	Division Series												
2012	Washington	N.L.	OF	5	23	2	3	1	1	1	2	0	.130

a Selected Rookie of the Year in National League for 2012.
b On disabled list from May 27 to July 1, 2013.

HARRISON, JOSH ISAIAH

Born, Cincinnati, Ohio, July 8, 1987.
Bats Right. Throws Right. Height, 5 feet, 8 inches. Weight, 185 pounds.

Year	Club	Lea	Pos	G	AB	R	H	2B	3B	HR	RBI	SB	Avg
2008	Boise	Northwest	2B-OF	33	114	27	40	11	2	1	25	12	.351
2008	Peoria	Midwest	2B-OF	31	122	15	32	4	1	1	4	6	.262
2009	Peoria	Midwest	OF-2B-3B	79	303	51	102	17	7	4	33	16	.337
2009	Daytona a	Fla.St.	OF-2B-3B	18	70	10	20	3	1	1	9	10	.286
2009	Lynchburg	Carolina	3B-2B-OF	34	141	15	38	8	1	1	13	4	.270
2010	Altoona	Eastern	3B-2B	135	520	74	156	33	3	4	75	19	.300
2011	Indianapolis	Int.	3B-2B-SS	62	226	35	70	15	2	5	23	13	.310
2011	Pittsburgh	N.L.	3B-2B	65	195	21	53	13	2	1	16	4	.272
2012	Pittsburgh	N.L.	2B-SS-3B-OF	104	249	34	58	9	5	3	16	7	.233
2013	Indianapolis	Int.	2B-SS-OF	64	268	50	85	29	5	4	34	19	.317
2013	Pittsburgh	N.L.	OF-2B-3B-SS	60	88	10	22	1	2	3	14	2	.250
Major League Totals			3 Yrs.	229	532	65	133	23	9	7	46	13	.250
	Division Series												
2013	Pittsburgh	N.L.	PH	2	0	1	0	0	0	0	0	0	.000

a Traded by Chicago Cubs to Pittsburgh Pirates with pitcher Kevin Hart and pitcher Jose Ascanio for pitcher John Grabow and pitcher Tom Gorzelanny, July 30, 2009.

HART, JON COREY (COREY)

Born, Bowling Green, Kentucky, March 24, 1982.
Bats Right. Throws Right. Height, 6 feet, 6 inches. Weight, 215 pounds.

Year	Club	Lea	Pos	G	AB	R	H	2B	3B	HR	RBI	SB	Avg
2000	Ogden	Pioneer	1B	57	216	32	62	9	1	2	30	6	.287
2001	Ogden	Pioneer	1B-OF	69	262	53	89	18	1	11	62	14	.340
2002	High Desert	Calif.	3B-1B	100	393	76	113	26	10	22	84	24	.288
2002	Huntsville	Southern	3B-1B	28	94	16	25	3	0	2	15	3	.266
2003	Huntsville	Southern	3B-OF	130	493	70	149	40	1	13	94	25	.302
2004	Indianapolis	Int.	OF-1B	121	440	68	124	29	8	15	67	17	.282
2004	Milwaukee	N.L.	DH	1	1	0	0	0	0	0	0	0	.000
2005	Milwaukee	N.L.	OF	21	57	9	11	2	1	2	7	2	.193
2005	Nashville	P.C.	OF-1B	113	429	85	132	29	9	17	69	31	.308
2006	Milwaukee	N.L.	OF-1B	87	237	32	67	13	2	9	33	5	.283
2007	Milwaukee	N.L.	OF	140	505	86	149	33	9	24	81	23	.295
2008	Milwaukee	N.L.	OF	157	612	76	164	45	6	20	91	23	.268
2009	Nashville	P.C.	OF	4	10	5	5	1	0	1	3	0	.500
2009	Milwaukee a	N.L.	OF	115	419	64	109	24	3	12	48	11	.260
2010	Milwaukee	N.L.	OF	145	558	91	158	34	4	31	102	7	.283
2011	Nashville	P.C.	OF	5	15	1	2	2	0	0	1	0	.133
2011	Milwaukee b	N.L.	OF	130	492	80	140	25	4	26	63	7	.285
2012	Milwaukee	N.L.	1B-OF	149	562	91	152	35	4	30	83	5	.270
2013	Milwaukee c-d	N.L.	INJURED—Did Not Play										
Major League Totals			9 Yrs.	945	3443	529	950	211	33	154	508	83	.276
	Division Series												
2008	Milwaukee	N.L.	OF	4	13	0	3	0	0	0	0	0	.231
2011	Milwaukee	N.L.	OF	5	21	4	5	0	0	1	3	0	.238
Division Series Totals				9	34	4	8	0	0	1	3	0	.235

Year	Club	Lea	Pos	G	AB	R	H	2B	3B	HR	RBI	SB	Avg
	Championship Series												
2011	Milwaukee	N.L.	OF	5	20	2	5	0	0	1	2	0	.250

a On disabled list from August 2 to September 8, 2009.
b On disabled list from March 22 to April 26, 2011.
c On disabled list from March 22 to October 31, 2013.
d Filed for free agency, October 31, 2013. Signed with Seattle Mariners, December 13, 2013.

HEADLEY, CHASE JORDAN

Born, Fountain, Colorado, May 9, 1984.
Bats Both. Throws Right. Height, 6 feet, 2 inches. Weight, 195 pounds.

Year	Club	Lea	Pos	G	AB	R	H	2B	3B	HR	RBI	SB	Avg
2005	Fort Wayne	Midwest	3B	4	15	2	3	0	0	0	1	0	.200
2005	Eugene	Northwest	3B	57	220	29	59	14	3	6	33	1	.268
2006	Lake Elsinore	Calif.	3B	129	484	79	141	33	0	12	73	4	.291
2007	San Antonio	Texas	3B	121	433	82	143	38	5	20	78	1	.330
2007	San Diego	N.L.	3B	8	18	1	4	1	0	0	0	0	.222
2008	Portland	P.C.	OF-3B	65	259	49	79	24	1	13	40	0	.305
2008	San Diego	N.L.	OF-3B	91	331	34	89	19	2	9	38	4	.269
2009	San Diego	N.L.	OF-3B-1B	156	543	62	142	31	2	12	64	10	.262
2010	San Diego	N.L.	3B	161	610	77	161	29	3	11	58	17	.264
2011	San Diego a	N.L.	3B	113	381	43	110	28	1	4	44	13	.289
2012	San Diego	N.L.	3B-1B	161	604	95	173	31	2	31	*115	17	.286
2013	Lake Elsinore	Calif.	3B	4	12	0	3	1	0	0	0	0	.250
2013	San Diego b	N.L.	3B	141	520	59	130	35	2	13	50	8	.250
Major League Totals			7 Yrs.	831	3007	371	809	174	12	80	369	69	.269

a On disabled list from August 7 to September 19, 2011.
b On disabled list from March 22 to April 17, 2013.

HECHAVARRIA (BARETTA), ADEINY

Born, Santiago de Cuba, Cuba, April 15, 1989.
Bats Right. Throws Right. Height, 5 feet, 11 inches. Weight, 180 pounds.

Year	Club	Lea	Pos	G	AB	R	H	2B	3B	HR	RBI	SB	Avg
2010	New Hampshire	Eastern	SS	61	253	36	69	11	1	3	34	6	.273
2010	Dunedin	Fla.St.	SS	41	161	21	31	7	3	1	7	7	.193
2011	New Hampshire	Eastern	SS	111	464	58	109	22	6	6	46	19	.235
2011	Las Vegas	P.C.	SS	25	108	16	42	6	2	2	11	1	.389
2012	Las Vegas	P.C.	SS-2B	102	443	78	138	20	6	6	63	8	.312
2012	Toronto a	A.L.	3B-SS-2B	41	126	10	32	8	0	2	15	0	.254
2013	Jupiter	Fla.St.	SS	2	7	0	3	1	0	0	1	1	.429
2013	Miami b	N.L.	SS	148	543	30	123	14	8	3	42	11	.227
Major League Totals			2 Yrs.	189	669	40	155	22	8	5	57	11	.232

a Traded to Miami Marlins with pitcher Henderson Alvarez, infielder Yunel Escobar, catcher Jeff Mathis, pitcher Anthony De Sclafani, outfielder Jake Marisnick and pitcher Justin Nicolino for outfielder Emilio Bonifacio, catcher John Buck, pitcher Mark Buehrle, pitcher Josh Johnson and infielder Jose Reyes, November 19, 2012.
b On disabled list from April 17 to May 2, 2013.

HEISEY, CHRISTOPHER J. (CHRIS)

Born, Lancaster, Pennsylvania, December 14, 1984.
Bats Right. Throws Right. Height, 6 feet. Weight, 215 pounds.

Year	Club	Lea	Pos	G	AB	R	H	2B	3B	HR	RBI	SB	Avg
2006	Billings	Pioneer	OF	70	245	46	70	10	0	6	37	11	.286
2007	Sarasota	Fla.St.	OF	12	43	6	15	1	0	1	5	3	.349
2007	Dayton	Midwest	OF	104	374	60	108	24	2	9	46	19	.289
2008	Sarasota	Fla.St.	OF	117	436	77	125	31	7	7	51	27	.287
2008	Chattanooga	Southern	OF	19	79	11	25	6	1	2	10	5	.316
2009	Louisville	Int.	OF	63	245	37	68	17	1	9	37	8	.278
2009	Carolina	Southern	OF	71	271	54	94	18	2	13	40	13	.347
2010	Louisville	Int.	OF	20	79	6	19	3	0	4	13	2	.241
2010	Cincinnati	N.L.	OF	97	201	33	51	10	1	8	21	1	.254
2011	Louisville	Int.	OF	4	12	1	1	0	0	1	2	0	.083
2011	Cincinnati a	N.L.	OF	120	279	44	71	9	1	18	50	6	.254
2012	Cincinnati	N.L.	OF	120	347	44	92	16	5	7	31	6	.265
2013	Pensacola	Southern	OF	1	0	0	0	0	0	0	0	0	.000
2013	Louisville	Int.	OF	6	20	1	4	1	0	0	1	0	.200
2013	Cincinnati b	N.L.	OF	87	224	29	53	11	1	9	23	3	.237
Major League Totals			4 Yrs.	424	1051	150	267	46	8	42	125	16	.254

Year	Club	Lea	Pos	G	AB	R	H	2B	3B	HR	RBI	SB	Avg
	Wild Card Playoff												
2013	Cincinnati	N.L.	PH	1	1	0	0	0	0	0	0	0	.000
	Division Series												
2010	Cincinnati	N.L.	OF	1	2	0	0	0	0	0	0	0	.000
2012	Cincinnati	N.L.	OF	4	3	1	0	0	0	0	0	0	.000
Division Series Totals				5	5	1	0	0	0	0	0	0	.000

a On disabled list from August 6 to September 1, 2011.
b On disabled list from April 28 to June 25, 2013.

HELTON, TODD LYNN

Born, Knoxville, Tennessee, August 20, 1973.
Bats Left. Throws Left. Height, 6 feet, 2 inches. Weight, 210 pounds.

Year	Club	Lea	Pos	G	AB	R	H	2B	3B	HR	RBI	SB	Avg
1995	Asheville	So. Atl.	1B	54	201	24	51	11	1	1	15	1	.254
1996	New Haven	Eastern	1B	93	319	46	106	24	2	7	51	2	.332
1996	Colo Sprngs	P.C.	1B-OF	21	71	13	25	4	1	2	13	0	.352
1997	Colo Sprngs	P.C.	1B-OF	99	392	87	138	31	2	16	88	3	.352
1997	Colorado	N.L.	OF-1B	35	93	13	26	2	1	5	11	0	.280
1998	Colorado	N.L.	1B	152	530	78	167	37	1	25	97	3	.315
1999	Colorado	N.L.	1B	159	578	114	185	39	5	35	113	7	.320
2000	Colorado	N.L.	1B	160	580	138	*216	*59	2	42	*147	5	*.372
2001	Colorado	N.L.	1B	159	587	132	197	54	2	49	146	7	.336
2002	Colorado	N.L.	1B	156	553	107	182	39	4	30	109	5	.329
2003	Colorado	N.L.	1B	160	583	135	209	49	5	33	117	0	.358
2004	Colorado	N.L.	1B	154	547	115	190	49	2	32	96	3	.347
2005	Colo Sprngs	P.C.	2B	2	5	1	3	2	0	0	1	0	.600
2005	Colorado a	N.L.	1B	144	509	92	163	45	2	20	79	3	.320
2006	Colo Sprngs	P.C.	1B	2	6	0	2	0	0	0	0	0	.333
2006	Colorado b	N.L.	1B	145	546	94	165	40	5	15	81	3	.302
2007	Colorado	N.L.	1B	154	557	86	178	42	2	17	91	0	.320
2008	Colorado c	N.L.	1B	83	299	39	79	16	0	7	29	0	.264
2009	Colorado	N.L.	1B	151	544	79	177	38	3	15	86	0	.325
2010	Casper	Pioneer	1B	3	10	1	5	1	0	0	5	0	.500
2010	Colorado d	N.L.	1B	118	398	48	102	18	1	8	37	0	.256
2011	Colorado	N.L.	1B	124	421	59	127	27	0	14	69	0	.302
2012	Grand Junction	Pioneer	1B	2	5	0	3	0	0	0	2	0	.600
2012	Colorado e	N.L.	1B	69	240	31	57	16	1	7	37	1	.237
2013	Colorado f-g	N.L.	1B	124	397	41	99	22	1	15	61	0	.249
Major League Totals			17 Yrs.	2247	7962	1401	2519	592	37	369	1406	37	.316
	Division Series												
2007	Colorado	N.L.	1B	3	12	1	1	0	1	0	0	0	.083
2009	Colorado	N.L.	1B	4	16	5	3	0	0	0	2	0	.188
Division Series Totals				7	28	6	4	0	1	0	2	0	.143
	Championship Series												
2007	Colorado	N.L.	1B	4	14	3	3	0	0	0	1	0	.214
	World Series Record												
2007	Colorado	N.L.	1B	4	15	2	5	2	0	0	1	0	.333

a On disabled list from July 26 to August 10, 2005.
b On disabled list from April 20 to May 5, 2006.
c On disabled list from July 3 to September 12, 2008.
d On disabled list from July 7 to August 3, 2010.
e On disabled list from July 9 to July 27 and August 6 to November 2, 2012.
f On disabled list from April 20 to May 5, 2013.
g Announced retirement, September 30, 2013.

HERRERA, JONATHAN ALEJANDRO

Born, Maracaibo, Venezuela, November 3, 1984.
Bats Both. Throws Right. Height, 5 feet, 9 inches. Weight, 150 pounds.

Year	Club	Lea	Pos	G	AB	R	H	2B	3B	HR	RBI	SB	Avg
2003	Casper	Pioneer	2B	39	159	27	49	7	1	1	25	12	.308
2004	Asheville	So.Atl.	SS	95	380	71	106	20	2	6	35	21	.279
2005	Modesto	Calif.	SS-2B	73	310	48	80	9	4	2	30	9	.258
2005	Asheville	So.Atl.	SS-2B	19	87	17	27	2	0	0	5	6	.310
2006	Modesto	Calif.	SS-2B-3B	127	487	87	151	20	8	7	77	34	.310
2007	Tulsa	Texas	SS	131	509	65	131	24	4	3	40	18	.257
2008	Colorado	N.L.	2B-SS	28	61	5	14	1	1	0	3	1	.230
2008	Colorado Springs a	P.C.	SS-2B	66	226	40	70	7	0	3	31	15	.310

Year	Club	Lea	Pos	G	AB	R	H	2B	3B	HR	RBI	SB	Avg
2009	Colorado Springs	P.C.	SS-2B	119	381	63	102	11	5	2	33	16	.268
2010	Colorado Springs	P.C.	SS-2B-3B	58	222	30	58	6	1	2	17	3	.261
2010	Colorado	N.L.	2B-3B-SS	76	222	34	63	6	2	1	21	2	.284
2011	Colorado b	N.L.	2B-SS-3B	104	281	28	68	5	1	3	14	4	.242
2012	Tulsa	Texas	2B-SS	5	17	2	3	0	0	1	1	0	.176
2012	Colorado Springs	P.C.	2B	4	12	1	2	1	0	0	1	0	.167
2012	Colorado c	N.L.	SS-2B-3B	86	225	29	59	9	1	3	12	4	.262
2013	Colorado d	N.L.	SS-2B-3B-OF	81	195	16	57	7	2	1	16	3	.292
Major League Totals			5 Yrs.	375	984	112	261	28	7	8	66	14	.265

a Not offered contract, December 12, 2008, re-signed with Colorado Rockies, December 13, 2008.
b On disabled list from September 6 to October 31, 2011.
c On disabled list from May 22 to June 23 and July 16 to July 31, 2012.
d Traded to Boston Red Sox for pitcher Franklin Morales, December 18, 2013.

HEYWARD, JASON ADENOLITH

Born, Ridgewood, New Jersey, August 9, 1989.
Bats Left. Throws Left. Height, 6 feet, 5 inches. Weight, 240 pounds.

Year	Club	Lea	Pos	G	AB	R	H	2B	3B	HR	RBI	SB	Avg
2007	Danville	Appal.	OF	4	16	3	5	1	0	0	1	0	.313
2007	Braves	Gulf Coast	OF	8	27	1	8	4	0	1	5	1	.296
2008	Myrtle Beach	Carolina	OF	7	22	3	4	2	0	0	4	0	.182
2008	Rome	So.Atl.	OF	120	449	88	145	27	6	11	52	15	.323
2009	Myrtle Beach	Carolina	OF	49	189	34	56	12	0	10	31	4	.296
2009	Gwinnett	Int.	OF	3	11	3	4	0	0	0	2	1	.364
2009	Mississippi	Southern	OF	47	162	32	57	13	4	7	30	5	.352
2010	Atlanta a	N.L.	OF	142	520	83	144	29	5	18	72	11	.277
2011	Gwinnett	Int.	OF	2	6	1	1	1	0	0	0	0	.167
2011	Atlanta b	N.L.	OF	128	396	50	90	18	2	14	42	9	.227
2012	Atlanta	N.L.	OF	158	587	93	158	30	6	27	82	21	.269
2013	Gwinnett	Int.	OF	6	20	1	6	1	0	0	6	1	.300
2013	Atlanta c	N.L.	OF	104	382	67	97	22	1	14	38	2	.254
Major League Totals			4 Yrs.	532	1885	293	489	99	14	73	234	43	.259
	Wild Card Playoff												
2012	Atlanta	N.L.	OF	1	5	0	1	1	0	0	0	0	.200
	Division Series												
2010	Atlanta	N.L.	OF	4	16	0	2	0	0	0	0	0	.125
2013	Atlanta	N.L.	OF	4	18	1	3	0	0	1	4	0	.167
Division Series Totals				8	34	1	5	0	0	1	4	0	.147

a On disabled list from June 27 to July 15, 2010.
b On disabled list from May 22 to June 15, 2011.
c On disabled list from April 21 to May 17 and August 22 to September 20, 2013.

HILL, AARON WALTER

Born, Visalia, California, March 21, 1982.
Bats Right. Throws Right. Height, 5 feet, 11 inches. Weight, 195 pounds.

Year	Club	Lea	Pos	G	AB	R	H	2B	3B	HR	RBI	SB	Avg
2003	Dunedin	Fla.St.	SS	32	119	26	34	7	0	0	11	1	.286
2003	Auburn	N.Y.-Penn.	SS	33	122	22	44	4	0	4	34	1	.361
2004	New Hampshire	Eastern	SS	135	479	78	134	26	2	11	80	3	.280
2005	Syracuse	Int.	SS	38	156	22	47	11	0	5	18	2	.301
2005	Toronto	A.L.	3B-2B-SS	105	361	49	99	25	3	3	40	2	.274
2006	Toronto	A.L.	2B-SS	155	546	70	159	28	3	6	50	5	.291
2007	Toronto	A.L.	2B	160	608	87	177	47	2	17	78	4	.291
2008	Toronto a	A.L.	2B	55	205	19	54	14	0	2	20	4	.263
2009	Toronto	A.L.	2B	158	*682	103	195	37	0	36	108	6	.286
2010	Toronto b	A.L.	2B	138	528	70	108	22	0	26	68	2	.205
2011	Dunedin	Fla.St.	2B	2	6	2	1	0	0	0	1	0	.167
2011	Toronto	A.L.	2B	104	396	38	89	15	1	6	45	16	.225
2011	Arizona c-d-e	N.L.	2B	33	124	23	39	12	2	2	16	5	.315
2012	Arizona	N.L.	2B	156	609	93	184	44	6	26	85	14	.302
2013	Reno	P.C.	2B	6	24	8	9	1	1	0	6	0	.375
2013	Arizona f	N.L.	2B	87	327	45	95	21	1	11	41	1	.291
Major League Totals			9 Yrs.	1151	4386	597	1199	265	18	135	551	59	.273
	Division Series												
2011	Arizona	N.L.	2B	5	18	3	5	0	0	1	1	0	.278

a On disabled list from June 5 to November 14, 2008.
b On disabled list from April 8 to April 23, 2010.

c On disabled list from April 20 to May 8, 2011.
d Traded to Arizona Diamondbacks with infielder John McDonald for infielder Kelly Johnson, August 23, 2011.
e Filed for free agency, October 31, 2011, re-signed with Arizona Diamondbacks, November 15, 2011.
f On disabled list from April 15 to June 25, 2013.

HOES, JEROME O'BRYAN (L.J.)

Born, Washington, District of Columbia, March 5, 1990.
Bats Right. Throws Right. Height, 6 feet. Weight, 190 pounds.

Year	Club	Lea	Pos	G	AB	R	H	2B	3B	HR	RBI	SB	Avg
2008	Orioles	Gulf Coast	2B-3B	48	159	36	49	4	3	1	18	10	.308
2009	Delmarva	So.Atl.	2B	119	431	42	112	19	0	2	47	20	.260
2010	Aberdeen	N.Y.-Penn.	2B	8	28	8	13	5	1	1	5	1	.464
2010	Frederick	Carolina	2B	97	353	52	98	19	2	3	44	10	.278
2010	Bowie	Eastern	DH	3	9	1	2	0	0	0	1	0	.222
2011	Frederick	Carolina	2B-OF	41	158	23	38	7	0	3	17	4	.241
2011	Bowie	Eastern	OF-3B-2B	95	344	47	105	17	1	6	54	16	.305
2012	Bowie	Eastern	OF	51	196	25	52	9	3	2	16	12	.265
2012	Norfolk	Int.	OF	82	317	54	95	14	4	3	38	8	.300
2012	Baltimore	A.L.	OF	2	1	0	0	0	0	0	0	0	.000
2013	Norfolk	Int.	OF	99	365	62	111	25	1	3	40	7	.304
2013	Baltimore-Houston a	A.L.	OF	47	170	24	48	7	2	1	10	7	.282
Major League Totals			2 Yrs.	49	171	24	48	7	2	1	10	7	.281

a Traded to Houston Astros with pitcher Josh Hader and a competitive balance draft choice for pitcher Bud Norris and an international draft choice, July 31, 2013.

HOLLIDAY, MATTHEW THOMAS (MATT)

Born, Stillwater, Oklahoma, January 15, 1980.
Bats Right. Throws Right. Height, 6 feet, 4 inches. Weight, 235 pounds.

Year	Club	Lea	Pos	G	AB	R	H	2B	3B	HR	RBI	SB	Avg
1998	Rockies	Arizona	3B	32	117	20	40	4	1	5	23	2	.342
1999	Asheville	So.Atl.	3B	121	444	76	117	28	0	16	64	10	.264
2000	Salem	Carolina	3B	123	460	64	126	28	2	7	72	11	.274
2001	Salem	Carolina	OF	72	255	36	70	16	1	11	52	11	.275
2002	Carolina	Southern	OF	130	463	79	128	19	2	10	64	16	.276
2003	Tulsa	Texas	OF	135	522	65	132	28	5	12	72	15	.253
2004	Colorado Springs	P.C.	OF	6	22	8	8	5	0	2	4	2	.364
2004	Colorado	N.L.	OF	121	400	65	116	31	3	14	57	3	.290
2005	Tulsa	Texas	OF	7	26	6	14	3	0	1	6	1	.538
2005	Colorado a	N.L.	OF	125	479	68	147	24	7	19	87	14	.307
2006	Colorado	N.L.	OF	155	602	119	196	45	5	34	114	10	.326
2007	Colorado	N.L.	OF	158	636	120	*216	*50	6	36	*137	11	*.340
2008	Colorado Springs	P.C.	OF	3	10	4	6	1	0	1	3	0	.600
2008	Colorado b-c	N.L.	OF	139	539	107	173	38	2	25	88	28	.321
2009	Oakland	A.L.	OF	93	346	52	99	23	1	11	54	12	.286
2009	St. Louis d-e	N.L.	OF	63	235	42	83	16	2	13	55	2	.353
2010	St. Louis	N.L.	OF	158	596	95	186	45	1	28	103	9	.312
2011	St. Louis f	N.L.	OF	124	446	83	132	36	0	22	75	2	.296
2012	St. Louis	N.L.	OF	157	599	95	177	36	2	27	102	4	.295
2013	St. Louis g	N.L.	OF	141	520	103	156	31	1	22	94	6	.300
Major League Totals			10 Yrs.	1434	5398	949	1681	375	30	251	966	101	.311
	Wild Card Playoff												
2012	St. Louis	N.L.	OF	1	3	2	2	0	0	1	1	0	.667
	Division Series												
2007	Colorado	N.L.	OF	3	13	2	3	0	0	2	3	0	.231
2009	St. Louis	N.L.	OF	3	12	1	2	0	0	1	1	0	.167
2011	St. Louis	N.L.	OF	4	9	2	2	0	0	0	0	0	.222
2012	St. Louis	N.L.	OF	5	21	2	4	1	0	0	4	0	.190
2013	St. Louis	N.L.	OF	5	20	4	6	1	0	1	2	0	.300
Division Series Totals				20	75	11	17	2	0	4	10	0	.227
	Championship Series												
2007	Colorado	N.L.	OF	4	15	3	5	0	0	2	4	0	.333
2011	St. Louis	N.L.	OF	6	23	6	10	2	0	1	5	0	.435
2012	St. Louis	N.L.	OF	6	25	1	5	0	0	0	2	1	.200
2013	St. Louis	N.L.	OF	6	25	2	5	2	0	1	3	0	.200
Championship Series Totals				22	88	12	25	4	0	4	14	1	.284
	World Series Record												
2007	Colorado	N.L.	OF	4	17	1	5	0	0	1	3	0	.294
2011	St. Louis	N.L.	OF	6	19	5	3	1	0	0	0	0	.158

Year	Club	Lea	Pos	G	AB	R	H	2B	3B	HR	RBI	SB	Avg
2013	St. Louis.............	N.L.	OF	6	24	4	6	1	1	2	5	0	.250
World Series Totals.............				16	60	10	14	2	1	3	8	0	.233

a On disabled list from June 9 to July 19, 2005.
b On disabled list from May 25 to June 10, 2008.
c Traded to Oakland Athletics for outfielder Carlos Gonzalez, pitcher Greg Smith and pitcher Huston Street, November 12, 2008.
d Traded to St. Louis Cardinals for pitcher Clayton Mortensen, infielder Brett Wallace and outfielder Shane Peterson, July 24, 2009.
e Filed for free agency, November 5, 2009, re-signed with St. Louis Cardinals, January 5, 2010.
f On disabled list from June 1 to June 16, 2011.
g On disabled list from July 12 to July 27, 2013.

HOSMER, ERIC JOHN

Born, South Miami, Florida, October 24, 1989.
Bats Left. Throws Left. Height, 6 feet, 4 inches. Weight, 230 pounds.

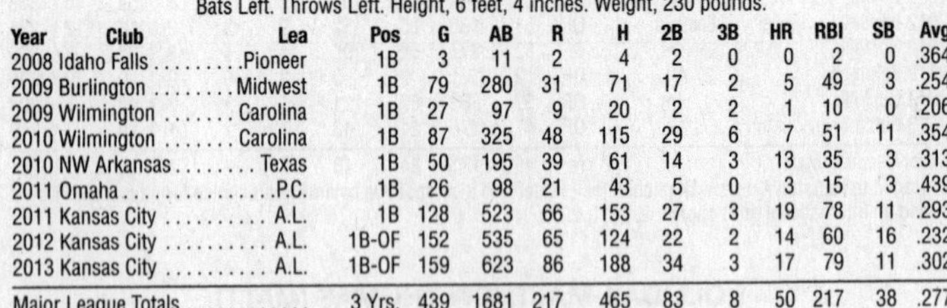

Year	Club	Lea	Pos	G	AB	R	H	2B	3B	HR	RBI	SB	Avg
2008	Idaho Falls.........	Pioneer	1B	3	11	2	4	2	0	0	2	0	.364
2009	Burlington	Midwest	1B	79	280	31	71	17	2	5	49	3	.254
2009	Wilmington	Carolina	1B	27	97	9	20	2	2	1	10	0	.206
2010	Wilmington	Carolina	1B	87	325	48	115	29	6	7	51	11	.354
2010	NW Arkansas........	Texas	1B	50	195	39	61	14	3	13	35	3	.313
2011	Omaha................	P.C.	1B	26	98	21	43	5	0	3	15	3	.439
2011	Kansas City	A.L.	1B	128	523	66	153	27	3	19	78	11	.293
2012	Kansas City	A.L.	1B-OF	152	535	65	124	22	2	14	60	16	.232
2013	Kansas City	A.L.	1B-OF	159	623	86	188	34	3	17	79	11	.302
Major League Totals			3 Yrs.	439	1681	217	465	83	8	50	217	38	.277

HOWARD, RYAN JAMES

Born, St. Louis, Missouri, November 19, 1979.
Bats Left. Throws Left. Height, 6 feet, 4 inches. Weight, 250 pounds.

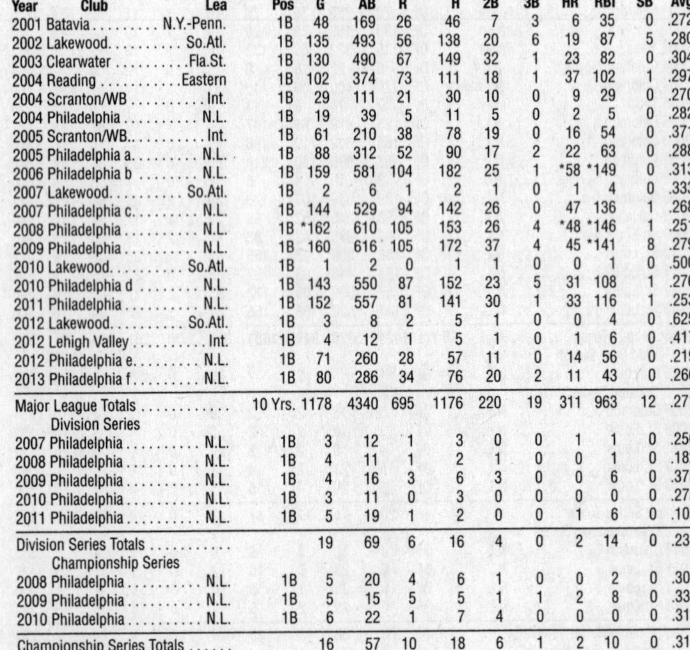

Year	Club	Lea	Pos	G	AB	R	H	2B	3B	HR	RBI	SB	Avg
2001	Batavia..........	N.Y.-Penn.	1B	48	169	26	46	7	3	6	35	0	.272
2002	Lakewood..........	So.Atl.	1B	135	493	56	138	20	6	19	87	5	.280
2003	Clearwater	Fla.St.	1B	130	490	67	149	32	1	23	82	0	.304
2004	Reading	Eastern	1B	102	374	73	111	18	1	37	102	1	.297
2004	Scranton/WB	Int.	1B	29	111	21	30	10	0	9	29	0	.270
2004	Philadelphia	N.L.	1B	19	39	5	11	5	0	2	5	0	.282
2005	Scranton/WB...........	Int.	1B	61	210	38	78	19	0	16	54	0	.371
2005	Philadelphia a..........	N.L.	1B	88	312	52	90	17	2	22	63	0	.288
2006	Philadelphia b	N.L.	1B	159	581	104	182	25	1	*58	*149	0	.313
2007	Lakewood..........	So.Atl.	1B	2	6	1	2	1	0	1	4	0	.333
2007	Philadelphia c.........	N.L.	1B	144	529	94	142	26	0	47	136	1	.268
2008	Philadelphia	N.L.	1B	*162	610	105	153	26	4	*48	*146	1	.251
2009	Philadelphia	N.L.	1B	160	616	105	172	37	4	45	*141	8	.279
2010	Lakewood..........	So.Atl.	1B	1	2	0	1	1	0	0	1	0	.500
2010	Philadelphia d	N.L.	1B	143	550	87	152	23	5	31	108	1	.276
2011	Philadelphia..........	N.L.	1B	152	557	81	141	30	1	33	116	1	.253
2012	Lakewood..........	So.Atl.	1B	3	8	2	5	1	0	0	4	0	.625
2012	Lehigh Valley	Int.	1B	4	12	1	5	1	0	1	6	0	.417
2012	Philadelphia e.........	N.L.	1B	71	260	28	57	11	0	14	56	0	.219
2013	Philadelphia f.........	N.L.	1B	80	286	34	76	20	2	11	43	0	.266
Major League Totals			10 Yrs.	1178	4340	695	1176	220	19	311	963	12	.271
	Division Series												
2007	Philadelphia..........	N.L.	1B	3	12	1	3	0	0	1	1	0	.250
2008	Philadelphia..........	N.L.	1B	4	11	1	2	1	0	0	1	0	.182
2009	Philadelphia..........	N.L.	1B	4	16	3	6	3	0	0	6	0	.375
2010	Philadelphia..........	N.L.	1B	3	11	0	3	0	0	0	0	0	.273
2011	Philadelphia..........	N.L.	1B	5	19	1	2	0	0	1	6	0	.105
Division Series Totals				19	69	6	16	4	0	2	14	0	.232
	Championship Series												
2008	Philadelphia..........	N.L.	1B	5	20	4	6	1	0	0	2	0	.300
2009	Philadelphia..........	N.L.	1B	5	15	5	5	1	1	2	8	0	.333
2010	Philadelphia..........	N.L.	1B	6	22	1	7	4	0	0	0	0	.318
Championship Series Totals				16	57	10	18	6	1	2	10	0	.316
	World Series Record												
2008	Philadelphia..........	N.L.	1B	5	21	3	6	1	0	3	6	0	.286

Year	Club	Lea	Pos	G	AB	R	H	2B	3B	HR	RBI	SB	Avg
2009	Philadelphia	N.L.	1B	6	23	3	4	2	0	1	3	1	.174
World Series Totals				11	44	6	10	3	0	4	9	1	.227

a Selected Rookie of the Year in National League for 2005.
b Selected Most Valuable Player in National League for 2006.
c On disabled list from May 10 to May 25, 2007.
d On disabled list from August 2 to August 21, 2010.
e On disabled list from March 26 to July 6, 2012.
f On disabled list from July 6 to November 1, 2013.

HUNDLEY, NICHOLAS JOHN (NICK)

Born, Corvallis, Oregon, September 8, 1983.
Bats Right. Throws Right. Height, 6 feet, 1 inch. Weight, 210 pounds.

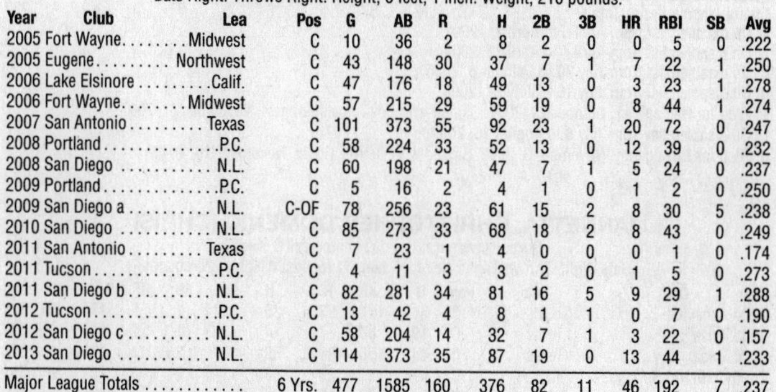

Year	Club	Lea	Pos	G	AB	R	H	2B	3B	HR	RBI	SB	Avg
2005	Fort Wayne	Midwest	C	10	36	2	8	2	0	0	5	0	.222
2005	Eugene	Northwest	C	43	148	30	37	7	1	7	22	1	.250
2006	Lake Elsinore	Calif.	C	47	176	18	49	13	0	3	23	1	.278
2006	Fort Wayne	Midwest	C	57	215	29	59	19	0	8	44	1	.274
2007	San Antonio	Texas	C	101	373	55	92	23	1	20	72	0	.247
2008	Portland	P.C.	C	58	224	33	52	13	0	12	39	0	.232
2008	San Diego	N.L.	C	60	198	21	47	7	1	5	24	0	.237
2009	Portland	P.C.	C	5	16	2	4	1	0	1	2	0	.250
2009	San Diego a	N.L.	C-OF	78	256	23	61	15	2	8	30	5	.238
2010	San Diego	N.L.	C	85	273	33	68	18	2	8	43	0	.249
2011	San Antonio	Texas	C	7	23	1	4	0	0	0	1	0	.174
2011	Tucson	P.C.	C	4	11	3	3	2	0	1	5	0	.273
2011	San Diego b	N.L.	C	82	281	34	81	16	5	9	29	1	.288
2012	Tucson	P.C.	C	13	42	4	8	1	1	0	7	0	.190
2012	San Diego c	N.L.	C	58	204	14	32	7	1	3	22	0	.157
2013	San Diego	N.L.	C	114	373	35	87	19	0	13	44	1	.233
Major League Totals			6 Yrs.	477	1585	160	376	82	11	46	192	7	.237

a On disabled list from June 18 to August 12, 2009.
b On disabled list from May 5 to June 8 and July 6 to August 12, 2011.
c On disabled list from August 16 to November 2, 2012.

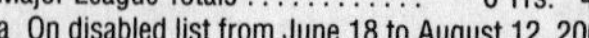

HUNTER, TORII KEDAR

Born, Pine Bluff, Arkansas, July 18, 1975.
Bats Right. Throws Right. Height, 6 feet, 2 inches. Weight, 215 pounds.

Year	Club	Lea	Pos	G	AB	R	H	2B	3B	HR	RBI	SB	Avg
1993	Twins	Gulf Coast	OF	28	100	6	19	3	0	0	8	4	.190
1994	Fort Wayne	Midwest	OF	91	335	57	98	17	1	10	50	8	.293
1995	Fort Myers	Fla.St.	OF	113	391	64	96	15	2	7	36	7	.246
1996	Fort Myers	Fla.St.	OF	4	16	1	3	0	0	0	1	1	.188
1996	New Britain	Eastern	OF	99	342	49	90	20	3	7	33	7	.263
1997	New Britain	Eastern	OF	127	471	57	109	22	2	8	56	8	.231
1997	Minnesota	A.L.	OF	1	0	0	0	0	0	0	0	0	.000
1998	New Britain	Eastern	OF	82	308	42	87	24	3	6	32	11	.282
1998	Salt Lake	P.C.	OF	26	92	15	31	7	0	4	20	2	.337
1998	Minnesota	A.L.	OF	6	17	0	4	1	0	0	2	0	.235
1999	Minnesota	A.L.	OF	135	384	52	98	17	2	9	35	10	.255
2000	Salt Lake	P.C.	OF	55	209	58	77	17	2	18	61	11	.368
2000	Minnesota	A.L.	OF	99	336	44	94	14	7	5	44	4	.280
2001	Minnesota a	A.L.	OF	148	564	82	147	32	5	27	92	9	.261
2002	Minnesota	A.L.	OF	148	561	89	162	37	4	29	94	23	.289
2003	Minnesota	A.L.	OF	154	581	83	145	31	4	26	102	6	.250
2004	Minnesota b	A.L.	OF	138	520	79	141	37	0	23	81	21	.271
2005	Minnesota c	A.L.	OF	98	372	63	100	24	1	14	56	23	.269
2006	Minnesota d	A.L.	OF	147	557	86	155	21	2	31	98	12	.278
2007	Minnesota e	A.L.	OF	160	600	94	172	45	1	28	107	18	.287
2008	Los Angeles	A.L.	OF	146	551	85	153	37	2	21	78	19	.278
2009	Rancho Cucamonga	Calif.	OF	3	9	3	3	0	0	1	3	1	.333
2009	Los Angeles f	A.L.	OF	119	451	74	135	26	1	22	90	18	.299
2010	Los Angeles	A.L.	OF	152	573	76	161	36	0	23	90	9	.281
2011	Los Angeles	A.L.	OF	156	580	80	152	24	2	23	82	5	.262
2012	Los Angeles g	A.L.	OF	140	534	81	167	24	1	16	92	9	.313
2013	Detroit	A.L.	OF	144	606	90	184	37	5	17	84	3	.304
Major League Totals			17 Yrs.	2091	7787	1158	2170	443	37	314	1227	189	.279

Year	Club	Lea	Pos	G	AB	R	H	2B	3B	HR	RBI	SB	Avg
	Division Series												
2002	Minnesota	A.L.	OF	5	20	4	6	4	0	0	2	0	.300
2003	Minnesota	A.L.	OF	4	14	3	6	0	1	1	2	0	.429
2004	Minnesota	A.L.	OF	4	17	5	6	1	0	1	2	2	.353
2006	Minnesota	A.L.	OF	3	11	1	3	1	0	1	2	0	.273
2008	Los Angeles	A.L.	OF	4	18	0	7	0	0	0	5	0	.389
2009	Los Angeles	A.L.	OF	3	10	2	2	1	0	1	3	0	.200
2013	Detroit	A.L.	OF	5	19	3	3	0	0	0	0	0	.158
Division Series Totals				28	109	18	33	7	1	4	16	2	.303
	Championship Series												
2002	Minnesota	A.L.	OF	5	18	2	3	2	0	0	0	0	.167
2009	Los Angeles	A.L.	OF	6	23	2	7	1	0	0	2	1	.304
2013	Detroit	A.L.	OF	6	26	2	6	2	0	0	2	0	.231
Championship Series Totals				17	67	6	16	5	0	0	4	1	.239

a On disabled list from April 6 to April 21, 2001.
b On disabled list from April 7 to April 25, 2004.
c On disabled list from July 30 to October 6, 2005.
d On disabled list from July 16 to July 31, 2006.
e Filed for free agency, October 29, 2007. Signed with Los Angeles Angels, November 21, 2007.
f On disabled list from July 8 to August 16, 2009.
g Filed for free agency, November 3, 2012. Signed with Detroit Tigers, November 16, 2012.

IANNETTA, CHRISTOPHER DOMENIC (CHRIS)

Born, Providence, Rhode Island, April 8, 1983.
Bats Right. Throws Right. Height, 5 feet, 11 inches. Weight, 225 pounds.

Year	Club	Lea	Pos	G	AB	R	H	2B	3B	HR	RBI	SB	Avg
2004	Asheville	So.Atl.	C	36	121	23	38	5	1	5	17	0	.314
2005	Tulsa	Texas	C	19	60	7	14	3	1	2	11	0	.233
2006	Tulsa	Texas	C	44	156	38	50	10	2	11	26	1	.321
2006	Colorado Springs	P.C.	C	47	151	23	53	11	2	3	22	0	.351
2006	Colorado	N.L.	C	21	77	12	20	4	0	2	10	0	.260
2007	Colorado Springs	P.C.	C	16	54	8	16	3	0	1	7	0	.296
2007	Colorado	N.L.	C	67	197	22	43	8	3	4	27	0	.218
2008	Colorado	N.L.	C-3B	104	333	50	88	22	2	18	65	0	.264
2009	Colorado Springs	P.C.	C	4	15	3	5	2	0	1	3	0	.333
2009	Colorado a	N.L.	C	93	289	41	66	15	2	16	52	0	.228
2010	Colorado Springs	P.C.	C-1B	17	63	17	22	7	0	5	21	0	.349
2010	Colorado	N.L.	C-1B-3B	61	188	20	37	6	1	9	27	1	.197
2011	Colorado b	N.L.	C-1B-3B	112	345	51	82	17	1	14	55	6	.238
2012	Salt Lake	P.C.	C	6	22	3	6	2	0	0	2	0	.273
2012	Los Angeles c	A.L.	C	79	221	27	53	6	1	9	26	1	.240
2013	Los Angeles	A.L.	C	115	325	40	73	15	0	11	39	0	.225
Major League Totals			8 Yrs.	652	1975	263	462	93	10	83	301	8	.234

a On disabled list from May 24 to June 9, 2009.
b Traded to Los Angeles Angels for pitcher Tyler Chatwood, November 30, 2011.
c On disabled list from May 10 to July 28, 2012.

IBANEZ, RAUL JAVIER

Born, New York, New York, June 2, 1972.
Bats Left. Throws Right. Height, 6 feet, 2 inches. Weight, 220 pounds.

Year	Club	Lea	Pos	G	AB	R	H	2B	3B	HR	RBI	SB	Avg
1992	Mariners	Arizona	DH-1B-C-OF	33	120	25	37	8	2	1	16	1	.308
1993	Appleton	Midwest	DH-1B-OF-C	52	157	26	43	9	0	5	21	0	.274
1993	Bellingham	Northwest	C	43	134	16	38	5	2	0	15	0	.284
1994	Appleton	Midwest	DH-C-1B-OF	91	327	55	102	30	3	7	59	10	.312
1995	Riverside	California	C-1B	95	361	59	120	23	9	20	108	4	.332
1996	Port City	Southern	OF-1B-C	19	76	12	28	8	1	1	13	3	.368
1996	Seattle	A.L.	DH	4	5	0	0	0	0	0	0	0	.000
1996	Tacoma	P.C.	OF-1B	111	405	59	115	20	3	11	47	7	.284
1997	Tacoma	P.C.	OF	111	438	84	133	30	5	15	84	7	.304
1997	Seattle	A.L.	OF	11	26	3	4	0	1	1	4	0	.154
1998	Tacoma	P.C.	OF	52	190	24	41	8	1	6	25	1	.216
1998	Seattle	A.L.	OF-1B	37	98	12	25	7	1	2	12	0	.255
1999	Tacoma	P.C.	OF	8	31	6	11	1	0	3	5	1	.355
1999	Seattle a	A.L.	OF-1B-C	87	209	23	54	7	0	9	27	5	.258
2000	Tacoma	P.C.	OF	10	40	3	10	4	0	0	6	0	.250
2000	Seattle b-c	A.L.	OF-1B	92	140	21	32	8	0	2	15	2	.229

Year	Club	Lea	Pos	G	AB	R	H	2B	3B	HR	RBI	SB	Avg
2001	Omaha	P.C.	OF-SS	8	27	3	4	1	0	2	5	0	.148
2001	Kansas City	A.L.	OF-1B-3B	104	279	44	78	11	5	13	54	0	.280
2002	Kansas City	A.L.	OF-1B	137	497	70	146	37	6	24	103	5	.294
2003	Kansas City d	A.L.	OF-1B	157	608	95	179	33	5	18	90	8	.294
2004	Tacoma	P.C.	OF	4	17	2	4	1	0	0	1	0	.235
2004	Seattle e	A.L.	OF-1B	123	481	67	146	31	1	16	62	1	.304
2005	Seattle	A.L.	DH-OF-1B	*162	614	92	172	32	2	20	89	9	.280
2006	Seattle	A.L.	OF	159	626	103	181	33	5	33	123	2	.289
2007	Seattle	A.L.	OF	149	573	80	167	35	5	21	105	0	.291
2008	Seattle f	A.L.	OF	162	635	85	186	43	3	23	110	2	.293
2009	Reading	Eastern	OF	1	2	1	0	0	0	0	0	0	.000
2009	Lehigh Valley	Int.	OF	2	5	1	2	1	0	0	2	0	.400
2009	Philadelphia g	N.L.	OF	134	500	93	136	32	3	34	93	4	.272
2010	Philadelphia	N.L.	OF-1B	155	561	75	154	37	5	16	83	4	.275
2011	Philadelphia h	N.L.	OF	144	535	65	131	31	1	20	84	2	.245
2012	New York i	A.L.	OF	130	384	50	92	19	3	19	62	3	.240
2013	Seattle j	A.L.	OF	124	454	54	110	20	2	29	65	0	.242
Major League Totals			18 Yrs.	2071	7225	1032	1993	416	48	300	1181	47	.276
	Division Series												
2000	Seattle	A.L.	OF	3	8	2	3	0	0	0	0	0	.375
2009	Philadelphia	N.L.	OF	4	13	2	4	1	0	0	5	0	.308
2010	Philadelphia	N.L.	OF	3	12	0	3	1	0	0	0	0	.250
2011	Philadelphia	N.L.	OF	4	15	1	3	0	0	1	4	0	.200
2012	New York	A.L.	DH	4	9	2	4	0	0	2	3	0	.444
Division Series Totals				18	57	7	17	2	0	3	12	0	.298
	Championship Series												
2000	Seattle	A.L.	OF	6	9	0	0	0	0	0	0	0	.000
2009	Philadelphia	N.L.	OF	5	18	4	3	1	0	1	4	0	.167
2010	Philadelphia	N.L.	OF	5	19	1	4	1	0	0	0	0	.211
2012	New York	A.L.	DH	4	13	1	3	1	0	1	2	0	.231
Championship Series Totals				20	59	6	10	3	0	2	6	0	.169
	World Series Record												
2009	Philadelphia	N.L.	OF-DH	6	23	2	7	4	0	1	4	0	.304

a On disabled list from May 18 to June 3, 1999.
b On disabled list from August 7 to August 21, 2000.
c Not offered contract, December 21, 2000. Signed with Kansas City Royals organization, January 13, 2001.
d Filed for free agency, October 27, 2003. Signed with Seattle Mariners, November 19, 2003.
e On disabled list from June 3 to July 10, 2004.
f Filed for free agency, October 30, 2008. Signed with Philadelphia Phillies, December 16, 2008.
g On disabled list from June 18 to July 10, 2009.
h Filed for free agency, October 30, 2011. Signed with New York Yankees, February 21, 2012.
i Filed for free agency, November 3, 2012. Signed with Seattle Mariners, December 26, 2012.
j Filed for free agency, October 31, 2013. Signed with Los Angeles Angels, December 27, 2013.

IGLESIAS (ALEMAN), JOSE ANTONIO

Born, Havana, Cuba, January 5, 1990.
Bats Right. Throws Right. Height, 5 feet, 11 inches. Weight, 175 pounds.

Year	Club	Lea	Pos	G	AB	R	H	2B	3B	HR	RBI	SB	Avg
2010	Portland	Eastern	SS	57	221	29	63	10	3	0	13	5	.285
2010	Lowell	N.Y.-Penn.	SS	13	40	8	14	2	2	0	7	2	.350
2011	Pawtucket	Int.	SS	101	357	35	84	9	0	1	31	12	.235
2011	Boston	A.L.	SS	10	6	3	2	0	0	0	0	0	.333
2012	Lowell	N.Y.-Penn.	SS	2	8	1	3	1	0	0	0	1	.375
2012	Pawtucket	Int.	SS	88	353	46	94	9	1	1	23	12	.266
2012	Boston	A.L.	SS	25	68	5	8	2	0	1	2	1	.118
2013	Pawtucket	Int.	SS-3B	33	119	17	24	2	0	4	15	5	.202
2013	Boston-Detroit a	A.L.	SS-3B-2B	109	350	39	106	16	2	3	29	5	.303
Major League Totals			3 Yrs.	144	424	47	116	18	2	4	31	6	.274
	Division Series												
2013	Detroit	A.L.	SS	5	12	0	1	0	0	0	0	0	.083
	Championship Series												
2013	Detroit	A.L.	SS	6	14	2	5	0	0	0	1	0	.357

a Traded to Detroit Tigers for outfielder Avisail Garcia and pitcher Brayan Villarreal, July 31, 2013.

INFANTE, OMAR RAFAEL

Born, Puerto La Cruz, Venezuela, December 26, 1981.
Bats Right. Throws Right. Height, 6 feet. Weight, 180 pounds.

Year	Club	Lea	Pos	G	AB	R	H	2B	3B	HR	RBI	SB	Avg
1999	Tigers	Gulf Coast	SS	21	75	9	20	0	0	0	4	4	.267
2000	Lakeland	Fla.St.	SS	79	259	35	71	11	0	2	24	11	.274
2000	West Michigan	Midwest	SS-2B	12	48	7	11	0	0	0	5	1	.229
2001	Erie	Eastern	SS	132	540	86	163	21	4	2	62	27	.302
2002	Toledo	Int.	SS	120	436	49	117	16	8	4	51	19	.268
2002	Detroit	A.L.	SS-2B	18	72	4	24	3	0	1	6	0	.333
2003	Toledo	Int.	SS	64	224	28	50	10	0	2	18	22	.223
2003	Detroit	A.L.	SS-3B-2B	69	221	24	49	6	1	0	8	6	.222
2004	Detroit	A.L.	2B-SS-3B-OF	142	503	69	133	27	9	16	55	13	.264
2005	Detroit	A.L.	2B-SS	121	406	36	90	28	2	9	43	8	.222
2006	Detroit	A.L.	2B-SS-3B	78	224	35	62	11	4	4	25	3	.277
2007	Toledo	Int.	SS-2B	10	38	3	14	2	0	0	4	1	.368
2007	Detroit a-b	A.L.	2B-OF-SS-3B	66	166	24	45	6	1	2	17	4	.271
2008	Richmond	Int.	OF	3	11	3	4	1	0	0	3	0	.364
2008	Atlanta c	N.L.	OF-3B-SS-2B	96	317	45	93	24	3	3	40	0	.293
2009	Rome	So.Atl.	2B-3B-SS-OF	5	17	1	5	0	0	0	0	1	.294
2009	Gwinnett	Int.	SS	1	3	1	1	0	0	1	2	0	.333
2009	Atlanta d	N.L.	2B-OF-3B-SS	70	203	24	62	9	1	2	27	2	.305
2010	Atlanta e	N.L.	2B-3B-OF-SS	134	471	65	151	15	3	8	47	7	.321
2011	Jupiter	Fla.St.	2B	1	5	0	3	0	0	0	0	0	.600
2011	Florida f	N.L.	2B	148	579	55	160	24	8	7	49	4	.276
2012	Miami	N.L.	2B	85	328	42	94	23	2	8	33	10	.287
2012	Detroit g	A.L.	2B-3B	64	226	27	58	7	5	4	20	7	.257
2013	West Michigan	Midwest	2B	2	5	0	2	0	0	0	0	0	.400
2013	Toledo	Int.	2B	5	19	1	4	0	0	0	1	0	.211
2013	Detroit h-i	A.L.	2B	118	453	54	144	24	3	10	51	5	.318
Major League Totals			12 Yrs.	1209	4169	504	1165	207	42	74	421	69	.279
Division Series													
2010	Atlanta	N.L.	3B-2B	4	18	1	4	1	0	0	0	0	.222
2012	Detroit	A.L.	2B	5	17	6	6	1	0	0	0	1	.353
2013	Detroit	A.L.	2B	5	18	0	4	1	0	0	3	0	.222
Division Series Totals				14	53	7	14	3	0	0	3	1	.264
Championship Series													
2006	Detroit	A.L.	DH	1	2	0	1	0	0	0	0	1	.500
2012	Detroit	A.L.	2B	4	18	3	4	0	0	0	0	1	.222
2013	Detroit	A.L.	2B	6	21	1	4	1	0	0	0	0	.190
Championship Series Totals				11	41	4	9	1	0	0	0	2	.220
World Series Record													
2006	Detroit	A.L.	PH	1	1	0	0	0	0	0	0	0	.000
2012	Detroit	A.L.	2B	4	15	0	5	0	0	0	0	0	.333
World Series Totals				5	16	0	5	0	0	0	0	0	.313

a Traded to Chicago Cubs for outfielder Jacque Jones, November 12, 2007.
b Traded to Atlanta Braves with pitcher Will Ohman for pitcher Jose Ascanio, December 4, 2007.
c On disabled list from March 21 to May 8 and July 7 to July 22, 2008.
d On disabled list from May 21 to August 11, 2009.
e Traded to Florida Marlins with pitcher Michael Dunn for infielder Dan Uggla, November 16, 2010.
f On disabled list from August 5 to August 20, 2011.
g Traded to Detroit Tigers with pitcher Anibal Sanchez for pitcher Jacob Turner, catcher Rob Brantley and pitcher Brian Flynn, July 23, 2012.
h On disabled list from July 4 to August 12, 2013.
i Filed for free agency, October 31, 2013. Signed with Kansas City Royals, December 16, 2013.

IZTURIS, CESAR DAVID

Born, Barquisimeto, Venezuela, February 10, 1980.
Bats Both. Throws Right. Height, 5 feet, 9 inches. Weight, 180 pounds.

Year	Club	Lea	Pos	G	AB	R	H	2B	3B	HR	RBI	SB	Avg
1997	St.Cathrnes	N.Y.-Penn.	2B-SS	70	231	32	44	3	0	1	11	6	.190
1998	Hagerstown	So.Atl.	SS-2B-3B	130	413	56	108	13	1	1	38	20	.262
1999	Dunedin	Fla.St.	SS-2B-3B	131	536	77	165	28	12	3	77	32	.308
2000	Syracuse	Int.	SS	132	435	54	95	16	5	0	27	21	.218
2001	Syracuse	Int.	SS-2B	87	342	32	100	16	3	2	35	24	.292
2001	Toronto a	A.L.	2B-SS	46	134	19	36	6	2	2	9	8	.269
2002	Los Angeles	N.L.	SS-2B	135	439	43	102	24	2	1	31	7	.232
2003	Los Angeles	N.L.	SS	158	558	47	140	21	6	1	40	10	.251
2004	Los Angeles	N.L.	SS	159	670	90	193	32	9	4	62	25	.288

Year	Club	Lea	Pos	G	AB	R	H	2B	3B	HR	RBI	SB	Avg
2005	Los Angeles b	N.L.	SS	106	444	48	114	19	2	2	31	8	.257
2006	Las Vegas	P.C.	SS-2B	15	59	9	16	3	0	0	3	0	.271
2006	LA-Chicago c-d	N.L.	3B-SS-2B	54	192	14	47	9	1	1	18	1	.245
2007	Chicago-Pitt. e-f	N.L.	SS-3B	110	314	31	81	14	2	0	16	3	.258
2008	St. Louis g-h	N.L.	SS-3B	135	414	50	109	10	3	1	24	24	.263
2009	Bowie	Eastern	SS	2	6	2	2	0	0	0	0	1	.333
2009	Baltimore i	A.L.	SS	114	387	34	99	14	4	2	30	12	.256
2010	Baltimore	A.L.	SS	150	473	42	109	13	1	1	28	11	.230
2011	Orioles	Gulf Coast	2B	1	2	0	0	0	0	0	0	0	.000
2011	Bowie	Eastern	2B-SS-3B	7	25	3	6	1	0	0	3	0	.240
2011	Baltimore j-k-l	A.L.	SS-2B-3B	18	30	4	6	0	0	0	1	0	.200
2012	Nashville	P.C.	SS	4	12	1	1	0	0	0	0	0	.083
2012	Milwaukee-Wash. m-n	N.L.	SS-3B-2B-1B	62	166	13	40	7	2	2	11	1	.241
2013	Cincinnati o-p	N.L.	SS-2B-3B	63	129	6	27	8	0	0	11	0	.209
Major League Totals			13 Yrs.	1310	4350	441	1103	177	34	17	312	110	.254
Division Series													
2004	Los Angeles	N.L.	SS	4	17	1	3	1	0	0	0	0	.176

a Traded to Los Angeles Dodgers with pitcher Paul Quantrill for pitcher Luke Prokopec and pitcher Chad Ricketts, December 13, 2001.
b On disabled list from June 30 to July 15 and August 23 to October 7, 2005.
c On disabled list from March 28 to June 20 and August 22 to September 6, 2006.
d Traded to Chicago Cubs for pitcher Greg Maddux, July 31, 2006.
e Sold to Pittsburgh Pirates, July 19, 2007.
f Filed for free agency, November 12, 2007. Signed with St. Louis Cardinals, November 30, 2007.
g On disabled list from June 21 to July 6, 2008.
h Filed for free agency, October 30, 2008. Signed with Baltimore Orioles, December 15, 2008.
i On disabled list from June 4 to July 10, 2009.
j Filed for free agency, November 1, 2010, re-signed with Baltimore Orioles, January 5, 2011.
k On disabled list from May 13 to August 5 and August 8 to September 29, 2011.
l Filed for free agency, October 30, 2011. Signed with Milwaukee Brewers organization, December 21, 2011.
m On disabled list from May 26 to June 22, 2012.
n Claimed on waivers by Washington Nationals, August 6, 2012.
o Filed for free agency, August 20, 2012. Signed with Cincinnati Reds organization, January 14, 2013.
p Filed for free agency, October 31, 2013. Signed with Houston Astros organization, January 13, 2014.

IZTURIS, MAICER

Born, Barquisimeto, Venezuela, September 12, 1980.
Bats Both. Throws Right. Height, 5 feet, 8 inches. Weight, 160 pounds.

Year	Club	Lea	Pos	G	AB	R	H	2B	3B	HR	RBI	SB	Avg
1998	Burlington	Appal.	SS	55	217	33	63	8	2	2	33	16	.290
1999	Columbus	So.Atl.	SS	57	220	46	66	5	3	4	23	14	.300
2000	Columbus	So.Atl.	SS	10	29	4	8	1	0	0	1	0	.276
2001	Kinston	Carolina	2B	114	433	47	104	16	6	1	39	32	.240
2002	Kinston	Carolina	2B	58	233	28	61	13	1	1	30	24	.262
2002	Akron	Eastern	2B	67	253	34	70	12	7	0	32	8	.277
2003	Akron	Eastern	2B-SS-OF	54	218	31	61	11	5	1	20	14	.280
2003	Buffalo	Int.	SS-2B	85	301	43	79	16	4	2	29	14	.262
2004	Edmonton	P.C.	SS-2B	99	376	65	127	19	2	3	36	14	.338
2004	Montreal a-b	N.L.	SS-2B	32	107	10	22	5	2	1	4	4	.206
2005	Salt Lake	P.C.	SS-3B-2B	10	31	10	14	4	0	0	2	4	.452
2005	Los Angeles c	A.L.	3B-SS-2B-OF	77	191	18	47	8	4	1	15	9	.246
2006	Salt Lake	P.C.	SS-3B-2B	9	36	5	11	5	1	0	5	1	.306
2006	Los Angeles d	A.L.	3B-SS-2B	104	352	64	103	21	3	5	44	14	.293
2007	Rancho Cucamonga	Calif.	3B	7	22	5	7	1	0	0	3	0	.318
2007	Salt Lake	P.C.	2B-SS	5	17	3	6	1	0	0	0	0	.353
2007	Los Angeles e	A.L.	3B-2B-SS	102	336	47	97	17	2	6	51	7	.289
2008	Rancho Cucamonga	Calif.	2B	1	2	0	1	0	0	0	0	0	.500
2008	Los Angeles f	A.L.	SS-2B-3B	79	290	44	78	14	2	3	37	11	.269
2009	Los Angeles	A.L.	2B-SS-3B-OF	114	387	74	116	22	3	8	65	13	.300
2010	Salt Lake	P.C.	3B-SS	2	7	1	2	0	0	0	1	0	.286
2010	Los Angeles g	A.L.	3B-2B-SS	61	212	27	53	13	1	3	27	7	.250
2011	Los Angeles	A.L.	2B-3B-SS	122	449	51	124	35	0	5	38	9	.276
2012	Los Angeles h	A.L.	3B-2B-SS	100	289	35	74	11	0	2	20	17	.256
2013	Toronto i	A.L.	2B-3B-SS	107	365	33	86	12	0	5	32	1	.236
Major League Totals			10 Yrs.	898	2978	403	800	158	17	39	333	92	.269
Division Series													
2007	Los Angeles	A.L.	3B	3	12	1	4	2	0	0	0	2	.333
2009	Los Angeles	A.L.	2B	2	7	1	1	0	0	0	1	1	.143
Division Series Totals				5	19	2	5	2	0	0	1	3	.263

Year	Club	Lea	Pos	G	AB	R	H	2B	3B	HR	RBI	SB	Avg
	Championship Series												
2005	Los Angeles	A.L.	SS	1	0	0	0	0	0	0	0	0	.000
2009	Los Angeles	A.L.	2B	4	10	1	1	1	0	0	1	0	.100
Championship Series Totals				5	10	1	1	1	0	0	1	0	.100

a Traded by Cleveland Indians to Montreal Expos with outfielder Ryan Church for pitcher Scott Stewart, January 5, 2004.
b Traded to Anaheim Angels with outfielder Juan Rivera for outfielder Jose Guillen, November 19, 2004.
c On disabled list from April 26 to June 18, 2005.
d On disabled list from April 24 to June 9, 2006.
e On disabled list from April 30 to May 15 and May 21 to July 3, 2007.
f On disabled list from April 28 to May 13 and August 14 to October 9, 2008.
g On disabled list from May 6 to May 25 and June 16 to July 18 and August 20 to September 27, 2010.
h Filed for free agency, November 3, 2012. Signed with Toronto Blue Jays, November 8, 2012.
i On disabled list from August 21 to October 31, 2013.

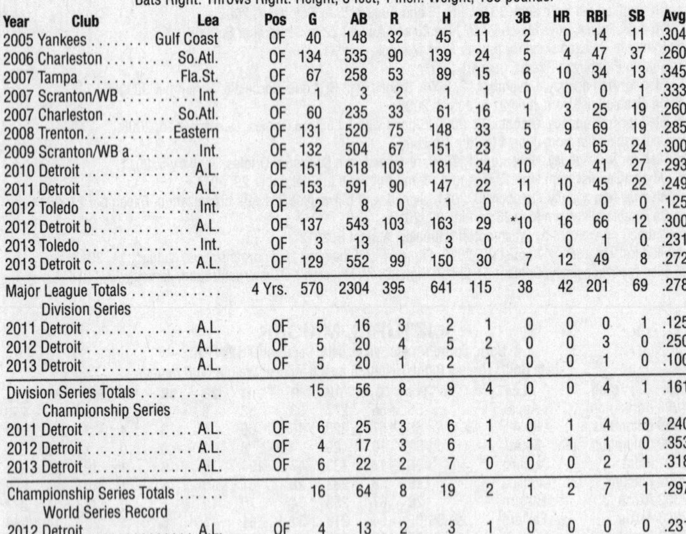

JACKSON, AUSTIN JARRIEL

Born, Denton, Texas, February 1, 1987.
Bats Right. Throws Right. Height, 6 feet, 1 inch. Weight, 185 pounds.

Year	Club	Lea	Pos	G	AB	R	H	2B	3B	HR	RBI	SB	Avg
2005	Yankees	Gulf Coast	OF	40	148	32	45	11	2	0	14	11	.304
2006	Charleston	So.Atl.	OF	134	535	90	139	24	5	4	47	37	.260
2007	Tampa	Fla.St.	OF	67	258	53	89	15	6	10	34	13	.345
2007	Scranton/WB	Int.	OF	1	3	2	1	1	0	0	0	1	.333
2007	Charleston	So.Atl.	OF	60	235	33	61	16	1	3	25	19	.260
2008	Trenton	Eastern	OF	131	520	75	148	33	5	9	69	19	.285
2009	Scranton/WB a	Int.	OF	132	504	67	151	23	9	4	65	24	.300
2010	Detroit	A.L.	OF	151	618	103	181	34	10	4	41	27	.293
2011	Detroit	A.L.	OF	153	591	90	147	22	11	10	45	22	.249
2012	Toledo	Int.	OF	2	8	0	1	0	0	0	0	0	.125
2012	Detroit b	A.L.	OF	137	543	103	163	29	*10	16	66	12	.300
2013	Toledo	Int.	OF	3	13	1	3	0	0	0	1	0	.231
2013	Detroit c	A.L.	OF	129	552	99	150	30	7	12	49	8	.272
Major League Totals			4 Yrs.	570	2304	395	641	115	38	42	201	69	.278
	Division Series												
2011	Detroit	A.L.	OF	5	16	3	2	1	0	0	0	1	.125
2012	Detroit	A.L.	OF	5	20	4	5	2	0	0	3	0	.250
2013	Detroit	A.L.	OF	5	20	1	2	1	0	0	1	0	.100
Division Series Totals				15	56	8	9	4	0	0	4	1	.161
	Championship Series												
2011	Detroit	A.L.	OF	6	25	3	6	1	0	1	4	0	.240
2012	Detroit	A.L.	OF	4	17	3	6	1	1	1	1	0	.353
2013	Detroit	A.L.	OF	6	22	2	7	0	0	0	2	1	.318
Championship Series Totals				16	64	8	19	2	1	2	7	1	.297
	World Series Record												
2012	Detroit	A.L.	OF	4	13	2	3	1	0	0	0	0	.231

a Traded by New York Yankees to Detroit Tigers with pitcher Phil Coke and pitcher Ian Kennedy for outfielder Curtis Granderson, December 9, 2009.
b On disabled list from May 17 to June 9, 2012.
c On disabled list from May 12 to June 14, 2013.

JASO, JOHN EDWARD

Born, Chula Vista, California, September 19, 1983.
Bats Left. Throws Right. Height, 6 feet, 2 inches. Weight, 205 pounds.

Year	Club	Lea	Pos	G	AB	R	H	2B	3B	HR	RBI	SB	Avg
2003	Hudson Valley	N.Y.-Penn.	C	47	154	20	34	7	0	2	20	2	.221
2004	Hudson Valley	N.Y.-Penn.	C-1B-SS	57	199	34	60	17	2	2	35	1	.302
2005	SW Michigan	Midwest	C-1B	92	332	61	102	25	1	14	50	3	.307
2006	Visalia	Calif.	C	95	366	58	113	22	0	10	55	1	.309
2007	Montgomery	Southern	C	109	380	62	120	24	2	12	71	2	.316
2008	Montgomery	Southern	C	85	284	51	77	13	2	7	43	1	.271
2008	Durham	Int.	C	31	108	14	30	7	0	5	24	1	.278
2008	Tampa Bay	A.L.	C	5	10	2	2	0	0	0	0	0	.200
2009	Durham	Int.	C	104	331	42	88	14	2	5	30	1	.266
2010	Durham	Int.	C	3	11	1	4	1	0	0	2	0	.364
2010	Tampa Bay	A.L.	C-1B	109	339	57	89	18	3	5	44	4	.263
2011	Durham	Int.	C	6	20	2	6	2	0	0	4	0	.300
2011	Tampa Bay a-b	A.L.	C	89	246	26	55	15	1	5	27	1	.224

Year	Club	Lea	Pos	G	AB	R	H	2B	3B	HR	RBI	SB	Avg
2012	Seattle	A.L.	DH-C	108	294	41	81	19	2	10	50	5	.276
2013	Oakland c-d-e	A.L.	C-1B	70	207	31	56	12	0	3	21	2	.271
Major League Totals			5 Yrs.	381	1096	157	283	64	6	23	142	12	.258
	Division Series												
2010	Tampa Bay	A.L.	C	3	10	0	3	0	0	0	1	0	.300
2011	Tampa Bay	A.L.	C	2	4	0	0	0	0	0	0	0	.000
Division Series Totals				5	14	0	3	0	0	0	1	0	.214

a On disabled list from July 15 to August 19, 2011.
b Traded to Seattle Mariners for pitcher Josh Lueke, November 27, 2011.
c Traded to Washington Nationals for outfielder Michael Morse, January 16, 2013.
d Traded to Oakland Athletics for pitcher A.J. Cole, pitcher Blake Treinen and player to be named later, January 16, 2013.
e On disabled list from July 25 to October 1, 2013.

JAY, JONATHAN HENRY (JON)

Born, Miami, Florida, March 15, 1985.
Bats Left. Throws Left. Height, 5 feet, 11 inches. Weight, 200 pounds.

Year	Club	Lea	Pos	G	AB	R	H	2B	3B	HR	RBI	SB	Avg
2006	Quad Cities	Midwest	OF	60	234	42	80	13	3	3	45	9	.342
2007	Palm Beach	Fla.St.	OF	32	126	19	36	8	0	2	10	5	.286
2007	Cardinals	Gulf Coast	DH	1	2	0	1	0	0	0	0	0	.500
2007	Springfield	Texas	OF	26	102	17	24	4	2	2	11	4	.235
2008	Memphis	P.C.	OF	16	58	8	20	4	1	1	10	0	.345
2008	Springfield	Texas	OF	96	372	57	114	17	3	11	47	10	.306
2009	Memphis	P.C.	OF-1B	136	505	72	142	23	2	10	54	20	.281
2010	Memphis	P.C.	OF-1B	42	165	31	53	16	0	4	32	13	.321
2010	St. Louis	N.L.	OF	105	287	47	86	19	2	4	27	2	.300
2011	St. Louis	N.L.	OF	159	455	56	135	24	2	10	37	6	.297
2012	Memphis	P.C.	OF	2	7	3	3	0	1	1	3	0	.429
2012	St. Louis a	N.L.	OF	117	443	70	135	22	4	4	40	19	.305
2013	St. Louis	N.L.	OF	157	548	75	151	27	2	7	67	10	.276
Major League Totals			4 Yrs.	538	1733	248	507	92	10	25	171	37	.293
	Wild Card Playoff												
2012	St. Louis	N.L.	OF	1	4	0	0	0	0	0	0	0	.000
	Division Series												
2011	St. Louis	N.L.	OF	5	12	0	2	0	0	0	2	0	.167
2012	St. Louis	N.L.	OF	5	20	4	4	0	1	0	4	2	.200
2013	St. Louis	N.L.	OF	5	16	5	3	0	0	0	2	1	.188
Division Series Totals				15	48	9	9	0	1	0	8	3	.188
	Championship Series												
2011	St. Louis	N.L.	OF	6	25	7	6	2	0	0	1	1	.240
2012	St. Louis	N.L.	OF	7	29	3	6	1	0	0	3	0	.207
2013	St. Louis	N.L.	OF	6	18	0	4	0	0	0	1	0	.222
Championship Series Totals				19	72	10	16	3	0	0	5	1	.222
	World Series Record												
2011	St. Louis	N.L.	OF	7	18	1	2	0	0	0	0	0	.111
2013	St. Louis	N.L.	OF	6	18	1	3	0	0	0	0	1	.167
World Series Totals				13	36	2	5	0	0	0	0	1	.139

a On disabled list from May 15 to June 22, 2012.

JENNINGS, DESMOND DELANE

Born, Birmingham, Alabama, October 30, 1986.
Bats Right. Throws Right. Height, 6 feet, 2 inches. Weight, 200 pounds.

Year	Club	Lea	Pos	G	AB	R	H	2B	3B	HR	RBI	SB	Avg
2006	Princeton	Appal.	OF	56	213	48	59	10	1	4	20	32	.277
2007	Columbus	So.Atl.	OF	99	387	75	122	21	5	9	37	45	.315
2008	Vero Beach	Fla.St.	OF	24	85	17	22	5	1	2	6	5	.259
2009	Montgomery	Southern	OF	100	383	69	121	25	8	8	45	37	.316
2009	Durham	Int.	OF	32	114	23	37	6	2	3	17	15	.325
2010	Durham	Int.	OF	109	399	82	111	25	6	3	36	37	.278
2010	Tampa Bay	A.L.	OF	17	21	5	4	1	1	0	2	2	.190
2011	Durham	Int.	OF	89	338	68	93	19	3	12	39	17	.275
2011	Tampa Bay	A.L.	OF	63	247	44	64	9	4	10	25	20	.259
2012	Charlotte	Fla.St.	OF	1	3	1	1	1	0	0	0	0	.333
2012	Durham	Int.	OF	3	12	1	2	0	0	0	0	0	.167
2012	Tampa Bay a	A.L.	OF	132	505	85	124	19	7	13	47	31	.246

Year	Club	Lea	Pos	G	AB	R	H	2B	3B	HR	RBI	SB	Avg
2013	Charlotte	Fla.St.	OF	1	3	1	1	0	0	0	0	1	.333
2013	Tampa Bay b	A.L.	OF	139	527	82	133	31	6	14	54	20	.252
Major League Totals			4 Yrs.	351	1300	216	325	60	18	37	128	73	.250
	Wild Card Playoff												
2013	Tampa Bay	A.L.	OF	1	3	0	2	1	0	0	2	0	.667
	Division Series												
2010	Tampa Bay	A.L.	OF	2	2	1	0	0	0	0	0	0	.000
2011	Tampa Bay	A.L.	OF	4	15	3	5	1	0	2	2	0	.333
2013	Tampa Bay	A.L.	OF	4	13	1	3	0	0	0	0	1	.231
Division Series Totals				10	30	5	8	1	0	2	2	1	.267

a On disabled list from May 12 to June 5, 2012.
b On disabled list from August 4 to August 19, 2013.

JETER, DEREK SANDERSON

Born, Pequannock, New Jersey, June 26, 1974.
Bats Right. Throws Right. Height, 6 feet, 3 inches. Weight, 195 pounds.

Year	Club	Lea	Pos	G	AB	R	H	2B	3B	HR	RBI	SB	Avg
1992	Tampa Yankees	Gulf C.	SS	47	173	19	35	10	0	3	25	2	.202
1992	Greensboro	So. Atl.	SS	11	37	4	9	0	0	1	4	0	.243
1993	Greensboro	So. Atl.	SS	128	515	85	152	14	11	5	71	18	.295
1994	Tampa	Fla. St.	SS	69	292	61	96	13	8	0	39	28	.329
1994	Albany	Eastern	SS	34	122	17	46	7	2	2	13	12	.377
1994	Columbus	Int.	SS	35	126	25	44	7	1	3	16	10	.349
1995	Columbus	Int.	SS	123	486	96	154	27	9	2	45	20	.317
1995	New York	A.L.	SS	15	48	5	12	4	1	0	7	0	.250
1996	New York a	A.L.	SS	157	582	104	183	25	6	10	78	14	.314
1997	New York	A.L.	SS	159	654	116	190	31	7	10	70	23	.291
1998	Columbus	Int.	SS	1	5	2	2	2	0	0	0	0	.400
1998	New York b	A.L.	SS	149	626	*127	203	25	8	19	84	30	.324
1999	New York	A.L.	SS	158	627	134	219	37	9	24	102	19	.349
2000	Tampa	Fla.St.	SS	1	3	2	2	1	0	0	0	0	.667
2000	New York c	A.L.	SS	148	593	119	201	31	4	15	73	22	.339
2001	New York d	A.L.	SS	150	614	110	191	35	3	21	74	27	.311
2002	New York	A.L.	SS	157	644	124	191	26	0	18	75	32	.297
2003	Trenton	Eastern	SS	5	18	2	8	1	1	0	5	0	.444
2003	New York e	A.L.	SS	119	482	87	156	25	3	10	52	11	.324
2004	New York	A.L.	SS	154	643	111	188	44	1	23	78	23	.292
2005	New York	A.L.	SS	159	654	122	202	25	5	19	70	14	.309
2006	New York	A.L.	SS	154	623	118	214	39	3	14	97	34	.343
2007	New York	A.L.	SS	156	639	102	206	39	4	12	73	15	.322
2008	New York	A.L.	SS	150	596	88	179	25	3	11	69	11	.300
2009	New York	A.L.	SS	153	634	107	212	27	1	18	66	30	.334
2010	New York f	A.L.	SS	157	663	111	179	30	3	10	67	18	.270
2011	Trenton	Eastern	SS	2	4	1	2	0	0	0	0	0	.500
2011	New York g	A.L.	SS	131	546	84	162	24	4	6	61	16	.297
2012	New York	A.L.	SS	159	*683	99	*216	32	0	15	58	9	.316
2013	Scranton/WB	Int.	SS	7	18	4	4	1	0	0	1	0	.222
2013	New York h	A.L.	SS	17	63	8	12	1	0	1	7	0	.190
Major League Totals			19 Yrs.	2602	10614	1876	3316	525	65	256	1261	348	.312
	Division Series												
1996	New York	A.L.	SS	4	17	2	7	1	0	0	1	0	.412
1997	New York	A.L.	SS	5	21	6	7	1	0	2	2	1	.333
1998	New York	A.L.	SS	3	9	0	1	0	0	0	0	0	.111
1999	New York	A.L.	SS	3	11	3	5	1	1	0	0	0	.455
2000	New York	A.L.	SS	5	19	1	4	0	0	0	2	0	.211
2001	New York	A.L.	SS	5	18	2	8	1	0	0	1	0	.444
2002	New York	A.L.	SS	4	16	6	8	0	0	2	3	0	.500
2003	New York	A.L.	SS	4	14	2	6	0	0	1	1	1	.429
2004	New York	A.L.	SS	4	19	3	6	1	0	1	4	1	.316
2005	New York	A.L.	SS	5	21	4	7	0	0	2	5	1	.333
2006	New York	A.L.	SS	4	16	4	8	4	0	1	1	0	.500
2007	New York	A.L.	SS	4	17	0	3	0	0	0	1	0	.176
2009	New York	A.L.	SS	3	10	4	4	2	0	1	2	0	.400
2010	New York	A.L.	SS	3	14	0	4	0	0	0	1	1	.286
2011	New York	A.L.	SS	5	24	6	6	1	0	0	2	1	.250
2012	New York	A.L.	SS-DH	5	22	4	8	1	1	0	2	0	.364
Division Series Totals				66	268	47	92	13	2	10	28	6	.343

Year	Club	Lea	Pos	G	AB	R	H	2B	3B	HR	RBI	SB	Avg
	Championship Series												
1996	New York	A.L.	SS	5	24	5	10	2	0	1	1	2	.417
1998	New York	A.L.	SS	6	25	3	5	1	1	0	2	3	.200
1999	New York	A.L.	SS	5	20	3	7	1	0	1	3	0	.350
2000	New York	A.L.	SS	6	22	6	7	0	0	2	5	1	.318
2001	New York	A.L.	SS	5	17	0	2	0	0	0	2	0	.118
2003	New York	A.L.	SS	7	30	3	7	2	0	1	2	1	.233
2004	New York	A.L.	SS	7	30	5	6	1	0	0	5	1	.200
2009	New York	A.L.	SS	6	27	5	7	0	0	2	3	0	.259
2010	New York	A.L.	SS	6	26	2	6	3	1	0	1	0	.231
2012	New York	A.L.	SS	1	5	0	1	0	0	0	0	0	.200
Championship Series Totals				54	226	32	58	10	2	7	24	8	.257
	World Series												
1996	New York	A.L.	SS	6	20	5	5	0	0	0	1	1	.250
1998	New York	A.L.	SS	4	17	4	6	0	0	0	1	0	.353
1999	New York	A.L.	SS	4	17	4	6	1	0	0	1	3	.353
2000	New York	A.L.	SS	5	22	6	9	2	1	2	2	0	.409
2001	New York	A.L.	SS	7	27	3	4	0	0	1	1	0	.148
2003	New York	A.L.	SS	6	26	5	9	3	0	0	2	0	.346
2009	New York	A.L.	SS	6	27	5	11	3	0	0	1	0	.407
World Series Totals				38	156	32	50	9	1	3	9	4	.321

a Selected Rookie of the Year in American League for 1996.
b On disabled list from June 4 to June 19, 1998.
c On disabled list from May 12 to May 26, 2000.
d On disabled list from March 23 to April 7, 2001.
e On disabled list from April 1 to May 13, 2003.
f Filed for free agency, November 1, 2010, re-signed with New York Yankees, December 7, 2010.
g On disabled list from June 14 to July 4, 2011.
h On disabled list from March 22 to July 11 and July 12 to July 28 and August 3 to August 26 and September 8 to November 4, 2013.

JOHNSON, CHRISTOPHER DALTON (CHRIS)

Born, Naples, Florida, October 1, 1984.
Bats Right. Throws Right. Height, 6 feet, 3 inches. Weight, 220 pounds.

Year	Club	Lea	Pos	G	AB	R	H	2B	3B	HR	RBI	SB	Avg
2006	Tri-City	N.Y.-Penn.	3B-1B	60	222	18	47	7	1	1	29	7	.212
2007	Salem	Carolina	3B-1B	60	224	24	59	11	0	6	38	1	.263
2007	Lexington	So.Atl.	3B-SS-1B	64	255	37	66	14	0	8	44	3	.259
2008	Round Rock	P.C.	3B	30	101	10	22	2	1	1	9	0	.218
2008	Corpus Christi	Texas	3B	84	330	43	107	24	0	12	58	5	.324
2009	Lancaster	Calif.	3B	4	16	5	7	5	0	0	6	0	.438
2009	Round Rock	P.C.	3B	104	384	48	108	20	5	13	42	2	.281
2009	Houston	N.L.	3B	11	22	1	2	0	0	0	1	0	.091
2010	Round Rock	P.C.	3B	38	149	26	49	10	1	8	33	0	.329
2010	Houston a	N.L.	3B	94	341	40	105	22	2	11	52	3	.308
2011	Oklahoma	P.C.	3B	21	81	18	22	7	0	4	15	1	.272
2011	Houston	N.L.	3B	107	378	32	95	21	3	7	42	2	.251
2012	Houston-Arizona b	N.L.	3B-1B-OF	136	488	48	137	28	5	15	76	5	.281
2013	Atlanta c	N.L.	3B-1B	142	514	54	165	34	0	12	68	0	.321
Major League Totals			5 Yrs.	490	1743	175	504	105	10	45	239	10	.289
	Division Series												
2013	Atlanta	N.L.	3B	4	16	1	7	0	0	0	5	0	.438

a On disabled list from April 18 to May 8, 2010.
b Traded to Arizona Diamondbacks for outfielder Marc Krauss and outfielder Bobby Borchering, July 29, 2012.
c Traded to Atlanta Braves with outfielder Justin Upton for outfielder Martin Prado, pitcher Randall Delgado, pitcher Zeke Spruill, infielder Nick Ahmed and infielder Brandon Drury, January 24, 2013.

JOHNSON, ELLIOT TYLER

Born, Safford, Arizona, March 9, 1984.
Bats Both. Throws Right. Height, 6 feet. Weight, 190 pounds.

Year	Club	Lea	Pos	G	AB	R	H	2B	3B	HR	RBI	SB	Avg
2002	Princeton	Appal.	2B-SS	42	152	21	40	10	1	1	13	14	.263
2003	Charleston	So.Atl.	2B-SS-OF	54	151	22	32	4	0	0	15	8	.212
2004	Charleston	So.Atl.	2B	126	503	92	132	22	7	6	41	43	.262
2005	Visalia	Calif.	2B	56	227	42	62	10	3	8	33	28	.273
2005	Montgomery	Southern	2B-SS	63	264	31	69	9	6	3	21	15	.261
2006	Montgomery	Southern	2B	122	494	69	139	21	10	15	50	20	.281

Year Club	Lea	Pos	G	AB	R	H	2B	3B	HR	RBI	SB	Avg
2007 Durham	Int.	2B	129	463	56	96	17	6	11	45	16	.207
2008 Tampa Bay	A.L.	SS-OF-2B	7	19	0	3	0	0	0	0	0	.158
2008 Durham	Int.	2B-SS-OF	107	387	49	101	26	5	9	50	15	.261
2009 Rays	Gulf Coast	2B	5	16	2	5	2	0	0	2	0	.313
2009 Durham	Int.	2B-3B-SS-OF	63	233	31	61	9	1	11	35	7	.262
2010 Durham	Int.	SS-OF-2B	109	427	72	136	24	5	11	56	30	.319
2011 Durham	Int.	SS	2	9	1	2	0	0	0	0	0	.222
2011 Tampa Bay a	A.L.	SS-2B-1B-OF	70	160	20	31	7	2	4	17	6	.194
2012 Tampa Bay	A.L.	SS-2B-3B-OF	123	297	32	72	10	2	6	33	18	.242
2013 Kansas City b	A.L.	2B-SS-3B-OF	79	162	19	29	2	1	2	9	14	.179
2013 Atlanta c-d	N.L.	2B-OF-3B-SS	32	92	8	24	5	2	0	10	8	.261
Major League Totals		4 Yrs.	311	730	79	159	24	7	12	69	46	.218
Division Series												
2011 Tampa Bay	A.L.	PH	1	0	0	0	0	0	0	0	0	.000
2013 Atlanta	N.L.	2B	4	14	1	1	0	1	0	0	0	.071
Division Series Totals			5	14	1	1	0	1	0	0	0	.071

a On disabled list from May 22 to June 12, 2011.
b Sent to Kansas City Royals to complete trade for Wil Myers, February 12, 2013.
c Claimed on waivers by Atlanta Braves, August 21, 2013.
d Not offered contract, December 2, 2013.

JOHNSON, KELLY ANDREW

Born, Austin, Texas, February 22, 1982.
Bats Left. Throws Right. Height, 6 feet, 1 inch. Weight, 205 pounds.

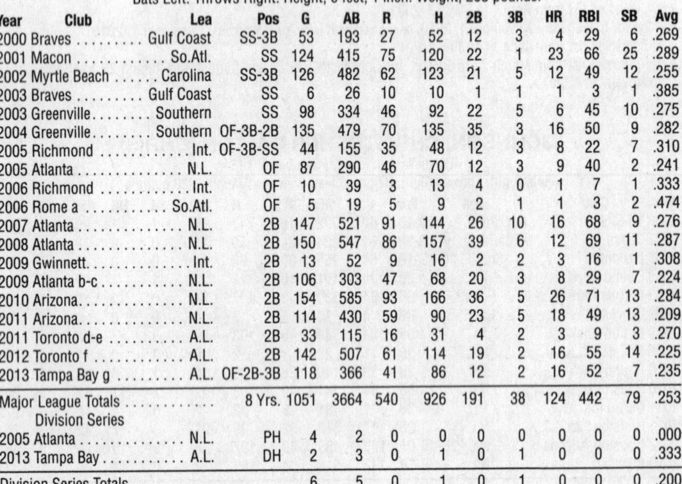

Year Club	Lea	Pos	G	AB	R	H	2B	3B	HR	RBI	SB	Avg
2000 Braves	Gulf Coast	SS-3B	53	193	27	52	12	3	4	29	6	.269
2001 Macon	So.Atl.	SS	124	415	75	120	22	1	23	66	25	.289
2002 Myrtle Beach	Carolina	SS-3B	126	482	62	123	21	5	12	49	12	.255
2003 Braves	Gulf Coast	SS	6	26	10	10	1	1	1	3	1	.385
2003 Greenville	Southern	SS	98	334	46	92	22	5	6	45	10	.275
2004 Greenville	Southern	OF-3B-2B	135	479	70	135	35	3	16	50	9	.282
2005 Richmond	Int.	OF-3B-SS	44	155	35	48	12	3	8	22	7	.310
2005 Atlanta	N.L.	OF	87	290	46	70	12	3	9	40	2	.241
2006 Richmond	Int.	OF	10	39	3	13	4	0	1	7	1	.333
2006 Rome a	So.Atl.	OF	5	19	5	9	2	1	1	3	2	.474
2007 Atlanta	N.L.	2B	147	521	91	144	26	10	16	68	9	.276
2008 Atlanta	N.L.	2B	150	547	86	157	39	6	12	69	11	.287
2009 Gwinnett	Int.	2B	13	52	9	16	2	2	3	16	1	.308
2009 Atlanta b-c	N.L.	2B	106	303	47	68	20	3	8	29	7	.224
2010 Arizona	N.L.	2B	154	585	93	166	36	5	26	71	13	.284
2011 Arizona	N.L.	2B	114	430	59	90	23	5	18	49	13	.209
2011 Toronto d-e	A.L.	2B	33	115	16	31	4	2	3	9	3	.270
2012 Toronto f	A.L.	2B	142	507	61	114	19	2	16	55	14	.225
2013 Tampa Bay g	A.L.	OF-2B-3B	118	366	41	86	12	2	16	52	7	.235
Major League Totals		8 Yrs.	1051	3664	540	926	191	38	124	442	79	.253
Division Series												
2005 Atlanta	N.L.	PH	4	2	0	0	0	0	0	0	0	.000
2013 Tampa Bay	A.L.	DH	2	3	0	1	0	1	0	0	0	.333
Division Series Totals			6	5	0	1	0	1	0	0	0	.200

a On disabled list from March 24 to November 1, 2006.
b On disabled list from July 3 to July 23, 2009.
c Not offered contract, December 12, 2009. Signed with Arizona Diamondbacks, December 30, 2009.
d Traded to Toronto Blue Jays for infielder Aaron Hill and infielder John McDonald, August 23, 2011.
e Filed for free agency, October 30, 2011. Accepted arbitration, December 7, 2011.
f Filed for free agency, November 3, 2012. Signed with Tampa Bay Rays, February 5, 2013.
g Filed for free agency, October 31, 2013. Signed with New York Yankees, December 6, 2013.

JOHNSON, REED CAMERON

Born, Riverside, California, December 8, 1976.
Bats Right. Throws Right. Height, 5 feet, 10 inches. Weight, 180 pounds.

Year Club	Lea	Pos	G	AB	R	H	2B	3B	HR	RBI	SB	Avg
1999 St. Catharines	N.Y.-Penn.	OF	60	189	24	44	8	2	2	23	5	.233
2000 Dunedin	Fla.St.	OF	36	133	26	42	9	2	4	28	3	.316
2000 Hagerstown	So.Atl.	OF	95	324	66	94	24	5	8	70	14	.290
2001 Tennessee	Southern	OF	136	554	104	174	29	4	13	74	42	.314
2002 Dunedin	Fla.St.	OF	8	33	7	9	3	0	0	6	0	.273
2002 Syracuse	Int.	OF	44	159	27	37	8	3	2	10	1	.233

Year	Club	Lea	Pos	G	AB	R	H	2B	3B	HR	RBI	SB	Avg
2003	Syracuse	Int.	OF	26	101	14	33	4	1	2	16	3	.327
2003	Toronto	A.L.	OF	114	412	79	121	21	2	10	52	5	.294
2004	Toronto	A.L.	OF	141	537	68	145	25	2	10	61	6	.270
2005	Toronto	A.L.	OF	142	398	55	107	21	6	8	58	5	.269
2006	Toronto	A.L.	OF	134	461	86	147	34	2	12	49	8	.319
2007	Dunedin	Fla.St.	OF	4	12	1	4	1	0	1	1	0	.333
2007	Syracuse	Int.	OF	2	8	1	3	0	0	0	1	0	.375
2007	Toronto a	A.L.	OF	79	275	31	65	13	2	2	14	4	.236
2008	Chicago b-c	N.L.	OF	109	333	52	101	21	0	6	50	5	.303
2009	Peoria	Midwest	OF	3	6	2	2	0	0	0	0	0	.333
2009	Chicago d-e	N.L.	OF	65	165	23	42	10	2	4	22	2	.255
2010	Inland Empire	Calif.	OF	2	6	2	3	1	0	0	0	0	.500
2010	Los Angeles f-g	N.L.	OF	102	202	24	53	11	2	2	15	2	.262
2011	Iowa	P.C.	OF	3	6	0	0	0	0	0	0	0	.000
2011	Chicago h-i	N.L.	OF	111	246	33	76	22	1	5	28	2	.309
2012	Chicago-Atlanta j-k	N.L.	OF	119	269	30	78	14	3	3	20	2	.290
2013	Atlanta l-m	N.L.	OF	74	123	13	30	7	1	1	11	0	.244
Major League Totals			11 Yrs.	1190	3421	494	965	199	23	63	380	41	.282
	Division Series												
2013	Atlanta	N.L.	PH	3	2	1	1	0	0	0	0	0	.500

a On disabled list from April 12 to July 6, 2007.
b Released by Toronto Blue Jays, March 23, 2008. Signed with Chicago Cubs, March 25, 2008.
c On disabled list from June 18 to July 3, 2008.
d On disabled list from June 21 to July 6 and July 30 to September 21, 2009.
e Filed for free agency, November 5, 2009. Signed with Los Angeles Dodgers, February 1, 2010.
f On disabled list from July 9 to August 4, 2010.
g Filed for free agency, November 1, 2010. Signed with Chicago Cubs organization, January 12, 2011.
h On disabled list from May 29 to June 14, 2011.
i Filed for free agency, October 30, 2011, re-signed with Chicago Cubs, January 3, 2012.
j Traded to Atlanta Braves with pitcher Paul Maholm and cash for pitcher Jaye Chapman and pitcher Arodys Vizcaino, July 31, 2012.
k Filed for free agency, November 3, 2012, re-signed with Atlanta Braves, December 6, 2012.
l On disabled list from July 29 to September 10, 2013.
m Filed for free agency, November 5, 2013.

JONES, ADAM LA MARQUE

Born, San Diego, California, August 1, 1985.
Bats Right. Throws Right. Height, 6 feet, 2 inches. Weight, 200 pounds.

Year	Club	Lea	Pos	G	AB	R	H	2B	3B	HR	RBI	SB	Avg
2003	Mariners	Arizona	SS	28	109	18	31	5	1	0	8	5	.284
2003	Everett	Northwest	SS	3	13	2	6	1	0	0	4	0	.462
2004	Wisconsin	Midwest	SS-3B	130	510	76	136	23	7	11	72	8	.267
2005	Inland Empire	Calif.	SS	68	271	43	80	20	5	8	46	4	.295
2005	San Antonio	Texas	SS-OF	63	228	33	68	10	3	7	20	9	.298
2006	Tacoma	P.C.	OF	96	380	69	109	19	4	16	62	13	.287
2006	Seattle	A.L.	OF	32	74	6	16	4	0	1	8	3	.216
2007	Tacoma	P.C.	OF	101	420	75	132	27	6	25	84	8	.314
2007	Seattle	A.L.	OF	41	65	16	16	2	1	2	4	2	.246
2008	Baltimore a-b	A.L.	OF	132	477	61	129	21	7	9	57	10	.270
2009	Baltimore c	A.L.	OF	119	473	83	131	22	3	19	70	10	.277
2010	Baltimore	A.L.	OF	149	581	76	165	25	5	19	69	7	.284
2011	Baltimore	A.L.	OF	151	567	68	159	26	2	25	83	12	.280
2012	Baltimore	A.L.	OF	*162	648	103	186	39	3	32	82	16	.287
2013	Baltimore	A.L.	OF	160	653	100	186	35	1	33	108	14	.285
Major League Totals			8 Yrs.	946	3538	513	988	174	22	140	481	74	.279
	Wild Card Playoff												
2012	Baltimore	A.L.	OF	1	3	0	0	0	0	0	1	0	.000
	Division Series												
2012	Baltimore	A.L.	OF	5	23	0	2	0	0	0	0	0	.087

a Traded to Baltimore Orioles with pitcher Tony Butler, pitcher Kam Mickolio, pitcher George Sherrill and pitcher Chris Tillman for pitcher Erik Bedard, February 8, 2008.
b On disabled list from August 3 to September 1, 2008.
c On disabled list from September 2 to November 6, 2009.

JONES, GARRETT THOMAS

Born, Harvey, Illinois, June 21, 1981.
Bats Left. Throws Left. Height, 6 feet, 4 inches. Weight, 245 pounds.

Year	Club	Lea	Pos	G	AB	R	H	2B	3B	HR	RBI	SB	Avg
1999	Braves	Gulf Coast	1B	46	170	17	41	3	0	3	18	1	.241
2000	Danville	Appal.	1B	40	138	12	24	7	2	0	16	0	.174
2001	Danville	Appal.	1B	40	149	13	43	11	0	3	23	0	.289
2002	Quad Cities a	Midwest	1B-OF	63	223	21	45	8	0	10	32	3	.202
2003	Fort Myers	Fla.St.	1B-OF	117	404	52	89	12	5	18	67	5	.220
2004	New Britain	Eastern	1B	122	450	68	140	33	2	30	92	11	.311
2004	Fort Myers	Fla.St.	1B	19	66	6	16	5	0	1	6	2	.242
2005	Rochester	Int.	1B-OF	134	488	71	119	22	2	24	72	5	.244
2006	Rochester	Int.	1B-OF	140	525	72	125	32	3	21	92	3	.238
2007	Rochester	Int.	OF-1B	107	400	57	112	32	3	13	70	2	.280
2007	Minnesota	A.L.	DH-1B-OF	31	77	7	16	2	1	2	5	1	.208
2008	Rochester b	Int.	1B-OF	138	527	82	147	33	3	23	92	9	.279
2009	Indianapolis	Int.	OF-1B	72	277	44	85	18	0	12	49	14	.307
2009	Pittsburgh	N.L.	OF-1B	82	314	45	92	21	1	21	44	10	.293
2010	Pittsburgh	N.L.	1B-OF	158	592	64	146	34	1	21	86	7	.247
2011	Pittsburgh	N.L.	OF-1B	148	423	51	103	30	1	16	58	6	.243
2012	Pittsburgh	N.L.	1B-OF	145	475	68	130	28	3	27	86	2	.274
2013	Pittsburgh c	N.L.	1B-OF	144	403	41	94	26	2	15	51	2	.233
Major League Totals			6 Yrs.	708	2284	276	581	141	9	102	330	28	.254
	Division Series												
2013	Pittsburgh	N.L.	PH	2	2	0	0	0	0	0	0	0	.000

a Released by Atlanta Braves, May 21, 2002. Signed with Minnesota Twins organization, May 24, 2002.
b Filed for free agency, November 3, 2008. Signed with Pittsburgh Pirates organization, December 16, 2008.
c Not offered contract, December 2, 2013. Signed with Miami Marlins, December 9, 2013.

JOYCE, MATTHEW R. (MATT)

Born, Tampa, Florida, August 3, 1984.
Bats Left. Throws Right. Height, 6 feet, 2 inches. Weight, 205 pounds.

Year	Club	Lea	Pos	G	AB	R	H	2B	3B	HR	RBI	SB	Avg
2005	Oneonta	N.Y.-Penn.	OF	65	245	51	81	10	4	4	45	9	.331
2006	West Michigan	Midwest	OF	122	465	75	120	30	5	11	86	5	.258
2007	Erie	Eastern	OF	130	456	61	117	33	3	17	70	4	.257
2008	Toledo	Int.	OF	56	200	36	54	13	2	13	41	2	.270
2008	Detroit a	A.L.	OF	92	242	40	61	16	3	12	33	0	.252
2009	Tampa Bay	A.L.	OF	11	32	3	6	1	0	3	7	1	.188
2009	Durham	Int.	OF	111	417	73	114	35	2	16	66	14	.273
2010	Charlotte	Fla.St.	OF	10	29	6	11	5	0	2	8	1	.379
2010	Durham	Int.	OF	25	92	18	27	8	0	3	12	1	.293
2010	Tampa Bay b	A.L.	OF	77	216	30	52	15	3	10	40	2	.241
2011	Tampa Bay	A.L.	OF	141	462	69	128	32	2	19	75	13	.277
2012	Charlotte	Fla.St.	OF	2	8	2	2	1	0	0	2	0	.250
2012	Durham	Int.	OF	1	2	0	0	0	0	0	0	0	.000
2012	Tampa Bay c	A.L.	OF	124	399	55	96	18	3	17	59	4	.241
2013	Tampa Bay	A.L.	OF	140	413	61	97	22	0	18	47	7	.235
Major League Totals			6 Yrs.	585	1764	258	440	104	11	79	261	27	.249
	Division Series												
2010	Tampa Bay	A.L.	OF	4	9	0	2	0	0	0	0	1	.222
2011	Tampa Bay	A.L.	OF	4	15	1	3	1	0	1	4	0	.200
2013	Tampa Bay	A.L.	OF-DH	4	8	0	0	0	0	0	0	0	.000
Division Series Totals				12	32	1	5	1	0	1	4	1	.156

a Traded to Tampa Bay Rays for pitcher Edwin Jackson, December 10, 2008.
b On disabled list from March 26 to May 31, 2010.
c On disabled list from June 20 to July 17, 2012.

KAWASAKI, MUNENORI

Born, Kagoshima, Japan, June 3, 1981.
Bats Left. Throws Right. Height, 5 feet, 10 inches. Weight, 165 pounds.

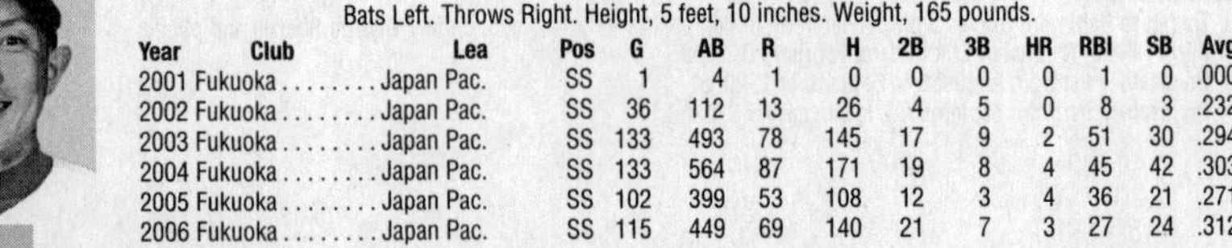

Year	Club	Lea	Pos	G	AB	R	H	2B	3B	HR	RBI	SB	Avg
2001	Fukuoka	Japan Pac.	SS	1	4	1	0	0	0	0	1	0	.000
2002	Fukuoka	Japan Pac.	SS	36	112	13	26	4	5	0	8	3	.232
2003	Fukuoka	Japan Pac.	SS	133	493	78	145	17	9	2	51	30	.294
2004	Fukuoka	Japan Pac.	SS	133	564	87	171	19	8	4	45	42	.303
2005	Fukuoka	Japan Pac.	SS	102	399	53	108	12	3	4	36	21	.271
2006	Fukuoka	Japan Pac.	SS	115	449	69	140	21	7	3	27	24	.312

Year Club	Lea	Pos	G	AB	R	H	2B	3B	HR	RBI	SB	Avg
2007 Fukuoka	Japan Pac.	SS	95	383	57	126	12	7	4	43	23	.329
2008 Fukuoka	Japan Pac.	SS	99	424	55	136	16	6	1	34	19	.321
2009 Fukuoka	Japan Pac.	SS	143	540	73	140	26	8	4	34	44	.259
2010 Fukuoka	Japan Pac.	SS	144	602	74	190	27	5	4	53	30	.316
2011 Fukuoka	Japan Pac.	SS	144	603	71	161	19	7	1	37	31	.267
2012 Seattle a-b	A.L.	SS-2B-3B	61	104	13	20	1	0	0	7	2	.192
2013 Toronto c	A.L.	SS-2B	96	240	27	55	6	5	1	24	7	.229
Major League Totals		2 Yrs.	157	344	40	75	7	5	1	31	9	.218

a Signed with Seattle Mariners organization, January 12, 2012.
b Released by Seattle Mariners, October 24, 2012. Signed with Toronto Blue Jays organization, March 2, 2013.
c Filed for free agency, November 1, 2013, re-signed with Toronto Blue Jays organization, December 24, 2013.

KELLY, DONALD THOMAS (DON)

Born, Butler, Pennsylvania, February 15, 1980.
Bats Left. Throws Right. Height, 6 feet, 4 inches. Weight, 190 pounds.

Year Club	Lea	Pos	G	AB	R	H	2B	3B	HR	RBI	SB	Avg
2001 Oneonta	N.Y.-Penn.	SS	67	262	41	75	8	3	0	25	8	.286
2002 West Michigan	Midwest	SS	128	455	72	130	21	5	1	59	9	.286
2003 Lakeland	Fla.St.	3B-SS-1B-2B	87	303	48	96	17	4	1	38	15	.317
2003 Erie	Eastern	SS-1B	22	83	14	22	5	1	1	13	0	.265
2004 Tigers	Gulf Coast	SS	3	10	2	4	0	0	0	0	1	.400
2004 Erie	Eastern	SS	28	101	17	23	6	2	0	9	3	.228
2005 Erie	Eastern	3B-SS	82	329	54	112	22	3	9	54	10	.340
2005 Toledo	Int.	SS-3B-OF	43	160	22	40	8	0	1	13	8	.250
2006 Erie	Eastern	2B-SS-3B-1B	58	207	30	57	11	1	0	24	5	.275
2006 Toledo a	Int.	SS-1B-2B	66	237	23	54	14	3	0	19	18	.228
2007 Pittsburgh	N.L.	SS-2B-OF	25	27	2	4	0	0	0	0	0	.148
2007 Indianapolis b	Int.	OF-SS-2B-3B	52	150	20	37	5	2	0	11	6	.247
2008 Tucson	P.C.	2B-SS-3B-OF	124	436	61	120	24	5	8	55	2	.275
2009 Toledo	Int.	OF-1B-3B-2B	105	372	57	123	20	6	6	40	27	.331
2009 Detroit c	A.L.	OF-3B-1B-2B	31	56	8	14	3	1	0	3	1	.250
2010 Detroit	A.L.	OF-1B-3B	119	238	30	58	4	0	9	27	3	.244
2011 Detroit	A.L.	OF-3B-1B-C	113	257	35	63	8	3	7	28	2	.245
2012 Toledo	Int.	3B-OF-1B	20	73	8	17	2	0	1	12	4	.233
2012 Detroit	A.L.	OF-1B-3B-2B	75	113	14	21	2	1	1	7	2	.186
2013 Detroit d	A.L.	OF-3B-1B-2B	112	216	33	48	6	1	6	23	2	.222
Major League Totals		6 Yrs.	475	907	122	208	23	6	23	88	10	.229
Division Series												
2011 Detroit	A.L.	OF-3B	4	11	3	4	0	0	1	2	0	.364
2012 Detroit	A.L.	PH	1	0	1	0	0	0	0	1	0	.000
2013 Detroit	A.L.	OF	3	5	0	2	0	0	0	0	0	.400
Division Series Totals			8	16	4	6	0	0	1	3	0	.375
Championship Series												
2011 Detroit	A.L.	OF-3B	5	9	0	2	1	0	0	0	0	.222
2012 Detroit	A.L.	PH	1	0	1	0	0	0	0	0	0	.000
2013 Detroit	A.L.	OF	6	6	0	0	0	0	0	0	0	.000
Championship Series Totals			12	15	1	2	1	0	0	0	0	.133
World Series Record												
2012 Detroit	A.L.	OF	2	1	0	0	0	0	0	0	0	.000

a Filed for free agency from Detroit Tigers, October 3, 2006. Signed with Pittsburgh Pirates organization, November 16, 2006.
b Filed for free agency, October 4, 2007. Signed with Arizona Diamondbacks organization, November 24, 2007.
c Filed for free agency, November 3, 2008. Signed with Detroit Tigers organization, January 14, 2009.
d Filed for free agency, October 31, 2012, re-signed with Detroit Tigers organization, January 11, 2013.

KEMP, MATTHEW RYAN (MATT)

Born, Midwest City, Oklahoma, September 23, 1984.
Bats Right. Throws Right. Height, 6 feet, 2 inches. Weight, 230 pounds.

Year Club	Lea	Pos	G	AB	R	H	2B	3B	HR	RBI	SB	Avg
2003 Dodgers	Gulf Coast	OF	42	159	11	43	5	2	1	17	2	.270
2004 Vero Beach	Fla.St.	OF	11	37	5	13	5	0	1	9	2	.351
2004 Columbus	So.Atl.	OF	112	423	67	122	22	8	17	66	8	.288
2005 Vero Beach	Fla.St.	OF	109	418	76	128	21	4	27	90	23	.306
2006 Jacksonville	Southern	OF	48	199	38	65	15	2	7	34	11	.327
2006 Las Vegas	P.C.	OF	44	182	37	67	14	6	3	36	14	.368
2006 Los Angeles	N.L.	OF	52	154	30	39	7	1	7	23	6	.253
2007 Las Vegas	P.C.	OF	39	161	32	53	16	3	4	20	9	.329

Year	Club	Lea	Pos	G	AB	R	H	2B	3B	HR	RBI	SB	Avg
2007	Los Angeles a	N.L.	OF	98	292	47	100	12	5	10	42	10	.342
2008	Los Angeles	N.L.	OF	155	606	93	176	38	5	18	76	35	.290
2009	Los Angeles	N.L.	OF	159	606	97	180	25	7	26	101	34	.297
2010	Los Angeles	N.L.	OF	*162	602	82	150	25	6	28	89	19	.249
2011	Los Angeles	N.L.	OF	161	602	*115	195	33	4	*39	*126	40	.324
2012	Rancho Cucamonga	Calif.	OF	4	14	2	6	1	0	0	4	0	.429
2012	Albuquerque	P.C.	OF	4	16	6	8	2	0	2	6	0	.500
2012	Los Angeles b	N.L.	OF	106	403	74	122	22	2	23	69	9	.303
2013	Rancho Cucamonga	Calif.	OF	5	18	0	0	0	0	0	0	0	.000
2013	Albuquerque	P.C.	OF	3	11	3	2	2	0	0	0	1	.182
2013	Los Angeles c	N.L.	OF	73	263	35	71	15	0	6	33	9	.270
	Major League Totals		8 Yrs.	966	3528	573	1033	177	30	157	559	162	.293
	Division Series												
2008	Los Angeles	N.L.	OF	3	13	0	2	2	0	0	1	0	.154
2009	Los Angeles	N.L.	OF	3	14	2	2	0	0	1	2	0	.143
	Division Series Totals			6	27	2	4	2	0	1	3	0	.148
	Championship Series												
2008	Los Angeles	N.L.	OF	5	15	1	5	1	0	0	0	0	.333
2009	Los Angeles	N.L.	OF	5	20	2	5	0	0	1	2	0	.250
	Championship Series Totals			10	35	3	10	1	0	1	2	0	.286

a On disabled list from April 10 to April 27, 2007.
b On disabled list from May 31 to July 13 and May 14 to May 29, 2012.
c On disabled list from May 30 to June 25 and July 6 to July 21 and July 22 to September 16, 2013.

KENDRICK, HOWARD JOSEPH (HOWIE)

Born, Jacksonville, Florida, July 12, 1983.
Bats Right. Throws Right. Height, 5 feet, 10 inches. Weight, 195 pounds.

Year	Club	Lea	Pos	G	AB	R	H	2B	3B	HR	RBI	SB	Avg
2002	Angels	Arizona	2B	42	157	24	50	6	4	0	13	12	.318
2003	Provo	Pioneer	2B	63	234	65	86	20	3	3	36	8	.368
2004	Angels	Arizona	2B	3	12	1	3	1	0	0	0	2	.250
2004	Cedar Rapids	Midwest	2B	75	313	66	115	24	6	10	49	15	.367
2005	Rancho Cucamonga	Calif.	2B	63	279	69	107	23	6	12	47	13	.384
2005	Arkansas	Texas	2B	46	190	35	65	20	2	7	42	12	.342
2006	Salt Lake	P.C.	2B-3B	69	290	57	107	25	6	13	62	11	.369
2006	Los Angeles	A.L.	1B-2B-3B	72	267	25	76	21	1	4	30	6	.285
2007	Rancho Cucamonga	Calif.	DH	1	4	0	1	0	0	0	0	0	.250
2007	Salt Lake	P.C.	2B	13	50	9	15	1	0	3	11	1	.300
2007	Los Angeles a	A.L.	2B	88	338	55	109	24	2	5	39	5	.322
2008	Rancho Cucamonga	Calif.	2B	2	6	3	5	0	0	2	2	1	.833
2008	Salt Lake	P.C.	2B	2	5	0	1	0	0	0	1	0	.200
2008	Los Angeles b	A.L.	2B	92	340	43	104	26	2	3	37	11	.306
2009	Salt Lake	P.C.	2B	20	78	11	27	6	1	2	11	4	.346
2009	Los Angeles	A.L.	2B	105	374	61	109	21	3	10	61	11	.291
2010	Los Angeles	A.L.	2B-1B-OF	158	616	67	172	41	4	10	75	14	.279
2011	Los Angeles c	A.L.	2B-OF-1B	140	537	86	153	30	6	18	63	14	.285
2012	Los Angeles	A.L.	2B-1B-OF	147	550	57	158	32	3	8	67	14	.287
2013	Los Angeles d	A.L.	2B-OF	122	478	55	142	21	4	13	54	6	.297
	Major League Totals		8 Yrs.	924	3500	449	1023	216	25	71	426	81	.292
	Division Series												
2007	Los Angeles	A.L.	2B	3	10	0	2	0	0	0	1	2	.200
2008	Los Angeles	A.L.	2B	4	17	0	2	0	0	0	0	0	.118
2009	Los Angeles	A.L.	2B	2	5	1	1	0	0	0	0	1	.200
	Division Series Totals			9	32	1	5	0	0	0	1	3	.156
	Championship Series												
2009	Los Angeles	A.L.	2B	4	14	3	4	0	1	1	1	0	.286

a On disabled list from April 18 to May 23 and July 8 to August 20, 2007.
b On disabled list from April 14 to May 30 and August 28 to September 22, 2008.
c On disabled list from May 20 to June 4, 2011.
d On disabled list from August 6 to September 10, 2013.

KEPPINGER, JEFFREY SCOTT (JEFF)

Born, Miami, Florida, April 21, 1980.
Bats Right. Throws Right. Height, 6 feet. Weight, 180 pounds.

Year	Club	Lea	Pos	G	AB	R	H	2B	3B	HR	RBI	SB	Avg
2002	Hickory	So.Atl.	2B	126	478	75	132	23	4	10	73	6	.276
2003	Lynchburg	Carolina	2B-3B-1B	92	342	55	111	21	2	3	51	3	.325

Year	Club	Lea	Pos	G	AB	R	H	2B	3B	HR	RBI	SB	Avg
2004	Altoona	Eastern	2B	82	323	45	108	17	2	1	33	10	.334
2004	Binghamton	Eastern	2B-3B	14	47	14	17	3	1	0	5	2	.362
2004	Norfolk	Int.	2B	6	19	1	6	1	0	0	2	0	.316
2004	New York a	N.L.	2B	33	116	9	33	2	0	3	9	2	.284
2005	Norfolk b	Int.	2B-3B-SS	64	255	40	86	15	3	3	29	5	.337
2006	Norfolk	Int.	2B-OF-3B	87	323	36	97	13	0	2	26	0	.300
2006	Omaha	P.C.	2B-3B-1B-SS	32	127	21	45	6	1	2	17	0	.354
2006	Kansas City c	A.L.	3B-1B-2B-OF	22	60	11	16	2	0	2	8	0	.267
2007	Sarasota	Fla.St.	3B-2B	3	12	1	4	2	0	0	1	0	.333
2007	Louisville	Int.	3B-2B-OF-1B	57	228	31	84	15	1	2	18	1	.368
2007	Cincinnati d-e	N.L.	SS-3B-2B-OF	67	241	39	80	16	2	5	32	2	.332
2008	Sarasota	Fla.St.	3B	2	7	1	2	0	0	0	1	0	.286
2008	Louisville	Int.	3B-SS	6	22	3	11	2	0	1	2	0	.500
2008	Cincinnati f	N.L.	SS-3B-1B-2B	121	459	45	122	24	2	3	43	3	.266
2009	Houston g	N.L.	3B-2B-SS-OF	107	305	35	78	13	3	7	29	0	.256
2010	Corpus Christi	Texas	2B	2	5	0	2	0	0	0	1	0	.400
2010	Houston h	N.L.	2B-SS	137	514	62	148	34	1	6	59	4	.288
2011	Corpus Christi	Texas	2B	4	16	4	7	1	0	1	2	0	.438
2011	Oklahoma	P.C.	2B	7	28	2	7	0	0	0	1	0	.250
2011	Houston-San Fran. i-j-k	N.L.	2B	99	379	39	105	20	0	6	35	0	.277
2012	Durham	Int.	3B-1B	6	21	4	6	1	0	0	1	0	.286
2012	Tampa Bay l-m	A.L.	3B-1B-2B	115	385	46	125	15	1	9	40	1	.325
2013	Chicago	A.L.	2B-3B-1B	117	423	38	107	13	1	4	40	0	.253
Major League Totals			9 Yrs.	818	2882	324	814	139	10	45	295	12	.282

a Traded by Pittsburgh Pirates to New York Mets with pitcher Kris Benson for infielder Ty Wigginton, pitcher Matt Peterson and infielder Jose Bautista, July 30, 2004.
b On disabled list from September 9 to October 31, 2005.
c Traded to Kansas City Royals for infielder Ruben Gotay, July 19, 2006.
d Traded to Cincinnati Reds for pitcher Russ Haltiwanger, January 11, 2007.
e On disabled list from March 23 to April 22, 2007.
f On disabled list from May 14 to June 22, 2008.
g Traded to Houston Astros for player to be named later, March 31, 2009. Cincinnati Reds received infielder Drew Sutton to complete trade, April 16, 2009.
h On disabled list from August 17 to September 1, 2010.
i On disabled list from March 22 to May 27, 2011.
j Traded to San Francisco Giants for pitcher Henry Sosa and pitcher Jason Stoffel, July 19, 2011.
k Not offered contract, December 12, 2011. Signed with Tampa Bay Rays, January 27, 2012.
l On disabled list from May 19 to June 22, 2012.
m Filed for free agency, November 3, 2012. Signed with Chicago White Sox, December 10, 2012.

KINSLER, IAN MICHAEL

Born, Tucson, Arizona, June 22, 1982.
Bats Right. Throws Right. Height, 6 feet. Weight, 200 pounds.

Year	Club	Lea	Pos	G	AB	R	H	2B	3B	HR	RBI	SB	Avg
2003	Spokane	Northwest	SS	51	188	32	52	10	6	1	15	11	.277
2004	Clinton	Midwest	SS	60	227	52	91	30	1	11	53	16	.401
2004	Frisco	Texas	SS	71	277	51	83	21	1	9	46	7	.300
2005	Oklahoma	P.C.	2B-SS-3B	131	530	102	145	28	2	23	94	19	.274
2006	Oklahoma	P.C.	2B	10	39	7	10	3	0	2	6	1	.256
2006	Texas a	A.L.	2B	120	423	65	121	27	1	14	55	11	.286
2007	Oklahoma	P.C.	2B	3	13	1	5	0	0	0	3	2	.385
2007	Texas b	A.L.	2B	130	483	96	127	22	2	20	61	23	.263
2008	Texas c	A.L.	2B	121	518	102	165	41	4	18	71	26	.319
2009	Frisco	Texas	2B	2	7	1	0	0	0	0	0	0	.000
2009	Texas d	A.L.	2B	144	566	101	143	32	4	31	86	31	.253
2010	Frisco	Texas	2B	6	19	3	5	0	1	0	6	2	.263
2010	Texas e	A.L.	2B	103	391	73	112	20	1	9	45	15	.286
2011	Texas	A.L.	2B	155	620	121	158	34	4	32	77	30	.255
2012	Texas	A.L.	2B-3B	157	655	105	168	42	5	19	72	21	.256
2013	Frisco	Texas	2B	2	8	0	0	0	0	0	0	0	.000
2013	Texas f-g	A.L.	2B	136	545	85	151	31	2	13	72	15	.277
Major League Totals			8 Yrs.	1066	4201	748	1145	249	23	156	539	172	.273
	Wild Card Playoff												
2012	Texas	A.L.	2B	1	3	1	2	0	0	0	0	0	.667
	Division Series												
2010	Texas	A.L.	2B	5	18	5	8	0	0	3	6	0	.444
2011	Texas	A.L.	2B	4	16	2	4	2	0	1	3	1	.250
Division Series Totals				9	34	7	12	2	0	4	9	1	.353

Year	Club	Lea	Pos	G	AB	R	H	2B	3B	HR	RBI	SB	Avg
	Championship Series												
2010	Texas	A.L.	2B	6	20	1	5	1	1	0	3	2	.250
2011	Texas	A.L.	2B	6	24	6	7	2	0	0	6	1	.292
Championship Series Totals				12	44	7	12	3	1	0	9	3	.273
	World Series Record												
2010	Texas	A.L.	2B	5	16	1	3	1	0	0	0	1	.188
2011	Texas	A.L.	2B	7	25	2	9	1	0	0	2	1	.360
World Series Totals				12	41	3	12	2	0	0	2	2	.293

a On disabled list from April 12 to May 25, 2006.
b On disabled list from July 2 to July 31, 2007.
c On disabled list from August 18 to November 14, 2008.
d On disabled list from July 29 to August 14, 2009.
e On disabled list from March 26 to April 30 and July 28 to September 1, 2010.
f On disabled list from May 18 to June 15, 2013.
g Traded to Detroit Tigers for infielder Prince Fielder and cash, November 20, 2013.

KIPNIS, JASON MICHAEL

Born, Northbrook, Illinois, April 3, 1987.
Bats Left. Throws Right. Height, 5 feet, 11 inches. Weight, 185 pounds.

Year	Club	Lea	Pos	G	AB	R	H	2B	3B	HR	RBI	SB	Avg
2009	Mahoning Valley	N.Y.-Penn.	OF	29	111	19	34	8	3	1	19	3	.306
2010	Kinston	Carolina	2B	54	203	33	61	12	3	6	31	2	.300
2010	Akron	Eastern	2B	79	315	63	98	20	5	10	43	7	.311
2011	Columbus	Int.	2B	92	343	65	96	16	9	12	55	12	.280
2011	Cleveland a	A.L.	2B	36	136	24	37	9	1	7	19	5	.272
2012	Cleveland	A.L.	2B	152	591	86	152	22	4	14	76	31	.257
2013	Cleveland	A.L.	2B	149	564	86	160	36	4	17	84	30	.284
Major League Totals			3 Yrs.	337	1291	196	349	67	9	38	179	66	.270
	Wild Card Playoff												
2013	Cleveland	A.L.	2B	1	4	0	0	0	0	0	0	0	.000

a On disabled list from August 14 to September 6, 2011.

KONERKO, PAUL HENRY

Born, Providence, Rhode Island, March 5, 1976.
Bats Right. Throws Right. Height, 6 feet, 2 inches. Weight, 220 pounds.

Year	Club	Lea	Pos	G	AB	R	H	2B	3B	HR	RBI	SB	Avg
1994	Yakima	Northwest	C	67	257	25	74	15	2	6	58	1	.288
1995	San Berndno	California	C	118	448	77	124	21	1	19	77	3	.277
1996	San Antonio	Texas	1B	133	470	78	141	23	2	29	86	1	.300
1996	Albuquerque	P.C.	1B	4	14	2	6	0	0	1	2	0	.429
1997	Albuquerque	P.C.	3B-1B-2B	130	483	97	156	31	1	37	127	2	.323
1997	Los Angeles	N.L.	1B-3B	6	7	0	1	0	0	0	0	0	.143
1998	Albuquerque	P.C.	OF-1B-3B	24	87	16	33	10	0	6	26	0	.379
1998	Indianapols	Int.	3B	39	150	25	49	8	0	8	39	1	.327
1998	Los Angeles-Cinc. a-b	N.L.	1B-3B-OF	75	217	21	47	4	0	7	29	0	.217
1999	Chicago	A.L.	1B-3B	142	513	71	151	31	4	24	81	1	.294
2000	Chicago	A.L.	1B-3B	143	524	84	156	31	1	21	97	1	.298
2001	Chicago	A.L.	1B	156	582	92	164	35	0	32	99	1	.282
2002	Chicago	A.L.	1B	151	570	81	173	30	0	27	104	0	.304
2003	Chicago	A.L.	1B	137	444	49	104	19	0	18	65	0	.234
2004	Chicago	A.L.	1B	155	563	84	156	22	0	41	117	1	.277
2005	Chicago c	A.L.	1B	158	575	98	163	24	0	40	100	0	.283
2006	Chicago	A.L.	1B	152	566	97	177	30	0	35	113	1	.313
2007	Chicago	A.L.	1B	151	549	71	142	34	0	31	90	0	.259
2008	Charlotte	Int.	1B	4	11	3	5	2	0	0	3	0	.455
2008	Chicago d	A.L.	1B	122	438	59	105	19	1	22	62	2	.240
2009	Chicago	A.L.	1B	152	546	75	151	30	1	28	88	1	.277
2010	Chicago e	A.L.	1B	149	548	89	171	30	1	39	111	0	.312
2011	Chicago	A.L.	1B	149	543	69	163	25	0	31	105	1	.300
2012	Chicago f	A.L.	1B	144	533	66	159	22	0	26	75	0	.298
2013	Birmingham	Southern	1B	3	10	1	4	0	0	0	1	0	.400
2013	Chicago g-h	A.L.	1B	126	467	41	114	16	0	12	54	0	.244
Major League Totals			17 Yrs.	2268	8185	1147	2297	402	8	434	1390	9	.281
	Division Series												
2000	Chicago	A.L.	1B	3	9	1	0	0	0	0	0	0	.000
2005	Chicago	A.L.	1B	3	12	3	3	0	0	2	4	0	.250
2008	Chicago	A.L.	1B	4	16	3	5	0	0	2	2	0	.313

Year Club	Lea	Pos	G	AB	R	H	2B	3B	HR	RBI	SB	Avg
Division Series Totals			10	37	7	8	0	0	4	6	0	.216
Championship Series												
2005 Chicago	A.L.	1B	5	21	2	6	1	0	2	7	0	.286
World Series Record												
2005 Chicago	A.L.	1B	4	16	1	4	1	0	1	4	0	.250

a Traded to Cincinnati Reds with pitcher Dennis Reyes for pitcher Jeff Shaw, July 4, 1998.
b Traded to Chicago White Sox for outfielder Mike Cameron, November 11, 1998.
c Filed for free agency, October 27, 2005, re-signed with Chicago White Sox, November 30, 2005.
d On disabled list from June 15 to July 8, 2008.
e Filed for free agency, November 1, 2010, re-signed with Chicago White Sox, December 8, 2010.
f On disabled list from August 10 to August 17, 2012.
g On disabled list from July 3 to July 22, 2013.
h Filed for free agency, October 31, 2013, re-signed with Chicago White Sox, December 4, 2013.

KOZMA, PETER MICHAEL (PETE)

Born, Tulsa, Oklahoma, April 11, 1988.
Bats Right. Throws Right. Height, 6 feet. Weight, 190 pounds.

Year Club	Lea	Pos	G	AB	R	H	2B	3B	HR	RBI	SB	Avg
2007 Cardinals	Gulf Coast	SS-OF	4	13	4	2	0	0	0	0	0	.154
2007 Johnson City	Appal.	SS	30	106	16	28	8	0	2	9	3	.264
2007 Batavia	N.Y.-Penn.	SS	8	27	1	4	0	1	0	2	1	.148
2008 Quad Cities	Midwest	SS-3B	99	377	58	107	20	4	5	40	12	.284
2008 Palm Beach	Fla.St.	SS	24	77	4	10	4	0	0	10	0	.130
2009 Palm Beach	Fla.St.	SS	18	73	8	23	5	0	0	8	1	.315
2009 Springfield	Texas	SS	113	407	52	88	15	3	6	37	4	.216
2010 Springfield	Texas	SS	132	503	69	122	28	2	13	72	13	.243
2011 St. Louis	N.L.	2B-SS-3B	16	17	2	3	1	0	0	1	0	.176
2011 Memphis	P.C.	SS-2B-3B	112	398	48	85	17	2	3	47	2	.214
2012 Memphis	P.C.	2B-SS	131	448	61	104	16	3	11	63	7	.232
2012 St. Louis	N.L.	SS-2B	26	72	11	24	5	3	2	14	2	.333
2013 St. Louis	N.L.	SS-OF	143	410	44	89	20	0	1	35	3	.217
Major League Totals		3 Yrs.	185	499	57	116	26	3	3	50	5	.232
Wild Card Playoff												
2012 St. Louis	N.L.	SS	1	4	1	0	0	0	0	0	0	.000
Division Series												
2012 St. Louis	N.L.	SS	5	16	4	4	1	0	1	5	0	.250
2013 St. Louis	N.L.	SS	4	10	1	4	1	0	0	1	1	.400
Division Series Totals			9	26	5	8	2	0	1	6	1	.308
Championship Series												
2012 St. Louis	N.L.	SS	7	22	3	5	1	0	0	2	1	.227
2013 St. Louis	N.L.	SS	6	15	1	1	0	0	0	1	0	.067
Championship Series Totals			13	37	4	6	1	0	0	3	1	.162
World Series Record												
2013 St. Louis	N.L.	SS	4	10	1	0	0	0	0	0	1	.000

KUBEL, JASON JAMES

Born, Belle Fourche, South Dakota, May 25, 1982.
Bats Left. Throws Right. Height, 5 feet, 11 inches. Weight, 200 pounds.

Year Club	Lea	Pos	G	AB	R	H	2B	3B	HR	RBI	SB	Avg
2000 Twins	Gulf Coast	OF	23	78	17	22	3	2	0	13	0	.282
2001 Twins	Gulf Coast	OF	37	124	14	41	10	4	1	30	3	.331
2002 Quad Cities	Midwest	OF	115	424	60	136	26	4	17	69	3	.321
2003 Fort Myers	Fla.St.	OF	116	420	56	125	20	4	5	82	4	.298
2004 New Britain	Eastern	OF	37	138	25	52	14	4	6	29	0	.377
2004 Rochester	Int.	OF	90	350	71	120	28	0	16	71	16	.343
2004 Minnesota	A.L.	OF	23	60	10	18	2	0	2	7	1	.300
2005 Minnesota a	A.L.	INJURED—Did Not Play										
2006 Rochester	Int.	OF	30	120	18	34	7	2	4	22	2	.283
2006 Minnesota	A.L.	OF	73	220	23	53	8	0	8	26	2	.241
2007 Minnesota	A.L.	OF	128	418	49	114	31	2	13	65	5	.273
2008 Minnesota	A.L.	DH-OF	141	463	74	126	22	5	20	78	0	.272
2009 Minnesota	A.L.	DH-OF	146	514	73	154	35	2	28	103	1	.300
2010 Minnesota	A.L.	OF	143	518	68	129	23	3	21	92	0	.249
2011 Fort Myers	Fla.St.	OF	2	3	0	0	0	0	0	1	0	.000
2011 Rochester	Int.	OF	5	18	3	6	1	0	1	2	0	.333
2011 Minnesota b-c	A.L.	OF	99	366	37	100	21	1	12	58	1	.273
2012 Arizona	N.L.	OF	141	506	75	128	30	4	30	90	1	.253

Year	Club	Lea	Pos	G	AB	R	H	2B	3B	HR	RBI	SB	Avg
2013	Arizona d	N.L.	OF	89	241	21	53	8	1	5	32	0	.220
2013	Cleveland e-f	A.L.	OF	8	18	0	3	1	0	0	0	0	.167
Major League Totals			9 Yrs.	991	3324	430	878	181	18	139	551	11	.264
	Division Series												
2004	Minnesota	A.L.	DH	2	7	0	1	1	0	0	0	0	.143
2009	Minnesota	A.L.	OF-DH	3	14	0	1	0	0	0	0	0	.071
2010	Minnesota	A.L.	OF	3	8	0	0	0	0	0	0	0	.000
Division Series Totals				8	29	0	2	1	0	0	0	0	.069

a On disabled list from March 15 to October 14, 2005.
b On disabled list from May 31 to July 22, 2011.
c Filed for free agency, October 30, 2011. Signed with Arizona Diamondbacks, December 20, 2011.
d On disabled list from April 13 to April 28, 2013.
e Traded to Cleveland Indians for player to be named later, August 30, 2013. Arizona Diamondbacks received pitcher Matt Langwell to complete trade, September 1, 2013.
f Filed for free agency, October 31, 2013. Signed with Minnesota Twins organization, December 13, 2013.

LAGARES, JUAN OSVALDO

Born, Constanza, Dominican Republic, March 17, 1989.
Bats Right. Throws Right. Height, 6 feet, 1 inch. Weight, 175 pounds.

Year	Club	Lea	Pos	G	AB	R	H	2B	3B	HR	RBI	SB	Avg
2007	Savannah	So.Atl.	SS	83	281	26	59	12	6	2	16	11	.210
2008	Brooklyn	N.Y.-Penn.	SS-3B	19	72	8	18	7	0	1	7	1	.250
2008	Savannah	So.Atl.	SS	46	181	14	46	9	0	2	17	3	.254
2009	Mets	Gulf Coast	OF	6	24	1	5	1	0	0	1	1	.208
2009	Savannah	So.Atl.	OF-SS-3B	47	168	23	46	6	2	0	13	9	.274
2010	Savannah	So.Atl.	OF	67	290	42	87	13	9	5	39	18	.300
2010	St. Lucie	Fla.St.	OF	33	133	16	31	5	0	2	16	7	.233
2011	St. Lucie	Fla.St.	OF	82	308	51	104	15	6	7	49	5	.338
2011	Binghamton	Eastern	OF	38	162	21	60	11	3	2	22	10	.370
2012	Binghamton	Eastern	OF	130	499	69	141	29	6	4	48	21	.283
2013	Las Vegas	P.C.	OF	17	78	13	27	3	2	3	9	2	.346
2013	New York	N.L.	OF	121	392	35	95	21	5	4	34	6	.242

LAKE, JUNIOR OSVALDO

Born, San Pedro de Macoris, Dominican Republic, March 27, 1990.
Bats Right. Throws Right. Height, 6 feet, 3 inches. Weight, 215 pounds.

Year	Club	Lea	Pos	G	AB	R	H	2B	3B	HR	RBI	SB	Avg
2008	Cubs	Arizona	SS-3B-2B	47	168	24	48	4	6	2	23	12	.286
2009	Peoria	Midwest	SS-2B-3B	131	463	71	115	19	7	7	42	10	.248
2010	Daytona	Fla.St.	SS-3B	120	394	56	104	18	4	9	46	13	.264
2011	Daytona	Fla.St.	SS	49	203	39	64	11	4	6	34	19	.315
2011	Tennessee	Southern	SS-3B	67	242	41	60	10	2	6	17	19	.248
2012	Tennessee	Southern	SS-3B	103	405	56	113	26	3	10	50	21	.279
2013	Iowa	P.C.	3B-OF	40	156	30	46	10	2	4	18	14	.295
2013	Chicago	N.L.	OF	64	236	26	67	16	0	6	16	4	.284

LA ROCHE, DAVID ADAM (ADAM)

Born, Orange Co., California, November 6, 1979.
Bats Left. Throws Left. Height, 6 feet, 3 inches. Weight, 200 pounds.

Year	Club	Lea	Pos	G	AB	R	H	2B	3B	HR	RBI	SB	Avg
2000	Danville	Appal.	1B	56	201	38	62	13	3	7	45	4	.308
2001	Myrtle Beach	Carolina	1B-OF	126	471	49	118	31	0	7	47	10	.251
2002	Myrtle Beach	Carolina	1B	69	250	30	84	17	0	9	53	0	.336
2002	Greenville	Southern	1B	45	173	17	50	9	0	4	19	1	.289
2003	Greenville	Southern	1B	61	219	42	62	12	1	12	37	1	.283
2003	Richmond	Int.	1B	72	264	33	78	21	0	8	35	1	.295
2004	Richmond	Int.	1B	4	11	1	2	0	0	1	2	0	.182
2004	Atlanta a	N.L.	1B	110	324	45	90	27	1	13	45	0	.278
2005	Atlanta	N.L.	1B	141	451	53	117	28	0	20	78	0	.259
2006	Atlanta b	N.L.	1B	149	492	89	140	38	1	32	90	0	.285
2007	Pittsburgh	N.L.	1B	152	563	71	153	42	0	21	88	1	.272
2008	Hickory	So.Atl.	1B	3	10	2	6	1	0	1	4	0	.600
2008	Pittsburgh c	N.L.	1B	136	492	66	133	32	3	25	85	1	.270
2009	Boston	A.L.	1B	6	19	2	5	2	0	1	3	0	.263
2009	Pittsburgh-Atlanta d-e-f	N.L.	1B	144	536	76	149	36	2	24	80	2	.278
2010	Arizona g	N.L.	1B	151	560	75	146	37	2	25	100	0	.261

Year	Club	Lea	Pos	G	AB	R	H	2B	3B	HR	RBI	SB	Avg
2011	Washington h	N.L.	1B	43	151	15	26	4	0	3	15	1	.172
2012	Washington i	N.L.	1B	154	571	76	155	35	1	33	100	1	.271
2013	Washington	N.L.	1B	152	511	70	121	19	3	20	62	4	.237
Major League Totals			10 Yrs.	1338	4670	638	1235	300	13	217	746	10	.264
	Division Series												
2004	Atlanta	N.L.	1B	5	17	1	4	1	0	1	4	0	.235
2005	Atlanta	N.L.	1B	3	8	2	4	1	0	1	6	0	.500
2012	Washington	N.L.	1B	5	17	4	3	0	0	2	2	0	.176
Division Series Totals				13	42	7	11	2	0	4	12	0	.262

a On disabled list from May 29 to July 2, 2004.
b Traded to Pittsburgh Pirates with outfielder Jamie Romak for pitcher Mike Gonzalez and infielder Brent Lillibridge, January 17, 2007.
c On disabled list from July 28 to August 14, 2008.
d Traded to Boston Red Sox for infielder Argenis Diaz and pitcher Hunter Strickland, July 22, 2009.
e Traded to Atlanta Braves for infielder Casey Kotchman, July 31, 2009.
f Filed for free agency, November 5, 2009. Signed with Arizona Diamondbacks, January 15, 2010.
g Filed for free agency, November 2, 2010. Signed with Washington Nationals, January 7, 2011.
h On disabled list from May 22 to October 31, 2011.
i Filed for free agency, November 3, 2012, re-signed with Washington Nationals, January 8, 2013.

LAWRIE, BRETT R.

Born, Langley, British Columbia, Canada, January 18, 1990.
Bats Right. Throws Right. Height, 6 feet. Weight, 215 pounds.

Year	Club	Lea	Pos	G	AB	R	H	2B	3B	HR	RBI	SB	Avg
2009	Wisconsin	Midwest	2B	105	372	48	102	18	5	13	65	19	.274
2009	Huntsville	Southern	2B	13	52	6	14	0	1	0	0	0	.269
2010	Huntsville a	Southern	2B	135	554	90	158	36	16	8	63	30	.285
2011	Dunedin	Fla.St.	3B	4	8	0	1	0	0	0	1	0	.125
2011	Las Vegas	P.C.	3B	69	292	64	103	24	6	18	61	13	.353
2011	Toronto b	A.L.	3B	43	150	26	44	8	4	9	25	7	.293
2012	Blue Jays	Gulf Coast	3B	1	1	0	0	0	0	0	0	0	.000
2012	Dunedin	Fla.St.	3B	1	3	0	0	0	0	0	0	0	.000
2012	Toronto c	A.L.	3B-SS	125	494	73	135	26	3	11	48	13	.273
2013	Lansing	Midwest	3B	2	6	1	0	0	0	0	0	0	.000
2013	Dunedin	Fla.St.	2B-3B	4	12	1	6	1	1	0	2	0	.500
2013	New Hampshire	Eastern	3B	3	9	3	3	0	0	0	0	0	.333
2013	Buffalo	Int.	2B	3	12	2	2	0	0	1	3	1	.167
2013	Toronto d	A.L.	3B-2B	107	401	41	102	18	3	11	46	9	.254
Major League Totals			3 Yrs.	275	1045	140	281	52	10	31	119	29	.269

a Traded by Milwaukee Brewers to Toronto Blue Jays for pitcher Shaun Marcum, December 6, 2010.
b On disabled list from September 22 to September 29, 2011.
c On disabled list from August 4 to September 7, 2012.
d On disabled list from March 22 to April 16 and May 28 to July 13, 2013.

LE MAHIEU, DAVID JOHN (D.J.)

Born, Visalia, California, July 13, 1988.
Bats Right. Throws Right. Height, 6 feet, 4 inches. Weight, 205 pounds.

Year	Club	Lea	Pos	G	AB	R	H	2B	3B	HR	RBI	SB	Avg
2009	Cubs	Arizona	2B-SS	3	12	2	5	0	1	0	4	1	.417
2009	Peoria	Midwest	SS-2B	38	152	19	48	4	2	0	30	2	.316
2010	Daytona	Fla.St.	2B-3B-SS	135	554	63	174	24	5	2	73	15	.314
2011	Tennessee	Southern	2B-3B	50	187	32	67	15	2	2	27	4	.358
2011	Iowa	P.C.	3B-2B-SS	58	227	23	65	7	1	3	23	5	.286
2011	Chicago a	N.L.	2B-3B-1B	37	60	3	15	2	0	0	4	0	.250
2012	Colorado Springs	P.C.	2B-3B-SS	61	255	33	80	14	2	1	31	13	.314
2012	Colorado	N.L.	2B-3B-SS-1B	81	229	26	68	12	4	2	22	1	.297
2013	Colorado Springs	P.C.	SS-2B-3B	33	143	34	52	8	5	1	22	8	.364
2013	Colorado	N.L.	2B-3B-1B-SS	109	404	39	113	21	3	2	28	18	.280
Major League Totals			3 Yrs.	227	693	68	196	35	7	4	54	19	.283

a Traded to Colorado Rockies with outfielder Tyler Colvin for pitcher Casey Weathers and infielder Ian Stewart, December 8, 2011.

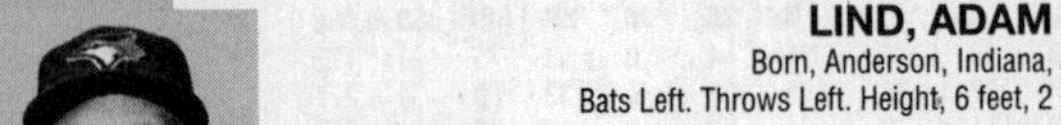

LIND, ADAM ALAN

Born, Anderson, Indiana, July 17, 1983.
Bats Left. Throws Left. Height, 6 feet, 2 inches. Weight, 195 pounds.

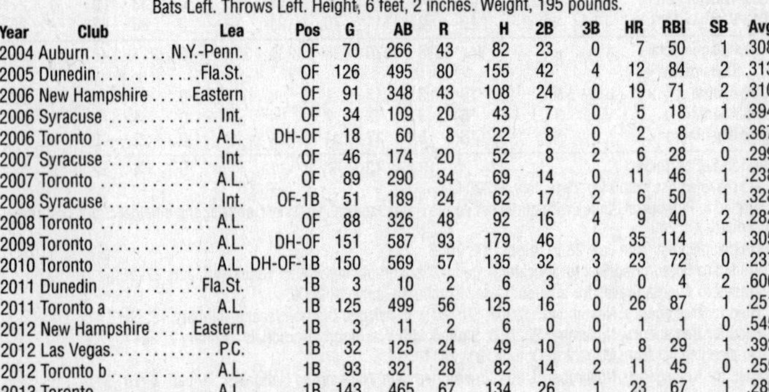

Year	Club	Lea	Pos	G	AB	R	H	2B	3B	HR	RBI	SB	Avg
2004	Auburn	N.Y.-Penn.	OF	70	266	43	82	23	0	7	50	1	.308
2005	Dunedin	Fla.St.	OF	126	495	80	155	42	4	12	84	2	.313
2006	New Hampshire	Eastern	OF	91	348	43	108	24	0	19	71	2	.310
2006	Syracuse	Int.	OF	34	109	20	43	7	0	5	18	1	.394
2006	Toronto	A.L.	DH-OF	18	60	8	22	8	0	2	8	0	.367
2007	Syracuse	Int.	OF	46	174	20	52	8	2	6	28	0	.299
2007	Toronto	A.L.	OF	89	290	34	69	14	0	11	46	1	.238
2008	Syracuse	Int.	OF-1B	51	189	24	62	17	2	6	50	1	.328
2008	Toronto	A.L.	OF	88	326	48	92	16	4	9	40	2	.282
2009	Toronto	A.L.	DH-OF	151	587	93	179	46	0	35	114	1	.305
2010	Toronto	A.L.	DH-OF-1B	150	569	57	135	32	3	23	72	0	.237
2011	Dunedin	Fla.St.	1B	3	10	2	6	3	0	0	4	2	.600
2011	Toronto a	A.L.	1B	125	499	56	125	16	0	26	87	1	.251
2012	New Hampshire	Eastern	1B	3	11	2	6	0	0	1	1	0	.545
2012	Las Vegas	P.C.	1B	32	125	24	49	10	0	8	29	1	.392
2012	Toronto b	A.L.	1B	93	321	28	82	14	2	11	45	0	.255
2013	Toronto	A.L.	1B	143	465	67	134	26	1	23	67	1	.288
Major League Totals			8 Yrs.	857	3117	391	838	172	10	140	479	6	.269

a On disabled list from May 8 to June 4, 2011.
b On disabled list from July 26 to August 26, 2012.

LOBATON, JOSE MANUEL

Born, Acarigua, Venezuela, October 21, 1984.
Bats Both. Throws Right. Height, 6 feet. Weight, 210 pounds.

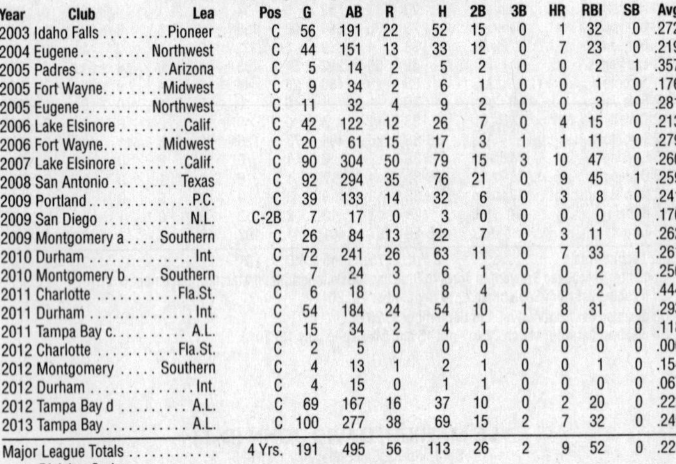

Year	Club	Lea	Pos	G	AB	R	H	2B	3B	HR	RBI	SB	Avg
2003	Idaho Falls	Pioneer	C	56	191	22	52	15	0	1	32	0	.272
2004	Eugene	Northwest	C	44	151	13	33	12	0	7	23	0	.219
2005	Padres	Arizona	C	5	14	2	5	2	0	0	2	1	.357
2005	Fort Wayne	Midwest	C	9	34	2	6	1	0	0	1	0	.176
2005	Eugene	Northwest	C	11	32	4	9	2	0	0	3	0	.281
2006	Lake Elsinore	Calif.	C	42	122	12	26	7	0	4	15	0	.213
2006	Fort Wayne	Midwest	C	20	61	15	17	3	1	1	11	0	.279
2007	Lake Elsinore	Calif.	C	90	304	50	79	15	3	10	47	0	.260
2008	San Antonio	Texas	C	92	294	35	76	21	0	9	45	1	.259
2009	Portland	P.C.	C	39	133	14	32	6	0	3	8	0	.241
2009	San Diego	N.L.	C-2B	7	17	0	3	0	0	0	0	0	.176
2009	Montgomery a	Southern	C	26	84	13	22	7	0	3	11	0	.262
2010	Durham	Int.	C	72	241	26	63	11	0	7	33	1	.261
2010	Montgomery b	Southern	C	7	24	3	6	1	0	0	2	0	.250
2011	Charlotte	Fla.St.	C	6	18	0	8	4	0	0	2	0	.444
2011	Durham	Int.	C	54	184	24	54	10	1	8	31	0	.293
2011	Tampa Bay c	A.L.	C	15	34	2	4	1	0	0	0	0	.118
2012	Charlotte	Fla.St.	C	2	5	0	0	0	0	0	0	0	.000
2012	Montgomery	Southern	C	4	13	1	2	1	0	0	1	0	.154
2012	Durham	Int.	C	4	15	0	1	1	0	0	0	0	.067
2012	Tampa Bay d	A.L.	C	69	167	16	37	10	0	2	20	0	.222
2013	Tampa Bay	A.L.	C	100	277	38	69	15	2	7	32	0	.249
Major League Totals			4 Yrs.	191	495	56	113	26	2	9	52	0	.228
	Division Series												
2013	Tampa Bay	A.L.	C	4	7	1	2	0	0	1	1	0	.286

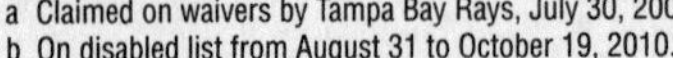

a Claimed on waivers by Tampa Bay Rays, July 30, 2009.
b On disabled list from August 31 to October 19, 2010.
c On disabled list from July 18 to September 2, 2011.
d On disabled list from April 13 to May 28, 2012.

LOMBARDOZZI, STEPHEN PAUL JR. (STEVE)

Born, Fulton, Maryland, September 20, 1988.
Bats Both. Throws Right. Height, 6 feet. Weight, 195 pounds.

Year	Club	Lea	Pos	G	AB	R	H	2B	3B	HR	RBI	SB	Avg
2008	Nationals	Gulf Coast	2B-SS	48	152	23	43	4	1	0	24	4	.283
2009	Hagerstown	So.Atl.	2B-SS	128	496	90	147	26	7	3	58	16	.296
2010	Potomac	Carolina	2B	110	440	71	129	30	9	1	38	20	.293
2010	Harrisburg	Eastern	2B	27	105	19	31	5	2	5	11	4	.295
2011	Harrisburg	Eastern	2B-SS	65	262	40	81	12	7	4	23	16	.309

Year Club	Lea	Pos	G	AB	R	H	2B	3B	HR	RBI	SB	Avg
2011 Syracuse	Int.	2B-SS-3B	69	294	46	91	13	2	4	29	14	.310
2011 Washington	N.L.	2B-3B-SS	13	31	3	6	1	0	0	1	0	.194
2012 Washington	N.L.	2B-OF-3B-SS	126	384	40	105	16	3	3	27	5	.273
2013 Washington a......	N.L.	2B-OF-3B	118	290	25	75	15	1	2	22	4	.259
Major League Totals		3 Yrs.	257	705	68	186	32	4	5	50	9	.264
Division Series												
2012 Washington	N.L.	PH	3	3	0	1	0	0	0	0	0	.333

a Traded to Detroit Tigers with pitcher Ian Krol and pitcher Robbie Ray for pitcher Doug Fister, December 2, 2013.

LONEY, JAMES ANTHONY

Born, Houston, Texas, May 7, 1984.
Bats Left. Throws Left. Height, 6 feet, 3 inches. Weight, 220 pounds.

Year Club	Lea	Pos	G	AB	R	H	2B	3B	HR	RBI	SB	Avg
2002 Vero Beach..........	Fla.St.	1B	17	67	6	20	6	0	0	5	0	.299
2002 Great Falls	Pioneer	1B	47	170	33	63	22	3	5	30	5	.371
2003 Vero Beach..........	Fla.St.	1B-OF	125	468	64	129	31	3	7	46	9	.276
2004 Jacksonville	Southern	1B	104	395	39	94	19	2	4	35	6	.238
2005 Jacksonville	Southern	1B-OF	138	504	74	143	31	2	11	65	1	.284
2006 Las Vegas.............	P.C.	1B-OF	98	366	64	139	33	2	8	67	9	.380
2006 Los Angeles	N.L.	1B-OF	48	102	20	29	6	5	4	18	1	.284
2007 Las Vegas.............	P.C.	1B-OF	58	233	28	65	19	1	1	32	2	.279
2007 Los Angeles	N.L.	1B-OF	96	344	41	114	18	4	15	67	0	.331
2008 Los Angeles	N.L.	1B	161	595	66	172	35	6	13	90	7	.289
2009 Los Angeles	N.L.	1B	158	576	73	162	25	2	13	90	7	.281
2010 Los Angeles	N.L.	1B	161	588	67	157	41	2	10	88	10	.267
2011 Los Angeles	N.L.	1B	158	531	56	153	30	1	12	65	4	.288
2012 Los Angeles	N.L.	1B	114	334	32	85	18	0	4	33	0	.254
2012 Boston a-b	A.L.	1B	30	100	5	23	2	0	2	8	0	.230
2013 Tampa Bay c..........	A.L.	1B	158	549	54	164	33	0	13	75	3	.299
Major League Totals		8 Yrs.	1084	3719	414	1059	208	20	86	534	32	.285
Wild Card Playoff												
2013 Tampa Bay	A.L.	1B	1	4	1	1	0	0	0	0	0	.250
Division Series												
2006 Los Angeles	N.L.	1B	1	4	0	3	0	0	0	3	0	.750
2008 Los Angeles	N.L.	1B	3	14	2	3	1	0	1	6	0	.214
2009 Los Angeles	N.L.	1B	3	12	0	3	0	0	0	0	0	.250
2013 Tampa Bay	A.L.	1B	4	12	0	5	2	0	0	2	0	.417
Division Series Totals			11	42	2	14	3	0	1	11	0	.333
Championship Series												
2008 Los Angeles	N.L.	1B	5	16	0	7	2	0	0	2	0	.438
2009 Los Angeles	N.L.	1B	5	17	3	6	0	0	2	3	0	.353
Championship Series Totals			10	33	3	13	2	0	2	5	0	.394

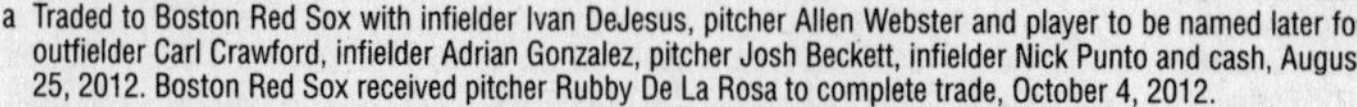

a Traded to Boston Red Sox with infielder Ivan DeJesus, pitcher Allen Webster and player to be named later for outfielder Carl Crawford, infielder Adrian Gonzalez, pitcher Josh Beckett, infielder Nick Punto and cash, August 25, 2012. Boston Red Sox received pitcher Rubby De La Rosa to complete trade, October 4, 2012.

b Filed for free agency, November 3, 2012. Signed with Tampa Bay Rays, December 6, 2012.

c Filed for free agency, October 31, 2013, re-signed with Tampa Bay Rays, January 3, 2014.

LONGORIA, EVAN MICHAEL

Born, Downey, California, October 7, 1985.
Bats Right. Throws Right. Height, 6 feet, 2 inches. Weight, 210 pounds.

Year Club	Lea	Pos	G	AB	R	H	2B	3B	HR	RBI	SB	Avg
2006 Visalia	Calif.	3B	28	110	22	36	8	0	8	28	1	.327
2006 Hudson Valley ...	N.Y.-Penn.	3B	8	33	5	14	1	1	4	11	1	.424
2006 Montgomery	Southern	3B	26	105	14	28	5	0	6	19	2	.267
2007 Durham	Int.	3B	31	104	19	28	8	0	5	19	0	.269
2007 Montgomery	Southern	3B	105	381	78	117	21	0	21	76	4	.307
2008 Durham	Int.	3B	7	25	2	5	0	0	0	1	0	.200
2008 Tampa Bay a-b........	A.L.	3B-SS	122	448	67	122	31	2	27	85	7	.272
2009 Tampa Bay	A.L.	3B	157	584	100	164	44	0	33	113	9	.281
2010 Tampa Bay	A.L.	3B	151	574	96	169	46	5	22	104	15	.294
2011 Montgomery	Southern	3B	4	15	5	4	0	0	3	3	0	.267
2011 Tampa Bay c..........	A.L.	3B	133	483	78	118	26	1	31	99	3	.244
2012 Durham	Int.	DH	10	30	0	6	0	0	0	3	0	.200
2012 Tampa Bay d	A.L.	3B	74	273	39	79	14	0	17	55	2	.289
2013 Tampa Bay	A.L.	3B	160	614	91	165	39	3	32	88	1	.269
Major League Totals		6 Yrs.	797	2976	471	817	200	11	162	544	37	.275

Year	Club	Lea	Pos	G	AB	R	H	2B	3B	HR	RBI	SB	Avg
	Wild Card Playoff												
2013	Tampa Bay	A.L.	3B	1	4	1	1	0	0	0	0	0	.250
	Division Series												
2008	Tampa Bay	A.L.	3B	4	15	2	4	0	0	2	3	1	.267
2010	Tampa Bay	A.L.	3B	5	20	2	4	2	0	1	2	0	.200
2011	Tampa Bay	A.L.	3B	4	16	2	3	0	0	1	3	0	.188
2013	Tampa Bay	A.L.	3B	4	13	1	2	0	0	1	3	0	.154
Division Series Totals				17	64	7	13	2	0	5	11	1	.203
	Championship Series												
2008	Tampa Bay	A.L.	3B	7	27	8	7	3	0	4	8	0	.259
	World Series Record												
2008	Tampa Bay	A.L.	3B	5	20	0	1	0	0	0	2	0	.050

a On disabled list from August 8 to September 6, 2008.
b Selected Rookie of the Year in American League for 2008.
c On disabled list from April 3 to May 3, 2011.
d On disabled list from May 1 to August 7, 2012.

LOUGH, DAVID DENNIS

Born, Akron, Ohio, January 20, 1986.
Bats Left. Throws Left. Height, 5 feet, 11 inches. Weight, 180 pounds.

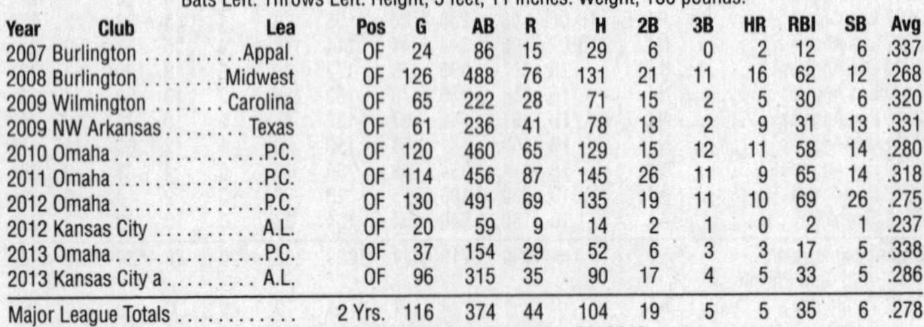

Year	Club	Lea	Pos	G	AB	R	H	2B	3B	HR	RBI	SB	Avg
2007	Burlington	Appal.	OF	24	86	15	29	6	0	2	12	6	.337
2008	Burlington	Midwest	OF	126	488	76	131	21	11	16	62	12	.268
2009	Wilmington	Carolina	OF	65	222	28	71	15	2	5	30	6	.320
2009	NW Arkansas	Texas	OF	61	236	41	78	13	2	9	31	13	.331
2010	Omaha	P.C.	OF	120	460	65	129	15	12	11	58	14	.280
2011	Omaha	P.C.	OF	114	456	87	145	26	11	9	65	14	.318
2012	Omaha	P.C.	OF	130	491	69	135	19	11	10	69	26	.275
2012	Kansas City	A.L.	OF	20	59	9	14	2	1	0	2	1	.237
2013	Omaha	P.C.	OF	37	154	29	52	6	3	3	17	5	.338
2013	Kansas City a	A.L.	OF	96	315	35	90	17	4	5	33	5	.286
Major League Totals			2 Yrs.	116	374	44	104	19	5	5	35	6	.278

a Traded to Baltimore Orioles for infielder Danny Valencia, December 18, 2013.

LOWRIE, JED CARLSON

Born, Salem, Oregon, April 17, 1984.
Bats Both. Throws Right. Height, 6 feet. Weight, 180 pounds.

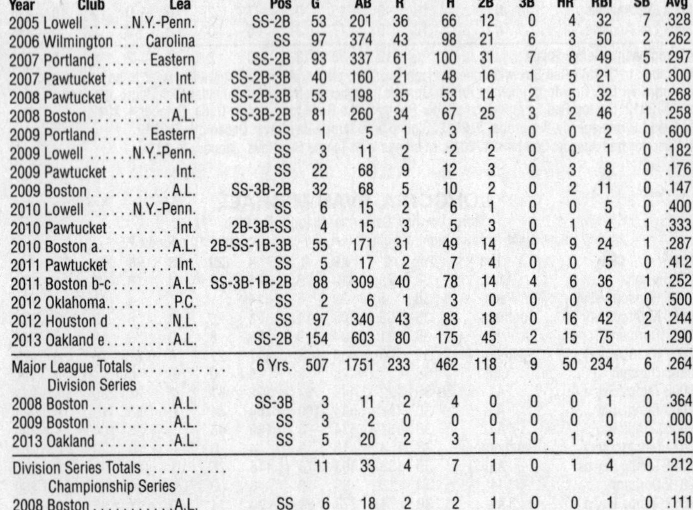

Year	Club	Lea	Pos	G	AB	R	H	2B	3B	HR	RBI	SB	Avg
2005	Lowell	N.Y.-Penn.	SS-2B	53	201	36	66	12	0	4	32	7	.328
2006	Wilmington	Carolina	SS	97	374	43	98	21	6	3	50	2	.262
2007	Portland	Eastern	SS-2B	93	337	61	100	31	7	8	49	5	.297
2007	Pawtucket	Int.	SS-2B-3B	40	160	21	48	16	1	5	21	0	.300
2008	Pawtucket	Int.	SS-2B-3B	53	198	35	53	14	2	5	32	1	.268
2008	Boston	A.L.	SS-3B-2B	81	260	34	67	25	3	2	46	1	.258
2009	Portland	Eastern	SS	1	5	1	3	1	0	0	2	0	.600
2009	Lowell	N.Y.-Penn.	SS	3	11	2	2	2	0	0	1	0	.182
2009	Pawtucket	Int.	SS	22	68	9	12	3	0	3	8	0	.176
2009	Boston	A.L.	SS-3B-2B	32	68	5	10	2	0	2	11	0	.147
2010	Lowell	N.Y.-Penn.	SS	6	15	2	6	1	0	0	5	0	.400
2010	Pawtucket	Int.	2B-3B-SS	4	15	3	5	3	0	1	4	1	.333
2010	Boston a	A.L.	2B-SS-1B-3B	55	171	31	49	14	0	9	24	1	.287
2011	Pawtucket	Int.	SS	5	17	2	7	4	0	0	5	0	.412
2011	Boston b-c	A.L.	SS-3B-1B-2B	88	309	40	78	14	4	6	36	1	.252
2012	Oklahoma	P.C.	SS	2	6	1	3	0	0	0	3	0	.500
2012	Houston d	N.L.	SS	97	340	43	83	18	0	16	42	2	.244
2013	Oakland e	A.L.	SS-2B	154	603	80	175	45	2	15	75	1	.290
Major League Totals			6 Yrs.	507	1751	233	462	118	9	50	234	6	.264
	Division Series												
2008	Boston	A.L.	SS-3B	3	11	2	4	0	0	0	1	0	.364
2009	Boston	A.L.	SS	3	2	0	0	0	0	0	0	0	.000
2013	Oakland	A.L.	SS	5	20	2	3	1	0	1	3	0	.150
Division Series Totals				11	33	4	7	1	0	1	4	0	.212
	Championship Series												
2008	Boston	A.L.	SS	6	18	2	2	1	0	0	1	0	.111

a On disabled list from March 26 to July 21, 2010.
b On disabled list from June 17 to August 8, 2011.

c Traded to Houston Astros with pitcher Kyle Weiland for pitcher Mark Melancon, December 14, 2011.
d On disabled list from March 29 to April 12 and July 15 to September 11, 2012.
e Traded to Oakland Athletics with pitcher Franklin Rodriguez for infielder Chris Carter, pitcher Brad Peacock and catcher Max Stassi, February 4, 2013.

LUCAS, EDWARD LEE (ED)

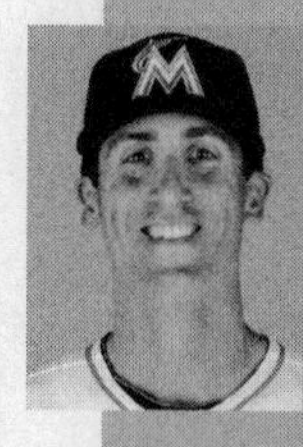

Born, Grand Rapids, Michigan, May 21, 1982.
Bats Right. Throws Right. Height, 6 feet, 3 inches. Weight, 210 pounds.

Year	Club	Lea	Pos	G	AB	R	H	2B	3B	HR	RBI	SB	Avg
2004	Idaho Falls	Pioneer	SS	41	154	30	48	6	1	0	29	7	.312
2004	Burlington	Midwest	3B-SS	24	89	12	18	5	1	0	10	2	.202
2005	Burlington	Midwest	3B-SS-1B-OF	113	425	52	124	12	4	1	36	29	.292
2006	High Desert	Calif.	3B-1B	124	455	71	128	26	4	8	66	19	.281
2007	Wichita	Texas	3B-1B	34	125	19	35	6	1	3	17	2	.280
2008	NW Arkansas	Texas	3B-OF-1B-2B	79	270	38	82	10	4	4	30	14	.304
2008	Omaha	P.C.	3B	16	47	7	6	0	0	0	0	0	.128
2009	NW Arkansas	Texas	3B-OF-1B-2B	103	355	61	103	22	2	10	58	18	.290
2009	Omaha	P.C.	OF	5	8	1	1	0	0	0	1	0	.125
2010	Omaha a	P.C.	SS-3B-2B-OF	99	352	52	108	20	1	13	50	7	.307
2011	Mississippi	Southern	SS-1B	42	159	32	43	6	0	7	26	0	.270
2011	Gwinnett b	Int.	2B-3B-SS-OF	81	262	25	57	14	1	3	29	4	.218
2012	Salt Lake c	P.C.	SS-2B-OF	118	412	61	108	20	2	12	52	5	.262
2013	New Orleans	P.C.	2B-SS-3B	46	181	26	55	12	0	5	14	2	.304
2013	Miami	N.L.	3B-1B-2B-SS	94	351	43	90	14	1	4	28	1	.256

a Filed for free agency from Kansas City Royals, November 6, 2010. Signed with Atlanta Braves organization, November 19, 2010.
b Filed for free agency, November 2, 2011. Signed with Los Angeles Angels organization, January 18, 2012.
c Filed for free agency, November 3, 2012. Signed with Miami Marlins organization, December 10, 2012.

LUCROY, JONATHAN CHARLES

Born, Eustis, Pennsylvania, June 13, 1986.
Bats Right. Throws Right. Height, 6 feet. Weight, 195 pounds.

Year	Club	Lea	Pos	G	AB	R	H	2B	3B	HR	RBI	SB	Avg
2007	Helena	Pioneer	C	61	234	35	80	18	2	4	39	0	.342
2008	Brevard County	Fla.St.	C	64	236	31	69	12	1	10	44	1	.292
2008	West Tenn	So.Atl.	C	65	239	45	74	16	1	10	33	8	.310
2009	Huntsville	Southern	C	125	419	61	112	32	2	9	66	1	.267
2010	Huntsville	Southern	C	10	42	8	19	3	0	0	5	0	.452
2010	Nashville	P.C.	C	21	80	8	19	4	0	2	11	0	.237
2010	Milwaukee	N.L.	C	75	277	24	70	9	0	4	26	4	.253
2011	Huntsville	Southern	C	4	11	3	3	1	0	0	4	1	.273
2011	Milwaukee a	N.L.	C	136	430	45	114	16	1	12	59	2	.265
2012	Wisconsin	Midwest	C	4	12	0	4	1	0	0	2	1	.333
2012	Nashville	P.C.	C	2	7	4	3	0	0	0	1	1	.429
2012	Milwaukee b	N.L.	C	96	316	46	101	17	4	12	58	4	.320
2013	Milwaukee	N.L.	C-1B	147	521	59	146	25	6	18	82	9	.280
Major League Totals			4 Yrs.	454	1544	174	431	67	11	46	225	19	.279
	Division Series												
2011	Milwaukee	N.L.	C	4	15	1	3	0	0	0	2	0	.200
	Championship Series												
2011	Milwaukee	N.L.	C	6	17	2	5	1	0	1	3	0	.294

a On disabled list from March 22 to April 11, 2011.
b On disabled list from May 28 to July 26, 2012.

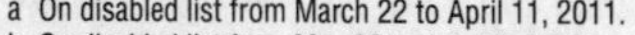

LUDWICK, RYAN ANDREW

Born, Satellite Beach, Florida, July 13, 1978.
Bats Right. Throws Left. Height, 6 feet, 3 inches. Weight, 220 pounds.

Year	Club	Lea	Pos	G	AB	R	H	2B	3B	HR	RBI	SB	Avg
1999	Modesto	Calif.	OF	43	171	28	47	11	3	4	34	2	.275
2000	Modesto	Calif.	OF	129	493	86	130	26	3	29	102	10	.264
2001	Sacramento	P.C.	OF	17	57	10	13	3	0	1	7	2	.228
2001	Midland	Texas	OF	119	443	82	119	23	3	25	96	9	.269
2002	Oklahoma	P.C.	OF	78	305	62	87	27	4	15	52	2	.285
2002	Texas a	A.L.	OF	23	81	10	19	6	0	1	9	2	.235
2003	Oklahoma	P.C.	OF	81	317	51	96	24	3	17	63	1	.303
2003	Texas-Cleveland b-c	A.L.	OF	47	162	17	40	8	1	7	26	2	.247
2004	Akron	Eastern	OF	8	26	4	7	2	0	1	5	0	.269
2004	Buffalo	Int.	OF	44	166	25	45	15	0	8	30	0	.271

Year	Club	Lea	Pos	G	AB	R	H	2B	3B	HR	RBI	SB	Avg
2004	Cleveland d	A.L.	OF	15	50	3	11	2	0	2	4	0	.220
2005	Cleveland	A.L.	OF	19	41	8	9	0	0	4	5	0	.220
2005	Buffalo	Int.	OF	54	188	27	36	10	2	4	16	0	.191
2006	Toledo e-f	Int.	OF	134	508	81	135	34	2	28	80	2	.266
2007	Memphis	P.C.	OF	29	106	27	36	8	0	8	36	1	.340
2007	St. Louis	N.L.	OF	120	303	42	81	22	0	14	52	4	.267
2008	St. Louis	N.L.	OF	152	538	104	161	40	3	37	113	4	.299
2009	St. Louis g	N.L.	OF	139	486	63	129	20	1	22	97	4	.265
2010	Memphis	P.C.	OF	3	9	2	3	1	0	2	5	0	.333
2010	St. Louis-San Diego h-i	N.L.	OF	136	490	63	123	27	2	17	69	0	.251
2011	Indianapolis	Int.	OF	4	13	3	5	1	0	1	5	0	.385
2011	San Diego-Pittsburgh j-k-l	N.L.	OF	139	490	56	116	23	0	13	75	1	.237
2012	Cincinnati m	N.L.	OF	125	422	53	116	28	1	26	80	0	.275
2013	Dayton	Midwest	DH	3	6	2	1	0	0	0	0	0	.167
2013	Louisville	Int.	OF	10	38	2	5	1	0	1	4	0	.132
2013	Cincinnati n	N.L.	OF	38	129	7	31	5	0	2	12	0	.240
Major League Totals			11 Yrs.	953	3192	426	836	181	8	145	542	17	.262
	Wild Card Playoff												
2013	Cincinnati	N.L.	OF	1	4	0	3	2	0	0	0	0	.750
	Division Series												
2009	St. Louis	N.L.	OF	3	12	1	4	0	0	0	1	0	.333
2012	Cincinnati	N.L.	OF	5	18	4	6	0	0	3	4	0	.333
Division Series Totals				8	30	5	10	0	0	3	5	0	.333

a Traded to Texas Rangers by Oakland Athletics with pitcher Mario Ramos, infielder Jason Hart and catcher Gerald Laird for pitcher Mike Venafro and infielder Carlos Pena, January 14, 2002.
b Traded to Cleveland Indians for outfielder Shane Spencer and pitcher Ricardo Rodriguez, July 18, 2003.
c On disabled list from September 9 to October 28, 2003.
d On disabled list from April 2 to July 5, 2004.
e Filed for free agency, October 28, 2005. Signed with Detroit Tigers organization, January 4, 2006.
f Filed for free agency, October 15, 2006. Signed with St. Louis Cardinals organization, December 1, 2006.
g On disabled list from May 13 to May 29, 2009.
h On disabled list from June 26 to July 24, 2010.
i Traded to San Diego Padres for pitcher Nick Greenwood and pitcher Corey Kluber, July 31, 2010.
j Sold to Pittsburgh Pirates, July 31, 2011.
k On disabled list from August 23 to September 7, 2011.
l Filed for free agency, October 30, 2011. Signed with Cincinnati Reds, February 8, 2012.
m Filed for free agency, November 3, 2012, re-signed with Cincinnati Reds, December 10, 2012.
n On disabled list from April 2 to August 12, 2013.

MACHADO, MANUEL AUTURO (MANNY)

Born, Hialeah, Florida, July 6, 1992.

Bats Right. Throws Right. Height, 6 feet, 3 inches. Weight, 185 pounds.

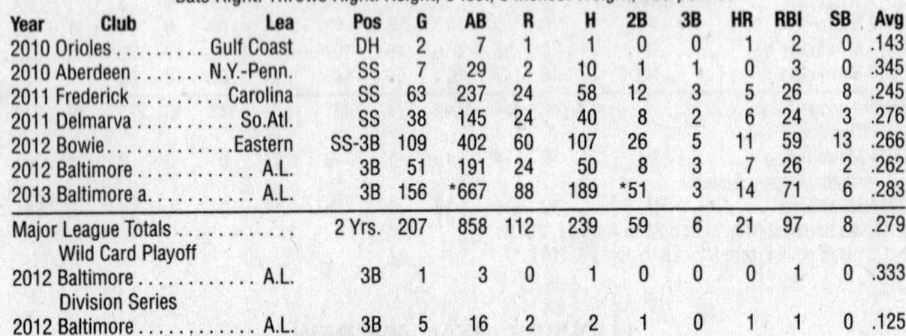

Year	Club	Lea	Pos	G	AB	R	H	2B	3B	HR	RBI	SB	Avg
2010	Orioles	Gulf Coast	DH	2	7	1	1	0	0	1	2	0	.143
2010	Aberdeen	N.Y.-Penn.	SS	7	29	2	10	1	1	0	3	0	.345
2011	Frederick	Carolina	SS	63	237	24	58	12	3	5	26	8	.245
2011	Delmarva	So.Atl.	SS	38	145	24	40	8	2	6	24	3	.276
2012	Bowie	Eastern	SS-3B	109	402	60	107	26	5	11	59	13	.266
2012	Baltimore	A.L.	3B	51	191	24	50	8	3	7	26	2	.262
2013	Baltimore a	A.L.	3B	156	*667	88	189	*51	3	14	71	6	.283
Major League Totals			2 Yrs.	207	858	112	239	59	6	21	97	8	.279
	Wild Card Playoff												
2012	Baltimore	A.L.	3B	1	3	0	1	0	0	0	1	0	.333
	Division Series												
2012	Baltimore	A.L.	3B	5	16	2	2	1	0	1	1	0	.125

a On disabled list from September 25 to November 1, 2013.

MALDONADO (VALDES), MARTIN

Born, Naguabo, Puerto Rico, August 16, 1986.

Bats Right. Throws Right. Height, 6 feet, 1 inch. Weight, 225 pounds.

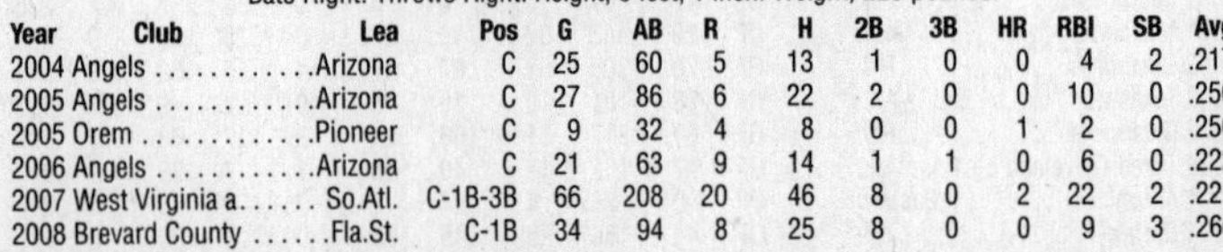

Year	Club	Lea	Pos	G	AB	R	H	2B	3B	HR	RBI	SB	Avg
2004	Angels	Arizona	C	25	60	5	13	1	0	0	4	2	.217
2005	Angels	Arizona	C	27	86	6	22	2	0	0	10	0	.256
2005	Orem	Pioneer	C	9	32	4	8	0	0	1	2	0	.250
2006	Angels	Arizona	C	21	63	9	14	1	1	0	6	0	.222
2007	West Virginia a	So.Atl.	C-1B-3B	66	208	20	46	8	0	2	22	2	.221
2008	Brevard County	Fla.St.	C-1B	34	94	8	25	8	0	0	9	3	.266

Year	Club	Lea	Pos	G	AB	R	H	2B	3B	HR	RBI	SB	Avg
2008	Huntsville	Southern	C	31	98	4	19	2	0	2	8	0	.194
2009	Brevard County	Fla.St.	C	81	251	25	50	9	0	2	21	2	.199
2009	Wisconsin	Midwest	C	7	19	1	2	0	0	0	2	1	.105
2009	Nashville	P.C.	C	7	18	1	6	1	0	0	3	0	.333
2010	Brevard County	Fla.St.	C	10	33	1	4	0	0	0	3	1	.121
2010	Nashville	P.C.	C	52	174	19	44	9	0	7	26	0	.253
2010	Huntsville	Southern	C	34	103	9	26	6	0	2	12	0	.252
2011	Huntsville	Southern	C	64	208	24	55	13	0	3	34	2	.264
2011	Nashville	P.C.	C	39	134	23	43	5	0	8	25	0	.321
2011	Milwaukee	N.L.	C	3	1	0	0	0	0	0	0	0	.000
2012	Nashville	P.C.	C	35	121	10	24	6	0	4	13	0	.198
2012	Milwaukee	N.L.	C-1B	78	233	22	62	9	0	8	30	1	.266
2013	Milwaukee	N.L.	C-1B	67	183	13	31	7	1	4	22	0	.169
Major League Totals			3 Yrs.	148	417	35	93	16	1	12	52	1	.223

a Released by Los Angeles Angels January 10, 2007. Signed with Milwaukee Brewers organization, January 24, 2007.

MARKAKIS, NICHOLAS WILLIAM (NICK)

Born, Woodstock, Georgia, November 17, 1983.
Bats Left. Throws Left. Height, 6 feet, 2 inches. Weight, 195 pounds.

Year	Club	Lea	Pos	G	AB	R	H	2B	3B	HR	RBI	SB	Avg
2003	Aberdeen	N.Y.-Penn.	OF	59	205	22	58	14	3	1	28	13	.283
2004	Delmarva	So.Atl.	OF	96	355	57	106	22	3	11	64	12	.299
2005	Frederick	Carolina	OF	91	350	59	105	25	1	12	62	2	.300
2005	Bowie	Eastern	OF	33	124	19	42	16	2	3	30	0	.339
2006	Baltimore	A.L.	OF	147	491	72	143	25	2	16	62	2	.291
2007	Baltimore	A.L.	OF	161	637	97	191	43	3	23	112	18	.300
2008	Baltimore	A.L.	OF	157	595	106	182	48	1	20	87	10	.306
2009	Baltimore	A.L.	OF	*161	642	94	188	45	2	18	101	6	.293
2010	Baltimore	A.L.	OF	160	629	79	187	45	3	12	60	7	.297
2011	Baltimore	A.L.	OF-1B	160	641	72	182	31	1	15	73	12	.284
2012	Bowie	Eastern	OF	3	10	4	3	1	0	2	4	0	.300
2012	Baltimore a	A.L.	OF	104	420	59	125	28	3	13	54	1	.298
2013	Baltimore	A.L.	OF	160	634	89	172	24	0	10	59	1	.271
Major League Totals			8 Yrs.	1210	4689	668	1370	289	15	127	608	57	.292

a On disabled list from June 1 to July 9, 2012.

MARTE, STARLING JAVIER

Born, Santo Domingo, Dominican Republic, October 9, 1988.
Bats Right. Throws Right. Height, 6 feet, 2 inches. Weight, 180 pounds.

Year	Club	Lea	Pos	G	AB	R	H	2B	3B	HR	RBI	SB	Avg
2009	Lynchburg	Carolina	SS	1	2	0	2	0	0	0	1	0	1.000
2009	Pirates	Gulf Coast	OF	2	7	1	0	0	0	0	0	0	.000
2009	West Virginia	So.Atl.	OF	54	221	41	69	9	5	3	34	24	.312
2010	Bradenton	Fla.St.	OF	60	222	41	70	16	5	0	33	22	.315
2010	Pirates	Gulf Coast	OF	8	26	6	9	3	0	2	5	4	.346
2011	Altoona	Eastern	OF	129	536	91	178	38	8	12	50	24	.332
2012	State College	N.Y.-Penn.	DH	1	5	0	0	0	0	0	0	0	.000
2012	Indianapolis	Int.	OF	99	388	64	111	21	13	12	62	21	.286
2012	Pittsburgh a	N.L.	OF	47	167	18	43	3	6	5	17	12	.257
2013	Pittsburgh b	N.L.	OF	135	510	83	143	26	10	12	35	41	.280
Major League Totals			2 Yrs.	182	677	101	186	29	16	17	52	53	.275
	Wild Card Playoff												
2013	Pittsburgh	N.L.	OF	1	5	1	2	1	0	0	0	0	.400
	Division Series												
2013	Pittsburgh	N.L.	OF	5	19	1	1	0	0	1	1	1	.053

a On disabled list from August 19 to September 7, 2012.
b On disabled list from August 19 to September 7, 2013.

MARTIN (TAPANES), LEONYS

Born, Corralillo, Villa Clara,Cuba, March 6, 1988.
Bats Left. Throws Right. Height, 6 feet, 1 inch. Weight, 190 pounds.

Year	Club	Lea	Pos	G	AB	R	H	2B	3B	HR	RBI	SB	Avg
2011	Rangers	Arizona	OF	4	15	2	4	0	2	0	1	0	.267
2011	Frisco	Texas	OF	29	112	24	39	9	2	4	24	10	.348
2011	Round Rock	P.C.	OF	40	175	27	46	7	1	0	17	9	.263

Year	Club	Lea	Pos	G	AB	R	H	2B	3B	HR	RBI	SB	Avg
2011	Texas	A.L.	OF	8	8	2	3	1	0	0	0	0	.375
2012	Round Rock	P.C.	OF	55	231	48	83	18	2	12	42	10	.359
2012	Texas	A.L.	OF	24	46	6	8	5	2	0	6	3	.174
2013	Texas	A.L.	OF	147	457	66	119	21	6	8	49	36	.260
Major League Totals			3 Yrs.	179	511	74	130	27	8	8	55	39	.254

MARTIN, RUSSELL NATHAN

Born, East York, Ontario, Canada, February 15, 1983.
Bats Right. Throws Right. Height, 5 feet, 10 inches. Weight, 210 pounds.

Year	Club	Lea	Pos	G	AB	R	H	2B	3B	HR	RBI	SB	Avg
2002	Dodgers	Gulf Coast	3B-SS	41	126	22	36	3	3	0	10	7	.286
2003	Ogden	Pioneer	C	52	188	25	51	13	0	6	36	3	.271
2003	South Georgia	So.Atl.	C-OF-3B	25	98	15	28	4	1	3	14	5	.286
2004	Vero Beach	Fla.St.	C	122	416	74	104	24	1	15	64	9	.250
2005	Jacksonville	Southern	C-OF	129	409	83	127	17	1	9	61	15	.311
2006	Las Vegas	P.C.	C	23	74	14	22	9	0	0	9	0	.297
2006	Los Angeles	N.L.	C	121	415	65	117	26	4	10	65	10	.282
2007	Los Angeles	N.L.	C	151	540	87	158	32	3	19	87	21	.293
2008	Los Angeles	N.L.	C-3B	155	553	87	155	25	0	13	69	18	.280
2009	Los Angeles	N.L.	C-3B	143	505	63	126	19	0	7	53	11	.250
2010	Los Angeles a-b	N.L.	C	97	331	45	82	13	0	5	26	6	.248
2011	New York	A.L.	C-3B-2B	125	417	57	99	17	0	18	65	8	.237
2012	New York c	A.L.	C	133	422	50	89	18	0	21	53	6	.211
2013	Pittsburgh	N.L.	C-3B-OF	127	438	51	99	21	0	15	55	9	.226
Major League Totals			8 Yrs.	1052	3621	505	925	171	7	108	473	89	.255
	Wild Card Playoff												
2013	Pittsburgh	N.L.	C	1	4	2	3	0	0	2	2	0	.750
	Division Series												
2006	Los Angeles	N.L.	C	3	12	2	4	0	0	0	0	0	.333
2008	Los Angeles	N.L.	C	3	13	2	4	3	0	1	5	0	.308
2009	Los Angeles	N.L.	C	3	9	0	1	0	0	0	1	0	.111
2011	New York	A.L.	C	5	17	3	3	1	0	0	0	0	.176
2012	New York	A.L.	C	5	17	2	3	1	0	1	1	0	.176
2013	Pittsburgh	N.L.	C	5	13	0	2	0	0	0	4	0	.154
Division Series Totals				24	81	9	17	5	0	2	11	0	.210
	Championship Series												
2008	Los Angeles	N.L.	C	5	17	3	2	0	0	0	1	1	.118
2009	Los Angeles	N.L.	C	5	16	2	4	1	0	0	2	0	.250
2012	New York	A.L.	C	4	14	1	2	0	0	0	0	0	.143
Championship Series Totals				14	47	6	8	1	0	0	3	1	.170

a On disabled list from August 4 to November 2, 2010.
b Not offered contract, December 2, 2010. Signed with New York Yankees, December 16, 2010.
c Filed for free agency, November 3, 2012. Signed with Pittsburgh Pirates, November 30, 2012.

MARTINEZ, JULIO DANIEL (J.D.)

Born, Miami, Florida, August 21, 1987.
Bats Right. Throws Right. Height, 6 feet, 3 inches. Weight, 200 pounds.

Year	Club	Lea	Pos	G	AB	R	H	2B	3B	HR	RBI	SB	Avg
2009	Greeneville	Appal.	OF-1B	19	77	17	31	9	1	5	23	0	.403
2009	Tri-City	N.Y.-Penn.	OF-1B	53	187	25	61	15	2	7	33	1	.326
2010	Lexington	So.Atl.	OF	88	348	83	126	31	3	15	64	3	.362
2010	Corpus Christi	Texas	OF	50	189	24	57	9	1	3	25	2	.302
2011	Corpus Christi	Texas	OF	88	317	50	107	25	1	13	72	1	.338
2011	Houston	N.L.	OF	53	208	29	57	13	0	6	35	0	.274
2012	Oklahoma	P.C.	OF	23	90	6	21	6	0	0	4	0	.233
2012	Houston	N.L.	OF	113	395	34	95	14	3	11	55	0	.241
2013	Corpus Christi	Texas	OF	5	20	1	6	2	0	1	5	0	.300
2013	Houston a	A.L.	OF	86	296	24	74	17	0	7	36	2	.250
Major League Totals			3 Yrs.	252	899	87	226	44	3	24	126	2	.251

a On disabled list from April 20 to May 7 and July 27 to September 13, 2013.

MARTINEZ, VICTOR JESUS

Born, Ciudad Bolivar, Venezuela, December 23, 1978.
Bats Both. Throws Right. Height, 6 feet, 2 inches. Weight, 210 pounds.

Year	Club	Lea	Pos	G	AB	R	H	2B	3B	HR	RBI	SB	Avg
1997	Maracay-1	Venzuelan	C	53	122	21	42	12	0	0	26	6	.344
1998	Guacara-2	Venzuelan	C	55	160	28	43	13	0	1	27	8	.269
1999	Mahoning Valley	N.Y.-Penn.	C	64	235	37	65	9	0	4	36	0	.277
2000	Kinston	Carolina	C	26	83	9	18	7	0	0	8	1	.217
2000	Columbus a	So.Atl.	C	21	70	11	26	9	1	2	12	0	.371
2001	Kinston	Carolina	C	114	420	59	138	33	2	10	57	3	.329
2002	Akron	Eastern	C	121	443	84	149	40	0	22	85	3	.336
2002	Cleveland	A.L.	C	12	32	2	9	1	0	1	5	0	.281
2003	Buffalo	Int.	C-1B	73	274	42	90	19	0	7	45	3	.328
2003	Akron	Eastern	C	3	12	1	4	2	0	0	2	0	.333
2003	Cleveland b	A.L.	C	49	159	15	46	4	0	1	16	1	.289
2004	Cleveland	A.L.	C	141	520	77	147	38	1	23	108	0	.283
2005	Cleveland	A.L.	C	147	547	73	167	33	0	20	80	0	.305
2006	Cleveland	A.L.	C-1B	153	572	82	181	37	0	16	93	0	.316
2007	Cleveland	A.L.	C-1B	147	562	78	169	40	0	25	114	0	.301
2008	Akron	Eastern	DH	2	6	1	2	0	0	1	1	0	.333
2008	Buffalo	Int.	C	6	20	2	6	2	0	0	2	0	.300
2008	Cleveland c	A.L.	C-1B	73	266	30	74	17	0	2	35	0	.278
2009	Cleveland-Boston d	A.L.	C-1B	155	588	88	178	33	1	23	108	1	.303
2010	Boston e-f	A.L.	C-1B	127	493	64	149	32	1	20	79	1	.302
2011	Toledo	Int.	DH	2	6	1	3	1	0	0	2	0	.500
2011	Detroit g	A.L.	DH-C-1B	145	540	76	178	40	0	12	103	1	.330
2012	Detroit h	A.L.	INJURED—Did Not Play										
2013	Detroit	A.L.	DH-1B-C	159	605	68	182	36	0	14	83	0	.301
Major League Totals			11 Yrs.	1308	4884	653	1480	311	3	157	824	4	.303
	Division Series												
2007	Cleveland	A.L.	C-1B	4	17	2	6	1	0	1	4	0	.353
2009	Boston	A.L.	C	3	11	0	2	0	0	0	2	0	.182
2011	Detroit	A.L.	DH	5	18	1	4	0	0	1	3	0	.222
2013	Detroit	A.L.	DH	5	20	5	9	2	0	1	2	0	.450
Division Series Totals				17	66	8	21	3	0	3	11	0	.318
	Championship Series												
2007	Cleveland	A.L.	C-1B	7	27	4	8	1	0	1	3	0	.296
2011	Detroit	A.L.	DH	6	22	3	6	0	1	1	2	0	.273
2013	Detroit	A.L.	DH	6	22	4	8	2	0	0	3	0	.364
Championship Series Totals				19	71	11	22	3	1	2	8	0	.310

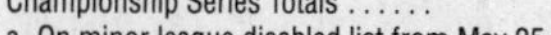

a On minor league disabled list from May 25 to July 19, 2000.
b On disabled list from August 9 to September 2, 2003.
c On disabled list from June 12 to August 29, 2008.
d Traded to Boston Red Sox for pitcher Justin Masterson, pitcher Nick Hagadone and pitcher Bryan Price, July 31, 2009.
e On disabled list from June 28 to July 26, 2010.
f Filed for free agency, November 1, 2010. Signed with Detroit Tigers, November 26, 2010.
g On disabled list from April 19 to May 4, 2011.
h On disabled list from March 12 to October 29, 2012.

MATHIS, JEFFERY STEPHEN (JEFF)

Born, Marianna, Florida, March 31, 1983.
Bats Right. Throws Right. Height, 6 feet. Weight, 180 pounds.

Year	Club	Lea	Pos	G	AB	R	H	2B	3B	HR	RBI	SB	Avg
2001	Angels	Arizona	C-OF	7	23	1	7	1	0	0	3	0	.304
2001	Provo	Pioneer	C	22	77	14	23	6	3	0	18	1	.299
2002	Cedar Rapids	Midwest	C	128	491	75	141	41	3	10	73	7	.287
2003	Rancho Cucamonga	Calif.	C	98	378	74	122	28	3	11	54	5	.323
2003	Arkansas	Texas	C	24	95	19	27	11	0	2	14	1	.284
2004	Arkansas	Texas	C	117	432	57	98	24	3	14	55	2	.227
2005	Salt Lake	P.C.	C	112	427	78	118	26	3	21	73	4	.276
2005	Los Angeles	A.L.	C	5	3	1	1	0	0	0	0	0	.333
2006	Salt Lake	P.C.	C	99	384	62	111	33	3	5	45	3	.289
2006	Los Angeles	A.L.	C	23	55	9	8	2	0	2	6	0	.145
2007	Salt Lake	P.C.	C	66	250	39	61	14	2	5	26	3	.244
2007	Los Angeles	A.L.	C	59	171	24	36	12	0	4	23	0	.211
2008	Los Angeles	A.L.	C	94	283	35	55	8	0	9	42	2	.194
2009	Los Angeles	A.L.	C	84	237	26	50	8	0	5	28	2	.211
2010	Salt Lake	P.C.	C	9	33	6	8	1	1	1	5	0	.242

Year	Club	Lea	Pos	G	AB	R	H	2B	3B	HR	RBI	SB	Avg
2010	Los Angeles a	A.L.	C	68	205	19	40	6	1	3	18	3	.195
2011	Los Angeles b	A.L.	C	93	247	18	43	12	0	3	22	1	.174
2012	Toronto c	A.L.	C-P	71	211	25	46	13	0	8	27	1	.218
2013	Jupiter	Fla.St.	C	4	14	1	4	2	0	0	4	0	.286
2013	Jacksonville	Southern	C	3	11	1	3	1	0	1	6	0	.273
2013	New Orleans	P.C.	C	2	9	1	2	1	0	1	2	0	.222
2013	Miami d	N.L.	C	73	232	14	42	7	1	5	29	0	.181
Major League Totals			9 Yrs.	570	1644	171	321	68	2	39	195	9	.195
	Division Series												
2007	Los Angeles	A.L.	C	2	3	0	0	0	0	0	1	0	.000
2008	Los Angeles	A.L.	C	1	2	0	1	0	0	0	0	0	.500
2009	Los Angeles	A.L.	C	2	3	0	1	0	0	0	0	0	.333
Division Series Totals				5	8	0	2	0	0	0	1	0	.250
	Championship Series												
2009	Los Angeles	A.L.	C	5	12	2	7	5	0	0	1	0	.583

a On disabled list from April 20 to June 17, 2010.
b Traded to Toronto Blue Jays for pitcher Brad Mills, December 3, 2011.
c Traded to Miami Marlins with pitcher Henderson Alvarez, infielder Yunel Escobar, infielder Adeiny Hechavarria, pitcher Anthony De Sclafani, outfielder Jake Marisnick and pitcher Justin Nicolino for outfielder Emilio Bonifacio, catcher John Buck, pitcher Mark Buehrle, pitcher Josh Johnson and infielder Jose Reyes, November 19, 2012.
d On disabled list from March 22 to May 14, 2013.

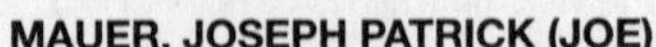

MAUER, JOSEPH PATRICK (JOE)

Born, St. Paul, Minnesota, April 19, 1983.
Bats Left. Throws Right. Height, 6 feet, 4 inches. Weight, 220 pounds.

Year	Club	Lea	Pos	G	AB	R	H	2B	3B	HR	RBI	SB	Avg
2001	Elizabethton	Appal.	C	32	110	14	44	6	2	0	14	4	.400
2002	Quad Cities	Midwest	C-1B	110	411	58	124	23	1	4	62	0	.302
2003	Fort Myers	Fla.St.	C-1B	62	233	25	78	13	1	1	44	3	.335
2003	New Britain	Eastern	C	73	276	48	94	17	1	4	41	0	.341
2004	Fort Myers	Fla.St.	C	2	6	0	4	0	0	0	2	0	.667
2004	Rochester	Int.	C	5	19	1	6	3	0	0	2	0	.316
2004	Minnesota a	A.L.	C	35	107	18	33	8	1	6	17	1	.308
2005	Minnesota	A.L.	C	131	489	61	144	26	2	9	55	13	.294
2006	Minnesota	A.L.	C	140	521	86	181	36	4	13	84	8	*.347
2007	Fort Myers	Fla.St.	C	1	3	0	0	0	0	0	0	0	.000
2007	Minnesota b	A.L.	C	109	406	62	119	27	3	7	60	7	.293
2008	Minnesota	A.L.	C	146	536	98	176	31	4	9	85	1	*.328
2009	Fort Myers	Fla.St.	C	5	15	2	6	2	0	0	4	0	.400
2009	Minnesota c-d	A.L.	C	138	523	94	191	30	1	28	96	4	*.365
2010	Minnesota	A.L.	C	137	510	88	167	43	1	9	75	1	.327
2011	Fort Myers	Fla.St.	C	7	23	3	6	2	0	1	6	0	.261
2011	Minnesota e	A.L.	C-1B-OF	82	296	38	85	15	0	3	30	0	.287
2012	Minnesota	A.L.	C-1B	147	545	81	174	31	4	10	85	8	.319
2013	Minnesota f	A.L.	C-1B	113	445	62	144	35	0	11	47	0	.324
Major League Totals			10 Yrs.	1178	4378	688	1414	282	20	105	634	43	.323
	Division Series												
2006	Minnesota	A.L.	C	3	11	0	2	0	0	0	0	0	.182
2009	Minnesota	A.L.	C	3	12	1	5	1	0	0	1	0	.417
2010	Minnesota	A.L.	C	3	12	0	3	0	0	0	0	0	.250
Division Series Totals				9	35	1	10	1	0	0	1	0	.286

a On disabled list from April 7 to June 2 and from July 16 to October 11, 2004.
b On disabled list from May 5 to June 8, 2007.
c On disabled list from March 27 to May 1, 2009.
d Selected Most Valuable Player in American League for 2009.
e On disabled list from April 13 to June 17 and September 15 to October 3, 2011.
f On disabled list from August 20 to October 1, 2013.

MAXWELL, JUSTIN ADAM

Born, Olney, Maryland, November 6, 1983.
Bats Right. Throws Right. Height, 6 feet, 5 inches. Weight, 235 pounds.

Year	Club	Lea	Pos	G	AB	R	H	2B	3B	HR	RBI	SB	Avg
2006	Vermont	N.Y.-Penn.	OF	74	271	36	73	11	3	4	33	20	.269
2006	Savannah	So.Atl.	OF	17	58	8	10	2	2	1	7	1	.172
2007	Hagerstown	So.Atl.	OF	56	209	51	63	12	2	14	40	14	.301
2007	Potomac	Carolina	OF	58	228	35	60	13	0	13	43	21	.263
2007	Washington	N.L.	OF	15	26	5	7	0	0	2	5	0	.269

Year	Club	Lea	Pos	G	AB	R	H	2B	3B	HR	RBI	SB	Avg
2008	Harrisburg a	Eastern	OF	43	146	35	34	6	3	7	28	13	.233
2009	Syracuse	Int.	OF	111	384	68	93	10	5	13	42	35	.242
2009	Washington	N.L.	OF	40	89	13	22	4	1	4	9	6	.247
2010	Syracuse	Int.	OF	66	230	34	66	17	0	6	21	16	.287
2010	Washington	N.L.	OF	67	104	16	15	6	0	3	12	5	.144
2011	Scranton-WB b-c	Int.	OF	48	177	36	46	8	1	16	35	11	.260
2012	Corpus Christi	Texas	OF	2	8	2	2	1	0	0	1	0	.250
2012	Oklahoma	P.C.	OF	3	10	1	2	1	0	0	0	0	.200
2012	Houston d-e	N.L.	OF	124	315	46	72	13	3	18	53	9	.229
2013	Corpus Christi	Texas	OF	6	21	1	1	0	0	0	2	1	.048
2013	Oklahoma	P.C.	OF	8	28	5	5	0	0	1	3	0	.179
2013	Houston-Kansas City f-g	A.L.	OF	75	234	35	59	16	3	7	25	6	.252
Major League Totals			5 Yrs.	321	768	115	175	39	7	34	104	26	.228

a On disabled list from September 2 to September 29, 2008.
b Traded to New York Yankees for pitcher Adam Olbrychowski, February 2, 2011.
c On disabled list from September 1 to October 12, 2011.
d Claimed on waivers by Houston Astros, April 8, 2012.
e On disabled list from June 26 to July 13, 2012.
f On disabled list from April 24 to June 18 and June 30 to July 13, 2013.
g Traded to Kansas City Royals for pitcher Kyle Smith, July 31, 2013.

MAYBERRY, JOHN CLAIBORN JR.

Born, Kansas City, Missouri, December 21, 1983.
Bats Right. Throws Right. Height, 6 feet, 6 inches. Weight, 230 pounds.

Year	Club	Lea	Pos	G	AB	R	H	2B	3B	HR	RBI	SB	Avg
2005	Spokane	Northwest	OF	71	265	51	67	16	0	11	26	7	.253
2006	Clinton	Midwest	OF	126	459	77	123	26	4	21	77	9	.268
2007	Bakersfield	Calif.	OF	63	244	47	56	15	1	16	45	9	.230
2007	Frisco	Texas	OF	69	245	35	59	10	0	14	38	7	.241
2008	Frisco a	Texas	OF	21	82	16	22	8	0	4	13	4	.268
2008	Oklahoma	P.C.	OF-1B	114	437	49	115	30	7	16	58	6	.263
2009	Lehigh Valley	Int.	OF	89	316	44	81	20	2	13	43	6	.256
2009	Philadelphia	N.L.	OF	39	57	8	12	3	0	4	8	0	.211
2010	Lehigh Valley	Int.	OF	128	495	75	132	25	1	15	65	20	.267
2010	Philadelphia	N.L.	OF	11	12	4	4	0	0	2	6	0	.333
2011	Lehigh Valley	Int.	OF-1B	28	113	16	30	8	0	4	15	2	.265
2011	Philadelphia	N.L.	OF-1B	104	267	37	73	17	1	15	49	8	.273
2012	Philadelphia	N.L.	OF-1B	149	441	53	108	24	0	14	46	1	.245
2013	Philadelphia	N.L.	OF-1B	134	353	47	80	23	1	11	39	5	.227
Major League Totals			5 Yrs.	437	1130	149	277	67	2	46	148	14	.245
Division Series													
2011	Philadelphia	N.L.	OF	2	4	0	0	0	0	0	0	0	.000

a Traded by Texas Rangers to Philadelphia Phillies for outfielder Greg Golson, November 20, 2008.

MAYBIN, CAMERON KEITH

Born, Asheville, North Carolina, April 4, 1987.
Bats Right. Throws Right. Height, 6 feet, 4 inches. Weight, 205 pounds.

Year	Club	Lea	Pos	G	AB	R	H	2B	3B	HR	RBI	SB	Avg
2006	West Michigan	Midwest	OF	101	385	59	117	20	6	9	69	27	.304
2007	Tigers	Gulf Coast	OF	2	7	1	4	0	0	0	1	0	.571
2007	Lakeland	Fla.St.	OF	83	296	58	90	14	5	10	44	25	.304
2007	Erie	Eastern	OF	6	20	9	8	1	0	4	8	0	.400
2007	Detroit a	A.L.	OF	24	49	8	7	3	0	1	2	5	.143
2008	Carolina	Southern	OF	108	390	73	108	15	8	13	49	21	.277
2008	Florida	N.L.	OF	8	32	9	16	2	0	0	2	4	.500
2009	New Orleans	P.C.	OF	82	298	44	95	18	8	3	39	8	.319
2009	Florida	N.L.	OF	54	176	30	44	12	2	4	13	1	.250
2010	Marlins	Gulf Coast	OF	3	11	4	4	1	0	1	5	0	.364
2010	New Orleans	P.C.	OF	33	130	21	44	6	2	4	23	5	.338
2010	Florida b	N.L.	OF	82	291	46	68	7	3	8	28	9	.234
2011	Tucson	P.C.	OF	3	10	1	2	1	0	0	1	1	.200
2011	San Diego c	N.L.	OF	137	516	82	136	24	8	9	40	40	.264
2012	San Diego	N.L.	OF	147	507	67	123	20	5	8	45	26	.243
2013	Tucson	P.C.	OF	15	46	7	12	1	0	4	5	1	.261
2013	San Diego d	N.L.	OF	14	51	7	8	1	0	1	5	4	.157
Major League Totals			7 Yrs.	466	1622	249	402	69	18	31	135	89	.248

a Traded to Florida Marlins with pitcher Burke Badenhop, pitcher Eulogio De La Cruz, pitcher Andrew Miller and catcher Mike Rabelo for pitcher Dontrelle Willis and infielder Miguel Cabrera, December 5, 2007.
b Traded to San Diego Padres for pitcher Edward Mujica and pitcher Ryan Webb, November 13, 2010.
c On disabled list from May 28 to June 13, 2011.
d On disabled list from April 16 to June 6 and June 10 to September 30, 2013.

MC CANN, BRIAN MICHAEL

Born, Athens, Georgia, February 20, 1984.
Bats Left. Throws Right. Height, 6 feet, 3 inches. Weight, 230 pounds.

Year Club	Lea	Pos	G	AB	R	H	2B	3B	HR	RBI	SB	Avg
2002 Braves	Gulf Coast	C	29	100	9	22	5	0	2	11	0	.220
2003 Rome	So.Atl.	C	115	424	40	123	31	3	12	71	7	.290
2004 Myrtle Beach	Carolina	C	111	385	45	107	35	0	16	66	2	.278
2005 Mississippi	Southern	C	48	166	27	44	13	2	6	26	2	.265
2005 Atlanta	N.L.	C	59	180	20	50	7	0	5	23	1	.278
2006 Rome	So.Atl.	DH	2	7	0	2	0	0	0	0	0	.286
2006 Atlanta a	N.L.	C	130	442	61	147	34	0	24	93	2	.333
2007 Atlanta	N.L.	C	139	504	51	136	38	0	18	92	0	.270
2008 Atlanta	N.L.	C	145	509	68	153	42	1	23	87	5	.301
2009 Myrtle Beach	Carolina	DH	2	6	1	2	2	0	0	1	0	.333
2009 Gwinnett	Int.	C	1	3	0	1	1	0	0	1	0	.333
2009 Atlanta b	N.L.	C	138	488	63	137	35	1	21	94	4	.281
2010 Atlanta	N.L.	C	143	479	63	129	25	0	21	77	5	.269
2011 Gwinnett	Int.	C	2	6	1	2	0	0	1	2	0	.333
2011 Atlanta c	N.L.	C	128	466	51	126	19	0	24	71	3	.270
2012 Atlanta	N.L.	C	121	439	44	101	14	0	20	67	3	.230
2013 Rome	So.Atl.	C	4	14	4	5	1	0	3	7	0	.357
2013 Gwinnett	Int.	C	3	9	1	3	0	0	1	2	0	.333
2013 Atlanta d-e	N.L.	C	102	356	43	91	13	0	20	57	0	.256
Major League Totals		9 Yrs.	1105	3863	464	1070	227	2	176	661	23	.277
Wild Card Playoff												
2012 Atlanta	N.L.	PH	1	0	0	0	0	0	0	0	0	.000
Division Series												
2005 Atlanta	N.L.	C	3	16	2	3	0	0	2	5	0	.188
2010 Atlanta	N.L.	C	4	14	2	6	1	0	1	3	0	.429
2013 Atlanta	N.L.	C	4	13	0	0	0	0	0	1	0	.000
Division Series Totals			11	43	4	9	1	0	3	9	0	.209

a On disabled list from May 24 to June 9, 2006.
b On disabled list from April 23 to May 8, 2009.
c On disabled list from July 27 to August 14, 2011.
d On disabled list from March 22 to May 6, 2013.
e Filed for free agency, October 31, 2013. Signed with New York Yankees, December 3, 2013.

MC CUTCHEN, ANDREW STEFAN

Born, Fort Meade, Florida, October 10, 1986.
Bats Right. Throws Right. Height, 5 feet, 11 inches. Weight, 175 pounds.

Year Club	Lea	Pos	G	AB	R	H	2B	3B	HR	RBI	SB	Avg
2005 Pirates	Gulf Coast	OF	45	158	36	47	9	3	2	30	13	.297
2005 Williamsport	N.Y.-Penn.	OF	13	52	12	18	3	1	0	5	4	.346
2006 Altoona	Eastern	OF	20	78	12	24	4	0	3	12	1	.308
2006 Hickory	So.Atl.	OF	114	453	77	132	20	4	14	62	22	.291
2007 Altoona	Eastern	OF	118	446	70	115	20	3	10	48	17	.258
2007 Indianapolis	Int.	OF	17	67	7	21	4	0	1	5	4	.313
2008 Indianapolis	Int.	OF	135	512	75	145	26	3	9	50	34	.283
2009 Indianapolis	Int.	OF	49	201	41	61	10	8	4	20	10	.303
2009 Pittsburgh	N.L.	OF	108	433	74	124	26	9	12	54	22	.286
2010 Pittsburgh	N.L.	OF	154	570	94	163	35	5	16	56	33	.286
2011 Pittsburgh	N.L.	OF	158	572	87	148	34	5	23	89	23	.259
2012 Pittsburgh	N.L.	OF	157	593	107	*194	29	6	31	96	20	.327
2013 Pittsburgh a	N.L.	OF	157	583	97	185	38	5	21	84	27	.317
Major League Totals		5 Yrs.	734	2751	459	814	162	30	103	379	125	.296
Wild Card Playoff												
2013 Pittsburgh	N.L.	OF	1	3	1	2	0	0	0	0	0	.667
Division Series												
2013 Pittsburgh	N.L.	OF	5	18	2	5	1	0	0	0	0	.278

a Selected Most Valuable Player in National League for 2013.

MC LOUTH, NATHAN RICHARD (NATE)

Born, Muskegon, Michigan, October 28, 1981.
Bats Left. Throws Right. Height, 5 feet, 11 inches. Weight, 185 pounds.

Year Club	Lea	Pos	G	AB	R	H	2B	3B	HR	RBI	SB	Avg
2001 Hickory............	So.Atl.	OF-2B	96	351	59	100	17	5	12	54	21	.285
2002 Lynchburg	Carolina	OF	114	393	58	96	23	4	9	46	20	.244
2003 Lynchburg	Carolina	OF	117	440	85	132	27	2	6	33	40	.300
2004 Altoona............	Eastern	OF	133	515	93	166	40	4	8	73	31	.322
2005 Indianapolis	Int.	OF	110	397	64	118	20	3	5	39	34	.297
2005 Pittsburgh	N.L.	OF	41	109	20	28	6	0	5	12	2	.257
2006 Pittsburgh a..........	N.L.	OF	106	270	50	63	16	2	7	16	10	.233
2007 Pittsburgh	N.L.	OF	137	329	62	85	21	3	13	38	22	.258
2008 Pittsburgh	N.L.	OF	152	597	113	165	*46	4	26	94	23	.276
2009 Rome..............	So.Atl.	OF	1	2	0	0	0	0	0	0	0	.000
2009 Mississippi.......	Southern	OF	2	3	1	0	0	0	0	0	0	.000
2009 Pittsburgh-Atlanta b-c ..	N.L.	OF	129	507	86	130	27	2	20	70	19	.256
2010 Gwinnett..............	Int.	OF	34	128	18	30	1	0	6	18	7	.234
2010 Atlanta d.............	N.L.	OF	85	242	30	46	12	1	6	24	7	.190
2011 Gwinnett..............	Int.	OF	3	6	2	3	0	0	0	1	0	.500
2011 Atlanta e-f	N.L.	OF	81	267	35	61	12	2	4	16	4	.228
2012 Norfolk...............	Int.	OF	47	180	29	44	5	2	10	33	5	.244
2012 Pittsburgh	N.L.	OF	34	57	4	8	2	0	0	2	0	.140
2012 Baltimore g-h.........	A.L.	OF	55	209	35	56	12	1	7	18	12	.268
2013 Baltimore i	A.L.	OF	146	531	76	137	31	4	12	36	30	.258
Major League Totals		9 Yrs.	966	3118	511	779	185	19	100	326	129	.250
Wild Card Playoff												
2012 Baltimore	A.L.	OF	1	4	1	1	0	0	0	2	1	.250
Division Series												
2010 Atlanta	N.L.	OF	3	2	0	1	0	0	0	0	0	.500
2012 Baltimore	A.L.	OF	5	22	2	7	1	0	1	3	2	.318
Division Series Totals			8	24	2	8	1	0	1	3	2	.333

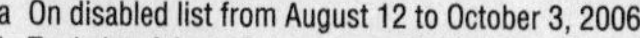

a On disabled list from August 12 to October 3, 2006.
b Traded to Atlanta Braves for outfielder Gorkys Hernandez, pitcher Jeff Locke and pitcher Charlie Morton, June 3, 2009.
c On disabled list from August 16 to September 4, 2009.
d On disabled list from June 10 to July 21, 2010.
e On disabled list from May 23 to June 19 and July 29 to October 30, 2011.
f Filed for free agency, October 31, 2011. Signed with Pittsburgh Pirates, December 7, 2011.
g Released by Pittsburgh Pirates, May 31, 2012. Signed with Baltimore Orioles organization, June 5, 2012.
h Filed for free agency, November 3, 2012, re-signed with Baltimore Orioles, December 13, 2012.
i Filed for free agency, October 31, 2013. Signed with Washington Nationals, December 12, 2013.

MERCER, JORDY JOE

Born, Seiling, Oklahoma, August 27, 1986.
Bats Right. Throws Right. Height, 6 feet, 3 inches. Weight, 210 pounds.

Year Club	Lea	Pos	G	AB	R	H	2B	3B	HR	RBI	SB	Avg
2008 State College	.N.Y.-Penn.	SS	6	24	5	6	1	1	1	2	1	.250
2008 Hickory.........	So.Atl.	SS	50	192	21	48	7	0	4	18	4	.250
2009 Lynchburg	Carolina	SS-3B	131	513	64	131	36	4	10	83	10	.255
2010 Altoona........	Eastern	3B-2B-SS-1B	126	485	67	137	31	2	3	65	7	.282
2011 Altoona........	Eastern	SS	72	265	40	71	17	1	13	48	6	.268
2011 Indianapolis	Int.	2B-SS-OF	60	226	39	54	13	1	6	21	3	.239
2012 Indianapolis	Int.	SS-2B-3B	56	209	28	60	14	1	4	27	3	.287
2012 Pittsburgh	N.L.	SS-2B-3B	42	62	7	13	5	1	1	5	0	.210
2013 Indianapolis	Int.	SS-2B-3B	26	96	11	32	6	1	1	19	3	.333
2013 Pittsburgh	N.L.	SS-2B-1B-3B	103	333	33	95	22	2	8	27	3	.285
Major League Totals		2 Yrs.	145	395	40	108	27	3	9	32	3	.273
Division Series												
2013 Pittsburgh	N.L.	SS	5	8	0	2	0	0	0	0	0	.250

MESORACO, DEVIN DOUGLAS

Born, Dubois, Pennsylvania, June 19, 1988.
Bats Right. Throws Right. Height, 6 feet, 1 inch. Weight, 230 pounds.

Year Club	Lea	Pos	G	AB	R	H	2B	3B	HR	RBI	SB	Avg
2007 Reds...........	Gulf Coast	C	40	137	16	30	4	0	1	8	2	.219
2008 Dayton	Midwest	C	83	306	29	80	13	1	9	42	2	.261
2009 Sarasota............	Fla.St.	C	92	312	32	71	22	1	8	37	0	.228
2010 Lynchburg	Carolina	C	43	158	24	53	11	2	10	31	2	.335

Year	Club	Lea	Pos	G	AB	R	H	2B	3B	HR	RBI	SB	Avg
2010	Carolina	Southern	C	56	187	42	55	11	3	13	31	1	.294
2010	Louisville	Int.	C	14	52	5	12	3	0	3	13	0	.231
2011	Louisville	Int.	C	120	436	60	126	36	2	15	71	1	.289
2011	Cincinnati	N.L.	C	18	50	5	9	3	0	2	6	0	.180
2012	Louisville	Int.	C	5	18	0	3	1	0	0	0	0	.167
2012	Cincinnati a	N.L.	C	54	165	17	35	8	0	5	14	1	.212
2013	Cincinnati	N.L.	C	103	323	31	77	13	0	9	42	0	.238
Major League Totals			3 Yrs.	175	538	53	121	24	0	16	62	1	.225
	Wild Card Playoff												
2013	Cincinnati	N.L.	C	1	1	0	0	0	0	0	0	0	.000

a On disabled list from August 1 to August 9, 2012.

MIDDLEBROOKS, WILLIAM SCOTT (WILL)

Born, Greenville, Texas, September 9, 1988.
Bats Right. Throws Right. Height, 6 feet, 4 inches. Weight, 225 pounds.

Year	Club	Lea	Pos	G	AB	R	H	2B	3B	HR	RBI	SB	Avg
2008	Lowell	N.Y.-Penn.	3B	59	209	21	53	17	2	1	21	10	.254
2009	Greenville	So.Atl.	3B	103	374	53	99	25	3	7	57	7	.265
2010	Salem	Carolina	3B	114	435	69	120	31	2	12	70	5	.276
2011	Portland	Eastern	3B	96	371	54	112	25	1	18	80	6	.302
2011	Pawtucket	Int.	3B	16	56	4	9	0	0	2	8	3	.161
2011	Lowell	N.Y.-Penn.	DH	4	12	4	4	1	0	3	6	1	.333
2012	Pawtucket	Int.	3B	24	93	18	31	3	1	9	27	3	.333
2012	Boston a	A.L.	3B	75	267	34	77	14	0	15	54	4	.288
2013	Pawtucket	Int.	3B	45	179	25	48	5	0	10	35	1	.268
2013	Boston b	A.L.	3B-2B-1B	94	348	41	79	18	0	17	49	3	.227
Major League Totals			2 Yrs.	169	615	75	156	32	0	32	103	7	.254
	Division Series												
2013	Boston	A.L.	3B	4	13	1	3	1	0	0	1	0	.231
	Championship Series												
2013	Boston	A.L.	3B	5	10	1	1	1	0	0	0	0	.100
	World Series Record												
2013	Boston	A.L.	3B	1	2	0	0	0	0	0	0	0	.000

a On disabled list from August 11 to November 2, 2012.
b On disabled list from May 24 to June 10, 2013.

MILLER, BRADLEY AUSTIN (BRAD)

Born, Orlando, Florida, October 18, 1989.
Bats Left. Throws Right. Height, 6 feet, 2 inches. Weight, 185 pounds.

Year	Club	Lea	Pos	G	AB	R	H	2B	3B	HR	RBI	SB	Avg
2011	Clinton	Midwest	SS	14	53	9	22	4	1	0	7	1	.415
2012	High Desert	Calif.	SS	97	410	89	139	33	5	11	56	19	.339
2012	Jackson	Southern	SS	40	147	21	47	7	2	4	12	4	.320
2013	Jackson	Southern	SS-2B-3B	42	153	27	45	7	1	6	25	4	.294
2013	Tacoma	P.C.	SS-2B	26	104	26	37	5	1	6	28	2	.356
2013	Seattle	A.L.	SS-2B-3B	76	306	41	81	11	6	8	36	5	.265

MOLINA (MATTA), JOSE BENJAMIN

Born, Bayamon, Puerto Rico, June 3, 1975.
Bats Right. Throws Right. Height, 6 feet, 1 inch. Weight, 250 pounds.

Year	Club	Lea	Pos	G	AB	R	H	2B	3B	HR	RBI	SB	Avg
1993	Cubs	Gulf Coast	C-1B	33	78	5	17	2	0	0	4	3	.218
1993	Daytona	Fla.St.	C	3	7	0	1	0	0	0	1	0	.143
1994	Peoria	Midwest	C	78	253	31	58	13	1	1	33	4	.229
1995	Daytona	Fla.St.	C	82	233	27	55	9	1	1	19	1	.236
1996	Rockford	Midwest	C	96	305	35	69	10	1	2	27	2	.226
1997	Iowa	A.A.	C	1	3	0	1	0	0	0	0	0	.333
1997	Daytona	Fla.St.	C	55	179	17	45	9	1	0	23	4	.251
1997	Orlando	Southern	C	37	99	10	17	3	0	1	15	0	.172
1998	West Tenn	Southern	C-1B	109	320	33	71	10	1	2	28	1	.222
1999	West Tenn	Southern	C	14	35	2	6	3	0	0	5	0	.171
1999	Iowa	P.C.	C	74	240	24	63	11	1	4	26	0	.262
1999	Chicago	N.L.	C	10	19	3	5	1	0	0	1	0	.263
2000	Iowa	P.C.	C-1B	76	248	22	58	9	0	1	17	1	.234
2001	Salt Lake	P.C.	C	61	213	29	64	11	1	5	31	1	.300
2001	Anaheim a-b	A.L.	C	15	37	8	10	3	0	2	4	0	.270

Year Club	Lea	Pos	G	AB	R	H	2B	3B	HR	RBI	SB	Avg
2002 Salt Lake	P.C.	C	79	290	30	89	14	2	4	43	0	.307
2002 Anaheim	A.L.	C	29	70	5	19	3	0	0	5	0	.271
2003 Anaheim	A.L.	C	53	114	12	21	4	0	0	6	0	.184
2004 Anaheim	A.L.	C-1B	73	203	26	53	10	2	3	25	4	.261
2005 Los Angeles	A.L.	C-1B	75	184	14	42	4	0	6	25	2	.228
2006 Los Angeles	A.L.	C-1B	78	225	18	54	17	0	4	22	1	.240
2007 Los Angeles-New York c-d	A.L.	C	69	191	18	49	13	0	1	19	2	.257
2008 New York	A.L.	C-1B	100	268	32	58	17	0	3	18	0	.216
2009 Scranton-WB	Int.	C	2	4	0	1	1	0	0	1	0	.250
2009 Trenton	Eastern	C	3	7	0	0	0	0	0	0	0	.000
2009 New York e	A.L.	C-1B-3B	52	138	15	30	4	0	1	11	0	.217
2010 Toronto f	A.L.	C	57	167	13	41	4	0	6	12	1	.246
2011 Toronto g	A.L.	C	55	171	19	48	12	1	3	15	2	.281
2012 Tampa Bay	A.L.	C	102	251	27	56	9	0	8	32	3	.223
2013 Tampa Bay h	A.L.	C	99	283	26	66	14	0	2	18	2	.233
Major League Totals		14 Yrs.	867	2321	236	552	115	3	39	213	17	.238
Wild Card Playoff												
2013 Tampa Bay	A.L.	C	1	3	0	0	0	0	0	0	0	.000
Division Series												
2004 Anaheim	A.L.	C	2	3	2	1	0	0	0	0	0	.333
2005 Los Angeles	A.L.	C	1	1	1	1	0	0	0	1	0	1.000
2009 New York	A.L.	C	1	1	0	0	0	0	0	0	0	.000
2013 Tampa Bay	A.L.	C	3	5	0	0	0	0	0	0	0	.000
Division Series Totals			7	10	3	2	0	0	0	1	0	.200
Championship Series												
2002 Anaheim	A.L.	C	3	1	0	0	0	0	0	0	0	.000
2005 Los Angeles	A.L.	C	1	3	0	1	0	0	0	0	0	.333
2009 New York	A.L.	C	2	3	0	1	0	0	0	0	0	.333
Championship Series Totals			6	7	0	2	0	0	0	0	0	.286
World Series Record												
2002 Anaheim	A.L.	C	3	0	0	0	0	0	0	0	0	.000
2009 New York	A.L.	C	2	2	0	0	0	0	0	0	0	.000
World Series Totals			5	2	0	0	0	0	0	0	0	.000

a Released by Chicago Cubs, November 27, 2000. Signed with Anaheim Angels organization, January 15, 2001.
b On disabled list from May 21 to July 2, 2001.
c Traded to New York Yankees for pitcher Jeff Kennard, July 21, 2007.
d Filed for free agency, October 30, 2007, re-signed with New York Yankees, December 3, 2007.
e On disabled list from May 8 to July 8, 2009.
f Filed for free agency, November 9, 2009. Signed with Toronto Blue Jays, February 19, 2010.
g Filed for free agency, October 30, 2011. Signed with Tampa Bay Rays, November 28, 2011.
h Filed for free agency, October 31, 2013, re-signed with Tampa Bay Rays, December 2, 2013.

MOLINA, YADIER BENJAMIN

Born, Bayamon, Puerto Rico, July 13, 1982.
Bats Right. Throws Right. Height, 5 feet, 11 inches. Weight, 225 pounds.

Year Club	Lea	Pos	G	AB	R	H	2B	3B	HR	RBI	SB	Avg
2001 Johnson City	Appal.	C	44	158	18	41	11	0	4	18	1	.259
2002 Peoria	Midwest	C	112	393	39	110	20	0	7	50	2	.280
2003 Tennessee	Southern	C	104	364	32	100	13	1	2	51	0	.275
2004 Memphis	P.C.	C	37	129	19	39	6	0	1	14	0	.302
2004 St. Louis	N.L.	C	51	135	12	36	6	0	2	15	0	.267
2005 St. Louis a	N.L.	C-1B	114	385	36	97	15	1	8	49	2	.252
2006 St. Louis	N.L.	C-1B	129	417	29	90	26	0	6	49	1	.216
2007 St. Louis b	N.L.	C-1B	111	353	30	97	15	0	6	40	1	.275
2008 St. Louis	N.L.	C-1B	124	444	37	135	18	0	7	56	0	.304
2009 St. Louis	N.L.	C-1B	140	481	45	141	23	1	6	54	9	.293
2010 St. Louis	N.L.	C-1B	136	465	34	122	19	0	6	62	8	.262
2011 St. Louis	N.L.	C-1B	139	475	55	145	32	1	14	65	4	.305
2012 St. Louis	N.L.	C-1B	138	505	65	159	28	0	22	76	12	.315
2013 St. Louis c	N.L.	C-1B	136	505	68	161	44	0	12	80	3	.319
Major League Totals		10 Yrs.	1218	4165	411	1183	226	3	89	546	40	.284
Wild Card Playoff												
2012 St. Louis	N.L.	C	1	4	0	0	0	0	0	1	0	.000
Division Series												
2005 St. Louis	N.L.	C	3	13	1	3	0	0	0	3	0	.231
2006 St. Louis	N.L.	C	4	13	0	4	1	0	0	1	0	.308
2009 St. Louis	N.L.	C	3	13	0	4	1	0	0	0	0	.308
2011 St. Louis	N.L.	C	5	19	1	4	0	0	0	1	1	.211

Year	Club	Lea	Pos	G	AB	R	H	2B	3B	HR	RBI	SB	Avg
2012	St. Louis.	N.L.	C	5	17	3	2	0	0	0	1	0	.118
2013	St. Louis.	N.L.	C	5	17	2	5	1	0	1	1	0	.294
Division Series Totals				25	92	7	22	3	0	1	7	1	.239
	Championship Series												
2004	St. Louis.	N.L.	C	1	4	0	1	0	0	0	0	0	.250
2005	St. Louis.	N.L.	C	6	22	1	7	3	0	0	0	0	.318
2006	St. Louis.	N.L.	C	7	23	2	8	1	0	2	6	0	.348
2011	St. Louis.	N.L.	C-1B	6	24	5	8	3	0	0	2	0	.333
2012	St. Louis.	N.L.	C	7	28	2	11	1	0	0	2	0	.393
2013	St. Louis.	N.L.	C	6	22	2	5	0	0	0	1	0	.227
Championship Series Totals				33	123	12	40	8	0	2	11	0	.325
	World Series Record												
2004	St. Louis.	N.L.	C	3	3	0	0	0	0	0	0	0	.000
2006	St. Louis.	N.L.	C	5	17	3	7	2	0	0	1	0	.412
2011	St. Louis.	N.L.	C	7	24	1	8	2	0	0	9	0	.333
2013	St. Louis.	N.L.	C	6	23	0	7	1	0	0	2	0	.304
World Series Totals.				21	67	4	22	5	0	0	12	0	.328

a On disabled list from July 9 to August 18, 2005.
b On disabled list from May 30 to June 28, 2007.
c On disabled list from July 31 to August 15, 2013.

MONTERO, MIGUEL ANGEL

Born, Caracas, Venezuela, July 9, 1983.
Bats Left. Throws Right. Height, 5 feet, 11 inches. Weight, 195 pounds.

Year	Club	Lea	Pos	G	AB	R	H	2B	3B	HR	RBI	SB	Avg
2002	Missoula	Pioneer	C-3B-1B	50	152	21	40	10	1	3	14	2	.263
2003	Missoula	Pioneer	C	59	196	24	59	10	2	4	32	2	.301
2004	South Bend	Midwest	C-1B-SS	115	403	47	106	22	2	11	59	8	.263
2005	Lancaster.	Calif.	C-1B	85	355	73	124	24	1	24	82	1	.349
2005	Tennessee	Southern	C-1B	30	108	13	27	1	2	2	13	1	.250
2006	Tennessee	Southern	C	81	289	24	78	18	0	10	46	0	.270
2006	Tucson	P.C.	C	36	134	21	43	5	0	7	29	1	.321
2006	Arizona.	N.L.	C	6	16	0	4	1	0	0	3	0	.250
2007	Arizona.	N.L.	C	84	214	30	48	7	0	10	37	0	.224
2008	Tucson	P.C.	C	11	32	3	9	2	0	1	5	0	.281
2008	Arizona a	N.L.	C	70	184	24	47	16	1	5	18	0	.255
2009	Arizona.	N.L.	C	128	425	61	125	30	0	16	59	1	.294
2010	Reno	P.C.	C	4	15	1	5	0	0	0	2	0	.333
2010	Arizona b	N.L.	C	85	297	36	79	20	2	9	43	0	.266
2011	Arizona.	N.L.	C	140	493	65	139	36	1	18	86	1	.282
2012	Arizona.	N.L.	C	141	486	65	139	25	2	15	88	0	.286
2013	D-Backs	Arizona	C	6	19	2	5	2	0	0	4	0	.263
2013	Arizona c	N.L.	C	116	413	44	95	14	0	11	42	0	.230
Major League Totals			8 Yrs.	770	2528	325	676	149	6	84	376	2	.267
	Division Series												
2007	Arizona.	N.L.	C	1	2	1	0	0	0	0	0	0	.000
2011	Arizona.	N.L.	C	5	20	3	6	2	0	0	2	0	.300
Division Series Totals				6	22	4	6	2	0	0	2	0	.273
	Championship Series												
2007	Arizona.	N.L.	C	3	5	0	2	0	0	0	0	0	.400

a On disabled list from March 23 to April 23, 2008.
b On disabled list from April 11 to June 12, 2010.
c On disabled list from July 29 to August 26, 2013.

MOORE, TYLER MICHAEL

Born, Brandon, Mississippi, January 30, 1987.
Bats Right. Throws Right. Height, 6 feet, 2 inches. Weight, 215 pounds.

Year	Club	Lea	Pos	G	AB	R	H	2B	3B	HR	RBI	SB	Avg
2008	Vermont.	N.Y.-Penn.	1B	71	265	17	53	10	0	6	28	1	.200
2009	Hagerstown	So.Atl.	1B	111	421	38	125	30	3	9	87	2	.297
2010	Potomac.	Carolina	1B	129	502	78	135	43	3	31	111	0	.269
2011	Harrisburg	Eastern	1B	137	519	70	140	35	4	31	90	2	.270
2012	Syracuse	Int.	1B-OF	29	101	15	31	6	1	9	26	1	.307
2012	Washington	N.L.	OF-1B	75	156	20	41	9	0	10	29	3	.263
2013	Syracuse	Int.	OF-1B	45	173	26	55	14	1	10	46	1	.318

Year	Club	Lea	Pos	G	AB	R	H	2B	3B	HR	RBI	SB	Avg
2013	Washington	N.L.	OF-1B	63	167	16	37	9	0	4	21	0	.222
Major League Totals			2 Yrs.	138	323	36	78	18	0	14	50	3	.241
Division Series													
2012	Washington	N.L.	PH	1	1	0	1	0	0	0	2	0	1.000

MORALES, KENDRYS

Born, Fomento, Cuba, June 20, 1983.
Bats Both. Throws Right. Height, 6 feet, 1 inch. Weight, 225 pounds.

Year	Club	Lea	Pos	G	AB	R	H	2B	3B	HR	RBI	SB	Avg
2005	Rancho Cucamonga	Calif.	1B-3B-OF	22	90	18	31	3	0	5	17	0	.344
2005	Arkansas	Texas	1B-OF	74	281	47	86	12	0	17	54	2	.306
2006	Salt Lake	P.C.	1B	66	256	41	82	13	1	12	52	0	.320
2006	Los Angeles	A.L.	1B	57	197	21	46	10	1	5	22	1	.234
2007	Salt Lake	P.C.	1B	64	255	42	87	20	1	5	37	0	.341
2007	Los Angeles	A.L.	1B-OF	43	119	12	35	10	0	4	15	0	.294
2008	Angels	Arizona	OF	5	21	4	11	3	0	1	10	0	.524
2008	Salt Lake	P.C.	1B-OF	78	317	46	108	19	0	15	64	1	.341
2008	Los Angeles	A.L.	OF-1B	27	61	7	13	2	0	3	8	0	.213
2009	Los Angeles	A.L.	1B	152	566	86	173	43	2	34	108	3	.306
2010	Los Angeles a	A.L.	1B	51	193	29	56	5	0	11	39	0	.290
2011	Los Angeles b	A.L.					INJURED—Did Not Play						
2012	Los Angeles c	A.L.	DH-1B	134	484	61	132	26	1	22	73	0	.273
2013	Seattle d	A.L.	DH-1B	156	602	64	167	34	0	23	80	0	.277
Major League Totals			7 Yrs.	620	2222	280	622	130	4	102	345	4	.280
Division Series													
2007	Los Angeles	A.L.	1B-DH	3	9	1	1	0	0	0	0	0	.111
2008	Los Angeles	A.L.	PH	4	4	0	2	1	0	0	0	0	.500
2009	Los Angeles	A.L.	1B	3	10	1	2	0	0	1	3	0	.200
Division Series Totals				10	23	2	5	1	0	1	3	0	.217
Championship Series													
2009	Los Angeles	A.L.	1B	6	24	1	4	0	0	1	4	0	.167

a On disabled list from May 30 to November 2, 2010.
b On disabled list from March 22 to October 30, 2011.
c Traded to Seattle Mariners for pitcher Jason Vargas, December 19, 2012.
d Filed for free agency, November 11, 2013.

MORELAND, MITCHELL AUSTIN (MITCH)

Born, Amory, Mississippi, September 6, 1985.
Bats Left. Throws Left. Height, 6 feet, 2 inches. Weight, 230 pounds.

Year	Club	Lea	Pos	G	AB	R	H	2B	3B	HR	RBI	SB	Avg
2007	Spokane	Northwest	1B-OF	27	108	10	28	7	1	2	15	1	.259
2008	Clinton	Midwest	1B-OF	123	466	64	151	37	4	18	99	2	.324
2009	Bakersfield	Calif.	1B-OF	43	170	34	58	19	0	8	26	1	.341
2009	Frisco	Texas	OF-1B	73	301	51	98	19	3	8	59	1	.326
2010	Oklahoma	P.C.	OF-1B	95	353	52	102	29	2	12	65	2	.289
2010	Texas	A.L.	1B-OF	47	145	20	37	4	0	9	25	3	.255
2011	Texas	A.L.	1B-OF	134	464	60	120	22	1	16	51	2	.259
2012	Frisco	Texas	1B	3	13	4	4	2	0	0	1	0	.308
2012	Round Rock	P.C.	1B	2	6	0	1	0	0	0	0	0	.167
2012	Texas a	A.L.	1B-OF	114	327	41	90	18	0	15	50	1	.275
2013	Frisco	Texas	1B	3	12	3	6	3	0	1	3	0	.500
2013	Texas b	A.L.	1B-OF	147	462	60	107	24	1	23	60	0	.232
Major League Totals			4 Yrs.	442	1398	181	354	68	2	63	186	6	.253
Wild Card Playoff													
2012	Texas	A.L.	PH	1	1	0	0	0	0	0	0	0	.000
Division Series													
2010	Texas	A.L.	1B	4	15	1	3	3	0	0	1	0	.200
2011	Texas	A.L.	1B	3	10	1	1	0	0	1	2	0	.100
Division Series Totals				7	25	2	4	3	0	1	3	0	.160
Championship Series													
2010	Texas	A.L.	1B	6	18	3	7	0	0	0	3	0	.389
2011	Texas	A.L.	1B	3	9	0	1	0	0	0	0	0	.111
Championship Series Totals				9	27	3	8	0	0	0	3	0	.296
World Series Record													
2010	Texas	A.L.	1B	5	13	1	6	1	0	1	3	0	.462

Year	Club	Lea	Pos	G	AB	R	H	2B	3B	HR	RBI	SB	Avg
2011	Texas	A.L.	1B	3	10	1	1	0	0	1	1	0	.100
World Series Totals				8	23	2	7	1	0	2	4	0	.304

a On disabled list from June 20 to July 30, 2012.
b On disabled list from June 6 to June 21, 2013.

MORNEAU, JUSTIN ERNEST GEORGE

Born, New Westminster, British Columbia, Canada, May 15, 1981.
Bats Left. Throws Right. Height, 6 feet, 4 inches. Weight, 225 pounds.

Year	Club	Lea	Pos	G	AB	R	H	2B	3B	HR	RBI	SB	Avg
1999	Twins	Gulf Coast	DH	17	53	3	16	5	0	0	9	0	.302
2000	Twins	Gulf Coast	1B-C-OF	52	194	47	78	21	0	10	58	3	.402
2000	Elizabethton	Appal.	C	6	23	4	5	0	0	1	3	0	.217
2001	Quad Cities	Midwest	1B	64	236	50	84	17	2	12	53	0	.356
2001	Fort Myers	Fla.St.	1B	53	197	25	58	10	3	4	40	0	.294
2001	New Britain	Eastern	1B	10	38	3	6	1	0	0	4	0	.158
2002	New Britain	Eastern	1B	126	494	72	147	31	4	16	80	7	.298
2003	New Britain	Eastern	1B	20	79	14	26	3	1	6	13	0	.329
2003	Rochester	Int.	1B	71	265	39	71	11	1	16	42	0	.268
2003	Minnesota	A.L.	DH-1B	40	106	14	24	4	0	4	16	0	.226
2004	Rochester	Int.	1B	72	288	51	88	23	0	22	63	1	.306
2004	Minnesota	A.L.	1B	74	280	39	76	17	0	19	58	0	.271
2005	Minnesota a	A.L.	1B	141	490	62	117	23	4	22	79	0	.239
2006	Minnesota b	A.L.	1B	157	592	97	190	37	1	34	130	3	.321
2007	Minnesota	A.L.	1B	157	590	84	160	31	3	31	111	1	.271
2008	Minnesota	A.L.	1B	*163	623	97	187	47	4	23	129	0	.300
2009	Minnesota	A.L.	1B	135	508	85	139	31	1	30	100	0	.274
2010	Minnesota c	A.L.	1B	81	296	53	102	25	1	18	56	0	.345
2011	Rochester	Int.	1B	7	30	8	11	4	0	1	8	0	.367
2011	Minnesota d	A.L.	1B	69	264	19	60	16	0	4	30	0	.227
2012	Minnesota e	A.L.	1B	134	505	63	135	26	2	19	77	1	.267
2013	Minnesota f	A.L.	1B	127	495	56	128	32	0	17	74	0	.259
2013	Pittsburgh g	N.L.	1B	25	77	6	20	4	0	0	3	0	.260
Major League Totals			11 Yrs.	1303	4826	675	1338	293	16	221	863	5	.277
	Wild Card Playoff												
2013	Pittsburgh	N.L.	1B	1	4	0	1	0	0	0	0	0	.250
	Division Series												
2004	Minnesota	A.L.	1B	4	17	1	4	2	0	0	2	0	.235
2006	Minnesota	A.L.	1B	3	12	3	5	1	0	2	2	0	.417
2013	Pittsburgh	N.L.	1B	5	20	4	6	1	0	0	0	0	.300
Division Series Totals				12	49	8	15	4	0	2	4	0	.306

a On disabled list from April 7 to April 22, 2005.
b Selected Most Valuable Player in American League for 2006.
c On disabled list from July 8 to November 2, 2010.
d On disabled list from June 10 to August 12 and September 12 to October 3, 2011.
e On disabled list from May 1 to May 16, 2012.
f Traded to Pittsburgh Pirates for outfielder Alex Presley and player to be named later, August 31, 2013. Minnesota Twins received pitcher Duke Welker to complete trade, October 5, 2013.
g Filed for free agency, October 31, 2013. Signed with Colorado Rockies, December 13, 2013.

MORRISON, JUSTIS LOGAN (LOGAN)

Born, Kansas City, Missouri, August 25, 1987.
Bats Left. Throws Left. Height, 6 feet, 3 inches. Weight, 235 pounds.

Year	Club	Lea	Pos	G	AB	R	H	2B	3B	HR	RBI	SB	Avg
2006	Marlins	Gulf Coast	1B	26	89	10	24	4	0	1	7	1	.270
2006	Jamestown	N.Y.-Penn.	1B	23	74	6	15	3	0	1	11	0	.203
2007	Greensboro	So.Atl.	1B	128	453	71	121	22	2	24	86	2	.267
2008	Jupiter	Fla.St.	1B	130	488	71	162	38	1	13	74	9	.332
2009	Jupiter	Fla.St.	1B	3	11	0	3	1	0	0	2	0	.273
2009	Jacksonville	Southern	1B-OF	79	278	48	77	18	2	8	47	9	.277
2010	Jupiter	Fla.St.	1B	5	21	3	8	2	2	0	2	0	.381
2010	New Orleans	P.C.	1B-OF	68	238	36	73	17	4	6	45	1	.307
2010	Florida	N.L.	OF	62	244	43	69	20	7	2	18	0	.283
2011	Jupiter	Fla.St.	OF	3	10	2	2	0	0	1	3	0	.200
2011	New Orleans	P.C.	OF	6	24	3	4	2	0	1	5	0	.167
2011	Florida a	N.L.	OF-1B	123	462	54	114	25	4	23	72	2	.247
2012	Miami b	N.L.	OF-1B	93	296	30	68	15	1	11	36	1	.230
2013	Jupiter	Fla.St.	1B	6	23	0	4	0	0	0	3	0	.174

Year	Club	Lea	Pos	G	AB	R	H	2B	3B	HR	RBI	SB	Avg
2013	Jacksonville	Southern	1B	10	33	5	6	0	0	2	7	0	.182
2013	Miami c-d	N.L.	1B	85	293	32	71	13	4	6	36	0	.242
Major League Totals			4 Yrs.	363	1295	159	322	73	16	42	162	3	.249

a On disabled list from April 20 to May 13, 2011.
b On disabled list from July 29 to October 31, 2012.
c On disabled list from March 31 to June 9, 2013.
d Traded to Seattle Mariners for pitcher Carter Capps, December 13, 2013.

MORSE, MICHAEL JOHN

Born, Fort Lauderdale, Florida, March 22, 1982.
Bats Right. Throws Right. Height, 6 feet, 4 inches. Weight, 230 pounds.

Year	Club	Lea	Pos	G	AB	R	H	2B	3B	HR	RBI	SB	Avg
2000	White Sox	Arizona	SS	45	180	32	46	6	1	2	24	5	.256
2001	Bristol	Appal.	SS	57	181	23	41	7	3	4	27	6	.227
2002	Kannapolis	So.Atl.	SS-3B	113	417	43	107	30	4	2	56	7	.257
2003	Winston-Salem	Carolina	SS	122	432	45	106	30	2	10	55	4	.245
2004	Birmingham	Southern	SS	54	209	30	60	9	5	11	38	0	.287
2004	San Antonio a	Texas	SS	41	157	18	43	10	1	6	33	0	.274
2005	Tacoma	P.C.	SS	49	182	20	46	12	2	4	23	1	.253
2005	Seattle	A.L.	SS-OF	72	230	27	64	10	1	3	23	3	.278
2006	Tacoma	P.C.	1B-3B-SS-OF	57	206	23	51	15	1	5	34	0	.248
2006	Seattle	A.L.	OF-3B-1B-SS	21	43	5	16	5	0	0	11	1	.372
2007	Mariners	Arizona	3B-SS	5	15	2	3	1	0	0	2	0	.200
2007	Tacoma	P.C.	3B-SS-OF	76	291	48	90	26	0	6	39	5	.309
2007	Seattle	A.L.	1B-3B-SS-OF	9	18	1	8	2	0	0	3	0	.444
2008	Seattle b	A.L.	OF	5	9	0	2	1	0	0	0	0	.222
2009	Tacoma	P.C.	SS-2B-3B-OF	66	260	38	81	14	0	10	52	0	.312
2009	Syracuse	Int.	1B-3B-OF-SS	44	165	21	56	12	3	6	34	2	.339
2009	Washington c	N.L.	1B-OF-3B	32	52	4	13	3	0	3	10	0	.250
2010	Syracuse	Int.	1B-OF-3B	15	51	12	13	2	0	3	8	0	.255
2010	Washington d	N.L.	OF-1B	98	266	36	77	12	2	15	41	0	.289
2011	Washington	N.L.	1B-OF	146	522	73	158	36	0	31	95	2	.303
2012	Hagerstown	So.Atl.	OF	1	4	1	2	0	0	0	0	0	.500
2012	Potomac	Carolina	OF	3	9	0	3	1	0	0	1	0	.333
2012	Harrisburg	Eastern	OF	3	8	1	3	2	0	1	4	0	.375
2012	Washington e	N.L.	OF-1B	102	406	53	118	17	1	18	62	0	.291
2013	Tacoma f	P.C.	OF	6	24	3	6	1	0	1	2	0	.250
2013	Seattle-Baltimore g-h-i	A.L.	OF-1B	88	312	34	67	13	0	13	27	0	.215
Major League Totals			9 Yrs.	573	1858	233	523	99	4	83	272	6	.281
Division Series													
2012	Washington	N.L.	OF	5	19	2	5	0	0	1	2	0	.263

a Traded by Chicago White Sox to Seattle Mariners with catcher Miguel Olivo and outfielder Jeremy Reed for pitcher Freddy Garcia, catcher Ben Davis and cash, June 27, 2004.
b On disabled list from April 14 to September 29, 2008.
c Traded to Washington Nationals for outfielder Ryan Langerhans, June 28, 2009.
d On disabled list from April 11 to May 16, 2010.
e On disabled list from March 26 to June 1, 2012.
f Traded to Seattle Mariners for catcher John Jaso, January 16, 2013.
g On disabled list from June 21 to July 29, 2013.
h Traded to Baltimore Orioles for outfielder Xavier Avery, August 30, 2013.
i Filed for free agency, October 31, 2013. Signed with San Francisco Giants, December 17, 2013.

MOSS, BRANDON DOUGLAS

Born, Monroe, Georgia, September 16, 1983.
Bats Left. Throws Right. Height, 6 feet. Weight, 210 pounds.

Year	Club	Lea	Pos	G	AB	R	H	2B	3B	HR	RBI	SB	Avg
2002	Red Sox	Gulf Coast	2B-3B	42	113	10	23	6	2	0	6	1	.204
2003	Lowell	N.Y.-Penn.	OF	65	228	29	54	15	4	7	34	7	.237
2004	Sarasota	Fla.St.	OF	23	83	16	35	2	1	2	10	2	.422
2004	Augusta	So.Atl.	OF	109	433	66	147	25	6	13	101	19	.339
2005	Portland	Eastern	OF	135	503	87	135	31	4	16	61	6	.268
2006	Portland	Eastern	OF	133	508	76	145	36	3	12	83	8	.285
2007	Pawtucket	Int.	OF-1B	133	493	66	139	41	2	16	78	3	.282
2007	Boston	A.L.	OF	15	25	6	7	2	1	0	1	0	.280
2008	Boston	A.L.	OF-1B	34	78	7	23	5	1	2	11	1	.295
2008	Pawtucket	Int.	1B-OF	43	163	29	46	8	4	8	30	2	.282
2008	Pittsburgh a-b	N.L.	OF	45	158	12	35	10	2	6	23	0	.222

Year	Club	Lea	Pos	G	AB	R	H	2B	3B	HR	RBI	SB	Avg
2009	Pittsburgh	N.L.	OF	133	385	47	91	20	4	7	41	1	.236
2010	Indianapolis	Int.	OF	136	500	73	133	32	2	22	96	12	.266
2010	Pittsburgh c	N.L.	OF	17	26	2	4	1	0	0	2	0	.154
2011	Lehigh Valley	Int.	OF	124	436	66	120	31	1	23	80	4	.275
2011	Philadelphia d	N.L.	OF	5	6	0	0	0	0	0	0	0	.000
2012	Sacramento	P.C.	OF-1B	51	196	32	56	11	1	15	33	4	.286
2012	Oakland	A.L.	1B-OF	84	265	48	77	18	0	21	52	1	.291
2013	Oakland	A.L.	1B-OF-3B	145	446	73	114	23	3	30	87	4	.256
Major League Totals			7 Yrs.	478	1389	195	351	79	11	66	217	7	.253
Division Series													
2012	Oakland	A.L.	1B	5	15	0	2	0	0	0	0	0	.133
2013	Oakland	A.L.	1B-DH	5	18	2	2	0	0	1	1	0	.111
Division Series Totals				10	33	2	4	0	0	1	1	0	.121

a On disabled list from May 3 to May 23, 2008.
b Traded to Pittsburgh Pirates with outfielder Manny Ramirez and pitcher Craig Hansen for outfielder Jason Bay, July 31, 2008.
c Filed for free agency, November 6, 2010. Signed with Philadelphia Phillies organization, November 19, 2010.
d Filed for free agency, October 18, 2011. Signed with Oakland Athletics organization, November 19, 2011.

MOUSTAKAS, MICHAEL CHRISTOPHER (MIKE)

Born, Los Angeles, California, September 11, 1988.
Bats Left. Throws Right. Height, 5 feet, 11 inches. Weight, 230 pounds.

Year	Club	Lea	Pos	G	AB	R	H	2B	3B	HR	RBI	SB	Avg
2007	Idaho Falls	Pioneer	SS	11	41	6	12	4	1	0	10	0	.293
2008	Burlington	Midwest	3B-SS	126	496	77	135	25	3	22	71	8	.272
2009	Wilmington	Carolina	3B	129	492	66	123	32	2	16	86	10	.250
2010	Omaha	P.C.	3B	52	225	36	66	16	0	15	48	2	.293
2010	NW Arkansas	Texas	3B	66	259	58	90	25	0	21	76	0	.347
2011	Omaha	P.C.	3B	55	223	38	64	15	1	10	44	1	.287
2011	Kansas City	A.L.	3B	89	338	26	89	18	1	5	30	2	.263
2012	Kansas City	A.L.	3B	149	563	69	136	34	1	20	73	5	.242
2013	Kansas City	A.L.	3B	136	472	42	110	26	0	12	42	2	.233
Major League Totals			3 Yrs.	374	1373	137	335	78	2	37	145	9	.244

MURPHY, DANIEL THOMAS

Born, Jacksonville, Florida, April 1, 1985.
Bats Left. Throws Right. Height, 6 feet, 3 inches. Weight, 205 pounds.

Year	Club	Lea	Pos	G	AB	R	H	2B	3B	HR	RBI	SB	Avg
2006	Mets	Gulf Coast	DH	8	18	2	1	0	0	0	0	0	.056
2006	Kingsport	Appal.	DH	9	33	2	9	0	0	2	7	0	.273
2006	Brooklyn	N.Y.-Penn.	DH	8	29	2	7	1	0	0	3	0	.241
2007	St. Lucie	Fla.St.	3B	135	502	68	143	34	3	11	78	6	.285
2008	Brooklyn	N.Y.-Penn.	DH	3	14	1	7	0	0	0	2	0	.500
2008	Binghamton	Eastern	3B-2B-1B-OF	95	357	56	110	26	1	13	67	14	.308
2008	New Orleans	P.C.	3B	1	4	2	1	0	0	0	0	0	.250
2008	New York	N.L.	OF	49	131	24	41	9	3	2	17	0	.313
2009	New York	N.L.	1B-OF	155	508	60	135	38	4	12	63	4	.266
2010	St. Lucie	Fla.St.	1B	3	11	2	8	1	0	1	6	0	.727
2010	Buffalo a	Int.	1B-2B	8	34	4	10	3	0	1	8	1	.294
2011	New York b	N.L.	1B-3B-2B-OF	109	391	49	125	28	2	6	49	5	.320
2012	New York	N.L.	2B-1B	156	571	62	166	40	3	6	65	10	.291
2013	New York	N.L.	2B-1B	161	658	92	188	38	4	13	78	23	.286
Major League Totals			5 Yrs.	630	2259	287	655	153	16	39	272	42	.290

a On disabled list from March 31 to May 24, 2010.
b On disabled list from August 8 to October 24, 2011.

MURPHY, DAVID MATTHEW

Born, Houston, Texas, October 18, 1981.
Bats Left. Throws Left. Height, 6 feet, 4 inches. Weight, 205 pounds.

Year	Club	Lea	Pos	G	AB	R	H	2B	3B	HR	RBI	SB	Avg
2003	Sarasota	Fla.St.	OF	45	153	18	37	5	1	1	18	6	.242
2003	Lowell	N.Y.-Penn.	OF	21	78	13	27	4	0	0	13	4	.346
2004	Sarasota	Fla.St.	OF	73	272	35	71	11	0	4	38	3	.261
2004	Red Sox	Gulf Coast	OF	5	18	3	5	1	0	0	1	1	.278
2005	Portland	Eastern	OF	135	484	71	133	25	4	14	75	13	.275

Year	Club	Lea	Pos	G	AB	R	H	2B	3B	HR	RBI	SB	Avg
2006	Portland	Eastern	OF	42	172	22	47	17	1	3	25	4	.273
2006	Pawtucket	Int.	OF	84	318	45	85	23	5	8	44	3	.267
2006	Boston	A.L.	OF	20	22	4	5	1	0	1	2	0	.227
2007	Oklahoma	P.C.	OF	2	7	0	2	0	0	0	0	0	.286
2007	Pawtucket	Int.	OF	100	400	50	112	20	5	9	47	8	.280
2007	Boston-Texas a	A.L.	OF	46	105	17	36	12	2	2	14	0	.343
2008	Texas b	A.L.	OF	108	415	64	114	28	3	15	74	7	.275
2009	Texas	A.L.	OF	128	432	61	116	24	1	17	57	9	.269
2010	Texas	A.L.	OF	138	419	54	122	26	2	12	65	14	.291
2011	Texas	A.L.	OF	120	404	46	111	14	2	11	46	11	.275
2012	Texas	A.L.	OF	147	457	65	139	29	3	15	61	10	.304
2013	Texas c	A.L.	OF-P	142	436	51	96	26	1	13	45	1	.220
Major League Totals			8 Yrs.	849	2690	362	739	160	14	86	364	52	.275
	Wild Card Playoff												
2012	Texas	A.L.	OF	1	2	0	0	0	0	0	0	0	.000
	Division Series												
2010	Texas	A.L.	OF	2	7	0	1	0	0	0	0	0	.143
2011	Texas	A.L.	OF	3	6	0	2	0	0	0	0	0	.333
Division Series Totals				5	13	0	3	0	0	0	0	0	.231
	Championship Series												
2010	Texas	A.L.	OF	6	13	6	3	1	0	1	2	0	.231
2011	Texas	A.L.	OF-DH	5	17	4	7	2	1	0	3	1	.412
Championship Series Totals				11	30	10	10	3	1	1	5	1	.333
	World Series Record												
2010	Texas	A.L.	OF	3	7	0	1	0	0	0	1	0	.143
2011	Texas	A.L.	OF	7	18	1	4	1	0	0	0	0	.222
World Series Totals				10	25	1	5	1	0	0	1	0	.200

a Traded to Texas Rangers with pitcher Kason Gabbard and outfielder Engle Beltre for pitcher Eric Gagne, July 31, 2007.

b On disabled list from August 7 to October 2, 2008.

c Filed for free agency, October 31, 2013. Signed with Cleveland Indians, November 25, 2013.

MYERS, WILLIAM BRADFORD (WIL)

Born, High Point, North Carolina, December 10, 1990.
Bats Right. Throws Right. Height, 6 feet, 1 inches. Weight, 205 pounds.

Year	Club	Lea	Pos	G	AB	R	H	2B	3B	HR	RBI	SB	Avg
2009	Burlington	Appal.	C	4	16	1	2	0	1	1	4	0	.125
2009	Idaho Falls	Pioneer	C	18	68	18	29	7	1	4	14	2	.426
2010	Burlington	Midwest	C	68	242	42	70	19	1	10	45	10	.289
2010	Wilmington	Carolina	C	58	205	28	71	18	2	4	38	2	.346
2011	NW Arkansas	Texas	OF	99	354	50	90	23	1	8	49	9	.254
2012	NW Arkansas	Texas	OF-3B	35	134	32	46	11	1	13	30	4	.343
2012	Omaha a	Pacific	OF-3B	99	388	66	118	15	5	24	79	2	.304
2013	Durham	Int.	OF	64	252	44	72	13	2	14	57	7	.286
2013	Tampa Bay b	A.L.	OF	88	335	50	98	23	0	13	53	5	.293
	Wild Card Playoff												
2013	Tampa Bay	A.L.	OF	1	4	0	1	0	0	0	0	0	.250
	Division Series												
2013	Tampa Bay	A.L.	OF	4	16	0	1	0	0	0	0	0	.063

a Traded by Kansas City Royals to Tampa Bay Rays with pitcher Mike Montgomery, pitcher Jake Odorizzi and infielder Patrick Leonard for pitcher James Shields, pitcher Wade Davis and player to be named later, December 9, 2012. Kansas City Royals received infielder Elliot Johnson to complete trade, February 12, 2013.

b Selected Rookie of the Year in American League for 2013.

NAPOLI, MICHAEL ANTHONY (MIKE)

Born, Hollywood, Florida, October 31, 1981.
Bats Right. Throws Right. Height, 6 feet. Weight, 205 pounds.

Year	Club	Lea	Pos	G	AB	R	H	2B	3B	HR	RBI	SB	Avg
2000	Butte	Pioneer	1B-C	10	26	3	6	2	0	0	3	1	.231
2001	Rancho Cucamonga	Calif.	C	7	20	3	4	0	0	1	4	0	.200
2001	Cedar Rapids	Midwest	C-1B	43	155	23	36	10	1	5	18	3	.232
2002	Cedar Rapids	Midwest	C-1B-3B	106	362	57	91	19	1	10	50	6	.251
2003	Rancho Cucamonga	Calif.	C-1B	47	165	28	44	10	1	4	26	5	.267
2004	Rancho Cucamonga	Calif.	C-1B-3B	132	482	94	136	29	4	29	118	9	.282
2005	Arkansas	Texas	C-1B	131	439	96	104	22	2	31	99	12	.237
2006	Salt Lake	P.C.	C-1B	21	78	12	19	6	0	3	10	1	.244
2006	Los Angeles	A.L.	C	99	268	47	61	13	0	16	42	2	.228

Year	Club	Lea	Pos	G	AB	R	H	2B	3B	HR	RBI	SB	Avg
2007	Los Angeles a	A.L.	C	75	219	40	54	11	1	10	34	5	.247
2008	Rancho Cucamonga	Calif.	C	5	14	3	8	3	0	1	4	0	.571
2008	Los Angeles b	A.L.	C	78	227	39	62	9	1	20	49	7	.273
2009	Los Angeles	A.L.	C	114	382	60	104	22	1	20	56	3	.272
2010	Los Angeles	A.L.	1B-C	140	453	60	108	24	1	26	68	4	.238
2011	Round Rock	P.C.	C-1B	4	15	3	4	1	0	3	9	0	.267
2011	Texas c-d-e	A.L.	C-1B	113	369	72	118	25	0	30	75	4	.320
2012	Texas f-g	A.L.	C-1B	108	352	53	80	9	2	24	56	1	.227
2013	Boston h	A.L.	1B	139	498	79	129	38	2	23	92	1	.259
Major League Totals			8 Yrs.	866	2768	450	716	151	8	169	472	27	.259
	Wild Card Playoff												
2012	Texas	A.L.	C-DH	1	3	0	0	0	0	0	0	0	.000
	Division Series												
2007	Los Angeles	A.L.	C	3	6	0	1	0	0	0	0	0	.167
2008	Los Angeles	A.L.	C	4	12	3	3	0	0	2	4	0	.250
2009	Los Angeles	A.L.	C	2	4	1	1	1	0	0	0	0	.250
2011	Texas	A.L.	C	4	14	3	5	0	0	1	4	1	.357
2013	Boston	A.L.	1B	4	13	1	2	1	0	0	1	0	.154
Division Series Totals				17	49	8	12	2	0	3	9	1	.245
	Championship Series												
2009	Los Angeles	A.L.	C	5	9	0	1	0	0	0	0	0	.111
2011	Texas	A.L.	C-1B-DH	6	24	6	7	0	0	0	1	0	.292
2013	Boston	A.L.	1B	6	20	4	6	2	0	2	2	0	.300
Championship Series Totals				17	53	10	14	2	0	2	3	0	.264
	World Series Record												
2011	Texas	A.L.	C-1B	7	20	2	7	1	0	2	10	0	.350
2013	Boston	A.L.	1B	5	13	0	2	1	0	0	4	0	.154
World Series Totals				12	33	2	9	2	0	2	14	0	.273

a On disabled list from July 2 to July 18 and July 28 to September 1, 2007.
b On disabled list from July 6 to August 8, 2008.
c Traded to Toronto Blue Jays with outfielder Juan Rivera for outfielder Vernon Wells, January 21, 2011.
d Traded to Texas Rangers for pitcher Frank Francisco, January 25, 2011.
e On disabled list from June 12 to July 4, 2011.
f On disabled list from August 11 to September 15, 2012.
g Filed for free agency, November 3, 2012. Signed with Boston Red Sox, January 22, 2013.
h Filed for free agency, October 31, 2013, re-signed with Boston Red Sox, December 12, 2013.

NAVA, DANIEL JAMES

Born, Redwood City, California, February 22, 1983.
Bats Both. Throws Left. Height, 5 feet, 10 inches. Weight, 200 pounds.

Year	Club	Lea	Pos	G	AB	R	H	2B	3B	HR	RBI	SB	Avg
2007	Chico a	Golden	OF	72	256	70	95	23	3	12	59	18	.371
2008	Lancaster b	Calif.	OF	85	323	54	110	27	1	10	59	4	.341
2009	Salem	Carolina	OF	29	109	18	37	12	1	1	13	0	.339
2009	Portland	Eastern	OF	32	118	25	43	10	1	4	23	0	.364
2010	Pawtucket	Int.	OF	77	284	41	82	16	1	10	48	4	.289
2010	Boston	A.L.	OF	60	161	23	39	14	1	1	26	1	.242
2011	Pawtucket	Int.	OF	121	441	69	118	27	2	10	48	10	.268
2012	Pawtucket	Int.	OF	29	99	20	31	7	1	4	18	1	.313
2012	Boston c	A.L.	OF	88	267	38	65	21	0	6	33	3	.243
2013	Boston	A.L.	OF-1B	134	458	77	139	29	0	12	66	0	.303
Major League Totals			3 Yrs.	282	886	138	243	64	1	19	125	4	.274
	Division Series												
2013	Boston	A.L.	OF	2	5	0	1	0	0	0	0	0	.200
Championship Series													
2013	Boston	A.L.	OF	2	6	0	2	0	0	0	0	0	.333
	World Series Record												
2013	Boston	A.L.	OF	5	14	1	2	1	0	0	2	0	.143

a Signed by independent Chico, 2007.
b Signed by Boston Red Sox organization, January 17, 2008.
c On disabled list from July 29 to August 21 and August 25 to September 9, 2012.

NAVARRO (VIVAS), DIONER FAVIAN

Born, Caracas, Venezuela, February 9, 1984.
Bats Both. Throws Right. Height, 5 feet, 10 inches. Weight, 205 pounds.

Year	Club	Lea	Pos	G	AB	R	H	2B	3B	HR	RBI	SB	Avg
2001	Yankees	Gulf Coast	C	43	143	27	40	10	1	2	22	6	.280
2002	Greensboro	So.Atl.	C	92	328	41	78	12	2	8	36	1	.238
2002	Tampa	Fla.St.	C	1	2	1	1	0	0	0	0	0	.500
2003	Tampa	Fla.St.	C	52	197	28	59	16	4	3	28	1	.299
2003	Trenton	Eastern	C	58	208	28	71	15	0	4	37	2	.341
2004	Trenton	Eastern	C	70	255	32	69	14	1	3	29	1	.271
2004	Columbus	Int.	C	40	136	18	34	8	2	1	16	1	.250
2004	New York a	A.L.	C	5	7	2	3	0	0	0	1	0	.429
2005	Las Vegas b	P.C.	C	75	241	31	64	12	0	6	29	2	.266
2005	Los Angeles	N.L.	C	50	176	21	48	9	0	3	14	0	.273
2006	Los Angeles c	N.L.	C	25	75	5	21	2	0	2	8	1	.280
2006	Las Vegas d	P.C.	C	11	40	3	7	2	0	0	2	1	.175
2006	Tampa Bay	A.L.	C	56	193	23	47	7	0	4	20	1	.244
2007	Tampa Bay	A.L.	C	119	388	46	88	19	2	9	44	3	.227
2008	Vero Beach	Fla.St.	C	4	10	4	4	1	0	1	4	1	.400
2008	Tampa Bay e	A.L.	C	120	427	43	126	27	0	7	54	0	.295
2009	Tampa Bay	A.L.	C	115	376	38	82	15	0	8	32	5	.218
2010	Durham	Int.	C	43	141	19	40	9	0	2	21	3	.284
2010	Tampa Bay f	A.L.	C	48	124	11	24	5	0	1	7	0	.194
2011	Chattanooga	Southern	C-1B	5	14	0	2	0	0	0	1	2	.143
2011	Los Angeles g-h	N.L.	C	64	176	13	34	6	1	5	17	0	.193
2012	Louisville	Int.	C	62	207	24	66	12	0	5	32	0	.319
2012	Cincinnati i	N.L.	C	24	69	6	20	3	1	2	12	0	.290
2013	Chicago j	N.L.	C	89	240	31	72	7	0	13	34	0	.300
Major League Totals			10 Yrs.	715	2251	239	565	100	4	54	243	10	.251
	Division Series												
2008	Tampa Bay	A.L.	C	4	15	1	6	3	0	0	3	0	.400
2012	Cincinnati	N.L.	C	2	4	0	1	0	0	0	0	0	.250
Division Series Totals				6	19	1	7	3	0	0	3	0	.368
	Championship Series												
2008	Tampa Bay	A.L.	C	7	26	1	5	0	0	0	2	0	.192
	World Series Record												
2008	Tampa Bay	A.L.	C	5	17	2	6	1	0	0	0	0	.353

a Traded to Arizona Diamondbacks with pitcher Javier Vazquez, pitcher Brad Halsey and cash for pitcher Randy Johnson, January 11, 2005.

b Traded to Los Angeles Dodgers with pitcher Danny Muegge, pitcher Beltran Perez and pitcher William Juarez for outfielder Shawn Green, January 11, 2005.

c On disabled list from May 5 to June 15, 2006.

d Traded to Tampa Bay Devil Rays with pitcher Jae Seo and player to be named later for pitcher Mark Hendrickson, catcher Toby Hall and cash, June 27, 2006.

e On disabled list from April 5 to April 22, 2008.

f Not offered contract, December 2, 2010. Signed with Los Angeles Dodgers, December 8, 2010.

g On disabled list from March 22 to April 25, 2011.

h Released by Los Angeles Dodgers, August 30, 2011. Signed with Cincinnati Reds organization, January 16, 2012.

i Filed for free agency, November 3, 2012. Signed with Chicago Cubs, November 16, 2012.

j Filed for free agency, October 31, 2013. Signed with Toronto Blue Jays, December 2, 2013.

NELSON, CHRISTOPHER L. (CHRIS)

Born, Escondido, California, September 3, 1985.
Bats Right. Throws Right. Height, 5 feet, 11 inches. Weight, 175 pounds.

Year	Club	Lea	Pos	G	AB	R	H	2B	3B	HR	RBI	SB	Avg
2004	Casper	Pioneer	SS	38	147	36	51	6	3	4	20	6	.347
2005	Asheville	So.Atl.	SS	79	315	51	76	13	3	3	38	7	.241
2006	Asheville	So.Atl.	SS	118	466	69	121	38	1	11	76	14	.260
2007	Modesto	Calif.	SS	133	529	97	153	42	7	19	99	27	.289
2008	Modesto	Calif.	SS	8	30	2	5	1	0	1	5	0	.167
2008	Tulsa	Texas	SS	73	283	38	67	18	2	3	42	6	.237
2009	Tulsa	Texas	SS-2B	29	107	21	30	5	2	4	17	5	.280
2010	Colorado Springs	P.C.	SS-2B-3B-OF	85	319	60	100	15	3	12	55	7	.313
2010	Colorado	N.L.	2B-3B	17	25	7	7	1	0	0	0	1	.280
2011	Colorado Springs	P.C.	SS-2B-3B	73	289	52	95	20	5	11	65	3	.329
2011	Colorado	N.L.	2B-3B-SS	63	180	20	45	10	1	4	16	3	.250
2012	Colorado Springs	P.C.	3B-2B	13	51	12	15	4	1	0	8	1	.294
2012	Colorado a	N.L.	3B-2B-SS	111	345	45	104	21	3	9	53	2	.301
2013	Salt Lake	P.C.	3B-SS-2B-OF	34	134	20	44	11	0	6	24	4	.328
2013	Colorado b-c	N.L.	3B	21	66	6	16	1	2	0	4	0	.242

Year	Club	Lea	Pos	G	AB	R	H	2B	3B	HR	RBI	SB	Avg
2013	New York-LA d-e....	A.L.	3B-2B	43	145	13	32	3	2	3	20	2	.221
Major League Totals			4 Yrs.	255	761	91	204	36	8	16	93	8	.268

a On disabled list from May 15 to May 31 and July 16 to August 6, 2012.
b Sold to New York Yankees, May 1, 2013.
c Claimed on waivers by Los Angeles Angels, May 18, 2013.
d On disabled list from August 29 to September 17, 2013.
e Not offered contract, December 2, 2013.

NIEVES, WILBERT (WIL)

Born, San Juan, Puerto Rico, September 25, 1977.
Bats Right. Throws Right. Height, 5 feet, 11 inches. Weight, 190 pounds.

Year	Club	Lea	Pos	G	AB	R	H	2B	3B	HR	RBI	SB	Avg
1996	Padres	Arizona	C-3B-OF	43	113	23	39	5	0	2	22	3	.345
1997	Clinton	Midwest	C	18	55	6	12	1	1	1	7	2	.218
1997	Padres	Arizona	DH-OF	8	27	2	8	2	0	0	2	1	.296
1998	Clinton	Midwest	C	115	380	47	97	22	0	3	55	7	.255
1999	Rancho Cucamonga....	Calif.	C	120	427	58	140	26	2	7	61	2	.328
2000	Rancho Cucamonga....	Calif.	C	31	101	16	26	5	0	0	9	2	.257
2000	Mobile	Southern	C-1B-2B	68	214	18	57	4	0	4	30	1	.266
2000	Las Vegas............	P.C.	DH	1	1	0	0	0	0	0	0	0	.000
2001	Mobile	Southern	C	95	330	28	99	24	0	3	41	1	.300
2002	Portland..............	P.C.	C-1B	70	237	24	73	20	2	7	29	0	.308
2002	San Diego a	N.L.	C	28	72	2	13	3	1	0	3	1	.181
2003	Salt Lake	P.C.	C-1B	102	361	48	102	16	2	4	38	1	.283
2004	Salt Lake b...........	P.C.	C-1B-3B	108	421	60	125	22	8	10	53	3	.297
2005	Columbus..............	Int.	C	102	380	45	110	22	3	4	37	1	.289
2005	New York	A.L.	C	3	4	0	0	0	0	0	0	0	.000
2006	Columbus..............	Int.	C	88	321	29	83	13	0	5	34	2	.259
2006	New York	A.L.	C	6	6	0	0	0	0	0	0	0	.000
2007	New York	A.L.	C-1B	26	61	6	10	4	0	0	8	0	.164
2007	Scranton/WB c..........	Int.	C	27	90	5	23	1	2	1	8	1	.256
2008	Columbus..............	Int.	C	9	25	3	6	1	0	0	2	1	.240
2008	Washington	N.L.	C	68	176	15	46	9	1	1	20	0	.261
2009	Washington	N.L.	C	72	224	20	58	6	0	1	26	1	.259
2010	Washington d..........	N.L.	C	59	158	10	32	8	0	3	16	0	.203
2011	Milwaukee	N.L.	C	20	50	2	7	2	0	0	0	0	.140
2011	Nashville	P.C.	C	23	88	3	15	2	0	1	6	0	.170
2011	Gwinnett e	Int.	C	21	71	8	20	2	0	1	6	1	.282
2012	Colorado Springs.......	P.C.	C	34	111	15	34	4	0	3	16	1	.306
2012	Colorado-Arizona f-g-h .	N.L.	C-1B	32	83	7	25	3	0	2	8	0	.301
2013	Arizona i.............	N.L.	C	71	195	16	58	11	0	1	22	0	.297
Major League Totals			10 Yrs.	385	1029	78	249	46	2	8	103	2	.242

a Claimed on waivers by Anaheim Angels, December 18, 2002.
b Traded to New York Yankees for pitcher Bret Prinz, March 29, 2005.
c Filed for free agency, October 9, 2007. Signed with Washington Nationals organization, February 6, 2008.
d Not offered contract, December 2, 2010. Signed with Milwaukee Brewers, December 10, 2010.
e Filed for free agency, November 2, 2011. Signed with Colorado Rockies organization, December 19, 2011.
f On disabled list from July 9 to August 1, 2012.
g Claimed on waivers by Arizona Diamondbacks, August 6, 2012.
h Not offered contract, November 30, 2012, re-signed with Arizona Diamondbacks, December 6, 2012.
i Filed for free agency, October 31, 2013. Signed with Philadelphia Phillies, December 5, 2013.

NIX, JAYSON TRUITT EDWARD

Born, Dallas, Texas, August 26, 1982.
Bats Right. Throws Right. Height, 5 feet, 11 inches. Weight, 195 pounds.

Year	Club	Lea	Pos	G	AB	R	H	2B	3B	HR	RBI	SB	Avg
2001	Casper	Pioneer	SS	42	153	28	45	10	1	5	24	1	.294
2002	Asheville........	So.Atl.	2B	132	487	73	120	29	2	14	79	14	.246
2003	Visalia	Calif.	2B	137	562	107	158	46	0	21	86	24	.281
2004	Tulsa	Texas	2B	123	456	58	97	17	1	14	58	14	.213
2005	Tulsa	Texas	2B	131	501	68	118	27	0	11	47	10	.236
2006	Colorado Springs...	P.C.	2B-3B	103	358	39	90	14	1	2	26	15	.251
2007	Colorado Springs...	P.C.	2B-3B	124	439	80	128	33	2	11	58	24	.292
2008	Colorado	N.L.	2B	22	56	2	7	2	0	0	2	1	.125
2008	Colorado Springs a .	P.C.	2B-3B	67	264	63	80	21	2	17	51	11	.303
2009	Birmingham...	Southern	SS	3	10	1	3	0	0	0	3	0	.300
2009	Charlotte	Int.	SS-2B	5	20	4	9	1	0	0	5	1	.450
2009	Chicago b..........	A.L.	2B-SS-3B-OF	94	255	36	57	11	0	12	32	10	.224

Year Club	Lea	Pos	G	AB	R	H	2B	3B	HR	RBI	SB	Avg
2010 Chicago-Cleveland c	A.L.	3B-2B-OF-SS	102	331	32	74	15	0	14	34	1	.224
2011 Dunedin	Fla.St.	3B	3	12	0	1	0	0	0	2	0	.083
2011 Toronto	A.L.	3B-2B-OF	46	136	15	23	5	1	4	16	4	.169
2011 Las Vegas d-e-f	P.C.	3B-SS-OF-2B	41	163	30	44	12	2	8	29	3	.270
2012 Scranton-WB	Int.	2B-3B-OF	8	30	5	7	4	0	0	4	0	.233
2012 New York	A.L.	3B-SS-2B-OF	74	177	24	43	13	0	4	18	6	.243
2013 Yankees1	Gulf Coast	3B	1	2	0	0	0	0	0	0	0	.000
2013 Tampa	Fla.St.	3B	3	10	1	1	1	0	0	1	0	.100
2013 New York g-h	A.L.	SS-3B-2B	87	267	32	63	9	1	3	24	13	.236
Major League Totals		6 Yrs.	425	1222	141	267	55	2	37	126	35	.218
Division Series												
2012 New York	A.L.	SS	2	4	0	2	1	0	0	0	0	.500
Championship Series												
2012 New York	A.L.	SS-3B	4	4	0	0	0	0	0	0	0	.000

a Filed for free agency, October 15, 2008. Signed with Chicago White Sox, October 24, 2008.
b On disabled list from March 27 to May 1, 2009.
c Claimed on waivers by Cleveland Indians, June 25, 2010.
d Sold to Toronto Blue Jays, March 29, 2011.
e On disabled list from April 23 to May 16, 2011.
f Filed for free agency, November 2, 2011. Signed with New York Yankees organization, November 22, 2011.
g On disabled list from July 2 to July 28 and August 22 to November 4, 2013.
h Not offered contract, December 2, 2013. Signed with Tampa Bay Rays organization, January 9, 2014.

NORRIS, DEREK RYAN

Born, Ryan, Kansas, February 14, 1989.
Bats Right. Throws Right. Height, 6 feet. Weight, 210 pounds.

Year Club	Lea	Pos	G	AB	R	H	2B	3B	HR	RBI	SB	Avg
2007 Nationals	Gulf Coast	C-1B	37	123	16	25	6	2	4	15	2	.203
2008 Vermont	N.Y.-Penn.	C	70	227	42	63	12	0	10	38	11	.278
2009 Hagerstown	So.Atl.	C	126	437	78	125	30	0	23	84	6	.286
2010 Potomac	Carolina	C	94	298	67	70	19	0	12	49	6	.235
2011 Harrisburg a	Eastern	C	104	334	75	70	17	1	20	46	13	.210
2012 Sacramento	P.C.	C	58	218	39	59	14	2	9	38	5	.271
2012 Oakland	A.L.	C	60	209	19	42	8	1	7	34	5	.201
2013 Sacramento	P.C.	C	3	14	3	6	0	0	2	4	0	.429
2013 Oakland b	A.L.	C-1B	98	264	41	65	16	0	9	30	5	.246
Major League Totals		2 Yrs.	158	473	60	107	24	1	16	64	10	.226
Division Series												
2012 Oakland	A.L.	C	5	12	0	1	0	0	0	0	0	.083
2013 Oakland	A.L.	C	1	1	0	0	0	0	0	0	0	.000
Division Series Totals			6	13	0	1	0	0	0	0	0	.077

a Traded by Washington Nationals to Oakland Athletics with pitcher A.J. Cole, pitcher Brad Peacock and pitcher Tom Milone for pitcher Gio Gonzalez and pitcher Robert Gilliam, December 23, 2011.
b On disabled list from August 21 to September 5, 2013.

NUNEZ (MENDEZ), EDUARDO MICHELLE

Born, Santo Domingo, Dominican Republic, June 15, 1987.
Bats Right. Throws Right. Height, 6 feet. Weight, 155 pounds.

Year Club	Lea	Pos	G	AB	R	H	2B	3B	HR	RBI	SB	Avg
2005 Staten Island	N.Y.-Penn.	SS	73	281	37	88	11	6	3	46	6	.313
2006 Tampa	Fla.St.	SS	37	147	17	27	5	3	4	26	6	.184
2006 Charleston	So.Atl.	SS-2B-3B	90	344	36	78	11	3	2	40	16	.227
2007 Charleston	So.Atl.	SS	91	328	36	78	10	2	1	28	20	.238
2007 Tampa	Fla.St.	SS	30	123	16	35	5	0	1	13	9	.285
2008 Tampa	Fla.St.	SS	94	373	45	101	18	3	6	42	14	.271
2009 Trenton	Eastern	SS	123	497	70	160	26	1	9	55	19	.322
2010 Scranton-WB	Int.	SS-3B-2B	118	464	55	134	25	3	4	50	23	.289
2010 New York	A.L.	3B-SS-2B	30	50	12	14	1	0	1	7	5	.280
2011 New York	A.L.	SS-3B-2B-OF	112	309	38	82	18	2	5	30	22	.265
2012 Yankees	Gulf Coast	SS	4	10	1	2	0	0	1	1	0	.200
2012 Tampa	Fla.St.	SS	2	7	2	2	0	0	0	0	1	.286
2012 Scranton-WB	Int.	SS	38	163	18	37	4	0	2	16	16	.227
2012 New York	A.L.	SS-3B-OF-2B	38	89	14	26	4	1	1	11	11	.292
2013 Charleston	So.Atl.	SS	2	5	1	2	0	0	0	0	1	.400
2013 Tampa	Fla.St.	SS	3	3	2	1	0	0	0	0	2	.333
2013 Trenton	Eastern	SS	2	8	1	3	0	0	0	1	0	.375

Year	Club	Lea	Pos	G	AB	R	H	2B	3B	HR	RBI	SB	Avg
2013	New York a	A.L.	SS-3B-2B	90	304	38	79	17	4	3	28	10	.260
Major League Totals			4 Yrs.	270	752	102	201	40	7	10	76	48	.267
	Division Series												
2011	New York	A.L.	PH	1	0	0	0	0	0	0	0	1	.000
2012	New York	A.L.	SS-DH	3	5	2	1	1	0	0	0	0	.200
Division Series Totals				4	5	2	1	1	0	0	0	1	.200
	Championship Series												
2012	New York	A.L.	SS	2	6	2	2	0	1	1	1	1	.333

a On disabled list from May 6 to July 6, 2013.

ORTIZ (ARIAS), DAVID AMERICO

Born, Santo Domingo, Dominican Republic, November 18, 1975.
Bats Left. Throws Left. Height, 6 feet, 4 inches. Weight, 230 pounds.

Year	Club	Lea	Pos	G	AB	R	H	2B	3B	HR	RBI	SB	Avg
1993	Seattle	Domincan	1B	61	201	37	53	17	1	7	31	1	.264
1994	Mariners	Arizona	1B	53	167	14	41	10	1	2	20	1	.246
1995	Mariners	Arizona	1B	48	184	30	61	18	4	4	37	2	.332
1996	Wisconsin a	Midwest	1B	129	485	89	156	34	2	18	93	3	.322
1997	Salt Lake	P.C.	1B	10	42	5	9	1	0	4	10	0	.214
1997	New Britain	Eastern	DH-1B	69	258	40	83	22	2	14	56	2	.322
1997	Fort Myers	Fla.St.	1B	61	239	45	79	15	0	13	58	2	.331
1997	Fort Myers	A.L.	1B	15	49	10	16	3	0	1	6	0	.327
1998	Salt Lake	P.C.	1B	11	37	5	9	3	0	2	6	0	.243
1998	Minnesota b	A.L.	1B	86	278	47	77	20	0	9	46	1	.277
1999	Salt Lake	P.C.	1B	130	476	85	150	35	3	30	110	2	.315
1999	Minnesota	A.L.	1B	10	20	1	0	0	0	0	0	0	.000
2000	Minnesota	A.L.	DH-1B	130	415	59	117	36	1	10	63	1	.282
2001	Twins	Gulf Coast	DH	4	10	3	4	0	0	0	1	1	.400
2001	Fort Myers	Fla.St.	1B	1	3	0	0	0	0	0	0	0	.000
2001	New Britain	Eastern	1B	9	37	3	9	4	0	0	1	0	.243
2001	Minnesota c	A.L.	DH-1B	89	303	46	71	17	1	18	48	1	.234
2002	Minnesota d-e	A.L.	DH-1B	125	412	52	112	32	1	20	75	1	.272
2003	Boston	A.L.	DH-1B	128	448	79	129	39	2	31	101	0	.288
2004	Boston	A.L.	DH-1B	150	582	94	175	47	3	41	139	0	.301
2005	Boston	A.L.	DH-1B	159	601	119	180	40	1	47	*148	1	.300
2006	Boston	A.L.	DH-1B	151	558	115	160	29	2	*54	*137	1	.287
2007	Boston	A.L.	DH-1B	149	549	116	182	52	1	35	117	3	.332
2008	Portland	Eastern	DH	3	8	2	2	0	0	0	1	0	.250
2008	Pawtucket	Int.	DH	3	9	4	3	0	0	3	5	0	.333
2008	Boston f	A.L.	DH	109	416	74	110	30	1	23	89	1	.264
2009	Boston	A.L.	DH-1B	150	541	77	129	35	1	28	99	0	.238
2010	Boston	A.L.	DH-1B	145	518	86	140	36	1	32	102	0	.270
2011	Boston g	A.L.	DH-1B	146	525	84	162	40	1	29	96	1	.309
2012	Boston h-i	A.L.	DH-1B	90	324	65	103	26	0	23	60	0	.318
2013	Pawtucket	Int.	DH	6	18	3	4	0	0	1	4	0	.222
2013	Boston j	A.L.	DH-1B	137	518	84	160	38	2	30	103	4	.309
Major League Totals			17 Yrs.	1969	7057	1208	2023	520	18	431	1429	15	.287
	Division Series												
2002	Minnesota	A.L.	DH	4	13	0	3	2	0	0	2	0	.231
2003	Boston	A.L.	DH	5	21	0	2	1	0	0	2	0	.095
2004	Boston	A.L.	DH	3	11	4	6	2	0	1	4	0	.545
2005	Boston	A.L.	DH	3	12	2	4	2	0	1	1	0	.333
2007	Boston	A.L.	DH	3	7	5	5	0	0	2	3	0	.714
2008	Boston	A.L.	DH	4	17	1	4	1	0	0	1	0	.235
2009	Boston	A.L.	DH	3	12	0	1	0	0	0	0	0	.083
2013	Boston	A.L.	DH	4	13	4	5	1	0	2	3	0	.385
Division Series Totals				29	106	16	30	9	0	6	16	0	.283
	Championship Series												
2002	Minnesota	A.L.	DH	5	16	0	5	1	0	0	2	0	.313
2003	Boston	A.L.	DH	7	26	4	7	1	0	2	6	0	.269
2004	Boston	A.L.	DH	7	31	6	12	0	1	3	11	0	.387
2007	Boston	A.L.	DH	7	24	7	7	3	0	1	3	0	.292
2008	Boston	A.L.	DH	7	26	3	4	1	1	1	4	0	.154
2013	Boston	A.L.	DH	6	22	1	2	0	0	1	4	0	.091
Championship Series Totals				39	145	21	37	6	2	8	30	0	.255
	World Series Record												
2004	Boston	A.L.	1B-DH	4	13	3	4	1	0	1	4	0	.308
2007	Boston	A.L.	1B-DH	4	15	4	5	3	0	0	4	0	.333

Year	Club	Lea	Pos	G	AB	R	H	2B	3B	HR	RBI	SB	Avg
2013	Boston	A.L.	1B-DH	6	16	7	11	2	0	2	6	0	.688
World Series Totals				14	44	14	20	6	0	3	14	0	.455

a Sent to Minnesota Twins by Seattle Mariners to complete trade for infielder Dave Hollins, September 13, 1996.
b On disabled list from May 10 to July 9, 1998.
c On disabled list from May 5 to July 21, 2001.
d On disabled list from April 20 to May 13, 2002.
e Released by Minnesota Twins, December 16, 2002. Signed with Boston Red Sox, January 22, 2003.
f On disabled list from June 1 to July 25, 2008.
g Filed for free agency, October 30, 2011. Accepted arbitration, December 7, 2011.
h On disabled list from July 17 to August 24 and August 25 to October 5, 2012.
i Filed for free agency, November 3, 2012, re-signed with Boston Red Sox, November 5, 2012.
j On disabled list from March 22 to April 20, 2013.

OVERBAY, LYLE STEFAN

Born, Centralia, Washington, January 28, 1977.
Bats Left. Throws Left. Height, 6 feet, 2 inches. Weight, 235 pounds.

Year	Club	Lea	Pos	G	AB	R	H	2B	3B	HR	RBI	SB	Avg
1999	Missoula	Pioneer	1B	75	306	66	105	25	7	12	101	10	.343
2000	South Bend	Midwest	1B	71	259	47	86	19	3	6	47	9	.332
2000	El Paso	Texas	1B	62	244	43	86	16	2	8	49	3	.352
2001	El Paso	Texas	1B-OF	138	532	82	187	49	3	13	100	5	.352
2001	Arizona	N.L.	PH	2	2	0	1	0	0	0	0	0	.500
2002	Tucson	P.C.	1B	134	525	83	180	40	0	19	109	0	.343
2002	Arizona	N.L.	PH	10	10	0	1	0	0	0	1	0	.100
2003	Tucson	P.C.	1B	35	119	24	34	11	0	4	16	0	.286
2003	Arizona a	N.L.	1B	86	254	23	70	20	0	4	28	1	.276
2004	Milwaukee	N.L.	1B	159	579	83	174	*53	1	16	87	2	.301
2005	Milwaukee b	N.L.	1B	158	537	80	148	34	1	19	72	1	.276
2006	Toronto	A.L.	1B	157	581	82	181	46	1	22	92	5	.312
2007	New Hampshire	Eastern	1B	4	15	2	4	1	0	1	5	0	.267
2007	Toronto c	A.L.	1B	122	425	49	102	30	2	10	44	2	.240
2008	Toronto	A.L.	1B	158	544	74	147	32	2	15	69	1	.270
2009	Toronto	A.L.	1B	132	423	57	112	35	1	16	64	0	.265
2010	Toronto d	A.L.	1B	154	534	75	130	37	2	20	67	1	.243
2011	Pittsburgh-Arizona e-f	N.L.	1B	121	394	43	92	21	1	9	47	2	.234
2012	Gwinnett	Int.	1B	7	22	3	6	3	0	0	3	0	.273
2012	Arizona-Atlanta g-h	N.L.	1B	65	116	12	30	10	0	2	10	0	.259
2013	New York i-j	A.L.	1B-OF	142	445	43	107	24	1	14	59	2	.240
Major League Totals			13 Yrs.	1466	4844	621	1295	342	12	147	640	17	.267
	Division Series												
2011	Arizona	N.L.	1B	2	4	0	0	0	0	0	0	0	.000

a Traded to Milwaukee Brewers with infielder Junior Spivey, infielder Craig Counsell, catcher Chad Moeller, pitcher Chris Capuano and pitcher Jorge De La Rosa for infielder Richie Sexson, pitcher Shane Nance and player to be named later, December 1, 2003. Arizona Diamondbacks received outfielder Gary Varner to complete trade, December 15, 2003.
b Traded to Toronto Blue Jays with pitcher Ty Taubenheim for pitcher Dave Bush, outfielder Gabe Gross and pitcher Zach Jackson, December 7, 2005.
c On disabled list from June 4 to July 12, 2007.
d Filed for free agency, November 1, 2010. Signed with Pittsburgh Pirates, December 14, 2010.
e Released by Pittsburgh Pirates, August 5, 2011. Signed with Arizona Diamondbacks, August 13, 2011.
f Filed for free agency, October 31, 2011, re-signed with Arizona Diamondbacks, December 9, 2011.
g Released by Arizona Diamondbacks, August 3, 2012. Signed with Atlanta Braves organization, August 20, 2012.
h Filed for free agency, November 3, 2012. Signed with Boston Red Sox organization, January 31, 2013.
i Released by Boston Red Sox, March 26, 2013. Signed with New York Yankees organization, March 26, 2013.
j Filed for free agency, October 31, 2013. Signed with Milwaukee Brewers organization, January 20, 2014.

OZUNA (IDELFONSO), MARCELL

Born, Santo Domingo, Dominican Republic, November 12, 1990.
Bats Right. Throws Right. Height, 6 feet, 1 inch. Weight, 220 pounds.

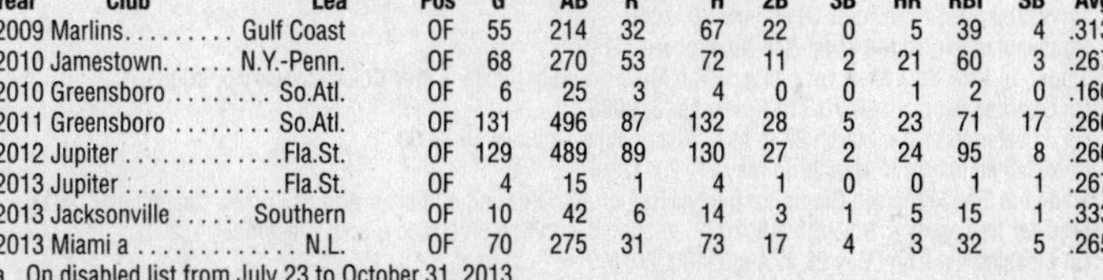

Year	Club	Lea	Pos	G	AB	R	H	2B	3B	HR	RBI	SB	Avg
2009	Marlins	Gulf Coast	OF	55	214	32	67	22	0	5	39	4	.313
2010	Jamestown	N.Y.-Penn.	OF	68	270	53	72	11	2	21	60	3	.267
2010	Greensboro	So.Atl.	OF	6	25	3	4	0	0	1	2	0	.160
2011	Greensboro	So.Atl.	OF	131	496	87	132	28	5	23	71	17	.266
2012	Jupiter	Fla.St.	OF	129	489	89	130	27	2	24	95	8	.266
2013	Jupiter	Fla.St.	OF	4	15	1	4	1	0	0	1	1	.267
2013	Jacksonville	Southern	OF	10	42	6	14	3	1	5	15	1	.333
2013	Miami a	N.L.	OF	70	275	31	73	17	4	3	32	5	.265

a On disabled list from July 23 to October 31, 2013.

PACHECO, JORDAN PATRICK

Born, Albuquerque, New Mexico, January 30, 1986.
Bats Right. Throws Right. Height, 6 feet, 1 inch. Weight, 200 pounds.

Year	Club	Lea	Pos	G	AB	R	H	2B	3B	HR	RBI	SB	Avg
2007	Tri-City	Northwest	2B-SS	8	31	5	8	2	0	0	3	0	.258
2007	Casper	Pioneer	3B-SS-2B	55	192	27	56	10	2	3	29	3	.292
2008	Tri-City	Northwest	C	54	214	25	60	8	3	1	35	3	.280
2009	Asheville	So.Atl.	C	117	451	67	145	30	4	13	79	12	.322
2010	Modesto	Calif.	C	104	390	59	125	27	3	5	70	5	.321
2010	Tulsa	Texas	C	21	78	11	26	5	0	1	19	1	.333
2011	Colorado Springs	P.C.	C-3B	97	363	57	101	21	3	3	50	2	.278
2011	Colorado	N.L.	1B-3B-C-2B	21	84	5	24	1	0	2	14	0	.286
2012	Colorado Springs	P.C.	3B-C	17	67	10	29	4	0	3	10	1	.433
2012	Colorado	N.L.	3B-1B-C	132	475	51	147	32	3	5	54	7	.309
2013	Colorado Springs	P.C.	C-1B	18	54	8	17	5	1	1	6	3	.315
2013	Colorado	N.L.	1B-C-OF	95	247	23	59	15	0	1	22	0	.239
Major League Totals			3 Yrs.	248	806	79	230	48	3	8	90	7	.285

PAGAN, ANGEL ANTHONY

Born, Rio Piedras, Puerto Rico, July 2, 1981.
Bats Both. Throws Right. Height, 6 feet, 1 inch. Weight, 195 pounds.

Year	Club	Lea	Pos	G	AB	R	H	2B	3B	HR	RBI	SB	Avg
2000	Kingsport	Appal.	OF	19	72	13	26	5	1	0	8	6	.361
2001	Brooklyn	N.Y.-Penn.	OF	62	238	46	75	10	2	0	15	30	.315
2001	Columbia	So.Atl.	OF	15	57	4	17	1	1	0	5	3	.298
2002	St. Lucie	Fla.St.	OF	16	67	12	23	2	1	1	7	10	.343
2002	Columbia	So.Atl.	OF	108	458	79	128	14	5	1	36	52	.279
2003	St. Lucie	Fla.St.	OF	113	441	64	110	15	5	1	33	35	.249
2004	Binghamton	Eastern	OF	112	448	71	129	25	8	4	63	29	.288
2004	Norfolk	Int.	OF	12	45	13	13	3	3	0	1	4	.289
2005	Norfolk	Int.	OF	129	516	69	140	20	10	8	40	27	.271
2006	Cubs	Arizona	OF	3	9	1	1	0	0	0	0	1	.111
2006	Iowa	P.C.	OF	4	15	2	4	1	0	0	0	1	.267
2006	Chicago a-b	N.L.	OF	77	170	28	42	6	2	5	18	4	.247
2007	Iowa	P.C.	OF	33	116	18	29	4	3	3	9	6	.250
2007	Chicago c-d	N.L.	OF	71	148	21	39	10	2	4	21	4	.264
2008	Mets	Gulf Coast	OF	2	5	1	3	1	0	0	0	2	.600
2008	Brooklyn	N.Y.-Penn.	OF	4	13	0	4	0	0	0	1	3	.308
2008	St. Lucie	Fla.St.	OF	1	4	1	0	0	0	0	0	0	.000
2008	New York e	N.L.	OF	31	91	12	25	7	1	0	13	4	.275
2009	St. Lucie	Fla.St.	OF	4	12	4	5	2	0	0	3	2	.417
2009	Buffalo	Int.	OF	3	14	2	4	0	2	0	2	0	.286
2009	New York f	N.L.	OF	88	343	54	105	22	11	6	32	14	.306
2010	New York	N.L.	OF	151	579	80	168	31	7	11	69	37	.290
2011	St. Lucie	Fla.St.	OF	8	31	6	7	1	1	1	2	0	.226
2011	New York g-h	N.L.	OF	123	478	68	125	24	4	7	56	32	.262
2012	San Francisco i	N.L.	OF	154	605	95	174	38	*15	8	56	29	.288
2013	Giants	Arizona	OF	4	11	3	2	0	1	0	0	0	.182
2013	San Jose	Calif.	OF	1	2	0	0	0	0	0	0	0	.000
2013	Fresno	P.C.	OF	5	18	1	5	0	0	0	3	0	.278
2013	San Francisco j	N.L.	OF	71	280	44	79	16	3	5	30	9	.282
Major League Totals			8 Yrs.	766	2694	402	757	154	45	46	295	133	.281
	Division Series												
2012	San Francisco	N.L.	OF	5	20	3	3	1	0	1	4	0	.150
	Championship Series												
2012	San Francisco	N.L.	OF	7	33	4	8	0	1	1	2	0	.242
	World Series Record												
2012	San Francisco	N.L.	OF	4	16	3	2	2	0	0	0	1	.125

a Sold to Chicago by New York Mets, January 25, 2006.
b On disabled list from April 16 to June 30, 2006.
c On disabled list from August 8 to November 1, 2007.
d Traded to New York Mets for pitcher Ryan Meyers and outfielder Corey Coles, January 5, 2008.
e On disabled list from May 13 to November 3, 2008.
f On disabled list from March 27 to May 16 and June 1 to July 10, 2009.
g On disabled list from April 22 to May 27, 2011.
h Traded to San Francisco Giants for pitcher Ramon Ramirez and outfielder Andres Torres, December 7, 2011.
i Filed for free agency, November 3, 2012, re-signed with San Francisco Giants, December 4, 2012.
j On disabled list from May 28 to August 30, 2013.

PARMELEE, CHRISTOPHER MATTHEW (CHRIS)

Born, Long Beach, California, February 24, 1988.
Bats Left. Throws Left. Height, 6 feet, 1 inch. Weight, 230 pounds.

Year	Club	Lea	Pos	G	AB	R	H	2B	3B	HR	RBI	SB	Avg
2006	Twins	Gulf Coast	OF-1B	45	154	29	43	7	4	8	32	3	.279
2006	Beloit	Midwest	1B	11	22	2	5	1	0	0	2	0	.227
2007	Beloit	Midwest	OF-1B	128	447	56	107	23	5	15	70	8	.239
2008	Beloit	Midwest	1B-OF	69	226	41	54	10	3	14	49	3	.239
2009	Fort Myers	Fla.St.	1B-OF	123	422	61	109	27	1	16	73	2	.258
2010	New Britain	Eastern	1B-OF	111	411	51	113	25	2	6	44	3	.275
2010	Fort Myers	Fla.St.	1B-OF	22	80	9	27	2	1	2	17	0	.338
2011	New Britain	Eastern	1B-OF	142	530	76	152	30	5	13	83	0	.287
2011	Minnesota	A.L.	1B	21	76	8	27	6	0	4	14	0	.355
2012	Rochester	Int.	1B	64	228	45	77	17	1	17	49	1	.338
2012	Minnesota	A.L.	1B-OF	64	192	18	44	10	2	5	20	0	.229
2013	Rochester	Int.	1B-OF	45	173	23	40	13	1	3	22	1	.231
2013	Minnesota	A.L.	OF-1B	101	294	21	67	13	0	8	24	1	.228
Major League Totals			3 Yrs.	186	562	47	138	29	2	17	57	1	.246

PARRA, GERARDO ENRIQUE

Born, Santa Barbara Del Zulia, Venezuela, May 6, 1987.
Bats Left. Throws Left. Height, 5 feet, 11 inches. Weight, 195 pounds.

Year	Club	Lea	Pos	G	AB	R	H	2B	3B	HR	RBI	SB	Avg
2006	Missoula	Pioneer	OF	69	271	46	89	18	4	4	43	23	.328
2007	Visalia	Calif.	OF	24	102	11	29	2	1	2	14	2	.284
2007	South Bend	Midwest	OF	110	444	64	142	25	4	6	57	24	.320
2008	Visalia	Calif.	OF	50	196	26	59	8	4	2	19	12	.301
2008	Mobile	Southern	OF	73	265	35	73	14	6	4	33	16	.275
2009	Mobile	Southern	OF	29	108	23	39	3	1	3	12	7	.361
2009	Arizona	N.L.	OF	120	455	59	132	21	8	5	60	5	.290
2010	Reno	P.C.	OF	9	36	8	15	4	0	1	7	3	.417
2010	Arizona	N.L.	OF	133	364	31	95	19	6	3	30	1	.261
2011	Arizona	N.L.	OF	141	445	55	130	20	8	8	46	15	.292
2012	Arizona	N.L.	OF	133	385	58	105	21	2	7	36	15	.273
2013	Arizona	N.L.	OF	156	601	79	161	43	4	10	48	10	.268
Major League Totals			5 Yrs.	683	2250	282	623	124	28	33	220	46	.277
	Division Series												
2011	Arizona	N.L.	OF	5	18	1	1	1	0	0	0	0	.056

PEDROIA, DUSTIN LUIS

Born, Woodland, California, August 17, 1983.
Bats Right. Throws Right. Height, 5 feet, 9 inches. Weight, 180 pounds.

Year	Club	Lea	Pos	G	AB	R	H	2B	3B	HR	RBI	SB	Avg
2004	Sarasota	Fla.St.	SS	30	107	23	36	8	3	2	14	0	.336
2004	Augusta	So.Atl.	SS	12	50	11	20	5	0	1	5	2	.400
2005	Portland	Eastern	2B-SS	66	256	39	83	19	2	8	40	7	.324
2005	Pawtucket	Int.	2B-SS	51	204	39	52	9	1	5	24	1	.255
2006	Pawtucket	Int.	SS-2B-3B	111	423	55	129	30	3	5	50	1	.305
2006	Boston	A.L.	2B-SS	31	89	5	17	4	0	2	7	0	.191
2007	Boston a	A.L.	2B	139	520	86	165	39	1	8	50	7	.317
2008	Boston b	A.L.	2B	157	653	*118	*213	*54	2	17	83	20	.326
2009	Boston	A.L.	2B	154	626	*115	185	48	1	15	72	20	.296
2010	Pawtucket	Int.	2B	2	6	1	1	0	0	0	0	0	.167
2010	Boston c	A.L.	2B	75	302	53	87	24	1	12	41	9	.288
2011	Boston	A.L.	2B	159	635	102	195	37	3	21	91	26	.307
2012	Boston d	A.L.	2B	141	563	81	163	39	3	15	65	20	.290
2013	Boston	A.L.	2B	160	641	91	193	42	2	9	84	17	.301
Major League Totals			8 Yrs.	1016	4029	651	1218	287	13	99	493	119	.302
	Division Series												
2007	Boston	A.L.	2B	3	13	2	2	2	0	0	1	0	.154
2008	Boston	A.L.	2B	4	17	0	1	1	0	0	1	0	.059
2009	Boston	A.L.	2B	3	12	1	2	1	0	0	2	0	.167
2013	Boston	A.L.	2B	4	17	2	4	1	0	0	5	0	.235
Division Series Totals				14	59	5	9	5	0	0	9	0	.153
	Championship Series												
2007	Boston	A.L.	2B	7	29	8	10	3	0	1	5	0	.345
2008	Boston	A.L.	2B	7	26	9	9	1	0	3	5	2	.346

Year	Club	Lea	Pos	G	AB	R	H	2B	3B	HR	RBI	SB	Avg
2013	Boston	A.L.	2B	6	22	1	6	1	0	0	1	1	.273
Championship Series Totals				20	77	18	25	5	0	4	11	3	.325
	World Series Record												
2007	Boston	A.L.	2B	4	18	2	5	1	0	1	4	0	.278
2013	Boston	A.L.	2B	6	24	5	5	2	0	0	1	0	.208
World Series Totals.............				10	42	7	10	3	0	1	5	0	.238

a Selected Rookie of the Year in American League for 2007.
b Selected Most Valuable Player in American League for 2008.
c On disabled list from June 26 to August 17 and August 19 to October 13, 2010.
d On disabled list from July 4 to July 19, 2012.

PENA, BRAYAN EDUARDO

Born, Havana, Cuba, January 7, 1982.
Bats Both. Throws Right. Height, 5 feet, 11 inches. Weight, 245 pounds.

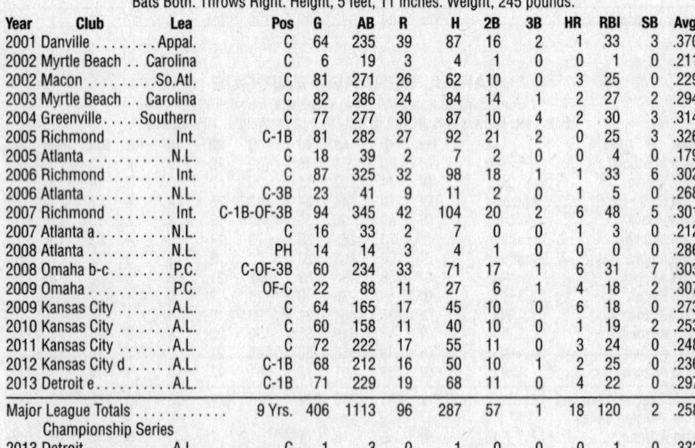

Year	Club	Lea	Pos	G	AB	R	H	2B	3B	HR	RBI	SB	Avg
2001	Danville	Appal.	C	64	235	39	87	16	2	1	33	3	.370
2002	Myrtle Beach ..	Carolina	C	6	19	3	4	1	0	0	1	0	.211
2002	Macon	So.Atl.	C	81	271	26	62	10	0	3	25	0	.229
2003	Myrtle Beach ..	Carolina	C	82	286	24	84	14	1	2	27	2	.294
2004	Greenville.....	Southern	C	77	277	30	87	10	4	2	30	3	.314
2005	Richmond	Int.	C-1B	81	282	27	92	21	2	0	25	3	.326
2005	Atlanta	N.L.	C	18	39	2	7	2	0	0	4	0	.179
2006	Richmond	Int.	C	87	325	32	98	18	1	1	33	6	.302
2006	Atlanta	N.L.	C-3B	23	41	9	11	2	0	1	5	0	.268
2007	Richmond	Int.	C-1B-OF-3B	94	345	42	104	20	2	6	48	5	.301
2007	Atlanta a..........	N.L.	C	16	33	2	7	0	0	1	3	0	.212
2008	Atlanta	N.L.	PH	14	14	3	4	1	0	0	0	0	.286
2008	Omaha b-c........	P.C.	C-OF-3B	60	234	33	71	17	1	6	31	7	.303
2009	Omaha	P.C.	OF-C	22	88	11	27	6	1	4	18	2	.307
2009	Kansas City	A.L.	C	64	165	17	45	10	0	6	18	0	.273
2010	Kansas City	A.L.	C	60	158	11	40	10	0	1	19	2	.253
2011	Kansas City	A.L.	C	72	222	17	55	11	0	3	24	0	.248
2012	Kansas City d......	A.L.	C-1B	68	212	16	50	10	1	2	25	0	.236
2013	Detroit e..........	A.L.	C-1B	71	229	19	68	11	0	4	22	0	.297
Major League Totals			9 Yrs.	406	1113	96	287	57	1	18	120	2	.258
	Championship Series												
2013	Detroit	A.L.	C	1	3	0	1	0	0	0	1	0	.333

a On disabled list from May 2 to May 17, 2007.
b On disabled list from May 5 to May 23, 2008.
c Claimed on waivers by Kansas City Royals, May 30, 2008.
d Filed for free agency, November 28, 2012. Signed with Detroit Tigers, December 10, 2012.
e Filed for free agency, October 31, 2013. Signed with Cincinnati Reds, November 12, 2013.

PENA, CARLOS FELIPE

Born, Santo Domingo, Dominican Republic, May 17, 1978.
Bats Left. Throws Left. Height, 6 feet, 2 inches. Weight, 210 pounds.

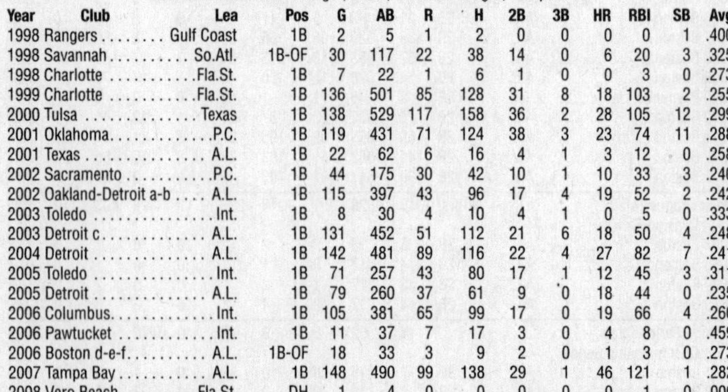

Year	Club	Lea	Pos	G	AB	R	H	2B	3B	HR	RBI	SB	Avg
1998	Rangers	Gulf Coast	1B	2	5	1	2	0	0	0	0	1	.400
1998	Savannah	So.Atl.	1B-OF	30	117	22	38	14	0	6	20	3	.325
1998	Charlotte	Fla.St.	1B	7	22	1	6	1	0	0	3	0	.273
1999	Charlotte	Fla.St.	1B	136	501	85	128	31	8	18	103	2	.255
2000	Tulsa	Texas	1B	138	529	117	158	36	2	28	105	12	.299
2001	Oklahoma.............	P.C.	1B	119	431	71	124	38	3	23	74	11	.288
2001	Texas	A.L.	1B	22	62	6	16	4	1	3	12	0	.258
2002	Sacramento	P.C.	1B	44	175	30	42	10	1	10	33	3	.240
2002	Oakland-Detroit a-b	A.L.	1B	115	397	43	96	17	4	19	52	2	.242
2003	Toledo	Int.	1B	8	30	4	10	4	1	0	5	0	.333
2003	Detroit c..............	A.L.	1B	131	452	51	112	21	6	18	50	4	.248
2004	Detroit	A.L.	1B	142	481	89	116	22	4	27	82	7	.241
2005	Toledo	Int.	1B	71	257	43	80	17	1	12	45	3	.311
2005	Detroit	A.L.	1B	79	260	37	61	9	0	18	44	0	.235
2006	Columbus.............	Int.	1B	105	381	65	99	17	0	19	66	4	.260
2006	Pawtucket	Int.	1B	11	37	7	17	3	0	4	8	0	.459
2006	Boston d-e-f...........	A.L.	1B-OF	18	33	3	9	2	0	1	3	0	.273
2007	Tampa Bay	A.L.	1B	148	490	99	138	29	1	46	121	1	.282
2008	Vero Beach..........	Fla.St.	DH	1	4	0	0	0	0	0	1	0	.000

Year	Club	Lea	Pos	G	AB	R	H	2B	3B	HR	RBI	SB	Avg
2008	Tampa Bay g	A.L.	1B	139	490	76	121	24	2	31	102	1	.247
2009	Tampa Bay h	A.L.	1B	135	471	91	107	25	2	*39	100	3	.227
2010	Charlotte	Fla.St.	DH	1	3	1	2	0	0	0	1	0	.667
2010	Tampa Bay i-j	A.L.	1B	144	484	64	95	18	0	28	84	5	.196
2011	Chicago k	N.L.	1B	153	493	72	111	27	3	28	80	2	.225
2012	Tampa Bay l	A.L.	1B	160	497	72	98	17	2	19	61	2	.197
2013	Omaha m	P.C.	1B	5	18	5	6	0	1	2	6	0	.333
2013	Houston-Kansas City n-o	A.L.	1B	89	280	38	58	13	1	8	25	1	.207
Major League Totals			13 Yrs.	1475	4890	741	1138	228	26	285	816	28	.233
	Division Series												
2008	Tampa Bay	A.L.	1B	3	10	0	5	0	0	0	2	2	.500
2010	Tampa Bay	A.L.	1B	4	14	4	4	1	1	1	4	0	.286
Division Series Totals				7	24	4	9	1	1	1	6	2	.375
	Championship Series												
2008	Tampa Bay	A.L.	1B	7	26	8	7	1	0	3	6	1	.269
	World Series Record												
2008	Tampa Bay	A.L.	1B	5	17	1	2	1	0	0	2	0	.118

a Traded to Oakland Athletics with pitcher Mike Venafro for pitcher Mario Ramos, outfielder Ryan Ludwick, infielder Jason Hart and catcher Gerald Laird, January 14, 2002.
b Traded to Detroit Tigers with pitcher Franklyn German and player to be named later for pitcher Jeff Weaver, July 5, 2002. Detroit Tigers received pitcher Jeremy Bonderman to complete trade, August 22, 2002.
c On disabled list from June 2 to June 27, 2003.
d Released by Detroit Tigers, March 26, 2006. Signed with New York Yankees organization, April 15, 2006.
e Filed for free agency, August 16, 2006. Signed with Boston Red Sox organization, August 17, 2006.
f Filed for free agency, October 13, 2006. Signed with Tampa Bay Devil Rays organization, February 1, 2007.
g On disabled list from June 4 to June 27, 2008.
h On disabled list from September 7 to November 19, 2009.
i On disabled list from August 1 to August 16, 2010.
j Filed for free agency, November 1, 2010. Signed with Chicago Cubs, December 8, 2010.
k Filed for free agency, October 30, 2011. Signed with Tampa Bay Rays, January 24, 2012.
l Filed for free agency, November 3, 2012. Signed with Houston Astros, December 17, 2012.
m Released by Houston Astros, July 31, 2013. Signed with Kansas City Royals organization, August 27, 2013.
n On disabled list from September 17 to October 31, 2013.
o Filed for free agency, October 31, 2013.

PENCE, HUNTER ANDREW

Born, Arlington, Texas, April 13, 1983.
Bats Right. Throws Right. Height, 6 feet, 4 inches. Weight, 210 pounds.

Year	Club	Lea	Pos	G	AB	R	H	2B	3B	HR	RBI	SB	Avg
2004	Tri-City	N.Y.-Penn.	OF	51	199	36	59	18	1	8	37	3	.296
2005	Lexington	So.Atl.	OF	80	302	59	102	14	3	25	60	8	.338
2005	Salem	Carolina	OF	41	151	24	46	8	1	6	30	1	.305
2006	Corpus Christi	Texas	OF	136	523	97	148	31	8	28	95	17	.283
2007	Round Rock	P.C.	OF	25	95	17	31	11	1	3	21	2	.326
2007	Houston a	N.L.	OF	108	456	57	147	30	9	17	69	11	.322
2008	Houston	N.L.	OF	157	595	78	160	34	4	25	83	11	.269
2009	Houston	N.L.	OF	159	585	76	165	26	5	25	72	14	.282
2010	Houston	N.L.	OF	156	614	93	173	29	3	25	91	18	.282
2011	Houston-Philadelphia b	N.L.	OF	154	606	84	190	38	5	22	97	8	.314
2012	Philadelphia-San Fran. c	N.L.	OF	160	617	87	156	26	4	24	104	5	.253
2013	San Francisco	N.L.	OF	*162	629	91	178	35	5	27	99	22	.283
Major League Totals			7 Yrs.	1056	4102	566	1169	218	35	165	615	89	.285
	Division Series												
2011	Philadelphia	N.L.	OF	5	19	3	4	0	0	0	4	0	.211
2012	San Francisco	N.L.	OF	5	20	0	4	0	0	0	0	1	.200
Division Series Totals				10	39	3	8	0	0	0	4	1	.205
	Championship Series												
2012	San Francisco	N.L.	OF	7	28	4	5	1	0	1	3	0	.179
	World Series Record												
2012	San Francisco	N.L.	OF	4	14	3	4	1	0	0	1	1	.286

a On disabled list from July 23 to August 21, 2007.
b Traded to Philadelphia Phillies with cash for infielder Jonathan Singleton, pitcher Jarred Cosart, pitcher Josh Zeid and player to be named later, July 30, 2011. Houston Astros received pitcher Domingo Santana to complete trade, August 15, 2011.
c Traded to San Francisco Giants with cash for outfielder Nate Schierholtz, catcher Tommy Joseph and pitcher Seth Rosin, July 31, 2012.

PENNINGTON, CLIFTON RANDOLPH (CLIFF)

Born, Corpus Christi, Texas, June 15, 1984.
Bats Both. Throws Right. Height, 5 feet, 11 inches. Weight, 190 pounds.

Year	Club	Lea	Pos	G	AB	R	H	2B	3B	HR	RBI	SB	Avg
2005	Kane County	Midwest	SS	69	290	49	80	15	0	3	29	25	.276
2006	Athletics	Arizona	SS	9	28	3	13	3	1	0	6	0	.464
2006	Stockton	Calif.	SS	46	177	36	36	7	0	2	21	7	.203
2007	Stockton	Calif.	SS-2B	68	286	50	73	17	3	6	36	9	.255
2007	Midland	Texas	SS-2B	70	271	41	68	13	2	2	21	8	.251
2008	Midland	Texas	SS-2B	50	204	42	53	7	2	0	18	20	.260
2008	Sacramento	P.C.	SS-2B-3B	65	236	47	70	9	3	2	16	11	.297
2008	Oakland	A.L.	2B-SS-3B	36	99	14	24	5	0	0	9	4	.242
2009	Sacramento	P.C.	SS-2B-3B-OF	99	360	48	95	22	3	3	40	27	.264
2009	Oakland	A.L.	SS	60	208	27	58	11	3	4	21	7	.279
2010	Oakland	A.L.	SS	156	508	64	127	26	8	6	46	29	.250
2011	Oakland	A.L.	SS	148	515	57	136	26	2	8	58	14	.264
2012	Sacramento	P.C.	SS	3	11	2	5	1	0	0	1	1	.455
2012	Oakland a-b	A.L.	SS-2B	125	418	50	90	18	2	6	28	15	.215
2013	Arizona	N.L.	SS-2B-3B	96	269	25	65	13	1	1	18	2	.242
Major League Totals			6 Yrs.	621	2017	237	500	99	16	25	180	71	.248
	Division Series												
2012	Oakland	A.L.	2B	5	14	1	4	0	0	0	1	0	.286

a On disabled list from July 20 to August 7, 2012.
b Traded to Arizona Diamondbacks with infielder Yordy Cabrera for outfielder Chris Young and cash, October 20, 2012.

PERALTA, JHONNY ANTONIO

Born, Santiago, Dominican Republic, May 28, 1982.
Bats Right. Throws Right. Height, 6 feet, 1 inch. Weight, 210 pounds.

Year	Club	Lea	Pos	G	AB	R	H	2B	3B	HR	RBI	SB	Avg
2001	Kinston	Carolina	SS	125	441	57	106	24	2	7	47	4	.240
2002	Akron	Eastern	SS	130	470	62	132	28	5	15	62	4	.281
2003	Buffalo	Int.	SS-3B	63	237	25	61	12	1	1	21	1	.257
2003	Cleveland	A.L.	SS-3B	77	242	24	55	10	1	4	21	1	.227
2004	Buffalo	Int.	SS-3B	138	556	109	181	44	2	15	86	8	.326
2004	Cleveland	A.L.	SS-3B	8	25	2	6	1	0	0	2	0	.240
2005	Cleveland	A.L.	SS	141	504	82	147	35	4	24	78	0	.292
2006	Cleveland	A.L.	SS	149	569	84	146	28	3	13	68	0	.257
2007	Cleveland	A.L.	SS	152	574	87	155	27	1	21	72	4	.270
2008	Cleveland	A.L.	SS-3B	154	605	104	167	42	4	23	89	3	.276
2009	Cleveland	A.L.	3B-SS	151	582	57	148	35	1	11	83	0	.254
2010	Cleveland-Detroit a-b	A.L.	3B-SS-1B	148	551	60	137	30	2	15	81	1	.249
2011	Detroit	A.L.	SS-1B	146	525	68	157	25	3	21	86	0	.299
2012	Detroit	A.L.	SS	150	531	58	127	32	3	13	63	1	.239
2013	Detroit c-d	A.L.	SS-OF	107	409	50	124	30	0	11	55	3	.303
Major League Totals			11 Yrs.	1383	5117	676	1369	295	22	156	698	13	.268
	Division Series												
2007	Cleveland	A.L.	SS	4	15	2	7	3	0	0	2	1	.467
2011	Detroit	A.L.	SS	5	18	0	4	2	0	0	1	0	.222
2012	Detroit	A.L.	SS	5	17	1	5	0	0	0	0	1	.294
2013	Detroit	A.L.	OF-SS	4	12	1	5	1	0	1	5	0	.417
Division Series Totals				18	62	4	21	6	0	1	8	2	.339
	Championship Series												
2007	Cleveland	A.L.	SS	7	27	4	7	2	0	2	8	0	.259
2011	Detroit	A.L.	SS	6	23	2	5	1	0	2	2	0	.217
2012	Detroit	A.L.	SS	4	18	3	7	1	0	2	3	0	.389
2013	Detroit	A.L.	OF-SS	6	21	1	6	3	0	0	1	0	.286
Championship Series Totals				23	89	10	25	7	0	6	14	0	.281
	World Series Record												
2012	Detroit	A.L.	SS	4	15	1	1	0	0	1	2	0	.067

a Traded to Detroit Tigers for pitcher Giovanni Soto, July 28, 2010.
b Filed for free agency, November 2, 2010, re-signed with Detroit Tigers, November 8, 2010.
c Suspended for 50 games for performance-enhancing drug use, August 5, 2013.
d Filed for free agency, October 31, 2013. Signed with St. Louis Cardinals, November 25, 2013.

PEREZ (DÍAZ), SALVADOR

Born, Valencia, Venezuela, May 10, 1990.
Bats Right. Throws Right. Height, 6 feet, 3 inches. Weight, 230 pounds.

Year	Club	Lea	Pos	G	AB	R	H	2B	3B	HR	RBI	SB	Avg
2007	Royals	Arizona	C	30	86	10	21	3	0	0	10	1	.244
2008	Burlington	Appal.	C-2B	13	40	4	13	0	1	0	10	0	.325
2008	Idaho Falls	Pioneer	C	12	43	7	17	3	1	1	6	0	.395
2009	Burlington	Midwest	C	36	127	10	24	6	0	0	7	0	.189
2009	Idaho Falls	Pioneer	C	57	226	33	71	14	3	2	37	0	.314
2010	Wilmington	Carolina	C	99	365	35	106	21	1	7	53	1	.290
2011	NW Arkansas	Texas	C	79	286	35	81	14	0	9	43	0	.283
2011	Omaha	P.C.	C	12	48	5	16	5	0	1	10	0	.333
2011	Kansas City	A.L.	C	39	148	20	49	8	2	3	21	0	.331
2012	Omaha	P.C.	C	12	50	11	17	2	0	0	7	0	.340
2012	Kansas City a	A.L.	C	76	289	38	87	16	0	11	39	0	.301
2013	Kansas City b	A.L.	C-1B	138	496	48	145	25	3	13	79	0	.292
Major League Totals			3 Yrs.	253	933	106	281	49	5	27	139	0	.301

a On disabled list from March 20 to June 22, 2012.
b On disabled list from August 4 to August 11, 2013.

PHEGLEY, JOSHUA AARON (JOSH)

Born, Terre Haute, Indiana, February 12, 1988.
Bats Right. Throws Right. Height, 5 feet, 10 inches. Weight, 220 pounds.

Year	Club	Lea	Pos	G	AB	R	H	2B	3B	HR	RBI	SB	Avg
2009	Kannapolis	So.Atl.	C	52	196	27	44	9	0	9	33	1	.224
2010	Bristol	Appal.	C	5	15	1	3	1	0	0	1	0	.200
2010	Winston-Salem	Carolina	C	25	89	16	26	3	0	3	12	0	.292
2010	Birmingham	Southern	C	18	72	7	21	4	0	2	13	0	.292
2011	Birmingham	Southern	C	94	364	43	88	21	2	7	50	1	.242
2011	Charlotte	Int.	C	22	79	9	19	4	0	2	6	0	.241
2012	Charlotte	Int.	C	102	394	40	105	22	1	6	48	3	.266
2013	Charlotte	Int.	C	61	231	39	73	18	1	15	41	1	.316
2013	Chicago	A.L.	C-2B	65	204	14	42	7	0	4	22	2	.206

PHILLIPS, BRANDON EMIL

Born, Raleigh, North Carolina, June 28, 1981.
Bats Right. Throws Right. Height, 6 feet. Weight, 195 pounds.

Year	Club	Lea	Pos	G	AB	R	H	2B	3B	HR	RBI	SB	Avg
1999	Expos	Gulf Coast	SS	47	169	23	49	11	3	1	21	12	.290
2000	Cape Fear	So.Atl.	SS-2B	126	484	74	117	17	8	11	72	23	.242
2001	Harrisburg	Eastern	SS-2B-3B	67	265	35	79	19	0	7	36	13	.298
2001	Jupiter	Fla.St.	SS	55	194	36	55	12	2	4	23	17	.284
2002	Harrisburg	Eastern	SS	60	245	40	80	13	2	9	35	6	.327
2002	Ottawa	Int.	SS	10	35	1	9	4	0	1	5	0	.257
2002	Buffalo	Int.	SS-2B	55	223	30	63	14	0	8	27	8	.283
2002	Cleveland a	A.L.	2B	11	31	5	8	3	1	0	4	0	.258
2003	Cleveland	A.L.	2B	112	370	36	77	18	1	6	33	4	.208
2003	Buffalo	Int.	2B	43	154	14	27	7	0	3	13	7	.175
2004	Buffalo	Int.	2B-SS	135	521	83	158	34	4	8	50	14	.303
2004	Cleveland	A.L.	2B	6	22	1	4	2	0	0	1	0	.182
2005	Cleveland	A.L.	2B-SS	6	9	1	0	0	0	0	0	0	.000
2005	Buffalo	Int.	SS	112	465	79	119	24	1	15	46	7	.256
2006	Cincinnati b	N.L.	2B-SS	149	536	65	148	28	1	17	75	25	.276
2007	Cincinnati	N.L.	2B-SS	158	650	107	187	26	6	30	94	32	.288
2008	Cincinnati c	N.L.	2B	141	559	80	146	24	7	21	78	23	.261
2009	Cincinnati	N.L.	2B	153	584	78	161	30	5	20	98	25	.276
2010	Cincinnati	N.L.	2B	155	626	100	172	33	5	18	59	16	.275
2011	Cincinnati	N.L.	2B	150	610	94	183	38	2	18	82	14	.300
2012	Cincinnati	N.L.	2B	147	580	86	163	30	1	18	77	15	.281
2013	Cincinnati	N.L.	2B	151	606	80	158	24	2	18	103	5	.261
Major League Totals			12 Yrs.	1339	5183	733	1407	256	31	166	704	159	.271
	Wild Card Playoff												
2013	Cincinnati	N.L.	2B	1	4	0	0	0	0	0	0	0	.000
	Division Series												
2010	Cincinnati	N.L.	2B	3	12	2	4	1	0	1	1	0	.333
2012	Cincinnati	N.L.	2B	5	24	1	9	3	0	1	7	1	.375
Division Series Totals				8	36	3	13	4	0	2	8	1	.361

a Traded to Cleveland Indians with infielder Lee Stevens, outfielder Grady Sizemore and pitcher Cliff Lee for pitcher Bartolo Colon and player to be named later, June 27, 2002. Montreal Expos received pitcher Tim Drew to complete trade, June 28, 2002.

b Traded to Cincinnati Reds for player to be named later, April 7, 2006. Cleveland Indians received pitcher Jeff Stevens to complete trade, June 13, 2006.

c On disabled list from September 12 to November 6, 2008.

PIERRE, JUAN D'VAUGHN

Born, Mobile, Alabama, August 14, 1977.
Bats Left. Throws Left. Height, 6 feet. Weight, 180 pounds.

Year Club	Lea	Pos	G	AB	R	H	2B	3B	HR	RBI	SB	Avg
1998 Portland	Northwest	OF	64	264	55	93	9	2	0	30	38	.352
1999 Asheville	So.Atl.	OF	140	585	93	187	28	5	1	55	66	.320
2000 Carolina	Southern	OF	107	439	63	143	16	4	0	32	46	.326
2000 Colorado Spgs	P.C.	OF	4	17	3	8	0	1	0	1	1	.471
2000 Colorado	N.L.	OF	51	200	26	62	2	0	0	20	7	.310
2001 Colorado	N.L.	OF	156	617	108	202	26	11	2	55	*46	.327
2002 Colorado a	N.L.	OF	152	592	90	170	20	5	1	35	47	.287
2003 Florida	N.L.	OF	*162	*668	100	204	28	7	1	41	*65	.305
2004 Florida	N.L.	OF	*162	*678	100	*221	22	*12	3	49	45	.326
2005 Florida b	N.L.	OF	*162	656	96	181	19	13	2	47	57	.276
2006 Chicago c	N.L.	OF	*162	*699	87	*204	32	13	3	40	58	.292
2007 Los Angeles	N.L.	OF	*162	668	96	196	24	8	0	41	64	.293
2008 Las Vegas	P.C.	OF	2	6	2	3	1	0	0	0	0	.500
2008 Los Angeles d	N.L.	OF	119	375	44	106	10	2	1	28	40	.283
2009 Los Angeles e	N.L.	OF	145	380	57	117	16	8	0	31	30	.308
2010 Chicago	A.L.	OF	160	651	96	179	18	3	1	47	*68	.275
2011 Chicago f	A.L.	OF	158	639	80	178	17	4	2	50	27	.279
2012 Philadelphia g	N.L.	OF	130	394	59	121	10	6	1	25	37	.307
2013 Miami h	N.L.	OF	113	308	36	76	11	2	1	8	23	.247
Major League Totals		14 Yrs.	1994	7525	1075	2217	255	94	18	517	614	.295
Division Series												
2003 Florida	N.L.	OF	4	19	5	5	1	0	0	3	1	.263
2008 Los Angeles	N.L.	OF	1	1	1	0	0	0	0	0	0	.000
2009 Los Angeles	N.L.	OF	3	0	1	0	0	0	0	0	0	.000
Division Series Totals			8	20	7	5	1	0	0	3	1	.250
Championship Series												
2003 Florida	N.L.	OF	7	33	5	10	1	2	0	1	1	.303
2008 Los Angeles	N.L.	OF	1	3	1	2	1	0	0	0	0	.667
2009 Los Angeles	N.L.	OF	4	2	1	0	0	0	0	0	0	.000
Championship Series Totals			12	38	7	12	2	2	0	1	1	.316
World Series Record												
2003 Florida	N.L.	OF	6	21	2	7	2	0	0	3	1	.333

a Traded to Florida Marlins with pitcher Mike Hampton for outfielder Preston Wilson, catcher Charles Johnson, pitcher Vic Darensbourg and infielder Pablo Ozuna, November 16, 2002.

b Traded to Chicago Cubs for pitcher Sergio Mitre, pitcher Ricky Nolasco and pitcher Renyel Pinto, December 7, 2005.

c Filed for free agency, October 29, 2006. Signed with Los Angeles Dodgers, November 22, 2006.

d On disabled list from June 30 to July 25, 2008.

e Traded with cash to Chicago White Sox for pitcher John Ely and pitcher Jon Link, December 15, 2009.

f Filed for free agency, October 30, 2011. Signed with Philadelphia Phillies organization, January 27, 2012.

g Filed for free agency, November 3, 2012. Signed with Miami Marlins, November 19, 2012.

h Filed for free agency, October 31, 2013.

PIERZYNSKI, ANTHONY JOHN (A.J.)

Born, Bridgehampton, New York, December 30, 1976.
Bats Left. Throws Right. Height, 6 feet, 3 inches. Weight, 235 pounds.

Year Club	Lea	Pos	G	AB	R	H	2B	3B	HR	RBI	SB	Avg
1994 Twins	Gulf Coast	C	43	152	21	44	8	1	1	19	0	.289
1995 Ft. Wayne	Midwest	C	22	84	10	26	5	1	2	14	0	.310
1995 Elizabethtn	Appal.	C-1B	56	205	29	68	13	1	7	45	0	.332
1996 Ft. Wayne	Midwest	C-OF	114	431	48	118	30	3	7	70	0	.274
1997 Ft. Myers	Fla.St.	C-1B	118	412	49	115	23	1	9	64	2	.279
1998 New Britain	Eastern	C	59	212	30	63	11	0	3	17	0	.297
1998 Salt Lake	P.C.	C	59	208	29	53	7	2	7	30	3	.255
1998 Minnesota	A.L.	C	7	10	1	3	0	0	0	1	0	.300
1999 Salt Lake	P.C.	C	67	228	29	59	10	0	1	25	0	.259
1999 Minnesota a	A.L.	C	9	22	3	6	2	0	0	3	0	.273
2000 New Britain	Eastern	C	62	228	36	68	17	2	4	34	0	.298

Year Club	Lea	Pos	G	AB	R	H	2B	3B	HR	RBI	SB	Avg
2000 Salt Lake	P.C.	C	41	155	22	52	14	1	4	25	1	.335
2000 Minnesota	A.L.	C	33	88	12	27	5	1	2	11	1	.307
2001 Minnesota	A.L.	C	114	381	51	110	33	2	7	55	1	.289
2002 Minnesota	A.L.	C	130	440	54	132	31	6	6	49	1	.300
2003 Minnesota b	A.L.	C	137	487	63	152	35	3	11	74	3	.312
2004 San Francisco c	N.L.	C	131	471	45	128	28	2	11	77	0	.272
2005 Chicago	A.L.	C	128	460	61	118	21	0	18	56	0	.257
2006 Chicago	A.L.	C	140	509	65	150	24	0	16	64	1	.295
2007 Chicago	A.L.	C	136	472	54	124	24	0	14	50	1	.263
2008 Chicago	A.L.	C	134	534	66	150	31	1	13	60	1	.281
2009 Chicago	A.L.	C	138	504	57	151	22	1	13	49	1	.300
2010 Chicago d	A.L.	C	128	474	43	128	29	0	9	56	3	.270
2011 Charlotte	Int.	C	3	10	2	2	0	0	0	1	0	.200
2011 Chicago e	A.L.	C	129	464	38	133	29	1	8	48	0	.287
2012 Chicago f	A.L.	C	135	479	68	133	18	4	27	77	0	.278
2013 Frisco	Texas	C	2	6	0	1	0	0	0	0	0	.167
2013 Texas g-h	A.L.	C	134	503	48	137	24	1	17	70	1	.272
Major League Totals		16 Yrs.	1763	6298	729	1782	356	22	172	800	14	.283
Division Series												
2002 Minnesota	A.L.	C	5	16	4	7	0	1	1	4	0	.438
2003 Minnesota	A.L.	C	4	13	1	3	0	0	1	1	0	.231
2005 Chicago	A.L.	C	3	9	5	4	2	0	2	4	1	.444
2008 Chicago	A.L.	C	4	13	1	5	1	0	0	1	0	.385
Division Series Totals			16	51	11	19	3	1	4	10	1	.373
Championship Series												
2002 Minnesota	A.L.	C	5	16	1	4	0	0	0	2	0	.250
2005 Chicago	A.L.	C	5	18	1	3	0	0	1	2	0	.167
Championship Series Totals			10	34	2	7	0	0	1	4	0	.206
World Series Record												
2005 Chicago	A.L.	C	4	15	3	4	2	0	0	3	1	.267

a On disabled list from August 24 to September 30, 1999.
b Traded to San Francisco Giants with cash for pitcher Joe Nathan, pitcher Boof Bonser and pitcher Francisco Liriano, November 14, 2003.
c Released by San Francisco Giants, December 16, 2004. Signed with Chicago White Sox, January 5, 2005.
d Filed for free agency, November 1, 2010, re-signed with Chicago White Sox, December 3, 2010.
e On disabled list from August 13 to September 2, 2011.
f Filed for free agency, November 3, 2012. Signed with Texas Rangers, December 26, 2012.
g On disabled list from May 6 to May 21, 2013.
h Filed for free agency, October 31, 2013. Signed with Boston Red Sox, December 3, 2013.

PINTO, JOSMIL OSWALDO

Born, Valencia, Venezuela, March 31, 1989.
Bats Right. Throws Right. Height, 5 feet, 11 inches. Weight, 210 pounds.

Year Club	Lea	Pos	G	AB	R	H	2B	3B	HR	RBI	SB	Avg
2008 Twins	Gulf Coast	C	24	85	14	28	9	3	1	14	1	.329
2009 Elizabethton	Appal.	C	53	205	34	68	14	2	13	55	0	.332
2010 Beloit	Midwest	C-3B	100	347	60	78	21	1	10	54	2	.225
2011 Beloit	Midwest	C	9	32	4	8	3	0	1	9	0	.250
2011 Fort Myers	Fla.St.	C	64	221	21	58	11	1	5	32	1	.262
2012 Fort Myers	Fla.St.	C	93	349	45	103	22	2	12	51	0	.295
2012 New Britain	Eastern	C	12	47	8	14	4	1	2	9	0	.298
2013 New Britain	Eastern	C	107	386	59	119	23	1	14	68	0	.308
2013 Rochester	Int.	C	19	70	6	22	9	0	1	6	0	.314
2013 Minnesota	A.L.	C	21	76	10	26	5	0	4	12	0	.342

PLOUFFE, TREVOR PATRICK

Born, West Hills, California, June 15, 1986.
Bats Right. Throws Right. Height, 6 feet, 2 inches. Weight, 200 pounds.

Year Club	Lea	Pos	G	AB	R	H	2B	3B	HR	RBI	SB	Avg
2004 Elizabethton	Appal.	SS	60	237	29	67	7	2	4	28	3	.283
2005 Beloit	Midwest	SS	127	466	58	104	18	0	13	60	8	.223
2006 Fort Myers	Fla.St.	SS-3B	125	455	60	112	26	4	4	45	8	.246
2007 New Britain	Eastern	SS	126	497	75	136	37	2	9	50	12	.274
2008 New Britain	Eastern	SS-3B	58	227	32	61	17	3	3	21	4	.269
2008 Rochester	Int.	3B-2B-SS	66	250	34	64	17	3	6	39	1	.256
2009 Rochester	Int.	SS	118	430	53	112	23	5	10	60	3	.260
2010 Rochester	Int.	SS-3B-2B	102	402	53	98	22	4	15	49	5	.244
2010 Minnesota	A.L.	SS-2B	22	41	7	6	1	0	2	6	0	.146

Year	Club	Lea	Pos	G	AB	R	H	2B	3B	HR	RBI	SB	Avg
2011	Rochester.........	Int.	SS-2B-1B-OF	51	192	33	60	11	3	15	33	3	.313
2011	Minnesota	A.L.	SS-2B-OF-1B	81	286	47	68	18	1	8	31	3	.238
2012	Rochester.........	Int.	3B	2	8	0	0	0	0	0	0	0	.000
2012	Minnesota a.......	A.L.	3B-OF-2B-1B	119	422	56	99	19	1	24	55	1	.235
2013	Rochester.........	Int.	3B	4	15	3	5	0	0	1	3	0	.333
2013	Minnesota b.......	A.L.	3B-1B	129	477	44	121	22	1	14	52	2	.254
Major League Totals			4 Yrs.	351	1226	154	294	60	3	48	144	6	.240

a On disabled list from July 21 to August 13, 2012.

b On disabled list from May 22 to May 29 and May 29 to June 15, 2013.

POLANCO, PLACIDO ENRIQUE

Born, Santo Domingo, Dominican Republic, October 10, 1975.

Bats Right. Throws Right. Height, 5 feet, 10 inches. Weight, 195 pounds.

Year	Club	Lea	Pos	G	AB	R	H	2B	3B	HR	RBI	SB	Avg
1994	Cardinals	Arizona	SS-2B	32	127	17	27	4	0	1	10	4	.213
1995	Peoria........	Midwest	SS-2B	103	361	43	96	7	4	2	41	7	.266
1996	St. Pete	Fla.St.	2B	137	540	65	157	29	5	0	51	4	.291
1997	Arkansas	Texas	2B	129	508	71	148	16	3	2	51	19	.291
1998	Memphis	P.C.	2B-SS	70	246	36	69	19	1	1	21	6	.280
1998	St. Louis..........	N.L.	SS-2B	45	114	10	29	3	2	1	11	2	.254
1999	Memphis	P.C.	2B	29	120	18	33	4	1	0	10	2	.275
1999	St. Louis..........	N.L.	2B-3B-SS	88	220	24	61	9	3	1	19	1	.277
2000	St. Louis a	N.L.	2B-3B-SS-1B	118	323	50	102	12	3	5	39	4	.316
2001	St. Louis..........	N.L.	3B-SS-2B	144	564	87	173	26	4	3	38	12	.307
2002	St. Louis-Phil. b....	N.L.	3B-SS-2B	147	548	75	158	32	2	9	49	5	.288
2003	Philadelphia c.......	N.L.	2B-3B	122	492	87	142	30	3	14	63	14	.289
2004	Reading	Eastern	2B	1	3	0	2	0	0	0	0	0	.667
2004	Scranton/WB	Int.	2B	1	3	1	0	0	0	0	0	0	.000
2004	Philadelphia d-e....	N.L.	2B-3B	126	503	74	150	21	0	17	55	7	.298
2005	Philadelphia	N.L.	2B-3B-OF-SS	43	158	26	50	7	0	3	20	0	.316
2005	Detroit f-g	A.L.	2B-3B	86	343	58	116	20	2	6	36	4	.338
2006	Detroit h..........	A.L.	2B	110	461	58	136	18	1	4	52	1	.295
2007	Detroit	A.L.	2B	142	587	105	200	36	3	9	67	7	.341
2008	Detroit	A.L.	2B	141	580	90	178	34	3	8	58	7	.307
2009	Detroit i	A.L.	2B	153	618	82	176	31	4	10	72	7	.285
2010	Phillies......	Gulf Coast	2B	1	3	1	3	1	0	0	2	0	1.000
2010	Clearwater	Fla.St.	3B	1	4	1	1	0	0	0	0	0	.250
2010	Philadelphia j	N.L.	3B-2B	132	554	76	165	27	2	6	52	5	.298
2011	Lehigh Valley	Int.	3B	2	6	0	0	0	0	0	0	0	.000
2011	Philadelphia k.......	N.L.	3B-2B	122	469	46	130	14	0	5	50	3	.277
2012	Clearwater	Fla.St.	3B	3	12	3	5	0	0	0	2	0	.417
2012	Philadelphia l-m....	N.L.	3B	90	303	28	78	15	0	2	19	0	.257
2013	Miami n-o	N.L.	3B	118	377	33	98	13	0	1	23	2	.260
Major League Totals			16 Yrs.	1927	7214	1009	2142	348	32	104	723	81	.297
	Division Series												
2000	St. Louis..........	N.L.	3B	3	10	1	3	0	0	0	3	1	.300
2001	St. Louis..........	N.L.	3B	5	15	1	4	0	0	0	1	1	.267
2006	Detroit	A.L.	2B	4	17	3	7	1	0	0	2	0	.412
2010	Philadelphia	N.L.	3B	2	9	1	1	0	0	0	0	0	.111
2011	Philadelphia	N.L.	3B	5	19	0	2	0	0	0	0	0	.105
Division Series Totals				19	70	6	17	1	0	0	6	2	.243
	Championship Series												
2000	St. Louis..........	N.L.	3B	4	5	0	1	0	0	0	0	0	.200
2006	Detroit	A.L.	2B	4	17	2	9	1	0	0	2	0	.529
2010	Philadelphia	N.L.	3B	6	20	3	5	2	0	0	5	1	.250
Championship Series Totals				14	42	5	15	3	0	0	7	1	.357
	World Series Record												
2006	Detroit	A.L.	2B	5	17	0	0	0	0	0	0	0	.000

a On disabled list from July 1 to July 15, 2000.

b Traded to Philadelphia Phillies with pitcher Bud Smith and pitcher Mike Timlin for infielder Scott Rolen and pitcher Doug Nickle, July 29, 2002.

c On disabled list from April 16 to May 1, 2003.

d On disabled list from May 8 to June 7, 2004.

e Filed for free agency, October 29, 2004, re-signed with Philadelphia Phillies, December 19, 2004.

f Traded to Detroit Tigers for pitcher Ugueth Urbina and infielder Ramon Martinez, June 8, 2005.

g On disabled list from July 12 to July 27, 2005.

h On disabled list from August 16 to September 22, 2006.

i Filed for free agency, November 5, 2009. Signed with Philadelphia Phillies, December 3, 2009.

j On disabled list from June 26 to July 17, 2010.
k On disabled list from July 5 to July 30 and August 7 to August 22, 2011.
l On disabled list from July 23 to August 20 and September 5 to October 5, 2012.
m Filed for free agency, November 3, 2012. Signed with Miami Marlins, December 20, 2012.
n On disabled list from August 19 to August 27, 2013.
o Filed for free agency, October 31, 2013.

POLLOCK, ALLEN LORENZ (A.J.)

Born, Hebron, Connecticut, December 5, 1987.
Bats Right. Throws Right. Height, 6 feet, 1 inch. Weight, 195 pounds.

Year Club	Lea	Pos	G	AB	R	H	2B	3B	HR	RBI	SB	Avg
2009 South Bend	Midwest	OF	63	255	36	69	12	3	3	22	10	.271
2010 a				INJURED—Did Not Play								
2011 Mobile	Southern	OF	133	550	103	169	41	5	8	73	36	.307
2012 Reno	P.C.	OF	106	428	65	136	25	3	3	52	21	.318
2012 Arizona	N.L.	OF	31	81	8	20	4	1	2	8	1	.247
2013 Arizona	N.L.	OF	137	443	64	119	28	5	8	38	12	.269
Major League Totals		2 Yrs.	168	524	72	139	32	6	10	46	13	.265

a On minor league disabled list from April 8 to September 7, 2010.

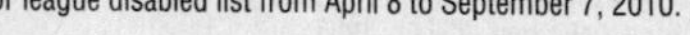

POSEY, GERALD DEMP (BUSTER)

Born, Leesburg, Georgia, March 27, 1987.
Bats Right. Throws Right. Height, 6 feet, 1 inch. Weight, 205 pounds.

Year Club	Lea	Pos	G	AB	R	H	2B	3B	HR	RBI	SB	Avg
2008 Giants	Arizona	C	7	26	8	10	3	1	1	4	0	.385
2008 Salem-Keizer	Northwest	C	3	11	2	3	2	0	0	2	0	.273
2009 San Jose	Calif.	C	80	291	63	95	23	0	13	58	6	.326
2009 Fresno	P.C.	C	35	131	21	42	8	1	5	22	0	.321
2009 San Francisco	N.L.	C	7	17	1	2	0	0	0	0	0	.118
2010 Fresno	P.C.	C-1B	47	172	31	60	13	2	6	32	1	.349
2010 San Francisco a	N.L.	C-1B	108	406	58	124	23	2	18	67	0	.305
2011 San Francisco b	N.L.	C-1B	45	162	17	46	5	0	4	21	3	.284
2012 San Francisco c	N.L.	C-1B	148	530	78	178	39	1	24	103	1	*.336
2013 San Francisco	N.L.	C-1B	148	520	61	153	34	1	15	72	2	.294
Major League Totals		5 Yrs.	456	1635	215	503	101	4	61	263	6	.308
Division Series												
2010 San Francisco	N.L.	C	4	16	3	6	1	0	0	0	1	.375
2012 San Francisco	N.L.	C-1B	5	19	3	4	0	0	2	5	0	.211
Division Series Totals			9	35	6	10	1	0	2	5	1	.286
Championship Series												
2010 San Francisco	N.L.	C	6	23	1	5	2	0	0	3	0	.217
2012 San Francisco	N.L.	C-1B	7	26	1	4	0	0	0	1	0	.154
Championship Series Totals			13	49	2	9	2	0	0	4	0	.184
World Series Record												
2010 San Francisco	N.L.	C	5	20	2	6	0	0	1	2	0	.300
2012 San Francisco	N.L.	C	4	15	1	4	0	0	1	3	0	.267
World Series Totals			9	35	3	10	0	0	2	5	0	.286

a Selected Rookie of the Year in National League for 2010.
b On disabled list from May 26 to October 31, 2011.
c Selected Most Valuable Player in National League for 2012.

PRADO, MARTIN MANUEL

Born, Maracay, Venezuela, October 27, 1983.
Bats Right. Throws Right. Height, 6 feet, 1 inch. Weight, 170 pounds.

Year Club	Lea	Pos	G	AB	R	H	2B	3B	HR	RBI	SB	Avg
2003 Braves	Gulf Coast	2B-3B	59	220	28	63	2	6	0	23	9	.286
2004 Rome	So.Atl.	2B	107	429	68	135	25	6	3	38	14	.315
2005 Myrtle Beach	Carolina	2B	75	297	44	91	13	3	4	34	9	.306
2005 Mississippi	Southern	2B	39	143	17	40	7	1	1	11	3	.280
2006 Richmond	Int.	2B-3B	60	241	30	68	12	1	2	23	2	.282
2006 Mississippi	Southern	2B-3B	43	176	17	49	6	2	1	15	2	.278
2006 Atlanta	N.L.	2B-3B	24	42	3	11	1	1	1	9	0	.262
2007 Richmond	Int.	2B-3B-SS	103	395	61	125	23	3	4	41	5	.316
2007 Atlanta	N.L.	2B-3B	28	59	5	17	3	0	0	2	0	.288
2008 Mississippi	Southern	2B-3B-SS-OF	5	19	2	5	2	0	0	3	0	.263
2008 Atlanta a	N.L.	3B-1B-2B-OF	78	228	36	73	18	4	2	33	3	.320

Year	Club	Lea	Pos	G	AB	R	H	2B	3B	HR	RBI	SB	Avg
2009	Atlanta	N.L.	2B-3B-1B-OF	128	450	64	138	38	0	11	49	1	.307
2010	Gwinnett	Int.	2B-3B	1	4	0	1	0	0	0	0	0	.250
2010	Atlanta b	N.L.	2B-3B-1B	140	599	100	184	40	3	15	66	5	.307
2011	Mississippi	Southern	3B	2	9	2	2	0	0	0	2	0	.222
2011	Gwinnett	Int.	3B-OF	6	17	2	3	0	0	0	1	0	.176
2011	Atlanta c	N.L.	OF-3B-1B	129	551	66	143	26	2	13	57	4	.260
2012	Atlanta	N.L.	OF-3B-SS-2B	156	617	81	186	42	6	10	70	17	.301
2013	Arizona d	N.L.	3B-2B-OF-SS	155	609	70	172	36	2	14	82	3	.282
Major League Totals			8 Yrs.	838	3155	425	924	204	18	66	368	33	.293
Wild Card Playoff													
2012	Atlanta	N.L.	OF	1	5	0	1	0	0	0	0	0	.200

a On disabled list from May 5 to July 3, 2008.
b On disabled list from July 31 to August 17, 2010.
c On disabled list from June 8 to July 15, 2011.
d Traded to Arizona Diamondbacks with pitcher Randall Delgado, pitcher Zeke Spruill, infielder Nick Ahmed and infielder Brandon Drury for outfielder Justin Upton and infielder Chris Johnson, January 24, 2013.

PRESLEY, ALEXANDER CRAWFORD (ALEX)

Born, Monroe, Louisiana, July 25, 1985.
Bats Left. Throws Left. Height, 5 feet, 9 inches. Weight, 190 pounds.

Year	Club	Lea	Pos	G	AB	R	H	2B	3B	HR	RBI	SB	Avg
2006	Williamsport	N.Y.-Penn.	OF	61	223	26	58	7	8	3	23	3	.260
2007	Hickory	So.Atl.	OF	121	495	79	145	22	8	11	63	18	.293
2008	Lynchburg	Carolina	OF	82	287	39	74	15	1	6	35	13	.258
2009	Lynchburg	Carolina	OF	115	417	51	107	17	11	4	37	9	.257
2010	Altoona	Eastern	OF	67	246	42	86	13	7	6	47	5	.350
2010	Indianapolis	Int.	OF	69	272	44	80	15	6	6	38	8	.294
2010	Pittsburgh	N.L.	OF	19	23	2	6	1	0	0	0	1	.261
2011	Bradenton	Fla.St.	OF	2	6	2	1	0	0	0	0	0	.167
2011	Indianapolis	Int.	OF	87	342	58	114	18	5	8	41	22	.333
2011	Pittsburgh a	N.L.	OF	52	215	27	64	12	6	4	20	9	.298
2012	Indianapolis	Int.	OF	40	153	24	47	3	4	5	22	7	.307
2012	Pittsburgh b	N.L.	OF	104	346	46	82	14	7	10	25	9	.237
2013	Indianapolis	Int.	OF	89	342	57	102	17	6	5	27	17	.298
2013	Pittsburgh	N.L.	OF	29	72	8	19	1	1	2	4	0	.264
2013	Minnesota c	A.L.	OF	28	113	9	32	4	1	1	11	1	.283
Major League Totals			4 Yrs.	232	769	92	203	32	15	17	60	20	.264

a On disabled list from July 23 to August 25, 2011.
b On disabled list from July 5 to July 16, 2012.
c Traded to Minnesota Twins with player to be named later for infielder Justin Morneau, August 31, 2013. Minnesota Twins received pitcher Duke Welker to complete trade, October 5, 2013.

PROFAR, JURICKSON BARTHELOMEUS

Born, Willemstad, Curacao, February 20, 1993.
Bats Both. Throws Right. Height, 6 feet. Weight, 165 pounds.

Year	Club	Lea	Pos	G	AB	R	H	2B	3B	HR	RBI	SB	Avg
2010	Spokane	Northwest	SS	63	252	42	63	19	0	4	23	8	.250
2011	Hickory	So.Atl.	SS	115	430	86	123	37	8	12	65	23	.286
2012	Frisco	Texas	SS-2B-3B	126	480	76	135	26	7	14	62	16	.281
2012	Texas	A.L.	2B-SS	9	17	2	3	2	0	1	2	0	.176
2013	Round Rock	P.C.	SS-2B	37	144	27	40	7	2	4	19	6	.278
2013	Texas	A.L.	2B-SS-3B	85	286	30	67	11	0	6	26	2	.234
Major League Totals			2 Yrs.	94	303	32	70	13	0	7	28	2	.231
Wild Card Playoff													
2012	Texas	A.L.	PH	1	1	0	1	0	0	0	0	0	1.000

PUIG (VALDES), YASIEL

Born, Cienfuegos, Cuba, December 7, 1990.
Bats Right. Throws Right. Height, 6 feet, 3 inches. Weight, 245 pounds.

Year	Club	Lea	Pos	G	AB	R	H	2B	3B	HR	RBI	SB	Avg
2012	Dodgers a-b	Arizona	OF	9	30	10	12	0	3	4	11	1	.400
2012	Rancho Cucamonga	Calif.	OF	14	52	10	17	2	0	1	4	7	.327
2013	Chattanooga	Southern	OF	40	147	26	46	12	3	8	37	13	.313
2013	Los Angeles	N.L.	OF	104	382	66	122	21	2	19	42	11	.319
Division Series													
2013	Los Angeles	N.L.	OF	4	17	5	8	1	0	0	2	0	.471

Year	Club	Lea	Pos	G	AB	R	H	2B	3B	HR	RBI	SB	Avg
	Championship Series												
2013	Los Angeles..........	N.L.	OF	6	22	1	5	0	1	0	2	0	.227

a Played in Cuba 2008-2011.
b Signed with Los Angeles Dodgers, June 29, 2012.

PUJOLS, JOSE ALBERTO (ALBERT)

Born, Santo Domingo, Dominican Republic, January 16, 1980.
Bats Right. Throws Right. Height, 6 feet, 3 inches. Weight, 225 pounds.

Year	Club	Lea	Pos	G	AB	R	H	2B	3B	HR	RBI	SB	Avg
2000	Potomac......	Carolina	3B	21	81	11	23	8	1	2	10	1	.284
2000	Peoria........	Midwest	3B	109	395	62	128	32	6	17	84	2	.324
2000	Memphis	P.C.	3B-OF	3	14	1	3	1	0	0	2	1	.214
2001	St. Louis a	N.L.	OF-3B-1B	161	590	112	194	47	4	37	130	1	.329
2002	St. Louis..........	N.L.	OF-3B-1B-SS	157	590	118	185	40	2	34	127	2	.314
2003	St. Louis..........	N.L.	OF-1B	157	591	*137	*212	*51	1	43	124	5	*.359
2004	St. Louis..........	N.L.	1B	154	592	*133	196	51	2	46	123	5	.331
2005	St. Louis b	N.L.	1B	161	591	*129	195	38	2	41	117	16	.330
2006	St. Louis c	N.L.	1B	143	535	119	177	33	1	49	137	7	.331
2007	St. Louis..........	N.L.	1B	158	565	99	185	38	1	32	103	2	.327
2008	St. Louis d-e	N.L.	1B-2B	148	524	100	187	44	0	37	116	7	.357
2009	St. Louis f	N.L.	1B	160	568	*124	186	45	1	*47	135	16	.327
2010	St. Louis..........	N.L.	1B	159	587	*115	183	39	1	*42	*118	14	.312
2011	St. Louis g-h	N.L.	1B-3B	147	579	105	173	29	0	37	99	9	.299
2012	Los Angeles.......	A.L.	1B-3B	154	607	85	173	50	0	30	105	8	.285
2013	Los Angeles i	A.L.	DH-1B	99	391	49	101	19	0	17	64	1	.258
Major League Totals			13 Yrs.	1958	7310	1425	2347	524	15	492	1498	93	.321
	Division Series												
2001	St. Louis..........	N.L.	1B-OF	5	18	1	2	0	0	1	2	0	.111
2002	St. Louis..........	N.L.	OF-1B-3B	3	10	3	3	0	1	0	3	0	.300
2004	St. Louis..........	N.L.	1B	4	15	4	5	0	0	2	5	0	.333
2005	St. Louis..........	N.L.	1B	3	9	4	5	2	0	0	2	0	.556
2006	St. Louis..........	N.L.	1B	4	15	3	5	1	0	1	3	0	.333
2009	St. Louis..........	N.L.	1B	3	10	0	3	0	0	0	1	0	.300
2011	St. Louis..........	N.L.	1B	5	20	2	7	3	0	0	1	1	.350
Division Series Totals				27	97	17	30	6	1	4	17	1	.309
	Championship Series												
2002	St. Louis..........	N.L.	OF-3B-1B	5	19	2	5	1	0	1	2	0	.263
2004	St. Louis..........	N.L.	1B	7	28	10	14	2	0	4	9	0	.500
2005	St. Louis..........	N.L.	1B	6	23	3	7	0	0	2	6	0	.304
2006	St. Louis..........	N.L.	1B	7	22	5	7	1	0	1	1	0	.318
2011	St. Louis..........	N.L.	1B	6	23	5	11	4	0	2	9	0	.478
Championship Series Totals				31	115	25	44	8	0	10	27	0	.383
	World Series Record												
2004	St. Louis..........	N.L.	1B	4	15	1	5	2	0	0	0	0	.333
2006	St. Louis..........	N.L.	1B	5	15	3	3	1	0	1	2	0	.200
2011	St. Louis..........	N.L.	1B	7	25	8	6	1	0	3	6	0	.240
World Series Totals.............				16	55	12	14	4	0	4	8	0	.255

a Selected Rookie of the Year in National League for 2001.
b Selected Most Valuable Player in National League for 2005.
c On disabled list from June 4 to June 22, 2006.
d On disabled list from June 11 to June 26, 2008.
e Selected Most Valuable Player in National League for 2008.
f Selected Most Valuable Player in National League for 2009.
g On disabled list from June 20 to July 5, 2011.
h Filed for free agency, October 30, 2011. Signed with Los Angeles Angels, December 10, 2011.
i On disabled list from July 27 to September 30, 2013.

PUNTO, NICHOLAS PAUL (NICK)

Born, San Diego, California, November 8, 1977.
Bats Both. Throws Right. Height, 5 feet, 9 inches. Weight, 185 pounds.

Year	Club	Lea	Pos	G	AB	R	H	2B	3B	HR	RBI	SB	Avg
1998	Batavia......	N.Y.-Penn.	SS-2B	72	279	51	69	9	4	1	20	19	.247
1999	Clearwater	Fla.St.	SS	106	400	65	122	18	6	1	48	16	.305
2000	Reading	Eastern	SS	121	456	77	116	15	4	5	47	33	.254
2001	Scranton-WB	Int.	SS	123	463	57	106	19	5	1	39	33	.229
2001	Philadelphia	N.L.	SS	4	5	0	2	0	0	0	0	0	.400
2002	Philadelphia	N.L.	2B-SS	9	6	0	1	0	0	0	0	0	.167

Year	Club	Lea	Pos	G	AB	R	H	2B	3B	HR	RBI	SB	Avg
2002	Scranton-WB	Int.	SS	115	443	74	120	12	5	1	29	42	.271
2003	Philadelphia	N.L.	2B-3B-SS	64	92	14	20	2	0	1	4	2	.217
2003	Scranton/WB a	Int.	SS	25	111	19	35	7	1	0	9	7	.315
2004	Minnesota	A.L.	2B-SS-3B-OF	38	91	17	23	0	0	2	12	6	.253
2004	Quad Cities b	Midwest	SS-2B-3B	4	16	4	7	1	0	1	6	1	.438
2005	Rochester	Int.	2B	4	15	2	3	1	0	0	1	0	.200
2005	Minnesota c	A.L.	2B-SS-3B-OF	112	394	45	94	18	4	4	26	13	.239
2006	Minnesota	A.L.	3B-SS-2B-OF	135	459	73	133	21	7	1	45	17	.290
2007	Minnesota	A.L.	3B-SS-2B	150	472	53	99	18	4	1	25	16	.210
2008	Fort Myers	Fla.St.	SS	3	12	0	3	0	0	0	1	1	.250
2008	Minnesota d-e	A.L.	SS-2B-3B-OF	99	338	43	96	19	4	2	28	15	.284
2009	Minnesota f	A.L.	2B-SS-3B	125	359	56	82	15	1	1	38	16	.228
2010	Minnesota g-h	A.L.	3B-SS-2B	88	252	24	60	11	1	1	20	6	.238
2011	Springfield	Texas	2B	7	24	3	8	1	0	0	2	1	.333
2011	Memphis	P.C.	2B-3B	5	15	2	3	0	0	0	0	0	.200
2011	St. Louis i-j	N.L.	2B-SS-3B	63	133	21	37	8	4	1	20	1	.278
2012	Boston	A.L.	3B-2B-SS-1B	65	125	14	25	6	0	1	10	5	.200
2012	Los Angeles k	N.L.	2B-3B	22	35	6	10	1	0	0	0	1	.286
2013	Los Angeles l	N.L.	SS-3B-2B	116	294	34	75	15	0	2	21	3	.255
Major League Totals			13 Yrs.	1090	3055	400	757	134	25	17	249	101	.248
	Division Series												
2006	Minnesota	A.L.	3B	3	12	0	2	0	0	0	0	0	.167
2009	Minnesota	A.L.	2B	3	9	0	4	1	0	0	1	0	.444
2011	St. Louis	N.L.	2B	3	6	0	1	0	0	0	0	0	.167
2013	Los Angeles	N.L.	SS	1	0	0	0	0	0	0	0	0	.000
Division Series Totals				10	27	0	7	1	0	0	1	0	.259
	Championship Series												
2011	St. Louis	N.L.	2B	6	15	0	2	0	0	0	3	0	.133
2013	Los Angeles	N.L.	SS	5	6	0	2	1	0	0	0	0	.333
Championship Series Totals				11	21	0	4	1	0	0	3	0	.190
	World Series Record												
2011	St. Louis	N.L.	2B	6	14	0	3	0	0	0	0	0	.214

a Traded to Minnesota Twins with pitcher Carlos Silva and cash for pitcher Eric Milton, December 3, 2003.
b On disabled list from May 9 to June 30 and July 27 to October 28, 2004.
c On disabled list from June 3 to July 3, 2005.
d On disabled list from May 8 to May 31 and June 6 to June 24, 2008.
e Filed for free agency, October 30, 2008, re-signed with Minnesota Twins, December 11, 2008.
f On disabled list from May 28 to June 12, 2009.
g On disabled list from April 16 to May 1 and July 29 to August 17 and August 20 to September 10, 2010.
h Filed for free agency, November 1, 2010. Signed with St. Louis Cardinals, January 21, 2011.
i On disabled list from March 22 to April 19 and May 18 to June 27 and July 29 to September 6, 2011.
j Filed for free agency, October 30, 2011. Signed with Boston Red Sox, December 14, 2011.
k Traded to Los Angeles Dodgers with outfielder Carl Crawford, infielder Adrian Gonzalez, pitcher Josh Beckett and cash for infielder James Loney, infielder Ivan DeJesus, pitcher Allen Webster and player to be named later, August 25, 2012. Boston Red Sox received pitcher Rubby De La Rosa to complete trade, October 4, 2012.
l Filed for free agency, October 31, 2013. Signed with Oakland Athletics, November 13, 2013.

QUENTIN, CARLOS JOSE

Born, Bellflower, California, August 28, 1982.
Bats Right. Throws Right. Height, 6 feet, 1 inch. Weight, 225 pounds.

Year	Club	Lea	Pos	G	AB	R	H	2B	3B	HR	RBI	SB	Avg
2004	Lancaster	Calif.	OF	65	242	64	75	14	1	15	51	5	.310
2004	El Paso	Texas	OF	60	210	39	75	19	0	6	38	0	.357
2005	Tucson	P.C.	OF	136	452	98	136	28	4	21	89	9	.301
2006	Tucson	P.C.	OF	85	318	66	92	30	3	9	52	5	.289
2006	Arizona	N.L.	OF	57	166	23	42	13	3	9	32	1	.253
2007	Tucson	P.C.	OF	33	115	30	40	12	1	4	27	0	.348
2007	Arizona a-b	N.L.	OF	81	229	29	49	16	0	5	31	2	.214
2008	Chicago	A.L.	OF	130	480	96	138	26	1	36	100	7	.287
2009	Kannapolis	So.Atl.	OF	2	3	0	1	1	0	0	1	0	.333
2009	Charlotte	Int.	OF	12	37	10	14	3	0	1	9	0	.378
2009	Chicago c	A.L.	OF	99	351	47	83	14	0	21	56	3	.236
2010	Chicago	A.L.	OF	131	453	73	110	25	2	26	87	2	.243
2011	Chicago d-e	A.L.	OF	118	421	53	107	31	0	24	77	1	.254
2012	Lake Elsinore	Calif.	OF	4	14	3	6	1	0	1	5	0	.429
2012	Tucson	P.C.	OF	5	14	5	4	0	0	1	4	0	.286
2012	San Diego f	N.L.	OF	86	284	44	74	21	0	16	46	0	.261
2013	San Diego g	N.L.	OF	82	276	42	76	21	0	13	44	0	.275
Major League Totals			8 Yrs.	784	2660	407	679	167	6	150	473	16	.255

a On disabled list from March 23 to April 16 and August 2 to September 1, 2007.
b Traded to Chicago White Sox for infielder Chris Carter, December 3, 2007.
c On disabled list from May 26 to July 20, 2009.
d On disabled list from August 21 to September 12, 2011.
e Traded to San Diego Padres for pitcher Simon Castro and pitcher Pedro Hernandez, December 31, 2011.
f On disabled list from April 3 to May 28, 2012.
g On disabled list from July 31 to September 30, 2013.

RABURN, RYAN NEIL

Born, Tampa, Florida, April 17, 1981.
Bats Right. Throws Right. Height, 6 feet. Weight, 185 pounds.

Year	Club	Lea	Pos	G	AB	R	H	2B	3B	HR	RBI	SB	Avg
2001	Tigers	Gulf Coast	3B	19	58	4	9	2	0	1	5	2	.155
2001	Oneonta	N.Y.-Penn.	3B-2B	44	171	25	62	17	8	8	42	1	.363
2002	Tigers	Gulf Coast	3B	8	30	4	9	3	1	1	5	0	.300
2002	West Michigan	Midwest	3B	40	150	27	33	10	1	6	28	0	.220
2003	West Michigan	Midwest	3B	16	57	14	20	7	0	3	12	1	.351
2003	Lakeland	Fla.St.	3B	95	325	52	72	14	3	12	56	2	.222
2004	Lakeland	Fla.St.	2B	3	11	1	3	1	0	1	3	0	.273
2004	Erie	Eastern	2B	98	366	66	110	29	4	16	63	3	.301
2004	Detroit	A.L.	2B	12	29	4	4	1	0	0	1	1	.138
2005	Toledo	Int.	2B-OF	130	471	62	119	22	4	19	64	8	.253
2006	Toledo	Int.	OF-2B	118	451	68	124	29	4	20	79	16	.275
2007	Toledo	Int.	OF-2B	85	315	60	92	21	3	17	64	12	.292
2007	Detroit	A.L.	OF-2B-3B	49	138	28	42	12	2	4	27	3	.304
2008	Toledo	Int.	OF	5	19	6	6	2	0	2	6	0	.316
2008	Detroit	A.L.	OF-3B-2B	92	182	26	43	10	1	4	20	3	.236
2009	Toledo	Int.	OF	12	47	11	12	3	0	5	9	2	.255
2009	Detroit	A.L.	OF-1B-3B	113	261	44	76	11	2	16	45	5	.291
2010	Toledo	Int.	OF	7	27	5	12	6	0	0	2	1	.444
2010	Detroit	A.L.	OF-2B-3B-1B	113	371	54	104	25	1	15	62	2	.280
2011	Detroit	A.L.	OF-2B-3B-1B	121	387	53	99	22	2	14	49	1	.256
2012	Toledo	Int.	2B-OF-1B	15	60	8	15	2	0	4	12	1	.250
2012	Detroit a-b	A.L.	OF-2B	66	205	14	35	14	0	1	12	1	.171
2013	Cleveland c	A.L.	OF-2B-P	87	243	40	66	18	0	16	55	0	.272
Major League Totals			8 Yrs.	653	1816	263	469	113	8	70	271	16	.258
	Wild Card Playoff												
2013	Cleveland	A.L.	OF	1	3	0	1	1	0	0	0	0	.333
	Division Series												
2011	Detroit	A.L.	OF-2B	3	5	0	2	0	0	0	1	0	.400
	Championship Series												
2011	Detroit	A.L.	OF	6	23	4	6	1	0	2	4	0	.261

a On disabled list from August 1 to September 1 and September 11 to October 29, 2012.
b Released by Detroit Tigers, November 20, 2012. Signed with Cleveland Indians organization, January 21, 2013.
c On disabled list from August 19 to September 3, 2013.

RAMIREZ, ALEXEI FERNANDO

Born, Pinar Del Rio, Cuba, September 22, 1981.
Bats Right. Throws Right. Height, 6 feet, 3 inches. Weight, 185 pounds.

Year	Club	Lea	Pos	G	AB	R	H	2B	3B	HR	RBI	SB	Avg
2008	Chicago a-b	A.L.	2B-SS-OF-3B	136	480	65	139	22	2	21	77	13	.290
2009	Chicago	A.L.	SS	148	542	71	150	14	1	15	68	14	.277
2010	Chicago	A.L.	SS	156	585	83	165	29	2	18	70	13	.282
2011	Chicago	A.L.	SS	158	614	81	165	31	2	15	70	7	.269
2012	Chicago	A.L.	SS	158	593	59	157	24	4	9	73	20	.265
2013	Chicago	A.L.	SS	158	637	68	181	39	2	6	48	30	.284
Major League Totals			6 Yrs.	914	3451	427	957	159	13	84	406	97	.277
	Division Series												
2008	Chicago	A.L.	2B	4	12	1	3	0	0	0	2	0	.250

a Played in Cuba 2001-2007.
b Signed with Chicago White Sox, January 1, 2008.

RAMIREZ (NIN), ARAMIS

Born, Santo Domingo, Dominican Republic, June 25, 1978.
Bats Right. Throws Right. Height, 6 feet, 1 inch. Weight, 215 pounds.

Year	Club	Lea	Pos	G	AB	R	H	2B	3B	HR	RBI	SB	Avg
1995	Pittsburgh	Domincan	3B	64	214	41	63	13	0	11	54	2	.294
1996	Erie	N.Y.-Penn.	3B	61	223	37	68	14	4	9	42	0	.305

Year Club	Lea	Pos	G	AB	R	H	2B	3B	HR	RBI	SB	Avg
1996 Augusta	So.Atl.	3B	6	20	3	4	1	0	1	2	0	.200
1997 Lynchburg	Carolina	3B	137	482	85	134	24	2	29	114	5	.278
1998 Nashville	P.C.	3B-SS	47	168	19	46	10	0	5	18	0	.274
1998 Pittsburgh a	N.L.	3B	72	251	23	59	9	1	6	24	0	.235
1999 Nashville	P.C.	3B	131	460	92	151	35	1	21	74	5	.328
1999 Pittsburgh	N.L.	3B	18	56	2	10	2	1	0	7	0	.179
2000 Nashville	P.C.	3B	44	167	28	59	12	2	4	26	2	.353
2000 Pittsburgh b	N.L.	3B	73	254	19	65	15	2	6	35	0	.256
2001 Pittsburgh	N.L.	3B	158	603	83	181	40	0	34	112	5	.300
2002 Pittsburgh	N.L.	3B	142	522	51	122	26	0	18	71	2	.234
2003 Pittsburgh-Chicago c-d .	N.L.	3B	159	607	75	165	32	2	27	106	2	.272
2004 Chicago	N.L.	3B	145	547	99	174	32	1	36	103	0	.318
2005 Chicago e	N.L.	3B	123	463	72	140	30	0	31	92	0	.302
2006 Chicago f	N.L.	3B	157	594	93	173	38	4	38	119	2	.291
2007 Chicago g	N.L.	3B	132	506	72	157	35	4	26	101	0	.310
2008 Chicago	N.L.	3B	149	554	97	160	44	1	27	111	2	.289
2009 Peoria	Midwest	3B	3	6	2	3	1	0	0	1	0	.500
2009 Chicago h	N.L.	3B	82	306	46	97	14	1	15	65	2	.317
2010 Peoria	Midwest	3B	2	6	1	1	0	0	0	1	0	.167
2010 Chicago i	N.L.	3B	124	465	61	112	21	1	25	83	0	.241
2011 Chicago j	N.L.	3B	149	565	80	173	35	1	26	93	1	.306
2012 Milwaukee	N.L.	3B	149	570	92	171	*50	3	27	105	9	.300
2013 Milwaukee k	N.L.	3B	92	304	43	86	18	0	12	49	0	.283
Major League Totals		16 Yrs.	1924	7167	1008	2045	441	22	354	1276	25	.285
Division Series												
2003 Chicago	N.L.	3B	5	18	2	5	1	0	1	3	0	.278
2007 Chicago	N.L.	3B	3	12	0	0	0	0	0	0	0	.000
2008 Chicago	N.L.	3B	3	11	1	2	1	0	0	0	0	.182
Division Series Totals			11	41	3	7	2	0	1	3	0	.171
Championship Series												
2003 Chicago	N.L.	3B	7	26	4	6	0	1	3	7	0	.231

a On disabled list from August 10 to September 4, 1998.
b On disabled list from August 29 to October 1, 2000.
c Traded to Chicago Cubs with outfielder Kenny Lofton for infielder Jose Hernandez, pitcher Matt Bruback and player to be named later, July 22, 2003.
d Pittsburgh Pirates received infielder Bobby Hill to complete trade, August 15, 2003.
e On disabled list from August 25 to October 3, 2005.
f Filed for free agency, October 30, 2006, re-signed with Chicago Cubs, November 12, 2006.
g On disabled list from June 7 to June 22, 2007.
h On disabled list from May 9 to July 6, 2009.
i On disabled list from June 8 to June 25, 2010.
j Filed for free agency, November 1, 2011. Signed with Milwaukee Brewers, December 12, 2011.
k On disabled list from April 6 to May 3 and July 7 to August 13, 2013.

RAMIREZ, HANLEY

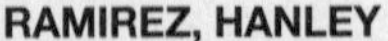

Born, Samana, Dominican Republic, December 23, 1983.
Bats Right. Throws Right. Height, 6 feet, 3 inches. Weight, 195 pounds.

Year Club	Lea	Pos	G	AB	R	H	2B	3B	HR	RBI	SB	Avg
2002 Red Sox	Gulf Coast	SS-2B-3B	45	164	29	56	11	3	6	26	8	.341
2002 Lowell	N.Y.-Penn.	SS	22	97	17	36	9	2	1	19	4	.371
2003 Augusta	So.Atl.	SS	111	422	69	116	24	3	8	50	36	.275
2004 Portland	Eastern	SS	32	129	26	40	7	2	5	15	12	.310
2004 Sarasota	Fla.St.	SS	62	239	33	74	8	4	1	24	12	.310
2004 Red Sox	Gulf Coast	SS-2B	6	20	5	8	0	1	0	7	1	.400
2005 Portland	Eastern	SS-2B-3B	122	465	66	126	21	7	6	52	26	.271
2005 Boston a	A.L.	SS	2	2	0	0	0	0	0	0	0	.000
2006 Florida b	N.L.	SS	158	633	119	185	46	11	17	59	51	.292
2007 Florida	N.L.	SS	154	639	125	212	48	6	29	81	51	.332
2008 Florida	N.L.	SS	153	589	*125	177	34	4	33	67	35	.301
2009 Florida	N.L.	SS	151	576	101	197	42	1	24	106	27	*.342
2010 Florida	N.L.	SS	142	543	92	163	28	2	21	76	32	.300
2011 Jupiter	Fla.St.	SS	6	21	6	10	1	1	0	4	1	.476
2011 Florida c	N.L.	SS	92	338	55	82	16	0	10	45	20	.243
2012 Miami-Los Angeles d .	N.L.	3B-SS	157	604	79	155	29	4	24	92	21	.257
2013 Rancho Cucamonga	Calif.	SS	5	15	1	5	2	0	0	6	0	.333
2013 Los Angeles e	N.L.	SS	86	304	62	105	25	2	20	57	10	.345
Major League Totals		9 Yrs.	1095	4228	758	1276	268	30	178	583	247	.302
Division Series												
2013 Los Angeles	N.L.	SS	4	16	4	8	4	1	1	6	1	.500

Year	Club	Lea	Pos	G	AB	R	H	2B	3B	HR	RBI	SB	Avg
	Championship Series												
2013	Los Angeles	N.L.	SS	5	15	1	2	0	0	0	1	0	.133

a Traded to Florida Marlins with pitcher Anibal Sanchez and pitcher Jesus Delgado for pitcher Josh Beckett, infielder Mike Lowell and pitcher Guillermo Mota, November 24, 2005.
b Selected Rookie of the Year in National League for 2006.
c On disabled list from May 30 to June 14 and August 3 to October 31, 2011.
d Traded to Los Angeles Dodgers with pitcher Randy Choate for pitcher Nathan Eovaldi and pitcher Scott McGough, July 25, 2012.
e On disabled list from March 22 to April 29 and May 4 to June 4, 2013.

RAMOS (CAMPOS), WILSON ABRAHAM

Born, Valencia, Venezuela, August 10, 1987.
Bats Right. Throws Right. Height, 6 feet. Weight, 220 pounds.

Year	Club	Lea	Pos	G	AB	R	H	2B	3B	HR	RBI	SB	Avg
2006	Twins	Gulf Coast	C-1B	46	154	18	44	12	1	3	26	4	.286
2007	Beloit	Midwest	C	73	292	40	85	17	1	8	42	1	.291
2008	Fort Myers	Fla.St.	C	126	452	50	130	23	2	13	78	0	.288
2009	Twins	Gulf Coast	C	5	19	4	6	1	1	3	6	0	.316
2009	New Britain	Eastern	C	54	205	31	65	16	0	4	29	0	.317
2010	Minnesota	A.L.	C	7	27	2	8	3	0	0	1	0	.296
2010	Rochester	Int.	C	71	278	25	67	14	0	5	30	1	.241
2010	Syracuse	Int.	C	20	79	14	25	3	1	3	8	0	.316
2010	Washington a	N.L.	C	15	52	3	14	4	0	1	4	0	.269
2011	Washington	N.L.	C	113	389	48	104	22	1	15	52	0	.267
2012	Washington b	N.L.	C	25	83	11	22	2	0	3	10	0	.265
2013	Nationals	Gulf Coast	C	2	3	0	0	0	0	0	0	0	.000
2013	Potomac	Carolina	C	3	10	0	0	0	0	0	0	0	.000
2013	Harrisburg	Eastern	C	2	4	1	2	1	0	0	0	0	.500
2013	Washington c	N.L.	C	78	287	29	78	9	0	16	59	0	.272
Major League Totals			4 Yrs.	238	838	93	226	40	1	35	126	0	.270

a Traded to Washington Nationals with pitcher Joe Testa and cash for pitcher Matt Capps, July 30, 2010.
b On disabled list from May 13 to November 2, 2012.
c On disabled list from April 14 to April 29 and May 16 to July 4, 2013.

RASMUS, COLBY RYAN

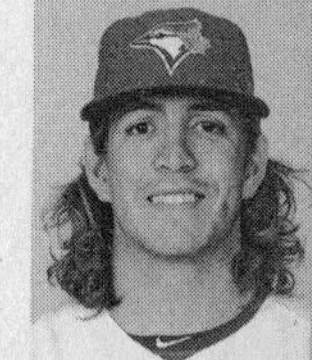

Born, Columbus, Georgia, August 11, 1986.
Bats Left. Throws Left. Height, 6 feet, 2 inches. Weight, 200 pounds.

Year	Club	Lea	Pos	G	AB	R	H	2B	3B	HR	RBI	SB	Avg
2005	Johnson City	Appal.	OF	62	216	47	64	16	5	7	27	13	.296
2006	Palm Beach	Fla.St.	OF	53	193	22	49	4	5	5	35	11	.254
2006	Quad Cities	Midwest	OF	78	303	49	94	22	3	11	50	17	.310
2007	Springfield	Texas	OF	128	472	93	130	37	3	29	72	18	.275
2008	Palm Beach	Fla.St.	OF	3	9	1	0	0	0	0	0	0	.000
2008	Cardinals	Gulf Coast	OF	3	9	1	5	1	0	1	2	0	.556
2008	Memphis	P.C.	OF	90	331	56	83	15	0	11	36	15	.251
2009	St. Louis	N.L.	OF	147	474	72	119	22	2	16	52	3	.251
2010	St. Louis	N.L.	OF	144	464	85	128	28	3	23	66	12	.276
2011	St. Louis	N.L.	OF	94	338	61	83	14	6	11	40	5	.246
2011	Toronto a-b	A.L.	OF	35	133	14	23	10	0	3	13	0	.173
2012	Toronto	A.L.	OF	151	565	75	126	21	5	23	75	4	.223
2013	Toronto c	A.L.	OF	118	417	57	115	26	1	22	66	0	.276
Major League Totals			5 Yrs.	689	2391	364	594	121	17	98	312	24	.248
	Division Series												
2009	St. Louis	N.L.	OF	3	9	1	4	3	0	0	1	0	.444

a Traded to Toronto Blue Jays with pitcher Trever Miller, pitcher Brian Tallet and pitcher P.J. Walters for pitcher Edwin Jackson, pitcher Octavio Dotel, pitcher Marc Rzepczynski, outfielder Corey Patterson and cash, July 27, 2011.
b On disabled list from August 24 to September 16, 2011.
c On disabled list from August 12 to September 13 and September 21 to October 1, 2013.

REDDICK, WILLIAM JOSHUA (JOSH)

Born, Savannah, Georgia, February 19, 1987.
Bats Left. Throws Right. Height, 6 feet, 2 inches. Weight, 180 pounds.

Year	Club	Lea	Pos	G	AB	R	H	2B	3B	HR	RBI	SB	Avg
2007	Greenville	So.Atl.	OF	94	369	60	113	17	6	18	72	8	.306
2007	Portland	Eastern	PH	1	1	0	0	0	0	0	0	0	.000
2008	Greenville	So.Atl.	OF	14	53	7	18	4	2	0	9	2	.340
2008	Lancaster	Calif.	OF	76	312	60	107	11	8	17	57	9	.343

Year	Club	Lea	Pos	G	AB	R	H	2B	3B	HR	RBI	SB	Avg
2008	Portland	Eastern	OF	34	117	22	25	4	2	6	25	3	.214
2009	Portland	Eastern	OF	63	256	47	71	17	3	13	29	5	.277
2009	Pawtucket	Int.	OF	18	71	1	9	0	2	0	6	0	.127
2009	Boston	A.L.	OF	27	59	5	10	4	0	2	4	0	.169
2010	Pawtucket	Int.	OF	114	451	59	120	28	4	18	65	4	.266
2010	Boston	A.L.	OF	29	62	5	12	3	1	1	5	1	.194
2011	Pawtucket	Int.	OF	52	191	37	44	9	1	14	36	4	.230
2011	Boston a	A.L.	OF	87	254	41	71	18	3	7	28	1	.280
2012	Oakland	A.L.	OF	156	611	85	148	29	5	32	85	11	.242
2013	Stockton	Calif.	OF	1	3	0	1	0	0	0	0	0	.333
2013	Sacramento	P.C.	OF	3	11	5	2	0	0	0	0	2	.182
2013	Oakland b	A.L.	OF	114	385	54	87	19	2	12	56	9	.226
Major League Totals			5 Yrs.	413	1371	190	328	73	11	54	178	22	.239
	Division Series												
2012	Oakland	A.L.	OF	5	17	2	2	0	0	1	1	0	.118
2013	Oakland	A.L.	OF	5	17	1	4	1	0	1	1	0	.235
Division Series Totals				10	34	3	6	1	0	2	2	0	.176

a Traded to Oakland Athletics with infielder Miles Head and pitcher Raul Alcantara for pitcher Andrew Bailey and outfielder Ryan Sweeney, December 28, 2011.

b On disabled list from May 7 to May 31 and August 26 to September 10, 2013.

REIMOLD, NOLAN GALLAGHER

Born, Greenville, Pennsylvania, October 12, 1983.

Bats Right. Throws Right. Height, 6 feet, 4 inches. Weight, 215 pounds.

Year	Club	Lea	Pos	G	AB	R	H	2B	3B	HR	RBI	SB	Avg
2005	Aberdeen	N.Y.-Penn.	OF-1B	50	180	33	53	15	2	9	30	2	.294
2005	Frederick	Carolina	OF	23	83	17	22	6	0	6	11	3	.265
2006	Frederick	Carolina	OF	119	415	73	106	26	0	19	75	14	.255
2007	Orioles	Gulf Coast	OF	9	30	4	7	4	1	0	8	0	.233
2007	Bowie	Eastern	OF	50	186	30	57	15	0	11	34	2	.306
2008	Bowie	Eastern	OF	139	507	87	144	29	3	25	84	7	.284
2009	Norfolk	Int.	OF	31	109	21	43	11	0	9	27	6	.394
2009	Baltimore a	A.L.	OF	104	358	49	100	18	2	15	45	8	.279
2010	Norfolk	Int.	OF-1B	94	337	52	84	12	0	10	37	9	.249
2010	Baltimore	A.L.	OF	39	116	9	24	5	0	3	14	0	.207
2011	Norfolk	Int.	OF	39	139	16	33	6	0	6	22	2	.237
2011	Baltimore	A.L.	OF	87	267	40	66	10	3	13	45	7	.247
2012	Baltimore b	A.L.	OF	16	67	10	21	6	0	5	10	1	.313
2013	Bowie	Eastern	OF	12	46	3	9	0	1	1	5	0	.196
2013	Baltimore c	A.L.	DH-OF	40	128	17	25	3	0	5	12	0	.195
Major League Totals			5 Yrs.	286	936	125	236	42	5	41	126	16	.252

a On disabled list from September 18 to October 13, 2009.

b On disabled list from May 1 to November 2, 2012.

c On disabled list from May 12 to July 2 and July 14 to November 1, 2013.

RENDON, ANTHONY MICHAEL

Born, Richmond, Texas, June 6, 1990.

Bats Right. Throws Right. Height, 6 feet. Weight, 195 pounds.

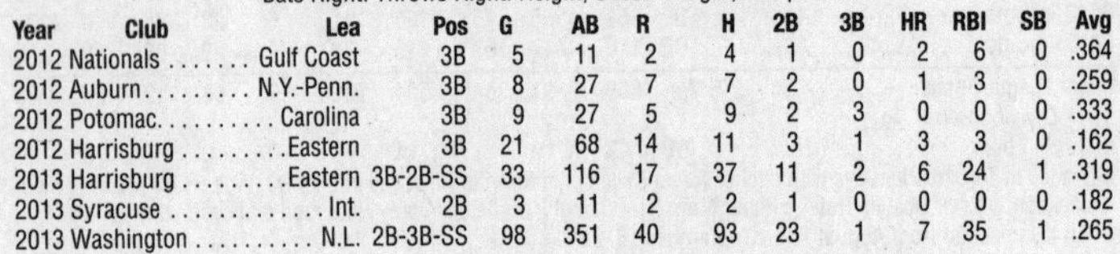

Year	Club	Lea	Pos	G	AB	R	H	2B	3B	HR	RBI	SB	Avg
2012	Nationals	Gulf Coast	3B	5	11	2	4	1	0	2	6	0	.364
2012	Auburn	N.Y.-Penn.	3B	8	27	7	7	2	0	1	3	0	.259
2012	Potomac	Carolina	3B	9	27	5	9	2	3	0	0	0	.333
2012	Harrisburg	Eastern	3B	21	68	14	11	3	1	3	3	0	.162
2013	Harrisburg	Eastern	3B-2B-SS	33	116	17	37	11	2	6	24	1	.319
2013	Syracuse	Int.	2B	3	11	2	2	1	0	0	0	0	.182
2013	Washington	N.L.	2B-3B-SS	98	351	40	93	23	1	7	35	1	.265

REVERE, BEN DANIEL

Born, Atlanta, Georgia, May 3, 1988.

Bats Left. Throws Right. Height, 5 feet, 9 inches. Weight, 170 pounds.

Year	Club	Lea	Pos	G	AB	R	H	2B	3B	HR	RBI	SB	Avg
2007	Twins	Gulf Coast	OF	50	191	46	62	6	10	0	29	21	.325
2008	Beloit	Midwest	OF	83	340	51	129	17	10	1	43	44	.379
2009	Fort Myers	Fla.St.	OF	121	466	75	145	13	4	2	48	45	.311
2010	New Britain	Eastern	OF	94	361	44	110	10	4	1	23	36	.305
2010	Minnesota	A.L.	OF	13	28	1	5	0	0	0	2	0	.179

Year	Club	Lea	Pos	G	AB	R	H	2B	3B	HR	RBI	SB	Avg
2011	Rochester	Int.	OF	32	132	15	40	3	1	1	9	8	.303
2011	Minnesota	A.L.	OF	117	450	56	120	9	5	0	30	34	.267
2012	Rochester	Int.	OF	23	94	9	31	1	0	0	6	6	.330
2012	Minnesota a	A.L.	OF	124	511	70	150	13	6	0	32	40	.294
2013	Philadelphia b	N.L.	OF	88	315	37	96	9	3	0	17	22	.305
Major League Totals			4 Yrs.	342	1304	164	371	31	14	0	81	96	.285

a Traded to Philadelphia Phillies for pitcher Trevor May and pitcher Vance Worley, December 6, 2012.
b On disabled list from July 14 to September 30, 2013.

REYES, JOSE BERNABE

Born, Villa Gonzalez, Dominican Republic, June 11, 1983.
Bats Both. Throws Right. Height, 6 feet. Weight, 200 pounds.

Year	Club	Lea	Pos	G	AB	R	H	2B	3B	HR	RBI	SB	Avg
2000	Kingsport	Appal.	SS-3B-2B-OF	49	132	22	33	3	3	0	8	10	.250
2001	Columbia	So.Atl.	SS	108	407	71	125	22	15	5	48	30	.307
2002	Binghamton	Eastern	SS	65	275	46	79	16	8	2	24	27	.287
2002	St. Lucie	Fla.St.	SS	69	288	58	83	10	11	6	38	31	.288
2003	Norfolk	Int.	SS	42	160	28	43	6	4	0	13	26	.269
2003	New York a	N.L.	SS	69	274	47	84	12	4	5	32	13	.307
2004	St. Lucie	Fla.St.	2B	6	23	3	6	2	0	0	1	2	.261
2004	Binghamton	Eastern	2B	4	18	2	2	0	0	0	3	3	.111
2004	New York b	N.L.	2B-SS	53	220	33	56	16	2	2	14	19	.255
2005	New York	N.L.	SS	161	*696	99	190	24	*17	7	58	*60	.273
2006	New York	N.L.	SS	153	647	*122	194	30	17	19	81	*64	.300
2007	New York	N.L.	SS	160	681	119	191	36	12	12	57	*78	.280
2008	New York	N.L.	SS	159	*688	113	*204	37	*19	16	68	56	.297
2009	New York c	N.L.	SS	36	147	18	41	7	2	2	15	11	.279
2010	St. Lucie	Fla.St.	SS	1	4	0	0	0	0	0	1	0	.000
2010	New York d	N.L.	SS	133	563	83	159	29	10	11	54	30	.282
2011	Brooklyn	N.Y.-Penn.	SS	1	3	1	1	1	0	0	0	0	.333
2011	Binghamton	Eastern	SS	3	9	3	3	0	0	1	1	0	.333
2011	New York e-f	N.L.	SS	126	537	101	181	31	*16	7	44	39	*.337
2012	Miami g	N.L.	SS	160	642	86	184	37	12	11	57	40	.287
2013	Dunedin	Fla.St.	SS	3	12	3	5	0	0	0	1	1	.417
2013	Buffalo	Int.	SS	4	17	3	7	1	0	0	1	1	.412
2013	Toronto h	A.L.	SS	93	382	58	113	20	0	10	37	15	.296
Major League Totals			11 Yrs.	1303	5477	879	1597	279	111	102	517	425	.292
	Division Series												
2006	New York	N.L.	SS	3	12	2	2	0	0	0	3	1	.167
	Championship Series												
2006	New York	N.L.	SS	7	32	5	9	1	1	1	2	2	.281

a On disabled list from September 1 to November 6, 2003.
b On disabled list from March 26 to June 19 and August 12 to September 24, 2004.
c On disabled list from May 21 to October 14, 2009.
d On disabled list from March 26 to April 8, 2010.
e On disabled list from July 3 to July 19 and August 8 to August 29, 2011.
f Filed for free agency, October 30, 2011. Signed with Florida Marlins, December 7, 2011.
g Traded to Toronto Blue Jays with outfielder Emilio Bonifacio, catcher John Buck, pitcher Mark Buehrle and pitcher Josh Johnson for pitcher Henderson Alvarez, infielder Yunel Escobar, infielder Adeiny Hechavarria, catcher Jeff Mathis, pitcher Anthony De Sclafani, outfielder Jake Marisnick and pitcher Justin Nicolino, November 19, 2012.
h On disabled list from April 13 to June 26, 2013.

REYNOLDS, MARK ANDREW

Born, Pikeville, Kentucky, August 3, 1983.
Bats Right. Throws Right. Height, 6 feet, 1 inch. Weight, 220 pounds.

Year	Club	Lea	Pos	G	AB	R	H	2B	3B	HR	RBI	SB	Avg
2004	Lancaster	Calif.	3B-SS	4	12	1	1	0	0	0	1	0	.083
2004	South Bend	Midwest	3B	4	15	0	1	1	0	0	0	0	.067
2004	Yakima	Northwest	SS-3B-2B	64	234	58	64	19	1	12	41	5	.274
2005	South Bend	Midwest	SS-3B	118	434	65	110	26	2	19	76	4	.253
2006	Lancaster	Calif.	SS-3B-2B-1B	76	273	64	92	18	2	23	77	1	.337
2006	Tennessee	Southern	OF-3B-2B	30	114	23	31	7	0	8	21	0	.272
2007	Mobile	Southern	3B-2B	37	134	28	41	9	2	6	22	2	.306
2007	Arizona	N.L.	3B-2B-OF	111	366	62	102	20	4	17	62	0	.279
2008	Arizona	N.L.	3B-1B	152	539	87	129	28	3	28	97	11	.239
2009	Arizona	N.L.	3B-1B	155	578	98	150	30	1	44	102	24	.260
2010	Arizona a	N.L.	3B-1B	145	499	79	99	17	2	32	85	7	.198
2011	Baltimore	A.L.	3B-1B	155	534	84	118	27	1	37	86	6	.221

Year	Club	Lea	Pos	G	AB	R	H	2B	3B	HR	RBI	SB	Avg
2012	Bowie	Eastern	3B	2	7	0	1	0	0	0	0	0	.143
2012	Baltimore b-c	A.L.	1B-3B	135	457	65	101	26	0	23	69	1	.221
2013	Cleveland-NY d-e	A.L.	1B-3B-2B	135	445	55	98	14	0	21	67	3	.220
Major League Totals			7 Yrs.	988	3418	530	797	162	11	202	568	52	.233
	Wild Card Playoff												
2012	Baltimore	A.L.	1B	1	3	0	0	0	0	0	0	1	.000
	Division Series												
2007	Arizona	N.L.	3B	3	10	2	2	0	0	1	1	0	.200
2012	Baltimore	A.L.	1B	5	19	0	3	0	0	0	1	0	.158
Division Series Totals				8	29	2	5	0	0	1	2	0	.172
	Championship Series												
2007	Arizona	N.L.	3B	4	16	1	2	0	0	1	1	0	.125

a Traded to Baltimore Orioles with player to be named later for pitcher Kam Mickolio and pitcher David Hernandez, December 6, 2010. Baltimore Orioles received catcher John Hester to complete trade, April 30, 2011.
b On disabled list from May 12 to May 28, 2012.
c Not offered contract, November 30, 2012. Signed with Cleveland Indians, December 18 , 2012.
d Released by Cleveland Indians, August 12, 2013. Signed with New York Yankees, August 16, 2013.
e Filed for free agency, October 31, 2013. Signed with Milwaukee Brewers organization, January 16, 2014.

RIOS, ALEXIS ISRAEL

Born, Coffee County, Alabama, February 18, 1981.
Bats Right. Throws Right. Height, 6 feet, 5 inches. Weight, 195 pounds.

Year	Club	Lea	Pos	G	AB	R	H	2B	3B	HR	RBI	SB	Avg
1999	Medicine Hat	Pioneer	OF	67	234	35	63	7	3	0	13	8	.269
2000	Hagerstown	So.Atl.	DH	22	74	5	17	3	1	0	5	2	.230
2000	Queens	N.Y.-Penn.	OF	50	206	22	55	9	2	1	25	5	.267
2001	Charleston-WV	So.Atl.	OF	130	480	40	126	20	9	2	58	22	.262
2002	Dunedin	Fla.St.	OF	111	456	60	139	22	8	3	61	14	.305
2003	New Haven	Eastern	OF	127	514	86	181	32	11	11	82	11	.352
2004	Syracuse	Int.	OF	46	185	14	48	10	1	3	23	2	.259
2004	Toronto	A.L.	OF	111	426	55	122	24	7	1	28	15	.286
2005	Toronto	A.L.	OF	146	481	71	126	23	6	10	59	14	.262
2006	Syracuse	Int.	OF	3	10	0	3	1	0	0	1	0	.300
2006	Toronto a	A.L.	OF	128	450	68	136	33	6	17	82	15	.302
2007	Toronto	A.L.	OF	161	643	114	191	43	7	24	85	17	.297
2008	Toronto	A.L.	OF	155	635	91	185	47	8	15	79	32	.291
2009	Toronto-Chicago b	A.L.	OF	149	582	63	144	31	2	17	71	24	.247
2010	Chicago	A.L.	OF	147	567	89	161	29	3	21	88	34	.284
2011	Chicago	A.L.	OF	145	537	64	122	22	2	13	44	11	.227
2012	Chicago	A.L.	OF	157	605	93	184	37	8	25	91	23	.304
2013	Chicago-Texas c	A.L.	OF	156	616	83	171	33	4	18	81	42	.278
Major League Totals			10 Yrs.	1455	5542	791	1542	322	53	161	708	227	.278

a On disabled list from June 28 to July 28, 2006.
b Claimed on waivers by Chicago White Sox, August 10, 2009.
c Traded to Texas Rangers with cash for player to be named later, August 9, 2013. Chicago White Sox received infielder Leury Garcia to complete trade, August 11, 2013.

RIVERA, RENE

Born, Bayamon, Puerto Rico, July 31, 1983.
Bats Right. Throws Right. Height, 5 feet, 10 inches. Weight, 230 pounds.

Year	Club	Lea	Pos	G	AB	R	H	2B	3B	HR	RBI	SB	Avg
2001	Mariners	Arizona	C	21	71	13	24	4	0	2	12	0	.338
2001	Everett	Northwest	C	15	45	3	4	1	0	2	3	0	.089
2002	Everett	Northwest	C	62	227	29	55	18	1	1	26	5	.242
2003	Wisconsin	Midwest	C	116	407	39	112	19	0	9	54	2	.275
2004	Inland Empire	Calif.	C	107	379	41	89	22	1	6	53	0	.235
2004	Tacoma	P.C.	C	4	15	3	6	1	0	1	1	0	.400
2004	Seattle	A.L.	C	2	3	0	0	0	0	0	0	0	.000
2005	San Antonio	Texas	C	57	212	20	59	14	1	2	21	1	.278
2005	Tacoma	P.C.	C	14	49	3	10	3	0	1	6	0	.204
2005	Seattle	A.L.	C	16	48	3	19	3	0	1	6	0	.396
2006	Tacoma	P.C.	C	1	3	1	2	1	0	0	0	0	.667
2006	Seattle	A.L.	C	35	99	8	15	4	0	2	4	1	.152
2007	West Tenn a	Southern	C	91	323	29	69	16	0	5	40	1	.214
2008	Jacksonville	Southern	1B-C	38	134	13	31	5	0	5	18	0	.231
2008	Las Vegas b	P.C.	C-1B	37	118	12	32	7	0	4	12	0	.271
2009	Buffalo	Int.	C-3B	68	240	22	56	14	0	9	30	0	.233

Year Club	Lea	Pos	G	AB	R	H	2B	3B	HR	RBI	SB	Avg
2010 Camden	Atlantic	C	22	82	10	23	6	0	7	19	0	.280
2010 Trenton	Eastern	C	25	94	13	30	10	0	5	17	0	.319
2010 Scranton/WB c-d-e	Int.	C	19	68	3	17	3	0	2	11	0	.250
2011 Rochester	Int.	C	43	149	15	40	12	0	5	24	0	.268
2011 Minnesota f	A.L.	C	45	104	9	15	3	0	1	5	0	.144
2012 Rochester g	Int.	C-1B	95	288	31	65	14	1	10	34	0	.226
2013 Tucson	P.C.	C-1B	74	251	36	86	18	0	5	38	0	.343
2013 San Diego	N.L.	C	23	67	4	17	3	1	0	7	0	.254
Major League Totals		5 Yrs.	121	321	24	66	13	1	4	22	1	.206

a Filed for free agency, October 29, 2007. Signed with Los Angeles Dodgers organization, November 29, 2007.
b Filed for free agency, November 3, 2008. Signed with New York Mets organization, November 20, 2008.
c Filed for free agency, November 9, 2009. Signed with Camden (Atlantic) April 2010.
d Signed with New York Yankees organization, May 21, 2010.
e Filed for free agency, November 6, 2010. Signed with Minnesota Twins organization, December 14, 2010.
f Filed for free agency, November 2, 2011, re-signed with Minnesota Twins organization, December 14, 2011.
g Filed for free agency, November 3, 2012. Signed with San Diego Padres organization, December 12, 2012.

RIZZO, ANTHONY VINCENT

Born, Ft. Lauderdale, Florida, August 8, 1989.
Bats Left. Throws Left. Height, 6 feet, 3 inches. Weight, 220 pounds.

Year Club	Lea	Pos	G	AB	R	H	2B	3B	HR	RBI	SB	Avg
2007 Red Sox	Gulf Coast	1B	6	21	6	6	0	0	1	3	0	.286
2008 Greenville	So.Atl.	1B	21	83	9	31	6	0	0	11	0	.373
2009 Salem	Carolina	1B	55	200	23	59	16	0	3	24	2	.295
2009 Greenville	So.Atl.	1B	64	245	40	73	21	0	9	42	2	.298
2010 Salem	Carolina	1B	29	117	26	29	12	0	5	20	3	.248
2010 Portland a	Eastern	1B	107	414	66	109	30	0	20	80	7	.263
2011 Tucson	P.C.	1B	93	356	64	118	34	1	26	101	7	.331
2011 San Diego	N.L.	1B	49	128	9	18	8	1	1	9	2	.141
2012 Iowa	P.C.	1B	70	257	48	88	18	2	23	62	2	.342
2012 Chicago b	N.L.	1B	87	337	44	96	15	0	15	48	3	.285
2013 Chicago	N.L.	1B	160	606	71	141	40	2	23	80	6	.233
Major League Totals		3 Yrs.	.296	1071	124	255	63	3	39	137	11	.238

a Traded by Boston Red Sox to San Diego Padres with pitcher Casey Kelly, outfielder Reymond Fuentes and player to be named later for infielder Adrian Gonzalez, December 5, 2010.
b Traded to Chicago Cubs with pitcher Zach Cates for pitcher Andrew Cashner and outfielder Kyung-Min Na, January 6, 2012. San Diego Padres received outfielder Eric Patterson to complete trade, December 16, 2012.

ROBERTS, BRIAN MICHAEL

Born, Durham, North Carolina, October 9, 1977.
Bats Both. Throws Right. Height, 5 feet, 9 inches. Weight, 175 pounds.

Year Club	Lea	Pos	G	AB	R	H	2B	3B	HR	RBI	SB	Avg
1999 Delmarva a	So.Atl.	SS	47	167	22	40	12	1	0	21	17	.240
2000 Frederick	Carolina	SS	48	163	27	49	6	3	0	16	13	.301
2000 Orioles b	Gulf Coast	SS	9	29	8	9	1	2	1	3	7	.310
2001 Bowie	Eastern	2B-SS	22	81	12	24	7	0	1	7	10	.296
2001 Rochester	Int.	SS	44	161	16	43	4	1	1	12	23	.267
2001 Baltimore	A.L.	SS-2B	75	273	42	69	12	3	2	17	12	.253
2002 Rochester	Int.	2B	78	313	49	86	9	7	3	30	22	.275
2002 Baltimore	A.L.	2B	38	128	18	29	6	0	1	11	9	.227
2003 Ottawa	Int.	2B-SS	44	178	36	56	13	1	0	15	19	.315
2003 Baltimore	A.L.	2B-SS	112	460	65	124	22	4	5	41	23	.270
2004 Baltimore	A.L.	2B	159	641	107	175	*50	2	4	53	29	.273
2005 Baltimore	A.L.	2B	143	561	92	176	45	7	18	73	27	.314
2006 Bowie	Eastern	2B	2	5	0	1	0	0	0	0	0	.200
2006 Baltimore c	A.L.	2B	138	563	85	161	34	3	10	55	36	.286
2007 Baltimore	A.L.	2B	156	621	103	180	42	5	12	57	*50	.290
2008 Baltimore	A.L.	2B	155	611	107	181	51	8	9	57	40	.296
2009 Baltimore	A.L.	2B	159	632	110	179	*56	1	16	79	30	.283
2010 Orioles	Gulf Coast	2B	5	15	1	8	1	0	0	0	0	.533
2010 Bowie	Eastern	2B	3	14	3	6	2	0	0	3	0	.429
2010 Baltimore d	A.L.	2B	59	230	28	64	14	0	4	15	12	.278
2011 Baltimore e	A.L.	2B	39	163	18	36	7	1	3	19	6	.221
2012 Aberdeen	N.Y.-Penn.	2B	1	4	1	0	0	0	0	0	0	.000
2012 Delmarva	So.Atl.	2B	2	5	0	1	0	0	0	0	0	.200
2012 Bowie	Eastern	2B	7	16	4	4	3	0	1	3	0	.250
2012 Norfolk	Int.	2B	5	21	2	5	2	0	0	1	0	.238
2012 Baltimore f	A.L.	2B	17	66	2	12	0	0	0	5	1	.182

Year	Club	Lea	Pos	G	AB	R	H	2B	3B	HR	RBI	SB	Avg
2013	Norfolk	Int.	2B	4	13	2	3	1	0	0	1	0	.231
2013	Baltimore g-h	A.L.	2B	77	265	33	66	12	1	8	39	3	.249
Major League Totals			13 Yrs.	1327	5214	810	1452	351	35	92	521	278	.278

a Drafted by Baltimore Orioles with choice received for Texas Rangers signing infielder Rafael Palmeiro, June 2, 1999.
b On disabled list from April 19 to July 13, 2000.
c On disabled list from April 30 to May 24, 2006.
d On disabled list from April 10 to July 23, 2010.
e On disabled list from May 17 to May 31 and May 31 to November 2, 2011.
f On disabled list from March 26 to June 12 and July 3 to November 2, 2012.
g On disabled list from April 5 to June 30, 2013.
h Filed for free agency, October 31, 2013. Signed with New York Yankees, January 13, 2014.

ROBINSON, DERRICK LAMAR

Born, Gainesville, Florida, September 28, 1987.
Bats Both. Throws Left. Height, 5 feet, 11 inches. Weight, 190 pounds.

Year	Club	Lea	Pos	G	AB	R	H	2B	3B	HR	RBI	SB	Avg
2006	Royals	Arizona	OF	54	176	25	41	6	3	1	24	20	.233
2007	Burlington	Midwest	OF	102	407	42	99	11	3	2	26	34	.243
2007	Wilmington	Carolina	OF	3	13	1	5	1	0	0	0	1	.385
2008	Wilmington	Carolina	OF	124	497	69	122	22	8	0	34	62	.245
2009	Wilmington	Carolina	OF	128	522	72	125	19	5	5	47	69	.239
2010	NW Arkansas	Texas	OF	127	511	74	146	26	8	2	48	50	.286
2011	NW Arkansas	Texas	OF	107	419	56	105	6	2	1	25	55	.251
2012	Omaha a	P.C.	OF	116	422	73	113	12	3	2	28	23	.268
2013	Louisville	Int.	OF	15	59	5	13	3	0	0	3	3	.220
2013	Cincinnati b	N.L.	OF	102	192	21	49	7	3	0	8	4	.255

a Not offered contract by Kansas City Royals, November 30, 2012. Signed with Cincinnati Reds organization, December 20, 2012.
b Not offered contract, December 2, 2013.

ROBINSON, SHANE M.

Born, Tampa, Florida, October 30, 1984.
Bats Right. Throws Right. Height, 5 feet, 9 inches. Weight, 160 pounds.

Year	Club	Lea	Pos	G	AB	R	H	2B	3B	HR	RBI	SB	Avg
2006	Quad Cities	Midwest	OF	63	252	41	71	9	2	0	21	13	.282
2007	Palm Beach	Fla.St.	OF	43	166	22	42	6	1	3	13	14	.253
2007	Cardinals	Gulf Coast	OF	4	11	1	2	0	0	0	1	0	.182
2008	Memphis	P.C.	OF	42	141	10	31	4	1	1	10	2	.220
2008	Springfield	Texas	OF	63	244	46	86	17	3	4	32	13	.352
2009	St. Louis	N.L.	OF	11	25	1	6	1	0	0	1	1	.240
2009	Memphis	P.C.	OF	100	345	46	82	18	3	5	40	16	.238
2010	Memphis	P.C.	OF	26	86	9	24	5	0	2	13	3	.279
2011	Cardinals	Gulf Coast	OF	6	22	4	3	2	1	0	0	0	.136
2011	Springfield	Texas	OF	7	31	8	15	2	0	3	8	0	.484
2011	Memphis	P.C.	OF	43	167	35	50	8	3	4	23	9	.299
2011	St. Louis	N.L.	OF	9	7	0	0	0	0	0	0	0	.000
2012	Memphis	P.C.	OF	18	70	15	21	4	2	0	3	5	.300
2012	St. Louis	N.L.	OF	102	166	20	42	8	0	3	16	1	.253
2013	Springfield	Texas	OF	3	10	0	2	0	0	0	0	0	.200
2013	St. Louis a	N.L.	OF	99	144	22	36	2	1	2	16	5	.250
Major League Totals			4 Yrs.	221	342	43	84	11	1	5	33	7	.246
	Wild Card Playoff												
2012	St. Louis	N.L.	OF	1	1	0	0	0	0	0	0	0	.000
	Division Series												
2012	St. Louis	N.L.	OF	3	1	1	0	0	0	0	0	0	.000
2013	St. Louis	N.L.	PH	1	1	0	0	0	0	0	0	0	.000
Division Series Totals				4	2	1	0	0	0	0	0	0	.000
	Championship Series												
2012	St. Louis	N.L.	OF	6	6	0	0	0	0	0	1	0	.000
2013	St. Louis	N.L.	OF	3	7	2	3	0	0	1	3	0	.429
Championship Series Totals				9	13	2	3	0	0	1	4	0	.231
	World Series Record												
2013	St. Louis	N.L.	OF	4	8	1	2	1	0	0	0	0	.250

a On disabled list from July 31 to August 15, 2013.

RODRIGUEZ, ALEXANDER EMMANUEL (ALEX)

Born, New York, New York, July 27, 1975.
Bats Right. Throws Right. Height, 6 feet, 3 inches. Weight, 225 pounds.

Year	Club	Lea	Pos	G	AB	R	H	2B	3B	HR	RBI	SB	Avg
1994	Appleton	Midwest	SS	65	248	49	79	17	6	14	55	16	.319
1994	Jacksonville	Southern	SS	17	59	7	17	4	1	1	8	2	.288
1994	Seattle	A.L.	SS	17	54	4	11	0	0	0	2	3	.204
1994	Calgary	P.C.	SS	32	119	22	37	7	4	6	21	2	.311
1995	Tacoma	P.C.	SS	54	214	37	77	12	3	15	45	2	.360
1995	Seattle	A.L.	SS	48	142	15	33	6	2	5	19	4	.232
1996	Tacoma a	P.C.	SS	2	5	0	1	0	0	0	0	0	.200
1996	Seattle	A.L.	SS	146	601	*141	215	*54	1	36	123	15	*.358
1997	Seattle b	A.L.	SS	141	587	100	176	40	3	23	84	29	.300
1998	Seattle	A.L.	SS	161	*686	123	*213	35	5	42	124	46	.310
1999	Seattle c	A.L.	SS	129	502	110	143	25	0	42	111	21	.285
2000	Seattle d-e	A.L.	SS	148	554	134	175	34	2	41	132	15	.316
2001	Texas	A.L.	SS	*162	632	*133	201	34	1	*52	135	18	.318
2002	Texas	A.L.	SS	*162	624	125	187	27	2	*57	*142	9	.300
2003	Texas	A.L.	SS	161	607	*124	181	30	6	*47	118	17	.298
2004	New York f-g	A.L.	3B-SS	155	601	112	172	24	2	36	106	28	.286
2005	New York h	A.L.	3B-SS	*162	605	*124	194	29	1	*48	130	21	.321
2006	New York	A.L.	3B	154	572	113	166	26	1	35	121	15	.290
2007	New York i-j	A.L.	3B	158	583	*143	183	31	0	*54	*156	24	.314
2008	New York k	A.L.	3B	138	510	104	154	33	0	35	103	18	.302
2009	New York l	A.L.	3B	124	444	78	127	17	1	30	100	14	.286
2010	New York m	A.L.	3B	137	522	74	141	29	2	30	125	4	.270
2011	Tampa	Fla.St.	DH	2	6	2	2	1	0	1	2	0	.333
2011	Scranton-WB	Int.	3B	2	5	0	2	0	0	0	1	0	.400
2011	New York n	A.L.	3B	99	373	67	103	21	0	16	62	4	.276
2012	Tampa	Fla.St.	3B	2	7	1	0	0	0	0	0	0	.000
2012	New York o	A.L.	3B	122	463	74	126	17	1	18	57	13	.272
2013	Charleston	So.Atl.	3B	2	4	0	0	0	0	0	0	0	.000
2013	Tampa	Fla.St.	3B	6	17	2	3	1	0	0	3	0	.176
2013	Trenton	Eastern	3B	4	9	3	3	0	0	2	5	0	.333
2013	Scranton/WB	Int.	3B	3	12	1	3	0	0	1	2	0	.250
2013	New York p-q	A.L.	3B	44	156	21	38	7	0	7	19	4	.244
Major League Totals			20 Yrs.	2568	9818	1919	2939	519	30	654	1969	322	.299
	Division Series												
1995	Seattle	A.L.	SS	1	1	1	0	0	0	0	0	0	.000
1997	Seattle	A.L.	SS	4	16	1	5	1	0	1	1	0	.313
2000	Seattle	A.L.	SS	3	13	0	4	0	0	0	2	0	.308
2004	New York	A.L.	3B	4	19	3	8	3	0	1	3	2	.421
2005	New York	A.L.	3B	5	15	2	2	1	0	0	0	1	.133
2006	New York	A.L.	3B	4	14	0	1	0	0	0	0	0	.071
2007	New York	A.L.	3B	4	15	2	4	0	0	1	1	0	.267
2009	New York	A.L.	3B	3	11	4	5	0	0	2	6	0	.455
2010	New York	A.L.	3B	3	11	1	3	0	0	0	1	1	.273
2011	New York	A.L.	3B	5	18	1	2	0	0	0	3	0	.111
2012	New York	A.L.	3B-DH	4	16	1	2	0	0	0	0	0	.125
Division Series Totals				40	149	16	36	5	0	5	17	4	.242
	Championship Series												
1995	Seattle	A.L.	PH	1	1	0	0	0	0	0	0	0	.000
2000	Seattle	A.L.	SS	6	22	4	9	2	0	2	5	1	.409
2004	New York	A.L.	3B	7	31	8	8	2	0	2	5	0	.258
2009	New York	A.L.	3B	6	21	6	9	2	0	3	6	1	.429
2010	New York	A.L.	3B	6	21	4	4	2	0	0	2	1	.190
2012	New York	A.L.	3B	3	9	0	1	0	0	0	0	0	.111

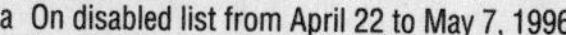

Year	Club	Lea	Pos	G	AB	R	H	2B	3B	HR	RBI	SB	Avg
Championship Series Totals				29	105	22	31	8	0	7	18	3	.295
	World Series Record												
2009	New York	A.L.	3B	6	20	5	5	3	0	1	6	1	.250

a On disabled list from April 22 to May 7, 1996.
b On disabled list from June 12 to June 27, 1997.
c On disabled list from April 7 to May 14, 1999.
d On disabled list from July 8 to July 23, 2000.
e Filed for free agency, October 30, 2000. Signed with Texas Rangers, December 11, 2000.
f Traded to New York Yankees for infielder Alfonso Soriano and player to be named later, February 16, 2004.
g Texas Rangers received infielder Joaquin Arias to complete trade, March 23, 2004.
h Selected Most Valuable Player in American League for 2005.
i Filed for free agency, October 29, 2007, re-signed with New York Yankees, December 13, 2007.
j Selected Most Valuable Player in American League for 2007.
k On disabled list from April 30 to May 20, 2008.

l On disabled list from March 27 to May 8, 2009.
m On disabled list from August 21 to September 5, 2010.
n On disabled list from July 14 to August 21, 2011.
o On disabled list from July 25 to September 3, 2012.
p On disabled list from February 13 to August 5, 2013.
q Suspended for 211 games for performance-enhancing drug use, August 5, 2013. After appeal, suspension changed to 162 games plus playoffs on January 11, 2014.

RODRIGUEZ, SEAN JOHN

Born, Miami, Florida, April 26, 1985.
Bats Right. Throws Right. Height, 6 feet, 1 inch. Weight, 215 pounds.

Year	Club	Lea	Pos	G	AB	R	H	2B	3B	HR	RBI	SB	Avg
2003	Angels	Arizona	SS-3B-2B-OF	54	216	30	58	8	5	2	25	11	.269
2004	Cedar Rapids	Midwest	2B-OF-3B-SS	57	196	35	49	8	4	4	17	14	.250
2004	Provo	Pioneer	SS-OF	64	225	64	76	14	4	10	55	9	.338
2005	Cedar Rapids	Midwest	SS-3B-OF-2B	124	448	86	112	29	3	14	45	27	.250
2006	Rancho Cucamonga	Calif.	SS-OF	116	455	78	137	29	5	24	77	15	.301
2006	Salt Lake	P.C.	SS	1	2	0	0	0	0	0	0	0	.000
2006	Arkansas	Texas	SS	18	65	16	23	5	0	5	9	0	.354
2007	Arkansas	Texas	SS-OF	136	508	84	129	31	2	17	73	15	.254
2008	Salt Lake	P.C.	2B-SS-OF	66	248	68	76	19	1	21	52	4	.306
2008	Los Angeles	A.L.	2B-SS-3B	59	167	18	34	8	1	3	10	3	.204
2009	Los Angeles	A.L.	OF-2B	12	25	4	5	0	0	2	4	0	.200
2009	Salt Lake	P.C.	2B-SS-OF	103	365	81	109	17	6	29	93	9	.299
2009	Durham a	Int.	2B-3B	5	20	6	4	2	0	1	5	0	.200
2010	Tampa Bay	A.L.	2B-OF-3B-SS	118	343	53	86	19	2	9	40	13	.251
2011	Tampa Bay	A.L.	SS-2B-3B-1B	131	373	45	83	20	3	8	36	11	.223
2012	Durham	Int.	2B-SS	2	6	2	3	2	0	1	4	0	.500
2012	Tampa Bay b	A.L.	3B-SS-2B	112	301	36	64	14	1	6	32	5	.213
2013	Tampa Bay	A.L.	OF-1B-SS-2B	96	195	21	48	10	1	5	23	1	.246
Major League Totals			6 Yrs.	528	1404	177	320	71	8	33	145	33	.228
	Division Series												
2010	Tampa Bay	A.L.	2B	4	10	2	2	0	0	0	0	0	.200
2011	Tampa Bay	A.L.	SS-2B	4	12	3	2	1	0	0	1	0	.167
2013	Tampa Bay	A.L.	OF-1B	4	6	1	1	0	0	1	1	0	.167
Division Series Totals				12	28	6	5	1	0	1	2	0	.179

a Sent to Tampa Bay Rays as player to be named later for pitcher Scott Kazmir, September 1, 2009.
b On disabled list from August 31 to September 15, 2012.

ROLLINS, JAMES CALVIN (JIMMY)

Born, Oakland, California, November 27, 1978.
Bats Both. Throws Right. Height, 5 feet, 8 inches. Weight, 170 pounds.

Year	Club	Lea	Pos	G	AB	R	H	2B	3B	HR	RBI	SB	Avg
1996	Martinsvlle	Appal.	SS	49	172	22	41	3	1	1	16	11	.238
1997	Piedmont	So.Atl.	SS	139	560	94	151	22	8	6	59	46	.270
1998	Clearwater	Fla.St.	SS	119	495	72	121	18	9	6	35	23	.244
1999	Reading	Eastern	SS	133	532	81	145	21	8	11	56	24	.273
1999	Scranton-WB	Int.	SS	4	13	0	1	1	0	0	0	1	.077
2000	Scranton-WB	Int.	SS	133	470	67	129	28	11	12	69	24	.274
2000	Philadelphia	N.L.	SS	14	53	5	17	1	1	0	5	3	.321
2001	Philadelphia	N.L.	SS	158	*656	97	180	29	*12	14	54	*46	.274
2002	Philadelphia	N.L.	SS-2B	154	*637	82	156	33	*10	11	60	31	.245
2003	Philadelphia	N.L.	SS	156	628	85	165	42	6	8	62	20	.263
2004	Philadelphia	N.L.	SS	154	657	119	190	43	*12	14	73	30	.289
2005	Philadelphia	N.L.	SS	158	677	115	196	38	11	12	54	41	.290
2006	Philadelphia	N.L.	SS	158	689	127	191	45	9	25	83	36	.277
2007	Philadelphia a	N.L.	SS	*162	*716	*139	212	38	*20	30	94	41	.296
2008	Clearwater	Fla.St.	SS	1	3	2	0	0	0	0	0	0	.000
2008	Philadelphia b	N.L.	SS	137	556	76	154	38	9	11	59	47	.277
2009	Philadelphia	N.L.	SS	155	*672	100	168	43	5	21	77	31	.250
2010	Clearwater	Fla.St.	SS	5	14	2	2	0	0	0	2	0	.143
2010	Philadelphia c	N.L.	SS	88	350	48	85	16	3	8	41	17	.243
2011	Philadelphia d-e	N.L.	SS	142	567	87	152	22	2	16	63	30	.268
2012	Philadelphia	N.L.	SS	156	632	102	158	33	5	23	68	30	.250
2013	Philadelphia	N.L.	SS	160	600	65	151	36	2	6	39	22	.252
Major League Totals			14 Yrs.	1952	8090	1247	2175	457	107	199	832	425	.269
	Division Series												
2007	Philadelphia	N.L.	SS	3	11	1	2	0	1	1	4	1	.182

Year	Club	Lea	Pos	G	AB	R	H	2B	3B	HR	RBI	SB	Avg
2008	Philadelphia	N.L.	SS	4	16	2	6	2	0	1	1	1	.375
2009	Philadelphia	N.L.	SS	4	19	1	5	1	0	0	0	0	.263
2010	Philadelphia	N.L.	SS	3	11	1	1	0	0	0	0	0	.091
2011	Philadelphia	N.L.	SS	5	20	6	9	4	0	0	0	2	.450
Division Series Totals				19	77	11	23	7	1	2	5	4	.299
	Championship Series												
2008	Philadelphia	N.L.	SS	5	21	4	3	0	0	1	1	2	.143
2009	Philadelphia	N.L.	SS	5	22	5	5	2	0	0	3	0	.227
2010	Philadelphia	N.L.	SS	6	23	0	6	1	0	0	4	2	.261
Championship Series Totals				16	66	9	14	3	0	1	8	4	.212
	World Series Record												
2008	Philadelphia	N.L.	SS	5	22	4	5	2	0	0	0	0	.227
2009	Philadelphia	N.L.	SS	6	23	3	5	0	0	0	2	3	.217
World Series Totals				11	45	7	10	2	0	0	2	3	.222

a Selected Most Valuable Player in National League for 2007.
b On disabled list from April 20 to May 9, 2008.
c On disabled list from April 13 to May 17 and May 22 to June 22, 2010.
d On disabled list from August 22 to September 8, 2011.
e Filed for free agency, October 30, 2011, re-signed with Philadelphia Phillies, December 19, 2011.

ROSALES, ADAM MARCOS

Born, Chicago, Illinois, May 20, 1983.
Bats Right. Throws Right. Height, 6 feet, 1 inch. Weight, 195 pounds.

Year	Club	Lea	Pos	G	AB	R	H	2B	3B	HR	RBI	SB	Avg
2005	Dayton	Midwest	SS	32	134	24	44	8	0	9	21	3	.328
2005	Billings	Pioneer	SS	34	140	29	45	14	0	5	25	2	.321
2006	Sarasota	Fla.St.	SS	34	122	15	26	8	2	2	14	3	.213
2006	Dayton	Midwest	SS	55	222	36	60	9	3	6	29	5	.270
2007	Sarasota	Fla.St.	1B-SS	69	248	47	73	23	5	5	48	9	.294
2007	Chattanooga	Southern	1B-3B-SS-OF	67	255	51	71	18	6	13	31	4	.278
2008	Louisville	Int.	3B-SS-1B-2B	117	432	70	124	29	7	11	58	7	.287
2008	Cincinnati	N.L.	3B-2B	18	29	0	6	1	0	0	2	1	.207
2009	Louisville	Int.	3B-SS-2B-1B	30	109	27	38	8	2	5	20	4	.349
2009	Cincinnati	N.L.	3B-1B-SS-2B	87	230	23	49	10	1	4	19	1	.213
2010	Oakland a	A.L.	2B-SS-1B-3B	80	255	31	69	8	2	7	31	2	.271
2011	Sacramento	P.C.	SS-2B-3B	40	147	23	39	5	1	3	22	1	.265
2011	Oakland	A.L.	SS-3B-1B-2B	24	61	5	6	0	0	2	8	0	.098
2012	Sacramento	P.C.	SS-2B-3B-OF	76	275	46	77	21	1	8	47	4	.280
2012	Oakland	A.L.	2B-SS-1B-3B	42	99	12	22	5	0	2	8	0	.222
2013	Stockton	Calif.	2B-SS	3	12	3	6	2	0	1	1	0	.500
2013	Sacramento	P.C.	SS-2B	9	38	4	8	2	0	0	6	1	.211
2013	Oakland-Texas b-c-d-e	A.L.	SS-2B-1B-3B	68	147	15	28	5	0	5	12	0	.190
Major League Totals			6 Yrs.	319	821	86	180	29	3	20	80	4	.219

a Traded to Oakland Athletics with outfielder Willy Taveras for infielder Aaron Miles, February 1, 2010.
b On disabled list from March 26 to April 25, 2013.
c Claimed on waivers by Texas Rangers, August 2, 2013.
d Claimed on waivers by Oakland Athletics, August 8, 2013.
e Claimed on waivers by Texas Rangers, August 12, 2013.

ROSARIO, WILIN ARISMENDY

Born, Bonao, Dominican Republic, February 23, 1989.
Bats Right. Throws Right. Height, 5 feet, 11 inches. Weight, 215 pounds.

Year	Club	Lea	Pos	G	AB	R	H	2B	3B	HR	RBI	SB	Avg
2007	Casper	Pioneer	C	34	115	11	24	4	0	2	9	2	.209
2008	Casper	Pioneer	C	66	263	48	83	15	3	12	49	4	.316
2009	Modesto	Calif.	C	58	203	17	54	12	2	4	33	2	.266
2010	Tulsa	Texas	C	73	270	42	77	13	1	19	52	1	.285
2011	Tulsa	Texas	C-1B	102	405	52	101	15	3	21	48	1	.249
2011	Colorado	N.L.	C	16	54	6	11	3	1	3	8	0	.204
2012	Colorado	N.L.	C-3B-1B	117	396	67	107	19	0	28	71	4	.270
2013	Colorado	N.L.	C-1B	121	449	63	131	22	1	21	79	4	.292
Major League Totals			3 Yrs.	254	899	136	249	44	2	52	158	8	.277

ROSS, CODY JOSEPH

Born, Portales, New Mexico, December 23, 1980.
Bats Right. Throws Left. Height, 5 feet, 9 inches. Weight, 205 pounds.

Year	Club	Lea	Pos	G	AB	R	H	2B	3B	HR	RBI	SB	Avg
1999	Tigers	Gulf Coast	OF	42	142	19	31	8	3	4	18	3	.218
2000	West Michigan	Midwest	OF	122	434	71	116	17	9	7	68	11	.267
2001	Lakeland	Fla.St.	OF	127	482	84	133	34	5	15	80	28	.276
2002	Erie	Eastern	OF	105	400	73	112	28	3	19	72	16	.280
2003	Toledo	Int.	OF	124	470	74	135	35	6	20	61	15	.287
2003	Detroit	A.L.	OF	6	19	1	4	1	0	1	5	0	.211
2004	Las Vegas a	P.C.	OF	60	238	44	65	17	2	14	49	2	.273
2005	Los Angeles	N.L.	OF	14	25	1	4	1	0	0	1	0	.160
2005	Las Vegas	P.C.	OF	115	393	79	105	21	4	22	63	4	.267
2006	L.A.-Cin.-Florida b-c-d-e	N.L.	OF	101	269	34	61	12	2	13	46	1	.227
2007	Jupiter	Fla.St.	OF	7	23	2	6	1	0	2	3	0	.261
2007	Florida f	N.L.	OF	66	173	35	58	19	0	12	39	2	.335
2008	Florida	N.L.	OF	145	461	59	120	29	5	22	73	6	.260
2009	Florida	N.L.	OF-P	151	559	73	151	37	1	24	90	5	.270
2010	Florida-San Francisco g	N.L.	OF	153	525	71	141	28	3	14	65	9	.269
2011	Fresno	P.C.	OF	2	6	1	3	1	0	0	2	0	.500
2011	San Francisco h-i	N.L.	OF	121	405	54	97	25	0	14	52	5	.240
2012	Pawtucket	Int.	OF	2	7	1	1	0	0	0	0	0	.143
2012	Boston j-k	A.L.	OF	130	476	70	127	34	1	22	81	2	.267
2013	Visalia	Calif.	OF	6	16	2	2	0	0	0	2	0	.125
2013	Reno	P.C.	OF	1	3	1	2	1	0	0	2	0	.667
2013	Arizona l	N.L.	OF	94	317	33	88	17	1	8	38	3	.278
Major League Totals			10 Yrs.	981	3229	431	851	203	13	130	490	33	.264
	Division Series												
2010	San Francisco	N.L.	OF	4	14	2	4	1	0	1	3	0	.286
	Championship Series												
2010	San Francisco	N.L.	OF	6	20	4	7	3	0	3	5	0	.350
	World Series Record												
2010	San Francisco	N.L.	OF	5	17	5	4	1	0	1	2	0	.235

a Traded to Los Angeles Dodgers for pitcher Steve Colyer and cash, April 1, 2004.
b Traded to Cincinnati Reds for player to be named later, April 24, 2006.
c Los Angeles Dodgers received pitcher Ben Kozlowski to complete trade, June 1, 2006.
d On disabled list from April 29 to May 23, 2006.
e Sold to Florida Marlins, May 27, 2006.
f On disabled list from May 6 to July 19, 2007.
g Claimed on waivers by San Francisco Giants, August 22, 2010.
h On disabled list from March 22 to April 20, 2011.
i Filed for free agency, October 30, 2011. Signed with Boston Red Sox, January 26, 2012.
j On disabled list from May 19 to June 19, 2012.
k Filed for free agency, November 3, 2012. Signed with Arizona Diamondbacks, December 22, 2012.
l On disabled list from March 22 to April 13 and August 12 to November 1, 2013.

ROSS, DAVID WADE

Born, Bainbridge, Georgia, March 19, 1977.
Bats Right. Throws Right. Height, 6 feet, 2 inches. Weight, 240 pounds.

Year	Club	Lea	Pos	G	AB	R	H	2B	3B	HR	RBI	SB	Avg
1998	Yakima	Northwest	C	59	191	31	59	14	1	6	25	2	.309
1999	Vero Beach	Fla.St.	C-1B-OF	114	375	47	85	19	1	7	39	5	.227
2000	San Bernardino	Calif.	C	51	191	27	49	11	1	7	21	3	.257
2000	San Antonio	Texas	C	24	67	11	14	2	1	3	12	1	.209
2001	Jacksonville	Southern	C	74	246	35	65	13	1	11	45	1	.264
2002	Las Vegas	P.C.	C	92	293	48	87	16	2	15	68	1	.297
2002	Los Angeles	N.L.	C	8	10	2	2	1	0	1	2	0	.200
2003	Las Vegas	P.C.	C	24	86	12	19	4	0	5	16	0	.221
2003	Los Angeles	N.L.	C	40	124	19	32	7	0	10	18	0	.258
2004	Los Angeles	N.L.	C	70	165	13	28	3	1	5	15	0	.170
2005	Indianapolis	Int.	C	6	19	1	4	1	0	0	1	0	.211
2005	Portland	P.C.	C	6	21	3	3	1	0	0	1	0	.143
2005	Pittsburgh-San Diego a-b	N.L.	C	51	125	11	30	8	1	3	15	0	.240
2006	Chattanooga	Southern	C	2	6	0	2	0	0	0	2	0	.333
2006	Cincinnati c-d	N.L.	C	90	247	37	63	15	1	21	52	0	.255
2007	Louisville	Int.	C	3	9	0	2	1	0	0	0	0	.222
2007	Cincinnati e	N.L.	C	112	311	32	63	10	0	17	39	0	.203
2008	Sarasota	Fla.St.	C	4	11	2	2	0	0	0	1	0	.182
2008	Louisville	Int.	C	9	30	4	5	1	1	1	2	0	.167
2008	Cincinnati	N.L.	C	52	134	17	31	9	0	3	13	0	.231

Year	Club	Lea	Pos	G	AB	R	H	2B	3B	HR	RBI	SB	Avg
2008	Pawtucket	Int.	C	6	28	4	7	1	0	1	3	0	.250
2008	Boston f-g-h	A.L.	C	8	8	1	1	0	0	0	0	0	.125
2009	Rome	So.Atl.	C	2	6	1	3	0	0	1	4	0	.500
2009	Atlanta i	N.L.	C	54	128	18	35	9	0	7	20	0	.273
2010	Atlanta	N.L.	C	59	121	15	35	13	2	2	28	0	.289
2011	Atlanta	N.L.	C	52	152	14	40	7	0	6	23	0	.263
2012	Atlanta j	N.L.	C	62	176	18	45	7	0	9	23	1	.256
2013	Portland	Eastern	C	3	6	3	2	2	0	0	2	0	.333
2013	Pawtucket	Int.	C	4	13	0	0	0	0	0	0	0	.000
2013	Boston k	A.L.	C	36	102	11	22	5	0	4	10	1	.216
Major League Totals			12 Yrs.	694	1803	208	427	94	5	88	258	2	.237
	Wild Card Playoff												
2012	Atlanta	N.L.	C	1	4	1	3	0	0	1	2	0	.750
	Division Series												
2004	Los Angeles	N.L.	C	2	3	0	0	0	0	0	0	0	.000
2008	Boston	A.L.	C	1	0	0	0	0	0	0	0	0	.000
2010	Atlanta	N.L.	C	2	0	0	0	0	0	0	0	0	.000
2013	Boston	A.L.	C	2	5	1	1	1	0	0	0	0	.200
Division Series Totals				7	8	1	1	1	0	0	0	0	.125
	Championship Series												
2013	Boston	A.L.	C	2	4	0	2	1	0	0	1	0	.500
	World Series Record												
2013	Boston	A.L.	C	4	16	1	3	1	0	0	1	0	.188

a Sold to Pittsburgh Pirates, March 30, 2005.
b Traded to San Diego Padres for infielder J.J. Furmaniak, July 28, 2005.
c Traded to Cincinnati Reds for pitcher Bobby Basham, March 21, 2006.
d On disabled list from July 8 to July 26, 2006.
e On disabled list from August 13 to August 28, 2007.
f On disabled list from March 30 to April 23, 2008.
g Released by Cincinnati Reds, August 19, 2008. Signed with Boston Red Sox organization, August 22, 2008.
h Filed for free agency, October 30, 2008. Signed with Atlanta Braves, December 5, 2008.
i On disabled list from April 1 to April 16, 2009.
j Filed for free agency, November 3, 2012. Signed with Boston Red Sox, November 14, 2012.
k On disabled list from May 12 to May 24 and June 18 to August 19, 2013.

RUF, DARIN CORTLAND

Born, Omaha, Nebraska, July 28, 1986.
Bats Right. Throws Right. Height, 6 feet, 3 inches. Weight, 220 pounds.

Year	Club	Lea	Pos	G	AB	R	H	2B	3B	HR	RBI	SB	Avg
2009	Phillies	Gulf Coast	1B	20	43	5	14	3	0	0	6	0	.326
2009	Williamsport	N.Y.-Penn.	1B	37	133	17	40	17	0	3	24	0	.301
2010	Lakewood	So.Atl.	1B	32	115	25	38	7	3	4	17	3	.330
2010	Clearwater	Fla.St.	1B-OF	97	368	45	102	34	2	5	50	2	.277
2011	Clearwater	Fla.St.	1B-OF-3B	133	484	72	149	43	1	17	82	0	.308
2012	Reading	Eastern	1B-OF	139	489	93	155	32	1	38	104	2	.317
2012	Philadelphia	N.L.	OF-1B	12	33	4	11	2	1	3	10	0	.333
2013	Lehigh Valley	Int.	OF-1B	83	305	44	81	22	0	7	46	1	.266
2013	Philadelphia	N.L.	OF-1B	73	251	36	62	11	0	14	30	0	.247
Major League Totals			2 Yrs.	85	284	40	73	13	1	17	40	0	.257

RUGGIANO, JUSTIN MARSHALL

Born, Austin, Texas, April 12, 1982.
Bats Right. Throws Right. Height, 6 feet, 2 inches. Weight, 205 pounds.

Year	Club	Lea	Pos	G	AB	R	H	2B	3B	HR	RBI	SB	Avg
2004	Ogden	Pioneer	OF	46	155	26	51	12	0	7	36	6	.329
2005	Vero Beach	Fla.St.	OF	71	242	47	75	15	4	9	37	16	.310
2005	Jacksonville	Southern	OF	53	161	23	55	10	1	6	29	8	.342
2006	Jacksonville	Southern	OF	89	292	51	76	19	3	9	45	10	.260
2006	Montgomery a	Southern	OF	31	108	25	36	14	3	4	27	4	.333
2007	Durham	Int.	OF	127	482	78	149	29	2	20	73	26	.309
2007	Tampa Bay	A.L.	OF	7	14	2	3	0	0	0	3	0	.214
2008	Durham	Int.	OF	66	257	49	81	18	3	11	51	20	.315
2008	Tampa Bay	A.L.	OF	45	76	9	15	4	0	2	7	2	.197
2009	Durham	Int.	OF	123	471	71	119	28	1	15	72	23	.253
2010	Durham	Int.	OF-3B	117	457	77	131	31	0	15	70	24	.287
2011	Durham	Int.	OF	43	168	29	51	13	1	7	34	12	.304
2011	Tampa Bay b	A.L.	OF	46	105	11	26	4	0	4	13	1	.248

Year	Club	Lea	Pos	G	AB	R	H	2B	3B	HR	RBI	SB	Avg
2012	Oklahoma	P.C.	OF-1B	39	117	21	38	13	1	5	29	5	.325
2012	Miami c-d	N.L.	OF	91	288	38	90	23	1	13	36	14	.313
2013	Miami e	N.L.	OF	128	424	49	94	18	1	18	50	15	.222
Major League Totals			5 Yrs.	317	907	109	228	49	2	37	109	32	.251

a Traded by Los Angeles Dodgers to Tampa Bay Devil Rays with catcher Dioner Navarro and pitcher Jae Seo for pitcher Mark Hendrickson, catcher Toby Hall and cash, June 27, 2006.
b On disabled list from August 7 to September 1, 2011.
c Filed for free agency, January 30, 2012. Signed with Houston Astros organization, February 6, 2012.
d Traded to Miami Marlins for catcher Jobduan Morales, May 26, 2012.
e Traded to Chicago Cubs for outfielder Brian Bogusevic, December 12, 2013.

RUIZ, CARLOS JOAQUIN

Born, David, Panama, January 22, 1979.
Bats Right. Throws Right. Height, 5 feet, 10 inches. Weight, 200 pounds.

Year	Club	Lea	Pos	G	AB	R	H	2B	3B	HR	RBI	SB	Avg
2000	Phillies	Gulf Coast	C	38	130	11	36	7	1	1	22	3	.277
2001	Lakewood	So.Atl.	C-OF	73	249	21	65	14	3	4	32	5	.261
2002	Clearwater	Fla.St.	C	92	342	35	73	18	3	5	32	3	.213
2003	Reading	Eastern	C-OF	52	169	22	45	6	0	2	16	1	.266
2003	Clearwater	Fla.St.	C	15	54	5	17	0	0	2	9	2	.315
2004	Reading	Eastern	C	101	349	45	99	15	2	17	50	8	.284
2005	Scranton-WB	Int.	C-1B	100	347	50	104	25	9	4	40	4	.300
2006	Scranton-WB	Int.	C	100	368	56	113	25	0	16	69	4	.307
2006	Philadelphia	N.L.	C	27	69	5	18	1	1	3	10	0	.261
2007	Philadelphia	N.L.	C	115	374	42	97	29	2	6	54	6	.259
2008	Philadelphia	N.L.	C-3B	117	320	47	70	14	0	4	31	1	.219
2009	Lehigh Valley	Int.	C	4	13	1	3	1	0	0	2	0	.231
2009	Philadelphia a	N.L.	C	107	322	32	82	26	1	9	43	3	.255
2010	Lakewood	So.Atl.	C	2	8	1	4	2	0	0	1	0	.500
2010	Lehigh Valley	Int.	C	1	2	0	0	0	0	0	0	0	.000
2010	Philadelphia b	N.L.	C	121	371	43	112	28	1	8	53	0	.302
2011	Clearwater	Fla.St.	C	1	3	1	1	0	0	0	0	0	.333
2011	Philadelphia c	N.L.	C-3B	132	410	49	116	23	0	6	40	1	.283
2012	Philadelphia d	N.L.	C	114	372	56	121	32	0	16	68	4	.325
2013	Clearwater	Fla.St.	C	2	8	1	1	0	0	1	3	0	.125
2013	Reading	Eastern	C	2	6	0	1	1	0	0	0	0	.167
2013	Lehigh Valley	Int.	C	2	5	1	1	0	0	0	0	0	.200
2013	Philadelphia e-f-g	N.L.	C	92	310	30	83	16	0	5	37	1	.268
Major League Totals			8 Yrs.	825	2548	304	699	169	5	57	336	16	.274
	Division Series												
2007	Philadelphia	N.L.	C	3	9	1	3	1	0	0	0	1	.333
2008	Philadelphia	N.L.	C	4	14	1	1	0	0	0	0	0	.071
2009	Philadelphia	N.L.	C	4	13	0	4	0	0	0	3	0	.308
2010	Philadelphia	N.L.	C	3	8	1	2	1	0	0	1	0	.250
2011	Philadelphia	N.L.	C	5	17	1	1	0	0	0	0	0	.059
Division Series Totals				19	61	4	11	2	0	0	4	1	.180
	Championship Series												
2008	Philadelphia	N.L.	C	5	16	3	5	1	0	0	1	0	.313
2009	Philadelphia	N.L.	C	5	13	4	5	1	0	1	4	1	.385
2010	Philadelphia	N.L.	C	6	18	2	3	0	0	1	1	0	.167
Championship Series Totals				16	47	9	13	2	0	2	6	1	.277
	World Series Record												
2008	Philadelphia	N.L.	C	5	16	2	6	2	0	1	3	1	.375
2009	Philadelphia	N.L.	C	6	18	4	6	2	1	1	2	0	.333
World Series Totals				11	34	6	12	4	1	2	5	1	.353

a On disabled list from April 11 to May 2, 2009.
b On disabled list from June 19 to July 10, 2010.
c On disabled list from April 28 to May 13, 2011.
d On disabled list from August 3 to September 7, 2012.
e Suspended for 25 games for performance-enhancing drug use, November 27, 2012.
f On disabled list from May 20 to June 18, 2013.
g Filed for free agency, October 31, 2013, re-signed with Philadelphia Phillies, November 19, 2013.

RUTLEDGE, JOSHUA ALAN (JOSH)

Born, Cullman, Alabama, April 21, 1989.
Bats Right. Throws Right. Height, 6 feet, 1 inch. Weight, 190 pounds.

Year	Club	Lea	Pos	G	AB	R	H	2B	3B	HR	RBI	SB	Avg
2010	Tri-City	Northwest	SS	11	39	6	5	0	0	0	4	1	.128
2011	Modesto	Calif.	SS	113	460	91	160	33	9	9	71	16	.348
2012	Tulsa	Texas	SS-2B	87	356	57	109	27	3	13	35	14	.306
2012	Colorado	N.L.	SS-2B	73	277	37	76	20	5	8	37	7	.274
2013	Colorado Springs	P.C.	SS-2B	38	143	24	53	17	1	4	24	1	.371
2013	Colorado	N.L.	2B-SS	88	285	45	67	6	1	7	19	12	.235
Major League Totals			2 Yrs.	161	562	82	143	26	6	15	56	19	.254

RYAN, BRENDAN WOOD

Born, Los Angeles, California, March 26, 1982.
Bats Right. Throws Right. Height, 6 feet, 2 inches. Weight, 195 pounds.

Year	Club	Lea	Pos	G	AB	R	H	2B	3B	HR	RBI	SB	Avg
2003	New Jersey	N.Y.-Penn.	SS-3B	53	193	20	60	14	4	0	13	11	.311
2004	Peoria	Midwest	SS	105	426	72	137	21	4	2	59	30	.322
2005	Palm Beach	Fla.St.	SS	49	188	29	57	17	0	1	16	8	.303
2005	Springfield	Texas	SS	43	154	28	42	8	1	2	9	6	.273
2006	Palm Beach	Fla.St.	SS	3	14	2	6	1	0	0	1	1	.429
2006	State College	N.Y.-Penn.	SS	8	34	5	8	0	0	0	3	1	.235
2006	Memphis	P.C.	SS	7	26	4	4	0	0	1	6	1	.154
2006	Springfield	Texas	SS	10	43	6	13	1	0	0	3	1	.302
2007	Memphis	P.C.	SS	81	323	55	88	9	5	1	15	17	.272
2007	St. Louis	N.L.	SS-3B-2B	67	180	30	52	9	0	4	12	7	.289
2008	Palm Beach	Fla.St.	SS	3	12	1	3	1	0	0	0	1	.250
2008	Springfield	Texas	3B-2B-SS	4	19	5	7	3	0	1	3	1	.368
2008	Memphis	P.C.	OF-2B-SS	21	80	13	19	5	0	3	10	1	.237
2008	St. Louis a	N.L.	SS-2B-3B-OF	80	197	30	48	9	0	0	10	7	.244
2009	Memphis	P.C.	SS	3	11	0	0	0	0	0	0	0	.000
2009	St. Louis b	N.L.	SS-2B	129	390	55	114	19	7	3	37	14	.292
2010	St. Louis c	N.L.	SS	139	439	50	98	19	3	2	36	11	.223
2011	Seattle d	A.L.	SS	123	436	51	108	19	3	3	39	13	.248
2012	Seattle	A.L.	SS	141	407	42	79	19	3	3	31	11	.194
2013	Seattle-New York e-f	A.L.	SS	104	319	30	63	12	0	4	22	4	.197
Major League Totals			7 Yrs.	783	2368	288	562	106	16	19	187	67	.237
	Division Series												
2009	St. Louis	N.L.	SS	3	12	0	1	1	0	0	0	0	.083

a On disabled list from March 21 to April 23, 2008.
b On disabled list from April 30 to May 15, 2009.
c Traded to Seattle Mariners for pitcher Maikel Cleto, December 12, 2010.
d On disabled list from August 4 to August 19, 2011.
e Traded to New York Yankees for player to be named later, September 11, 2013.
f Filed for free agency, October 31, 2013, re-signed with New York Yankees, December 2, 2013.

SALTALAMACCHIA, JARROD SCOTT

Born, West Palm Beach, Florida, May 2, 1985.
Bats Both. Throws Right. Height, 6 feet, 4 inches. Weight, 235 pounds.

Year	Club	Lea	Pos	G	AB	R	H	2B	3B	HR	RBI	SB	Avg
2003	Braves	Gulf Coast	C-3B	46	134	23	32	11	2	2	14	0	.239
2004	Rome	So.Atl.	C	91	323	42	88	19	2	10	51	1	.272
2005	Myrtle Beach	Carolina	C	129	459	70	144	35	1	19	81	4	.314
2006	Mississippi	Southern	C	92	313	30	72	18	1	9	39	0	.230
2007	Mississippi	Southern	C	22	81	18	25	7	0	6	13	2	.309
2007	Atlanta	N.L.	C-1B	47	141	11	40	6	0	4	12	0	.284
2007	Texas a	A.L.	1B-C	46	167	28	42	7	1	7	21	0	.251
2008	Oklahoma	P.C.	C	15	55	10	16	3	1	2	13	0	.291
2008	Texas	A.L.	C	61	198	27	50	13	0	3	26	0	.253
2009	Frisco	Texas	C	2	4	1	0	0	0	0	0	0	.000
2009	Texas b	A.L.	C	84	283	34	66	12	0	9	34	0	.233
2010	Oklahoma	P.C.	C	63	238	37	58	11	2	11	33	1	.244
2010	Pawtucket	Int.	C-1B	9	36	5	10	5	0	1	6	0	.278
2010	Texas-Boston c-d	A.L.	C-1B	12	24	2	4	3	0	0	2	0	.167
2011	Boston	A.L.	C	103	358	52	84	23	3	16	56	1	.235
2012	Boston	A.L.	C-1B	121	405	55	90	17	1	25	59	0	.222
2013	Boston e	A.L.	C	121	425	68	116	40	0	14	65	4	.273
Major League Totals			7 Yrs.	595	2001	277	492	121	5	78	275	5	.246

Year	Club	Lea	Pos	G	AB	R	H	2B	3B	HR	RBI	SB	Avg
	Division Series												
2013	Boston	A.L.	C	3	10	1	3	1	0	0	3	0	.300
	Championship Series												
2013	Boston	A.L.	C	5	16	0	3	0	0	0	2	0	.188
	World Series Record												
2013	Boston	A.L.	C	2	6	0	0	0	0	0	0	0	.000

a Traded to Texas Rangers with infielder Elvis Andrews, pitcher Neftali Feliz, pitcher Matt Harrison and pitcher Beau James for infielder Mark Teixeira and pitcher Ron Mahay, July 31, 2007.
b On disabled list from August 16 to September 2, 2009.
c On disabled list from April 8 to April 27 and August 16 to September 1, 2010.
d Traded to Boston Red Sox for pitcher Roman Mendez, infielder Chris McGuiness, player to be named later and cash, July 31, 2010. Texas Rangers received catcher Michael Thomas to complete trade, August 14, 2010.
e Filed for free agency, October 31, 2013. Signed with Miami Marlins, December 6, 2013.

SANCHEZ, GABRIEL (GABY)

Born, Miami, Florida, September 2, 1983.
Bats Right. Throws Right. Height, 6 feet, 2 inches. Weight, 225 pounds.

Year	Club	Lea	Pos	G	AB	R	H	2B	3B	HR	RBI	SB	Avg
2005	Jamestown	N.Y.-Penn.	3B-1B-C	62	234	34	83	16	0	5	42	11	.355
2006	Jupiter	Fla.St.	1B-3B-C	16	55	13	10	3	1	1	7	1	.182
2006	Marlins	Gulf Coast	1B	3	6	1	2	1	0	0	3	0	.333
2006	Greensboro	So.Atl.	1B-C	55	189	43	60	12	0	14	40	6	.317
2007	Jupiter	Fla.St.	1B-3B-C	133	473	89	132	40	3	9	70	6	.279
2008	Carolina	Southern	1B-3B	133	478	70	150	42	1	17	92	17	.314
2008	Florida	N.L.	1B	5	8	0	3	2	0	0	1	0	.375
2009	New Orleans	P.C.	1B-3B	85	318	55	92	11	0	16	56	5	.289
2009	Florida	N.L.	1B	21	21	2	5	0	0	2	3	0	.238
2010	Florida	N.L.	1B	151	572	72	156	37	3	19	85	5	.273
2011	Florida	N.L.	1B	159	572	72	152	35	0	19	78	3	.266
2012	New Orleans	P.C.	1B	34	116	20	35	7	0	5	18	2	.302
2012	Miami-Pittsburgh a	N.L.	1B	105	299	30	65	16	0	7	30	1	.217
2013	Pittsburgh	N.L.	1B-3B	136	264	29	67	18	0	7	36	1	.254
Major League Totals			6 Yrs.	577	1736	205	448	108	3	54	233	10	.258
	Division Series												
2013	Pittsburgh	N.L.	1B	2	2	0	0	0	0	0	0	0	.000

a Traded to Pittsburgh Pirates with pitcher Kyle Kaminska for outfielder Gorkys Hernandez and a competitive balance draft pick, July 31, 2012.

SANCHEZ, HECTOR ENRIQUE

Born, Maracay, Venezuela, November 17, 1989.
Bats Both. Throws Right. Height, 5 feet, 11 inches. Weight, 225 pounds.

Year	Club	Lea	Pos	G	AB	R	H	2B	3B	HR	RBI	SB	Avg
2009	Giants	Arizona	C	33	117	13	35	8	1	1	22	0	.299
2010	Augusta	So.Atl.	C	89	310	29	85	20	1	5	31	0	.274
2011	Fresno	P.C.	C	46	153	15	40	9	0	1	26	0	.261
2011	San Jose	Calif.	C-1B	52	212	31	64	14	1	11	58	0	.302
2011	San Francisco	N.L.	C	13	31	0	8	2	0	0	1	0	.258
2012	Fresno	P.C.	C	4	15	0	1	0	0	0	1	0	.067
2012	San Francisco a	N.L.	C	74	218	22	61	15	0	3	34	0	.280
2013	Giants	Arizona	C	1	3	0	1	1	0	0	2	0	.333
2013	San Jose	Calif.	C	4	12	1	3	1	0	0	3	0	.250
2013	Fresno	P.C.	C	32	85	10	23	4	0	3	11	0	.271
2013	San Francisco b	N.L.	C	63	129	8	32	4	0	3	19	0	.248
Major League Totals			3 Yrs.	150	378	30	101	21	0	6	54	0	.267
	Division Series												
2012	San Francisco	N.L.	C	1	2	1	1	0	0	0	0	0	.500
	Championship Series												
2012	San Francisco	N.L.	C	2	5	0	0	0	0	0	0	0	.000
	World Series Record												
2012	San Francisco	N.L.	DH	1	4	0	0	0	0	0	0	0	.000

a On disabled list from July 18 to August 2, 2012.
b On disabled list from July 9 to July 24, 2013.

SANDOVAL, PABLO E.

Born, Puerto Cabello, Venezuela, August 11, 1986.
Bats Both. Throws Right. Height, 5 feet, 11 inches. Weight, 245 pounds.

Year Club Lea	Pos	G	AB	R	H	2B	3B	HR	RBI	SB	Avg
2004 Giants... Arizona	C	46	177	21	47	9	5	0	26	4	.266
2005 Salem-Keizer... Northwest	3B-1B-C	75	294	46	97	15	2	3	50	2	.330
2006 Augusta... So.Atl.	1B-3B	117	438	43	116	20	1	1	49	3	.265
2007 San Jose... Calif.	C-1B	102	401	56	115	33	5	11	52	3	.287
2008 San Jose... Calif.	C-1B	68	273	61	98	25	2	12	59	2	.359
2008 Connecticut... Eastern	C-1B	44	175	29	59	13	0	8	37	0	.337
2008 San Francisco... N.L.	1B-3B-C	41	145	24	50	10	1	3	24	0	.345
2009 San Francisco... N.L.	3B-1B-C	153	572	79	189	44	5	25	90	5	.330
2010 San Francisco... N.L.	3B-1B	152	563	61	151	34	3	13	63	3	.268
2011 San Jose... Calif.	3B	1	3	1	0	0	0	0	0	0	.000
2011 Fresno... P.C.	3B-1B	5	18	4	5	0	0	2	7	0	.278
2011 San Francisco a... N.L.	3B-1B	117	426	55	134	26	3	23	70	2	.315
2012 San Jose... Calif.	3B	6	22	1	6	2	0	1	1	0	.273
2012 Fresno... P.C.	3B	3	11	3	3	1	0	2	2	0	.273
2012 San Francisco b... N.L.	3B-1B	108	396	59	112	25	2	12	63	1	.283
2013 San Jose... Calif.	3B	2	6	2	4	0	0	2	2	0	.667
2013 San Francisco c... N.L.	3B	141	525	52	146	27	2	14	79	0	.278
Major League Totals...	6 Yrs.	712	2627	330	782	166	16	90	389	11	.298
Division Series											
2010 San Francisco... N.L.	3B	2	6	0	1	0	0	0	0	0	.167
2012 San Francisco... N.L.	3B	5	21	2	7	2	0	1	3	0	.333
Division Series Totals...		7	27	2	8	2	0	1	3	0	.296
Championship Series											
2010 San Francisco... N.L.	3B	3	8	0	2	1	0	0	2	0	.250
2012 San Francisco... N.L.	3B	7	29	4	9	2	0	2	6	0	.310
Championship Series Totals...		10	37	4	11	3	0	2	8	0	.297
World Series Record											
2010 San Francisco... N.L.	DH	1	3	0	0	0	0	0	0	0	.000
2012 San Francisco... N.L.	3B	4	16	3	8	1	0	3	4	0	.500
World Series Totals...		5	19	3	8	1	0	3	4	0	.421

a On disabled list from April 30 to June 14, 2011.
b On disabled list from May 3 to June 9 and July 25 to August 13, 2012.
c On disabled list from June 9 to June 24, 2013.

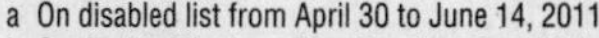

SANTANA, CARLOS

Born, Santo Domingo, Dominican Republic, April 8, 1986.
Bats Both. Throws Right. Height, 5 feet, 11 inches. Weight, 190 pounds.

Year Club Lea	Pos	G	AB	R	H	2B	3B	HR	RBI	SB	Avg
2005 Dodgers... Gulf Coast	3B-OF-C-2B	32	78	14	23	4	1	1	14	0	.295
2006 Vero Beach... Fla.St.	3B-OF	54	198	16	53	10	2	3	18	0	.268
2006 Ogden... Pioneer	OF-3B	37	132	31	40	5	1	7	27	4	.303
2007 Great Lakes... Midwest	C-3B-OF	86	292	32	65	20	1	7	36	5	.223
2008 Inland Empire... Calif.	C-OF-1B-2B	99	350	88	113	34	4	14	96	7	.323
2008 Kinston... Carolina	C	29	105	34	37	5	1	6	19	3	.352
2008 Akron a... Eastern	C	2	8	3	1	0	0	1	2	0	.125
2009 Akron... Eastern	C	130	428	91	124	30	2	23	97	2	.290
2010 Columbus... Int.	C	57	196	39	62	14	1	13	51	6	.316
2010 Cleveland b... A.L.	C	46	150	23	39	13	0	6	22	3	.260
2011 Cleveland... A.L.	C-1B	155	552	84	132	35	2	27	79	5	.239
2012 Lake County... Midwest	DH	1	4	1	1	0	0	1	2	0	.250
2012 Cleveland c... A.L.	C-1B-OF	143	507	72	128	27	2	18	76	3	.252
2013 Cleveland... A.L.	C-1B	154	541	75	145	39	1	20	74	3	.268
Major League Totals...	4 Yrs.	498	1750	254	444	114	5	71	251	14	.254
Wild Card Playoff											
2013 Cleveland... A.L.	DH	1	4	0	2	1	0	0	0	0	.500

a Traded by Los Angeles Dodgers to Cleveland Indians with pitcher Jonathan Meloan for infielder Casey Blake, July 26, 2008.
b On disabled list from August 3 to November 9, 2010.
c On disabled list from May 26 to June 5, 2012.

SANTIAGO, RAMON D.

Born, Las Matas de Farfan, Dominican Republic, August 31, 1979.
Bats Both. Throws Right. Height, 5 feet, 11 inches. Weight, 150 pounds.

Year Club	Lea	Pos	G	AB	R	H	2B	3B	HR	RBI	SB	Avg
1999 Tigers	Gulf Coast	SS	35	134	25	43	9	2	0	11	20	.321
1999 Oneonta	N.Y.-Penn.	SS	12	50	9	17	1	2	1	8	5	.340
2000 West Michigan	Midwest	SS	98	379	69	103	15	1	1	42	39	.272
2001 Lakeland	Fla.St.	DH	120	429	64	115	15	3	2	46	34	.268
2002 Erie	Eastern	SS	22	75	9	21	0	2	1	7	6	.280
2002 Toledo	Int.	SS	9	28	8	12	1	0	2	6	0	.429
2002 Detroit	A.L.	SS	65	222	33	54	5	5	4	20	8	.243
2003 Detroit	A.L.	SS-2B	141	444	41	100	18	1	2	29	10	.225
2004 Tacoma	P.C.	SS-2B	71	243	35	47	7	2	1	24	9	.193
2004 Seattle a	A.L.	SS	19	39	8	7	1	0	0	2	0	.179
2005 Tacoma	P.C.	2B-SS-3B-C	129	441	68	111	22	3	10	50	18	.252
2005 Seattle	A.L.	2B-SS	8	8	2	1	0	0	0	0	0	.125
2006 Toledo	Int.	2B-SS	25	83	13	21	6	0	2	12	2	.253
2006 Detroit b	A.L.	SS-2B-3B	43	80	9	18	1	1	0	3	2	.225
2007 Toledo	Int.	SS-2B	91	365	40	96	19	4	3	30	8	.263
2007 Detroit	A.L.	SS	32	67	10	19	5	1	0	7	3	.284
2008 Toledo	Int.	SS	8	28	3	6	2	0	0	3	0	.214
2008 Detroit c	A.L.	SS-2B-3B	58	124	30	35	6	2	4	18	1	.282
2009 Detroit	A.L.	SS-2B-3B	93	262	29	70	6	2	7	35	1	.267
2010 Detroit	A.L.	SS-2B	112	320	38	84	9	1	3	22	2	.262
2011 Detroit d	A.L.	2B-SS-3B	101	258	29	67	11	3	5	30	0	.260
2012 Detroit	A.L.	2B-SS-3B	93	228	19	47	7	1	2	17	1	.206
2013 Detroit e	A.L.	2B-3B-SS	80	205	27	46	8	1	1	14	0	.224
Major League Totals		12 Yrs.	845	2257	275	548	77	18	28	197	28	.243
Division Series												
2011 Detroit	A.L.	2B	4	14	0	2	1	0	0	2	0	.143
2013 Detroit	A.L.	3B	3	0	0	0	0	0	0	0	0	.000
Division Series Totals			7	14	0	2	1	0	0	2	0	.143
Championship Series												
2006 Detroit	A.L.	SS	3	7	0	0	0	0	0	0	0	.000
2011 Detroit	A.L.	2B	6	24	1	9	1	0	0	0	0	.375
2013 Detroit	A.L.	3B	2	0	0	0	0	0	0	0	0	.000
Championship Series Totals			11	31	1	9	1	0	0	0	0	.290
World Series Record												
2006 Detroit	A.L.	SS	3	5	0	1	0	0	0	0	0	.200
2012 Detroit	A.L.	PH	1	1	0	0	0	0	0	0	0	.000
World Series Totals			4	6	0	1	0	0	0	0	0	.167

a Traded to Seattle Mariners with infielder Juan Gonzalez for infielder Carlos Guillen, January 8, 2004.
b Released by Seattle Mariners, November 18, 2005. Signed with Detroit Tigers organization, January 4, 2006.
c On disabled list from June 5, to July 8, 2008.
d Filed for free agency, October 30, 2011, re-signed with Detroit Tigers November 30, 2011.
e Filed for free agency, October 31, 2013.

SATIN, JOSHUA (JOSH)

Born, Hidden Hills, California, December 23, 1984.
Bats Right. Throws Right. Height, 6 feet, 2 inches. Weight, 200 pounds.

Year Club	Lea	Pos	G	AB	R	H	2B	3B	HR	RBI	SB	Avg
2008 Kingsport	Appal.	2B	3	12	3	7	2	0	1	2	0	.583
2008 Brooklyn	N.Y.-Penn.	2B-SS-3B	45	143	21	40	10	2	4	13	0	.280
2009 Savannah	So.Atl.	2B-1B-3B	125	440	62	125	38	0	7	60	0	.284
2009 St. Lucie	Fla.St.	2B	7	22	6	8	2	0	1	5	0	.364
2010 St. Lucie	Fla.St.	2B-1B	58	209	27	66	15	0	5	35	1	.316
2010 Binghamton	Eastern	2B-1B-3B	79	286	49	88	24	1	7	39	1	.308
2011 Binghamton	Eastern	2B-3B-1B	94	338	60	110	35	2	11	60	2	.325
2011 Buffalo	Int.	3B-1B-2B	38	145	17	46	8	0	1	16	1	.317
2011 New York	N.L.	1B-3B	15	25	3	5	1	0	0	2	0	.200
2012 New York	N.L.	DH	1	1	0	0	0	0	0	0	0	.000
2012 Buffalo	Int.	1B-2B-3B	131	441	72	126	25	1	14	60	3	.286
2013 Las Vegas	P.C.	1B-OF	60	220	46	67	14	0	9	32	0	.305
2013 New York	N.L.	1B-3B	75	190	23	53	15	0	3	17	1	.279
Major League Totals		3 Yrs.	91	216	26	58	16	0	3	19	1	.269

SAUNDERS, MICHAEL EDWARD BRETT

Born, Victoria, British Columbia, Canada, November 19, 1986.
Bats Left. Throws Right. Height, 6 feet, 4 inches. Weight, 210 pounds.

Year	Club	Lea	Pos	G	AB	R	H	2B	3B	HR	RBI	SB	Avg
2005	Everett	Northwest	OF	56	196	24	53	13	3	7	39	2	.270
2006	Wisconsin	Midwest	OF	104	359	48	86	10	8	4	39	22	.240
2007	High Desert	Calif.	OF	108	431	91	129	25	4	14	77	27	.299
2007	West Tenn	Southern	OF	15	52	8	15	1	2	1	7	2	.288
2008	Tacoma	P.C.	OF	24	95	12	23	4	1	3	16	1	.242
2008	West Tenn	Southern	OF	67	248	46	72	18	3	8	30	11	.290
2009	Tacoma	P.C.	OF	64	248	58	77	15	2	13	32	6	.310
2009	Seattle	A.L.	OF	46	122	13	27	1	3	0	4	4	.221
2010	Tacoma	P.C.	OF	21	80	6	16	1	0	0	5	4	.200
2010	Seattle	A.L.	OF	100	289	29	61	11	2	10	33	6	.211
2011	Tacoma	P.C.	OF	64	236	51	68	11	3	7	38	10	.288
2011	Seattle	A.L.	OF	58	161	16	24	5	0	2	8	6	.149
2012	Seattle	A.L.	OF	139	507	71	125	31	3	19	57	21	.247
2013	Tacoma	P.C.	OF	3	11	2	2	1	1	0	2	0	.182
2013	Seattle a	A.L.	OF	132	406	59	96	23	3	12	46	13	.236
Major League Totals			5 Yrs.	475	1485	188	333	71	11	43	148	50	.224

a On disabled list from April 11 to April 29, 2013.

SCHAFER, JORDAN JAMES

Born, Hammond, Indiana, September 4, 1986.
Bats Left. Throws Left. Height, 6 feet, 1 inch. Weight, 200 pounds.

Year	Club	Lea	Pos	G	AB	R	H	2B	3B	HR	RBI	SB	Avg
2005	Braves	Gulf Coast	OF	49	182	18	37	12	3	3	19	13	.203
2006	Rome	So.Atl.	OF	114	388	49	93	15	7	8	60	15	.240
2007	Rome	So.Atl.	OF	30	129	16	48	15	2	5	20	4	.372
2007	Myrtle Beach	Carolina	OF	106	436	70	128	34	8	10	43	19	.294
2008	Mississippi a	Southern	OF	84	297	46	80	18	6	10	51	12	.269
2009	Atlanta	N.L.	OF	50	167	18	34	8	0	2	8	2	.204
2009	Gwinnett	Int.	OF	9	35	6	8	0	0	2	3	3	.229
2010	Gwinnett	Int.	OF	52	189	16	38	5	1	1	8	9	.201
2010	Rome	So.Atl.	OF	6	22	4	6	2	0	0	1	2	.273
2010	Mississippi b	Southern	OF	18	63	7	11	3	0	0	5	1	.175
2011	Oklahoma	P.C.	OF	5	20	4	10	2	0	0	3	3	.500
2011	Gwinnett	Int.	OF	42	164	21	42	8	0	1	21	6	.256
2011	Atlanta-Houston c-d	N.L.	OF	82	302	46	73	10	3	2	13	22	.242
2012	Astros	Gulf Coast	OF	1	2	0	1	0	0	0	0	0	.500
2012	Oklahoma	P.C.	OF	4	13	2	2	0	0	0	0	2	.154
2012	Houston e-f	N.L.	OF	106	313	40	66	10	2	4	23	27	.211
2013	Gwinnett	Int.	OF	8	32	0	2	2	0	0	2	0	.063
2013	Atlanta g	N.L.	OF	94	231	32	57	8	3	3	21	22	.247
Major League Totals			4 Yrs.	332	1013	136	230	36	8	11	65	73	.227
	Division Series												
2013	Atlanta	N.L.	OF	1	1	0	0	0	0	0	0	0	.000

a Suspended for 50 games for performance enhancing drug use, April 8, 2008.
b On disabled list from September 4 to October 9, 2009. On disabled list from March 26 to May 17, 2010.
c Traded to Houston Astros with pitcher Juan Abreu, pitcher Paul Clemens and pitcher Brett Oberholtzer for outfielder Michael Bourn and cash, July 31, 2011.
d On disabled list from July 27 to August 22, 2011.
e On disabled list from August 7 to September 1, 2012.
f Claimed on waivers by Atlanta Braves, November 1, 2012.
g On disabled list from July 4 to August 10, 2013.

SCHAFER, LOGAN EDWARD

Born, San Jose, California, September 8, 1986.
Bats Left. Throws Left. Height, 6 feet, 1 inch. Weight, 180 pounds.

Year	Club	Lea	Pos	G	AB	R	H	2B	3B	HR	RBI	SB	Avg
2008	Helena	Pioneer	OF-3B	8	25	4	6	0	1	2	8	1	.240
2008	West Virginia	So.Atl.	OF	43	181	25	50	13	2	0	20	3	.276
2009	Brevard County	Fla.St.	OF	113	457	76	143	31	6	6	58	16	.313
2009	Huntsville	Southern	OF	7	23	4	5	0	1	0	0	1	.217
2010	Brevard County	Fla.St.	OF	7	23	7	4	2	0	0	1	0	.174
2011	Brevard County	Fla.St.	OF	9	36	4	11	0	0	0	1	1	.306
2011	Huntsville	Southern	OF	50	189	31	57	9	4	0	19	10	.302
2011	Nashville	P.C.	OF	40	169	31	56	13	2	5	23	5	.331

Year	Club	Lea	Pos	G	AB	R	H	2B	3B	HR	RBI	SB	Avg
2011	Milwaukee	N.L.	OF	8	3	1	1	0	0	0	0	0	.333
2012	Nashville	P.C.	OF	124	464	72	129	23	9	11	40	16	.278
2012	Milwaukee	N.L.	OF	16	23	3	7	1	2	0	5	0	.304
2013	Milwaukee	N.L.	OF	134	298	29	63	15	3	4	33	7	.211
Major League Totals			3 Yrs.	158	324	33	71	16	5	4	38	7	.219

SCHIERHOLTZ, NATHAN JOHN (NATE)

Born, Reno, Nevada, February 15, 1984.
Bats Left. Throws Right. Height, 6 feet, 2 inches. Weight, 215 pounds.

Year	Club	Lea	Pos	G	AB	R	H	2B	3B	HR	RBI	SB	Avg
2003	Giants	Arizona	3B-1B	11	45	5	18	0	2	0	5	4	.400
2003	Salem-Keizer	Northwest	3B	35	124	23	38	6	2	3	29	0	.306
2004	San Jose	Calif.	3B-OF	62	258	39	76	18	9	3	31	3	.295
2004	Hagerstown	So.Atl.	3B	59	235	41	70	22	0	15	54	1	.298
2005	San Jose	Calif.	OF	128	502	83	160	37	8	15	86	5	.319
2006	Connecticut	Eastern	OF	125	470	55	127	25	7	14	54	8	.270
2007	Fresno	P.C.	OF	109	411	67	137	31	7	16	68	10	.333
2007	San Francisco	N.L.	OF	39	112	9	34	5	3	0	10	3	.304
2008	Fresno	P.C.	OF	93	350	62	112	22	10	18	73	9	.320
2008	San Francisco	N.L.	OF	19	75	12	24	8	1	1	5	0	.320
2009	Fresno	P.C.	OF	5	18	2	4	1	0	0	1	1	.222
2009	San Francisco a	N.L.	OF	116	285	33	76	19	2	5	29	3	.267
2010	San Francisco	N.L.	OF	137	227	34	55	13	3	3	17	4	.242
2011	San Francisco b	N.L.	OF	115	335	42	93	22	1	9	41	7	.278
2012	Lehigh Valley	Int.	OF	4	17	1	2	0	0	0	1	0	.118
2012	San Fran.-Philadelphia c-d-e	N.L.	OF	114	241	20	62	8	5	6	21	3	.257
2013	Chicago	N.L.	OF	137	462	56	116	32	3	21	68	6	.251
Major League Totals			7 Yrs.	677	1737	206	460	107	18	45	191	26	.265
	Division Series												
2010	San Francisco	N.L.	OF	4	4	0	1	0	0	0	0	0	.250
	Championship Series												
2010	San Francisco	N.L.	OF	4	3	1	0	0	0	0	0	0	.000
	World Series Record												
2010	San Francisco	N.L.	OF	3	5	1	1	0	0	0	1	0	.200

a On disabled list from July 27 to August 12, 2009.
b On disabled list from August 22 to September 29, 2011.
c Traded to Philadelphia Phillies with catcher Tommy Joseph and pitcher Seth Rosin for outfielder Hunter Pence and cash, July 31, 2012.
d On disabled list from August 13 to September 1, 2012.
e Not offered contract, November 30, 2012. Signed with Chicago Cubs, December 21, 2012.

SCHUMAKER, JARED MICHAEL (SKIP)

Born, Torrance, California, February 3, 1980.
Bats Left. Throws Right. Height, 5 feet, 10 inches. Weight, 195 pounds.

Year	Club	Lea	Pos	G	AB	R	H	2B	3B	HR	RBI	SB	Avg
2001	New Jersey	N.Y.-Penn.	OF	49	162	22	41	10	1	0	14	11	.253
2002	Potomac	Carolina	OF	136	551	71	158	22	4	2	44	26	.287
2003	Tennessee	Southern	OF	91	342	43	86	20	3	2	22	6	.251
2004	Tennessee	Southern	OF-3B	138	516	78	163	29	6	4	43	19	.316
2005	Memphis	P.C.	OF	115	443	66	127	24	3	7	34	14	.287
2005	St. Louis	N.L.	OF	27	24	9	6	1	0	0	1	1	.250
2006	Memphis	P.C.	OF	95	369	47	113	13	3	3	27	11	.306
2006	St. Louis	N.L.	OF	28	54	3	10	1	0	1	2	2	.185
2007	Memphis	P.C.	OF	59	232	34	71	16	0	7	31	2	.306
2007	St. Louis	N.L.	OF	88	177	19	59	12	2	2	19	1	.333
2008	St. Louis	N.L.	OF	153	540	87	163	22	5	8	46	8	.302
2009	St. Louis	N.L.	2B-OF	153	532	85	161	34	1	4	35	2	.303
2010	St. Louis	N.L.	2B-OF	137	476	66	126	18	1	5	42	5	.265
2011	St. Louis a-b	N.L.	2B-OF-P	117	367	34	104	19	0	2	38	0	.283
2012	Memphis	P.C.	2B-OF	7	21	5	6	2	0	0	0	1	.286
2012	St. Louis c-d	N.L.	2B-OF	107	272	37	75	14	4	1	28	1	.276
2013	Los Angeles e	N.L.	OF-2B-P	125	319	31	84	16	0	2	30	2	.263
Major League Totals			9 Yrs.	935	2761	371	788	137	13	25	241	22	.285
	Division Series												
2009	St. Louis	N.L.	2B-OF	2	6	1	2	1	0	0	1	0	.333
2011	St. Louis	N.L.	OF-2B	5	10	1	6	2	0	0	3	0	.600
2012	St. Louis	N.L.	PH	4	4	0	0	0	0	0	1	0	.000

Year Club	Lea	Pos	G	AB	R	H	2B	3B	HR	RBI	SB	Avg
2013 Los Angeles..........	N.L.	OF	4	13	0	3	0	0	0	2	0	.231
Division Series Totals............			15	33	2	11	3	0	0	7	0	.333
Championship Series												
2012 St. Louis.............	N.L.	2B	5	5	0	0	0	0	0	0	0	.000
2013 Los Angeles..........	N.L.	OF	4	6	0	0	0	0	0	0	0	.000
Championship Series Totals......			9	11	0	0	0	0	0	0	0	.000
World Series Record												
2011 St. Louis.............	N.L.	OF	6	11	1	2	0	0	0	1	0	.182

a On disabled list from April 16 to May 23, 2011.
b Not offered contract, December 12, 2011, re-signed with St. Louis Cardinals, December 12, 2011.
c On disabled list from April 1 to April 20 and May 31 to June 19, 2012.
d Traded to Los Angeles Dodgers for infielder Jake Lemmerman, December 12, 2012.
e Filed for free agency, October 31, 2013. Signed with Cincinnati Reds, November 26, 2013.

SCOTT, LUKE BRANDON

Born, DeLeon Springs, Florida, June 25, 1978.
Bats Left. Throws Right. Height, 6 feet. Weight, 210 pounds.

Year Club	Lea	Pos	G	AB	R	H	2B	3B	HR	RBI	SB	Avg
2001 Kinston a.....	Carolina				INJURED — Did Not Play							
2002 Kinston.......	Carolina	OF-1B	48	163	22	39	7	1	8	30	2	.239
2002 Columbus.......	So.Atl.	OF	49	171	28	44	15	4	7	32	9	.257
2003 Kinston.......	Carolina	OF	67	241	37	67	12	1	13	44	6	.278
2003 Akron.........	Eastern	OF	50	183	21	50	13	1	7	37	0	.273
2004 Salem........	Carolina	OF	66	241	45	67	20	1	8	35	6	.278
2004 Round Rock b ...	Texas	OF	63	208	45	62	17	0	19	62	0	.298
2005 Round Rock.......	P.C.	OF	103	398	69	114	25	4	31	87	2	.286
2005 Houston..........	N.L.	OF	34	80	6	15	4	2	0	4	1	.188
2006 Round Rock.......	P.C.	OF	87	318	63	95	15	1	20	63	6	.299
2006 Houston..........	N.L.	OF	65	214	31	72	19	6	10	37	2	.336
2007 Houston c	N.L.	OF	132	369	49	94	28	5	18	64	3	.255
2008 Baltimore.........	A.L.	OF	148	475	67	122	29	2	23	65	2	.257
2009 Delmarva.......	So.Atl.	OF	2	4	1	3	0	0	1	1	0	.750
2009 Baltimore d	A.L.	DH-OF-1B	128	449	61	116	26	1	25	77	0	.258
2010 Orioles......	Gulf Coast	OF	3	9	1	2	0	0	0	2	0	.222
2010 Baltimore e........	A.L.	DH-1B-OF	131	447	70	127	29	1	27	72	2	.284
2011 Bowie.........	Eastern	DH	3	10	5	5	1	0	3	7	0	.500
2011 Baltimore f-g	A.L.	OF-1B	64	209	24	46	11	0	9	22	1	.220
2012 Charlotte	Fla.St.	1B	8	26	6	8	1	0	2	6	0	.308
2012 Durham	Int.	DH	2	8	3	3	0	0	2	4	0	.375
2012 Tampa Bay h-i	A.L.	DH-1B	96	314	35	72	22	1	14	55	5	.229
2013 Charlotte	Fla.St.	DH	5	18	2	4	1	0	0	2	0	.222
2013 Durham	Int.	DH	3	12	2	4	0	0	0	0	0	.333
2013 Tampa Bay j-k	A.L.	DH-OF-1B	91	253	27	61	13	2	9	40	1	.241
Major League Totals............		9 Yrs.	889	2810	370	725	181	20	135	436	17	.258
Division Series												
2005 Houston..........	N.L.	OF	2	2	1	0	0	0	0	0	0	.000
World Series Record												
2005 Houston..........	N.L.	PH	0	0	0	0	0	0	0	0	0	.000

a On disabled list from June 21 to September 14, 2001.
b Traded by Cleveland Indians to Houston Astros with outfielder Willy Taveras for pitcher Jeriome Robertston, March 31, 2004.
c Traded to Baltimore Orioles with pitcher Troy Patton, pitcher Matt Albers, pitcher Dennis Sarfate and infielder Michael Costanzo for infielder Miguel Tejada, December 12, 2007.
d On disabled list from May 11 to May 27, 2009.
e On disabled list from July 1 to July 19, 2010.
f On disabled list from July 3 to July 22 and July 23 to November 2, 2011.
g Not offered contract, December 12, 2011. Signed with Tampa Bay Rays, January 12, 2012.
h On disabled list from June 9 to June 28 and July 21 to August 21, 2012.
i Filed for free agency, November 3, 2012, re-signed with Tampa Bay Rays, February 6, 2013.
j On disabled list from March 24 to April 30 and August 15 to September 1, 2013.
k Filed for free agency, October 31, 2013. Signed with SK Wyverns (Korea), December 18, 2013.

SCUTARO, MARCOS (MARCO)

Born, San Felipe, Venezuela, October 30, 1975.
Bats Right. Throws Right. Height, 5 feet, 10 inches. Weight, 190 pounds.

Year Club	Lea	Pos	G	AB	R	H	2B	3B	HR	RBI	SB	Avg
1995 Cleveland...	Dominican	3B	66	262	71	103	18	6	0	38	32	.393
1996 Columbus.......	So.Atl.	2B-SS-3B	85	315	66	79	12	3	10	45	6	.251

Year	Club	Lea	Pos	G	AB	R	H	2B	3B	HR	RBI	SB	Avg
1997	Buffalo	A.A.	2B-3B-SS	21	57	8	15	3	0	1	6	0	.263
1997	Kinston	Carolina	2B-3B	97	378	58	103	17	6	10	59	23	.272
1998	Buffalo	Int.	2B-3B	8	26	3	6	3	0	0	4	0	.231
1998	Akron	Eastern	2B-SS	124	462	68	146	27	6	11	62	33	.316
1999	Buffalo	Int.	2B-SS	129	462	76	126	24	2	8	51	21	.273
2000	Buffalo	Int.	2B-SS	124	425	67	117	20	5	5	54	9	.275
2000	Indianapolis a	Int.	2B-SS	4	13	5	7	1	1	1	3	1	.538
2001	Indianapolis	Int.	2B-3B-SS	132	495	87	146	29	3	11	50	11	.295
2002	Norfolk	Int.	2B-SS-OF-3B	97	354	48	113	22	6	7	28	7	.319
2002	New York b	N.L.	2B-SS-3B-OF	27	36	2	8	0	1	1	6	0	.222
2003	Norfolk	Int.	3B-2B-SS-OF	70	244	42	76	18	3	9	32	11	.311
2003	New York c	N.L.	2B-SS	48	75	10	16	4	0	2	6	2	.213
2004	Oakland	A.L.	2B-SS-3B	137	455	50	124	32	1	7	43	0	.273
2005	Oakland	A.L.	SS-2B-3B-OF	118	381	48	94	22	3	9	37	5	.247
2006	Oakland	A.L.	SS-2B-3B-OF	117	365	52	97	21	6	5	41	5	.266
2007	Oakland d	A.L.	SS-3B-2B-OF	104	338	49	88	13	0	7	41	2	.260
2008	Toronto	A.L.	SS-2B-3B-1B	145	517	76	138	23	1	7	60	7	.267
2009	Toronto e	A.L.	SS-2B	144	574	100	162	35	1	12	60	14	.282
2010	Boston	A.L.	SS-2B	150	632	92	174	38	0	11	56	5	.275
2011	Pawtucket	Int.	2B-SS	3	11	4	5	1	0	0	0	0	.455
2011	Boston f	A.L.	SS-2B	113	395	59	118	26	1	7	54	4	.299
2012	Colorado-San Fran. g-h-i	N.L.	2B-SS-3B	156	620	87	190	32	4	7	74	9	.306
2013	San Francisco	N.L.	2B	127	488	57	145	23	3	2	31	2	.297
Major League Totals			12 Yrs.	1386	4876	682	1354	269	21	77	509	55	.278
	Division Series												
2006	Oakland	A.L.	SS	3	12	1	4	4	0	0	6	0	.333
2012	San Francisco	N.L.	2B	5	20	2	3	1	0	0	1	0	.150
Division Series Totals				8	32	3	7	5	0	0	7	0	.219
	Championship Series												
2006	Oakland	A.L.	SS	4	15	0	1	0	0	0	0	0	.067
2012	San Francisco	N.L.	2B	7	28	6	14	3	0	0	4	0	.500
Championship Series Totals				11	43	6	15	3	0	0	4	0	.349
	World Series Record												
2012	San Francisco	N.L.	2B	4	16	3	4	0	0	0	3	0	.250

a Sent by Cleveland Indians to Milwaukee Brewers as player to be named later in Richie Sexson trade, August 30, 2000.
b Claimed on waivers by New York Mets, April 3, 2002.
c Claimed on waivers by Oakland Athletics, October 9, 2003.
d Traded to Toronto Blue Jays for pitcher Kristian Bell and pitcher Graham Godfrey, November 18, 2007.
e Filed for free agency, November 6, 2009. Signed with Boston Red Sox, December 4, 2009.
f On disabled list from May 8 to June 7, 2011.
g Traded to Colorado Rockies for pitcher Clayton Mortensen, January 21, 2012.
h Traded to San Francisco Giants with cash for infielder Charlie Culberson, July 28, 2012.
i Filed for free agency, November 3, 2012, re-signed with San Francisco Giants, December 4, 2012.

SEAGER, KYLE DUERR

Born, Charlotte, North Carolina, November 3, 1987.

Bats Left. Throws Right. Height, 5 feet, 10 inches. Weight, 175 pounds.

Year	Club	Lea	Pos	G	AB	R	H	2B	3B	HR	RBI	SB	Avg
2009	Mariners	Arizona	2B	1	3	0	0	0	0	0	0	0	.000
2009	Clinton	Midwest	2B-3B-SS	41	153	17	42	8	0	1	22	4	.275
2009	High Desert	Calif.	2B	2	5	1	0	0	0	0	0	0	.000
2010	High Desert	Calif.	2B-3B-SS	135	557	126	192	40	3	14	74	13	.345
2011	Jackson	Southern	2B-SS-3B	66	266	33	83	25	1	4	37	8	.312
2011	Tacoma	P.C.	3B-2B-SS	24	106	24	41	8	2	3	17	3	.387
2011	Seattle	A.L.	3B-SS-2B	53	182	22	47	13	0	3	13	3	.258
2012	Seattle	A.L.	3B-2B	155	594	62	154	35	1	20	86	13	.259
2013	Seattle	A.L.	3B	160	615	79	160	32	2	22	69	9	.260
Major League Totals			3 Yrs.	368	1391	163	361	80	3	45	168	25	.260

SEGURA, JEAN CARLOS ENRIQUE

Born, San Juan, Dominican Republic, March 17, 1990.

Bats Right. Throws Right. Height, 5 feet, 10 inches. Weight, 165 pounds.

Year	Club	Lea	Pos	G	AB	R	H	2B	3B	HR	RBI	SB	Avg
2008	Angels	Arizona	2B-OF	11	36	13	9	0	0	0	4	1	.250
2009	Salt Lake	P.C.	2B	7	19	2	8	2	0	0	2	0	.421
2009	Orem	Pioneer	2B	36	162	33	56	10	4	3	21	11	.346

Year	Club	Lea	Pos	G	AB	R	H	2B	3B	HR	RBI	SB	Avg
2010	Cedar Rapids	Midwest	2B	130	515	89	161	24	12	10	79	50	.313
2011	Angels	Arizona	SS	8	30	5	11	4	0	1	5	0	.367
2011	Inland Empire	Calif.	SS	44	185	26	52	9	4	3	21	18	.281
2012	Arkansas	Texas	SS-2B	94	374	50	110	10	5	7	40	33	.294
2012	Huntsville	Southern	SS	8	30	7	13	3	0	0	4	4	.433
2012	Los Angeles	A.L.	SS	1	3	0	0	0	0	0	0	0	.000
2012	Milwaukee a	N.L.	SS	44	148	19	39	4	3	0	14	7	.264
2013	Milwaukee	N.L.	SS	146	588	74	173	20	10	12	49	44	.294
Major League Totals			2 Yrs.	191	739	93	212	24	13	12	63	51	.287

a Traded to Milwaukee Brewers with pitcher Ariel Pena and pitcher Johnny Hellweg for pitcher Zack Greinke, July 27, 2012.

SHUCK, JACK BURDETT (J.B.)

Born, Westerville, Ohio, June 18, 1987.
Bats Left. Throws Left. Height, 5 feet, 11 inches. Weight, 195 pounds.

Year	Club	Lea	Pos	G	AB	R	H	2B	3B	HR	RBI	SB	Avg
2008	Tri-City	N.Y.-Penn.	OF	65	263	51	79	12	5	4	24	8	.300
2009	Lancaster	Calif.	OF	133	556	98	175	30	11	1	36	18	.315
2010	Corpus Christi	Texas	OF	101	389	52	116	14	2	2	28	9	.298
2010	Round Rock	P.C.	OF	36	139	15	38	2	2	0	7	7	.273
2011	Oklahoma	P.C.	OF	108	354	60	105	11	7	0	30	20	.297
2011	Houston	N.L.	OF	37	81	9	22	2	1	0	3	2	.272
2012	Oklahoma a	P.C.	OF-1B	115	315	49	94	11	3	0	33	12	.298
2013	Los Angeles	A.L.	OF	129	437	60	128	20	3	2	39	8	.293
Major League Totals			2 Yrs.	166	518	69	150	22	4	2	42	10	.290

a Released by Houston Astros, November 2, 2012. Signed with Los Angeles Angels organization, November 15, 2012.

SIMMONS, ANDRELTON A.

Born, Mundo-Novo, Curacao, September 4, 1989.
Bats Right. Throws Right. Height, 6 feet, 2 inches. Weight, 170 pounds.

Year	Club	Lea	Pos	G	AB	R	H	2B	3B	HR	RBI	SB	Avg
2010	Danville	Appal.	SS	62	239	36	66	11	1	2	26	18	.276
2011	Lynchburg	Carolina	SS	131	517	69	161	35	6	1	52	26	.311
2012	Mississippi	Southern	SS	44	174	29	51	9	2	3	21	10	.293
2012	Atlanta a	N.L.	SS	49	166	17	48	8	2	3	19	1	.289
2013	Atlanta	N.L.	SS	157	606	76	150	27	6	17	59	6	.248
Major League Totals			2 Yrs.	206	772	93	198	35	8	20	78	7	.256
	Wild Card Playoff												
2012	Atlanta	N.L.	SS	1	4	0	1	0	0	0	0	0	.250
	Division Series												
2013	Atlanta	N.L.	SS	4	12	0	3	1	0	0	2	0	.250

a On disabled list from July 13 to September 10, 2012.

SMITH, GARRY SETH (SETH)

Born, Jackson, Mississippi, September 30, 1982.
Bats Left. Throws Left. Height, 6 feet, 3 inches. Weight, 215 pounds.

Year	Club	Lea	Pos	G	AB	R	H	2B	3B	HR	RBI	SB	Avg
2004	Tri-Cities	Northwest	OF	9	27	6	7	1	1	2	5	0	.259
2004	Casper	Pioneer	OF	56	233	46	86	21	3	9	61	9	.369
2005	Modesto	Calif.	OF	129	533	87	160	45	6	9	72	5	.300
2006	Tulsa	Texas	OF	130	524	79	154	46	4	15	71	4	.294
2007	Colorado Springs	P.C.	OF	129	451	68	143	32	6	17	82	7	.317
2007	Colorado	N.L.	OF	7	8	4	5	0	1	0	0	0	.625
2008	Colorado Springs	P.C.	OF	68	248	55	80	16	2	10	53	11	.323
2008	Colorado	N.L.	OF	67	108	13	28	7	0	4	15	1	.259
2009	Colorado	N.L.	OF	133	335	61	98	20	4	15	55	4	.293
2010	Colorado	N.L.	OF	133	358	55	88	19	5	17	52	2	.246
2011	Colorado a	N.L.	OF	147	476	67	135	32	9	15	59	10	.284
2012	Sacramento	P.C.	DH	1	3	0	2	0	0	0	0	0	.667
2012	Oakland b	A.L.	OF	125	383	55	92	23	2	14	52	2	.240
2013	Oakland c	A.L.	OF	117	368	49	93	27	0	8	40	0	.253
Major League Totals			7 Yrs.	729	2036	304	539	128	21	73	273	19	.265
	Division Series												
2007	Colorado	N.L.	PH	2	2	1	1	0	0	0	0	0	.500
2009	Colorado	N.L.	OF	3	5	0	1	0	0	0	0	0	.200
2012	Oakland	A.L.	DH	5	15	3	2	1	0	1	3	0	.133

Year	Club	Lea	Pos	G	AB	R	H	2B	3B	HR	RBI	SB	Avg
2013	Oakland	A.L.	DH	4	16	1	5	0	0	1	2	0	.313
Division Series Totals				14	38	5	9	1	0	2	5	0	.237
	Championship Series												
2007	Colorado	N.L.	PH	2	2	1	1	1	0	0	2	0	.500
	World Series Record												
2007	Colorado	N.L.	PH	2	2	0	1	0	0	0	0	0	.500

a Traded to Oakland Athletics for pitcher Guillermo Moscoso and pitcher Josh Outman, January 16, 2012.
b On disabled list from August 3 to August 21, 2012.
c Traded to San Diego Padres for pitcher Luke Gregerson, December 3, 2013.

SMOAK, JUSTIN KYLE

Born, Goose Creek, South Carolina, December 5, 1986.
Bats Both. Throws Left. Height, 6 feet, 4 inches. Weight, 220 pounds.

Year	Club	Lea	Pos	G	AB	R	H	2B	3B	HR	RBI	SB	Avg
2008	Clinton	Midwest	1B	14	56	9	17	3	0	3	6	0	.304
2009	Rangers	Arizona	1B	2	6	3	4	0	1	2	5	0	.667
2009	Oklahoma	P.C.	1B	54	197	25	48	11	0	4	23	0	.244
2009	Frisco	Texas	1B	50	183	30	60	10	0	6	29	0	.328
2010	Oklahoma	P.C.	1B	15	50	10	15	6	0	2	5	0	.300
2010	Tacoma	P.C.	1B	35	133	23	36	7	0	7	25	0	.271
2010	Texas-Seattle a	A.L.	1B	100	348	40	76	14	0	13	48	1	.218
2011	Tacoma	P.C.	1B	4	11	1	0	0	0	0	0	0	.000
2011	Seattle b	A.L.	1B	123	427	38	100	24	0	15	55	0	.234
2012	Tacoma	P.C.	1B	20	66	10	16	6	1	0	4	1	.242
2012	Seattle	A.L.	1B	132	483	49	105	14	0	19	51	1	.217
2013	Tacoma	P.C.	1B	5	21	2	5	2	0	0	1	0	.238
2013	Seattle c	A.L.	1B	131	454	53	108	19	0	20	50	0	.238
Major League Totals			4 Yrs.	486	1712	180	389	71	0	67	204	2	.227

a Traded to Seattle Mariners with pitcher Blake Beavan, pitcher Josh Lueke and infielder Matt Lawson for pitcher Cliff Lee, pitcher Mark Lowe and cash, July 9, 2010.
b On disabled list from August 13 to September 1, 2011.
c On disabled list from May 30 to June 18, 2013.

SNIDER, TRAVIS JAMES

Born, Kirkland, Washington, February 2, 1988.
Bats Left. Throws Left. Height, 5 feet, 11 inches. Weight, 245 pounds.

Year	Club	Lea	Pos	G	AB	R	H	2B	3B	HR	RBI	SB	Avg
2006	Pulaski	Appal.	OF	54	194	36	63	12	1	11	41	6	.325
2007	Lansing	Midwest	OF	118	457	72	143	35	7	16	93	3	.313
2008	Dunedin	Fla.St.	DH	17	61	15	17	5	0	4	7	1	.279
2008	New Hampshire	Eastern	OF	98	362	65	95	21	0	17	67	1	.262
2008	Syracuse	Int.	OF	18	64	9	22	5	0	2	17	1	.344
2008	Toronto	A.L.	OF	24	73	9	22	6	0	2	13	0	.301
2009	Las Vegas	P.C.	OF	48	175	32	59	13	1	14	40	2	.337
2009	Toronto	A.L.	OF	77	241	34	58	14	1	9	29	1	.241
2010	Blue Jays	Gulf Coast	OF	4	14	2	4	0	0	0	1	1	.286
2010	Dunedin	Fla.St.	DH	1	4	0	0	0	0	0	0	0	.000
2010	New Hampshire	Eastern	OF	20	81	14	24	5	0	5	17	3	.296
2010	Toronto a	A.L.	OF	82	298	36	76	20	0	14	32	6	.255
2011	Las Vegas	P.C.	OF	61	248	47	81	22	2	4	42	12	.327
2011	Toronto	A.L.	OF	49	187	23	42	14	0	3	30	9	.225
2012	Dunedin	Fla.St.	OF	5	22	3	5	1	0	0	1	2	.227
2012	Las Vegas	P.C.	OF	56	209	49	70	16	0	13	56	2	.335
2012	Toronto	A.L.	OF	10	36	6	9	2	0	3	8	0	.250
2012	Pittsburgh b	N.L.	OF	50	128	17	32	5	1	1	9	2	.250
2013	Altoona	Eastern	OF	2	6	1	2	0	0	0	0	0	.333
2013	Indianapolis	Int.	OF	8	32	4	11	1	0	0	5	1	.344
2013	Pittsburgh c	N.L.	OF	111	261	28	56	12	2	5	25	2	.215
Major League Totals			6 Yrs.	403	1224	153	295	73	4	37	146	20	.241
	Wild Card Playoff												
2013	Pittsburgh	N.L.	PH	1	1	0	0	0	0	0	0	0	.000

a On disabled list from May 15 to July 17, 2010.
b Traded to Pittsburgh Pirates for pitcher Brad Lincoln, July 31, 2012.
c On disabled list from July 28 to September 1, 2013.

SOGARD, ERIC SIDNEY

Born, Phoenix, Arizona, May 22, 1986.
Bats Left. Throws Right. Height, 5 feet, 10 inches. Weight, 190 pounds.

Year	Club	Lea	Pos	G	AB	R	H	2B	3B	HR	RBI	SB	Avg
2007	Eugene	Northwest	2B-SS	31	125	20	32	9	0	2	18	4	.256
2007	Fort Wayne	Midwest	2B	22	83	7	21	2	0	2	15	2	.253
2007	Portland	P.C.	DH	1	3	0	0	0	0	0	0	0	.000
2008	Lake Elsinore	Calif.	2B-3B	133	536	97	165	42	3	10	87	16	.308
2009	San Antonio a	Texas	2B	117	457	79	134	25	3	6	51	10	.293
2010	Sacramento	P.C.	2B-SS-3B	137	514	82	154	28	6	5	65	14	.300
2010	Oakland	A.L.	2B	4	7	0	3	0	0	0	0	0	.429
2011	Sacramento	P.C.	SS	79	315	55	94	16	2	5	37	13	.298
2011	Oakland	A.L.	SS-3B-2B	27	70	7	14	3	0	2	4	0	.200
2012	Oakland b	A.L.	SS-3B-2B	37	102	8	17	3	1	2	7	2	.167
2012	Sacramento	P.C.	2B-SS-3B	37	157	29	52	5	2	5	22	11	.331
2013	Oakland	A.L.	2B-SS	130	368	45	98	24	3	2	35	10	.266
Major League Totals			4 Yrs.	198	547	60	132	30	4	6	46	12	.241
	Division Series												
2013	Oakland	A.L.	2B	4	9	0	0	0	0	0	0	0	.000

a Traded by San Diego Padres to Oakland Athletics with infielder Kevin Kouzmanoff for outfielder Aaron Cunningham and outfielder Scott Hairston, January 16, 2010.
b On disabled list from August 10 to October 15, 2012.

SOLANO (PRECIADO), DONOVAN

Born, Barranquilla, Colombia, December 17, 1987.
Bats Right. Throws Right. Height, 5 feet, 9 inches. Weight, 190 pounds.

Year	Club	Lea	Pos	G	AB	R	H	2B	3B	HR	RBI	SB	Avg
2005	Johnson City	Appal.	SS-2B	45	145	27	38	4	0	0	11	3	.262
2005	New Jersey	N.Y.-Penn.	SS-3B-2B	22	77	7	19	5	0	0	11	1	.247
2006	State College	N.Y.-Penn.	3B-2B-SS	44	149	22	42	2	0	0	13	2	.282
2007	Palm Beach	Fla.St.	SS-3B-2B	50	163	17	34	2	1	0	11	0	.209
2007	Quad Cities	Midwest	3B-SS	82	292	31	75	8	0	0	30	5	.257
2008	Palm Beach	Fla.St.	SS-3B-2B-OF	107	402	56	115	15	4	1	31	1	.286
2008	Springfield	Texas	SS-2B	26	106	11	28	5	0	1	11	2	.264
2009	Memphis	P.C.	SS-2B-3B	52	164	22	52	7	0	0	14	3	.317
2009	Springfield	Texas	3B-2B-SS	64	251	27	52	7	1	1	16	1	.207
2010	Memphis	P.C.	SS-2B-3B	102	330	41	84	12	1	4	27	2	.255
2011	Memphis	P.C.	2B-SS-3B	81	229	22	65	21	1	1	23	2	.284
2011	Springfield a	Texas	2B-3B-SS	27	101	5	23	7	0	2	10	0	.228
2012	New Orleans	P.C.	2B-SS	36	141	14	37	7	1	0	14	4	.262
2012	Miami	N.L.	2B-3B-OF-SS	93	285	29	84	11	3	2	28	7	.295
2013	Jupiter	Fla.St.	3B-2B-SS	4	14	0	6	1	0	0	1	0	.429
2013	New Orleans	P.C.	2B-3B-SS	17	66	8	25	3	1	2	9	0	.379
2013	Miami b	N.L.	2B-3B	102	361	33	90	13	1	3	34	3	.249
Major League Totals			2 Yrs.	195	646	62	174	24	4	5	62	10	.269

a Filed for free agency from St. Louis Cardinals, November 2, 2011. Signed with Miami Marlins organization, November 22, 2011.
b On disabled list from May 6 to June 9, 2013.

SORIANO, ALFONSO GUILLEARD

Born, San Pedro de Macoris, Dominican Republic, January 7, 1976.
Bats Right. Throws Right. Height, 6 feet, 1 inch. Weight, 180 pounds.

Year	Club	Lea	Pos	G	AB	R	H	2B	3B	HR	RBI	SB	Avg
1995	Hiroshima	Dominican	SS	63	227	52	83	12	3	4	55	8	.366
1996	Hiroshima	Japan East.	SS	57	131	11	28	0	0	0	13	0	.214
1997	Hiroshima	Japan Cent.	SS	9	17	2	2	0	0	0	2	0	.118
1998 a						Did Not Play							
1999	Norwich	Eastern	SS	89	361	57	110	20	3	15	68	24	.305
1999	Yankees	Gulf Coast	SS	5	19	7	5	2	0	1	5	0	.263
1999	Columbus	Int.	SS	20	82	8	15	5	1	2	11	1	.183
1999	New York b	A.L.	SS	9	8	2	1	0	0	1	1	0	.125
2000	Columbus	Int.	SS-2B	111	459	90	133	32	6	12	66	14	.290
2000	New York	A.L.	3B-SS-2B	22	50	5	9	3	0	2	3	2	.180
2001	New York	A.L.	2B	158	574	77	154	34	3	18	73	43	.268
2002	New York	A.L.	2B	156	*696	*128	*209	51	2	39	102	41	.300
2003	New York	A.L.	2B	156	*682	114	198	36	5	38	91	35	.290
2004	Texas c-d	A.L.	2B	145	608	77	170	32	4	28	91	18	.280
2005	Texas e	A.L.	2B	156	637	102	171	43	2	36	104	30	.268
2006	Washington f	N.L.	OF	159	647	119	179	41	2	46	95	41	.277

Year	Club	Lea	Pos	G	AB	R	H	2B	3B	HR	RBI	SB	Avg
2007	Chicago g	N.L.	OF-2B	135	579	97	173	42	5	33	70	19	.299
2008	Azl Cubs	Arizona	DH	1	2	1	0	0	0	0	0	0	.000
2008	Iowa	P.C.	OF	1	3	0	1	0	0	0	0	0	.333
2008	Chicago h	N.L.	OF-2B	109	453	76	127	27	0	29	75	19	.280
2009	Chicago i	N.L.	OF-2B-3B	117	477	64	115	25	1	20	55	9	.241
2010	Chicago	N.L.	OF	147	496	67	128	40	3	24	79	5	.258
2011	Iowa	P.C.	OF	3	13	3	1	0	0	0	0	0	.077
2011	Chicago j	N.L.	OF	137	475	50	116	27	1	26	88	2	.244
2012	Chicago	N.L.	OF	151	561	68	147	33	2	32	108	6	.262
2013	Chicago	N.L.	OF	93	362	47	92	24	1	17	51	10	.254
2013	New York k	A.L.	OF	58	219	37	56	8	0	17	50	8	.256
Major League Totals			15 Yrs.	1908	7524	1130	2045	466	31	406	1136	288	.272
	Division Series												
2001	New York	A.L.	2B	5	18	2	4	0	0	0	3	2	.222
2002	New York	A.L.	2B	4	17	2	2	1	0	1	2	1	.118
2003	New York	A.L.	2B	4	19	2	7	1	0	0	4	2	.368
2007	Chicago	N.L.	OF	3	14	0	2	0	0	0	0	0	.143
2008	Chicago	N.L.	OF	3	14	0	1	0	0	0	0	0	.071
Division Series Totals				19	82	6	16	2	0	1	9	5	.195
	Championship Series												
2001	New York	A.L.	2B	5	15	5	6	0	0	1	2	2	.500
2003	New York	A.L.	2B	7	30	0	4	1	0	0	3	2	.133
Championship Series Totals				12	45	5	10	1	0	1	5	4	.222
	World Series Record												
2001	New York	A.L.	2B	7	25	1	6	0	0	1	2	0	.240
2003	New York	A.L.	2B-OF	6	22	2	5	0	0	1	2	1	.227
World Series Totals				13	47	3	11	0	0	2	4	1	.234

a Signed by New York Yankees as free agent, September 29, 1998.
b On disabled list from July 15 to August 15, 1999.
c Traded to Texas Rangers with player to be named later for infielder Alex Rodriguez, February 16, 2004.
d Texas Rangers received infielder Joaquin Arias to complete trade, March 23, 2004.
e Traded to Washington Nationals for outfielder Brad Wilkerson, outfielder Terrmel Sledge and pitcher Armando Galarraga, December 13, 2005.
f Filed for free agency, October 29, 2006. Signed with Chicago Cubs, November 20, 2006.
g On disabled list from August 6 to August 28, 2007.
h On disabled list from April 16 to May 1 and June 12 to July 23, 2008.
i On disabled list from September 4 to October 14, 2009.
j On disabled list from May 31 to June 15, 2011.
k Traded to New York Yankees with cash for pitcher Corey Black, July 26, 2013.

SOTO, GEOVANY

Born, San Juan, Puerto Rico, January 20, 1983.
Bats Right. Throws Right. Height, 6 feet, 1 inch. Weight, 230 pounds.

Year	Club	Lea	Pos	G	AB	R	H	2B	3B	HR	RBI	SB	Avg
2001	Cubs	Arizona	C-1B-3B-OF	41	150	18	39	16	0	1	20	1	.260
2002	Cubs	Arizona	C-1B	44	156	24	42	10	2	3	24	0	.269
2002	Boise	Northwest	C	1	5	1	2	0	0	0	0	0	.400
2003	Daytona	Fla.St.	C-3B	89	297	26	72	12	2	2	38	0	.242
2004	West Tenn	Southern	C-1B	104	332	47	90	16	0	9	48	1	.271
2005	Iowa	P.C.	C	91	292	30	74	14	0	4	39	0	.253
2005	Chicago	N.L.	PH	1	1	0	0	0	0	0	0	0	.000
2006	Iowa	P.C.	C	108	342	34	93	21	0	6	38	0	.272
2006	Chicago	N.L.	C	11	25	1	5	1	0	0	2	0	.200
2007	Iowa	P.C.	C-1B	110	385	75	136	31	3	26	109	0	.353
2007	Chicago	N.L.	C	18	54	12	21	6	0	3	8	0	.389
2008	Chicago a	N.L.	C	141	494	66	141	35	2	23	86	0	.285
2009	Azl Cubs	Arizona	DH	1	3	0	1	1	0	0	2	0	.333
2009	Tennessee	Southern	C	3	9	2	3	0	0	2	4	0	.333
2009	Chicago b	N.L.	C	102	331	27	72	19	1	11	47	1	.218
2010	Chicago c	N.L.	C	105	322	47	90	19	0	17	53	0	.280
2011	Tennessee	Southern	C	2	7	0	0	0	0	0	0	0	.000
2011	Chicago d	N.L.	C	125	421	46	96	26	0	17	54	0	.228
2012	Iowa	P.C.	C	5	16	1	3	2	0	0	0	0	.188
2012	Chicago	N.L.	C	52	176	26	35	6	1	6	14	0	.199
2012	Texas e-f-g	A.L.	C	47	148	19	29	6	0	5	25	1	.196
2013	Texas h	A.L.	C-3B	54	163	20	40	9	0	9	22	1	.245
Major League Totals			9 Yrs.	656	2135	264	529	127	4	91	311	3	.248

Year	Club	Lea	Pos	G	AB	R	H	2B	3B	HR	RBI	SB	Avg
	Wild Card Playoff												
2012	Texas	A.L.	C	1	2	0	0	0	0	0	0	0	.000
	Division Series												
2007	Chicago	N.L.	C	2	6	1	1	0	0	1	2	0	.167
2008	Chicago	N.L.	C	3	11	0	2	1	0	0	0	0	.182
Division Series Totals				5	17	1	3	1	0	1	2	0	.176

a Selected Rookie of the Year in National League for 2008.
b On disabled list from July 7 to August 7, 2009.
c On disabled list from August 7 to August 23 and September 19 to October 6, 2010.
d On disabled list from May 11 to May 29, 2011.
e On disabled list from May 17 to June 18, 2012.
f Traded to Texas Rangers with cash for pitcher Jacob Brigham and cash, July 31, 2012.
g Not offered contract, November 30, 2012, re-signed with Texas Rangers, December 2, 2012.
h Filed for free agency, October 31, 2013, re-signed with Texas Rangers, November 5, 2013.

SPAN, KEIUNTA DENARD (DENARD)

Born, Tampa, Florida, February 17, 1984.
Bats Left. Throws Left. Height, 6 feet. Weight, 205 pounds.

Year	Club	Lea	Pos	G	AB	R	H	2B	3B	HR	RBI	SB	Avg
2003	Elizabethton	Appal.	OF	50	207	34	56	5	1	1	18	14	.271
2004	Twins	Gulf Coast	OF	5	16	1	6	2	0	0	1	0	.375
2004	Quad Cities	Midwest	OF	64	240	29	64	4	3	0	14	15	.267
2005	New Britain	Eastern	OF	68	267	47	76	6	5	0	26	10	.285
2005	Fort Myers	Fla.St.	OF	49	186	38	63	3	3	1	19	13	.339
2006	New Britain	Eastern	OF	134	536	80	153	16	6	2	45	24	.285
2007	Rochester	Int.	OF	139	487	59	130	20	7	3	55	25	.267
2008	Rochester	Int.	OF	40	156	32	53	11	1	3	14	15	.340
2008	Minnesota	A.L.	OF	93	347	70	102	16	7	6	47	18	.294
2009	Rochester	Int.	OF	2	6	1	2	1	0	0	0	1	.333
2009	Minnesota a	A.L.	OF	145	578	97	180	16	*10	8	68	23	.311
2010	Minnesota	A.L.	OF	153	629	85	166	24	10	3	58	26	.264
2011	Rochester	Int.	OF	10	39	4	8	1	0	0	2	3	.205
2011	Minnesota b	A.L.	OF	70	284	37	75	11	5	2	16	6	.264
2012	Minnesota c-d	A.L.	OF	128	516	71	146	38	4	4	41	17	.283
2013	Washington	N.L.	OF	153	610	75	170	28	*11	4	47	20	.279
Major League Totals			6 Yrs.	742	2964	435	839	133	47	27	277	110	.283
	Division Series												
2009	Minnesota	A.L.	OF	3	15	1	6	1	0	0	1	1	.400
2010	Minnesota	A.L.	OF	3	13	0	4	0	0	0	0	0	.308
Division Series Totals				6	28	1	10	1	0	0	1	1	.357

a On disabled list from June 10 to June 25, 2009.
b On disabled list from June 10 to June 23 and June 23 to August 2 and August 14 to September 21, 2011.
c On disabled list from August 28 to September 12, 2012.
d Traded to Washington Nationals for pitcher Alex Meyer, November 29, 2012.

STANTON, GIANCARLO CRUZ-MICHAEL

Born, Panorama, California, November 8, 1989.
Bats Right. Throws Right. Height, 6 feet, 5 inches. Weight, 235 pounds.

Year	Club	Lea	Pos	G	AB	R	H	2B	3B	HR	RBI	SB	Avg
2007	Marlins	Gulf Coast	OF	8	26	6	7	2	0	0	1	0	.269
2007	Jamestown	N.Y.-Penn.	OF	9	30	2	2	1	0	1	2	0	.067
2008	Greensboro	So.Atl.	OF	125	468	89	137	26	3	39	97	4	.293
2009	Jupiter	Fla.St.	OF	50	180	27	53	9	3	12	39	2	.294
2009	Jacksonville	Southern	OF	79	299	49	69	15	2	16	53	1	.231
2010	Jacksonville	Southern	OF	53	192	42	60	13	2	21	52	1	.313
2010	Florida	N.L.	OF	100	359	45	93	21	1	22	59	5	.259
2011	Florida	N.L.	OF	150	516	79	135	30	5	34	87	5	.262
2012	Jupiter	Fla.St.	OF	4	16	2	5	1	0	2	5	0	.313
2012	Miami a	N.L.	OF	123	449	75	130	30	1	37	86	6	.290
2013	Jupiter	Fla.St.	OF	5	15	0	0	0	0	0	0	1	.000
2013	Miami b	N.L.	OF	116	425	62	106	26	0	24	62	1	.249
Major League Totals			4 Yrs.	489	1749	261	464	107	7	117	294	17	.265

a On disabled list from July 8 to August 7, 2012.
b On disabled list from April 30 to June 10, 2013.

STEWART, CHRISTOPHER DAVID (CHRIS)

Born, Fontana, California, February 19, 1982.
Bats Right. Throws Right. Height, 6 feet, 4 inches. Weight, 210 pounds.

Year	Club	Lea	Pos	G	AB	R	H	2B	3B	HR	RBI	SB	Avg
2002	Bristol	Appal.	C	42	158	25	44	9	0	1	12	0	.278
2003	Winston-Salem	Carolina	C	76	217	18	45	8	2	2	27	1	.207
2004	Birmingham	Southern	C-3B	83	260	26	60	11	2	1	17	2	.231
2004	Charlotte	Int.	C	5	14	1	1	1	0	0	1	0	.071
2005	Birmingham	Southern	C	95	311	39	89	21	0	11	51	3	.286
2006	Charlotte	Int.	C-1B-3B	89	272	40	72	17	3	4	28	3	.265
2006	Chicago a	A.L.	C	6	8	0	0	0	0	0	0	0	.000
2007	Texas	A.L.	C	17	37	4	9	2	0	0	3	0	.243
2007	Oklahoma b	P.C.	C	45	153	18	37	8	0	2	21	0	.242
2008	New York	A.L.	C	1	3	0	0	0	0	0	0	0	.000
2008	Scranton/WB c	Int.	C	86	272	32	76	19	0	2	24	2	.279
2009	Scranton/WB d-e-f	Int.	C	78	232	33	65	11	0	1	18	1	.280
2010	Portland	P.C.	C-1B	85	266	31	66	14	2	7	39	1	.248
2010	San Diego g	N.L.	C-1B	2	0	0	0	0	0	0	0	0	.000
2011	Fresno	P.C.	C-1B	33	95	9	21	5	0	0	10	3	.221
2011	San Francisco	N.L.	C-1B	67	162	20	33	8	0	3	10	0	.204
2012	New York h	A.L.	C	55	141	15	34	8	0	1	13	2	.241
2013	New York i	A.L.	C-1B	109	294	28	62	6	0	4	25	4	.211
Major League Totals			7 Yrs.	257	645	67	138	24	0	8	51	6	.214
	Championship Series												
2012	New York	A.L.	C	1	0	0	0	0	0	0	0	0	.000

a Traded by Chicago White Sox to Texas Rangers for pitcher John Lujan, January 12, 2007.
b Released by Texas Rangers, March 27, 2008. Signed with New York Yankees organization, April 3, 2008.
c Filed for free agency, November 3, 2008. Signed with Chicago White Sox organization, December 16, 2008.
d Sold to New York Yankees, March 22, 2009.
e Filed for free agency, June 2, 2009, re-signed with New York Yankees organization, June 2, 2009.
f Filed for free agency, November 9, 2009. Signed with San Diego Padres organization, December 17, 2009.
g Filed for free agency, October 8, 2010. Signed with San Francisco Giants organization, January 11, 2011.
h Traded to New York Yankees for pitcher George Kontos, April 4, 2012.
i Traded to Pittsburgh Pirates for player to be named later, December 2, 2013. New York Yankees received pitcher Kyle Haynes to complete trade, December 11, 2013.

STUBBS, ANDREW ROBERT (DREW)

Born, Texarkana, Texas, October 4, 1984.
Bats Right. Throws Right. Height, 6 feet, 4 inches. Weight, 205 pounds.

Year	Club	Lea	Pos	G	AB	R	H	2B	3B	HR	RBI	SB	Avg
2006	Billings	Pioneer	OF	56	210	39	53	7	3	6	24	19	.252
2007	Dayton	Midwest	OF	129	497	93	134	29	5	12	43	23	.270
2008	Sarasota	Fla.St.	OF	86	303	49	79	21	4	5	38	27	.261
2008	Louisville	Int.	OF	19	75	14	22	4	2	2	10	3	.293
2008	Chattanooga	Southern	OF	26	92	12	29	8	0	0	9	3	.315
2009	Louisville	Int.	OF	107	411	57	110	25	2	3	39	46	.268
2009	Cincinnati	N.L.	OF	42	180	27	48	5	1	8	17	10	.267
2010	Cincinnati	N.L.	OF	150	514	91	131	19	6	22	77	30	.255
2011	Cincinnati	N.L.	OF	158	604	92	147	22	3	15	44	40	.243
2012	Dayton	Midwest	OF	3	10	0	1	0	0	0	1	0	.100
2012	Cincinnati a-b	N.L.	OF	136	493	75	105	13	2	14	40	30	.213
2013	Cleveland c	A.L.	OF	146	430	59	100	21	2	10	45	17	.233
Major League Totals			5 Yrs.	632	2221	344	531	80	14	69	223	127	.239
	Division Series												
2010	Cincinnati	N.L.	OF	3	9	0	1	0	0	0	0	0	.111
2012	Cincinnati	N.L.	OF	5	19	4	4	1	1	0	1	0	.211
Division Series Totals				8	28	4	5	1	1	0	1	0	.179

a On disabled list from June 15 to June 25, 2012.
b Traded to Cleveland Indians with infielder Didi Gregorius for outfielder Shin-Soo Choo and infielder Jason Donald, December 11, 2012.
c Traded to Colorado Rockies for pitcher Josh Outman, December 18, 2013.

SUZUKI, ICHIRO

Born, Kasugai, Japan, October 22, 1973.
Bats Left. Throws Right. Height, 5 feet, 9 inches. Weight, 170 pounds.

Year	Club	Lea	Pos	G	AB	R	H	2B	3B	HR	RBI	SB	Avg
1992	Orix	Japan Pac.	OF	40	95	9	24	5	0	0	5	3	.253
1993	Orix	Japan Pac.	OF	43	64	4	12	2	0	1	2	0	.188
1994	Orix	Japan Pac.	OF	130	546	111	210	41	5	13	54	29	.385

Year Club	Lea	Pos	G	AB	R	H	2B	3B	HR	RBI	SB	Avg
1995 Orix	Japan Pac.	OF	130	524	104	179	23	4	25	80	49	.342
1996 Orix	Japan Pac.	OF	130	542	104	193	24	4	16	84	35	.356
1997 Orix	Japan Pac.	OF	135	536	94	185	31	4	17	91	39	.345
1998 Orix	Japan Pac.	OF	135	506	79	181	36	3	13	71	11	.358
1999 Orix	Japan Pac.	OF	103	411	80	141	27	2	21	68	12	.343
2000 Orix a	Japan Pac.	OF	105	395	73	153	22	1	12	73	21	.387
2001 Seattle b-c	A.L.	OF	157	*692	127	*242	34	8	8	69	*56	*.350
2002 Seattle	A.L.	OF	157	647	111	208	27	8	8	51	31	.321
2003 Seattle	A.L.	OF	159	679	111	212	29	8	13	62	34	.312
2004 Seattle	A.L.	OF	161	*704	101	*262	24	5	8	60	36	*.372
2005 Seattle	A.L.	OF	*162	679	111	206	21	12	15	68	33	.303
2006 Seattle	A.L.	OF	161	*695	110	*224	20	9	9	49	45	.322
2007 Seattle	A.L.	OF	161	*678	111	*238	22	7	6	68	37	.351
2008 Seattle	A.L.	OF	162	*686	103	*213	20	7	6	42	43	.310
2009 Seattle d	A.L.	OF	146	639	88	*225	31	4	11	46	26	.352
2010 Seattle	A.L.	OF	*162	*680	74	*214	30	3	6	43	42	.315
2011 Seattle	A.L.	OF	*161	*677	80	184	22	3	5	47	40	.272
2012 Seattle-New York e-f	A.L.	OF	*162	629	77	178	28	6	9	55	29	.283
2013 New York	A.L.	OF	150	520	57	136	15	3	7	35	20	.262
Major League Totals		13 Yrs.	2061	8605	1261	2742	323	83	111	695	472	.319
Division Series												
2001 Seattle	A.L.	OF	5	20	4	12	1	0	0	2	1	.600
2012 New York	A.L.	OF	5	23	2	5	2	0	0	3	1	.217
Division Series Totals			10	43	6	17	3	0	0	5	2	.395
Championship Series												
2001 Seattle	A.L.	OF	5	18	3	4	1	0	0	1	2	.222
2012 New York	A.L.	OF	4	17	1	6	0	0	1	2	0	.353
Championship Series Totals			9	35	4	10	1	0	1	3	2	.286

a Signed by Seattle Mariners as free agent, November 18, 2000.
b Selected Rookie of the Year in American League for 2001.
c Selected Most Valuable Player in American League for 2001.
d On disabled list from March 31 to April 15, 2009.
e Traded to New York Yankees with cash for pitcher D.J. Mitchell and pitcher Danny Farquar, July 23, 2012.
f Filed for free agency, November 3, 2012, re-signed with New York Yankees, December 19, 2012.

SUZUKI, KURT KIYOSHI

Born, Wailuku, Hawaii, October 4, 1983.
Bats Right. Throws Right. Height, 6 feet. Weight, 205 pounds.

Year Club	Lea	Pos	G	AB	R	H	2B	3B	HR	RBI	SB	Avg
2004 Vancouver	Northwest	C	46	175	27	52	10	3	3	31	0	.297
2005 Stockton	Calif.	C	114	441	85	122	26	5	12	65	5	.277
2006 Midland	Texas	C-1B	99	376	64	107	26	1	7	55	5	.285
2007 Sacramento	P.C.	C	55	211	32	59	9	0	3	27	0	.280
2007 Oakland	A.L.	C	68	213	27	53	13	0	7	39	0	.249
2008 Oakland	A.L.	C	148	530	54	148	25	1	7	42	2	.279
2009 Oakland	A.L.	C	147	570	74	156	37	1	15	88	8	.274
2010 Sacramento	P.C.	C	3	8	4	3	2	0	1	5	0	.375
2010 Oakland a	A.L.	C	131	495	55	120	18	2	13	71	3	.242
2011 Oakland	A.L.	C	134	460	54	109	26	0	14	44	2	.237
2012 Oakland	A.L.	C	75	262	19	57	15	0	1	18	1	.218
2012 Washington b	N.L.	C	43	146	17	39	5	0	5	25	1	.267
2013 Washington	N.L.	C	79	252	19	56	11	1	3	25	2	.222
2013 Oakland c-d	A.L.	C	15	33	6	10	2	0	2	7	0	.303
Major League Totals		7 Yrs.	840	2961	325	748	152	5	67	359	19	.253
Division Series												
2012 Washington	N.L.	C	5	17	0	4	0	0	0	2	0	.235

a On disabled list from April 24 to May 16, 2010.
b Traded to Washington Nationals with cash for pitcher David Freitas, August 3, 2012.
c Traded to Oakland Athletics with cash for pitcher Dakota Bacus, August 23, 2013.
d Filed for free agency, November 1, 2013. Signed with Minnesota Twins, December 23, 2013.

SWEENEY, RYAN JOSEPH

Born, Cedar Rapids, Iowa, February 20, 1985.
Bats Left. Throws Left. Height, 6 feet, 4 inches. Weight, 225 pounds.

Year Club	Lea	Pos	G	AB	R	H	2B	3B	HR	RBI	SB	Avg
2003 Bristol	Appal.	OF	19	67	11	21	3	0	2	5	3	.313
2003 Great Falls	Pioneer	OF	10	34	0	12	2	0	0	4	0	.353
2004 Winston-Salem	Carolina	OF	134	515	71	146	22	3	7	66	8	.283

Year Club	Lea	Pos	G	AB	R	H	2B	3B	HR	RBI	SB	Avg
2005 Birmingham......	Southern	OF	113	429	64	128	22	3	1	47	6	.298
2006 Charlotte	Int.	OF	118	449	64	133	25	3	13	70	7	.296
2006 Chicago	A.L.	OF	18	35	1	8	0	0	0	5	0	.229
2007 Chicago	A.L.	OF	15	45	5	9	3	0	1	5	0	.200
2007 Charlotte	Int.	OF	105	397	50	107	17	2	10	47	8	.270
2008 Sacramento a..........	P.C.	OF	8	34	5	14	4	0	1	5	0	.412
2008 Athletics...........	Arizona	DH	1	3	0	0	0	0	0	0	0	.000
2008 Oakland b............	A.L.	OF	115	384	53	110	18	2	5	45	9	.286
2009 Oakland c............	A.L.	OF	134	484	68	142	31	3	6	53	6	.293
2010 Oakland d............	A.L.	OF	82	303	41	89	20	2	1	36	1	.294
2011 Oakland e............	A.L.	OF	108	264	34	70	11	3	1	25	1	.265
2012 Portland...........	Eastern	OF	2	7	0	1	0	0	0	0	0	.143
2012 Boston f-g-h..........	A.L.	OF	63	204	22	53	19	2	0	16	0	.260
2013 Cubs..............	Arizona	OF	4	14	4	4	2	0	0	2	0	.286
2013 Kane County.......	Midwest	OF	1	4	0	1	0	0	0	0	0	.250
2013 Iowa..................	P.C.	OF	23	83	12	28	2	2	6	16	1	.337
2013 Chicago i	N.L.	OF	70	192	19	51	13	2	6	19	1	.266
Major League Totals		8 Yrs.	605	1911	243	532	115	14	20	204	18	.278

a Traded to Oakland Athletics with pitcher Gio Gonzalez and pitcher Fautino de los Santos for outfielder Nick Swisher, January 3, 2008.
b On disabled list from May 29 to June 13 and August 13 to August 28, 2008.
c On disabled list from June 3 to June 18, 2009.
d On disabled list from July 12 to November 4, 2010.
e Traded to Boston Red Sox with pitcher Andrew Bailey for outfielder Josh Reddick, infielder Miles Head and pitcher Raul Alcantara, December 28, 2011.
f On disabled list from May 21 to May 28 and June 17 to July 7 and July 31 to November 2, 2012.
g Not offered contract, November 30, 2012, re-signed with Boston Red Sox organization, January 25, 2013.
h Released by Boston Red Sox, March 30, 2013. Signed with Chicago Cubs organization, April 2, 2013.
i On disabled list from June 30 to September 1, 2013.

SWISHER, NICHOLAS THOMPSON (NICK)

Born, Columbus, Ohio, January 25, 1980.
Bats Both. Throws Left. Height, 6 feet. Weight, 215 pounds.

Year Club	Lea	Pos	G	AB	R	H	2B	3B	HR	RBI	SB	Avg
2002 Visalia	California	OF	49	183	22	44	13	2	4	23	3	.240
2002 Vancouver	Northwest	OF	13	44	10	11	3	0	2	12	3	.250
2003 Modesto.........	California	OF-1B	51	189	38	56	14	2	10	43	0	.296
2003 Midland	Texas	OF-1B	76	287	36	66	24	2	5	43	0	.230
2004 Sacramento	P.C.	OF-1B	125	443	109	119	28	2	29	92	3	.269
2004 Oakland	A.L.	OF-1B	20	60	11	15	4	0	2	8	0	.250
2005 Sacramento	P.C.	OF-1B	6	23	4	9	3	0	0	1	0	.391
2005 Oakland a............	A.L.	OF-1B	131	462	66	109	32	1	21	74	0	.236
2006 Oakland	A.L.	1B-OF	157	556	106	141	24	2	35	95	1	.254
2007 Oakland b............	A.L.	OF-1B	150	539	84	141	36	1	22	78	3	.262
2008 Chicago c............	A.L.	OF-1B	153	497	86	109	21	1	24	69	3	.219
2009 New York	A.L.	OF-1B-P	150	498	84	124	35	1	29	82	0	.249
2010 New York	A.L.	OF-1B	150	566	91	163	33	3	29	89	1	.288
2011 New York	A.L.	OF-1B	150	526	81	137	30	0	23	85	2	.260
2012 New York d...........	A.L.	OF-1B	148	537	75	146	36	0	24	93	2	.272
2013 Cleveland	A.L.	1B-OF	145	549	74	135	27	2	22	63	1	.246
Major League Totals		10 Yrs.	1354	4790	758	1220	278	11	231	736	13	.255
Wild Card Playoff												
2013 Cleveland	A.L.	1B	1	4	0	0	0	0	0	0	0	.000
Division Series												
2006 Oakland	A.L.	1B	3	10	3	3	2	0	0	1	0	.300
2008 Chicago	A.L.	OF-1B	3	4	1	1	0	0	0	0	0	.250
2009 New York	A.L.	OF	3	12	0	1	1	0	0	1	0	.083
2010 New York	A.L.	OF	3	12	3	4	2	0	1	1	0	.333
2011 New York	A.L.	OF	5	19	1	4	0	0	1	1	0	.211
2012 New York	A.L.	OF	5	18	0	2	0	0	0	1	0	.111
Division Series Totals			22	75	8	15	5	0	2	5	0	.200
Championship Series												
2006 Oakland	A.L.	1B	4	10	0	1	0	0	0	0	0	.100
2009 New York	A.L.	OF	6	20	2	3	0	0	0	0	0	.150
2010 New York	A.L.	OF-1B	6	22	3	2	1	0	1	1	0	.091
2012 New York	A.L.	OF	3	12	0	3	2	0	0	1	0	.250
Championship Series Totals			19	64	5	9	3	0	1	2	0	.141
World Series Record												
2009 New York	A.L.	OF	5	15	3	2	1	0	1	1	0	.133

a On disabled list from May 2 to May 25, 2005.
b Traded to Chicago White Sox for pitcher Gio Gonzalez, pitcher Fautino de los Santos and outfielder Ryan Sweeney, January 3, 2008.
c Traded to New York Yankees with pitcher Kaneoka Texeira for infielder Wilson Betemit, pitcher Jeff Marquez and pitcher Jhonny Nunez, November 13, 2008.
d Filed for free agency, November 3, 2012. Signed with Cleveland Indians, January 3, 2013.

TABATA, JOSE NICOLAS

Born, El Tigre, Venezuela, August 12, 1988.
Bats Right. Throws Right. Height, 5 feet, 11 inches. Weight, 210 pounds.

Year Club	Lea	Pos	G	AB	R	H	2B	3B	HR	RBI	SB	Avg
2005 Yankees	Gulf Coast	OF	44	156	30	49	5	1	3	25	22	.314
2006 Charleston	So.Atl.	OF	86	319	50	95	22	1	5	51	15	.298
2007 Tampa	Fla.St.	OF	103	411	56	126	16	2	5	54	15	.307
2008 Altoona	Eastern	OF	22	89	16	31	6	2	3	13	8	.348
2008 Trenton	Eastern	OF	79	294	40	73	9	0	3	36	10	.248
2008 Pirates a	Gulf Coast	OF	4	11	4	5	1	0	2	7	0	.455
2009 Altoona	Eastern	OF	61	228	31	69	15	1	2	25	7	.303
2009 Indianapolis	Int.	OF	32	134	21	37	7	1	3	10	4	.276
2010 Indianapolis	Int.	OF	53	224	42	69	13	2	3	19	25	.308
2010 Pittsburgh	N.L.	OF	102	405	61	121	21	4	4	35	19	.299
2011 Bradenton	Fla.St.	OF	4	8	1	1	1	0	0	1	0	.125
2011 Indianapolis	Int.	OF	9	33	6	11	6	0	0	2	0	.333
2011 Pittsburgh b	N.L.	OF	91	334	53	89	18	1	4	21	16	.266
2012 Indianapolis	Int.	OF	41	158	21	47	9	0	0	15	5	.297
2012 Pittsburgh	N.L.	OF	103	333	43	81	20	3	3	16	8	.243
2013 Indianapolis	Int.	OF	9	28	1	5	1	0	0	0	1	.179
2013 Pittsburgh c	N.L.	OF	106	308	35	87	17	5	6	33	3	.282
Major League Totals		4 Yrs.	402	1380	192	378	76	13	17	105	46	.274
Division Series												
2013 Pittsburgh	N.L.	OF	4	4	0	0	0	0	0	0	0	.000

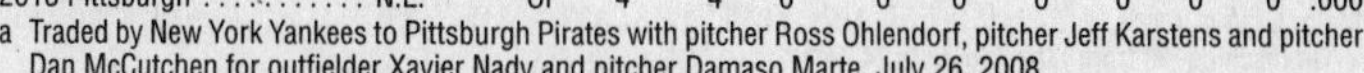

a Traded by New York Yankees to Pittsburgh Pirates with pitcher Ross Ohlendorf, pitcher Jeff Karstens and pitcher Dan McCutchen for outfielder Xavier Nady and pitcher Damaso Marte, July 26, 2008.
b On disabled list from June 27 to August 16, 2011.
c On disabled list from May 25 to July 3, 2013.

TEIXEIRA, MARK CHARLES

Born, Annapolis, Maryland, April 11, 1980.
Bats Both. Throws Right. Height, 6 feet, 3 inches. Weight, 220 pounds.

Year Club	Lea	Pos	G	AB	R	H	2B	3B	HR	RBI	SB	Avg
2002 Charlotte	Fla.St.	3B	38	150	32	48	10	2	9	41	2	.320
2002 Tulsa	Texas	3B	48	171	31	54	11	3	10	28	3	.316
2003 Texas	A.L.	1B-OF-3B	146	529	66	137	29	5	26	84	1	.259
2004 Frisco	Texas	1B	1	3	0	0	0	0	0	0	0	.000
2004 Texas a	A.L.	1B-OF	145	545	101	153	34	2	38	112	4	.281
2005 Texas	A.L.	1B	*162	644	112	194	41	3	43	144	4	.301
2006 Texas	A.L.	1B	*162	628	99	177	45	1	33	110	2	.282
2007 Frisco	Texas	1B	1	2	0	0	0	0	0	0	0	.000
2007 Texas	A.L.	1B	78	286	48	85	24	1	13	49	0	.297
2007 Atlanta b-c	N.L.	1B	54	208	38	66	9	1	17	56	0	.317
2008 Atlanta	N.L.	1B	103	381	63	108	27	0	20	78	0	.283
2008 Los Angeles d-e	A.L.	1B	54	193	39	69	14	0	13	43	2	.358
2009 New York	A.L.	1B	156	609	103	178	43	3	*39	*122	2	.292
2010 New York	A.L.	1B	158	601	*113	154	36	0	33	108	0	.256
2011 New York	A.L.	1B	156	589	90	146	26	1	39	111	4	.248
2012 New York	A.L.	1B	123	451	66	113	27	1	24	84	2	.251
2013 Trenton	Eastern	1B	2	5	0	1	0	0	0	0	0	.200
2013 New York f	A.L.	1B	15	53	5	8	1	0	3	12	0	.151
Major League Totals		11 Yrs.	1512	5717	943	1588	356	18	341	1113	21	.278
Division Series												
2008 Los Angeles	A.L.	1B	4	15	4	7	0	0	0	1	0	.467
2009 New York	A.L.	1B	3	12	3	2	0	0	1	1	0	.167
2010 New York	A.L.	1B	3	13	2	4	1	0	1	3	0	.308
2011 New York	A.L.	1B	5	18	2	3	2	0	0	1	0	.167
2012 New York	A.L.	1B	5	17	1	6	0	0	0	1	1	.353
Division Series Totals			20	75	12	22	3	0	2	7	1	.293
Championship Series												
2009 New York	A.L.	1B	6	27	2	6	1	0	0	4	0	.222
2010 New York	A.L.	1B	4	14	1	0	0	0	0	0	0	.000

Year	Club	Lea	Pos	G	AB	R	H	2B	3B	HR	RBI	SB	Avg
2012	New York	A.L.	1B	4	15	1	3	1	0	0	0	0	.200
Championship Series Totals				14	56	4	9	2	0	0	4	0	.161
	World Series Record												
2009	New York	A.L.	1B	6	22	5	3	1	0	1	3	0	.136

a On disabled list from April 13 to April 29, 2004.
b On disabled list from June 9 to July 13, 2007.
c Traded to Atlanta Braves with pitcher Ron Mahay for catcher Jarrod Saltalamacchia, infielder Elvis Andrus, pitcher Neftali Feliz, pitcher Matt Harrison and pitcher Beau James, July 31, 2007.
d Traded to Los Angeles Angels for infielder Casey Kotchman and pitcher Steve Marek, July 29, 2008.
e Filed for free agency, October 30, 2008. Signed with New York Yankees, January 6, 2009.
f On disabled list from March 22 to May 31 and June 16 to November 4, 2013.

TEJADA, RUBEN DARIO

Born, Veraguas, Panama, September 1, 1989.
Bats Right. Throws Right. Height, 5 feet, 11 inches. Weight, 160 pounds.

Year	Club	Lea	Pos	G	AB	R	H	2B	3B	HR	RBI	SB	Avg
2007	Mets	Gulf Coast	SS-2B	35	120	13	34	4	3	0	16	2	.283
2008	St. Lucie	Fla.St.	SS	131	497	55	114	19	4	2	37	8	.229
2009	Binghamton	Eastern	SS-2B	134	488	59	141	24	3	5	46	19	.289
2010	Buffalo	Int.	SS-2B	65	218	25	61	11	0	1	16	1	.280
2010	New York	N.L.	2B-SS	78	216	28	46	12	0	1	15	2	.213
2011	Buffalo	Int.	SS-2B	54	207	26	51	7	3	3	21	4	.246
2011	New York	N.L.	2B-SS	96	328	31	93	15	1	0	36	5	.284
2012	St. Lucie	Fla.St.	SS	2	9	1	1	1	0	0	0	0	.111
2012	Buffalo	Int.	SS	6	20	3	4	1	0	0	2	0	.200
2012	New York a	N.L.	SS	114	464	53	134	26	0	1	25	4	.289
2013	Mets	Gulf Coast	SS	3	9	1	3	1	0	0	2	0	.333
2013	Las Vegas	P.C.	SS-2B	60	240	38	69	14	1	2	24	1	.287
2013	New York b	N.L.	SS	57	208	20	42	12	0	0	10	2	.202
Major League Totals			4 Yrs.	345	1216	132	315	65	1	2	86	13	.259

a On disabled list from May 7 to June 24, 2012.
b On disabled list from May 30 to July 6, 2013.

TERDOSLAVICH, JOSEPH T. (JOEY)

Born, Sarasota, Florida, September 9, 1988.
Bats Both. Throws Right. Height, 6 feet. Weight, 200 pounds.

Year	Club	Lea	Pos	G	AB	R	H	2B	3B	HR	RBI	SB	Avg
2010	Danville	Appal.	1B-3B-OF	49	189	27	56	10	2	2	24	3	.296
2010	Rome	So.Atl.	3B-1B	21	79	7	25	9	0	0	10	0	.316
2011	Lynchburg	Carolina	1B-3B	131	483	72	138	52	2	20	82	2	.286
2012	Mississippi	Southern	1B-3B	78	298	43	94	24	5	5	51	4	.315
2012	Gwinnett	Int.	3B	53	194	19	35	4	0	4	20	3	.180
2013	Gwinnett	Int.	OF-1B	85	321	48	102	24	1	18	58	3	.318
2013	Atlanta	N.L.	OF-1B	55	79	11	17	4	0	0	4	1	.215

TORREALBA, YORVIT ADOLFO

Born, Caracas, Venezuela, July 19, 1978.
Bats Right. Throws Right. Height, 5 feet, 11 inches. Weight, 200 pounds.

Year	Club	Lea	Pos	G	AB	R	H	2B	3B	HR	RBI	SB	Avg
1995	Bellingham	Northwest	C	26	71	2	11	3	0	0	8	0	.155
1996	San Jose	Calif.	C	2	5	0	0	0	0	0	0	0	.000
1996	Burlington	Midwest	C	1	4	0	0	0	0	0	0	0	.000
1996	Bellingham	Northwest	C	48	150	23	40	4	0	1	10	4	.267
1997	Bakersfield	Calif.	C	119	446	52	122	15	3	4	40	4	.274
1998	San Jose	Calif.	C	21	70	10	20	2	0	0	10	2	.286
1998	Shreveport	Texas	C	59	196	18	46	7	0	0	13	0	.235
1998	Fresno	P.C.	C	4	11	1	2	1	0	0	1	0	.182
1999	San Jose	Calif.	C	19	73	10	23	3	0	2	14	0	.315
1999	Shreveport	Texas	C	65	217	25	53	10	1	4	19	0	.244
1999	Fresno	P.C.	C	17	63	9	16	2	0	2	10	0	.254
2000	Shreveport	Texas	C	108	398	50	114	21	1	4	32	2	.286
2001	Fresno	P.C.	C	115	394	56	108	23	3	8	36	2	.274
2001	San Francisco	N.L.	C	3	4	0	2	0	1	0	2	0	.500
2002	San Francisco	N.L.	C	53	136	17	38	10	0	2	14	0	.279
2003	San Francisco	N.L.	C-OF	66	200	22	52	10	2	4	29	1	.260
2004	San Francisco	N.L.	C	64	172	19	39	7	3	6	23	2	.227

Year Club	Lea	Pos	G	AB	R	H	2B	3B	HR	RBI	SB	Avg
2005 San Francisco	N.L.	C	34	93	18	21	8	0	1	7	1	.226
2005 Seattle a-b	A.L.	C	42	108	14	26	4	0	2	8	0	.241
2006 Colorado Springs	P.C.	C	10	36	0	6	2	0	0	2	0	.167
2006 Colorado c	N.L.	C	65	223	23	55	16	3	7	43	4	.247
2007 Colorado d	N.L.	C	113	396	47	101	22	1	8	47	2	.255
2008 Colorado e	N.L.	C	70	236	19	58	17	0	6	31	0	.246
2009 Colorado Springs	P.C.	C-1B	4	15	1	4	0	0	0	1	0	.267
2009 Colorado f	N.L.	C	64	213	27	62	11	1	2	31	1	.291
2010 San Diego g	N.L.	C	95	325	31	88	14	0	7	37	7	.271
2011 Texas	A.L.	C	113	396	40	108	27	1	7	37	0	.273
2012 New Hampshire h	Eastern	C	4	12	1	5	0	0	0	1	1	.417
2012 Texas-Toronto	A.L.	C-1B	59	189	19	44	8	0	4	14	1	.233
2012 Milwaukee i-j	N.L.	C	5	5	0	0	0	0	0	0	0	.000
2013 Colorado k-l	N.L.	C-1B	61	179	10	43	8	0	0	16	0	.240
Major League Totals		13 Yrs.	907	2875	306	737	162	12	56	339	19	.256
Division Series												
2003 San Francisco	N.L.	C	2	3	0	0	0	0	0	1	0	.000
2007 Colorado	N.L.	C	3	10	3	5	1	0	0	3	0	.500
2009 Colorado	N.L.	C	4	14	1	5	2	0	1	4	0	.357
2011 Texas	A.L.	DH	1	3	0	0	0	0	0	0	0	.000
Division Series Totals			10	30	4	10	3	0	1	8	0	.333
Championship Series												
2007 Colorado	N.L.	C	4	15	2	3	1	0	1	4	0	.200
2011 Texas	A.L.	C-DH	3	9	1	4	1	0	0	0	0	.444
Championship Series Totals			7	24	3	7	2	0	1	4	0	.292
World Series Record												
2007 Colorado	N.L.	C	4	14	0	2	0	0	0	1	0	.143
2011 Texas	A.L.	C	3	5	0	2	0	0	0	0	0	.400
World Series Totals			7	19	0	4	0	0	0	1	0	.211

a Traded to Seattle Mariners with pitcher Jesse Foppert for outfielder Randy Winn, July 31, 2005.
b Traded to Colorado Rockies for player to be named later, December 7, 2005. Seattle Mariners received pitcher Marcos Carvajal to complete trade, December 8, 2005.
c On disabled list from March 24 to June 2 and September 10 to November 1, 2006.
d Filed for free agency, October 31, 2007, re-signed with Colorado Rockies, November 29, 2007.
e On disabled list from August 26 to October 1, 2008.
f Filed for free agency, November 6, 2009. Signed with San Diego Padres, February 9, 2010.
g Filed for free agency, November 1, 2010. Signed with Texas Rangers, December 19, 2010.
h Released by Texas Rangers, August 8, 2012. Signed with Toronto Blue Jays organization, August 15, 2012.
i Sold to Milwaukee Brewers, September 21, 2012.
j Filed for free agency, October 17, 2012. Signed with Colorado Rockies organization, January 24, 2013.
k On disabled list from August 19 to August 27, 2013.
l Filed for free agency, October 31, 2013.

TORRES, ANDRES VUNGO

Born, Aguadilla, Puerto Rico, January 26, 1978.
Bats Both. Throws Right. Height, 5 feet, 10 inches. Weight, 190 pounds.

Year Club	Lea	Pos	G	AB	R	H	2B	3B	HR	RBI	SB	Avg
1998 Jamestown	N.Y.-Penn.	OF	48	192	28	45	2	6	1	21	13	.234
1999 West Michigan	Midwest	OF	117	407	72	96	20	5	2	34	39	.236
2000 Lakeland	Fla.St.	OF	108	398	82	118	11	11	3	33	65	.296
2000 Jacksonville	Southern	OF	14	54	3	8	0	0	0	0	2	.148
2001 Erie	Eastern	OF	64	252	54	74	16	3	1	23	19	.294
2002 Toledo	Int.	OF	115	462	80	123	17	8	4	42	42	.266
2002 Detroit	A.L.	OF	19	70	7	14	1	1	0	3	2	.200
2003 Toledo	Int.	OF	70	271	36	69	13	3	2	16	27	.255
2003 Detroit	A.L.	OF	59	168	23	37	4	3	1	9	5	.220
2004 Detroit	A.L.	OF	3	0	1	0	0	0	0	0	1	.000
2004 Charlotte	Int.	OF	87	322	49	95	11	4	8	26	23	.295
2004 Bristol a-b	Appal.	OF	6	22	8	8	0	0	1	2	5	.364
2005 Oklahoma	P.C.	OF	15	63	12	19	3	1	0	1	6	.302
2005 Texas c	A.L.	OF	8	19	2	3	1	0	0	1	1	.158
2006 Rochester	Int.	OF	116	348	46	82	17	9	2	30	19	.236
2007 Erie	Eastern	OF	85	305	53	89	15	11	6	35	17	.292
2007 Toledo d-e	Int.	OF	42	168	23	49	6	9	4	17	5	.292
2008 Iowa f	P.C.	OF	118	409	91	125	27	10	11	51	29	.306
2009 Azl Giants	Arizona	OF	3	6	1	2	1	0	0	1	1	.333
2009 San Jose	Calif.	OF	3	10	0	1	1	0	0	0	0	.100
2009 Fresno	P.C.	OF	11	43	7	13	1	1	1	2	1	.302

Year	Club	Lea	Pos	G	AB	R	H	2B	3B	HR	RBI	SB	Avg
2009	San Francisco g	N.L.	OF	75	152	30	41	6	8	6	23	6	.270
2010	San Francisco	N.L.	OF	139	507	84	136	43	8	16	63	26	.268
2011	Fresno	P.C.	OF	13	55	10	15	2	2	4	11	1	.273
2011	San Francisco h-i	N.L.	OF	112	348	50	77	24	1	4	19	19	.221
2012	St. Lucie	Fla.St.	OF	3	12	3	4	1	0	0	1	2	.333
2012	Buffalo	Int.	OF	2	7	1	1	0	0	0	0	1	.143
2012	New York j-k	N.L.	OF	132	374	47	86	17	7	3	35	13	.230
2013	San Francisco l-m	N.L.	OF	103	272	33	68	17	1	2	21	4	.250
Major League Totals			9 Yrs.	650	1910	277	462	113	29	32	174	77	.242
	Division Series												
2010	San Francisco	N.L.	OF	4	16	0	2	0	0	0	0	1	.125
	Championship Series												
2010	San Francisco	N.L.	OF	6	20	2	7	0	0	0	0	0	.350
	World Series Record												
2010	San Francisco	N.L.	OF	5	22	4	7	4	0	1	3	1	.318

a Filed for free agency, April 22, 2004. Signed with Chicago White Sox organization, April 26, 2004.
b Filed for free agency, October 15, 2004. Signed with Texas Rangers organization, November 19, 2004.
c Filed for free agency, October 6, 2005. Signed with Minnesota Twins organization, December 20, 2005.
d Filed for free agency, October 15, 2006. Signed with Detroit Tigers organization, March 2, 2007.
e Filed for free agency, October 29, 2007. Signed with Chicago Cubs organization, November 20, 2007.
f Filed for free agency, November 3, 2008. Signed with San Francisco Giants organization, January 9, 2009.
g On disabled list from April 28 to May 26 July 31 to September 1, 2009.
h On disabled list from April 10 to May 10 and August 13 to August 28, 2011.
i Traded to New York Mets with pitcher Ramon Ramirez for outfielder Angel Pagan, December 7, 2011.
j On disabled list from April 6 to April 30, 2012.
k Not offered contract, November 30, 2012. Signed with San Francisco Giants, December 13, 2012.
l On disabled list from August 22 to November 2, 2013.
m Filed for free agency, November 2, 2013.

TROUT, MICHAEL NELSON (MIKE)

Born, Vineland, New Jersey, August 7, 1991.
Bats Right. Throws Right. Height, 6 feet, 1 inch. Weight, 200 pounds.

Year	Club	Lea	Pos	G	AB	R	H	2B	3B	HR	RBI	SB	Avg
2009	Angels	Arizona	OF	39	164	29	59	7	7	1	25	13	.360
2009	Cedar Rapids	Midwest	OF	5	15	1	4	0	0	0	0	0	.267
2010	Rancho Cucamonga	Calif.	OF	50	196	30	60	9	2	4	19	11	.306
2010	Cedar Rapids	Midwest	OF	81	312	76	113	19	7	6	39	45	.362
2011	Arkansas	Texas	OF	91	353	82	115	18	13	11	38	33	.326
2011	Los Angeles	A.L.	OF	40	123	20	27	6	0	5	16	4	.220
2012	Salt Lake	P.C.	OF	20	77	21	31	4	5	1	13	6	.403
2012	Los Angeles a	A.L.	OF	139	559	*129	182	27	8	30	83	*49	.326
2013	Los Angeles	A.L.	OF	157	589	*109	190	39	9	27	97	33	.323
Major League Totals			3 Yrs.	336	1271	258	399	72	17	62	196	86	.314

a Selected Rookie of the Year in American League for 2012.

TRUMBO, MARK DANIEL

Born, Anaheim, California, January 16, 1986.
Bats Right. Throws Right. Height, 6 feet, 4 inches. Weight, 220 pounds.

Year	Club	Lea	Pos	G	AB	R	H	2B	3B	HR	RBI	SB	Avg
2005	Orem	Pioneer	1B	71	299	45	82	23	1	10	45	2	.274
2006	Cedar Rapids	Midwest	1B	118	428	43	94	19	0	13	59	5	.220
2007	Cedar Rapids	Midwest	1B	128	471	57	128	27	2	14	76	10	.272
2008	Rancho Cucamonga	Calif.	1B	103	407	70	115	28	2	26	68	7	.283
2008	Arkansas	Texas	1B	32	123	13	34	7	1	6	25	1	.276
2009	Arkansas	Texas	1B-OF	137	533	54	155	35	3	15	88	6	.291
2010	Salt Lake	P.C.	1B-OF	139	532	103	160	29	5	36	122	3	.301
2010	Los Angeles	A.L.	1B-OF	8	15	2	1	0	0	0	2	0	.067
2011	Los Angeles	A.L.	1B-OF	149	539	65	137	31	1	29	87	9	.254
2012	Los Angeles	A.L.	OF-1B-3B	144	544	66	146	19	3	32	95	4	.268
2013	Los Angeles a	A.L.	1B-OF-3B	159	620	85	145	30	2	34	100	5	.234
Major League Totals			4 Yrs.	460	1718	218	429	80	6	95	284	18	.250

a Traded to Arizona Diamondbacks with player to be named later for pitcher Tyler Skaggs and pitcher Hector Santiago, December 10, 2013. Arizona Diamondbacks received pitcher A.J. Schlugel to complete trade, December 13, 2013.

TUIASOSOPO, MATTHEW P. (MATT)

Born, Bellevue, Washington, May 10, 1986.
Bats Right. Throws Right. Height, 6 feet, 2 inches. Weight, 225 pounds.

Year	Club	Lea	Pos	G	AB	R	H	2B	3B	HR	RBI	SB	Avg
2004	Mariners	Arizona	SS	20	68	18	28	5	2	4	12	1	.412
2004	Everett	Northwest	SS	29	101	18	25	6	1	2	14	4	.248
2005	Wisconsin	Midwest	SS-3B	107	409	72	113	21	3	6	45	8	.276
2006	Inland Empire	Calif.	SS-3B	59	232	31	71	14	0	1	34	5	.306
2006	San Antonio	Texas	3B	62	216	16	40	4	0	1	10	2	.185
2007	West Tenn	Southern	3B	129	446	74	116	27	5	9	57	4	.260
2008	Tacoma	P.C.	3B	111	437	87	123	32	2	13	73	4	.281
2008	Seattle	A.L.	3B	14	44	1	7	2	1	0	2	0	.159
2009	Mariners	Arizona	3B	9	27	9	11	0	0	1	3	0	.407
2009	Tacoma	P.C.	3B-2B	59	226	43	59	15	0	11	35	3	.261
2009	Seattle	A.L.	2B	7	22	2	5	1	0	1	2	0	.227
2010	Tacoma	P.C.	3B-OF-2B-SS	38	143	26	36	6	0	5	21	2	.252
2010	Seattle	A.L.	OF-3B-1B-SS	50	127	12	22	5	0	4	11	0	.173
2011	Tacoma	P.C.	1B-OF-2B-3B	116	439	73	99	20	6	14	77	11	.226
2012	Buffalo a-b	Int.	3B-OF-1B-2B	131	418	47	101	14	0	12	57	3	.242
2013	Toledo	Int.	OF	2	5	3	2	1	0	0	0	0	.400
2013	Detroit c-d	A.L.	OF-1B-3B	81	164	26	40	7	0	7	30	0	.244
Major League Totals			4 Yrs.	152	357	41	74	15	1	12	45	0	.207

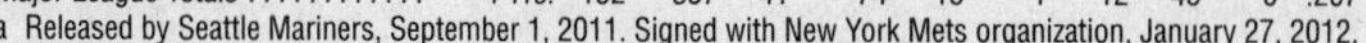

a Released by Seattle Mariners, September 1, 2011. Signed with New York Mets organization, January 27, 2012.
b Filed for free agency, November 3, 2012. Signed with Detroit Tigers organization, November 26, 2012.
c On disabled list from June 20 to July 5, 2013.
d Claimed on waivers by Arizona Diamondbacks, November 1, 2013.

TULOWITZKI, TROY TREVER

Born, Santa Clara, California, October 10, 1984.
Bats Right. Throws Right. Height, 6 feet, 3 inches. Weight, 205 pounds.

Year	Club	Lea	Pos	G	AB	R	H	2B	3B	HR	RBI	SB	Avg
2005	Modesto	Calif.	SS	22	94	17	25	6	0	4	14	1	.266
2006	Tulsa	Texas	SS	104	423	75	123	34	2	13	61	6	.291
2006	Colorado	N.L.	SS	25	96	15	23	2	0	1	6	3	.240
2007	Colorado	N.L.	SS	155	609	104	177	33	5	24	99	7	.291
2008	Modesto	Calif.	SS	5	12	3	4	3	0	0	1	0	.333
2008	Tulsa	Texas	SS	5	21	5	7	0	0	2	3	0	.333
2008	Colorado Springs	P.C.	SS	2	7	2	3	1	0	0	1	1	.429
2008	Colorado a	N.L.	SS	101	377	48	99	24	2	8	46	1	.263
2009	Colorado	N.L.	SS	151	543	101	161	25	9	32	92	20	.297
2010	Tulsa	Texas	SS	2	7	1	1	1	0	0	1	0	.143
2010	Colorado Springs	P.C.	SS	2	4	1	1	0	0	0	0	0	.250
2010	Colorado b	N.L.	SS	122	470	89	148	32	3	27	95	11	.315
2011	Colorado	N.L.	SS	143	537	81	162	36	2	30	105	9	.302
2012	Tulsa	Texas	SS	3	10	1	3	1	0	1	2	0	.300
2012	Colorado Springs	P.C.	SS	6	17	2	6	1	0	2	4	0	.353
2012	Colorado c	N.L.	SS	47	181	33	52	8	2	8	27	2	.287
2013	Colorado Springs	P.C.	SS	2	5	2	4	0	0	0	0	0	.800
2013	Colorado d	N.L.	SS	126	446	72	139	27	0	25	82	1	.312
Major League Totals			8 Yrs.	870	3259	543	961	187	23	155	552	54	.295
Division Series													
2007	Colorado	N.L.	SS	3	12	1	2	1	0	1	2	0	.167
2009	Colorado	N.L.	SS	4	16	0	4	2	0	0	3	0	.250
Division Series Totals				7	28	1	6	3	0	1	5	0	.214
Championship Series													
2007	Colorado	N.L.	SS	4	16	1	3	0	0	0	0	0	.188
World Series Record													
2007	Colorado	N.L.	SS	4	13	1	3	2	0	0	1	0	.231

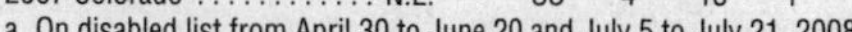

a On disabled list from April 30 to June 20 and July 5 to July 21, 2008.
b On disabled list from June 18 to July 27, 2010.
c On disabled list from May 30 to October 5, 2012.
d On disabled list from June 14 to July 11, 2013.

TURNER, JUSTIN MATTHEW

Born, Long Beach, California, November 23, 1984.
Bats Right. Throws Right. Height, 5 feet, 11 inches. Weight, 210 pounds.

Year	Club	Lea	Pos	G	AB	R	H	2B	3B	HR	RBI	SB	Avg
2006	Billings	Pioneer	2B-OF-3B-SS	60	231	53	78	16	3	6	41	12	.338
2007	Dayton	Midwest	2B-SS-3B	117	466	70	145	25	4	10	59	12	.311
2007	Sarasota	Fla.St.	2B	6	20	2	4	0	0	0	0	0	.200
2008	Sarasota	Fla.St.	2B	33	136	23	43	8	1	0	11	3	.316
2008	Chattanooga a	Southern	2B-3B	78	280	45	81	14	1	8	42	2	.289
2009	Norfolk	Int.	2B-3B-SS	108	387	54	116	28	0	2	43	9	.300
2009	Baltimore	A.L.	3B-2B	12	18	2	3	0	0	0	3	0	.167
2010	Baltimore	A.L.	2B-SS	5	9	0	0	0	0	0	0	0	.000
2010	Norfolk	Int.	2B-3B-SS	23	84	11	21	8	0	1	8	2	.250
2010	New York	N.L.	2B-3B	4	8	1	1	1	0	0	0	0	.125
2010	Buffalo b	Int.	2B-SS-3B	78	312	58	104	22	1	11	35	5	.333
2011	Buffalo	Int.	2B-3B	10	40	6	12	3	2	0	2	0	.300
2011	New York	N.L.	2B-3B-SS	117	435	49	113	30	0	4	51	7	.260
2012	Buffalo	Int.	2B-SS	2	8	0	2	0	0	0	0	0	.250
2012	New York c	N.L.	2B-1B-3B-SS	94	171	20	46	13	1	2	19	1	.269
2013	Mets	Gulf Coast	DH	1	4	0	0	0	0	0	0	0	.000
2013	Brooklyn	N.Y.-Penn.	SS-2B	3	10	2	3	1	0	0	0	0	.300
2013	St. Lucie	Fla.St.	2B	1	1	0	0	0	0	0	0	0	.000
2013	Binghamton	Eastern	2B-SS	4	15	5	6	2	0	0	1	0	.400
2013	New York d-e	N.L.	3B-SS-1B-2B	86	200	12	56	13	1	2	16	0	.280
Major League Totals			5 Yrs.	318	841	84	219	57	2	8	89	8	.260

a Traded by Cincinnati Reds to Baltimore Orioles with outfielder Ryan Freel and infielder Brandon Waring for catcher Ramon Hernandez and cash, December 9, 2008.
b Claimed on waivers by New York Mets, May 25, 2010.
c On disabled list from May 29 to June 16, 2012.
d On disabled list from June 17 to July 22, 2013.
e Not offered contract, December 2, 2013.

UGGLA, DANIEL COOLEY (DAN)

Born, Louisville, Kentucky, March 11, 1980.
Bats Right. Throws Right. Height, 5 feet, 11 inches. Weight, 200 pounds.

Year	Club	Lea	Pos	G	AB	R	H	2B	3B	HR	RBI	SB	Avg
2001	Yakima	Northwest	2B	72	278	39	77	21	0	5	40	8	.277
2002	Lancaster	Calif.	2B-3B	54	184	21	42	7	2	3	16	3	.228
2002	South Bend	Midwest	3B-2B	53	171	16	34	5	1	2	10	0	.199
2003	Lancaster	Calif.	3B-2B	134	534	104	155	31	7	23	90	24	.290
2004	Lancaster	Calif.	2B-3B-SS-1B	37	140	29	47	13	3	6	38	2	.336
2004	El Paso	Texas	3B-OF-2B	83	295	29	76	12	2	4	30	10	.258
2005	Tennessee a	Southern	2B-3B-1B-SS	135	498	88	148	33	3	21	87	15	.297
2006	Florida	N.L.	2B	154	611	105	172	26	7	27	90	6	.282
2007	Florida	N.L.	2B	159	632	113	155	49	3	31	88	2	.245
2008	Florida	N.L.	2B	146	531	97	138	37	1	32	92	5	.260
2009	Florida	N.L.	2B	158	564	84	137	27	1	31	90	2	.243
2010	Florida b	N.L.	2B	159	589	100	169	31	0	33	105	4	.287
2011	Atlanta	N.L.	2B	161	600	88	140	22	1	36	82	1	.233
2012	Atlanta	N.L.	2B	154	523	86	115	29	0	19	78	4	.220
2013	Gwinnett	Int.	2B	2	7	1	2	0	0	1	1	0	.286
2013	Atlanta c	N.L.	2B	136	448	60	80	10	3	22	55	2	.179
Major League Totals			8 Yrs.	1227	4498	733	1106	231	16	231	680	26	.246
	Wild Card Playoff												
2012	Atlanta	N.L.	2B	1	4	1	0	0	0	0	0	0	.000

a Selected by Florida Marlins from Arizona Diamondbacks in Rule V draft, December 8, 2005.
b Traded to Atlanta Braves for infielder Omar Infante and pitcher Michael Dunn, November 16, 2010.
c On disabled list from August 13 to August 28, 2013.

UPTON, JUSTIN IRVIN

Born, Norfolk, Virginia, August 25, 1987.
Bats Right. Throws Right. Height, 6 feet, 3 inches. Weight, 205 pounds.

Year	Club	Lea	Pos	G	AB	R	H	2B	3B	HR	RBI	SB	Avg
2006	South Bend	Midwest	OF	113	438	71	115	28	1	12	66	15	.263
2007	Visalia	Calif.	OF	32	126	27	43	6	2	5	17	9	.341
2007	Mobile	Southern	OF	71	259	48	80	17	4	13	53	10	.309
2007	Arizona	N.L.	OF	43	140	17	31	8	3	2	11	2	.221
2008	Tucson	P.C.	OF	15	61	13	17	3	1	3	10	2	.279
2008	Arizona a	N.L.	OF	108	356	52	89	19	6	15	42	1	.250

Year	Club	Lea	Pos	G	AB	R	H	2B	3B	HR	RBI	SB	Avg
2009	Visalia	Calif.	OF	2	8	1	2	0	0	1	6	1	.250
2009	Arizona b	N.L.	OF	138	526	84	158	30	7	26	86	20	.300
2010	Arizona	N.L.	OF	133	495	73	135	27	3	17	69	18	.273
2011	Arizona	N.L.	OF	159	592	105	171	39	5	31	88	21	.289
2012	Arizona	N.L.	OF	150	554	107	155	24	4	17	67	18	.280
2013	Atlanta c	N.L.	OF	149	558	94	147	27	2	27	70	8	.263
Major League Totals			7 Yrs.	880	3221	532	886	174	30	135	433	88	.275
Division Series													
2007	Arizona	N.L.	OF	2	5	2	3	0	0	0	1	1	.600
2011	Arizona	N.L.	OF	5	20	3	4	0	0	2	3	0	.200
2013	Atlanta	N.L.	OF	4	14	2	2	1	0	0	0	0	.143
Division Series Totals				11	39	7	9	1	0	2	4	1	.231
Championship Series													
2007	Arizona	N.L.	OF	4	9	0	2	1	1	0	0	0	.222

a On disabled list from July 9 to August 29, 2008.
b On disabled list from August 6 to August 26, 2009.
c Traded to Atlanta Braves with infielder Chris Johnson for outfielder Martin Prado, pitcher Randall Delgado, pitcher Zeke Spruill, infielder Nick Ahmed and infielder Brandon Drury, January 24, 2013.

UPTON, MELVIN EMANUEL (B.J.)

Born, Norfolk, Virginia, August 21, 1984.
Bats Right. Throws Right. Height, 6 feet, 3 inches. Weight, 180 pounds.

Year	Club	Lea	Pos	G	AB	R	H	2B	3B	HR	RBI	SB	Avg
2003	Charleston	So.Atl.	SS	101	384	70	116	22	6	7	46	38	.302
2003	Orlando	Southern	SS	29	105	14	29	8	0	1	16	2	.276
2004	Montgomery	Southern	SS	29	104	21	34	7	1	2	15	3	.327
2004	Durham	Int.	SS	69	264	65	82	17	1	12	36	17	.311
2004	Tampa Bay	A.L.	SS-3B-OF	45	159	19	41	8	2	4	12	4	.258
2005	Durham	Int.	SS	139	545	98	165	36	6	18	74	44	.303
2006	Durham	Int.	SS-3B	106	398	72	107	18	4	8	41	46	.269
2006	Tampa Bay	A.L.	3B	50	175	20	43	5	0	1	10	11	.246
2007	Vero Beach	Fla.St.	2B-OF	7	17	4	4	0	0	1	3	0	.235
2007	Durham	Int.	2B	2	7	1	3	0	0	1	1	0	.429
2007	Tampa Bay a	A.L.	OF-2B	129	474	86	142	25	1	24	82	22	.300
2008	Tampa Bay	A.L.	OF	145	531	85	145	37	2	9	67	44	.273
2009	Charlotte	Fla.St.	OF	3	9	1	4	0	0	0	2	4	.444
2009	Tampa Bay b	A.L.	OF	144	560	79	135	33	4	11	55	42	.241
2010	Tampa Bay	A.L.	OF	154	536	89	127	38	4	18	62	42	.237
2011	Tampa Bay	A.L.	OF	153	560	82	136	27	4	23	81	36	.243
2012	Charlotte	Fla.St.	OF	4	11	1	1	0	0	0	1	2	.091
2012	Montgomery	Southern	OF	3	10	1	2	0	0	0	1	0	.200
2012	Tampa Bay c-d	A.L.	OF	146	573	79	141	29	3	28	78	31	.246
2013	Gwinnett	Int.	OF	3	12	3	4	3	0	0	2	0	.333
2013	Atlanta e	N.L.	OF	126	391	30	72	14	0	9	26	12	.184
Major League Totals			9 Yrs.	1092	3959	569	982	216	20	127	473	244	.248
Division Series													
2008	Tampa Bay	A.L.	OF	4	18	5	5	0	1	3	4	0	.278
2010	Tampa Bay	A.L.	OF	5	21	0	4	2	0	0	2	2	.190
2011	Tampa Bay	A.L.	OF	4	14	3	4	3	0	0	0	1	.286
2013	Atlanta	N.L.	OF	3	3	1	0	0	0	0	0	0	.000
Division Series Totals				16	56	9	13	5	1	3	6	3	.232
Championship Series													
2008	Tampa Bay	A.L.	OF	7	28	8	9	1	0	4	11	2	.321
World Series Record													
2008	Tampa Bay	A.L.	OF	5	20	3	5	0	0	0	1	4	.250

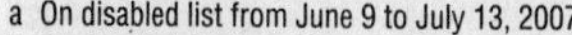

a On disabled list from June 9 to July 13, 2007.
b On disabled list from March 27 to April 13, 2009.
c On disabled list from March 26 to April 20, 2012.
d Filed for free agency, November 3, 2012. Signed with Atlanta Braves, November 29, 2012.
e On disabled list from July 13 to August 3, 2013.

URIBE (TENA), JUAN C.

Born, Bani, Dominican Republic, July 22, 1979.
Bats Right. Throws Right. Height, 6 feet. Weight, 220 pounds.

Year	Club	Lea	Pos	G	AB	R	H	2B	3B	HR	RBI	SB	Avg
1997	Colorado	Domincan	SS	65	234	32	63	12	0	0	29	7	.269
1998	Rockies	Arizona	SS	40	148	25	41	5	3	0	17	8	.277

Year	Club	Lea	Pos	G	AB	R	H	2B	3B	HR	RBI	SB	Avg
1999	Asheville	So.Atl.	SS	125	430	57	115	28	3	9	46	11	.267
2000	Salem	Carolina	SS	134	485	64	124	22	7	13	65	22	.256
2001	Carolina	Southern	SS	3	13	1	3	1	0	0	1	1	.231
2001	Colo Sprngs	P.C.	SS	74	281	40	87	27	7	7	48	11	.310
2001	Colorado	N.L.	SS	72	273	32	82	15	11	8	53	3	.300
2002	Colorado	N.L.	SS	155	566	69	136	25	7	6	49	9	.240
2003	Visalia	California	2B-SS	2	9	4	5	1	0	0	1	0	.556
2003	Tulsa	Texas	2B-3B-SS-OF	5	20	3	5	2	0	1	4	0	.250
2003	Colorado a-b	N.L.	SS-2B-OF	87	316	45	80	19	3	10	33	7	.253
2004	Chicago	A.L.	2B-SS-3B	134	502	82	142	31	6	23	74	9	.283
2005	Chicago	A.L.	SS	146	481	58	121	23	3	16	71	4	.252
2006	Chicago	A.L.	SS	132	463	53	109	28	2	21	71	1	.235
2007	Chicago	A.L.	SS	150	513	55	120	18	2	20	68	1	.234
2008	Charlotte	Int.	2B-SS	3	11	0	2	0	0	0	2	0	.182
2008	Chicago c-d	A.L.	3B-2B-SS	110	324	38	80	22	1	7	40	1	.247
2009	San Francisco e	N.L.	3B-SS-2B	122	398	50	115	26	4	16	55	3	.289
2010	San Francisco f	N.L.	SS-3B-2B	148	521	64	129	24	2	24	85	1	.248
2011	Rancho Cucamonga	Calif.	2B	3	8	2	4	1	0	0	0	0	.500
2011	Los Angeles g	N.L.	3B-2B-SS	77	270	21	55	12	0	4	28	2	.204
2012	Rancho Cucamonga	Calif.	3B	3	10	1	3	0	1	1	3	0	.300
2012	Los Angeles h	N.L.	3B-SS	66	162	15	31	9	0	2	17	0	.191
2013	Los Angeles i	N.L.	3B-1B	132	388	47	108	22	2	12	50	5	.278
Major League Totals			13 Yrs.	1531	5177	629	1308	274	43	169	694	46	.253
	Division Series												
2005	Chicago	A.L.	SS	3	10	4	4	1	0	1	4	0	.400
2008	Chicago	A.L.	3B	4	12	0	2	0	0	0	1	1	.167
2010	San Francisco	N.L.	SS-3B	4	14	0	1	0	0	0	1	0	.071
2013	Los Angeles	N.L.	3B	4	16	4	6	1	0	2	4	0	.375
Division Series Totals				15	52	8	13	2	0	3	10	1	.250
	Championship Series												
2005	Chicago	A.L.	SS	5	16	1	4	1	0	0	0	0	.250
2010	San Francisco	N.L.	SS-3B	5	14	1	3	0	0	1	3	0	.214
2013	Los Angeles	N.L.	3B	6	23	0	3	0	0	0	3	0	.130
Championship Series Totals				16	53	2	10	1	0	1	6	0	.189
	World Series Record												
2005	Chicago	A.L.	SS	4	16	2	4	3	0	0	2	1	.250
2010	San Francisco	N.L.	3B	5	19	3	3	0	0	1	5	0	.158
World Series Totals				9	35	5	7	3	0	1	7	1	.200

a On disabled list from March 18 to June 3, 2003.
b Traded to Chicago White Sox for infielder Aaron Miles, December 2, 2003.
c On disabled list from May 16 to May 31, 2008.
d Filed for free agency, October 30, 2008. Signed with San Francisco Giants organization, January 29, 2009.
e Filed for free agency, November 5, 2009, re-signed with San Francisco Giants, January 5, 2010.
f Filed for free agency, November 1, 2010. Signed with Los Angeles Dodgers, November 30, 2010.
g On disabled list from May 21 to June 6 and July 24 to September 30, 2011.
h On disabled list from May 14 to June 11, 2012.
i Filed for free agency, October 31, 2013, re-signed with Los Angeles Dodgers, December 24, 2013.

UTLEY, CHASE CAMERON

Born, Pasadena, California, December 17, 1978.
Bats Left. Throws Right. Height, 6 feet, 1 inch. Weight, 200 pounds.

Year	Club	Lea	Pos	G	AB	R	H	2B	3B	HR	RBI	SB	Avg
2000	Batavia	N.Y.-Penn.	2B	40	153	21	47	13	1	2	22	5	.307
2001	Clearwater	Fla.St.	2B	122	467	65	120	25	2	16	59	19	.257
2002	Scranton/W.B.	Int.	3B	125	464	73	122	39	1	17	70	8	.263
2003	Scranton/W.B.	Int.	2B	113	431	80	139	26	2	18	77	10	.323
2003	Philadelphia	N.L.	2B	43	134	13	32	10	1	2	21	2	.239
2004	Scranton/WB	Int.	2B	33	123	23	35	8	1	6	25	4	.285
2004	Philadelphia	N.L.	2B-1B	94	267	36	71	11	2	13	57	4	.266
2005	Philadelphia	N.L.	2B-1B	147	543	93	158	39	6	28	105	16	.291
2006	Philadelphia	N.L.	2B-1B	160	658	*131	203	40	4	32	102	15	.309
2007	Reading	Eastern	2B	3	10	0	1	0	0	0	0	0	.100
2007	Philadelphia a	N.L.	2B-1B	132	530	104	176	48	5	22	103	9	.332
2008	Philadelphia	N.L.	2B-1B	159	607	113	177	41	4	33	104	14	.292
2009	Philadelphia	N.L.	2B	156	571	112	161	28	4	31	93	23	.282
2010	Clearwater	Fla.St.	2B	4	12	1	3	0	2	0	1	0	.250
2010	Philadelphia b	N.L.	2B	115	425	75	117	20	2	16	65	13	.275
2011	Clearwater	Fla.St.	2B	9	32	4	9	2	0	1	4	1	.281

Year	Club	Lea	Pos	G	AB	R	H	2B	3B	HR	RBI	SB	Avg
2011	Philadelphia c	N.L.	2B	103	398	54	103	21	6	11	44	14	.259
2012	Clearwater	Fla.St.	2B	9	32	3	5	0	0	1	5	1	.156
2012	Lehigh Valley	Int.	2B	1	5	1	2	0	0	1	1	0	.400
2012	Philadelphia d	N.L.	2B	83	301	48	77	15	2	11	45	11	.256
2013	Reading	Eastern	2B	2	9	0	0	0	0	0	0	0	.000
2013	Philadelphia e	N.L.	2B	131	476	73	135	25	6	18	69	8	.284
Major League Totals			11 Yrs.	1323	4910	852	1410	298	42	217	808	129	.287
	Division Series												
2007	Philadelphia	N.L.	2B	3	11	0	2	0	0	0	0	0	.182
2008	Philadelphia	N.L.	2B	4	15	1	2	1	0	0	2	0	.133
2009	Philadelphia	N.L.	2B	4	14	5	6	0	0	1	1	2	.429
2010	Philadelphia	N.L.	2B	3	11	3	3	0	0	1	4	1	.273
2011	Philadelphia	N.L.	2B	5	16	5	7	2	1	0	1	0	.438
Division Series Totals				19	67	14	20	3	1	2	8	3	.299
	Championship Series												
2008	Philadelphia	N.L.	2B	5	17	4	6	2	0	1	3	0	.353
2009	Philadelphia	N.L.	2B	5	19	3	4	0	0	0	1	0	.211
2010	Philadelphia	N.L.	2B	6	22	5	4	1	0	0	1	3	.182
Championship Series Totals				16	58	12	14	3	0	1	5	3	.241
	World Series Record												
2008	Philadelphia	N.L.	2B	5	18	5	3	0	0	2	4	3	.167
2009	Philadelphia	N.L.	2B	6	21	7	6	1	0	5	8	1	.286
World Series Totals				11	39	12	9	1	0	7	12	4	.231

a On disabled list from July 27 to August 27, 2007.
b On disabled list from June 29 to August 17, 2010.
c On disabled list from March 22 to May 23, 2011.
d On disabled list from March 26 to June 27, 2012.
e On disabled list from May 21 to June 21, 2013.

VALBUENA, LUIS ADAN

Born, Caja Seca, Venezuela, November 30, 1985.
Bats Left. Throws Right. Height, 5 feet, 10 inches. Weight, 195 pounds.

Year	Club	Lea	Pos	G	AB	R	H	2B	3B	HR	RBI	SB	Avg
2005	Everett	Northwest	2B	74	287	47	75	10	3	12	51	14	.261
2005	Tacoma	P.C.	2B	3	4	0	0	0	0	0	0	0	.000
2006	Inland Empire	Calif.	2B-SS-3B	43	163	18	41	10	1	2	10	1	.252
2006	Wisconsin	Midwest	2B	89	325	45	93	16	6	3	38	21	.286
2007	West Tenn	Southern	2B	122	444	55	106	23	3	11	44	10	.239
2008	West Tenn	Southern	2B-3B	70	240	43	73	12	2	9	40	8	.304
2008	Tacoma	P.C.	2B-3B	58	212	41	64	9	0	2	20	10	.302
2008	Seattle a	A.L.	2B-SS	18	49	6	12	5	0	0	1	0	.245
2009	Columbus	Int.	2B-SS-3B	22	78	15	25	4	2	3	13	3	.321
2009	Cleveland	A.L.	2B-SS-3B	103	368	52	92	25	3	10	31	2	.250
2010	Columbus	Int.	SS-3B-2B	25	96	23	30	8	1	6	20	2	.313
2010	Cleveland	A.L.	2B-3B-SS-OF	91	275	22	53	12	0	2	24	1	.193
2011	Columbus	Int.	SS-3B-OF-2B	113	420	64	127	22	0	17	75	6	.302
2011	Cleveland b	A.L.	2B-OF-SS	17	43	4	9	0	0	1	1	1	.209
2012	Iowa	P.C.	SS-2B-3B	58	211	38	64	17	1	8	31	1	.303
2012	Chicago c	N.L.	3B-2B	90	265	26	58	20	0	4	28	0	.219
2013	Cubs	Arizona	3B	2	7	2	5	2	0	0	3	1	.714
2013	Kane County	Midwest	3B	1	3	0	1	0	0	0	0	0	.333
2013	Chicago d	N.L.	3B-2B-OF	108	331	34	72	15	1	12	37	1	.218
Major League Totals			6 Yrs.	427	1331	144	296	77	4	29	122	5	.222

a Traded to Cleveland Indians with pitcher Joe Smith for outfielder Franklin Gutierrez, December 10, 2008.
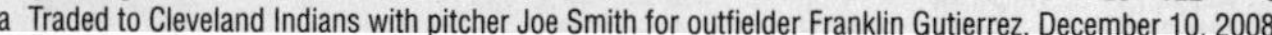
b Sold to Toronto Blue Jays, November 26, 2011.
c Claimed on waivers by Chicago Cubs, April 4, 2012.
d On disabled list from August 3 to September 1, 2013.

VALENCIA, DANIEL PAUL (DANNY)

Born, Miami, Florida, September 19, 1984.
Bats Right. Throws Right. Height, 6 feet, 2 inches. Weight, 220 pounds.

Year	Club	Lea	Pos	G	AB	R	H	2B	3B	HR	RBI	SB	Avg
2006	Elizabethton	Appal.	1B-3B	48	190	30	59	13	0	8	29	0	.311
2007	Beloit	Midwest	3B-1B	66	242	44	73	15	0	11	35	3	.302
2007	Fort Myers	Fla.St.	3B	61	230	28	67	8	2	6	31	1	.291
2008	Fort Myers	Fla.St.	3B-SS	60	220	35	74	19	3	5	44	2	.336

Year	Club	Lea	Pos	G	AB	R	H	2B	3B	HR	RBI	SB	Avg
2008	New Britain	Eastern	3B-1B	69	266	40	77	18	2	10	32	2	.289
2009	New Britain	Eastern	3B	57	218	44	62	14	4	7	29	0	.284
2009	Rochester	Int.	3B	71	269	35	77	24	0	7	41	0	.286
2010	Rochester	Int.	3B	49	185	22	54	15	0	0	24	2	.292
2010	Minnesota	A.L.	3B	85	299	30	93	18	1	7	40	2	.311
2011	Minnesota	A.L.	3B	154	564	63	139	28	2	15	72	2	.246
2012	Rochester	Int.	3B	69	268	30	67	17	1	7	37	1	.250
2012	Pawtucket	Int.	3B	13	49	3	15	3	0	1	8	0	.306
2012	Minnesota-Boston a-b	A.L.	3B	44	154	14	29	6	1	3	21	0	.188
2013	Norfolk	Int.	3B-1B-OF	65	262	40	75	20	1	14	51	1	.286
2013	Baltimore c	A.L.	DH-3B	52	161	20	49	14	1	8	23	0	.304
	Major League Totals		4 Yrs.	335	1178	127	310	66	5	33	156	4	.263
	Division Series												
2010	Minnesota	A.L.	3B	3	9	1	2	1	0	0	2	0	.222

a Traded to Boston Red Sox for outfielder Jeremias Pineda, August 5, 2012.
b Sold to Baltimore Orioles, November 28, 2012.
c Traded to Kansas City Royals for outfielder David Lough, December 18, 2013.

VAN SLYKE, SCOTT T.

Born, Chesterfield, Missouri, July 24, 1986.
Bats Right. Throws Right. Height, 6 feet, 5 inches. Weight, 250 pounds.

Year	Club	Lea	Pos	G	AB	R	H	2B	3B	HR	RBI	SB	Avg
2005	Dodgers	Gulf Coast	OF	24	85	15	24	4	1	2	15	4	.282
2006	Ogden	Pioneer	OF-1B	45	156	18	40	5	2	2	17	5	.256
2007	Great Lakes	Midwest	OF-1B	104	351	38	89	18	1	2	35	4	.254
2008	Great Lakes	Midwest	OF	22	61	4	9	4	0	0	7	0	.148
2008	Inland Empire	Calif.	OF	48	176	29	46	9	2	5	26	7	.261
2009	Inland Empire	Calif.	OF	132	496	75	146	42	4	23	100	10	.294
2009	Albuquerque	P.C.	OF	3	6	1	1	0	0	0	0	0	.167
2010	Inland Empire	Calif.	OF	48	189	34	58	12	2	9	35	3	.307
2010	Chattanooga	Southern	OF	65	217	28	51	7	3	4	29	4	.235
2010	Albuquerque	P.C.	OF	12	38	5	11	4	0	1	5	0	.289
2011	Chattanooga	Southern	OF-1B	130	457	81	159	45	4	20	92	6	.348
2012	Los Angeles	N.L.	OF-1B	27	54	4	9	2	0	2	7	1	.167
2012	Albuquerque	P.C.	OF-1B	95	358	68	117	34	1	18	67	5	.327
2013	Rancho Cucamonga	Calif.	OF	2	7	2	3	0	0	0	0	0	.429
2013	Albuquerque	P.C.	1B-OF	61	204	55	71	17	2	12	48	8	.348
2013	Los Angeles a	N.L.	OF-1B	53	129	13	31	8	0	7	19	1	.240
	Major League Totals		2 Yrs.	80	183	17	40	10	0	9	26	2	.219
	Division Series												
2013	Los Angeles	N.L.	PH	1	0	0	0	0	0	0	0	0	.000
	Championship Series												
2013	Los Angeles	N.L.	OF	1	0	0	0	0	0	0	0	0	.000

a On disabled list from June 11 to June 28, 2013.

VENABLE, WILLIAM DION (WILL)

Born, Greenbrae, California, October 29, 1982.
Bats Left. Throws Left. Height, 6 feet, 2 inches. Weight, 205 pounds.

Year	Club	Lea	Pos	G	AB	R	H	2B	3B	HR	RBI	SB	Avg
2005	Padres	Arizona	OF	15	59	13	19	4	2	1	12	4	.322
2005	Eugene	Northwest	OF	42	139	17	30	5	2	2	14	2	.216
2006	Fort Wayne	Midwest	OF	124	472	86	148	34	5	11	91	18	.314
2007	San Antonio	Texas	OF	134	515	66	143	19	3	8	68	21	.278
2008	Portland	P.C.	OF	120	442	70	129	26	4	14	58	7	.292
2008	San Diego	N.L.	OF	28	110	16	29	4	2	2	10	1	.264
2009	Portland	P.C.	OF	53	200	33	52	10	3	12	30	1	.260
2009	San Diego	N.L.	OF	95	293	38	75	14	2	12	38	6	.256
2010	Lake Elsinore	Calif.	OF	5	14	0	1	1	0	0	0	1	.071
2010	San Antonio	Texas	OF	2	6	2	2	0	0	0	1	2	.333
2010	San Diego a	N.L.	OF-1B	131	392	60	96	11	7	13	51	29	.245
2011	Tucson	P.C.	OF	14	58	14	16	3	2	3	11	3	.276
2011	San Diego	N.L.	OF	121	370	49	91	14	7	9	44	26	.246
2012	San Diego	N.L.	OF	148	417	62	110	26	8	9	45	24	.264
2013	San Diego	N.L.	OF	151	481	64	129	22	8	22	53	22	.268
	Major League Totals		6 Yrs.	674	2063	289	530	91	34	67	241	108	.257

a On disabled list from July 2 to July 21, 2010.

VICIEDO (PEREZ), DAYAN

Born, Remedios, Cuba, March 10, 1989.
Bats Right. Throws Right. Height, 5 feet, 11 inches. Weight, 240 pounds.

Year Club Lea	Pos	G	AB	R	H	2B	3B	HR	RBI	SB	Avg
2009 Birmingham a .... Southern	3B-1B	130	504	72	141	20	0	12	78	5	.280
2010 Charlotte .... Int.	1B-3B	86	343	42	94	15	0	20	47	1	.274
2010 Chicago .... A.L.	3B-1B	38	104	17	32	7	0	5	13	1	.308
2011 Charlotte .... Int.	OF-1B	119	452	60	134	28	0	20	78	2	.296
2011 Chicago b............. A.L.	OF-1B	29	102	11	26	3	0	1	6	1	.255
2012 Chicago .... A.L.	OF	147	505	64	129	18	1	25	78	0	.255
2013 Charlotte .... Int.	OF	4	15	2	3	0	0	0	0	0	.200
2013 Chicago c............. A.L.	OF	124	441	43	117	23	3	14	56	0	.265
Major League Totals	4 Yrs.	338	1152	135	304	51	4	45	153	2	.264

a Played in Cuba 2006 and 2007.
b On disabled list from March 22 to April 6, 2011.
c On disabled list from April 19 to May 10, 2013.

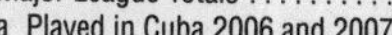

VICTORINO, SHANE PATRICK

Born, Wailuku, Hawaii, November 30, 1980.
Bats Both. Throws Right. Height, 5 feet, 9 inches. Weight, 180 pounds.

Year Club Lea	Pos	G	AB	R	H	2B	3B	HR	RBI	SB	Avg
1999 Great Falls ....Pioneer	OF	55	225	53	63	7	6	2	25	20	.280
2000 Yakima......... Northwest	2B-SS	61	236	32	58	7	2	2	20	21	.246
2001 Vero Beach..........Fla.St.	OF	2	6	2	1	0	0	0	0	0	.167
2001 Wilmington .... So.Atl.	OF	112	435	71	123	21	9	4	32	47	.283
2002 Jacksonville ...... Southern	OF	122	481	61	124	15	1	4	34	45	.258
2003 Jacksonville ...... Southern	OF	66	266	37	75	9	4	2	15	16	.282
2003 Las Vegas..............P.C.	OF	11	41	6	16	1	2	1	9	0	.390
2003 San Diego a .... N.L.	OF	36	73	8	11	2	0	0	4	7	.151
2004 Las Vegas..............P.C.	OF-2B	55	200	28	47	9	1	3	20	7	.235
2004 Jacksonville b .... Southern	OF	75	293	70	96	13	7	16	43	9	.328
2005 Scranton/WB .... Int.	OF	126	494	93	153	25	16	18	70	17	.310
2005 Philadelphia .... N.L.	OF	21	17	5	5	0	0	2	8	0	.294
2006 Philadelphia .... N.L.	OF	153	415	70	119	19	8	6	46	4	.287
2007 Lakewood.......... So.Atl.	DH	1	5	1	1	0	0	0	0	0	.200
2007 Reading ....Eastern	OF	2	6	0	2	0	0	0	1	1	.333
2007 Philadelphia c......... N.L.	OF	131	456	78	128	23	3	12	46	37	.281
2008 Clearwater ....Fla.St.	OF	2	5	1	2	0	0	0	1	0	.400
2008 Reading ....Eastern	OF	1	3	0	1	0	0	0	0	0	.333
2008 Lehigh Valley .... Int.	OF	2	8	0	3	0	0	0	0	0	.375
2008 Philadelphia d .... N.L.	OF	146	570	102	167	30	8	14	58	36	.293
2009 Philadelphia .... N.L.	OF	156	620	102	181	39	*13	10	62	25	.292
2010 Lehigh Valley .... Int.	OF	2	6	1	4	0	1	1	3	0	.667
2010 Philadelphia e.......... N.L.	OF	147	587	84	152	26	10	18	69	34	.259
2011 Lakewood.......... So.Atl.	OF	2	6	1	1	0	0	0	2	0	.167
2011 Reading ....Eastern	OF	4	15	2	5	1	0	1	3	1	.333
2011 Philadelphia f.......... N.L.	OF	132	519	95	145	27	*16	17	61	19	.279
2012 Philadelphia-L.A g-h.... N.L.	OF	154	595	72	152	29	7	11	55	39	.255
2013 Pawtucket .... Int.	OF	1	4	1	2	0	0	1	1	0	.500
2013 Boston i .... A.L.	OF	122	477	82	140	26	2	15	61	21	.294
Major League Totals	10 Yrs.	1198	4329	698	1200	221	67	105	470	222	.277
Division Series											
2007 Philadelphia .... N.L.	OF	3	9	2	2	0	0	1	1	1	.222
2008 Philadelphia .... N.L.	OF	4	14	2	5	3	0	1	5	3	.357
2009 Philadelphia .... N.L.	OF	4	17	4	6	1	0	1	1	1	.353
2010 Philadelphia .... N.L.	OF	3	13	2	3	1	0	0	3	1	.231
2011 Philadelphia .... N.L.	OF	5	19	2	6	1	0	0	2	0	.316
2013 Boston .... A.L.	OF	4	14	2	6	0	0	0	3	1	.429
Division Series Totals		23	86	14	28	6	0	3	15	7	.326
Championship Series											
2008 Philadelphia .... N.L.	OF	5	18	2	4	0	1	1	6	0	.222
2009 Philadelphia .... N.L.	OF	5	19	4	7	1	1	2	6	1	.368
2010 Philadelphia .... N.L.	OF	6	24	3	5	1	0	0	2	1	.208
2013 Boston .... A.L.	OF	6	24	2	3	1	0	1	5	1	.125
Championship Series Totals		22	85	11	19	3	2	4	19	3	.224
World Series Record											
2008 Philadelphia .... N.L.	OF	5	20	1	5	0	0	0	2	0	.250
2009 Philadelphia .... N.L.	OF	6	22	3	4	1	0	0	2	0	.182

Year	Club	Lea	Pos	G	AB	R	H	2B	3B	HR	RBI	SB	Avg
2013	Boston	A.L.	OF	4	13	2	2	1	0	0	4	0	.154
World Series Totals				15	55	6	11	2	0	0	8	0	.200

a Selected by San Diego Padres from Los Angeles Dodgers in Rule V draft, December 16, 2002. Returned to Los Angeles Dodgers, May 28, 2003.
b Selected by Philadelphia Phillies in Rule V draft, December 13, 2004.
c On disabled list from July 31 to August 22, 2007.
d On disabled list from April 13 to April 29, 2008.
e On disabled list from July 28 to August 12, 2010.
f On disabled list from May 20 to June 3 and July 4 to July 19, 2011.
g Traded to Los Angeles Dodgers for pitcher Josh Lindblom, pitcher Ethan Martin and player to be named later, July 31, 2012. Philadelphia Phillies received infielder Stefan Jarrin to complete trade, September 28, 2012.
h Filed for free agency, November 3, 2012. Signed with Boston Red Sox, December 13, 2012.
i On disabled list from May 21 to June 8, 2013.

VILLAR (ROQUE), JONATHAN RAFAEL

Born, LaVega, Dominican Republic, May 2, 1991.
Bats Both. Throws Right. Height, 6 feet, 1 inch. Weight, 195 pounds.

Year	Club	Lea	Pos	G	AB	R	H	2B	3B	HR	RBI	SB	Avg
2009	Phillies	Gulf Coast	SS	31	94	14	26	7	1	0	14	11	.277
2009	Williamsport	N.Y.-Penn.	SS	11	39	6	9	1	1	0	5	6	.231
2010	Lakewood	So.Atl.	SS	100	371	61	101	18	4	2	36	38	.272
2010	Lancaster a	Calif.	SS	32	129	18	29	6	2	3	19	7	.225
2011	Lancaster	Calif.	SS	47	174	26	45	7	4	4	26	20	.259
2011	Corpus Christi	Texas	SS	83	324	52	75	16	2	10	26	14	.231
2012	Corpus Christi	Texas	SS	86	326	54	85	7	2	11	50	39	.261
2013	Oklahoma	P.C.	SS	91	339	47	94	16	8	8	41	31	.277
2013	Houston	A.L.	SS	58	210	26	51	9	2	1	8	18	.243

a Traded by Philadelphia Phillies to Houston Astros with pitcher J.A.Happ and outfielder Anthony Gose for pitcher Roy Oswalt and cash, July 29, 2010.

VOTTO, JOSEPH DANIEL (JOEY)

Born, Toronto, Ontario, Canada, September 10, 1983.
Bats Left. Throws Right. Height, 6 feet, 3 inches. Weight, 220 pounds.

Year	Club	Lea	Pos	G	AB	R	H	2B	3B	HR	RBI	SB	Avg
2002	Reds	Gulf Coast	3B-C-OF	50	175	29	47	13	3	9	33	7	.269
2003	Dayton	Midwest	1B	60	195	19	45	8	0	1	20	2	.231
2003	Billings	Pioneer	1B	70	240	47	76	17	3	6	37	4	.317
2004	Potomac	Carolina	1B	24	84	11	25	7	0	5	20	1	.298
2004	Dayton	Midwest	1B	111	391	60	118	26	2	14	73	9	.302
2005	Sarasota	Fla.St.	1B	124	464	64	119	23	2	17	83	4	.256
2006	Chattanooga	Southern	1B	136	508	85	162	46	2	22	77	24	.319
2007	Louisville	Int.	1B-OF	133	496	74	146	21	2	22	92	17	.294
2007	Cincinnati	N.L.	1B-OF	24	84	11	27	7	0	4	17	1	.321
2008	Cincinnati	N.L.	1B	151	526	69	156	32	3	24	84	7	.297
2009	Dayton	Midwest	1B	2	7	3	3	0	0	1	3	1	.429
2009	Sarasota	Fla.St.	1B	1	2	0	0	0	0	0	0	0	.000
2009	Cincinnati a	N.L.	1B	131	469	82	151	38	1	25	84	4	.322
2010	Cincinnati b	N.L.	1B	150	547	106	177	36	2	37	113	16	.324
2011	Cincinnati	N.L.	1B	161	599	101	185	*40	3	29	103	8	.309
2012	Dayton	Midwest	1B	3	5	1	1	0	0	0	1	0	.200
2012	Louisville	Int.	1B	2	6	1	1	0	0	1	1	0	.167
2012	Cincinnati c	N.L.	1B	111	374	59	126	44	0	14	56	5	.337
2013	Cincinnati	N.L.	1B	*162	581	101	177	30	3	24	73	6	.305
Major League Totals			7 Yrs.	890	3180	529	999	227	12	157	530	47	.314
	Wild Card Playoff												
2013	Cincinnati	N.L.	1B	1	4	0	0	0	0	0	0	0	.000
	Division Series												
2010	Cincinnati	N.L.	1B	3	10	0	1	0	0	0	1	0	.100
2012	Cincinnati	N.L.	1B	5	18	3	7	0	0	0	0	0	.389
Division Series Totals				8	28	3	8	0	0	0	1	0	.286

a On disabled list from May 30 to June 23, 2009.
b Selected Most Valuable Player in National League for 2010.
c On disabled list from July 17 to September 4, 2012.

WALKER, NEIL MARTIN

Born, Pittsburgh, Pennsylvania, September 10, 1985.
Bats Both. Throws Right. Height, 6 feet, 3 inches. Weight, 210 pounds.

Year	Club	Lea	Pos	G	AB	R	H	2B	3B	HR	RBI	SB	Avg
2004	Pirates	Gulf Coast	C	52	192	28	52	12	3	4	20	3	.271
2004	Williamsport	N.Y.-Penn.	C	8	33	2	10	3	0	0	7	1	.303
2005	Lynchburg	Carolina	C	9	42	4	11	2	1	0	12	0	.262
2005	Hickory	So.Atl.	C	120	485	78	146	33	2	12	68	7	.301
2006	Lynchburg	Carolina	C	72	264	32	75	22	1	3	35	3	.284
2006	Altoona	Eastern	C	10	31	5	5	0	0	2	3	0	.161
2007	Altoona	Eastern	3B	117	431	77	124	30	3	13	66	9	.288
2007	Indianapolis	Int.	3B	19	64	7	13	3	0	0	0	1	.203
2008	Indianapolis	Int.	3B	133	505	69	122	25	7	16	80	10	.242
2009	Pirates	Gulf Coast	3B	8	30	2	5	2	0	1	1	0	.167
2009	Indianapolis	Int.	3B	95	356	38	94	31	2	14	69	5	.264
2009	Pittsburgh	N.L.	3B	17	36	5	7	1	0	0	0	1	.194
2010	Indianapolis	Int.	2B-OF-1B-3B	43	168	25	54	18	2	6	26	10	.321
2010	Pittsburgh	N.L.	2B-3B	110	426	57	126	29	3	12	66	2	.296
2011	Pittsburgh	N.L.	2B	159	596	76	163	36	4	12	83	9	.273
2012	Pittsburgh	N.L.	2B	129	472	62	132	27	0	14	69	7	.280
2013	Altoona	Eastern	2B	4	12	0	5	1	0	0	1	0	.417
2013	Indianapolis	Int.	2B	3	9	0	2	1	0	0	0	0	.222
2013	Pittsburgh a	N.L.	2B	133	478	62	120	24	4	16	53	1	.251
Major League Totals			5 Yrs.	548	2008	262	548	117	11	54	271	20	.273
	Wild Card Playoff												
2013	Pittsburgh	N.L.	2B	1	5	1	2	1	0	0	1	0	.400
	Division Series												
2013	Pittsburgh	N.L.	2B	5	19	0	0	0	0	0	0	0	.000

a On disabled list from April 27 to May 13 and July 7 to July 23, 2013.

WALLACE, BRETT ALEXANDER

Born, Marin, California, August 26, 1986.
Bats Left. Throws Right. Height, 6 feet, 2 inches. Weight, 205 pounds.

Year	Club	Lea	Pos	G	AB	R	H	2B	3B	HR	RBI	SB	Avg
2008	Quad Cities	Midwest	3B	41	153	28	50	8	1	5	25	0	.327
2008	Springfield	Texas	3B	13	49	13	18	5	0	3	11	0	.367
2009	Memphis	P.C.	3B-1B	62	222	22	65	11	0	6	19	0	.293
2009	Sacramento	P.C.	3B-1B	44	182	32	55	10	0	9	28	1	.302
2009	Springfield a-b	Texas	3B	32	128	22	36	5	0	5	16	0	.281
2010	Las Vegas	P.C.	1B	95	385	64	116	24	1	18	61	1	.301
2010	Houston c	N.L.	1B	51	144	14	32	6	1	2	13	0	.222
2011	Oklahoma	P.C.	1B	28	104	16	37	10	0	1	24	1	.356
2011	Houston	N.L.	1B	115	336	37	87	22	0	5	29	1	.259
2012	Oklahoma	P.C.	3B-1B-SS	86	310	54	93	16	0	16	57	0	.300
2012	Houston	N.L.	1B-3B	66	229	24	58	10	1	9	24	0	.253
2013	Oklahoma	P.C.	1B-3B	60	233	36	76	16	2	11	37	1	.326
2013	Houston	A.L.	1B-3B	79	262	35	58	14	1	13	36	1	.221
Major League Totals			4 Yrs.	311	971	110	235	52	3	29	102	2	.242

a Traded by St. Louis Cardinals to Oakland Athletics with pitcher Clayton Mortensen and outfielder Shane Peterson for outfielder Matt Holliday, July 24, 2009.
b Traded to Toronto Blue Jays for pitcher Michael Taylor, December 16, 2009.
c Traded to Houston Astros for outfielder Anthony Gose, July 29, 2010.

WEEKS, JEMILE NYKIWA

Born, Orlando, Florida, January 26, 1987.
Bats Both. Throws Right. Height, 5 feet, 9 inches. Weight, 160 pounds.

Year	Club	Lea	Pos	G	AB	R	H	2B	3B	HR	RBI	SB	Avg
2008	Kane County	Midwest	2B	19	74	11	22	3	1	1	8	6	.297
2009	Stockton	Calif.	2B	50	201	29	60	9	2	7	31	5	.299
2009	Midland	Texas	2B	30	105	10	25	5	0	2	13	4	.238
2010	Athletics	Arizona	2B	10	36	9	11	2	1	0	1	5	.306
2010	Midland	Texas	2B	67	273	43	73	14	7	3	33	11	.267
2011	Sacramento	P.C.	2B	45	184	30	59	6	4	3	22	10	.321
2011	Oakland	A.L.	2B	97	406	50	123	26	8	2	36	22	.303
2012	Sacramento	P.C.	2B	10	45	5	15	4	0	0	10	1	.333
2012	Oakland	A.L.	2B	118	444	54	98	15	8	2	20	16	.221
2013	Sacramento	P.C.	2B-OF-SS	130	520	96	141	19	10	4	40	17	.271

Year	Club	Lea	Pos	G	AB	R	H	2B	3B	HR	RBI	SB	Avg
2013	Oakland a	A.L.	2B-OF	8	9	3	1	0	0	0	0	0	.111
Major League Totals			3 Yrs.	223	859	107	222	41	16	4	56	38	.258

a Traded to Baltimore Orioles with player to be named later for pitcher Jim Johnson, December 3, 2013. Baltimore Orioles received catcher David Freitas to complete trade, December 12, 2013.

WEEKS, RICKIE DARNELL

Born, Altamonte Springs, Florida, September 13, 1982.
Bats Right. Throws Right. Height, 6 feet. Weight, 205 pounds.

Year	Club	Lea	Pos	G	AB	R	H	2B	3B	HR	RBI	SB	Avg
2003	Brewers	Arizona	DH	1	4	0	2	0	0	0	4	1	.500
2003	Beloit	Midwest	2B	20	63	13	22	8	1	1	16	2	.349
2003	Milwaukee	N.L.	2B	7	12	1	2	1	0	0	0	0	.167
2004	Huntsville	Southern	2B	133	479	67	124	35	6	8	42	11	.259
2005	Nashville	P.C.	2B	55	203	43	65	14	9	12	48	10	.320
2005	Milwaukee	N.L.	2B	96	360	56	86	13	2	13	42	15	.239
2006	Milwaukee a	N.L.	2B	95	359	73	100	15	3	8	34	19	.279
2007	Nashville	P.C.	2B	6	22	5	10	3	1	0	3	1	.455
2007	Milwaukee b	N.L.	2B	118	409	87	96	21	6	16	36	25	.235
2008	Milwaukee c	N.L.	2B	129	475	89	111	22	7	14	46	19	.234
2009	Milwaukee d	N.L.	2B	37	147	28	40	5	2	9	24	2	.272
2010	Milwaukee	N.L.	2B	160	*651	112	175	32	4	29	83	11	.269
2011	Milwaukee e	N.L.	2B	118	453	77	122	26	2	20	49	9	.269
2012	Milwaukee	N.L.	2B	157	588	85	135	29	4	21	63	16	.230
2013	Milwaukee f	N.L.	2B	104	350	40	73	20	1	10	24	7	.209
Major League Totals			10 Yrs.	1021	3804	648	940	184	31	140	401	123	.247
	Division Series												
2008	Milwaukee	N.L.	2B	3	4	0	0	0	0	0	0	0	.000
2011	Milwaukee	N.L.	2B	5	18	0	1	0	1	0	1	0	.056
Division Series Totals				8	22	0	1	0	1	0	1	0	.045
	Championship Series												
2011	Milwaukee	N.L.	2B	6	23	5	5	1	0	2	3	0	.217

a On disabled list from July 29 to October 31, 2006.
b On disabled list from May 30 to June 18, 2007.
c On disabled list from June 7 to June 22, 2008.
d On disabled list from May 17 to November 6, 2009.
e On disabled list from July 28 to September 8, 2011.
f On disabled list from August 8 to October 31, 2013.

WELLS, VERNON M.

Born, Shreveport, Louisiana, December 8, 1978.
Bats Right. Throws Right. Height, 6 feet, 1 inch. Weight, 225 pounds.

Year	Club	Lea	Pos	G	AB	R	H	2B	3B	HR	RBI	SB	Avg
1997	St.Catherines	N.Y.-Penn.	OF	66	264	52	81	20	1	10	31	8	.307
1998	Hagerstown	So.Atl.	OF	134	509	86	145	35	2	11	65	13	.285
1999	Dunedin	Fla.St.	OF	70	265	43	91	16	2	11	43	13	.343
1999	Knoxville	Southern	OF	26	106	18	36	6	2	3	17	6	.340
1999	Syracuse	Int.	OF	33	129	20	40	8	1	4	21	5	.310
1999	Toronto	A.L.	OF	24	88	8	23	5	0	1	8	1	.261
2000	Syracuse	Int.	OF	127	493	76	120	31	7	16	66	23	.243
2000	Toronto	A.L.	OF	3	2	0	0	0	0	0	0	0	.000
2001	Syracuse	Int.	OF	107	413	57	116	27	4	12	52	15	.281
2001	Toronto a	A.L.	OF	30	96	14	30	8	0	1	6	5	.313
2002	Toronto	A.L.	OF	159	608	87	167	34	4	23	100	9	.275
2003	Toronto	A.L.	OF	161	678	118	*215	*49	5	33	117	4	.317
2004	Toronto b	A.L.	OF	134	536	82	146	34	2	23	67	9	.272
2005	Toronto	A.L.	OF	156	620	78	167	30	3	28	97	8	.269
2006	Toronto	A.L.	OF	154	611	91	185	40	5	32	106	17	.303
2007	Toronto c	A.L.	OF	149	584	85	143	36	4	16	80	10	.245
2008	Dunedin	Fla.St.	OF	2	8	3	4	0	0	0	4	0	.500
2008	Syracuse	Int.	OF	2	6	0	0	0	0	0	0	0	.000
2008	Toronto d	A.L.	OF	108	427	63	128	22	1	20	78	4	.300
2009	Toronto	A.L.	OF	158	630	84	164	37	3	15	66	17	.260
2010	Toronto	A.L.	OF	157	590	79	161	44	3	31	88	6	.273
2011	Inland Empire	Calif.	OF	2	5	3	1	1	0	0	3	0	.200
2011	Los Angeles e-f	A.L.	OF	131	505	60	110	15	4	25	66	9	.218
2012	Salt Lake	P.C.	OF	7	26	2	8	1	0	2	3	3	.308
2012	Los Angeles g	A.L.	OF	77	243	36	56	9	0	11	29	3	.230
2013	New York h-i	A.L.	OF-1B-2B	130	424	45	99	16	0	11	50	7	.233
Major League Totals			15 Yrs.	1731	6642	930	1794	379	34	270	958	109	.270

a On disabled list from April 14 to 24, 2001.
b On disabled list from June 16 to July 16, 2004.
c On disabled list from September 22 to November 13, 2007.
d On disabled list from May 10 to June 7 and July 10 to August 10, 2008.
e Traded to Los Angeles Angels for catcher Mike Napoli and outfielder Juan Rivera, January 21, 2011.
f On disabled list from May 10 to June 7, 2011.
g On disabled list from May 21 to July 27, 2012.
h Traded to New York Yankees for outfielder Exicardo Cayones and pitcher Kramer Sneed, March 26, 2013.
i Released by New York Yankees, January 15, 2014.

WERTH, JAYSON RICHARD GOWAN

Born, Springfield, Illinois, May 20, 1979.
Bats Right. Throws Right. Height, 6 feet, 5 inches. Weight, 220 pounds.

Year Club	Lea	Pos	G	AB	R	H	2B	3B	HR	RBI	SB	Avg
1997 Orioles.........	Gulf Coast	C-1B-OF	32	88	16	26	6	0	1	8	7	.295
1998 Delmarva..........	So.Atl.	C	120	408	71	108	20	3	8	53	21	.265
1998 Bowie.............	Eastern	C	5	19	2	3	2	0	0	1	1	.158
1999 Frederick	Carolina	C	66	236	41	72	10	1	3	30	16	.305
1999 Bowie.............	Eastern	C-OF	35	121	18	33	5	1	1	11	7	.273
2000 Frederick	Carolina	C	24	83	16	23	3	0	2	18	5	.277
2000 Bowie a	Eastern	C-OF	85	276	47	63	16	2	5	26	9	.228
2001 Dunedin............	Fla.St.	C	21	70	9	14	3	0	2	14	1	.200
2001 Tennessee	Southern	C-1B	104	369	51	105	23	1	18	69	12	.285
2002 Syracuse	Int.	OF-C	127	443	65	114	25	2	18	82	24	.257
2002 Toronto	A.L.	OF	15	46	4	12	2	1	0	6	1	.261
2003 Dunedin............	Fla.St.	OF	18	62	10	23	5	0	4	18	1	.371
2003 Toronto	A.L.	OF	26	48	7	10	4	0	2	10	1	.208
2003 Syracuse b............	Int.	OF	64	236	37	56	19	1	9	34	11	.237
2004 Los Angeles..........	N.L.	OF	89	290	56	76	11	3	16	47	4	.262
2004 Las Vegas c-d	P.C.	OF	14	51	13	21	2	1	5	20	2	.412
2005 Las Vegas.............	P.C.	OF	15	49	9	18	0	0	3	10	6	.367
2005 Los Angeles e.........	N.L.	OF	102	337	46	79	22	2	7	43	11	.234
2006 Los Angeles f-g	N.L.			INJURED—Did Not Play								
2007 Clearwater	Fla.St.	OF	4	13	3	1	0	0	0	0	0	.077
2007 Philadelphia h	N.L.	OF-1B	94	255	43	76	11	3	8	49	7	.298
2008 Clearwater	Fla.St.	OF	2	6	0	1	0	0	0	0	0	.167
2008 Philadelphia i	N.L.	OF	134	418	73	114	16	3	24	67	20	.273
2009 Philadelphia	N.L.	OF	159	571	98	153	26	1	36	99	20	.268
2010 Philadelphia j	N.L.	OF	156	554	106	164	*46	2	27	85	13	.296
2011 Washington	N.L.	OF	150	561	69	130	26	1	20	58	19	.232
2012 Potomac..........	Carolina	OF	2	6	2	3	1	0	0	1	0	.500
2012 Syracuse	Int.	OF	7	21	4	5	2	0	0	4	0	.238
2012 Washington k..........	N.L.	OF	81	300	42	90	21	3	5	31	8	.300
2013 Potomac..........	Carolina	OF	6	18	6	10	1	0	2	8	0	.556
2013 Washington l	N.L.	OF	129	462	84	147	24	0	25	82	10	.318
Major League Totals		11 Yrs.	1135	3842	628	1051	209	19	170	577	114	.274
Division Series												
2004 Los Angeles..........	N.L.	OF	4	14	3	4	1	0	2	3	0	.286
2007 Philadelphia	N.L.	OF	2	3	0	0	0	0	0	0	0	.000
2008 Philadelphia	N.L.	OF	4	16	3	5	3	1	1	1	1	.313
2009 Philadelphia	N.L.	OF	4	14	5	5	0	1	2	4	0	.357
2010 Philadelphia	N.L.	OF	3	12	2	2	0	0	0	1	1	.167
2012 Washington	N.L.	OF	5	21	3	5	1	0	1	1	0	.238
Division Series Totals			22	80	16	21	5	2	6	10	2	.262
Championship Series												
2008 Philadelphia	N.L.	OF	5	21	2	4	1	0	0	0	0	.190
2009 Philadelphia	N.L.	OF	5	18	5	4	0	0	3	6	0	.222
2010 Philadelphia	N.L.	OF	6	18	3	4	1	0	2	5	0	.222
Championship Series Totals			16	57	10	12	2	0	5	11	0	.211
World Series Record												
2008 Philadelphia	N.L.	OF	5	18	4	8	3	0	1	3	3	.444
2009 Philadelphia	N.L.	OF	6	19	3	5	0	0	2	3	0	.263
World Series Totals............			11	37	7	13	3	0	3	6	3	.351

a Traded to Toronto Blue Jays by Baltimore Orioles for pitcher John Bale, December 11, 2000.
b On disabled list from March 21 to April 11, 2003.
c Traded to Los Angeles Dodgers for pitcher Jason Frasor, March 30, 2004.
d On disabled list from April 6 to June 4, 2004.
e On disabled list from March 25 to May 25 and from July 27 to August 11, 2005.
f On disabled list from April 1 to November 2, 2006.
g Not offered contract, December 12, 2006. Signed with Philadelphia Phillies, December 19, 2006.
h On disabled list from June 29 to August 1, 2007.

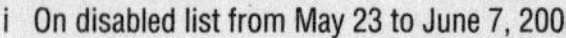

i On disabled list from May 23 to June 7, 2008.
j Filed for free agency, November 1, 2010. Signed with Washington Nationals, December 5, 2010.
k On disabled list from May 7 to August 2, 2012.
l On disabled list from May 3 to June 4, 2013.

WIETERS, MATTHEW RICHARD (MATT)

Born, Goose Creek, South Carolina, May 21, 1986.
Bats Both. Throws Right. Height, 6 feet, 5 inches. Weight, 230 pounds.

Year	Club	Lea	Pos	G	AB	R	H	2B	3B	HR	RBI	SB	Avg
2008	Frederick	Carolina	C	69	229	48	79	8	0	15	40	1	.345
2008	Bowie	Eastern	C	61	208	41	76	14	2	12	51	1	.365
2009	Norfolk	Int.	C	39	141	25	43	9	2	5	30	0	.305
2009	Baltimore	A.L.	C	96	354	35	102	15	1	9	43	0	.288
2010	Baltimore a	A.L.	C	130	446	37	111	22	1	11	55	0	.249
2011	Baltimore	A.L.	C-1B	139	500	72	131	28	0	22	68	1	.262
2012	Baltimore	A.L.	C	144	526	67	131	27	1	23	83	3	.249
2013	Baltimore	A.L.	C	148	523	59	123	29	0	22	79	2	.235
Major League Totals			5 Yrs.	657	2349	270	598	121	3	87	328	6	.255
	Wild Card Playoff												
2012	Baltimore	A.L.	C	1	4	0	0	0	0	0	0	0	.000
	Division Series												
2012	Baltimore	A.L.	C	5	20	2	3	1	0	0	0	0	.150

a On disabled list from July 10 to July 25, 2010.

WILLINGHAM, JOSHUA DAVID (JOSH)

Born, Florence, Alabama, February 17, 1979.
Bats Right. Throws Right. Height, 6 feet, 1 inch. Weight, 215 pounds.

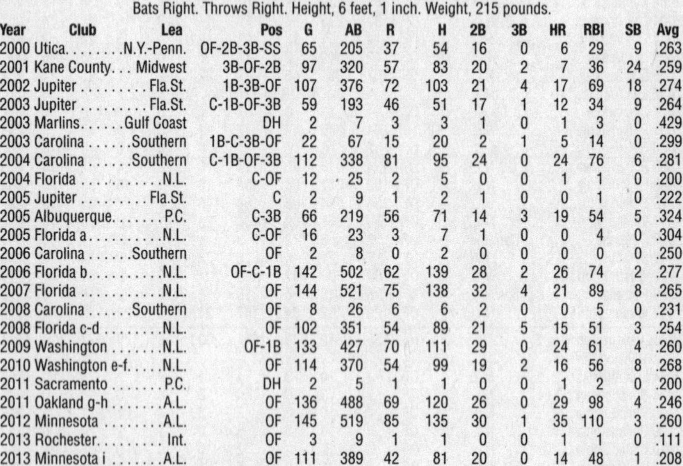

Year	Club	Lea	Pos	G	AB	R	H	2B	3B	HR	RBI	SB	Avg
2000	Utica	N.Y.-Penn.	OF-2B-3B-SS	65	205	37	54	16	0	6	29	9	.263
2001	Kane County	Midwest	3B-OF-2B	97	320	57	83	20	2	7	36	24	.259
2002	Jupiter	Fla.St.	1B-3B-OF	107	376	72	103	21	4	17	69	18	.274
2003	Jupiter	Fla.St.	C-1B-OF-3B	59	193	46	51	17	1	12	34	9	.264
2003	Marlins	Gulf Coast	DH	2	7	3	3	1	0	1	3	0	.429
2003	Carolina	Southern	1B-C-3B-OF	22	67	15	20	2	1	5	14	0	.299
2004	Carolina	Southern	C-1B-OF-3B	112	338	81	95	24	0	24	76	6	.281
2004	Florida	N.L.	C-OF	12	25	2	5	0	0	1	1	0	.200
2005	Jupiter	Fla.St.	C	2	9	1	2	1	0	0	1	0	.222
2005	Albuquerque	P.C.	C-3B	66	219	56	71	14	3	19	54	5	.324
2005	Florida a	N.L.	C-OF	16	23	3	7	1	0	0	4	0	.304
2006	Carolina	Southern	OF	2	8	0	2	0	0	0	0	0	.250
2006	Florida b	N.L.	OF-C-1B	142	502	62	139	28	2	26	74	2	.277
2007	Florida	N.L.	OF	144	521	75	138	32	4	21	89	8	.265
2008	Carolina	Southern	OF	8	26	6	6	2	0	0	5	0	.231
2008	Florida c-d	N.L.	OF	102	351	54	89	21	5	15	51	3	.254
2009	Washington	N.L.	OF-1B	133	427	70	111	29	0	24	61	4	.260
2010	Washington e-f	N.L.	OF	114	370	54	99	19	2	16	56	8	.268
2011	Sacramento	P.C.	DH	2	5	1	1	0	0	1	2	0	.200
2011	Oakland g-h	A.L.	OF	136	488	69	120	26	0	29	98	4	.246
2012	Minnesota	A.L.	OF	145	519	85	135	30	1	35	110	3	.260
2013	Rochester	Int.	OF	3	9	1	1	0	0	1	1	0	.111
2013	Minnesota i	A.L.	OF	111	389	42	81	20	0	14	48	1	.208
Major League Totals			10 Yrs.	1055	3615	516	924	206	14	181	592	33	.256

a On disabled list from June 30 to September 2, 2005.
b On disabled list from June 7 to June 22, 2006.
c On disabled list from April 28 to June 23, 2008.
d Traded to Washington Nationals with pitcher Scott Olsen for infielder Emilio Bonifacio, pitcher P.J. Dean and infielder Jake Smolinkski, November 11, 2008.

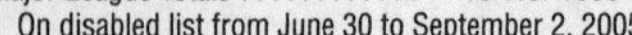

e On disabled list from August 18 to November 10, 2010.
f Traded to Oakland Athletics for pitcher Henry Rodriguez and outfielder Corey Brown, December 16, 2010.
g On disabled list from June 18 to July 7, 2011.
h Filed for free agency, October 30, 2011. Signed with Minnesota Twins, December 15, 2011.
i On disabled list from July 1 to August 9, 2013.

WONG, KOLTEN KAHA

Born, Hilo, Hawaii, October 10, 1990.
Bats Left. Throws Right. Height, 5 feet, 9 inches. Weight, 185 pounds.

Year	Club	Lea	Pos	G	AB	R	H	2B	3B	HR	RBI	SB	Avg
2011	Quad Cities	Midwest	2B	47	194	39	65	15	2	5	25	9	.335
2012	Springfield	Texas	2B	126	523	79	150	23	6	9	52	21	.287

Year	Club	Lea	Pos	G	AB	R	H	2B	3B	HR	RBI	SB	Avg
2013	Memphis	P.C.	2B	107	412	68	125	21	8	10	45	20	.303
2013	St. Louis	N.L.	2B	32	59	6	9	1	0	0	0	3	.153
	Division Series												
2013	St. Louis	N.L.	PH	2	2	0	0	0	0	0	0	0	.000
	Championship Series												
2013	St. Louis	N.L.	2B	3	3	0	0	0	0	0	0	0	.000
	World Series Record												
2013	St. Louis	N.L.	2B	2	1	0	1	0	0	0	0	1	1.000

WRIGHT, DAVID ALLEN

Born, Norfolk, Virginia, December 20, 1982.
Bats Right. Throws Right. Height, 6 feet. Weight, 215 pounds.

Year	Club	Lea	Pos	G	AB	R	H	2B	3B	HR	RBI	SB	Avg
2001	Kingsport	Appal.	3B	35	116	27	35	7	0	4	16	9	.302
2002	Columbia	So.Atl.	3B	135	496	85	132	30	2	11	93	21	.266
2003	St. Lucie	Fla.St.	3B	133	466	69	126	39	2	15	75	19	.270
2004	Binghamton	Eastern	3B	60	223	44	81	27	0	10	40	20	.363
2004	Norfolk	Int.	3B	31	114	18	34	8	0	8	17	2	.298
2004	New York	N.L.	3B	69	263	41	77	17	1	14	40	6	.293
2005	New York	N.L.	3B	160	575	99	176	42	1	27	102	17	.306
2006	New York	N.L.	3B	154	582	96	181	40	5	26	116	20	.311
2007	New York	N.L.	3B	160	604	113	196	42	1	30	107	34	.325
2008	New York	N.L.	3B	160	626	115	189	42	2	33	124	15	.302
2009	New York a	N.L.	3B	144	535	88	164	39	3	10	72	27	.307
2010	New York	N.L.	3B	157	587	87	166	36	3	29	103	19	.283
2011	St. Lucie	Fla.St.	3B	6	21	9	10	3	0	0	2	1	.476
2011	New York b	N.L.	3B-SS	102	389	60	99	23	1	14	61	13	.254
2012	New York	N.L.	3B-SS	156	581	91	178	41	2	21	93	15	.306
2013	New York c	N.L.	3B	112	430	63	132	23	6	18	58	17	.307
Major League Totals			10 Yrs.	1374	5172	853	1558	345	25	222	876	183	.301
	Division Series												
2006	New York	N.L.	3B	3	12	1	4	2	0	0	4	0	.333
	Championship Series												
2006	New York	N.L.	3B	7	25	2	4	1	0	1	2	0	.160

a On disabled list from August 16 to September 1, 2009.
b On disabled list from May 16 to July 22, 2011.
c On disabled list from August 3 to September 20, 2013.

YELICH, CHRISTIAN STEPHEN

Born, Thousand Oaks, California, December 5, 1991.
Bats Left. Throws Right. Height, 6 feet, 4 inches. Weight, 195 pounds.

Year	Club	Lea	Pos	G	AB	R	H	2B	3B	HR	RBI	SB	Avg
2010	Marlins	Gulf Coast	OF	6	24	3	9	1	1	0	3	1	.375
2010	Greensboro	So.Atl.	OF	6	23	2	8	2	0	0	2	0	.348
2011	Greensboro	So.Atl.	OF	122	461	73	144	32	1	15	77	32	.312
2012	Marlins	Gulf Coast	OF	1	4	0	1	0	0	0	0	0	.250
2012	Jupiter	Fla.St.	OF	106	397	76	131	29	5	12	48	20	.330
2013	Marlins	Gulf Coast	OF	5	17	2	5	0	1	0	0	0	.294
2013	Jupiter	Fla.St.	OF	7	26	3	6	0	0	2	4	0	.231
2013	Jacksonville	Southern	OF	49	193	33	54	13	6	7	29	5	.280
2013	Miami	N.L.	OF	62	240	34	69	12	1	4	16	10	.287

YOUNG, CHRISTOPHER BRANDON (CHRIS)

Born, Houston, Texas, September 5, 1983.
Bats Right. Throws Right. Height, 6 feet, 2 inches. Weight, 200 pounds.

Year	Club	Lea	Pos	G	AB	R	H	2B	3B	HR	RBI	SB	Avg
2002	White Sox	Arizona	OF	55	184	26	40	13	1	5	17	7	.217
2003	Bristol	Appal.	OF	64	238	47	69	18	3	7	28	21	.290
2003	Great Falls	Pioneer	OF	10	34	5	6	3	0	0	0	0	.176
2004	Kannapolis	So.Atl.	OF	136	467	83	122	31	5	24	56	31	.261
2005	Birmingham a	Southern	OF	126	466	100	129	41	3	26	77	32	.277
2006	Tucson	P.C.	OF	100	402	78	111	32	4	21	77	17	.276
2006	Arizona	N.L.	OF	30	70	10	17	4	0	2	10	2	.243
2007	Arizona	N.L.	OF	148	569	85	135	29	3	32	68	27	.237
2008	Arizona	N.L.	OF	160	625	85	155	42	7	22	85	14	.248
2009	Reno	P.C.	OF	13	54	17	20	5	1	3	9	2	.370
2009	Arizona	N.L.	OF	134	433	54	92	28	4	15	42	11	.212

Year Club	Lea	Pos	G	AB	R	H	2B	3B	HR	RBI	SB	Avg
2010 Arizona	N.L.	OF	156	584	94	150	33	0	27	91	28	.257
2011 Arizona	N.L.	OF	156	567	89	134	38	3	20	71	22	.236
2012 Visalia	Calif.	OF	3	13	3	4	3	0	1	7	0	.308
2012 Reno	P.C.	OF	1	2	0	0	0	0	0	1	0	.000
2012 Arizona b-c...........	N.L.	OF	101	325	36	75	24	0	14	41	8	.231
2013 Sacramento	P.C.	OF	1	1	1	1	0	0	0	0	1	1.000
2013 Oakland d-e	A.L.	OF	107	335	46	67	18	3	12	40	10	.200
Major League Totals		8 Yrs.	992	3508	499	825	216	20	144	448	122	.235
Division Series												
2007 Arizona...............	N.L.	OF	3	11	3	3	0	0	2	4	1	.273
2011 Arizona...............	N.L.	OF	5	18	5	7	1	0	3	4	2	.389
Division Series Totals			8	29	8	10	1	0	5	8	3	.345
Championship Series												
2007 Arizona...............	N.L.	OF	4	14	1	4	1	0	0	1	0	.286

a Traded to Arizona Diamondbacks by Chicago White Sox with pitcher Orlando Hernandez and pitcher Luis Vizcaino for pitcher Javier Vazquez, December 20, 2005.
b On disabled list from April 18 to May 18, 2012.
c Traded to Oakland Athletics with cash for infielder Cliff Pennington and infielder Yordy Cabrera, October 20, 2012.
d On disabled list from April 30 to May 18, 2013.
e Filed for free agency, November 1, 2013. Signed with New York Mets, November 26, 2013.

YOUNG, DELMON DAMARCUS

Born, Birmingham, Alabama, September 14, 1985.
Bats Right. Throws Right. Height, 6 feet, 3 inches. Weight, 205 pounds.

Year Club	Lea	Pos	G	AB	R	H	2B	3B	HR	RBI	SB	Avg
2004 Charleston	So.Atl.	OF	131	513	95	165	26	5	25	116	21	.322
2005 Durham	Int.	OF	52	228	33	65	13	3	6	28	7	.285
2005 Montgomery	Southern	OF	84	330	59	111	13	4	20	71	25	.336
2006 Durham	Int.	OF	86	342	50	108	22	4	8	59	22	.316
2006 Tampa Bay...........	A.L.	OF	30	126	16	40	9	1	3	10	2	.317
2007 Tampa Bay a..........	A.L.	OF	*162	645	65	186	38	0	13	93	10	.288
2008 Minnesota	A.L.	OF	152	575	80	167	28	4	10	69	14	.290
2009 Minnesota	A.L.	OF	108	395	50	112	16	2	12	60	2	.284
2010 Minnesota	A.L.	OF	153	570	77	170	46	1	21	112	5	.298
2011 Rochester.............	Int.	OF	9	31	5	9	3	0	2	5	0	.290
2011 Minnesota-Detroit b-c ..	A.L.	OF	124	473	54	127	21	1	12	64	1	.268
2012 Detroit d.............	A.L.	DH-OF	151	574	54	153	27	1	18	74	0	.267
2013 Clearwater	Fla.St.	OF	3	13	1	6	1	0	0	1	0	.462
2013 Montgomery	Southern	DH	7	30	4	7	0	0	1	3	0	.233
2013 Lehigh Valley	Int.	OF	4	17	2	5	1	0	0	1	0	.294
2013 Philadelphia e-f	N.L.	OF	80	272	22	71	13	0	8	31	0	.261
2013 Tampa Bay g	A.L.	DH-OF	23	62	8	16	3	0	3	7	0	.258
Major League Totals		8 Yrs.	983	3692	426	1042	201	10	100	520	34	.282
Wild Card Playoff												
2013 Tampa Bay...........	A.L.	DH	1	3	1	1	0	0	1	1	0	.333
Division Series												
2009 Minnesota	A.L.	OF	3	12	1	1	1	0	0	0	1	.083
2010 Minnesota	A.L.	OF	3	12	1	4	0	1	0	0	0	.333
2011 Detroit	A.L.	OF	5	19	4	6	0	0	3	3	0	.316
2012 Detroit	A.L.	DH	5	17	0	4	0	0	0	2	0	.235
2013 Tampa Bay...........	A.L.	DH	4	8	0	2	0	0	0	2	0	.250
Division Series Totals			20	68	6	17	1	1	3	7	1	.250
Championship Series												
2011 Detroit	A.L.	OF	4	15	2	2	0	0	2	3	0	.133
2012 Detroit	A.L.	DH	4	17	3	6	1	0	2	6	0	.353
Championship Series Totals			8	32	5	8	1	0	4	9	0	.250
World Series Record												
2012 Detroit	A.L.	OF-DH	4	14	2	5	1	0	1	1	0	.357

a Traded to Minnesota Twins with infielder Brendan Harris and outfielder Jason Pridie for infielder Jason Bartlett, pitcher Matt Garza and pitcher Eduardo Morlan, November 28, 2007.
b On disabled list from April 19 to May 13 and June 26 to July 11, 2011.
c Traded to Detroit Tigers for pitcher Cole Nelson and player to be named later, August 15, 2011. Minnesota Twins received pitcher Lester Oliveros to complete trade, August 16, 2011.
d Filed for free agency, November 3, 2012. Signed with Philadelphia Phillies, January 22, 2013.
e On disabled list from March 22 to April 30, 2013.
f Released by Philadelphia Phillies, August 14, 2013. Signed with Tampa Bay Rays organization, August 22, 2013.
g Filed for free agency, October 31, 2013. Signed with Baltimore Orioles organization, January 13, 2014.

YOUNG, ERIC ORLANDO JR.

Born, New Brunswick, New Jersey, May 25, 1985.
Bats Both. Throws Right. Height, 5 feet, 10 inches. Weight, 180 pounds.

Year Club	Lea	Pos	G	AB	R	H	2B	3B	HR	RBI	SB	Avg
2004 Casper	Pioneer	2B	23	87	20	23	5	1	0	7	14	.264
2005 Casper	Pioneer	2B	63	219	48	66	7	7	3	25	25	.301
2006 Asheville	So.Atl.	2B	128	482	92	142	28	6	5	49	87	.295
2007 Modesto	Calif.	2B	130	540	113	157	29	11	8	63	73	.291
2008 Tulsa	Texas	2B-OF	105	403	74	117	24	4	3	33	46	.290
2009 Colorado Springs	P.C.	2B-OF	119	472	118	141	21	10	7	43	58	.299
2009 Colorado	N.L.	2B-OF	30	57	7	14	1	0	1	1	4	.246
2010 Tulsa	Texas	2B	4	13	2	3	0	0	0	0	0	.231
2010 Colorado Springs	P.C.	2B-OF	33	123	20	31	5	1	1	9	10	.252
2010 Colorado a	N.L.	2B-OF	51	172	26	42	5	1	0	8	17	.244
2011 Colorado Springs	P.C.	OF-2B	58	223	61	81	18	9	2	28	17	.363
2011 Colorado	N.L.	OF-2B	77	198	34	49	4	3	0	10	27	.247
2012 Colorado b	N.L.	OF	98	174	36	55	7	2	4	15	14	.316
2013 Colorado-New York c	N.L.	OF-2B	148	539	70	134	27	7	2	32	*46	.249
Major League Totals		5 Yrs.	404	1140	173	294	44	13	7	66	108	.258
Division Series												
2009 Colorado	N.L.	PH	2	1	0	0	0	0	0	0	0	.000

a On disabled list from May 13 to July 31, 2010.
b On disabled list from August 20 to October 5, 2012.
c Traded to New York Mets for pitcher Collin McHugh, June 19, 2013.

YOUNG, MICHAEL BRIAN

Born, Covina, California, October 19, 1976.
Bats Right. Throws Right. Height, 6 feet, 1 Inch. Weight, 200 pounds.

Year Club	Lea	Pos	G	AB	R	H	2B	3B	HR	RBI	SB	Avg
1997 St.Catherines	N.Y.-Penn.	SS-2B	74	276	49	85	18	3	9	48	9	.308
1998 Hagerstown	So.Atl.	2B-SS-OF	140	522	86	147	33	5	16	87	16	.282
1999 Dunedin	Fla.St.	2B	129	495	86	155	36	3	5	83	30	.313
2000 Tennessee	Southern	2B-SS	91	345	51	95	24	5	6	47	16	.275
2000 Tulsa	Texas	SS	43	188	30	60	13	5	1	32	9	.319
2000 Texas a	A.L.	2B	2	2	0	0	0	0	0	0	0	.000
2001 Oklahoma	P.C.	2B-SS	47	189	28	55	8	0	8	28	3	.291
2001 Texas	A.L.	2B	106	386	57	96	18	4	11	49	3	.249
2002 Texas	A.L.	2B-SS-3B	156	573	77	150	26	8	9	62	6	.262
2003 Texas	A.L.	2B-SS	160	666	106	204	33	9	14	72	13	.306
2004 Texas	A.L.	SS	160	690	114	216	33	9	22	99	12	.313
2005 Texas	A.L.	SS	159	668	*114	*221	40	5	24	91	5	*.331
2006 Texas	A.L.	SS	*162	691	93	217	52	3	14	103	7	.314
2007 Texas	A.L.	SS	156	639	80	201	37	1	9	94	13	.315
2008 Texas	A.L.	SS	155	645	102	183	36	2	12	82	10	.284
2009 Texas	A.L.	3B	135	541	76	174	36	2	22	68	8	.322
2010 Texas	A.L.	3B	157	656	99	186	36	3	21	91	4	.284
2011 Texas	A.L.	DH-3B-1B-2B	159	631	88	*213	41	6	11	106	6	.338
2012 Texas b	A.L.	DH-1B-3B-2B	156	611	79	169	27	3	8	67	2	.277
2013 Philadelphia-LA c-d	N.L.	3B-1B-2B-SS	147	519	52	145	26	5	8	46	1	.279
Major League Totals		14 Yrs.	1970	7918	1137	2375	441	60	185	1030	90	.300
Wild Card Playoff												
2012 Texas	A.L.	1B	1	4	0	2	0	0	0	0	0	.500
Division Series												
2010 Texas	A.L.	3B	5	20	1	3	0	0	1	3	0	.150
2011 Texas	A.L.	DH-1B	4	15	1	2	0	0	0	0	0	.133
2013 Los Angeles	N.L.	PH	3	3	0	1	0	0	0	0	0	.333
Division Series Totals			12	38	2	6	0	0	1	3	0	.158
Championship Series												
2010 Texas	A.L.	3B	6	27	3	9	3	0	0	4	0	.333
2011 Texas	A.L.	1B-DH	6	28	3	7	3	0	1	7	0	.250
2013 Los Angeles	N.L.	1B-SS	6	7	0	0	0	0	0	0	0	.000
Championship Series Totals			18	62	6	16	6	0	1	11	0	.258
World Series Record												
2010 Texas	A.L.	3B	5	20	0	5	0	0	0	0	0	.250
2011 Texas	A.L.	1B-DH	7	27	3	7	4	0	1	5	0	.259
World Series Totals			12	47	3	12	4	0	1	5	0	.255

a Traded by Toronto Blue Jays to Texas Rangers with pitcher Darwin Cubillan for pitcher Esteban Loaiza, July 19, 2000.
b Traded to Philadelphia Phillies for pitcher Josh Lindblom and pitcher Lisalverto Bonilla, December 9, 2012.
c Traded to Los Angeles Dodgers with cash for pitcher Rob Rasmussen, August 31, 2013.
d Filed for free agency, October 31, 2013.

ZIMMERMAN, RYAN WALLACE

Born, Washington, North Carolina, September 28, 1984.
Bats Right. Throws Right. Height, 6 feet, 3 inches. Weight, 230 pounds.

Year	Club	Lea	Pos	G	AB	R	H	2B	3B	HR	RBI	SB	Avg
2005	Savannah	So.Atl.	1B-SS	4	17	5	8	2	1	2	6	0	.471
2005	Harrisburg	Eastern	3B-SS	63	233	40	76	20	0	9	32	1	.326
2005	Washington	N.L.	3B-SS	20	58	6	23	10	0	0	6	0	.397
2006	Washington	N.L.	3B	157	614	84	176	47	3	20	110	11	.287
2007	Washington	N.L.	3B	*162	653	99	174	43	5	24	91	4	.266
2008	Potomac	Carolina	DH	2	10	1	3	2	0	0	0	0	.300
2008	Columbus	Int.	3B	4	15	4	4	1	0	1	3	0	.267
2008	Washington a	N.L.	3B	106	428	51	121	24	1	14	51	1	.283
2009	Washington	N.L.	3B	157	610	110	178	37	3	33	106	2	.292
2010	Washington	N.L.	3B	142	525	85	161	32	0	25	85	4	.307
2011	Hagerstown	So.Atl.	2B	1	2	2	2	1	1	0	1	0	1.000
2011	Potomac	Carolina	3B	3	10	0	4	2	0	0	1	0	.400
2011	Syracuse	Int.	3B	2	9	1	2	0	0	0	1	0	.222
2011	Washington b	N.L.	3B	101	395	52	114	21	2	12	49	3	.289
2012	Washington c	N.L.	3B	145	578	93	163	36	1	25	95	5	.282
2013	Potomac	Carolina	3B	1	3	0	0	0	0	0	0	0	.000
2013	Washington d	N.L.	3B	147	568	84	156	26	2	26	79	6	.275
Major League Totals			9 Yrs.	1137	4429	664	1266	276	17	179	672	36	.286
	Division Series												
2012	Washington	N.L.	3B	5	21	3	8	1	0	2	4	0	.381

a On disabled list from May 26 to July 22, 2008.
b On disabled list from April 10 to June 14, 2011.
c On disabled list from April 21 to May 8, 2012.
d On disabled list from April 18 to May 3, 2013.

ZOBRIST, BENJAMIN THOMAS (BEN)

Born, Eureka, Illinois, May 26, 1981.
Bats Both. Throws Right. Height, 6 feet, 3 inches. Weight, 200 pounds.

Year	Club	Lea	Pos	G	AB	R	H	2B	3B	HR	RBI	SB	Avg
2004	Tri-City	N.Y.-Penn.	SS	68	257	50	87	14	3	4	45	15	.339
2005	Salem	Carolina	SS	42	141	25	47	12	1	3	13	2	.333
2005	Lexington	So.Atl.	SS	68	247	45	75	17	2	2	32	16	.304
2006	Corpus Christi	Texas	SS-3B	83	315	57	103	25	6	3	30	9	.327
2006	Durham	Int.	SS	18	69	12	21	3	1	0	6	4	.304
2006	Tampa Bay a	A.L.	SS	52	183	10	41	6	2	2	18	2	.224
2007	Durham	Int.	SS	61	222	42	62	14	2	7	22	8	.279
2007	Tampa Bay b	A.L.	SS	31	97	8	15	2	0	1	9	2	.155
2008	Vero Beach	Fla.St.	2B-3B-SS	4	14	1	4	1	0	0	2	0	.286
2008	Durham	Int.	SS-3B-2B	20	71	15	26	3	0	4	13	4	.366
2008	Tampa Bay c	A.L.	SS-OF-2B-3B	62	198	32	50	10	2	12	30	3	.253
2009	Tampa Bay	A.L.	2B-OF-SS-1B	152	501	91	149	28	7	27	91	17	.297
2010	Tampa Bay	A.L.	OF-2B-1B-3B	151	541	77	129	28	2	10	75	24	.238
2011	Tampa Bay	A.L.	2B-OF	156	588	99	158	46	6	20	91	19	.269
2012	Tampa Bay	A.L.	OF-2B-SS	157	560	88	151	39	7	20	74	14	.270
2013	Tampa Bay	A.L.	2B-OF-SS	157	612	77	168	36	3	12	71	11	.275
Major League Totals			8 Yrs.	918	3280	482	861	195	29	104	459	92	.262
	Wild Card Playoff												
2013	Tampa Bay	A.L.	2B	1	4	1	1	0	0	0	0	0	.250
	Division Series												
2010	Tampa Bay	A.L.	OF-2B-1B	5	20	2	6	2	0	1	2	0	.300
2011	Tampa Bay	A.L.	2B	4	17	2	4	0	0	0	0	0	.235
2013	Tampa Bay	A.L.	2B	4	14	2	2	0	0	1	1	0	.143
Division Series Totals				13	51	6	12	2	0	2	3	0	.235
	Championship Series												
2008	Tampa Bay	A.L.	OF-SS	3	4	0	0	0	0	0	0	0	.000
	World Series Record												
2008	Tampa Bay	A.L.	OF	4	7	0	1	0	0	0	0	0	.143

a Traded by Houston Astros to Tampa Bay Devil Rays with pitcher Mitch Talbot for infielder Aubrey Huff and cash, July 12, 2006.
b On disabled list from August 19 to November 12, 2007.
c On disabled list from March 25 to May 13, 2008.

PITCHERS

ADAMS, JON MICHAEL (MIKE)

Born, Corpus Christi, Texas, July 29, 1978.
Bats Right. Throws Right. Height, 6 feet, 5 inches. Weight, 190 pounds.

Year Club	Lea	G	IP	W	L	Pct	SO	BB	H	ERA	SAVES
2001 Ogden	Pioneer	23	32	2	2	.500	44	6	26	2.81	12
2002 High Desert	Calif.	10	14	2	1	.667	23	7	9	2.57	5
2002 Beloit	Midwest	11	15⅓	0	0	.000	21	2	13	2.93	5
2002 Huntsville	Southern	13	18⅔	1	0	1.000	17	12	14	3.38	1
2003 Huntsville	Southern	45	74⅓	3	7	.300	83	33	58	3.15	14
2004 Indianapolis	Int.	10	31	2	0	1.000	37	4	23	2.61	0
2004 Milwaukee	N.L.	46	53	2	3	.400	39	14	50	3.40	0
2005 Milwaukee	N.L.	13	13⅓	0	1	.000	14	10	12	2.70	1
2005 Nashville	P.C.	26	36	3	4	.429	45	12	35	5.75	2
2006 Milwaukee	N.L.	2	2⅓	0	0	.000	1	2	4	11.57	0
2006 Nashville	P.C.	15	16⅓	1	1	.500	18	8	17	3.31	2
2006 Norfolk	Int.	13	14⅔	0	0	.000	12	7	13	4.91	0
2006 Buffalo	Int.	3	4⅔	0	0	.000	3	0	4	1.93	0
2006 Portland a-b-c	P.C.	17	23⅔	0	2	.000	15	7	29	4.18	0
2007				INJURED—Did Not Play							
2008 Portland	P.C.	12	14⅔	3	1	.750	16	9	21	5.52	0
2008 San Diego d	N.L.	54	65⅓	2	3	.400	74	19	49	2.48	0
2009 San Antonio	Texas	4	4	1	0	1.000	6	2	3	2.25	0
2009 Portland	P.C.	4	5	0	0	.000	0	1	4	5.40	0
2009 San Diego e	N.L.	37	37	0	0	.000	45	8	14	0.73	0
2010 San Antonio	Texas	1	1	0	0	.000	1	0	0	0.00	0
2010 San Diego f	N.L.	70	66⅔	4	1	.800	73	23	48	1.75	0
2011 San Diego	N.L.	48	48	3	1	.750	49	9	26	1.13	1
2011 Texas g	A.L.	27	25⅔	2	3	.400	25	5	18	2.10	1
2012 Texas h	A.L.	61	52⅓	5	3	.625	45	17	56	3.27	1
2013 Philadelphia i	N.L.	28	25	1	4	.200	23	11	23	3.96	0
Major League Totals	9 Yrs.	386	388⅔	19	19	.500	388	118	300	2.39	4
Division Series											
2011 Texas	A.L.	3	2	0	0	.000	1	3	1	4.50	0
Championship Series											
2011 Texas	A.L.	5	4⅓	1	0	1.000	4	1	5	2.08	0
World Series Record											
2011 Texas	A.L.	3	2	1	0	1.000	1	2	5	4.50	0

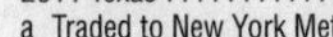

a Traded to New York Mets for pitcher Jeremi Gonzalez, May 26, 2006.
b Claimed on waivers by Cleveland Indians, July 6, 2006.
c Traded to San Diego Padres for pitcher Brian Sikorski, July 18, 2006.
d Released by San Diego Padres, March 14, 2007, re-signed with San Diego Padres organization, April 12, 2007.
e On disabled list from April 1 to June 8 and August 22 to September 17, 2009.
f On disabled list from July 12 to August 7, 2010.
g Traded to Texas Rangers for pitcher Robert Erlin and pitcher Joseph Wieland, July 31, 2011.
h Filed for free agency, November 3, 2012. Signed with Philadelphia Phillies, December 20, 2012.
i On disabled list from May 11 to May 26 and June 20 to November 1, 2013.

AFFELDT, JEREMY DAVID

Born, Phoenix, Arizona, June 6, 1979.
Bats Left. Throws Left. Height, 6 feet, 4 inches. Weight, 225 pounds.

Year Club	Lea	G	IP	W	L	Pct	SO	BB	H	ERA	SAVES
1997 Royals	Gulf Coast	10	40	2	0	1.000	36	21	34	4.50	0
1998 Royals	Gulf Coast	12	56	4	3	.571	67	24	50	2.89	0
1998 Lansing	Midwest	6	17	0	3	.000	8	12	27	9.53	0
1999 Charleston-WV	So.Atl.	27	143⅓	7	7	.500	111	80	140	3.83	0
2000 Wilmington	Carolina	27	147⅓	5	15	.250	92	59	158	4.09	0
2001 Wichita	Texas	25	145⅓	10	6	.625	128	46	153	3.90	0
2002 Wichita	Texas	3	6	0	0	.000	3	3	1	1.50	0
2002 Kansas City a	A.L.	34	77⅔	3	4	.429	67	37	85	4.64	0
2003 Kansas City b	A.L.	36	126	7	6	.538	98	38	126	3.93	4
2004 Omaha	P.C.	4	4	0	0	.000	5	0	2	0.00	3
2004 Kansas City c	A.L.	38	76⅓	3	4	.429	49	32	91	4.95	13
2005 Omaha	P.C.	9	8⅓	0	1	.000	9	6	9	6.48	0
2005 Kansas City d	A.L.	49	49⅔	0	2	.000	39	29	56	5.26	0

Year	Club	Lea	G	IP	W	L	Pct	SO	BB	H	ERA	SAVES
2006	Kansas City	A.L.	27	70	4	6	.400	28	42	71	5.91	0
2006	Colorado e	N.L.	27	27⅓	4	2	.667	20	13	30	6.91	1
2007	Colorado f	N.L.	75	59	4	3	.571	46	33	47	3.51	0
2008	Cincinnati g	N.L.	74	78⅓	1	1	.500	80	25	78	3.33	0
2009	San Francisco	N.L.	74	62⅓	2	2	.500	55	31	42	1.73	0
2010	San Jose	Calif.	2	3	0	0	.000	4	1	2	0.00	0
2010	San Francisco h	N.L.	53	50	4	3	.571	44	24	56	4.14	4
2011	San Francisco	N.L.	67	61⅔	3	2	.600	54	24	47	2.63	3
2012	San Francisco i-j	N.L.	67	63⅓	1	2	.333	57	23	57	2.70	3
2013	San Francisco k	N.L.	39	33⅔	1	5	.167	21	17	27	3.74	0
Major League Totals		12 Yrs.	660	835⅓	37	42	.468	658	368	814	4.00	28
	Division Series											
2007	Colorado	N.L.	1	1	0	0	.000	2	0	1	9.00	0
2012	San Francisco	N.L.	3	3⅔	0	0	.000	2	1	3	0.00	0
Division Series Totals			4	4⅔	0	0	.000	4	1	4	1.93	0
	Championship Series											
2007	Colorado	N.L.	2	1⅓	0	0	.000	0	0	0	0.00	0
2010	San Francisco	N.L.	3	2⅔	0	0	.000	4	1	0	3.38	0
2012	San Francisco	N.L.	5	4⅔	0	0	.000	4	1	2	0.00	0
Championship Series Totals			10	8⅔	0	0	.000	8	2	2	1.04	0
	World Series Record											
2007	Colorado	N.L.	4	3	0	0	.000	2	1	2	0.00	0
2010	San Francisco	N.L.	2	1⅓	0	0	.000	0	1	1	6.75	0
2012	San Francisco	N.L.	2	2	0	0	.000	4	1	0	0.00	0
World Series Totals			8	6⅓	0	0	.000	6	3	3	1.42	0

a On disabled list from June 9 to August 1, 2002.
b On disabled list from April 20 to May 6, 2003.
c On disabled list from June 27 to August 21, 2004.
d On disabled list from April 16 to June 4 and June 19 to July 7, 2005.
e Traded to Colorado Rockies with pitcher Denny Bautista for infielder Ryan Shealy and pitcher Scott Dohmann, July 31, 2006.
f Filed for free agency, October 29, 2007. Signed with Cincinnati Reds, January 23, 2008.
g Filed for free agency, October 30, 2008. Signed with San Francisco Giants, November 17, 2008.
h On disabled list from July 21 to August 18, 2010.
i On disabled list from April 28 to May 13, 2012.
j Filed for free agency, November 3, 2012, re-signed with San Francisco Giants, November 14, 2012.
k On disabled list from April 15 to May 3 and July 21 to September 12, 2013.

ALBERS, MATTHEW JAMES (MATT)

Born, Houston, Texas, January 20, 1983.
Bats Left. Throws Right. Height, 6 feet. Weight, 205 pounds.

Year	Club	Lea	G	IP	W	L	Pct	SO	BB	H	ERA	SAVES
2002	Martinsville	Appal.	13	59⅔	2	3	.400	72	38	61	5.13	0
2003	Tri-City	N.Y.-Penn.	15	86⅓	5	4	.556	94	25	69	2.92	0
2004	Lexington	So.Atl.	22	111⅓	8	3	.727	140	57	95	3.31	0
2005	Salem	Carolina	28	148⅔	8	12	.400	146	62	161	4.66	0
2006	Corpus Christi	Texas	19	116	10	2	.833	95	47	96	2.17	0
2006	Round Rock	P.C.	4	25	2	1	.667	26	10	24	3.96	0
2006	Houston	N.L.	4	15	0	2	.000	11	7	17	6.00	0
2007	Round Rock	P.C.	9	53	2	3	.400	43	22	50	3.74	0
2007	Houston a	N.L.	31	110⅔	4	11	.267	71	50	127	5.86	0
2008	Aberdeen	N.Y.-Penn.	2	2	0	0	.000	4	1	1	0.00	0
2008	Baltimore b	A.L.	28	49	3	3	.500	26	22	43	3.49	0
2009	Norfolk	Int.	10	12⅔	1	0	1.000	12	5	19	5.68	0
2009	Baltimore	A.L.	56	67	3	6	.333	49	36	80	5.51	0
2010	Baltimore c	A.L.	62	75⅔	5	3	.625	49	34	78	4.52	0
2011	Pawtucket	Int.	2	3	0	0	.000	2	0	1	0.00	0
2011	Boston d	A.L.	56	64⅔	4	4	.500	68	31	62	4.73	0
2012	Boston	A.L.	40	39⅓	2	0	1.000	25	15	30	2.29	0
2012	Arizona e-f	N.L.	23	21	1	1	.500	19	7	16	2.57	0
2013	Cleveland g	A.L.	56	63	3	1	.750	35	23	57	3.14	0
Major League Totals		8 Yrs.	356	505⅓	25	31	.446	353	225	510	4.49	0

a Traded to Baltimore Orioles with pitcher Troy Patton, outfielder Luke Scott, pitcher Dennis Sarfate and infielder Michael Costanzo for infielder Miguel Tejada, December 12, 2007.
b On disabled list from June 26 to October 21, 2008.
c Not offered contract, December 2, 2010. Signed with Boston Red Sox, December 16, 2010.
d On disabled list from April 8 to April 21, 2011.
e Traded to Arizona Diamondbacks with outfielder Scott Podsednik for pitcher Craig Breslow, July 31, 2012.

f Traded to Cleveland Indians with pitcher Trevor Bauer and pitcher Bryan Shaw for infielder Lars Anderson, infielder Didi Gregorius and pitcher Tony Sipp, December 11, 2012.
g Filed for free agency, October 31, 2013. Signed with Houston Astros, December 17, 2013.

ALBURQUERQUE, ALBERTO JOSE (AL)

Born, San Pedro de Macoris, Dominican Republic, June 10, 1986.
Bats Right. Throws Right. Height, 6 feet. Weight, 195 pounds.

Year Club	Lea	G	IP	W	L	Pct	SO	BB	H	ERA	SAVES
2005 a				INJURED—Did Not Play							
2006 Cubs	Arizona	8	12 2/3	0	2	.000	15	10	10	5.68	0
2007 Boise	Northwest	10	41	3	2	.600	49	17	42	3.73	1
2007 Peoria	Midwest	11	25 1/3	1	4	.200	20	12	36	9.24	0
2008 b				INJURED—Did Not Play							
2009 Daytona	Fla.St.	24	34 2/3	1	0	1.000	44	14	26	2.08	2
2009 Tulsa c	Texas	23	26 1/3	1	3	.250	31	13	23	3.76	0
2010 Tulsa d	Texas	25	34 1/3	2	4	.333	32	19	32	4.98	3
2011 Toledo	Int.	4	4 2/3	0	0	.000	10	2	5	1.93	0
2011 Detroit e	A.L.	41	43 1/3	6	1	.857	67	29	21	1.87	0
2012 Lakeland	Fla.St.	4	3 1/3	0	0	.000	9	1	5	5.40	0
2012 Toledo	Int.	9	10 2/3	1	0	1.000	18	4	9	1.69	0
2012 Detroit f	A.L.	8	13 1/3	0	0	.000	18	8	6	0.68	0
2013 Toledo	Int.	10	14 1/3	0	1	.000	27	13	9	3.14	1
2013 Detroit	A.L.	53	49	4	3	.571	70	34	39	4.59	0
Major League Totals	3 Yrs.	102	105 2/3	10	4	.714	155	71	66	2.98	0
Division Series											
2011 Detroit	A.L.	2	0 1/3	0	0	.000	0	1	2	81.00	0
2012 Detroit	A.L.	2	1 1/3	1	0	1.000	1	0	0	0.00	0
2013 Detroit	A.L.	1	0 2/3	0	1	.000	2	1	2	13.50	0
Division Series Totals		5	2 1/3	1	1	.500	3	2	4	15.43	0
Championship Series											
2011 Detroit	A.L.	2	1 2/3	0	0	.000	2	2	0	0.00	0
2013 Detroit	A.L.	6	4	0	0	.000	7	2	2	2.25	0
Championship Series Totals		8	5 2/3	0	0	.000	9	4	2	1.59	0
World Series Record											
2012 Detroit	A.L.	1	2	0	0	.000	2	0	1	4.50	0

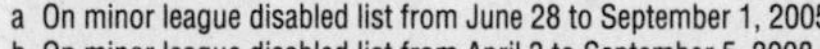

a On minor league disabled list from June 28 to September 1, 2005.
b On minor league disabled list from April 3 to September 5, 2008.
c Traded by Chicago Cubs to Colorado Rockies for outfielder Jeff Baker, July 2, 2009.
d Filed for free agency, November 6, 2010. Signed with Detroit Tigers organization, November 19, 2010.
e On disabled list from June 30 to July 16 and August 12 to September 4, 2011.
f On disabled list from April 4 to August 23, 2012.

ALLEN, CODY EDWARD

Born, Orlando, Florida, November 20, 1988.
Bats Right. Throws Right. Height, 6 feet, 1 inch. Weight, 210 pounds.

Year Club	Lea	G	IP	W	L	Pct	SO	BB	H	ERA	SAVES
2011 Mahoning Valley	N.Y.-Penn.	14	33 2/3	3	1	.750	42	9	21	2.14	0
2011 Lake County	Midwest	7	17	2	0	1.000	28	5	10	0.00	0
2011 Kinston	Carolina	1	3	0	0	.000	3	0	1	0.00	0
2011 Akron	Eastern	1	1	0	0	.000	2	0	3	18.00	0
2012 Carolina	Carolina	2	4	0	0	.000	8	0	1	0.00	0
2012 Akron	Eastern	5	7 2/3	0	0	.000	10	0	2	1.17	1
2012 Columbus	Int.	24	31 2/3	3	2	.600	35	9	22	2.27	2
2012 Cleveland	A.L.	27	29	0	1	.000	27	15	29	3.72	0
2013 Cleveland	A.L.	77	70 1/3	6	1	.857	88	26	62	2.43	2
Major League Totals	2 Yrs.	104	99 1/3	6	2	.750	115	41	91	2.81	2
Wild Card Playoff											
2013 Cleveland	A.L.	1	0 1/3	0	0	.000	1	0	1	0.00	0

ALVAREZ, HENDERSON JAVIER

Born, Valencia, Venezuela, April 18, 1990.
Bats Right. Throws Right. Height, 6 feet, 1 inch. Weight, 210 pounds.

Year Club	Lea	G	IP	W	L	Pct	SO	BB	H	ERA	SAVES
2008 Blue Jays	Gulf Coast	12	46 1/3	1	4	.200	34	6	63	5.63	0
2009 Lansing	Midwest	23	124 1/3	9	6	.600	92	19	121	3.47	0
2010 Dunedin	Fla.St.	23	112 1/3	8	7	.533	78	27	137	4.33	0
2011 Dunedin	Fla.St.	2	8 1/3	0	1	.000	4	1	11	6.48	0

Year	Club	Lea	G	IP	W	L	Pct	SO	BB	H	ERA	SAVES
2011	New Hampshire	Eastern	15	88	8	4	.667	66	17	81	2.86	0
2011	Toronto	A.L.	10	63⅔	1	3	.250	40	8	64	3.53	0
2012	Toronto a	A.L.	31	187⅓	9	14	.391	79	54	216	4.85	0
2013	Jupiter	Fla.St.	2	10	1	0	1.000	2	1	9	2.70	0
2013	Jacksonville	Southern	2	14⅓	1	0	1.000	13	0	5	0.00	0
2013	Miami b-c	N.L.	17	102⅔	5	6	.455	57	27	90	3.59	0
Major League Totals		3 Yrs.	58	353⅔	15	23	.395	176	89	370	4.25	0

a Traded to Miami Marlins with infielder Yunel Escobar, infielder Adeiny Hechavarria, catcher Jeff Mathis, pitcher Anthony De Sclafani, outfielder Jake Marisnick and pitcher Justin Nicolino for outfielder Emilio Bonifacio, catcher John Buck, pitcher Mark Buehrle, pitcher Josh Johnson and infielder Jose Reyes, November 19, 2012.

b On disabled list from March 27 to July 4, 2013.

c Pitched no-hit, no-run game against Detroit Tigers, September 29, 2013.

ANDERSON, BRETT FRANKLIN

Born, Midland, Texas, February 1, 1988.
Bats Left. Throws Left. Height, 6 feet, 4 inches. Weight, 235 pounds.

Year	Club	Lea	G	IP	W	L	Pct	SO	BB	H	ERA	SAVES
2007	Visalia	Calif.	9	39	3	3	.500	40	11	50	4.85	0
2007	South Bend a	Midwest	14	81⅓	8	4	.667	85	10	76	2.21	0
2008	Stockton	Calif.	14	74	9	4	.692	80	18	68	4.14	0
2008	Midland	Texas	6	31	2	1	.667	38	9	27	2.61	0
2009	Oakland	A.L.	30	175⅓	11	11	.500	150	45	180	4.06	0
2010	Athletics	Arizona	2	6	0	0	.000	6	0	11	3.00	0
2010	Sacramento	P.C.	3	13⅓	1	0	1.000	12	3	19	4.05	0
2010	Oakland	A.L.	19	112⅓	7	6	.538	75	22	112	2.80	0
2011	Oakland	A.L.	13	83⅓	3	6	.333	61	25	86	4.00	0
2012	Stockton	Calif.	1	2	0	0	.000	0	0	4	9.00	0
2012	Sacramento	P.C.	5	23⅓	1	1	.500	18	5	27	4.24	0
2012	Oakland b	A.L.	6	35	4	2	.667	25	7	29	2.57	0
2013	Stockton	Calif.	1	3⅓	0	1	.000	6	2	5	13.50	0
2013	Midland	Texas	1	3⅔	0	1	.000	3	4	6	14.73	0
2013	Sacramento	P.C.	1	2⅓	0	0	.000	2	3	3	7.71	0
2013	Oakland c-d	A.L.	16	44⅔	1	4	.200	46	21	51	6.04	3
Major League Totals		5 Yrs.	84	450⅔	26	29	.473	357	120	458	3.81	3
	Division Series											
2012	Oakland	A.L.	1	6	1	0	1.000	6	2	2	0.00	0
2013	Oakland	A.L.	1	0⅓	0	0	.000	1	1	1	27.00	0
Division Series Totals			2	6⅓	1	0	1.000	7	3	3	1.42	0

a Traded by Arizona Diamondbacks to Oakland Athletics with outfielder Carlos Gonzalez, pitcher Dana Eveland, pitcher Greg Smith, infielder Chris Carter and outfielder Aaron Cunningham for pitcher Danny Haren and pitcher Connor Robertson, December 14, 2007.

b On disabled list from March 13 to August 20, 2012.

c On disabled list from May 1 to August 28, 2013.

d Traded to Colorado Rockies for pitcher Drew Pomeranz and pitcher Chris Jensen, December 10, 2013.

ARCHER, CHRISTOPHER ALAN (CHRIS)

Born, Raleigh, North Carolina, September 26, 1988.
Bats Right. Throws Right. Height, 6 feet, 3 inches. Weight, 200 pounds.

Year	Club	Lea	G	IP	W	L	Pct	SO	BB	H	ERA	SAVES
2006	Indians	Gulf Coast	7	19⅓	0	3	.000	21	17	17	7.45	0
2006	Burlington	Appal.	1	1⅔	0	0	.000	1	1	2	10.80	0
2007	Indians	Gulf Coast	12	52⅔	1	7	.125	48	21	56	5.64	0
2007	Lake County	So.Atl.	1	4	0	0	.000	5	3	5	9.00	0
2008	Lake County a	So.Atl.	27	115⅓	4	8	.333	106	84	92	4.29	0
2009	Peoria	Midwest	27	109	6	4	.600	119	66	78	2.81	0
2010	Daytona	Fla.St.	15	72⅓	7	1	.875	82	26	54	2.86	0
2010	Tennessee	Southern	13	70	8	2	.800	67	39	48	1.80	0
2011	Montgomery	Southern	25	134⅓	8	7	.533	118	80	136	4.42	0
2011	Durham b	Int.	2	13	1	0	1.000	12	6	11	0.69	0
2012	Durham	Int.	25	128	7	9	.438	139	62	99	3.66	0
2012	Tampa Bay	A.L.	6	29⅓	1	3	.250	36	13	23	4.60	0
2013	Durham	Int.	10	50	5	3	.625	52	23	50	3.96	0
2013	Tampa Bay	A.L.	23	128⅔	9	7	.563	101	38	107	3.22	0
Major League Totals		2 Yrs.	29	158	10	10	.500	137	51	130	3.47	0
	Division Series											
2013	Tampa Bay	A.L.	2	1⅔	0	0	.000	2	0	1	0.00	0

a Traded by Cleveland Indians to Chicago Cubs with pitcher Jeff Stevens and pitcher John Gaub for infielder Mark DeRosa, December 31, 2008.

b Traded to Tampa Bay Rays with infielder Hak-Ju Lee, outfielder Brandon Guyer, catcher Robinson Chirinos and outfielder Sam Fuld for outfielder Fernando Perez, pitcher Matt Garza and pitcher Zachary Rosscup, January 8, 2011.

ARRIETA, JACOB JOSEPH (JAKE)

Born, Farmington, Missouri, March 6, 1986.
Bats Right. Throws Right. Height, 6 feet, 4 inches. Weight, 225 pounds.

Year	Club	Lea	G	IP	W	L	Pct	SO	BB	H	ERA	SAVES
2008	Frederick	Carolina	20	113	6	5	.545	120	51	80	2.87	0
2009	Bowie	Eastern	11	59	6	3	.667	70	23	45	2.59	0
2009	Norfolk	Int.	17	91 2/3	5	8	.385	78	33	97	3.93	0
2010	Norfolk	Int.	12	73	6	2	.750	64	34	48	1.85	0
2010	Baltimore	A.L.	18	100 1/3	6	6	.500	52	48	106	4.66	0
2011	Baltimore a	A.L.	22	119 1/3	10	8	.556	93	59	115	5.05	0
2012	Norfolk	Int.	10	56	5	4	.556	54	28	46	4.02	0
2012	Baltimore	A.L.	24	114 2/3	3	9	.250	109	35	122	6.20	0
2013	Iowa	P.C.	7	30 1/3	2	2	.500	39	16	32	3.56	0
2013	Norfolk	Int.	9	49	5	3	.625	38	14	45	4.41	0
2013	Baltimore	A.L.	5	23 2/3	1	2	.333	23	17	25	7.23	0
2013	Chicago b	N.L.	9	51 2/3	4	2	.667	37	24	34	3.66	0
Major League Totals		4 Yrs.	78	409 2/3	24	27	.471	314	183	402	5.23	0

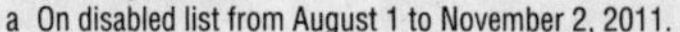

a On disabled list from August 1 to November 2, 2011.

b Traded to Chicago Cubs with pitcher Pedro Strop for catcher Steve Clevinger and pitcher Scott Feldman, July 2, 2013.

ARROYO, BRONSON ANTHONY

Born, Key West, Florida, February 24, 1977.
Bats Right. Throws Right. Height, 6 feet, 5 inches. Weight, 190 pounds.

Year	Club	Lea	G	IP	W	L	Pct	SO	BB	H	ERA	SAVES
1995	Pirates	Gulf Coast	13	61 1/3	5	4	.556	48	9	72	4.26	1
1996	Augusta	So.Atl.	26	135 2/3	8	6	.571	107	36	123	3.52	0
1997	Lynchburg	Carolina	24	160 1/3	12	4	.750	121	33	154	3.31	0
1998	Carolina a	Southern	23	127	9	8	.529	90	51	158	5.46	0
1999	Altoona	Eastern	25	153	15	4	.789	100	58	167	3.65	0
1999	Nashville	P.C.	3	13	0	2	.000	11	10	22	10.38	0
2000	Nashville	P.C.	13	88 2/3	8	2	.800	52	25	82	3.65	0
2000	Pittsburgh	N.L.	20	71 2/3	2	6	.250	50	36	88	6.40	0
2000	Lynchburg	Carolina	1	7	0	0	.000	3	2	8	3.86	0
2001	Pittsburgh	N.L.	24	88 1/3	5	7	.417	39	34	99	5.09	0
2001	Nashville	P.C.	9	66 1/3	6	2	.750	49	15	63	3.93	0
2002	Nashville	P.C.	22	143	8	6	.571	116	28	126	2.96	0
2002	Pittsburgh	N.L.	9	27	2	1	.667	22	15	30	4.00	0
2003	Pawtucket	Int.	24	149 2/3	12	6	.667	155	23	148	3.43	0
2003	Boston b	A.L.	6	17 1/3	0	0	.000	14	4	10	2.08	1
2004	Boston	A.L.	32	178 2/3	10	9	.526	142	47	171	4.03	0
2005	Boston	A.L.	35	205 1/3	14	10	.583	100	54	213	4.51	0
2006	Cincinnati c	N.L.	35	*240 2/3	14	11	.560	184	64	222	3.29	0
2007	Cincinnati	N.L.	34	210 2/3	9	15	.375	156	63	232	4.23	0
2008	Cincinnati	N.L.	34	200	15	11	.577	163	68	219	4.77	0
2009	Cincinnati	N.L.	33	220 1/3	15	13	.536	127	65	214	3.84	0
2010	Cincinnati	N.L.	33	215 2/3	17	10	.630	121	59	188	3.88	0
2011	Cincinnati	N.L.	32	199	9	12	.429	108	45	227	5.07	0
2012	Cincinnati	N.L.	32	202	12	10	.545	129	35	209	3.74	0
2013	Cincinnati d	N.L.	32	202	14	12	.538	124	34	199	3.79	0
Major League Totals		14 Yrs.	391	2278 2/3	138	127	.521	1479	623	2321	4.19	1
	Division Series											
2004	Boston	A.L.	1	6	0	0	.000	7	2	3	3.00	0
2005	Boston	A.L.	1	1	0	0	.000	1	2	2	18.00	0
2010	Cincinnati	N.L.	1	5 1/3	0	0	.000	2	3	4	1.69	0
2012	Cincinnati	N.L.	1	7	1	0	1.000	4	1	1	0.00	0
Division Series Totals			4	19 1/3	1	0	1.000	14	8	10	2.33	0
	Championship Series											
2003	Boston	A.L.	3	3 1/3	0	0	.000	5	2	2	2.70	0
2004	Boston	A.L.	3	4	0	0	.000	3	2	8	15.75	0
Championship Series Totals			6	7 1/3	0	0	.000	8	4	10	9.82	0
	World Series Record											
2004	Boston	A.L.	2	2 2/3	0	0	.000	4	1	4	6.75	0

a On minor league disabled list from May 18 to June 7 and June 18 to July 4, 1998.

b Claimed on waivers by Boston Red Sox, February 4, 2003.
c Traded to Cincinnati Reds for outfielder Wily Mo Pena, March 20, 2006.
d Filed for free agency, October 31, 2013.

ATCHISON, SCOTT BARHAM

Born, Denton, Texas, March 29, 1976.
Bats Right. Throws Right. Height, 6 feet, 2 inches. Weight, 200 pounds.

Year	Club	Lea	G	IP	W	L	Pct	SO	BB	H	ERA	SAVES
1999	Wisconsin	Midwest	15	81 2/3	4	5	.444	85	25	67	3.42	0
2000	Lancaster	Calif.	19	97 2/3	5	5	.500	77	21	117	3.69	0
2000	Tacoma	P.C.	5	26	1	1	.500	18	6	22	3.81	0
2001	San Antonio	Texas	24	136	9	10	.474	83	28	171	4.24	0
2002	Tacoma	P.C.	27	124 1/3	5	10	.333	112	31	123	4.63	2
2003	Tacoma	P.C.	39	108 2/3	6	9	.400	83	37	114	4.31	1
2004	Tacoma	P.C.	40	69 1/3	5	3	.625	76	26	71	4.15	7
2004	Seattle	A.L.	25	30 2/3	2	3	.400	36	14	29	3.52	0
2005	Mariners	Arizona	4	5	0	0	.000	9	1	7	5.40	0
2005	San Antonio	Texas	5	6	0	0	.000	8	2	3	0.00	0
2005	Tacoma	P.C.	10	13	0	0	.000	17	5	13	4.15	0
2005	Seattle a	A.L.	6	6 2/3	0	0	.000	9	1	7	6.75	0
2006	Tacoma b	P.C.	30	50	4	0	1.000	39	15	49	2.34	1
2007	Fresno	P.C.	38	53 2/3	3	2	.600	51	8	44	2.01	4
2007	San Francisco c	N.L.	22	30 2/3	0	0	.000	25	10	32	4.11	0
2008	Hanshin	Japan Pac.	42	104 2/3	7	6	.538	85	26	104	3.70	0
2009	Hanshin d	Japan Pac.	75	90	5	3	.625	81	20	60	1.70	0
2010	Pawtucket	Int.	11	13 1/3	1	0	1.000	17	5	13	4.05	0
2010	Boston	A.L.	43	60	2	3	.400	41	19	58	4.50	0
2011	Pawtucket	Int.	36	61 1/3	6	2	.750	72	9	50	2.64	5
2011	Boston	A.L.	17	30 1/3	1	0	1.000	17	6	31	3.26	1
2012	Pawtucket	Int.	2	2	0	0	.000	2	0	3	13.50	0
2012	Boston e-f	A.L.	42	51 1/3	2	1	.667	36	9	42	1.58	0
2013	Mets	Gulf Coast	2	2	0	1	.000	3	0	3	4.50	0
2013	St. Lucie	Fla.St.	1	1	0	0	.000	1	0	0	0.00	1
2013	Binghamton	Eastern	4	4	1	0	1.000	4	0	2	0.00	0
2013	New York g-h	N.L.	50	45 1/3	3	3	.500	28	12	45	4.37	0
Major League Totals		7 Yrs.	205	255	10	10	.500	192	71	244	3.64	1

a On disabled list from April 2 to September 3, 2005.
b Filed for free agency, October 15, 2006. Signed with San Francisco Giants organization, November 13, 2006.
c Filed for free agency, November 28, 2007. Signed with Boston Red Sox organization, December 12, 2007.
d Sold to Hanshin (Japan), December 19, 2007. Signed with Boston Red Sox, December 5, 2009.
e On disabled list from July 14 to September 12, 2012.
f Not offered contract, November 30, 2012. Signed with New York Mets organization, January 29, 2013.
g On disabled list from May 14 to June 18 and June 19 to July 14, 2013.
h Not offered contract, December 2, 2013. Signed with Cleveland Indians organization, January 6, 2014.

AVILAN, LUIS ARMANDO

Born, Caracas, Venezuela, July 19, 1989.
Bats Left. Throws Left. Height, 6 feet, 2 inches. Weight, 220 pounds.

Year	Club	Lea	G	IP	W	L	Pct	SO	BB	H	ERA	SAVES
2008	Braves	Gulf Coast	10	38 1/3	0	3	.000	49	15	31	2.58	0
2009	Danville	Appal.	14	38 1/3	0	2	.000	34	17	25	3.05	2
2010	Myrtle Beach	Carolina	31	48	4	3	.571	37	18	42	3.94	9
2010	Rome	So.Atl.	10	20 2/3	2	1	.667	21	9	15	2.61	0
2011	Mississippi	Southern	36	106 1/3	4	8	.333	78	36	113	4.57	1
2012	Mississippi	Southern	16	61 1/3	3	6	.333	55	31	50	3.23	1
2012	Atlanta	N.L.	31	36	1	0	1.000	33	10	27	2.00	0
2013	Atlanta	N.L.	75	65	5	0	1.000	38	22	40	1.52	0
Major League Totals		2 Yrs.	106	101	6	0	1.000	71	32	67	1.69	0
Division Series												
2013	Atlanta	N.L.	4	2 2/3	0	0	.000	1	1	3	0.00	0

AXELROD, DYLAN

Born, Santa Barbara, California, July 30, 1985.
Bats Right. Throws Right. Height, 6 feet. Weight, 185 pounds.

Year	Club	Lea	G	IP	W	L	Pct	SO	BB	H	ERA	SAVES
2007	Padres	Arizona	11	11 2/3	0	2	.000	15	4	15	5.40	2
2007	Fort Wayne	Midwest	10	21 1/3	2	1	.667	15	4	18	1.27	0

Year	Club	Lea	G	IP	W	L	Pct	SO	BB	H	ERA	SAVES
2008	Fort Wayne	Midwest	23	27⅓	1	1	.500	25	7	26	3.62	0
2008	Lake Elsinore	Calif.	32	49⅓	2	1	.667	55	19	51	5.29	0
2009	Lake Elsinore a	Calif.	11	12	0	0	.000	6	5	12	4.50	0
2009	Windy City	Frontier	22	61	3	1	.750	60	14	51	2.21	6
2009	Kannapolis b	So.Atl.	2	4⅓	0	0	.000	3	1	3	2.08	0
2009	Winston-Salem c	Carolina	5	28⅓	2	1	.667	17	4	29	1.91	0
2010	Winston-Salem	Carolina	23	99⅓	8	3	.727	84	12	95	1.99	0
2010	Birmingham	Southern	2	10	0	1	.000	8	3	8	2.70	0
2011	Birmingham	Southern	11	59⅓	3	2	.600	57	14	52	3.34	0
2011	Charlotte	Int.	15	91⅓	6	1	.857	75	21	74	2.27	0
2011	Chicago	A.L.	4	18⅔	1	0	1.000	19	9	18	2.89	0
2012	Charlotte	Int.	16	97	7	5	.583	92	31	81	2.88	0
2012	Chicago	A.L.	14	51	2	2	.500	40	21	56	5.47	0
2013	Chicago d	A.L.	30	128⅓	4	11	.267	73	43	170	5.68	0
Major League Totals		3 Yrs.	48	198	7	13	.350	132	73	244	5.36	0

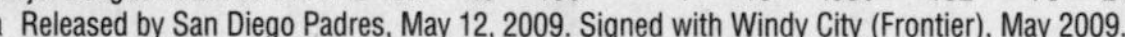

a Released by San Diego Padres, May 12, 2009. Signed with Windy City (Frontier), May 2009.
b Signed with Chicago White Sox organization, August 2, 2009.
c Filed for free agency, November 9, 2009, re-signed with Chicago White Sox organization, November 23, 2009.
d Not offered contract, December 2, 2013, re-signed with Chicago White Sox organization, January 15, 2014.

AXFORD, JOHN BERTON

Born, Simcoe, Ontario, Canada, April 1, 1983.
Bats Right. Throws Right. Height, 6 feet, 5 inches. Weight, 195 pounds.

Year	Club	Lea	G	IP	W	L	Pct	SO	BB	H	ERA	SAVES
2007	Tampa	Fla.St.	5	11⅓	0	0	.000	15	7	6	2.38	2
2007	Scranton/WB	Int.	1	0⅔	0	0	.000	1	1	2	13.50	0
2007	Staten Island	N.Y.-Penn.	8	24⅓	1	1	.50C	30	15	13	2.22	2
2007	Charleston	So.Atl.	13	26⅔	0	3	.000	21	22	29	4.39	0
2008	Brevard County a	Fla.St.	26	95	5	10	.333	89	73	86	4.55	0
2009	Brevard County	Fla.St.	19	27⅔	4	1	.800	43	16	14	1.63	0
2009	Huntsville	Southern	4	7⅔	0	0	.000	9	3	7	3.52	1
2009	Nashville	P.C.	22	33	5	0	1.000	37	19	23	3.55	0
2009	Milwaukee	N.L.	7	7⅔	0	0	.000	9	6	5	3.52	1
2010	Nashville	P.C.	12	13⅓	3	2	.600	19	5	14	2.03	2
2010	Milwaukee	N.L.	50	58	8	2	.800	76	27	42	2.48	24
2011	Milwaukee	N.L.	74	73⅔	2	2	.500	86	25	59	1.95	*46
2012	Milwaukee	N.L.	75	69⅓	5	8	.385	93	39	61	4.67	35
2013	Milwaukee-St. Louis b-c	N.L.	75	65	7	7	.500	65	26	73	4.02	0
Major League Totals		5 Yrs.	281	273⅔	22	19	.537	329	123	240	3.29	106
	Division Series											
2011	Milwaukee	N.L.	3	4	1	0	1.000	5	2	3	2.25	1
2013	St. Louis	N.L.	2	1⅓	0	0	.000	0	2	0	0.00	0
Division Series Totals			5	5⅓	1	0	1.000	5	4	3	1.69	1
	Championship Series											
2011	Milwaukee	N.L.	3	3	0	0	.000	4	0	2	0.00	2
2013	St. Louis	N.L.	2	2	0	0	.000	4	1	2	4.50	0
Championship Series Totals			5	5	0	0	.000	8	1	4	1.80	2
	World Series Record											
2013	St. Louis	N.L.	2	2⅓	0	0	.000	5	1	0	0.00	0

a Released by New York Yankees, December 14, 2007. Signed with Milwaukee Brewers organization, March 4, 2008.
b Traded to St. Louis Cardinals for player to be named later, August 30, 2013. Milwaukee Brewers received pitcher Michael Blazek to complete trade, September 2, 2013.
c Not offered contract, December 2, 2013. Signed with Cleveland Indians, December 19, 2013.

AYALA, LUIS IGNACIO

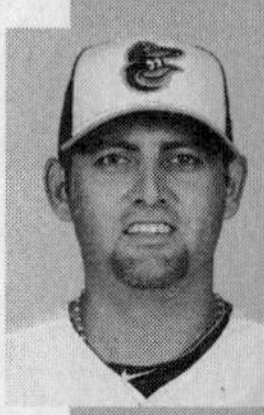

Born, Los Mochis, Mexico, January 12, 1978.
Bats Right. Throws Right. Height, 6 feet, 2 inches. Weight, 190 pounds.

Year	Club	Lea	G	IP	W	L	Pct	SO	BB	H	ERA	SAVES
1997	Saltillo	Mexican	37	62	7	5	.583	30	21	76	4.62	0
1998	Saltillo	Mexican	47	83	7	8	.467	29	45	105	5.62	7
1999	Saltillo a	Mexican	61	79	7	3	.700	28	22	54	1.71	41
2000	Saltillo	Mexican	55	65	5	3	.625	38	13	69	2.76	25
2001	Salem	Carolina	13	13⅓	0	1	.000	10	5	19	4.05	7
2001	Saltillo b	Mexican	33	40	1	2	.333	34	11	34	2.03	21
2002	Saltillo	Mexican	49	54	3	5	.375	43	15	43	1.68	23
2002	Ottawa c-d-e	Int.	6	7⅔	0	0	.000	6	4	7	3.52	0
2003	Expos	Gulf Coast	2	3⅔	0	0	.000	2	2	2	0.00	0

Year	Club	Lea	G	IP	W	L	Pct	SO	BB	H	ERA	SAVES
2003	Montreal f	N.L.	65	71	10	3	.769	46	13	65	2.92	5
2004	Montreal	N.L.	81	90 1/3	6	12	.333	63	15	92	2.69	2
2005	Washington	N.L.	68	71	8	7	.533	40	14	75	2.66	1
2006	Washington g	N.L.	INJURED—Did Not Play									
2007	Potomac	Carolina	3	2 2/3	0	0	.000	1	1	1	0.00	0
2007	Columbus	Int.	5	7	0	0	.000	5	2	4	1.29	0
2007	Washington h	N.L.	44	42 1/3	2	2	.500	28	12	43	3.19	1
2008	Washington-New York i	N.L.	81	75 2/3	2	10	.167	50	24	86	5.71	9
2009	Minnesota	A.L.	28	32 1/3	1	2	.333	21	8	38	4.18	0
2009	New Orleans	P.C.	9	10	0	0	.000	10	3	4	0.00	4
2009	Florida j-k-l	N.L.	10	7 2/3	0	3	.000	7	6	12	11.74	0
2010	Albuquerque	P.C.	14	14	1	3	.250	10	7	14	4.50	4
2010	Colorado Springs	P.C.	4	7 1/3	1	1	.500	4	0	8	4.91	0
2010	Reno m-n-o	P.C.	18	26 1/3	0	6	.000	17	11	38	7.86	0
2011	Scranton-WB	Int.	3	5	0	0	.000	7	0	6	1.80	0
2011	New York p-q	A.L.	52	56	2	2	.500	39	20	51	2.09	0
2012	Baltimore	A.L.	66	75	5	5	.500	51	14	81	2.64	1
2013	Mississippi	Southern	3	3	0	0	.000	2	0	2	0.00	0
2013	Gwinnett	Int.	8	8 1/3	0	1	.000	8	5	9	6.48	0
2013	Baltimore	A.L.	2	2	1	0	1.000	2	0	4	9.00	0
2013	Atlanta r-s-t	N.L.	37	31	1	1	.500	20	13	34	2.90	0
Major League Totals		9 Yrs.	534	554 1/3	38	47	.447	367	139	581	3.34	19
	Division Series											
2011	New York	A.L.	2	1 1/3	0	0	.000	0	0	3	6.75	0
2012	Baltimore	A.L.	1	0 1/3	0	0	.000	1	0	2	0.00	0
2013	Atlanta	N.L.	3	2	0	0	.000	3	2	1	0.00	0
Division Series Totals			6	3 2/3	0	0	.000	4	2	6	2.45	0

a Sold to Colorado Rockies by Saltillo (Mexican), October 14, 1999.
b Sold to Saltillo (Mexican), May 15, 2001.
c Sold to Montreal Expos, August 18, 2002.
d Filed for free agency, October 15, 2002. Signed with Arizona Diamondbacks organization, October 23, 2002.
e Selected by Montreal Expos organization in Rule V draft, December 16, 2002.
f On disabled list from June 22 to July 21, 2003.
g On disabled list from March 24 to October 9, 2006.
h On disabled list from March 28 to June 20, 2007.
i Traded to New York Mets for player to be named later, August 17, 2008. Washington Nationals received infielder Anderson Hernandez to complete trade, August 20, 2008.
j Filed for free agency, October 31, 2008. Signed with Minnesota Twins, February 18, 2009.
k Released by Minnesota Twins, June 30, 2009. Signed with Florida Marlins organization, July 2, 2009.
l Filed for free agency, September 4, 2009. Signed with Los Angeles Dodgers organization, December 17, 2009.
m Released by Los Angeles Dodgers, May 17, 2010. Signed with Arizona Diamondbacks organization, May 20, 2010.
n Released by Arizona Diamondbacks, July 16, 2010. Signed with Colorado Rockies organization, August 27, 2010.
o Released by Colorado Rockies, November 22, 2010. Signed with New York Yankees organization, February 11, 2011.
p On disabled list from April 13 to May 11, 2011.
q Filed for free agency, October 30, 2011. Signed with Baltimore Orioles, February 10, 2012.
r Traded to Atlanta Braves for pitcher Chris Jones, April 10, 2013.
s On disabled list from April 25 to July 5, 2013.
t Filed for free agency, October 31, 2013.

BADENHOP, BURKE HEINRICH

Born, Atlanta, Georgia, February 8, 1983.

Bats Right. Throws Right. Height, 6 feet, 5 inches. Weight, 220 pounds.

Year	Club	Lea	G	IP	W	L	Pct	SO	BB	H	ERA	SAVES
2005	Oneonta	N.Y.-Penn.	14	77	6	4	.600	55	26	69	2.92	0
2006	West Michigan	Midwest	27	171	14	3	.824	124	31	170	2.84	0
2007	Erie	Eastern	3	18 2/3	2	0	1.000	12	3	8	1.45	0
2007	Lakeland a	Fla.St.	23	135 1/3	10	6	.625	78	34	130	3.13	0
2008	Carolina	Southern	1	6 1/3	1	0	1.000	3	0	6	0.00	0
2008	Florida	N.L.	13	47 1/3	2	3	.400	35	21	55	6.08	0
2008	Marlins	Gulf Coast	1	3	0	0	.000	2	0	1	0.00	0
2009	Marlins	Gulf Coast	2	3	0	1	.000	4	0	2	0.00	0
2009	Jupiter	Fla.St.	2	8	0	0	.000	8	1	2	0.00	0
2009	New Orleans	P.C.	2	9 1/3	0	1	.000	6	4	14	6.75	0
2009	Florida b	N.L.	35	72	7	4	.636	57	24	71	3.75	0
2010	New Orleans	P.C.	12	16	0	1	.000	9	7	16	2.81	0
2010	Florida	N.L.	53	67 2/3	2	5	.286	47	21	62	3.99	1
2011	New Orleans	P.C.	11	14 2/3	1	1	.500	10	7	20	6.75	1
2011	Florida c	N.L.	50	63 2/3	2	3	.400	51	24	65	4.10	1

Year	Club	Lea	G	IP	W	L	Pct	SO	BB	H	ERA	SAVES
2012	Tampa Bay d	A.L.	66	$62\frac{1}{3}$	3	2	.600	42	12	63	3.03	0
2013	Milwaukee e	N.L.	63	$62\frac{1}{3}$	2	3	.400	42	12	62	3.47	1
Major League Totals		6 Yrs.	280	$375\frac{1}{3}$	18	20	.474	274	114	378	3.98	3

a Traded by Detroit Tigers to Florida Marlins with pitcher Eulogio De La Cruz, pitcher Andrew Miller, catcher Mike Rabelo and outfielder Cameron Maybin for pitcher Dontrelle Willis and infielder Miguel Cabrera, December 5, 2007.
b On disabled list from August 2 to September 1, 2009.
c Traded to Tampa Bay Rays for catcher Jake Jefferies, December 12, 2011.
d Traded to Milwaukee Brewers for outfielder Raul Mondesi, December 1, 2012.
e Traded to Boston Red Sox for pitcher Luis Ortega, November 22, 2013.

BAILEY, DAVID DEWITT (HOMER)

Born, LaGrange, Texas, May 3, 1986.
Bats Right. Throws Right. Height, 6 feet, 4 inches. Weight, 210 pounds.

Year	Club	Lea	G	IP	W	L	Pct	SO	BB	H	ERA	SAVES
2004	Reds	Gulf Coast	6	$12\frac{1}{3}$	0	1	.000	9	3	14	4.38	0
2005	Dayton	Midwest	28	$103\frac{2}{3}$	8	4	.667	125	62	89	4.43	0
2006	Sarasota	Fla.St.	13	$70\frac{2}{3}$	3	5	.375	79	22	49	3.31	0
2006	Chattanooga	Southern	13	68	7	1	.875	77	28	50	1.59	0
2007	Louisville	Int.	12	$67\frac{1}{3}$	6	3	.667	59	32	49	3.07	0
2007	Sarasota	Fla.St.	2	8	0	1	.000	7	5	15	10.13	0
2007	Cincinnati	N.L.	9	$45\frac{1}{3}$	4	2	.667	28	28	43	5.76	0
2008	Cincinnati	N.L.	8	$36\frac{1}{3}$	0	6	.000	18	17	59	7.93	0
2008	Louisville	Int.	19	$111\frac{1}{3}$	4	7	.364	96	46	118	4.77	0
2009	Louisville	Int.	14	$89\frac{2}{3}$	8	5	.615	82	27	87	2.71	0
2009	Cincinnati	N.L.	20	$113\frac{1}{3}$	8	5	.615	86	52	115	4.53	0
2010	Dayton	Midwest	1	4	0	1	.000	5	1	4	6.75	0
2010	Louisville	Int.	4	19	2	0	1.000	15	5	15	2.37	0
2010	Cincinnati a	N.L.	19	109	4	3	.571	100	40	109	4.46	0
2011	Louisville	Int.	6	30	2	1	.667	22	6	34	3.00	0
2011	Cincinnati b	N.L.	22	132	9	7	.563	106	33	136	4.43	0
2012	Cincinnati	N.L.	33	208	13	10	.565	168	52	206	3.68	0
2013	Cincinnati c	N.L.	32	209	11	12	.478	199	54	181	3.49	0
Major League Totals		7 Yrs.	143	853	49	45	.521	705	276	849	4.25	0
	Division Series											
2010	Cincinnati	N.L.	1	2	0	0	.000	2	0	2	0.00	0
2012	Cincinnati	N.L.	1	7	0	0	.000	10	1	1	1.29	0
Division Series Totals			2	9	0	0	.000	12	1	3	1.00	0

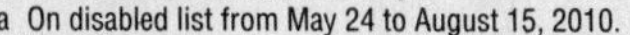

a On disabled list from May 24 to August 15, 2010.
b On disabled list from March 24 to May 5 and May 27 to June 26, 2011.
c Pitched no-hit, no-run game against San Francisco Giants, July 2, 2013.

BALFOUR, GRANT ROBERT

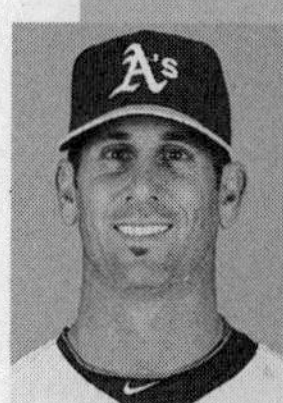

Born, Sydney, New South Wales, Australia, December 30, 1977.
Bats Right. Throws Right. Height, 6 feet, 2 inches. Weight, 190 pounds.

Year	Club	Lea	G	IP	W	L	Pct	SO	BB	H	ERA	SAVES
1997	Twins	Gulf Coast	13	67	2	4	.333	43	20	73	3.76	0
1998	Elizabethtn	Appal.	13	$77\frac{2}{3}$	7	2	.778	75	27	70	3.36	0
1999	Quad Cities	Midwest	19	$91\frac{2}{3}$	8	5	.615	95	37	66	3.53	1
2000	Fort Myers	Fla.St.	35	89	8	5	.615	90	34	91	4.25	6
2001	New Britain	Eastern	35	50	2	1	.667	72	22	26	1.08	13
2001	Minnesota	A.L.	2	$2\frac{2}{3}$	0	0	.000	2	3	3	13.50	0
2001	Edmonton	P.C.	11	$16\frac{1}{3}$	2	2	.500	17	10	18	5.51	0
2002	Edmonton	P.C.	58	$71\frac{1}{3}$	2	4	.333	88	30	60	4.16	8
2003	Rochester	Int.	21	71	5	2	.714	87	16	48	2.41	5
2003	Minnesota	A.L.	17	26	1	0	1.000	30	14	23	4.15	0
2004	Minnesota a	A.L.	36	$39\frac{1}{3}$	4	1	.800	42	21	35	4.35	0
2005	Minnesota b	A.L.	INJURED—Did Not Play									
2006	Sarasota	Fla.St.	5	$5\frac{2}{3}$	0	0	.000	7	3	8	7.94	0
2006	Reds	Gulf Coast	2	$1\frac{1}{3}$	0	0	.000	2	3	1	13.50	0
2006	Dayton c-d	Midwest	2	2	0	0	.000	3	0	0	0.00	0
2007	Huntsville	Southern	8	$11\frac{1}{3}$	0	0	.000	21	4	8	2.38	2
2007	Nashville	P.C.	24	32	1	1	.500	47	11	17	1.69	5
2007	Milwaukee e-f	N.L.	3	$2\frac{2}{3}$	0	2	.000	3	4	4	20.25	0
2007	Tampa Bay	A.L.	22	22	1	0	1.000	27	16	26	6.14	0
2008	Durham	Int.	15	$23\frac{2}{3}$	1	0	1.000	39	10	5	0.38	8
2008	Tampa Bay	A.L.	51	$58\frac{1}{3}$	6	2	.750	82	24	28	1.54	4
2009	Tampa Bay	A.L.	73	$67\frac{1}{3}$	5	4	.556	69	33	59	4.81	4
2010	Charlotte	Fla.St.	2	$1\frac{2}{3}$	0	1	.000	2	3	2	10.80	0

Year	Club	Lea	G	IP	W	L	Pct	SO	BB	H	ERA	SAVES
2010	Tampa Bay g-h	A.L.	57	55 1/3	2	1	.667	56	17	43	2.28	0
2011	Sacramento	P.C.	1	1	0	0	.000	0	1	2	9.00	0
2011	Oakland i	A.L.	62	62	5	2	.714	59	20	44	2.47	2
2012	Oakland	A.L.	75	74 2/3	3	2	.600	72	28	41	2.53	24
2013	Oakland j	A.L.	65	62 2/3	1	3	.250	72	27	48	2.59	38
Major League Totals		10 Yrs.	463	473	28	17	.622	514	207	354	3.27	72
	Division Series											
2004	Minnesota	A.L.	2	2 2/3	0	0	.000	2	0	0	0.00	0
2008	Tampa Bay	A.L.	3	3 1/3	0	0	.000	4	1	2	0.00	0
2010	Tampa Bay	A.L.	3	3 2/3	0	0	.000	1	0	2	0.00	0
2012	Oakland	A.L.	2	1 2/3	0	1	.000	2	1	3	5.40	1
2013	Oakland	A.L.	3	3	1	0	1.000	3	1	0	0.00	1
Division Series Totals			13	14 1/3	1	1	.500	12	3	7	0.63	2
	Championship Series											
2008	Tampa Bay	A.L.	4	2 1/3	0	0	.000	1	4	5	19.29	0
	World Series Record											
2008	Tampa Bay	A.L.	3	3	0	0	.000	2	3	4	3.00	0

a On disabled list from April 4 to May 14 and August 2 to August 17, 2004.
b On disabled list from March 25 to October 14, 2005.
c Filed for free agency, October 15, 2005. Signed with Cincinnati Reds organization, January 12, 2006.
d On disabled list from March 31 to October 3, 2006.
e Claimed on waivers by Milwaukee Brewers, October 5, 2006.
f Traded to Tampa Bay Devil Rays for pitcher Seth McClung, July 27, 2007.
g On disabled list from July 30 to September 1, 2010.
h Filed for free agency, November 1, 2010. Signed with Oakland Athletics, January 18, 2011.
i On disabled list from June 22 to July 7, 2011.
j Filed for free agency, October 31, 2013.

BASTARDO, ANTONIO FRANCISCO

Born, Hato Mayor, Dominican Republic, September 21, 1985.
Bats Right. Throws Left. Height, 5 feet, 11 inches. Weight, 195 pounds.

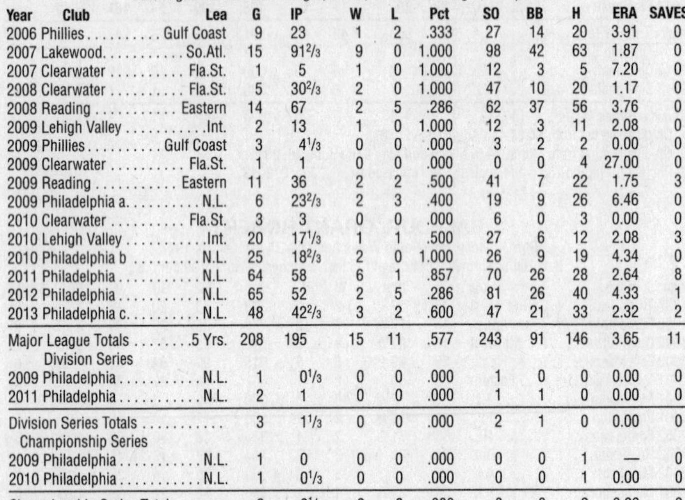

Year	Club	Lea	G	IP	W	L	Pct	SO	BB	H	ERA	SAVES
2006	Phillies	Gulf Coast	9	23	1	2	.333	27	14	20	3.91	0
2007	Lakewood	So.Atl.	15	91 2/3	9	0	1.000	98	42	63	1.87	0
2007	Clearwater	Fla.St.	1	5	1	0	1.000	12	3	5	7.20	0
2008	Clearwater	Fla.St.	5	30 2/3	2	0	1.000	47	10	20	1.17	0
2008	Reading	Eastern	14	67	2	5	.286	62	37	56	3.76	0
2009	Lehigh Valley	Int.	2	13	1	0	1.000	12	3	11	2.08	0
2009	Phillies	Gulf Coast	3	4 1/3	0	0	.000	3	2	2	0.00	0
2009	Clearwater	Fla.St.	1	1	0	0	.000	0	0	4	27.00	0
2009	Reading	Eastern	11	36	2	2	.500	41	7	22	1.75	3
2009	Philadelphia a	N.L.	6	23 2/3	2	3	.400	19	9	26	6.46	0
2010	Clearwater	Fla.St.	3	3	0	0	.000	6	0	3	0.00	0
2010	Lehigh Valley	Int.	20	17 1/3	1	1	.500	27	6	12	2.08	3
2010	Philadelphia b	N.L.	25	18 2/3	2	0	1.000	26	9	19	4.34	0
2011	Philadelphia	N.L.	64	58	6	1	.857	70	26	28	2.64	8
2012	Philadelphia	N.L.	65	52	2	5	.286	81	26	40	4.33	1
2013	Philadelphia c	N.L.	48	42 2/3	3	2	.600	47	21	33	2.32	2
Major League Totals		5 Yrs.	208	195	15	11	.577	243	91	146	3.65	11
	Division Series											
2009	Philadelphia	N.L.	1	0 1/3	0	0	.000	1	0	0	0.00	0
2011	Philadelphia	N.L.	2	1	0	0	.000	1	1	0	0.00	0
Division Series Totals			3	1 1/3	0	0	.000	2	1	0	0.00	0
	Championship Series											
2009	Philadelphia	N.L.	1	0	0	0	.000	0	0	1	—	0
2010	Philadelphia	N.L.	1	0 1/3	0	0	.000	0	0	1	0.00	0
Championship Series Totals			2	0 1/3	0	0	.000	0	0	2	0.00	0

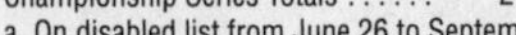

a On disabled list from June 26 to September 3, 2009.
b On disabled list from June 16 to July 15, 2010.
c Suspended for 50 games for performance-enhancing drug use, August 5, 2013.

BEACHY, BRANDON ALAN

Born, Kokomo, Indiana, September 3, 1986.
Bats Right. Throws Right. Height, 6 feet, 3 inches. Weight, 215 pounds.

Year	Club	Lea	G	IP	W	L	Pct	SO	BB	H	ERA	SAVES
2008	Danville	Appal.	6	12	2	0	1.000	16	2	12	2.25	0
2009	Rome	So.Atl.	12	17 2/3	0	0	.000	17	4	20	5.60	0

Year	Club	Lea	G	IP	W	L	Pct	SO	BB	H	ERA	SAVES
2009	Mississippi	Southern	1	1	0	0	.000	0	0	1	0.00	0
2009	Myrtle Beach	Carolina	22	58	4	3	.571	47	15	59	3.41	1
2010	Mississippi	Southern	27	73 2/3	3	1	.750	100	22	53	1.47	1
2010	Gwinnett	Int.	8	45 2/3	2	0	1.000	48	6	40	2.17	1
2010	Atlanta	N.L.	3	15	0	2	.000	15	7	16	3.00	0
2011	Gwinnett	Int.	1	5	1	0	1.000	8	2	4	1.80	0
2011	Atlanta a	N.L.	25	141 2/3	7	3	.700	169	46	125	3.68	0
2012	Atlanta b	N.L.	13	81	5	5	.500	68	29	49	2.00	0
2013	Rome	So.Atl.	1	5	1	0	1.000	3	1	3	0.00	0
2013	Mississippi	Southern	1	5	1	0	1.000	4	1	6	5.40	0
2013	Gwinnett	Int.	7	30	1	4	.200	26	18	23	3.00	0
2013	Atlanta c	N.L.	5	30	2	1	.667	23	4	27	4.50	0
Major League Totals		4 Yrs.	46	267 2/3	14	11	.560	275	86	217	3.23	0

a On disabled list from May 14 to June 22, 2011.
b On disabled list from June 16 to October 10, 2012.
c On disabled list from March 22 to July 29 and August 21 to October 1, 2013.

BECKETT, JOSHUA PATRICK (JOSH)

Born, Spring, Texas, May 15, 1980.
Bats Right. Throws Right. Height, 6 feet, 5 inches. Weight, 220 pounds.

Year	Club	Lea	G	IP	W	L	Pct	SO	BB	H	ERA	SAVES
2000	Kane County	Midwest	13	59 1/3	2	3	.400	61	15	45	2.12	0
2001	Brevard County	Fla.St.	13	65 2/3	6	0	1.000	101	15	32	1.23	0
2001	Portland	Eastern	13	74 1/3	8	1	.889	102	19	50	1.82	0
2001	Florida	N.L.	4	24	2	2	.500	24	11	14	1.50	0
2002	Marlins	Gulf Coast	1	4	0	0	.000	7	1	5	4.50	0
2002	Jupiter	Fla.St.	1	6	1	0	1.000	12	1	4	0.00	0
2002	Florida a	N.L.	23	107 2/3	6	7	.462	113	44	93	4.10	0
2003	Carolina	Southern	1	4	0	0	.000	7	0	4	4.50	0
2003	Jupiter	Fla.St.	1	3	0	0	.000	5	0	2	0.00	0
2003	Florida b	N.L.	24	142	9	8	.529	152	56	132	3.04	0
2004	Florida c	N.L.	26	156 2/3	9	9	.500	152	54	137	3.79	0
2005	Florida d-e	N.L.	29	178 2/3	15	8	.652	166	58	153	3.38	0
2006	Boston	A.L.	33	204 2/3	16	11	.593	158	74	191	5.01	0
2007	Boston f	A.L.	30	200 2/3	*20	7	.741	194	40	189	3.27	0
2008	Boston g	A.L.	27	174 1/3	12	10	.545	172	34	173	4.03	0
2009	Boston	A.L.	32	212 1/3	17	6	.739	199	55	198	3.86	0
2010	Pawtucket	Int.	2	8	0	0	.000	7	1	7	4.50	0
2010	Boston h	A.L.	21	127 2/3	6	6	.500	116	45	151	5.78	0
2011	Boston	A.L.	30	193	13	7	.650	175	52	146	2.89	0
2012	Boston	A.L.	21	127 1/3	5	11	.313	94	38	131	5.23	0
2012	Los Angeles i-j	N.L.	7	43	2	3	.400	38	14	43	2.93	0
2013	Los Angeles k	N.L.	8	43 1/3	0	5	.000	41	15	50	5.19	0
Major League Totals		13 Yrs.	315	1935 1/3	132	100	.569	1794	590	1801	3.94	0
	Division Series											
2003	Florida	N.L.	1	7	0	1	.000	9	5	2	1.29	0
2007	Boston	A.L.	1	9	1	0	1.000	8	0	4	0.00	0
2008	Boston	A.L.	1	5	0	0	.000	6	4	9	7.20	0
2009	Boston	A.L.	1	6 2/3	0	1	.000	3	1	5	5.40	0
Division Series Totals			4	27 2/3	1	2	.333	26	10	20	2.93	0
	Championship Series											
2003	Florida	N.L.	3	19 1/3	1	0	1.000	19	2	11	3.26	0
2007	Boston	A.L.	2	14	2	0	1.000	18	1	9	1.93	0
2008	Boston	A.L.	2	9 1/3	1	0	1.000	8	2	13	9.64	0
Championship Series Totals			7	42 2/3	4	0	1.000	45	5	33	4.22	0
	World Series Record											
2003	Florida	N.L.	2	16 1/3	1	1	.500	19	5	8	1.10	0
2007	Boston	A.L.	1	7	1	0	1.000	9	1	6	1.29	0
World Series Totals			3	23 1/3	2	1	.667	28	6	14	1.16	0

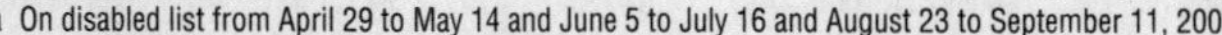

a On disabled list from April 29 to May 14 and June 5 to July 16 and August 23 to September 11, 2002.
b On disabled list from May 8 to July 1, 2003.
c On disabled list from May 31 to June 17 and from June 18 to July 5 and July 6 to July 30, 2004.
d On disabled list from June 15 to June 30 and July 6 to July 23, 2005.
e Traded to Boston Red Sox with infielder Mike Lowell and pitcher Guillermo Mota for infielder Hanley Ramirez, pitcher Anibal Sanchez and pitcher Jesus Delgado, November 24, 2005.
f On disabled list from May 14 to May 29, 2007.
g On disabled list from March 19 to April 6 and August 18 to September 5, 2008.
h On disabled list from May 19 to July 23, 2010.

i On disabled list from June 12 to June 30, 2012.
j Traded to Los Angeles Dodgers with outfielder Carl Crawford, infielder Adrian Gonzalez, infielder Nick Punto and cash for infielder James Loney, infielder Ivan DeJesus, pitcher Allen Webster and player to be named later, August 25, 2012. Boston Red Sox received pitcher Rubby De La Rosa to complete trade, October 4, 2012.
k On disabled list from May 14 to October 31, 2013.

BEDARD, ERIK JOSEPH

Born, Navan, Ontario,Canada, March 5, 1979.
Bats Left. Throws Left. Height, 6 feet, 1 inch. Weight, 200 pounds.

Year Club	Lea	G	IP	W	L	Pct	SO	BB	H	ERA	SAVES
1999 Orioles	Gulf Coast	8	29	2	1	.667	41	13	20	1.86	0
2000 Delmarva	So.Atl.	29	111	9	4	.692	131	35	98	3.57	2
2001 Orioles	Gulf Coast	2	6	0	1	.000	7	3	4	3.00	0
2001 Frederick	Carolina	17	96⅓	9	2	.818	130	26	68	2.15	0
2002 Bowie	Eastern	13	68⅔	6	3	.667	66	30	43	1.97	0
2002 Baltimore	A.L.	2	0⅔	0	0	.000	1	0	2	13.50	0
2003 Orioles	Gulf Coast	3	8	0	0	.000	11	2	4	1.13	0
2003 Aberdeen	N.Y.-Penn.	2	7⅔	0	0	.000	13	1	7	2.35	0
2003 Frederick a	Carolina	1	3⅔	0	1	.000	2	1	5	7.36	0
2004 Baltimore	A.L.	27	137⅓	6	10	.375	121	71	149	4.59	0
2004 Ottawa	Int.	2	5	0	1	.000	3	3	8	7.20	0
2005 Bowie	Eastern	1	2	0	1	.000	4	1	2	9.00	0
2005 Delmarva	So.Atl.	1	5	1	0	1.000	9	1	3	0.00	0
2005 Baltimore b	A.L.	24	141⅔	6	8	.429	125	57	139	4.00	0
2006 Baltimore	A.L.	33	196⅓	15	11	.577	171	69	196	3.76	0
2007 Baltimore c	A.L.	28	182	13	5	.722	221	57	141	3.16	0
2008 Seattle d-e	A.L.	15	81	6	4	.600	72	37	70	3.67	0
2009 Seattle f-g	A.L.	15	83	5	3	.625	90	34	65	2.82	0
2010 Mariners	Arizona	2	6⅔	0	0	.000	11	0	7	2.70	0
2010 Tacoma h	P.C.	1	4⅓	0	0	.000	3	3	3	0.00	0
2011 Seattle-Boston i-j-k	A.L.	24	129⅓	5	9	.357	125	48	118	3.62	0
2012 Pittsburgh l	N.L.	24	125⅔	7	14	.333	118	56	129	5.01	0
2013 Houston m	A.L.	32	151	4	12	.250	138	75	149	4.59	1
Major League Totals	10 Yrs.	224	1228	67	76	.469	1182	504	1158	3.94	1

a On disabled list from March 28 to September 29, 2003.
b On disabled list from May 22 to July 18, 2005.
c On disabled list from September 9 to October 23, 2007.
d Traded to Seattle Mariners for pitcher Tony Butler, outfielder Adam Jones, pitcher Kam Mickolio, pitcher George Sherrill and pitcher Chris Tillman, February 8, 2008.
e On disabled list from April 9 to April 26 and July 5 to October 1, 2008.
f On disabled list from June 8 to July 7 and July 26 to November 6, 2009.
g Filed for free agency, November 6, 2009, re-signed with Seattle Mariners, February 6, 2010.
h On disabled list from March 26 to November 3, 2010.
i On disabled list from June 29 to July 29, 2011.
j Traded to Boston Red Sox with pitcher Josh Fields for outfielder Trayvon Robinson and outfielder Chih-Hsien Chiang, July 31, 2011.
k Filed for free agency, October 30, 2011. Signed with Pittsburgh Pirates, December 7, 2011.
l Released by Pittsburgh Pirates, August 28, 2012. Signed with Houston Astros organization, January 21, 2013.
m Filed for free agency, October 31, 2013.

BELISARIO, RONALD J.

Born, Maracay, Venezuela, December 31, 1982.
Bats Right. Throws Right. Height, 6 feet, 3 inches. Weight, 245 pounds.

Year Club	Lea	G	IP	W	L	Pct	SO	BB	H	ERA	SAVES
2001 Marlins	Gulf Coast	13	73	4	6	.400	54	20	62	2.34	0
2002 Kane County	Midwest	23	140⅓	6	5	.545	98	56	131	3.46	0
2003 Jupiter	Fla.St.	6	18⅓	1	2	.333	13	8	20	4.91	0
2003 Greensboro	So.Atl.	10	48	5	1	.833	45	18	41	3.00	0
2004 Jupiter	Fla.St.	6	8⅔	1	1	.500	7	5	2	0.00	1
2004 Marlins	Gulf Coast	2	2	0	0	.000	2	0	1	0.00	0
2004 Carolina	Southern	15	73	3	5	.375	58	43	75	5.55	0
2005 a				Did Not Play							
2006 b				Did Not Play							
2007 Lynchburg	Carolina	19	34⅓	0	3	.000	19	13	38	4.46	4
2007 Altoona	Eastern	18	24⅔	1	0	1.000	21	14	23	3.28	0
2008 Altoona	Eastern	38	57	4	4	.500	36	25	63	4.74	9
2009 Inland Empire	Calif.	2	2	0	0	.000	3	1	2	0.00	0
2009 Los Angeles c-d	N.L.	69	70⅔	4	3	.571	64	29	52	2.04	0
2010 Inland Empire	Calif.	2	2	0	0	.000	1	2	1	4.50	0

Year Club	Lea	G	IP	W	L	Pct	SO	BB	H	ERA	SAVES
2010 Los Angeles	N.L.	59	$55\frac{1}{3}$	3	1	.750	38	19	52	5.04	2
2011					Did Not Play						
2012 Rancho Cucamonga	Calif.	2	3	0	1	.000	1	0	6	12.00	0
2012 Albuquerque	P.C.	2	$1\frac{2}{3}$	0	0	.000	0	2	2	0.00	0
2012 Los Angeles	N.L.	68	71	8	1	.889	69	29	47	2.54	1
2013 Los Angeles e	N.L.	77	68	5	7	.417	49	28	72	3.97	1
Major League Totals	4 Yrs.	273	265	20	12	.625	220	105	223	3.29	4
Division Series											
2009 Los Angeles	N.L.	2	$1\frac{1}{3}$	0	0	.000	0	0	0	0.00	0
2013 Los Angeles	N.L.	3	1	0	0	.000	1	1	2	9.00	0
Division Series Totals		5	$2\frac{1}{3}$	0	0	.000	1	1	2	3.86	0
Championship Series											
2009 Los Angeles	N.L.	4	$3\frac{1}{3}$	0	0	.000	0	1	5	10.80	0
2013 Los Angeles	N.L.	4	$2\frac{2}{3}$	0	0	.000	1	1	1	6.75	0
Championship Series Totals		8	6	0	0	.000	1	2	6	9.00	0

a On minor league disabled list April 7 to September 15, 2005.
b Filed for free agency from Florida Marlins, October 15, 2006. Signed with Pittsburgh Pirates organization, November 9, 2006.
c Filed for free agency, October 30, 2008. Signed with Los Angeles Dodgers organization, January 16, 2009.
d On disabled list from July 6 to August 8, 2009.
e Not offered contract, December 2, 2013. Signed with Chicago White Sox, December 19, 2013.

BELISLE, MATTHEW THOMAS (MATT)

Born, Austin, Texas, June 6, 1980.
Bats Right. Throws Right. Height, 6 feet, 3 inches. Weight, 225 pounds.

Year Club	Lea	G	IP	W	L	Pct	SO	BB	H	ERA	SAVES
1999 Danville	Appal.	14	$71\frac{1}{3}$	2	5	.286	60	23	86	4.67	0
2000 Myrtle Beach	Carolina	12	$78\frac{2}{3}$	3	4	.429	71	11	72	3.43	0
2000 Macon	So.Atl.	15	$102\frac{1}{3}$	9	5	.643	97	18	79	2.37	0
2001 a					INJURED—Did Not Play						
2002 Greenville	Southern	26	$159\frac{1}{3}$	5	9	.357	123	39	162	4.35	0
2003 Greenville	Southern	21	$125\frac{1}{3}$	6	8	.429	94	42	128	3.52	0
2003 Richmond	Int.	3	20	1	1	.500	10	0	17	2.25	0
2003 Louisville	Int.	4	26	1	3	.250	15	5	31	3.81	0
2003 Cincinnati b	N.L.	6	$8\frac{2}{3}$	1	1	.500	6	2	10	5.19	0
2004 Louisville	Int.	28	$162\frac{2}{3}$	9	11	.450	106	51	192	5.26	0
2005 Cincinnati	N.L.	60	$85\frac{2}{3}$	4	8	.333	59	26	101	4.41	1
2006 Dayton	Midwest	2	4	1	0	1.000	3	0	3	0.00	1
2006 Chattanooga	Southern	2	$3\frac{1}{3}$	0	0	.000	4	0	3	0.00	0
2006 Louisville	Int.	8	9	1	0	1.000	9	1	4	0.00	0
2006 Cincinnati c	N.L.	30	40	2	0	1.000	26	19	43	3.60	0
2007 Louisville	Int.	1	6	0	1	.000	7	2	7	3.00	0
2007 Cincinnati	N.L.	30	$177\frac{2}{3}$	8	9	.471	125	43	212	5.32	0
2008 Sarasota	Fla.St.	1	$8\frac{2}{3}$	1	0	1.000	3	0	2	0.00	0
2008 Chattanooga	Southern	1	9	1	0	1.000	3	0	7	2.00	0
2008 Cincinnati	N.L.	6	$29\frac{2}{3}$	1	4	.200	14	6	47	7.28	0
2008 Louisville d-e	Int.	26	38	5	1	.833	27	11	43	4.26	4
2009 Colorado Springs	P.C.	33	$58\frac{1}{3}$	1	1	.500	47	15	58	3.09	9
2009 Colorado f	N.L.	24	31	3	1	.750	22	5	35	5.52	0
2010 Colorado	N.L.	76	92	7	5	.583	91	16	84	2.93	1
2011 Colorado	N.L.	74	72	10	4	.714	58	14	77	3.25	0
2012 Colorado	N.L.	*80	80	3	8	.273	69	18	91	3.71	3
2013 Colorado	N.L.	72	73	5	7	.417	62	15	76	4.32	0
Major League Totals	10 Yrs.	458	$689\frac{2}{3}$	44	47	.484	532	164	776	4.37	5
Division Series											
2009 Colorado	N.L.	2	2	0	0	.000	2	1	0	0.00	0

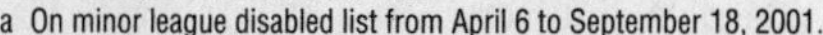

a On minor league disabled list from April 6 to September 18, 2001.
b Sent by Atlanta Braves to Cincinnati Reds as player to be named later for pitcher Kent Mercker, August 14, 2003.
c On disabled list from May 28 to June 27 and July 10 to August 20, 2006.
d On disabled list from March 21 to April 21, 2008.
e On disabled list from September 9 to November 6, 2008.
f Not offered contract, December 12, 2008, re-signed with Colorado Rockies organization, January 14, 2009.

BELL, HEATH JUSTIN

Born, Oceanside, California, September 29, 1977.
Bats Right. Throws Right. Height, 6 feet, 3 inches. Weight, 240 pounds.

Year	Club	Lea	G	IP	W	L	Pct	SO	BB	H	ERA	SAVES
1998	Kingsport	Appal.	22	46	1	0	1.000	61	11	40	2.54	8
1999	Columbia	So.Atl.	55	62 1/3	1	7	.125	68	17	47	2.60	25
2000	St. Lucie	Fla.St.	48	60	5	1	.833	75	21	43	2.55	23
2001	Binghamton	Eastern	43	61 1/3	3	1	.750	55	19	82	6.02	4
2002	Binghamton	Eastern	24	38	1	0	1.000	49	6	22	1.18	6
2002	Norfolk	Int.	22	31 2/3	3	4	.429	28	9	38	4.26	5
2003	Norfolk	Int.	40	49 2/3	2	3	.400	54	8	54	4.71	3
2004	Binghamton	Eastern	1	2	0	0	.000	0	0	2	0.00	0
2004	Norfolk	Int.	45	55 2/3	3	1	.750	68	24	42	3.23	16
2004	New York	N.L.	17	24 1/3	0	2	.000	27	6	22	3.33	0
2005	Norfolk	Int.	13	26 2/3	1	0	1.000	29	5	15	1.69	6
2005	New York	N.L.	42	46 2/3	1	3	.250	43	13	56	5.59	0
2006	Norfolk	Int.	30	35	3	3	.500	56	8	27	1.29	12
2006	New York a	N.L.	22	37	0	0	.000	35	11	51	5.11	0
2007	San Diego	N.L.	81	93 2/3	6	4	.600	102	30	60	2.02	2
2008	San Diego	N.L.	74	78	6	6	.500	71	28	66	3.58	0
2009	San Diego	N.L.	68	69 2/3	6	4	.600	79	24	54	2.71	*42
2010	San Diego	N.L.	67	70	6	1	.857	86	28	56	1.93	47
2011	San Diego b	N.L.	64	62 2/3	3	4	.429	51	21	51	2.44	43
2012	Miami c	N.L.	73	63 2/3	4	5	.444	59	29	70	5.09	19
2013	Arizona d	N.L.	69	65 2/3	5	2	.714	72	16	74	4.11	15
Major League Totals		10 Yrs.	577	611 1/3	37	31	.544	625	206	560	3.39	168

a Traded to San Diego Padres with pitcher Royce Ring for pitcher Jon Adkins and outfielder Ben Johnson, November 15, 2006.

b Filed for free agency, October 30, 2011. Signed with Florida Marlins, December 5, 2011.

c Traded to Arizona Diamondbacks with cash for infielder Yordy Cabrera, October 20, 2012.

d Traded to Tampa Bay Rays with pitcher David Holmberg and cash for pitcher Justin Choate and player to be named later, December 3, 2013.

BENOIT (PENA), JOAQUIN ANTONIO

Born, Santiago, Dominican Republic, July 26, 1977.
Bats Right. Throws Right. Height, 6 feet, 3 inches. Weight, 220 pounds.

Year	Club	Lea	G	IP	W	L	Pct	SO	BB	H	ERA	SAVES
1996	Texas	Dominican	14	75	6	5	.545	63	23	63	2.28	0
1997	Rangers	Gulf Coast	10	44	3	3	.500	38	11	40	2.05	0
1998	Savannah	So.Atl.	15	80	4	3	.571	68	18	79	3.83	0
1999	Charlotte	Fla.St.	22	105	7	4	.636	83	50	117	5.31	0
2000	Tulsa	Texas	16	82 1/3	4	4	.500	72	30	73	3.83	0
2001	Tulsa	Texas	4	21 2/3	1	0	1.000	23	6	23	3.32	0
2001	Oklahoma	P.C.	24	131	9	5	.643	142	73	113	4.19	0
2001	Texas	A.L.	1	5	0	0	.000	4	3	8	10.80	0
2002	Oklahoma	P.C.	16	98 2/3	8	4	.667	103	37	74	3.56	0
2002	Texas	A.L.	17	84 2/3	4	5	.444	59	58	91	5.31	1
2002	Charlotte	Fla.St.	1	5	0	0	.000	8	3	1	0.00	0
2003	Oklahoma	P.C.	6	33	2	1	.667	31	11	28	3.82	0
2003	Texas a	A.L.	25	105	8	5	.615	87	51	99	5.49	0
2004	Texas	A.L.	28	103	3	5	.375	95	31	113	5.68	0
2004	Frisco b	Texas	1	2	0	0	.000	6	0	0	0.00	0
2005	Oklahoma	P.C.	3	5	0	1	.000	2	4	4	5.40	0
2005	Rangers	Arizona	1	2	0	0	.000	4	1	0	0.00	0
2005	Texas c	A.L.	32	87	4	4	.500	78	38	69	3.72	0
2006	Texas	A.L.	56	79 2/3	1	1	.500	85	38	68	4.86	0
2007	Texas	A.L.	70	82	7	4	.636	87	28	68	2.85	6
2008	Frisco	Texas	3	1 2/3	0	0	.000	2	4	4	16.20	0
2008	Oklahoma	P.C.	2	3	1	0	1.000	3	0	1	0.00	0
2008	Texas d	A.L.	44	45	3	2	.600	43	35	40	5.00	1
2009	Texas e-f	A.L.			INJURED—Did Not Play							
2010	Durham	Int.	8	9 2/3	0	1	.000	17	3	8	2.79	2
2010	Tampa Bay g	A.L.	63	60 1/3	1	2	.333	75	11	30	1.34	1
2011	Detroit	A.L.	66	61	4	3	.571	63	17	47	2.95	2
2012	Detroit	A.L.	73	71	5	3	.625	84	22	59	3.68	2
2013	Detroit h	A.L.	66	67	4	1	.800	73	22	47	2.01	24
Major League Totals		12 Yrs.	541	850 2/3	44	35	.557	833	354	739	4.11	37
	Division Series											
2010	Tampa Bay	A.L.	3	3 2/3	1	0	1.000	3	0	0	0.00	0
2011	Detroit	A.L.	2	3 2/3	0	0	.000	6	1	4	2.45	0

Year Club	Lea	G	IP	W	L	Pct	SO	BB	H	ERA	SAVES
2012 Detroit	A.L.	3	3	0	0	.000	2	1	4	6.00	0
2013 Detroit	A.L.	3	$3\frac{1}{3}$	0	0	.000	6	1	3	5.40	2
Division Series Totals		11	$13\frac{2}{3}$	1	0	1.000	17	3	11	3.29	2
Championship Series											
2011 Detroit	A.L.	3	4	0	0	.000	3	2	0	0.00	0
2012 Detroit	A.L.	1	$0\frac{2}{3}$	0	0	.000	0	0	1	0.00	0
2013 Detroit	A.L.	3	$2\frac{1}{3}$	0	0	.000	4	0	4	7.71	1
Championship Series Totals		7	7	0	0	.000	7	2	5	2.57	1
World Series Record											
2012 Detroit	A.L.	2	$1\frac{2}{3}$	0	0	.000	3	0	1	0.00	0

a On disabled list from June 1 to June 22, 2003.
b On disabled list from August 23 to September 7, 2004.
c On disabled list from March 25 to May 2 and June 9 to June 28, 2005.
d On disabled list from July 3 to August 6, 2008.
e On disabled list from April 5 to November 5, 2009.
f Filed for free agency, November 5, 2009. Signed with Tampa Bay Rays organization, February 15, 2010.
g Filed for free agency, November 1, 2010. Signed with Detroit Tigers, November 19, 2010.
h Filed for free agency, October 31, 2013. Signed with San Diego Padres, December 28, 2013.

BETANCOURT, RAFAEL JOSE

Born, Cumana, Venezuela, April 29, 1975.
Bats Right. Throws Right. Height, 6 feet, 2 inches. Weight, 200 pounds.

Year Club	Lea	G	IP	W	L	Pct	SO	BB	H	ERA	SAVES
1997 Michigan	Midwest	27	$32\frac{1}{3}$	0	3	.000	52	2	26	1.95	11
1998 Red Sox	Gulf Coast	4	5	0	2	.000	4	1	6	7.20	0
1998 Sarasota	Fla.St.	20	28	3	1	.750	33	6	22	3.54	2
1998 Trenton	Eastern	7	$9\frac{1}{3}$	0	0	.000	9	3	9	6.75	0
1999 Sarasota	Fla.St.	6	7	0	0	.000	6	1	5	0.00	4
1999 Trenton a	Eastern	39	$54\frac{2}{3}$	6	2	.750	57	10	50	3.62	13
2000 Yokohama	Japan Cen.	11	29	1	2	.333	16	11	30	4.08	0
2000 Searex b	Japan East.	20	23	1	0	1.000	29	6	17	1.17	6
2001 Trenton	Eastern	16	24	0	1	.000	27	3	28	5.63	4
2002				INJURED—Did Not Play							
2003 Akron	Eastern	31	$45\frac{1}{3}$	0	0	.000	75	13	33	1.39	16
2003 Buffalo	Int.	4	$6\frac{2}{3}$	0	0	.000	6	2	6	4.05	1
2003 Cleveland c	A.L.	33	38	2	2	.500	36	13	27	2.13	1
2004 Akron	Eastern	1	1	0	0	.000	2	1	0	0.00	0
2004 Cleveland d	A.L.	68	$66\frac{2}{3}$	5	6	.455	76	18	71	3.92	4
2005 Cleveland e	A.L.	54	$67\frac{2}{3}$	4	3	.571	73	17	57	2.79	1
2006 Akron f	Eastern	1	1	0	0	.000	2	1	0	0.00	0
2007 Cleveland	A.L.	68	$79\frac{1}{3}$	5	1	.833	80	9	51	1.47	3
2008 Cleveland	A.L.	69	71	3	4	.429	64	25	76	5.07	4
2009 Columbus	Int.	3	$3\frac{1}{3}$	1	0	1.000	4	1	0	0.00	0
2009 Cleveland g-h-i	A.L.	29	$30\frac{2}{3}$	1	2	.333	32	15	25	3.52	1
2009 Colorado	N.L.	32	$25\frac{1}{3}$	3	1	.750	29	5	17	1.78	1
2010 Colorado	N.L.	72	$62\frac{1}{3}$	5	1	.833	89	8	52	3.61	1
2011 Colorado	N.L.	68	$62\frac{1}{3}$	2	0	1.000	73	8	46	2.89	8
2012 Colorado	N.L.	60	$57\frac{2}{3}$	1	4	.200	57	12	53	2.81	31
2013 Colorado Springs	P.C.	1	1	0	0	.000	1	0	2	9.00	0
2013 Colorado j-k	N.L.	32	$28\frac{2}{3}$	2	5	.286	27	11	26	4.08	16
Major League Totals	11 Yrs.	635	$646\frac{1}{3}$	36	33	.522	684	152	553	3.19	74
Division Series											
2007 Cleveland	A.L.	2	2	0	0	.000	3	0	1	0.00	0
2009 Colorado	N.L.	3	$2\frac{1}{3}$	0	0	.000	3	1	2	3.86	0
Division Series Totals		5	$4\frac{1}{3}$	0	0	.000	6	1	3	2.08	0
Championship Series											
2007 Cleveland	A.L.	5	8	0	0	.000	6	1	6	6.75	0

a Sold by Boston Red Sox to Yokohama, November 18,1999.
b Sold to Boston Red Sox, December 13, 2000.
c Filed for free agency, October 15, 2001. Signed with Cleveland Indians organization, January 20, 2003.
d On disabled list from June 26 to July 11, 2004.
e On disabled list from June 30 to July 18, 2005.
f On disabled list from April 20 to May 16, 2006.
g On disabled list from June 1 to July 9, 2009.
h Traded to Colorado Rockies for pitcher Connor Graham, July 23, 2009.
i Filed for free agency, November 14, 2009. Accepted arbitration, December 7, 2009.
j On disabled list from June 1 to June 28 and July 15 to August 17 and August 23 to September 30, 2013.
k Filed for free agency, November 1, 2013.

BILLINGSLEY, CHAD RYAN

Born, Defiance, Ohio, July 29, 1984.
Bats Right. Throws Right. Height, 6 feet. Weight, 245 pounds.

Year	Club	Lea	G	IP	W	L	Pct	SO	BB	H	ERA	SAVES
2003	Ogden	Pioneer	11	54	5	4	.556	62	15	49	2.83	0
2004	Vero Beach	Fla.St.	18	92	7	4	.636	111	49	68	2.35	0
2004	Jacksonville	Southern	8	42 1/3	4	0	1.000	47	22	32	2.98	0
2005	Jacksonville	Southern	28	146	13	6	.684	162	50	116	3.51	0
2006	Las Vegas	P.C.	13	70 2/3	6	3	.667	78	32	57	3.95	0
2006	Los Angeles	N.L.	18	90	7	4	.636	59	58	92	3.80	0
2007	Los Angeles	N.L.	43	147	12	5	.706	141	64	131	3.31	0
2008	Los Angeles	N.L.	35	200 2/3	16	10	.615	201	80	188	3.14	0
2009	Los Angeles	N.L.	33	196 1/3	12	11	.522	179	86	173	4.03	0
2010	Los Angeles a	N.L.	31	191 2/3	12	11	.522	171	69	176	3.57	0
2011	Los Angeles	N.L.	32	188	11	11	.500	152	84	189	4.21	0
2012	Los Angeles b	N.L.	25	149 2/3	10	9	.526	128	45	148	3.55	0
2013	Rancho Cucamonga	Calif.	1	4	0	0	.000	2	3	7	6.75	0
2013	Los Angeles c	N.L.	2	12	1	0	1.000	6	5	12	3.00	0
Major League Totals		8 Yrs.	219	1175 1/3	81	61	.570	1037	491	1109	3.65	0
	Division Series											
2006	Los Angeles	N.L.	2	2	0	0	.000	3	0	1	0.00	0
2008	Los Angeles	N.L.	1	6 2/3	1	0	1.000	7	1	5	1.35	0
Division Series Totals			3	8 2/3	1	0	1.000	10	1	6	1.04	0
	Championship Series											
2008	Los Angeles	N.L.	2	5	0	2	.000	9	7	12	18.00	0
2009	Los Angeles	N.L.	1	3 1/3	0	0	.000	3	2	2	5.40	0
Championship Series Totals			3	8 1/3	0	2	.000	12	9	14	12.96	0

a On disabled list from June 12 to June 28, 2010.
b On disabled list from July 8 to July 23 and August 25 to October 29, 2012.
c On disabled list from March 22 to April 10 and April 16 to October 31, 2013.

BLACKLEY, TRAVIS JARROD

Born, Melbourne, Victoria,Australia, November 4, 1982.
Bats Left. Throws Left. Height, 6 feet, 3 inches. Weight, 205 pounds.

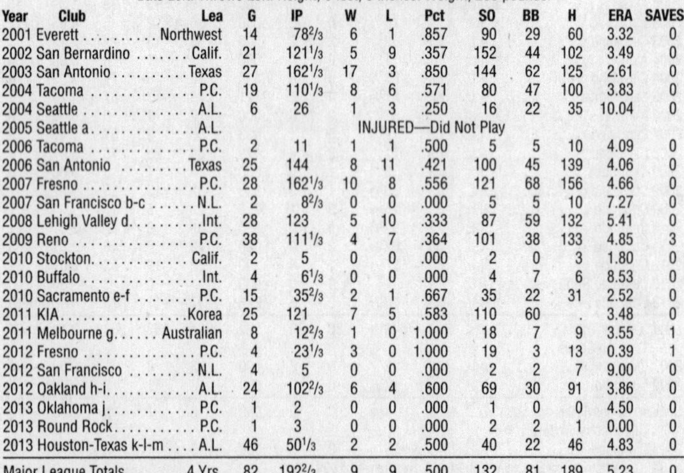

Year	Club	Lea	G	IP	W	L	Pct	SO	BB	H	ERA	SAVES
2001	Everett	Northwest	14	78 2/3	6	1	.857	90	29	60	3.32	0
2002	San Bernardino	Calif.	21	121 1/3	5	9	.357	152	44	102	3.49	0
2003	San Antonio	Texas	27	162 1/3	17	3	.850	144	62	125	2.61	0
2004	Tacoma	P.C.	19	110 1/3	8	6	.571	80	47	100	3.83	0
2004	Seattle	A.L.	6	26	1	3	.250	16	22	35	10.04	0
2005	Seattle a	A.L.				INJURED—Did Not Play						
2006	Tacoma	P.C.	2	11	1	1	.500	5	5	10	4.09	0
2006	San Antonio	Texas	25	144	8	11	.421	100	45	139	4.06	0
2007	Fresno	P.C.	28	162 1/3	10	8	.556	121	68	156	4.66	0
2007	San Francisco b-c	N.L.	2	8 2/3	0	0	.000	5	5	10	7.27	0
2008	Lehigh Valley d	Int.	28	123	5	10	.333	87	59	132	5.41	0
2009	Reno	P.C.	38	111 1/3	4	7	.364	101	38	133	4.85	3
2010	Stockton	Calif.	2	5	0	0	.000	2	0	3	1.80	0
2010	Buffalo	Int.	4	6 1/3	0	0	.000	4	7	6	8.53	0
2010	Sacramento e-f	P.C.	15	35 2/3	2	1	.667	35	22	31	2.52	0
2011	KIA	Korea	25	121	7	5	.583	110	60	.	3.48	0
2011	Melbourne g	Australian	8	12 2/3	1	0	1.000	18	7	9	3.55	1
2012	Fresno	P.C.	4	23 1/3	3	0	1.000	19	3	13	0.39	1
2012	San Francisco	N.L.	4	5	0	0	.000	2	2	7	9.00	0
2012	Oakland h-i	A.L.	24	102 2/3	6	4	.600	69	30	91	3.86	0
2013	Oklahoma j	P.C.	1	2	0	0	.000	1	0	0	4.50	0
2013	Round Rock	P.C.	1	3	0	0	.000	2	2	1	0.00	0
2013	Houston-Texas k-l-m	A.L.	46	50 1/3	2	2	.500	40	22	46	4.83	0
Major League Totals		4 Yrs.	82	192 2/3	9	9	.500	132	81	189	5.23	0

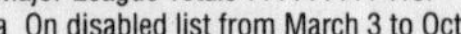

a On disabled list from March 3 to October 31, 2005.
b Traded to San Francisco Giants for outfielder Jason Ellison, April 1, 2007.
c Selected by Philadelphia Phillies in Rule V draft, December 6, 2007.
d Filed for free agency, October 14, 2008. Signed with Arizona Diamonbacks, December 29, 2008.
e Filed for free agency, October 5, 2009. Signed with New York Mets organization, February 4, 2010.
f Released by New York Mets, May 2, 2010. Signed with Oakland Athletics organization, November 5, 2010.
g Released by Oakland Athletics, December 20, 2010. Signed with KIA Tigers (Korea) for 2011.
h Signed with San Francisco Giants organization, February 16, 2012.
i Claimed on waivers by Oakland Athletics, May 15, 2012.
j Traded to Houston Astros for outfielder Jake Goebbert, April 4, 2013.

k On disabled list from April 5 to April 20, 2013.
l Sold to Texas Rangers, August 14, 2013.
m Filed for free agency, November 4, 2013. Signed with Rakuten Golden Eagles (Japan), January 1, 2014.

BLANTON, JOSEPH MATTHEW (JOE)

Born, Bowling Green, Kentucky, December 11, 1980.
Bats Right. Throws Right. Height, 6 feet, 3 inches. Weight, 255 pounds.

Year Club	Lea	G	IP	W	L	Pct	SO	BB	H	ERA	SAVES
2002 Modesto	California	2	6	0	1	.000	6	6	8	7.50	0
2002 Vancouver	Northwest	4	14 1/3	1	1	.500	15	2	11	3.14	0
2003 Kane County	Midwest	21	133	8	7	.533	144	19	110	2.57	0
2003 Midland	Texas	7	35 2/3	3	1	.750	30	7	21	1.26	1
2004 Sacramento	P.C.	28	176 1/3	11	8	.579	143	34	199	4.19	0
2004 Oakland	A.L.	3	8	0	0	.000	6	2	6	5.63	0
2005 Oakland	A.L.	33	201 1/3	12	12	.500	116	67	178	3.53	0
2006 Oakland	A.L.	32	194 1/3	16	12	.571	107	58	241	4.82	0
2007 Oakland	A.L.	34	230	14	10	.583	140	40	*240	3.95	0
2008 Oakland	A.L.	20	127	5	12	.294	62	35	145	4.96	0
2008 Philadelphia a	N.L.	13	70 2/3	4	0	1.000	49	31	66	4.20	0
2009 Philadelphia	N.L.	31	195 1/3	12	8	.600	163	59	198	4.05	0
2010 Lakewood	So.Atl.	1	2	0	0	.000	2	0	0	0.00	0
2010 Reading	Eastern	2	8	0	1	.000	5	2	9	5.63	0
2010 Philadelphia b	N.L.	29	175 2/3	9	6	.600	134	43	206	4.82	0
2011 Lakewood	So.Atl.	1	1	0	0	.000	0	0	0	0.00	0
2011 Philadelphia c	N.L.	11	41 1/3	1	2	.333	35	9	52	5.01	0
2012 Philadelphia-Los Angeles d-e	N.L.	31	191	10	13	.435	166	34	207	4.71	0
2013 Los Angeles	A.L.	28	132 2/3	2	14	.125	108	34	180	6.04	0
Major League Totals	10 Yrs.	265	1567 1/3	85	89	.489	1086	412	1719	4.51	0
Division Series											
2008 Philadelphia	N.L.	1	6	1	0	1.000	7	0	5	1.50	0
2009 Philadelphia	N.L.	2	3 2/3	0	0	.000	1	0	4	4.91	0
2011 Philadelphia	N.L.	1	1	0	0	.000	0	0	0	0.00	0
Division Series Totals		4	10 2/3	1	0	1.000	8	0	9	2.53	0
Championship Series											
2006 Oakland	A.L.	1	2	0	0	.000	2	2	0	0.00	0
2008 Philadelphia	N.L.	1	5	0	0	.000	4	4	7	5.40	0
2009 Philadelphia	N.L.	1	6	0	0	.000	2	2	6	4.50	0
2010 Philadelphia	N.L.	1	4 2/3	0	0	.000	3	1	5	5.79	0
Championship Series Totals		4	17 2/3	0	0	.000	11	9	18	4.58	0
World Series Record											
2008 Philadelphia	N.L.	1	6	1	0	1.000	7	2	4	3.00	0
2009 Philadelphia	N.L.	1	6	0	0	.000	7	2	5	6.00	0
World Series Totals		2	12	1	0	1.000	14	4	9	4.50	0

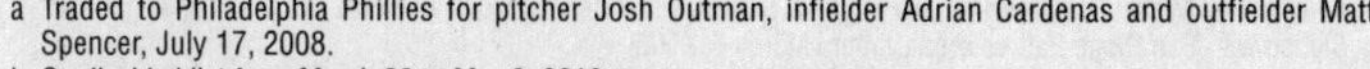

a Traded to Philadelphia Phillies for pitcher Josh Outman, infielder Adrian Cardenas and outfielder Matt Spencer, July 17, 2008.
b On disabled list from March 26 to May 3, 2010.
c On disabled list from April 24 to May 9 and May 16 to September 5, 2011.
d Traded to Los Angeles Dodgers for player to be named later, August 3, 2012. Philadelphia Phillies received pitcher Ryan O'Sullivan to complete trade, August 16, 2012.
e Filed for free agency, November 3, 2012. Signed with Los Angeles Angels, December 12, 2012.

BLEVINS, JERRY RICHARD

Born, Johnson City, Tennessee, September 6, 1983.
Bats Left. Throws Left. Height, 6 feet, 6 inches. Weight, 175 pounds.

Year Club	Lea	G	IP	W	L	Pct	SO	BB	H	ERA	SAVES
2004 Boise	Northwest	23	33 1/3	6	1	.857	42	21	17	1.62	5
2005 Peoria	Midwest	48	76 1/3	3	7	.300	96	38	75	5.54	14
2006 Daytona	Fla.St.	8	11	0	1	.000	9	4	18	9.00	1
2006 Boise	Northwest	16	22 1/3	1	2	.333	19	8	27	6.04	0
2006 West Tenn	Southern	5	6 1/3	0	0	.000	8	1	5	1.42	1
2007 Daytona	Fla.St.	15	23 2/3	1	0	1.000	32	5	13	0.38	6
2007 Tennessee	Southern	23	29 1/3	2	2	.500	37	8	23	1.53	3
2007 Midland	Texas	17	21 2/3	1	3	.250	29	5	18	3.32	1
2007 Sacramento	P.C.	1	2 2/3	1	0	1.000	4	0	1	0.00	0
2007 Oakland a	A.L.	6	4 2/3	0	1	.000	3	2	8	9.64	0
2008 Sacramento	P.C.	28	32 1/3	2	2	.500	36	6	31	2.78	10
2008 Oakland	A.L.	36	37 2/3	1	3	.250	35	13	32	3.11	0
2009 Sacramento	P.C.	45	63 1/3	5	3	.625	62	18	65	3.84	2

Year	Club	Lea	G	IP	W	L	Pct	SO	BB	H	ERA	SAVES
2009	Oakland	A.L.	20	22 1/3	0	0	.000	23	6	19	4.84	0
2010	Oakland	A.L.	63	48 2/3	2	1	.667	46	18	54	3.70	1
2011	Sacramento	P.C.	27	29 2/3	2	0	1.000	35	7	25	4.85	0
2011	Oakland	A.L.	26	28 1/3	0	0	.000	26	14	24	2.86	0
2012	Oakland	A.L.	63	65 1/3	5	1	.833	54	25	45	2.48	1
2013	Oakland b	A.L.	67	60	5	0	1.000	52	17	47	3.15	0
Major League Totals		7 Yrs.	281	267	13	6	.684	239	95	229	3.30	2
	Division Series											
2012	Oakland	A.L.	3	3 2/3	0	0	.000	0	0	1	0.00	0

a Traded by Chicago Cubs to Oakland Athletics with catcher Rob Bowen for catcher Jason Kendall and cash, July 17, 2007.

b Traded to Washington Nationals for outfielder Billy Burns, December 11, 2013.

BRESLOW, CRAIG ANDREW

Born, New Haven, Connecticut, August 8, 1980.

Bats Left. Throws Left. Height, 6 feet, 1 inch. Weight, 185 pounds.

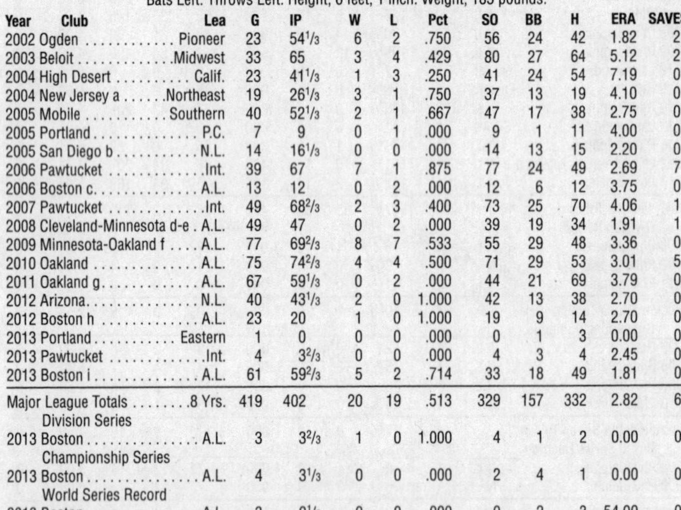

Year	Club	Lea	G	IP	W	L	Pct	SO	BB	H	ERA	SAVES
2002	Ogden	Pioneer	23	54 1/3	6	2	.750	56	24	42	1.82	2
2003	Beloit	Midwest	33	65	3	4	.429	80	27	64	5.12	2
2004	High Desert	Calif.	23	41 1/3	1	3	.250	41	24	54	7.19	0
2004	New Jersey a	Northeast	19	26 1/3	3	1	.750	37	13	19	4.10	0
2005	Mobile	Southern	40	52 1/3	2	1	.667	47	17	38	2.75	0
2005	Portland	P.C.	7	9	0	1	.000	9	1	11	4.00	0
2005	San Diego b	N.L.	14	16 1/3	0	0	.000	14	13	15	2.20	0
2006	Pawtucket	Int.	39	67	7	1	.875	77	24	49	2.69	7
2006	Boston c	A.L.	13	12	0	2	.000	12	6	12	3.75	0
2007	Pawtucket	Int.	49	68 2/3	2	3	.400	73	25	70	4.06	1
2008	Cleveland-Minnesota d-e	A.L.	49	47	0	2	.000	39	19	34	1.91	1
2009	Minnesota-Oakland f	A.L.	77	69 2/3	8	7	.533	55	29	48	3.36	0
2010	Oakland	A.L.	75	74 2/3	4	4	.500	71	29	53	3.01	5
2011	Oakland g	A.L.	67	59 1/3	0	2	.000	44	21	69	3.79	0
2012	Arizona	N.L.	40	43 1/3	2	0	1.000	42	13	38	2.70	0
2012	Boston h	A.L.	23	20	1	0	1.000	19	9	14	2.70	0
2013	Portland	Eastern	1	0	0	0	.000	0	1	3	0.00	0
2013	Pawtucket	Int.	4	3 2/3	0	0	.000	4	3	4	2.45	0
2013	Boston i	A.L.	61	59 2/3	5	2	.714	33	18	49	1.81	0
Major League Totals		8 Yrs.	419	402	20	19	.513	329	157	332	2.82	6
	Division Series											
2013	Boston	A.L.	3	3 2/3	1	0	1.000	4	1	2	0.00	0
	Championship Series											
2013	Boston	A.L.	4	3 1/3	0	0	.000	2	4	1	0.00	0
	World Series Record											
2013	Boston	A.L.	3	0 1/3	0	0	.000	0	2	3	54.00	0

a Released by Milwaukee Brewers, July 6, 2004. Signed with independent New Jersey (Northeast), July 2004.

b Signed with San Diego Padres organization, March 6, 2005.

c Not offered contract, December 21, 2005. Signed with Boston Red Sox organization, February 1, 2006.

d Claimed on waivers by Cleveland Indians, March 23, 2008.

e Claimed on waivers by Minnesota Twins, May 29, 2008.

f Claimed on waivers by Oakland Athletics, May 20, 2009.

g Traded to Arizona Diamondbacks with pitcher Trevor Cahill for outfielder Collin Cowgill, pitcher Jarrod Parker and pitcher Ryan Cook, December 9, 2011.

h Traded to Boston Red Sox for pitcher Matt Albers and outfielder Scott Podsednik, July 31, 2012.

i On disabled list from March 22 to May 6, 2013.

BROTHERS, REX COLEMAN

Born, Murfreesboro, Tennessee, December 18, 1987.

Bats Left. Throws Left. Height, 6 feet. Weight, 205 pounds.

Year	Club	Lea	G	IP	W	L	Pct	SO	BB	H	ERA	SAVES
2009	Tri-City	Northwest	8	10 2/3	2	0	1.000	18	5	10	3.38	0
2009	Asheville	So.Atl.	9	10 2/3	0	0	.000	10	3	6	3.38	0
2010	Modesto	Calif.	33	37	0	2	.000	43	19	20	2.68	3
2010	Tulsa	Texas	24	23	2	1	.667	27	18	14	3.91	4
2011	Colorado Springs	P.C.	25	28	3	2	.600	45	15	29	2.89	0
2011	Colorado	N.L.	48	40 2/3	1	2	.333	59	20	33	2.88	1
2012	Colorado Springs	P.C.	4	5 1/3	0	0	.000	13	3	3	1.69	1
2012	Colorado	N.L.	75	67 2/3	8	2	.800	83	37	63	3.86	0
2013	Colorado	N.L.	72	67 1/3	2	1	.667	76	36	51	1.74	19
Major League Totals		3 Yrs.	195	175 2/3	11	5	.688	218	93	147	2.82	20

BROXTON, JONATHAN ROY

Born, Augusta, Georgia, June 16, 1984.
Bats Right. Throws Right. Height, 6 feet, 4 inches. Weight, 290 pounds.

Year	Club	Lea	G	IP	W	L	Pct	SO	BB	H	ERA	SAVES
2002	Great Falls	Pioneer	11	$29^{1}/_{3}$	2	0	1.000	33	16	22	2.76	2
2003	South Bend	So.Atl.	9	$37^{1}/_{3}$	4	2	.667	30	22	27	3.13	0
2004	Vero Beach	Fla.St.	23	$128^{1}/_{3}$	11	6	.647	144	43	110	3.23	0
2005	Jacksonville	Southern	33	$96^{2}/_{3}$	5	3	.625	107	31	79	3.17	5
2005	Los Angeles	N.L.	14	$13^{2}/_{3}$	1	0	1.000	22	12	13	5.93	0
2006	Las Vegas	P.C.	11	$11^{1}/_{3}$	1	0	1.000	18	3	6	0.00	5
2006	Los Angeles	N.L.	68	$76^{1}/_{3}$	4	1	.800	97	33	61	2.59	3
2007	Los Angeles	N.L.	83	82	4	4	.500	99	25	69	2.85	2
2008	Los Angeles	N.L.	70	69	3	5	.375	88	27	54	3.13	14
2009	Los Angeles	N.L.	73	76	7	2	.778	114	29	44	2.61	36
2010	Los Angeles	N.L.	64	$62^{1}/_{3}$	5	6	.455	73	28	64	4.04	22
2011	Albuquerque	P.C.	2	2	0	0	.000	5	1	2	4.50	0
2011	Los Angeles a-b	N.L.	14	$12^{2}/_{3}$	1	2	.333	10	9	15	5.68	7
2012	Kansas City	A.L.	35	$35^{2}/_{3}$	1	2	.333	25	14	36	2.27	23
2012	Cincinnati c-d	N.L.	25	$22^{1}/_{3}$	3	3	.500	20	3	20	2.82	4
2013	Louisville	Int.	2	2	0	0	.000	3	0	5	0.00	0
2013	Cincinnati e	N.L.	34	$30^{2}/_{3}$	2	2	.500	25	12	27	4.11	0
Major League Totals		9 Yrs.	480	$480^{2}/_{3}$	31	27	.534	573	192	403	3.16	111
	Division Series											
2006	Los Angeles	N.L.	2	2	0	1	.000	3	2	5	13.50	0
2008	Los Angeles	N.L.	3	$3^{1}/_{3}$	0	0	.000	5	2	0	0.00	1
2009	Los Angeles	N.L.	3	$3^{2}/_{3}$	0	0	.000	4	0	4	2.45	1
2012	Cincinnati	N.L.	3	3	0	1	.000	4	1	4	0.00	0
Division Series Totals			11	12	0	2	.000	16	5	13	3.00	2
	Championship Series											
2008	Los Angeles	N.L.	2	$2^{1}/_{3}$	0	0	.000	2	1	3	3.86	0
2009	Los Angeles	N.L.	3	3	0	1	.000	1	1	2	6.00	1
Championship Series Totals			5	$5^{1}/_{3}$	0	1	.000	3	2	5	5.06	1

a On disabled list from May 4 to September 30, 2011.
b Filed for free agency, October 30, 2011. Signed with Kansas City Royals, November 29, 2011.
c Traded to Cincinnati Reds for pitcher Donnie Joseph and pitcher J.C. Sulbaran, July 31, 2012.
d Filed for free agency, November 3, 2012, re-signed with Cincinnati Reds, November 28, 2012.
e On disabled list from June 14 to August 7 and August 22 to November 1, 2013.

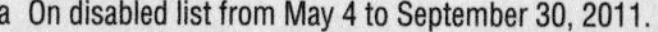

BUCHHOLZ, CLAY DANIEL

Born, Nederland, Texas, August 14, 1984.
Bats Left. Throws Right. Height, 6 feet, 3 inches. Weight, 190 pounds.

Year	Club	Lea	G	IP	W	L	Pct	SO	BB	H	ERA	SAVES
2005	Lowell	N.Y.-Penn.	15	$41^{1}/_{3}$	0	1	.000	45	9	34	2.61	0
2006	Wilmington	Carolina	3	16	2	0	1.000	23	4	10	1.13	0
2006	Greenville	So.Atl.	21	103	9	4	.692	117	29	78	2.62	0
2007	Portland	Eastern	16	$86^{2}/_{3}$	7	2	.778	116	22	55	1.77	0
2007	Pawtucket	Int.	8	$38^{2}/_{3}$	1	3	.250	55	13	32	3.96	0
2007	Boston a	A.L.	4	$22^{2}/_{3}$	3	1	.750	22	10	14	1.59	0
2008	Portland	Eastern	2	15	1	0	1.000	18	1	7	1.80	0
2008	Pawtucket	Int.	9	$43^{2}/_{3}$	4	2	.667	43	17	36	2.47	0
2008	Boston b	A.L.	16	76	2	9	.182	72	41	93	6.75	0
2009	Pawtucket	Int.	17	99	7	2	.778	89	30	67	2.36	0
2009	Boston	A.L.	16	92	7	4	.636	68	36	91	4.21	0
2010	Pawtucket	Int.	1	$3^{2}/_{3}$	0	0	.000	2	1	4	4.91	0
2010	Boston c	A.L.	28	$173^{2}/_{3}$	17	7	.708	120	67	142	2.33	0
2011	Boston d	A.L.	14	$82^{2}/_{3}$	6	3	.667	60	31	76	3.48	0
2012	Pawtucket	Int.	1	$2^{1}/_{3}$	0	0	.000	3	2	1	0.00	0
2012	Boston e	A.L.	29	$189^{1}/_{3}$	11	8	.579	129	64	187	4.56	0
2013	Lowell	N.Y.-Penn.	1	$0^{2}/_{3}$	0	0	.000	1	3	1	13.50	0
2013	Pawtucket	Int.	1	$3^{1}/_{3}$	0	0	.000	2	0	7	2.70	0
2013	Boston f	A.L.	16	$108^{1}/_{3}$	12	1	.923	96	36	75	1.74	0
Major League Totals		7 Yrs.	123	$744^{2}/_{3}$	58	33	.637	567	285	678	3.60	0
	Division Series											
2009	Boston	A.L.	1	5	0	0	.000	3	1	6	3.60	0
2013	Boston	A.L.	1	6	0	0	.000	5	3	7	4.50	0
Division Series Totals			2	11	0	0	.000	8	4	13	4.09	0
	Championship Series											
2013	Boston	A.L.	2	$10^{2}/_{3}$	0	0	.000	10	2	12	5.91	0

Year	Club	Lea	G	IP	W	L	Pct	SO	BB	H	ERA	SAVES
	World Series Record											
2013	Boston	A.L.	1	4	0	0	.000	2	3	3	0.00	0

a Pitched no-hit, no-run game against Baltimore Orioles, September 1, 2007.
b On disabled list from May 13 to May 31, 2008.
c On disabled list from June 27 to July 21, 2010.
d On disabled list from June 17 to September 28, 2011.
e On disabled list from June 20 to July 14, 2012.
f On disabled list from June 9 to September 10, 2013.

BUEHRLE, MARK ANTHONY

Born, St. Charles, Missouri, March 23, 1979.
Bats Left. Throws Left. Height, 6 feet, 2 inches. Weight, 225 pounds.

Year	Club	Lea	G	IP	W	L	PCT	SO	BB	H	ERA	SAVES
1999	Burlington	Midwest	20	$98\frac{2}{3}$	7	4	.636	91	16	105	4.10	3
2000	Birmingham	Southern	16	$118\frac{2}{3}$	8	4	.667	68	17	95	2.28	0
2000	Chicago	A.L.	28	$51\frac{1}{3}$	4	1	.800	37	19	55	4.21	0
2001	Chicago	A.L.	32	$221\frac{1}{3}$	16	8	.667	126	48	188	3.29	0
2002	Chicago	A.L.	34	239	19	12	.613	134	61	236	3.58	0
2003	Chicago	A.L.	35	$230\frac{1}{3}$	14	14	.500	119	61	250	4.14	0
2004	Chicago	A.L.	35	*$245\frac{1}{3}$	16	10	.615	165	51	257	3.89	0
2005	Chicago	A.L.	33	*$236\frac{2}{3}$	16	8	.667	149	40	*240	3.12	0
2006	Chicago	A.L.	32	204	12	13	.480	98	48	*247	4.99	0
2007	Chicago a	A.L.	30	201	10	9	.526	115	45	208	3.63	0
2008	Chicago	A.L.	34	$218\frac{2}{3}$	15	12	.556	140	52	*240	3.79	0
2009	Chicago b	A.L.	33	$213\frac{1}{3}$	13	10	.565	105	45	222	3.84	0
2010	Chicago	A.L.	33	$210\frac{1}{3}$	13	13	.500	99	49	*246	4.28	0
2011	Chicago c	A.L.	31	$205\frac{1}{3}$	13	9	.591	109	45	221	3.59	0
2012	Miami d	N.L.	31	$202\frac{1}{3}$	13	13	.500	125	40	197	3.74	0
2013	Toronto	A.L.	33	$203\frac{2}{3}$	12	10	.545	139	51	223	4.15	0
Major League Totals		14 Yrs.	454	$2882\frac{2}{3}$	186	142	.567	1660	655	3030	3.84	0
	Division Series											
2000	Chicago	A.L.	1	$0\frac{1}{3}$	0	0	.000	1	0	2	0.00	0
2005	Chicago	A.L.	1	7	1	0	1.000	2	1	8	5.14	0
2008	Chicago	A.L.	1	7	0	1	.000	3	0	10	6.43	0
Division Series Totals			3	$14\frac{1}{3}$	1	1	.500	6	1	20	5.65	0
	Championship Series											
2005	Chicago	A.L.	1	9	1	0	1.000	4	0	5	1.00	0
	World Series Record											
2005	Chicago	A.L.	2	$7\frac{1}{3}$	0	0	.000	6	0	7	4.91	1

a Pitched no-hit, no-run game against Texas Rangers, April 18, 2007.
b Pitched no-hit, no-run perfect game against Tampa Bay Rays, July 23, 2009.
c Filed for free agency, October 30, 2011. Signed with Florida Marlins, December 9, 2011.
d Traded to Toronto Blue Jays with outfielder Emilio Bonifacio, catcher John Buck, pitcher Josh Johnson and infielder Jose Reyes for pitcher Henderson Alvarez, infielder Yunel Escobar, infielder Adeiny Hechavarria, catcher Jeff Mathis, pitcher Anthony De Sclafani, outfielder Jake Marisnick and pitcher Justin Nicolino, November 19, 2012.

BUMGARNER, MADISON KYLE

Born, Hickory, North Carolina, August 1, 1989.
Bats Right. Throws Left. Height, 6 feet, 4 inches. Weight, 215 pounds.

Year	Club	Lea	G	IP	W	L	Pct	SO	BB	H	ERA	SAVES
2008	Augusta	So.Atl.	24	$141\frac{2}{3}$	15	3	.833	164	21	111	1.46	0
2009	San Jose	Calif.	5	$24\frac{1}{3}$	3	1	.750	23	4	20	1.48	0
2009	Connecticut	Eastern	20	107	9	1	.900	69	30	80	1.93	0
2009	San Francisco	N.L.	4	10	0	0	.000	10	3	8	1.80	0
2010	Fresno	P.C.	14	$82\frac{2}{3}$	7	1	.875	59	22	88	3.16	0
2010	San Francisco	N.L.	18	111	7	6	.538	86	26	119	3.00	0
2011	San Francisco	N.L.	33	$204\frac{2}{3}$	13	13	.500	191	46	202	3.21	0
2012	San Francisco	N.L.	32	$208\frac{1}{3}$	16	11	.593	191	49	183	3.37	0
2013	San Francisco	N.L.	31	$201\frac{1}{3}$	13	9	.591	199	62	146	2.77	0
Major League Totals		5 Yrs.	118	$735\frac{1}{3}$	49	39	.557	677	186	658	3.08	0
	Division Series											
2010	San Francisco	N.L.	1	6	1	0	1.000	5	1	6	3.00	0
2012	San Francisco	N.L.	1	$4\frac{1}{3}$	0	1	.000	4	1	7	8.31	0
Division Series Totals			2	$10\frac{1}{3}$	1	1	.500	9	2	13	5.23	0
	Championship Series											
2010	San Francisco	N.L.	2	$6\frac{2}{3}$	0	0	.000	7	2	9	4.05	0

Year	Club	Lea	G	IP	W	L	Pct	SO	BB	H	ERA	SAVES
2012	San Francisco	N.L.	1	3²/₃	0	1	.000	2	1	8	14.73	0
Championship Series Totals			3	10¹/₃	0	1	.000	9	3	17	7.84	0
	World Series Record											
2010	San Francisco	N.L.	1	8	1	0	1.000	6	2	3	0.00	0
2012	San Francisco	N.L.	1	7	1	0	1.000	8	2	2	0.00	0
World Series Totals			2	15	2	0	1.000	14	4	5	0.00	0

BURNETT, ALLAN JAMES (A.J.)

Born, North Little Rock, Arkansas, January 3, 1977.
Bats Right. Throws Right. Height, 6 feet, 4 inches. Weight, 230 pounds.

Year	Club	Lea	G	IP	W	L	Pct	SO	BB	H	ERA	SAVES
1995	Mets	Gulf Coast	9	33²/₃	2	3	.400	26	23	27	4.28	0
1996	Kingsport	Appal.	12	58	4	0	1.000	68	54	31	3.88	0
1997	Mets	Gulf Coast	3	11¹/₃	0	1	.000	15	8	8	3.18	0
1997	Pittsfield	N.Y.-Penn.	9	44	3	1	.750	48	35	28	4.70	0
1998	Kane County a	Midwest	20	119	10	4	.714	186	45	74	1.97	0
1999	Portland	Eastern	26	120²/₃	6	12	.333	121	71	132	5.52	0
1999	Florida	N.L.	7	41¹/₃	4	2	.667	33	25	37	3.48	0
2000	Brevard County	Fla.St.	2	7¹/₃	0	0	.000	6	6	4	3.68	0
2000	Calgary	P.C.	1	5	0	0	.000	6	3	0	0.00	0
2000	Florida b	N.L.	13	82²/₃	3	7	.300	57	44	80	4.79	0
2001	Brevard County	Fla.St.	2	9¹/₃	0	0	.000	10	4	4	1.93	0
2001	Florida c-d	N.L.	27	173¹/₃	11	12	.478	128	83	145	4.05	0
2002	Florida e	N.L.	31	204¹/₃	12	9	.571	203	90	153	3.30	0
2003	Florida f	N.L.	4	23	0	2	.000	21	18	18	4.70	0
2004	Jupiter	Fla.St.	1	4	0	0	.000	4	2	2	0.00	0
2004	Albuquerque	P.C.	1	3¹/₃	0	0	.000	6	2	7	10.80	0
2004	Florida g	N.L.	20	120	7	6	.538	113	38	102	3.68	0
2005	Florida h	N.L.	32	209	12	12	.500	198	79	184	3.44	0
2006	Dunedin	Fla.St.	2	8	0	0	.000	6	2	9	3.38	0
2006	New Hampshire	Eastern	1	6	1	0	1.000	9	3	2	1.50	0
2006	Syracuse	Int.	1	5	1	0	1.000	7	1	0	0.00	0
2006	Toronto i	A.L.	21	135²/₃	10	8	.556	118	39	138	3.98	0
2007	Syracuse	Int.	1	5	0	0	.000	7	1	3	1.80	0
2007	Toronto j	A.L.	25	165²/₃	10	8	.556	176	66	131	3.75	0
2008	Toronto k	A.L.	35	221¹/₃	18	10	.643	*231	86	211	4.07	0
2009	New York	A.L.	33	207	13	9	.591	195	*97	193	4.04	0
2010	New York	A.L.	33	186²/₃	10	15	.400	145	78	204	5.26	0
2011	New York	A.L.	33	190¹/₃	11	11	.500	173	83	190	5.15	0
2012	Bradenton	Fla.St.	2	6¹/₃	0	2	.000	9	2	7	8.53	0
2012	Indianapolis	Int.	1	4	0	1	.000	0	4	7	11.25	0
2012	Pittsburgh l-m	N.L.	31	202¹/₃	16	10	.615	180	62	189	3.51	0
2013	Pittsburgh n-o	N.L.	30	191	10	11	.476	209	67	165	3.30	0
Major League Totals		15 Yrs.	375	2353²/₃	147	132	.527	2180	955	2140	3.99	0
	Division Series											
2009	New York	A.L.	1	6	0	0	.000	6	5	3	1.50	0
2011	New York	A.L.	1	5²/₃	1	0	1.000	3	4	4	1.59	0
2013	Pittsburgh	N.L.	1	2	0	1	.000	0	4	6	31.50	0
Division Series Totals			3	13²/₃	1	1	.500	9	13	13	5.93	0
	Championship Series											
2009	New York	A.L.	2	12¹/₃	0	0	.000	7	5	11	5.84	0
2010	New York	A.L.	1	6	0	1	.000	4	3	6	7.50	0
Championship Series Totals			3	18¹/₃	0	1	.000	11	8	17	6.38	0
	World Series Record											
2009	New York	A.L.	2	9	1	1	.500	11	6	8	7.00	0

a Traded to Florida Marlins by New York Mets with pitcher Jesus Sanchez and outfielder Robert Stratton for pitcher Al Leiter and infielder Ralph Milliard, February 6, 1998.
b On disabled list from March 17 to July 19, 2000.
c On disabled list from March 23 to May 7, 2001.
d Pitched no-hit, no-run game against San Diego Padres, May 12, 2001.
e On disabled list from August 19 to September 14, 2002.
f On disabled list from March 21 to April 9 and April 26 to September 29, 2003.
g On disabled list from March 26 to June 3, 2004.
h Filed for free agency, October 27, 2005. Signed with Toronto Blue Jays, December 6, 2005.
i On disabled list from March 24 to April 15 and April 22 to June 22, 2006.
j On disabled list from June 13 to June 28 and June 29 to August 12, 2007.
k Filed for free agency, November 13, 2008. Signed with New York Yankees, December 18, 2008.

l Traded to Pittsburgh Pirates with cash for outfielder Exicardo Cayones and pitcher Diego Moreno, February 20, 2012.
m On disabled list from March 26 to April 21, 2012.
n On disabled list from June 9 to July 7, 2013.
o Filed for free agency, October 31, 2013.

BURNETT, SEAN RICHARD

Born, Dunedin, Florida, September 17, 1982.
Bats Left. Throws Left. Height, 5 feet, 11 inches. Weight, 190 pounds.

Year Club	Lea	G	IP	W	L	Pct	SO	BB	H	ERA	SAVES
2000 Pirates	Gulf Coast	8	31	2	1	.667	24	3	31	4.06	0
2001 Hickory	So.Atl.	26	$161\frac{1}{3}$	11	8	.579	134	33	164	2.62	0
2002 Lynchburg	Carolina	26	$155\frac{1}{3}$	13	4	.765	96	33	118	1.80	0
2003 Altoona	Eastern	27	$159\frac{2}{3}$	14	6	.700	86	29	158	3.21	0
2004 Nashville	P.C.	10	47	1	5	.167	25	17	58	5.36	0
2004 Pittsburgh a	N.L.	13	$71\frac{2}{3}$	5	5	.500	30	28	86	5.02	0
2005 Pittsburgh b	N.L.				INJURED—Did Not Play						
2006 Indianapolis	Int.	25	$120\frac{1}{3}$	8	11	.421	46	46	136	5.16	0
2007 Indianapolis	Int.	15	$70\frac{1}{3}$	4	5	.444	31	39	83	4.48	0
2008 Indianapolis	Int.	12	$17\frac{1}{3}$	1	1	.500	15	8	9	1.04	3
2008 Pittsburgh	N.L.	58	$56\frac{2}{3}$	1	1	.500	42	34	57	4.76	0
2009 Pittsburgh-Washington c	N.L.	71	$57\frac{2}{3}$	2	3	.400	43	28	36	3.12	1
2010 Washington	N.L.	73	63	1	7	.125	62	20	52	2.14	3
2011 Washington	N.L.	69	$56\frac{2}{3}$	5	5	.500	33	21	54	3.81	4
2012 Washington d	N.L.	70	$56\frac{2}{3}$	1	2	.333	57	12	58	2.38	2
2013 Inland Empire	Calif.	1	1	0	0	.000	0	0	1	9.00	0
2013 Los Angeles e	A.L.	13	$9\frac{2}{3}$	0	0	.000	7	4	9	0.93	0
Major League Totals	7 Yrs.	367	372	15	23	.395	274	147	352	3.51	10
Division Series											
2012 Washington	N.L.	2	1	0	0	.000	1	1	3	27.00	0

a On disabled list from August 22 to October 4, 2004.
b On disabled list from April 2 to October 3, 2005.
c Traded to Washington Nationals with outfielder Nyjer Morgan for outfielder Lastings Milledge and pitcher Joel Hanrahan, June 30, 2009.
d Filed for free agency, November 3, 2012. Signed with Los Angeles Angels, December 5, 2012.
e On disabled list from April 27 to May 21 and May 27 to November 4, 2013.

BURTON, LEVI JARED (JARED)

Born, Westminster, South Carolina, June 2, 1981.
Bats Right. Throws Right. Height, 6 feet, 5 inches. Weight, 225 pounds.

Year Club	Lea	G	IP	W	L	Pct	SO	BB	H	ERA	SAVES
2002 Vancouver	Northwest	13	$37\frac{2}{3}$	0	4	.000	38	14	32	3.58	1
2003 Kane County	Midwest	15	$31\frac{2}{3}$	2	1	.667	33	7	19	2.27	1
2004 Athletics	Arizona	5	$21\frac{2}{3}$	1	0	1.000	15	4	21	4.15	0
2004 Modesto	Calif.	10	32	3	2	.600	25	20	34	4.78	0
2005 Stockton	Calif.	52	$55\frac{1}{3}$	4	4	.500	67	20	44	2.60	24
2006 Midland a	Texas	53	74	6	5	.545	66	27	71	4.14	1
2007 Chattanooga	Southern	4	$5\frac{1}{3}$	0	1	.000	3	5	10	11.81	0
2007 Louisville	Int.	10	14	1	0	1.000	13	4	11	0.64	1
2007 Cincinnati b	N.L.	47	43	4	2	.667	36	22	28	2.51	0
2008 Louisville	Int.	2	2	0	0	.000	1	2	1	4.50	0
2008 Cincinnati c	N.L.	54	$58\frac{2}{3}$	5	1	.833	58	25	56	3.22	0
2009 Dayton	Midwest	1	1	1	0	1.000	3	0	1	0.00	0
2009 Louisville	Int.	10	11	3	0	1.000	10	3	8	0.82	0
2009 Cincinnati d	N.L.	53	$59\frac{1}{3}$	1	0	1.000	45	23	61	4.40	0
2010 Louisville	Int.	33	38	3	2	.600	34	16	29	2.61	4
2010 Cincinnati	N.L.	4	$3\frac{1}{3}$	0	0	.000	1	0	0	0.00	0
2011 Reds	Arizona	3	4	0	1	.000	6	0	7	9.00	0
2011 Louisville	Int.	11	13	2	0	1.000	11	5	12	4.15	0
2011 Cincinnati e-f	N.L.	6	$4\frac{2}{3}$	0	0	.000	3	3	6	3.86	0
2012 Minnesota	A.L.	64	62	3	2	.600	55	16	41	2.18	5
2013 Minnesota	A.L.	71	66	2	9	.182	61	22	61	3.82	2
Major League Totals	7 Yrs.	299	297	15	14	.517	259	111	253	3.24	7

a Selected by Cincinnati Reds from Oakland Athletics in Rule V draft, December 7, 2006.
b On disabled list from April 8 to May 9, 2007 and from June 11 to July 7, 2007.
c On disabled list from July 11 to September 2, 2008.
d On disabled list from July 25 to August 10, 2009.
e On disabled list from March 29 to August 22, 2011.
f Filed for free agency, November 1, 2011. Signed with Minnesota Twins organization, November 11, 2011.

CAHILL, TREVOR JOHN

Born, Oceanside, California, March 1, 1988.
Bats Right. Throws Right. Height, 6 feet, 3 inches. Weight, 210 pounds.

Year Club	Lea	G	IP	W	L	Pct	SO	BB	H	ERA	SAVES
2006 Athletics	Arizona	4	9	0	0	.000	11	7	2	3.00	0
2007 Kane County	Midwest	20	105 1/3	11	4	.733	117	40	85	2.73	0
2008 Stockton	Calif.	14	87 1/3	5	4	.556	103	31	52	2.78	0
2008 Midland	Texas	7	37	6	1	.857	33	19	24	2.19	0
2009 Oakland	A.L.	32	178 2/3	10	13	.435	90	72	185	4.63	0
2010 Sacramento	P.C.	2	8 2/3	1	0	1.000	8	5	7	1.04	0
2010 Oakland a	A.L.	30	196 2/3	18	8	.692	118	63	155	2.97	0
2011 Oakland b	A.L.	34	207 2/3	12	14	.462	147	82	214	4.16	0
2012 Arizona	N.L.	32	200	13	12	.520	156	74	184	3.78	0
2013 D-Backs	Arizona	1	5	0	0	.000	9	2	1	0.00	0
2013 Reno	P.C.	3	16 2/3	0	2	.000	13	9	16	5.94	0
2013 Arizona c	N.L.	26	146 2/3	8	10	.444	102	65	143	3.99	0
Major League Totals	5 Yrs.	154	929 2/3	61	57	.517	613	356	881	3.89	0

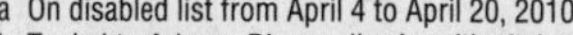

a On disabled list from April 4 to April 20, 2010.
b Traded to Arizona Diamondbacks with pitcher Craig Breslow for outfielder Collin Cowgill, pitcher Jarrod Parker and pitcher Ryan Cook, December 9, 2011.
c On disabled list from July 1 to August 17, 2013.

CAIN, MATTHEW THOMAS (MATT)

Born, Dothan, Alabama, October 1, 1984.
Bats Right. Throws Right. Height, 6 feet, 3 inches. Weight, 235 pounds.

Year Club	Lea	G	IP	W	L	Pct	SO	BB	H	ERA	SAVES
2002 Giants	Arizona	8	19 1/3	0	1	.000	20	11	13	3.72	0
2003 Hagerstown	So.Atl.	14	74	4	4	.500	90	24	57	2.55	0
2004 San Jose	Calif.	13	72 2/3	7	1	.875	89	17	58	1.86	0
2004 Norwich	Eastern	15	86	6	4	.600	72	40	73	3.35	0
2005 Fresno	P.C.	26	145 2/3	10	5	.667	176	73	118	4.39	0
2005 San Francisco	N.L.	7	46 1/3	2	1	.667	30	19	24	2.33	0
2006 San Francisco	N.L.	32	190 2/3	13	12	.520	179	87	157	4.15	0
2007 San Francisco	N.L.	32	200	7	16	.304	163	79	173	3.65	0
2008 San Francisco	N.L.	34	217 2/3	8	14	.364	186	91	206	3.76	0
2009 San Francisco	N.L.	33	217 2/3	14	8	.636	171	73	184	2.89	0
2010 San Francisco	N.L.	33	223 1/3	13	11	.542	177	61	181	3.14	0
2011 San Francisco	N.L.	33	221 2/3	12	11	.522	179	63	177	2.88	0
2012 San Francisco a	N.L.	32	219 1/3	16	5	.762	193	51	177	2.79	0
2013 San Francisco b	N.L.	30	184 1/3	8	10	.444	158	55	158	4.00	0
Major League Totals	9 Yrs.	266	1721	93	88	.514	1436	579	1437	3.35	0
Division Series											
2010 San Francisco	N.L.	1	6 2/3	0	0	.000	6	2	7	0.00	0
2012 San Francisco	N.L.	2	10 2/3	1	1	.500	9	3	11	5.06	0
Division Series Totals		3	17 1/3	1	1	.500	15	5	18	3.12	0
Championship Series											
2010 San Francisco	N.L.	1	7	1	0	1.000	5	3	2	0.00	0
2012 San Francisco	N.L.	2	12 1/3	1	1	.500	6	2	11	2.19	0
Championship Series Totals		3	19 1/3	2	1	.667	11	5	13	1.40	0
World Series Record											
2010 San Francisco	N.L.	1	7 2/3	1	0	1.000	2	2	4	0.00	0
2012 San Francisco	N.L.	1	7	0	0	.000	5	2	5	3.86	0
World Series Totals		2	14 2/3	1	0	1.000	7	4	9	1.84	0

a Pitched no-hit, no-run perfect game against Houston Astros, June 13, 2012.
b On disabled list from August 23 to September 7, 2013.

CAPPS, CARTER LEWIS

Born, Kinston, North Carolina, August 7, 1990.
Bats Right. Throws Right. Height, 6 feet, 5 inches. Weight, 220 pounds.

Year Club	Lea	G	IP	W	L	Pct	SO	BB	H	ERA	SAVES
2011 Clinton	Midwest	4	18	1	1	.500	21	10	19	6.00	0
2012 Jackson	Southern	38	50	2	3	.400	72	12	40	1.26	19
2012 Tacoma	P.C.	1	1 1/3	0	0	.000	3	0	0	0.00	0
2012 Seattle	A.L.	18	25	0	0	.000	28	11	25	3.96	0
2013 Tacoma	P.C.	7	11	0	0	.000	9	4	6	1.64	0
2013 Seattle a	A.L.	53	59	3	3	.500	66	23	73	5.49	0
Major League Totals	2 Yrs.	71	84	3	3	.500	94	34	98	5.04	0

a Traded to Miami Marlins for outfielder Logan Morrison, December 13, 2013.

CAPUANO, CHRISTOPHER FRANK (CHRIS)

Born, Springfield, Massachusetts, August 19, 1978.
Bats Left. Throws Left. Height, 6 feet, 3 inches. Weight, 225 pounds.

Year Club	Lea	G	IP	W	L	Pct	SO	BB	H	ERA	SAVES
2000 South Bend	Midwest	18	101 2/3	10	4	.714	105	45	68	2.21	0
2001 El Paso	Texas	28	159 1/3	10	11	.476	167	75	184	5.31	0
2002 Tucson	P.C.	6	36 1/3	4	1	.800	29	11	30	2.72	0
2003 Tucson	P.C.	23	142 2/3	9	5	.643	108	43	133	3.34	0
2003 Arizona a	N.L.	9	33	2	4	.333	23	11	27	4.64	0
2004 Milwaukee	N.L.	17	88 1/3	6	8	.429	80	37	91	4.99	0
2004 Beloit	Midwest	1	2 2/3	0	0	.000	4	1	3	3.38	0
2004 Indianapolis	Int.	2	8 2/3	0	1	.000	9	5	10	8.31	0
2004 High Desert b	Calif.	1	2	0	1	.000	2	3	6	27.00	0
2005 Milwaukee	N.L.	35	219	18	12	.600	176	91	212	3.99	0
2006 Milwaukee	N.L.	34	221 1/3	11	12	.478	174	47	229	4.03	0
2007 Milwaukee c	N.L.	29	150	5	12	.294	132	54	170	5.10	0
2008 Milwaukee d-e	N.L.			INJURED—Did Not Play							
2009 Brewers	Arizona	3	3	0	0	.000	4	2	5	6.00	0
2009 Helena	Pioneer	2	4	0	0	.000	3	0	2	0.00	0
2010 Brevard County	Fla.St.	3	14 2/3	2	0	1.000	17	0	12	1.23	0
2010 Nashville	P.C.	4	25	1	1	.500	16	4	21	1.80	0
2010 Milwaukee f	N.L.	24	66	4	4	.500	54	21	65	3.95	0
2011 New York g	N.L.	33	186	11	12	.478	168	53	198	4.55	0
2012 Los Angeles	N.L.	33	198 1/3	12	12	.500	162	54	188	3.72	0
2013 Albuquerque	P.C.	2	9 1/3	0	0	.000	9	3	8	1.93	0
2013 Los Angeles h-i	N.L.	24	105 2/3	4	7	.364	81	24	125	4.26	0
Major League Totals	9 Yrs.	238	1267 2/3	73	83	.468	1050	392	1305	4.27	0
Division Series											
2013 Los Angeles	N.L.	1	3	1	0	1.000	3	3	0	0.00	0

a Traded to Milwaukee Brewers with infielder Junior Spivey, infielder Craig Counsell, infielder Lyle Overbay, catcher Chad Moeller and pitcher Jorge DeRosa for infielder Richie Sexson, pitcher Shane Nance and player to be named later, December 1, 2003. Arizona Diamondbacks received outfielder Noochie Varner to complete trade, December 15, 2003.
b On disabled list from April 19 to May 26 and May 27 to June 12 and August 25 to October 6, 2004.
c On disabled list from June 9 to July 1, 2007.
d On disabled list from March 21 to September 29, 2008.
e Not offered contract, December 12, 2008, re-signed with Milwaukee Brewers organization, December 16, 2008.
f Filed for free agency, November 1, 2010. Signed with New York Mets, January 3, 2011.
g Filed for free agency, October 30, 2011. Signed with Los Angeles Dodgers, December 2, 2011.
h On disabled list from April 17 to May 6 and May 30 to June 19, 2013.
i Filed for free agency, October 31, 2013.

CARPENTER, DARRELL DAVID (DAVID)

Born, Morgantown, West Virginia, July 15, 1985.
Bats Right. Throws Right. Height, 6 feet, 2 inches. Weight, 215 pounds.

Year Club	Lea	G	IP	W	L	Pct	SO	BB	H	ERA	SAVES
2008 Cardinals	Gulf Coast	9	8 2/3	0	0	.000	9	6	9	1.04	3
2008 Johnson City	Appal.	6	6	0	0	.000	8	1	7	3.00	0
2009 Quad Cities	Midwest	52	67 1/3	5	3	.625	77	36	61	4.28	12
2010 Palm Beach a	Fla.St.	49	53 1/3	5	3	.625	50	15	45	2.36	20
2010 Lancaster	Calif.	6	7 2/3	1	1	.500	8	4	8	3.52	0
2011 Corpus Christi	Texas	14	14	0	1	.000	17	3	14	4.50	5
2011 Oklahoma	P.C.	19	19	0	0	.000	21	6	15	0.00	9
2011 Houston	N.L.	34	27 2/3	1	3	.250	29	13	28	2.93	1
2012 Houston	N.L.	30	29 2/3	0	2	.000	27	14	43	6.07	0
2012 Oklahoma	P.C.	7	8 2/3	1	0	1.000	6	0	7	2.08	3
2012 Las Vegas b	P.C.	16	17 2/3	0	1	.000	19	7	15	3.57	1
2012 Toronto c-d	A.L.	3	2 2/3	0	0	.000	4	2	8	30.38	0
2013 Gwinnett	Int.	6	15 1/3	1	2	.333	11	4	17	3.52	0
2013 Atlanta	N.L.	56	65 2/3	4	1	.800	74	20	45	1.78	0
Major League Totals	3 Yrs.	123	125 2/3	5	6	.455	134	49	124	3.65	1
Division Series											
2013 Atlanta	N.L.	3	2 2/3	0	1	.000	3	1	3	13.50	0

a Traded by St. Louis Cardinals to Houston Astros for infielder Pedro Feliz and cash, August 19, 2010.
b Traded to Toronto Blue Jays with pitcher Brandon Lyon and pitcher J.A. Happ for pitcher Francisco Cordero, outfielder Ben Francisco, pitcher Joseph Musgrove, pitcher Asher Wojciechowski, pitcher David Rollins, catcher Carlos Perez and player to be named later, July 20, 2012. Houston received pitcher Kevin Comer to complete trade, August 16, 2012.
c Traded to Boston Red Sox with manager John Farrell for infielder Mike Aviles, October 21, 2012.
d Claimed on waivers by Atlanta Braves, November 30, 2012.

CARRASCO, CARLOS LUIS

Born, Barquisimeto, Venezuela, March 21, 1987.
Bats Right. Throws Right. Height, 6 feet, 3 inches. Weight, 210 pounds.

Year	Club	Lea	G	IP	W	L	Pct	SO	BB	H	ERA	SAVES
2004	Phillies	Gulf Coast	11	48	5	4	.556	34	15	53	3.56	0
2005	Phillies	Gulf Coast	2	5	0	0	.000	2	1	3	1.80	0
2005	Batavia	N.Y.-Penn.	4	15 1/3	0	3	.000	12	5	29	13.50	0
2005	Lakewood	So.Atl.	13	62 2/3	1	7	.125	46	28	78	7.04	0
2006	Lakewood	So.Atl.	26	159 1/3	12	6	.667	159	65	103	2.26	0
2007	Clearwater	Fla.St.	12	69 2/3	6	2	.750	53	22	49	2.84	0
2007	Reading	Eastern	14	70 1/3	6	4	.600	49	46	65	4.86	0
2008	Reading	Eastern	20	114 2/3	7	7	.500	109	45	109	4.32	0
2008	Lehigh Valley	Int.	6	36 2/3	2	2	.500	46	13	37	1.72	0
2009	Lehigh Valley	Int.	20	114 2/3	6	9	.400	112	38	118	5.18	0
2009	Columbus	Int.	6	42 1/3	5	1	.833	36	7	31	3.19	0
2009	Cleveland a	A.L.	5	22 1/3	0	4	.000	11	11	40	8.87	0
2010	Columbus	Int.	25	150 1/3	10	6	.625	133	46	139	3.65	0
2010	Cleveland	A.L.	7	44 2/3	2	2	.500	38	14	47	3.83	0
2011	Akron	Eastern	1	3 2/3	0	0	.000	3	3	4	9.82	0
2011	Cleveland b	A.L.	21	124 2/3	8	9	.471	85	40	130	4.62	0
2012	Cleveland c	A.L.					INJURED—Did Not Play					
2013	Columbus	Int.	16	71 2/3	3	1	.750	79	21	59	3.14	1
2013	Cleveland	A.L.	15	46 2/3	1	4	.200	30	18	64	6.75	0
Major League Totals		4 Yrs.	48	238 1/3	11	19	.367	164	83	281	5.29	0

a Traded by Philadelphia Phillies to Cleveland Indians with catcher Lou Marson, pitcher Jason Knapp and infielder Jason Donald for pitcher Cliff Lee and outfielder Ben Francisco, July 29, 2009.
b On disabled list from April 25 to May 11 and August 4 to November 2, 2011.
c On disabled list from March 15 to November 2, 2012.

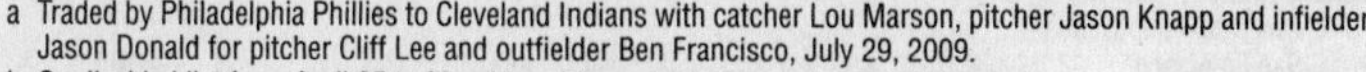

CASHNER, ANDREW BURTON

Born, Conroe, Texas, September 11, 1986.
Bats Right. Throws Right. Height, 6 feet, 6 inches. Weight, 210 pounds.

Year	Club	Lea	G	IP	W	L	Pct	SO	BB	H	ERA	SAVES
2008	Cubs	Arizona	1	1	0	0	.000	2	0	1	0.00	0
2008	Daytona	Fla.St.	1	2 2/3	0	1	.000	1	4	4	13.50	0
2008	Boise	Northwest	6	16 1/3	1	1	.500	16	19	19	4.96	0
2009	Daytona	Fla.St.	12	42	0	0	.000	34	15	31	1.50	0
2009	Tennessee	Southern	12	58 1/3	3	4	.429	41	27	45	3.39	0
2010	Tennessee	Southern	6	36	3	1	.750	42	13	22	2.75	0
2010	Iowa	P.C.	5	21	3	0	1.000	17	2	17	0.86	0
2010	Chicago	N.L.	53	54 1/3	2	6	.250	50	30	55	4.80	0
2011	Tennessee	Southern	3	2 2/3	0	1	.000	6	0	3	6.75	0
2011	Iowa	P.C.	2	2	0	0	.000	2	0	0	0.00	0
2011	Chicago a-b	N.L.	7	10 2/3	0	0	.000	8	4	3	1.69	0
2012	San Antonio	Texas	3	14 1/3	2	0	1.000	22	3	10	1.88	0
2012	Tucson	P.C.	3	9	0	1	.000	8	2	8	3.00	0
2012	San Diego c	N.L.	33	46 1/3	3	4	.429	52	19	42	4.27	0
2013	San Diego	N.L.	31	175	10	9	.526	128	47	151	3.09	0
Major League Totals		4 Yrs.	124	286 1/3	15	19	.441	238	100	251	3.55	0

a On disabled list from April 8 to September 5, 2011.
b Traded to San Diego Padres with outfielder Kyung-Min Na for infielder Anthony Rizzo and pitcher Zach Cates, January 6, 2012.
c On disabled list from July 4 to September 1, 2012.

CASILLA, SANTIAGO

Born, Don Gregorio, Dominican Republic, June 25, 1980.
Bats Right. Throws Right. Height, 6 feet. Weight, 200 pounds.

Year	Club	Lea	G	IP	W	L	Pct	SO	BB	H	ERA	SAVES
2001	Athletics	Arizona	12	47 1/3	4	2	.667	50	6	37	2.85	0
2002	Athletics	Arizona	13	59	2	1	.667	66	17	56	2.44	1
2002	Vancouver	Northwest	3	12 1/3	0	3	.000	16	7	15	7.30	0
2003	Kane County	Midwest	14	42 1/3	0	1	.000	28	19	40	2.55	0
2004	Kane County	Midwest	25	30	1	0	1.000	49	6	16	0.30	16
2004	Midland	Texas	13	18	2	0	1.000	32	15	10	1.50	2
2004	Sacramento	P.C.	11	13 2/3	1	2	.333	21	9	10	3.95	1
2004	Oakland	A.L.	4	5 2/3	0	0	.000	5	9	5	12.71	0
2005	Midland	Texas	10	16 2/3	0	0	.000	30	9	9	1.08	6
2005	Sacramento	P.C.	44	48 1/3	3	6	.333	73	20	45	4.47	20
2005	Oakland a	A.L.	3	3	0	0	.000	1	1	2	3.00	0

Year	Club	Lea	G	IP	W	L	Pct	SO	BB	H	ERA	SAVES
2006	Oakland	A.L.	2	2 1/3	0	0	.000	2	2	2	11.57	0
2006	Sacramento	P.C.	25	33	2	0	1.000	32	10	25	3.27	4
2007	Sacramento	P.C.	22	24	2	1	.667	29	14	18	4.13	3
2007	Oakland	A.L.	46	50 2/3	3	1	.750	52	23	43	4.44	2
2008	Stockton	Calif.	1	1	0	0	.000	2	0	0	0.00	0
2008	Sacramento	P.C.	2	2 2/3	0	0	.000	5	1	3	3.38	0
2008	Oakland b	A.L.	51	50 1/3	2	1	.667	43	20	60	3.93	2
2009	Stockton	Calif.	1	1	0	0	.000	0	0	0	0.00	0
2009	Sacramento	P.C.	1	1	0	0	.000	0	0	0	0.00	0
2009	Oakland c	A.L.	46	48 1/3	1	2	.333	35	25	61	5.96	0
2010	Fresno	P.C.	4	4	0	0	.000	7	2	2	0.00	2
2010	San Francisco	N.L.	52	55 1/3	7	2	.778	56	26	40	1.95	2
2011	San Jose	Calif.	2	3	0	0	.000	1	2	3	0.00	0
2011	Fresno	P.C.	4	5	0	0	.000	4	1	3	1.80	0
2011	San Francisco d	N.L.	49	51 2/3	2	2	.500	45	25	33	1.74	6
2012	San Francisco	N.L.	73	63 1/3	7	6	.538	55	22	55	2.84	25
2013	San Jose	Calif.	5	5	0	0	.000	2	5	7	5.40	0
2013	San Francisco e	N.L.	57	50	7	2	.778	38	25	39	2.16	2
Major League Totals		10 Yrs.	383	380 2/3	29	16	.644	332	178	340	3.43	39
Division Series												
2010	San Francisco	N.L.	1	1 2/3	0	0	.000	2	0	1	0.00	0
2012	San Francisco	N.L.	5	3 1/3	0	0	.000	5	1	6	2.70	0
Division Series Totals			6	5	0	0	.000	7	1	7	1.80	0
Championship Series												
2010	San Francisco	N.L.	2	1 2/3	0	0	.000	2	1	2	5.40	0
2012	San Francisco	N.L.	4	2 1/3	0	0	.000	3	0	2	0.00	0
Championship Series Totals			6	4	0	0	.000	5	1	4	2.25	0
World Series Record												
2010	San Francisco	N.L.	1	1 1/3	0	0	.000	1	0	0	0.00	0
2012	San Francisco	N.L.	2	1 1/3	1	0	1.000	0	0	0	0.00	0
World Series Totals			3	2 2/3	1	0	1.000	1	0	0	0.00	0

a Played under name of Jairo Garcia 2001-2005.
b On disabled list from May 16 to June 19, 2008.
c Released by Oakland Athletics, December 10, 2009. Signed with San Francisco Giants organization, January 21, 2010.
d On disabled list from April 6 to May 28, 2011.
e On disabled list from May 21 to July 13, 2013.

CECIL, BRETT AARION

Born, Dunkirk, Maryland, July 2, 1986.

Bats Right. Throws Left. Height, 6 feet, 2 inches. Weight, 225 pounds.

Year	Club	Lea	G	IP	W	L	Pct	SO	BB	H	ERA	SAVES
2007	Auburn	N.Y.-Penn.	14	49 2/3	1	0	1.000	56	11	36	1.27	0
2008	New Hampshire	Eastern	18	77 2/3	6	2	.750	87	23	66	2.55	0
2008	Dunedin	Fla.St.	4	10 1/3	0	0	.000	11	2	6	1.74	0
2008	Syracuse	Int.	6	30 2/3	2	3	.400	31	16	28	4.11	0
2009	Las Vegas	P.C.	9	49	1	5	.167	32	19	53	5.69	0
2009	Toronto	A.L.	18	93 1/3	7	4	.636	69	38	116	5.30	0
2010	Las Vegas	P.C.	2	11	2	0	1.000	11	2	13	2.45	0
2010	Toronto	A.L.	28	172 2/3	15	7	.682	117	54	175	4.22	0
2011	Las Vegas	P.C.	12	78 2/3	8	2	.800	63	24	89	5.26	0
2011	Toronto	A.L.	20	123 2/3	4	11	.267	87	42	122	4.73	0
2012	New Hampshire	Eastern	9	42 2/3	3	2	.600	34	14	44	3.38	0
2012	Las Vegas	P.C.	6	39 2/3	1	2	.333	33	7	36	2.50	0
2012	Toronto	A.L.	21	61 1/3	2	4	.333	51	23	70	5.72	0
2013	Toronto a	A.L.	60	60 2/3	5	1	.833	70	23	44	2.82	1
Major League Totals		5 Yrs.	147	511 2/3	33	27	.550	394	180	527	4.56	1

a On disabled list from September 13 to October 31, 2013.

CHACIN (MOLINA), JHOULYS JOSE

Born, Maracaibo, Venezuela, January 7, 1988.

Bats Right. Throws Right. Height, 6 feet, 3 inches. Weight, 215 pounds.

Year	Club	Lea	G	IP	W	L	Pct	SO	BB	H	ERA	SAVES
2007	Casper	Pioneer	16	73	6	5	.545	77	26	85	3.13	0
2008	Asheville	So.Atl.	16	111 1/3	10	1	.909	98	30	82	1.86	0
2008	Modesto	Calif.	12	66 1/3	8	2	.800	62	12	61	2.31	0

Year	Club	Lea	G	IP	W	L	Pct	SO	BB	H	ERA	SAVES
2009	Tulsa	Texas	18	103 1/3	8	6	.571	86	35	87	3.14	0
2009	Colorado Springs	P.C.	4	14 1/3	1	2	.333	11	13	11	3.77	0
2009	Colorado	N.L.	9	11	0	1	.000	13	11	6	4.91	0
2010	Colorado Springs	P.C.	7	35 2/3	3	2	.600	34	17	27	1.51	0
2010	Colorado	N.L.	28	137 1/3	9	11	.450	138	61	114	3.28	0
2011	Colorado	N.L.	31	194	11	14	.440	150	*87	168	3.62	0
2012	Modesto	Calif.	1	2 1/3	0	1	.000	1	0	7	19.29	0
2012	Tulsa	Texas	2	9	0	1	.000	7	2	9	6.00	0
2012	Colorado Springs	P.C.	2	13 2/3	1	1	.500	5	5	10	2.63	0
2012	Colorado a	N.L.	14	69	3	5	.375	45	32	80	4.43	0
2013	Colorado b	N.L.	31	197 1/3	14	10	.583	126	61	188	3.47	0
Major League Totals		5 Yrs.	113	608 2/3	37	41	.474	472	252	556	3.61	0

a On disabled list from May 2 to August 21, 2012.
b On disabled list from April 20 to May 5, 2013.

CHAMBERLAIN, JUSTIN LOUIS (JOBA)

Born, Lincoln, Nebraska, September 23, 1985.
Bats Right. Throws Right. Height, 6 feet, 2 inches. Weight, 230 pounds.

Year	Club	Lea	G	IP	W	L	Pct	SO	BB	H	ERA	SAVES
2007	Tampa	Fla.St.	7	40	4	0	1.000	51	11	25	2.03	0
2007	Trenton	Eastern	8	40 1/3	4	2	.667	66	15	32	3.35	0
2007	Scranton-WB	Int.	3	8	1	0	1.000	18	1	5	0.00	0
2007	New York	A.L.	19	24	2	0	1.000	34	6	12	0.38	1
2008	New York a	A.L.	42	100 1/3	4	3	.571	118	39	87	2.60	0
2009	New York	A.L.	32	157 1/3	9	6	.600	133	76	167	4.75	0
2010	New York	A.L.	73	71 1/3	3	4	.429	77	22	71	4.40	3
2011	New York b	A.L.	27	28 2/3	2	0	1.000	24	7	23	2.83	0
2012	Yankees	Gulf Coast	3	4	0	0	.000	6	0	0	0.00	0
2012	Tampa	Fla.St.	3	4	0	1	.000	1	1	3	2.25	0
2012	Trenton	Eastern	1	1 1/3	1	0	1.000	3	0	1	0.00	0
2012	New York c	A.L.	22	20 2/3	1	0	1.000	22	6	26	4.35	0
2013	Scranton/WB	Int.	1	1	0	0	.000	0	0	2	0.00	0
2013	New York d-e	A.L.	45	42	2	1	.667	38	26	47	4.93	1
Major League Totals		7 Yrs.	260	444 2/3	23	14	.622	446	182	433	3.85	5
	Division Series											
2007	New York	A.L.	2	3 2/3	0	0	.000	4	3	3	4.91	0
2009	New York	A.L.	3	1 2/3	0	0	.000	1	0	2	0.00	0
2012	New York	A.L.	1	1	0	0	.000	1	0	1	0.00	0
Division Series Totals			6	6 1/3	0	0	.000	6	3	6	2.84	0
	Championship Series											
2009	New York	A.L.	4	1 2/3	0	0	.000	2	0	5	5.40	0
2010	New York	A.L.	3	3 1/3	0	0	.000	3	2	4	2.70	0
2012	New York	A.L.	3	1 1/3	0	0	.000	0	0	3	0.00	0
Championship Series Totals			10	6 1/3	0	0	.000	5	2	12	2.84	0
	World Series Record											
2009	New York	A.L.	3	3	1	0	1.000	4	1	2	3.00	0

a On disabled list from August 5 to September 2, 2008.
b On disabled list from June 8 to October 12, 2011.
c On disabled list from March 26 to July 31, 2012.
d On disabled list from April 28 to May 28, 2013.
e Filed for free agency, October 31, 2013. Signed with Detroit Tigers, December 13, 2013.

CHAPMAN, ALBERTIN AROLDIS (AROLDIS)

Born, Holguin, Cuba, February 28, 1988.
Bats Left. Throws Left. Height, 6 feet, 4 inches. Weight, 185 pounds.

Year	Club	Lea	G	IP	W	L	Pct	SO	BB	H	ERA	SAVES
2010	Louisville	Int.	39	95 2/3	9	6	.600	125	52	77	3.57	8
2010	Cincinnati a	N.L.	15	13 1/3	2	2	.500	19	5	9	2.03	0
2011	Carolina	Southern	5	7 1/3	1	1	.500	11	6	5	6.14	0
2011	Louisville	Int.	4	5 2/3	0	1	.000	9	2	9	11.12	0
2011	Cincinnati b	N.L.	54	50	4	1	.800	71	41	24	3.60	1
2012	Cincinnati	N.L.	68	71 2/3	5	5	.500	122	23	35	1.51	38
2013	Cincinnati	N.L.	68	63 2/3	4	5	.444	112	29	37	2.54	38
Major League Totals		4 Yrs.	205	198 2/3	15	13	.536	324	98	105	2.40	77
	Division Series											
2010	Cincinnati	N.L.	2	1 2/3	0	1	.000	1	0	3	0.00	0

Year	Club	Lea	G	IP	W	L	Pct	SO	BB	H	ERA	SAVES
2012	Cincinnati	N.L.	3	3	0	0	.000	3	2	2	3.00	0
Division Series Totals			5	4²/₃	0	1	.000	4	2	5	1.93	0

a Played in Cuba 2005 through 2009. Signed with Cincinnati Reds, January 12, 2010.
b On disabled list from May 16 to June 24, 2011.

CHATWOOD, TYLER COLE

Born, Fontana, California, December 16, 1989.
Bats Right. Throws Right. Height, 6 feet. Weight, 185 pounds.

Year	Club	Lea	G	IP	W	L	Pct	SO	BB	H	ERA	SAVES
2008	Angels	Arizona	11	38	1	2	.333	48	36	25	3.08	0
2009	Cedar Rapids	Midwest	24	116 1/3	8	7	.533	106	66	99	4.02	0
2010	Rancho Cucamonga	Calif.	14	81 1/3	8	3	.727	70	36	71	1.77	0
2010	Salt Lake	P.C.	1	5 1/3	1	0	1.000	3	0	9	6.35	0
2010	Arkansas	Texas	12	68 1/3	4	6	.400	36	27	72	3.82	0
2011	Salt Lake	P.C.	4	16	1	2	.333	11	11	21	5.06	0
2011	Los Angeles a	A.L.	27	142	6	11	.353	74	71	166	4.75	0
2012	Tulsa	Texas	4	24	1	1	.500	22	7	17	3.00	0
2012	Colorado Springs	P.C.	9	37 1/3	0	2	.000	31	19	52	5.79	0
2012	Colorado	N.L.	19	64 2/3	5	6	.455	41	33	74	5.43	1
2013	Colorado Springs	P.C.	6	34	2	1	.667	33	7	37	2.91	0
2013	Colorado b	N.L.	20	111 1/3	8	5	.615	66	41	118	3.15	0
Major League Totals		3 Yrs.	66	318	19	22	.463	181	145	358	4.33	1

a Traded to Colorado Rockies for catcher Chris Iannetta, November 30, 2011.
b On disabled list from August 1 to September 1, 2013.

CHAVEZ, JESSE DAVID

Born, Victorville, California, August 21, 1983.
Bats Right. Throws Right. Height, 6 feet, 2 inches. Weight, 160 pounds.

Year	Club	Lea	G	IP	W	L	Pct	SO	BB	H	ERA	SAVES
2003	Spokane	Northwest	17	55 1/3	2	2	.500	48	31	63	4.55	1
2004	Clinton	Midwest	27	123	6	10	.375	96	35	149	4.68	0
2005	Bakersfield	Calif.	11	24 1/3	0	0	.000	31	9	16	2.22	2
2005	Frisco	Texas	31	57	4	3	.571	27	25	71	5.68	1
2006	Frisco	Texas	38	59	2	5	.286	70	28	54	4.42	4
2006	Indianapolis	Int.	12	17	2	1	.667	15	9	18	4.24	0
2006	Oklahoma a	P.C.	1	2	0	0	.000	3	0	3	4.50	0
2007	Indianapolis	Int.	46	80 1/3	3	3	.500	65	17	94	3.92	2
2008	Indianapolis	Int.	51	68 2/3	2	6	.250	70	22	58	3.80	14
2008	Pittsburgh	N.L.	15	15	0	1	.000	16	9	20	6.60	0
2009	Pittsburgh b-c	N.L.	73	67 1/3	1	4	.200	47	22	69	4.01	0
2010	Atlanta	N.L.	28	36 2/3	3	2	.600	29	12	40	5.89	0
2010	Kansas City d	A.L.	23	26	2	3	.400	16	11	29	5.88	0
2011	Omaha	P.C.	45	57 2/3	2	4	.333	54	16	63	3.75	16
2011	Kansas City e	A.L.	4	7 2/3	0	0	.000	8	5	12	10.57	0
2012	Las Vegas	P.C.	19	95	8	5	.615	86	20	90	3.98	1
2012	Sacramento	P.C.	2	10	0	0	.000	9	2	8	1.80	1
2012	Toronto-Oakland f	A.L.	13	24 2/3	1	1	.500	30	11	34	9.85	0
2013	Sacramento	P.C.	5	30	2	2	.500	26	5	35	2.70	0
2013	Oakland	A.L.	35	57 1/3	2	4	.333	55	20	50	3.92	1
Major League Totals		6 Yrs.	191	234 2/3	9	15	.375	201	90	254	5.48	1

a Traded by Texas Rangers to Pittsburgh Pirates for pitcher Kip Wells, July 31, 2006.
b Traded to Tampa Bay Rays for infielder Akinori Iwamura, November 3, 2009.
c Traded to Atlanta Braves for pitcher Rafael Soriano, December 11, 2009.
d Traded to Kansas City Royals with outfielder Gregor Blanco and pitcher Tim Collins for outfielder Rick Ankiel, pitcher Kyle Farnsworth and cash, July 31, 2010.
e Claimed on waivers by Toronto Blue Jays, October 21, 2011.
f Sold to Oakland Athletics, August 24, 2012.

CHEN, BRUCE KASTULO

Born, Panama City, Panama, June 19, 1977.
Bats Left. Throws Left. Height, 6 feet, 2 inches. Weight, 215 pounds.

Year	Club	Lea	G	IP	W	L	Pct	SO	BB	H	ERA	SAVES
1994	Braves	Gulf Coast	9	42 2/3	1	4	.200	26	3	42	3.80	1
1995	Danville	Appal.	14	70 1/3	4	4	.500	56	19	78	3.97	0
1996	Eugene	Northwest	11	35 2/3	4	1	.800	55	14	23	2.27	0
1997	Macon	So.Atl.	28	146 1/3	12	7	.632	182	44	120	3.51	0

Year	Club	Lea	G	IP	W	L	Pct	SO	BB	H	ERA	SAVES
1998	Greenville	Southern	24	139⅓	13	7	.650	164	48	106	3.29	0
1998	Richmond	Int.	4	24	2	1	.667	29	19	17	1.88	0
1998	Atlanta	N.L.	4	20⅓	2	0	1.000	17	9	23	3.98	0
1999	Richmond	Int.	14	78	6	3	.667	90	26	73	3.81	0
1999	Atlanta	N.L.	16	51	2	2	.500	45	27	38	5.47	0
2000	Richmond	Int.	1	6	1	0	1.000	6	1	5	0.00	0
2000	Atlanta-Philadelphia a	N.L.	37	134	7	4	.636	112	46	116	3.29	0
2001	Reading	Eastern	1	6	1	0	1.000	7	0	3	0.00	0
2001	Scranton-WB	Int.	3	18⅔	1	0	1.000	14	5	14	3.86	0
2001	Philadelphia-New York b	N.L.	27	146	7	7	.500	126	59	146	4.87	0
2002	NY-Montreal-Cincinnati c-d	N.L.	55	77⅔	2	5	.286	80	43	85	5.56	0
2003	Houston	N.L.	11	12	0	0	.000	8	8	14	6.00	0
2003	Boston	A.L.	5	12⅓	0	1	.000	12	2	12	5.11	0
2003	Pawtucket e-f-g	Int.	16	85	5	5	.500	73	15	80	4.24	1
2004	Syracuse	Int.	3	10⅓	0	1	.000	8	5	17	8.71	0
2004	Ottawa	Int.	22	95	4	3	.571	108	30	85	3.22	0
2004	Baltimore h	A.L.	8	47⅔	2	1	.667	32	16	39	3.02	0
2005	Baltimore	A.L.	34	197⅓	13	10	.565	133	63	187	3.83	0
2006	Baltimore	A.L.	40	98⅔	0	7	.000	70	35	137	6.93	0
2007	Texas	A.L.	5	10	0	0	.000	7	6	11	7.20	0
2007	Oklahoma i	P.C.	4	16	1	1	.500	12	3	17	5.63	0
2008						Did Not Play						
2009	Omaha	P.C.	14	82	4	2	.667	69	23	57	3.40	0
2009	Kansas City j-k-l	A.L.	17	62⅓	1	6	.143	45	25	74	5.78	0
2010	Omaha	P.C.	3	20⅔	0	1	.000	20	5	13	1.31	0
2010	Kansas City m	A.L.	33	140⅓	12	7	.632	98	57	136	4.17	1
2011	NW Arkansas	Texas	1	2	0	1	.000	2	0	5	18.00	0
2011	Omaha	P.C.	2	9	0	0	.000	8	1	11	6.00	0
2011	Kansas City n-o	A.L.	25	155	12	8	.600	97	50	152	3.77	0
2012	Kansas City	A.L.	34	191⅔	11	14	.440	140	47	215	5.07	0
2013	Kansas City p	A.L.	34	121	9	4	.692	78	36	107	3.27	0
Major League Totals		15 Yrs.	385	1477⅓	80	76	.513	1100	529	1492	4.49	1

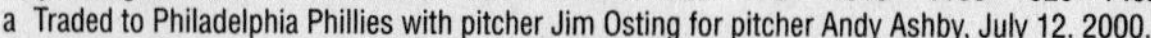

a Traded to Philadelphia Phillies with pitcher Jim Osting for pitcher Andy Ashby, July 12, 2000.
b Traded to New York Mets with pitcher Adam Walker for pitcher Turk Wendell and pitcher Dennis Cook, July 27, 2001.
c Traded to Montreal Expos with pitcher Dicky Gonzalez, infielder Luis Figueroa and player to be named later for pitcher Scott Strickland, pitcher Paul Seubel and outfielder Matt Watson, April 5, 2002. Montreal Expos received pitcher Saul Rivera to complete trade, July 14, 2002.
d Traded to Cincinnati Reds for pitcher Jim Brower, June 14, 2002.
e Released by Cincinnati Reds, March 12, 2003. Signed with Houston Astros organization, March 14, 2003.
f Claimed on waivers by Boston Red Sox, May 7, 2003.
g Filed for free agency, October 3, 2003. Signed with Toronto Blue Jays organization, November 26, 2003.
h Sold to Baltimore Orioles, May 1, 2004.
i Filed for free agency, October 29, 2006. Signed with Texas Rangers organization, February 6, 2007.
j Filed for free agency, October 15, 2007. Signed with Kansas City Royals organization, March 1, 2009.
k On disabled list from September 23 to November 6, 2009.
l Filed for free agency, November 6, 2009, re-signed with Kansas City Royals organization, December 11, 2009.
m Filed for free agency, November 1, 2010, re-signed with Kansas City Royals, January 15, 2011.
n On disabled list from May 6 to June 24, 2011.
o Filed for free agency, October 30, 2011, re-signed with Kansas City Royals, November 22, 2011.
p Filed for free agency, October 31, 2013.

CHEN, WEI-YIN

Born, Kaohsiung City, Taiwan, July 21, 1985.
Bats Left. Throws Left. Height, 6 feet. Weight, 195 pounds.

Year	Club	Lea	G	IP	W	L	Pct	SO	BB	H	ERA	SAVES
2005	Chunichi	Japan Cent.	10	19⅓	0	0	.000	20	6	29	6.16	1
2006-2007						Did Not Play						
2008	Chunichi	Japan Cent.	39	114⅔	7	6	.538	107	33	101	2.90	0
2009	Chunichi	Japan Cent.	24	164	8	4	.667	146	40	113	1.54	0
2010	Chunichi	Japan Cent.	29	188	13	10	.565	153	49	166	2.87	0
2011	Chunichi a	Japan Cent.	25	164⅔	8	10	.444	94	31	138	2.67	0
2012	Baltimore	A.L.	32	192⅔	12	11	.522	154	57	186	4.02	0
2013	Baltimore b	A.L.	23	137	7	7	.500	104	39	142	4.07	0
Major League Totals		2 Yrs.	55	329⅔	19	18	.514	258	96	328	4.04	0
	Division Series											
2012	Baltimore	A.L.	1	6⅓	1	0	1.000	3	1	8	1.42	0

a Signed with Baltimore Orioles, December 10, 2011.
b On disabled list from May 13 to July 10, 2013.

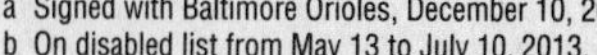

CHOATE, RANDOL DOYLE (RANDY)

Born, San Antonio, Texas, September 5, 1975.
Bats Left. Throws Left. Height, 6 feet, 3 inches. Weight, 200 pounds.

Year	Club	Lea	G	IP	W	L	Pct	SO	BB	H	ERA	SAVES
1997	Oneonta	N.Y.-Penn.	10	$62^1/_3$	5	1	.833	61	12	49	1.73	0
1998	Tampa	Fla.St.	13	70	1	8	.111	55	22	83	5.27	0
1998	Greensboro	So.Atl.	8	39	1	5	.167	32	7	46	3.00	0
1999	Tampa	Fla.St.	47	50	2	2	.500	62	24	51	4.50	1
2000	Columbus	Int.	33	$35^1/_3$	2	0	1.000	37	14	34	2.04	1
2000	New York	A.L.	22	17	0	1	.000	12	8	14	4.76	0
2001	New York	A.L.	37	$48^1/_3$	3	1	.750	35	27	34	3.35	0
2001	Columbus	Int.	4	$4^1/_3$	1	1	.500	4	3	7	2.08	0
2002	New York	A.L.	18	$22^1/_3$	0	0	.000	17	15	18	6.04	0
2002	Columbus	Int.	31	$36^2/_3$	3	2	.600	32	15	25	1.72	1
2003	Columbus	Int.	54	$71^1/_3$	3	5	.375	56	24	75	3.91	1
2003	New York a	A.L.	5	$3^2/_3$	0	0	.000	0	1	7	7.36	0
2004	Arizona	N.L.	74	$50^2/_3$	2	4	.333	49	28	52	4.62	0
2004	Tucson b	P.C.	15	$12^2/_3$	0	0	.000	7	8	10	5.68	1
2005	Arizona	N.L.	8	7	0	0	.000	4	5	8	9.00	0
2005	Tucson	P.C.	47	40	1	1	.500	20	22	44	3.38	3
2006	Tucson	P.C.	43	$45^2/_3$	6	0	1.000	44	10	39	2.17	8
2006	Arizona	N.L.	30	16	0	1	.000	12	3	21	3.94	0
2007	Arizona	N.L.	2	0	0	0	.000	0	0	3	0.00	0
2007	Tucson c-d-e	P.C.	55	$63^1/_3$	3	1	.750	61	16	68	2.98	3
2008	Brevard County	Fla.St.	1	1	0	0	.000	1	0	0	0.00	0
2008	Nashville f-g	P.C.	26	39	0	4	.000	31	20	42	5.08	2
2009	Durham	Int.	21	$19^1/_3$	3	0	1.000	15	9	16	3.72	0
2009	Tampa Bay	A.L.	61	$36^1/_3$	1	0	1.000	28	11	28	3.47	5
2010	Tampa Bay h	A.L.	*85	$44^2/_3$	4	3	.571	40	17	41	4.23	0
2011	Florida i	N.L.	54	$24^2/_3$	1	1	.500	31	13	13	1.82	0
2012	Miami-Los Angeles j-k	N.L.	*80	$38^2/_3$	0	0	.000	38	18	29	3.03	1
2013	St. Louis	N.L.	64	$35^1/_3$	2	1	.667	28	11	26	2.29	0
Major League Totals		13 Yrs.	540	$344^2/_3$	13	12	.520	294	157	294	3.84	6
	Division Series											
2000	New York	A.L.	1	$1^1/_3$	0	0	.000	1	1	0	6.75	0
2010	Tampa Bay	A.L.	3	1	0	0	.000	0	0	0	0.00	0
2013	St. Louis	N.L.	1	$0^2/_3$	0	0	.000	0	0	0	0.00	0
Division Series Totals			5	3	0	0	.000	1	1	0	3.00	0
	Championship Series											
2000	New York	A.L.	1	$0^1/_3$	0	0	.000	1	0	0	0.00	0
2013	St. Louis	N.L.	4	2	0	0	.000	1	0	0	0.00	0
Championship Series Totals			5	$2^1/_3$	0	0	.000	2	0	0	0.00	0
	World Series Record											
2001	New York	A.L.	2	$3^2/_3$	0	0	.000	2	1	7	2.45	0
2013	St. Louis	N.L.	4	$0^2/_3$	0	0	.000	0	1	1	0.00	0
World Series Totals			6	$4^1/_3$	0	0	.000	2	2	8	2.08	0

a Traded to Montreal Expos with infielder Nick Johnson and outfielder Juan Rivera for pitcher Javier Vazquez, December 4, 2003.
b Traded to Arizona Diamondbacks for pitcher John Patterson, March 25, 2004.
c Filed for free agency, October 31, 2006. Signed with Minnesota Twins organization, January 29, 2007.
d Released by Minnesota Twins, March 23, 2007. Signed with Arizona Diamondbacks organization, April 17, 2007.
e Filed for free agency, October 4, 2007. Signed with Milwaukee Brewers, November 13, 2007.
f On disabled list from March 21 to July 10, 2008.
g Filed for free agency, October 1, 2008. Signed with Tampa Bay Rays organization, December 23, 2008.
h Filed for free agency, November 1, 2010. Signed with Florida Marlins organization, December 15, 2010.
i On disabled list from August 16 to October 31, 2011.
j Traded to Los Angeles Dodgers with infielder Hanley Ramirez for pitcher Nathan Eovaldi and pitcher Scott McGough, July 25, 2012.
k Filed for free agency, November 3, 2012. Signed with St. Louis Cardinals, December 7, 2012.

CINGRANI, ANTHONY MICHAEL (TONY)

Born, New Lenox, Illinois, July 5, 1989.
Bats Left. Throws Left. Height, 6 feet, 4 inches. Weight, 215 pounds.

Year	Club	Lea	G	IP	W	L	Pct	SO	BB	H	ERA	SAVES
2011	Billings	Pioneer	13	$51^1/_3$	3	2	.600	80	6	35	1.75	0
2012	Bakersfield	Calif.	10	$56^2/_3$	5	1	.833	71	13	39	1.11	0
2012	Pensacola	Southern	16	$89^1/_3$	5	3	.625	101	39	59	2.12	0
2012	Cincinnati	N.L.	3	5	0	0	.000	9	2	4	1.80	0
2013	Louisville	Int.	6	$31^1/_3$	3	0	1.000	49	11	14	1.15	0

Year	Club	Lea	G	IP	W	L	Pct	SO	BB	H	ERA	SAVES
2013	Cincinnati a	N.L.	23	$104\frac{2}{3}$	7	4	.636	120	43	72	2.92	0
Major League Totals		2 Yrs.	26	$109\frac{2}{3}$	7	4	.636	129	45	76	2.87	0

a On disabled list from August 21 to September 5, 2013.

CISHEK, STEVEN R. (STEVE)

Born, Falmouth, Massachusetts, June 18, 1986.
Bats Right. Throws Right. Height, 6 feet, 6 inches. Weight, 215 pounds.

Year	Club	Lea	G	IP	W	L	Pct	SO	BB	H	ERA	SAVES
2007	Jamestown	N.Y.-Penn.	25	$32\frac{1}{3}$	1	2	.333	30	19	20	1.95	9
2008	Greensboro	So.Atl.	50	$75\frac{1}{3}$	3	5	.375	75	34	69	4.66	2
2009	Jupiter	Fla.St.	37	57	3	4	.429	45	16	36	2.84	2
2010	Jupiter	Fla.St.	26	35	0	6	.000	28	19	29	2.83	4
2010	Jacksonville	Southern	22	$31\frac{1}{3}$	3	1	.750	34	10	30	4.31	2
2010	Florida	N.L.	3	$4\frac{1}{3}$	0	0	.000	3	1	1	0.00	0
2011	New Orleans	P.C.	15	23	1	1	.500	19	12	18	2.35	0
2011	Florida	N.L.	45	$54\frac{2}{3}$	2	1	.667	55	19	45	2.63	3
2012	Miami	N.L.	68	$63\frac{2}{3}$	5	2	.714	68	29	54	2.69	15
2013	Miami	N.L.	69	$69\frac{2}{3}$	4	6	.400	74	22	53	2.33	34
Major League Totals		4 Yrs.	185	$192\frac{1}{3}$	11	9	.550	200	71	153	2.48	52

CLAIBORNE, PRESTON MICHAEL

Born, Dallas, Texas, January 21, 1988.
Bats Right. Throws Right. Height, 6 feet, 2 inches. Weight, 225 pounds.

Year	Club	Lea	G	IP	W	L	Pct	SO	BB	H	ERA	SAVES
2010	Staten Island	N.Y.-Penn.	19	$23\frac{2}{3}$	1	2	.333	30	8	20	2.28	2
2010	Tampa	Fla.St.	5	$7\frac{1}{3}$	0	1	.000	6	4	7	3.68	0
2011	Tampa	Fla.St.	38	81	3	7	.300	75	30	73	3.11	5
2012	Trenton	Eastern	30	$48\frac{2}{3}$	2	2	.500	49	24	33	2.22	5
2012	Scranton/WB	Int.	20	$33\frac{1}{3}$	4	0	1.000	29	12	31	4.05	1
2013	Tampa	Fla.St.	1	1	0	0	.000	1	1	0	0.00	0
2013	Scranton/WB	Int.	8	$10\frac{1}{3}$	0	0	.000	10	1	14	3.48	3
2013	New York	A.L.	44	$50\frac{1}{3}$	0	2	.000	42	14	51	4.11	0

CLEMENS, PAUL

Born, Columbia, South Carolina, February 14, 1988.
Bats Right. Throws Right. Height, 6 feet, 4 inches. Weight, 195 pounds.

Year	Club	Lea	G	IP	W	L	Pct	SO	BB	H	ERA	SAVES
2008	Braves	Gulf Coast	1	3	1	0	1.000	2	0	1	0.00	0
2008	Danville	Appal.	12	$58\frac{1}{3}$	3	3	.500	57	18	57	3.39	1
2008	Rome	So.Atl.	1	4	0	1	.000	0	2	7	9.00	0
2009	Rome	So.Atl.	26	$85\frac{1}{3}$	6	5	.545	64	49	105	5.91	3
2010	Rome	So.Atl.	8	19	2	0	1.000	16	8	11	1.42	1
2010	Myrtle Beach	Carolina	27	$75\frac{2}{3}$	0	4	.000	65	28	83	3.69	2
2011	Mississippi a	Southern	20	$108\frac{2}{3}$	6	5	.545	93	44	103	3.73	0
2011	Corpus Christi	Texas	5	$30\frac{2}{3}$	2	1	.667	26	12	23	2.35	0
2011	Oklahoma	P.C.	1	$4\frac{2}{3}$	0	1	.000	6	6	4	15.43	0
2012	Corpus Christi	Texas	7	$41\frac{2}{3}$	3	2	.600	37	11	41	3.46	0
2012	Oklahoma	P.C.	20	$101\frac{2}{3}$	8	8	.500	68	32	145	6.73	0
2013	Oklahoma	P.C.	6	30	3	2	.600	16	11	27	4.50	0
2013	Houston	A.L.	35	$73\frac{1}{3}$	4	7	.364	49	26	82	5.40	0

a Traded to by Atlanta Braves to Houston Astros with outfielder Jordan Schafer, pitcher Juan Abreu and pitcher Brett Oberholtzer for outfielder Michael Bourn and cash, July 31, 2011.

CLIPPARD, TYLER LEE

Born, Lexington, Kentucky, February 14, 1985.
Bats Right. Throws Right. Height, 6 feet, 4 inches. Weight, 200 pounds.

Year	Club	Lea	G	IP	W	L	Pct	SO	BB	H	ERA	SAVES
2003	Yankees	Gulf Coast	11	$43\frac{2}{3}$	3	3	.500	56	5	33	2.89	0
2004	Battle Creek	Midwest	26	149	10	10	.500	145	32	153	3.44	0
2005	Tampa	Fla.St.	26	$147\frac{1}{3}$	10	9	.526	169	34	118	3.18	0
2005	Columbus	Int.	1	1	0	0	.000	2	0	0	0.00	0
2005	Charleston	So.Atl.	1	6	0	1	.000	10	0	9	7.50	0
2006	Trenton	Eastern	28	$166\frac{1}{3}$	12	10	.545	175	55	118	3.35	0
2007	New York	A.L.	6	27	3	1	.750	18	17	29	6.33	0
2007	Scranton/WB	Int.	14	$69\frac{1}{3}$	4	4	.500	55	35	82	4.15	0

Year	Club	Lea	G	IP	W	L	Pct	SO	BB	H	ERA	SAVES
2007	Trenton a	Eastern	6	26 2/3	2	1	.667	28	12	22	5.40	0
2008	Washington	N.L.	2	10 1/3	1	1	.500	8	7	12	4.35	0
2008	Columbus	Int.	27	143	6	13	.316	125	66	129	4.66	0
2009	Syracuse	Int.	24	39	4	1	.800	42	15	20	0.92	1
2009	Washington	N.L.	41	60 1/3	4	2	.667	67	32	36	2.69	0
2010	Washington	N.L.	78	91	11	8	.579	112	41	69	3.07	1
2011	Washington	N.L.	72	88 1/3	3	0	1.000	104	26	48	1.83	0
2012	Washington	N.L.	74	72 2/3	2	6	.250	84	29	55	3.72	32
2013	Washington	N.L.	72	71	6	3	.667	73	24	37	2.41	0
Major League Totals		7 Yrs.	345	420 2/3	30	21	.588	466	176	286	3.00	33
	Division Series											
2012	Washington	N.L.	3	3	0	0	.000	5	1	1	3.00	0

a Traded to Washington Nationals for pitcher Jonathan Albaladejo, December 5, 2007.

COBB, ALEXANDER MILLER (ALEX)

Born, Boston, Massachusetts, October 7, 1987.
Bats Right. Throws Right. Height, 6 feet, 2 inches. Weight, 195 pounds.

Year	Club	Lea	G	IP	W	L	Pct	SO	BB	H	ERA	SAVES
2006	Princeton	Appal.	6	8 2/3	0	0	.000	8	3	9	5.19	0
2007	Hudson Valley	N.Y.-Penn.	16	81 1/3	5	6	.455	62	31	78	3.54	0
2008	Columbus	So.Atl.	25	139 2/3	9	7	.563	97	35	113	3.29	0
2009	Charlotte	Fla.St.	24	124 2/3	8	5	.615	107	31	116	3.03	0
2010	Montgomery	Southern	23	119 2/3	7	5	.583	128	35	120	2.71	0
2011	Durham	Int.	12	67 1/3	5	1	.833	70	16	61	1.87	0
2011	Tampa Bay a	A.L.	9	52 2/3	3	2	.600	37	21	49	3.42	0
2012	Durham	Int.	8	41 1/3	1	4	.200	44	18	44	4.14	0
2012	Tampa Bay	A.L.	23	136 1/3	11	9	.550	106	40	130	4.03	0
2013	Charlotte	Fla.St.	3	8 1/3	0	1	.000	8	4	8	4.32	0
2013	Tampa Bay b	A.L.	22	143 1/3	11	3	.786	134	45	120	2.76	0
Major League Totals		3 Yrs.	54	332 1/3	25	14	.641	277	106	299	3.39	0
	Wild Card Playoff											
2013	Tampa Bay	A.L.	1	6 2/3	1	0	1.000	5	1	8	0.00	0
	Division Series											
2013	Tampa Bay	A.L.	1	5	0	0	.000	5	2	5	3.60	0

a On disabled list from August 7 to October 5, 2011.
b On disabled list from June 16 to August 15, 2013.

COKE, PHILLIP DOUGLAS (PHIL)

Born, Sonora, California, July 19, 1982.
Bats Left. Throws Left. Height, 6 feet, 1 inch. Weight, 210 pounds.

Year	Club	Lea	G	IP	W	L	Pct	SO	BB	H	ERA	SAVES
2003	Yankees	Gulf Coast	10	12	0	0	.000	5	3	13	3.75	0
2004	Yankees	Gulf Coast	7	11 1/3	0	1	.000	13	3	18	3.97	0
2004	Staten Island	N.Y.-Penn.	3	8	0	0	.000	7	3	9	6.75	0
2005	Charleston	So.Atl.	24	103	8	11	.421	68	34	122	5.42	0
2006	Tampa	Fla.St.	22	110	5	7	.417	88	35	101	3.60	0
2006	Charleston	So.Atl.	5	17	0	1	.000	19	4	10	0.53	1
2007	Tampa	Fla.St.	17	99	7	3	.700	76	37	93	3.09	0
2008	Trenton	Eastern	23	118 1/3	9	4	.692	115	39	105	2.51	0
2008	Scranton-WB	Int.	14	17 1/3	2	2	.500	22	5	19	4.67	0
2008	New York	A.L.	12	14 2/3	1	0	1.000	14	2	8	0.61	0
2009	New York a	A.L.	72	60	4	3	.571	49	20	44	4.50	2
2010	Detroit	A.L.	74	64 2/3	7	5	.583	53	26	67	3.76	2
2011	Toledo	Int.	1	5 1/3	0	0	.000	6	2	8	5.06	0
2011	Detroit b	A.L.	48	108 2/3	3	9	.250	69	40	118	4.47	1
2012	Detroit	A.L.	66	54	2	3	.400	51	18	71	4.00	1
2013	Toledo	Int.	6	6	1	0	1.000	9	1	5	0.00	0
2013	Detroit c	A.L.	49	38 1/3	0	5	.000	30	21	43	5.40	1
Major League Totals		6 Yrs.	321	340 1/3	17	25	.405	266	127	351	4.20	7
	Division Series											
2009	New York	A.L.	2	0 2/3	0	0	.000	1	0	0	0.00	0
2011	Detroit	A.L.	1	1	0	0	.000	1	1	3	27.00	0
2012	Detroit	A.L.	3	1 2/3	0	0	.000	1	2	1	0.00	0
Division Series Totals			6	3 1/3	0	0	.000	3	3	4	8.10	0
	Championship Series											
2009	New York	A.L.	2	0 2/3	0	0	.000	1	1	1	0.00	0
2011	Detroit	A.L.	4	3 1/3	0	0	.000	2	1	3	2.70	1

Year	Club	Lea	G	IP	W	L	Pct	SO	BB	H	ERA	SAVES
2012	Detroit	A.L.	4	5 2/3	0	0	.000	4	0	3	0.00	2
2013	Detroit	A.L.	4	1	0	0	.000	0	0	1	9.00	0
Championship Series Totals			14	10 2/3	0	0	.000	7	2	8	1.69	3
	World Series Record											
2009	New York	A.L.	2	1 1/3	0	0	.000	1	0	3	13.50	0
2012	Detroit	A.L.	3	3 1/3	0	1	.000	8	0	2	2.70	0
World Series Totals			5	4 2/3	0	1	.000	9	0	5	5.79	0

a Traded to Detroit Tigers with outfielder Austin Jackson and pitcher Ian Kennedy for outfielder Curtis Granderson, December 9, 2009.

b On disabled list from May 24 to June 8, 2011.

c On disabled list from April 26 to May 11, 2013.

COLE, GERRIT ALAN

Born, Newport Beach, California, September 8, 1990.
Bats Right. Throws Right. Height, 6 feet, 4 inches. Weight, 240 pounds.

Year	Club	Lea	G	IP	W	L	Pct	SO	BB	H	ERA	SAVES
2012	Bradenton	Fla.St.	13	67	5	1	.833	69	21	53	2.55	0
2012	Altoona	Eastern	12	59	3	6	.333	60	23	54	2.90	0
2012	Indianapolis	Int.	1	6	1	0	1.000	7	1	6	4.50	0
2013	Indianapolis	Int.	12	68	5	3	.625	47	28	44	2.91	0
2013	Pittsburgh	N.L.	19	117 1/3	10	7	.588	100	28	109	3.22	0
	Division Series											
2013	Pittsburgh	N.L.	2	11	1	1	.500	10	2	5	2.45	0

COLLINS, TIMOTHY MICHAEL (TIM)

Born, Worcester, Massachusetts, August 21, 1989.
Bats Left. Throws Left. Height, 5 feet, 7 inches. Weight, 165 pounds.

Year	Club	Lea	G	IP	W	L	Pct	SO	BB	H	ERA	SAVES
2007	Blue Jays	Gulf Coast	7	6	0	0	.000	7	2	6	4.50	0
2008	Lansing	Midwest	39	68 1/3	4	2	.667	98	32	36	1.58	14
2009	Dunedin	Fla.St.	40	64 2/3	7	4	.636	99	28	47	2.37	3
2009	New Hampshire	Eastern	9	12 2/3	2	3	.400	17	7	12	5.68	0
2010	New Hampshire	Eastern	35	43	1	0	1.000	73	16	27	2.51	9
2010	Mississippi a	Southern	6	8	0	0	.000	14	3	4	1.13	2
2010	Omaha b	P.C.	15	20 1/3	2	1	.667	21	8	9	1.33	4
2011	Kansas City	A.L.	68	67	4	4	.500	60	48	52	3.63	0
2012	Kansas City	A.L.	72	69 2/3	5	4	.556	93	34	55	3.36	0
2013	Kansas City	A.L.	66	53 1/3	3	6	.333	52	28	49	3.54	0
Major League Totals		3 Yrs.	206	190	12	14	.462	205	110	156	3.51	0

a Traded by Toronto Blue Jays to Atlanta Braves with infielder Alex Gonzalez and infielder Tyler Pastornicky for infielder Yunel Escobar and pitcher Jo-Jo Reyes, July 14, 2010.

b Traded to Kansas City Royals with outfielder Gregor Blanco and pitcher Jesse Chavez for outfielder Rick Ankiel, pitcher Kyle Farnsworth and cash, July 31, 2010.

COLLMENTER, JOSHUA MICHAEL (JOSH)

Born, Homer, Michigan, February 7, 1986.
Bats Right. Throws Right. Height, 6 feet, 2 inches. Weight, 235 pounds.

Year	Club	Lea	G	IP	W	L	Pct	SO	BB	H	ERA	SAVES
2007	Yakima	Northwest	14	66 1/3	6	3	.667	57	21	60	2.71	0
2008	South Bend	Midwest	27	145 1/3	12	8	.600	123	47	126	3.41	0
2009	Visalia	Calif.	27	145 1/3	8	10	.444	152	55	127	4.15	0
2010	Visalia	Calif.	3	15	2	0	1.000	21	3	11	2.40	0
2010	Reno	P.C.	10	57 2/3	4	3	.571	39	26	64	5.77	0
2010	Mobile	Southern	12	79 1/3	8	3	.727	73	22	61	1.82	0
2011	Reno	P.C.	1	6	1	0	1.000	7	2	2	1.50	0
2011	Arizona	N.L.	31	154 1/3	10	10	.500	100	28	137	3.38	0
2012	D-Backs	Arizona	3	8	0	0	.000	11	0	5	0.00	0
2012	Arizona a	N.L.	28	90 1/3	5	3	.625	80	22	92	3.69	0
2013	Arizona	N.L.	49	92	5	5	.500	85	33	79	3.13	0
Major League Totals		3 Yrs.	108	336 2/3	20	18	.526	265	83	308	3.40	0
	Division Series											
2011	Arizona	N.L.	1	7	1	0	1.000	6	2	2	1.29	0

a On disabled list from August 9 to September 1, 2012.

COLON, BARTOLO

Born, Altamira, Dominican Republic, May 24, 1973.
Bats Right. Throws Right. Height, 6 feet. Weight, 265 pounds.

Year	Club	Lea	G	IP	W	L	Pct	SO	BB	H	ERA	SAVES
1993	Cleveland	Dominican	11	66	6	1	.857	43	33	44	2.59	1
1994	Burlington	Appal.	12	66	7	4	.636	84	44	46	3.14	0
1995	Kinston	Carolina	21	128⅔	13	3	.813	152	39	91	1.96	0
1996	Canton-Akrn	Eastern	13	62	2	2	.500	56	25	44	1.74	0
1996	Buffalo	A.A.	8	15	0	0	.000	19	8	16	6.00	0
1997	Buffalo	A.A.	10	56⅔	7	1	.875	54	23	45	2.22	0
1997	Cleveland	A.L.	19	94	4	7	.364	66	45	107	5.65	0
1998	Cleveland	A.L.	31	204	14	9	.609	158	79	205	3.71	0
1999	Cleveland	A.L.	32	205	18	5	.783	161	76	185	3.95	0
2000	Cleveland	A.L.	30	188	15	8	.652	212	98	163	3.88	0
2000	Buffalo a	Int.	1	5	1	0	1.000	4	0	6	1.80	0
2001	Cleveland	A.L.	34	222⅓	14	12	.538	201	90	220	4.09	0
2002	Cleveland	A.L.	16	116⅓	10	4	.714	75	31	104	2.55	0
2002	Montreal b	N.L.	17	117	10	4	.714	74	39	115	3.31	0
2003	Chicago c-d	A.L.	34	242	15	13	.536	173	67	223	3.87	0
2004	Anaheim	A.L.	34	208⅓	18	12	.600	158	71	215	5.01	0
2005	Los Angeles	A.L.	33	222⅔	*21	8	.724	157	43	215	3.48	0
2006	Rancho Cucamonga	Calif.	1	4	0	0	.000	3	1	2	0.00	0
2006	Salt Lake	P.C.	2	11⅔	0	1	.000	3	2	14	6.17	0
2006	Los Angeles e	A.L.	10	56⅓	1	5	.167	31	11	71	5.11	0
2007	Rancho Cucamonga	Calif.	2	9⅔	1	0	1.000	10	1	6	1.86	0
2007	Salt Lake	P.C.	3	15	2	0	1.000	8	3	12	2.40	0
2007	Los Angeles f-g	A.L.	19	99⅓	6	8	.429	76	29	132	6.34	0
2008	Pawtucket	Int.	9	31⅔	3	1	.750	21	6	23	2.27	0
2008	Boston h-i	A.L.	7	39	4	2	.667	27	10	44	3.92	0
2009	Kannapolis	So.Atl.	1	7	0	1	.000	8	1	7	2.57	0
2009	Charlotte	Int.	2	12	1	1	.500	1	4	10	3.75	0
2009	Chicago j-k	A.L.	12	62⅓	3	6	.333	38	21	69	4.19	0
2010							Did not play					
2011	New York l-m-n	A.L.	29	164⅓	8	10	.444	135	40	172	4.00	0
2012	Oakland o-p-q	A.L.	24	152⅓	10	9	.526	91	23	161	3.43	0
2013	Oakland r-s	A.L.	30	190⅓	18	6	.750	117	29	193	2.65	0
Major League Totals		16 Yrs.	411	2583⅔	189	128	.596	1950	802	2594	3.94	0
	Division Series											
1998	Cleveland	A.L.	1	5⅔	0	0	.000	3	3	5	1.59	0
1999	Cleveland	A.L.	2	9	0	1	.000	12	4	11	9.00	0
2001	Cleveland	A.L.	2	14⅔	1	1	.500	13	6	12	1.84	0
2004	Anaheim	A.L.	1	6	0	0	.000	3	3	7	4.50	0
2005	Los Angeles	A.L.	2	8	0	1	.000	7	1	10	4.50	0
2013	Oakland	A.L.	1	6	0	1	.000	4	0	10	4.50	0
Division Series Totals			9	49⅓	1	4	.200	42	17	55	4.20	0
	Championship Series											
1998	Cleveland	A.L.	1	9	1	0	1.000	3	4	4	1.00	0

a On disabled list from April 16 to May 11, 2000.
b Traded to Montreal Expos with player to be named later for infielder Lee Stevens, infielder Brandon Phillips, outfielder Grady Sizemore and pitcher Cliff Lee, June 27, 2002. Montreal Expos received pitcher Tim Drew to complete trade, June 28, 2002.
c Traded with infielder Jorge Nunez to Chicago White Sox for pitcher Rocky Biddle, pitcher Orlando Hernandez, outfielder Jeff Liefer and cash, January 15, 2003.
d Filed for free agency, October 27, 2003. Signed with Anaheim Angels, December 9, 2003.
e On disabled list from April 16 to June 18 and July 30 to October 2, 2006.
f On disabled list from March 23 to April 21, 2007.
g On disabled list from July 24 to September 9, 2007.
h Filed for free agency, October 29, 2007. Signed with Boston Red Sox organization, February 25, 2008.
i On disabled list from June 17 to September 7, 2008.
j Filed for free agency, October 31, 2008. Signed with Chicago White Sox, January 15, 2009.
k On disabled list from June 8 to July 23, 2009.
l Released by Chicago White Sox, September 16, 2009. Signed with New York Yankees organization, January 26, 2011.
m On disabled list from June 12 to July 2, 2011.
n Filed for free agency, October 30, 2011. Signed with Oakland Athletics, January 24, 2012.
o On disabled list from June 18 to July 3, 2012.
p Filed for free agency, November 3, 2012, re-signed with Oakland Athletics, November 3, 2012.
q Suspended for 50 games for performance-enhancing drug use, August 22, 2012.
r On disabled list from August 14 to August 29, 2013.
s Filed for free agency, October 31, 2013. Signed with New York Mets, December 14, 2013.

COOK, RYAN WILLIAM

Born, Clovis, California, June 30, 1987.
Bats Right. Throws Right. Height, 6 feet, 3 inches. Weight, 215 pounds.

Year	Club	Lea	G	IP	W	L	Pct	SO	BB	H	ERA	SAVES
2008	Yakima	Northwest	7	33	2	2	.500	23	11	37	4.64	0
2009	South Bend	Midwest	25	$142\frac{2}{3}$	11	11	.500	103	44	140	3.66	0
2010	Visalia	Calif.	20	$108\frac{1}{3}$	4	7	.364	100	36	110	4.24	0
2010	Reno	P.C.	1	5	0	0	.000	5	2	7	10.80	0
2010	Mobile	Southern	3	$18\frac{2}{3}$	1	1	.500	12	10	13	2.89	0
2011	Mobile	Southern	34	44	1	4	.200	50	14	28	2.25	13
2011	Reno	P.C.	14	17	0	1	.000	12	8	13	2.12	6
2011	Arizona a	N.L.	12	$7\frac{2}{3}$	0	1	.000	7	8	11	7.04	0
2012	Oakland	A.L.	71	$73\frac{1}{3}$	6	2	.750	80	27	42	2.09	14
2013	Oakland	A.L.	71	$67\frac{1}{3}$	6	4	.600	67	25	62	2.54	2
Major League Totals		3 Yrs.	154	$148\frac{1}{3}$	12	7	.632	154	60	115	2.55	16
	Division Series											
2012	Oakland	A.L.	4	$3\frac{1}{3}$	1	0	1.000	4	1	4	8.10	0
2013	Oakland	A.L.	1	$0\frac{2}{3}$	0	0	.000	1	1	1	27.00	0
Division Series Totals			5	4	1	0	1.000	5	2	5	11.25	0

a Traded to Oakland Athletics with outfielder Collin Cowgill and pitcher Jarrod Parker for pitcher Craig Breslow and pitcher Trevor Cahill, December 9, 2011.

CORBIN, PATRICK A.

Born, Clay, New York, July 19, 1989.
Bats Left. Throws Left. Height, 6 feet, 2 inches. Weight, 185 pounds.

Year	Club	Lea	G	IP	W	L	Pct	SO	BB	H	ERA	SAVES
2009	Orem	Pioneer	13	$46\frac{1}{3}$	4	2	.667	46	11	59	5.05	0
2010	Rancho Cucamonga	Calif.	11	$60\frac{1}{3}$	5	3	.625	64	18	57	3.88	0
2010	Visalia	Calif.	8	26	0	1	.000	30	9	17	1.38	0
2010	Cedar Rapids a	Midwest	9	$58\frac{1}{3}$	8	0	1.000	42	10	52	3.86	0
2011	Mobile	Southern	26	$160\frac{1}{3}$	9	8	.529	142	40	172	4.21	0
2012	Mobile	Southern	4	27	2	0	1.000	25	8	22	1.67	0
2012	Reno	P.C.	9	$52\frac{1}{3}$	3	2	.600	55	15	57	3.44	0
2012	Arizona	N.L.	22	107	6	8	.429	86	25	117	4.54	1
2013	Arizona	N.L.	32	$208\frac{1}{3}$	14	8	.636	178	54	189	3.41	0
Major League Totals		2 Yrs.	54	$315\frac{1}{3}$	20	16	.556	264	79	306	3.80	1

a Traded from Los Angeles Angels to Arizona Diamondbacks with pitcher Joe Saunders, pitcher Rafael Rodriguez and player to be named later for pitcher Danny Haren, July 25, 2010. Arizona Diamondbacks received pitcher Tyler Skaggs to complete trade, August 7, 2010.

CORREIA, KEVIN JOHN

Born, San Diego, California, August 24, 1980.
Bats Right. Throws Right. Height, 6 feet, 3 inches. Weight, 200 pounds.

Year	Club	Lea	G	IP	W	L	Pct	SO	BB	H	ERA	SAVES
2002	Salem-Keizer	Northwest	10	$37\frac{2}{3}$	2	2	.500	31	14	37	4.54	0
2003	Norwich	Eastern	16	$86\frac{1}{3}$	6	6	.500	73	30	80	3.65	0
2003	San Francisco	N.L.	10	$39\frac{1}{3}$	3	1	.750	28	18	41	3.66	0
2003	Fresno	P.C.	3	19	1	0	1.000	23	2	16	2.84	0
2004	Fresno	P.C.	29	$105\frac{1}{3}$	3	7	.300	70	35	118	4.53	0
2004	San Francisco	N.L.	12	19	0	1	.000	14	10	25	8.05	0
2005	San Jose	California	1	7	0	1	.000	7	5	5	2.57	0
2005	Fresno	P.C.	31	46	3	2	.600	35	23	50	6.07	7
2005	San Francisco	N.L.	16	$58\frac{1}{3}$	2	5	.286	44	31	61	4.63	0
2006	San Francisco	N.L.	48	$69\frac{2}{3}$	2	0	1.000	57	22	64	3.49	0
2007	San Francisco	N.L.	59	$101\frac{2}{3}$	4	7	.364	80	40	94	3.45	0
2008	San Jose	Calif.	1	$3\frac{1}{3}$	0	0	.000	1	1	1	0.00	0
2008	Fresno	P.C.	2	12	1	0	1.000	15	0	8	1.50	0
2008	San Francisco a-b	N.L.	25	110	3	8	.273	66	47	141	6.05	0
2009	San Diego	N.L.	33	198	12	11	.522	142	64	194	3.91	0
2010	San Diego c	N.L.	28	145	10	10	.500	115	64	152	5.40	0
2011	Pittsburgh d	N.L.	27	154	12	11	.522	77	39	175	4.79	0
2012	Pittsburgh e	N.L.	32	171	12	11	.522	89	46	176	4.21	0
2013	Minnesota	A.L.	31	$185\frac{1}{3}$	9	13	.409	101	45	218	4.18	0
Major League Totals		11 Yrs.	321	$1251\frac{1}{3}$	69	78	.469	813	426	1341	4.49	0

a On disabled list from April 27 to June 15, 2008.
b Filed for free agency, October 14, 2008. Signed with San Diego Padres organization, December 24, 2008.
c Filed for free agency, November 1, 2010. Signed with Pittsburgh Pirates, December 7, 2010.
d On disabled list from August 20 to November 1, 2011.
e Filed for free agency, November 3, 2012. Signed with Minnesota Twins, December 13, 2012.

COSART, JARRED LYNN

Born, League City, Texas, May 25, 1990.
Bats Right. Throws Right. Height, 6 feet, 3 inches. Weight, 180 pounds.

Year	Club	Lea	G	IP	W	L	Pct	SO	BB	H	ERA	SAVES
2009	Phillies	Gulf Coast	7	24 1/3	2	2	.500	25	7	12	2.22	0
2010	Lakewood	So.Atl.	14	71 1/3	7	3	.700	77	16	60	3.79	0
2011	Clearwater	Fla.St.	20	108	9	8	.529	79	43	98	3.92	0
2011	Corpus Christi a	Texas	7	36 1/3	1	2	.333	22	13	33	4.71	0
2012	Corpus Christi	Texas	15	87	5	5	.500	68	38	83	3.52	0
2012	Oklahoma	P.C.	6	27 2/3	1	2	.333	24	13	26	2.60	0
2013	Oklahoma	P.C.	18	93	7	4	.636	93	50	74	3.29	0
2013	Houston	A.L.	10	60	1	1	.500	33	35	46	1.95	0

a Traded by Philadelphia Phillies to Houston Astros with infielder Jonathan Singleton, pitcher Josh Zeid and player to be named later for outfielder Hunter Pence and cash, July 30, 2011. Houston Astros received pitcher Domingo Santana to complete trade, August 15, 2011.

COTTS, NEAL JAMES

Born, Belleville, Illinois, March 25, 1980.
Bats Left. Throws Left. Height, 6 feet, 2 inches. Weight, 200 pounds.

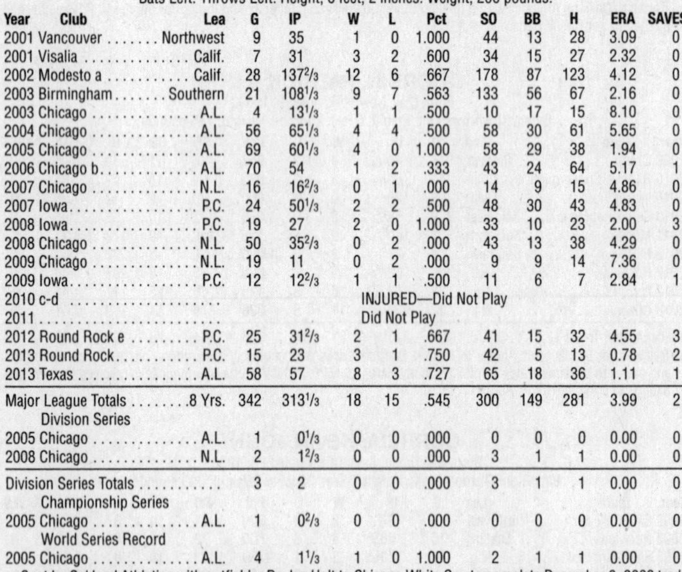

Year	Club	Lea	G	IP	W	L	Pct	SO	BB	H	ERA	SAVES
2001	Vancouver	Northwest	9	35	1	0	1.000	44	13	28	3.09	0
2001	Visalia	Calif.	7	31	3	2	.600	34	15	27	2.32	0
2002	Modesto a	Calif.	28	137 2/3	12	6	.667	178	87	123	4.12	0
2003	Birmingham	Southern	21	108 1/3	9	7	.563	133	56	67	2.16	0
2003	Chicago	A.L.	4	13 1/3	1	1	.500	10	17	15	8.10	0
2004	Chicago	A.L.	56	65 1/3	4	4	.500	58	30	61	5.65	0
2005	Chicago	A.L.	69	60 1/3	4	0	1.000	58	29	38	1.94	0
2006	Chicago b	A.L.	70	54	1	2	.333	43	24	64	5.17	1
2007	Chicago	N.L.	16	16 2/3	0	1	.000	14	9	15	4.86	0
2007	Iowa	P.C.	24	50 1/3	2	2	.500	48	30	43	4.83	0
2008	Iowa	P.C.	19	27	2	0	1.000	33	10	23	2.00	3
2008	Chicago	N.L.	50	35 2/3	0	2	.000	43	13	38	4.29	0
2009	Chicago	N.L.	19	11	0	2	.000	9	9	14	7.36	0
2009	Iowa	P.C.	12	12 2/3	1	1	.500	11	6	7	2.84	1
2010	c-d						INJURED—Did Not Play					
2011							Did Not Play					
2012	Round Rock e	P.C.	25	31 2/3	2	1	.667	41	15	32	4.55	3
2013	Round Rock	P.C.	15	23	3	1	.750	42	5	13	0.78	2
2013	Texas	A.L.	58	57	8	3	.727	65	18	36	1.11	1
Major League Totals		8 Yrs.	342	313 1/3	18	15	.545	300	149	281	3.99	2
	Division Series											
2005	Chicago	A.L.	1	0 1/3	0	0	.000	0	0	0	0.00	0
2008	Chicago	N.L.	2	1 2/3	0	0	.000	3	1	1	0.00	0
Division Series Totals			3	2	0	0	.000	3	1	1	0.00	0
	Championship Series											
2005	Chicago	A.L.	1	0 2/3	0	0	.000	0	0	0	0.00	0
	World Series Record											
2005	Chicago	A.L.	4	1 1/3	1	0	1.000	2	1	1	0.00	0

a Sent by Oakland Athletics with outfielder Daylan Holt to Chicago White Sox to complete December 3, 2002 trade for Keith Foulke, December 16, 2002.

b Traded to Chicago Cubs for pitcher David Aardsma and pitcher Carlos Vazquez, November 16, 2006.

c Not offered contract, December 12, 2009. Signed with Pittsburgh Pirates organization, January 4, 2010.

d Released by Pittsburgh Pirates, September 13, 2010. Signed with New York Yankees organization, November 29, 2010.

e Released by New York Yankees, February 16, 2011. Signed with Texas Rangers organization, March 5, 2012.

CRAIN, JESSE ALAN

Born, Toronto, Ontario, Canada, July 5, 1981.
Bats Right. Throws Right. Height, 6 feet, 1 inch. Weight, 205 pounds.

Year	Club	Lea	G	IP	W	L	Pct	SO	BB	H	ERA	SAVES
2002	Elizabethton	Appal.	9	15 2/3	2	1	.667	18	7	4	0.57	2
2002	Quad Cities	Midwest	9	12	1	1	.500	11	4	6	1.50	1
2003	New Britain	Eastern	22	39	1	1	.500	56	10	13	0.69	9
2003	Fort Myers	Fla.St.	10	19	2	1	.667	25	5	10	2.84	0
2003	Rochester	Int.	23	26	3	1	.750	33	10	24	3.12	10
2004	Rochester	Int.	41	50 2/3	3	2	.600	64	17	38	2.49	19
2004	Minnesota	A.L.	22	27	3	0	1.000	14	12	17	2.00	0
2005	Minnesota	A.L.	75	79 2/3	12	5	.706	25	29	61	2.71	1
2006	Minnesota	A.L.	68	76 2/3	4	5	.444	60	18	79	3.52	1

Year Club	Lea	G	IP	W	L	Pct	SO	BB	H	ERA	SAVES
2007 Minnesota a	A.L.	18	16 1/3	1	2	.333	10	4	19	5.51	0
2008 Minnesota	A.L.	66	62 2/3	5	4	.556	50	24	62	3.59	0
2009 Rochester	Int.	12	17 2/3	1	0	1.000	22	8	13	2.55	1
2009 Minnesota b	A.L.	56	51 2/3	7	4	.636	43	27	48	4.70	0
2010 Minnesota c	A.L.	71	68	1	1	.500	62	27	53	3.04	1
2011 Chicago	A.L.	67	65 1/3	8	3	.727	70	31	50	2.62	1
2012 Charlotte	Int.	2	2	0	0	.000	3	0	0	0.00	0
2012 Chicago d	A.L.	51	48	2	3	.400	60	23	29	2.44	0
2013 Chicago e-f-g	A.L.	38	36 2/3	2	3	.400	46	11	31	0.74	0
Major League Totals	10 Yrs.	532	532	45	30	.600	440	206	449	3.05	4
Division Series											
2004 Minnesota	A.L.	1	0 1/3	0	0	.000	0	0	1	0.00	0
2006 Minnesota	A.L.	2	1	0	0	.000	1	1	3	9.00	0
2010 Minnesota	A.L.	1	0 1/3	0	1	.000	0	0	3	54.00	0
Division Series Totals		4	1 2/3	0	1	.000	1	1	7	16.20	0

a On disabled list from May 16 to October 10, 2007.
b On disabled list from April 18 to May 4, 2009.
c Filed for free agency, November 1, 2010. Signed with Chicago White Sox, December 20, 2010.
d On disabled list from April 21 to May 15 and July 4 to July 21, 2012.
e Traded to Tampa Bay Rays with cash for player to be named later, July 29, 2013. Chicago White Sox received pitcher Sean Bierman to complete trade, October 15, 2013.
f On disabled list from June 30 to September 23 and September 30 to October 31, 2013.
g Filed for free agency, October 31, 2013. Signed with Houston Astros, December 31, 2013.

CROW, AARON JAMES

Born, Topeka, Kansas, November 10, 1986.
Bats Right. Throws Right. Height, 6 feet, 3 inches. Weight, 190 pounds.

Year Club	Lea	G	IP	W	L	Pct	SO	BB	H	ERA	SAVES
2008 Fort Worth	Amer. Assoc.	1	1	0	0	.000	0	0	1	0.00	0
2009 Fort Worth	Amer. Assoc.	3	17	3	0	1.000	17	5	11	1.06	0
2010 Wilmington	Carolina	7	44	2	3	.400	53	6	51	5.93	0
2010 NW Arkansas	Texas	22	119 1/3	7	7	.500	90	59	130	5.66	0
2011 Kansas City	A.L.	57	62	4	4	.500	65	31	55	2.76	0
2012 Kansas City	A.L.	73	64 2/3	3	1	.750	65	22	54	3.48	2
2013 Kansas City	A.L.	57	48	7	5	.583	44	22	49	3.38	1
Major League Totals	3 Yrs.	187	174 2/3	14	10	.583	174	75	158	3.19	3

CUETO (ORTIZ), JOHNNY

Born, San Pedro de Macoris, Dominican Republic, February 15, 1985.
Bats Right. Throws Right. Height, 5 feet, 10 inches. Weight, 185 pounds.

Year Club	Lea	G	IP	W	L	Pct	SO	BB	H	ERA	SAVES
2005 Sarasota	Fla.St.	2	6	0	1	.000	6	2	5	3.00	0
2005 Reds	Gulf Coast	13	43	2	2	.500	38	8	49	5.02	1
2006 Sarasota	Fla.St.	12	61 2/3	7	2	.778	61	23	48	3.50	0
2006 Dayton	Midwest	14	76 1/3	8	1	.889	82	15	52	2.59	0
2007 Sarasota	Fla.St.	14	78 1/3	4	5	.444	72	21	72	3.33	0
2007 Louisville	Int.	4	22	2	1	.667	21	2	22	2.05	0
2007 Chattanooga	Southern	10	61	6	3	.667	77	11	52	3.10	0
2008 Cincinnati	N.L.	31	174	9	14	.391	158	68	178	4.81	0
2009 Cincinnati a	N.L.	30	171 1/3	11	11	.500	132	61	172	4.41	0
2010 Cincinnati	N.L.	31	185 2/3	12	7	.632	138	56	181	3.64	0
2011 Louisville	Int.	4	14 1/3	0	2	.000	13	6	19	6.28	0
2011 Cincinnati b	N.L.	24	156	9	5	.643	104	47	123	2.31	0
2012 Cincinnati	N.L.	33	217	19	9	.679	170	49	205	2.78	0
2013 Dayton	Midwest	2	8	1	0	1.000	8	0	7	1.13	0
2013 Cincinnati c	N.L.	11	60 2/3	5	2	.714	51	18	46	2.82	0
Major League Totals	6 Yrs.	160	964 2/3	65	48	.575	753	299	905	3.53	0
Wild Card Playoff											
2013 Cincinnati	N.L.	1	3 1/3	0	1	.000	0	1	8	10.80	0
Division Series											
2010 Cincinnati	N.L.	1	5	0	1	.000	2	1	5	1.80	0
2012 Cincinnati	N.L.	1	0 1/3	0	0	.000	1	0	0	0.00	0
Division Series Totals		2	5 1/3	0	1	.000	3	1	5	1.69	0

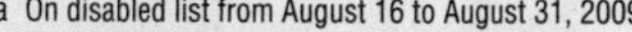

a On disabled list from August 16 to August 31, 2009.
b On disabled list from March 22 to May 8, 2011.
c On disabled list from April 14 to May 20 and June 1 to June 16 and June 29 to September 16, 2013.

DANKS, JOHN WILLIAM

Born, Austin, Texas, April 15, 1985.
Bats Left. Throws Left. Height, 6 feet, 1 inch. Weight, 200 pounds.

Year Club	Lea	G	IP	W	L	Pct	SO	BB	H	ERA	SAVES
2003 Rangers	Arizona	5	13	1	0	1.000	22	4	6	0.69	0
2003 Spokane	Northwest	5	12 2/3	0	2	.000	13	7	12	8.53	0
2004 Stockton	Calif.	13	55	1	4	.200	48	26	62	5.24	0
2004 Clinton	Midwest	14	49 2/3	3	2	.600	64	14	38	2.17	0
2005 Bakersfield	Calif.	10	57 2/3	3	3	.500	53	16	50	2.50	0
2005 Frisco	Texas	18	98 1/3	4	10	.286	85	34	117	5.49	0
2006 Oklahoma	P.C.	14	70 2/3	4	5	.444	72	34	67	4.33	0
2006 Frisco a	Texas	13	69 1/3	5	4	.556	82	22	74	4.15	0
2007 Chicago	A.L.	26	139	6	13	.316	109	54	160	5.50	0
2008 Chicago	A.L.	33	195	12	9	.571	159	57	182	3.32	0
2009 Chicago	A.L.	32	200 1/3	13	11	.542	149	73	184	3.77	0
2010 Chicago	A.L.	32	213	15	11	.577	162	70	189	3.72	0
2011 Charlotte	Int.	2	9	1	0	1.000	6	2	9	2.00	0
2011 Chicago b	A.L.	27	170 1/3	8	12	.400	135	46	182	4.33	0
2012 Charlotte	Int.	1	4	0	0	.000	1	1	4	2.25	0
2012 Chicago c	A.L.	9	53 2/3	3	4	.429	30	23	57	5.70	0
2013 Birmingham	Southern	1	7	1	0	1.000	1	1	5	2.57	0
2013 Charlotte	Int.	3	15 2/3	1	0	1.000	14	12	13	3.45	0
2013 Chicago d	A.L.	22	138 1/3	4	14	.222	89	27	151	4.75	0
Major League Totals	7 Yrs.	181	1109 2/3	61	74	.452	833	350	1105	4.20	0
Division Series											
2008 Chicago	A.L.	1	6 2/3	1	0	1.000	7	3	7	4.05	0

a Traded to Chicago White Sox by Texas Rangers with pitcher Nick Masset and pitcher Jacob Rasner for pitcher Brandon McCarthy and outfielder David Paisano, December 23, 2006.
b On disabled list from June 26 to July 20, 2011.
c On disabled list from May 20 to October 29, 2012.
d On disabled list from March 22 to May 24, 2013.

DARVISH, SEFAT FARID YU (YU)

Born, Osaka, Japan, August 16, 1986.
Bats Right. Throws Right. Height 6 feet, 5 inches. Weight, 187 pounds.

Year Club	Lea	G	IP	W	L	Pct	SO	BB	H	ERA	SAVES
2005 Nippon Ham	Japan Pac.	14	94 1/3	5	5	.500	52	48	97	3.53	0
2006 Nippon Ham	Japan Pac.	25	149 2/3	12	5	.706	115	64	128	2.89	0
2007 Nippon Ham	Japan Pac.	26	207 2/3	15	5	.750	210	49	123	1.82	0
2008 Nippon Ham	Japan Pac.	25	200 2/3	16	4	.800	208	44	136	1.80	0
2009 Nippon Ham	Japan Pac.	23	182	15	5	.750	167	45	118	1.73	0
2010 Nippon Ham	Japan Pac.	26	202	12	8	.600	222	47	158	1.78	0
2011 Nippon Ham	Japan Pac.	28	232	18	6	.750	276	36	156	1.44	0
2012 Texas a	A.L.	29	191 1/3	16	9	.640	221	89	156	3.90	0
2013 Texas b	A.L.	32	209 2/3	13	9	.591	*277	80	145	2.83	0
Major League Totals	2 Yrs.	61	401	29	18	.617	498	169	301	3.34	0
Wild Card Playoff											
2012 Texas	A.L.	1	6 2/3	0	1	.000	7	0	5	2.70	0

a Signed with Texas Rangers, January 18, 2012.
b On disabled list from July 7 to July 22, 2013.

DAVIS, WADE ALLEN

Born, Lake Wales, Florida, September 7, 1985.
Bats Right. Throws Right. Height, 6 feet, 5 inches. Weight, 220 pounds.

Year Club	Lea	G	IP	W	L	Pct	SO	BB	H	ERA	SAVES
2004 Princeton	Appal.	13	57 2/3	3	5	.375	38	19	71	5.93	0
2005 Hudson Valley	N.Y.-Penn.	15	86	7	4	.636	97	23	75	2.72	0
2006 SW Michigan	Midwest	27	146	7	12	.368	165	64	124	3.02	0
2007 Vero Beach	Fla.St.	13	78 1/3	3	0	1.000	88	21	54	1.84	0
2007 Montgomery	Southern	14	80	7	3	.700	81	30	74	3.15	0
2008 Durham	Int.	9	53	4	2	.667	55	24	39	2.72	0
2008 Montgomery	Southern	19	107 2/3	9	6	.600	81	42	104	3.85	0
2009 Durham	Int.	28	158 2/3	10	8	.556	140	60	139	3.40	0
2009 Tampa Bay	A.L.	6	36 1/3	2	2	.500	36	13	33	3.72	0
2010 Tampa Bay a	A.L.	29	168	12	10	.545	113	62	165	4.07	0
2011 Tampa Bay b	A.L.	29	184	11	10	.524	105	63	190	4.45	0
2012 Tampa Bay c	A.L.	54	70 1/3	3	0	1.000	87	29	48	2.43	0
2013 Wilmington	Carolina	1	2	0	0	.000	5	0	1	0.00	0

Year	Club	Lea	G	IP	W	L	Pct	SO	BB	H	ERA	SAVES
2013	Kansas City	A.L.	31	135⅓	8	11	.421	114	58	169	5.32	0
Major League Totals		5 Yrs.	149	594	36	33	.522	455	225	605	4.26	0
	Division Series											
2010	Tampa Bay	A.L.	1	5	1	0	1.000	7	3	7	3.60	0
2011	Tampa Bay	A.L.	2	2⅓	0	0	.000	1	1	1	0.00	0
Division Series Totals			3	7⅓	1	0	1.000	8	4	8	2.45	0

a On disabled list from August 6 to August 24, 2010.
b On disabled list from July 7 to July 22, 2011.
c Traded to Kansas City Royals with pitcher James Shields and player to be named later for pitcher Mike Montgomery, pitcher Jake Odorizzi, infielder Patrick Leonard and outfielder Wil Myers, December 9, 2012.

DEDUNO (LAKE), SAMUEL

Born, LaRomana, Dominican Republic, July 2, 1983.
Bats Right. Throws Right. Height, 6 feet, 3 inches. Weight, 190 pounds.

Year	Club	Lea	G	IP	W	L	Pct	SO	BB	H	ERA	SAVES
2004	Casper	Pioneer	15	76⅓	6	4	.600	118	32	62	3.18	0
2005	Asheville	So.Atl.	20	89⅔	8	8	.500	110	65	82	5.62	0
2006	Modesto	Calif.	27	146⅓	5	8	.385	167	92	121	4.80	0
2007	Modesto	Calif.	2	11	1	1	.500	8	7	9	6.55	0
2007	Tulsa	Texas	21	124	5	8	.385	121	66	120	5.44	0
2008	a		INJURED—Did Not Play									
2009	Tulsa	Texas	24	133	12	4	.750	123	72	94	2.57	0
2009	Colorado Springs	P.C.	1	5⅔	0	1	.000	8	4	5	6.35	0
2010	Tri-City	Northwest	4	16⅓	0	2	.000	20	5	18	5.51	0
2010	Colorado Springs	P.C.	6	30⅔	3	1	.750	29	18	20	2.93	0
2010	Colorado	N.L.	4	2⅔	0	0	.000	3	1	3	3.38	0
2011	San Diego b	N.L.	2	3	0	0	.000	4	3	5	3.00	0
2011	Tucson c	P.C.	40	105⅓	4	6	.400	85	58	101	3.93	0
2012	Rochester	Int.	9	42	1	2	.333	46	22	27	2.14	0
2012	Minnesota d	A.L.	15	79	6	5	.545	57	53	69	4.44	0
2013	Rochester	Int.	3	16⅔	0	0	.000	17	10	14	2.70	0
2013	Minnesota e	A.L.	18	108	8	8	.500	67	41	105	3.83	0
Major League Totals		4 Yrs.	39	192⅔	14	13	.519	131	98	182	4.06	0

a On minor league disabled list from June 17 to October 20, 2008.
b Claimed on waivers by San Diego Padres from Colorado Rockies, February 1, 2011.
c Filed for free agency, November 2, 2011. Signed with Minnesota Twins organization, November 18, 2011.
d Filed for free agency, November 3, 2012, re-signed with Minnesota Twins organization, November 20, 2012.
e On disabled list from August 30 to November 1, 2013.

DE FRATUS, JUSTIN ANDREW

Born, Oxnard, California, October 21, 1987.
Bats Both. Throws Right. Height, 6 feet, 4 inches. Weight, 220 pounds.

Year	Club	Lea	G	IP	W	L	Pct	SO	BB	H	ERA	SAVES
2007	Phillies	Gulf Coast	10	46	2	3	.400	34	3	51	4.30	0
2008	Williamsport	N.Y.-Penn.	14	83⅓	6	5	.545	74	25	87	3.67	0
2009	Lakewood	So.Atl.	36	110	5	6	.455	101	16	108	3.19	3
2010	Clearwater	Fla.St.	29	40⅓	2	0	1.000	43	11	31	1.79	15
2010	Reading	Eastern	20	24⅔	1	0	1.000	28	5	17	2.19	6
2011	Reading	Eastern	23	34⅓	4	0	1.000	43	14	28	2.10	8
2011	Lehigh Valley	Int.	28	41	2	3	.400	56	11	35	3.73	7
2011	Philadelphia	N.L.	5	4	1	0	1.000	3	3	1	2.25	0
2012	Phillies	Gulf Coast	2	2	0	0	.000	3	0	1	0.00	0
2012	Clearwater	Fla.St.	2	2	0	0	.000	1	0	2	0.00	0
2012	Lehigh Valley	Int.	17	21⅔	0	1	.000	22	3	15	2.49	3
2012	Philadelphia	N.L.	13	10⅔	0	0	.000	8	5	7	3.38	0
2013	Lehigh Valley	Int.	13	19	3	0	1.000	17	6	18	1.89	0
2013	Philadelphia	N.L.	58	46⅔	3	3	.500	42	25	45	3.86	0
Major League Totals		3 Yrs.	76	61⅓	4	3	.571	53	33	53	3.67	0

DELABAR, STEVEN EDWARD (STEVE)

Born, Fort Knox, Kentucky, July 17, 1983.
Bats Right. Throws Right. Height, 6 feet, 5 inches. Weight, 220 pounds.

Year	Club	Lea	G	IP	W	L	Pct	SO	BB	H	ERA	SAVES
2004	Padres	Arizona	14	45⅓	3	4	.429	39	21	51	4.37	0
2004	Eugene	Northwest	3	17	1	1	.500	11	3	13	2.65	0
2005	Eugene	Northwest	16	75⅔	4	6	.400	59	18	84	4.76	0

Year	Club	Lea	G	IP	W	L	Pct	SO	BB	H	ERA	SAVES
2006	Fort Wayne	Midwest	27	145	8	9	.471	118	65	129	3.41	0
2007	Lake Elsinore	Calif.	20	29	2	6	.250	33	16	26	5.59	0
2007	Fort Wayne	Midwest	21	68	2	5	.286	48	46	63	5.96	0
2008	Fort Wayne	Midwest	11	13 2/3	2	1	.667	12	5	17	5.27	0
2008	Florence	Frontier	4	6	0	0	.000	7	2	6	2.84	0
2008	Brockton a-b	Can-Amer.	11	69	3	3	.500	43	16	67	3.01	0
2009	Brockton	Can-Amer.	12	26	3	3	.500	23	12	23	3.76	0
2010							Did Not Play					
2011	High Desert	Calif.	7	12 1/3	1	1	.500	20	8	12	4.38	3
2011	Jackson	Southern	23	30 2/3	1	3	.250	30	26	23	2.05	12
2011	Tacoma	P.C.	10	13	1	1	.500	18	6	11	0.69	0
2011	Seattle c	A.L.	6	7	1	1	.500	7	4	5	2.57	0
2012	Tacoma	P.C.	9	12	0	1	.000	12	12	11	3.75	1
2012	Seattle-Toronto d	A.L.	61	66	4	3	.571	92	26	46	3.82	0
2013	Blue Jays	Gulf Coast	1	1	0	0	.000	0	0	0	0.00	0
2013	Dunedin	Fla.St.	1	1	0	0	.000	0	0	0	0.00	0
2013	Toronto e	A.L.	55	58 2/3	5	5	.500	82	29	50	3.22	1
Major League Totals		3 Yrs.	122	131 2/3	10	9	.526	181	59	101	3.49	1

a Released by San Diego Padres, May 23, 2008. Signed with Florence, June 2008.
b Signed with Brockton, June 2008.
c Signed with Seattle Mariners organization, April 19, 2011.
d Traded to Toronto Blue Jays for outfielder Eric Thames, July 31, 2012.
e On disabled list from August 3 to September 1, 2013.

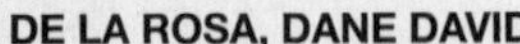

DE LA ROSA, DANE DAVID

Born, Torrance, California, February 1, 1983.
Bats Right. Throws Right. Height, 6 feet, 7 inches. Weight, 245 pounds.

Year	Club	Lea	G	IP	W	L	Pct	SO	BB	H	ERA	SAVES
2003	Yankees	Gulf Coast	5	9	0	0	.000	12	6	5	3.00	0
2004	Yankees	Gulf Coast	14	34 1/3	2	0	1.000	32	12	25	2.88	1
2004	Staten Island a	N.Y.-Penn.	1	1 2/3	0	0	.000	1	2	1	0.00	0
2005	Yuma b	Golden	23	67	1	6	.143	54	38	76	6.45	0
2006							Did Not Play					
2007	Long Beach c	Golden	39	46	2	4	.333	53	16	42	3.69	16
2007	Helena d	Pioneer	1	2	0	0	.000	3	1	1	0.00	0
2008	Orange County e	Golden	32	35	2	2	.500	40	13	35	4.41	14
2009	El Paso f	Amer.Assoc.	15	36	1	4	.200	37	20	51	8.07	1
2009	Victoria	Golden	6	4	0	1	.000	3	2	4	2.45	1
2009	Southern Maryland g	Atlantic	18	24	1	1	.500	32	7	16	1.11	3
2010	Charlotte	Fla.St.	2	3	0	0	.000	5	0	4	3.00	0
2010	Montgomery	Southern	47	73	9	3	.750	75	26	66	1.97	4
2011	Durham	Int.	52	70 1/3	6	5	.545	83	26	63	3.20	6
2011	Tampa Bay	A.L.	7	7 1/3	0	0	.000	8	3	10	9.82	0
2012	Durham	Int.	54	67 2/3	0	4	.000	87	42	36	2.79	20
2012	Tampa Bay	A.L.	5	5	0	0	.000	5	2	7	12.60	0
2013	Salt Lake h	P.C.	3	3 1/3	1	0	1.000	1	2	1	2.70	1
2013	Los Angeles	A.L.	75	72 1/3	6	1	.857	65	28	56	2.86	2
Major League Totals		3 Yrs.	87	84 2/3	6	1	.857	78	33	73	4.04	2

a Released by New York Yankees, December 18, 2004.
b Signed with Yuma (Golden), May 2005.
c Signed with Long Beach (Golden), June 2007.
d Signed with Milwaukee Brewers organization, September 4, 2007.
e Released by Milwaukee Brewers, March 28, 2008. Signed with Orange County (Golden), May 2008.
f Signed with El Paso (American Association), May 2009.
g Signed with Tampa Bay Rays organization, November 11, 2009.
h Traded to Los Angeles Angels for pitcher Steve Geltz, March 27, 2013.

DE LA ROSA, JORGE ALBERTO

Born, Monterrey, Mexico, April 5, 1981.
Bats Left. Throws Left. Height, 6 feet, 1 inch. Weight, 220 pounds.

Year	Club	Lea	G	IP	W	L	Pct	SO	BB	H	ERA	SAVES
1998	Arizona	Dominican	13	14	1	0	1.000	21	8	8	4.50	1
1999	Diamondbacks	Arizona	8	14	0	0	.000	17	3	12	3.21	2
1999	High Desert	Calif.	2	3	0	0	.000	3	2	1	0.00	0
1999	Missoula	Pioneer	13	14 2/3	0	1	.000	14	9	22	7.98	2
2000	Monterrey a	Mexican	37	39	3	2	.600	50	32	38	6.28	1
2001	Trenton	Eastern	29	37	1	3	.250	27	20	56	5.84	0
2001	Sarasota b	Fla.St.	12	29 2/3	0	1	.000	27	12	13	1.21	2
2002	Trenton	Eastern	4	18	1	2	.333	15	9	17	5.50	0

Year	Club	Lea	G	IP	W	L	Pct	SO	BB	H	ERA	SAVES
2002	Sarasota	Fla.St.	23	120 2/3	7	7	.500	95	52	105	3.65	0
2003	Portland	Eastern	22	99 2/3	6	3	.667	102	36	87	2.80	1
2003	Pawtucket c-d	Int.	5	24	1	2	.333	17	12	27	3.75	0
2004	Indianapolis	Int.	20	85 2/3	5	6	.455	86	36	80	4.52	0
2004	Milwaukee	N.L.	5	22 2/3	0	3	.000	5	14	29	6.35	0
2005	Milwaukee	N.L.	38	42 1/3	2	2	.500	42	38	48	4.46	0
2006	Milwaukee	N.L.	18	30 1/3	2	2	.500	31	22	32	8.60	0
2006	Huntsville	Southern	6	30	3	1	.750	23	3	31	2.40	0
2006	Kansas City e	A.L.	10	48 2/3	3	4	.429	36	32	49	5.18	0
2007	Wichita	Texas	3	5 2/3	0	1	.000	7	4	10	11.12	0
2007	Kansas City	A.L.	26	130	8	12	.400	82	53	160	5.82	0
2008	Omaha	P.C.	4	22	3	0	1.000	23	7	18	1.64	0
2008	Colorado f	N.L.	28	130	10	8	.556	128	62	128	4.92	0
2009	Colorado	N.L.	33	185	16	9	.640	193	83	172	4.38	0
2010	Colorado Springs	P.C.	3	14 2/3	1	2	.333	15	4	17	5.52	0
2010	Colorado g	N.L.	20	121 2/3	8	7	.533	113	55	105	4.22	0
2011	Colorado	N.L.	10	59	5	2	.714	52	22	48	3.51	0
2012	Grand Junction	Pioneer	1	3	0	0	.000	5	0	3	0.00	0
2012	Modesto	Calif.	2	5 2/3	0	0	.000	7	3	7	4.76	0
2012	Tulsa	Texas	2	5	0	0	.000	5	3	8	9.00	0
2012	Colorado Springs	P.C.	2	6 2/3	0	1	.000	5	3	9	9.45	0
2012	Colorado h	N.L.	3	10 2/3	0	2	.000	6	2	17	9.28	0
2013	Colorado	N.L.	30	167 2/3	16	6	.727	112	62	170	3.49	0
Major League Totals		10 Yrs.	221	948	70	57	.551	800	445	958	4.70	0

a Sold by Arizona Diamondbacks to Monterrey, April 2, 2000.
b Sold to Boston Red Sox, February 22, 2001.
c Traded by Boston Red Sox to Arizona Diamondbacks with pitcher Casey Fossum, pitcher Brandon Lyon and outfielder Michael Goss for pitcher Curt Schilling, November 28, 2003.
d Traded to Milwaukee Brewers with infielder Junior Spivey, infielder Craig Counsell, infielder Lyle Overbay, catcher Chad Moeller and pitcher Chris Capuano for infielder Richie Sexson, pitcher Shane Nance and player to be named later, December 1, 2003. Arizona Diamondbacks received outfielder Noochie Varner to complete trade, December 15, 2003.
e Traded to Kansas City Royals for infielder Tony Graffanino, July 25, 2006.
f Sent to Colorado Rockies as player to be named later for pitcher Ramon Ramirez, April 30, 2008.
g Filed for free agency, November 1, 2010, re-signed with Colorado Rockies, December 3, 2010.
h On disabled list from March 26 to September 20, 2012.

DELGADO, RANDALL ENRIQUE

Born, Las Tablas, Panama, February 9, 1990.
Bats Right. Throws Right. Height, 6 feet, 3 inches. Weight, 200 pounds.

Year	Club	Lea	G	IP	W	L	Pct	SO	BB	H	ERA	SAVES
2008	Danville	Appal.	14	69	3	8	.273	81	30	63	3.13	0
2009	Rome	So.Atl.	25	124	5	10	.333	141	49	123	4.35	0
2010	Myrtle Beach	Carolina	20	117 1/3	4	7	.364	120	32	89	2.76	0
2010	Mississippi	Southern	8	43 2/3	3	5	.375	42	20	36	4.74	0
2011	Mississippi	Southern	21	117 1/3	5	5	.500	110	46	116	3.84	0
2011	Gwinnett	Int.	4	21 2/3	2	2	.500	25	11	19	4.15	0
2011	Atlanta	N.L.	7	35	1	1	.500	18	14	29	2.83	0
2012	Gwinnett	Int.	8	44 1/3	4	3	.571	51	21	47	4.06	0
2012	Atlanta	N.L.	18	92 2/3	4	9	.308	76	42	89	4.37	0
2013	Reno	P.C.	13	64	2	5	.286	57	35	69	5.91	0
2013	Arizona a	N.L.	20	116 1/3	5	7	.417	79	23	116	4.26	0
Major League Totals		3 Yrs.	45	244	10	17	.370	173	79	234	4.09	0

a Traded to Arizona Diamondbacks with outfielder Martin Prado, pitcher Zeke Spruill, infielder Nick Ahmed and infielder Brandon Drury for outfielder Justin Upton and infielder Chris Johnson, January 24, 2013.

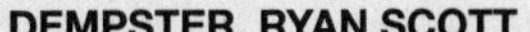

DEMPSTER, RYAN SCOTT

Born, Sechelt, British Columbia, Canada, May 3, 1977.
Bats Right. Throws Right. Height, 6 feet, 2 inches. Weight, 215 pounds.

Year	Club	Lea	G	IP	W	L	Pct	SO	BB	H	ERA	SAVES
1995	Rangers	Gulf Coast	8	34 1/3	3	1	.750	37	17	34	2.36	0
1995	Hudson Val.	N.Y.-Penn.	1	5 2/3	1	0	1.000	6	1	7	3.18	0
1996	Chston-SC	So.Atl.	23	144 1/3	7	11	.389	141	58	120	3.30	0
1996	Kane County a	Midwest	4	26 1/3	2	1	.667	16	18	18	2.73	0
1997	Brevard Cty	Fla.St.	28	165 1/3	10	9	.526	131	46	190	4.90	0
1998	Portland	Eastern	7	44 2/3	4	3	.571	33	15	34	3.22	0
1998	Florida	N.L.	14	54 2/3	1	5	.167	35	38	72	7.08	0
1998	Charlotte	Int.	5	33	3	1	.750	24	12	33	3.27	0

Year	Club	Lea	G	IP	W	L	Pct	SO	BB	H	ERA	SAVES
1999	Calgary	P.C.	5	30 2/3	1	1	.500	29	10	30	4.99	0
1999	Florida	N.L.	25	147	7	8	.467	126	93	146	4.71	0
2000	Florida	N.L.	33	226 1/3	14	10	.583	209	97	210	3.66	0
2001	Florida	N.L.	34	211 1/3	15	12	.556	171	112	218	4.94	0
2002	Florida-Cincinnati b	N.L.	33	209	10	13	.435	153	93	228	5.38	0
2003	Cincinnati	N.L.	22	115 2/3	3	7	.300	84	70	134	6.54	0
2003	Louisville c	Int.	2	13 2/3	1	1	.500	9	3	13	3.29	0
2004	Lansing	Midwest	5	18 1/3	0	0	.000	21	2	20	1.96	0
2004	Iowa	P.C.	6	21	1	1	.500	20	10	19	3.86	0
2004	Chicago d-e	N.L.	23	20 2/3	1	1	.500	18	13	16	3.92	2
2005	Chicago	N.L.	63	92	5	3	.625	89	49	83	3.13	33
2006	Chicago	N.L.	74	75	1	9	.100	67	36	77	4.80	24
2007	Iowa	P.C.	2	2	0	0	.000	4	1	1	0.00	0
2007	Chicago f	N.L.	66	66 2/3	2	7	.222	55	30	59	4.72	28
2008	Chicago g	N.L.	33	206 2/3	17	6	.739	187	76	174	2.96	0
2009	Chicago h	N.L.	31	200	11	9	.550	172	65	196	3.65	0
2010	Chicago	N.L.	34	215 1/3	15	12	.556	208	86	198	3.85	0
2011	Chicago	N.L.	34	202 1/3	10	14	.417	191	82	211	4.80	0
2012	Chicago	N.L.	16	104	5	5	.500	83	27	81	2.25	0
2012	Texas i-j-k	A.L.	12	69	7	3	.700	70	25	74	5.09	0
2013	Boston	A.L.	32	171 1/3	8	9	.471	157	79	170	4.57	0
Major League Totals		16 Yrs.	579	2387	132	133	.498	2075	1071	2347	4.35	87
	Division Series											
2007	Chicago	N.L.	1	1	0	0	.000	2	0	0	0.00	0
2008	Chicago	N.L.	1	4 2/3	0	1	.000	2	7	4	7.71	0
2013	Boston	A.L.	1	1	0	0	.000	2	0	1	0.00	0
Division Series Totals			3	6 2/3	0	1	.000	6	7	5	5.40	0
	Championship Series											
2013	Boston	A.L.	1	1	0	0	.000	0	0	1	0.00	0
	World Series Record											
2013	Boston	A.L.	1	1	0	0	.000	1	0	2	9.00	0

a Traded by Texas Rangers to Florida Marlins with player to be named later for pitcher John Burkett, August 8, 1996. Florida Marlins received pitcher Rick Helling to complete trade, September 3, 1996.

b Traded to Cincinnati Reds for outfielder Juan Encarnacion, infielder Wilton Guerrero and pitcher Ryan Snare, July 11, 2002.

c On disabled list from May 23 to June 7 and July 29 to November 3, 2003.

d Waived by Cincinnati Reds, November 4, 2003. Signed with Chicago Cubs, January 21, 2004.

e On disabled list from March 26 to August 1, 2004.

f On disabled list from June 23 to July 20, 2007.

g Filed for free agency, October 30, 2008, re-signed with Chicago Cubs, November 18, 2008.

h On disabled list from July 7 to July 28, 2009.

i On disabled list from April 18 to May 3 and June 16 to July 8, 2012.

j Traded to Texas Rangers for pitcher Kyle Hendricks and infielder Christian Villanueva, July 31, 2012.

k Filed for free agency, November 3, 2012. Signed with Boston Red Sox, December 19, 2012.

DETWILER, ROSS EMERY

Born, St.Louis, Missouri, March 6, 1986.
Bats Right. Throws Right. Height, 6 feet, 5 inches. Weight, 185 pounds.

Year	Club	Lea	G	IP	W	L	Pct	SO	BB	H	ERA	SAVES
2007	Nationals	Gulf Coast	4	12	0	0	.000	15	3	11	2.25	0
2007	Potomac	Carolina	5	21 1/3	2	2	.500	13	9	27	4.22	0
2007	Washington	N.L.	1	1	0	0	.000	1	0	0	0.00	0
2008	Potomac	Carolina	26	124	8	8	.500	114	57	140	4.86	0
2009	Harrisburg	Eastern	6	27 1/3	0	3	.000	28	10	28	2.96	0
2009	Syracuse	Int.	10	49 1/3	4	2	.667	42	20	56	3.10	0
2009	Washington	N.L.	15	75 2/3	1	6	.143	43	33	87	5.00	0
2010	Potomac	Carolina	2	6	0	0	.000	6	1	6	1.50	0
2010	Harrisburg	Eastern	7	32 2/3	2	2	.500	31	7	38	2.48	0
2010	Syracuse	Int.	1	5	1	0	1.000	2	1	5	1.80	0
2010	Washington a	N.L.	8	29 2/3	1	3	.250	17	14	34	4.25	0
2011	Syracuse	Int.	16	87 1/3	6	6	.500	63	32	98	4.53	0
2011	Washington	N.L.	15	66	4	5	.444	41	20	63	3.00	0
2012	Washington	N.L.	33	164 1/3	10	8	.556	105	52	149	3.40	0
2013	Potomac	Carolina	1	3 2/3	0	0	.000	4	0	7	2.45	0
2013	Washington b	N.L.	13	71 1/3	2	7	.222	39	14	92	4.04	0
Major League Totals		6 Yrs.	85	408	18	29	.383	246	133	425	3.79	0
	Division Series											
2012	Washington	N.L.	1	6	0	0	.000	2	3	3	0.00	0

a On disabled list from April 4 to June 21 and August 6 to September 7, 2010.

b On disabled list from May 16 to June 13 and July 4 to November 4, 2013.

DIAMOND, SCOTT MICHAEL

Born, Guelph, Ontario, Canada, July 30, 1986.
Bats Left. Throws Left. Height, 6 feet, 3 inches. Weight, 220 pounds.

Year	Club	Lea	G	IP	W	L	Pct	SO	BB	H	ERA	SAVES
2008	Myrtle Beach	Carolina	17	100	12	2	.857	85	28	95	2.79	0
2008	Rome	So.Atl.	9	$52\frac{2}{3}$	3	1	.750	38	11	47	3.08	0
2009	Mississippi	Southern	23	131	5	10	.333	111	53	152	3.50	0
2010	Gwinnett	Int.	10	$56\frac{1}{3}$	4	1	.800	33	15	53	3.36	0
2010	Mississippi a	Southern	17	$102\frac{1}{3}$	4	6	.400	90	39	113	3.52	0
2011	Rochester	Int.	23	123	4	14	.222	90	36	158	5.56	0
2011	Minnesota b	A.L.	7	39	1	5	.167	19	17	51	5.08	0
2012	Rochester	Int.	6	$34\frac{2}{3}$	4	1	.800	26	7	35	2.60	0
2012	Minnesota	A.L.	27	173	12	9	.571	90	31	184	3.54	0
2013	Fort Myers	Fla.St.	1	5	0	0	.000	3	0	6	7.20	0
2013	Rochester	Int.	6	41	4	0	1.000	19	9	33	2.41	0
2013	Minnesota c	A.L.	24	131	6	13	.316	52	36	163	5.43	0
Major League Totals		3 Yrs.	58	343	19	27	.413	161	84	398	4.43	0

a Selected by Minnesota Twins from Atlanta Braves in Rule V draft, December 9, 2010.
b Retained by Minnesota Twins from Atlanta Braves for pitcher Billy Bullock, March 28, 2011.
c On disabled list from March 22 to April 13, 2013.

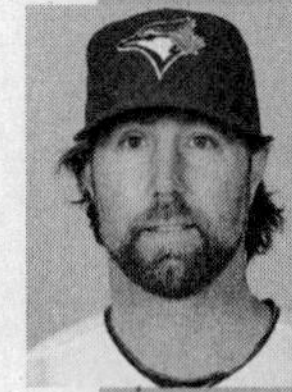

DICKEY, ROBERT ALAN (R.A.)

Born, Nashville, Tennessee, October 29, 1974.
Bats Right. Throws Right. Height, 6 feet, 3 inches. Weight, 220 pounds.

Year	Club	Lea	G	IP	W	L	Pct	SO	BB	H	ERA	SAVES
1997	Charlotte	Fla.St.	8	35	1	4	.200	32	12	51	6.94	0
1998	Charlotte	Fla.St.	57	60	1	5	.167	53	22	58	3.30	38
1999	Oklahoma	P.C.	6	$22\frac{2}{3}$	2	2	.500	17	7	23	4.37	0
1999	Tulsa	Texas	35	95	6	7	.462	59	40	105	4.55	10
2000	Oklahoma	P.C.	30	$158\frac{1}{3}$	8	9	.471	85	65	167	4.49	1
2001	Oklahoma	P.C.	24	163	11	7	.611	120	45	164	3.75	0
2001	Texas	A.L.	4	12	0	1	.000	4	7	13	6.75	0
2002	Oklahoma	P.C.	37	154	8	7	.533	109	47	176	4.09	0
2003	Oklahoma	P.C.	3	15	1	1	.500	4	3	14	1.20	0
2003	Texas	A.L.	38	$116\frac{2}{3}$	9	8	.529	94	38	135	5.09	1
2004	Frisco	Texas	4	$13\frac{2}{3}$	1	1	.500	9	1	16	1.98	0
2004	Texas a	A.L.	25	$104\frac{1}{3}$	6	7	.462	57	33	136	5.61	1
2005	Oklahoma	P.C.	19	$121\frac{2}{3}$	10	6	.625	81	39	152	5.99	0
2005	Texas b	A.L.	9	$29\frac{2}{3}$	1	2	.333	15	17	29	6.67	0
2006	Texas	A.L.	1	$3\frac{1}{3}$	0	1	.000	1	1	8	18.90	0
2006	Oklahoma	P.C.	22	$131\frac{2}{3}$	9	8	.529	61	46	134	4.92	1
2007	Nashville c-d-e	P.C.	31	$169\frac{1}{3}$	13	6	.684	119	60	159	3.72	0
2008	Tacoma	P.C.	7	$49\frac{2}{3}$	2	5	.286	30	8	58	3.44	0
2008	Seattle f-g	A.L.	32	$112\frac{1}{3}$	5	8	.385	58	51	124	5.21	0
2009	Rochester	Int.	5	$33\frac{1}{3}$	2	1	.667	18	9	39	5.13	0
2009	Minnesota h	A.L.	35	$64\frac{1}{3}$	1	1	.500	42	30	74	4.62	0
2010	Buffalo	Int.	8	$60\frac{2}{3}$	4	2	.667	37	8	55	2.23	0
2010	New York	N.L.	27	$174\frac{1}{3}$	11	9	.550	104	42	165	2.84	0
2011	New York	N.L.	33	$208\frac{2}{3}$	8	13	.381	134	54	202	3.28	0
2012	New York i-j	N.L.	34	*$233\frac{2}{3}$	20	6	.769	*230	54	192	2.73	0
2013	Toronto	A.L.	34	$224\frac{2}{3}$	14	13	.519	177	71	207	4.21	0
Major League Totals		11 Yrs.	272	1284	75	69	.521	916	398	1285	4.02	2

a On disabled list from June 25 to July 19 and July 30 to August 23, 2004.
b On disabled list from April 13 to May 25, 2005.
c Filed for free agency, October 11, 2006. Signed with Milwaukee Brewers organization, January 10, 2007.
d Filed for free agency, October 29, 2007. Signed with Minnesota Twins organization, November 29, 2007.
e Selected by Seattle Mariners in Rule V draft, December 6, 2007.
f Seattle retained rights to Dickey for catcher Jair Fernandez, March 29, 2008.
g Filed for free agency, December 9, 2008. Signed with Minnesota Twins organization, December 26, 2008.
h Filed for free agency, October 6, 2009. Signed with New York Mets organization, December 23, 2009.
i Selected Cy Young Award Winner in National League for 2012.
j Traded to Toronto Blue Jays with catcher Josh Thole and catcher Mike Nickeas for catcher John Buck, pitcher Noah Syndergaard, catcher Travis D'Arnaud and outfielder Wuilmer Becerra, December 17, 2012.

DIEKMAN, JACOB TANNER (JAKE)

Born, Wymore, Nebraska, January 21, 1987.
Bats Left. Throws Left. Height, 6 feet, 4 inches. Weight, 200 pounds.

Year	Club	Lea	G	IP	W	L	Pct	SO	BB	H	ERA	SAVES
2007	Phillies	Gulf Coast	10	37	1	3	.250	35	13	29	2.92	0
2007	Williamsport	N.Y.-Penn.	3	16	2	1	.667	11	8	10	2.25	0
2008	Williamsport	N.Y.-Penn.	8	45	1	4	.200	43	25	41	4.40	0
2008	Lakewood	So.Atl.	19	96 1/3	3	5	.375	53	47	120	5.42	0
2009	Lakewood	So.Atl.	32	55 2/3	2	0	1.000	52	28	59	4.04	2
2010	Lakewood	So.Atl.	21	23 2/3	2	0	1.000	30	15	16	1.90	0
2010	Clearwater	Fla.St.	24	32	0	2	.000	26	23	22	3.66	0
2011	Reading	Eastern	53	65	0	1	.000	83	44	47	3.05	3
2012	Lehigh Valley	Int.	25	26 2/3	1	1	.500	37	13	19	1.69	7
2012	Philadelphia	N.L.	32	27 1/3	1	1	.500	35	20	25	3.95	0
2013	Lehigh Valley	Int.	30	30	1	0	1.000	37	24	31	5.70	11
2013	Philadelphia	N.L.	45	38 1/3	1	4	.200	41	16	34	2.58	0
Major League Totals		2 Yrs.	77	65 2/3	2	5	.286	76	36	59	3.15	0

DOOLITTLE, SEAN ROBERT

Born, Rapid City, South Dakota, September 26, 1986.
Bats Left. Throws Left. Height, 6 feet, 3 inches. Weight, 210 pounds.

Year	Club	Lea	G	IP	W	L	Pct	SO	BB	H	ERA	SAVES
2010	a-b					INJURED—Did Not Play						
2011	Athletics	Arizona	1	1	0	0	.000	2	1	0	9.00	0
2012	Stockton	Calif.	6	10 1/3	0	0	.000	21	2	5	0.87	0
2012	Midland	Texas	8	11	0	0	.000	19	4	2	0.82	1
2012	Sacramento	P.C.	2	3 2/3	0	0	.000	8	1	1	0.00	0
2012	Oakland	A.L.	44	47 1/3	2	1	.667	60	11	40	3.04	1
2013	Oakland	A.L.	70	69	5	5	.500	60	13	53	3.13	2
Major League Totals		2 Yrs.	114	116 1/3	7	6	.538	120	24	93	3.09	3
	Division Series											
2012	Oakland	A.L.	3	2 2/3	0	0	.000	5	0	5	3.38	0
2013	Oakland	A.L.	4	4 1/3	0	1	.000	6	2	3	4.15	0
Division Series Totals			7	7	0	1	.000	11	2	8	3.86	0

a Played first base in Oakland Athletics system from 2007 through 2009.
b On minor league disabled list from April 8 to September 23, 2010.

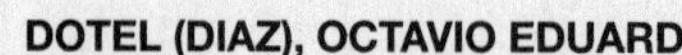

DOTEL (DIAZ), OCTAVIO EDUARDO

Born, Santo Domingo, Dominican Republic, November 25, 1973.
Bats Right. Throws Right. Height, 6 feet. Weight, 215 pounds.

Year	Club	Lea	G	IP	W	L	Pct	SO	BB	H	ERA	SAVES
1993	Mets	Dominican	15	59 1/3	6	2	.750	48	38	46	4.10	0
1994	Mets	Dominican	15	81 1/3	5	0	1.000	95	31	84	4.32	0
1995	Mets	Gulf Coast	13	74 1/3	7	4	.636	86	17	48	2.18	0
1995	St. Lucie	Fla.St.	3	8	1	0	1.000	9	4	10	5.63	0
1996	Columbia	So.Atl.	22	115 1/3	11	3	.786	142	49	89	3.59	0
1997	Mets	Gulf Coast	3	9 1/3	0	0	.000	7	2	9	0.96	1
1997	St. Lucie	Fla.St.	9	50	5	2	.714	39	23	44	2.52	0
1997	Binghamton	Eastern	12	55 2/3	3	4	.429	40	38	66	5.98	0
1998	Binghamton	Eastern	10	68 2/3	4	2	.667	82	24	41	1.97	0
1998	Norfolk	Int.	17	99	8	6	.571	118	43	82	3.45	0
1999	Norfolk	Int.	13	70 1/3	5	2	.714	90	34	52	3.84	0
1999	New York a	N.L.	19	85 1/3	8	3	.727	85	49	69	5.38	0
2000	Houston	N.L.	50	125	3	7	.300	142	61	127	5.40	16
2001	Houston	N.L.	61	105	7	5	.583	145	47	79	2.66	2
2002	Houston	N.L.	83	97 1/3	6	4	.600	118	27	58	1.85	6
2003	Houston	N.L.	76	87	6	4	.600	97	31	53	2.48	4
2004	Houston	N.L.	32	34 2/3	0	4	.000	50	15	27	3.12	14
2004	Oakland b-c	A.L.	45	50 2/3	6	2	.750	72	18	41	4.09	22
2005	Oakland d-e	A.L.	15	15 1/3	1	2	.333	16	11	10	3.52	7
2006	Staten Island	N.Y.-Penn.	1	1	0	0	.000	1	0	2	0.00	0
2006	Yankees	Gulf Coast	3	3	0	0	.000	6	1	0	0.00	0
2006	Tampa	Fla.St.	2	2	0	0	.000	2	0	1	0.00	0
2006	Trenton	Eastern	2	2	0	0	.000	3	0	1	0.00	0
2006	Columbus	Int.	5	5 1/3	0	0	.000	8	0	6	3.38	0
2006	New York f-g	A.L.	14	10	0	0	.000	7	11	18	10.80	0
2007	Wichita	Texas	3	3	0	1	.000	4	0	2	3.00	1
2007	Kansas City	A.L.	24	23	2	1	.667	29	11	24	3.91	11

Year Club	Lea	G	IP	W	L	Pct	SO	BB	H	ERA	SAVES
2007 Atlanta h-i-j	N.L.	9	7 2/3	0	0	.000	12	1	5	4.70	0
2008 Chicago	A.L.	72	67	4	4	.500	92	29	52	3.76	1
2009 Chicago k	A.L.	62	62 1/3	3	3	.500	75	36	54	3.32	0
2010 Pitt-LA-Col l-m-n	N.L.	68	64	3	4	.429	75	32	52	4.08	22
2011 Toronto	A.L.	36	29 1/3	2	1	.667	30	12	20	3.68	1
2011 St. Louis o-p-q	N.L.	29	24 2/3	3	3	.500	32	5	16	3.28	2
2012 Detroit r	A.L.	57	58	5	3	.625	62	12	50	3.57	1
2013 Tigers	Gulf Coast	2	2	0	0	.000	2	0	0	0.00	0
2013 Lakeland	Fla.St.	5	4 2/3	0	1	.000	2	0	9	7.71	0
2013 Toledo	Int.	3	1 1/3	0	0	.000	3	2	3	13.50	0
2013 Detroit s-t	A.L.	6	4 2/3	0	0	.000	4	4	10	13.50	0
Major League Totals	15 Yrs.	758	951	59	50	.541	1143	412	765	3.78	109
Division Series											
1999 New York	N.L.	1	0 1/3	0	0	.000	0	2	1	54.00	0
2001 Houston	N.L.	2	3 1/3	0	0	.000	5	0	5	5.40	0
2008 Chicago	A.L.	4	1 1/3	0	0	.000	3	0	2	13.50	0
2011 St. Louis	N.L.	3	2 2/3	1	0	1.000	4	0	0	0.00	0
2012 Detroit	A.L.	2	1	0	0	.000	2	1	0	0.00	0
Division Series Totals		12	8 2/3	1	0	1.000	14	3	8	6.23	0
Championship Series											
1999 New York	N.L.	1	3	1	0	1.000	5	2	4	3.00	0
2011 St. Louis	N.L.	4	4	1	0	1.000	5	1	2	2.25	0
2012 Detroit	A.L.	2	2 1/3	0	0	.000	3	2	0	0.00	0
Championship Series Totals		7	9 1/3	2	0	1.000	13	5	6	1.93	0
World Series Record											
2011 St. Louis	N.L.	5	3 2/3	0	1	.000	5	1	3	4.91	0
2012 Detroit	A.L.	2	1 2/3	0	0	.000	1	2	0	0.00	0
World Series Totals		7	5 1/3	0	1	.000	6	3	3	3.38	0

a Traded with Roger Cedeno and Kyle Kessel to Houston for Mike Hampton and Derek Bell, December 23, 1999.
b Traded to Kansas City Royals with catcher John Buck for outfielder Carlos Beltran, June 24, 2004.
c Traded to Oakland Athletics with cash for pitcher Mike Wood and infielder Mark Teahen, June 24, 2004.
d On disabled list from May 19 to October 28, 2005.
e Filed for free agency, October 28, 2005. Signed with New York Yankees, December 29, 2005.
f On disabled list from March 24 to August 16, 2006.
g Filed for free agency, October 28, 2006. Signed with Kansas City Royals, December 8, 2006.
h On disabled list from March 30 to May 22, 2007 and August 8 to September 20, 2007.
i Traded to Atlanta Braves for pitcher Kyle Davies, July 31, 2007.
j Filed for free agency, November 6, 2007. Signed with Chicago White Sox, January 22, 2008.
k Filed for free agency, November 9, 2009. Signed with Pittsburgh Pirates, January 21, 2010.
l Traded to Los Angeles Dodgers for pitcher James McDonald and outfielder Andrew Lambo, July 31, 2010.
m Traded to Colorado Rockies for player to be named later, September 18, 2010. Los Angeles Dodgers received outfielder Anthony Jackson to complete trade, November 15, 2010.
n Filed for free agency, November 3, 2010. Signed with Toronto Blue Jays, January 4, 2011.
o On disabled list from March 22 to April 8, 2011.
p Traded to St. Louis Cardinals with pitcher Edwin Jackson, pitcher Marc Rzepczynski, outfielder Corey Patterson and cash for outfielder Colby Rasmus, pitcher Trever Miller, pitcher Brian Tallet and pitcher P.J. Walters, July 27, 2011.
q Filed for free agency, October 31, 2011. Signed with Detroit Tigers, December 9, 2011.
r On disabled list from June 3 to June 19, 2012.
s On disabled list from April 20 to October 31, 2013.
t Filed for free agency, October 31, 2013.

DOUBRONT, FELIX ANTONIO

Born, Carabobo, Venezuela, October 23, 1987.
Bats Left. Throws Left. Height, 6 feet, 2 inches. Weight, 165 pounds.

Year Club	Lea	G	IP	W	L	Pct	SO	BB	H	ERA	SAVES
2006 Red Sox	Gulf Coast	11	53 2/3	2	3	.400	36	13	41	2.52	0
2006 Lowell	N.Y.-Penn.	2	11	2	0	1.000	7	3	7	4.91	0
2007 Lowell	N.Y.-Penn.	8	35	1	3	.250	25	11	41	5.66	0
2007 Greenville	So.Atl.	11	42 1/3	3	7	.300	22	17	63	8.93	0
2008 Lancaster	Calif.	3	14	1	1	.500	20	4	15	3.86	0
2008 Greenville	So.Atl.	23	115 1/3	12	8	.600	118	24	115	3.67	0
2009 Portland	Eastern	26	121	8	6	.571	101	52	119	3.35	0
2010 Portland	Eastern	8	43	4	0	1.000	38	17	39	2.51	0
2010 Pawtucket	Int.	9	37	4	3	.571	34	16	36	3.16	0
2010 Boston	A.L.	12	25	2	2	.500	23	10	27	4.32	2
2011 Portland	Eastern	1	5	1	0	1.000	9	0	4	1.80	0
2011 Lowell	N.Y.-Penn.	1	2	0	0	.000	4	0	0	0.00	0
2011 Pawtucket	Int.	18	70 1/3	2	5	.286	61	26	65	4.22	0
2011 Boston a	A.L.	11	10 1/3	0	0	.000	6	8	12	6.10	1

Year	Club	Lea	G	IP	W	L	Pct	SO	BB	H	ERA	SAVES
2012	Boston b	A.L.	29	161	11	10	.524	167	71	162	4.86	0
2013	Boston	A.L.	29	162⅓	11	6	.647	139	71	161	4.32	0
Major League Totals		4 Yrs.	81	358⅔	24	18	.571	335	160	362	4.62	3
	Championship Series											
2013	Boston	A.L.	2	2⅓	0	0	.000	1	2	1	0.00	0
	World Series Record											
2013	Boston	A.L.	2	4⅔	1	0	1.000	3	1	2	1.93	0

a On disabled list from March 22 to April 8, 2011.
b On disabled list from August 10 to August 25, 2012.

DOWNS, SCOTT JEREMY

Born, Louisville, Kentucky, March 17, 1976.
Bats Left. Throws Left. Height, 6 feet, 2 inches. Weight, 210 pounds.

Year	Club	Lea	G	IP	W	L	Pct	SO	BB	H	ERA	SAVES
1997	Williamsprt.	N.Y.-Penn.	5	23	0	2	.000	28	7	15	2.74	0
1997	Rockford	Midwest	5	36	3	0	1.000	43	8	17	1.25	0
1998	Daytona a	Fla.St.	27	161⅔	8	9	.471	117	55	179	3.90	0
1999	New Britain	Eastern	6	19⅔	0	0	.000	22	10	33	8.69	0
1999	Daytona	Fla.St.	7	48	5	0	1.000	41	11	41	1.88	0
1999	Fort Myers	Fla.St.	2	9⅔	0	1	.000	9	6	7	0.00	0
1999	West Tenn b	Southern	13	80	8	1	.889	101	28	56	1.35	0
2000	Chicago-Montreal c-d	N.L.	19	97	4	3	.571	63	40	122	5.29	0
2001	Montreal e	N.L.			INJURED—Did Not Play							
2002	Brevard County	Fla.St.	7	9	0	0	.000	7	2	7	3.00	1
2002	Ottawa f	Int.	17	23⅓	2	1	.667	15	3	31	5.79	0
2003	Edmonton	P.C.	21	121⅔	8	9	.471	54	39	119	4.29	0
2003	Montreal	N.L.	1	3	0	1	.000	4	3	5	15.00	0
2004	Edmonton	P.C.	22	135⅓	10	6	.625	67	26	143	3.52	0
2004	Montreal g	N.L.	12	63	3	6	.333	38	23	79	5.14	0
2005	Syracuse	Int.	7	39⅓	2	3	.400	35	3	45	4.81	0
2005	Toronto	A.L.	26	94	4	3	.571	75	34	93	4.31	0
2006	Toronto	A.L.	59	77	6	2	.750	61	30	73	4.09	1
2007	Toronto	A.L.	*81	58	4	2	.667	57	24	47	2.17	1
2008	Toronto h	A.L.	66	70⅔	0	3	.000	57	27	54	1.78	5
2009	Dunedin	Fla.St.	3	2⅓	0	0	.000	2	1	3	3.86	0
2009	Toronto i	A.L.	48	46⅔	1	3	.250	43	13	46	3.09	9
2010	Toronto j	A.L.	67	61⅓	5	5	.500	48	14	47	2.64	0
2011	Inland Empire	Calif.	2	2	1	1	.500	1	1	5	9.00	0
2011	Los Angeles k	A.L.	60	53⅔	6	3	.667	35	15	39	1.34	1
2012	Los Angeles l	A.L.	57	45⅔	1	1	.500	32	17	43	3.15	9
2013	Los Angeles	A.L.	43	29⅓	2	3	.400	22	11	26	1.84	0
2013	Atlanta m-n	N.L.	25	14	2	1	.667	15	8	19	3.86	0
Major League Totals		12 Yrs.	564	713⅓	38	36	.514	550	259	693	3.48	26

a Sent by Chicago Cubs to Minnesota Twins as player to be named later for pitcher Mike Morgan, November 3, 1998.
b Traded to Chicago Cubs with pitcher Rick Aguilera for pitcher Jason Ryan and pitcher Kyle Lohse, May 21, 1999.
c Traded to Montreal Expos for outfielder Rondell White, July 31, 2000.
d On disabled list from August 9 to October 1, 2000.
e On disabled list from March 23 to November 14, 2001.
f On disabled list from March 27 to June 10, 2002.
g Released by Montreal Expos, November 29, 2004. Signed with Toronto Blue Jays organization, December 16, 2004.
h On disabled list from September 20 to October 2, 2008.
i On disabled list from June 17 to July 8 and August 1 to August 24, 2009.
j Filed for free agency, November 1, 2010. Signed with Los Angeles Angels, December 10, 2010.
k On disabled list from March 22 to April 11 and April 14 to April 29, 2011.
l On disabled list from July 28 to August 18, 2012.
m Traded to Atlanta Braves for pitcher Cory Rasmus, July 29, 2013.
n Filed for free agency, October 31, 2013. Signed with Chicago White Sox, January 2, 2014.

DRABEK, KYLE JORDAN

Born, The Woodlands, Texas, December 8, 1987.
Bats Right. Throws Right. Height, 6 feet, 1 inch. Weight, 190 pounds.

Year	Club	Lea	G	IP	W	L	Pct	SO	BB	H	ERA	SAVES
2006	Phillies	Gulf Coast	6	23⅓	1	3	.250	14	11	33	7.71	0
2007	Lakewood	So.Atl.	11	54	5	1	.833	46	23	50	4.33	0
2008	Phillies	Gulf Coast	4	12	0	1	.000	6	6	6	2.25	0
2008	Williamsport	N.Y.-Penn.	4	20⅓	1	2	.333	10	6	11	2.21	0
2009	Reading	Eastern	15	96⅓	8	2	.800	76	31	92	3.64	0
2009	Clearwater a	Fla.St.	10	61⅔	4	1	.800	74	19	49	2.48	0

Year	Club	Lea	G	IP	W	L	Pct	SO	BB	H	ERA	SAVES
2010	New Hampshire	Eastern	27	162	14	9	.609	132	68	126	2.94	0
2010	Toronto	A.L.	3	17	0	3	.000	12	5	18	4.76	0
2011	Las Vegas	P.C.	15	75	5	4	.556	45	41	111	7.44	0
2011	Toronto	A.L.	18	78 2/3	4	5	.444	51	55	87	6.06	0
2012	Toronto b	A.L.	13	71 1/3	4	7	.364	47	47	67	4.67	0
2013	Dunedin	Fla.St.	8	20 2/3	0	1	.000	20	3	14	2.61	0
2013	New Hampshire	Eastern	2	8	0	1	.000	3	1	4	3.38	0
2013	Buffalo	Int.	4	14 1/3	1	2	.333	12	2	14	3.77	0
2013	Toronto c	A.L.	3	2 1/3	0	0	.000	3	2	4	7.71	0
Major League Totals		4 Yrs.	37	169 1/3	8	15	.348	113	109	176	5.37	0

a Traded by Philadelphia Phillies to Toronto Blue Jays with pitcher Michael Taylor and catcher Travis D'Arnaud for pitcher Roy Halladay, December 16, 2009.
b On disabled list from June 14 to October 31, 2012.
c On disabled list from February 25 to July 5, 2013.

DUENSING, BRIAN MATTHEW

Born, Marysville, Kansas, February 22, 1983.
Bats Left. Throws Left. Height, 5 feet, 11 inches. Weight, 195 pounds.

Year	Club	Lea	G	IP	W	L	Pct	SO	BB	H	ERA	SAVES
2005	Elizabethton	Appal.	12	50 1/3	4	3	.571	55	16	49	2.32	0
2006	New Britain	Eastern	10	49 1/3	1	2	.333	30	18	51	3.65	0
2006	Fort Myers	Fla.St.	7	40 1/3	2	5	.286	33	8	47	4.24	0
2006	Beloit	Midwest	11	70 1/3	2	3	.400	55	14	68	2.94	0
2007	New Britain	Eastern	9	50 2/3	4	1	.800	38	7	47	2.66	0
2007	Rochester	Int.	19	116 2/3	11	5	.688	86	30	115	3.24	0
2008	Rochester	Int.	25	138 2/3	5	11	.313	77	34	150	4.28	0
2009	Rochester	Int.	13	75 1/3	4	6	.400	44	19	87	4.66	0
2009	Minnesota	A.L.	24	84	5	2	.714	53	31	84	3.64	0
2010	Minnesota	A.L.	53	130 2/3	10	3	.769	78	35	122	2.62	0
2011	Minnesota	A.L.	32	161 2/3	9	14	.391	115	52	193	5.23	0
2012	Minnesota	A.L.	55	109	4	12	.250	69	27	126	5.12	0
2013	Minnesota	A.L.	73	61	6	2	.750	56	22	68	3.98	1
Major League Totals		5 Yrs.	237	546 1/3	34	33	.507	371	167	593	4.20	1
	Division Series											
2009	Minnesota	A.L.	1	4 2/3	0	1	.000	3	1	7	9.64	0
2010	Minnesota	A.L.	1	3 1/3	0	1	.000	1	1	7	13.50	0
Division Series Totals			2	8	0	2	.000	4	2	14	11.25	0

DUFFY, DANIEL RICHARD (DANNY)

Born, Goleta, California, December 21, 1988.
Bats Left. Throws Left. Height, 6 feet, 3 inches. Weight, 200 pounds.

Year	Club	Lea	G	IP	W	L	Pct	SO	BB	H	ERA	SAVES
2007	Royals	Arizona	11	37 1/3	2	3	.400	63	17	24	1.45	0
2008	Burlington	Midwest	17	81 2/3	8	4	.667	102	25	56	2.20	0
2009	Wilmington	Carolina	24	126 2/3	9	3	.750	125	41	108	2.98	0
2010	Royals	Arizona	2	2 2/3	0	0	.000	4	1	2	3.38	0
2010	Idaho Falls	Pioneer	2	6	0	1	.000	6	0	4	1.50	0
2010	Wilmington	Carolina	3	14	0	0	.000	18	7	8	2.57	0
2010	NW Arkansas	Texas	7	39 2/3	5	2	.714	41	9	38	2.95	0
2011	Omaha	P.C.	8	42	3	1	.750	48	10	37	3.43	0
2011	Kansas City	A.L.	20	105 1/3	4	8	.333	87	51	119	5.64	0
2012	Kansas City a	A.L.	6	27 2/3	2	2	.500	28	18	26	3.90	0
2013	NW Arkansas	Texas	4	16	0	2	.000	28	5	16	3.94	0
2013	Omaha	P.C.	12	53	3	0	1.000	59	25	50	4.08	0
2013	Kansas City b	A.L.	5	24 1/3	2	0	1.000	22	14	19	1.85	0
Major League Totals		3 Yrs.	31	157 1/3	8	10	.444	137	83	164	4.75	0

a On disabled list from May 14 to November 2, 2012.
b On disabled list from March 31 to June 25 and September 8 to September 30, 2013.

DUNN, MICHAEL GLEN

Born, Farmington, New Mexico, May 23, 1985.
Bats Left. Throws Left. Height, 6 feet, 1 inch. Weight, 195 pounds.

Year	Club	Lea	G	IP	W	L	Pct	SO	BB	H	ERA	SAVES
2006	Yankees	Gulf Coast	11	24 2/3	3	0	1.000	26	9	13	0.73	4
2006	Staten Island	N.Y.-Penn.	3	6 1/3	0	0	.000	7	7	3	5.68	0
2007	Charleston	So.Atl.	27	144 2/3	12	5	.706	138	45	136	3.42	0

Year	Club	Lea	G	IP	W	L	Pct	SO	BB	H	ERA	SAVES
2008	Trenton	Eastern	1	1 2/3	1	0	1.000	2	1	1	0.00	0
2008	Tampa	Fla.St.	30	124 2/3	4	7	.364	118	58	124	4.55	1
2009	Trenton	Eastern	26	53 1/3	3	3	.500	76	32	41	3.71	2
2009	Scranton/WB	Int.	12	20	1	0	1.000	23	14	17	2.25	0
2009	New York a	A.L.	4	4	0	0	.000	5	5	3	6.75	0
2010	Gwinnett	Int.	38	47 1/3	2	0	1.000	64	25	31	1.52	7
2010	Atlanta b	N.L.	25	19	2	0	1.000	27	17	15	1.89	0
2011	Florida	N.L.	72	63	5	6	.455	68	31	51	3.43	0
2012	New Orleans	P.C.	12	17 2/3	1	1	.500	24	7	19	4.58	0
2012	Miami	N.L.	60	44	0	3	.000	47	29	49	4.91	1
2013	Miami	N.L.	75	67 2/3	3	4	.429	72	28	53	2.66	2
Major League Totals		5 Yrs.	236	197 2/3	10	13	.435	219	110	171	3.41	3
Division Series												
2010	Atlanta	N.L.	3	1 1/3	0	0	.000	2	0	2	0.00	0

a Traded to Atlanta Braves with outfielder Melky Cabrera, pitcher Arodys Vizcaino and cash for pitcher Javier Vazquez and pitcher Boone Logan, December 22, 2009.

b Traded to Florida Marlins with infielder Omar Infante for infielder Dan Uggla, November 16, 2010.

EOVALDI, NATHAN EDWARD

Born, Houston, Texas, February 13, 1990.

Bats Right. Throws Right. Height, 6 feet, 3 inches. Weight, 195 pounds.

Year	Club	Lea	G	IP	W	L	Pct	SO	BB	H	ERA	SAVES
2008	Dodgers	Gulf Coast	6	8	0	1	.000	9	3	6	1.13	1
2008	Ogden	Pioneer	1	2 2/3	0	0	.000	2	0	1	0.00	0
2009	Great Lakes	Midwest	26	96 1/3	3	5	.375	71	41	95	3.27	1
2010	Dodgers	Arizona	3	8 1/3	0	1	.000	10	4	6	4.32	0
2010	Inland Empire	Calif.	16	85	3	5	.375	58	33	99	4.45	0
2010	Ogden	Pioneer	1	5	1	0	1.000	4	0	3	1.80	0
2011	Chattanooga	Southern	20	103	6	5	.545	99	46	76	2.62	0
2011	Los Angeles	N.L.	10	34 2/3	1	2	.333	23	20	28	3.63	0
2012	Chattanooga	Southern	9	35	2	2	.500	30	13	30	3.09	0
2012	Los Angeles-Miami a	N.L.	22	119 1/3	4	13	.235	78	47	133	4.30	0
2013	Jupiter	Fla.St.	2	9	0	1	.000	6	2	9	3.00	0
2013	Jacksonville	Southern	3	11 2/3	1	0	1.000	9	4	13	5.40	0
2013	Miami b	N.L.	18	106 1/3	4	6	.400	78	40	100	3.39	0
Major League Totals		3 Yrs.	50	260 1/3	9	21	.300	179	107	261	3.84	0

a Traded to Miami Marlins with pitcher Scott McGough for infielder Hanley Ramirez and pitcher Randy Choate, July 25, 2012.

b On disabled list from March 24 to June 18, 2013.

ESTRADA, MARCO RENE

Born, Sonora, Mexico, July 5, 1983.

Bats Right. Throws Right. Height, 6 feet. Weight, 180 pounds.

Year	Club	Lea	G	IP	W	L	Pct	SO	BB	H	ERA	SAVES
2005	Vermont	N.Y.-Penn.	9	33 2/3	1	3	.250	37	16	31	5.08	1
2006	Nationals	Gulf Coast	5	23 2/3	2	0	1.000	27	6	14	1.52	0
2006	Savannah	So.Atl.	8	37	1	4	.200	29	14	44	5.59	0
2007	Hagerstown	So.Atl.	8	36	1	5	.167	35	17	39	5.25	0
2007	Nationals	Gulf Coast	4	11 1/3	0	0	.000	13	3	19	3.18	0
2007	Potomac	Carolina	11	58 1/3	5	3	.625	54	17	67	4.94	0
2008	Harrisburg	Eastern	13	74 1/3	6	3	.667	67	32	62	2.66	0
2008	Columbus	Int.	12	65 1/3	3	3	.500	52	21	73	3.58	0
2008	Washington	N.L.	11	12 2/3	0	0	.000	10	5	17	7.82	0
2009	Syracuse	Int.	27	136 1/3	9	5	.643	98	33	133	3.63	0
2009	Washington	N.L.	4	7 1/3	0	1	.000	9	4	6	6.14	0
2010	Nashville	P.C.	7	40	1	2	.333	33	11	30	3.15	0
2010	Milwaukee a-b	N.L.	7	11 1/3	0	0	.000	13	6	14	9.53	0
2011	Milwaukee	N.L.	43	92 2/3	4	8	.333	88	29	83	4.08	0
2012	Nashville	P.C.	2	8	0	0	.000	5	5	7	1.13	0
2012	Milwaukee c	N.L.	29	138 1/3	5	7	.417	143	29	129	3.64	0
2013	Brewers	Arizona	1	2 2/3	0	0	.000	4	0	3	3.38	0
2013	Wisconsin	Midwest	1	2 2/3	0	1	.000	5	1	8	20.25	0
2013	Nashville	P.C.	1	2 2/3	0	0	.000	2	2	3	6.75	0
2013	Milwaukee d	N.L.	21	128	7	4	.636	118	29	109	3.87	0
Major League Totals		6 Yrs.	115	390 1/3	16	20	.444	381	102	358	4.17	0
Division Series												
2011	Milwaukee	N.L.	2	3	0	0	.000	5	0	3	0.00	0

Year	Club	Lea	G	IP	W	L	Pct	SO	BB	H	ERA	SAVES
	Championship Series											
2011	Milwaukee	N.L.	2	3	0	0	.000	4	2	4	12.00	0

a Claimed on waivers by Milwaukee Brewers, February 3, 2010.
b On disabled list from June 1 to October 5, 2010.
c On disabled list from May 24 to June 26, 2012.
d On disabled list from June 4 to August 7, 2013.

FARNSWORTH, KYLE LYNN

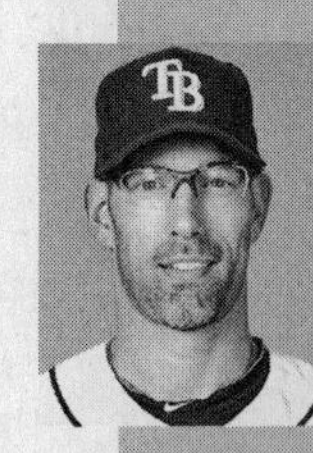

Born, Wichita, Kansas, April 14, 1976.
Bats Right. Throws Right. Height, 6 feet, 4 inches. Weight, 230 pounds.

Year	Club	Lea	G	IP	W	L	Pct	SO	BB	H	ERA	SAVES
1995	Cubs	Gulf Coast	16	31	3	2	.600	18	11	22	0.87	1
1996	Rockford	Midwest	20	112	9	6	.600	82	35	122	3.70	0
1997	Daytona	Fla.St.	27	$156\frac{1}{3}$	10	10	.500	105	47	178	4.09	0
1998	West Tenn	Southern	13	$81\frac{1}{3}$	8	2	.800	73	21	70	2.77	0
1998	Iowa	P.C.	18	$102\frac{2}{3}$	5	9	.357	79	36	129	6.93	0
1999	Iowa	P.C.	6	$39\frac{1}{3}$	2	2	.500	29	9	38	3.20	0
1999	Chicago	N.L.	27	130	5	9	.357	70	52	140	5.05	0
2000	Chicago	N.L.	46	77	2	9	.182	74	50	90	6.43	1
2000	Iowa	P.C.	22	$25\frac{1}{3}$	0	2	.000	22	18	24	3.20	9
2001	Chicago	N.L.	76	82	4	6	.400	107	29	65	2.74	2
2002	Iowa	P.C.	2	3	0	1	.000	2	0	3	6.00	0
2002	Chicago a	N.L.	45	$46\frac{2}{3}$	4	6	.400	46	24	53	7.33	1
2003	Chicago	N.L.	77	$76\frac{1}{3}$	3	2	.600	92	36	53	3.30	0
2004	Chicago b	N.L.	72	$66\frac{2}{3}$	4	5	.444	78	33	67	4.72	0
2005	Detroit	A.L.	46	$42\frac{2}{3}$	1	1	.500	55	20	29	2.32	6
2005	Atlanta c-d-e	N.L.	26	$27\frac{1}{3}$	0	0	.000	32	7	15	1.98	10
2006	New York	A.L.	72	66	3	6	.333	75	28	62	4.36	6
2007	New York	A.L.	64	60	2	1	.667	48	27	60	4.80	0
2008	New York-Detroit f-g	A.L.	61	$60\frac{1}{3}$	2	3	.400	61	22	70	4.48	1
2009	Omaha	P.C.	2	2	0	0	.000	2	0	0	0.00	0
2009	NW Arkansas	Texas	3	$3\frac{2}{3}$	0	0	.000	3	1	1	0.00	0
2009	Kansas City h	A.L.	41	$37\frac{1}{3}$	1	5	.167	42	14	43	4.58	0
2010	Kansas City	A.L.	37	$44\frac{2}{3}$	3	0	1.000	36	12	40	2.42	0
2010	Atlanta i-j	N.L.	23	20	0	2	.000	25	7	15	5.40	0
2011	Tampa Bay	A.L.	63	$57\frac{2}{3}$	5	1	.833	51	12	45	2.18	25
2012	Charlotte	Fla.St.	4	4	0	0	.000	2	0	3	2.25	0
2012	Durham	Int.	2	2	0	0	.000	4	0	2	0.00	0
2012	Tampa Bay k-l	A.L.	34	27	1	6	.143	25	14	22	4.00	0
2013	Indianapolis	Int.	6	$6\frac{2}{3}$	1	1	.500	3	4	7	4.05	0
2013	Tampa Bay	A.L.	39	$29\frac{2}{3}$	2	0	1.000	19	7	37	5.76	0
2013	Pittsburgh m-n	N.L.	9	$8\frac{2}{3}$	1	1	.500	9	3	6	1.04	2
Major League Totals		15 Yrs.	858	960	43	63	.406	945	397	912	4.26	54
	Division Series											
2003	Chicago	N.L.	3	$2\frac{2}{3}$	0	0	.000	2	1	1	0.00	0
2005	Atlanta	N.L.	2	3	0	0	.000	4	1	2	9.00	0
2006	New York	A.L.	2	2	0	0	.000	1	1	1	0.00	0
2007	New York	A.L.	1	1	0	0	.000	2	0	1	0.00	0
2010	Atlanta	N.L.	2	2	1	0	1.000	1	1	1	0.00	0
Division Series Totals			10	$10\frac{2}{3}$	1	0	1.000	10	4	6	2.53	0
	Championship Series											
2003	Chicago	N.L.	5	$5\frac{1}{3}$	0	0	.000	7	2	6	10.13	0

a On disabled list from April 10 to June 4, 2002.
b On disabled list from August 28 to September 12, 2004.
c Traded to Detroit Tigers for pitcher Roberto Novoa, infielder Scott Moore and outfielder Clarence Flowers, February 9, 2005.
d Traded to Atlanta Braves for pitcher Roman Colon and pitcher Zach Miner, July 26, 2005.
e Filed for free agency, October 31, 2005. Signed with New York Yankees, December 5, 2005.
f Traded to Detroit Tigers for catcher Ivan Rodriguez, July 30, 2008.
g Filed for free agency, November 3, 2008. Signed with Kansas City Royals, December 13, 2008.
h On disabled list from June 25 to August 18, 2009.
i Traded to Atlanta Braves with outfielder Rick Ankiel and cash for outfielder Gregor Blanco, pitcher Jesse Chavez and pitcher Tim Collins, July 31, 2010.
j Filed for free agency, November 1, 2010. Signed with Tampa Bay Rays, January 15, 2011.
k On disabled list from April 1 to June 30, 2012.
l Filed for free agency, November 3, 2012, re-signed with Tampa Bay Rays, February 5, 2013.
m Filed for free agency, August 10, 2013. Signed with Pittsburgh Pirates organization, August 16, 2013.
n Filed for free agency, October 31, 2013.

FARQUHAR, DANIEL ANDRES (DANNY)

Born, Pembroke Pines, Florida, February 17, 1987.
Bats Right. Throws Right. Height, 5 feet, 11 inches. Weight, 180 pounds.

Year	Club	Lea	G	IP	W	L	Pct	SO	BB	H	ERA	SAVES
2008	Auburn	N.Y.-Penn.	12	26⅓	2	2	.500	27	6	20	2.39	0
2008	Lansing	Midwest	3	6	0	0	.000	4	2	0	0.00	0
2009	Dunedin	Fla.St.	17	17	1	0	1.000	23	11	10	0.53	7
2009	New Hampshire	Eastern	37	45⅔	1	4	.200	51	30	31	2.36	15
2010	New Hampshire a	Eastern	53	76⅔	4	3	.571	79	42	50	3.52	17
2011	Sacramento	P.C.	4	8	0	0	.000	9	3	7	0.00	1
2011	Las Vegas b	P.C.	50	51⅔	4	5	.444	43	18	63	4.70	14
2011	Toronto	A.L.	3	2	0	0	.000	1	2	4	13.50	0
2012	New Hampshire	Eastern	20	30⅓	0	1	.000	33	10	28	2.97	1
2012	Sacramento c	P.C.	5	8	1	2	.333	6	6	10	10.13	0
2012	Trenton d	Eastern	6	11	1	0	1.000	14	0	2	0.00	4
2012	Scranton/WB	Int.	1	2	0	0	.000	1	0	0	0.00	0
2012	Tacoma e	P.C.	12	16⅔	1	0	1.000	16	5	9	0.54	4
2013	Tacoma	P.C.	15	20	0	1	.000	30	4	17	2.25	6
2013	Seattle	A.L.	46	55⅔	0	3	.000	79	22	44	4.20	16
Major League Totals		2 Yrs.	49	57⅔	0	3	.000	80	24	48	4.53	16

a Traded by Toronto Blue Jays to Oakland Athletics with pitcher Trystan Magnuson for outfielder Rajai Davis, November 17, 2010.
b Traded to Toronto Blue Jays for pitcher David Purcey, April 18, 2011.
c Claimed on waivers by Oakland Athletics, June 9, 2012.
d Claimed on waivers by New York Yankees, June 26, 2012.
e Traded to Seattle Mariners with pitcher D.J. Mitchell for outfielder Ichiro Suzuki and cash, July 23, 2012.

FELDMAN, SCOTT WAYNE

Born, Kailua, Hawaii, February 7, 1983.
Bats Left. Throws Right. Height, 6 feet, 5 inches. Weight, 210 pounds.

Year	Club	Lea	G	IP	W	L	Pct	SO	BB	H	ERA	SAVES
2003	Rangers	Arizona	3	6⅓	1	1	.500	7	1	4	4.26	0
2004	Rangers	Arizona	4	7	0	0	.000	5	1	2	0.00	0
2005	Bakersfield	Calif.	6	9	0	0	.000	11	2	5	0.00	3
2005	Frisco	Texas	46	61	1	2	.333	41	23	43	2.36	14
2005	Texas	A.L.	8	9⅓	0	1	.000	4	2	9	0.96	0
2006	Oklahoma	P.C.	23	27⅓	2	2	.500	24	9	20	1.98	4
2006	Texas	A.L.	36	41⅓	0	2	.000	30	10	42	3.92	0
2007	Oklahoma	P.C.	21	30	1	1	.500	24	12	28	4.50	2
2007	Texas	A.L.	29	39	1	2	.333	19	32	44	5.77	0
2008	Frisco	Texas	2	12⅔	2	0	1.000	4	2	11	4.26	0
2008	Texas	A.L.	28	151⅓	6	8	.429	74	56	161	5.29	0
2009	Texas	A.L.	34	189⅔	17	8	.680	113	65	178	4.08	0
2010	Oklahoma	P.C.	1	4	0	0	.000	3	0	5	4.50	0
2010	Texas a	A.L.	29	141⅓	7	11	.389	75	45	181	5.48	0
2011	Frisco	Texas	2	9	1	0	1.000	8	2	5	3.00	0
2011	Round Rock	P.C.	8	40⅔	2	1	.667	24	9	48	4.43	0
2011	Texas b	A.L.	11	32	2	1	.667	22	10	25	3.94	0
2012	Texas c	A.L.	29	123⅔	6	11	.353	96	32	139	5.09	0
2013	Chicago	N.L.	15	91	7	6	.538	67	25	79	3.46	0
2013	Baltimore d-e	A.L.	15	90⅔	5	6	.455	65	31	80	4.27	0
Major League Totals		9 Yrs.	234	909⅓	51	56	.477	565	308	938	4.62	0
	Division Series											
2011	Texas	A.L.	1	3	0	0	.000	4	0	2	0.00	0
	Championship Series											
2011	Texas	A.L.	3	5⅔	1	0	1.000	5	0	1	0.00	0
	World Series Record											
2011	Texas	A.L.	5	5	0	0	.000	2	6	5	9.00	0

a On disabled list from August 22 to September 7, 2010.
b On disabled list from March 22 to July 14, 2011.
c Filed for free agency, November 3, 2012. Signed with Chicago Cubs, November 27, 2012.
d Traded to Baltimore Orioles with catcher Steve Clevenger for pitcher Jake Arrieta and pitcher Pedro Strop, July 2, 2013.
e Filed for free agency, October 31, 2013. Signed with Houston Astros, December 6, 2013.

FELIZ (ANTONIO), NEFTALI

Born, Azua, Dominican Republic, May 2, 1988.
Bats Right. Throws Right. Height, 6 feet, 3 inches. Weight, 225 pounds.

Year	Club	Lea	G	IP	W	L	Pct	SO	BB	H	ERA	SAVES
2006	Braves	Gulf Coast	11	29	0	2	.000	42	14	20	4.03	2
2007	Danville	Appal.	8	27 1/3	2	0	1.000	28	12	18	1.98	0
2007	Spokane a	Northwest	8	15	0	2	.000	27	12	13	3.60	0
2008	Clinton	Midwest	17	82	6	3	.667	106	28	55	2.52	0
2008	Frisco	Texas	10	45 1/3	4	3	.571	47	23	34	2.98	0
2009	Oklahoma	P.C.	25	77 1/3	4	6	.400	75	30	69	3.49	0
2009	Texas	A.L.	20	31	1	0	1.000	39	8	13	1.74	2
2010	Texas b	A.L.	70	69 1/3	4	3	.571	71	18	43	2.73	40
2011	Frisco	Texas	1	1	0	0	.000	3	0	1	0.00	0
2011	Texas	A.L.	64	62 1/3	2	3	.400	54	30	42	2.74	32
2012	Texas c	A.L.	8	42 2/3	3	1	.750	37	23	28	3.16	0
2012	Frisco	Texas	1	2	0	1	.000	4	2	1	0.00	0
2012	Round Rock	P.C.	2	4 2/3	0	1	.000	4	3	4	1.93	0
2013	Rangers	Arizona	2	2	0	0	.000	4	2	1	0.00	0
2013	Round Rock	P.C.	6	8 2/3	0	0	.000	9	2	4	0.00	0
2013	Texas d	A.L.	6	4 2/3	0	0	.000	4	2	5	0.00	0
Major League Totals		5 Yrs.	168	210	10	7	.588	205	81	131	2.61	74
	Division Series											
2010	Texas	A.L.	2	1 1/3	0	0	.000	2	3	2	6.75	0
2011	Texas	A.L.	3	3 1/3	0	0	.000	2	2	2	2.70	3
Division Series Totals			5	4 2/3	0	0	.000	4	5	4	3.86	3
	Championship Series											
2010	Texas	A.L.	3	3	0	0	.000	5	2	0	0.00	0
2011	Texas	A.L.	4	4 1/3	0	0	.000	3	2	1	0.00	1
Championship Series Totals			7	7 1/3	0	0	.000	8	4	1	0.00	1
	World Series Record											
2010	Texas	A.L.	2	3	0	0	.000	4	0	1	0.00	1
2011	Texas	A.L.	4	3 2/3	0	0	.000	7	4	2	4.91	2
World Series Totals			6	6 2/3	0	0	.000	11	4	3	2.70	3

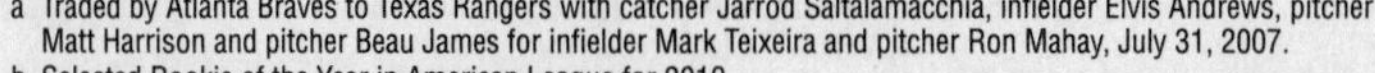

a Traded by Atlanta Braves to Texas Rangers with catcher Jarrod Saltalamacchia, infielder Elvis Andrews, pitcher Matt Harrison and pitcher Beau James for infielder Mark Teixeira and pitcher Ron Mahay, July 31, 2007.
b Selected Rookie of the Year in American League for 2010.
c On disabled list from May 19 to October 31, 2012.
d On disabled list from March 24 to September 1, 2013.

FERNANDEZ, JOSE

Born, Santa Clara, Cuba, July 31, 1992.
Bats Right. Throws Right. Height, 6 feet, 2 inches. Weight, 240 pounds.

Year	Club	Lea	G	IP	W	L	Pct	SO	BB	H	ERA	SAVES
2011	Marlins	Gulf Coast	1	2	0	0	.000	3	1	1	0.00	0
2011	Jamestown	N.Y.-Penn.	1	2 1/3	0	1	.000	4	3	4	19.29	0
2012	Greensboro	So.Atl.	14	79	7	0	1.000	99	18	51	1.59	0
2012	Jupiter	Fla.St.	11	55	7	1	.875	59	17	38	1.96	0
2013	Miami a	N.L.	28	172 2/3	12	6	.667	187	58	111	2.19	0

a Selected Rookie of the Year in National League for 2013.

FIEN, CASEY MICHAEL

Born, Santa Rosa, California, October 21, 1983.
Bats Right. Throws Right. Height, 6 feet, 2 inches. Weight, 195 pounds.

Year	Club	Lea	G	IP	W	L	Pct	SO	BB	H	ERA	SAVES
2006	Oneonta	N.Y.-Penn.	20	42 2/3	1	1	.500	37	8	39	2.74	1
2007	West Michigan	Midwest	39	61	6	1	.857	77	10	55	3.10	6
2008	Erie	Eastern	40	45 2/3	3	3	.500	42	12	38	2.96	12
2008	Toledo	Int.	12	15	2	0	1.000	17	4	14	2.40	1
2009	Toledo	Int.	42	58	2	1	.667	66	15	51	3.41	14
2009	Detroit	A.L.	9	11 1/3	0	1	.000	9	6	13	7.94	0
2010	Toledo	Int.	44	62 1/3	3	3	.500	44	13	54	2.60	8
2010	Detroit a-b-c-d	A.L.	2	2 2/3	0	0	.000	0	0	4	10.13	0
2011	Astros	Gulf Coast	2	2	1	0	1.000	3	0	1	0.00	0
2011	Oklahoma e	P.C.	21	24 1/3	2	2	.500	24	8	28	4.81	3
2012	Rochester	Int.	33	46	2	5	.286	42	14	39	4.30	9
2012	Minnesota	A.L.	35	35	2	1	.667	32	9	25	2.06	0
2013	Minnesota	A.L.	73	62	5	2	.714	73	12	51	3.92	0
Major League Totals		4 Yrs.	119	111	7	4	.636	114	27	93	3.89	0

a Claimed on waivers by Boston Red Sox, March 1, 2010.
b Claimed on waivers by Toronto Blue Jays, March 4, 2010.
c Released by Blue Jays, March 17, 2010. Signed with Detroit Tigers organization, March 19, 2010.
d Filed for free agency, October 5, 2010. Signed with Houston Astros organization, November 5, 2010.
e Released by Houston Astros, August 2, 2011. Signed with Minnesota Twins organization, January 3, 2012.

FIGARO (FIGARO), ALFREDO

Born, Samana, Dominican Republic, July 7, 1984.
Bats Right. Throws Right. Height, 6 feet. Weight, 175 pounds.

Year Club	Lea	G	IP	W	L	Pct	SO	BB	H	ERA	SAVES
2006 Tigers a	Gulf Coast	14	$38^{1}/_{3}$	3	1	.750	31	12	29	0.70	1
2007 Oneonta	N.Y.-Penn.	11	$53^{1}/_{3}$	4	2	.667	40	16	56	3.38	0
2007 Lakeland	Fla.St.	5	$22^{2}/_{3}$	0	2	.000	6	6	26	4.76	0
2008 West Michigan	Midwest	19	123	12	2	.857	96	30	99	2.05	0
2008 Lakeland	Fla.St.	6	$29^{1}/_{3}$	0	5	.000	23	12	37	4.91	0
2009 Erie	Eastern	16	80	6	3	.667	69	23	67	3.60	0
2009 Detroit b	A.L.	5	17	2	2	.500	16	10	23	6.35	0
2010 Toledo	Int.	23	124	10	6	.625	112	39	142	4.14	0
2010 Detroit c-d	A.L.	8	$14^{2}/_{3}$	0	2	.000	5	8	18	6.75	0
2011 Orix	Japan Pac.	24	$123^{2}/_{3}$	8	6	.571	90	36	126	3.42	0
2012 Orix	Japan Pac.	11	64	0	5	.000	37	19	64	3.09	0
2013 Brewers e	Arizona	1	$2^{1}/_{3}$	0	0	.000	4	0	1	0.00	0
2013 Nashville	P.C.	3	13	1	0	1.000	8	9	14	2.77	0
2013 Milwaukee f	N.L.	33	74	3	3	.500	54	15	77	4.14	1
Major League Totals	3 Yrs.	46	$105^{2}/_{3}$	5	7	.417	75	33	118	4.85	1

a Released by Los Angeles Dodgers, October 11, 2004. Signed with Detroit Tigers organization, March 7, 2005.
b On disabled list from June 28 to September 16, 2009.
c Released by Detroit Tigers, December 14, 2010.
d Signed with Orix (Japan), December 14, 2010.
e Signed with Milwaukee Brewers organization, January 31, 2013.
f On disabled list from June 24 to July 24, 2013.

FISTER, DOUGLAS WILDES (DOUG)

Born, Merced, California, February 4, 1984.
Bats Left. Throws Right. Height, 6 feet, 8 inches. Weight, 200 pounds.

Year Club	Lea	G	IP	W	L	Pct	SO	BB	H	ERA	SAVES
2006 Everett	Northwest	20	40	3	5	.375	35	11	35	2.25	4
2007 West Tenn	Southern	24	131	7	8	.467	85	32	156	4.60	0
2008 West Tenn	Southern	31	$134^{1}/_{3}$	6	14	.300	104	45	155	5.43	0
2009 West Tenn	Southern	2	$5^{2}/_{3}$	1	0	1.000	5	1	2	0.00	0
2009 Tacoma	P.C.	22	$106^{1}/_{3}$	6	4	.600	79	11	132	3.81	0
2009 Seattle	A.L.	11	61	3	4	.429	36	15	63	4.13	0
2010 Tacoma	P.C.	1	4	0	0	.000	3	0	4	4.50	0
2010 Seattle a	A.L.	28	171	6	14	.300	93	32	187	4.11	0
2011 Seattle-Detroit b	A.L.	32	$216^{1}/_{3}$	11	13	.458	146	37	193	2.83	0
2012 Toledo	Int.	1	4	0	0	.000	5	1	2	0.00	0
2012 Detroit c	A.L.	26	$161^{2}/_{3}$	10	10	.500	137	37	156	3.45	0
2013 Detroit d	A.L.	33	$208^{2}/_{3}$	14	9	.609	159	44	229	3.67	0
Major League Totals	5 Yrs.	130	$818^{2}/_{3}$	44	50	.468	571	165	828	3.53	0
Division Series											
2011 Detroit	A.L.	2	$9^{2}/_{3}$	1	1	.500	10	4	12	6.52	0
2012 Detroit	A.L.	1	7	0	0	.000	8	2	6	2.57	0
2013 Detroit	A.L.	1	6	0	0	.000	1	1	7	4.50	0
Division Series Totals		4	$22^{2}/_{3}$	1	1	.500	19	7	25	4.76	0
Championship Series											
2011 Detroit	A.L.	1	$7^{1}/_{3}$	1	0	1.000	3	0	7	2.45	0
2012 Detroit	A.L.	1	$6^{1}/_{3}$	0	0	.000	5	4	6	0.00	0
2013 Detroit	A.L.	1	6	1	0	1.000	7	1	8	1.50	0
Championship Series Totals		3	$19^{2}/_{3}$	2	0	1.000	15	5	21	1.37	0
World Series Record											
2012 Detroit	A.L.	1	6	0	1	.000	3	1	4	1.50	0

a On disabled list from June 1 to June 25, 2010.
b Traded to Detroit Tigers with pitcher David Pauley for pitcher Charlie Furbush, outfielder Casper Wells, infielder Francisco Martinez and player to be named later, July 30, 2011. Seattle Mariners received pitcher Chance Ruffin to complete trade, August 17, 2011.
c On disabled list from April 8 to May 7 and May 29 to June 16, 2012.
d Traded to Washington Nationals for pitcher Ian Krol, infielder Steve Lombardozzi and pitcher Robbie Ray, December 2, 2013.

FLOYD, GAVIN CHRISTOPHER

Born, Annapolis, Maryland, January 27, 1983.
Bats Right. Throws Right. Height, 6 feet, 4 inches. Weight, 230 pounds.

Year Club	Lea	G	IP	W	L	Pct	SO	BB	H	ERA	SAVES
2002 Lakewood	So.Atl.	27	166	11	10	.524	140	64	119	2.77	0
2003 Clearwater	Fla.St.	24	138	7	8	.467	115	45	128	3.00	0
2004 Reading	Eastern	20	119	6	6	.500	94	46	93	2.57	0
2004 Scranton-WB	Int.	5	30 2/3	1	3	.250	18	9	39	4.99	0
2004 Philadelphia	N.L.	6	28 1/3	2	0	1.000	24	16	25	3.49	0
2005 Scranton-WB	Int.	24	137 1/3	6	9	.400	97	66	155	6.16	0
2005 Philadelphia	N.L.	7	26	1	2	.333	17	16	30	10.04	0
2006 Philadelphia	N.L.	11	54 1/3	4	3	.571	34	32	70	7.29	0
2006 Scranton-WB a	Int.	17	115	7	4	.636	85	38	117	4.23	0
2007 Charlotte	Int.	17	106 2/3	7	3	.700	96	35	93	3.12	0
2007 Chicago	A.L.	16	70	1	5	.167	49	19	85	5.27	0
2008 Chicago	A.L.	33	206 1/3	17	8	.680	145	70	190	3.84	0
2009 Chicago	A.L.	30	193	11	11	.500	163	59	178	4.06	0
2010 Chicago	A.L.	31	187 1/3	10	13	.435	151	58	199	4.08	0
2011 Chicago	A.L.	31	193 2/3	12	13	.480	151	45	180	4.37	0
2012 Chicago b	A.L.	29	168	12	11	.522	144	63	166	4.29	0
2013 Chicago c-d	A.L.	5	24 1/3	0	4	.000	25	12	27	5.18	0
Major League Totals	10 Yrs.	199	1151 1/3	70	70	.500	903	390	1150	4.48	0
Division Series											
2008 Chicago	A.L.	1	3	0	1	.000	4	2	5	12.00	0

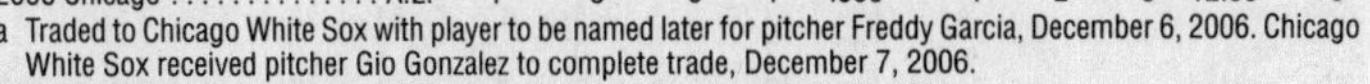

a Traded to Chicago White Sox with player to be named later for pitcher Freddy Garcia, December 6, 2006. Chicago White Sox received pitcher Gio Gonzalez to complete trade, December 7, 2006.
b On disabled list from July 8 to July 23 and August 27 to September 12, 2012.
c On disabled list from April 28 to October 24, 2013.
d Filed for free agency, October 31, 2013. Signed with Atlanta Braves, December 16, 2013.

FRANCIS, JEFFREY WILLIAM (JEFF)

Born, Vancouver, British Columbia, Canada, January 8, 1981.
Bats Left. Throws Left. Height, 6 feet, 5 inches. Weight, 220 pounds.

Year Club	Lea	G	IP	W	L	Pct	SO	BB	H	ERA	SAVES
2002 Tri-City	Northwest	4	10 2/3	0	0	.000	16	4	5	0.00	0
2002 Asheville	So.Atl.	4	20	0	0	.000	23	4	16	1.80	0
2003 Visalia	Calif.	27	160 2/3	12	9	.571	153	45	135	3.47	0
2004 Tulsa	Texas	17	113 2/3	13	1	.929	147	22	73	1.98	0
2004 Colorado Springs	P.C.	7	41	3	2	.600	49	7	35	2.85	0
2004 Colorado	N.L.	7	36 2/3	3	2	.600	32	13	42	5.15	0
2005 Colorado	N.L.	33	183 2/3	14	12	.538	128	70	228	5.68	0
2006 Colorado	N.L.	32	199	13	11	.542	117	69	187	4.16	0
2007 Colorado	N.L.	34	215 1/3	17	9	.654	165	63	234	4.22	0
2008 Tulsa	Texas	3	14 1/3	1	0	1.000	19	2	12	0.63	0
2008 Colorado a	N.L.	24	143 2/3	4	10	.286	94	49	164	5.01	0
2009 Colorado b	N.L.			INJURED—Did Not Play							
2010 Tulsa	Texas	2	11 2/3	0	0	.000	5	2	11	1.54	0
2010 Colorado Springs	P.C.	1	3	0	0	.000	3	1	1	0.00	0
2010 Colorado c-d	N.L.	20	104 1/3	4	6	.400	67	23	119	5.00	0
2011 Kansas City e	A.L.	31	183	6	16	.273	91	39	224	4.82	0
2012 Louisville	Int.	12	77 1/3	3	6	.333	65	18	84	3.72	0
2012 Colorado f-g	N.L.	24	113	6	7	.462	76	22	145	5.58	0
2013 Colorado Springs	P.C.	11	37 1/3	2	2	.500	33	9	42	4.34	0
2013 Colorado h-i	N.L.	23	70 1/3	3	5	.375	63	24	89	6.27	0
Major League Totals	9 Yrs.	228	1249	70	78	.473	833	372	1432	4.94	0
Division Series											
2007 Colorado	N.L.	1	6	1	0	1.000	8	2	4	3.00	0
Championship Series											
2007 Colorado	N.L.	1	6 2/3	1	0	1.000	4	1	7	1.35	0
World Series Record											
2007 Colorado	N.L.	1	4	0	1	.000	3	3	10	13.50	0

a On disabled list from June 29 to August 6, 2008.
b On disabled list from March 27 to November 13, 2009.
c On disabled list from April 2 to May 16 and August 12 to September 7, 2010.
d Filed for free agency, November 3, 2010. Signed with Kansas City Royals, January 14, 2011.
e Filed for free agency, October 30, 2011. Signed with Cincinnati Reds organization, February 8, 2012.
f Released by Cincinnati Reds, June 4, 2012. Signed with Colorado Rockies, June 9, 2012.
g Filed for free agency, November 3, 2012, re-signed with Colorado Rockies, December 19, 2012.
h On disabled list from May 15 to June 8, 2013.
i Filed for free agency, October 31, 2013. Signed with Cincinnati Reds organization, January 13, 2014.

FRANCISCO, FRANKLIN (FRANK)

Born, Santo Domingo, Dominican Republic, September 11, 1979.
Bats Right. Throws Right. Height, 6 feet, 2 inches. Weight, 235 pounds.

Year	Club	Lea	G	IP	W	L	Pct	SO	BB	H	ERA	SAVES
1997					INJURED—Did Not Play							
1998	Co-op	Dominican	16	48	0	5	.000	53	76	44	10.31	0
1999	Red Sox	Gulf Coast	12	53 1/3	2	4	.333	48	35	58	4.56	0
2000	Red Sox	Gulf Coast	1	1	0	0	.000	1	2	2	18.00	0
2001	Augusta	So.Atl.	37	68	4	3	.571	90	30	40	2.91	2
2002	Winston-Salem	Carolina	6	25 2/3	0	4	.000	25	18	31	8.06	0
2002	Trenton	Eastern	9	16	2	2	.500	18	16	10	5.63	0
2002	Sarasota a	Fla.St.	16	53	1	5	.167	58	27	33	2.55	0
2003	Winston-Salem	Carolina	16	78 1/3	7	3	.700	67	36	59	3.56	0
2003	Frisco b	Texas	7	35 1/3	2	3	.400	22	18	43	8.41	0
2004	Frisco	Texas	15	17 2/3	1	3	.250	30	10	7	2.55	6
2004	Texas	A.L.	45	51 1/3	5	1	.833	60	28	36	3.33	0
2005	Oklahoma	P.C.	2	3	0	0	.000	4	2	2	3.00	1
2005	Frisco c	Texas	4	3 1/3	0	1	.000	3	2	4	8.10	0
2006	Frisco	Texas	13	14 2/3	0	0	.000	22	4	10	1.84	0
2006	Spokane	Northwest	4	4	0	0	.000	6	0	3	0.00	0
2006	Texas d	A.L.	8	7 1/3	0	1	.000	6	2	8	4.91	0
2007	Oklahoma	P.C.	5	6	1	0	1.000	14	3	0	0.00	2
2007	Texas	A.L.	59	59 1/3	1	1	.500	49	38	57	4.55	0
2008	Oklahoma	P.C.	8	9	0	0	.000	16	3	3	0.00	5
2008	Texas	A.L.	58	63 1/3	3	5	.375	83	26	47	3.13	5
2009	Frisco	Texas	2	2	0	0	.000	1	0	1	0.00	0
2009	Texas e	A.L.	51	49 1/3	2	3	.400	57	15	40	3.83	25
2010	Texas f-g	A.L.	56	52 2/3	6	4	.600	60	18	49	3.76	2
2011	Dunedin	Fla.St.	5	5	0	1	.000	6	4	6	10.80	0
2011	Toronto h-i-j	A.L.	54	50 2/3	1	4	.200	53	18	49	3.55	17
2012	Binghamton	Eastern	5	4 2/3	0	0	.000	4	1	6	3.86	1
2012	New York k	N.L.	48	42 1/3	1	3	.250	47	21	47	5.53	23
2013	Mets	Gulf Coast	5	5	0	2	.000	7	0	5	1.80	0
2013	St. Lucie	Fla.St.	5	5	0	0	.000	6	2	1	0.00	0
2013	Binghamton	Eastern	2	2	0	0	.000	1	1	2	0.00	0
2013	New York l-m	N.L.	8	6 1/3	1	0	1.000	6	3	4	4.26	1
Major League Totals		9 Yrs.	387	382 2/3	20	22	.476	421	169	337	3.93	73

a Traded to Chicago White Sox by Boston Red Sox with pitcher Byeong An for pitcher Bob Howry, July 31, 2002.
b Sent to Texas Rangers as one of the players to be named later for outfielder Carl Everett, July 23, 2003.
c On disabled list from March 25 to October 12, 2005.
d On disabled list from March 24 to June 19, 2006.
e On disabled list from May 7 to May 22 and June 4 to June 20 and July 11 to August 2, 2009.
f On disabled list from August 28 to November 1, 2010.
g Filed for free agency, November 1, 2010, accepted arbitration to remain with Texas Rangers, November 30, 2010.
h Traded to Toronto Blue Jays for catcher Mike Napoli, January 25, 2011.
i On disabled list from March 22 to April 19, 2011.
j Filed for free agency, October 30, 2011. Signed with New York Mets, December 19, 2011.
k On disabled list from June 23 to August 3, 2012.
l On disabled list from March 22 to September 7, 2013.
m Filed for free agency, October 31, 2013.

FRASOR, JASON ANDREW

Born, Chicago, Illinois, August 9, 1977.
Bats Right. Throws Right. Height, 5 feet, 10 inches. Weight, 170 pounds.

Year	Club	Lea	G	IP	W	L	Pct	SO	BB	H	ERA	SAVES
1999	Oneonta	N.Y.-Penn.	12	58 2/3	3	3	.500	69	22	36	1.69	0
1999	West Michigan	Midwest	4	24	2	1	.667	33	9	17	2.63	0
2000	West Michigan	Midwest	14	71 1/3	5	3	.625	65	29	55	3.28	0
2001	West Michigan a	Midwest			INJURED—Did Not Play							
2002	Lakeland b	Fla.St.	24	117	5	6	.455	87	46	112	3.54	0
2003	Vero Beach	Fla.St.	15	24 1/3	1	0	1.000	36	4	16	1.85	6
2003	Jacksonville	Southern	35	36 2/3	1	0	1.000	50	14	33	2.95	17
2004	Syracuse	Int.	3	4	0	0	.000	6	5	1	2.25	0
2004	Toronto c	A.L.	63	68 1/3	4	6	.400	54	36	64	4.08	17
2005	Toronto	A.L.	67	74 2/3	3	5	.375	62	28	67	3.25	1
2006	Syracuse	Int.	18	20 1/3	3	1	.750	33	13	21	3.98	1
2006	Toronto	A.L.	51	50	3	2	.600	51	17	47	4.32	0
2007	Toronto	A.L.	51	57	1	5	.167	59	23	47	4.58	3
2008	Toronto	A.L.	49	47 1/3	1	2	.333	42	32	36	4.18	0
2009	Toronto	A.L.	61	57 2/3	7	3	.700	56	16	43	2.50	11

Year Club	Lea	G	IP	W	L	Pct	SO	BB	H	ERA	SAVES
2010 Toronto d	A.L.	69	63 2/3	3	4	.429	65	27	61	3.68	4
2011 Toronto-Chicago e-f	A.L.	64	60	3	3	.500	57	26	58	3.60	0
2012 Dunedin	Fla.St.	2	2	0	0	.000	4	0	0	0.00	0
2012 Toronto g-h	A.L.	50	43 2/3	1	1	.500	53	22	42	4.12	0
2013 Texas i	A.L.	61	49	4	3	.571	48	20	36	2.57	0
Major League Totals	10 Yrs.	586	571 1/3	30	34	.469	547	247	501	3.67	36

a On minor league disabled list, April 5 to September 14, 2001.
b Sent by Detroit Tigers to Los Angeles Dodgers as player to be named later for infielder Hiram Bocachica, September 18, 2002.
c Traded to Toronto Blue Jays for outfielder Jayson Werth, March 30, 2004.
d Filed for free agency, November 1, 2010, accepted arbitration to remain with Toronto Blue Jays, November 30, 2010.
e Traded to Chicago White Sox with pitcher Zach Stewart for pitcher Edwin Jackson and infielder Mark Teahen, July 27, 2011.
f Traded to Toronto Blue Jays for pitcher Daniel Webb and pitcher Myles Jaye, January 1, 2012.
g On disabled list from July 17 to September 3, 2012.
h Filed for free agency, November 3, 2012. Signed with Texas Rangers, January 3, 2013.
i Filed for free agency, October 31, 2013, re-signed with Texas Rangers, November 4, 2013.

FRIERI (GUTIERREZ), ERNESTO

Born, Bolivar, Colombia, July 19, 1985.
Bats Right. Throws Right. Height, 6 feet, 2 inches. Weight, 200 pounds.

Year Club	Lea	G	IP	W	L	Pct	SO	BB	H	ERA	SAVES
2005 Lake Elsinore	Calif.	2	3 1/3	0	0	.000	3	1	3	2.70	0
2005 Padres	Arizona	17	46 1/3	7	1	.875	59	29	21	1.17	0
2006 Fort Wayne	Midwest	1	1	0	0	.000	1	5	1	9.00	0
2006 Lake Elsinore	Calif.	2	6	0	0	.000	4	3	8	6.00	0
2006 Eugene	Northwest	27	37 2/3	3	3	.500	38	15	31	3.82	2
2007 Fort Wayne	Midwest	40	64 2/3	1	2	.333	65	23	48	2.64	0
2007 Lake Elsinore	Calif.	13	21 2/3	1	0	1.000	27	6	11	1.25	1
2008 Portland	P.C.	1	6	1	0	1.000	7	2	2	1.50	0
2008 Lake Elsinore	Calif.	33	123 2/3	8	6	.571	108	32	125	4.00	0
2008 San Antonio	Texas	2	11	1	0	1.000	10	2	7	4.09	0
2009 San Antonio	Texas	27	140 1/3	10	9	.526	118	62	125	3.59	0
2009 San Diego	N.L.	2	2	0	0	.000	2	1	0	0.00	0
2010 Portland	P.C.	34	37 2/3	3	1	.750	49	18	14	1.43	17
2010 San Diego	N.L.	33	31 2/3	1	1	.500	41	17	18	1.71	0
2011 Tucson	P.C.	4	3 1/3	1	0	1.000	5	2	3	2.70	0
2011 San Diego a	N.L.	59	63	1	2	.333	76	34	51	2.71	0
2012 San Diego	N.L.	11	11 2/3	1	0	1.000	18	4	9	2.31	0
2012 Los Angeles b	A.L.	56	54 1/3	4	2	.667	80	26	26	2.32	23
2013 Los Angeles	A.L.	67	68 2/3	2	4	.333	98	30	55	3.80	37
Major League Totals	5 Yrs.	228	231 1/3	9	9	.500	315	112	159	2.76	60

a On disabled list from August 8 to August 21, 2011.
b Traded to Los Angeles Angels for infielder Alexi Amarista and pitcher Donn Roach, May 3, 2012.

FURBUSH, CHARLES RODERICK (CHARLIE)

Born, South Portland, Maine, April 11, 1986.
Bats Left. Throws Left. Height, 6 feet, 5 inches. Weight, 215 pounds.

Year Club	Lea	G	IP	W	L	Pct	SO	BB	H	ERA	SAVES
2007 Tigers	Gulf Coast	4	16	2	0	1.000	23	3	11	2.81	0
2007 West Michigan	Midwest	8	45 2/3	4	1	.800	46	11	40	2.17	0
2008 a				INJURED—Did Not Play							
2009 Lakeland	Fla.St.	24	111 1/3	6	7	.462	93	32	111	3.96	0
2010 Erie	Eastern	5	33 1/3	1	0	1.000	37	10	31	3.24	0
2010 Lakeland	Fla.St.	13	77	4	5	.444	109	14	68	3.39	0
2010 Toledo	Int.	9	48 2/3	3	4	.429	37	16	59	6.29	0
2011 Toledo	Int.	10	54	5	3	.625	61	16	35	3.17	0
2011 Detroit-Seattle b	A.L.	28	85 1/3	4	10	.286	67	30	97	5.48	0
2012 Tacoma	P.C.	7	10	1	0	1.000	13	3	7	3.60	0
2012 Seattle c	A.L.	48	46 1/3	5	2	.714	53	16	28	2.72	0
2013 Seattle	A.L.	71	65	2	6	.250	80	29	48	3.74	0
Major League Totals	3 Yrs.	147	196 2/3	11	18	.379	200	75	173	4.26	0

a On minor league disabled list from April 3 to September 8, 2008.
b Traded to Seattle Mariners with outfielder Casper Wells, infielder Francisco Martinez and player to be named later for pitcher Doug Fister and pitcher David Pauley, July 30, 2011. Seattle Mariners received pitcher Chance Ruffin to complete trade, August 17, 2011.
c On disabled list from July 18 to August 17, 2012.

GALLARDO, YOVANI

Born, La Piedad, Mexico, February 27, 1986.
Bats Right. Throws Right. Height, 6 feet, 1 inch. Weight, 210 pounds.

Year	Club	Lea	G	IP	W	L	Pct	SO	BB	H	ERA	SAVES
2004	Brewers	Arizona	6	19⅓	0	0	.000	23	4	14	0.47	0
2004	Beloit	Midwest	2	7⅓	0	1	.000	8	4	12	12.27	0
2005	West Virginia	So.Atl.	26	121⅓	8	3	.727	110	51	100	2.74	1
2006	Brevard County	Fla.St.	13	77⅔	6	3	.667	103	23	54	2.09	0
2006	Huntsville	Southern	13	77⅓	5	2	.714	85	28	50	1.63	0
2007	Nashville	P.C.	13	77⅔	8	3	.727	110	28	53	2.90	0
2007	Milwaukee	N.L.	20	110⅓	9	5	.643	101	37	103	3.67	0
2008	Nashville	P.C.	3	15⅔	0	1	.000	18	5	20	5.17	0
2008	Milwaukee a	N.L.	4	24	0	0	.000	20	8	22	1.88	0
2009	Milwaukee	N.L.	30	185⅔	13	12	.520	204	94	150	3.73	0
2010	Milwaukee b	N.L.	31	185	14	7	.667	200	75	178	3.84	0
2011	Milwaukee	N.L.	33	207⅓	17	10	.630	207	59	193	3.52	0
2012	Milwaukee	N.L.	33	204	16	9	.640	204	81	185	3.66	0
2013	Milwaukee c	N.L.	31	180⅔	12	10	.545	144	66	180	4.18	0
Major League Totals		7 Yrs.	182	1097	81	53	.604	1080	420	1011	3.72	0
	Division Series											
2008	Milwaukee	N.L.	2	7	0	1	.000	4	5	4	0.00	0
2011	Milwaukee	N.L.	2	14	1	0	1.000	14	3	10	1.29	0
Division Series Totals			4	21	1	1	.500	18	8	14	0.86	0
	Championship Series											
2011	Milwaukee	N.L.	1	5	0	1	.000	2	5	8	7.20	0

a On disabled list from March 21 to April 20 and May 2 to September 23, 2008.
b On disabled list from July 5 to July 22, 2010.
c On disabled list from July 31 to August 17, 2013.

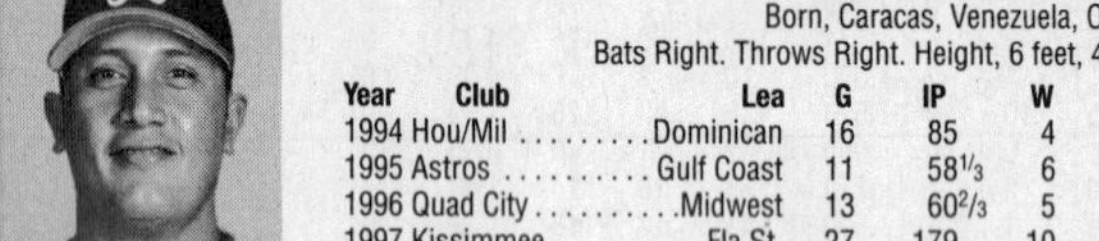

GARCIA, FREDDY ANTONIO

Born, Caracas, Venezuela, October 6, 1976.
Bats Right. Throws Right. Height, 6 feet, 4 inches. Weight, 250 pounds.

Year	Club	Lea	G	IP	W	L	Pct	SO	BB	H	ERA	SAVES
1994	Hou/Mil	Dominican	16	85	4	6	.400	68	38	80	5.29	0
1995	Astros	Gulf Coast	11	58⅓	6	3	.667	58	14	60	4.47	0
1996	Quad City	Midwest	13	60⅔	5	4	.556	50	27	57	3.12	0
1997	Kissimmee	Fla.St.	27	179	10	8	.556	131	49	165	2.56	0
1998	Jackson	Texas	19	119⅓	6	7	.462	115	58	94	3.24	0
1998	New Orleans	P.C.	2	14⅓	1	0	1.000	13	1	14	3.14	0
1998	Tacoma a	P.C.	5	32⅔	3	1	.750	30	13	30	3.86	0
1999	Seattle	A.L.	33	201⅓	17	8	.680	170	90	205	4.07	0
2000	Seattle	A.L.	21	124⅓	9	5	.643	79	64	112	3.91	0
2000	Everett	Northwest	2	10	0	0	.000	15	2	11	4.50	0
2000	Tacoma b	P.C.	1	7	1	0	1.000	11	2	5	2.57	0
2001	Seattle	A.L.	34	*238⅔	18	6	.750	163	69	199	*3.05	0
2002	Seattle	A.L.	34	223⅔	16	10	.615	181	63	227	4.39	0
2003	Seattle	A.L.	33	201⅓	12	14	.462	144	71	196	4.51	0
2004	Seattle-Chicago c	A.L.	31	210	13	11	.542	184	64	192	3.81	0
2005	Chicago	A.L.	33	228	14	8	.636	146	60	225	3.87	0
2006	Chicago d	A.L.	33	216⅓	17	9	.654	135	48	228	4.53	0
2007	Philadelphia	N.L.	11	58	1	5	.167	50	19	74	5.90	0
2007	Phillies	Gulf Coast	1	2	0	0	.000	2	0	2	4.50	0
2007	Clearwater e	Fla.St.	2	6⅓	0	0	.000	8	1	5	0.00	0
2008	Lakeland	Fla.St.	1	2	0	0	.000	1	1	3	0.00	0
2008	Toledo	Int.	1	3	0	0	.000	4	0	2	0.00	0
2008	Detroit f	A.L.	3	15	1	1	.500	12	6	11	4.20	0
2009	Buffalo	Int.	2	11	0	2	.000	6	5	12	8.18	0
2009	Kannapolis	So.Atl.	1	3	0	0	.000	3	1	2	0.00	0
2009	Bristol	Appal.	2	11	0	0	.000	7	0	6	1.64	0
2009	Charlotte	Int.	1	6	0	1	.000	9	0	8	3.00	0
2009	Chicago g-h	A.L.	9	56	3	4	.429	37	12	56	4.34	0
2010	Chicago i	A.L.	28	157	12	6	.667	89	45	171	4.64	0
2011	Scranton-WB	Int.	1	4	1	0	1.000	0	1	8	4.50	0
2011	New York j-k	A.L.	26	146⅔	12	8	.600	96	45	152	3.62	0
2012	New York l	A.L.	30	107⅓	7	6	.538	89	35	112	5.20	0
2013	Gwinnett m	Int.	1	3⅔	0	1	.000	1	5	7	19.64	0
2013	Norfolk	Int.	13	82⅓	8	3	.727	61	15	73	2.84	0
2013	Baltimore n	A.L.	11	53	3	5	.375	26	12	60	5.77	0
2013	Atlanta o-p	N.L.	6	27⅓	1	2	.333	20	5	23	1.65	0
Major League Totals		15 Yrs.	376	2264	156	108	.591	1621	708	2243	4.15	0

Year Club	Lea	G	IP	W	L	Pct	SO	BB	H	ERA	SAVES
Division Series											
2000 Seattle	A.L.	1	3 1/3	0	0	.000	2	3	6	10.80	0
2001 Seattle	A.L.	2	11 2/3	1	1	.500	13	3	13	3.86	0
2005 Chicago	A.L.	1	5	1	0	1.000	1	4	5	5.40	0
2011 New York	A.L.	1	5 1/3	0	1	.000	6	0	6	5.06	0
2013 Atlanta	N.L.	1	6	0	0	.000	6	2	8	3.00	0
Division Series Totals		6	31 1/3	2	2	.500	28	12	38	4.88	0
Championship Series											
2000 Seattle	A.L.	2	11 2/3	2	0	1.000	11	4	10	1.54	0
2001 Seattle	A.L.	1	7 1/3	0	1	.000	6	4	7	3.68	0
2005 Chicago	A.L.	1	9	1	0	1.000	5	1	6	2.00	0
Championship Series Totals		4	28	3	1	.750	22	9	23	2.25	0
World Series Record											
2005 Chicago	A.L.	1	7	1	0	1.000	7	3	4	0.00	0

a Traded by Houston Astros to Seattle Mariners with infielder Carlos Guillen and player to be named later for pitcher Randy Johnson, July 31, 1998. Seattle Mariners received pitcher John Halama to complete trade, October 1, 1998.
b On disabled list from April 22 to July 6, 2000.
c Traded to Chicago White Sox with catcher Ben Davis and cash for catcher Miguel Olivo, outfielder Jeremy Reed and infielder Michael Morse, June 27, 2004.
d Traded to Philadelphia Phillies for pitcher Gavin Floyd and player to be named later, December 6, 2006. Chicago White Sox received pitcher Gio Gonzalez to complete trade, December 7, 2006.
e On disabled list from March 23 to April 16 and June 9 to October 31, 2007.
f Filed for free agency, October 31, 2007. Signed with Detroit Tigers organization, August 12, 2008.
g Filed for free agency, October 30, 2008. Signed with New York Mets organization, January 22, 2009.
h Released by New York Mets, April 28, 2009. Signed with Chicago White Sox organization, June 9, 2009.
i Filed for free agency, November 1, 2010. Signed with New York Yankees organization, February 1, 2011.
j On disabled list from August 8 to August 29, 2011.
k Filed for free agency, October 30, 2011, re-signed with New York Yankees, December 9, 2011.
l Filed for free agency, November 3, 2012. Signed with San Diego Padres organization, January 28, 2013.
m Released by San Diego Padres, March 24, 2013. Signed with Baltimore Orioles organization, March 29, 2013.
n Filed for free agency, June 27, 2013, re-signed with Baltimore Orioles organization, June 27, 2013.
o Sold to Atlanta Braves, August 23, 2013.
p Filed for free agency, October 31, 2013.

GARCIA, JAIME OMAR

Born, Reynosa, Mexico, July 8, 1986.
Bats Left. Throws Left. Height, 6 feet, 2 inches. Weight, 215 pounds.

Year Club	Lea	G	IP	W	L	Pct	SO	BB	H	ERA	SAVES
2006 Palm Beach	Fla.St.	12	77 1/3	5	4	.556	51	16	84	3.84	0
2006 Quad Cities	Midwest	13	77 2/3	5	4	.556	80	18	67	2.90	0
2007 Springfield	Texas	18	103 1/3	5	9	.357	97	45	93	3.75	0
2008 Springfield	Texas	6	35	3	2	.600	41	16	26	2.06	0
2008 Memphis	P.C.	13	71	4	4	.500	59	26	74	4.44	0
2008 St. Louis a	N.L.	10	16	1	1	.500	8	8	14	5.63	0
2009 Palm Beach	Fla.St.	3	12 2/3	0	1	.000	16	4	4	0.71	0
2009 Cardinals	Gulf Coast	2	4	0	1	.000	3	1	4	4.50	0
2009 Memphis b	P.C.	4	21	2	0	1.000	22	9	17	3.86	0
2010 St. Louis	N.L.	28	163 1/3	13	8	.619	132	64	151	2.70	0
2011 St. Louis	N.L.	32	194 2/3	13	7	.650	156	50	207	3.56	0
2012 Cardinals	Gulf Coast	1	2 1/3	0	0	.000	1	0	4	0.00	0
2012 Springfield	Texas	2	10 1/3	1	0	1.000	11	0	8	5.23	0
2012 Memphis	P.C.	1	5	0	1	.000	8	3	4	3.60	0
2012 St. Louis c	N.L.	20	121 2/3	7	7	.500	98	30	136	3.92	0
2013 St. Louis d	N.L.	9	55 1/3	5	2	.714	43	15	57	3.58	0
Major League Totals	5 Yrs.	99	551	39	25	.609	437	167	565	3.45	0
Division Series											
2011 St. Louis	N.L.	1	7	0	1	.000	3	2	6	3.86	0
2012 St. Louis	N.L.	1	2	0	0	.000	3	3	2	4.50	0
Division Series Totals		2	9	0	1	.000	6	5	8	4.00	0
Championship Series											
2011 St. Louis	N.L.	2	8 2/3	0	1	.000	8	3	13	7.27	0
World Series Record											
2011 St. Louis	N.L.	2	10	0	0	.000	10	3	8	1.80	0

a On disabled list from August 27 to October 8, 2008.
b On disabled list from March 27 to August 20, 2009.
c On disabled list from June 6 to August 19, 2012.
d On disabled list from May 18 to November 1, 2013.

GARZA, MATTHEW SCOTT (MATT)

Born, Selma, California, November 11, 1983.
Bats Right. Throws Right. Height, 6 feet, 4 inches. Weight, 205 pounds.

Year Club	Lea	G	IP	W	L	Pct	SO	BB	H	ERA	SAVES
2005 Elizabethton	Appal.	4	$19\frac{2}{3}$	1	1	.500	25	6	14	3.66	0
2006 Fort Myers	Fla.St.	8	$44\frac{1}{3}$	5	1	.833	53	11	27	1.42	0
2006 New Britain	Eastern	10	$57\frac{1}{3}$	6	2	.750	68	14	40	2.51	0
2006 Rochester	Int.	5	34	3	1	.750	33	7	20	1.85	0
2006 Minnesota	A.L.	10	50	3	6	.333	38	23	62	5.76	0
2007 Rochester	Int.	16	92	4	6	.400	95	31	93	3.62	0
2007 Minnesota a	A.L.	16	83	5	7	.417	67	32	96	3.69	0
2008 Vero Beach	Fla.St.	1	$3\frac{2}{3}$	0	0	.000	4	3	8	9.82	0
2008 Tampa Bay b	A.L.	30	$184\frac{2}{3}$	11	9	.550	128	59	170	3.70	0
2009 Tampa Bay	A.L.	32	203	8	12	.400	189	79	177	3.95	0
2010 Tampa Bay c-d	A.L.	33	$204\frac{2}{3}$	15	10	.600	150	63	193	3.91	1
2011 Chicago e	N.L.	31	198	10	10	.500	197	63	186	3.32	0
2012 Chicago f	N.L.	18	$103\frac{2}{3}$	5	7	.417	96	32	90	3.91	0
2013 Tennessee	Southern	2	6	0	1	.000	2	4	4	1.50	0
2013 Iowa	P.C.	2	$9\frac{1}{3}$	1	0	1.000	9	0	6	0.96	0
2013 Chicago g	N.L.	11	71	6	1	.857	62	20	61	3.17	0
2013 Texas h-i	A.L.	13	$84\frac{1}{3}$	4	5	.444	74	22	89	4.38	0
Major League Totals	8 Yrs.	194	$1182\frac{1}{3}$	67	67	.500	1001	393	1124	3.84	1
Division Series											
2008 Tampa Bay	A.L.	1	6	0	1	.000	4	4	7	7.50	0
2010 Tampa Bay	A.L.	1	6	0	0	.000	4	2	5	1.50	0
Division Series Totals		2	12	0	1	.000	8	6	12	4.50	0
Championship Series											
2008 Tampa Bay	A.L.	2	13	2	0	1.000	14	6	8	1.38	0
World Series Record											
2008 Tampa Bay	A.L.	1	6	0	0	.000	7	2	6	6.00	0

a Traded to Tampa Bay Devil Rays with infielder Jason Bartlett and pitcher Eduardo Morlan for infielder Brendan Harris, outfielder Jason Pridie and outfielder Delmon Young, November 28, 2007.
b On disabled list from April 9 to April 25, 2008.
c Pitched no-hit, no-run game against Detroit Tigers, July 26, 2010.
d Traded to Chicago Cubs with outfielder Fernando Perez and pitcher Zachary Rosscup for infielder Hak-Ju Lee, outfielder Brandon Guyer, pitcher Chris Archer, catcher Robinson Chirinos and outfielder Sam Fuld, January 8, 2011.
e On disabled list from May 24 to June 6, 2011.
f On disabled list from July 28 to November 2, 2012.
g On disabled list from March 22 to May 21, 2013.
h Traded to Texas Rangers for pitcher J.C. Edwards, pitcher Justin Grimm, infielder Mike Olt and player to be named later, July 22, 2013. Chicago Cubs received pitcher Neil Ramirez to complete trade, August 23, 2013.
i Filed for free agency, October 31, 2013.

GAUDIN, CHAD EDWARD

Born, Metairie, Louisiana, March 24, 1983.
Bats Right. Throws Right. Height, 5 feet, 10 inches. Weight, 185 pounds.

Year Club	Lea	G	IP	W	L	Pct	SO	BB	H	ERA	SAVES
2002 Charleston-SC	So.Atl.	26	$119\frac{1}{3}$	4	6	.400	106	37	106	2.26	1
2003 Bakersfield	Calif.	14	$80\frac{1}{3}$	5	3	.625	70	23	63	2.13	0
2003 Orlando	Southern	3	19	2	0	1.000	23	3	8	0.47	0
2003 Tampa Bay	A.L.	15	40	2	0	1.000	23	16	37	3.60	0
2004 Tampa Bay	A.L.	26	$42\frac{2}{3}$	1	2	.333	30	16	59	4.85	0
2004 Durham a	Int.	17	$47\frac{2}{3}$	1	3	.250	52	17	48	4.72	2
2005 Toronto	A.L.	5	13	1	3	.250	12	6	31	13.15	0
2005 Syracuse b	Int.	23	$150\frac{1}{3}$	9	8	.529	113	35	140	3.35	0
2006 Sacramento	P.C.	4	$24\frac{1}{3}$	3	0	1.000	26	8	14	0.37	0
2006 Oakland	A.L.	55	64	4	2	.667	36	42	51	3.09	2
2007 Oakland	A.L.	34	$199\frac{1}{3}$	11	13	.458	154	100	205	4.42	0
2008 Oakland	A.L.	26	$62\frac{2}{3}$	5	3	.625	44	17	63	3.59	0
2008 Chicago c-d	N.L.	24	$27\frac{1}{3}$	4	2	.667	27	10	29	6.26	0
2009 Portland	P.C.	2	$8\frac{2}{3}$	0	0	.000	10	2	4	0.00	0
2009 San Diego	N.L.	20	$105\frac{1}{3}$	4	10	.286	105	56	105	5.13	0
2009 New York e-f	A.L.	11	42	2	0	1.000	34	20	41	3.43	0
2010 Oakland-New York g-h-i	A.L.	42	$65\frac{1}{3}$	1	4	.200	53	25	73	5.65	0
2011 Washington j	N.L.	10	$8\frac{1}{3}$	1	1	.500	10	8	12	6.48	0
2011 Potomac	Carolina	1	1	0	0	.000	0	0	0	0.00	0
2011 Hagerstown	So.Atl.	1	2	0	0	.000	0	0	2	0.00	0
2011 Syracuse	Int.	6	$12\frac{1}{3}$	0	2	.000	14	3	17	4.38	0
2011 Las Vegas k	P.C.	6	$29\frac{1}{3}$	2	3	.400	13	9	37	6.14	0
2012 Miami l-m	N.L.	46	$69\frac{1}{3}$	4	2	.667	57	26	72	4.54	0

Year Club	Lea	G	IP	W	L	Pct	SO	BB	H	ERA	SAVES
2013 San Francisco n-o	N.L.	30	97	5	2	.714	88	40	81	3.06	0
Major League Totals	11 Yrs.	344	836¹/₃	45	44	.506	673	382	859	4.44	2
Championship Series											
2006 Oakland	A.L.	3	3¹/₃	0	0	.000	1	3	2	0.00	0
2009 New York	A.L.	1	1	0	0	.000	0	0	0	0.00	0
Championship Series Totals		4	4¹/₃	0	0	.000	1	3	2	0.00	0

a Traded to Toronto Blue Jays for catcher Kevin Cash, December 13, 2004.
b Traded to Oakland Athletics for player to be named later, December 5, 2005. Toronto Blue Jays received outfielder Dustin Majewski to complete trade, December 8, 2005.
c On disabled list from March 19 to April 8, 2008.
d Traded to Chicago Cubs with pitcher Rich Harden for pitcher Sean Gallagher, outfielder Matt Murton, outfielder Eric Patterson and catcher Josh Donaldson, July 8, 2008.
e Released by Chicago Cubs, April 5, 2009. Signed with San Diego Padres organization, April 12, 2009.
f Sold to New York Yankees, August 6, 2009.
g Released by New York Yankees, March 25, 2010. Signed with Oakland Athletics, March 28, 2010.
h Released by Oakland Athletics, May 21, 2010. Signed with New York Yankees, May 26, 2010.
i Filed for free agency, November 2, 2010. Signed with Washington Nationals organization, December 17, 2011.
j On disabled list from April 26 to July 19, 2011.
k Released by Washington Nationals, July 21, 2011. Signed with Toronto Blue Jays organization, July 30, 2011.
l Filed for free agency, November 2, 2011. Signed with Miami Marlins organization, January 4, 2012.
m Filed for free agency, November 3, 2012. Signed with San Francisco Giants organization, December 13, 2012.
n On disabled list from June 21 to July 7 and August 17 to October 1, 2013.
o Filed for free agency, October 31, 2013. Signed with Philadelphia Phillies organization, January 21, 2014.

GAUSMAN, KEVIN JOHN

Born, Centennial, Colorado, January 6, 1991.
Bats Right. Throws Right. Height, 6 feet, 3 inches. Weight, 190 pounds.

Year Club	Lea	G	IP	W	L	Pct	SO	BB	H	ERA	SAVES
2012 Aberdeen	N.Y.-Penn.	2	6	0	0	.000	5	0	1	0.00	0
2012 Frederick	Carolina	3	9	0	1	.000	8	1	10	6.00	0
2013 Bowie	Eastern	8	46¹/₃	2	4	.333	49	5	44	3.11	0
2013 Norfolk	Int.	8	35²/₃	1	2	.333	33	9	36	4.04	0
2013 Baltimore	A.L.	20	47²/₃	3	5	.375	49	13	51	5.66	0

GEE, DILLON KYLE

Born, Cleburne, Texas, April 28, 1986.
Bats Right. Throws Right. Height, 6 feet, 1 inch. Weight, 205 pounds.

Year Club	Lea	G	IP	W	L	Pct	SO	BB	H	ERA	SAVES
2007 Brooklyn	N.Y.-Penn.	14	62	3	1	.750	56	9	57	2.47	0
2008 St. Lucie	Fla.St.	21	127¹/₃	8	6	.571	94	19	117	3.25	0
2008 Binghamton	Eastern	4	27	2	0	1.000	20	5	18	1.33	0
2009 Buffalo	Int.	9	48¹/₃	1	3	.250	42	16	47	4.10	0
2010 Buffalo	Int.	28	161¹/₃	13	8	.619	165	41	174	4.96	0
2010 New York	N.L.	5	33	2	2	.500	17	15	25	2.18	0
2011 Buffalo	Int.	2	11²/₃	1	1	.500	8	5	7	4.63	0
2011 New York	N.L.	30	160²/₃	13	6	.684	114	71	150	4.43	0
2012 New York a	N.L.	17	109²/₃	6	7	.462	97	29	108	4.10	0
2013 New York	N.L.	32	199	12	11	.522	142	47	208	3.62	0
Major League Totals	4 Yrs.	84	502¹/₃	33	26	.559	370	162	491	3.89	0

a On disabled list from July 8 to October 29, 2012.

GERMEN, GONZALEZ GERMAN

Born, LaRomana, Dominican Republic, September 23, 1987.
Bats Right. Throws Right. Height, 6 feet, 2 inches. Weight, 200 pounds.

Year Club	Lea	G	IP	W	L	Pct	SO	BB	H	ERA	SAVES
2009 Mets	Gulf Coast	2	6	0	1	.000	7	0	6	6.00	0
2010 Kingsport	Appal.	10	61	2	5	.286	54	11	64	3.69	0
2010 Savannah	So.Atl.	2	13	1	0	1.000	10	1	11	2.77	0
2011 Savannah	So.Atl.	26	119	7	7	.500	111	35	126	3.93	0
2012 St. Lucie	Fla.St.	5	26²/₃	3	0	1.000	21	8	25	3.04	0
2012 Binghamton	Eastern	20	119²/₃	8	12	.400	97	33	127	4.59	0
2012 Buffalo	Int.	1	7	1	0	1.000	3	2	7	5.14	0
2013 Las Vegas	P.C.	35	44	3	3	.500	51	11	47	5.52	4
2013 New York	N.L.	29	34¹/₃	1	2	.333	33	16	32	3.93	1

GOMEZ, JEANMAR ALEJANDRO

Born, Caracas, Venezuela, February 10, 1988.
Bats Right. Throws Right. Height, 6 feet, 3 inches. Weight, 200 pounds.

Year	Club	Lea	G	IP	W	L	Pct	SO	BB	H	ERA	SAVES
2006	Indians	Gulf Coast	11	54⅓	4	3	.571	34	12	50	2.48	0
2007	Lake County	So.Atl.	27	140⅔	11	7	.611	94	46	152	4.80	0
2008	Kinston	Carolina	27	138⅓	5	9	.357	110	46	154	4.55	0
2009	Kinston	Carolina	4	24	2	2	.500	15	5	17	2.63	0
2009	Akron	Eastern	22	123⅓	10	4	.714	109	40	117	3.43	0
2010	Columbus	Int.	20	116	8	8	.500	78	42	129	5.20	0
2010	Cleveland	A.L.	11	57⅔	4	5	.444	34	22	73	4.68	0
2011	Mahoning Valley	N.Y.-Penn.	1	4	0	0	.000	3	0	5	2.25	0
2011	Columbus	Int.	21	137⅔	10	7	.588	107	49	123	2.55	0
2011	Cleveland	A.L.	11	58⅓	5	3	.625	31	15	73	4.47	0
2012	Columbus	Int.	11	69⅓	6	5	.545	54	17	75	4.41	0
2012	Cleveland a	A.L.	20	90⅔	5	8	.385	47	34	95	5.96	0
2013	Indianapolis	Int.	2	8	1	0	1.000	7	4	3	1.13	0
2013	Pittsburgh b	N.L.	34	80⅔	3	0	1.000	53	28	65	3.35	0
Major League Totals		4 Yrs.	76	287⅓	17	16	.515	165	99	306	4.67	0
	Division Series											
2013	Pittsburgh	N.L.	1	4	0	0	.000	0	2	3	0.00	0

a Traded to Pittsburgh Pirates for outfielder Quincy Latimore, January 9, 2013.
b On disabled list from June 3 to June 26, 2013.

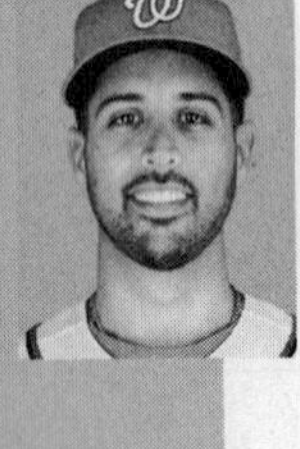

GONZALEZ, GIOVANY ARAMIS (GIO)

Born, Hialeah, Florida, September 19, 1985.
Bats Right. Throws Left. Height, 5 feet, 11 inches. Weight, 195 pounds.

Year	Club	Lea	G	IP	W	L	Pct	SO	BB	H	ERA	SAVES
2004	Bristol	Appal.	7	24	1	2	.333	36	8	17	2.25	0
2004	Kannapolis	So.Atl.	8	40⅔	1	2	.333	34	20	39	3.76	0
2005	Winston-Salem	Carolina	13	73⅓	8	3	.727	79	25	61	3.56	0
2005	Kannapolis a	So.Atl.	11	57⅔	5	3	.625	84	22	36	1.87	0
2006	Reading b	Eastern	27	154⅔	7	12	.368	166	81	140	4.66	0
2007	Birmingham	Southern	27	150	9	7	.563	185	57	116	3.18	0
2008	Sacramento	P.C.	23	123	8	7	.533	128	61	106	4.24	0
2008	Oakland c	A.L.	10	34	1	4	.200	34	25	32	7.68	0
2009	Sacramento	P.C.	12	61	4	1	.800	71	34	42	2.51	0
2009	Oakland	A.L.	20	98⅔	6	7	.462	109	56	113	5.75	0
2010	Oakland	A.L.	33	200⅔	15	9	.625	171	92	171	3.23	0
2011	Oakland d	A.L.	32	202	16	12	.571	197	*91	175	3.12	0
2012	Washington	N.L.	32	199⅓	*21	8	.724	207	76	149	2.89	0
2013	Washington	N.L.	32	195⅔	11	8	.579	192	76	169	3.36	0
Major League Totals		6 Yrs.	159	930⅓	70	48	.593	910	416	809	3.59	0
	Division Series											
2012	Washington	N.L.	2	10	0	0	.000	10	11	6	4.50	0

a Sent by Chicago White Sox to Philadelphia as player to be named later for infielder Jim Thome, December 8, 2005.
b Sent to Chicago White Sox as player to be named later for pitcher Freddy Garcia, December 7, 2006.
c Traded to Oakland Athletics with pitcher Fautino de los Santos and outfielder Ryan Sweeney for outfielder Nick Swisher, January 3, 2008.
d Traded to Washington Nationals with pitcher Robert Gilliam for pitcher A.J. Cole, pitcher Brad Peacock, catcher Derek Norris and pitcher Tom Milone, December 23, 2011.

GONZALEZ, MICHAEL VELA (MIKE)

Born, Corpus Christi, Texas, May 23, 1978.

Bats Right. Throws Left. Height, 6 feet, 2 inches. Weight, 215 pounds.

Year	Club	Lea	G	IP	W	L	Pct	SO	BB	H	ERA	SAVES
1997	Pirates	Gulf Coast	7	29	2	0	1.000	33	8	21	2.48	0
1997	Augusta	So.Atl.	4	19⅓	1	1	.500	22	8	11	1.86	0
1998	Lynchburg	Carolina	7	28⅓	0	3	.000	22	13	40	6.67	0
1998	Augusta	So.Atl.	11	50⅔	4	2	.667	72	26	43	2.84	0
1999	Lynchburg	Carolina	20	112	10	4	.714	119	63	98	4.02	0
1999	Altoona	Eastern	7	26⅔	2	3	.400	31	19	34	8.10	0
2000	Pirates	Gulf Coast	2	6	1	0	1.000	7	4	8	4.50	0
2000	Lynchburg	Carolina	12	56	4	3	.571	53	34	57	4.66	0
2001	Lynchburg	Carolina	14	30⅔	2	2	.500	32	7	28	2.93	0
2001	Altoona	Eastern	14	87⅓	5	4	.556	66	36	81	3.71	0
2002	Altoona	Eastern	16	85⅓	8	4	.667	82	47	77	3.80	0
2002	Pirates	Gulf Coast	2	13⅓	2	0	1.000	14	3	5	0.00	0
2003	Lynchburg	Carolina	5	7	0	1	.000	9	5	7	5.14	0
2003	Altoona	Eastern	5	7⅓	0	0	.000	10	2	4	1.23	1

Year	Club	Lea	G	IP	W	L	Pct	SO	BB	H	ERA	SAVES
2003	Pawtucket	Int.	2	1⅔	0	0	.000	2	1	2	0.00	1
2003	Nashville	P.C.	7	10	0	0	.000	10	4	9	4.50	2
2003	Pittsburgh a-b	N.L.	16	8⅓	0	1	.000	6	6	7	7.56	0
2004	Nashville	P.C.	14	20	2	0	1.000	35	7	12	0.90	2
2004	Pittsburgh	N.L.	47	43⅓	3	1	.750	55	6	32	1.25	1
2005	Indianapolis	Int.	2	3⅓	0	0	.000	5	0	0	0.00	0
2005	Pittsburgh c	N.L.	51	50	1	3	.250	58	31	35	2.70	3
2006	Pittsburgh d	N.L.	54	54	3	4	.429	64	31	42	2.17	24
2007	Atlanta e-f	N.L.	18	17	2	0	1.000	13	8	15	1.59	2
2008	Mississippi	Southern	4	5	0	0	.000	4	0	7	0.00	0
2008	Richmond	Int.	5	6	1	0	1.000	8	1	5	1.50	1
2008	Atlanta g	N.L.	36	33⅔	0	3	.000	44	14	26	4.28	14
2009	Atlanta h	N.L.	80	74⅓	5	4	.556	90	33	56	2.42	10
2010	Orioles	Gulf Coast	2	2	0	0	.000	3	0	1	0.00	0
2010	Bowie	Eastern	4	4	1	0	1.000	4	1	2	2.25	0
2010	Aberdeen	N.Y.-Penn.	4	5	0	1	.000	5	0	7	5.40	0
2010	Norfolk	Int.	2	1⅔	0	0	.000	4	2	3	10.80	0
2010	Baltimore i	A.L.	29	24⅔	1	3	.250	31	14	18	4.01	1
2011	Baltimore-Texas j-k	A.L.	56	53⅓	2	2	.500	51	21	51	4.39	1
2012	Syracuse	Int.	1	1⅓	0	0	.000	2	0	0	0.00	0
2012	Washington l	N.L.	47	35⅔	0	0	.000	39	16	31	3.03	0
2013	Milwaukee m	N.L.	75	50	0	3	.000	60	25	58	4.68	0
Major League Totals		11 Yrs.	509	444⅓	17	24	.415	511	205	371	3.14	56
	Division Series											
2011	Texas	A.L.	2	0⅔	0	0	.000	2	0	1	0.00	0
2012	Washington	N.L.	1	1	0	0	.000	1	0	1	9.00	0
Division Series Totals			3	1⅔	0	0	.000	3	0	2	5.40	0
	Championship Series											
2011	Texas	A.L.	3	0⅔	0	0	.000	0	0	1	0.00	0
	World Series Record											
2011	Texas	A.L.	3	3	0	0	.000	2	1	1	6.00	0

a Traded to Boston Red Sox with pitcher Scott Sauerbeck for pitcher Brandon Lyon and pitcher Anastacio Martinez, July 22, 2003.
b Traded to Pittsburgh Pirates with infielder Freddy Sanchez and cash for pitcher Jeff Suppan, pitcher Brandon Lyon and pitcher Anastacio Martinez, July 31, 2003.
c On disabled list from June 23 to August 16, 2005.
d On disabled list from August 25 to October 3, 2006.
e Traded to Atlanta Braves with infielder Brent Lillibridge for infielder Adam LaRoche and outfielder Jamie Romak, January 17, 2007.
f On disabled list from May 16 to November 13, 2007.
g On disabled list from March 21 to June 18, 2008.
h Filed for free agency, November 5, 2009. Signed with Baltimore Orioles, December 18, 2009.
i On disabled list from April 10 to July 21, 2010.
j Traded to Texas Rangers for player to be named later, August 31, 2011. Baltimore Orioles received pitcher Pedro Strop to complete trade, September 1, 2011.
k Filed for free agency, October 30, 2011. Signed with Washington Nationals organization, May 8, 2012.
l Filed for free agency, November 3, 2012. Signed with Milwaukee Brewers, January 7, 2013.
m Filed for free agency, October 31, 2013.

GONZALEZ (MARTIN), MIGUEL ANGEL

Born, Guadalajara, Mexico, May 27, 1984.
Bats Right. Throws Right. Height, 6 feet, 1 inch. Weight, 170 pounds.

Year	Club	Lea	G	IP	W	L	Pct	SO	BB	H	ERA	SAVES
2005	Angels	Arizona	3	4	1	0	1.000	7	0	0	0.00	0
2005	Rancho Cucamonga	Calif.	2	4⅔	0	0	.000	3	2	0	0.00	0
2005	Cedar Rapids	Midwest	28	44	2	5	.286	42	8	47	4.70	8
2006	Rancho Cucamonga	Calif.	14	26⅓	1	0	1.000	24	2	17	1.71	1
2006	Arkansas	Texas	31	53⅓	0	2	.000	38	17	41	3.88	4
2007	Arkansas	Texas	30	130⅔	8	4	.667	81	42	128	3.38	1
2008-2009 a-b-c			INJURED—Did Not Play									
2010	Salem	Carolina	17	73⅓	6	4	.600	47	18	82	4.54	0
2011	Salem	Carolina	2	5	0	1	.000	4	2	5	1.80	0
2011	Portland	Eastern	15	46⅔	0	5	.000	45	19	55	6.17	0
2011	Pawtucket d	Int.	1	5	0	1	.000	5	2	2	1.80	0
2012	Norfolk	Int.	14	44⅔	3	2	.600	53	10	22	1.61	1
2012	Baltimore	A.L.	18	105⅓	9	4	.692	77	35	92	3.25	0
2013	Baltimore e	A.L.	30	171⅓	11	8	.579	120	53	157	3.78	0
Major League Totals		2 Yrs.	48	276⅔	20	12	.625	197	88	249	3.58	0
	Division Series											
2012	Baltimore	A.L.	1	7	0	0	.000	8	0	5	1.29	0

a On minor league disabled list from April 3 to September 22, 2008.
b Selected by Boston Red Sox from Los Angeles Angels in Rule V draft, December 11, 2008.
c On disabled list from March 27 to November 6, 2009.
d Released by Boston Red Sox, December 20, 2011. Signed with Baltimore Orioles organization, February 15, 2012.
e On disabled list from May 4 to May 21, 2013.

GORZELANNY, THOMAS STEPHEN (TOM)

Born, Evergreen Park, Illinois, July 12, 1982.
Bats Left. Throws Left. Height, 6 feet, 2 inches. Weight, 205 pounds.

Year	Club	Lea	G	IP	W	L	Pct	SO	BB	H	ERA	SAVES
2003	Williamsport	N.Y.-Penn.	8	$30\frac{1}{3}$	1	2	.333	22	10	23	1.78	0
2004	Lynchburg	Carolina	10	$55\frac{2}{3}$	3	5	.375	61	19	54	4.85	0
2004	Hickory	So.Atl.	16	93	7	2	.778	106	34	63	2.23	0
2005	Altoona	Eastern	23	$129\frac{2}{3}$	8	5	.615	124	46	114	3.26	0
2005	Pittsburgh	N.L.	3	6	0	1	.000	3	3	10	12.00	0
2006	Indianapolis	Int.	16	$99\frac{2}{3}$	6	5	.545	94	27	67	2.35	0
2006	Pittsburgh a	N.L.	11	$61\frac{2}{3}$	2	5	.286	40	31	50	3.79	0
2007	Pittsburgh	N.L.	32	$201\frac{2}{3}$	14	10	.583	135	68	214	3.88	0
2008	Indianapolis	Int.	7	35	3	1	.750	33	4	28	2.06	0
2008	Pittsburgh b	N.L.	21	$105\frac{1}{3}$	6	9	.400	67	70	120	6.66	0
2009	Indianapolis	Int.	15	87	4	3	.571	85	30	73	2.48	0
2009	Pittsburgh-Chicago c	N.L.	22	47	7	3	.700	47	17	45	5.55	0
2010	Chicago d	N.L.	29	$136\frac{1}{3}$	7	9	.438	119	68	136	4.09	1
2011	Syracuse	Int.	1	4	0	1	.000	3	1	5	9.00	0
2011	Washington e	N.L.	30	105	4	6	.400	95	33	102	4.03	0
2012	Washington f	N.L.	45	72	4	2	.667	62	30	65	2.88	1
2013	Milwaukee g	N.L.	43	$85\frac{1}{3}$	3	6	.333	83	31	77	3.90	0
Major League Totals		9 Yrs.	236	$820\frac{1}{3}$	47	51	.480	651	351	819	4.36	2
	Division Series											
2012	Washington	N.L.	1	$0\frac{1}{3}$	0	0	.000	0	0	1	0.00	0

a On disabled list from August 18 to September 16, 2006.
b On disabled list from September 24 to November 13, 2008.
c Traded to Chicago Cubs with pitcher John Grabow for pitcher Kevin Hart, pitcher Jose Ascanio and infielder Josh Harrison, July 30, 2009.
d Traded to Washington Nationals for outfielder Michael Burgess, pitcher Graham Hicks and pitcher A.J. Morris, January 19, 2011.
e On disabled list from May 24 to June 19, 2011.
f Not offered contract, November 30, 2012. Signed with Milwaukee Brewers, December 21, 2012.
g On disabled list from May 8 to May 24, 2013.

GRAY, SONNY DOUGLAS

Born, Nashville, Tennessee, November 7, 1989.
Bats Right. Throws Right. Height, 5 feet, 11 inches. Weight, 200 pounds.

Year	Club	Lea	G	IP	W	L	Pct	SO	BB	H	ERA	SAVES
2011	Athletics	Arizona	1	2	0	1	.000	2	0	4	4.50	0
2011	Midland	Texas	5	20	1	0	1.000	18	6	15	0.45	0
2012	Midland	Texas	26	148	6	9	.400	97	57	148	4.14	0
2012	Sacramento	P.C.	1	4	0	0	.000	2	1	10	9.00	0
2013	Sacramento	P.C.	20	$118\frac{1}{3}$	10	7	.588	118	39	117	3.42	0
2013	Oakland	A.L.	12	64	5	3	.625	67	20	51	2.67	0
	Division Series											
2013	Oakland	A.L.	2	13	0	1	.000	12	6	10	2.08	0

GREGERSON, LUKAS JOHN (LUKE)

Born, Park Ridge, Illinois, May 14, 1984.
Bats Left. Throws Right. Height, 6 feet, 3 inches. Weight, 200 pounds.

Year	Club	Lea	G	IP	W	L	Pct	SO	BB	H	ERA	SAVES
2006	Johnson City	Appal.	15	$16\frac{1}{3}$	0	1	.000	24	6	14	3.86	5
2006	State College	N.Y.-Penn.	12	$15\frac{2}{3}$	6	1	.857	22	9	9	1.72	4
2007	Palm Beach	Fla.St.	53	64	3	4	.429	69	20	42	1.97	29
2007	Springfield	Texas	1	1	0	0	.000	3	0	1	0.00	0
2008	Springfield	Texas	57	$75\frac{1}{3}$	7	6	.538	78	26	62	3.35	10
2009	San Diego a-b	N.L.	72	75	2	4	.333	93	31	62	3.24	1
2010	San Diego	N.L.	80	$78\frac{1}{3}$	4	7	.364	89	18	47	3.22	2
2011	Tucson	P.C.	2	$1\frac{1}{3}$	0	0	.000	2	2	3	20.25	0
2011	San Diego c	N.L.	61	$55\frac{2}{3}$	3	3	.500	34	19	57	2.75	0
2012	San Diego	N.L.	77	$71\frac{2}{3}$	2	0	1.000	72	21	57	2.39	9

Year	Club	Lea	G	IP	W	L	Pct	SO	BB	H	ERA	SAVES
2013	San Diego d	N.L.	73	66⅓	6	8	.429	64	18	49	2.71	4
Major League Totals		5 Yrs.	363	347	17	22	.436	352	107	272	2.88	16

a Sent by St. Louis Cardinals to San Diego Padres as player to be named later for Khalil Greene, March 23, 2009.
b On disabled list from June 8 to July 6, 2009.
c On disabled list from June 9 to July 5, 2011.
d Traded to Oakland Athletics for outfielder Seth Smith, December 3, 2013.

GREGG, KEVIN MARSCHALL

Born, Corvallis, Oregon, June 20, 1978.
Bats Both. Throws Right. Height, 6 feet, 6 inches. Weight, 245 pounds.

Year	Club	Lea	G	IP	W	L	Pct	SO	BB	H	ERA	SAVES
1996	Athletics	Arizona	11	40⅔	3	3	.500	48	21	30	3.10	0
1997	Visalia	Calif.	25	115⅓	6	8	.429	136	74	116	5.70	0
1998	Modesto	Calif.	30	144	8	7	.533	141	76	139	3.81	1
1999	Visalia	Calif.	13	64	4	4	.500	48	23	60	3.80	1
1999	Midland	Texas	16	91⅓	4	7	.364	66	31	75	3.74	0
1999	Vancouver	P.C.	1	5	1	0	1.000	4	2	6	3.60	0
2000	Midland	Texas	28	140⅔	5	14	.263	97	73	171	6.40	0
2001	Midland	Texas	44	81⅓	5	5	.500	72	40	88	4.54	1
2002	Visalia	Calif.	3	17⅓	2	1	.667	11	9	8	2.08	0
2002	Midland	Texas	11	37⅔	3	3	.500	45	18	31	4.30	0
2002	Sacramento a	P.C.	16	58⅔	2	5	.286	45	23	82	7.52	0
2003	Arkansas	Texas	15	66⅓	4	3	.571	60	19	60	3.53	0
2003	Salt Lake	P.C.	15	91⅔	7	4	.636	75	18	90	4.03	0
2003	Anaheim	A.L.	5	24⅔	2	0	1.000	14	8	18	3.28	0
2004	Anaheim	A.L.	55	87⅔	5	2	.714	84	28	86	4.21	1
2005	Salt Lake	P.C.	7	34⅔	3	1	.750	36	10	36	3.89	0
2005	Los Angeles	A.L.	33	64⅓	1	2	.333	52	29	70	5.04	0
2006	Salt Lake	P.C.	3	10	1	0	1.000	8	4	5	0.00	0
2006	Los Angeles b	A.L.	32	78⅓	3	4	.429	71	21	88	4.14	0
2007	Florida	N.L.	74	84	0	5	.000	87	40	63	3.54	32
2008	Florida c	N.L.	72	68⅔	7	8	.467	58	37	51	3.41	29
2009	Chicago	N.L.	72	68⅔	5	6	.455	71	30	60	4.72	23
2010	Toronto d	A.L.	63	59	2	6	.250	58	30	52	3.51	37
2011	Baltimore e	A.L.	63	59⅔	0	3	.000	53	40	58	4.37	22
2012	Baltimore f	A.L.	40	43⅔	3	2	.600	37	24	50	4.95	0
2013	Chicago g-h	N.L.	62	62	2	6	.250	56	32	53	3.48	33
Major League Totals		11 Yrs.	571	700⅔	30	44	.405	641	319	649	4.07	177
	Division Series											
2004	Anaheim	A.L.	1	2	0	0	.000	0	1	3	0.00	0
	Championship Series											
2005	Los Angeles	A.L.	1	2	0	0	.000	3	1	1	0.00	0

a Filed for free agency from Oakland Athletics, October 15, 2002. Signed with Anaheim Angels organization, November 20, 2002.
b Traded to Florida Marlins for pitcher Chris Resop, November 20, 2006.
c Traded to Chicago Cubs for pitcher Jose Ceda, November 13, 2008.
d Filed for free agency, November 9, 2009. Signed with Toronto Blue Jays, February 5, 2010.
e Filed for free agency, November 4, 2010. Signed with Baltimore Orioles, January 5, 2011.
f Released by Baltimore Orioles, September 14, 2012. Signed with Los Angeles Dodgers organization, February 10, 2013.
g Released by Los Angeles Dodgers, April 3, 2013. Signed with Chicago Cubs organization, April 14, 2013.
h Filed for free agency, October 31, 2013.

GREINKE, DONALD ZACKARY (ZACK)

Born, Orlando, Florida, October 21, 1983.
Bats Right. Throws Right. Height, 6 feet, 2 inches. Weight, 185 pounds.

Year	Club	Lea	G	IP	W	L	Pct	SO	BB	H	ERA	SAVES
2002	Wilmington	Carolina	1	2	0	0	.000	0	0	1	0.00	0
2002	Royals	Gulf Coast	3	4⅔	0	0	.000	4	3	3	1.93	0
2002	Spokane	Northwest	2	4⅔	0	0	.000	5	0	9	7.71	0
2003	Wilmington	Carolina	14	87	11	1	.917	78	13	56	1.14	0
2003	Wichita	Texas	9	53	4	3	.571	34	5	58	3.23	0
2004	Omaha	P.C.	6	28⅔	1	1	.500	23	6	25	2.51	0
2004	Kansas City	A.L.	24	145	8	11	.421	100	26	143	3.97	0
2005	Kansas City	A.L.	33	183	5	17	.227	114	53	233	5.80	0
2006	Wichita	Texas	18	105⅔	8	3	.727	94	27	96	4.34	0
2006	Kansas City a	A.L.	3	6⅓	1	0	1.000	5	3	7	4.26	0
2007	Kansas City	A.L.	52	122	7	7	.500	106	36	122	3.69	1

Year	Club	Lea	G	IP	W	L	Pct	SO	BB	H	ERA	SAVES
2008	Kansas City	A.L.	32	202 1/3	13	10	.565	183	56	202	3.47	0
2009	Kansas City b	A.L.	33	229 1/3	16	8	.667	242	51	195	*2.16	0
2010	Kansas City c	A.L.	33	220	10	14	.417	181	55	219	4.17	0
2011	Brevard County	Fla.St.	1	3	0	0	.000	4	0	1	0.00	0
2011	Nashville	P.C.	2	7 2/3	0	1	.000	9	2	10	4.70	0
2011	Milwaukee d	N.L.	28	171 2/3	16	6	.727	201	45	161	3.83	0
2012	Milwaukee	N.L.	21	123	9	3	.750	122	28	120	3.44	0
2012	Los Angeles e-f	A.L.	13	89 1/3	6	2	.750	78	26	80	3.53	0
2013	Rancho Cucamonga	Calif.	1	4 1/3	0	0	.000	4	0	6	6.23	0
2013	Los Angeles g	N.L.	28	177 2/3	15	4	*.789	148	46	152	2.63	0
Major League Totals		10 Yrs.	300	1669 2/3	106	82	.564	1480	425	1634	3.65	1
	Division Series											
2011	Milwaukee	N.L.	1	5	0	0	.000	7	0	8	7.20	0
2013	Los Angeles	N.L.	1	6	0	1	.000	3	0	4	3.00	0
Division Series Totals			2	11	0	1	.000	10	0	12	4.91	0
	Championship Series											
2011	Milwaukee	N.L.	2	11 2/3	1	1	.500	6	4	15	6.17	0
2013	Los Angeles	N.L.	2	15	1	0	1.000	14	2	10	2.40	0
Championship Series Totals			4	26 2/3	2	1	.667	20	6	25	4.05	0

a On disabled list from April 1 to June 21, 2006.
b Selected Cy Young Award Winner in American League for 2009.
c Traded to Milwaukee Brewers with infielder Yuniesky Betancourt for outfielder Lorenzo Cain, infielder Alcides Escobar, pitcher Jeremy Jeffress and pitcher Jake Odorizzi, December 19, 2010.
d On disabled list from March 26 to May 3, 2011.
e Traded to Los Angeles Angels for infielder Jean Segura, pitcher Ariel Pena and pitcher Johnny Hellweg, July 27, 2012.
f Filed for free agency, November 3, 2012. Signed with Los Angeles Dodgers, December 10, 2012.
g On disabled list from April 12 to May 15, 2013.

GRIFFIN, ARTHUR JOSEPH (A.J.)

Born, El Cajon, California, January 28, 1988.
Bats Right. Throws Right. Height, 6 feet, 5 inches. Weight, 230 pounds.

Year	Club	Lea	G	IP	W	L	Pct	SO	BB	H	ERA	SAVES
2010	Athletics	Arizona	4	5	0	0	.000	6	0	1	0.00	0
2010	Vancouver	Northwest	20	21 1/3	1	1	.500	27	7	14	2.95	15
2011	Stockton	Calif.	12	70 2/3	5	3	.625	82	14	64	3.57	0
2011	Burlington	Midwest	8	52	4	0	1.000	46	5	36	1.56	0
2011	Sacramento	P.C.	1	6	0	1	.000	8	2	6	3.00	0
2011	Midland	Texas	6	32	2	3	.400	20	11	39	6.47	0
2012	Midland	Texas	7	43 1/3	3	1	.750	44	7	31	2.49	0
2012	Sacramento	P.C.	10	58 2/3	4	2	.667	47	11	48	3.07	0
2012	Oakland a	A.L.	15	82 1/3	7	1	.875	64	19	74	3.06	0
2013	Oakland	A.L.	32	200	14	10	.583	171	54	171	3.83	0
Major League Totals		2 Yrs.	47	282 1/3	21	11	.656	235	73	245	3.60	0
	Division Series											
2012	Oakland	A.L.	1	5	0	0	.000	1	0	7	3.60	0

a On disabled list from August 5 to September 1, 2012.

GRILLI, JASON MICHAEL

Born, Royal Oak, Michigan, November 11, 1976.
Bats Right. Throws Right. Height, 6 feet, 4 inches. Weight, 225 pounds.

Year	Club	Lea	G	IP	W	L	Pct	SO	BB	H	ERA	SAVES
1998	Shreveport	Texas	21	123 1/3	7	10	.412	100	37	113	3.79	0
1998	Fresno	P.C.	8	42	2	3	.400	37	18	49	5.14	0
1999	Calgary	P.C.	8	41	1	5	.167	27	23	56	7.68	0
1999	Fresno a	P.C.	19	100 2/3	7	5	.583	76	39	124	5.54	0
2000	Calgary	P.C.	8	41 1/3	1	4	.200	21	23	58	7.19	0
2000	Florida	N.L.	1	6 2/3	1	0	1.000	3	2	11	5.40	0
2001	Florida	N.L.	6	26 2/3	2	2	.500	17	11	30	6.07	0
2001	Calgary	P.C.	8	47	1	2	.333	35	20	46	4.02	0
2001	Marlins	Gulf Coast	2	4	0	0	.000	6	0	2	0.00	0
2001	Brevard County	Fla.St.	3	13 2/3	2	0	1.000	14	5	12	1.98	0
2001	Portland	Eastern	1	4	0	1	.000	3	0	3	2.25	0
2002	Calgary	P.C.	1	5 2/3	0	1	.000	8	3	3	1.59	0
2003	Jupiter	Fla.St.	7	42 2/3	4	2	.667	30	6	38	2.53	0
2003	Albuquerque b	P.C.	12	66 2/3	6	2	.750	38	30	64	3.38	0
2004	Charlotte	Int.	25	152 2/3	9	9	.500	101	58	163	4.83	0
2004	Chicago	A.L.	8	45	2	3	.400	26	20	52	7.40	0

Year	Club	Lea	G	IP	W	L	Pct	SO	BB	H	ERA	SAVES
2005	Toledo c	Int.	28	167⅓	12	9	.571	120	58	170	4.09	0
2005	Detroit	A.L.	3	16	1	1	.500	5	6	14	3.38	0
2006	Detroit	A.L.	51	62	2	3	.400	31	25	61	4.21	0
2007	Detroit	A.L.	57	79⅔	5	3	.625	62	32	81	4.74	0
2008	Detroit	A.L.	9	13⅔	0	1	.000	10	7	12	3.29	0
2008	Colorado d	N.L.	51	61⅓	3	2	.600	59	31	55	2.93	1
2009	Colorado	N.L.	22	19⅓	0	1	.000	22	13	29	6.05	1
2009	Frisco	Texas	1	1	0	0	.000	1	1	0	0.00	0
2009	Texas e-f-g	A.L.	30	26⅓	2	2	.500	27	14	21	4.78	0
2010	h.				INJURED—Did Not Play							
2011	Lehigh Valley i	Int.	28	32⅔	4	1	.800	43	12	26	1.93	3
2011	Pittsburgh j	N.L.	28	32⅔	2	1	.667	37	15	24	2.48	1
2012	Pittsburgh k	N.L.	64	58⅔	1	6	.143	90	22	45	2.91	2
2013	Altoona	Eastern	2	2	0	0	.000	4	0	2	0.00	0
2013	Pittsburgh l	N.L.	54	50	0	2	.000	74	13	40	2.70	33
Major League Totals		11 Yrs.	384	498	21	27	.438	463	211	475	4.17	38
	Wild Card Playoff											
2013	Pittsburgh	N.L.	1	1	0	0	.000	1	0	0	0.00	0
	Division Series											
2006	Detroit	A.L.	1	0⅓	0	0	.000	0	0	0	0.00	0
2013	Pittsburgh	N.L.	3	2⅓	0	0	.000	3	0	3	0.00	1
Division Series Totals			4	2⅔	0	0	.000	3	0	3	0.00	1
	Championship Series											
2006	Detroit	A.L.	2	1	0	0	.000	1	3	1	0.00	0
	World Series Record											
2006	Detroit	A.L.	2	1⅔	0	0	.000	0	1	0	0.00	0

a Traded by San Francisco Giants to Florida Marlins with pitcher Nathan Bump for pitcher Livan Hernandez, July 24, 1999.
b Selected by Chicago White Sox in Rule V draft, December 15, 2003.
c Released by Chicago White Sox, January 28, 2005. Signed with Detroit Tigers organization, February 10, 2005.
d Traded to Colorado Rockies for pitcher Zachary Simons, April 30, 2008.
e Sold to Texas Rangers, June 9, 2009.
f On disabled list from August 2 to August 22, 2009.
g Filed for free agency, October 22, 2009. Signed with Cleveland Indians organization, December 2, 2009.
h On minor league disabled list from April 8 to September 19, 2010.
i Filed for free agency, November 6, 2010. Signed with Philadelphia Phillies organization, February 1, 2011.
j Released by Philadelphia Phillies, July 20, 2011. Signed with Pittsburgh Pirates, July 21, 2011.
k Filed for free agency, November 3, 2012, re-signed with Pittsburgh Pirates, December 12, 2012.
l On disabled list from July 23 to September 3, 2013.

GUERRIER, MATTHEW OLSON (MATT)

Born, Cleveland, Ohio, August 2, 1978.
Bats Right. Throws Right. Height, 6 feet, 3 inches. Weight, 195 pounds.

Year	Club	Lea	G	IP	W	L	Pct	SO	BB	H	ERA	SAVES
1999	Bristol	Appal.	21	25⅔	5	0	1.000	37	14	18	1.05	10
1999	Winston-Salem	Carolina	4	3⅓	0	0	.000	5	0	3	5.40	2
2000	Winston-Salem	Carolina	30	34⅔	0	3	.000	35	12	25	1.30	19
2000	Birmingham	Southern	23	23⅓	3	1	.750	19	12	17	2.70	7
2001	Birmingham	Southern	15	98⅔	11	3	.786	75	32	85	3.10	0
2001	Charlotte	Int.	12	81⅓	7	1	.875	43	18	75	3.54	0
2002	Nashville a	P.C.	27	157	7	12	.368	130	47	154	4.59	0
2003	Nashville b	P.C.	20	105⅓	4	6	.400	78	18	108	4.53	0
2004	Rochester	Int.	24	144	5	10	.333	97	25	135	3.19	0
2004	Minnesota	A.L.	9	19	0	1	.000	11	6	22	5.68	0
2005	Minnesota	A.L.	43	71⅔	0	3	.000	46	24	71	3.39	0
2006	New Britain	Eastern	4	8⅔	2	0	1.000	10	3	3	1.04	0
2006	Minnesota c	A.L.	39	69⅔	1	0	1.000	37	21	78	3.36	1
2007	Minnesota	A.L.	73	88	2	4	.333	68	21	71	2.35	1
2008	Minnesota	A.L.	*76	76⅓	6	9	.400	59	37	84	5.19	1
2009	Minnesota	A.L.	*79	76⅓	5	1	.833	47	16	58	2.36	1
2010	Minnesota d	A.L.	74	71	5	7	.417	42	22	56	3.17	1
2011	Los Angeles	N.L.	70	66⅓	4	3	.571	50	25	59	4.07	1
2012	Rancho Cucamonga	Calif.	5	5	0	0	.000	5	0	3	3.60	0
2012	Los Angeles e	N.L.	16	14	0	2	.000	9	7	8	3.86	0
2013	Los Angeles-Chicago f-g-h	N.L.	49	42⅔	4	4	.500	30	17	43	4.01	0
Major League Totals		10 Yrs.	528	595	27	34	.443	399	196	550	3.51	6
	Division Series											
2006	Minnesota	A.L.	1	1	0	0	.000	0	0	0	0.00	0

Year	Club	Lea	G	IP	W	L	Pct	SO	BB	H	ERA	SAVES
2009	Minnesota	A.L.	2	2	0	0	.000	2	0	0	0.00	0
2010	Minnesota	A.L.	2	$1\frac{2}{3}$	0	0	.000	2	1	1	0.00	0
Division Series Totals			5	$4\frac{2}{3}$	0	0	.000	4	1	1	0.00	0

a Traded by Chicago White Sox to Pittsburgh Pirates for pitcher Damaso Marte and infielder Edwin Yan, March 27, 2002.
b Claimed on waivers by Minnesota Twins, November 20, 2003.
c On disabled list from June 9 to August 1, 2006.
d Filed for free agency, November 1, 2010. Signed with Los Angeles Dodgers, December 16, 2010.
e On disabled list from April 19 to August 30, 2012.
f Traded to Chicago Cubs for pitcher Carlos Marmol, July 2, 2013.
g On disabled list from August 8 to October 31, 2013.
h Filed for free agency, October 31, 2013.

GUTHRIE, JEREMY SHANE

Born, Roseburg, Oregon, April 8, 1979.
Bats Right. Throws Right. Height, 6 feet, 1 inch. Weight, 200 pounds.

Year	Club	Lea	G	IP	W	L	Pct	SO	BB	H	ERA	SAVES
2003	Akron	Eastern	10	$62\frac{2}{3}$	6	2	.750	35	14	44	1.44	0
2003	Buffalo	Int.	18	$96\frac{2}{3}$	4	9	.308	62	30	129	6.52	0
2004	Buffalo	Int.	4	$19\frac{1}{3}$	1	2	.333	10	18	23	7.91	0
2004	Akron	Eastern	23	$130\frac{1}{3}$	8	8	.500	94	42	145	4.21	0
2004	Cleveland	A.L.	6	$11\frac{2}{3}$	0	0	.000	7	6	9	4.63	0
2005	Cleveland	A.L.	1	6	0	0	.000	3	2	9	6.00	0
2005	Buffalo	Int.	25	$136\frac{1}{3}$	12	10	.545	100	49	152	5.08	0
2006	Buffalo	Int.	21	$123\frac{1}{3}$	9	5	.643	88	48	104	3.14	0
2006	Cleveland	A.L.	9	$19\frac{1}{3}$	0	0	.000	14	15	24	6.98	0
2007	Baltimore a	A.L.	32	$175\frac{1}{3}$	7	5	.583	123	47	165	3.70	0
2008	Baltimore b	A.L.	30	$190\frac{2}{3}$	10	12	.455	120	58	176	3.63	0
2009	Baltimore	A.L.	33	200	10	*17	.370	110	60	224	5.04	0
2010	Baltimore	A.L.	32	$209\frac{1}{3}$	11	14	.440	119	50	193	3.83	0
2011	Baltimore	A.L.	34	208	9	*17	.346	130	66	213	4.33	0
2012	Modesto	Calif.	1	4	0	0	.000	4	1	3	0.00	0
2012	Colorado c-d	N.L.	19	$90\frac{2}{3}$	3	9	.250	45	31	122	6.35	0
2012	Kansas City e-f	A.L.	14	91	5	3	.625	56	19	84	3.16	0
2013	Kansas City	A.L.	33	$211\frac{2}{3}$	15	12	.556	111	59	*236	4.04	0
Major League Totals		10 Yrs.	243	$1413\frac{2}{3}$	70	89	.440	838	413	1455	4.24	0

a Claimed on waivers by Baltimore Orioles, January 29, 2007.
b On disabled list from September 6 to September 27, 2008.
c Traded to Colorado Rockies for pitcher Jason Hammel and pitcher Matt Lindstrom, February 6, 2012.
d On disabled list from April 23 to May 15, 2012.
e Traded to Kansas City Royals for pitcher Jonathan Sanchez, July 20, 2012.
f Filed for free agency, November 3, 2012, re-signed with Kansas City Royals, November 20, 2012.

GUTIERREZ, JUAN CARLOS

Born, Puerto La Cruz, Venezuela, July 14, 1983.
Bats Right. Throws Right. Height, 6 feet, 3 inches. Weight, 245 pounds.

Year	Club	Lea	G	IP	W	L	Pct	SO	BB	H	ERA	SAVES
2003	Martinsville	Appal.	16	34	1	2	.333	30	13	42	4.76	2
2004	Greeneville	Appal.	13	$65\frac{2}{3}$	8	2	.800	59	30	74	3.70	0
2005	Lexington	So.Atl.	22	$120\frac{2}{3}$	9	5	.643	100	43	106	3.21	0
2005	Salem	Carolina	3	12	1	1	.500	9	8	10	3.00	0
2006	Corpus Christi	Texas	20	$103\frac{2}{3}$	8	4	.667	106	34	94	3.04	0
2007	Round Rock	P.C.	26	156	5	10	.333	108	63	154	4.15	0
2007	Houston a	N.L.	7	$21\frac{1}{3}$	1	1	.500	16	6	25	5.91	0
2008	Tucson	P.C.	25	$116\frac{2}{3}$	5	11	.313	87	44	152	6.09	0
2009	Arizona	N.L.	65	71	4	3	.571	66	30	67	4.06	9
2010	Arizona b	N.L.	58	$56\frac{2}{3}$	0	6	.000	47	23	55	5.08	15
2011	Arizona c-d	N.L.	20	$18\frac{1}{3}$	0	0	.000	23	9	22	5.40	0
2012	Royals	Arizona	4	$4\frac{2}{3}$	0	1	.000	6	1	11	17.36	0
2012	NW Arkansas	Texas	5	5	0	0	.000	5	2	8	9.00	3
2012	Omaha e	P.C.	10	11	0	1	.000	7	3	13	8.18	0
2013	Kansas City-Los Angeles f	A.L.	53	$55\frac{1}{3}$	1	5	.167	45	20	56	4.23	0
Major League Totals		5 Yrs.	203	$222\frac{2}{3}$	6	15	.286	197	88	225	4.65	24

a Traded to Arizona Diamondbacks with pitcher Chad Qualls and outfielder Chris Burke for pitcher Jose Valverde, December 14, 2007.
b On disabled list from August 3 to August 18, 2010.
c On disabled list from May 25 to October 13, 2011.

d Released by Arizona Diamondbacks, October 13, 2011. Signed with Kansas City Royals organization, December 13, 2011.
e Claimed on waivers by Los Angeles Angels, July 24, 2013.
f Not offered contract, December 2, 2013. Signed with San Francisco Giants organization, January 6, 2014.

HALLADAY, HARRY LEROY (ROY)

Born, Denver, Colorado, May 14, 1977.
Bats Right. Throws Right. Height, 6 feet, 6 inches. Weight, 225 pounds.

Year Club	Lea	G	IP	W	L	Pct	SO	BB	H	ERA	SAVES
1995 Blue Jays........	Gulf Coast	10	$50^{1}/_{3}$	3	5	.375	48	16	35	3.40	0
1996 Dunedin............	Fla.St.	27	$164^{2}/_{3}$	15	7	.682	109	46	158	2.73	0
1997 Knoxville	Southern	7	$36^{2}/_{3}$	2	3	.400	30	11	46	5.40	0
1997 Syracuse	Int.	22	$125^{2}/_{3}$	7	10	.412	64	53	132	4.58	0
1998 Syracuse	Int.	21	$116^{1}/_{3}$	9	5	.643	71	53	107	3.79	0
1998 Toronto	A.L.	2	14	1	0	1.000	13	2	9	1.93	0
1999 Toronto	A.L.	36	$149^{1}/_{3}$	8	7	.533	82	79	156	3.92	1
2000 Syracuse	Int.	11	$73^{2}/_{3}$	2	3	.400	38	21	85	5.50	0
2000 Toronto	A.L.	19	$67^{2}/_{3}$	4	7	.364	44	42	107	10.64	0
2001 Dunedin............	Fla.St.	13	$22^{2}/_{3}$	0	1	.000	15	3	28	3.97	2
2001 Tennessee	Southern	5	34	2	1	.667	29	6	25	2.12	0
2001 Syracuse	Int.	2	14	1	0	1.000	13	0	12	3.21	0
2001 Toronto	A.L.	17	$105^{1}/_{3}$	5	3	.625	96	25	97	3.16	0
2002 Toronto	A.L.	34	$*239^{1}/_{3}$	19	7	.731	168	62	223	2.93	0
2003 Toronto a..............	A.L.	36	*266	*22	7	*.759	204	32	*253	3.25	0
2004 Toronto b..............	A.L.	21	133	8	8	.500	95	39	140	4.20	0
2005 Toronto c..............	A.L.	19	$141^{2}/_{3}$	12	4	.750	108	18	118	2.41	0
2006 Toronto	A.L.	32	220	16	5	*.762	132	34	208	3.19	0
2007 Toronto d..............	A.L.	31	$225^{1}/_{3}$	16	7	.696	139	48	232	3.71	0
2008 Toronto	A.L.	34	*246	20	11	.645	206	39	220	2.78	0
2009 Toronto e-f..............	A.L.	32	239	17	10	.630	208	35	234	2.79	0
2010 Philadelphia g-h-i.......	N.L.	33	$*250^{2}/_{3}$	*21	10	.677	219	30	*231	2.44	0
2011 Philadelphia...........	N.L.	32	$233^{2}/_{3}$	19	6	.760	220	35	208	2.35	0
2012 Clearwater	Fla.St.	1	3	0	0	.000	4	0	3	0.00	0
2012 Philadelphia j..........	N.L.	25	$156^{1}/_{3}$	11	8	.579	132	36	155	4.49	0
2013 Phillies..........	Gulf Coast	1	6	0	0	.000	4	3	6	4.50	0
2013 Lakewood...........	So.Atl.	1	6	0	0	.000	4	3	7	1.50	0
2013 Philadelphia k-l-m......	N.L.	13	62	4	5	.444	51	36	55	6.82	0
Major League Totals	16 Yrs.	416	$2749^{1}/_{3}$	203	105	.659	2117	592	2646	3.38	1
Division Series											
2010 Philadelphia...........	N.L.	1	9	1	0	1.000	8	1	0	0.00	0
2011 Philadelphia...........	N.L.	2	16	1	1	.500	15	2	9	2.25	0
Division Series Totals		3	25	2	1	.667	23	3	9	1.44	0
Championship Series											
2010 Philadelphia...........	N.L.	2	13	1	1	.500	12	2	14	4.15	0

a Selected Cy Young Award Winner in American League for 2003.
b On disabled list from May 28 to June 12 and from July 17 to September 21, 2004.
c On disabled list from July 9 to October 3, 2005.
d On disabled list from May 11 to May 31, 2007.
e On disabled list from June 13 to June 28, 2009.
f Traded to Philadelphia Phillies for pitcher Kyle Drabek, pitcher Michael Taylor and catcher Travis D'Arnaud, December 16, 2009.
g Pitched no-hit, no-run perfect game against Florida Marlins, May 29, 2010.
h Pitched no-hit, no-run game against Cincinnati Reds in divisional playoff, October 6, 2010.
i Selected Cy Young Award Winner in National League for 2010.
j On disabled list from May 28 to July 17, 2012.
k On disabled list from May 6 to August 25, 2013.
l Filed for free agency, October 31, 2013. Signed with Toronto Blue Jays organization, December 9, 2013.
m Announced retirement, December 9, 2013.

HAMELS, COLBERT RICHARD (COLE)

Born, San Diego, California, December 27, 1983.
Bats Left. Throws Left. Height, 6 feet, 4 inches. Weight, 195 pounds.

Year Club	Lea	G	IP	W	L	Pct	SO	BB	H	ERA	SAVES
2003 Clearwater	Fla.St.	5	$26^{1}/_{3}$	0	2	.000	32	14	29	2.73	0
2003 Lakewood...........	So.Atl.	13	$74^{2}/_{3}$	6	1	.857	115	25	32	0.84	0
2004 Clearwater	Fla.St.	4	16	1	0	1.000	24	4	10	1.13	0
2005 Reading	Eastern	3	19	2	0	1.000	19	12	10	2.37	0
2005 Clearwater	Fla.St.	3	16	2	0	1.000	18	7	7	2.25	0
2006 Lakewood...........	So.Atl.	1	$5^{2}/_{3}$	0	0	.000	3	2	3	1.59	0

Year Club	Lea	G	IP	W	L	Pct	SO	BB	H	ERA	SAVES
2006 Clearwater	Fla.St.	4	20 1/3	1	1	.500	29	9	16	1.77	0
2006 Scranton/WB	Int.	3	23	2	0	1.000	36	1	10	0.39	0
2006 Philadelphia a	N.L.	23	132 1/3	9	8	.529	145	48	117	4.08	0
2007 Philadelphia b	N.L.	28	183 1/3	15	5	.750	177	43	163	3.39	0
2008 Philadelphia	N.L.	33	227 1/3	14	10	.583	196	53	193	3.09	0
2009 Philadelphia	N.L.	32	193 2/3	10	11	.476	168	43	206	4.32	0
2010 Philadelphia	N.L.	33	208 2/3	12	11	.522	211	61	185	3.06	0
2011 Philadelphia c	N.L.	32	216	14	9	.609	194	44	169	2.79	0
2012 Philadelphia	N.L.	31	215 1/3	17	6	.739	216	52	190	3.05	0
2013 Philadelphia	N.L.	33	220	8	14	.364	202	50	205	3.60	0
Major League Totals	8 Yrs.	245	1596 2/3	99	74	.572	1509	394	1428	3.38	0
Division Series											
2007 Philadelphia	N.L.	1	6 2/3	0	1	.000	7	4	3	4.05	0
2008 Philadelphia	N.L.	1	8	1	0	1.000	9	1	2	0.00	0
2009 Philadelphia	N.L.	1	5	0	1	.000	5	0	7	7.20	0
2010 Philadelphia	N.L.	1	9	1	0	1.000	9	0	5	0.00	0
2011 Philadelphia	N.L.	1	6	1	0	1.000	8	3	5	0.00	0
Division Series Totals		5	34 2/3	3	2	.600	38	8	22	1.82	0
Championship Series											
2008 Philadelphia	N.L.	2	14	2	0	1.000	13	5	11	1.93	0
2009 Philadelphia	N.L.	2	9 2/3	1	0	1.000	7	2	13	6.52	0
2010 Philadelphia	N.L.	1	6	0	1	.000	8	1	5	4.50	0
Championship Series Totals		5	29 2/3	3	1	.750	28	8	29	3.94	0
World Series Record											
2008 Philadelphia	N.L.	2	13	1	0	1.000	8	3	10	2.77	0
2009 Philadelphia	N.L.	1	4 1/3	0	1	.000	3	2	5	10.38	0
World Series Totals		3	17 1/3	1	1	.500	11	5	15	4.67	0

a On disabled list from May 19 to June 6, 2006.
b On disabled list from August 17 to September 18, 2007.
c On disabled list from August 13 to August 29, 2011.

HAMMEL, JASON AARON

Born, Greenville, South Carolina, September 2, 1982.
Bats Right. Throws Right. Height, 6 feet, 6 inches. Weight, 220 pounds.

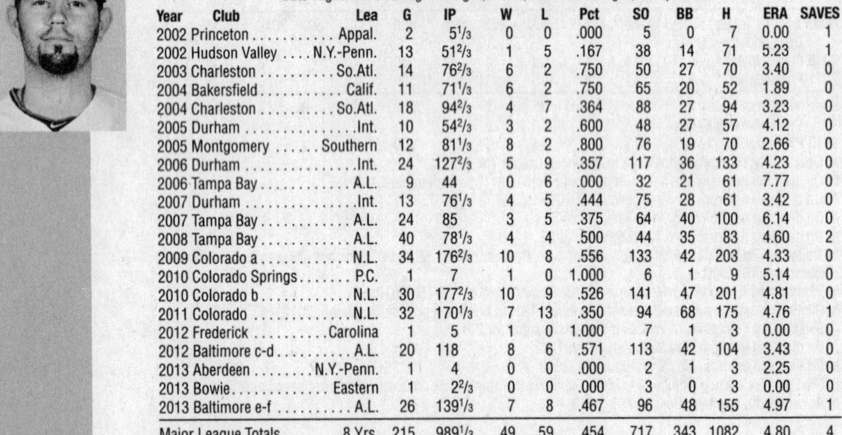

Year Club	Lea	G	IP	W	L	Pct	SO	BB	H	ERA	SAVES
2002 Princeton	Appal.	2	5 1/3	0	0	.000	5	0	7	0.00	1
2002 Hudson Valley	N.Y.-Penn.	13	51 2/3	1	5	.167	38	14	71	5.23	1
2003 Charleston	So.Atl.	14	76 2/3	6	2	.750	50	27	70	3.40	0
2004 Bakersfield	Calif.	11	71 1/3	6	2	.750	65	20	52	1.89	0
2004 Charleston	So.Atl.	18	94 2/3	4	7	.364	88	27	94	3.23	0
2005 Durham	Int.	10	54 2/3	3	2	.600	48	27	57	4.12	0
2005 Montgomery	Southern	12	81 1/3	8	2	.800	76	19	70	2.66	0
2006 Durham	Int.	24	127 2/3	5	9	.357	117	36	133	4.23	0
2006 Tampa Bay	A.L.	9	44	0	6	.000	32	21	61	7.77	0
2007 Durham	Int.	13	76 1/3	4	5	.444	75	28	61	3.42	0
2007 Tampa Bay	A.L.	24	85	3	5	.375	64	40	100	6.14	0
2008 Tampa Bay	A.L.	40	78 1/3	4	4	.500	44	35	83	4.60	2
2009 Colorado a	N.L.	34	176 2/3	10	8	.556	133	42	203	4.33	0
2010 Colorado Springs	P.C.	1	7	1	0	1.000	6	1	9	5.14	0
2010 Colorado b	N.L.	30	177 2/3	10	9	.526	141	47	201	4.81	0
2011 Colorado	N.L.	32	170 1/3	7	13	.350	94	68	175	4.76	1
2012 Frederick	Carolina	1	5	1	0	1.000	7	1	3	0.00	0
2012 Baltimore c-d	A.L.	20	118	8	6	.571	113	42	104	3.43	0
2013 Aberdeen	N.Y.-Penn.	1	4	0	0	.000	2	1	3	2.25	0
2013 Bowie	Eastern	1	2 2/3	0	0	.000	3	0	3	0.00	0
2013 Baltimore e-f	A.L.	26	139 1/3	7	8	.467	96	48	155	4.97	1
Major League Totals	8 Yrs.	215	989 1/3	49	59	.454	717	343	1082	4.80	4
Division Series											
2009 Colorado	N.L.	1	3 2/3	0	0	.000	5	3	4	9.82	0
2012 Baltimore	A.L.	2	11 1/3	0	1	.000	11	6	8	3.18	0
Division Series Totals		3	15	0	1	.000	16	9	12	4.80	0

a Traded to Colorado Rockies for pitcher Aneury Rodriguez, April 4, 2009.
b On disabled list from April 27 to May 15, 2010.
c Traded to Baltimore Orioles with pitcher Matt Lindstrom for pitcher Jeremy Guthrie, February 6, 2012.
d On disabled list from July 15 to September 6, 2012.
e On disabled list from July 29 to September 5, 2013.
f Filed for free agency, October 31, 2013.

HAND, DONOVAN JAY

Born, Tecumseh, Alabama, April 20, 1986.
Bats Right. Throws Right. Height, 6 feet, 3 inches. Weight, 210 pounds.

Year	Club	Lea	G	IP	W	L	Pct	SO	BB	H	ERA	SAVES
2007	Helena	Pioneer	7	33	2	2	.500	26	4	31	3.55	0
2007	West Virginia	So.Atl.	10	25	1	2	.333	17	0	32	2.16	4
2008	Brevard County	Fla.St.	10	58 1/3	4	2	.667	36	10	49	2.31	0
2008	Huntsville	Southern	16	81 1/3	3	4	.429	41	26	101	5.09	0
2009	Huntsville	Southern	27	98 2/3	8	5	.615	51	21	102	3.56	1
2010	Huntsville	Southern	27	50 1/3	2	1	.667	38	8	57	2.86	2
2010	Nashville	P.C.	21	25 1/3	2	0	1.000	11	5	29	4.62	0
2011	Huntsville	Southern	9	11 1/3	0	0	.000	12	1	16	2.38	1
2011	Nashville	P.C.	39	55	2	6	.250	32	21	66	3.60	1
2012	Nashville	P.C.	44	79 2/3	3	3	.500	54	18	90	3.84	0
2013	Nashville	P.C.	20	35 2/3	3	1	.750	38	11	34	3.28	0
2013	Milwaukee	N.L.	31	68 1/3	1	5	.167	37	21	71	3.69	0

HANSON, THOMAS J. (TOMMY)

Born, Tulsa, Oklahoma, August 28, 1986.
Bats Right. Throws Right. Height, 6 feet, 6 inches. Weight, 220 pounds.

Year	Club	Lea	G	IP	W	L	Pct	SO	BB	H	ERA	SAVES
2006	Danville	Appal.	13	51 2/3	4	1	.800	56	9	42	2.09	0
2007	Myrtle Beach	Carolina	11	60	3	3	.500	64	32	53	4.20	0
2007	Rome	So.Atl.	15	73	2	6	.250	90	26	51	2.59	0
2008	Myrtle Beach	Carolina	7	40	3	1	.750	49	11	15	0.90	0
2008	Mississippi	Southern	18	98	8	4	.667	114	41	70	3.03	0
2009	Gwinnett	Int.	11	66 1/3	3	3	.500	90	17	40	1.49	0
2009	Atlanta	N.L.	21	127 2/3	11	4	.733	116	46	105	2.89	0
2010	Atlanta	N.L.	34	202 2/3	10	11	.476	173	56	182	3.33	0
2011	Atlanta a	N.L.	22	130	11	7	.611	142	46	106	3.60	0
2012	Gwinnett	Int.	1	5	1	0	1.000	5	2	3	0.00	0
2012	Atlanta b-c	N.L.	31	174 2/3	13	10	.565	161	71	183	4.48	0
2013	Inland Empire	Calif.	1	3 1/3	0	1	.000	6	1	3	5.40	0
2013	Salt Lake	P.C.	4	19 2/3	0	2	.000	15	6	23	5.49	0
2013	Los Angeles d-e	A.L.	15	73	4	3	.571	56	30	83	5.42	0
Major League Totals		5 Yrs.	123	708	49	35	.583	648	249	659	3.80	0
	Division Series											
2010	Atlanta	N.L.	1	4	0	0	.000	5	1	5	9.00	0

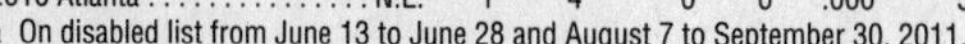

a On disabled list from June 13 to June 28 and August 7 to September 30, 2011.
b On disabled list from July 31 to August 17, 2012.
c Traded to Los Angeles Angels for pitcher Jordan Walden, November 30, 2012.
d On disabled list from June 21 to July 23, 2013.
e Not offered contract, December 2, 2013.

HAPP, JAMES ANTHONY (J.A.)

Born, Spring Valley, Illinois, October 19, 1982.
Bats Left. Throws Left. Height, 6 feet, 6 inches. Weight, 200 pounds.

Year	Club	Lea	G	IP	W	L	Pct	SO	BB	H	ERA	SAVES
2004	Batavia	N.Y.-Penn.	11	35 2/3	1	2	.333	37	18	22	2.02	0
2005	Reading	Eastern	1	6	1	0	1.000	8	2	3	1.50	0
2005	Lakewood	So.Atl.	14	72 1/3	4	4	.500	70	26	57	2.36	0
2006	Reading	Eastern	12	74 2/3	6	2	.750	81	29	58	2.65	0
2006	Clearwater	Fla.St.	13	80	3	7	.300	77	19	63	2.81	0
2006	Scranton/WB	Int.	1	6	1	0	1.000	4	1	3	1.50	0
2007	Philadelphia	N.L.	1	4	0	1	.000	5	2	7	11.25	0
2007	Ottawa	Int.	24	118 1/3	4	6	.400	117	62	118	5.02	0
2008	Lehigh Valley	Int.	24	135	8	7	.533	151	48	116	3.60	0
2008	Philadelphia	N.L.	8	31 2/3	1	0	1.000	26	14	28	3.69	0
2009	Philadelphia	N.L.	35	166	12	4	.750	119	56	149	2.93	0
2010	Clearwater	Fla.St.	1	3	0	1	.000	2	0	3	6.00	0
2010	Reading	Eastern	3	12 1/3	1	0	1.000	10	4	18	8.03	0
2010	Lehigh Valley	Int.	5	22 1/3	0	1	.000	22	15	26	4.84	0
2010	Philadelphia-Houston a-b	N.L.	16	87 1/3	6	4	.600	70	47	73	3.40	0
2011	Oklahoma	P.C.	3	18	1	0	1.000	16	9	11	1.50	0
2011	Houston	N.L.	28	156 1/3	6	15	.286	134	83	157	5.35	0
2012	Houston	N.L.	18	104 1/3	7	9	.438	98	39	112	4.83	0
2012	Toronto c-d	A.L.	10	40 1/3	3	2	.600	46	17	35	4.69	0
2013	Blue Jays	Gulf Coast	1	3	0	0	.000	0	0	4	0.00	0
2013	Dunedin	Fla.St.	1	5	0	0	.000	7	0	3	0.00	0

Year	Club	Lea	G	IP	W	L	Pct	SO	BB	H	ERA	SAVES
2013	Buffalo	Int.	3	13 1/3	0	2	.000	13	8	17	6.75	0
2013	Toronto e	A.L.	18	92 2/3	5	7	.417	77	45	91	4.56	0
Major League Totals		7 Yrs.	134	682 2/3	40	42	.488	575	303	652	4.25	0
	Division Series											
2009	Philadelphia	N.L.	2	3	0	0	.000	4	2	6	9.00	0
	Championship Series											
2008	Philadelphia	N.L.	1	3	0	0	.000	2	2	4	3.00	0
2009	Philadelphia	N.L.	3	0 2/3	0	0	.000	0	3	0	0.00	0
Championship Series Totals			4	3 2/3	0	0	.000	2	5	4	2.45	0
	World Series Record											
2009	Philadelphia	N.L.	2	2 2/3	0	0	.000	4	1	2	3.38	0

a On disabled list from April 16 to July 6, 2010.

b Traded to Houston Astros with outfielder Anthony Gose and infielder Jonathan Villar for pitcher Roy Oswalt and cash, July 29, 2010.

c Traded to Toronto Blue Jays with pitcher Brandon Lyon and pitcher David Carpenter for pitcher Francisco Cordero, outfielder Ben Francisco, pitcher Joseph Musgrove, pitcher Asher Wojciechowski, pitcher David Rollins, catcher Carlos Perez and player to be named later, July 20, 2012. Houston Astros received pitcher Kevin Comer to complete trade, August 16, 2012.

d On disabled list from September 4 to October 31, 2012.

e On disabled list from May 8 to August 5, 2013.

HARANG, AARON MICHAEL

Born, San Diego, California, May 9, 1978.

Bats Right. Throws Right. Height, 6 feet, 7 inches. Weight, 270 pounds.

Year	Club	Lea	G	IP	W	L	Pct	SO	BB	H	ERA	SAVES
1999	Pulaski	Appal.	16	78 1/3	9	2	.818	87	17	64	2.30	1
2000	Charlotte a	Fla.St.	28	157	13	5	.722	136	50	128	3.32	0
2001	Midland	Texas	27	150	10	8	.556	112	37	173	4.14	0
2002	Midland	Texas	3	16 2/3	2	0	1.000	21	7	12	1.08	0
2002	Sacramento	P.C.	8	38 2/3	3	3	.500	39	9	41	3.26	0
2002	Oakland	A.L.	16	78 1/3	5	4	.556	64	45	78	4.83	0
2003	Louisville	Int.	1	3	0	1	.000	4	2	5	15.00	0
2003	Sacramento	P.C.	12	69 2/3	8	2	.800	60	17	62	2.71	0
2003	Oakland	A.L.	7	30 1/3	1	3	.250	16	9	41	5.34	0
2003	Cincinnati b	N.L.	9	46	4	3	.571	26	10	48	5.28	0
2004	Louisville	Int.	1	3	0	1	.000	3	3	9	12.00	0
2004	Cincinnati c	N.L.	28	161	10	9	.526	125	53	177	4.86	0
2005	Cincinnati	N.L.	32	211 2/3	11	13	.458	163	51	217	3.83	0
2006	Cincinnati	N.L.	36	234 1/3	*16	11	.593	*216	56	242	3.76	0
2007	Cincinnati	N.L.	34	231 2/3	16	6	.727	218	52	213	3.73	0
2008	Louisville	Int.	1	6	1	0	1.000	6	0	5	0.00	0
2008	Cincinnati d	N.L.	30	184 1/3	6	*17	.261	153	50	205	4.78	0
2009	Cincinnati e	N.L.	26	162 1/3	6	14	.300	142	43	186	4.21	0
2010	Louisville	Int.	2	11	0	2	.000	10	2	14	9.00	0
2010	Cincinnati f-g	N.L.	22	111 2/3	6	7	.462	82	38	139	5.32	0
2011	Lake Elsinore	Calif.	1	4	0	1	.000	7	1	5	6.75	0
2011	San Diego h-i	N.L.	28	170 2/3	14	7	.667	124	58	175	3.64	0
2012	Los Angeles	N.L.	31	179 2/3	10	10	.500	131	85	167	3.61	0
2013	Seattle j-k	A.L.	22	120 1/3	5	11	.313	87	28	133	5.76	0
2013	Las Vegas	P.C.	1	4	0	0	.000	5	1	7	4.50	0
2013	New York l-m	N.L.	4	23	0	1	.000	26	12	20	3.52	0
Major League Totals		12 Yrs.	325	1945 1/3	110	116	.487	1573	590	2041	4.28	0

a Traded by Texas Rangers to Oakland Athletics with pitcher Ryan Cullen for infielder Randy Velarde, November 17, 2000.

b Traded to Cincinnati Reds with pitcher Joe Valentine and pitcher Jeff Bruksch for outfielder Jose Guillen, July 30, 2003.

c On disabled list from June 2 to June 26, 2004.

d On disabled list from July 9 to August 10, 2008.

e On disabled list from August 21 to October 14, 2009.

f On disabled list from July 1 to August 31, 2010.

g Filed for free agency, November 3, 2010. Signed with San Diego Padres, December 6, 2010.

h On disabled list from June 10 to July 9, 2011.

i Filed for free agency, October 31, 2011. Signed with Los Angeles Dodgers, December 8, 2011.

j Traded to Colorado Rockies for catcher Ramon Hernandez, April 6, 2013.

k Traded to Seattle Mariners for pitcher Steve Hensley, April 11, 2013.

l Released by Seattle Mariners, August 30, 2013. Signed with New York Mets organization, September 1, 2013.

m Filed for free agency, October 31, 2013.

HAREN, DANIEL JOHN (DAN)

Born, Monterey Park, California, September 17, 1980.
Bats Right. Throws Right. Height, 6 feet, 5 inches. Weight, 220 pounds.

Year	Club	Lea	G	IP	W	L	Pct	SO	BB	H	ERA	SAVES
2001	New Jersey	N.Y.-Penn.	12	52 1/3	3	3	.500	57	8	47	3.10	1
2002	Potomac	Carolina	14	92	3	6	.333	82	19	90	3.62	0
2002	Peoria	Midwest	14	101 2/3	7	3	.700	89	12	89	1.95	0
2003	Memphis	P.C.	8	45 2/3	2	1	.667	35	8	50	4.93	0
2003	Tennessee	Southern	8	55	6	0	1.000	49	6	36	0.82	0
2003	St. Louis	N.L.	14	72 2/3	3	7	.300	43	22	84	5.08	0
2004	Memphis	P.C.	21	128	11	4	.733	150	33	136	4.15	0
2004	St. Louis a	N.L.	14	46	3	3	.500	32	17	45	4.50	0
2005	Oakland	A.L.	34	217	14	12	.538	163	53	212	3.73	0
2006	Oakland	A.L.	34	223	14	13	.519	176	45	224	4.12	0
2007	Oakland b	A.L.	34	222 2/3	15	9	.625	192	55	214	3.07	0
2008	Arizona	N.L.	33	216	16	8	.667	206	40	204	3.33	0
2009	Arizona	N.L.	33	229 1/3	14	10	.583	223	38	192	3.14	0
2010	Arizona	N.L.	21	141	7	8	.467	141	29	161	4.60	0
2010	Los Angeles c	A.L.	14	94	5	4	.556	75	25	84	2.87	0
2011	Los Angeles	A.L.	35	238 1/3	16	10	.615	192	33	211	3.17	0
2012	Inland Empire	Calif.	1	5	0	0	.000	2	0	7	3.60	0
2012	Los Angeles d-e	A.L.	30	176 2/3	12	13	.480	142	38	190	4.33	0
2013	Washington f-g	N.L.	31	169 2/3	10	14	.417	151	31	179	4.67	1
Major League Totals		11 Yrs.	327	2046 1/3	129	111	.538	1736	426	2000	3.74	1
	Division Series											
2004	St. Louis	N.L.	1	2	1	0	1.000	3	1	1	0.00	0
2006	Oakland	A.L.	1	6	1	0	1.000	2	1	9	3.00	0
Division Series Totals			2	8	2	0	1.000	5	2	10	2.25	0
	Championship Series											
2004	St. Louis	N.L.	2	1 2/3	0	0	.000	2	0	3	10.80	0
2006	Oakland	A.L.	1	5	0	0	.000	7	2	7	5.40	0
Championship Series Totals			3	6 2/3	0	0	.000	9	2	10	6.75	0
	World Series Record											
2004	St. Louis	N.L.	2	4 2/3	0	0	.000	2	3	4	0.00	0

a Traded to Oakland Athletics with pitcher Kiko Calero and catcher Daric Barton for pitcher Mark Mulder, December 18, 2004.

b Traded to Arizona Diamondbacks with pitcher Connor Robertson for pitcher Brett Anderson, pitcher Dana Eveland, pitcher Greg Smith, infielder Chris Carter, outfielder Aaron Cunningham and outfielder Carlos Gonzalez, December 14, 2007.

c Traded to Los Angeles Angels for pitcher Joe Saunders, pitcher Rafael Rodriguez, pitcher Patrick Corbin and player to be named later, July 25, 2010. Arizona Diamondbacks received pitcher Tyler Skaggs to complete trade, August 7, 2010.

d On disabled list from July 5 to July 22, 2012.

e Filed for free agency, November 3, 2012. Signed with Washington Nationals, December 7, 2012.

f On disabled list from June 23 to July 8, 2013.

g Filed for free agency, October 31, 2013. Signed with Los Angeles Dodgers, November 25, 2013.

HARRELL, LUCAS WILLIAM BRADLEY

Born, Springfield, Missouri, June 3, 1985.
Bats Both. Throws Right. Height, 6 feet, 2 inches. Weight, 210 pounds.

Year	Club	Lea	G	IP	W	L	Pct	SO	BB	H	ERA	SAVES
2004	Bristol	Appal.	13	48 1/3	3	5	.375	33	32	53	5.59	0
2005	Kannapolis	So.Atl.	26	133 1/3	7	11	.389	85	71	128	3.65	0
2006	Winston-Salem	Carolina	17	91 2/3	7	2	.778	70	44	58	2.45	0
2006	Birmingham	Southern	3	9 2/3	0	2	.000	4	14	12	10.24	0
2007	a				INJURED—Did Not Play							
2008	Bristol	Appal.	1	3	0	0	.000	5	1	3	3.00	0
2008	Kannapolis	So.Atl.	3	10 2/3	1	1	.500	7	4	13	5.91	0
2008	Birmingham	Southern	11	54 2/3	3	3	.500	34	19	56	3.46	0
2009	Charlotte	Int.	11	65 2/3	4	1	.800	42	37	58	3.29	0
2009	Birmingham	Southern	14	80 1/3	8	3	.727	51	32	78	3.25	0
2010	Charlotte	Int.	26	137 2/3	10	10	.500	84	61	141	4.58	0
2010	Chicago	A.L.	8	24	1	0	1.000	15	17	34	4.88	0
2011	Chicago	A.L.	3	5	0	0	.000	5	1	11	7.20	0
2011	Charlotte	Int.	13	74 1/3	7	3	.700	56	26	67	3.27	0
2011	Oklahoma	P.C.	9	52 1/3	5	2	.714	38	24	42	1.72	0
2011	Houston b	N.L.	6	13	0	2	.000	10	7	12	3.46	0
2012	Houston	N.L.	32	193 2/3	11	11	.500	140	78	185	3.76	0
2013	Houston	A.L.	36	153 2/3	6	*17	.261	89	*88	174	5.86	0

Year Club	Lea	G	IP	W	L	Pct	SO	BB	H	ERA	SAVES
Major League Totals	4 Yrs.	85	389 1/3	18	30	.375	259	191	416	4.69	0

a On minor league disabled list from April 5 to September 17, 2007.
b Claimed on waivers by Houston Astros, July 8, 2011.

HARRIS, WILLIAM TAYLOR (WILL)

Born, Houston, Texas, August 28, 1984.
Bats Right. Throws Right. Height, 6 feet, 4 inches. Weight, 225 pounds.

Year Club	Lea	G	IP	W	L	Pct	SO	BB	H	ERA	SAVES
2006 Tri-City	Northwest	22	31	2	3	.400	42	9	20	1.16	6
2007 Asheville	So.Atl.	38	47 2/3	1	2	.333	68	13	38	1.32	1
2008 Modesto	Calif.	49	61 2/3	3	5	.375	70	20	51	2.77	3
2009 Tri-City	Northwest	1	1	0	0	.000	2	0	1	0.00	0
2010 a				INJURED—Did Not Play							
2011 Modesto	Calif.	33	47	3	2	.600	55	21	45	5.55	0
2012 Tulsa	Texas	31	34 1/3	2	1	.667	46	12	26	2.62	1
2012 Colorado Springs	P.C.	13	17 2/3	2	0	1.000	20	1	9	1.02	0
2012 Colorado	N.L.	20	17 2/3	1	1	.500	19	6	27	8.15	0
2013 Reno b	P.C.	12	11 2/3	0	0	.000	23	6	12	4.63	2
2013 Arizona c	N.L.	61	52 2/3	4	1	.800	53	15	50	2.91	0
Major League Totals	2 Yrs.	81	70 1/3	5	2	.714	72	21	77	4.22	0

a On minor league disabled list from June 18 to September 28, 2010.
b Claimed on waivers by Oakland Athletics, April 3, 2013.
c Claimed on waivers by Arizona Diamondbacks, April 6, 2013.

HARRISON, MATTHEW REID (MATT)

Born, Durham, North Carolina, August 16, 1985.
Bats Left. Throws Left. Height, 6 feet, 4 inches. Weight, 225 pounds.

Year Club	Lea	G	IP	W	L	Pct	SO	BB	H	ERA	SAVES
2003 Braves	Gulf Coast	11	39	3	1	.750	33	9	40	3.69	1
2004 Danville	Appal.	13	66	4	4	.500	49	10	72	4.09	0
2005 Rome	So.Atl.	27	167	12	7	.632	118	30	151	3.23	0
2006 Myrtle Beach	Carolina	13	81 1/3	8	4	.667	60	16	77	3.10	0
2006 Mississippi	Southern	13	77 1/3	3	4	.429	54	17	83	3.61	0
2007 Mississippi a	Southern	20	116 2/3	5	7	.417	78	34	118	3.39	0
2008 Frisco	Texas	9	46	3	2	.600	35	14	49	3.33	0
2008 Oklahoma	P.C.	6	38	3	1	.750	20	14	40	3.55	0
2008 Texas	A.L.	15	83 2/3	9	3	.750	42	31	100	5.49	0
2009 Frisco	Texas	3	9	0	1	.000	7	4	9	3.00	0
2009 Texas b	A.L.	11	63 1/3	4	5	.444	34	23	81	6.11	0
2010 Frisco	Texas	2	3	0	0	.000	4	0	3	3.00	1
2010 Oklahoma	P.C.	1	4 1/3	0	1	.000	4	1	9	6.23	0
2010 Texas c	A.L.	37	78 1/3	3	2	.600	46	39	80	4.71	2
2011 Texas	A.L.	31	185 2/3	14	9	.609	126	57	180	3.39	0
2012 Texas	A.L.	32	213 1/3	18	11	.621	133	59	210	3.29	0
2013 Frisco	Texas	2	5	0	1	.000	5	2	5	1.80	0
2013 Round Rock	P.C.	1	3	0	1	.000	0	2	3	9.00	0
2013 Texas d	A.L.	2	10 2/3	0	2	.000	12	7	14	8.44	0
Major League Totals	6 Yrs.	128	635	48	32	.600	393	216	665	4.15	2
Division Series											
2011 Texas	A.L.	2	5 2/3	1	0	1.000	9	3	6	4.76	0
Championship Series											
2011 Texas	A.L.	1	5	0	0	.000	3	3	3	3.60	0
World Series Record											
2011 Texas	A.L.	2	7 2/3	0	2	.000	4	3	11	7.04	0

a Traded to Texas Rangers with catcher Jarrod Saltalamacchia, infielder Elvis Andrus, pitcher Neftali Feliz and pitcher Beau James for infielder Mark Teixeira and pitcher Ron Mahay, July 31, 2007.
b On disabled list from May 26 to June 17 and June 24 to November 13, 2009.
c On disabled list from May 7 to May 29, 2010.
d On disabled list from April 7 to November 4, 2013.

HARVEY, MATTHEW EDWARD (MATT)

Born, New London, Connecticut, March 27, 1989.
Bats Right. Throws Right. Height, 6 feet, 4 inches. Weight, 225 pounds.

Year Club	Lea	G	IP	W	L	Pct	SO	BB	H	ERA	SAVES
2011 Binghamton	Eastern	12	59 2/3	5	3	.625	64	23	58	4.53	0
2011 St. Lucie	Fla.St.	14	76	8	2	.800	92	24	67	2.37	0

Year	Club	Lea	G	IP	W	L	Pct	SO	BB	H	ERA	SAVES
2012	Buffalo	Int.	20	110	7	5	.583	112	48	97	3.68	0
2012	New York	N.L.	10	59 1/3	3	5	.375	70	26	42	2.73	0
2013	New York a	N.L.	26	178 1/3	9	5	.643	191	31	135	2.27	0
Major League Totals		2 Yrs.	36	237 2/3	12	10	.545	261	57	177	2.39	0

a On disabled list from August 27 to October 31, 2013.

HAWKINS, LA TROY (LA TROY)

Born, Gary, Indiana, December 21, 1972.

Bats Right. Throws Right. Height, 6 feet, 5 inches. Weight, 220 pounds.

Year	Club	Lea	G	IP	W	L	Pct	SO	BB	H	ERA	SAVES
1991	Twins	Gulf Coast	11	55	4	3	.571	47	26	62	4.75	0
1992	Twins	Gulf Coast	6	36 1/3	3	2	.600	35	10	36	3.22	0
1992	Elizabethtn	Appal.	5	26 2/3	0	1	.000	36	11	21	3.38	0
1993	Ft. Wayne	Midwest	26	157 1/3	15	5	.750	179	41	110	2.06	0
1994	Ft. Myers	Fla.St.	6	38 2/3	4	0	1.000	36	6	32	2.33	0
1994	Nashville	Southern	11	73 1/3	9	2	.818	53	28	50	2.33	0
1994	Salt Lake	P.C.	12	81 2/3	5	4	.556	37	33	92	4.08	0
1995	Salt Lake	P.C.	22	144 1/3	9	7	.563	74	40	150	3.55	0
1995	Minnesota	A.L.	6	27	2	3	.400	9	12	39	8.67	0
1996	Minnesota	A.L.	7	26 1/3	1	1	.500	24	9	42	8.20	0
1996	Salt Lake	P.C.	20	137 2/3	9	8	.529	99	31	138	3.92	0
1997	Salt Lake	P.C.	14	76	9	4	.692	53	16	100	5.45	0
1997	Minnesota	A.L.	20	103 1/3	6	12	.333	58	47	134	5.84	0
1998	Minnesota	A.L.	33	190 1/3	7	14	.333	105	61	227	5.25	0
1999	Minnesota	A.L.	33	174 1/3	10	14	.417	103	60	238	6.66	0
2000	Minnesota	A.L.	66	87 2/3	2	5	.286	59	32	85	3.39	14
2001	Minnesota	A.L.	62	51 1/3	1	5	.167	36	39	59	5.96	28
2002	Minnesota	A.L.	65	80 1/3	6	0	1.000	63	15	63	2.13	0
2003	Minnesota a	A.L.	74	77 1/3	9	3	.750	75	15	69	1.86	2
2004	Chicago	N.L.	77	82	5	4	.556	69	14	72	2.63	25
2005	Fresno	P.C.	2	2	0	0	.000	1	0	2	0.00	0
2005	Chicago-San Fran. b-c-d	N.L.	66	56 1/3	2	8	.200	43	24	58	3.83	6
2006	Baltimore e	A.L.	60	60 1/3	3	2	.600	27	15	73	4.48	0
2007	Colorado Springs	P.C.	4	4	1	0	1.000	5	2	2	2.25	0
2007	Colorado f-g	N.L.	62	55 1/3	2	5	.286	29	16	52	3.42	0
2008	New York	A.L.	33	41	1	1	.500	23	17	42	5.71	0
2008	Houston h-i	N.L.	24	21	2	0	1.000	25	5	11	0.43	1
2009	Houston j-k	N.L.	65	63 1/3	1	4	.200	45	16	60	2.13	11
2010	Brewers	Arizona	2	3 2/3	0	0	.000	5	0	4	2.45	0
2010	Nashville	P.C.	4	6 1/3	0	0	.000	1	0	4	0.00	1
2010	Milwaukee l	N.L.	18	16	0	3	.000	18	6	21	8.44	0
2011	Brevard County	Fla.St.	3	3 2/3	0	0	.000	5	0	6	4.91	0
2011	Nashville	P.C.	2	1 1/3	0	0	.000	1	2	1	0.00	0
2011	Milwaukee m-n	N.L.	52	48 1/3	3	1	.750	28	10	50	2.42	0
2012	Inland Empire	Calif.	1	1	0	0	.000	2	0	2	9.00	0
2012	Salt Lake	P.C.	2	2	0	0	.000	1	1	1	0.00	0
2012	Los Angeles o-p	A.L.	48	42	2	3	.400	23	13	45	3.64	1
2013	New York q	N.L.	72	70 2/3	3	2	.600	55	10	71	2.93	13
Major League Totals		19 Yrs.	943	1374 1/3	68	90	.430	917	436	1511	4.37	101
	Division Series											
2002	Minnesota	A.L.	3	2 1/3	0	0	.000	5	0	0	0.00	0
2003	Minnesota	A.L.	3	3	1	0	1.000	5	0	5	6.00	0
2007	Colorado	N.L.	1	1	0	0	.000	0	1	0	0.00	0
2011	Milwaukee	N.L.	1	1	0	0	.000	1	2	0	0.00	0
Division Series Totals			8	7 1/3	1	0	1.000	11	3	5	2.45	0
	Championship Series											
2002	Minnesota	A.L.	4	1 1/3	0	0	.000	1	1	4	20.25	0
2007	Colorado	N.L.	2	2	0	0	.000	1	0	1	0.00	0
2011	Milwaukee	N.L.	3	3	0	0	.000	2	2	2	0.00	0
Championship Series Totals			9	6 1/3	0	0	.000	4	3	7	4.26	0
	World Series Record											
2007	Colorado	N.L.	2	2	0	0	.000	2	0	1	4.50	0

a Filed for free agency, October 27, 2003. Signed with Chicago Cubs, December 3, 2003.
b Traded to San Francisco Giants for pitcher Jerome Williams and pitcher David Aardsma, May 28, 2005.
c On disabled list from June 10 to July 4, 2005.
d Traded to Baltimore Orioles for pitcher Steve Kline, December 6, 2005.
e Filed for free agency, October 31, 2006. Signed with Colorado Rockies, December 5, 2006.
f On disabled list from April 21 to May 22, 2007.

g Filed for free agency, November 1, 2007. Signed with New York Yankees, December 21, 2007.
h Traded to Houston Astros for infielder Matt Cusick and cash, July 30, 2008.
i Filed for free agency, October 31, 2008, re-signed with Houston Astros, November 11, 2008.
j On disabled list from July 28 to August 12, 2009.
k Filed for free agency, November 6, 2009. Signed with Milwaukee Brewers, December 16, 2009.
l On disabled list from May 7 to July 29 and August 11 to October 5, 2010.
m On disabled list from March 22 to April 21, 2011.
n Filed for free agency, October 30, 2011. Signed with Los Angeles Angels, December 8, 2011.
o On disabled list from May 7 to June 9, 2012.
p Filed for free agency, November 3, 2012. Signed with New York Mets organization, January 31, 2013.
q Filed for free agency, October 31, 2013. Signed with Los Angeles Dodgers, November 19, 2013.

HEFNER, JEREMY SCOTT

Born, Perkins, Oklahoma, March 11, 1986.
Bats Right. Throws Right. Height, 6 feet, 4 inches. Weight, 215 pounds.

Year	Club	Lea	G	IP	W	L	Pct	SO	BB	H	ERA	SAVES
2007	Eugene	Northwest	17	62⅓	2	5	.286	74	20	51	3.90	0
2008	Lake Elsinore	Calif.	1	5	0	0	.000	6	2	3	3.60	0
2008	Fort Wayne	Midwest	29	140⅓	10	5	.667	144	41	117	3.33	0
2009	Lake Elsinore	Calif.	27	150⅔	14	9	.609	142	38	165	4.12	0
2009	Portland	P.C.	1	5⅓	0	0	.000	5	2	7	3.38	0
2010	San Antonio	Texas	28	167⅔	11	8	.579	115	51	156	2.95	0
2011	Tucson a-b	P.C.	28	157⅓	9	7	.563	120	61	178	4.98	0
2012	Buffalo	Int.	10	61⅔	5	2	.714	37	10	55	2.77	0
2012	New York	N.L.	26	93⅔	4	7	.364	62	18	110	5.09	0
2013	New York c-d	N.L.	24	130⅔	4	8	.333	99	37	132	4.34	0
Major League Totals		2 Yrs.	50	224⅓	8	15	.348	161	55	242	4.65	0

a Claimed on waivers from San Diego Padres by Pittsburgh Pirates, November 18, 2011.
b Claimed on waivers by New York Mets, December 12, 2011.
c On disabled list from August 10 to October 31, 2013.
d Not offered contract, December 2, 2013, re-signed with New York Mets organization, January 8, 2014.

HELLICKSON, JEREMY ROBERT

Born, Des Moines, Iowa, April 8, 1987.
Bats Right. Throws Right. Height, 6 feet, 1 inch. Weight, 185 pounds.

Year	Club	Lea	G	IP	W	L	Pct	SO	BB	H	ERA	SAVES
2005	Princeton	Appal.	4	6	0	0	.000	11	1	6	6.00	0
2006	Hudson Valley	N.Y.-Penn.	15	77⅔	3	3	.500	96	16	55	2.43	0
2007	Columbus	So.Atl.	21	111⅓	13	3	.813	106	34	87	2.67	0
2008	Vero Beach	Fla.St.	14	76⅔	7	1	.875	83	5	64	2.00	0
2008	Montgomery	Southern	13	75⅓	4	4	.500	79	15	84	3.94	0
2009	Durham	Int.	9	57⅓	6	1	.857	70	15	31	2.51	0
2009	Montgomery	Southern	11	56⅔	3	1	.750	62	14	41	2.38	0
2010	Charlotte	Fla.St.	1	1⅔	0	0	.000	4	2	4	21.60	0
2010	Durham	Int.	21	117⅔	12	3	.800	123	35	103	2.45	0
2010	Tampa Bay	A.L.	10	36⅓	4	0	1.000	33	8	32	3.47	0
2011	Tampa Bay a	A.L.	29	189	13	10	.565	117	72	146	2.95	0
2012	Tampa Bay b	A.L.	31	177	10	11	.476	124	59	163	3.10	0
2013	Tampa Bay	A.L.	32	174	12	10	.545	135	50	185	5.17	0
Major League Totals		4 Yrs.	102	576⅓	39	31	.557	409	189	526	3.70	0
	Division Series											
2011	Tampa Bay	A.L.	1	4	0	1	.000	1	1	4	6.75	0
2013	Tampa Bay	A.L.	1	1	0	0	.000	0	2	1	0.00	0
Division Series Totals			2	5	0	1	.000	1	3	5	5.40	0

a Selected Rookie of the Year in American League for 2011.
b On disabled list from June 15 to June 30, 2012.

HENDERSON, JAMES DUFFY (JIM)

Born, Calgary, Alberta, Canada, October 21, 1982.
Bats Left. Throws Right. Height, 6 feet, 5 inches. Weight, 190 pounds.

Year	Club	Lea	G	IP	W	L	Pct	SO	BB	H	ERA	SAVES
2003	Expos	Gulf Coast	4	8	0	0	.000	3	1	6	2.25	1
2003	Vermont	N.Y.-Penn.	15	24⅔	1	1	.500	13	15	32	6.93	0
2004	Vermont	N.Y.-Penn.	14	76⅓	2	6	.250	39	27	61	2.59	0
2005	Savannah	So.Atl.	26	149⅔	9	11	.450	76	50	166	5.47	0
2006	Potomac	Carolina	25	52	2	2	.500	56	22	44	4.50	1
2006	Savannah a	So.Atl.	3	5⅓	0	1	.000	6	0	6	3.38	0

Year	Club	Lea	G	IP	W	L	Pct	SO	BB	H	ERA	SAVES
2007	Iowa	P.C.	8	13	3	0	1.000	6	6	16	5.54	0
2007	Tennessee	Southern	42	58	4	3	.571	49	25	50	1.86	10
2008	Iowa	P.C.	3	3	0	0	.000	4	5	2	15.00	0
2008	Tennessee	Southern	5	$6^1/_3$	0	1	.000	4	1	5	0.00	1
2009	Brevard County	Fla.St.	15	$29^1/_3$	3	0	1.000	20	14	16	2.76	4
2009	Wisconsin	Midwest	26	$25^1/_3$	0	0	.000	26	8	19	1.07	17
2009	Huntsville b	Southern	5	7	1	0	1.000	5	4	8	2.57	0
2010	Huntsville c	Southern	45	61	4	5	.444	60	35	49	5.46	7
2011	Nashville	P.C.	20	$30^1/_3$	3	1	.750	30	23	24	5.93	0
2011	Huntsville	Southern	22	$30^2/_3$	4	1	.800	39	8	22	2.64	5
2012	Nashville	P.C.	35	48	4	3	.571	56	22	36	1.69	15
2012	Milwaukee	N.L.	36	$30^2/_3$	1	3	.250	45	13	26	3.52	3
2013	Wisconsin	Midwest	1	1	0	0	.000	3	0	1	0.00	0
2013	Milwaukee d	N.L.	61	60	5	5	.500	75	24	44	2.70	28
Major League Totals		2 Yrs.	97	$90^2/_3$	6	8	.429	120	37	70	2.98	31

a Selected by Chicago Cubs from Washington Nationals in Rule V draft, December 7, 2006.
b Released by Chicago Cubs, March 13, 2009. Signed with Milwaukee Brewers organization, April 1, 2009.
c Filed for free agency, November 6, 2010, re-signed with Milwaukee Brewers organization, December 21, 2010.
d On disabled list from May 25 to June 9, 2013.

HERNANDEZ, DAVID JESUS

Born, Sacramento, California, May 13, 1985.
Bats Right. Throws Right. Height, 6 feet, 3 inches. Weight, 215 pounds.

Year	Club	Lea	G	IP	W	L	Pct	SO	BB	H	ERA	SAVES
2005	Aberdeen	N.Y.-Penn.	12	$41^2/_3$	1	2	.333	47	17	41	3.89	0
2006	Delmarva	So.Atl.	28	$145^1/_3$	7	8	.467	154	71	134	4.15	0
2007	Frederick	Carolina	28	$145^1/_3$	7	11	.389	168	47	139	4.95	0
2008	Bowie	Eastern	27	141	10	4	.714	166	71	112	2.68	0
2009	Bowie	Eastern	1	4	0	0	.000	4	1	2	2.25	0
2009	Norfolk	Int.	11	$57^1/_3$	3	2	.600	79	18	42	3.30	0
2009	Baltimore	A.L.	20	$101^1/_3$	4	10	.286	68	46	118	5.42	0
2010	Bowie	Eastern	2	2	0	0	.000	3	0	1	0.00	0
2010	Baltimore a-b	A.L.	41	$79^1/_3$	8	8	.500	72	42	72	4.31	2
2011	Arizona	N.L.	74	$69^1/_3$	5	3	.625	77	30	49	3.38	11
2012	Arizona	N.L.	72	$68^1/_3$	2	3	.400	98	22	48	2.50	4
2013	Reno	P.C.	9	$9^2/_3$	0	0	.000	12	5	6	0.93	2
2013	Arizona	N.L.	62	$62^1/_3$	5	6	.455	66	24	50	4.48	2
Major League Totals		5 Yrs.	269	$380^2/_3$	24	30	.444	381	164	337	4.14	19
Division Series												
2011	Arizona	N.L.	4	5	0	0	.000	5	0	2	3.60	0

a On disabled list from August 5 to September 7, 2010.
b Traded to Arizona Diamondbacks with pitcher Kam Mickolio for infielder Mark Reynolds and player to be named later, December 6, 2010. Baltimore Orioles received catcher John Hester to complete trade, April 30, 2011.

HERNANDEZ, FELIX ABRAHAM

Born, Valencia, Venezuela, April 8, 1986.
Bats Right. Throws Right. Height, 6 feet, 3 inches. Weight, 230 pounds.

Year	Club	Lea	G	IP	W	L	Pct	SO	BB	H	ERA	SAVES
2003	Wisconsin	Midwest	2	14	0	0	.000	18	3	9	1.93	0
2003	Everett	Northwest	11	55	7	2	.778	73	24	43	2.29	0
2004	Inland Empire	California	16	92	9	3	.750	114	26	85	2.74	0
2004	San Antonio	Texas	10	$57^1/_3$	5	1	.833	58	21	47	3.30	0
2005	Tacoma	P.C.	19	88	9	4	.692	100	48	62	2.25	0
2005	Seattle	A.L.	12	$84^1/_3$	4	4	.500	77	23	61	2.67	0
2006	Seattle	A.L.	31	191	12	14	.462	176	60	195	4.52	0
2007	Seattle a	A.L.	30	$190^1/_3$	14	7	.667	165	53	209	3.92	0
2008	Seattle b	A.L.	31	$200^2/_3$	9	11	.450	175	80	198	3.45	0
2009	Seattle	A.L.	34	$238^2/_3$	*19	5	*.792	217	71	200	2.49	0
2010	Seattle c	A.L.	34	*$249^2/_3$	13	12	.520	232	70	194	*2.27	0
2011	Seattle	A.L.	33	$233^2/_3$	14	14	.500	222	67	218	3.47	0
2012	Seattle d	A.L.	33	232	13	9	.591	223	56	209	3.06	0
2013	Seattle	A.L.	31	$204^1/_3$	12	10	.545	216	46	185	3.04	0
Major League Totals		9 Yrs.	269	$1824^2/_3$	110	86	.561	1703	526	1669	3.20	0

a On disabled list from April 19 to May 15, 2007.
b On disabled list from June 24 to July 11, 2008.
c Selected Cy Young Award Winner in American League for 2010.
d Pitched no-hit, no-run perfect game against Tampa Bay Rays, August 15, 2012.

HERNANDEZ (HEREDIA), ROBERTO

Born, Santo Domingo, Dominican Republic, August 30, 1980.
Bats Right. Throws Right. Height, 6 feet, 4 inches. Weight, 230 pounds.
(Played under name of Fausto Carmona 2002-2011)

Year	Club	Lea	G	IP	W	L	Pct	SO	BB	H	ERA	SAVES
2002	Burlington	Appal.	13	76⅓	2	4	.333	42	10	89	3.30	1
2002	Mahoning Valley	N.Y.-Penn.	3	4	0	0	.000	0	1	2	0.00	0
2003	Lake County	So.Atl.	24	148⅓	17	4	.810	83	14	117	2.06	0
2003	Akron	Eastern	1	6	0	0	.000	3	0	8	4.50	0
2004	Kinston	Carolina	13	70	5	2	.714	57	20	68	2.83	0
2004	Akron	Eastern	15	87	4	8	.333	63	21	114	4.97	0
2004	Buffalo	Int.	1	6	1	0	1.000	2	3	6	6.00	0
2005	Akron	Eastern	14	90⅔	6	5	.545	57	20	100	4.07	0
2005	Buffalo	Int.	13	83	7	4	.636	49	15	76	3.25	0
2006	Buffalo	Int.	6	27⅔	1	3	.250	28	8	28	5.53	0
2006	Cleveland	A.L.	38	74⅔	1	10	.091	58	31	88	5.42	0
2007	Cleveland	A.L.	32	215	19	8	.704	137	61	199	3.06	0
2008	Lake County	So.Atl.	1	4	0	0	.000	3	0	1	0.00	0
2008	Akron	Eastern	1	5	1	0	1.000	2	0	9	1.80	0
2008	Cleveland a	A.L.	22	120⅔	8	7	.533	58	70	126	5.44	0
2009	Lake County	So.Atl.	1	6⅓	1	0	1.000	7	1	1	0.00	0
2009	Akron	Eastern	1	7	1	0	1.000	5	0	4	1.29	0
2009	Columbus	Int.	5	33	1	3	.250	27	6	32	3.55	0
2009	Cleveland	A.L.	24	125⅓	5	12	.294	79	70	151	6.32	0
2010	Cleveland	A.L.	33	210⅓	13	14	.481	124	72	203	3.77	0
2011	Cleveland b	A.L.	32	188⅔	7	15	.318	109	60	205	5.25	0
2012	Lake County	Midwest	2	12⅓	1	1	.500	13	1	12	3.65	0
2012	Columbus	Int.	2	12	1	0	1.000	7	3	13	4.50	0
2012	Cleveland c	A.L.	3	14⅓	0	3	.000	2	3	17	7.53	0
2013	Tampa Bay d	A.L.	32	151	6	13	.316	113	38	164	4.89	1
Major League Totals		8 Yrs.	216	1100	59	82	.418	680	405	1153	4.67	1
	Division Series											
2007	Cleveland	A.L.	1	9	0	0	.000	5	2	3	1.00	0
	Championship Series											
2007	Cleveland	A.L.	2	6	0	1	.000	7	9	10	16.50	0

a On disabled list from May 24 to July 26, 2008.
b On disabled list from July 3 to July 18, 2011.
c Filed for free agency, November 3, 2012. Signed with Tampa Bay Rays, December 18, 2012.
d Filed for free agency, October 31, 2013. Signed with Philadelphia Phillies, December 18, 2013.

HERRERA, KELVIN DE JESUS

Born, Tenares, Dominican Republic, December 31, 1989.
Bats Right. Throws Right. Height, 5 feet, 10 inches. Weight, 190 pounds.

Year	Club	Lea	G	IP	W	L	Pct	SO	BB	H	ERA	SAVES
2008	Burlington	Appal.	11	50⅔	2	2	.500	45	5	48	1.42	0
2008	Burlington	Midwest	3	12⅔	2	0	1.000	7	2	13	2.13	0
2009	Burlington	Midwest	1	5	1	0	1.000	1	0	3	0.00	0
2010	Burlington	Midwest	8	41⅓	2	3	.400	40	15	38	4.35	0
2011	Wilmington	Carolina	8	14⅔	2	1	.667	12	2	8	0.61	1
2011	NW Arkansas	Texas	23	36	4	0	1.000	40	6	22	1.75	7
2011	Omaha	P.C.	14	17	1	0	1.000	18	7	12	2.12	6
2011	Kansas City	A.L.	2	2	0	1	.000	0	0	2	13.50	0
2012	Kansas City	A.L.	76	84⅓	4	3	.571	77	21	79	2.35	3
2013	NW Arkansas	Texas	2	2	0	0	.000	5	0	1	0.00	0
2013	Omaha	P.C.	10	16	0	1	.000	22	6	6	1.13	2
2013	Kansas City	A.L.	59	58⅓	5	7	.417	74	21	48	3.86	2
Major League Totals		3 Yrs.	137	144⅔	9	11	.450	151	42	129	3.11	5

HILL, RICHARD JOSEPH (RICH)

Born, Boston, Massachusetts, March 11, 1980.
Bats Left. Throws Left. Height, 6 feet, 5 inches. Weight, 220 pounds.

Year	Club	Lea	G	IP	W	L	Pct	SO	BB	H	ERA	SAVES
2002	Boise	Northwest	6	14	0	2	.000	12	14	15	8.36	0
2003	Boise	Northwest	14	68⅓	1	6	.143	99	32	57	4.35	0
2003	Lansing	Midwest	15	29⅓	0	1	.000	50	36	14	2.76	0
2004	Daytona	Fla.St.	28	109⅓	7	6	.538	136	72	88	4.03	0
2005	West Tenn	Southern	10	57⅔	4	3	.571	90	21	42	3.28	0
2005	Peoria	Midwest	1	8	1	0	1.000	12	0	5	1.13	0
2005	Iowa	P.C.	11	65	6	1	.857	92	14	53	3.60	0

Year Club	Lea	G	IP	W	L	Pct	SO	BB	H	ERA	SAVES
2005 Chicago	N.L.	10	23⅔	0	2	.000	21	17	25	9.13	0
2006 Iowa	P.C.	15	100	7	1	.875	135	21	62	1.80	0
2006 Chicago	N.L.	17	99⅓	6	7	.462	90	39	83	4.17	0
2007 Chicago	N.L.	32	195	11	8	.579	183	63	170	3.92	0
2008 Iowa	P.C.	7	26	2	4	.333	32	28	22	5.88	0
2008 Cubs	Arizona	3	9⅓	1	1	.500	11	5	5	2.89	0
2008 Daytona	Fla.St.	3	12⅓	1	2	.333	14	11	12	8.03	0
2008 Chicago a	N.L.	5	19⅔	1	0	1.000	15	18	13	4.12	0
2009 Frederick b	Carolina	1	3	0	1	.000	3	0	1	3.00	0
2009 Norfolk	Int.	3	13⅓	1	1	.500	14	9	5	1.35	0
2009 Baltimore c	A.L.	14	57⅔	3	3	.500	46	40	68	7.80	0
2010 Memphis d	P.C.	23	46	4	3	.571	47	30	35	4.30	0
2010 Pawtucket e	Int.	19	53	3	1	.750	55	29	45	3.74	0
2010 Boston f	A.L.	6	4	1	0	1.000	3	1	5	0.00	0
2011 Pawtucket	Int.	10	16	1	0	1.000	18	5	8	1.13	1
2011 Boston g-h	A.L.	9	8	0	0	.000	12	3	3	0.00	0
2012 Greenville	So.Atl.	2	2	0	0	.000	5	0	2	4.50	0
2012 Salem	Carolina	3	4	0	0	.000	8	1	1	0.00	0
2012 Red Sox	Gulf Coast	2	1⅓	0	1	.000	3	2	0	13.50	0
2012 Portland	Eastern	1	1	0	0	.000	1	0	1	0.00	0
2012 Pawtucket	Int.	8	8	1	0	1.000	10	2	3	1.13	0
2012 Boston i-j	A.L.	25	19⅔	1	0	1.000	21	11	17	1.83	0
2013 Cleveland k	A.L.	63	38⅔	1	2	.333	51	29	38	6.28	0
Major League Totals	9 Yrs.	181	465⅔	24	22	.522	442	221	422	4.74	0
Division Series											
2007 Chicago	N.L.	1	3	0	1	.000	3	2	6	9.00	0

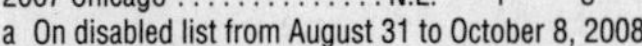

a On disabled list from August 31 to October 8, 2008.
b Sold to Baltimore Orioles, February 2, 2009.
c On disabled list from March 29 to May 16 and July 28 to October 30, 2009.
d Filed for free agency, November 3, 2009. Signed with St. Louis Cardinals organization, January 26, 2010.
e Filed for free agency, June 28, 2010. Signed with Boston Red Sox organization, June 30, 2010.
f Filed for free agency, October 8, 2010, re-signed with Boston Red Sox organization, December 16, 2010.
g On disabled list from June 2 to October 31, 2011.
h Not offered contract, December 12, 2011, re-signed with Boston Red Sox organization, December 13, 2011.
i On disabled list from March 26 to April 27 and June 9 to September 1, 2012.
j Not offered contract, November 30, 2012. Signed with Cleveland Indians organization, February 7, 2013.
k Filed for free agency, October 31, 2013.

HOCHEVAR, LUKE ANTHONY

Born, Denver, Colorado, September 15, 1983.
Bats Right. Throws Right. Height, 6 feet, 5 inches. Weight, 205 pounds.

Year Club	Lea	G	IP	W	L	Pct	SO	BB	H	ERA	SAVES
2006 Burlington	Midwest	4	15⅓	0	1	.000	16	2	8	1.17	0
2007 Wichita	Texas	17	94	3	6	.333	94	26	110	4.69	0
2007 Omaha	P.C.	10	58	1	3	.250	44	21	53	5.12	0
2007 Kansas City	A.L.	4	12⅔	0	1	.000	5	4	11	2.13	0
2008 Omaha	P.C.	3	17⅓	1	1	.500	12	6	11	2.60	0
2008 Kansas City a	A.L.	22	129	6	12	.333	72	47	143	5.51	0
2009 Omaha	P.C.	8	48	5	1	.833	36	12	41	1.50	0
2009 Kansas City	A.L.	25	143	7	13	.350	106	46	167	6.55	0
2010 Omaha	P.C.	2	5	0	0	.000	4	1	3	1.80	0
2010 Kansas City b	A.L.	18	103	6	6	.500	76	37	110	4.81	0
2011 Kansas City	A.L.	31	198	11	11	.500	128	62	192	4.68	0
2012 Kansas City	A.L.	32	185⅓	8	16	.333	144	61	202	5.73	0
2013 Kansas City	A.L.	58	70⅓	5	2	.714	82	17	41	1.92	2
Major League Totals	7 Yrs.	190	841⅓	43	61	.413	613	274	866	5.10	2

a On disabled list from August 20 to November 14, 2008.
b On disabled list from June 12 to September 3, 2010.

HOLLAND, DEREK LANE

Born, Newark, Ohio, October 9, 1986.
Bats Both. Throws Left. Height, 6 feet, 2 inches. Weight, 185 pounds.

Year Club	Lea	G	IP	W	L	Pct	SO	BB	H	ERA	SAVES
2007 Spokane	Northwest	16	67	4	5	.444	83	21	57	3.22	0
2008 Bakersfield	Calif.	5	31	3	1	.750	37	5	20	3.19	0
2008 Clinton	Midwest	17	93⅔	7	0	1.000	91	29	77	2.40	0
2008 Frisco	Texas	4	26	3	0	1.000	29	6	14	0.69	0
2009 Oklahoma	P.C.	1	4	0	1	.000	5	3	5	9.00	0

Year Club	Lea	G	IP	W	L	Pct	SO	BB	H	ERA	SAVES
2009 Texas	A.L.	33	138⅓	8	13	.381	107	47	160	6.12	0
2010 Rangers	Arizona	1	3	0	0	.000	6	0	0	0.00	0
2010 Oklahoma	P.C.	11	62⅔	6	2	.750	51	18	50	1.87	0
2010 Texas a	A.L.	14	57⅓	3	4	.429	54	24	55	4.08	0
2011 Texas	A.L.	32	198	16	5	.762	162	67	201	3.95	0
2012 Round Rock	P.C.	2	9	0	2	.000	5	2	11	6.00	0
2012 Texas b	A.L.	29	175⅓	12	7	.632	145	52	162	4.67	0
2013 Texas	A.L.	33	213	10	9	.526	189.	64	210	3.42	0
Major League Totals	5 Yrs.	141	782	49	38	.563	657	254	788	4.36	0
Wild Card Playoff											
2012 Texas	A.L.	1	0⅓	0	0	.000	1	0	1	0.00	0
Division Series											
2010 Texas	A.L.	2	4⅔	0	0	.000	4	1	6	5.79	0
2011 Texas	A.L.	2	6⅓	1	0	1.000	2	2	7	1.42	0
Division Series Totals		4	11	1	0	1.000	6	3	13	3.27	0
Championship Series											
2010 Texas	A.L.	2	5⅔	1	0	1.000	4	2	3	0.00	0
2011 Texas	A.L.	2	7⅓	0	0	.000	5	4	11	8.59	0
Championship Series Totals		4	13	1	0	1.000	9	6	14	4.85	0
World Series Record											
2010 Texas	A.L.	2	1	0	0	.000	1	4	0	27.00	0
2011 Texas	A.L.	2	10⅓	1	0	1.000	7	2	4	0.87	0
World Series Totals		4	11⅓	1	0	1.000	8	6	4	3.18	0

a On disabled list from May 31 to August 1, 2010.
b On disabled list from June 6 to July 7, 2012.

HOLLAND, GREGORY SCOTT (GREG)

Born, Morganton, North Carolina, November 20, 1985.
Bats Right. Throws Right. Height, 5 feet, 11 inches. Weight, 200 pounds.

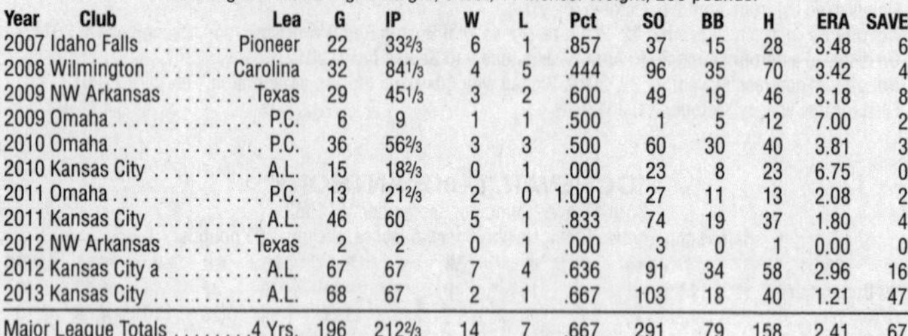

Year Club	Lea	G	IP	W	L	Pct	SO	BB	H	ERA	SAVES
2007 Idaho Falls	Pioneer	22	33⅔	6	1	.857	37	15	28	3.48	6
2008 Wilmington	Carolina	32	84⅓	4	5	.444	96	35	70	3.42	4
2009 NW Arkansas	Texas	29	45⅓	3	2	.600	49	19	46	3.18	8
2009 Omaha	P.C.	6	9	1	1	.500	1	5	12	7.00	2
2010 Omaha	P.C.	36	56⅔	3	3	.500	60	30	40	3.81	3
2010 Kansas City	A.L.	15	18⅔	0	1	.000	23	8	23	6.75	0
2011 Omaha	P.C.	13	21⅔	2	0	1.000	27	11	13	2.08	2
2011 Kansas City	A.L.	46	60	5	1	.833	74	19	37	1.80	4
2012 NW Arkansas	Texas	2	2	0	1	.000	3	0	1	0.00	0
2012 Kansas City a	A.L.	67	67	7	4	.636	91	34	58	2.96	16
2013 Kansas City	A.L.	68	67	2	1	.667	103	18	40	1.21	47
Major League Totals	4 Yrs.	196	212⅔	14	7	.667	291	79	158	2.41	67

a On disabled list from April 21 to May 12, 2012.

HOOVER, JAMES ALLEN (J.J.)

Born, Pittsburgh, Pennsylvania, August 13, 1987.
Bats Right. Throws Right. Height, 6 feet, 3 inches. Weight, 230 pounds.

Year Club	Lea	G	IP	W	L	Pct	SO	BB	H	ERA	SAVES
2008 Danville	Appal.	2	4⅔	1	0	1.000	6	1	4	0.00	0
2009 Myrtle Beach	Carolina	1	3	0	0	.000	2	5	3	9.00	0
2009 Rome	So.Atl.	25	134⅓	7	6	.538	148	25	135	3.35	1
2010 Myrtle Beach	Carolina	24	132⅔	11	6	.647	118	35	126	3.26	0
2010 Mississippi	Southern	4	20⅔	3	1	.750	34	15	15	3.48	0
2011 Gwinnett	Int.	12	18⅔	1	1	.500	31	12	12	3.38	1
2011 Mississippi	Southern	31	87	2	5	.286	86	28	65	2.48	1
2012 Louisville a	Int.	30	37	4	0	1.000	55	12	15	1.22	13
2012 Cincinnati	N.L.	28	30⅔	1	0	1.000	31	13	17	2.05	1
2013 Cincinnati	N.L.	69	66	5	5	.500	67	26	47	2.86	3
Major League Totals	2 Yrs.	97	96⅔	6	5	.545	98	39	64	2.61	4
Wild Card Playoff											
2013 Cincinnati	N.L.	1	0⅔	0	0	.000	0	0	0	0.00	0
Division Series											
2012 Cincinnati	N.L.	2	2⅔	0	0	.000	2	2	0	0.00	0

a Traded by Atlanta Braves to Cincinnati Reds for infielder Juan Francisco, April 1, 2012.

HOWELL, JAMES PHILLIP (J.P.)

Born, Modesto, California, April 25, 1983.
Bats Left. Throws Left. Height, 6 feet. Weight, 190 pounds.

Year Club	Lea	G	IP	W	L	Pct	SO	BB	H	ERA	SAVES
2004 Idaho Falls	Pioneer	6	26	3	1	.750	38	12	16	2.77	0
2005 High Desert	Calif.	8	46	3	1	.750	48	24	33	1.96	0
2005 Wichita	Texas	3	18	2	0	1.000	23	5	12	2.50	0
2005 Omaha	P.C.	7	37 2/3	3	1	.750	29	19	40	4.06	0
2005 Kansas City	A.L.	15	72 2/3	3	5	.375	54	39	73	6.19	0
2006 Omaha	P.C.	8	36	3	2	.600	33	14	39	4.75	0
2006 Durham	Int.	10	55	5	3	.625	49	15	53	2.62	0
2006 Tampa Bay a	A.L.	8	42 1/3	1	3	.250	33	14	52	5.10	0
2007 Durham	Int.	21	128	7	8	.467	145	34	110	3.38	0
2007 Tampa Bay	A.L.	10	51	1	6	.143	49	21	69	7.59	0
2008 Tampa Bay	A.L.	64	89 1/3	6	1	.857	92	39	62	2.22	3
2009 Tampa Bay	A.L.	69	66 2/3	7	5	.583	79	33	47	2.83	17
2010 Tampa Bay b-c	A.L.			INJURED—Did Not Play							
2011 Durham	Int.	4	3 2/3	0	0	.000	5	1	5	0.00	0
2011 Tampa Bay	A.L.	46	30 2/3	2	3	.400	26	18	30	6.16	1
2011 Charlotte d	Fla.St.	3	3 1/3	0	1	.000	4	1	3	2.70	0
2012 Tampa Bay e	A.L.	55	50 1/3	1	0	1.000	42	22	39	3.04	0
2013 Los Angeles f	N.L.	67	62	4	1	.800	54	23	42	2.03	0
Major League Totals	8 Yrs.	334	465	25	24	.510	429	209	414	4.10	21
Division Series											
2008 Tampa Bay	A.L.	3	4 1/3	0	0	.000	6	0	2	0.00	0
2011 Tampa Bay	A.L.	1	0	0	0	.000	0	0	1	—	0
2013 Los Angeles	N.L.	3	2 1/3	0	0	.000	3	1	1	0.00	0
Division Series Totals		7	6 2/3	0	0	.000	9	1	4	0.00	0
Championship Series											
2008 Tampa Bay	A.L.	6	5 1/3	0	1	.000	6	3	5	3.38	0
2013 Los Angeles	N.L.	4	3 2/3	0	0	.000	3	2	4	2.45	0
Championship Series Totals		10	9	0	1	.000	9	5	9	3.00	0
World Series Record											
2008 Tampa Bay	A.L.	3	2 1/3	0	2	.000	5	1	2	7.71	0

a Traded to Tampa Bay Devil Rays for outfielder Joey Gathright and infielder Fernando Cortez, June 20, 2006.
b On disabled list from March 26 to November 2, 2010.
c Not offered contract, December 2, 2010, re-signed with Tampa Bay Rays, December 13, 2010.
d On disabled list from March 22 to May 20, 2011.
e Filed for free agency, November 3, 2012. Signed with Los Angeles Dodgers, January 7, 2013.
f Filed for free agency, October 31, 2013, re-signed with Los Angeles Dodgers, December 20, 2013.

HUDSON, TIMOTHY ADAM (TIM)

Born, Columbus, Georgia, July 14, 1975.
Bats Right. Throws Right. Height, 6 feet, I Inch. Weight, 170 pounds.

Year Club	Lea	G	IP	W	L	Pct	SO	BB	H	ERA	SAVES
1997 Sou Oregon	Northwest	8	28 2/3	3	1	.750	37	15	12	2.51	0
1998 Modesto	California	8	37 2/3	4	0	1.000	48	18	19	1.67	0
1998 Huntsville	Southern	22	134 2/3	10	9	.526	104	71	136	4.54	0
1999 Midland	Texas	3	18	3	0	1.000	18	3	9	0.50	0
1999 Vancouver	P.C.	8	49	4	0	1.000	61	21	38	2.20	0
1999 Oakland	A.L.	21	136 1/3	11	2	.846	132	62	121	3.23	0
2000 Oakland	A.L.	32	202 1/3	*20	6	*.769	169	82	169	4.14	0
2001 Oakland	A.L.	35	235	18	9	.667	181	71	216	3.37	0
2002 Oakland	A.L.	34	238 1/3	15	9	.625	152	62	237	2.98	0
2003 Oakland	A.L.	34	240	16	7	.696	162	61	197	2.70	0
2004 Sacramento	P.C.	1	3	0	0	.000	3	2	2	6.00	0
2004 Oakland a-b	A.L.	27	188 2/3	12	6	.667	103	44	194	3.53	0
2005 Atlanta c	N.L.	29	192	14	9	.609	115	65	194	3.52	0
2006 Atlanta	N.L.	35	218 1/3	13	12	.520	141	79	235	4.86	0
2007 Atlanta	N.L.	34	224 1/3	16	10	.615	132	53	221	3.33	0
2008 Atlanta d	N.L.	23	142	11	7	.611	85	40	125	3.17	0
2009 Myrtle Beach	Carolina	2	4 2/3	0	1	.000	3	2	5	5.79	0
2009 Gwinnett	Int.	4	18 2/3	1	0	1.000	11	2	24	3.38	0
2009 Atlanta e	N.L.	7	42 1/3	2	1	.667	30	13	49	3.61	0
2010 Atlanta	N.L.	34	228 2/3	17	9	.654	139	74	189	2.83	0
2011 Atlanta	N.L.	33	215	16	10	.615	158	56	189	3.22	0
2012 Rome	So.Atl.	2	7	0	2	.000	1	1	13	7.71	0
2012 Gwinnett	Int.	2	10 2/3	2	0	1.000	8	5	8	0.84	0
2012 Atlanta f	N.L.	28	179	16	7	.696	102	48	168	3.62	0

Year	Club	Lea	G	IP	W	L	Pct	SO	BB	H	ERA	SAVES
2013	Atlanta g-h	N.L.	21	131⅓	8	7	.533	95	36	120	3.97	0
Major League Totals		15 Yrs.	427	2813⅔	205	111	.649	1896	846	2624	3.44	0
	Division Series											
2000	Oakland	A.L.	1	8	0	1	.000	5	4	6	3.38	0
2001	Oakland	A.L.	2	9⅔	1	0	1.000	5	1	8	0.93	0
2002	Oakland	A.L.	2	8⅔	0	1	.000	8	4	13	6.23	0
2003	Oakland	A.L.	2	7⅔	0	0	.000	6	1	10	3.52	0
2005	Atlanta	N.L.	2	13⅔	0	1	.000	8	6	13	5.27	0
2010	Atlanta	N.L.	1	7	0	0	.000	5	4	4	0.00	0
Division Series Totals			10	54⅔	1	3	.250	37	20	54	3.46	0

a On disabled list from June 23 to August 7, 2004.
b Traded to Atlanta Braves for pitcher Juan Cruz, pitcher Dan Meyer and outfielder Charles Thomas, December 16, 2004.
c On disabled list from June 14 to July 16, 2005.
d On disabled list from July 27 to November 3, 2008.
e On disabled list from February 24 to September 1, 2009.
f On disabled list from April 3 to April 29, 2012.
g On disabled list from July 25 to October 31, 2013.
h Filed for free agency, October 31, 2013. Signed with San Francisco Giants, November 19, 2013.

HUGHES, PHILIP JOSEPH

Born, Mission Viejo, California, June 24, 1986.
Bats Right. Throws Right. Height, 6 feet, 5 inches. Weight, 220 pounds.

Year	Club	Lea	G	IP	W	L	Pct	SO	BB	H	ERA	SAVES
2004	Yankees	Gulf Coast	3	5	0	0	.000	8	0	4	0.00	0
2005	Tampa	Fla.St.	5	17⅔	2	0	1.000	21	4	8	3.06	0
2005	Charleston	So.Atl.	12	68⅔	7	1	.875	72	16	46	1.97	0
2006	Trenton	Eastern	21	116	10	3	.769	138	32	73	2.25	0
2006	Tampa	Fla.St.	5	30	2	3	.400	30	2	19	1.80	0
2007	Tampa	Fla.St.	1	2	0	0	.000	3	2	0	0.00	0
2007	Trenton	Eastern	2	7	0	0	.000	11	2	5	1.29	0
2007	Scranton-WB	Int.	5	28⅔	4	1	.800	28	8	16	2.20	0
2007	New York a	A.L.	13	72⅔	5	3	.625	58	29	64	4.46	0
2008	Charleston	So.Atl.	2	6⅔	2	0	1.000	6	2	3	0.00	0
2008	Scranton-WB	Int.	6	29	1	0	1.000	31	9	34	5.90	0
2008	New York b	A.L.	8	34	0	4	.000	23	15	43	6.62	0
2009	Scranton/WB	Int.	3	19⅓	3	0	1.000	19	3	17	1.86	0
2009	New York	A.L.	51	86	8	3	.727	96	28	68	3.03	3
2010	New York	A.L.	31	176⅓	18	8	.692	146	58	162	4.19	0
2011	Staten Island	N.Y.-Penn.	1	4⅓	0	0	.000	7	1	3	2.08	0
2011	Trenton	Eastern	2	9⅔	1	0	1.000	11	4	6	1.86	0
2011	New York c	A.L.	17	74⅔	5	5	.500	47	27	84	5.79	0
2012	New York	A.L.	32	191⅓	16	13	.552	165	46	196	4.23	0
2013	New York d-e	A.L.	30	145⅔	4	14	.222	121	42	170	5.19	0
Major League Totals		7 Yrs.	182	780⅔	56	50	.528	656	245	787	4.53	3
	Division Series											
2007	New York	A.L.	2	5⅔	1	0	1.000	6	0	3	1.59	0
2009	New York	A.L.	3	2	0	0	.000	3	1	5	9.00	0
2010	New York	A.L.	1	7	1	0	1.000	6	1	4	0.00	0
2011	New York	A.L.	2	2⅓	0	0	.000	4	0	2	0.00	0
2012	New York	A.L.	1	6⅔	0	0	.000	8	3	4	1.35	0
Division Series Totals			9	23⅔	2	0	1.000	27	5	18	1.52	0
	Championship Series											
2009	New York	A.L.	3	2⅔	0	1	.000	3	1	4	3.38	0
2010	New York	A.L.	2	8⅔	0	2	.000	6	7	14	11.42	0
2012	New York	A.L.	1	3	0	1	.000	1	3	3	3.00	0
Championship Series Totals			6	14⅓	0	4	.000	10	11	21	8.16	0
	World Series Record											
2009	New York	A.L.	3	1⅔	0	0	.000	1	2	2	16.20	0

a On disabled list from May 2 to August 4, 2007.
b On disabled list from April 30 to July 30, 2008.
c On disabled list from April 15 to July 6, 2011.
d On disabled list from March 22 to April 6, 2013.
e Filed for free agency, October 31, 2013. Signed with Minnesota Twins, December 5, 2013.

HUNTER, RAYMOND THOMAS (TOMMY)

Born, Tuscaloosa, Alabama, July 3, 1986.
Bats Right. Throws Right. Height, 6 feet, 3 inches. Weight, 255 pounds.

Year Club	Lea	G	IP	W	L	Pct	SO	BB	H	ERA	SAVES
2007 Spokane	Northwest	10	17⅔	2	3	.400	13	1	15	2.55	1
2008 Bakersfield	Calif.	9	58⅓	5	4	.556	50	8	63	3.55	0
2008 Frisco	Texas	8	52⅓	4	2	.667	28	17	52	3.78	0
2008 Texas	A.L.	3	11	0	2	.000	9	3	23	16.36	0
2008 Oklahoma	P.C.	8	53	4	2	.667	28	9	55	2.89	0
2009 Frisco	Texas	5	21⅔	1	0	1.000	16	4	30	4.98	0
2009 Oklahoma	P.C.	8	49⅓	3	2	.600	35	16	53	3.83	0
2009 Texas	A.L.	19	112	9	6	.600	64	33	113	4.10	0
2010 Oklahoma	P.C.	6	26⅔	1	2	.333	14	11	28	4.05	0
2010 Texas a	A.L.	23	128	13	4	.765	68	33	126	3.73	0
2011 Frisco	Texas	1	4	0	0	.000	5	1	3	4.50	0
2011 Round Rock	P.C.	8	26⅔	2	2	.500	16	3	37	5.06	1
2011 Texas-Baltimore b-c	A.L.	20	84⅔	4	4	.500	45	15	100	4.68	0
2012 Bowie	Eastern	2	10	1	0	1.000	6	1	3	0.00	1
2012 Norfolk	Int.	3	19⅓	2	1	.667	14	5	20	4.66	0
2012 Baltimore	A.L.	33	133⅔	7	8	.467	77	27	161	5.45	0
2013 Baltimore	A.L.	68	86⅓	6	5	.545	68	14	71	2.81	4
Major League Totals	6 Yrs.	166	555⅔	39	29	.574	331	125	594	4.47	4
Division Series											
2010 Texas	A.L.	1	4	0	1	.000	7	0	6	4.50	0
2012 Baltimore	A.L.	2	1⅓	0	0	.000	1	0	0	0.00	0
Division Series Totals		3	5⅓	0	1	.000	8	0	6	3.38	0
Championship Series											
2010 Texas	A.L.	1	3⅓	0	0	.000	5	0	5	8.10	0
World Series Record											
2010 Texas	A.L.	1	4	0	1	.000	1	1	5	4.50	0

a On disabled list from March 26 to April 28, 2010.
b On disabled list from March 25 to July 1, 2011.
c Traded to Baltimore Orioles with infielder Chris Davis for pitcher Koji Uehara and cash, July 30, 2011.

IWAKUMA, HISASHI

Born, Tokyo, Japan, April 12, 1981.
Bats Right. Throws Right. Height, 6 feet, 3 inches. Weight, 190 pounds.

Year Club	Lea	G	IP	W	L	Pct	SO	BB	H	ERA	SAVES
2001 Kintetsu	Japan Pac.	9	43⅔	4	2	.667	25	13	46	4.53	0
2002 Kintetsu	Japan Pac.	23	141⅓	8	7	.533	131	42	132	3.69	0
2003 Kintetsu	Japan Pac.	27	195⅔	15	10	.600	149	48	201	3.45	0
2004 Kintetsu	Japan Pac.	21	158⅔	15	2	.882	123	30	149	3.10	0
2005 Rakuten	Japan Pac.	27	182⅓	9	15	.375	124	40	218	4.99	0
2006 Rakuten	Japan Pac.	6	38⅔	1	2	.333	16	12	43	3.72	0
2007 Rakuten	Japan Pac.	16	90	5	5	.500	84	23	95	3.40	0
2008 Rakuten	Japan Pac.	28	201⅔	21	4	.840	159	36	161	1.87	0
2009 Rakuten	Japan Pac.	24	169	13	6	.684	121	43	179	3.25	0
2010 Rakuten	Japan Pac.	28	201	10	9	.526	153	36	184	2.82	0
2011 Rakuten	Japan Pac.	17	119	6	7	.462	90	19	106	2.42	0
2012 Seattle a	A.L.	30	125⅓	9	5	.643	101	43	117	3.16	2
2013 Seattle	A.L.	33	219⅔	14	6	.700	185	42	179	2.66	0
Major League Totals	2 Yrs.	63	345	23	11	.676	286	85	296	2.84	2

a Signed with Seattle Mariners, January 5, 2012.

JACKSON, EDWIN

Born, Neu-Ulm, West Germany, September 9, 1983.
Bats Right. Throws Right. Height, 6 feet, 3 inches. Weight, 210 pounds.

Year Club	Lea	G	IP	W	L	Pct	SO	BB	H	ERA	SAVES
2001 Dodgers	Gulf Coast	12	22	2	1	.667	23	19	14	2.45	0
2002 South Bend	So.Atl.	19	104⅔	5	2	.714	85	33	79	1.98	0
2003 Jacksonville	Southern	27	148⅓	7	7	.500	157	53	121	3.70	0
2003 Los Angeles	N.L.	4	22	2	1	.667	19	11	17	2.45	0
2004 Las Vegas	P.C.	19	90⅔	6	4	.600	70	55	90	5.86	0
2004 Los Angeles a	N.L.	8	24⅔	2	1	.667	16	11	31	7.30	0
2005 Jacksonville	Southern	11	62	6	4	.600	44	18	52	3.48	0
2005 Las Vegas	P.C.	12	55⅓	3	7	.300	33	37	76	8.62	0
2005 Los Angeles	N.L.	7	28⅔	2	2	.500	13	17	31	6.28	0
2006 Durham	Int.	22	73	3	7	.300	66	35	84	5.55	5

Year	Club	Lea	G	IP	W	L	Pct	SO	BB	H	ERA	SAVES
2006	Tampa Bay b	A.L.	23	36⅓	0	0	.000	27	25	42	5.45	0
2007	Tampa Bay	A.L.	32	161	5	15	.250	128	88	195	5.76	0
2008	Tampa Bay c	A.L.	32	183⅓	14	11	.560	108	77	199	4.42	0
2009	Detroit d	A.L.	33	214	13	9	.591	161	70	200	3.62	0
2010	Arizona e-f	N.L.	21	134⅓	6	10	.375	104	60	141	5.16	0
2010	Chicago	A.L.	11	75	4	2	.667	77	18	73	3.24	0
2011	Chicago	A.L.	19	121⅔	7	7	.500	97	39	134	3.92	0
2011	St. Louis g-h-i	N.L.	13	78	5	2	.714	51	23	91	3.58	0
2012	Washington j	N.L.	31	189⅔	10	11	.476	168	58	173	4.03	0
2013	Chicago	N.L.	31	175⅓	8	*18	.308	135	59	197	4.98	0
Major League Totals		11 Yrs.	265	1444	78	89	.467	1104	556	1524	4.47	0
	Division Series											
2011	St. Louis	N.L.	1	6	1	0	1.000	4	1	5	3.00	0
2012	Washington	N.L.	2	6	0	1	.000	6	3	9	7.50	0
Division Series Totals			3	12	1	1	.500	10	4	14	5.25	0
	Championship Series											
2008	Tampa Bay	N.L.	2	2⅓	0	0	.000	4	2	0	0.00	0
2011	St. Louis	N.L.	2	6⅓	0	0	.000	5	1	11	8.53	0
Championship Series Totals			4	8⅔	0	0	.000	9	3	11	6.23	0
	World Series Record											
2008	Tampa Bay c	N.L.	1	2	0	0	.000	1	1	2	4.50	0
2011	St. Louis	N.L.	1	5⅓	0	1	.000	3	7	3	5.06	0
World Series Totals			2	7⅓	0	1	.000	4	8	5	4.91	0

a On disabled list from July 9 to September 7, 2004.
b Traded to Tampa Bay Devil Rays with pitcher Chuck Tiffany for pitcher Danys Baez and pitcher Lance Carter, January 14, 2006.
c Traded to Detroit Tigers for outfielder Matt Joyce, December 10, 2008.
d Traded to Arizona Diamondbacks with pitcher Ian Kennedy for pitcher Daniel Schlereth and pitcher Max Scherzer, December 9, 2009.
e Pitched no-hit, no-run game against Tampa Bay Rays, June 25, 2010.
f Traded to Chicago White Sox for pitcher Daniel Hudson and pitcher David Holmberg, July 30, 2010.
g Traded to Toronto Blue Jays with infielder Mark Teahen for pitcher Jason Frasor and pitcher Zach Stewart, July 27, 2011.
h Traded to St. Louis Cardinals with pitcher Octavio Dotel, pitcher Marc Rzepczynski, outfielder Corey Patterson and cash for outfielder Colby Rasmus, pitcher Trever Miller, pitcher Brian Tallet and pitcher P.J. Walters, July 27, 2011.
i Filed for free agency, October 30, 2011. Signed with Washington Nationals, February 2, 2012.
j Filed for free agency, November 3, 2012. Signed with Chicago Cubs, January 2, 2013.

JANSEN, KENLEY JERONIMO

Born, Curacao, Netherlands Antilles, September 30, 1987.
Bats Both. Throws Right. Height, 6 feet, 6 inches. Weight, 220 pounds.

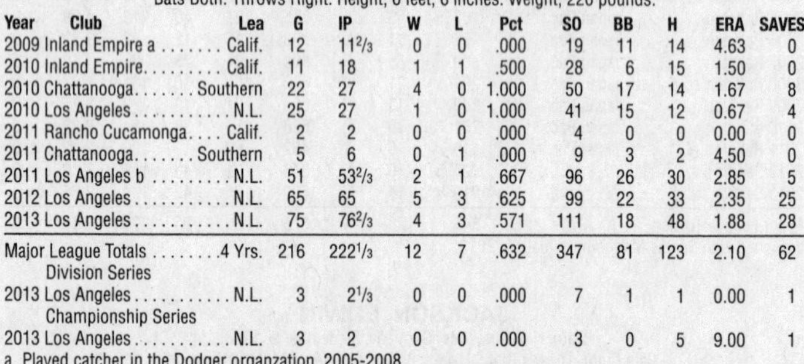

Year	Club	Lea	G	IP	W	L	Pct	SO	BB	H	ERA	SAVES
2009	Inland Empire a	Calif.	12	11⅔	0	0	.000	19	11	14	4.63	0
2010	Inland Empire	Calif.	11	18	1	1	.500	28	6	15	1.50	0
2010	Chattanooga	Southern	22	27	4	0	1.000	50	17	14	1.67	8
2010	Los Angeles	N.L.	25	27	1	0	1.000	41	15	12	0.67	4
2011	Rancho Cucamonga	Calif.	2	2	0	0	.000	4	0	0	0.00	0
2011	Chattanooga	Southern	5	6	0	1	.000	9	3	2	4.50	0
2011	Los Angeles b	N.L.	51	53⅔	2	1	.667	96	26	30	2.85	5
2012	Los Angeles	N.L.	65	65	5	3	.625	99	22	33	2.35	25
2013	Los Angeles	N.L.	75	76⅔	4	3	.571	111	18	48	1.88	28
Major League Totals		4 Yrs.	216	222⅓	12	7	.632	347	81	123	2.10	62
	Division Series											
2013	Los Angeles	N.L.	3	2⅓	0	0	.000	7	1	1	0.00	1
	Championship Series											
2013	Los Angeles	N.L.	3	2	0	0	.000	3	0	5	9.00	1

a Played catcher in the Dodger organzation, 2005-2008.
b On disabled list from May 29 to June 17 and July 27 to August 25, 2011.

JANSSEN, ROBERT CASEY (CASEY)

Born, Orange, California, September 17, 1981.
Bats Right. Throws Right. Height, 6 feet, 4 inches. Weight, 205 pounds.

Year	Club	Lea	G	IP	W	L	Pct	SO	BB	H	ERA	SAVES
2004	Auburn	N.Y.-Penn.	10	50	3	1	.750	45	10	47	3.60	0
2005	New Hampshire	Eastern	9	43	3	3	.500	47	4	49	2.93	0
2005	Dunedin	Fla.St.	10	59⅔	6	1	.857	51	12	46	2.26	0
2005	Lansing	Midwest	7	46	4	0	1.000	38	4	27	1.37	0

Year	Club	Lea	G	IP	W	L	Pct	SO	BB	H	ERA	SAVES
2006	Syracuse	Int.	9	$42^{2}/_{3}$	1	5	.167	32	8	47	4.85	0
2006	Toronto	A.L.	19	94	6	10	.375	44	21	103	5.07	0
2007	Toronto	A.L.	70	$72^{2}/_{3}$	2	3	.400	39	20	67	2.35	6
2008	Toronto a	A.L.			INJURED—Did Not Play							
2009	Blue Jays	Gulf Coast	1	1	0	0	.000	0	0	2	9.00	0
2009	Dunedin	Fla.St.	4	13	0	0	.000	10	2	6	0.69	0
2009	New Hampshire	Eastern	6	15	1	0	1.000	12	5	12	2.40	0
2009	Las Vegas	P.C.	7	$6^{2}/_{3}$	0	0	.000	7	1	4	5.40	0
2009	Toronto b	A.L.	21	40	2	4	.333	24	14	59	5.85	1
2010	Toronto	A.L.	56	$68^{2}/_{3}$	5	2	.714	63	21	74	3.67	0
2011	New Hampshire	Eastern	5	5	0	0	.000	7	1	1	0.00	0
2011	Las Vegas	P.C.	1	2	0	0	.000	3	0	1	0.00	0
2011	Toronto c	A.L.	55	$55^{2}/_{3}$	6	0	1.000	53	14	47	2.26	2
2012	Toronto	A.L.	62	$63^{2}/_{3}$	1	1	.500	67	11	44	2.54	22
2013	Toronto	A.L.	56	$52^{2}/_{3}$	4	1	.800	50	13	39	2.56	34
Major League Totals		7 Yrs.	339	$447^{1}/_{3}$	26	21	.553	340	114	433	3.48	65

a On disabled list from March 17 to November 14, 2008.
b On disabled list from March 27 to April 30 and June 14 to July 23, 2009.
c On disabled list from June 16 to July 19, 2011.

JENNINGS, DANIEL LEE (DAN)

Born, Berkeley, California, April 17, 1987.
Bats Left. Throws Left. Height, 6 feet, 3 inches. Weight, 210 pounds.

Year	Club	Lea	G	IP	W	L	Pct	SO	BB	H	ERA	SAVES
2008	Jamestown	N.Y.-Penn.	13	$58^{2}/_{3}$	1	4	.200	62	18	79	3.53	0
2009	Greensboro	So.Atl.	34	$49^{1}/_{3}$	1	2	.333	54	21	42	2.74	0
2009	Jupiter	Fla.St.	8	$11^{2}/_{3}$	0	0	.000	13	4	5	0.00	6
2009	Jacksonville	Southern	3	$1^{2}/_{3}$	0	0	.000	2	1	2	0.00	0
2010	Jacksonville	Southern	37	$52^{2}/_{3}$	4	2	.667	44	26	49	2.56	0
2011	Jacksonville	Southern	21	$25^{2}/_{3}$	4	1	.800	29	11	26	3.16	2
2011	New Orleans	P.C.	24	$30^{2}/_{3}$	1	3	.250	27	17	34	7.04	2
2012	New Orleans	P.C.	42	$51^{2}/_{3}$	1	3	.250	48	16	48	3.14	2
2012	Miami	N.L.	22	19	1	0	1.000	8	11	18	1.89	0
2013	New Orleans	P.C.	18	25	4	2	.667	25	11	19	1.80	1
2013	Miami	N.L.	47	$40^{2}/_{3}$	2	4	.333	38	16	39	3.76	0
Major League Totals		2 Yrs.	69	$59^{2}/_{3}$	3	4	.429	46	27	57	3.17	0

JEPSEN, KEVIN MARTIN

Born, Anaheim, California, July 26, 1984.
Bats Right. Throws Right. Height, 6 feet, 3 inches. Weight, 235 pounds.

Year	Club	Lea	G	IP	W	L	Pct	SO	BB	H	ERA	SAVES
2002	Angels	Arizona	8	$26^{1}/_{3}$	1	3	.250	19	12	29	6.84	0
2003	Cedar Rapids	Midwest	10	51	6	3	.667	42	28	32	2.65	0
2004	Cedar Rapids	Midwest	27	$144^{1}/_{3}$	8	10	.444	136	77	122	3.43	0
2005	Angels	Arizona	7	$14^{2}/_{3}$	0	1	.000	17	11	8	5.52	0
2005	Rancho Cucamonga	Calif.	4	$12^{2}/_{3}$	0	1	.000	11	10	19	10.66	0
2006	Rancho Cucamonga	Calif.	47	$50^{1}/_{3}$	4	4	.500	46	34	51	3.58	16
2007	Rancho Cucamonga	Calif.	44	$53^{2}/_{3}$	1	5	.167	50	38	61	4.19	3
2008	Arkansas	Texas	25	$31^{2}/_{3}$	2	1	.667	35	18	22	1.42	11
2008	Salt Lake	P.C.	15	23	1	3	.250	21	12	17	2.35	2
2008	Los Angeles	A.L.	9	$8^{1}/_{3}$	0	1	.000	7	4	8	4.32	0
2009	Salt Lake	P.C.	14	18	1	0	1.000	20	16	30	9.00	2
2009	Los Angeles a	A.L.	54	$54^{2}/_{3}$	6	4	.600	48	19	63	4.94	1
2010	Los Angeles	A.L.	68	59	2	4	.333	61	29	54	3.97	0
2011	Los Angeles	A.L.	16	13	1	2	.333	6	9	21	7.62	0
2011	Salt Lake	P.C.	24	$28^{1}/_{3}$	1	3	.250	20	8	32	4.45	7
2012	Salt Lake	P.C.	23	25	2	2	.500	35	9	18	3.24	2
2012	Los Angeles	A.L.	49	$44^{2}/_{3}$	3	2	.600	38	12	39	3.02	2
2013	Inland Empire	Calif.	1	1	0	0	.000	0	0	0	0.00	0
2013	Salt Lake	P.C.	2	2	0	0	.000	1	2	2	13.50	0
2013	Los Angeles b	A.L.	45	36	1	3	.250	36	14	41	4.50	0
Major League Totals		6 Yrs.	241	$215^{2}/_{3}$	13	16	.448	196	87	226	4.34	3
Division Series												
2009	Los Angeles	A.L.	2	$1^{1}/_{3}$	0	0	.000	1	0	3	6.75	0
Championship Series												
2009	Los Angeles	A.L.	3	$3^{2}/_{3}$	1	0	1.000	2	2	5	2.45	0

a On disabled list from April 19 to May 4, 2009.
b On disabled list from April 13 to May 26 and August 22 to November 4, 2013.

JIMENEZ, UBALDO

Born, Nagua, Dominican Republic, January 22, 1984.
Bats Right. Throws Right. Height, 6 feet, 4 inches. Weight, 200 pounds.

Year	Club	Lea	G	IP	W	L	Pct	SO	BB	H	ERA	SAVES
2002	Casper	Pioneer	14	62	3	5	.375	65	29	72	6.53	0
2003	Visalia	Calif.	1	5	1	0	1.000	7	1	3	0.00	0
2003	Asheville	So.Atl.	27	$153^2/_3$	10	6	.625	138	67	129	3.46	0
2004	Visalia	Calif.	9	$44^1/_3$	4	1	.800	61	12	29	2.23	0
2005	Modesto	Calif.	14	$72^1/_3$	5	3	.625	78	40	61	3.98	0
2005	Tulsa	Texas	12	63	2	5	.286	53	31	58	5.43	0
2006	Tulsa	Texas	13	$73^1/_3$	9	2	.818	86	40	49	2.45	0
2006	Colorado Springs	P.C.	13	$78^1/_3$	5	2	.714	64	43	74	5.06	0
2006	Colorado	N.L.	2	$7^2/_3$	0	0	.000	3	3	5	3.52	0
2007	Colorado Springs	P.C.	19	103	8	5	.615	89	62	110	5.85	0
2007	Colorado	N.L.	15	82	4	4	.500	68	37	70	4.28	0
2008	Colorado	N.L.	34	$198^2/_3$	12	12	.500	172	103	182	3.99	0
2009	Colorado	N.L.	33	218	15	12	.556	198	85	183	3.47	0
2010	Colorado	N.L.	33	$221^2/_3$	19	8	*.704	214	92	164	2.88	0
2011	Colorado	N.L.	21	123	6	9	.400	118	51	118	4.46	0
2011	Cleveland a-b	A.L.	11	$65^1/_3$	4	4	.500	62	27	68	5.10	0
2012	Cleveland	A.L.	31	$176^2/_3$	9	*17	.346	143	95	190	5.40	0
2013	Cleveland c	A.L.	32	$182^2/_3$	13	9	.591	194	80	163	3.30	0
Major League Totals		8 Yrs.	212	$1275^2/_3$	82	75	.522	1172	573	1143	3.92	0
	Division Series											
2007	Colorado	N.L.	1	$6^1/_3$	0	0	.000	5	4	3	1.42	0
2009	Colorado	N.L.	2	12	0	1	.000	11	3	15	5.25	0
Division Series Totals			3	$18^1/_3$	0	1	.000	16	7	18	3.93	0
	Championship Series											
2007	Colorado	N.L.	1	5	0	0	.000	6	4	5	1.80	0
	World Series Record											
2007	Colorado	N.L.	1	$4^2/_3$	0	1	.000	2	5	3	3.86	0

a On disabled list from April 2 to April 19, 2011.
b Traded to Cleveland Indians for pitcher Alex White, pitcher Joseph Gardner, outfielder Matt McBride and player to be named later, July 31, 2011. Colorado Rockies received pitcher Drew Pomeranz to complete trade, August 17, 2011.
c Filed for free agency, October 31, 2013.

JOHNSON, ERIK CRAIG

Born, Mountain View, California, December 30, 1989.
Bats Right. Throws Right. Height, 6 feet, 3 inches. Weight, 235 pounds.

Year	Club	Lea	G	IP	W	L	Pct	SO	BB	H	ERA	SAVES
2011	Great Falls	Pioneer	2	2	0	0	.000	2	1	4	4.50	0
2012	Kannapolis	So.Atl.	9	43	2	2	.500	39	19	39	2.30	0
2012	Winston-Salem	Carolina	8	$49^1/_3$	4	3	.571	48	10	43	2.74	0
2013	Birmingham	Southern	14	$84^2/_3$	8	2	.800	74	21	57	2.23	0
2013	Charlotte	Int.	10	$57^1/_3$	4	1	.800	57	19	43	1.57	0
2013	Chicago	A.L.	5	$27^2/_3$	3	2	.600	18	11	32	3.25	0

JOHNSON, JAMES ROBERT (JIM)

Born, Johnson City, New York, June 27, 1983.
Bats Right. Throws Right. Height, 6 feet, 5 inches. Weight, 230 pounds.

Year	Club	Lea	G	IP	W	L	Pct	SO	BB	H	ERA	SAVES
2001	Orioles	Gulf Coast	7	$18^2/_3$	0	1	.000	19	7	17	3.86	0
2002	Bluefield	Appal.	11	$55^2/_3$	4	2	.667	36	16	52	4.37	0
2003	Bluefield	Appal.	11	$51^1/_3$	3	2	.600	46	18	62	3.68	0
2004	Frederick	Carolina	1	3	0	0	.000	6	1	6	9.00	0
2004	Delmarva	So.Atl.	20	$106^2/_3$	8	7	.533	93	30	97	3.29	0
2005	Frederick	Carolina	28	$159^2/_3$	12	9	.571	168	64	139	3.49	1
2005	Bowie	Eastern	1	7	0	0	.000	6	2	3	0.00	0
2006	Baltimore	A.L.	1	3	0	1	.000	0	3	9	24.00	0
2006	Bowie	Eastern	27	156	13	6	.684	124	57	165	4.44	0
2007	Baltimore	A.L.	1	2	0	0	.000	1	2	3	9.00	0
2007	Norfolk	Int.	26	148	6	12	.333	109	48	164	4.07	0
2008	Norfolk	Int.	1	4	0	1	.000	2	1	2	2.25	0
2008	Baltimore a	A.L.	54	$68^2/_3$	2	4	.333	38	28	54	2.23	1
2009	Baltimore	A.L.	64	70	4	6	.400	49	23	73	4.11	10
2010	Orioles	Gulf Coast	4	4	0	0	.000	5	1	5	6.75	0
2010	Frederick	Carolina	2	3	0	0	.000	1	0	6	3.00	0
2010	Bowie	Eastern	4	5	0	0	.000	6	0	2	1.80	0

Year	Club	Lea	G	IP	W	L	Pct	SO	BB	H	ERA	SAVES
2010	Norfolk	Int.	1	1	0	0	.000	0	0	1	0.00	0
2010	Baltimore b	A.L.	26	26⅓	1	1	.500	22	5	32	3.42	1
2011	Baltimore	A.L.	69	91	6	5	.545	58	21	80	2.67	9
2012	Baltimore	A.L.	71	68⅔	2	1	.667	41	15	55	2.49	*51
2013	Baltimore c	A.L.	74	70⅓	3	8	.273	56	18	72	2.94	*50
Major League Totals		8 Yrs.	360	400	18	26	.409	265	115	378	3.11	122
	Wild Card Playoff											
2012	Baltimore	A.L.	1	1	0	0	.000	0	1	2	0.00	0
	Division Series											
2012	Baltimore	A.L.	4	4⅓	0	1	.000	4	0	6	10.38	2

a On disabled list from September 1 to October 2, 2008.
b On disabled list from May 28 to August 27, 2010.
c Traded to Oakland Athletics for infielder Jemile Weeks and player to be named later, December 3, 2013. Baltimore Orioles received pitcher David Freitas to complete trade, December 12, 2013.

JOHNSON, JOSHUA MICHAEL (JOSH)

Born, Minneapolis, Minnesota, January 31, 1984.
Bats Left. Throws Right. Height, 6 feet, 7 inches. Weight, 230 pounds.

Year	Club	Lea	G	IP	W	L	Pct	SO	BB	H	ERA	SAVES
2002	Marlins	Gulf Coast	4	15	2	0	1.000	11	3	8	0.60	0
2003	Greensboro	So.Atl.	17	82⅓	4	7	.364	59	29	69	3.61	0
2004	Jupiter	Fla.St.	23	114⅓	5	12	.294	103	47	124	3.38	0
2005	Carolina	Southern	26	139⅔	12	4	.750	113	50	139	3.87	0
2005	Florida	N.L.	4	12⅓	0	0	.000	10	10	11	3.65	0
2006	Florida	N.L.	31	157	12	7	.632	133	68	136	3.10	0
2007	Carolina	Southern	2	10⅓	0	0	.000	9	5	8	1.74	0
2007	Florida	N.L.	4	15⅔	0	3	.000	14	12	26	7.47	0
2007	Jupiter a	Fla.St.	3	11⅓	0	0	.000	13	0	9	0.79	0
2008	Greensboro	So.Atl.	1	5	0	1	.000	7	0	8	3.60	0
2008	Jupiter	Fla.St.	1	5⅓	0	0	.000	2	2	6	5.06	0
2008	Carolina	Southern	3	19	1	1	.500	14	3	22	3.32	0
2008	Florida b	N.L.	14	87⅓	7	1	.875	77	27	91	3.61	0
2009	Florida	N.L.	33	209	15	5	.750	191	58	184	3.23	0
2010	Florida	N.L.	28	183⅔	11	6	.647	186	48	155	*2.30	0
2011	Florida c	N.L.	9	60⅓	3	1	.750	56	20	39	1.64	0
2012	Miami d	N.L.	31	191⅓	8	14	.364	165	65	180	3.81	0
2013	Dunedin	Fla.St.	1	3	0	0	.000	5	0	3	3.00	0
2013	Buffalo	Int.	2	8⅔	0	1	.000	6	4	9	6.23	0
2013	Toronto e-f	A.L.	16	81⅓	2	8	.200	83	30	105	6.20	0
Major League Totals		9 Yrs.	170	998	58	45	.563	915	338	927	3.40	0

a On disabled list from March 23 to June 18 and July 5 to November 12, 2007.
b On disabled list from March 21 to July 10, 2008.
c On disabled list from May 17 to October 31, 2011.
d Traded to Toronto Blue Jays with outfielder Emilio Bonifacio, catcher John Buck, pitcher Mark Buehrle and infielder Jose Reyes for pitcher Henderson Alvarez, infielder Yunel Escobar, infielder Adeiny Hechavarria, catcher Jeff Mathis, pitcher Anthony De Sclafani, outfielder Jake Marisnick and pitcher Justin Nicolino, November 19, 2012.
e On disabled list from April 29 to June 4 and August 7 to October 31, 2013.
f Filed for free agency, October 31, 2013. Signed with San Diego Padres, November 20, 2013.

JONES, NATHAN ANDREW (NATE)

Born, Covington, Kentucky, January 28, 1986.
Bats Right. Throws Right. Height, 6 feet, 5 inches. Weight, 185 pounds.

Year	Club	Lea	G	IP	W	L	Pct	SO	BB	H	ERA	SAVES
2007	Bristol	Appal.	13	47⅓	0	4	.000	42	29	44	5.13	0
2008	Bristol	Appal.	4	6⅔	1	0	1.000	12	2	6	1.35	0
2008	Winston-Salem	Carolina	2	2⅔	0	0	.000	1	2	1	3.38	0
2008	Kannapolis	So.Atl.	18	56⅔	1	7	.125	71	35	63	6.83	0
2009	Winston-Salem	Carolina	32	49⅓	2	1	.667	43	13	44	3.65	0
2009	Kannapolis	So.Atl.	13	18⅔	2	0	1.000	25	9	8	2.41	1
2010	Winston-Salem	Carolina	28	152⅓	11	6	.647	109	56	176	4.08	0
2011	Birmingham	Southern	42	63⅓	2	3	.400	67	27	58	3.27	12
2012	Chicago	A.L.	65	71⅔	8	0	1.000	65	32	67	2.39	0
2013	Chicago	A.L.	70	78	4	5	.444	89	26	69	4.15	0
Major League Totals		2 Yrs.	135	149⅔	12	5	.706	154	58	136	3.31	0

KAZMIR, SCOTT EDWARD

Born, Houston, Texas, January 24, 1984.
Bats Left. Throws Left. Height, 6 feet. Weight, 185 pounds.

Year	Club	Lea	G	IP	W	L	Pct	SO	BB	H	ERA	SAVES
2002	Brooklyn	N.Y.-Penn.	5	18	0	1	.000	34	7	5	0.50	0
2003	Capital City	So.Atl.	18	76 1/3	4	4	.500	105	28	50	2.36	0
2003	St. Lucie	Fla.St.	7	33	1	2	.333	40	16	29	3.27	0
2004	St. Lucie	Fla.St.	11	50	1	2	.333	51	22	49	3.42	0
2004	Binghamton	Eastern	4	26	2	1	.667	29	9	16	1.73	0
2004	Montgomery a	Southern	4	25	1	2	.333	24	11	14	1.44	0
2004	Tampa Bay	A.L.	8	33 1/3	2	3	.400	41	21	33	5.67	0
2005	Tampa Bay	A.L.	32	186	10	9	.526	174	*100	172	3.77	0
2006	Tampa Bay b	A.L.	24	144 2/3	10	8	.556	163	52	132	3.24	0
2007	Tampa Bay	A.L.	34	206 2/3	13	9	.591	*239	89	196	3.48	0
2008	Vero Beach	Fla.St.	2	7 2/3	0	1	.000	7	0	8	4.70	0
2008	Durham	Int.	1	5	0	0	.000	3	1	3	1.80	0
2008	Tampa Bay c	A.L.	27	152 1/3	12	8	.600	166	70	123	3.49	0
2009	Charlotte	Fla.St.	1	4 2/3	0	0	.000	5	1	3	0.00	0
2009	Durham	Int.	1	6	1	0	1.000	5	0	5	1.50	0
2009	Tampa Bay-LA d-e	A.L.	26	147 1/3	10	9	.526	117	60	149	4.89	0
2010	Rancho Cucamonga	Calif.	1	6 1/3	0	0	.000	6	0	8	4.26	0
2010	Los Angeles f	A.L.	28	150	9	15	.375	93	79	158	5.94	0
2011	Los Angeles g	A.L.	1	1 2/3	0	0	.000	0	2	5	27.00	0
2011	Salt Lake h	P.C.	5	15 1/3	0	5	.000	14	20	22	17.02	0
2012	Sugarland	Atlantic	14	64	3	6	.333	51	33	74	5.34	0
2013	Columbus i	Int.	1	5	1	0	1.000	5	0	5	0.00	0
2013	Cleveland j-k	A.L.	29	158	10	9	.526	162	47	162	4.04	0
Major League Totals		9 Yrs.	209	1180	76	70	.521	1155	520	1130	4.16	0
	Division Series											
2008	Tampa Bay	A.L.	1	5 1/3	1	0	1.000	4	2	8	3.38	0
2009	Los Angeles	A.L.	1	6	0	0	.000	1	3	5	7.50	0
Division Series Totals			2	11 1/3	1	0	1.000	5	5	13	5.56	0
	Championship Series											
2008	Tampa Bay	A.L.	2	10 1/3	0	0	.000	9	6	8	4.35	0
2009	Los Angeles	A.L.	2	4 2/3	0	1	.000	3	5	6	7.71	0
Championship Series Totals			4	15	0	1	.000	12	11	14	5.40	0
	World Series Record											
2008	Tampa Bay	A.L.	2	10	0	1	.000	9	10	10	4.50	0

a Traded by New York Mets to Tampa Bay Devil Rays with pitcher Jose Diaz for pitcher Victor Zambrano and pitcher Bartolome Fortunado, July 30, 2004.
b On disabled list from July 31 to August 8 and August 23 to October 2, 2006.
c On disabled list from March 25 to May 4, 2008.
d On disabled list from May 21 to June 26, 2009.
e Traded to Los Angeles Angels for pitcher Alexander Torres, infielder Matthew Sweeney and player to be named later, August 28, 2009. Tampa Bay Rays received infielder Sean Rodriguez to complete trade, September 1, 2009.
f On disabled list from March 31 to April 15 and July 11 to August 7, 2010.
g On disabled list from April 4 to June 15, 2011.
h Released by Anaheim Angels, June 15, 2011. Signed with Sugarland (Atlantic), July 7, 2012.
i Signed with Cleveland Indians organization, January 8, 2013.
j On disabled list from April 2 to April 20, 2013.
k Filed for free agency, October 31, 2013. Signed with Oakland Athletics, December 2, 2013.

KELLEY, SHAWN ANDREW

Born, Louisville, Kentucky, April 26, 1984.
Bats Right. Throws Right. Height, 6 feet, 2 inches. Weight, 215 pounds.

Year	Club	Lea	G	IP	W	L	Pct	SO	BB	H	ERA	SAVES
2007	Wisconsin	Midwest	9	12	1	1	.500	14	4	16	2.25	0
2007	Everett	Northwest	3	3	1	0	1.000	4	0	2	3.00	0
2008	High Desert	Calif.	12	12	0	0	.000	12	3	8	0.00	3
2008	Wisconsin	Midwest	8	7 2/3	0	0	.000	12	2	10	3.52	3
2008	West Tenn	Southern	29	42 2/3	3	1	.750	44	17	31	2.11	9
2009	Mariners	Arizona	2	2	0	0	.000	3	0	0	0.00	0
2009	Tacoma	P.C.	1	1	0	0	.000	0	0	0	0.00	0
2009	Seattle a	A.L.	41	46	5	4	.556	41	9	45	4.50	0
2010	Tacoma	P.C.	3	3 2/3	0	0	.000	6	3	1	4.91	1
2010	Seattle b	A.L.	22	25	3	1	.750	26	12	26	3.96	0
2011	Jackson	Southern	3	3	0	1	.000	3	0	4	0.00	0
2011	Tacoma	P.C.	12	14 2/3	1	0	1.000	15	6	11	1.84	0
2011	Seattle c	A.L.	10	12 2/3	0	0	.000	10	3	7	0.00	0
2012	Tacoma	P.C.	14	20	2	0	1.000	25	4	9	0.90	6

Year	Club	Lea	G	IP	W	L	Pct	SO	BB	H	ERA	SAVES
2012	Seattle	A.L.	47	44 1/3	2	4	.333	45	15	43	3.25	0
2013	New York d.	A.L.	57	53 1/3	4	2	.667	71	23	47	4.39	0
Major League Totals		5 Yrs.	177	181 1/3	14	11	.560	193	62	168	3.77	0

a On disabled list from May 6 to July 3, 2009.
b On disabled list from June 16 to October 8, 2010.
c On disabled list from March 2 to August 9, 2011.
d Traded to New York Yankees for outfielder Abraham Almonte, February 13, 2013.

KELLY, JOSEPH WILLIAM (JOE)

Born, Anaheim, California, June 9, 1988.
Bats Right. Throws Right. Height, 6 feet, 1 inch. Weight, 185 pounds.

Year	Club	Lea	G	IP	W	L	Pct	SO	BB	H	ERA	SAVES
2009	Batavia	N.Y.-Penn.	16	30 1/3	2	3	.400	30	11	33	4.75	1
2010	Quad Cities	Midwest	26	103 1/3	6	8	.429	92	45	103	4.62	1
2011	Palm Beach	Fla.St.	12	72 2/3	5	2	.714	62	34	56	2.60	0
2011	Springfield	Texas	11	59 1/3	6	4	.600	51	25	70	5.01	0
2012	Memphis	P.C.	12	72 1/3	2	5	.286	45	21	75	2.86	0
2012	St. Louis	N.L.	24	107	5	7	.417	75	36	112	3.53	0
2013	St. Louis	N.L.	37	124	10	5	.667	79	44	124	2.69	0
Major League Totals		2 Yrs.	61	231	15	12	.556	154	80	236	3.08	0
	Division Series											
2012	St. Louis	N.L.	3	3 2/3	0	0	.000	3	1	0	0.00	0
2013	St. Louis	N.L.	1	5 1/3	0	0	.000	5	4	5	3.38	0
Division Series Totals			4	9	0	0	.000	8	5	5	2.00	0
	Championship Series											
2012	St. Louis	N.L.	4	4	0	0	.000	2	3	6	4.50	0
2013	St. Louis	N.L.	2	11	0	1	.000	8	2	13	4.91	0
Championship Series Totals			6	15	0	1	.000	10	5	19	4.80	0
	World Series Record											
2013	St. Louis	N.L.	1	5 1/3	0	0	.000	6	3	2	3.38	0

KENDRICK, KYLE RODNEY

Born, Houston, Texas, August 26, 1984.
Bats Right. Throws Right. Height, 6 feet, 3 inches. Weight, 190 pounds.

Year	Club	Lea	G	IP	W	L	Pct	SO	BB	H	ERA	SAVES
2003	Phillies	Gulf Coast	9	31 1/3	0	4	.000	26	12	40	5.46	0
2004	Batavia	N.Y.-Penn.	13	70 2/3	2	8	.200	53	18	94	5.48	0
2004	Lakewood	So.Atl.	15	66 2/3	3	8	.273	36	33	85	6.07	0
2005	Clearwater	Fla.St.	1	4	0	1	.000	1	2	5	0.00	0
2005	Batavia	N.Y.-Penn.	14	91 1/3	5	4	.556	70	22	94	3.74	0
2005	Lakewood	So.Atl.	5	22 2/3	0	3	.000	11	10	38	9.13	0
2006	Clearwater	Fla.St.	21	130	9	7	.563	79	37	117	3.53	0
2006	Lakewood	So.Atl.	7	46	3	2	.600	54	15	34	2.15	0
2007	Reading	Eastern	12	81 1/3	4	7	.364	50	18	82	3.21	0
2007	Philadelphia	N.L.	20	121	10	4	.714	49	25	129	3.87	0
2008	Philadelphia	N.L.	31	155 2/3	11	9	.550	68	57	194	5.49	0
2009	Lehigh Valley	Int.	24	143	9	7	.563	62	35	133	3.34	0
2009	Philadelphia	N.L.	9	26 1/3	3	1	.750	15	9	27	3.42	0
2010	Philadelphia	N.L.	33	180 2/3	11	10	.524	84	49	199	4.73	0
2011	Philadelphia	N.L.	34	114 2/3	8	6	.571	59	30	110	3.22	0
2012	Philadelphia	N.L.	37	159 1/3	11	12	.478	116	49	154	3.90	0
2013	Philadelphia a.	N.L.	30	182	10	13	.435	110	47	207	4.70	0
Major League Totals		7 Yrs.	194	939 2/3	64	55	.538	501	266	1020	4.38	0
	Division Series											
2007	Philadelphia	N.L.	1	3 2/3	0	1	.000	2	2	5	12.27	0

a On disabled list from September 14 to November 1, 2013.

KENNEDY, IAN PATRICK

Born, Huntington Beach, California, December 19, 1984.
Bats Right. Throws Right. Height, 6 feet. Weight, 195 pounds.

Year	Club	Lea	G	IP	W	L	Pct	SO	BB	H	ERA	SAVES
2006	Staten Island	N.Y.-Penn.	1	2 2/3	0	0	.000	2	2	2	0.00	0
2007	Tampa	Fla.St.	11	63	6	1	.857	72	22	39	1.29	0
2007	Trenton	Eastern	9	48 2/3	5	1	.833	57	17	27	2.59	0
2007	Scranton/WB	Int.	6	34 2/3	1	1	.500	34	11	25	2.08	0

Year	Club	Lea	G	IP	W	L	Pct	SO	BB	H	ERA	SAVES
2007	New York	A.L.	3	19	1	0	1.000	15	9	13	1.89	0
2008	Yankees	Gulf Coast	1	3	1	0	1.000	7	0	3	3.00	0
2008	Tampa	Fla.St.	1	5	0	0	.000	4	1	2	0.00	0
2008	New York	A.L.	10	39⅔	0	4	.000	27	26	50	8.17	0
2008	Scranton/WB a	Int.	13	69	5	3	.625	72	17	52	2.35	0
2009	Scranton/WB	Int.	4	22⅔	1	0	1.000	25	7	18	1.59	0
2009	New York b-c	A.L.	1	1	0	0	.000	1	2	0	0.00	0
2010	Arizona	N.L.	32	194	9	10	.474	168	70	163	3.80	0
2011	Arizona	N.L.	33	222	*21	4	*.840	198	55	186	2.88	0
2012	Arizona	N.L.	33	208⅓	15	12	.556	187	55	216	4.02	0
2013	Arizona-San Diego d	N.L.	31	181⅓	7	10	.412	163	73	180	4.91	0
Major League Totals		7 Yrs.	143	865⅓	53	40	.570	759	290	808	4.00	0
	Division Series											
2011	Arizona	N.L.	2	12⅔	0	1	.000	8	3	13	4.26	0

a On disabled list from May 28 to June 24, 2008.
b Traded to Detroit Tigers with outfielder Austin Jackson and pitcher Phil Coke for outfielder Curtis Granderson, December 9, 2009.
c Traded to Arizona Diamondbacks with pitcher Edwin Jackson for pitcher Daniel Schlereth and pitcher Max Scherzer, December 9, 2009.
d Traded to San Diego Padres for pitcher Joe Thatcher, pitcher Matt Stites and a competitive balance draft choice, July 31, 2013.

KERSHAW, CLAYTON EDWARD

Born, Dallas, Texas, March 19, 1988.
Bats Left. Throws Left. Height, 6 feet, 3 inches. Weight, 220 pounds.

Year	Club	Lea	G	IP	W	L	Pct	SO	BB	H	ERA	SAVES
2006	Dodgers	Gulf Coast	10	37	2	0	1.000	54	5	28	1.95	1
2007	Great Lakes	Midwest	20	97⅓	7	5	.583	134	50	72	2.77	0
2007	Jacksonville	Southern	5	24⅔	1	2	.333	29	17	17	3.65	0
2008	Jacksonville	Southern	13	61⅓	2	3	.400	59	19	39	1.91	0
2008	Los Angeles	N.L.	22	107⅔	5	5	.500	100	52	109	4.26	0
2009	Los Angeles	N.L.	31	171	8	8	.500	185	91	119	2.79	0
2010	Los Angeles	N.L.	32	204⅓	13	10	.565	212	81	160	2.91	0
2011	Los Angeles a	N.L.	33	233⅓	*21	5	.808	*248	54	174	*2.28	0
2012	Los Angeles	N.L.	33	227⅔	14	9	.609	229	63	170	*2.53	0
2013	Los Angeles b	N.L.	33	236	16	9	.640	*232	52	164	*1.83	0
Major League Totals		6 Yrs.	184	1180	77	46	.626	1206	393	896	2.60	0
	Division Series											
2009	Los Angeles	N.L.	1	6⅔	0	0	.000	4	1	9	2.70	0
2013	Los Angeles	N.L.	2	13	1	0	1.000	18	4	6	0.69	0
Division Series Totals			3	19⅔	1	0	1.000	22	5	15	1.37	0
	Championship Series											
2008	Los Angeles	N.L.	2	2	0	0	.000	1	2	1	4.50	0
2009	Los Angeles	N.L.	2	6⅔	0	1	.000	6	6	5	9.45	0
2013	Los Angeles	N.L.	2	10	0	2	.000	10	3	12	6.30	0
Championship Series Totals			6	18⅔	0	3	.000	17	11	18	7.23	0

a Selected Cy Young Award Winner in National League for 2011.
b Selected Cy Young Award Winner in National League for 2013.

KEUCHEL, DALLAS

Born, Tulsa, Oklahoma, January 1, 1988.
Bats Left. Throws Left. Height, 6 feet, 3 inches. Weight, 210 pounds.

Year	Club	Lea	G	IP	W	L	Pct	SO	BB	H	ERA	SAVES
2009	Tri-City	N.Y.-Penn.	11	56⅔	2	3	.400	44	9	52	2.70	0
2010	Lancaster	Calif.	19	120⅔	5	8	.385	97	25	129	3.36	0
2010	Corpus Christi	Texas	9	53⅔	2	6	.250	36	11	59	4.70	0
2011	Oklahoma	P.C.	7	36	1	1	.500	15	12	52	7.50	0
2011	Corpus Christi	Texas	20	127⅔	9	7	.563	76	27	116	3.17	0
2012	Oklahoma	P.C.	16	91⅓	6	4	.600	50	20	92	3.90	0
2012	Houston	N.L.	16	85⅓	3	8	.273	38	39	93	5.27	0
2013	Oklahoma	P.C.	1	6	1	0	1.000	5	0	3	0.00	0
2013	Houston	A.L.	31	153⅔	6	10	.375	123	52	184	5.15	0
Major League Totals		2 Yrs.	47	239	9	18	.333	161	91	277	5.20	0

KIMBREL, CRAIG MICHAEL

Born, Huntsville, Alabama, May 28, 1988.
Bats Right. Throws Right. Height, 5 feet, 11 inches. Weight, 205 pounds.

Year Club	Lea	G	IP	W	L	Pct	SO	BB	H	ERA	SAVES
2008 Danville	Appal.	12	19	1	2	.333	27	10	5	0.47	6
2008 Myrtle Beach	Carolina	2	$3^{2}/_{3}$	0	0	.000	3	1	5	0.00	0
2008 Rome	So.Atl.	10	$12^{2}/_{3}$	2	0	1.000	26	4	6	0.71	4
2009 Myrtle Beach	Carolina	19	$26^{1}/_{3}$	0	2	.000	45	28	18	5.47	2
2009 Gwinnett	Int.	2	2	0	0	.000	3	4	0	0.00	0
2009 Rome	So.Atl.	16	20	0	0	.000	38	6	9	0.90	10
2009 Mississippi	Southern	12	$11^{2}/_{3}$	2	1	.667	17	7	3	0.77	6
2010 Gwinnett	Int.	48	$55^{2}/_{3}$	3	2	.600	83	35	28	1.62	23
2010 Atlanta	N.L.	21	$20^{2}/_{3}$	4	0	1.000	40	16	9	0.44	1
2011 Atlanta a	N.L.	79	77	4	3	.571	127	32	48	2.10	*46
2012 Atlanta	N.L.	63	$62^{2}/_{3}$	3	1	.750	116	14	27	1.01	*42
2013 Atlanta	N.L.	68	67	4	3	.571	98	20	39	1.21	*50
Major League Totals	4 Yrs.	231	$227^{1}/_{3}$	15	7	.682	381	82	123	1.39	139
Wild Card Playoff											
2012 Atlanta	N.L.	1	1	0	0	.000	1	0	0	0.00	0
Division Series											
2010 Atlanta	N.L.	4	$4^{1}/_{3}$	0	1	.000	7	1	1	2.08	0
2013 Atlanta	N.L.	1	$1^{1}/_{3}$	0	0	.000	2	2	0	0.00	1
Division Series Totals		5	$5^{2}/_{3}$	0	1	.000	9	3	1	1.59	1

a Selected Rookie of the Year in National League for 2011.

KINTZLER, BRANDON LEE

Born, Las Vegas, Nevada, August 1, 1984.
Bats Right. Throws Right. Height, 6 feet, 1 inch. Weight, 185 pounds.

Year Club	Lea	G	IP	W	L	Pct	SO	BB	H	ERA	SAVES
2004 Padres	Arizona	21	34	3	2	.600	38	9	36	2.38	6
2004 Eugene	Northwest	3	3	0	0	.000	4	0	3	0.00	3
2005 Padres	Arizona	8	11	2	0	1.000	17	4	15	4.09	1
2005 Eugene	Northwest	3	$3^{1}/_{3}$	0	0	.000	1	0	3	0.00	0
2005 Fort Wayne	Midwest	19	$23^{1}/_{3}$	1	2	.333	19	7	20	3.09	0
2006 a						Did Not Play					
2007 Winnipeg	Northern	29	77	5	2	.714	41	13	78	4.07	1
2008 Winnipeg	Northern	20	112	7	6	.538	73	36	139	4.65	0
2009 St. Paul b	Amer.Assoc.	14	81	8	3	.727	46	24	89	2.79	0
2009 Huntsville c	Southern	9	$35^{2}/_{3}$	1	2	.333	32	9	41	4.54	0
2010 Huntsville	Southern	20	$22^{1}/_{3}$	1	0	1.000	23	1	11	0.40	10
2010 Nashville	P.C.	22	$26^{2}/_{3}$	3	0	1.000	21	6	19	2.36	6
2010 Milwaukee	N.L.	7	$7^{1}/_{3}$	0	1	.000	9	4	10	7.36	0
2011 Nashville	P.C.	1	1	0	0	.000	2	0	0	0.00	0
2011 Milwaukee	N.L.	9	$14^{2}/_{3}$	1	1	.500	15	3	14	3.68	0
2012 Brevard County	Fla.St.	6	6	0	1	.000	9	3	7	3.00	0
2012 Huntsville	Southern	31	$35^{2}/_{3}$	0	2	.000	20	12	35	3.28	9
2012 Nashville	P.C.	8	$11^{2}/_{3}$	0	1	.000	11	2	8	1.54	0
2012 Milwaukee	N.L.	14	$16^{2}/_{3}$	3	0	1.000	14	7	18	3.78	0
2013 Milwaukee	N.L.	71	77	3	3	.500	58	16	66	2.69	0
Major League Totals	4 Yrs.	101	$115^{2}/_{3}$	7	5	.583	96	30	108	3.27	0

a Released by San Diego Padres, April 1, 2006. Signed with Winnipeg (Northern), May 2007.
b Signed with St. Paul (American Association), May 2009.
c Signed with Milwaukee Brewers organization, July 24, 2009.

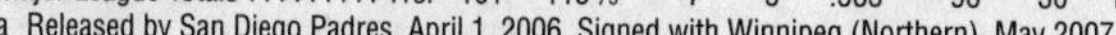

KLUBER, COREY SCOTT

Born, Birmingham, Alabama, April 10, 1986.
Bats Right. Throws Right. Height, 6 feet, 4 inches. Weight, 215 pounds.

Year Club	Lea	G	IP	W	L	Pct	SO	BB	H	ERA	SAVES
2007 Eugene	Northwest	10	$33^{1}/_{3}$	1	1	.500	33	15	28	3.51	0
2008 Fort Wayne	Midwest	10	56	4	3	.571	72	13	49	3.21	0
2008 Lake Elsinore	Calif.	19	$85^{1}/_{3}$	2	5	.286	75	34	93	6.01	0
2009 Lake Elsinore	Calif.	19	109	7	9	.438	124	36	110	4.54	0
2009 San Antonio	Texas	9	45	2	4	.333	35	34	45	4.60	0
2010 San Antonio a	Texas	22	$122^{2}/_{3}$	6	6	.500	136	40	121	3.45	0
2010 Akron b	Eastern	5	$26^{1}/_{3}$	2	2	.500	21	10	38	3.76	0
2010 Columbus	Int.	2	11	1	1	.500	8	6	10	3.27	0
2011 Columbus	Int.	27	$150^{2}/_{3}$	7	11	.389	143	70	153	5.56	0
2011 Cleveland	A.L.	3	$4^{1}/_{3}$	0	0	.000	5	3	6	8.31	0

Year	Club	Lea	G	IP	W	L	Pct	SO	BB	H	ERA	SAVES
2012	Columbus	Int.	21	125⅓	11	7	.611	128	49	121	3.59	0
2012	Cleveland	A.L.	12	63	2	5	.286	54	18	76	5.14	0
2013	Columbus	Int.	2	12⅓	1	1	.500	12	3	14	6.57	0
2013	Cleveland c	A.L.	26	147⅓	11	5	.688	136	33	153	3.85	0
Major League Totals		3 Yrs.	41	214⅔	13	10	.565	195	54	235	4.32	0

a Traded by San Diego Padres to St. Louis Cardinals with pitcher Nick Greenwood for outfielder Ryan Ludwick, July 31, 2010.

b Traded to Cleveland Indians for pitcher Jake Westbrook and cash, July 31, 2010.

c On disabled list from August 6 to September 7, 2013.

KOEHLER, THOMAS R. (TOM)

Born, Bronx, New York, June 29, 1986.
Bats Right. Throws Right. Height, 6 feet, 2 inches. Weight, 235 pounds.

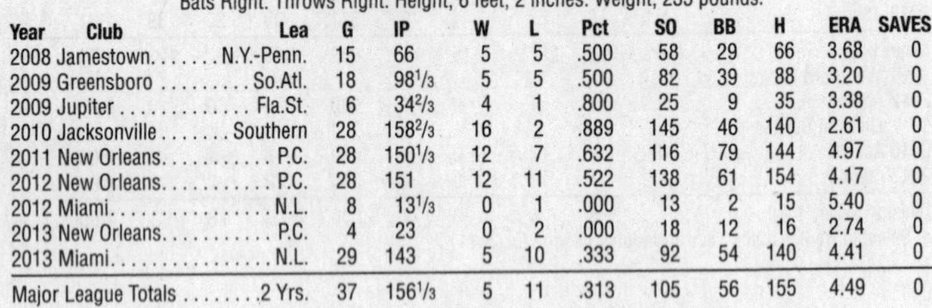

Year	Club	Lea	G	IP	W	L	Pct	SO	BB	H	ERA	SAVES
2008	Jamestown	N.Y.-Penn.	15	66	5	5	.500	58	29	66	3.68	0
2009	Greensboro	So.Atl.	18	98⅓	5	5	.500	82	39	88	3.20	0
2009	Jupiter	Fla.St.	6	34⅔	4	1	.800	25	9	35	3.38	0
2010	Jacksonville	Southern	28	158⅔	16	2	.889	145	46	140	2.61	0
2011	New Orleans	P.C.	28	150⅓	12	7	.632	116	79	144	4.97	0
2012	New Orleans	P.C.	28	151	12	11	.522	138	61	154	4.17	0
2012	Miami	N.L.	8	13⅓	0	1	.000	13	2	15	5.40	0
2013	New Orleans	P.C.	4	23	0	2	.000	18	12	16	2.74	0
2013	Miami	N.L.	29	143	5	10	.333	92	54	140	4.41	0
Major League Totals		2 Yrs.	37	156⅓	5	11	.313	105	56	155	4.49	0

KOHN, MICHAEL THOMAS

Born, Camden, South Carolina, June 26, 1986.
Bats Right. Throws Right. Height, 6 feet. Weight, 200 pounds.

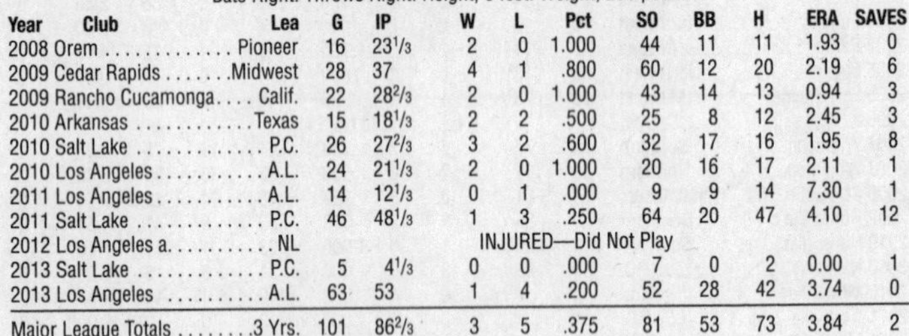

Year	Club	Lea	G	IP	W	L	Pct	SO	BB	H	ERA	SAVES
2008	Orem	Pioneer	16	23⅓	2	0	1.000	44	11	11	1.93	0
2009	Cedar Rapids	Midwest	28	37	4	1	.800	60	12	20	2.19	6
2009	Rancho Cucamonga	Calif.	22	28⅔	2	0	1.000	43	14	13	0.94	3
2010	Arkansas	Texas	15	18⅓	2	2	.500	25	8	12	2.45	3
2010	Salt Lake	P.C.	26	27⅔	3	2	.600	32	17	16	1.95	8
2010	Los Angeles	A.L.	24	21⅓	2	0	1.000	20	16	17	2.11	1
2011	Los Angeles	A.L.	14	12⅓	0	1	.000	9	9	14	7.30	1
2011	Salt Lake	P.C.	46	48⅓	1	3	.250	64	20	47	4.10	12
2012	Los Angeles a	NL	INJURED—Did Not Play									
2013	Salt Lake	P.C.	5	4⅓	0	0	.000	7	0	2	0.00	1
2013	Los Angeles	A.L.	63	53	1	4	.200	52	28	42	3.74	0
Major League Totals		3 Yrs.	101	86⅔	3	5	.375	81	53	73	3.84	2

a On disabled list from March 26 to November 2, 2012.

KONTOS, GEORGE NICHOLAS

Born, Lincolnwood, Illinois, June 12, 1985.
Bats Right. Throws Right. Height, 6 feet, 3 inches. Weight, 225 pounds.

Year	Club	Lea	G	IP	W	L	Pct	SO	BB	H	ERA	SAVES
2006	Staten Island	N.Y.-Penn.	14	78⅓	7	3	.700	82	19	64	2.64	0
2007	Tampa	Fla.St.	19	94	4	6	.400	101	30	95	4.02	0
2008	Trenton	Eastern	27	151⅔	6	11	.353	152	57	134	3.68	0
2009	Trenton	Eastern	4	20⅓	1	1	.500	24	9	19	2.66	0
2009	Scranton-WB	Int.	9	51	3	4	.429	39	21	44	3.35	0
2010	Trenton	Eastern	17	32	0	2	.000	28	11	30	3.38	0
2010	Tampa	Fla.St.	5	10⅓	0	1	.000	8	3	7	2.61	0
2010	Scranton-WB	Int.	2	2⅔	0	1	.000	2	1	5	10.13	0
2011	Scranton-WB	Int.	40	89⅓	4	4	.500	91	26	72	2.62	2
2011	New York a	A.L.	7	6	0	0	.000	6	3	4	3.00	0
2012	Fresno	P.C.	23	31⅔	2	0	1.000	26	7	24	1.71	1
2012	San Francisco b	N.L.	44	43⅔	2	1	.667	44	12	34	2.47	0
2013	Fresno	P.C.	18	23⅔	3	2	.600	26	3	19	4.18	4
2013	San Francisco	N.L.	52	55⅓	2	2	.500	47	18	60	4.39	0
Major League Totals		3 Yrs.	103	105	4	3	.571	97	33	98	3.51	0
	Division Series											
2012	San Francisco	N.L.	4	3⅔	0	0	.000	2	0	2	0.00	0
	Championship Series											
2012	San Francisco	N.L.	3	1⅓	0	0	.000	0	0	2	13.50	0

Year	Club	Lea	G	IP	W	L	Pct	SO	BB	H	ERA	SAVES
	World Series Record											
2012	San Francisco	N.L.	1	$0\frac{1}{3}$	0	0	.000	0	1	2	54.00	0

a Selected by San Diego Padres from New York Yankees in Rule V draft, December 9, 2010. Returned by San Diego Padres, March 14, 2011.

b Traded to San Francisco Giants for catcher Chris Stewart, April 4, 2012.

KURODA, HIROKI

Born, Osaka, Japan, February 10, 1975.
Bats Right. Throws Right. Height, 6 feet, 1 inch. Weight, 210 pounds.

Year	Club	Lea	G	IP	W	L	Pct	SO	BB	H	ERA	SAVES
1997	Hiroshima	Japan Cent.	23	135	6	9	.400	64	63	147	4.40	0
1998	Hiroshima	Japan Cent.	18	45	1	4	.200	25	24	53	6.60	0
1999	Hiroshima	Japan Cent.	21	$87\frac{2}{3}$	5	8	.385	55	39	106	6.78	0
2000	Hiroshima	Japan Cent.	29	144	9	6	.600	116	61	147	4.31	0
2001	Hiroshima	Japan Cent.	27	190	12	8	.600	146	45	175	3.03	0
2002	Hiroshima	Japan Cent.	23	$164\frac{1}{3}$	10	10	.500	144	34	166	3.67	0
2003	Hiroshima	Japan Cent.	28	$205\frac{2}{3}$	13	9	.591	137	45	197	3.11	0
2004	Hiroshima	Japan Cent.	21	147	7	9	.438	138	29	187	4.65	0
2005	Hiroshima	Japan Cent.	29	$212\frac{2}{3}$	15	12	.556	165	42	183	3.17	0
2006	Hiroshima	Japan Cent.	26	$189\frac{1}{3}$	13	6	.684	144	21	169	1.85	1
2007	Hiroshima a	Japan Cent.	26	$179\frac{2}{3}$	12	8	.600	123	42	176	3.56	0
2008	Los Angeles b	N.L.	31	$183\frac{1}{3}$	9	10	.474	116	42	181	3.73	0
2009	Los Angeles c	N.L.	21	$117\frac{1}{3}$	8	7	.533	87	24	110	3.76	0
2010	Los Angeles d	N.L.	31	$196\frac{1}{3}$	11	13	.458	159	48	180	3.39	0
2011	Los Angeles e	N.L.	32	202	13	16	.448	161	49	196	3.07	0
2012	New York f	A.L.	33	$219\frac{2}{3}$	16	11	.593	167	51	205	3.32	0
2013	New York g	A.L.	32	$201\frac{1}{3}$	11	13	.458	150	43	191	3.31	0
Major League Totals		6 Yrs.	180	1120	68	70	.493	840	257	1063	3.40	0
	Division Series											
2008	Los Angeles	N.L.	1	$6\frac{1}{3}$	1	0	1.000	4	2	6	0.00	0
2012	New York	A.L.	1	$8\frac{1}{3}$	0	0	.000	3	1	5	2.16	0
Division Series Totals			2	$14\frac{2}{3}$	1	0	1.000	7	3	11	1.23	0
	Championship Series											
2008	Los Angeles	N.L.	1	6	1	0	1.000	3	1	5	3.00	0
2009	Los Angeles	N.L.	1	$1\frac{1}{3}$	0	1	.000	1	0	6	40.50	0
2012	New York	A.L.	1	$7\frac{2}{3}$	0	1	.000	11	0	5	3.52	0
Championship Series Totals			3	15	1	2	.333	15	1	16	6.60	0

a Signed with Los Angeles Dodgers, December 16, 2007.

b On disabled list from June 13 to July 2, 2008.

c On disabled list from April 7 to June 1 and August 16 to September 6, 2009.

d Filed for free agency, November 1, 2010, re-signed with Los Angeles Dodgers, November 15, 2010.

e Filed for free agency, October 30, 2011. Signed with New York Yankees, January 26, 2012.

f Filed for free agency, November 3, 2012, re-signed with New York Yankees, November 20, 2012.

g Filed for free agency, October 31, 2013, re-signed with New York Yankees, December 7, 2013.

LACKEY, JOHN DERRAN

Born, Abilene, Texas, October 23, 1978.
Bats Right. Throws Right. Height, 6 feet, 6 inches. Weight, 235 pounds.

Year	Club	Lea	G	IP	W	L	Pct	SO	BB	H	ERA	SAVES
1999	Boise	Northwest	15	$81\frac{1}{3}$	6	2	.750	77	50	81	4.98	0
2000	Cedar Rapids	Midwest	5	$30\frac{1}{3}$	3	2	.600	21	5	20	2.08	0
2000	Lake Elsinore	Calif.	15	$100\frac{2}{3}$	6	6	.500	74	42	94	3.40	0
2000	Erie	Eastern	8	$57\frac{1}{3}$	6	1	.857	43	9	58	3.30	0
2001	Arkansas	Texas	18	$127\frac{1}{3}$	9	7	.563	94	29	106	3.46	0
2001	Salt Lake	P.C.	10	$57\frac{2}{3}$	3	4	.429	42	16	75	6.71	0
2002	Salt Lake	P.C.	16	$101\frac{2}{3}$	8	2	.800	82	28	89	2.57	0
2002	Anaheim	A.L.	18	$108\frac{1}{3}$	9	4	.692	69	33	113	3.66	0
2003	Anaheim	A.L.	33	204	10	16	.385	151	66	223	4.63	0
2004	Anaheim	A.L.	33	$198\frac{1}{3}$	14	13	.519	144	60	215	4.67	0
2005	Los Angeles	A.L.	33	209	14	5	.737	199	71	208	3.44	0
2006	Los Angeles	A.L.	33	$217\frac{2}{3}$	13	11	.542	190	72	203	3.56	0
2007	Los Angeles	A.L.	33	224	19	9	.679	179	52	219	*3.01	0
2008	Rancho Cucamonga	Calif.	3	9	0	0	.000	11	2	8	4.00	0
2008	Los Angeles a	A.L.	24	$163\frac{1}{3}$	12	5	.706	130	40	161	3.75	0
2009	Salt Lake	P.C.	2	$9\frac{2}{3}$	0	1	.000	8	1	6	2.79	0
2009	Los Angeles b-c	A.L.	27	$176\frac{1}{3}$	11	8	.579	139	47	177	3.83	0
2010	Boston	A.L.	33	215	14	11	.560	156	72	233	4.40	0

Year	Club	Lea	G	IP	W	L	Pct	SO	BB	H	ERA	SAVES
2011	Pawtucket	Int.	1	5 2/3	0	0	.000	4	0	3	1.59	0
2011	Boston d	A.L.	28	160	12	12	.500	108	56	203	6.41	0
2012	Boston e	A.L.				INJURED—Did Not Play						
2013	Portland	Eastern	1	3 2/3	0	0	.000	5	2	3	0.00	0
2013	Boston f	A.L.	29	189 1/3	10	13	.435	161	40	179	3.52	0
Major League Totals		11 Yrs.	324	2065 1/3	138	107	.563	1626	609	2134	4.05	0
	Division Series											
2002	Anaheim	A.L.	1	3	0	0	.000	3	1	3	0.00	0
2005	Los Angeles	A.L.	2	11 1/3	0	0	.000	9	9	7	2.38	0
2007	Los Angeles	A.L.	1	6	0	1	.000	4	2	9	6.00	0
2008	Los Angeles	A.L.	2	13 2/3	0	1	.000	6	4	11	2.63	0
2009	Los Angeles	A.L.	1	7 1/3	1	0	1.000	4	1	4	0.00	0
2013	Boston	A.L.	1	5 1/3	1	0	1.000	6	3	7	6.75	0
Division Series Totals			8	46 2/3	2	2	.500	32	20	41	2.89	0
	Championship Series											
2002	Anaheim	A.L.	1	7	1	0	1.000	7	0	3	0.00	0
2005	Los Angeles	A.L.	1	5	0	1	.000	3	1	8	9.00	0
2009	Los Angeles	A.L.	2	12 1/3	0	1	.000	10	6	15	3.65	0
2013	Boston	A.L.	1	6 2/3	1	0	1.000	8	0	4	0.00	0
Championship Series Totals			5	31	2	2	.500	28	7	30	2.90	0
	World Series Record											
2002	Anaheim	A.L.	3	12 1/3	1	0	1.000	7	5	15	4.38	0
2013	Boston	A.L.	3	14	1	1	.500	11	3	14	2.57	0
World Series Totals			6	26 1/3	2	1	.667	18	8	29	3.42	0

a On disabled list from March 21 to May 14, 2008.
b On disabled list from March 27 to May 16, 2009.
c Filed for free agency, November 5, 2009. Signed with Boston Red Sox, December 16, 2009.
d On disabled list from May 12 to June 5, 2011.
e On disabled list from February 21 to November 2, 2012.
f On disabled list from April 7 to April 28, 2013.

LATOS, MATHEW ADAM (MAT)

Born, Alexandria, Virginia, December 9, 1987.
Bats Right. Throws Right. Height, 6 feet, 6 inches. Weight, 225 pounds.

Year	Club	Lea	G	IP	W	L	Pct	SO	BB	H	ERA	SAVES
2007	Eugene	Northwest	16	56 1/3	1	4	.200	74	22	58	3.83	0
2008	Padres	Arizona	5	14	1	0	1.000	23	2	12	3.21	0
2008	Fort Wayne	Midwest	7	24 2/3	0	3	.000	23	8	24	3.28	0
2008	Eugene	Northwest	3	17 1/3	2	0	1.000	23	3	13	1.04	0
2009	Fort Wayne	Midwest	4	25 1/3	3	0	1.000	27	3	10	0.36	0
2009	San Antonio	Texas	9	47	5	1	.833	46	9	32	1.91	0
2009	San Diego	N.L.	10	50 2/3	4	5	.444	39	23	43	4.62	0
2010	San Diego a	N.L.	31	184 2/3	14	10	.583	189	50	150	2.92	0
2011	San Diego b-c	N.L.	31	194 1/3	9	14	.391	185	62	168	3.47	0
2012	Cincinnati	N.L.	33	209 1/3	14	4	.778	185	64	179	3.48	0
2013	Cincinnati	N.L.	32	210 2/3	14	7	.667	187	58	197	3.16	0
Major League Totals		5 Yrs.	137	849 2/3	55	40	.579	785	257	737	3.35	0
	Division Series											
2012	Cincinnati	N.L.	2	8 1/3	0	1	.000	5	2	11	6.48	0

a On disabled list from July 9 to July 24, 2010.
b On disabled list from March 22 to April 11, 2011.
c Traded to Cincinnati Reds for pitcher Edinson Volquez, pitcher Brad Boxberger, catcher Yasmani Grandal and infielder Yonder Alonso, December 17, 2011.

LEAGUE, BRANDON PAUL

Born, Sacramento, California, March 16, 1983.
Bats Right. Throws Right. Height, 6 feet, 3 inches. Weight, 200 pounds.

Year	Club	Lea	G	IP	W	L	Pct	SO	BB	H	ERA	SAVES
2001	Medicine Hat	Pioneer	9	38 2/3	2	2	.500	38	11	36	4.66	0
2002	Auburn	N.Y.-Penn.	16	85 2/3	7	2	.778	72	23	80	3.15	0
2003	Dunedin	Fla.St.	13	66 1/3	4	3	.571	34	20	76	4.75	0
2003	Charleston	So.Atl.	12	70 2/3	2	3	.400	61	18	58	1.91	0
2004	New Hampshire	Eastern	41	104	6	4	.600	90	41	92	3.38	2
2004	Toronto	A.L.	3	4 2/3	1	0	1.000	2	1	3	0.00	0
2005	Syracuse	Int.	19	63	4	4	.500	35	18	78	5.71	0
2005	Toronto	A.L.	20	35 2/3	1	0	1.000	17	20	42	6.56	0

Year	Club	Lea	G	IP	W	L	Pct	SO	BB	H	ERA	SAVES
2006	Syracuse	Int.	31	54 2/3	3	2	.600	43	15	57	2.14	8
2006	Toronto	A.L.	33	42 2/3	1	2	.333	29	9	34	2.53	1
2007	Syracuse	Int.	11	12	0	0	.000	10	6	12	3.00	0
2007	Blue Jays	Gulf Coast	1	1	0	0	.000	1	0	1	0.00	0
2007	Dunedin	Fla.St.	4	6	0	0	.000	6	2	5	4.50	0
2007	New Hampshire	Eastern	6	7 2/3	1	1	.500	7	7	5	3.52	0
2007	Toronto a	A.L.	14	11 2/3	0	0	.000	7	7	19	6.17	0
2008	Syracuse	Int.	20	34 1/3	2	3	.400	32	10	36	3.93	2
2008	Toronto	A.L.	31	33	1	2	.333	23	15	28	2.18	1
2009	Toronto b	A.L.	67	74 2/3	3	6	.333	76	21	72	4.58	0
2010	Seattle	A.L.	70	79	9	7	.563	56	27	67	3.42	6
2011	Seattle	A.L.	65	61 1/3	1	5	.167	45	10	56	2.79	37
2012	Seattle	A.L.	46	44 2/3	0	5	.000	27	19	48	3.63	9
2012	Los Angeles c	N.L.	28	27 1/3	2	1	.667	27	14	17	2.30	6
2013	Los Angeles	N.L.	58	54 1/3	6	4	.600	28	15	69	5.30	14
Major League Totals		10 Yrs.	435	469	25	32	.439	337	158	455	3.80	74

a On disabled list from March 31 to July 15 and August 5 to September 4, 2007.
b Traded to Seattle Mariners with outfielder Johermyn Chavez for pitcher Brandon Morrow, December 23, 2009.
c Traded to Los Angeles Dodgers for pitcher Logan Bawcom and outfielder Leon Landry, July 31, 2012.

LEAKE, MICHAEL RAYMOND (MIKE)

Born, San Diego, California, November 12, 1987.
Bats Right. Throws Right. Height, 6 feet, 1 inch. Weight, 190 pounds.

Year	Club	Lea	G	IP	W	L	Pct	SO	BB	H	ERA	SAVES
2010	Cincinnati a	N.L.	24	138 1/3	8	4	.667	91	49	158	4.23	0
2011	Louisville	Int.	2	7 1/3	0	1	.000	5	0	12	9.82	0
2011	Cincinnati	N.L.	29	167 2/3	12	9	.571	118	38	159	3.86	0
2012	Cincinnati	N.L.	30	179	8	9	.471	116	41	201	4.58	0
2013	Cincinnati	N.L.	31	192 1/3	14	7	.667	122	48	193	3.37	0
Major League Totals		4 Yrs.	114	677 1/3	42	29	.592	447	176	711	3.99	0
	Division Series											
2012	Cincinnati	N.L.	1	4 1/3	0	1	.000	1	2	6	10.38	0

a On disabled list from August 25 to September 10, 2010.

LE CURE, SAMUEL R. (SAM)

Born, Jefferson City, Missouri, May 4, 1984.
Bats Right. Throws Right. Height, 6 feet, 1 inch. Weight, 205 pounds.

Year	Club	Lea	G	IP	W	L	Pct	SO	BB	H	ERA	SAVES
2005	Billings	Pioneer	13	41 1/3	5	1	.833	44	15	43	3.27	0
2006	Sarasota	Fla.St.	27	141 2/3	7	12	.368	115	46	130	3.43	0
2007	Sarasota	Fla.St.	1	5	1	0	1.000	8	0	2	1.80	0
2007	Chattanooga	Southern	21	110	7	5	.583	104	46	119	4.17	0
2008	Chattanooga	Southern	27	155 1/3	9	7	.563	128	58	147	3.42	0
2009	Louisville	Int.	25	143 1/3	10	8	.556	125	44	143	4.46	0
2010	Louisville	Int.	15	98	8	3	.727	87	23	98	3.67	0
2010	Cincinnati	N.L.	15	48	2	5	.286	37	25	50	4.50	0
2011	Louisville	Int.	4	6 2/3	0	1	.000	6	2	5	1.35	1
2011	Cincinnati a	N.L.	43	77 2/3	2	1	.667	73	21	57	3.71	0
2012	Cincinnati	N.L.	48	57 1/3	3	3	.500	61	23	46	3.14	0
2013	Cincinnati	N.L.	63	61	2	1	.667	66	24	50	2.66	1
Major League Totals		4 Yrs.	169	244	9	10	.474	237	93	203	3.47	1
	Wild Card Playoff											
2013	Cincinnati	N.L.	1	1	0	0	.000	0	0	1	0.00	0
	Division Series											
2012	Cincinnati	N.L.	3	4	1	0	1.000	5	2	2	0.00	0

a On disabled list from May 29 to June 22, 2011.

LEE, CLIFTON PHIFER (CLIFF)

Born, Benton, Arkansas, August 30, 1978.
Bats Left. Throws Left. Height, 6 feet, 3 inches. Weight, 190 pounds.

Year	Club	Lea	G	IP	W	L	Pct	SO	BB	H	ERA	SAVES
2000	Cape Fear	So.Atl.	11	44 2/3	1	4	.200	63	36	50	5.24	0
2001	Jupiter	Fla.St.	21	109 2/3	6	7	.462	179	46	78	2.79	0
2002	Harrisburg	Eastern	15	86 1/3	7	2	.778	105	23	61	3.23	0
2002	Akron	Eastern	3	16 2/3	2	1	.667	18	10	11	5.40	0
2002	Buffalo	Int.	8	43	3	2	.600	30	22	36	3.77	0

Year	Club	Lea	G	IP	W	L	Pct	SO	BB	H	ERA	SAVES
2002	Cleveland a-b	A.L.	2	10 1/3	0	1	.000	6	8	6	1.74	0
2003	Buffalo	Int.	11	63 1/3	6	1	.857	61	31	62	3.27	0
2003	Kinston	Carolina	1	4 1/3	0	0	.000	4	3	0	0.00	0
2003	Akron	Eastern	2	12	1	0	1.000	13	4	7	1.50	0
2003	Cleveland c	A.L.	9	52 1/3	3	3	.500	44	20	41	3.61	0
2004	Cleveland	A.L.	33	179	14	8	.636	161	81	188	5.43	0
2005	Cleveland	A.L.	32	202	18	5	*.783	143	52	194	3.79	0
2006	Cleveland	A.L.	33	200 2/3	14	11	.560	129	58	224	4.40	0
2007	Kinston	Carolina	1	2	0	0	.000	4	0	1	0.00	0
2007	Akron	Eastern	1	5	1	0	1.000	7	1	2	0.00	0
2007	Buffalo	Int.	8	41	1	3	.250	50	25	32	3.51	0
2007	Cleveland d	A.L.	20	97 1/3	5	8	.385	66	36	112	6.29	0
2008	Cleveland e	A.L.	31	223 1/3	*22	3	*.880	170	34	214	*2.54	0
2009	Cleveland f-g	A.L.	22	152	7	9	.438	107	33	165	3.14	0
2009	Philadelphia	N.L.	12	79 2/3	7	4	.636	74	10	80	3.39	0
2010	Tacoma	P.C.	1	6	0	0	.000	4	0	3	0.00	0
2010	Seattle-Texas h-i-j	A.L.	28	212 1/3	12	9	.571	185	18	195	3.18	0
2011	Philadelphia	N.L.	32	232 2/3	17	8	.680	238	42	197	2.40	0
2012	Philadelphia k	N.L.	30	211	6	9	.400	207	28	207	3.16	0
2013	Philadelphia	N.L.	31	222 2/3	14	8	.636	222	32	193	2.87	0
Major League Totals		12 Yrs.	315	2075 1/3	139	86	.618	1752	452	2016	3.51	0
	Division Series											
2009	Philadelphia	N.L.	2	16 1/3	1	0	1.000	10	3	11	1.10	0
2010	Texas	A.L.	2	16	2	0	1.000	21	0	11	1.13	0
2011	Philadelphia	N.L.	1	6	0	1	.000	9	2	12	7.50	0
Division Series Totals			5	38 1/3	3	1	.750	40	5	34	2.11	0
	Championship Series											
2009	Philadelphia	N.L.	1	8	1	0	1.000	10	0	3	0.00	0
2010	Texas	A.L.	1	8	1	0	1.000	13	1	2	0.00	0
Championship Series Totals			2	16	2	0	1.000	23	1	5	0.00	0
	World Series Record											
2009	Philadelphia	N.L.	2	16	2	0	1.000	13	3	13	2.81	0
2010	Texas	A.L.	2	11 2/3	0	2	.000	13	1	14	6.94	0
World Series Totals			4	27 2/3	2	2	.500	26	4	27	4.55	0

a Traded to Cleveland Indians with infielder Lee Stevens, infielder Brandon Phillips and outfielder Grady Sizemore for pitcher Bartolo Colon and player to be named later, June 27, 2002.
b Montreal Expos received pitcher Tim Drew to complete trade, June 28, 2002.
c On disabled list from March 29 to May 30, 2003.
d On disabled list from March 23 to May 3, 2007.
e Selected Cy Young Award Winner in American League for 2008.
f Traded to Philadelphia Phillies with outfielder Ben Francisco for catcher Lou Marson, pitcher Jason Knapp, infielder Jason Donald and pitcher Carlos Carrasco, July 29, 2009.
g Traded to Seattle Mariners for outfielder J.C. Ramirez, pitcher Phillippe Aumont and outfielder Tyson Gillies, December 16, 2009.
h On disabled list from March 26 to April 30, 2010.
i Traded to Texas Rangers with pitcher Mark Lowe and cash for infielder Justin Smoak, pitcher Blake Beavan, pitcher Josh Lueke and infielder Matt Lawson, July 9, 2010.
j Filed for free agency, November 1, 2010. Signed with Philadelphia Phillies, December 15, 2010.
k On disabled list from April 19 to May 9, 2012.

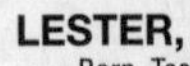
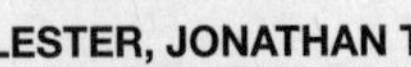

LESTER, JONATHAN TYLER (JON)

Born, Tacoma, Washington, January 7, 1984.
Bats Left. Throws Left. Height, 6 feet, 2 inches. Weight, 190 pounds.

Year	Club	Lea	G	IP	W	L	Pct	SO	BB	H	ERA	SAVES
2002	Red Sox	Gulf Coast	1	0 2/3	0	1	.000	1	1	5	13.50	0
2003	Augusta	So.Atl.	24	106	6	9	.400	71	44	102	3.65	0
2004	Sarasota	Fla.St.	21	90 1/3	7	6	.538	97	37	82	4.28	0
2004	Red Sox	Gulf Coast	1	1	0	0	.000	1	2	0	0.00	0
2005	Portland	Eastern	26	148 1/3	11	6	.647	163	57	114	2.61	0
2006	Pawtucket	Int.	11	46 2/3	3	4	.429	43	25	43	2.70	0
2006	Boston a	A.L.	15	81 1/3	7	2	.778	60	43	91	4.76	0
2007	Greenville	So.Atl.	3	13	0	0	.000	15	2	11	2.08	0
2007	Portland	Eastern	1	6	1	0	1.000	4	4	5	1.50	0
2007	Pawtucket	Int.	14	71 2/3	4	5	.444	51	31	67	3.89	0
2007	Boston b	A.L.	12	63	4	0	1.000	50	31	61	4.57	0
2008	Boston c	A.L.	33	210 1/3	16	6	.727	152	66	202	3.21	0
2009	Boston	A.L.	32	203 1/3	15	8	.652	225	64	186	3.41	0
2010	Boston	A.L.	32	208	19	9	.679	225	83	167	3.25	0

Year Club	Lea	G	IP	W	L	Pct	SO	BB	H	ERA	SAVES
2011 Boston d	A.L.	31	191⅔	15	9	.625	182	75	166	3.47	0
2012 Boston	A.L.	33	205⅓	9	14	.391	166	68	216	4.82	0
2013 Boston	A.L.	33	213⅓	15	8	.652	177	67	209	3.75	0
Major League Totals	8 Yrs.	221	1376⅓	100	56	.641	1237	497	1298	3.76	0
Division Series											
2008 Boston	A.L.	2	14	1	0	1.000	11	3	10	0.00	0
2009 Boston	A.L.	1	6	0	1	.000	5	4	4	4.50	0
2013 Boston	A.L.	1	7⅔	1	0	1.000	7	3	3	2.35	0
Division Series Totals		4	27⅔	2	1	.667	23	10	17	1.63	0
Championship Series											
2007 Boston	A.L.	2	3⅔	0	0	.000	5	1	3	4.91	0
2008 Boston	A.L.	2	12⅔	0	2	.000	15	2	14	4.97	0
2013 Boston	A.L.	2	11⅔	1	1	.500	7	4	13	2.31	0
Championship Series Totals		6	28	1	3	.250	27	7	30	3.86	0
World Series Record											
2007 Boston	A.L.	1	5⅔	1	0	1.000	3	3	3	0.00	0
2013 Boston	A.L.	2	15⅓	2	0	1.000	15	1	9	0.59	0
World Series Totals		3	21	3	0	1.000	18	4	12	0.43	0

a On disabled list from August 24 to November 6, 2006.
b On disabled list from March 23 to June 11, 2007.
c Pitched no-hit, no-run game against Kansas City Royals, May 19, 2008.
d On disabled list from July 6 to July 25, 2011.

LEWIS, COLBY PRESTON

Born, Bakersfield, California, August 2, 1979.
Bats Right. Throws Right. Height, 6 feet, 4 inches. Weight, 230 pounds.

Year Club	Lea	G	IP	W	L	Pct	SO	BB	H	ERA	SAVES
1999 Pulaski	Appal.	14	64⅔	7	3	.700	84	27	46	1.95	0
2000 Charlotte	Fla.St.	28	163⅔	11	10	.524	153	45	169	4.07	0
2001 Charlotte	Fla.St.	1	4⅓	1	0	1.000	8	0	0	0.00	0
2001 Tulsa	Texas	25	156	10	10	.500	162	62	150	4.50	0
2002 Texas	A.L.	15	34⅓	1	3	.250	28	26	42	6.29	0
2002 Oklahoma	P.C.	20	106⅔	5	6	.455	99	28	100	3.63	0
2003 Texas	A.L.	26	127	10	9	.526	88	70	163	7.30	0
2003 Oklahoma	P.C.	7	47⅔	5	1	.833	43	19	36	3.02	0
2004 Texas a-b	A.L.	3	15⅓	1	1	.500	11	13	13	4.11	0
2005 Detroit c	A.L.			INJURED—Did Not Play							
2006 Toledo	Int.	24	147⅔	6	7	.462	104	36	154	3.96	0
2006 Detroit d	A.L.	2	3	0	0	.000	5	1	8	3.00	0
2007 Sacramento	P.C.	15	95⅔	8	3	.727	97	23	70	1.88	0
2007 Oakland e-f	A.L.	26	37⅔	0	2	.000	23	14	44	6.45	0
2008 Hiroshima g	Japan Cent.	26	178	15	8	.652	183	27	151	2.68	0
2009 Hiroshima	Japan Cent.	29	176⅓	11	9	.550	186	19	156	2.96	0
2010 Texas h	A.L.	32	201	12	13	.480	196	65	174	3.72	0
2011 Texas	A.L.	32	200⅓	14	10	.583	169	56	187	4.40	0
2012 Texas i	A.L.	16	105	6	6	.500	93	14	99	3.43	0
2013 Frisco	Texas	5	18	0	1	.000	15	4	23	7.00	0
2013 Round Rock	P.C.	2	6	0	1	.000	4	4	10	9.00	0
2013 Texas j-k	A.L.			INJURED—Did Not Play							
Major League Totals	8 Yrs.	152	723⅔	44	44	.500	613	259	730	4.76	0
Division Series											
2010 Texas	A.L.	1	5	0	0	.000	5	5	2	0.00	0
2011 Texas	A.L.	1	6	1	0	1.000	6	2	1	1.50	0
Division Series Totals		2	11	1	0	1.000	11	7	3	0.82	0
Championship Series											
2010 Texas	A.L.	2	13⅔	2	0	1.000	13	6	9	1.98	0
2011 Texas	A.L.	1	5⅔	0	1	.000	6	2	8	6.35	0
Championship Series Totals		3	19⅓	2	1	.667	19	8	17	3.26	0
World Series Record											
2010 Texas	A.L.	1	7⅔	1	0	1.000	6	2	5	2.35	0
2011 Texas	A.L.	2	12	0	0	.000	8	5	7	2.25	0
World Series Totals		3	19⅔	1	0	1.000	14	7	12	2.29	0

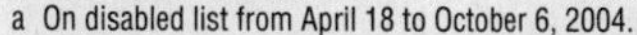

a On disabled list from April 18 to October 6, 2004.
b Claimed on waivers by Detroit Tigers, October 8, 2004.
c On disabled list from April 2 to October 31, 2005.
d Filed for free agency, October 2, 2006. Signed with Washington Nationals organization, November 6, 2006.

e Released by Washington Nationals, March 19, 2007. Signed with Oakland Athletics organization, March 29, 2007.
f Claimed on waivers by Kansas City Royals, November 2, 2007.
g Released by Kansas City Royals, December 4, 2007. Signed with Hiroshima (Japan) for 2008.
h Signed with Texas Rangers, January 14, 2010.
i On disabled list from June 24 to July 18 and July 19 to October 29, 2012.
j On disabled list from March 22 to October 31, 2013.
k Filed for free agency, October 31, 2013, re-signed with Texas Rangers organization, November 23, 2013.

LINCECUM, TIMOTHY LEROY (TIM)

Born, Bellevue, Washington, June 15, 1984.
Bats Left. Throws Right. Height, 5 feet, 11 inches. Weight, 160 pounds.

Year Club	Lea	G	IP	W	L	Pct	SO	BB	H	ERA	SAVES
2006 San Jose	Calif.	6	$27\frac{2}{3}$	2	0	1.000	48	12	13	1.95	0
2006 Salem-Keizer	Northwest	2	4	0	0	.000	10	0	1	0.00	0
2007 Fresno	P.C.	5	31	4	0	1.000	46	11	12	0.29	0
2007 San Francisco	N.L.	24	$146\frac{1}{3}$	7	5	.583	150	65	122	4.00	0
2008 San Francisco a	N.L.	34	227	18	5	*.783	*265	84	182	2.62	0
2009 San Francisco b	N.L.	32	$225\frac{1}{3}$	15	7	.682	*261	68	168	2.48	0
2010 San Francisco	N.L.	33	$212\frac{1}{3}$	16	10	.615	*231	76	194	3.43	0
2011 San Francisco	N.L.	33	217	13	14	.481	220	86	176	2.74	0
2012 San Francisco	N.L.	33	186	10	*15	.400	190	90	183	5.18	0
2013 San Francisco c	N.L.	32	$197\frac{2}{3}$	10	14	.417	193	76	184	4.37	0
Major League Totals	7 Yrs.	221	$1411\frac{2}{3}$	89	70	.560	1510	545	1209	3.46	0
Division Series											
2010 San Francisco	N.L.	1	9	1	0	1.000	14	1	2	0.00	0
2012 San Francisco	N.L.	2	$6\frac{1}{3}$	1	0	1.000	8	0	3	1.42	0
Division Series Totals		3	$15\frac{1}{3}$	2	0	1.000	22	1	5	0.59	0
Championship Series											
2010 San Francisco	N.L.	3	$14\frac{1}{3}$	1	1	.500	16	4	12	3.14	0
2012 San Francisco	N.L.	2	$6\frac{2}{3}$	0	1	.000	4	4	6	5.40	0
Championship Series Totals		5	21	1	2	.333	20	8	18	3.86	0
World Series Record											
2010 San Francisco	N.L.	2	$13\frac{2}{3}$	2	0	1.000	13	4	11	3.29	0
2012 San Francisco	N.L.	2	$4\frac{2}{3}$	0	0	.000	8	1	0	0.00	0
World Series Totals.............		4	$18\frac{1}{3}$	2	0	1.000	21	5	11	2.45	0

a Selected Cy Young Award Winner in National League for 2008.
b Selected Cy Young Award Winner in National League for 2009.
c Pitched no-hit, no-run game against San Diego Padres, July 13, 2013.

LINCOLN, BRAD ERIC

Born, Lake Jackson, Texas, May 25, 1985.
Bats Left. Throws Right. Height, 6 feet. Weight, 210 pounds.

Year Club	Lea	G	IP	W	L	Pct	SO	BB	H	ERA	SAVES
2006 Pirates	Gulf Coast	2	$7\frac{2}{3}$	0	0	.000	9	1	6	0.00	0
2006 Hickory.............	So.Atl.	4	16	1	2	.333	10	6	25	6.75	0
2007 a........................					INJURED—Did Not Play						
2008 Hickory.............	So.Atl.	11	62	5	5	.500	46	6	72	4.65	0
2008 Lynchburg	Carolina	8	$41\frac{2}{3}$	1	5	.167	29	11	42	4.75	0
2009 Altoona............	Eastern	13	75	1	5	.167	65	18	63	2.28	0
2009 Indianapolis	Int.	12	$61\frac{1}{3}$	6	2	.750	42	10	72	4.70	0
2010 Indianapolis	Int.	17	94	7	5	.583	84	24	83	4.12	0
2010 Pittsburgh	N.L.	11	$52\frac{2}{3}$	1	4	.200	25	15	66	6.66	0
2011 Indianapolis	Int.	19	$111\frac{2}{3}$	7	8	.467	94	21	115	4.19	0
2011 Pittsburgh b............	N.L.	12	$47\frac{2}{3}$	2	3	.400	29	16	54	4.72	0
2012 Indianapolis	Int.	2	12	1	0	1.000	9	0	10	2.25	0
2012 Pittsburgh	N.L.	28	$59\frac{1}{3}$	4	2	.667	60	14	51	2.73	1
2012 Toronto c	A.L.	24	$28\frac{2}{3}$	1	0	1.000	28	10	29	5.65	0
2013 Buffalo	Int.	23	$26\frac{1}{3}$	3	2	.600	29	8	22	2.05	5
2013 Toronto d	A.L.	22	$31\frac{2}{3}$	1	2	.333	25	22	28	3.98	0
Major League Totals	4 Yrs.	97	220	9	11	.450	167	77	228	4.66	1

a On minor league disabled list from April 5 to September 7, 2007.
b On disabled list from March 22 to April 11, 2011.
c Traded to Toronto Blue Jays for outfielder Travis Snider, July 31, 2012.
d Traded to Philadelphia Phillies for catcher Erik Kratz and pitcher Rob Rasmussen, December 3, 2013.

LINDSTROM, MATTHEW JAMES (MATT)

Born, Rexburg, Idaho, February 11, 1980.
Bats Right. Throws Right. Height, 6 feet, 4 inches. Weight, 210 pounds.

Year	Club	Lea	G	IP	W	L	Pct	SO	BB	H	ERA	SAVES
2002	Kingsport	Appal.	12	48⅓	0	6	.000	39	21	56	4.84	0
2003	Brooklyn	N.Y.-Penn.	14	65⅓	7	3	.700	52	27	61	3.44	0
2003	Capital City	So.Atl.	12	56⅔	2	3	.400	50	33	46	2.86	0
2004	St. Lucie	Fla.St.	14	79⅔	5	5	.500	50	20	83	3.73	0
2004	Capital City	So.Atl.	12	56	3	2	.600	64	10	47	3.21	0
2005	Binghamton	Eastern	35	73⅓	2	5	.286	58	55	90	5.40	0
2006	Binghamton	Eastern	35	40⅔	2	4	.333	54	14	42	3.76	11
2006	St. Lucie a	Fla.St.	11	18	1	0	1.000	16	7	14	2.50	2
2007	Florida	N.L.	71	67	3	4	.429	62	21	66	3.09	0
2008	Albuquerque	P.C.	3	4	0	0	.000	4	1	5	9.00	0
2008	Florida	N.L.	66	57⅓	3	3	.500	43	26	57	3.14	5
2009	Jupiter	Fla.St.	2	2	0	0	.000	1	0	1	0.00	0
2009	Jacksonville	Southern	2	2	0	1	.000	3	0	2	9.00	0
2009	Florida b-c	N.L.	54	47⅓	2	1	.667	39	24	54	5.89	15
2010	Corpus Christi	Texas	1	1	0	0	.000	1	0	0	0.00	0
2010	Houston d-e	N.L.	58	53⅓	2	5	.286	43	20	68	4.39	23
2011	Colorado Springs	P.C.	2	2	0	0	.000	4	0	4	13.50	0
2011	Colorado f	N.L.	63	54	2	2	.500	36	14	52	3.00	2
2012	Orioles	Gulf Coast	2	2	0	0	.000	2	0	2	4.50	0
2012	Bowie	Eastern	2	2⅓	0	0	.000	1	1	4	3.86	0
2012	Baltimore g-h	A.L.	34	36⅓	1	0	1.000	30	12	35	2.72	0
2012	Arizona i-j	N.L.	12	10⅔	0	0	.000	10	2	10	2.53	0
2013	Chicago	A.L.	76	60⅔	2	4	.333	46	23	64	3.12	0
Major League Totals		7 Yrs.	434	386⅔	15	19	.441	309	142	406	3.56	45

a Traded to Florida Marlins by New York Mets with pitcher Henry Owens for pitcher Adam Bostick and pitcher Jason Vargas, November 20, 2006.
b On disabled list from June 24 to August 1, 2009.
c Traded to Houston Astros for infielder Luis Bryan and pitcher Robert Bono, December 9, 2009.
d On disabled list from August 17 to September 1, 2010.
e Traded to Colorado Rockies for pitcher Wes Musick and pitcher Jonnathan Aristil, December 23, 2010.
f On disabled list from August 10 to August 26, 2011.
g Traded to Baltimore Orioles with pitcher Jason Hammel for pitcher Jeremy Guthrie, February 6, 2012.
h On disabled list from May 11 to June 27, 2012.
i Traded to Arizona Diamondbacks with cash for pitcher Joe Saunders and cash, August 26, 2012.
j Filed for free agency, November 3, 2012. Signed with Chicago White Sox, January 25, 2013.

LIRIANO, FRANCISCO CASILLAS

Born, San Cristobal, Dominican Republic, October 26, 1983.
Bats Left. Throws Left. Height, 6 feet, 2 inches. Weight, 225 pounds.

Year	Club	Lea	G	IP	W	L	Pct	SO	BB	H	ERA	SAVES
2001	Giants	Arizona	13	62	5	4	.556	67	24	51	3.63	0
2001	Salem-Keizer	Northwest	2	9	0	0	.000	12	1	7	5.00	0
2002	Hagerstown	So.Atl.	16	80	3	6	.333	85	31	61	3.49	0
2003	Giants	Arizona	4	8⅓	0	1	.000	9	6	5	4.32	0
2003	San Jose a	Calif.	1	0⅔	0	1	.000	0	2	5	54.00	0
2004	New Britain	Eastern	7	39⅔	3	2	.600	49	17	45	3.18	0
2004	Fort Myers	Fla.St.	21	117	6	7	.462	125	43	118	4.00	0
2005	New Britain	Eastern	13	76⅔	3	5	.375	92	26	70	3.64	0
2005	Rochester	Int.	14	91	9	2	.818	112	24	56	1.78	0
2005	Minnesota	A.L.	6	23⅔	1	2	.333	33	7	19	5.70	0
2006	Minnesota b	A.L.	28	121	12	3	.800	144	32	89	2.16	1
2007	Minnesota c	A.L.	INJURED—Did Not Play									
2008	Fort Myers	Fla.St.	1	5⅓	0	1	.000	8	2	6	6.75	0
2008	Rochester	Int.	19	118	10	2	.833	113	31	102	3.28	0
2008	Minnesota	A.L.	14	76	6	4	.600	67	32	74	3.91	0
2009	Minnesota d	A.L.	29	136⅔	5	13	.278	122	65	147	5.80	0
2010	Minnesota	A.L.	31	191⅔	14	10	.583	201	58	184	3.62	0
2011	Minnesota e-f	A.L.	26	134⅓	9	10	.474	112	75	125	5.09	0
2012	Minnesota-Chicago g-h	A.L.	34	156⅔	6	12	.333	167	87	143	5.34	0
2013	Bradenton	Fla.St.	1	3	0	0	.000	6	0	0	0.00	0
2013	Altoona	Eastern	1	2⅔	0	1	.000	4	3	4	13.50	0
2013	Indianapolis	Int.	3	16	2	0	1.000	23	1	15	3.38	0
2013	Pittsburgh i	N.L.	26	161	16	8	.667	163	63	134	3.02	0
Major League Totals		8 Yrs.	194	1001	69	62	.527	1009	419	915	4.18	1
Wild Card Playoff												
2013	Pittsburgh	N.L.	1	7	1	0	1.000	5	1	4	1.29	0

Year Club	Lea	G	IP	W	L	Pct	SO	BB	H	ERA	SAVES
Division Series											
2009 Minnesota	A.L.	1	2	0	0	.000	1	1	1	4.50	0
2010 Minnesota	A.L.	1	5 2/3	0	0	.000	7	3	6	6.35	0
2013 Pittsburgh	N.L.	1	6	0	0	.000	5	2	3	3.00	0
Division Series Totals		3	13 2/3	0	0	.000	13	6	10	4.61	0

a Traded by San Francisco Giants to Minnesota Twins with pitcher Joe Nathan and pitcher Boof Bonser for catcher A.J. Pierzynski, November 14, 2003.
b On disabled list from August 8 to September 11, 2006.
c On disabled list from March 24 to October 10, 2007.
d On disabled list from August 18 to September 9, 2009.
e Pitched no-hit, no-run game against Chicago White Sox, May 3, 2011.
f On disabled list from May 30 to June 7 and August 26 to September 16, 2011.
g Traded to Chicago White Sox for infielder Eduardo Escobar and pitcher Pedro Hernandez, July 29, 2012.
h Filed for free agency, November 3, 2012. Signed with Pittsburgh Pirates, February 8, 2013.
i On disabled list from March 22 to May 11, 2013.

LOCKE, JEFFREY ALAN (JEFF)

Born, Center Conway, New Hampshire, November 20, 1987.
Bats Left. Throws Left. Height, 6 feet, 1 inch. Weight, 215 pounds.

Year Club	Lea	G	IP	W	L	Pct	SO	BB	H	ERA	SAVES
2006 Braves	Gulf Coast	10	32	4	3	.571	38	5	38	4.22	0
2007 Danville	Appal.	13	61	7	1	.875	74	8	48	2.66	1
2008 Rome	So.Atl.	25	139 2/3	5	12	.294	113	38	150	4.06	0
2009 Lynchburg	Carolina	17	81 2/3	4	4	.500	56	18	98	4.08	0
2009 Myrtle Beach a	Carolina	10	45 2/3	1	4	.200	43	26	47	5.52	0
2010 Altoona	Eastern	10	57 2/3	3	2	.600	56	12	57	3.59	0
2010 Bradenton	Fla.St.	17	86 1/3	9	3	.750	83	14	82	3.54	0
2011 Altoona	Eastern	23	125	7	8	.467	114	46	118	4.03	0
2011 Indianapolis	Int.	5	28 1/3	1	2	.333	25	9	25	2.22	0
2011 Pittsburgh	N.L.	4	16 2/3	0	3	.000	5	10	21	6.48	0
2012 Indianapolis	Int.	24	141 2/3	10	5	.667	131	43	126	2.48	0
2012 Pittsburgh	N.L.	8	34 1/3	1	3	.250	34	11	36	5.50	0
2013 Pittsburgh	N.L.	30	166 1/3	10	7	.588	125	*84	146	3.52	0
Major League Totals	3 Yrs.	42	217 1/3	11	13	.458	164	105	203	4.06	0

a Traded by Atlanta Braves to Pittsburgh Pirates with outfielder Gorkys Hernandez and pitcher Charlie Morton for outfielder Nate McLouth, June 3, 2009.

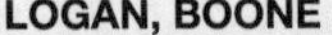

LOGAN, BOONE

Born, San Antonio, Texas, August 13, 1984.
Bats Right. Throws Left. Height, 6 feet, 5 inches. Weight, 215 pounds.

Year Club	Lea	G	IP	W	L	Pct	SO	BB	H	ERA	SAVES
2003 Great Falls	Pioneer	16	67	3	3	.500	48	31	76	6.58	0
2004 Great Falls	Pioneer	18	64 1/3	3	7	.300	48	31	74	5.60	1
2005 Winston-Salem	Carolina	4	5 1/3	0	0	.000	5	4	7	5.06	0
2005 Great Falls	Pioneer	21	35 1/3	1	1	.500	29	4	34	3.31	2
2006 Charlotte	Int.	38	42 2/3	3	1	.750	57	12	35	3.38	11
2006 Chicago	A.L.	21	17 1/3	0	0	.000	15	15	21	8.31	1
2007 Charlotte	Int.	4	8 1/3	0	1	.000	11	4	8	2.16	1
2007 Chicago	A.L.	68	50 2/3	2	1	.667	35	20	59	4.97	0
2008 Charlotte	Int.	5	9	0	1	.000	7	6	10	6.00	0
2008 Chicago a	A.L.	55	42 1/3	2	3	.400	42	14	57	5.95	0
2009 Gwinnett	Int.	29	35 2/3	4	2	.667	39	17	26	3.28	2
2009 Atlanta b	N.L.	20	17 1/3	1	1	.500	10	9	21	5.19	0
2010 Scranton/WB	Int.	14	21 1/3	0	1	.000	23	4	18	2.11	0
2010 New York	A.L.	51	40	2	0	1.000	38	20	34	2.93	0
2011 New York	A.L.	64	41 2/3	5	3	.625	46	13	43	3.46	0
2012 New York	A.L.	*80	55 1/3	7	2	.778	68	28	48	3.74	1
2013 New York c	A.L.	61	39	5	2	.714	50	13	33	3.23	0
Major League Totals	8 Yrs.	420	303 2/3	24	12	.667	304	132	316	4.39	2
Division Series											
2010 New York	A.L.	2	1	0	0	.000	0	0	1	0.00	0
2011 New York	A.L.	3	2 1/3	0	0	.000	6	0	1	0.00	0
2012 New York	A.L.	2	0 2/3	0	0	.000	1	0	0	0.00	0
Division Series Totals		7	4	0	0	.000	7	0	2	0.00	0
Championship Series											
2010 New York	A.L.	3	0 2/3	0	0	.000	1	1	2	27.00	0
2012 New York	A.L.	3	3	0	0	.000	1	0	3	0.00	0
Championship Series Totals		6	3 2/3	0	0	.000	2	1	5	4.91	0

a Traded to Atlanta Braves with pitcher Javier Vazquez for catcher Tyler Flowers, infielder Jonathan Gilmore, infielder Brent Lillibridge and pitcher Santos Rodriguez, December 4, 2008.
b Traded to New York Yankees with pitcher Javier Vazquez for outfielder Melky Cabrera, pitcher Arodys Vizcaino, pitcher Michael Dunn and cash, December 22, 2009.
c Filed for free agency, October 31, 2013. Signed with Colorado Rockies, December 16, 2013.

LOHSE, KYLE MATTHEW

Born, Chico, California, October 4, 1978.
Bats Right. Throws Right. Height, 6 feet, 2 inches. Weight, 210 pounds.

Year Club	Lea	G	IP	W	L	Pxt	SO	BB	H	ERA	SAVES
1997 Cubs	Arizona	12	47 2/3	2	2	.500	49	22	46	3.02	0
1998 Rockford	Midwest	28	170 2/3	13	8	.619	121	45	158	3.22	0
1999 New Britain	Eastern	11	70 1/3	3	4	.429	41	23	87	5.89	0
1999 Daytona	Fla.St.	9	53	5	3	.625	41	16	48	2.89	0
1999 Fort Myers a	Fla.St.	7	41 2/3	2	3	.400	33	9	47	5.18	0
2000 New Britain	Eastern	28	167	3	18	.143	124	55	196	6.04	0
2001 New Britain	Eastern	6	38	3	1	.750	32	4	32	2.37	0
2001 Edmonton	P.C.	8	49	4	2	.667	48	13	50	3.12	0
2001 Minnesota	A.L.	19	90 1/3	4	7	.364	64	29	102	5.68	0
2002 Minnesota	A.L.	32	180 2/3	13	8	.619	124	70	181	4.23	0
2003 Minnesota	A.L.	33	201	14	11	.560	130	45	211	4.61	0
2004 Minnesota	A.L.	35	194	9	13	.409	111	76	240	5.34	0
2005 Minnesota	A.L.	31	178 2/3	9	13	.409	86	44	211	4.18	0
2006 Rochester	Int.	4	24	2	1	.667	12	6	15	1.50	0
2006 Minnesota	A.L.	22	63 2/3	2	5	.286	46	25	80	7.07	0
2006 Cincinnati b	N.L.	12	63	3	5	.375	51	19	70	4.57	0
2007 Cincinnati-Philadelphia c-d	N.L.	34	192 2/3	9	12	.429	122	57	207	4.62	0
2008 St. Louis	N.L.	33	200	15	6	.714	119	49	211	3.78	0
2009 Springfield	Texas	1	4 2/3	0	0	.000	3	4	3	3.86	0
2009 Memphis	P.C.	1	6	1	0	1.000	6	2	2	0.00	0
2009 St. Louis e	N.L.	23	117 2/3	6	10	.375	77	36	125	4.74	0
2010 Springfield	Texas	1	5	0	1	.000	4	0	12	9.00	0
2010 Memphis	P.C.	3	14	1	0	1.000	14	2	9	3.21	0
2010 St. Louis f	N.L.	18	92	4	8	.333	54	35	129	6.55	0
2011 St. Louis	N.L.	30	188 1/3	14	8	.636	111	42	178	3.39	0
2012 St. Louis g	N.L.	33	211	16	3	*.842	143	38	192	2.86	0
2013 Milwaukee	N.L.	32	198 2/3	11	10	.524	125	36	196	3.35	0
Major League Totals	13 Yrs.	387	2171 2/3	129	119	.520	1363	601	2333	4.35	0
Wild Card Playoff											
2012 St. Louis	N.L.	1	5 2/3	1	0	1.000	6	1	6	3.18	0
Division Series											
2002 Minnesota	A.L.	2	4	0	0	.000	5	0	2	0.00	0
2003 Minnesota	A.L.	1	5	0	1	.000	5	2	6	5.40	0
2004 Minnesota	A.L.	1	2	0	1	.000	3	0	1	4.50	0
2007 Philadelphia	N.L.	1	1 2/3	0	0	.000	1	0	1	6.75	0
2011 St. Louis	N.L.	1	5 1/3	0	1	.000	4	1	7	8.44	0
2012 St. Louis	N.L.	1	7	0	0	.000	5	1	2	1.29	0
Division Series Totals		7	24 2/3	0	3	.000	23	4	19	4.01	0
Championship Series											
2002 Minnesota	A.L.	1	1	0	0	.000	1	0	0	0.00	0
2011 St. Louis	N.L.	1	4 1/3	0	1	.000	3	0	6	6.23	0
2012 St. Louis	N.L.	2	7 2/3	1	1	.500	3	6	13	7.04	0
Championship Series Totals		4	13	1	2	.333	7	6	19	6.23	0
World Series Record											
2011 St. Louis	N.L.	1	3	0	0	.000	3	2	5	9.00	0

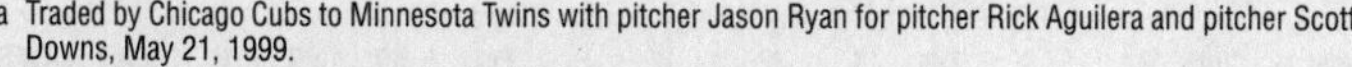

a Traded by Chicago Cubs to Minnesota Twins with pitcher Jason Ryan for pitcher Rick Aguilera and pitcher Scott Downs, May 21, 1999.
b Traded to Cincinnati Reds for pitcher Zach Ward, July 31, 2006.
c Traded to Philadelphia Phillies for pitcher Matt Maloney, July 30, 2007.
d Filed for free agency, October 31, 2007. Signed with St. Louis Cardinals, March 14, 2008.
e On disabled list from June 4 to July 12 and August 22 to September 6, 2009.
f On disabled list from May 23 to August 15, 2010.
g Filed for free agency, November 3, 2012. Signed with Milwaukee Brewers, March 25, 2013.

LOPEZ, JAVIER ALFONSO

Born, San Juan, Puerto Rico, July 11, 1977.
Bats Left. Throws Left. Height, 6 feet, 4 inches. Weight, 225 pounds.

Year Club	Lea	G	IP	W	L	Pct	SO	BB	H	ERA	SAVES
1998 South Bend	Midwest	16	44	2	4	.333	31	30	60	6.55	0
1999 South Bend	Midwest	20	99	4	6	.400	70	43	122	6.00	0
2000 High Desert	Calif.	30	136 1/3	4	8	.333	98	57	152	5.22	2
2001 Lancaster	Calif.	17	24	1	3	.250	18	5	30	2.63	1
2001 El Paso	Texas	22	40	1	0	1.000	21	14	64	7.43	0
2002 El Paso a	Texas	61	46 1/3	2	2	.500	47	16	34	2.72	6
2003 Colorado b	N.L.	75	58 1/3	4	1	.800	40	12	58	3.70	1
2004 Colorado Springs	P.C.	8	9	0	1	.000	9	2	10	4.00	0
2004 Colorado	N.L.	64	40 2/3	1	2	.333	20	26	45	7.52	0
2005 Tucson	P.C.	27	24 1/3	0	1	.000	16	12	17	2.22	2
2005 Colorado-Arizona c	N.L.	32	16 1/3	1	1	.500	12	11	26	11.02	2
2006 Charlotte d	Int.	26	33	2	1	.667	26	6	28	0.55	12
2006 Pawtucket	Int.	13	16 2/3	0	0	.000	12	8	20	4.86	4
2006 Boston e	A.L.	27	16 2/3	1	0	1.000	11	10	13	2.70	1
2007 Pawtucket	Int.	17	16 2/3	2	1	.667	15	8	19	3.78	0
2007 Boston	A.L.	61	40 2/3	2	1	.667	26	18	36	3.10	0
2008 Boston	A.L.	70	59 1/3	2	0	1.000	38	27	53	2.43	0
2009 Boston	A.L.	14	11 2/3	0	2	.000	5	9	20	9.26	0
2009 Pawtucket f	Int.	38	39 2/3	1	1	.500	23	13	35	3.18	0
2010 Pittsburgh-San Francisco g	N.L.	77	57 2/3	4	2	.667	38	20	50	2.34	0
2011 San Francisco	N.L.	70	53	5	2	.714	40	26	42	2.72	1
2012 San Francisco	N.L.	70	36	3	0	1.000	28	14	37	2.50	7
2013 San Francisco h	N.L.	69	39 1/3	4	2	.667	37	12	30	1.83	1
Major League Totals	11 Yrs.	629	429 2/3	27	13	.675	295	185	410	3.64	13
Division Series											
2007 Boston	A.L.	1	0 1/3	0	0	.000	0	0	0	0.00	0
2008 Boston	A.L.	1	1	0	1	.000	1	0	3	9.00	0
2010 San Francisco	N.L.	2	0 2/3	0	0	.000	2	0	0	0.00	0
2012 San Francisco	N.L.	2	0 2/3	0	0	.000	0	0	0	0.00	0
Division Series Totals		6	2 2/3	0	1	.000	3	0	3	3.38	0
Championship Series											
2007 Boston	A.L.	3	2	0	0	.000	0	2	3	18.00	0
2008 Boston	A.L.	2	1 2/3	0	0	.000	0	0	3	0.00	0
2010 San Francisco	N.L.	5	4 1/3	1	0	1.000	4	1	1	2.08	0
2012 San Francisco	N.L.	3	2 1/3	0	0	.000	4	2	0	0.00	0
Championship Series Totals		13	10 1/3	1	0	1.000	8	5	7	4.35	0
World Series Record											
2007 Boston	A.L.	1	0	0	0	.000	0	0	2	INF	0
2010 San Francisco	N.L.	2	0 2/3	0	0	.000	0	0	0	0.00	0
World Series Totals		3	0 2/3	0	0	.000	0	0	2	27.00	0

a Selected by Boston Red Sox from Arizona Diamondbacks in Rule V draft, December 16, 2002.
b Traded to Colorado Rockies for player to be named later, March 28, 2003. Boston Red Sox received pitcher Ryan Cameron to complete trade, March 29, 2003.
c Claimed on waivers by Arizona Diamondbacks, April 14, 2005.
d Filed for free agency, October 15, 2005. Signed with Chicago White Sox organization, January 19, 2006.
e Traded to Boston Red Sox for pitcher David Riske, June 15, 2006.
f Filed for free agency, October 5, 2009. Signed with Pittsburgh Pirates, December 18, 2009.
g Traded to San Francisco Giants for pitcher Joe Martinez and outfielder John Bowker, July 31, 2010.
h Filed for free agency, October 31, 2013, re-signed with San Francisco Giants, November 21, 2013.

LOPEZ, WILTON

Born, Leon, Nicaragua, July 19, 1983.
Bats Right. Throws Right. Height, 6 feet. Weight, 190 pounds.

Year Club	Lea	G	IP	W	L	Pct	SO	BB	H	ERA	SAVES
2002-03						Did Not Play					
2004 Tampa	Fla.St.	1	2	0	0	.000	2	1	2	4.50	0
2004 Yankees	Gulf Coast	4	5 2/3	1	0	1.000	6	0	2	0.00	1
2004 Battle Creek	Midwest	2	1 2/3	0	1	.000	2	1	4	0.00	0
2004 Staten Island	N.Y.-Penn.	2	3	0	0	.000	2	1	5	12.00	0
2005-06						Did Not Play					
2007 Lake Elsinore	Calif.	22	20 2/3	2	1	.667	19	1	35	6.10	3
2007 Fort Wayne a	Midwest	22	30	1	0	1.000	17	2	34	3.30	0
2008 Lake Elsinore	Calif.	30	30 2/3	2	1	.667	26	4	34	2.64	12
2008 Portland	P.C.	1	1	0	0	.000	1	2	1	9.00	0
2008 San Antonio	Texas	27	38 1/3	0	2	.000	24	9	41	4.93	0

Year	Club	Lea	G	IP	W	L	Pct	SO	BB	H	ERA	SAVES
2009	Corpus Christi	Texas	29	110 1/3	4	5	.444	69	13	133	4.73	0
2009	Houston b	N.L.	8	19 1/3	0	2	.000	9	8	32	8.38	0
2010	Round Rock	P.C.	3	5	2	1	.667	2	0	8	5.40	0
2010	Houston	N.L.	68	67	5	2	.714	50	5	66	2.96	1
2011	Houston c	N.L.	73	71	2	6	.250	56	18	72	2.79	0
2012	Oklahoma	P.C.	2	2	0	0	.000	1	0	4	13.50	0
2012	Houston d-e	N.L.	64	66 1/3	6	3	.667	54	8	61	2.17	10
2013	Colorado	N.L.	75	75 1/3	3	4	.429	48	18	88	4.06	0
Major League Totals		5 Yrs.	288	299	16	17	.485	217	57	319	3.37	11

a Released by New York Yankees, March 1, 2007. Signed with San Diego Padres organization, March 3, 2007.
b Claimed on waivers by Houston Astros, April 10, 2009.
c On disabled list from April 14 to May 3, 2011.
d On disabled list from June 11 to July 9, 2012.
e Traded to Colorado Rockies with player to be named later for pitcher Alex White and pitcher Alex Gillingham, December 4, 2012. Colorado Rockies received outfielder Jose Monzon to complete trade, May 1, 2013.

LOUP, AARON CHRISTOPHER

Born, Raceland, Louisiana, December 19, 1987.
Bats Left. Throws Left. Height, 5 feet, 11 inches. Weight, 210 pounds.

Year	Club	Lea	G	IP	W	L	Pct	SO	BB	H	ERA	SAVES
2009	Blue Jays	Gulf Coast	13	16 1/3	2	1	.667	19	3	17	3.86	3
2010	Lansing	Midwest	35	73 1/3	3	2	.600	73	22	79	4.54	2
2011	Dunedin	Fla.St.	48	65 2/3	4	3	.571	56	27	67	4.66	5
2012	New Hampshire	Eastern	37	45 1/3	0	3	.000	43	14	46	2.78	3
2012	Toronto	A.L.	33	30 2/3	0	2	.000	21	2	26	2.64	0
2013	Toronto	A.L.	64	69 1/3	4	6	.400	53	13	66	2.47	2
Major League Totals		2 Yrs.	97	100	4	8	.333	74	15	92	2.52	2

LYLES, JORDAN HORTON

Born, Florence, North Carolina, October 19, 1990.
Bats Right. Throws Right. Height, 6 feet, 4 inches. Weight, 210 pounds.

Year	Club	Lea	G	IP	W	L	Pct	SO	BB	H	ERA	SAVES
2008	Greeneville	Appal.	13	49 2/3	3	3	.500	64	10	44	3.99	0
2008	Tri-City	N.Y.-Penn.	2	5 2/3	0	0	.000	4	7	7	6.35	0
2009	Lexington	So.Atl.	26	144 2/3	7	11	.389	167	38	134	3.24	0
2010	Round Rock	P.C.	6	31 2/3	0	3	.000	22	11	48	5.40	0
2010	Corpus Christi	Texas	21	127	7	9	.438	115	35	133	3.12	0
2011	Oklahoma	P.C.	12	62 1/3	3	3	.500	42	17	64	3.61	0
2011	Houston	N.L.	20	94	2	8	.200	67	26	107	5.36	0
2012	Oklahoma	P.C.	7	40 2/3	5	0	1.000	33	8	41	3.54	0
2012	Houston	N.L.	25	141 1/3	5	12	.294	99	42	159	5.09	0
2013	Oklahoma	P.C.	6	23 2/3	2	2	.500	11	6	30	5.32	0
2013	Houston a	A.L.	27	141 2/3	7	9	.438	93	49	165	5.59	1
Major League Totals		3 Yrs.	72	377	14	29	.326	259	117	431	5.35	1

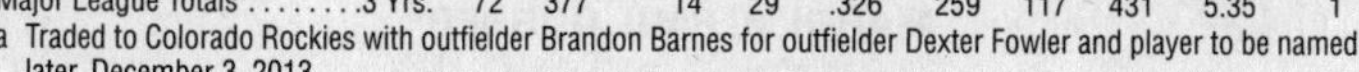

a Traded to Colorado Rockies with outfielder Brandon Barnes for outfielder Dexter Fowler and player to be named later, December 3, 2013.

LYNN, MICHAEL LANCE (LANCE)

Born, Indianapolis, Indiana, May 12, 1987.
Bats Right. Throws Right. Height, 6 feet, 5 inches. Weight, 250 pounds.

Year	Club	Lea	G	IP	W	L	Pct	SO	BB	H	ERA	SAVES
2008	Quad Cities	Midwest	2	8	0	1	.000	7	2	8	2.25	0
2008	Batavia	N.Y.-Penn.	6	18 2/3	1	0	1.000	22	4	12	0.96	0
2009	Palm Beach	Fla.St.	5	15 2/3	0	0	.000	17	3	16	2.30	0
2009	Memphis	P.C.	1	6 2/3	0	0	.000	9	3	5	2.70	0
2009	Springfield	Texas	22	126 1/3	11	4	.733	98	51	117	2.92	0
2010	Memphis	P.C.	29	164	13	10	.565	141	62	164	4.77	0
2011	Memphis	P.C.	12	75	7	3	.700	64	25	79	3.84	0
2011	St. Louis a	N.L.	18	34 2/3	1	1	.500	40	11	25	3.12	1
2012	St. Louis	N.L.	35	176	18	7	.720	180	64	168	3.78	0
2013	St. Louis	N.L.	33	201 2/3	15	10	.600	198	76	189	3.97	0
Major League Totals		3 Yrs.	86	412 1/3	34	18	.654	418	151	382	3.82	1
	Wild Card Playoff											
2012	St. Louis	N.L.	1	0 1/3	0	0	.000	0	0	0	0.00	0
	Division Series											
2012	St. Louis	N.L.	3	3 1/3	1	1	.500	6	2	4	8.10	0

Year	Club	Lea	G	IP	W	L	Pct	SO	BB	H	ERA	SAVES
2013	St. Louis	N.L.	1	4 1/3	0	1	.000	6	3	7	10.38	0
Division Series Totals			4	7 2/3	1	2	.333	12	5	11	9.39	0
	Championship Series											
2011	St. Louis	N.L.	5	5 1/3	1	0	1.000	1	2	3	0.00	0
2012	St. Louis	N.L.	2	7 1/3	0	1	.000	9	4	9	4.91	0
2013	St. Louis	N.L.	2	7 1/3	2	0	1.000	6	4	7	2.45	0
Championship Series Totals			9	20	3	1	.750	16	10	19	2.70	0
	World Series Record											
2011	St. Louis	N.L.	5	5 2/3	1	0	1.000	4	3	7	6.35	0
2013	St. Louis	N.L.	2	5 2/3	0	1	.000	5	4	5	4.76	0
World Series Totals			7	11 1/3	1	1	.500	9	7	12	5.56	0

a On disabled list from August 10 to October 9, 2011.

MACHI, JEAN MANUEL

Born, El Tigre, Venezuela, February 1, 1982.
Bats Right. Throws Right. Height, 6 feet. Weight, 260 pounds.

Year	Club	Lea	G	IP	W	L	Pct	SO	BB	H	ERA	SAVES
2002	Phillies	Gulf Coast	10	27	2	0	1.000	22	16	11	1.00	1
2003	Batavia	N.Y.-Penn.	8	32	2	4	.333	19	13	30	4.78	0
2004	Tronconero 1 a	VSL	9	41	2	2	.500	39	10	29	2.18	0
2005	Visalia	Calif.	31	97	3	11	.214	106	58	113	6.03	3
2005	Montgomery	Southern	1	0 2/3	0	0	.000	0	1	4	54.00	0
2006	Montgomery b	Southern	49	71 2/3	6	1	.857	68	37	68	2.64	16
2007	New Hampshire	Eastern	48	81 2/3	2	4	.333	56	24	68	3.53	2
2008	New Hampshire	Eastern	21	69 2/3	2	6	.250	51	40	74	4.65	1
2009	Altoona c	Eastern	28	34 2/3	2	3	.400	25	13	28	2.08	6
2009	Indianapolis	Int.	13	17	1	1	.500	12	6	8	2.12	6
2010	Indianapolis	Int.	58	59 2/3	5	5	.500	58	32	51	3.92	23
2011	Mexico City d-e	Mexican	48	55	2	1	.750	37	17	54	2.30	15
2011	Fresno	P.C.	3	4	1	1	.500	6	0	5	9.00	0
2012	Fresno	P.C.	53	56 2/3	2	1	.667	44	17	67	3.97	15
2012	San Francisco	N.L.	8	6 2/3	0	0	.000	4	1	7	6.75	0
2013	Fresno	P.C.	16	18 1/3	3	1	.750	19	3	13	0.98	2
2013	San Francisco	N.L.	51	53	3	1	.750	51	12	46	2.38	0
Major League Totals		2 Yrs.	59	59 2/3	3	1	.750	55	13	53	2.87	0

a Selected by Tampa Bay Devil Rays from Philadelphia Phillies in Rule V draft, December 13, 2004.
b Filed for free agency, October 15, 2006. Signed with Toronto Blue Jays organization, October 31, 2006.
c Released by Toronto Blue Jays, November 12, 2008. Signed with Pittsburgh Pirates organization, February 13, 2009.
d Filed for free agency, November 6, 2010. Signed with San Francisco Giants organization, February 9, 2011.
e Loaned to Mexico City, April 7 to September 6, 2011.

MAHOLM, PAUL GURNER

Born, Greenwood, Mississippi, June 25, 1982.
Bats Left. Throws Left. Height, 6 feet, 2 inches. Weight, 230 pounds.

Year	Club	Lea	G	IP	W	L	Pct	SO	BB	H	ERA	SAVES
2003	Williamsport	N.Y.-Penn.	8	34 1/3	2	1	.667	32	10	25	1.83	0
2004	Lynchburg	Carolina	8	44	1	3	.250	28	15	39	1.84	0
2004	Pirates	Gulf Coast	1	4	0	0	.000	2	1	5	2.25	0
2004	Hickory	So.Atl.	3	12 1/3	0	2	.000	12	10	17	9.49	0
2005	Altoona	Eastern	16	81 2/3	6	2	.750	75	26	73	3.20	0
2005	Indianapolis	Int.	6	35 2/3	1	1	.500	21	12	40	3.53	0
2005	Pittsburgh	N.L.	6	41 1/3	3	1	.750	26	17	31	2.18	0
2006	Pittsburgh	N.L.	30	176	8	10	.444	117	81	202	4.76	0
2007	Pittsburgh	N.L.	29	177 2/3	10	15	.400	105	49	204	5.02	0
2008	Pittsburgh	N.L.	31	206 1/3	9	9	.500	139	63	201	3.71	0
2009	Pittsburgh	N.L.	31	194 2/3	8	9	.471	119	60	221	4.44	0
2010	Pittsburgh	N.L.	32	185 1/3	9	15	.375	102	62	228	5.10	0
2011	Pittsburgh a-b	N.L.	26	162 1/3	6	14	.300	97	50	160	3.66	0
2012	Chicago-Atlanta c	N.L.	32	189	13	11	.542	140	53	178	3.67	0
2013	Rome	So.Atl.	1	5 2/3	1	0	1.000	6	0	4	1.59	0
2013	Atlanta d-e	N.L.	26	153	10	11	.476	105	47	169	4.41	0
Major League Totals		9 Yrs.	243	1485 2/3	76	95	.444	950	482	1594	4.28	0

a On disabled list from August 18 to October 31, 2011.
b Filed for free agency, October 31, 2011. Signed with Chicago Cubs organization, January 10, 2012.

c Traded to Atlanta Braves with outfielder Reed Johnson and cash for pitcher Jaye Chapman and pitcher Arodys Vizcaino, July 31, 2012.
d On disabled list from July 21 to August 22, 2013.
e Filed for free agency, October 31, 2013.

MANESS, MICHAEL SETH (SETH)

Born, Pinehurst, North Carolina, October 14, 1988.
Bats Right. Throws Right. Height, 6 feet. Weight, 190 pounds.

Year	Club	Lea	G	IP	W	L	Pct	SO	BB	H	ERA	SAVES
2011	Batavia	N.Y.-Penn.	10	39 2/3	0	1	.000	31	3	27	0.91	0
2011	Quad Cities	Midwest	2	5	1	0	1.000	3	0	4	1.80	0
2011	Palm Beach	Fla.St.	3	8 1/3	1	0	1.000	8	2	7	4.32	0
2012	Palm Beach	Fla.St.	7	46	3	1	.750	29	1	45	2.15	0
2012	Springfield	Texas	20	123 2/3	11	3	.786	83	9	122	3.27	0
2013	Memphis	P.C.	4	25	2	2	.500	18	3	34	4.32	0
2013	St. Louis	N.L.	66	62	5	2	.714	35	13	65	2.32	1
	Division Series											
2013	St. Louis	N.L.	2	1 1/3	0	0	.000	0	0	1	0.00	0
	Championship Series											
2013	St. Louis	N.L.	3	1 1/3	0	0	.000	1	0	2	0.00	0
	World Series Record											
2013	St. Louis	N.L.	4	2 1/3	0	0	.000	2	0	3	3.86	0

MARMOL, CARLOS AGUSTIN

Born, Bonao, Dominican Republic, October 14, 1982.
Bats Right. Throws Right. Height, 6 feet, 2 inches. Weight, 180 pounds.

Year	Club	Lea	G	IP	W	L	Pct	SO	BB	H	ERA	SAVES
2002	Cubs	Arizona	1	1	0	0	.000	1	1	1	0.00	0
2003	Cubs	Arizona	15	64 1/3	3	5	.375	74	37	59	4.76	0
2004	Lansing	Midwest	26	154 2/3	14	8	.636	154	53	131	3.20	0
2005	Daytona	Fla.St.	13	72 1/3	6	2	.750	71	37	60	2.99	0
2005	West Tenn	Southern	14	81 1/3	3	4	.429	70	40	70	3.65	0
2006	West Tenn	Southern	11	58	3	2	.600	67	25	42	2.33	0
2006	Iowa	P.C.	2	3	0	0	.000	1	1	4	9.00	0
2006	Chicago a	N.L.	19	77	5	7	.417	59	59	71	6.08	0
2007	Iowa	P.C.	8	41	4	1	.800	48	12	30	3.95	0
2007	Chicago	N.L.	59	69 1/3	5	1	.833	96	35	41	1.43	1
2008	Chicago	N.L.	82	87 1/3	2	4	.333	114	41	40	2.68	7
2009	Chicago	N.L.	79	74	2	4	.333	93	65	43	3.41	15
2010	Chicago	N.L.	77	77 2/3	2	3	.400	138	52	40	2.55	38
2011	Chicago	N.L.	75	74	2	6	.250	99	48	54	4.01	34
2012	Iowa	P.C.	2	2	0	0	.000	4	2	1	0.00	0
2012	Chicago b	N.L.	61	55 1/3	3	3	.500	72	45	40	3.42	20
2013	Rancho Cucamonga	Calif.	3	3	0	0	.000	4	1	4	6.00	1
2013	Chattanooga	Southern	2	2	0	0	.000	2	1	0	0.00	0
2013	Chicago-Los Angeles c-d	N.L.	52	49	2	4	.333	59	40	40	4.41	2
Major League Totals		8 Yrs.	504	563 2/3	23	32	.418	730	385	369	3.46	117
	Division Series											
2007	Chicago	N.L.	2	3	0	1	.000	6	3	3	9.00	0
2008	Chicago	N.L.	2	2 2/3	0	0	.000	3	0	3	6.75	0
Division Series Totals			4	5 2/3	0	1	.000	9	3	6	7.94	0
	Championship Series											
2013	Los Angeles	N.L.	2	3 2/3	0	0	.000	5	1	1	0.00	0

a On disabled list from August 19 to September 4, 2006.
b On disabled list from May 12 to May 28, 2012.
c Traded to Los Angeles Dodgers for pitcher Matt Guerrier, July 2, 2013.
d Filed for free agency, October 31, 2013.

MARQUIS, JASON SCOTT

Born, Manhasset, New York, August 21, 1978.
Bats Left. Throws Right. Height, 6 feet, 1 inch. Weight, 210 pounds.

Year	Club	Lea	G	IP	W	L	Pct	SO	BB	H	ERA	SAVES
1996	Danville	Appal.	7	23 1/3	1	1	.500	24	7	30	4.63	0
1997	Macon	So.Atl.	28	141 2/3	14	10	.583	121	55	156	4.38	0
1998	Danville	Carolina	22	114 2/3	2	12	.143	135	41	120	4.87	0
1999	Myrtle Beach	Carolina	6	32	3	0	1.000	41	17	22	0.28	0
1999	Greenville a	Southern	12	55	3	4	.429	35	29	52	4.58	0
2000	Greenville	Southern	11	68	4	2	.667	49	23	68	3.57	0

Year Club	Lea	G	IP	W	L	Pct	SO	BB	H	ERA	SAVES
2000 Atlanta	N.L.	15	23 1/3	1	0	1.000	17	12	23	5.01	0
2000 Richmond	Int.	6	20	0	3	.000	18	13	26	9.00	0
2001 Atlanta	N.L.	38	129 1/3	5	6	.455	98	59	113	3.48	0
2002 Richmond	Int.	1	5	0	1	.000	6	1	5	3.60	0
2002 Atlanta b	N.L.	22	114 1/3	8	9	.471	84	49	127	5.04	0
2003 Richmond	Int.	15	94	8	4	.667	75	34	93	3.35	0
2003 Atlanta c	N.L.	21	40 2/3	0	0	.000	19	18	43	5.53	1
2004 St. Louis	N.L.	32	201 1/3	15	7	.682	138	70	215	3.71	0
2005 St. Louis	N.L.	33	207	13	14	.481	100	69	206	4.13	0
2006 St. Louis d	N.L.	33	194 1/3	14	*16	.467	96	75	221	6.02	0
2007 Chicago	N.L.	34	191 2/3	12	9	.571	109	76	190	4.60	0
2008 Chicago e	N.L.	29	167	11	9	.550	91	70	172	4.53	0
2009 Colorado f	N.L.	33	216	15	13	.536	115	80	218	4.04	0
2010 Nationals	Gulf Coast	1	3	0	0	.000	4	0	2	0.00	0
2010 Potomac	Carolina	1	3 2/3	0	0	.000	3	1	6	7.36	0
2010 Harrisburg	Eastern	1	3 1/3	0	0	.000	3	1	5	8.10	0
2010 Syracuse	Int.	2	11	0	0	.000	11	3	7	4.09	0
2010 Washington g	N.L.	13	58 2/3	2	9	.182	31	24	76	6.60	0
2011 Washington-Arizona h-i-j	N.L.	23	132	8	6	.571	76	43	154	4.43	0
2012 San Antonio	Texas	1	7	1	0	1.000	5	2	5	1.29	0
2012 New Britain	Eastern	2	14	1	0	1.000	11	0	12	1.93	0
2012 Minnesota	A.L.	7	34	2	4	.333	12	14	52	8.47	0
2012 San Diego k-l-m	N.L.	15	93 2/3	6	7	.462	79	28	94	4.04	0
2013 San Diego n-o	N.L.	20	117 2/3	9	5	.643	72	68	111	4.05	0
Major League Totals	14 Yrs.	368	1921	121	114	.515	1137	755	2015	4.56	1
Division Series											
2004 St. Louis	N.L.	1	3 1/3	0	0	.000	0	4	4	8.10	0
2008 Chicago	N.L.	1	1	0	0	.000	1	0	1	9.00	0
2009 Colorado	N.L.	1	1	0	0	.000	0	0	1	0.00	0
Division Series Totals		3	5 1/3	0	0	.000	1	4	6	6.75	0
Championship Series											
2001 Atlanta	N.L.	2	2	0	0	.000	3	2	2	0.00	0
2004 St. Louis	N.L.	1	4	0	0	.000	2	2	5	6.75	0
2005 St. Louis	N.L.	3	5 1/3	0	1	.000	4	3	6	3.38	0
Championship Series Totals		6	11 1/3	0	1	.000	9	7	13	3.97	0
World Series Record											
2004 St. Louis	N.L.	2	7	0	1	.000	4	7	6	3.86	0

a On disabled list from July 5 to 31, 1999.
b On disabled list from April 15 to May 11, 2002.
c Traded to St. Louis Cardinals with pitcher Ray King and pitcher Adam Wainwright for catcher Eli Marrero and outfielder J.D. Drew, December 13, 2003.
d Filed for free agency, October 30, 2006. Signed with Chicago Cubs, December 19, 2006.
e Traded to Colorado Rockies for pitcher Luis Vizcaino, January 6, 2009.
f Filed for free agency, November 5, 2009. Signed with Washington Nationals, December 22, 2009.
g On disabled list from April 19 to August 8, 2010.
h Traded to Arizona Diamondbacks for infielder Zachary Walters, July 30, 2011.
i On disabled list from August 15 to October 30, 2011.
j Filed for free agency, October 31, 2011. Signed with Minnesota Twins, December 22, 2011.
k Released by Minnesota Twins, May 26, 2012. Signed with San Diego Padres organization, May 29, 2012.
l On disabled list from August 23 to October 15, 2012.
m Filed for free agency, November 3, 2012, re-signed with San Diego Padres, December 3, 2012.
n On disabled list from July 20 to October 31, 2013.
o Filed for free agency, October 31, 2013.

MARSHALL, SEAN CHRISTOPHER

Born, Richmond, Virginia, August 30, 1982.

Bats Left. Throws Left. Height, 6 feet, 7 inches. Weight, 220 pounds.

Year Club	Lea	G	IP	W	L	Pct	SO	BB	H	ERA	SAVES
2003 Lansing	Midwest	1	7	1	0	1.000	11	0	5	0.00	0
2003 Boise	Northwest	14	73 2/3	5	6	.455	88	23	66	2.57	0
2004 Lansing	Midwest	7	48 2/3	2	0	1.000	51	4	29	1.11	0
2004 West Tenn	Southern	6	29	2	2	.500	23	12	36	5.90	0
2005 Daytona	Fla.St.	12	69	4	4	.500	61	26	63	2.74	0
2005 West Tenn	Southern	4	25	0	1	.000	24	5	16	2.52	0
2006 Iowa	P.C.	4	21 2/3	0	2	.000	21	14	17	3.32	0
2006 Chicago a	N.L.	24	125 2/3	6	9	.400	77	59	132	5.59	0
2007 Daytona	Fla.St.	1	6	1	0	1.000	4	1	7	3.00	0
2007 Iowa	P.C.	4	24 2/3	2	0	1.000	15	8	17	1.82	0
2007 Chicago	N.L.	21	103 1/3	7	8	.467	67	35	107	3.92	0

Year Club	Lea	G	IP	W	L	Pct	SO	BB	H	ERA	SAVES
2008 Iowa	P.C.	7	31 2/3	1	1	.500	25	6	26	3.41	0
2008 Chicago	N.L.	34	65 1/3	3	5	.375	58	23	60	3.86	1
2009 Chicago	N.L.	55	85 1/3	3	7	.300	68	32	91	4.32	0
2010 Chicago	N.L.	80	74 2/3	7	5	.583	90	25	58	2.65	1
2011 Chicago b	N.L.	78	75 2/3	6	6	.500	79	17	66	2.26	5
2012 Cincinnati	N.L.	73	61	5	5	.500	74	16	55	2.51	9
2013 Louisville	Int.	2	2	0	0	.000	4	0	2	0.00	0
2013 Cincinnati c	N.L.	16	10 1/3	0	1	.000	10	2	4	1.74	0
Major League Totals	8 Yrs.	381	601 1/3	37	46	.446	523	209	573	3.77	16
Wild Card Playoff											
2013 Cincinnati	N.L.	1	0	0	0	.000	0	2	1	INF	0
Division Series											
2008 Chicago	N.L.	2	3 1/3	0	0	.000	5	1	2	2.70	0
2012 Cincinnati	N.L.	3	4	0	0	.000	3	0	0	0.00	0
Division Series Totals		5	7 1/3	0	0	.000	8	1	2	1.23	0

a On disabled list from July 23 to September 1, 2006.

b Traded to Cincinnati Reds for pitcher Travis Wood, outfielder Dave Sappelt and infielder Ronald Torreyes, December 23, 2011.

c On disabled list from April 8 to April 26 and May 21 to September 16, 2013.

MASTERSON, JUSTIN DANIEL

Born, Kingston, Jamaica, March 22, 1985.

Bats Right. Throws Right. Height, 6 feet, 6 inches. Weight, 250 pounds.

Year Club	Lea	G	IP	W	L	Pct	SO	BB	H	ERA	SAVES
2006 Lowell	N.Y.-Penn.	14	31 2/3	3	1	.750	33	2	20	0.85	0
2007 Lancaster	Calif.	17	95 2/3	8	5	.615	56	22	103	4.33	0
2007 Portland	Eastern	10	58	4	3	.571	59	18	49	4.34	0
2008 Portland	Eastern	8	38 1/3	1	3	.250	37	16	37	4.23	0
2008 Pawtucket	Int.	4	9 1/3	1	0	1.000	8	1	6	2.89	0
2008 Boston	A.L.	36	88 1/3	6	5	.545	68	40	68	3.16	0
2009 Boston-Cleveland a	A.L.	42	129 1/3	4	10	.286	119	60	128	4.52	0
2010 Cleveland	A.L.	34	180	6	13	.316	140	73	197	4.70	0
2011 Cleveland	A.L.	34	216	12	10	.545	158	65	211	3.21	0
2012 Cleveland	A.L.	34	206 1/3	11	15	.423	159	88	212	4.93	0
2013 Cleveland	A.L.	32	193	14	10	.583	195	76	156	3.45	0
Major League Totals	6 Yrs.	212	1013	53	63	.457	839	402	972	4.03	0
Wild Card Playoff											
2013 Cleveland	A.L.	1	2	0	0	.000	2	0	1	0.00	0
Division Series											
2008 Boston	A.L.	4	4	0	0	.000	3	3	6	2.25	0
Championship Series											
2008 Boston	A.L.	5	5 2/3	1	0	1.000	6	2	4	1.59	0

a Traded to Cleveland Indians with pitcher Nick Hagadone and pitcher Bryan Price for catcher Victor Martinez, July 31, 2009.

MATUSZ, BRIAN ROBERT

Born, Grand Junction, Colorado, February 11, 1987.

Bats Left. Throws Left. Height, 6 feet, 5 inches. Weight, 200 pounds.

Year Club	Lea	G	IP	W	L	Pct	SO	BB	H	ERA	SAVES
2009 Frederick	Carolina	11	66 2/3	4	2	.667	75	21	56	2.16	0
2009 Bowie	Eastern	8	46 1/3	7	0	1.000	46	11	31	1.55	0
2009 Baltimore	A.L.	8	44 2/3	5	2	.714	38	14	52	4.63	0
2010 Baltimore	A.L.	32	175 2/3	10	12	.455	143	63	173	4.30	0
2011 Frederick	Carolina	1	4	0	0	.000	2	2	2	2.25	0
2011 Bowie	Eastern	1	6	0	0	.000	1	1	3	0.00	0
2011 Norfolk	Int.	9	54 2/3	2	3	.400	41	19	51	3.46	0
2011 Baltimore a	A.L.	12	49 2/3	1	9	.100	38	24	81	10.69	0
2012 Norfolk	Int.	10	47	2	1	.667	32	15	43	4.21	1
2012 Baltimore	A.L.	34	98	6	10	.375	81	41	112	4.87	0
2013 Baltimore	A.L.	65	51	2	1	.667	50	16	43	3.53	0
Major League Totals	5 Yrs.	151	419	24	34	.414	350	158	461	5.13	0
Wild Card Playoff											
2012 Baltimore	A.L.	1	0 1/3	0	0	.000	1	0	0	0.00	0
Division Series											
2012 Baltimore	A.L.	5	4 1/3	0	1	.000	5	2	2	2.08	0

a On disabled list from April 3 to June 1, 2011.

MAZZARO, VINCENT MICHAEL (VIN)

Born, Hackensack, New Jersey, September 27, 1986.
Bats Right. Throws Right. Height, 6 feet, 1 inch. Weight, 220 pounds.

Year	Club	Lea	G	IP	W	L	Pct	SO	BB	H	ERA	SAVES
2006	Kane County	Midwest	24	119⅓	9	9	.500	81	42	146	5.05	0
2007	Stockton	Calif.	28	153⅔	9	12	.429	115	71	159	5.33	0
2008	Midland	Texas	22	137⅓	12	3	.800	104	36	115	1.90	0
2008	Sacramento	P.C.	6	33⅔	3	3	.500	27	9	49	6.15	0
2009	Oakland	A.L.	17	91⅓	4	9	.308	59	39	120	5.32	0
2009	Sacramento a	P.C.	10	56⅔	2	2	.500	44	17	42	2.38	0
2010	Sacramento	P.C.	7	37⅓	3	1	.750	38	17	35	3.13	0
2010	Oakland b	A.L.	24	122⅓	6	8	.429	79	50	127	4.27	0
2011	Omaha	P.C.	22	123⅔	7	2	.778	107	60	140	4.29	0
2011	Kansas City	A.L.	7	28⅓	1	1	.500	10	15	39	8.26	0
2012	Omaha	P.C.	22	67	2	2	.500	62	20	69	3.63	5
2012	Kansas City c	A.L.	18	44	4	3	.571	26	19	55	5.73	0
2013	Indianapolis	Int.	3	7	1	0	1.000	9	1	3	0.00	0
2013	Pittsburgh	N.L.	57	73⅔	8	2	.800	46	21	68	2.81	1
Major League Totals		5 Yrs.	123	359⅔	23	23	.500	220	144	409	4.73	1
Division Series												
2013	Pittsburgh	N.L.	3	1⅔	0	0	.000	2	0	0	0.00	0

a On disabled list from September 8 to November 4, 2009.

b Traded to Kansas City Royals with pitcher Justin Marks for outfielder David DeJesus, November 10, 2010.

c Traded to Pittsburgh Pirates with infielder Clint Robinson for pitcher Luis Rico and pitcher Luis Santos, November 28, 2012.

MC ALLISTER, ZACHARY TAYLOR (ZACH)

Born, Chillicothe, Illinois, December 8, 1987.
Bats Right. Throws Right. Height, 6 feet, 6 inches. Weight, 240 pounds.

Year	Club	Lea	G	IP	W	L	Pct	SO	BB	H	ERA	SAVES
2006	Yankees	Gulf Coast	11	35	5	2	.714	28	12	35	3.09	0
2007	Staten Island	N.Y.-Penn.	16	71⅓	4	6	.400	75	28	80	5.17	0
2008	Tampa	Fla.St.	15	88⅔	8	6	.571	62	13	74	1.83	1
2008	Charleston	So.Atl.	10	62⅓	6	3	.667	53	8	59	2.45	0
2009	Trenton	Eastern	22	121	7	5	.583	96	33	98	2.23	0
2010	Columbus	Int.	3	17	1	2	.333	11	7	20	6.88	0
2010	Scranton-WB a	Int.	24	132⅔	8	10	.444	88	38	165	5.09	0
2011	Columbus	Int.	25	154⅔	12	3	.800	128	31	155	3.32	0
2011	Cleveland	A.L.	4	17⅔	0	1	.000	14	7	26	6.11	0
2012	Columbus	Int.	11	63⅓	5	2	.714	52	19	59	2.98	0
2012	Cleveland	A.L.	22	125⅓	6	8	.429	110	38	133	4.24	0
2013	Akron	Eastern	1	3⅓	0	0	.000	5	1	4	5.40	0
2013	Columbus	Int.	1	6	1	0	1.000	2	2	2	0.00	0
2013	Cleveland b	A.L.	24	134⅓	9	9	.500	101	49	134	3.75	0
Major League Totals		3 Yrs.	50	277⅓	15	18	.455	225	94	293	4.12	0

a Sent by New York Yankees to Cleveland Indians as player to be named later for outfielder Austin Kearns, August 20, 2010.

b On disabled list from June 3 to July 23, 2013.

MC CARTHY, BRANDON PATRICK

Born, Glendale, California, July 7, 1983.
Bats Right. Throws Right. Height, 6 feet, 7 inches. Weight, 200 pounds.

Year	Club	Lea	G	IP	W	L	Pct	SO	BB	H	ERA	SAVES
2002	White Sox	Arizona	14	78⅓	4	4	.500	79	15	78	2.76	0
2003	Great Falls	Pioneer	16	101	9	4	.692	125	15	105	3.65	0
2004	Kannapolis	So.Atl.	15	94	8	5	.615	113	21	80	3.64	0
2004	Winston-Salem	Carolina	8	52	6	0	1.000	60	3	31	2.08	0
2004	Birmingham	Southern	4	26	3	1	.750	29	6	23	3.46	0
2005	Charlotte	Int.	20	119⅓	7	7	.500	130	32	104	3.92	0
2005	Chicago	A.L.	12	67	3	2	.600	48	17	62	4.03	0
2006	Chicago a	A.L.	53	84⅔	4	7	.364	69	33	77	4.68	0
2007	Oklahoma	P.C.	1	4⅓	0	0	.000	6	0	3	0.00	0
2007	Texas b	A.L.	23	101⅔	5	10	.333	59	48	111	4.87	0
2008	Rangers	Arizona	2	5	0	0	.000	5	1	7	3.60	0
2008	Oklahoma	P.C.	5	26⅔	1	1	.500	23	8	21	3.38	0
2008	Texas c	A.L.	5	22	1	1	.500	10	8	20	4.09	0
2009	Oklahoma	P.C.	5	21⅔	0	1	.000	22	9	20	4.15	0
2009	Texas d	A.L.	17	97⅓	7	4	.636	65	36	96	4.62	0
2010	Oklahoma e-f	P.C.	11	56⅓	4	2	.667	44	11	51	3.36	0

Year	Club	Lea	G	IP	W	L	Pct	SO	BB	H	ERA	SAVES
2011	Stockton	Calif.	2	10	1	0	1.000	8	0	7	0.00	0
2011	Oakland g	A.L.	25	170 2/3	9	9	.500	123	25	168	3.32	0
2012	Sacramento	P.C.	2	9 2/3	0	1	.000	11	3	9	5.59	0
2012	Oakland h-i	A.L.	18	111	8	6	.571	73	24	115	3.24	0
2013	Reno	P.C.	2	10 1/3	0	0	.000	4	3	15	6.97	0
2013	Arizona j	N.L.	22	135	5	11	.313	76	21	161	4.53	0
Major League Totals		8 Yrs.	175	789 1/3	42	50	.457	523	212	810	4.10	0

a Traded to Texas Rangers with outfielder David Paisano for pitcher John Danks, pitcher Jacob Rasner and pitcher Nick Masset, December 23, 2006.
b On disabled list from June 10 to July 2 and August 11 to September 11, 2007.
c On disabled list from March 30 to August 7, 2008.
d On disabled list from June 5 to September 1, 2009.
e On disabled list from July 29 to November 3, 2010.
f Filed for free agency, November 5, 2010. Signed with Oakland Athletics, December 14, 2010.
g On disabled list from May 19 to July 3, 2011.
h On disabled list from May 18 to June 2 and June 20 to August 10, 2012.
i Filed for free agency, November 3, 2012. Signed with Arizona Diamondbacks, December 11, 2012.
j On disabled list from May 31 to August 4, 2013.

MC DONALD, JAMES ZELL

Born, Long Beach, California, October 19, 1984.
Bats Left. Throws Right. Height, 6 feet, 5 inches. Weight, 195 pounds.

Year	Club	Lea	G	IP	W	L	Pct	SO	BB	H	ERA	SAVES
2003	Dodgers	Gulf Coast	12	48 2/3	2	4	.333	47	15	39	3.33	0
2004	a				Did Not Pitch							
2005	Ogden	Pioneer	4	6	0	0	.000	9	2	4	1.50	0
2006	Columbus	So.Atl.	30	142 1/3	5	10	.333	146	65	119	3.98	0
2007	Inland Empire	Calif.	16	82	6	7	.462	104	21	79	3.95	0
2007	Jacksonville	Southern	10	52 2/3	7	2	.778	64	16	42	1.71	0
2008	Jacksonville	Southern	22	118 2/3	5	3	.625	113	46	98	3.19	0
2008	Las Vegas	P.C.	5	22 1/3	2	1	.667	28	7	17	3.63	0
2008	Los Angeles	N.L.	4	6	0	0	.000	2	1	5	0.00	0
2009	Albuquerque	P.C.	6	30 1/3	1	0	1.000	40	14	21	3.26	0
2009	Los Angeles	N.L.	45	63	5	5	.500	54	34	60	4.00	0
2010	Dodgers	Arizona	2	5 2/3	0	0	.000	8	3	3	1.59	0
2010	Albuquerque	P.C.	12	63 1/3	6	1	.857	57	24	64	4.41	0
2010	Los Angeles-Pittsburgh b	N.L.	15	71 2/3	4	6	.400	68	29	70	4.02	0
2011	Pittsburgh	N.L.	31	171	9	9	.500	142	78	176	4.21	0
2012	Pittsburgh	N.L.	30	171	12	8	.600	151	69	147	4.21	0
2013	Pirates	Gulf Coast	3	5 2/3	0	0	.000	5	1	5	6.35	0
2013	Bradenton	Fla.St.	1	2	0	0	.000	1	0	4	9.00	0
2013	Altoona	Eastern	2	4 2/3	0	1	.000	2	5	4	5.79	0
2013	Indianapolis	Int.	4	20 2/3	1	3	.250	12	9	26	6.53	0
2013	Pittsburgh c-d	N.L.	6	29 2/3	2	2	.500	25	20	29	5.76	0
Major League Totals		6 Yrs.	131	512 1/3	32	30	.516	442	231	487	4.20	0
	Championship Series											
2008	Los Angeles	N.L.	2	5 1/3	0	0	.000	7	2	3	0.00	0

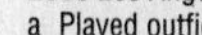

a Played outfield for Dodgers in the Gulf Coast League.
b Traded to Pittsburgh Pirates with outfielder Andrew Lambo for pitcher Octavio Dotel, July 31, 2010.
c On disabled list from May 1 to September 7, 2013.
d Filed for free agency, September 14, 2013.

MC GEE, JACOB DANIEL (JAKE)

Born, San Jose, California, August 6, 1986.
Bats Left. Throws Left. Height, 6 feet, 3 inches. Weight, 230 pounds.

Year	Club	Lea	G	IP	W	L	Pct	SO	BB	H	ERA	SAVES
2004	Princeton	Appal.	12	56 2/3	4	1	.800	53	25	49	3.97	0
2005	Hudson Valley	N.Y.-Penn.	15	76 2/3	5	4	.556	89	23	64	3.64	0
2006	SW Michigan	Midwest	26	134	7	9	.438	171	65	103	2.96	0
2007	Vero Beach	Fla.St.	21	116 2/3	5	4	.556	145	39	86	2.93	0
2007	Montgomery	Southern	5	23 1/3	3	2	.600	30	13	19	4.24	0
2008	Montgomery	Southern	15	77 2/3	6	4	.600	65	37	65	3.94	0
2009	Charlotte	Fla.St.	11	22 1/3	0	2	.000	26	9	26	6.45	0
2009	Rays	Gulf Coast	5	7 2/3	0	2	.000	14	3	5	3.52	0
2010	Montgomery	Southern	19	88 1/3	3	7	.300	100	33	81	3.57	0
2010	Durham	Int.	11	17 1/3	1	1	.500	27	3	9	0.52	1
2010	Tampa Bay	A.L.	8	5	0	0	.000	6	3	2	1.80	0
2011	Durham	Int.	24	33 1/3	4	2	.667	38	8	30	2.70	9

Year	Club	Lea	G	IP	W	L	Pct	SO	BB	H	ERA	SAVES
2011	Tampa Bay	A.L.	37	28	5	2	.714	27	12	30	4.50	0
2012	Tampa Bay	A.L.	69	55 1/3	5	2	.714	73	11	33	1.95	0
2013	Tampa Bay	A.L.	71	62 2/3	5	3	.625	75	22	52	4.02	1
Major League Totals		4 Yrs.	185	151	15	7	.682	181	48	117	3.28	1
	Wild Card Playoff											
2013	Tampa Bay	A.L.	1	0 1/3	0	0	.000	1	0	0	0.00	0
	Division Series											
2011	Tampa Bay	A.L.	1	0 1/3	0	0	.000	0	0	0	0.00	0
2013	Tampa Bay	A.L.	3	2 2/3	0	1	.000	2	3	3	6.75	0
Division Series Totals			4	3	0	1	.000	2	3	3	6.00	0

MEDINA, YOERVIS JOSE

Born, Puerto Cabello, Venezuela, July 27, 1988.

Bats Right. Throws Right. Height, 6 feet, 3 inches. Weight, 245 pounds.

Year	Club	Lea	G	IP	W	L	Pct	SO	BB	H	ERA	SAVES
2010	Everett	Northwest	8	40 2/3	3	2	.600	48	15	49	4.20	0
2010	Clinton	Midwest	6	36	5	0	1.000	42	12	30	2.50	0
2010	Tacoma	P.C.	1	5 2/3	1	0	1.000	4	4	3	0.00	0
2011	Mariners	Arizona	1	5	0	0	.000	9	1	7	7.20	0
2011	High Desert	Calif.	20	101	1	13	.071	73	38	139	6.50	0
2011	Jackson	Southern	4	25	0	1	.000	17	9	23	4.68	0
2012	Jackson	Southern	46	69 1/3	5	5	.500	77	35	63	3.25	5
2013	Tacoma	P.C.	4	6	0	1	.000	7	3	2	1.50	0
2013	Seattle	A.L.	63	68	4	6	.400	71	40	49	2.91	1

MEDLEN, KRISTOPHER ALLEN (KRIS)

Born, Artesia, California, October 7, 1985.

Bats Both. Throws Right. Height, 5 feet, 10 inches. Weight, 190 pounds.

Year	Club	Lea	G	IP	W	L	Pct	SO	BB	H	ERA	SAVES
2006	Danville	Appal.	20	22	1	0	1.000	36	2	14	0.41	10
2007	Myrtle Beach	Carolina	18	24	2	0	1.000	28	7	22	1.13	2
2007	Rome	So.Atl.	17	20 2/3	0	1	.000	33	3	13	0.87	8
2007	Mississippi	Southern	3	2 1/3	0	0	.000	2	2	4	11.57	1
2008	Mississippi	Southern	36	120 1/3	7	8	.467	120	27	121	3.52	1
2009	Gwinnett	Int.	8	37 2/3	5	0	1.000	44	10	20	1.19	0
2009	Atlanta	N.L.	37	67 2/3	3	5	.375	72	30	65	4.26	0
2010	Atlanta a	N.L.	31	107 2/3	6	2	.750	83	21	108	3.68	0
2011	Atlanta b	N.L.	2	2 1/3	0	0	.000	2	0	1	0.00	0
2012	Gwinnett	Int.	3	13 1/3	0	2	.000	12	6	15	4.72	0
2012	Atlanta	N.L.	50	138	10	1	.909	120	23	103	1.57	1
2013	Atlanta	N.L.	32	197	15	12	.556	157	47	194	3.11	0
Major League Totals		5 Yrs.	152	512 2/3	34	20	.630	434	121	471	2.95	1
	Wild Card Playoff											
2012	Atlanta	N.L.	1	6 1/3	0	1	.000	4	0	3	2.84	0
	Division Series											
2013	Atlanta	N.L.	1	4	0	1	.000	4	1	9	11.25	0

a On disabled list from August 5 to November 4, 2010.

b On disabled list from March 27 to September 24, 2011.

MEJIA, JENRRY MANUEL

Born, Azua, Dominican Republic, October 11, 1989.

Bats Right. Throws Right. Height, 6 feet. Weight, 205 pounds.

Year	Club	Lea	G	IP	W	L	Pct	SO	BB	H	ERA	SAVES
2008	Mets	Gulf Coast	3	15	2	0	1.000	15	3	9	0.60	0
2008	Brooklyn	N.Y.-Penn.	11	56 2/3	3	2	.600	52	23	42	3.49	0
2009	St. Lucie	Fla.St.	9	50 1/3	4	1	.800	44	16	41	1.97	0
2009	Binghamton	Eastern	10	44 1/3	0	5	.000	47	23	44	4.47	0
2010	Mets	Gulf Coast	1	3	0	0	.000	3	1	4	3.00	0
2010	St. Lucie	Fla.St.	1	4	0	0	.000	7	0	1	0.00	0
2010	Binghamton	Eastern	6	27 1/3	2	0	1.000	26	14	19	1.32	0
2010	Buffalo	Int.	1	8	0	0	.000	9	1	5	1.13	0
2010	New York	N.L.	33	39	0	4	.000	22	20	46	4.62	0
2011	Buffalo	Int.	5	28 1/3	1	2	.333	21	14	16	2.86	0
2012	St. Lucie	Fla.St.	2	11	1	0	1.000	8	2	7	2.45	0
2012	Binghamton	Eastern	2	8	0	0	.000	8	3	11	5.63	0
2012	Buffalo	Int.	26	73 2/3	3	4	.429	39	24	75	3.54	0

Year	Club	Lea	G	IP	W	L	Pct	SO	BB	H	ERA	SAVES
2012	New York	N.L.	5	16	1	2	.333	8	9	20	5.63	0
2013	Mets	Gulf Coast	2	5²/₃	0	0	.000	3	2	8	3.18	0
2013	St. Lucie	Fla.St.	2	8	0	0	.000	14	4	10	4.50	0
2013	Binghamton	Eastern	2	11	2	0	1.000	9	4	6	0.82	0
2013	New York a	N.L.	5	27¹/₃	1	2	.333	27	4	28	2.30	0
Major League Totals		3 Yrs.	43	82¹/₃	2	8	.200	57	33	94	4.04	0

a On disabled list from March 22 to July 26 and August 18 to October 31, 2013.

MELANCON, MARK DAVID

Born, Wheat Ridge, Colorado, March 28, 1985.
Bats Right. Throws Right. Height, 6 feet, 2 inches. Weight, 215 pounds.

Year	Club	Lea	G	IP	W	L	Pct	SO	BB	H	ERA	SAVES
2006	Staten Island	N.Y.-Penn.	7	7²/₃	0	1	.000	8	2	9	3.52	2
2007	a						INJURED—Did Not Play					
2008	Trenton	Eastern	19	49²/₃	6	0	1.000	47	12	32	1.81	2
2008	Tampa	Fla.St.	13	25¹/₃	1	0	1.000	20	6	26	2.84	0
2008	Scranton/WB	Int.	12	20	1	1	.500	22	4	11	2.70	1
2009	Scranton/WB	Int.	32	53	4	0	1.000	54	11	37	2.89	3
2009	New York	A.L.	13	16¹/₃	0	1	.000	10	10	13	3.86	0
2010	Round Rock	P.C.	3	4¹/₃	1	0	1.000	2	1	5	0.00	1
2010	Scranton/WB	Int.	40	56¹/₃	6	1	.857	58	31	63	3.67	6
2010	New York	A.L.	2	4	0	0	.000	3	0	7	9.00	0
2010	Houston b	N.L.	20	17¹/₃	2	0	1.000	19	8	12	3.12	0
2011	Houston c	N.L.	71	74¹/₃	8	4	.667	66	26	65	2.78	20
2012	Pawtucket	Int.	21	21²/₃	0	0	.000	27	3	15	0.83	11
2012	Boston d	A.L.	41	45	0	2	.000	41	12	45	6.20	1
2013	Pittsburgh	N.L.	72	71	3	2	.600	70	8	60	1.39	16
Major League Totals		5 Yrs.	219	228	13	9	.591	209	64	202	3.24	37
Division Series												
2013	Pittsburgh	N.L.	4	3²/₃	1	0	1.000	2	1	5	9.82	0

a On minor league disabled list from April 5 to September 16, 2007.
b Traded to Houston Astros with infielder Jimmy Paredes for infielder Lance Berkman and cash, July 31, 2010.
c Traded to Boston Red Sox for infielder Jed Lowrie and pitcher Kyle Weiland, December 14, 2011.
d Traded to Pittsburgh Pirates with infielder Ivan DeJesus, pitcher Stolmy Pimentel and outfielder Jerry Sands for pitcher Joel Hanrahan and infielder Brock Holt, December 26, 2012.

MILEY, ALLEN WADE (WADE)

Born, Hammond, Louisiana, November 13, 1986.
Bats Left. Throws Left. Height, 6 feet, 1 inch. Weight, 220 pounds.

Year	Club	Lea	G	IP	W	L	Pct	SO	BB	H	ERA	SAVES
2008	Yakima	Northwest	7	11	1	1	.500	11	5	11	4.91	0
2009	Visalia	Calif.	3	15	1	1	.500	11	4	18	4.80	0
2009	South Bend	Midwest	21	113²/₃	5	9	.357	91	29	127	4.12	0
2010	Visalia	Calif.	14	80¹/₃	4	5	.444	50	37	81	3.25	0
2010	Mobile	Southern	13	72²/₃	5	2	.714	63	28	60	1.98	0
2011	Mobile	Southern	14	75¹/₃	4	2	.667	46	28	74	4.78	0
2011	Reno	P.C.	8	54¹/₃	4	1	.800	56	16	53	3.64	0
2011	Arizona	N.L.	8	40	4	2	.667	25	18	48	4.50	0
2012	Arizona	N.L.	32	194²/₃	16	11	.593	144	37	193	3.33	0
2013	Arizona	N.L.	33	202²/₃	10	10	.500	147	66	201	3.55	0
Major League Totals		3 Yrs.	73	437¹/₃	30	23	.566	316	121	442	3.54	0

MILLER, ANDREW MARK

Born, Gainesville, Florida, May 21, 1985.
Bats Left. Throws Left. Height, 6 feet, 6 inches. Weight, 210 pounds.

Year	Club	Lea	G	IP	W	L	Pct	SO	BB	H	ERA	SAVES
2006	Lakeland	Fla.St.	3	5	0	0	.000	9	1	2	0.00	0
2006	Detroit	A.L.	8	10¹/₃	0	1	.000	6	10	8	6.10	0
2007	Lakeland	Fla.St.	7	41¹/₃	1	4	.200	28	15	43	3.48	0
2007	Erie	Eastern	4	30²/₃	2	0	1.000	24	5	22	0.59	0
2007	Toledo	Int.	2	6	0	0	.000	9	5	6	9.00	0
2007	Detroit a-b	A.L.	13	64	5	5	.500	56	39	73	5.63	0
2008	Marlins	Gulf Coast	1	1	0	1	.000	0	1	2	18.00	0
2008	Carolina	Southern	1	5²/₃	0	0	.000	6	4	2	3.18	0
2008	Jupiter	Fla.St.	4	12²/₃	1	0	1.000	11	1	10	0.71	0
2008	Florida c	N.L.	29	107¹/₃	6	10	.375	89	56	120	5.87	0

Year	Club	Lea	G	IP	W	L	Pct	SO	BB	H	ERA	SAVES
2009	Jupiter	Fla.St.	1	4	0	0	.000	5	1	3	2.25	0
2009	Jacksonville	Southern	1	6	0	0	.000	5	2	5	1.50	0
2009	Marlins	Gulf Coast	2	7	0	0	.000	10	4	8	2.57	0
2009	New Orleans	P.C.	3	11 2/3	1	2	.333	16	13	9	7.71	0
2009	Florida d	N.L.	20	80	3	5	.375	59	43	85	4.84	0
2010	Jupiter	Fla.St.	3	15 2/3	1	1	.500	23	15	8	1.72	0
2010	Jacksonville	Southern	18	85 1/3	1	8	.111	66	61	98	6.01	0
2010	Florida e	N.L.	9	32 2/3	1	5	.167	28	26	51	8.54	0
2011	Pawtucket f	Int.	13	65 2/3	3	3	.500	61	35	42	2.47	0
2011	Boston	A.L.	17	65	6	3	.667	50	41	77	5.54	0
2012	Greenville	So.Atl.	2	2	0	0	.000	3	0	2	0.00	0
2012	Pawtucket	Int.	10	11	0	0	.000	23	14	4	5.73	1
2012	Boston g	A.L.	53	40 1/3	3	2	.600	51	20	28	3.35	0
2013	Boston h	A.L.	37	30 2/3	1	2	.333	48	17	25	2.64	0
Major League Totals		8 Yrs.	186	430 1/3	25	33	.431	387	252	467	5.33	0

a On disabled list from August 4 to August 24, 2007.
b Traded to Florida Marlins with pitcher Burke Badenhop, pitcher Eulogio De La Cruz, catcher Mike Rabelo and outfielder Cameron Maybin for pitcher Dontrelle Willis and infielder Miguel Cabrera, December 5, 2007.
c On disabled list from July 14 to September 1, 2008.
d On disabled list from April 21 to May 16, 2009.
e Traded to Boston Red Sox for pitcher Dustin Richardson, November 12, 2010.
f Not offered contract, December 2, 2010, re-signed with Boston Red Sox organization, December 16, 2010.
g On disabled list from March 26 to May 6, 2012.
h On disabled list from July 7 to November 4, 2013.

MILLER, SHELBY CHARLES

Born, Houston, Texas, October 10, 1990.
Bats Right. Throws Right. Height, 6 feet, 3 inches. Weight, 215 pounds.

Year	Club	Lea	G	IP	W	L	Pct	SO	BB	H	ERA	SAVES
2009	Quad Cities	Midwest	2	3	0	0	.000	2	2	5	6.00	0
2010	Quad Cities	Midwest	24	104 1/3	7	5	.583	140	33	97	3.62	0
2011	Palm Beach	Fla.St.	9	53	2	3	.400	81	20	40	2.89	0
2011	Springfield	Texas	16	86 2/3	9	3	.750	89	33	72	2.70	0
2012	Memphis	P.C.	27	136 2/3	11	10	.524	160	50	138	4.74	0
2012	St. Louis	N.L.	6	13 2/3	1	0	1.000	16	4	9	1.32	0
2013	St. Louis	N.L.	31	173 1/3	15	9	.625	169	57	152	3.06	0
Major League Totals		2 Yrs.	37	187	16	9	.640	185	61	161	2.94	0
	Division Series											
2013	St. Louis	N.L.	1	1	0	0	.000	1	0	1	9.00	0
	Championship Series											
2012	St. Louis	N.L.	2	3 1/3	0	0	.000	4	1	4	5.40	0

MILONE, TOM

Born, Saugas, California, February 16, 1987.
Bats Left. Throws Left. Height, 6 feet, 1 inch. Weight, 205 pounds.

Year	Club	Lea	G	IP	W	L	Pct	SO	BB	H	ERA	SAVES
2008	Vermont	N.Y.-Penn.	6	21 2/3	1	3	.250	22	3	27	4.57	0
2008	Hagerstown	So.Atl.	7	37 1/3	0	3	.000	27	6	36	2.89	0
2009	Potomac	Carolina	27	151 1/3	12	5	.706	106	36	144	2.91	0
2010	Harrisburg	Eastern	27	158	12	5	.706	155	23	161	2.85	0
2011	Syracuse	Int.	24	148 1/3	12	6	.667	155	16	137	3.22	0
2011	Washington a	N.L.	5	26	1	0	1.000	15	4	28	3.81	0
2012	Oakland	A.L.	31	190	13	10	.565	137	36	207	3.74	0
2013	Sacramento	P.C.	2	10 1/3	0	0	.000	15	1	16	1.74	0
2013	Oakland	A.L.	28	156 1/3	12	9	.571	126	39	160	4.14	0
Major League Totals		3 Yrs.	64	372 1/3	26	19	.578	278	79	395	3.92	0
	Division Series											
2012	Oakland	A.L.	1	6	0	0	.000	6	1	5	1.50	0

a Traded to Oakland Athletics with pitcher A.J. Cole, pitcher Brad Peacock and catcher Derek Norris for pitcher Gio Gonzalez and pitcher Robert Gilliam, December 23, 2011.

MINOR, MICHAEL DAVID (MIKE)

Born, Chapel Hill, Tennessee, December 26, 1987.
Bats Right. Throws Left. Height, 6 feet, 3 inches. Weight, 205 pounds.

Year	Club	Lea	G	IP	W	L	Pct	SO	BB	H	ERA	SAVES
2009	Rome	So.Atl.	4	14	0	1	.000	17	0	10	0.64	0
2010	Mississippi	Southern	15	87	2	6	.250	109	34	74	4.03	0

Year	Club	Lea	G	IP	W	L	Pct	SO	BB	H	ERA	SAVES
2010	Gwinnett	Int.	6	33⅓	4	1	.800	37	12	19	1.89	0
2010	Atlanta	N.L.	9	40⅔	3	2	.600	43	11	53	5.98	0
2011	Gwinnett	Int.	16	100⅔	4	5	.444	99	27	93	3.13	0
2011	Atlanta	N.L.	15	82⅔	5	3	.625	77	30	93	4.14	0
2012	Atlanta	N.L.	30	179⅓	11	10	.524	145	56	151	4.12	0
2013	Atlanta	N.L.	32	204⅔	13	9	.591	181	46	177	3.21	0
Major League Totals		4 Yrs.	86	507⅓	32	24	.571	446	143	474	3.90	0
Division Series												
2013	Atlanta	N.L.	1	6⅓	1	0	1.000	5	1	8	1.42	0

MOORE, MATTHEW CODY (MATT)

Born, Fort Walton Beach, Florida, June 18, 1989.
Bats Left. Throws Left. Height, 6 feet, 2 inches. Weight, 205 pounds.

Year	Club	Lea	G	IP	W	L	Pct	SO	BB	H	ERA	SAVES
2007	Princeton	Appal.	8	20⅓	0	0	.000	29	16	12	2.66	0
2008	Princeton	Appal.	12	54⅓	2	2	.500	77	19	30	1.66	0
2009	Bowling Green	So.Atl.	26	123	8	5	.615	176	70	86	3.15	0
2010	Charlotte	Fla.St.	26	144⅔	6	11	.353	208	61	109	3.36	0
2011	Montgomery	Southern	18	102⅓	8	3	.727	131	28	68	2.20	0
2011	Durham	Int.	9	52⅔	4	0	1.000	79	18	33	1.37	0
2011	Tampa Bay	A.L.	3	9⅓	1	0	1.000	15	3	9	2.89	0
2012	Tampa Bay	A.L.	31	177⅓	11	11	.500	175	81	158	3.81	0
2013	Durham	Int.	1	4	0	0	.000	2	2	8	9.00	0
2013	Tampa Bay a	A.L.	27	150⅓	17	4	.810	143	76	119	3.29	0
Major League Totals		3 Yrs.	61	337	29	15	.659	333	160	286	3.55	0
Division Series												
2011	Tampa Bay	A.L.	2	10	1	0	1.000	8	3	3	0.90	0
2013	Tampa Bay	A.L.	2	6⅓	0	1	.000	7	3	9	9.95	0
Division Series Totals			4	16⅓	1	1	.500	15	6	12	4.41	0

a On disabled list from July 29 to September 3, 2013.

MORRIS, AVERY BRYAN (BRYAN)

Born, Woodbury, Tennessee, March 28, 1987.
Bats Left. Throws Right. Height, 6 feet, 3 inches. Weight, 225 pounds.

Year	Club	Lea	G	IP	W	L	Pct	SO	BB	H	ERA	SAVES
2006	Ogden	Pioneer	14	59⅔	4	5	.444	79	40	64	5.13	0
2007	a				INJURED — Did Not Play							
2008	Great Lakes	Midwest	17	81⅔	2	4	.333	72	31	74	3.20	0
2008	Hickory b	So.Atl.	3	14⅓	0	2	.000	11	12	17	5.02	0
2009	Lynchburg	Carolina	15	72⅔	4	9	.308	32	34	87	5.57	0
2010	Bradenton	Fla.St.	8	44⅔	3	0	1.000	40	7	37	0.60	0
2010	Altoona	Eastern	19	89	6	4	.600	84	31	87	4.25	0
2011	Altoona	Eastern	35	78	3	4	.429	64	33	72	3.35	3
2012	Indianapolis	Int.	46	81	2	2	.500	79	17	76	2.67	5
2012	Pittsburgh	N.L.	5	5	0	0	.000	6	2	2	1.80	0
2013	Indianapolis	Int.	5	6⅓	0	0	.000	4	1	5	1.42	5
2013	Pittsburgh	N.L.	55	65	5	7	.417	37	28	57	3.46	0
Major League Totals		2 Yrs.	60	70	5	7	.417	43	30	59	3.34	0
Division Series												
2013	Pittsburgh	N.L.	1	1	0	0	.000	1	0	1	0.00	0

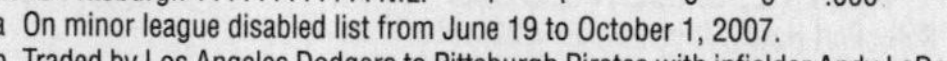

a On minor league disabled list from June 19 to October 1, 2007.
b Traded by Los Angeles Dodgers to Pittsburgh Pirates with infielder Andy LaRoche for outfielder Manny Ramirez, July 31, 2008.

MORROW, BRANDON JOHN

Born, Santa Rosa, California, July 26, 1984.
Bats Right. Throws Right. Height, 6 feet, 3 inches. Weight, 190 pounds.

Year	Club	Lea	G	IP	W	L	Pct	SO	BB	H	ERA	SAVES
2006	Mariners	Arizona	7	13	0	2	.000	13	9	10	2.77	0
2006	Inland Empire	Calif.	1	3	0	0	.000	4	0	0	0.00	0
2007	Seattle	A.L.	60	63⅓	3	4	.429	66	50	56	4.12	0
2008	West Tenn	Southern	6	7⅓	0	0	.000	8	6	3	0.00	0
2008	Tacoma	P.C.	6	23⅓	1	2	.333	26	11	17	5.01	0
2008	Seattle	A.L.	45	64⅔	3	4	.429	75	34	40	3.34	10
2009	Tacoma	P.C.	10	55	5	3	.625	40	23	50	3.60	0
2009	Seattle a-b	A.L.	26	69⅔	2	4	.333	63	44	66	4.39	6

Year	Club	Lea	G	IP	W	L	Pct	SO	BB	H	ERA	SAVES
2010	Toronto	A.L.	26	146 1/3	10	7	.588	178	66	136	4.49	0
2011	Dunedin	Fla.St.	3	9 1/3	0	2	.000	11	6	13	7.71	0
2011	Toronto c	A.L.	30	179 1/3	11	11	.500	203	69	162	4.72	0
2012	Dunedin	Fla.St.	2	6	0	0	.000	6	3	8	1.50	0
2012	New Hampshire	Eastern	3	14 1/3	1	0	1.000	12	3	10	2.51	0
2012	Toronto d	A.L.	21	124 2/3	10	7	.588	108	41	98	2.96	0
2013	Dunedin	Fla.St.	1	2	0	0	.000	0	1	5	13.50	0
2013	Toronto e	A.L.	10	54 1/3	2	3	.400	42	18	63	5.63	0
Major League Totals		7 Yrs.	218	702 1/3	41	40	.506	735	322	621	4.22	16

a On disabled list from April 24 to May 9, 2009.
b Traded to Toronto Blue Jays for pitcher Brandon League and outfielder Johermyn Chavez, December 23, 2009.
c On disabled list from March 22 to April 21, 2011.
d On disabled list from June 12 to August 25, 2012.
e On disabled list from June 1 to October 31, 2013.

MORTON, CHARLES ALFRED (CHARLIE)

Born, Flemington, New Jersey, November 12, 1983.
Bats Right. Throws Right. Height, 6 feet, 4 inches. Weight, 235 pounds.

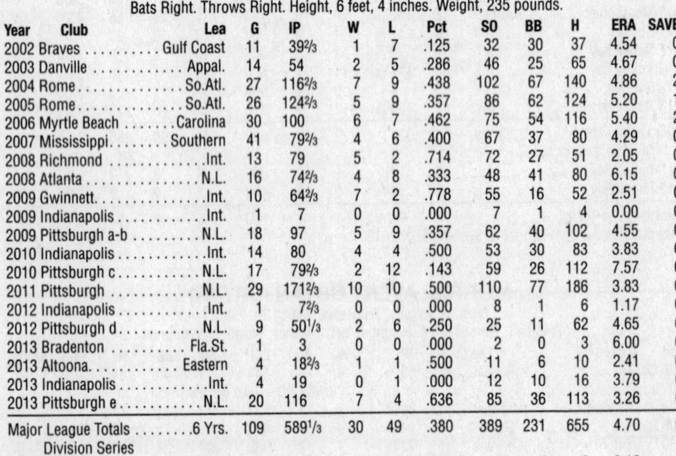

Year	Club	Lea	G	IP	W	L	Pct	SO	BB	H	ERA	SAVES
2002	Braves	Gulf Coast	11	39 2/3	1	7	.125	32	30	37	4.54	0
2003	Danville	Appal.	14	54	2	5	.286	46	25	65	4.67	0
2004	Rome	So.Atl.	27	116 2/3	7	9	.438	102	67	140	4.86	2
2005	Rome	So.Atl.	26	124 2/3	5	9	.357	86	62	124	5.20	1
2006	Myrtle Beach	Carolina	30	100	6	7	.462	75	54	116	5.40	2
2007	Mississippi	Southern	41	79 2/3	4	6	.400	67	37	80	4.29	0
2008	Richmond	Int.	13	79	5	2	.714	72	27	51	2.05	0
2008	Atlanta	N.L.	16	74 2/3	4	8	.333	48	41	80	6.15	0
2009	Gwinnett	Int.	10	64 2/3	7	2	.778	55	16	52	2.51	0
2009	Indianapolis	Int.	1	7	0	0	.000	7	1	4	0.00	0
2009	Pittsburgh a-b	N.L.	18	97	5	9	.357	62	40	102	4.55	0
2010	Indianapolis	Int.	14	80	4	4	.500	53	30	83	3.83	0
2010	Pittsburgh c	N.L.	17	79 2/3	2	12	.143	59	26	112	7.57	0
2011	Pittsburgh	N.L.	29	171 2/3	10	10	.500	110	77	186	3.83	0
2012	Indianapolis	Int.	1	7 2/3	0	0	.000	8	1	6	1.17	0
2012	Pittsburgh d	N.L.	9	50 1/3	2	6	.250	25	11	62	4.65	0
2013	Bradenton	Fla.St.	1	3	0	0	.000	2	0	3	6.00	0
2013	Altoona	Eastern	4	18 2/3	1	1	.500	11	6	10	2.41	0
2013	Indianapolis	Int.	4	19	0	1	.000	12	10	16	3.79	0
2013	Pittsburgh e	N.L.	20	116	7	4	.636	85	36	113	3.26	0
Major League Totals		6 Yrs.	109	589 1/3	30	49	.380	389	231	655	4.70	0
	Division Series											
2013	Pittsburgh	N.L.	1	5 2/3	0	1	.000	4	4	3	3.18	0

a On disabled list from March 27 to April 11, 2009.
b Traded to Pittsburgh Pirates with outfielder Gorkys Hernandez and pitcher Jeff Locke for outfielder Nate McLouth, June 3, 2009.
c On disabled list from May 28 to July 2, 2010.
d On disabled list from March 29 to April 14 and May 30 to October 31, 2012.
e On disabled list from March 22 to June 13, 2013.

MOTTE, JASON LOUIS

Born, Port Huron, Michigan, June 22, 1982.
Bats Right. Throws Right. Height, 6 feet. Weight, 195 pounds.

Year	Club	Lea	G	IP	W	L	Pct	SO	BB	H	ERA	SAVES
2006	Quad Cities	Midwest	8	12 2/3	1	1	.500	13	3	16	4.97	0
2006	State College a	N.Y.-Penn.	21	26 1/3	1	2	.333	25	4	30	3.08	8
2007	Palm Beach	Fla.St.	9	10	1	0	1.000	6	1	7	0.90	3
2007	Springfield	Texas	44	49	3	3	.500	63	22	36	2.20	8
2008	Memphis	P.C.	63	66 2/3	4	3	.571	110	26	64	3.24	9
2008	St. Louis	N.L.	12	11	0	0	.000	16	3	5	0.82	1
2009	St. Louis	N.L.	69	56 2/3	4	4	.500	54	23	57	4.76	0
2010	Memphis	P.C.	2	2 2/3	0	0	.000	2	1	2	3.38	0
2010	St. Louis b	N.L.	56	52 1/3	4	2	.667	54	18	41	2.24	2
2011	St. Louis	N.L.	78	68	5	2	.714	63	16	49	2.25	9
2012	St. Louis	N.L.	67	72	4	5	.444	86	17	49	2.75	*42
2013	St. Louis c	N.L.			INJURED — Did Not Play							
Major League Totals		5 Yrs.	282	260	17	13	.567	273	77	201	2.87	54

Year Club	Lea	G	IP	W	L	Pct	SO	BB	H	ERA	SAVES
Wild Card Playoff											
2012 St. Louis	N.L.	1	1 1/3	0	0	.000	1	1	2	0.00	1
Division Series											
2009 St. Louis	N.L.	1	1	0	0	.000	0	0	0	0.00	0
2011 St. Louis	N.L.	3	3 1/3	0	0	.000	3	0	1	0.00	2
2012 St. Louis	N.L.	2	3	1	0	1.000	1	0	3	3.00	0
Division Series Totals		6	7 1/3	1	0	1.000	4	0	4	1.23	2
Championship Series											
2011 St. Louis	N.L.	4	4 2/3	0	0	.000	4	0	0	0.00	2
2012 St. Louis	N.L.	3	4	0	0	.000	0	0	2	2.25	2
Championship Series Totals		7	8 2/3	0	0	.000	4	0	2	1.04	4
World Series Record											
2011 St. Louis	N.L.	5	4 1/3	0	1	.000	1	1	4	6.23	1

a Played catcher 2003-2006.
b On disabled list from August 3 to August 30, 2010.
c On disabled list from March 22 to November 4, 2013.

MUJICA, EDWARD JOSE

Born, Valencia, Venezuela, May 10, 1984.
Bats Right. Throws Right. Height, 6 feet, 2 inches. Weight, 215 pounds.

Year Club	Lea	G	IP	W	L	Pct	SO	BB	H	ERA	SAVES
2003 Burlington	Appal.	14	55 2/3	2	6	.250	41	20	57	4.37	0
2004 Lake County	So.Atl.	26	124	7	7	.500	89	32	130	4.65	2
2005 Kinston	Carolina	25	26	1	0	1.000	32	2	17	2.08	14
2005 Akron	Eastern	27	34 1/3	2	1	.667	33	5	36	2.88	10
2006 Akron	Eastern	12	19	1	0	1.000	17	9	11	0.00	8
2006 Buffalo	Int.	22	32 2/3	3	1	.750	29	5	31	2.48	5
2006 Cleveland	A.L.	10	18 1/3	0	1	.000	12	0	25	2.95	0
2007 Buffalo	Int.	34	37 2/3	2	1	.667	44	9	35	5.02	14
2007 Cleveland	A.L.	10	13	0	0	.000	7	2	19	8.31	0
2008 Buffalo	Int.	18	26	0	2	.000	27	10	29	4.15	4
2008 Cleveland	A.L.	33	38 2/3	3	2	.600	27	10	46	6.75	0
2009 San Diego a	N.L.	67	93 2/3	3	5	.375	76	19	101	3.94	2
2010 San Diego b	N.L.	59	69 2/3	2	1	.667	72	6	59	3.62	0
2011 Florida	N.L.	67	76	9	6	.600	63	14	64	2.96	0
2012 Jupiter	Fla.St.	2	3	0	0	.000	2	0	0	0.00	0
2012 Miami-St. Louis c-d	N.L.	70	65 1/3	0	3	.000	47	12	56	3.03	2
2013 St. Louis e	N.L.	65	64 2/3	2	1	.667	46	5	60	2.78	37
Major League Totals	8 Yrs.	381	439 1/3	19	19	.500	350	68	430	3.75	41
Wild Card Playoff											
2012 St. Louis	N.L.	1	0 2/3	0	0	.000	0	0	2	13.50	0
Division Series											
2012 St. Louis	N.L.	3	3	0	0	.000	1	1	3	3.00	0
2013 St. Louis	N.L.	1	1	0	0	.000	0	0	0	0.00	0
Division Series Totals		4	4	0	0	.000	1	1	3	2.25	0
Championship Series											
2012 St. Louis	N.L.	5	4	1	0	1.000	3	0	4	0.00	0
2013 St. Louis	N.L.	1	1	0	0	.000	0	0	1	9.00	0
Championship Series Totals		6	5	1	0	1.000	3	0	5	1.80	0

a Sold to San Diego Padres, April 1, 2009.
b Traded to Florida Marlins with pitcher Ryan Webb for outfielder Cameron Maybin, November 13, 2010.
c On disabled list from June 30 to July 18, 2012.
d Traded to St. Louis Cardinals for infielder Zack Cox, July 31, 2012.
e Filed for free agency, October 31, 2013. Signed with Boston Red Sox, December 7, 2013.

NATHAN, JOSEPH MICHAEL (JOE)

Born, Houston, Texas, November 22, 1974.
Bats Right. Throws Right. Height, 6 feet, 4 inches. Weight, 220 pounds.

Year Club	Lea	G	IP	W	L	Pct	SO	BB	H	ERA	SAVES
1995 San Francisco a	N.L.				Did Not Play						
1996					Did Not Play						
1997 Salem-Keizer	Northwest	18	62	2	1	.667	44	26	53	2.47	2
1998 Shreveport	Texas	4	15 1/3	1	3	.250	10	9	20	8.80	0
1998 San Jose	California	22	122	8	6	.571	118	48	100	3.32	0
1999 Shreveport	Texas	2	8 2/3	0	1	.000	7	7	5	3.12	0
1999 San Francisco	N.L.	19	90 1/3	7	4	.636	54	46	84	4.18	1

Year Club	Lea	G	IP	W	L	Pct	SO	BB	H	ERA	SAVES
1999 Fresno	P.C.	13	74⅔	6	4	.600	82	36	68	4.46	0
2000 San Francisco	N.L.	20	93⅓	5	2	.714	61	63	89	5.21	0
2000 San Jose	California	1	5	0	1	.000	2	1	4	3.60	0
2000 Bakersfield	California	1	5⅓	1	0	1.000	6	7	2	5.06	0
2000 Fresno b	P.C.	3	14⅓	0	2	.000	9	7	15	4.40	0
2001 Fresno	P.C.	10	46⅓	0	5	.000	21	33	63	7.77	0
2001 Shreveport	Texas	21	62⅓	3	6	.333	33	37	73	6.93	0
2002 Fresno	P.C.	31	146⅓	6	12	.333	117	74	167	5.60	0
2002 San Francisco	N.L.	4	3⅔	0	0	.000	2	0	1	0.00	0
2003 San Francisco c	N.L.	78	79	12	4	.750	83	33	51	2.96	0
2004 Minnesota	A.L.	73	72⅓	1	2	.333	89	23	48	1.62	44
2005 Minnesota	A.L.	69	70	7	4	.636	94	22	46	2.70	43
2006 Minnesota	A.L.	64	68⅓	7	0	1.000	95	16	38	1.58	36
2007 Minnesota	A.L.	68	71⅔	4	2	.667	77	19	54	1.88	37
2008 Minnesota	A.L.	68	67⅔	1	2	.333	74	18	43	1.33	39
2009 Minnesota	A.L.	70	68⅔	2	2	.500	89	22	42	2.10	47
2010 Minnesota d	A.L.			INJURED—Did Not Play							
2011 Rochester	Int.	3	3	0	0	.000	5	1	2	0.00	0
2011 Minnesota e-f	A.L.	48	44⅔	2	1	.667	43	14	38	4.84	14
2012 Texas	A.L.	66	64⅓	3	5	.375	78	13	55	2.80	37
2013 Texas g	A.L.	67	64⅔	6	2	.750	73	22	36	1.39	43
Major League Totals	13 Yrs.	714	858⅔	57	30	.655	912	311	625	2.76	341
Wild Card Playoff											
2012 Texas	A.L.	1	1	0	0	.000	1	1	2	18.00	0
Division Series											
2003 San Francisco	N.L.	2	0⅓	0	1	.000	1	1	4	81.00	0
2004 Minnesota	A.L.	3	5	0	1	.000	6	5	2	3.60	1
2006 Minnesota	A.L.	1	0⅔	0	0	.000	1	0	1	0.00	0
2009 Minnesota	A.L.	2	2	0	0	.000	2	1	5	9.00	0
Division Series Totals		8	8	0	2	.000	10	7	12	7.88	1

a Played shortstop in 1995.
b On disabled list from May 13 to June 5 and July 14 to August 18, 2000.
c Traded to Minnesota Twins with pitcher Boof Bonser and pitcher Francisco Liriano for catcher A.J. Pierzynski, November 14, 2003.
d On disabled list from March 26 to November 3, 2010.
e On disabled list from May 28 to June 24, 2011.
f Filed for free agency, October 30, 2011. Signed with Texas Rangers, November 21, 2011.
g Filed for free agency, November 1, 2013. Signed with Detroit Tigers, December 3, 2013.

NESHEK, PATRICK J. (PAT)

Born, Madison, Wisconsin, September 4, 1980.
Bats Both. Throws Right. Height, 6 feet, 3 inches. Weight, 210 pounds.

Year Club	Lea	G	IP	W	L	Pct	SO	BB	H	ERA	SAVES
2002 Elizabethton	Appal.	23	27⅓	0	2	.000	41	6	13	0.99	15
2003 Quad Cities	Midwest	28	34⅓	3	2	.600	53	11	20	0.52	14
2003 Fort Myers	Fla.St.	20	29⅓	4	1	.800	29	6	22	2.15	2
2003 New Britain	Eastern	5	7⅔	1	1	.500	5	3	7	5.87	1
2004 Fort Myers	Fla.St.	16	18⅓	0	1	.000	19	2	16	2.95	10
2004 New Britain	Eastern	26	35⅓	2	1	.667	38	18	34	3.82	2
2005 New Britain	Eastern	55	82⅓	6	4	.600	95	21	69	2.19	24
2006 Rochester	Int.	33	60	6	2	.750	87	14	41	1.95	14
2006 Minnesota	A.L.	32	37	4	2	.667	53	6	23	2.19	0
2007 Minnesota	A.L.	74	70⅓	7	2	.778	74	27	44	2.94	0
2008 Minnesota a	A.L.	15	13⅓	0	1	.000	15	4	12	4.72	0
2009 Minnesota b	A.L.			INJURED—Did Not Play							
2010 Fort Myers	Fla.St.	2	2	0	0	.000	2	2	3	13.50	0
2010 Rochester	Int.	30	39⅓	5	1	.833	25	13	40	3.89	1
2010 Minnesota c	A.L.	11	9	0	1	.000	9	8	7	5.00	0
2011 Tucson d	P.C.	24	26⅓	1	2	.333	13	10	29	4.10	3
2011 San Diego e	N.L.	25	24⅔	1	1	.500	20	22	19	4.01	0
2012 Norfolk	Int.	35	44	3	2	.600	49	7	42	2.66	11
2012 Oakland f	A.L.	24	19⅔	2	1	.667	16	6	10	1.37	0
2013 Sacramento	P.C.	2	2	0	0	.000	2	0	2	0.00	0
2013 Oakland g	A.L.	45	40⅓	2	1	.667	29	15	40	3.35	0
Major League Totals	7 Yrs.	226	214⅓	16	9	.640	216	88	155	3.07	0
Division Series											
2006 Minnesota	A.L.	2	1	0	1	.000	1	0	1	9.00	0
2012 Oakland	A.L.	1	0⅔	0	0	.000	1	0	0	0.00	0
Division Series Totals		3	1⅔	0	1	.000	2	0	1	5.40	0

a On disabled list from May 9 to October 1, 2008.
b On disabled list from February 21 to November 10, 2009.
c On disabled list from April 29 to June 5, 2010.
d Claimed on waivers by San Diego Padres, March 20, 2011.
e Filed for free agency, September 29, 2011. Signed with Baltimore Orioles organization, January 30, 2012.
f Sold to Oakland Athletics, August 3, 2012.
g Filed for free agency, November 5, 2013.

NICASIO, JUAN RAMON

Born, San Francisco de Macoris, Dominican Republic, August 31, 1986.
Bats Right. Throws Right. Height, 6 feet, 3 inches. Weight, 230 pounds.

Year Club	Lea	G	IP	W	L	Pct	SO	BB	H	ERA	SAVES
2007 Casper	Pioneer	13	$43\frac{1}{3}$	0	3	.000	33	13	48	4.36	0
2008 Tri-City	Northwest	12	54	2	4	.333	61	19	46	4.50	0
2009 Asheville	So.Atl.	18	112	9	3	.750	115	23	110	2.41	0
2010 Modesto	Calif.	28	$177\frac{1}{3}$	12	10	.545	171	31	186	3.91	0
2011 Tulsa	Texas	9	$56\frac{2}{3}$	5	1	.833	63	10	48	2.22	0
2011 Colorado a	N.L.	13	$71\frac{2}{3}$	4	4	.500	58	18	73	4.14	0
2012 Colorado b	N.L.	11	58	2	3	.400	54	22	72	5.28	0
2013 Colorado Springs	P.C.	2	11	1	0	1.000	8	1	8	0.82	0
2013 Colorado	N.L.	31	$157\frac{2}{3}$	9	9	.500	119	64	168	5.14	0
Major League Totals	3 Yrs.	55	$287\frac{1}{3}$	15	16	.484	231	104	313	4.92	0

a On disabled list from August 6 to October 31, 2011.
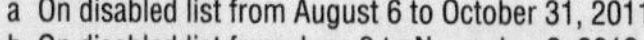
b On disabled list from June 3 to November 2, 2012.

NIESE, JONATHON JOSEPH

Born, Lima, Ohio, October 27, 1986.
Bats Left. Throws Left. Height, 6 feet, 4 inches. Weight, 215 pounds.

Year Club	Lea	G	IP	W	L	Pct	SO	BB	H	ERA	SAVES
2005 Mets	Gulf Coast	7	$24\frac{2}{3}$	1	0	1.000	24	10	23	3.65	0
2006 St. Lucie	Fla.St.	2	10	0	2	.000	10	5	8	4.50	0
2006 Hagerstown	So.Atl.	25	$123\frac{2}{3}$	11	9	.550	132	62	121	3.93	0
2007 St. Lucie	Fla.St.	27	$134\frac{1}{3}$	11	7	.611	110	31	151	4.29	0
2008 Binghamton	Eastern	22	$124\frac{1}{3}$	6	7	.462	112	44	118	3.04	0
2008 New Orleans	P.C.	7	$39\frac{2}{3}$	5	1	.833	32	14	34	3.40	0
2008 New York	N.L.	3	14	1	1	.500	11	8	20	7.07	0
2009 Buffalo	Int.	16	$94\frac{1}{3}$	5	6	.455	82	26	95	3.82	0
2009 New York a	N.L.	5	$25\frac{2}{3}$	1	1	.500	18	9	27	4.21	0
2010 Buffalo	Int.	1	6	0	0	.000	3	0	8	3.00	0
2010 New York b	N.L.	30	$173\frac{2}{3}$	9	10	.474	148	62	192	4.20	0
2011 New York c	N.L.	27	$157\frac{1}{3}$	11	11	.500	138	44	178	4.40	0
2012 New York	N.L.	30	$190\frac{1}{3}$	13	9	.591	155	49	174	3.40	0
2013 Mets	Gulf Coast	1	2	0	0	.000	1	0	3	4.50	0
2013 St. Lucie	Fla.St.	1	4	0	0	.000	4	1	2	0.00	0
2013 Binghamton	Eastern	1	5	1	0	1.000	6	3	4	3.60	0
2013 New York d	N.L.	24	143	8	8	.500	105	48	158	3.71	0
Major League Totals	6 Yrs.	119	704	43	40	.518	575	220	749	3.99	0

a On disabled list from August 6 to November 12, 2009.
b On disabled list from May 17 to June 5, 2010.
c On disabled list from August 24 to September 30, 2011.
d On disabled list from June 21 to August 11, 2013.

NOLASCO, CARLOS ENRIQUE (RICKY)

Born, Corona, California, December 13, 1982.
Bats Right. Throws Right. Height, 6 feet, 2 inches. Weight, 220 pounds.

Year Club	Lea	G	IP	W	L	Pct	SO	BB	H	ERA	SAVES
2001 Cubs	Arizona	5	18	1	0	1.000	23	5	11	1.50	0
2002 Boise	Northwest	15	$90\frac{2}{3}$	7	2	.778	92	25	72	2.48	0
2003 Daytona	Fla.St.	26	149	11	5	.688	136	48	129	2.96	0
2004 Iowa	P.C.	9	$40\frac{2}{3}$	2	3	.400	28	16	68	9.30	0
2004 West Tenn	Southern	19	107	6	4	.600	115	37	104	3.70	0
2005 West Tenn a	Southern	27	$161\frac{2}{3}$	14	3	.824	173	46	151	2.89	0
2006 Florida	N.L.	35	140	11	11	.500	99	41	157	4.82	0
2007 Florida	N.L.	5	$21\frac{1}{3}$	1	2	.333	11	9	26	5.48	0
2007 Marlins	Gulf Coast	2	$3\frac{1}{3}$	0	0	.000	8	0	4	2.70	0
2007 Jupiter	Fla.St.	5	12	1	1	.500	9	1	10	0.75	0
2007 Carolina	Southern	1	3	0	1	.000	2	1	2	6.00	0

Year	Club	Lea	G	IP	W	L	Pct	SO	BB	H	ERA	SAVES
2007	Albuquerque b	P.C.	4	$15\frac{1}{3}$	0	2	.000	15	4	29	14.09	0
2008	Florida	N.L.	34	$212\frac{1}{3}$	15	8	.652	186	42	192	3.52	0
2009	New Orleans	P.C.	2	15	1	1	.500	12	3	12	2.40	0
2009	Florida	N.L.	31	185	13	9	.591	195	44	188	5.06	0
2010	Florida c	N.L.	26	$157\frac{2}{3}$	14	9	.609	147	33	169	4.51	0
2011	Florida	N.L.	33	206	10	12	.455	148	44	*244	4.67	0
2012	Miami	N.L.	31	191	12	13	.480	125	47	214	4.48	0
2013	Miami-Los Angeles d-e	N.L.	34	$199\frac{1}{3}$	13	11	.542	165	46	195	3.70	0
Major League Totals		8 Yrs.	229	$1312\frac{2}{3}$	89	75	.543	1076	306	1385	4.37	0
	Championship Series											
2013	Los Angeles	N.L.	1	4	0	1	.000	4	1	3	6.75	0

a Traded by Chicago Cubs to Florida Marlins with pitcher Sergio Mitre and pitcher Renyel Pinto for outfielder Juan Pierre, December 7, 2005.

b On disabled list from April 7 to May 1 and May 18 to August 20, 2007.

c On disabled list from September 1 to November 5, 2010.

d Traded to Los Angeles Dodgers for pitcher Steve Ames, pitcher Josh Wall and pitcher Angel Sanchez, July 6, 2013.

e Filed for free agency, October 31, 2013. Signed with Minnesota Twins, December 3, 2013.

NORRIS, DAVID STEFAN (BUD)

Born, Greenbrae, California, March 2, 1985.
Bats Right. Throws Right. Height, 6 feet. Weight, 225 pounds.

Year	Club	Lea	G	IP	W	L	Pct	SO	BB	H	ERA	SAVES
2006	Tri-City	N.Y.-Penn.	15	38	2	0	1.000	46	13	28	3.79	2
2007	Salem	Carolina	1	6	1	0	1.000	2	1	4	1.50	0
2007	Lexington	So.Atl.	22	$96\frac{2}{3}$	2	8	.200	117	41	85	4.75	0
2008	Corpus Christi	Texas	19	80	3	8	.273	84	31	89	4.05	0
2009	Round Rock	P.C.	19	120	4	9	.308	112	53	104	2.63	0
2009	Houston	N.L.	11	$55\frac{2}{3}$	6	3	.667	54	25	59	4.53	0
2010	Round Rock	P.C.	3	$14\frac{2}{3}$	1	0	1.000	14	6	16	3.07	0
2010	Houston a	N.L.	27	$153\frac{2}{3}$	9	10	.474	158	77	151	4.92	0
2011	Houston	N.L.	31	186	6	11	.353	176	70	177	3.77	0
2012	Oklahoma	P.C.	1	5	1	0	1.000	7	3	3	3.60	0
2012	Houston b	N.L.	29	$168\frac{1}{3}$	7	13	.350	165	66	165	4.65	0
2013	Houston-Baltimore c	A.L.	32	$176\frac{2}{3}$	10	12	.455	147	67	196	4.18	0
Major League Totals		5 Yrs.	130	$740\frac{1}{3}$	38	49	.437	700	305	748	4.36	0

a On disabled list from May 24 to June 27, 2010.

b On disabled list from June 13 to June 29, 2012.

c Traded to Baltimore Orioles with an international draft choice, outfielder L.J. Hoes, pitcher Josh Hader and a competitive balance draft choice, July 31, 2013.

NOVA (GUANCE), IVAN MANUEL

Born, San Cristobal, Dominican Republic, January 12, 1987.
Bats Right. Throws Right. Height, 6 feet, 4 inches. Weight, 225 pounds..

Year	Club	Lea	G	IP	W	L	Pct	SO	BB	H	ERA	SAVES
2006	Yankees	Gulf Coast	10	43	3	0	1.000	36	7	36	2.72	1
2007	Charleston	So.Atl.	21	$99\frac{1}{3}$	6	8	.429	54	31	121	4.98	0
2008	Tampa	Fla.St.	26	$148\frac{2}{3}$	8	13	.381	109	46	168	4.36	0
2009	Trenton	Eastern	12	$72\frac{1}{3}$	5	4	.556	47	31	65	2.36	0
2009	Scranton-WB a	Int.	12	67	1	4	.200	43	28	72	5.10	0
2010	Scranton-WB	Int.	23	145	12	3	.800	115	48	135	2.86	0
2010	New York	A.L.	10	42	1	2	.333	26	17	44	4.50	0
2011	Scranton-WB	Int.	3	16	1	2	.333	18	2	16	3.38	0
2011	New York	A.L.	28	$165\frac{1}{3}$	16	4	.800	98	57	163	3.70	0
2012	New York b	A.L.	28	$170\frac{1}{3}$	12	8	.600	153	56	194	5.02	0
2013	Scranton/WB	Int.	3	$17\frac{2}{3}$	2	0	1.000	17	4	15	2.04	0
2013	New York c	A.L.	23	$139\frac{1}{3}$	9	6	.600	116	44	135	3.10	0
Major League Totals		4 Yrs.	89	517	38	20	.655	393	174	536	4.04	0
	Division Series											
2011	New York	A.L.	2	$8\frac{1}{3}$	1	1	.500	8	4	7	4.32	0

a Selected by San Diego Padres from New York Yankees in Rule V draft, December 11, 2008. Returned to New York Yankees, March 25, 2009.

b On disabled list from August 22 to September 15, 2012.

c On disabled list from April 27 to May 24, 2013.

OBERHOLTZER, BRETT R.

Born, Christiana, Delaware, July 1, 1989.

Bats Left. Throws Left. Height, 6 feet, 1 inch. Weight, 235 pounds.

Year Club	Lea	G	IP	W	L	Pct	SO	BB	H	ERA	SAVES
2008 Braves	Gulf Coast	10	37⅓	4	1	.800	32	10	34	2.89	0
2009 Danville	Appal.	12	67	6	2	.750	56	6	46	2.01	0
2010 Rome	So.Atl.	4	23	0	2	.000	19	5	22	1.96	0
2010 Myrtle Beach	Carolina	22	112⅔	6	6	.500	107	18	123	4.15	2
2011 Mississippi	Southern	21	127⅔	9	9	.500	93	42	119	3.74	0
2011 Corpus Christi a	Texas	6	27⅓	2	3	.400	28	10	28	5.27	0
2012 Corpus Christi	Texas	13	77	5	3	.625	68	21	81	4.21	0
2012 Oklahoma	P.C.	15	89⅔	5	7	.417	69	19	105	4.52	0
2013 Oklahoma	P.C.	16	80⅓	6	6	.500	72	25	77	4.37	0
2013 Houston	A.L.	13	71⅔	4	5	.444	45	13	66	2.76	0

a Traded by Atlanta Braves to Houston Astros with outfielder Jordan Schafer, pitcher Juan Abreu and pitcher Paul Clemens for outfielder Michael Bourn and cash, July 31, 2011.

O'DAY, DARREN CHRISTOPHER

Born, Jacksonville, Florida, October 22, 1982.

Bats Right. Throws Right. Height, 6 feet, 4 inches. Weight, 225 pounds.

Year Club	Lea	G	IP	W	L	Pct	SO	BB	H	ERA	SAVES
2006 Cedar Rapids	Midwest	17	23⅓	3	1	.750	14	2	20	2.70	1
2006 Orem	Pioneer	14	14⅓	0	1	.000	15	5	11	2.51	7
2007 Rancho Cucamonga	Calif.	24	24	4	0	1.000	26	6	10	0.75	11
2007 Arkansas	Texas	29	29⅓	3	4	.429	22	14	27	3.99	10
2008 Salt Lake	P.C.	21	33	2	2	.500	30	7	29	3.27	7
2008 Los Angeles a	A.L.	30	43⅓	0	1	.000	29	14	49	4.57	0
2009 New York	N.L.	4	3	0	0	.000	2	1	5	0.00	0
2009 Texas b	A.L.	64	55⅔	2	1	.667	54	17	36	1.94	2
2010 Texas	A.L.	72	62	6	2	.750	45	12	43	2.03	0
2011 Frisco	Texas	1	1	0	0	.000	1	0	1	9.00	0
2011 Round Rock	P.C.	17	20⅓	1	0	1.000	26	4	16	2.21	1
2011 Texas c-d	A.L.	16	16⅔	0	1	.000	18	5	17	5.40	0
2012 Baltimore	A.L.	69	67	7	1	.875	69	14	49	2.28	0
2013 Baltimore	A.L.	68	62	5	3	.625	59	15	47	2.18	2
Major League Totals	6 Yrs.	323	309⅔	20	9	.690	276	78	246	2.62	4
Wild Card Playoff											
2012 Baltimore	A.L.	1	2	0	0	.000	1	0	1	0.00	0
Division Series											
2010 Texas	A.L.	4	2	0	0	.000	4	0	2	0.00	0
2012 Baltimore	A.L.	4	5	0	0	.000	4	1	0	0.00	0
Division Series Totals		8	7	0	0	.000	8	1	2	0.00	0
Championship Series											
2010 Texas	A.L.	3	0⅔	0	1	.000	1	1	1	13.50	0
World Series Record											
2010 Texas	A.L.	4	2	0	0	.000	3	0	3	13.50	0

a Selected by New York Mets in Rule V draft, December 11, 2008.

b Claimed on waivers by Texas Rangers, April 22, 2009.

c On disabled list from April 27 to July 2 and August 25 to September 13, 2011.

d Claimed on waivers by Baltimore Orioles, November 2, 2011.

O'FLAHERTY, ERIC GEORGE

Born, Walla Walla, Washington, February 5, 1985.

Bats Left. Throws Left. Height, 6 feet, 2 inches. Weight, 220 pounds.

Year Club	Lea	G	IP	W	L	Pct	SO	BB	H	ERA	SAVES
2003 Mariners	Arizona	13	27⅔	3	0	1.000	20	7	17	1.95	0
2003 Everett	Northwest	3	10⅔	1	0	1.000	7	3	8	3.38	0
2004 Wisconsin	Midwest	12	57⅓	3	3	.500	38	23	83	6.12	0
2005 Wisconsin	Midwest	45	69⅔	4	4	.500	51	30	73	3.75	13
2006 Inland Empire	Calif.	16	28⅔	0	1	.000	33	6	31	3.45	1
2006 San Antonio	Texas	25	39⅓	2	2	.500	36	15	45	1.14	7
2006 Tacoma	P.C.	2	3⅔	1	0	1.000	4	1	3	0.00	0
2006 Seattle	A.L.	15	11	0	0	.000	6	6	18	4.09	0
2007 Tacoma	P.C.	6	8	0	0	.000	8	4	5	1.13	3
2007 Seattle	A.L.	56	52⅓	7	1	.875	36	20	45	4.47	0
2008 Seattle	A.L.	7	6⅔	0	1	.000	4	4	16	20.25	0
2008 West Tenn	Southern	1	2	0	0	.000	2	0	1	0.00	0
2008 Tacoma a	P.C.	14	16⅓	1	0	1.000	19	9	23	4.96	2

Year	Club	Lea	G	IP	W	L	Pct	SO	BB	H	ERA	SAVES
2009	Atlanta	N.L.	78	56 1/3	2	1	.667	39	18	52	3.04	0
2010	Gwinnett	Int.	3	4	0	0	.000	5	1	1	0.00	0
2010	Atlanta b	N.L.	56	44	3	2	.600	36	18	37	2.45	0
2011	Atlanta	N.L.	78	73 2/3	2	4	.333	67	21	59	0.98	0
2012	Atlanta	N.L.	64	57 1/3	3	0	1.000	46	19	47	1.73	0
2013	Atlanta c-d	N.L.	19	18	3	0	1.000	11	5	12	2.50	0
Major League Totals		8 Yrs.	373	319 1/3	20	9	.690	245	111	286	2.85	0
	Wild Card Playoff											
2012	Atlanta	N.L.	1	1	0	0	.000	0	0	2	0.00	0

a Claimed on waivers by Atlanta Braves, November 20, 2008.
b On disabled list from July 10 to August 20, 2010.
c On disabled list from May 18 to October 31, 2013.
d Filed for free agency, October 31, 2013.

OGANDO, ALEXI

Born, San Pedro de Macoris, Dominican Republic, October 5, 1983.
Bats Right. Throws Right. Height, 6 feet, 4 inches. Weight, 185 pounds.

Year	Club	Lea	G	IP	W	L	Pct	SO	BB	H	ERA	SAVES
2010	Texas a-b-c	A.L.	44	41 2/3	4	1	.800	39	16	31	1.30	0
2011	Texas	A.L.	31	169	13	8	.619	126	43	149	3.51	0
2012	Round Rock	P.C.	2	3	0	0	.000	5	0	1	0.00	0
2012	Texas d	A.L.	58	66	2	0	1.000	66	17	49	3.27	3
2013	Frisco	Texas	1	6	1	0	1.000	4	0	4	0.00	0
2013	Round Rock	P.C.	3	13	0	1	.000	4	4	12	6.23	0
2013	Texas e	A.L.	23	104 1/3	7	4	.636	72	41	87	3.11	0
Major League Totals		4 Yrs.	156	381	26	13	.667	303	117	316	3.12	3
	Division Series											
2010	Texas	A.L.	1	0 1/3	0	0	.000	0	0	1	0.00	0
2011	Texas	A.L.	3	2 2/3	0	0	.000	2	0	1	0.00	0
Division Series Totals			4	3	0	0	.000	2	0	2	0.00	0
	Championship Series											
2010	Texas	A.L.	2	2	0	0	.000	2	1	3	4.50	0
2011	Texas	A.L.	4	7 2/3	2	0	1.000	10	2	3	1.17	0
Championship Series Totals			6	9 1/3	2	0	1.000	12	3	6	1.86	0
	World Series Record											
2010	Texas	A.L.	2	3 2/3	0	0	.000	6	0	1	0.00	0
2011	Texas	A.L.	6	2 2/3	0	0	.000	3	7	7	10.13	0
World Series Totals			8	6 1/3	0	0	.000	9	7	8	4.26	0

a Played as an outfielder in the Arizona and Northern Leagues in 2003-2004.
b Confined to the Dominican Republic with visa problems 2005-2009.
c Selected by Texas Rangers from Oakland Athletics in Rule V draft. December 8, 2005.
d On disabled list from June 11 to July 17, 2012.
e On disabled list from May 16 to June 5 and June 6 to July 23 and August 14 to September 3, 2013.

OLIVER, DARREN CHRISTOPHER

Born, Rio Linda, California, October 6, 1970.
Bats Right. Throws Left. Height, 6 feet, 2 inches. Weight, 200 pounds.

Year	Club	Lea	G	IP	W	L	Pct	SO	BB	H	ERA	SAVES
1988	Rangers	Gulf Coast	12	54 1/3	5	1	.833	59	18	39	2.15	0
1989	Gastonia	So.Atl.	24	122 1/3	8	7	.533	108	82	86	3.16	0
1990	Rangers	Gulf Coast	3	6	0	0	.000	7	1	1	0.00	0
1990	Gastonia	So.Atl.	1	2	0	0	.000	2	4	1	13.50	0
1991	Charlotte	Fla.St.	2	8	0	1	.000	12	3	6	4.50	0
1992	Charlotte	Fla.St.	8	25	1	0	1.000	33	10	11	0.72	2
1992	Tulsa	Texas	3	14 1/3	0	1	.000	14	4	15	3.14	0
1993	Tulsa	Texas	46	73 1/3	7	5	.583	77	41	51	1.96	6
1993	Texas	A.L.	2	3 1/3	0	0	.000	4	1	2	2.70	0
1994	Okla City	A.A.	6	7 1/3	0	0	.000	6	3	1	0.00	1
1994	Texas	A.L.	43	50	4	0	1.000	50	35	40	3.42	2
1995	Texas a	A.L.	17	49	4	2	.667	39	32	47	4.22	0
1996	Charlotte	Fla.St.	2	12	0	1	.000	9	3	8	3.00	0
1996	Texas	A.L.	30	173 2/3	14	6	.700	112	76	190	4.66	0
1997	Texas	A.L.	32	201 1/3	13	12	.520	104	82	213	4.20	0
1998	Oklahoma	P.C.	1	5	0	0	.000	1	1	2	0.00	0
1998	Texas b	A.L.	19	103 1/3	6	7	.462	58	43	140	6.53	0
1998	St. Louis c	N.L.	10	57	4	4	.500	29	23	64	4.26	0
1999	St. Louis	N.L.	30	196 1/3	9	9	.500	119	74	197	4.26	0

Year	Club	Lea	G	IP	W	L	Pct	SO	BB	H	ERA	SAVES
2000	Texas	A.L.	21	108	2	9	.182	49	42	151	7.42	0
2000	Oklahoma	P.C.	7	32	2	1	.667	28	14	22	1.97	0
2000	Tulsa d-e	Texas	1	4 2/3	0	1	.000	5	2	10	11.57	0
2001	Texas	A.L.	28	154	11	11	.500	104	65	189	6.02	0
2001	Oklahoma	P.C.	1	3	0	0	.000	3	0	3	0.00	0
2001	Tulsa f-g	Texas	1	5	0	1	.000	5	2	4	5.40	0
2002	Memphis	P.C.	5	16	0	2	.000	9	17	17	7.87	0
2002	Boston h	A.L.	14	58	4	5	.444	32	27	70	4.66	0
2003	Colorado i	N.L.	33	180 1/3	13	11	.542	88	61	201	5.04	0
2004	Florida-Houston j-k-l	N.L.	27	72 2/3	3	3	.500	46	21	87	5.94	0
2005	Iowa	P.C.	3	13 1/3	0	3	.000	10	5	28	13.50	0
2005	Tucson m-n-o-p	P.C.	4	18 1/3	1	0	1.000	8	3	33	6.38	0
2006	New York q	N.L.	45	81	4	1	.800	60	21	70	3.44	0
2007	Los Angeles	A.L.	61	64 1/3	3	1	.750	51	23	58	3.78	0
2008	Los Angeles r	A.L.	54	72	7	1	.875	48	16	67	2.88	0
2009	Los Angeles s-t	A.L.	63	73	5	1	.833	65	22	61	2.71	0
2010	Texas	A.L.	64	61 2/3	1	2	.333	65	15	53	2.48	1
2011	Texas u	A.L.	61	51	5	5	.500	44	11	47	2.29	2
2012	Toronto	A.L.	62	56 2/3	3	4	.429	52	15	43	2.06	2
2013	Dunedin	Fla.St.	2	2	0	0	.000	4	0	0	0.00	0
2013	Toronto v-w	A.L.	50	49	3	4	.429	40	15	47	3.86	0
Major League Totals		20 Yrs.	766	1915 2/3	118	98	.546	1259	720	2037	4.51	7
	Division Series											
1996	Texas	A.L.	1	8	0	1	.000	3	2	6	3.38	0
2006	New York	N.L.	1	1 1/3	0	0	.000	0	0	3	20.25	0
2007	Los Angeles	A.L.	1	0 2/3	0	0	.000	0	0	2	27.00	0
2008	Los Angeles	A.L.	2	1 1/3	0	0	.000	1	1	0	0.00	0
2009	Los Angeles	A.L.	3	2 1/3	1	0	1.000	2	0	1	0.00	0
2010	Texas	A.L.	3	4 1/3	0	1	.000	5	1	3	4.15	0
2011	Texas	A.L.	2	1 1/3	0	0	.000	1	0	3	6.75	0
Division Series Totals			13	19 1/3	1	2	.333	12	4	18	5.12	0
	Championship Series											
2006	New York	N.L.	1	6	0	0	.000	3	1	3	0.00	0
2009	Los Angeles	A.L.	5	6 1/3	0	0	.000	6	4	6	4.26	0
2010	Texas	A.L.	3	2 1/3	0	0	.000	1	3	1	7.71	1
2011	Texas	A.L.	3	2 1/3	0	0	.000	2	0	0	0.00	0
Championship Series Totals			12	17 1/3	0	0	.000	12	8	10	2.60	1
	World Series Record											
2010	Texas	A.L.	2	2 2/3	0	0	.000	4	0	3	3.38	0
2011	Texas	A.L.	3	2 1/3	1	0	1.000	3	0	3	11.57	0
World Series Totals			5	5	1	0	1.000	7	0	6	7.20	0

a On disabled list from June 27 to October 2, 1995.
b On disabled list from June 11 to June 26, 1998.
c Traded to St. Louis Cardinals with infielder Fernando Tatis and player to be named later for infielder Royce Clayton and pitcher Todd Stottlemyre, July 31, 1998. St. Louis Cardinals received infielder Mark Little to complete trade, August 9, 1998.
d Filed for free agency, October 29, 1999. Signed with Texas Rangers, January 27, 2000.
e On disabled list from June 17 to July 19 and July 31 to August 31, 2000.
f On disabled list from May 8 to June 6, 2001.
g Traded to Boston Red Sox for outfielder Carl Everett, December 12, 2001.
h Released by Boston Red Sox, July 2, 2002. Signed with St. Louis Cardinals organization, July 20, 2002.
i Released by St. Louis Cardinals, August 13, 2002. Signed with Colorado Rockies organization, January 29, 2003.
j Filed for free agency, October 26, 2003. Signed with Florida Marlins, January 28, 2004.
k Sold to Houston Astros, July 22, 2004.
l On disabled list from August 6 to September 6, 2004.
m Filed for free agency, November 8, 2004. Signed with Colorado Rockies organization, January 22, 2005.
n Released by Colorado Rockies, March 31, 2005. Signed with Arizona Diamondbacks organization, April 12, 2005.
o Released by Arizona Diamondbacks, May 3, 2005. Signed with Chicago Cubs organization, May 7, 2005.
p Released by Chicago Cubs, May 20, 2005. Signed with New York Mets organization, December 16, 2005.
q Filed for free agency, October 31, 2006. Signed with Los Angeles Angels, December 11, 2006.
r Filed for free agency, October 31, 2008, re-signed with Los Angeles Angels, January 17, 2009.
s On disabled list from April 19 to May 4, 2009.
t Filed for free agency, November 5, 2009. Signed with Texas Rangers, December 22, 2009.
u Filed for free agency, October 30, 2011. Signed with Toronto Blue Jays, January 9, 2012.
v On disabled list from May 19 to June 10, 2013.
w Filed for free agency, October 31, 2013.

ONDRUSEK, LOGAN JARED

Born, Hallettsville, Texas, February 13, 1985.
Bats Right. Throws Right. Height, 6 feet, 8 inches. Weight, 225 pounds.

Year	Club	Lea	G	IP	W	L	Pct	SO	BB	H	ERA	SAVES
2005	Billings	Pioneer	15	$55^1/_3$	1	6	.143	46	19	72	6.02	0
2006	Dayton	Midwest	27	$52^2/_3$	4	5	.444	47	19	48	3.42	0
2006	Billings	Pioneer	1	1	0	1	.000	3	1	4	27.00	0
2006	Chattanooga	Southern	1	4	0	0	.000	7	3	0	0.00	0
2007	Sarasota	Fla.St.	31	124	7	10	.412	86	48	131	4.43	1
2008	Sarasota	Fla.St.	40	$79^2/_3$	1	7	.125	58	32	93	4.97	1
2008	Louisville	Int.	1	$1^1/_3$	0	0	.000	1	2	1	0.00	0
2009	Sarasota	Fla.St.	13	$18^2/_3$	2	0	1.000	12	7	7	0.96	0
2009	Louisville	Int.	19	$20^2/_3$	0	0	.000	11	2	16	1.74	12
2009	Carolina	Southern	24	$32^2/_3$	2	1	.667	24	12	21	1.65	7
2010	Louisville	Int.	14	$19^2/_3$	0	1	.000	14	3	21	4.12	1
2010	Cincinnati	N.L.	60	$58^2/_3$	5	0	1.000	39	20	49	3.68	0
2011	Cincinnati a	N.L.	66	$61^1/_3$	5	5	.500	41	28	55	3.23	0
2012	Louisville	Int.	3	4	0	1	.000	5	4	8	9.00	0
2012	Cincinnati	N.L.	63	$54^2/_3$	5	2	.714	39	31	51	3.46	2
2013	Pensacola	Southern	3	$2^1/_3$	0	0	.000	1	0	1	0.00	0
2013	Louisville	Int.	6	8	0	0	.000	6	2	4	0.00	1
2013	Cincinnati	N.L.	52	55	3	1	.750	53	16	53	4.09	0
Major League Totals		4 Yrs.	241	$229^2/_3$	18	8	.692	172	95	208	3.61	2
	Wild Card Playoff											
2013	Cincinnati	N.L.	1	1	0	0	.000	1	0	1	9.00	0
	Division Series											
2010	Cincinnati	N.L.	2	2	0	0	.000	0	1	0	0.00	0

a On disabled list from August 8 to August 26, 2011.

OTTAVINO, ADAM ROBERT

Born, New York, New York, November 22, 1985.
Bats Left. Throws Right. Height, 6 feet, 5 inches. Weight, 230 pounds.

Year	Club	Lea	G	IP	W	L	Pct	SO	BB	H	ERA	SAVES
2006	Quad Cities	Midwest	8	$36^2/_3$	2	3	.400	38	19	28	3.44	0
2006	State College	N.Y.-Penn.	6	$28^2/_3$	2	2	.500	26	13	23	3.14	0
2007	Palm Beach	Fla.St.	27	$143^1/_3$	12	8	.600	128	63	130	3.08	0
2008	Springfield	Texas	24	$115^1/_3$	3	7	.300	96	52	133	5.23	0
2009	Memphis	P.C.	27	144	7	12	.368	119	82	141	4.75	0
2010	Memphis	P.C.	9	$47^2/_3$	5	3	.625	43	12	43	3.97	0
2010	St. Louis a	N.L.	5	$22^1/_3$	0	2	.000	12	9	37	8.46	0
2011	Memphis	P.C.	26	141	7	8	.467	120	71	154	4.85	0
2012	Colorado Springs	P.C.	13	$19^2/_3$	0	0	.000	25	7	22	3.20	0
2012	Colorado b	N.L.	53	79	5	1	.833	81	34	76	4.56	0
2013	Colorado	N.L.	51	$78^1/_3$	1	3	.250	78	31	73	2.64	0
Major League Totals		3 Yrs.	109	$179^2/_3$	6	6	.500	171	74	186	4.21	0

a On disabled list from July 4 to September 29, 2010.
b Claimed on waivers by Colorado Rockies, April 3, 2012.

OUTMAN, JOSHUA STEPHEN (JOSH)

Born, St.Louis, Missouri, September 14, 1984.
Bats Left. Throws Left. Height, 6 feet, 1 inch. Weight, 205 pounds.

Year	Club	Lea	G	IP	W	L	Pct	SO	BB	H	ERA	SAVES
2005	Batavia	N.Y.-Penn.	11	$29^1/_3$	2	1	.667	31	14	23	2.76	0
2006	Lakewood	So.Atl.	27	$155^1/_3$	14	6	.700	161	75	119	2.95	0
2007	Clearwater	Fla.St.	20	$117^1/_3$	10	4	.714	117	54	104	2.45	0
2007	Reading	Eastern	7	42	2	3	.400	34	23	38	4.50	0
2008	Reading	Eastern	33	$70^1/_3$	5	4	.556	66	37	68	3.20	1
2008	Midland a	Texas	4	$12^2/_3$	1	0	1.000	5	3	13	4.26	0
2008	Sacramento	P.C.	5	$15^1/_3$	1	0	1.000	15	5	9	1.76	0
2008	Oakland	A.L.	6	$25^2/_3$	1	2	.333	19	8	34	4.56	0
2009	Oakland b	A.L.	14	$67^1/_3$	4	1	.800	53	25	53	3.48	0
2010	Oakland c	A.L.	INJURED — Did Not Play									
2011	Sacramento	P.C.	17	$78^1/_3$	8	3	.727	72	47	77	3.91	0
2011	Oakland	A.L.	13	$58^1/_3$	3	5	.375	35	23	62	3.70	0
2012	Modesto d	Calif.	1	1	0	0	.000	1	0	0	0.00	0
2012	Colorado Springs	P.C.	2	2	0	0	.000	1	0	1	0.00	0
2012	Tulsa	Texas	14	$69^1/_3$	2	5	.286	71	30	64	3.63	0
2012	Colorado e	N.L.	27	$40^2/_3$	1	3	.250	40	20	47	8.19	0
2013	Colorado Springs	P.C.	5	$10^2/_3$	1	0	1.000	14	4	8	0.84	0

Year Club	Lea	G	IP	W	L	Pct	SO	BB	H	ERA	SAVES
2013 Colorado f	N.L.	61	54	3	0	1.000	53	23	56	4.33	0
Major League Totals	5 Yrs.	121	246	12	11	.522	200	99	252	4.61	0

a Traded by Philadelphia Phillies to Oakland Athletics with infielder Adrian Cardenas and outfielder Matt Spencer for pitcher Joe Blanton, July 17, 2008.
b On disabled list from June 20 to November 4, 2009.
c On disabled list from March 26 to November 4, 2010.
d Traded to Colorado Rockies with pitcher Guillermo Moscoso for outfielder Seth Smith, January 16, 2012.
e On disabled list from March 30 to May 11, 2012.
f Traded to Cleveland Indians for outfielder Drew Stubbs, December 18, 2013.

PAPELBON, JONATHAN ROBERT

Born, Baton Rouge, Louisiana, November 23, 1980.
Bats Right. Throws Right. Height, 6 feet, 4 inches. Weight, 230 pounds.

Year Club	Lea	G	IP	W	L	Pct	SO	BB	H	ERA	SAVES
2003 Lowell	N.Y.-Penn.	13	32 2/3	1	2	.333	36	9	43	6.34	0
2004 Sarasota	Fla.St.	24	129 2/3	12	7	.632	153	43	97	2.64	0
2005 Portland	Eastern	14	87	5	2	.714	83	23	59	2.48	0
2005 Pawtucket	Int.	7	27 2/3	1	2	.333	27	3	21	2.93	1
2005 Boston	A.L.	17	34	3	1	.750	34	17	33	2.65	0
2006 Boston	A.L.	59	68 1/3	4	2	.667	75	13	40	0.92	35
2007 Boston	A.L.	59	58 1/3	1	3	.250	84	15	30	1.85	37
2008 Boston	A.L.	67	69 1/3	5	4	.556	77	8	58	2.34	41
2009 Boston	A.L.	66	68	1	1	.500	76	24	54	1.85	38
2010 Boston	A.L.	65	67	5	7	.417	76	28	57	3.90	37
2011 Boston a	A.L.	63	64 1/3	4	1	.800	87	10	50	2.94	31
2012 Philadelphia	N.L.	70	70	5	6	.455	92	18	56	2.44	38
2013 Philadelphia	N.L.	61	61 2/3	5	1	.833	57	11	59	2.92	29
Major League Totals	9 Yrs.	527	561	33	26	.559	658	144	437	2.41	286
Division Series											
2005 Boston	A.L.	2	4	0	0	.000	2	0	2	0.00	0
2007 Boston	A.L.	1	1 1/3	1	0	1.000	1	2	0	0.00	0
2008 Boston	A.L.	3	5	1	0	1.000	7	1	2	0.00	1
2009 Boston	A.L.	2	2	0	1	.000	1	2	4	13.50	0
Division Series Totals		8	12 1/3	2	1	.667	11	5	8	2.19	1
Championship Series											
2007 Boston	A.L.	3	5	0	0	.000	3	2	3	0.00	1
2008 Boston	A.L.	4	5 1/3	0	0	.000	6	1	1	0.00	2
Championship Series Totals		7	10 1/3	0	0	.000	9	3	4	0.00	3
World Series Record											
2007 Boston	A.L.	3	4 1/3	0	0	.000	3	0	2	0.00	3

a Filed for free agency, October 30, 2011. Signed with Philadelphia Phillies, November 14, 2011.

PARKER, JARROD BRENT

Born, Fort Wayne, Indiana, November 24, 1988.
Bats Right. Throws Right. Height, 6 feet, 1 inch. Weight, 195 pounds.

Year Club	Lea	G	IP	W	L	Pct	SO	BB	H	ERA	SAVES
2008 South Bend	Midwest	24	117 2/3	12	5	.706	117	33	113	3.44	0
2009 Visalia	Calif.	4	19	1	0	1.000	21	4	12	0.95	0
2009 Mobile	Southern	16	78 1/3	4	6	.400	74	34	82	3.68	0
2010 a						INJURED—Did Not Play					
2011 Mobile	Southern	26	130 2/3	11	8	.579	112	55	112	3.79	0
2011 Arizona b	N.L.	1	5 2/3	0	0	.000	1	1	4	0.00	0
2012 Sacramento	P.C.	4	20 2/3	1	0	1.000	21	6	22	2.18	0
2012 Oakland	A.L.	29	181 1/3	13	8	.619	140	63	166	3.47	0
2013 Oakland	A.L.	32	197	12	8	.600	134	63	178	3.97	0
Major League Totals	3 Yrs.	62	384	25	16	.610	275	127	348	3.68	0
Division Series											
2011 Arizona	N.L.	1	0 1/3	0	0	.000	0	1	2	27.00	0
2012 Oakland	A.L.	2	12 2/3	0	2	.000	11	2	14	4.26	0
2013 Oakland	A.L.	1	5	1	0	1.000	1	1	5	5.40	0
Division Series Totals		4	18	1	2	.333	12	4	21	5.00	0

a On minor league disabled list from April 8 to September 7, 2010.
b Traded to Oakland Athletics with outfielder Collin Cowgill and pitcher Ryan Cook for pitcher Craig Breslow and pitcher Trevor Cahill, December 9, 2011.

PARKER, RICHARD BLAKE (BLAKE)

Born, Fayetteville, Arkansas, June 19, 1985.
Bats Right. Throws Right. Height, 6 feet, 3 inches. Weight, 225 pounds.

Year	Club	Lea	G	IP	W	L	Pct	SO	BB	H	ERA	SAVES
2007	Cubs	Arizona	11	15	1	0	1.000	14	3	10	1.80	2
2007	Boise	Northwest	8	11 1/3	1	0	1.000	10	7	15	3.18	0
2008	Peoria	Midwest	23	47 1/3	3	0	1.000	51	18	32	1.33	3
2008	Daytona	Fla.St.	20	21 1/3	1	2	.333	21	10	17	3.38	9
2008	Iowa	P.C.	2	3	0	0	.000	3	2	1	6.00	0
2009	Tennessee	Southern	10	12 1/3	0	0	.000	19	8	8	1.46	3
2009	Iowa	P.C.	45	51	2	3	.400	58	27	36	3.00	22
2010	Tennessee	Southern	13	17	0	1	.000	25	6	11	2.65	5
2010	Iowa	P.C.	35	49 1/3	1	4	.200	42	28	52	4.74	2
2011	Tennessee	Southern	16	24	1	2	.333	20	13	20	4.13	3
2011	Iowa	P.C.	37	51 1/3	3	3	.500	60	27	37	2.81	4
2012	Iowa	P.C.	21	23 2/3	1	1	.500	22	6	16	3.42	6
2012	Chicago a-b	N.L.	7	6	0	0	.000	6	5	10	6.00	0
2013	Iowa	P.C.	16	17 2/3	0	1	.000	26	10	8	2.04	7
2013	Chicago	N.L.	49	46 1/3	1	2	.333	55	15	39	2.72	1
Major League Totals		2 Yrs.	56	52 1/3	1	2	.333	61	20	49	3.10	1

a On disabled list from June 6 to August 28 and September 7 to October 26, 2012.
b Filed for free agency, November 6, 2012, re-signed with Chicago Cubs organization, November 7, 2012.

PARNELL, ROBERT ALLEN (BOBBY)

Born, Salisbury, North Carolina, September 8, 1984.
Bats Right. Throws Right. Height, 6 feet, 4 inches. Weight, 200 pounds.

Year	Club	Lea	G	IP	W	L	Pct	SO	BB	H	ERA	SAVES
2005	Brooklyn	N.Y.-Penn.	15	73	2	3	.400	67	29	48	1.73	0
2006	St. Lucie	Fla.St.	3	11 2/3	0	1	.000	13	9	16	9.26	0
2006	Hagerstown	So.Atl.	18	93 2/3	5	10	.333	84	40	84	4.04	0
2007	Binghamton	Eastern	17	88 2/3	5	5	.500	74	38	98	4.77	0
2007	St. Lucie	Fla.St.	12	55 1/3	3	3	.500	62	22	56	3.25	0
2008	Binghamton	Eastern	24	127 2/3	10	6	.625	91	57	126	4.30	0
2008	New Orleans	P.C.	5	20 1/3	2	2	.500	23	9	25	6.64	0
2008	New York	N.L.	6	5	0	0	.000	3	2	3	5.40	0
2009	New York	N.L.	68	88 1/3	4	8	.333	74	46	101	5.30	1
2010	Buffalo	Int.	24	41 1/3	1	1	.500	42	17	36	4.14	4
2010	New York	N.L.	41	35	0	1	.000	33	8	41	2.83	0
2011	St. Lucie	Fla.St.	1	1	0	0	.000	0	1	0	0.00	0
2011	Buffalo	Int.	8	8	0	0	.000	11	2	7	3.38	1
2011	New York a	N.L.	60	59 1/3	4	6	.400	64	27	60	3.64	6
2012	New York	N.L.	74	68 2/3	5	4	.556	61	20	65	2.49	7
2013	New York b	N.L.	49	50	5	5	.500	44	12	38	2.16	22
Major League Totals		6 Yrs.	298	306 1/3	18	24	.429	279	115	308	3.55	36

a On disabled list from April 20 to May 30, 2011.
b On disabled list from July 31 to October 31, 2013.

PARRA, MANUEL ALEX (MANNY)

Born, Carmichael, California, October 30, 1982.
Bats Left. Throws Left. Height, 6 feet, 3 inches. Weight, 205 pounds.

Year	Club	Lea	G	IP	W	L	Pct	SO	BB	H	ERA	SAVES
2002	Brewers	Arizona	1	2	0	0	.000	4	0	1	4.50	0
2002	Ogden	Pioneer	11	47 2/3	3	1	.750	51	10	59	3.21	0
2003	Beloit	Midwest	23	138 2/3	11	2	.846	117	24	127	2.73	0
2004	High Desert	Calif.	13	67 1/3	5	2	.714	64	19	76	3.48	0
2004	Huntsville	Southern	3	6	0	1	.000	10	0	5	3.00	0
2005	Huntsville	Southern	16	91	5	6	.455	86	21	111	3.96	0
2006	Brevard County	Fla.St.	15	54 2/3	1	3	.250	61	32	47	2.96	0
2006	Huntsville	Southern	6	31 1/3	3	0	1.000	29	8	26	2.87	0
2007	Huntsville	Southern	13	80 2/3	7	3	.700	81	26	70	2.68	0
2007	Nashville	P.C.	4	26	3	1	.750	25	7	15	1.73	0
2007	Milwaukee a	N.L.	9	26 1/3	0	1	.000	26	12	25	3.76	0
2008	Milwaukee	N.L.	32	166	10	8	.556	147	75	181	4.39	0
2009	Nashville	P.C.	4	24 2/3	1	2	.333	19	13	16	2.92	0
2009	Milwaukee	N.L.	27	140	11	11	.500	116	77	179	6.36	0
2010	Milwaukee	N.L.	42	122	3	10	.231	129	63	135	5.02	0
2011	Wisconsin	Midwest	1	2	1	0	1.000	4	0	0	0.00	0
2011	Nashville b	P.C.	7	10 1/3	0	1	.000	8	5	12	6.10	0
2012	Milwaukee c	N.L.	62	58 2/3	2	3	.400	61	35	62	5.06	0

Year	Club	Lea	G	IP	W	L	Pct	SO	BB	H	ERA	SAVES
2013	Pensacola	Southern	3	5	0	0	.000	5	1	3	0.00	0
2013	Cincinnati d-e	N.L.	57	46	2	3	.400	56	15	40	3.33	0
Major League Totals		6 Yrs.	229	559	28	36	.438	535	277	622	4.97	0
	Wild Card Playoff											
2013	Cincinnati	N.L.	1	$0^2/_3$	0	0	.000	1	0	1	0.00	0
	Division Series											
2008	Milwaukee	N.L.	2	$2^1/_3$	0	0	.000	3	1	2	0.00	0

a On disabled list from August 31 to September 21, 2007.
b On disabled list from March 26 to October 25, 2011.
c Not offered contract, November 30, 2012. Signed with Cincinnati Reds, February 1, 2013.
d On disabled list from April 24 to May 24, 2013.
e Filed for free agency, October 31, 2013, re-signed with Cincinnati Reds, November 27, 2013.

PATTON, TROY JAMIESON

Born, Spring, Texas, September 3, 1985.
Bats Both. Throws Left. Height, 6 feet, 1 inch. Weight, 180 pounds.

Year	Club	Lea	G	IP	W	L	Pct	SO	BB	H	ERA	SAVES
2004	Greeneville	Appal.	6	28	2	2	.500	32	5	23	1.93	0
2005	Salem	Carolina	10	41	1	4	.200	38	8	34	2.63	0
2005	Lexington	So.Atl.	15	$78^2/_3$	5	2	.714	94	20	59	1.94	0
2006	Salem	Carolina	19	$101^1/_3$	7	7	.500	102	37	92	2.93	0
2006	Corpus Christi	Texas	8	$45^1/_3$	2	5	.286	37	13	48	4.37	0
2007	Corpus Christi	Texas	16	$102^1/_3$	6	6	.500	69	33	96	2.99	0
2007	Round Rock	P.C.	8	49	4	2	.667	25	11	44	4.59	0
2007	Houston a	N.L.	3	$12^2/_3$	0	2	.000	8	4	10	3.55	0
2008	b				INJURED—Did Not Play							
2009	Bowie	Eastern	11	$63^1/_3$	6	2	.750	47	18	50	1.99	0
2009	Norfolk	Int.	9	$44^2/_3$	1	3	.250	26	14	62	6.45	0
2010	Norfolk	Int.	25	136	8	11	.421	89	43	144	4.43	0
2010	Baltimore	A.L.	1	$0^2/_3$	0	0	.000	1	1	1	0.00	0
2011	Norfolk	Int.	17	$44^1/_3$	4	1	.800	30	12	44	1.83	0
2011	Baltimore	A.L.	20	30	2	1	.667	22	5	25	3.00	0
2012	Baltimore c	A.L.	54	$55^2/_3$	1	0	1.000	49	12	45	2.43	0
2013	Baltimore d	A.L.	56	56	2	0	1.000	42	16	57	3.70	0
Major League Totals		5 Yrs.	134	155	5	3	.625	122	38	138	3.08	0
	Division Series											
2012	Baltimore	A.L.	3	2	0	0	.000	3	2	3	4.50	0

a Traded to Baltimore Orioles with outfielder Luke Scott, pitcher Matt Albers, pitcher Dennis Sarfate and infielder Michael Costanzo for infielder Miguel Tejada, December 12, 2007.
b On disabled list from March 21 to October 21, 2008.
c On disabled list from August 13 to September 21, 2012.
d Suspended for 25 games for performance-enhancing drug use, December 20, 2013.

PAXTON, JAMES ALSTON

Born, Richmond, British Columbia, Canada, November 6, 1988.
Bats Left. Throws Left. Height, 6 feet, 4 inches. Weight, 220 pounds.

Year	Club	Lea	G	IP	W	L	Pct	SO	BB	H	ERA	SAVES
2010	Grand Prairie	Amer.Assoc.	4	17	1	2	.333	18	7	15	4.24	0
2011	Clinton	Midwest	10	56	3	3	.500	80	30	45	2.73	0
2011	Jackson	Southern	7	39	3	0	1.000	51	13	28	1.85	0
2012	Jackson	Southern	21	$106^1/_3$	9	4	.692	110	54	96	3.05	0
2013	Tacoma	P.C.	28	$145^2/_3$	8	11	.421	131	58	158	4.45	0
2013	Seattle	A.L.	4	24	3	0	1.000	21	7	15	1.50	0

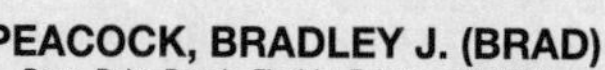

PEACOCK, BRADLEY J. (BRAD)

Born, Palm Beach, Florida, February 2, 1988.
Bats Right. Throws Right. Height, 6 feet, 1 inch. Weight, 175 pounds.

Year	Club	Lea	G	IP	W	L	Pct	SO	BB	H	ERA	SAVES
2007	Nationals	Gulf Coast	13	$39^1/_3$	1	1	.500	34	15	38	3.89	0
2008	Vermont	N.Y.-Penn.	14	75	4	7	.364	54	27	67	3.12	0
2008	Hagerstown	So.Atl.	8	$33^2/_3$	0	5	.000	23	21	38	9.09	0
2009	Hagerstown	So.Atl.	19	100	5	8	.385	77	32	104	4.05	0
2009	Potomac	Carolina	8	$47^2/_3$	3	3	.500	27	10	46	4.34	0
2010	Potomac	Carolina	19	$103^1/_3$	4	9	.308	118	25	109	4.44	0
2010	Harrisburg	Eastern	7	$38^2/_3$	2	2	.500	30	22	33	4.66	0
2011	Harrisburg	Eastern	16	$98^2/_3$	10	2	.833	129	23	62	2.01	0
2011	Syracuse	Int.	9	48	5	1	.833	48	24	36	3.19	0

Year	Club	Lea	G	IP	W	L	Pct	SO	BB	H	ERA	SAVES
2011	Washington a	N.L.	3	12	2	0	1.000	4	6	7	0.75	0
2012	Sacramento	P.C.	28	134 2/3	12	9	.571	139	66	147	6.01	0
2013	Oklahoma	P.C.	14	79	6	2	.750	76	22	65	2.73	0
2013	Houston b	A.L.	18	83 1/3	5	6	.455	77	37	78	5.18	0
Major League Totals		2 Yrs.	21	95 1/3	7	6	.538	81	43	85	4.63	0

a Traded to Oakland Athletics with pitcher A.J. Cole, pitcher Derek Norris and pitcher Tom Milone for pitcher Gio Gonzalez and pitcher Robert Gilliam, December 23, 2011.

b Traded to Houston Astros with infielder Chris Carter and catcher Max Stassi for infielder Jed Lowrie and pitcher Franklin Rodriguez, February 4, 2013.

PEAVY, JACOB EDWARD (JAKE)

Born, Mobile, Alabama, May 3, 1981.

Bats Right. Throws Right. Height, 6 feet, 1 inch. Weight, 195 pounds.

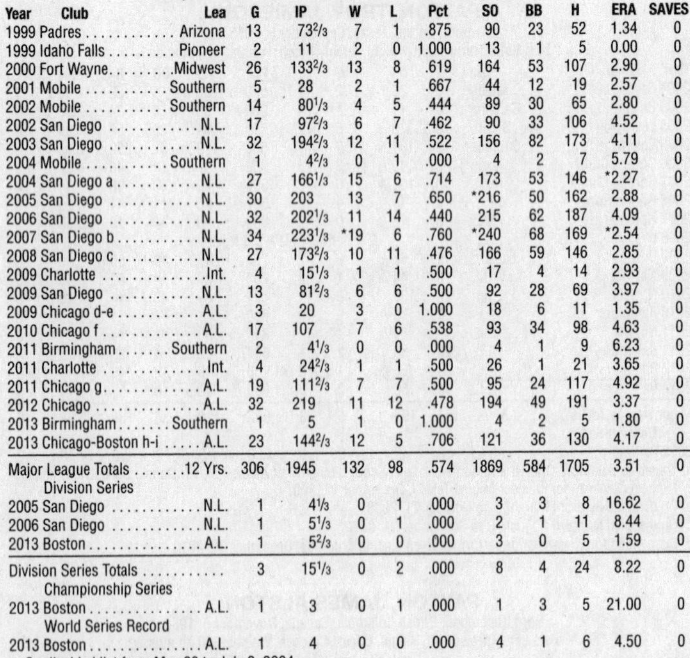

Year	Club	Lea	G	IP	W	L	Pct	SO	BB	H	ERA	SAVES
1999	Padres	Arizona	13	73 2/3	7	1	.875	90	23	52	1.34	0
1999	Idaho Falls	Pioneer	2	11	2	0	1.000	13	1	5	0.00	0
2000	Fort Wayne	Midwest	26	133 2/3	13	8	.619	164	53	107	2.90	0
2001	Mobile	Southern	5	28	2	1	.667	44	12	19	2.57	0
2002	Mobile	Southern	14	80 1/3	4	5	.444	89	30	65	2.80	0
2002	San Diego	N.L.	17	97 2/3	6	7	.462	90	33	106	4.52	0
2003	San Diego	N.L.	32	194 2/3	12	11	.522	156	82	173	4.11	0
2004	Mobile	Southern	1	4 2/3	0	1	.000	4	2	7	5.79	0
2004	San Diego a	N.L.	27	166 1/3	15	6	.714	173	53	146	*2.27	0
2005	San Diego	N.L.	30	203	13	7	.650	*216	50	162	2.88	0
2006	San Diego	N.L.	32	202 1/3	11	14	.440	215	62	187	4.09	0
2007	San Diego b	N.L.	34	223 1/3	*19	6	.760	*240	68	169	*2.54	0
2008	San Diego c	N.L.	27	173 2/3	10	11	.476	166	59	146	2.85	0
2009	Charlotte	Int.	4	15 1/3	1	1	.500	17	4	14	2.93	0
2009	San Diego	N.L.	13	81 2/3	6	6	.500	92	28	69	3.97	0
2009	Chicago d-e	A.L.	3	20	3	0	1.000	18	6	11	1.35	0
2010	Chicago f	A.L.	17	107	7	6	.538	93	34	98	4.63	0
2011	Birmingham	Southern	2	4 1/3	0	0	.000	4	1	9	6.23	0
2011	Charlotte	Int.	4	24 2/3	1	1	.500	26	1	21	3.65	0
2011	Chicago g	A.L.	19	111 2/3	7	7	.500	95	24	117	4.92	0
2012	Chicago	A.L.	32	219	11	12	.478	194	49	191	3.37	0
2013	Birmingham	Southern	1	5	1	0	1.000	4	2	5	1.80	0
2013	Chicago-Boston h-i	A.L.	23	144 2/3	12	5	.706	121	36	130	4.17	0
Major League Totals		12 Yrs.	306	1945	132	98	.574	1869	584	1705	3.51	0
	Division Series											
2005	San Diego	N.L.	1	4 1/3	0	1	.000	3	3	8	16.62	0
2006	San Diego	N.L.	1	5 1/3	0	1	.000	2	1	11	8.44	0
2013	Boston	A.L.	1	5 2/3	0	0	.000	3	0	5	1.59	0
Division Series Totals			3	15 1/3	0	2	.000	8	4	24	8.22	0
	Championship Series											
2013	Boston	A.L.	1	3	0	1	.000	1	3	5	21.00	0
	World Series Record											
2013	Boston	A.L.	1	4	0	0	.000	4	1	6	4.50	0

a On disabled list from May 20 to July 2, 2004.

b Selected Cy Young Award Winner in National League for 2007.

c On disabled list from May 15 to June 12, 2008.

d Traded to Chicago White Sox for pitcher Aaron Poreda, pitcher Clayton Richard, pitcher Adam Russell and pitcher Dexter Carter, July 31, 2009.

e On disabled list from June 9 to September 19, 2009.

f On disabled list from July 7 to November 2, 2010.

g On disabled list from March 22 to May 11, 2011.

h On disabled list from June 5 to July 19, 2013.

i Traded to Boston Red Sox for pitcher Francellis Montas, infielder Cleuluis Rondon, pitcher Jeffrey Wendelken and outfielder Avisail Garcia, July 31, 2013.

PELFREY, MICHAEL ALAN (MIKE)

Born, Wright-Patterson AFB, Ohio, January 14, 1984.

Bats Right. Throws Right. Height, 6 feet, 7 inches. Weight, 250 pounds.

Year	Club	Lea	G	IP	W	L	Pct	SO	BB	H	ERA	SAVES
2006	St. Lucie	Fla.St.	4	22	2	1	.667	26	2	17	1.64	0
2006	Binghamton	Eastern	12	66 1/3	4	2	.667	77	26	60	2.71	0
2006	New York	N.L.	4	21 1/3	2	1	.667	13	12	25	5.48	0
2006	Norfolk	Int.	2	8	1	0	1.000	6	5	4	2.25	0
2007	St. Lucie	Fla.St.	1	6	0	0	.000	2	3	5	3.00	0

Year	Club	Lea	G	IP	W	L	Pct	SO	BB	H	ERA	SAVES
2007	New Orleans	P.C.	14	74	3	6	.333	56	26	74	4.01	0
2007	New York	N.L.	15	72 2/3	3	8	.273	45	39	85	5.57	0
2008	New York	N.L.	32	200 2/3	13	11	.542	110	64	209	3.72	0
2009	New York	N.L.	31	184 1/3	10	12	.455	107	66	213	5.03	0
2010	New York	N.L.	34	204	15	9	.625	113	68	213	3.66	1
2011	New York	N.L.	34	193 2/3	7	13	.350	105	65	220	4.74	0
2012	New York a-b	N.L.	3	19 2/3	0	0	.000	13	4	24	2.29	0
2013	Cedar Rapids	Midwest	1	6	1	0	1.000	6	0	2	3.00	0
2013	Minnesota c-d	A.L.	29	152 2/3	5	13	.278	101	53	184	5.19	0
Major League Totals		8 Yrs.	182	1049	55	67	.451	607	371	1173	4.48	1

a On disabled list from April 22 to October 29, 2012.
b Not offered contract, November 30, 2012. Signed with Minnesota Twins, December 20, 2012.
c On disabled list from June 19 to July 4, 2013.
d Filed for free agency, October 31, 2013. Signed with Minnesota Twins, December 23, 2013.

PERALTA (GUTIERREZ), JOEL

Born, Bonao, Dominican Republic, March 23, 1976.
Bats Right. Throws Right. Height, 5 feet, 11 inches. Weight, 195 pounds.

Year	Club	Lea	G	IP	W	L	Pct	SO	BB	H	ERA	SAVES
2000	Boise	Northwest	4	8 1/3	0	0	.000	9	5	12	6.48	0
2000	Butte a	Pioneer	10	19	2	1	.667	17	10	24	6.63	1
2001	Cedar Rapids	Midwest	41	42 1/3	0	0	.000	53	5	27	2.13	23
2001	Arkansas	Texas	9	10	0	1	.000	14	5	15	6.30	2
2002	Cedar Rapids	Midwest	41	47 1/3	5	0	1.000	53	11	28	0.95	21
2002	Arkansas	Texas	12	17 2/3	0	0	.000	11	10	25	6.62	0
2003	Salt Lake	P.C.	1	0	0	0	.000	0	1	0	0.00	0
2003	Arkansas	Texas	47	52 1/3	5	4	.556	48	12	39	2.24	20
2004	Angels	Arizona	2	4 1/3	0	0	.000	9	0	1	2.08	0
2004	Rancho Cucamonga	Calif.	1	2	0	0	.000	1	1	5	9.00	0
2004	Salt Lake	P.C.	39	56	4	2	.667	68	18	64	4.98	1
2005	Los Angeles	A.L.	28	34 2/3	1	0	1.000	30	14	28	3.89	0
2005	Salt Lake b	P.C.	19	20	4	1	.800	18	6	11	2.70	10
2006	Omaha	P.C.	6	7 2/3	1	0	1.000	8	3	8	2.35	2
2006	Kansas City	A.L.	64	73 2/3	1	3	.250	57	17	74	4.40	1
2007	Kansas City	A.L.	62	87 2/3	1	3	.250	66	19	93	3.80	1
2008	Omaha	P.C.	10	18 2/3	1	0	1.000	19	6	9	0.00	2
2008	Kansas City	A.L.	40	52 2/3	1	2	.333	38	14	56	5.98	0
2009	Colorado Springs	P.C.	31	36 2/3	6	0	1.000	32	11	31	2.45	4
2009	Colorado c-d	N.L.	27	24 2/3	0	3	.000	22	12	27	6.20	0
2010	Syracuse	Int.	28	33 1/3	2	0	1.000	38	7	24	1.08	20
2010	Washington e	N.L.	39	49	1	0	1.000	49	9	30	2.02	0
2011	Tampa Bay	A.L.	71	67 2/3	3	4	.429	61	18	44	2.93	6
2012	Tampa Bay f	A.L.	76	67	2	6	.250	84	17	49	3.63	2
2013	Tampa Bay	A.L.	*80	71 1/3	3	8	.273	74	34	47	3.41	1
Major League Totals		9 Yrs.	487	528 1/3	13	29	.310	481	154	448	3.87	11
	Wild Card Playoff											
2013	Tampa Bay	A.L.	1	1	0	0	.000	1	0	1	0.00	0
	Division Series											
2011	Tampa Bay	A.L.	3	2 1/3	0	0	.000	0	2	1	0.00	0
2013	Tampa Bay	A.L.	2	2 1/3	0	0	.000	3	1	2	0.00	0
Division Series Totals			5	4 2/3	0	0	.000	3	3	3	0.00	0

a Released by Oakland Athletics, July 4, 1998. Signed with Anaheim Angels organization, February 25, 1999.
b Claimed on waivers by Kansas City Royals, October 7, 2005.
c Released by Kansas City Royals, March 31, 2009. Signed with Colorado Rockies organization, April 8, 2009.
d Filed for free agency, October 26, 2009. Signed with Washington Nationals organization, December 15, 2009.
e Not offered contract, December 2, 2010. Signed with Tampa Bay Rays, December 17, 2010.
f Filed for free agency, November 3, 2012, re-signed with Tampa Bay Rays, November 19, 2012.

PERALTA, WILY

Born, Samana, Dominican Republic, May 8, 1989.
Bats Right. Throws Right. Height, 6 feet, 2 inches. Weight, 245 pounds.

Year	Club	Lea	G	IP	W	L	Pct	SO	BB	H	ERA	SAVES
2006	Brewers	Arizona	14	38	2	5	.286	28	20	51	6.63	0
2007	a				INJURED—Did Not Play							
2008	Helena	Pioneer	15	29 1/3	1	1	.500	36	8	23	3.07	2
2008	West Virginia	So.Atl.	2	5	0	1	.000	3	3	6	10.80	0
2009	Wisconsin	Midwest	27	103 2/3	4	4	.500	118	46	91	3.47	1
2010	Brevard County	Fla.St.	19	105	6	3	.667	75	40	102	3.86	0

Year	Club	Lea	G	IP	W	L	Pct	SO	BB	H	ERA	SAVES
2010	Huntsville	Southern	8	$42\frac{1}{3}$	2	3	.400	29	24	43	3.61	0
2011	Huntsville	Southern	21	$119\frac{2}{3}$	9	7	.563	117	48	106	3.46	0
2011	Nashville	P.C.	5	31	2	0	1.000	40	11	21	2.03	0
2012	Nashville	P.C.	28	$146\frac{2}{3}$	7	11	.389	143	78	154	4.66	0
2012	Milwaukee	N.L.	6	29	2	1	.667	23	11	24	2.48	0
2013	Milwaukee	N.L.	32	$183\frac{1}{3}$	11	15	.423	129	73	187	4.37	0
Major League Totals		2 Yrs.	38	$212\frac{1}{3}$	13	16	.448	152	84	211	4.11	0

a On minor league disabled list from June 22 to August 31, 2007.

PEREZ (JIMENEZ), MARTIN

Born, Guanare, Venezuela, April 4, 1991.

Bats Left. Throws Left. Height, 6 feet. Weight, 180 pounds.

Year	Club	Lea	G	IP	W	L	Pct	SO	BB	H	ERA	SAVES
2008	Spokane	Northwest	15	$61\frac{2}{3}$	1	2	.333	53	28	66	3.65	0
2009	Hickory	So.Atl.	22	$93\frac{2}{3}$	5	5	.500	105	33	82	2.31	1
2009	Frisco	Texas	5	21	1	3	.250	14	5	29	5.57	0
2010	Frisco	Texas	24	$99\frac{2}{3}$	5	8	.385	101	50	117	5.96	0
2011	Round Rock	P.C.	10	49	4	4	.500	37	20	72	6.43	0
2011	Frisco	Texas	17	$88\frac{1}{3}$	4	2	.667	83	36	80	3.16	0
2012	Round Rock	P.C.	22	127	7	6	.538	69	56	122	4.25	0
2012	Texas	A.L.	12	38	1	4	.200	25	15	47	5.45	0
2013	Frisco	Texas	2	$7\frac{1}{3}$	0	1	.000	2	2	14	11.05	0
2013	Round Rock	P.C.	6	36	5	1	.833	28	8	29	1.75	0
2013	Texas a	A.L.	20	$124\frac{1}{3}$	10	6	.625	84	37	129	3.62	0
Major League Totals		2 Yrs.	32	$162\frac{1}{3}$	11	10	.524	109	52	176	4.05	0

a On disabled list from March 22 to May 12, 2013.

PEREZ (MARTINEZ), OLIVER

Born, Culiacan, Mexico, August 15, 1981.

Bats Left. Throws Left. Height, 6 feet, 3 inches. Weight, 220 pounds.

Year	Club	Lea	G	IP	W	L	Pct	SO	BB	H	ERA	SAVES
1999	Padres	Arizona	15	$28\frac{1}{3}$	1	2	.333	37	16	28	5.08	3
2000	Idaho Falls	Pioneer	5	$24\frac{1}{3}$	3	1	.750	27	9	24	4.07	0
2001	Fort Wayne	Midwest	19	$101\frac{1}{3}$	8	5	.615	98	43	84	3.46	0
2001	Lake Elsinore	Calif.	9	53	2	4	.333	62	25	45	2.72	0
2002	Lake Elsinore	Calif.	9	$48\frac{2}{3}$	3	3	.500	66	24	36	1.85	0
2002	Mobile	Southern	4	23	1	0	1.000	34	16	11	1.17	0
2002	San Diego	N.L.	16	90	4	5	.444	94	48	71	3.50	0
2003	Portland	P.C.	8	$47\frac{2}{3}$	3	3	.500	48	12	44	3.02	0
2003	San Diego-Pittsburgh a	N.L.	24	$126\frac{2}{3}$	4	10	.286	141	77	129	5.47	0
2004	Pittsburgh	N.L.	30	196	12	10	.545	239	81	145	2.98	0
2005	Indianapolis	Int.	3	10	0	1	.000	4	12	14	9.90	0
2005	Pittsburgh	N.L.	20	103	7	5	.583	97	70	102	5.85	0
2006	Indianapolis	Int.	6	32	1	3	.250	34	11	28	5.63	0
2006	Norfolk	Int.	4	$19\frac{1}{3}$	1	2	.333	26	12	18	6.05	0
2006	Pittsburgh-New York b	N.L.	22	$112\frac{2}{3}$	3	13	.188	102	68	129	6.55	0
2007	Mets	Gulf Coast	1	4	0	0	.000	7	0	2	0.00	0
2007	New York	N.L.	29	177	15	10	.600	174	79	153	3.56	0
2008	New York	N.L.	34	194	10	7	.588	180	*105	167	4.22	0
2009	St. Lucie	Fla.St.	1	3	0	1	.000	3	1	7	6.00	0
2009	Brooklyn	N.Y.-Penn.	1	5	1	0	1.000	6	1	2	0.00	0
2009	Buffalo	Int.	2	$9\frac{1}{3}$	0	2	.000	9	9	8	3.86	0
2009	New York c	N.L.	14	66	3	4	.429	62	58	69	6.82	0
2010	St. Lucie	Fla.St.	2	$11\frac{2}{3}$	1	1	.500	14	4	7	4.63	0
2010	Buffalo	Int.	2	$11\frac{2}{3}$	0	0	.000	10	7	10	2.31	0
2010	New York	N.L.	17	$46\frac{1}{3}$	0	5	.000	37	42	54	6.80	0
2011	Harrisburg d	Eastern	16	$75\frac{2}{3}$	3	5	.375	58	27	78	3.09	0
2012	Tacoma e	P.C.	22	31	2	2	.500	42	19	33	4.65	1
2012	Seattle f	A.L.	33	$29\frac{2}{3}$	1	3	.250	24	10	27	2.12	0
2013	Seattle g	A.L.	61	53	3	3	.500	74	26	50	3.74	2
Major League Totals		11 Yrs.	300	$1194\frac{1}{3}$	62	75	.453	1224	664	1096	4.53	2
	Championship Series											
2006	New York	N.L.	2	$11\frac{2}{3}$	1	0	1.000	7	3	13	4.63	0

a Traded to Pittsburgh Pirates with outfielder Jason Bay and player to be named later for outfielder Brian Giles, August 26, 2003. Pittsburgh Pirates received pitcher Cory Stewart to complete trade, October 2, 2003.

b Traded to New York Mets with pitcher Roberto Hernandez for outfielder Xavier Nady, July 31, 2006.

c Filed for free agency, October 30, 2008, re-signed with New York Mets, February 3, 2009.

d Released by New York Mets, March 21, 2011. Signed with Washington Nationals organization, March 25, 2011.
e Filed for free agency, November 2, 2011. Signed with Seattle Mariners organization, January 23, 2012.
f Filed for free agency, November 3, 2012, re-signed with Seattle Mariners, November 3, 2012.
g Filed for free agency, October 31, 2013.

PERKINS, GLEN WESTON

Born, St.Paul, Minnesota, March 2, 1983.
Bats Left. Throws Left. Height, 5 feet, 11 inches. Weight, 210 pounds.

Year Club	Lea	G	IP	W	L	Pct	SO	BB	H	ERA	SAVES
2004 Elizabethton	Appal.	3	12	1	0	1.000	22	4	8	2.25	0
2004 Quad Cities	Midwest	9	48 1/3	2	1	.667	49	12	33	1.30	0
2005 Fort Myers	Fla.St.	10	55	3	2	.600	66	13	41	2.13	0
2005 New Britain	Eastern	14	79	4	4	.500	67	35	80	4.90	0
2006 New Britain	Eastern	23	117 1/3	4	11	.267	131	45	109	3.91	0
2006 Rochester	Int.	1	4 1/3	0	1	.000	3	5	6	2.08	0
2006 Minnesota	A.L.	4	5 2/3	0	0	.000	6	0	3	1.59	0
2007 Rochester	Int.	1	6	0	0	.000	2	1	2	1.50	0
2007 Fort Myers	Fla.St.	1	1	0	0	.000	0	0	3	27.00	0
2007 Twins	Gulf Coast	3	5	0	0	.000	6	2	3	1.80	0
2007 New Britain	Eastern	3	7 1/3	0	2	.000	7	7	11	11.05	0
2007 Minnesota a	A.L.	19	28 2/3	0	0	.000	20	12	23	3.14	0
2008 Rochester	Int.	7	33 1/3	2	1	.667	27	19	28	2.97	0
2008 Minnesota	A.L.	26	151	12	4	.750	74	39	183	4.41	0
2009 Fort Myers	Fla.St.	2	11	1	0	1.000	9	1	8	2.45	0
2009 Minnesota b	A.L.	18	96 1/3	6	7	.462	45	23	120	5.89	0
2009 Twins	Gulf Coast	1	1	0	0	.000	0	0	0	0.00	0
2010 Rochester	Int.	26	124	4	9	.308	98	36	160	5.81	0
2010 Minnesota	A.L.	13	21 2/3	1	1	.500	14	5	29	5.82	0
2011 Rochester	Int.	2	3	0	0	.000	2	0	4	0.00	0
2011 Minnesota c	A.L.	65	61 2/3	4	4	.500	65	21	55	2.48	2
2012 Minnesota	A.L.	70	70 1/3	3	1	.750	78	16	57	2.56	16
2013 Minnesota	A.L.	61	62 2/3	2	0	1.000	77	15	43	2.30	36
Major League Totals	8 Yrs.	276	498	28	17	.622	379	131	513	3.89	54
Division Series											
2006 Minnesota	A.L.	1	0 1/3	0	0	.000	0	0	2	0.00	0

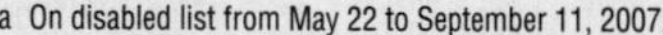

a On disabled list from May 22 to September 11, 2007.
b On disabled list from May 19 to June 16 and August 9 to August 30, 2009.
c On disabled list from May 22 to June 17, 2011.

PETTIBONE, HARRY JONATHAN (JONATHAN)

Born, Placentia, California, July 19, 1990.
Bats Left. Throws Right. Height, 6 feet, 6 inches. Weight, 225 pounds.

Year Club	Lea	G	IP	W	L	Pct	SO	BB	H	ERA	SAVES
2008 Phillies	Gulf Coast	1	1	0	1	.000	0	1	3	0.00	0
2009 Williamsport	N.Y.-Penn.	9	35 1/3	2	4	.333	36	16	37	5.35	0
2010 Lakewood	So.Atl.	24	131 1/3	8	6	.571	84	41	114	3.49	0
2011 Clearwater	Fla.St.	27	161	10	11	.476	115	34	149	2.96	0
2012 Reading	Eastern	19	117 1/3	9	7	.563	81	27	115	3.30	0
2012 Lehigh Valley	Int.	7	42 1/3	4	1	.800	32	22	31	2.55	0
2013 Reading	Eastern	1	5	0	0	.000	4	1	5	5.40	0
2013 Lehigh Valley	Int.	4	17 1/3	0	2	.000	10	5	26	6.75	0
2013 Philadelphia a	N.L.	18	100 1/3	5	4	.556	66	38	109	4.04	0

a On disabled list from July 29 to November 4, 2013.

PETTITTE, ANDREW EUGENE (ANDY)

Born, Baton Rouge, Louisiana, June 15, 1972.
Bats Left. Throws Left. Height, 6 feet, 5 inches. Weight, 225 pounds.

Year Club	Lea	G	IP	W	L	Pct	SO	BB	H	ERA	SAVES
1991 Yankees	Gulf Coast	6	36 2/3	4	1	.800	51	8	16	0.98	0
1991 Oneonta	N.Y.-Penn.	6	33	2	2	.500	32	16	33	2.18	0
1992 Greensboro	So.Atl.	27	168	10	4	.714	130	55	141	2.20	0
1993 Pr William	Carolina	26	159 2/3	11	9	.550	129	47	146	3.04	0
1993 Albany	Eastern	1	5	1	0	1.000	6	2	5	3.60	0
1994 Albany	Eastern	11	73	7	2	.778	50	18	60	2.71	0
1994 Columbus	Int.	16	96 2/3	7	2	.778	61	21	101	2.98	0
1995 Columbus	Int.	2	11 2/3	0	0	.000	8	0	7	0.00	0
1995 New York	A.L.	31	175	12	9	.571	114	63	183	4.17	0
1996 New York	A.L.	35	221	*21	8	.724	162	72	229	3.87	0

Year	Club	Lea	G	IP	W	L	Pct	SO	BB	H	ERA	SAVES
1997	New York	A.L.	35	240 1/3	18	7	.720	166	65	233	2.88	0
1998	New York	A.L.	33	216 1/3	16	11	.593	146	87	226	4.24	0
1999	Tampa	Fla.St.	1	5	1	0	1.000	8	2	4	0.00	0
1999	New York a	A.L.	31	191 2/3	14	11	.560	121	89	216	4.70	0
2000	New York b	A.L.	32	204 2/3	19	9	.679	125	80	219	4.35	0
2001	New York c	A.L.	31	200 2/3	15	10	.600	164	41	224	3.99	0
2002	Tampa	Fla.St.	2	5	0	0	.000	4	0	3	0.00	0
2002	Norwich	Eastern	1	6 1/3	0	0	.000	5	0	2	1.42	0
2002	New York d	A.L.	22	134 2/3	13	5	.722	97	32	144	3.27	0
2003	New York e	A.L.	33	208 1/3	21	8	.724	180	50	227	4.02	0
2004	Round Rock	Texas	2	8	0	0	.000	9	2	4	2.25	0
2004	Houston f	N.L.	15	83	6	4	.600	79	31	71	3.90	0
2005	Houston	N.L.	33	222 1/3	17	9	.654	171	41	188	2.39	0
2006	Houston g	N.L.	36	214 1/3	14	13	.519	178	70	238	4.20	0
2007	New York	A.L.	36	215 1/3	15	9	.625	141	69	238	4.05	0
2008	New York h	A.L.	33	204	14	14	.500	158	55	233	4.54	0
2009	New York	A.L.	32	194 2/3	14	8	.636	148	76	193	4.16	0
2010	New York i	A.L.	21	129	11	3	.786	101	41	123	3.28	0
2011	j				RETIRED—Did Not Play							
2012	Tampa	Fla.St.	2	7	0	0	.000	5	0	4	1.29	0
2012	Trenton	Eastern	1	5	0	1	.000	3	1	7	5.40	0
2012	Scranton-WB	Int.	1	5	0	1	.000	5	2	8	5.40	0
2012	New York k-l-m	A.L.	12	75 1/3	5	4	.556	69	21	65	2.87	0
2013	New York n-o	A.L.	30	185 1/3	11	11	.500	128	48	198	3.74	0
Major League Totals		18 Yrs.	531	3316	256	153	.626	2448	1031	3448	3.85	0
	Division Series											
1995	New York	A.L.	1	7	0	0	.000	0	3	9	5.14	0
1996	New York	A.L.	1	6 1/3	0	0	.000	3	6	4	5.68	0
1997	New York	A.L.	2	11 2/3	0	2	.000	5	1	15	8.49	0
1998	New York	A.L.	1	7	1	0	1.000	8	0	3	1.29	0
1999	New York	A.L.	1	7 1/3	1	0	1.000	5	0	7	1.23	0
2000	New York	A.L.	2	11 1/3	1	0	1.000	7	3	15	3.97	0
2001	New York	A.L.	1	6 1/3	0	1	.000	4	2	7	1.42	0
2002	New York	A.L.	1	3	0	0	.000	1	0	8	12.00	0
2003	New York	A.L.	1	7	1	0	1.000	10	3	4	1.29	0
2005	Houston	N.L.	1	7	1	0	1.000	6	2	4	3.86	0
2007	New York	A.L.	1	6 1/3	0	0	.000	5	2	7	0.00	0
2009	New York	A.L.	1	6 1/3	1	0	1.000	7	1	3	1.42	0
2010	New York	A.L.	1	7	1	0	1.000	4	1	5	2.57	0
2012	New York	A.L.	1	7	0	1	.000	5	1	7	3.86	0
Division Series Totals			16	100 2/3	7	4	.636	70	25	98	3.67	0
	Championship Series											
1996	New York	A.L.	2	15	1	0	1.000	7	5	10	3.60	0
1998	New York	A.L.	1	4 2/3	0	1	.000	1	3	8	11.57	0
1999	New York	A.L.	1	7 1/3	1	0	1.000	5	1	8	2.45	0
2000	New York	A.L.	1	6 2/3	1	0	1.000	2	1	9	2.70	0
2001	New York	A.L.	2	14 1/3	2	0	1.000	8	2	11	2.51	0
2003	New York	A.L.	2	11 2/3	1	0	1.000	10	4	17	4.63	0
2005	Houston	N.L.	2	12 1/3	0	1	.000	6	4	15	5.11	0
2009	New York	A.L.	2	12 2/3	1	0	1.000	8	2	14	2.84	0
2010	New York	A.L.	1	7	0	1	.000	5	0	5	2.57	0
2012	New York	A.L.	1	6 2/3	0	0	.000	5	3	7	2.70	0
Championship Series Totals			15	98 1/3	7	3	.700	57	25	104	3.75	0
	World Series Record											
1996	New York	A.L.	2	10 2/3	1	1	.500	5	4	11	5.91	0
1998	New York	A.L.	1	7 1/3	1	0	1.000	4	3	5	0.00	0
1999	New York	A.L.	1	3 2/3	0	0	.000	1	1	10	12.27	0
2000	New York	A.L.	2	13 2/3	0	0	.000	9	4	16	1.98	0
2001	New York	A.L.	2	9	0	2	.000	9	2	12	10.00	0
2003	New York	A.L.	2	15 2/3	1	1	.500	14	4	12	0.57	0
2005	Houston	N.L.	1	6	0	0	.000	4	0	8	3.00	0
2009	New York	A.L.	2	11 2/3	2	0	1.000	10	8	9	5.40	0
World Series Totals			13	77 2/3	5	4	.556	56	26	83	4.06	0

a On disabled list from March 26 to April 17, 1999.

b On disabled list from April 8 to April 25, 2000.

c On disabled list from June 16 to July 1, 2001.

d On disabled list from April 16 to June 14, 2002.

e Filed for free agency, November 6, 2003. Signed with Houston Astros, December 11, 2003.

f On disabled list from April 7 to April 29 and from May 27 to June 29 and from August 18 to October 28, 2004.

g Filed for free agency, November 6, 2006. Signed with New York Yankees, December 8, 2006.

h On disabled list from March 21 to April 5, 2008.

i On disabled list from July 19 to September 17, 2010.

j Announced retirement, February 4, 2011.
k Signed with New York Yankees organization, March 16, 2012.
l On disabled list from June 28 to September 19, 2012.
m Filed for free agency, November 3, 2012, re-signed with New York Yankees, November 28, 2012.
n On disabled list from May 17 to June 3, 2013.
o Announced retirement, September 20, 2013.

PHELPS, DAVID EDWARD

Born, St.Louis, Missouri, October 9, 1986.
Bats Right. Throws Right. Height, 6 feet, 2 inches. Weight, 200 pounds.

Year	Club	Lea	G	IP	W	L	Pct	SO	BB	H	ERA	SAVES
2008	Staten Island	N.Y.-Penn.	15	72 2/3	8	2	.800	52	18	67	2.72	0
2009	Tampa	Fla.St.	7	38 1/3	3	1	.750	32	6	34	1.17	0
2009	Charleston	So.Atl.	19	112 2/3	10	3	.769	90	25	117	2.80	0
2010	Trenton	Eastern	14	88 1/3	6	0	1.000	84	23	63	2.04	0
2010	Scranton-WB	Int.	12	70 1/3	4	2	.667	57	13	76	3.07	0
2011	Yankees	Gulf Coast	2	7	1	1	.500	5	1	4	0.00	0
2011	Scranton-WB	Int.	18	107 1/3	6	6	.500	90	26	115	3.19	0
2012	Tampa	Fla.St.	2	5 1/3	0	0	.000	5	1	7	0.00	0
2012	Trenton	Eastern	1	6 2/3	1	0	1.000	11	1	1	0.00	0
2012	Scranton-WB	Int.	1	6 2/3	1	0	1.000	7	3	4	0.00	0
2012	New York	A.L.	33	99 2/3	4	4	.500	96	38	81	3.34	0
2013	Trenton	Eastern	2	7 2/3	0	0	.000	12	5	5	3.52	0
2013	New York a	A.L.	22	86 2/3	6	5	.545	79	35	88	4.98	0
Major League Totals		2 Yrs.	55	186 1/3	10	9	.526	175	73	169	4.11	0
	Division Series											
2012	New York	A.L.	1	1 1/3	0	1	.000	1	0	2	6.75	0
	Championship Series											
2012	New York	A.L.	2	2	0	1	.000	1	1	5	9.00	0

a On disabled list from July 5 to September 14, 2013.

PINEDA, MICHAEL FRANCISCO

Born, Yaguate, Dominican Republic, January 18, 1989.
Bats Right. Throws Right. Height, 6 feet, 7 inches. Weight, 260 pounds.

Year	Club	Lea	G	IP	W	L	Pct	SO	BB	H	ERA	SAVES
2008	Wisconsin	Midwest	26	138 1/3	8	6	.571	128	35	109	1.95	0
2009	Mariners	Arizona	2	3	0	0	.000	4	0	2	0.00	0
2009	High Desert	Calif.	10	44 1/3	4	2	.667	48	6	29	2.84	0
2010	Tacoma	P.C.	12	62 1/3	3	3	.500	76	17	54	4.76	0
2010	West Tenn	Southern	13	77	8	1	.889	78	17	67	2.22	0
2011	Seattle	A.L.	28	171	9	10	.474	173	55	133	3.74	0
2012	New York a-b	A.L.	INJURED—Did Not Play									
2013	New York c	A.L.	INJURED—Did Not Play									

a Traded to New York Yankees with pitcher Juan Campos for catcher Jesus Montero and pitcher Hector Noesi, January 17, 2012.
b On disabled list from March 31 to October 31, 2012.
c On disabled list from March 16 to July 7, 2013.

POMERANZ, THOMAS ANDREW (DREW)

Born, Collierville, Tennessee, November 22, 1988.
Bats Right. Throws Left. Height, 6 feet, 5 inches. Weight, 230 pounds.

Year	Club	Lea	G	IP	W	L	Pct	SO	BB	H	ERA	SAVES
2011	Kinston	Carolina	15	77	3	2	.600	95	32	56	1.87	0
2011	Tulsa	Texas	2	10	1	0	1.000	7	0	2	0.00	0
2011	Akron	Eastern	3	14	0	1	.000	17	6	10	2.57	0
2011	Colorado a	N.L.	4	18 1/3	2	1	.667	13	5	19	5.40	0
2012	Tulsa	Texas	1	4	0	0	.000	4	1	4	0.00	0
2012	Colorado Springs	P.C.	9	46 2/3	4	4	.500	46	20	52	2.51	0
2012	Colorado	N.L.	22	96 2/3	2	9	.182	83	46	97	4.93	0
2013	Tulsa	Texas	1	5 1/3	0	1	.000	5	1	10	11.81	0
2013	Colorado Springs	P.C.	15	85 2/3	8	1	.889	96	33	83	4.20	0
2013	Colorado b-c	N.L.	8	21 2/3	0	4	.000	19	19	25	6.23	0
Major League Totals		3 Yrs.	34	136 2/3	4	14	.222	115	70	141	5.20	0

a Sent by Cleveland Indians to Colorado Rockies as player to be named later for pitcher Ubaldo Jimenez, August 17, 2011.
b On disabled list from July 23 to September 6, 2013.
c Traded to Oakland Athletics with pitcher Chris Jensen for pitcher Brett Anderson and cash, December 10, 2013.

PORCELLO, FREDERICK ALFRED (RICK)

Born, Morristown, New Jersey, December 27, 1988.
Bats Right. Throws Right. Height, 6 feet, 5 inches. Weight, 200 pounds.

Year Club	Lea	G	IP	W	L	Pct	SO	BB	H	ERA	SAVES
2008 Lakeland	Fla.St.	24	125	8	6	.571	72	33	116	2.66	0
2009 Detroit	A.L.	31	$170\frac{2}{3}$	14	9	.609	89	52	176	3.96	0
2010 Toledo	Int.	4	28	1	2	.333	19	10	24	3.21	0
2010 Detroit	A.L.	27	$162\frac{2}{3}$	10	12	.455	84	38	188	4.92	0
2011 Detroit	A.L.	31	182	14	9	.609	104	46	210	4.75	0
2012 Detroit	A.L.	31	$176\frac{1}{3}$	10	12	.455	107	44	*226	4.59	0
2013 Detroit	A.L.	32	177	13	8	.619	142	42	185	4.32	0
Major League Totals	5 Yrs.	152	$868\frac{2}{3}$	61	50	.550	526	222	985	4.51	0
Division Series											
2011 Detroit	A.L.	1	6	0	1	.000	5	1	5	6.00	0
2012 Detroit	A.L.	1	$0\frac{1}{3}$	0	0	.000	0	0	0	0.00	0
2013 Detroit	A.L.	1	0	0	0	.000	0	0	1	INF	0
Division Series Totals		3	$6\frac{1}{3}$	0	1	.000	5	1	6	5.68	0
Championship Series											
2011 Detroit	A.L.	3	9	0	0	.000	7	1	10	4.00	0
2013 Detroit	A.L.	1	0	0	1	.000	0	0	2	INF	0
Championship Series Totals		4	9	0	1	.000	7	1	12	4.00	0
World Series Record											
2012 Detroit	A.L.	1	1	0	0	.000	1	0	0	0.00	0

PRESSLY, THOMAS RYAN (RYAN)

Born, Dallas, Texas, December 15, 1988.
Bats Right. Throws Right. Height, 6 feet, 3 inches. Weight, 205 pounds.

Year Club	Lea	G	IP	W	L	Pct	SO	BB	H	ERA	SAVES
2008 Red Sox	Gulf Coast	10	$40\frac{1}{3}$	1	4	.200	34	21	41	3.79	0
2009 Lowell	N.Y.-Penn.	13	$59\frac{2}{3}$	6	4	.600	64	25	48	3.17	0
2010 Greenville	So.Atl.	26	$113\frac{2}{3}$	5	7	.417	96	43	110	3.72	0
2011 Salem	Carolina	26	130	6	11	.353	72	53	125	4.50	0
2012 Salem	Carolina	20	76	5	3	.625	61	26	86	6.28	0
2012 Portland a	Eastern	14	$27\frac{2}{3}$	2	2	.500	21	10	23	2.93	0
2013 Minnesota	A.L.	49	$76\frac{2}{3}$	3	3	.500	49	27	71	3.87	0

a Selected by Minnesota Twins from Boston Red Sox in Rule V draft, December 6, 2012.

PRICE, DAVID TAYLOR

Born, Murfreesboro, Tennessee, August 26, 1985.
Bats Left. Throws Left. Height, 6 feet, 6 inches. Weight, 225 pounds.

Year Club	Lea	G	IP	W	L	Pct	SO	BB	H	ERA	SAVES
2008 Vero Beach	Fla.St.	6	$34\frac{2}{3}$	4	0	1.000	37	7	28	1.82	0
2008 Montgomery	Southern	9	57	7	0	1.000	55	16	42	1.89	0
2008 Durham	Int.	4	18	1	1	.500	17	9	22	4.50	0
2008 Tampa Bay	A.L.	5	14	0	0	.000	12	4	9	1.93	0
2009 Durham	Int.	8	$34\frac{1}{3}$	1	4	.200	35	18	28	3.93	0
2009 Tampa Bay	A.L.	23	$128\frac{1}{3}$	10	7	.588	102	54	119	4.42	0
2010 Tampa Bay	A.L.	32	$208\frac{2}{3}$	19	6	*.760	188	79	170	2.72	0
2011 Tampa Bay	A.L.	34	$224\frac{1}{3}$	12	13	.480	218	63	192	3.49	0
2012 Tampa Bay a	A.L.	31	211	*20	5	*.800	205	59	173	*2.56	0
2013 Charlotte	Fla.St.	2	$7\frac{1}{3}$	1	0	1.000	12	3	4	1.23	0
2013 Tampa Bay b	A.L.	27	$186\frac{2}{3}$	10	8	.556	151	27	178	3.33	0
Major League Totals	6 Yrs.	152	973	71	39	.645	876	286	841	3.19	0
Division Series											
2010 Tampa Bay	A.L.	2	$12\frac{2}{3}$	0	2	.000	14	0	17	4.97	0
2011 Tampa Bay	A.L.	1	$6\frac{2}{3}$	0	1	.000	3	1	7	4.05	0
2013 Tampa Bay	A.L.	1	7	0	1	.000	5	2	9	9.00	0
Division Series Totals		4	$26\frac{1}{3}$	0	4	.000	22	3	33	5.81	0
Championship Series											
2008 Tampa Bay	A.L.	3	$2\frac{1}{3}$	1	0	1.000	4	2	0	0.00	1
World Series Record											
2008 Tampa Bay	A.L.	2	$3\frac{1}{3}$	0	0	.000	4	2	2	2.70	0

a Selected Cy Young Award Winner in American League for 2012.
b On disabled list from May 16 to July 2, 2013.

PRYOR, STEPHEN MICHAEL

Born, Donelson, Tennessee, July 23, 1989.
Bats Right. Throws Right. Height, 6 feet, 4 inches. Weight, 245 pounds.

Year	Club	Lea	G	IP	W	L	Pct	SO	BB	H	ERA	SAVES
2010	Clinton	Midwest	12	17	0	2	.000	29	6	17	3.71	1
2010	Everett	Northwest	11	18 1/3	0	0	.000	26	7	7	0.49	4
2011	High Desert	Calif.	22	27	1	0	1.000	34	26	28	7.67	4
2011	Jackson	Southern	17	22 2/3	2	1	.667	27	7	9	1.19	6
2012	High Desert	Calif.	2	2 2/3	0	0	.000	3	3	0	6.75	0
2012	Jackson	Southern	11	16	1	0	1.000	24	5	7	1.13	7
2012	Tacoma	P.C.	16	20	0	0	.000	20	11	11	0.00	3
2012	Seattle a	A.L.	26	23	3	1	.750	27	13	22	3.91	0
2013	Everett	Northwest	1	0 2/3	0	0	.000	1	0	3	27.00	0
2013	Tacoma	P.C.	4	3	0	0	.000	1	2	5	15.00	0
2013	Seattle b	A.L.	7	7 1/3	0	0	.000	7	1	3	0.00	0
Major League Totals		2 Yrs.	33	30 1/3	3	1	.750	34	14	25	2.97	0

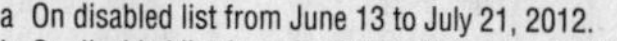

a On disabled list from June 13 to July 21, 2012.
b On disabled list from April 15 to November 1, 2013.

PUTZ, JOSEPH JASON (J.J.)

Born, Trenton, Michigan, February 2, 1977.
Bats Right. Throws Right. Height, 6 feet, 5 inches. Weight, 250 pounds.

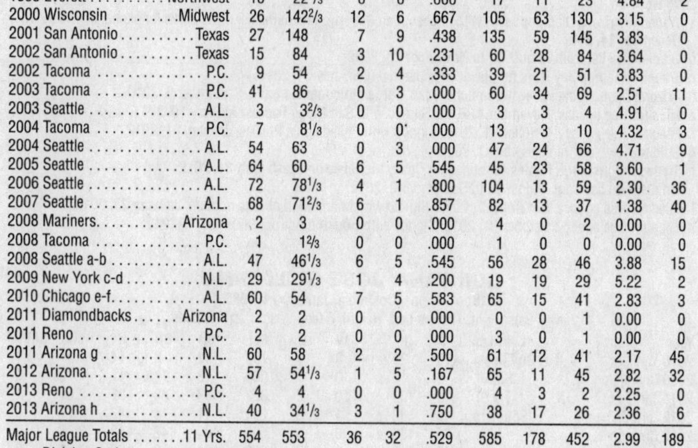

Year	Club	Lea	G	IP	W	L	Pct	SO	BB	H	ERA	SAVES
1999	Everett	Northwest	10	22 1/3	0	0	.000	17	11	23	4.84	2
2000	Wisconsin	Midwest	26	142 2/3	12	6	.667	105	63	130	3.15	0
2001	San Antonio	Texas	27	148	7	9	.438	135	59	145	3.83	0
2002	San Antonio	Texas	15	84	3	10	.231	60	28	84	3.64	0
2002	Tacoma	P.C.	9	54	2	4	.333	39	21	51	3.83	0
2003	Tacoma	P.C.	41	86	0	3	.000	60	34	69	2.51	11
2003	Seattle	A.L.	3	3 2/3	0	0	.000	3	3	4	4.91	0
2004	Tacoma	P.C.	7	8 1/3	0	0	.000	13	3	10	4.32	3
2004	Seattle	A.L.	54	63	0	3	.000	47	24	66	4.71	9
2005	Seattle	A.L.	64	60	6	5	.545	45	23	58	3.60	1
2006	Seattle	A.L.	72	78 1/3	4	1	.800	104	13	59	2.30	36
2007	Seattle	A.L.	68	71 2/3	6	1	.857	82	13	37	1.38	40
2008	Mariners	Arizona	2	3	0	0	.000	4	0	2	0.00	0
2008	Tacoma	P.C.	1	1 2/3	0	0	.000	1	0	0	0.00	0
2008	Seattle a-b	A.L.	47	46 1/3	6	5	.545	56	28	46	3.88	15
2009	New York c-d	N.L.	29	29 1/3	1	4	.200	19	19	29	5.22	2
2010	Chicago e-f	A.L.	60	54	7	5	.583	65	15	41	2.83	3
2011	Diamondbacks	Arizona	2	2	0	0	.000	0	0	1	0.00	0
2011	Reno	P.C.	2	2	0	0	.000	3	0	1	0.00	0
2011	Arizona g	N.L.	60	58	2	2	.500	61	12	41	2.17	45
2012	Arizona	N.L.	57	54 1/3	1	5	.167	65	11	45	2.82	32
2013	Reno	P.C.	4	4	0	0	.000	4	3	2	2.25	0
2013	Arizona h	N.L.	40	34 1/3	3	1	.750	38	17	26	2.36	6
Major League Totals		11 Yrs.	554	553	36	32	.529	585	178	452	2.99	189
Division Series												
2011	Arizona	N.L.	3	2 1/3	0	1	.000	0	1	3	3.86	0

a On disabled list from April 2 to April 22 and June 12 to July 20, 2008.
b Traded to New York Mets with pitcher Sean Green and outfielder Jeremy Reed for pitcher Aaron Heilman, outfielder Endy Chavez, pitcher Jason Vargas, infielder Mike Carp, outfielder Ezequiel Carrera and pitcher Maikel Cleto, December 10, 2008.
c On disabled list from June 5 to November 7, 2009.
d Filed for free agency, November 7, 2009. Signed with Chicago White Sox, December 11, 2009.
e On disabled list from August 25 to September 9, 2010.
f Filed for free agency, November 1, 2010. Signed with Arizona Diamondbacks, December 7, 2010.
g On disabled list from June 29 to July 26, 2011.
h On disabled list from May 8 to June 29 and August 24 to September 16, 2013.

QUALLS, CHAD MICHAEL

Born, Lomita, California, August 17, 1978.
Bats Right. Throws Right. Height, 6 feet, 5 inches. Weight, 220 pounds.

Year	Club	Lea	G	IP	W	L	Pct	SO	BB	H	ERA	SAVES
2001	Michigan	Midwest	26	162	15	6	.714	125	31	149	3.72	0
2002	Round Rock	Texas	29	163	6	13	.316	142	67	174	4.36	0
2003	Round Rock	Texas	28	175 1/3	8	11	.421	132	61	174	3.85	0
2004	New Orleans	P.C.	32	106 2/3	3	6	.333	72	30	134	5.57	1
2004	Houston	N.L.	25	33	4	0	1.000	24	8	34	3.55	1

Year Club	Lea	G	IP	W	L	Pct	SO	BB	H	ERA	SAVES
2005 Houston	N.L.	77	79 2/3	6	4	.600	60	23	73	3.28	0
2006 Houston	N.L.	81	88 2/3	7	3	.700	56	28	76	3.76	0
2007 Houston a	N.L.	79	82 2/3	6	5	.545	78	25	84	3.05	5
2008 Arizona	N.L.	77	73 2/3	4	8	.333	71	18	61	2.81	9
2009 Arizona b	N.L.	51	52	2	2	.500	45	7	53	3.63	24
2010 Arizona	N.L.	43	38	1	4	.200	34	15	61	8.29	12
2010 Tampa Bay c-d-e	A.L.	27	21	2	0	1.000	15	6	24	5.57	0
2011 San Diego f	N.L.	77	74 1/3	6	8	.429	43	20	73	3.51	0
2012 Indianapolis	Int.	1	1	0	0	.000	3	0	0	0.00	0
2012 New York	A.L.	8	7 1/3	1	0	1.000	2	3	10	6.14	0
2012 Phil.-Pittsburgh g-h-i-j	N.L.	52	45	1	1	.500	25	11	53	5.20	0
2013 Miami k	N.L.	66	62	5	2	.714	49	19	57	2.61	0
Major League Totals	10 Yrs.	663	657 1/3	45	37	.549	502	183	659	3.79	51
Division Series											
2004 Houston	N.L.	4	4	0	0	.000	3	1	4	6.75	0
2005 Houston	N.L.	2	3	0	0	.000	1	2	5	6.00	0
2010 Tampa Bay	A.L.	2	1 2/3	0	0	.000	0	0	4	10.80	0
Division Series Totals		8	8 2/3	0	0	.000	4	3	13	7.27	0
Championship Series											
2004 Houston	N.L.	2	4	0	1	.000	4	2	8	11.25	0
2005 Houston	N.L.	4	4 2/3	1	0	1.000	4	0	0	0.00	0
Championship Series Totals		6	8 2/3	1	1	.500	8	2	8	5.19	0
World Series Record											
2005 Houston	N.L.	3	5 1/3	0	0	.000	5	2	3	1.69	0

a Traded to Arizona Diamondbacks with pitcher Juan Gutierrez and outfielder Chris Burke for pitcher Jose Valverde, December 14, 2007.
b On disabled list from August 31 to November 20, 2009.
c Traded to Tampa Bay Rays for player to be named later, July 31, 2010.
d Arizona Diamondbacks received pitcher Matt Gorgen to complete trade, September 9, 2010.
e Filed for free agency, November 1, 2010. Signed with San Diego Padres, January 19, 2011.
f Filed for free agency, October 31, 2011. Signed with Philadelphia Phillies, January 31, 2012.
g Sold to New York Yankees, July 1, 2012.
h Traded to Pittsburgh Pirates for outfielder Casey McGehee and cash, July 31, 2012.
i On disabled list from August 25 to September 9, 2012.
j Filed for free agency, November 3, 2012. Signed with Miami Marlins organization, January 25, 2013.
k Filed for free agency, October 31, 2013. Signed with Houston Astros, December 7, 2013.

QUINTANA, JOSE GUILLERMO

Born, Arjona, Colombia, January 24, 1989.
Bats Right. Throws Left. Height, 6 feet. Weight, 215 pounds.

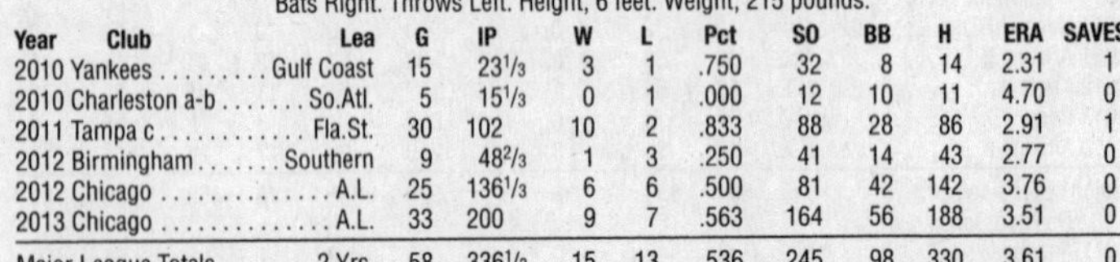

Year Club	Lea	G	IP	W	L	Pct	SO	BB	H	ERA	SAVES
2010 Yankees	Gulf Coast	15	23 1/3	3	1	.750	32	8	14	2.31	1
2010 Charleston a-b	So.Atl.	5	15 1/3	0	1	.000	12	10	11	4.70	0
2011 Tampa c	Fla.St.	30	102	10	2	.833	88	28	86	2.91	1
2012 Birmingham	Southern	9	48 2/3	1	3	.250	41	14	43	2.77	0
2012 Chicago	A.L.	25	136 1/3	6	6	.500	81	42	142	3.76	0
2013 Chicago	A.L.	33	200	9	7	.563	164	56	188	3.51	0
Major League Totals	2 Yrs.	58	336 1/3	15	13	.536	245	98	330	3.61	0

a Released by New York Mets, July 11, 2007. Signed with New York Yankees organization, March 10, 2008.
b Filed for free agency, November 6, 2010, re-signed with New York Yankees organization, December 14, 2010.
c Filed for free agency, November 2, 2011. Signed with Chicago White Sox organization, November 9, 2011.

RAMIREZ, ERASMO JOSE

Born, Rivas, Nicaragua, May 2, 1990.
Bats Right. Throws Right. Height, 5 feet, 11 inches. Weight, 205 pounds.

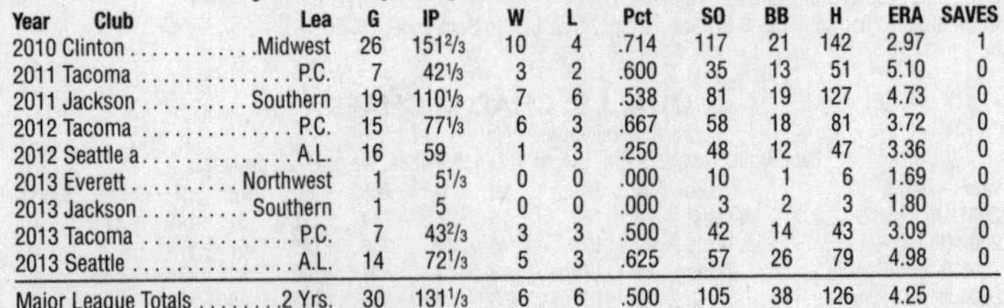

Year Club	Lea	G	IP	W	L	Pct	SO	BB	H	ERA	SAVES
2010 Clinton	Midwest	26	151 2/3	10	4	.714	117	21	142	2.97	1
2011 Tacoma	P.C.	7	42 1/3	3	2	.600	35	13	51	5.10	0
2011 Jackson	Southern	19	110 1/3	7	6	.538	81	19	127	4.73	0
2012 Tacoma	P.C.	15	77 1/3	6	3	.667	58	18	81	3.72	0
2012 Seattle a	A.L.	16	59	1	3	.250	48	12	47	3.36	0
2013 Everett	Northwest	1	5 1/3	0	0	.000	10	1	6	1.69	0
2013 Jackson	Southern	1	5	0	0	.000	3	2	3	1.80	0
2013 Tacoma	P.C.	7	43 2/3	3	3	.500	42	14	43	3.09	0
2013 Seattle	A.L.	14	72 1/3	5	3	.625	57	26	79	4.98	0
Major League Totals	2 Yrs.	30	131 1/3	6	6	.500	105	38	126	4.25	0

a On disabled list from July 1 to August 5, 2012.

RAMOS, ALEJANDRO HINOJOS (A.J.)

Born, Lubbock, Texas, September 20, 1986.
Bats Right. Throws Right. Height, 5 feet, 10 inches. Weight, 210 pounds.

Year	Club	Lea	G	IP	W	L	Pct	SO	BB	H	ERA	SAVES
2009	Jamestown	N.Y.-Penn.	25	33 2/3	2	2	.500	50	14	22	2.14	9
2010	Greensboro	So.Atl.	49	58 1/3	3	7	.300	78	32	40	3.70	28
2011	Jupiter	Fla.St.	49	50 2/3	1	4	.200	71	19	37	1.78	25
2012	Jacksonville	Southern	55	68 2/3	3	3	.500	89	21	36	1.44	21
2012	Miami	N.L.	11	9 1/3	0	0	.000	13	4	8	3.86	0
2013	Miami	N.L.	68	80	3	4	.429	86	43	58	3.15	0
Major League Totals		2 Yrs.	79	89 1/3	3	4	.429	99	47	66	3.22	0

RAMOS, CESAR

Born, Los Angeles, California, June 22, 1984.
Bats Left. Throws Left. Height, 6 feet, 2 inches. Weight, 205 pounds.

Year	Club	Lea	G	IP	W	L	Pct	SO	BB	H	ERA	SAVES
2005	Eugene	Northwest	6	20 2/3	0	1	.000	13	7	27	6.53	0
2005	Fort Wayne	Midwest	7	38 2/3	3	2	.600	32	7	42	4.19	0
2006	Lake Elsinore	Calif.	26	141	7	8	.467	70	44	161	3.70	0
2007	San Antonio	Texas	27	163 2/3	13	9	.591	90	43	153	3.41	0
2008	Portland	P.C.	28	149 2/3	9	11	.450	105	57	183	5.29	0
2009	Padres	Arizona	4	8	0	1	.000	8	0	8	2.25	0
2009	Lake Elsinore	Calif.	2	9	1	0	1.000	6	5	9	1.00	0
2009	Portland	P.C.	15	76 2/3	5	6	.455	45	31	84	3.99	0
2009	San Diego	N.L.	5	14 2/3	0	1	.000	10	4	19	3.07	0
2010	Portland	P.C.	30	96	6	7	.462	63	43	90	3.28	0
2010	San Diego a	N.L.	14	8 1/3	0	1	.000	9	4	18	11.88	0
2011	Durham	Int.	4	4	2	0	1.000	1	2	5	4.50	0
2011	Tampa Bay	A.L.	59	43 2/3	0	1	.000	31	25	36	3.92	0
2012	Durham	Int.	25	62	5	5	.500	46	16	58	3.77	1
2012	Tampa Bay	A.L.	17	30	1	0	1.000	29	10	19	2.10	0
2013	Tampa Bay	A.L.	48	67 1/3	2	2	.500	53	22	66	4.14	1
Major League Totals		5 Yrs.	143	164	3	5	.375	132	65	158	4.01	1

a Traded to Tampa Bay Rays with pitcher Adam Russell, pitcher Brandon Gomes and infielder Cole Figueroa for infielder Jason Bartlett and cash, December 17, 2010.

REDMOND, TODD RICHARD

Born, St.Petersburg, Florida, May 17, 1985.
Bats Right. Throws Right. Height, 6 feet, 3 inches. Weight, 235 pounds.

Year	Club	Lea	G	IP	W	L	Pct	SO	BB	H	ERA	SAVES
2005	Williamsport	N.Y.-Penn.	15	72 2/3	1	2	.333	63	21	62	1.98	0
2006	Hickory	So.Atl.	27	160 1/3	13	6	.684	148	33	137	2.75	0
2007	Lynchburg	Carolina	25	142 2/3	7	12	.368	95	32	151	4.54	0
2007	Altoona	Eastern	3	17 1/3	1	1	.500	12	3	15	3.12	0
2008	Mississippi a	Southern	28	166 1/3	13	5	.722	133	33	164	3.52	0
2009	Gwinnett	Int.	27	145	9	6	.600	106	47	152	4.41	0
2010	Gwinnett	Int.	28	162 2/3	9	10	.474	142	44	156	4.26	0
2011	Gwinnett	Int.	28	169 2/3	10	8	.556	142	47	152	2.92	0
2012	Gwinnett	Int.	18	105 2/3	6	6	.500	96	28	107	3.58	0
2012	Louisville b	Int.	8	43	2	5	.286	40	11	43	3.77	0
2012	Cincinnati	N.L.	1	3 1/3	0	1	.000	2	5	7	10.80	0
2013	Buffalo	Int.	6	26 2/3	3	1	.750	29	5	29	5.06	0
2013	Toronto c-d	A.L.	17	77	4	3	.571	76	23	70	4.32	0
Major League Totals		2 Yrs.	18	80 1/3	4	4	.500	78	28	77	4.59	0

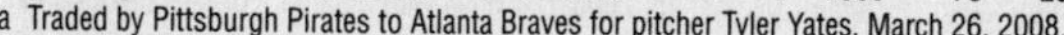

a Traded by Pittsburgh Pirates to Atlanta Braves for pitcher Tyler Yates, March 26, 2008.
b Traded to Cincinnati Reds for catcher Paul Janish, July 14, 2012.
c Claimed on waivers by Baltimore Orioles, February 8, 2013.
d Claimed on waivers by Toronto Blue Jays, March 22, 2013.

REED, ADDISON DEVON

Born, Montclair, California, December 27, 1988.
Bats Left. Throws Right. Height, 6 feet, 4 inches. Weight, 220 pounds.

Year	Club	Lea	G	IP	W	L	Pct	SO	BB	H	ERA	SAVES
2010	Great Falls	Pioneer	13	30	1	0	1.000	44	6	17	1.80	1
2011	Kannapolis	So.Atl.	4	8	0	0	.000	11	1	4	1.13	0
2011	Winston-Salem	Carolina	15	28 1/3	2	0	1.000	39	4	21	1.59	1
2011	Birmingham	Southern	13	20 2/3	0	1	.000	33	6	10	0.87	2

Year	Club	Lea	G	IP	W	L	Pct	SO	BB	H	ERA	SAVES
2011	Charlotte	Int.	11	$21\frac{1}{3}$	0	0	.000	28	3	8	1.27	2
2011	Chicago	A.L.	6	$7\frac{1}{3}$	0	0	.000	12	1	10	3.68	0
2012	Chicago	A.L.	62	55	3	2	.600	54	18	57	4.75	29
2013	Chicago a	A.L.	68	$71\frac{1}{3}$	5	4	.556	72	23	56	3.79	40
Major League Totals		3 Yrs.	136	$133\frac{2}{3}$	8	6	.571	138	42	123	4.17	69

a Traded to Arizona Diamondbacks for infielder Matt Davidson, December 16, 2013.

REYNOLDS, MATTHEW PAUL (MATT)

Born, Knoxville, Tennessee, October 2, 1984.
Bats Left. Throws Left. Height, 6 feet, 5 inches. Weight, 240 pounds.

Year	Club	Lea	G	IP	W	L	Pct	SO	BB	H	ERA	SAVES
2007	Tri-City	Northwest	20	35	1	4	.200	27	4	37	3.60	0
2008	Asheville	So.Atl.	42	57	6	2	.750	53	14	49	2.53	2
2009	Modesto	Calif.	39	49	5	3	.625	58	8	32	1.29	3
2009	Tulsa	Texas	21	$25\frac{2}{3}$	1	2	.333	29	9	23	4.21	1
2010	Colorado Springs	P.C.	50	55	1	3	.250	67	16	49	2.62	7
2010	Colorado	N.L.	21	18	1	0	1.000	17	5	10	2.00	0
2011	Colorado	N.L.	73	$50\frac{2}{3}$	1	2	.333	50	18	48	4.09	0
2012	Colorado a	N.L.	71	$57\frac{1}{3}$	3	1	.750	51	17	65	4.40	0
2013	Arizona b	N.L.	30	$27\frac{1}{3}$	0	2	.000	23	5	25	1.98	2
Major League Totals		4 Yrs.	195	$153\frac{1}{3}$	5	5	.500	141	45	148	3.58	2

a Traded to Arizona Diamondbacks for infielder Ryan Wheeler, November 20, 2012.
b On disabled list from June 10 to November 1, 2013.

RICE, SCOTT ADAM

Born, Simi Valley, California, September 21, 1981.
Bats Left. Throws Left. Height, 6 feet, 6 inches. Weight, 225 pounds.

Year	Club	Lea	G	IP	W	L	Pct	SO	BB	H	ERA	SAVES
1999	Orioles	Gulf Coast	9	$17\frac{1}{3}$	1	4	.200	14	20	26	10.38	0
2000	Orioles	Gulf Coast	13	57	1	6	.143	34	48	61	5.21	0
2001	Bluefield	Appal.	12	$63\frac{1}{3}$	4	3	.571	53	28	58	4.12	0
2002	Aberdeen	N.Y.-Penn.	11	$56\frac{1}{3}$	1	7	.125	41	24	66	4.47	1
2002	Delmarva	So.Atl.	18	40	0	6	.000	22	21	45	5.40	3
2003	Delmarva	So.Atl.	32	$47\frac{2}{3}$	4	1	.800	53	12	21	0.94	5
2003	Frederick	Carolina	25	31	1	3	.250	27	14	34	3.19	0
2004	Bowie	Eastern	41	96	6	5	.545	61	40	94	3.66	1
2005	Bowie a	Eastern	57	$74\frac{1}{3}$	4	1	.800	42	32	68	3.27	1
2006	Ottawa b	Int.	52	$65\frac{1}{3}$	3	4	.429	38	28	65	3.86	1
2007	Rangers	Arizona	4	4	0	0	.000	7	1	2	0.00	0
2007	Clinton	Midwest	3	4	0	0	.000	4	3	1	0.00	0
2007	Frisco	Texas	1	2	0	0	.000	0	0	4	0.00	0
2008	Long Island c-d	Atlantic	7	10	2	2	.500	11	5	23	15.68	0
2009	San Antonio e	Texas	25	$29\frac{1}{3}$	1	4	.200	21	22	33	7.36	0
2009	Newark f	Atlantic	9	13	2	1	.667	9	8	19	9.00	0
2010	Tulsa g	Texas	35	$46\frac{2}{3}$	2	0	1.000	33	18	23	0.96	4
2010	Colorado Springs h	P.C.	23	$22\frac{2}{3}$	0	1	.000	15	15	27	6.75	3
2011	York i	Atlantic	15	15	1	0	1.000	15	4	9	2.45	1
2011	Chattanooga j	Southern	34	$50\frac{2}{3}$	4	4	.500	42	17	42	1.95	1
2012	Albuquerque k	P.C.	54	$59\frac{1}{3}$	2	3	.400	47	22	58	4.40	9
2013	New York l	N.L.	73	51	4	5	.444	41	27	42	3.71	0

a Filed for free agency from Baltimore Orioles, October 15, 2005, re-signed with Baltimore Orioles organization, December 1, 2005.
b Filed for free agency, October 15, 2006. Signed with Texas Rangers organization, November 29, 2006.
c Filed for free agency, October 29, 2007. Signed with Los Angeles Dodgers organization, March 2, 2008.
d Released by Los Angeles Dodgers, March 28, 2008. Signed with Long Island (Atlantic), April 2008.
e Signed with San Diego Padres organization, May 20, 2009.
f Released by San Diego Padres, August 7, 2009. Signed with Newark (Atlantic), August 2009.
g Signed with Colorado Rockies organization, March 6, 2010.
h Filed for free agency, November 6, 2010. Signed with Chicago Cubs organization, November 17, 2010.
i Released by Chicago Cubs, March 23, 2011. Signed with York (Atlantic), April 2011.
j Signed with Los Angeles Dodgers organization, June 7, 2011.
k Filed for free agency, November 3, 2012. Signed with New York Mets organization, November 16, 2012.
l On disabled list from September 9 to October 31, 2013.

RICHARD, CLAYTON COLBY

Born, Lafayette, Indiana, September 12, 1983.
Bats Left. Throws Left. Height, 6 feet, 5 inches. Weight, 240 pounds.

Year	Club	Lea	G	IP	W	L	Pct	SO	BB	H	ERA	SAVES
2005	Great Falls	Pioneer	10	41	2	1	.667	39	12	37	2.85	0
2005	Kannapolis	So.Atl.	3	10 1/3	0	1	.000	8	1	14	5.23	0
2006	Winston-Salem	Carolina	4	23 2/3	1	3	.250	12	6	29	4.56	0
2006	Kannapolis	So.Atl.	18	95 2/3	6	6	.500	54	28	117	3.67	0
2007	Winston-Salem	Carolina	28	161 1/3	8	12	.400	99	59	159	3.63	0
2008	Birmingham	Southern	13	83 2/3	6	6	.500	53	16	66	2.47	0
2008	Charlotte	Int.	7	44	6	0	1.000	33	4	33	2.45	0
2008	Chicago a	A.L.	13	47 2/3	2	5	.286	29	13	61	6.04	0
2009	Chicago	A.L.	26	89	4	3	.571	66	37	94	4.65	0
2009	San Diego b	N.L.	12	64	5	2	.714	48	34	60	4.08	0
2010	San Diego	N.L.	33	201 2/3	14	9	.609	153	78	206	3.75	0
2011	San Diego c	N.L.	18	99 2/3	5	9	.357	53	38	104	3.88	0
2012	San Diego	N.L.	33	218 2/3	14	14	.500	107	42	*228	3.99	0
2013	Tucson	P.C.	2	12	0	1	.000	12	0	10	2.25	0
2013	San Diego d-e	N.L.	12	52 2/3	2	5	.286	24	21	65	7.01	0
Major League Totals		6 Yrs.	147	773 1/3	46	47	.495	480	263	818	4.33	0
	Division Series											
2008	Chicago	A.L.	2	6 1/3	0	0	.000	6	3	5	1.42	0

a On disabled list from March 22 to May 29, 2008.
b Traded to San Diego Padres with pitcher Aaron Poreda, pitcher Adam Russell and pitcher Dexter Carter for pitcher Jake Peavy, July 31, 2009.
c On disabled list from July 5 to October 28, 2011.
d On disabled list from May 5 to May 27 and June 22 to October 30, 2013.
e Filed for free agency, October 28, 2013.

RICHARDS, GARRETT THOMAS

Born, Riverside, California, May 27, 1988.
Bats Right. Throws Right. Height, 6 feet, 3 inches. Weight, 215 pounds.

Year	Club	Lea	G	IP	W	L	Pct	SO	BB	H	ERA	SAVES
2009	Orem	Pioneer	8	35 1/3	3	1	.750	30	4	37	1.53	0
2010	Rancho Cucamonga	Calif.	7	34 2/3	4	1	.800	41	9	38	3.89	0
2010	Cedar Rapids	Midwest	19	108 1/3	8	4	.667	108	34	92	3.41	0
2011	Arkansas	Texas	22	143	12	2	.857	103	40	123	3.15	0
2011	Los Angeles a	A.L.	7	14	0	2	.000	9	7	16	5.79	0
2012	Salt Lake	P.C.	14	77	7	3	.700	65	35	87	4.21	0
2012	Los Angeles	A.L.	30	71	4	3	.571	47	34	77	4.69	1
2013	Los Angeles	A.L.	47	145	7	8	.467	101	44	151	4.16	1
Major League Totals		3 Yrs.	84	230	11	13	.458	157	85	244	4.42	2

a On disabled list from August 16 to September 6, 2011.

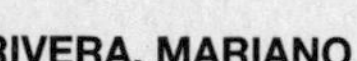

RIVERA, MARIANO

Born, Panama City, Panama, November 29, 1969.
Bats Right. Throws Right. Height, 6 feet, 2 inches. Weight, 195 pounds.

Year	Club	Lea	G	IP	W	L	Pct	SO	BB	H	ERA	SAVES
1990	Yankees	Gulf Coast	22	52	5	1	.833	58	7	17	0.17	1
1991	Greensboro	So. Atl.	29	114 2/3	4	9	.308	123	36	103	2.75	0
1992	Ft. Lauderdale	Fla. St.	10	59 1/3	5	3	.625	42	5	40	2.28	0
1993	Yankees	Gulf Coast	2	4	0	1	.000	6	1	2	2.25	0
1993	Greensboro	So. Atl.	10	39 1/3	1	0	1.000	32	15	31	2.06	0
1994	Tampa	Fla. St.	7	36 2/3	3	0	1.000	27	12	34	2.21	0
1994	Albany	Eastern	9	63 1/3	3	0	1.000	39	8	58	2.27	0
1994	Columbus	Int.	6	31	4	2	.667	23	10	34	5.81	0
1995	Columbus	Int.	7	30	2	2	.500	30	3	25	2.10	0
1995	New York	A.L.	19	67	5	3	.625	51	30	71	5.51	0
1996	New York	A.L.	61	107 2/3	8	3	.727	130	34	73	2.09	5
1997	New York	A.L.	66	71 2/3	6	4	.600	68	20	65	1.88	43
1998	New York a	A.L.	54	61 1/3	3	0	1.000	36	17	48	1.91	36
1999	New York	A.L.	66	69	4	3	.571	52	18	43	1.83	*45
2000	New York	A.L.	66	75 2/3	7	4	.636	58	25	58	2.85	36
2001	New York	A.L.	71	80 2/3	4	6	.400	83	12	61	2.34	*50
2002	Yankees	Gulf Coast	1	2	0	0	.000	2	1	2	0.00	0
2002	New York b	A.L.	45	46	1	4	.200	41	11	35	2.74	28
2003	New York c	A.L.	64	70 2/3	5	2	.714	63	10	61	1.66	40
2004	New York	A.L.	74	78 2/3	4	2	.667	66	20	65	1.94	*53
2005	New York	A.L.	71	78 1/3	7	4	.636	80	18	50	1.38	43

Year	Club	Lea	G	IP	W	L	Pct	SO	BB	H	ERA	SAVES
2006	New York	A.L.	63	75	5	5	.500	55	11	61	1.80	34
2007	New York d	A.L.	67	$71\frac{1}{3}$	3	4	.429	74	12	68	3.15	30
2008	New York	A.L.	64	$70\frac{2}{3}$	6	5	.545	77	6	41	1.40	39
2009	New York	A.L.	66	$66\frac{1}{3}$	3	3	.500	72	12	48	1.76	44
2010	New York e	A.L.	61	60	3	3	.500	45	11	39	1.80	33
2011	New York	A.L.	64	$61\frac{1}{3}$	1	2	.333	60	8	47	1.91	44
2012	New York f-g	A.L.	9	$8\frac{1}{3}$	1	1	.500	8	2	6	2.16	5
2013	New York h	A.L.	64	64	6	2	.750	54	9	58	2.11	44
Major League Totals		19 Yrs.	1115	$1283\frac{2}{3}$	82	60	.577	1173	286	998	2.21	652
	Division Series											
1995	New York	A.L.	3	$5\frac{1}{3}$	1	0	1.000	8	1	3	0.00	0
1996	New York	A.L.	2	$4\frac{2}{3}$	0	0	.000	1	1	0	0.00	0
1997	New York	A.L.	2	2	0	0	.000	1	0	2	4.50	1
1998	New York	A.L.	3	$3\frac{1}{3}$	0	0	.000	2	1	1	0.00	2
1999	New York	A.L.	2	3	0	0	.000	3	0	1	0.00	2
2000	New York	A.L.	3	5	0	0	.000	2	0	2	0.00	3
2001	New York	A.L.	3	5	0	0	.000	4	0	4	0.00	2
2002	New York	A.L.	1	1	0	0	.000	0	0	1	0.00	1
2003	New York	A.L.	2	4	0	0	.000	4	0	0	0.00	2
2004	New York	A.L.	4	$5\frac{2}{3}$	1	0	1.000	2	0	2	0.00	0
2005	New York	A.L.	2	3	0	0	.000	2	1	1	3.00	2
2006	New York	A.L.	1	1	0	0	.000	0	0	1	0.00	0
2007	New York	A.L.	3	$4\frac{2}{3}$	0	0	.000	6	1	2	0.00	0
2009	New York	A.L.	3	$3\frac{2}{3}$	0	0	.000	7	1	4	0.00	1
2010	New York	A.L.	3	$3\frac{1}{3}$	0	0	.000	1	0	2	0.00	2
2011	New York	A.L.	2	$1\frac{1}{3}$	0	0	.000	1	0	0	0.00	0
Division Series Totals			39	56	2	0	1.000	44	6	26	0.32	18
	Championship Series											
1996	New York	A.L.	2	4	1	0	1.000	5	1	6	0.00	0
1998	New York	A.L.	4	$5\frac{2}{3}$	0	0	.000	5	1	0	0.00	1
1999	New York	A.L.	3	$4\frac{2}{3}$	1	0	1.000	3	0	5	0.00	2
2000	New York	A.L.	3	$4\frac{2}{3}$	0	0	.000	1	0	4	1.93	1
2001	New York	A.L.	4	$4\frac{2}{3}$	1	0	1.000	3	1	2	1.93	2
2003	New York	A.L.	4	8	1	0	1.000	6	0	5	1.13	2
2004	New York	A.L.	5	7	0	0	.000	6	2	6	1.29	2
2009	New York	A.L.	5	7	0	0	.000	4	2	3	1.29	2
2010	New York	A.L.	3	3	0	0	.000	1	0	2	0.00	1
Championship Series Totals			33	$48\frac{2}{3}$	4	0	1.000	34	7	33	0.92	13
	World Series Record											
1996	New York	A.L.	4	$5\frac{2}{3}$	0	0	.000	4	3	4	1.59	0
1998	New York	A.L.	3	$4\frac{1}{3}$	0	0	.000	4	0	5	0.00	3
1999	New York	A.L.	3	$4\frac{2}{3}$	1	0	1.000	3	1	3	0.00	2
2000	New York	A.L.	4	6	0	0	.000	7	1	4	3.00	2
2001	New York	A.L.	4	$6\frac{1}{3}$	1	1	.500	7	1	6	1.42	0
2003	New York	A.L.	2	4	0	0	.000	4	0	2	0.00	1
2009	New York	A.L.	4	$5\frac{1}{3}$	0	0	.000	3	2	3	0.00	2
World Series Totals			24	$36\frac{1}{3}$	2	1	.667	32	8	27	0.99	11

a On disabled list from April 6 to April 24, 1998.
b On disabled list from June 9 to June 25 and July 21 to August 8 and August 18 to September 20, 2002.
c On disabled list from March 25 to April 29, 2003.
d Filed for free agency, October 30, 2007, re-signed with New York Yankees, December 17, 2007.
e Filed for free agency, November 1, 2010, re-signed with New York Yankees, December 14, 2010.
f On disabled list from May 4 to October 29, 2012.
g Filed for free agency, November 3, 2012, re-signed with New York Yankees, November 30, 2012.
h Announced retirement, October 31, 2013.

ROBERTSON, DAVID

Born, Birmingham, Alabama, April 9, 1985.
Bats Right. Throws Right. Height, 5 feet, 11 inches. Weight, 190 pounds.

Year	Club	Lea	G	IP	W	L	Pct	SO	BB	H	ERA	SAVES
2007	Trenton	Eastern	2	4	0	0	.000	9	2	2	2.25	0
2007	Tampa	Fla.St.	18	$33\frac{1}{3}$	3	1	.750	37	15	18	1.08	1
2007	Charleston	So.Atl.	24	47	5	2	.714	67	15	25	0.77	3
2008	Trenton	Eastern	9	$18\frac{2}{3}$	0	0	.000	26	6	8	0.96	2
2008	Scranton/WB	Int.	21	35	4	0	1.000	51	17	20	2.06	1
2008	New York	A.L.	25	$30\frac{1}{3}$	4	0	1.000	36	15	29	5.34	0
2009	Scranton/WB	Int.	8	$14\frac{2}{3}$	0	3	.000	25	6	10	1.84	2
2009	New York	A.L.	45	$43\frac{2}{3}$	2	1	.667	63	23	36	3.30	1

Year Club	Lea	G	IP	W	L	Pct	SO	BB	H	ERA	SAVES
2010 New York	A.L.	64	61⅓	4	5	.444	71	33	59	3.82	1
2011 New York	A.L.	70	66⅔	4	0	1.000	100	35	40	1.08	1
2012 Scranton-WB	Int.	2	2	0	0	.000	2	0	0	0.00	0
2012 New York a	A.L.	65	60⅔	2	7	.222	81	19	52	2.67	2
2013 New York	A.L.	70	66⅓	5	1	.833	77	18	51	2.04	3
Major League Totals	6 Yrs.	339	329	21	14	.600	428	143	267	2.76	8
Division Series											
2009 New York	A.L.	1	1	1	0	1.000	0	0	1	0.00	0
2010 New York	A.L.	2	0⅔	0	0	.000	1	1	0	0.00	0
2011 New York	A.L.	2	2	0	0	.000	2	0	0	0.00	0
2012 New York	A.L.	4	4⅓	1	0	1.000	5	0	1	0.00	0
Division Series Totals		9	8	2	0	1.000	8	1	2	0.00	0
Championship Series											
2009 New York	A.L.	2	2	1	0	1.000	1	2	1	0.00	0
2010 New York	A.L.	4	2⅔	0	0	.000	4	1	8	20.25	0
2012 New York	A.L.	2	2	0	0	.000	2	0	2	4.50	0
Championship Series Totals		8	6⅔	1	0	1.000	7	3	11	9.45	0
World Series Record											
2009 New York	A.L.	2	2⅓	0	0	.000	2	1	2	0.00	0

a On disabled list from May 14 to June 14, 2012.

RODNEY, FERNANDO

Born, Samana, Dominican Republic, March 17, 1977.
Bats Right. Throws Right. Height, 5 feet, 11 inches. Weight, 220 pounds.

Year Club	Lea	G	IP	W	L	Pct	SO	BB	H	ERA	SAVES
1998 Detroit	Dominican	11	32	1	3	.250	37	19	25	3.38	1
1999 Lakeland	Fla.St.	4	6⅓	1	0	1.000	5	1	7	1.42	2
1999 Tigers	Gulf Coast	22	30	3	3	.500	39	21	20	2.40	9
2000 West Michigan	Midwest	22	82⅔	6	4	.600	56	35	74	2.94	0
2001 Erie	Eastern	4	6⅓	0	0	.000	8	3	7	4.26	1
2001 Lakeland	Fla.St.	16	55⅓	4	2	.667	44	19	53	3.42	0
2001 Tigers	Gulf Coast	1	1	0	0	.000	1	1	0	0.00	0
2002 Erie	Eastern	21	20⅓	1	0	1.000	18	5	14	1.33	11
2002 Detroit	A.L.	20	18	1	3	.250	10	10	25	6.00	0
2002 Toledo	Int.	20	22⅓	1	1	.500	25	9	13	0.81	4
2003 Toledo	Int.	38	40⅔	1	1	.500	58	13	22	1.33	23
2003 Detroit	A.L.	27	29⅔	1	3	.250	33	17	35	6.07	3
2004 Detroit a	A.L.			INJURED—Did Not Play							
2005 Toledo	Int.	3	3	0	0	.000	4	1	2	3.00	0
2005 Detroit b	A.L.	39	44	2	3	.400	42	17	39	2.86	9
2006 Detroit	A.L.	63	71⅔	7	4	.636	65	34	51	3.52	7
2007 Toledo	Int.	4	3	0	0	.000	4	2	4	0.00	0
2007 Detroit c	A.L.	48	50⅔	2	6	.250	54	21	46	4.26	1
2008 Toledo	Int.	4	5⅓	1	0	1.000	8	5	3	6.75	0
2008 Detroit d	A.L.	38	40⅓	0	6	.000	49	30	34	4.91	13
2009 Detroit e	A.L.	73	75⅔	2	5	.286	61	41	70	4.40	37
2010 Los Angeles	A.L.	72	68	4	3	.571	53	35	70	4.24	14
2011 Inland Empire	Calif.	2	2	0	0	.000	3	1	2	9.00	0
2011 Los Angeles f-g	A.L.	39	32	3	5	.375	26	28	26	4.50	3
2012 Tampa Bay	A.L.	76	74⅔	2	2	.500	76	15	43	0.60	48
2013 Tampa Bay h	A.L.	68	66⅔	5	4	.556	82	36	53	3.38	37
Major League Totals	11 Yrs.	563	571⅓	29	44	.397	551	284	492	3.70	172
Wild Card Playoff											
2013 Tampa Bay	A.L.	1	1	0	0	.000	2	0	0	0.00	0
Division Series											
2013 Tampa Bay	A.L.	2	1⅓	1	0	1.000	2	3	1	13.50	0
Championship Series											
2006 Detroit	A.L.	3	3⅔	0	0	.000	4	1	1	0.00	0
World Series Record											
2006 Detroit	A.L.	4	4	0	0	.000	5	4	5	4.50	0

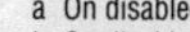

a On disabled list from March 26 to October 4, 2004.
b On disabled list from March 29 to June 9, 2005.
c On disabled list from May 21 to June 5 and June 24 to August 4, 2007.
d On disabled list from March 30 to June 16, 2008.
e Filed for free agency, November 5, 2009. Signed with Los Angeles Angels, December 24, 2009.
f On disabled list from June 9 to July 22, 2011.
g Filed for free agency, October 30, 2011. Signed with Tampa Bay Rays, January 4, 2012.
h Filed for free agency, October 31, 2013.

RODRIGUEZ, FRANCISCO JOSE

Born, Caracas, Venezuela, January 7, 1982.
Bats Right. Throws Right. Height, 6 feet. Weight, 195 pounds.

Year Club	Lea	G	IP	W	L	Pct	SO	BB	H	ERA	SAVES
1999 Boise	Northwest	1	5	1	0	1.000	6	1	3	5.40	0
1999 Butte	Pioneer	12	51 2/3	1	1	.500	69	21	33	3.31	0
2000 Lake Elsinore	California	13	64	4	4	.500	79	32	43	2.81	0
2001 Rancho Cucamonga	California	20	113 2/3	5	7	.417	147	55	127	5.38	0
2002 Arkansas	Texas	23	41 1/3	3	3	.500	61	15	32	1.96	9
2002 Salt Lake	P.C.	27	42	2	3	.400	59	13	30	2.57	6
2002 Anaheim	A.L.	5	5 2/3	0	0	.000	13	2	3	0.00	0
2003 Anaheim	A.L.	59	86	8	3	.727	95	35	50	3.03	2
2004 Anaheim	A.L.	69	84	4	1	.800	123	33	51	1.82	12
2005 Los Angeles a	A.L.	66	67 1/3	2	5	.286	91	32	45	2.67	*45
2006 Los Angeles	A.L.	69	73	2	3	.400	98	28	52	1.73	*47
2007 Los Angeles	A.L.	64	67 1/3	5	2	.714	90	34	50	2.81	40
2008 Los Angeles b	A.L.	*76	68 1/3	2	3	.400	77	34	54	2.24	*62
2009 New York	N.L.	70	68	3	6	.333	73	38	51	3.71	35
2010 New York	N.L.	53	57 1/3	4	2	.667	67	21	45	2.20	25
2011 New York-Milwaukee c-d-e	N.L.	73	71 2/3	6	2	.750	79	26	67	2.64	23
2012 Milwaukee f	N.L.	78	72	2	7	.222	72	31	65	4.38	3
2013 Brevard County	Fla.St.	2	2	0	0	.000	4	1	0	0.00	0
2013 Nashville	P.C.	2	2	0	0	.000	3	2	1	0.00	0
2013 Milwaukee	N.L.	25	24 2/3	1	1	.500	26	9	17	1.09	10
2013 Baltimore g-h	A.L.	23	22	2	1	.667	28	5	25	4.50	0
Major League Totals	12 Yrs.	730	767 1/3	41	36	.532	932	328	575	2.70	304
Division Series											
2002 Anaheim	A.L.	3	5 2/3	2	0	1.000	8	2	2	3.18	0
2004 Anaheim	A.L.	2	4 2/3	0	2	.000	5	3	4	3.86	0
2005 Los Angeles	A.L.	3	3 1/3	0	0	.000	2	0	5	2.70	2
2007 Los Angeles	A.L.	1	0 1/3	0	0	.000	1	1	1	54.00	0
2008 Los Angeles	A.L.	2	2 1/3	0	1	.000	2	2	5	7.71	0
2011 Milwaukee	N.L.	2	2	0	0	.000	4	3	2	0.00	0
Division Series Totals		13	18 1/3	2	3	.400	22	11	19	4.42	2
Championship Series											
2002 Anaheim	A.L.	4	4 1/3	2	0	1.000	7	2	2	0.00	0
2005 Los Angeles	A.L.	2	2 1/3	0	0	.000	3	3	2	0.00	1
2011 Milwaukee	N.L.	3	3	0	0	.000	4	1	3	3.00	0
Championship Series Totals		9	9 2/3	2	0	1.000	14	6	7	0.93	1
World Series Record											
2002 Anaheim	A.L.	4	8 2/3	1	1	.500	13	1	6	2.08	0

a On disabled list from May 15 to June 1, 2005.
b Filed for free agency, November 3, 2008. Signed with New York Mets, December 10, 2008.
c Traded to Milwaukee Brewers with cash for two players to be named later, July 13, 2011. New York Mets received pitcher Daniel Ray Herrera and pitcher Adrian Rosario to complete trade, September 1, 2011.
d On disabled list from May 10 to October 30, 2011.
e Filed for free agency, October 30, 2011. Accepted arbitration, December 7, 2011.
f Filed for free agency, November 3, 2012, re-signed with Milwaukee Brewers organization, April 17, 2013.
g Traded to Baltimore Orioles for infielder Nick Delmonico, July 23, 2013.
h Filed for free agency, October 31, 2013.

RODRIGUEZ, STEVEN FRANCIS (PACO)

Born, Miami, Florida, April 16, 1991.
Bats Left. Throws Left. Height, 6 feet, 3 inches. Weight, 220 pounds.

Year Club	Lea	G	IP	W	L	Pct	SO	BB	H	ERA	SAVES
2012 Great Lakes	Midwest	6	6	0	0	.000	10	0	4	0.00	2
2012 Chattanooga	Southern	15	13 2/3	1	0	1.000	22	6	7	1.32	3
2012 Los Angeles	N.L.	11	6 2/3	0	1	.000	6	4	3	1.35	0
2013 Los Angeles	N.L.	76	54 1/3	3	4	.429	63	19	30	2.32	2
Major League Totals	2 Yrs.	87	61	3	5	.375	69	23	33	2.21	2
Division Series											
2013 Los Angeles	N.L.	2	0 2/3	0	0	.000	1	2	4	27.00	0

RODRIGUEZ, WANDY FULTON

Born, Santiago Rodriguez, Dominican Republic, January 18, 1979.
Bats Both. Throws Left. Height, 5 feet, 11 inches. Weight, 160 pounds.

Year	Club	Lea	G	IP	W	L	Pct	SO	BB	H	ERA	SAVES
2001	Martinsville	Appal.	12	74	4	3	.571	67	20	54	1.58	0
2002	Lexington	So.Atl.	28	159⅓	11	4	.733	137	44	167	3.78	0
2003	Salem	Carolina	20	111	8	7	.533	72	41	102	3.49	0
2004	Round Rock	Texas	26	142⅔	11	6	.647	115	57	159	4.48	0
2005	Corpus Christi	Texas	1	3⅓	0	0	.000	3	2	3	2.70	0
2005	Round Rock	P.C.	8	46⅓	4	2	.667	48	16	43	3.69	0
2005	Houston	N.L.	25	128⅔	10	10	.500	80	53	135	5.53	0
2006	Round Rock	P.C.	5	26	2	2	.500	13	13	32	6.92	0
2006	Houston	N.L.	30	135⅔	9	10	.474	98	63	154	5.64	0
2007	Houston	N.L.	31	182⅔	9	13	.409	158	62	179	4.58	0
2008	Corpus Christi	Texas	1	6	0	0	.000	0	1	4	1.50	0
2008	Houston a	N.L.	25	137⅓	9	7	.563	131	44	136	3.54	0
2009	Houston	N.L.	33	205⅔	14	12	.538	193	63	192	3.02	0
2010	Houston	N.L.	32	195	11	12	.478	178	68	183	3.60	0
2011	Corpus Christi	Texas	1	4	0	0	.000	2	1	6	2.25	0
2011	Houston b	N.L.	30	191	11	11	.500	166	69	182	3.49	0
2012	Houston-Pittsburgh c	N.L.	34	205⅔	12	13	.480	139	56	205	3.76	0
2013	Indianapolis	Int.	1	4	0	0	.000	5	1	4	2.25	0
2013	Pittsburgh d	N.L.	12	62⅔	6	4	.600	46	12	58	3.59	0
Major League Totals		9 Yrs.	252	1444⅓	91	92	.497	1189	490	1424	4.01	0
	Division Series											
2005	Houston	N.L.	1	1	0	0	.000	2	0	1	9.00	0
	World Series Record											
2005	Houston	N.L.	2	3⅔	0	1	.000	2	5	4	2.45	0

a On disabled list from April 20 to May 28, 2008.
b On disabled list from May 23 to June 13, 2011.
c Traded to Pittsburgh Pirates with cash for pitcher Rudy Owens, pitcher Colton Cain and outfielder Robbie Grossman, July 25, 2012.
d On disabled list from June 6 to November 1, 2013.

ROENICKE, JOSHUA JAMES (JOSH)

Born, Baltimore, Maryland, August 4, 1982.
Bats Right. Throws Right. Height, 6 feet, 3 inches. Weight, 200 pounds.

Year	Club	Lea	G	IP	W	L	Pct	SO	BB	H	ERA	SAVES
2006	Reds	Gulf Coast	7	7⅔	1	0	1.000	9	3	8	1.17	0
2006	Billings	Pioneer	14	15⅔	1	0	1.000	24	12	10	6.32	6
2007	Sarasota	Fla.St.	27	27⅔	2	1	.667	41	15	23	3.25	16
2007	Chattanooga	Southern	19	19	1	1	.500	15	6	12	0.95	8
2008	Chattanooga	Southern	22	22	4	2	.667	28	12	21	3.27	10
2008	Louisville	Int.	35	39	2	0	1.000	43	14	34	2.54	3
2008	Cincinnati	N.L.	5	3	0	0	.000	6	2	6	9.00	0
2009	Louisville	Int.	27	28	1	0	1.000	32	6	30	2.57	12
2009	Cincinnati	N.L.	11	13⅓	0	0	.000	14	4	13	2.70	0
2009	Toronto a	A.L.	13	17⅔	0	0	.000	19	12	19	7.13	0
2010	Las Vegas	P.C.	36	59⅓	9	1	.900	54	25	61	3.64	1
2010	Toronto	A.L.	16	19	1	0	1.000	18	13	18	5.68	0
2011	Las Vegas	P.C.	16	22⅓	1	3	.250	20	15	25	6.04	0
2011	Colorado Springs	P.C.	23	30⅔	0	1	.000	22	7	30	3.52	0
2011	Colorado b	N.L.	19	16⅔	0	0	.000	12	7	14	3.78	0
2012	Colorado c	N.L.	63	88⅔	4	2	.667	54	43	85	3.25	1
2013	Minnesota	A.L.	63	62	3	1	.750	45	36	63	4.35	1
Major League Totals		6 Yrs.	190	220⅓	8	3	.727	168	117	218	4.17	2

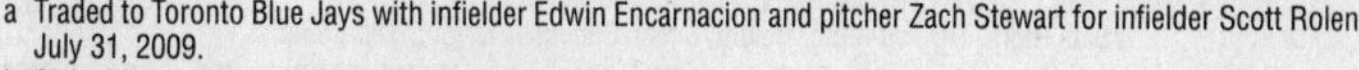

a Traded to Toronto Blue Jays with infielder Edwin Encarnacion and pitcher Zach Stewart for infielder Scott Rolen, July 31, 2009.
b Claimed on waivers by Colorado Rockies, June 2, 2011.
c Claimed on waivers by Minnesota Twins, November 2, 2012.

ROGERS, ESMIL ANTONIO

Born, Santo Domingo, Dominican Republic, August 14, 1985.
Bats Right. Throws Right. Height, 6 feet, 1 inch. Weight, 190 pounds.

Year	Club	Lea	G	IP	W	L	Pct	SO	BB	H	ERA	SAVES
2006	Casper	Pioneer	15	63⅓	3	6	.333	40	24	78	6.96	0
2007	Asheville	So.Atl.	19	117⅔	7	4	.636	90	42	125	3.75	0
2008	Modesto	Calif.	25	143⅔	9	7	.563	116	45	146	3.95	0
2009	Tulsa	Texas	15	94⅓	8	2	.800	83	19	87	2.48	0

Year	Club	Lea	G	IP	W	L	Pct	SO	BB	H	ERA	SAVES
2009	Colorado Springs	P.C.	12	60²/₃	3	5	.375	46	35	77	7.42	0
2009	Colorado	N.L.	1	4	0	0	.000	3	2	3	4.50	0
2010	Colorado Springs	P.C.	12	61	3	3	.500	53	19	62	5.75	0
2010	Colorado	N.L.	28	72	2	3	.400	66	26	94	6.13	0
2011	Tulsa	Texas	1	4	0	1	.000	2	1	5	2.25	0
2011	Colorado Springs	P.C.	5	23	1	2	.333	15	5	36	6.26	0
2011	Colorado a	N.L.	18	83	6	6	.500	63	47	110	7.05	0
2012	Colorado	N.L.	23	25²/₃	0	2	.000	29	18	36	8.06	0
2012	Cleveland b-c	A.L.	44	53	3	1	.750	54	12	47	3.06	0
2013	Toronto	A.L.	44	137²/₃	5	9	.357	96	44	152	4.77	0
Major League Totals		5 Yrs.	158	375¹/₃	16	21	.432	311	149	442	5.52	0

a On disabled list from May 2 to July 25, 2011.
b Sold to Cleveland Indians, June 12, 2012.
c Traded to Toronto Blue Jays for infielder Mike Aviles and catcher Yan Gomes, November 3, 2012.

ROMO, SERGIO FRANCISCO

Born, Brawley, California, March 4, 1983.
Bats Right. Throws Right. Height, 5 feet, 11 inches. Weight, 190 pounds.

Year	Club	Lea	G	IP	W	L	Pct	SO	BB	H	ERA	SAVES
2005	Salem-Keizer	Northwest	15	68²/₃	7	1	.875	65	9	70	2.75	0
2006	Augusta	So.Atl.	31	103¹/₃	10	2	.833	95	19	78	2.53	4
2007	San Jose	Calif.	41	66¹/₃	6	2	.750	106	15	35	1.36	9
2008	Connecticut	Eastern	24	27	1	3	.250	30	7	22	4.00	11
2008	Fresno	P.C.	3	6	0	0	.000	7	2	3	0.00	0
2008	San Francisco	N.L.	29	34	3	1	.750	33	8	16	2.12	0
2009	San Jose	Calif.	3	4²/₃	0	0	.000	6	2	2	0.00	0
2009	Fresno	P.C.	3	3	0	0	.000	3	0	2	0.00	0
2009	San Francisco a	N.L.	45	34	5	2	.714	41	11	30	3.97	2
2010	San Francisco	N.L.	68	62	5	3	.625	70	14	46	2.18	0
2011	Giants	Arizona	1	1	0	0	.000	3	0	1	0.00	0
2011	San Francisco b	N.L.	65	48	3	1	.750	70	5	29	1.50	1
2012	San Francisco	N.L.	69	55¹/₃	4	2	.667	63	10	37	1.79	14
2013	San Francisco	N.L.	65	60¹/₃	5	8	.385	58	12	53	2.54	38
Major League Totals		6 Yrs.	341	293²/₃	25	17	.595	335	60	211	2.27	55
	Division Series											
2010	San Francisco	N.L.	2	0²/₃	1	0	1.000	0	0	3	40.50	0
2012	San Francisco	N.L.	3	4¹/₃	1	0	1.000	1	1	2	2.08	1
Division Series Totals			5	5	2	0	1.000	1	1	5	7.20	1
	Championship Series											
2010	San Francisco	N.L.	3	2¹/₃	0	0	.000	3	1	2	0.00	0
2012	San Francisco	N.L.	4	3¹/₃	0	0	.000	3	0	2	0.00	0
Championship Series Totals			7	5²/₃	0	0	.000	6	1	4	0.00	0
	World Series Record											
2010	San Francisco	N.L.	1	0²/₃	0	0	.000	1	0	1	0.00	0
2012	San Francisco	N.L.	3	3	0	0	.000	5	0	0	0.00	3
World Series Totals			4	3²/₃	0	0	.000	6	0	1	0.00	3

a On disabled list from March 26 to May 30, 2009.
b On disabled list from August 10 to August 28, 2011.

RONDON, HECTOR LUIS

Born, Guatire, Venezuela, February 26, 1988.
Bats Right. Throws Right. Height, 6 feet, 3 inches. Weight, 180 pounds.

Year	Club	Lea	G	IP	W	L	Pct	SO	BB	H	ERA	SAVES
2006	Indians	Gulf Coast	11	52²/₃	3	4	.429	32	3	62	5.13	0
2007	Lake County	So.Atl.	27	136	7	10	.412	113	27	143	4.37	0
2008	Kinston	Carolina	27	145	11	6	.647	145	42	130	3.60	0
2009	Akron	Eastern	15	72	7	5	.583	73	16	60	2.75	0
2009	Columbus	Int.	12	74¹/₃	4	5	.444	64	13	83	4.00	0
2010	Columbus	Int.	7	31²/₃	1	3	.250	33	10	48	8.53	0
2011	Mahoning Valley	N.Y.-Penn.	2	3	0	0	.000	2	0	3	3.00	0
2012	Indians	Arizona	2	3	0	0	.000	6	1	0	0.00	0
2012	Akron a	Eastern	2	4	0	0	.000	3	1	4	2.25	0
2013	Chicago	N.L.	45	54²/₃	2	1	.667	44	25	52	4.77	0

a Selected by Chicago Cubs from Cleveland Indians in Rule V draft, December 6, 2012.

ROSENTHAL, TREVOR JORDAN

Born, Lees Summit, Missouri, May 29, 1990.
Bats Right. Throws Right. Height, 6 feet, 2 inches. Weight, 190 pounds.

Year Club	Lea	G	IP	W	L	Pct	SO	BB	H	ERA	SAVES
2009 Cardinals	Gulf Coast	14	24	4	1	.800	26	10	25	4.88	0
2010 Johnson City	Appal.	10	32	3	0	1.000	30	7	23	2.25	1
2011 Quad Cities	Midwest	22	120⅓	7	7	.500	133	39	111	4.11	0
2012 Springfield	Texas	17	94	8	6	.571	83	37	67	2.78	0
2012 Memphis	P.C.	3	15	0	0	.000	21	5	11	4.20	0
2012 St. Louis	N.L.	19	22⅔	0	2	.000	25	7	14	2.78	0
2013 St. Louis	N.L.	74	75⅓	2	4	.333	108	20	63	2.63	3
Major League Totals	2 Yrs.	93	98	2	6	.250	133	27	77	2.66	3
Division Series											
2012 St. Louis	N.L.	3	3⅓	0	0	.000	6	0	1	0.00	0
2013 St. Louis	N.L.	2	2	0	0	.000	2	1	1	0.00	1
Division Series Totals		5	5⅓	0	0	.000	8	1	2	0.00	1
Championship Series											
2012 St. Louis	N.L.	4	5⅓	0	0	.000	9	2	1	0.00	0
2013 St. Louis	N.L.	4	5	0	0	.000	7	1	2	0.00	2
Championship Series Totals		8	10⅓	0	0	.000	16	3	3	0.00	2
World Series Record											
2013 St. Louis	N.L.	4	4⅔	1	0	1.000	9	1	1	0.00	1

ROSS, ROBERT CHARLES (ROBBIE)

Born, Lexington, Kentucky, June 24, 1989.
Bats Left. Throws Left. Height, 5 feet, 11 inches. Weight, 185 pounds.

Year Club	Lea	G	IP	W	L	Pct	SO	BB	H	ERA	SAVES
2009 Spokane	Northwest	15	74⅓	4	4	.500	76	17	68	2.66	0
2010 Bakersfield	Calif.	11	52	4	4	.500	49	17	67	5.37	0
2010 Hickory	So.Atl.	16	94	8	7	.533	62	20	89	2.59	0
2011 Myrtle Beach	Carolina	21	123⅓	9	4	.692	98	28	102	2.26	0
2011 Frisco	Texas	6	38	1	1	.500	36	5	33	2.61	0
2012 Texas a	A.L.	58	65	6	0	1.000	47	23	55	2.22	0
2013 Texas	A.L.	65	62⅓	4	2	.667	58	19	63	3.03	0
Major League Totals	2 Yrs.	123	127⅓	10	2	.833	105	42	118	2.62	0

a On disabled list from August 30 to September 15, 2012.

ROSS, TYSON WILLIAM

Born, Berkeley, California, April 22, 1987.
Bats Right. Throws Right. Height, 6 feet, 6 inches. Weight, 230 pounds.

Year Club	Lea	G	IP	W	L	Pct	SO	BB	H	ERA	SAVES
2008 Kane County	Midwest	6	19⅓	0	1	.000	16	5	16	4.66	0
2009 Stockton	Calif.	18	86⅓	5	6	.455	82	33	78	4.17	0
2009 Midland	Texas	9	50	5	4	.556	31	20	40	3.96	0
2010 Oakland	A.L.	26	39⅓	1	4	.200	32	20	39	5.49	1
2010 Sacramento	P.C.	6	25⅓	2	1	.667	30	13	22	3.55	0
2011 Oakland	A.L.	9	36	3	3	.500	24	13	33	2.75	0
2011 Stockton	Calif.	1	1	0	0	.000	1	1	2	9.00	0
2011 Sacramento a	P.C.	9	36⅔	3	2	.600	34	22	52	7.61	0
2012 Sacramento	P.C.	15	78⅓	6	2	.750	64	29	69	2.99	0
2012 Oakland b	A.L.	18	73⅓	2	11	.154	46	37	96	6.50	0
2013 Tucson	P.C.	4	11⅔	1	1	.500	9	6	12	4.63	0
2013 San Diego c	N.L.	35	125	3	8	.273	119	44	100	3.17	0
Major League Totals	4 Yrs.	88	273⅔	9	26	.257	221	114	268	4.34	1

a On disabled list from May 20 to July 24, 2011.
b Traded to San Diego Padres with infielder A.J. Kirby-Jones for infielder Andy Parrino and pitcher Andrew Werner, November 16, 2012.
c On disabled list from April 18 to May 5, 2013.

RUSIN, CHRISTOPHER PATRICK (CHRIS)

Born, Detroit, Michigan, October 22, 1986.
Bats Left. Throws Left. Height, 6 feet, 2 inches. Weight, 195 pounds.

Year Club	Lea	G	IP	W	L	Pct	SO	BB	H	ERA	SAVES
2009 Cubs	Arizona	2	5	0	0	.000	2	3	1	0.00	0
2009 Boise	Northwest	8	31	0	4	.000	27	9	33	3.48	0
2010 Daytona	Fla.St.	20	91	4	3	.571	84	15	79	3.36	0

Year	Club	Lea	G	IP	W	L	Pct	SO	BB	H	ERA	SAVES
2010	Tennessee	Southern	4	19	2	1	.667	15	4	21	1.89	0
2011	Iowa	P.C.	11	62 2/3	5	2	.714	46	14	70	4.02	0
2011	Tennessee	Southern	15	76	3	2	.600	49	16	80	3.91	0
2012	Tennessee	Southern	1	3	0	0	.000	1	0	0	0.00	0
2012	Iowa	P.C.	25	140 1/3	8	9	.471	94	53	146	4.55	0
2012	Chicago	N.L.	7	29 2/3	2	3	.400	21	11	38	6.37	0
2013	Iowa	P.C.	19	121	8	7	.533	69	27	113	3.35	0
2013	Chicago	N.L.	13	66 1/3	2	6	.250	36	24	66	3.93	0
Major League Totals		2 Yrs.	20	96	4	9	.308	57	35	104	4.69	0

RUSSELL, JAMES CLAYTON

Born, Cincinnati, Ohio, January 8, 1986.
Bats Left. Throws Left. Height, 6 feet, 4 inches. Weight, 205 pounds.

Year	Club	Lea	G	IP	W	L	Pct	SO	BB	H	ERA	SAVES
2007	Cubs	Arizona	1	2	0	0	.000	2	0	0	0.00	0
2007	Peoria	Midwest	2	7	0	0	.000	9	4	3	0.00	0
2008	Daytona	Fla.St.	8	41	2	2	.500	24	13	36	3.51	0
2008	Tennessee	Southern	18	86 1/3	4	8	.333	62	25	111	6.36	0
2009	Iowa	P.C.	26	65 2/3	3	3	.500	46	19	71	3.43	0
2009	Tennessee	Southern	11	37	2	3	.400	26	9	45	5.11	0
2010	Iowa	P.C.	5	11	0	0	.000	10	4	11	5.73	0
2010	Chicago	N.L.	57	49	1	1	.500	42	11	55	4.96	0
2011	Chicago	N.L.	64	67 2/3	1	6	.143	43	14	76	4.12	0
2012	Chicago	N.L.	77	69 1/3	7	1	.875	55	23	67	3.25	2
2013	Chicago	N.L.	74	52 2/3	1	6	.143	37	18	46	3.59	0
Major League Totals		4 Yrs.	272	238 2/3	10	14	.417	177	66	244	3.92	2

RYU, HYUN-JIN

Born, Incheon, Korea, March 25, 1987.
Bats Left. Throws Left. Height, 6 feet, 2 inches. Weight, 215 pounds.

Year	Club	Lea	G	IP	W	L	Pct	SO	BB	H	ERA	SAVES
2006	Hanwha	Korea	30	201 2/3	18	6	.750	204	52	159	2.23	1
2007	Hanwha	Korea	30	211	17	7	.708	178	68	195	2.94	0
2008	Hanwha	Korea	26	165 2/3	14	7	.667	143	67	144	3.31	0
2009	Hanwha	Korea	28	189 1/3	13	12	.520	188	67	180	3.57	0
2010	Hanwha	Korea	25	192 2/3	16	4	.800	187	45	149	1.82	0
2011	Hanwha	Korea	24	126	11	7	.611	128	38	101	3.36	0
2012	Hanwha a	Korea	27	182 2/3	9	9	.500	210	46	153	2.66	0
2013	Los Angeles	N.L.	30	192	14	8	.636	154	49	182	3.00	0
	Division Series											
2013	Los Angeles	N.L.	1	3	0	0	.000	1	1	6	12.00	0
	Championship Series											
2013	Los Angeles	N.L.	1	7	1	0	1.000	4	1	3	0.00	0

a Signed with Los Angeles Dodgers, December 9, 2012.

SABATHIA, CARSTEN CHARLES (CC)

Born, Vallejo, California, July 21, 1980.
Bats Left. Throws Left. Height, 6 feet, 7 inches. Weight, 290 pounds.

Year	Club	Lea	G	IP	W	L	Pct	SO	BB	H	ERA	SAVES
1998	Burlington	Appal.	5	18	1	0	1.000	35	8	20	4.50	0
1999	Kinston	Carolina	7	32	3	3	.500	29	19	30	5.34	0
1999	Mahoning Valley	N.Y.-Penn.	6	19 2/3	0	0	.000	27	12	9	1.83	0
1999	Columbus a	So.Atl.	3	16 2/3	2	0	1.000	20	5	8	1.08	0
2000	Kinston	Carolina	10	56	3	2	.600	69	24	48	3.54	0
2000	Akron	Eastern	17	90 1/3	3	7	.300	90	48	75	3.59	0
2001	Cleveland	A.L.	33	180 1/3	17	5	.773	171	95	149	4.39	0
2002	Cleveland	A.L.	33	210	13	11	.542	149	88	198	4.37	0
2003	Cleveland	A.L.	30	197 2/3	13	9	.591	141	66	190	3.60	0
2004	Cleveland	A.L.	30	188	11	10	.524	139	72	176	4.12	0
2005	Akron	Eastern	2	9	0	1	.000	9	2	4	1.00	0
2005	Cleveland b	A.L.	31	196 2/3	15	10	.600	161	62	185	4.03	0
2006	Buffalo	Int.	1	5	1	0	1.000	5	1	6	1.80	0
2006	Cleveland c	A.L.	28	192 2/3	12	11	.522	172	44	182	3.22	0
2007	Cleveland d	A.L.	34	*241	19	7	.731	209	37	238	3.21	0
2008	Cleveland	A.L.	18	122 1/3	6	8	.429	123	34	117	3.83	0
2008	Milwaukee e-f	N.L.	17	130 2/3	11	2	.846	128	25	106	1.65	0

Year	Club	Lea	G	IP	W	L	Pct	SO	BB	H	ERA	SAVES
2009	New York	A.L.	34	230	*19	8	.704	197	67	197	3.37	0
2010	New York	A.L.	34	$237\frac{2}{3}$	*21	7	.750	197	74	209	3.18	0
2011	New York	A.L.	33	$237\frac{1}{3}$	19	8	.704	230	61	230	3.00	0
2012	New York g	A.L.	28	200	15	6	.714	197	44	184	3.38	0
2013	New York h	A.L.	32	211	14	13	.519	175	65	224	4.78	0
Major League Totals		13 Yrs.	415	$2775\frac{1}{3}$	205	115	.641	2389	834	2585	3.60	0
	Division Series											
2001	Cleveland	A.L.	1	6	1	0	1.000	5	5	6	3.00	0
2007	Cleveland	A.L.	1	5	1	0	1.000	5	6	4	5.40	0
2008	Milwaukee	N.L.	1	$3\frac{2}{3}$	0	1	.000	5	4	6	12.27	0
2009	New York	A.L.	1	$6\frac{2}{3}$	1	0	1.000	8	0	8	1.35	0
2010	New York	A.L.	1	6	1	0	1.000	5	3	5	4.50	0
2011	New York	A.L.	3	$8\frac{2}{3}$	0	0	.000	11	8	10	6.23	0
2012	New York	A.L.	2	$17\frac{2}{3}$	2	0	1.000	16	3	12	1.53	0
Division Series Totals			10	$53\frac{2}{3}$	6	1	.857	55	29	51	3.86	0
	Championship Series											
2007	Cleveland	A.L.	2	$10\frac{1}{3}$	0	2	.000	9	7	17	10.45	0
2009	New York	A.L.	2	16	2	0	1.000	12	3	9	1.13	0
2010	New York	A.L.	2	10	1	0	1.000	10	4	17	6.30	0
2012	New York	A.L.	1	$3\frac{2}{3}$	0	1	.000	3	2	11	12.27	0
Championship Series Totals			7	40	3	3	.500	34	16	54	5.85	0
	World Series Record											
2009	New York	A.L.	2	$13\frac{2}{3}$	0	1	.000	12	6	11	3.29	0

a On disabled list from April 1 through June 20, 1999.
b On disabled list from March 25 to April 17, 2005.
c On disabled list from April 3 to May 2, 2006.
d Selected Cy Young Award Winner in American League for 2007.
e Traded to Milwaukee Brewers for outfielder Matt LaPorta, pitcher Zach Jackson, pitcher Rob Bryson and player to be named later, July 7, 2008. Cleveland Indians received outfielder Michael Brantley to complete trade, October 3, 2008.
f Filed for free agency, November 1, 2008. Signed with New York Yankees, December 18, 2008.
g On disabled list from June 28 to July 17 and August 9 to August 24, 2012.
h On disabled list from September 21 to November 4, 2013.

SALAZAR, DANNY DARIEL

Born, Santo Domingo, Dominican Republic, January 11, 1990.
Bats Right. Throws Right. Height, 6 feet. Weight, 190 pounds.

Year	Club	Lea	G	IP	W	L	Pct	SO	BB	H	ERA	SAVES
2008	Indians	Gulf Coast	11	$53\frac{1}{3}$	4	2	.667	43	13	46	2.87	0
2009	Lake County	So.Atl.	21	$107\frac{1}{3}$	5	7	.417	65	40	114	4.44	0
2010	Lake County	Midwest	7	$32\frac{1}{3}$	1	1	.500	23	13	34	4.45	0
2011	Indians	Arizona	5	$6\frac{2}{3}$	0	0	.000	11	2	6	2.70	0
2011	Lake County	Midwest	3	8	0	2	.000	7	2	8	3.38	0
2012	Carolina	Carolina	16	$53\frac{2}{3}$	1	2	.333	53	19	46	2.68	0
2012	Akron	Eastern	6	34	4	0	1.000	23	8	25	1.85	0
2013	Akron	Eastern	7	$33\frac{2}{3}$	2	3	.400	51	10	27	2.67	0
2013	Columbus	Int.	14	$59\frac{1}{3}$	4	2	.667	78	14	44	2.73	1
2013	Cleveland	A.L.	10	52	2	3	.400	65	15	44	3.12	0
	Wild Card Playoff											
2013	Cleveland	A.L.	1	4	0	1	.000	4	2	4	6.75	0

SALE, CHRISTOPHER (CHRIS)

Born, Lakeland, Florida, March 30, 1989.
Bats Left. Throws Left. Height, 6 feet, 5 inches. Weight, 170 pounds.

Year	Club	Lea	G	IP	W	L	Pct	SO	BB	H	ERA	SAVES
2010	Winston-Salem	Carolina	4	4	0	0	.000	4	2	3	2.25	0
2010	Charlotte	Int.	7	$6\frac{1}{3}$	0	0	.000	15	4	3	2.84	0
2010	Chicago	A.L.	21	$23\frac{1}{3}$	2	1	.667	32	10	15	1.93	4
2011	Chicago	A.L.	58	71	2	2	.500	79	27	52	2.79	8
2012	Chicago	A.L.	30	192	17	8	.680	192	51	167	3.05	0
2013	Chicago	A.L.	30	$214\frac{1}{3}$	11	14	.440	226	46	184	3.07	0
Major League Totals		4 Yrs.	139	$500\frac{2}{3}$	32	25	.561	529	134	418	2.97	12

SAMARDZIJA, JEFFREY ALAN (JEFF)

Born, Merrillville, Indiana, January 23, 1985.
Bats Right. Throws Right. Height, 6 feet, 5 inches. Weight, 225 pounds.

Year Club	Lea	G	IP	W	L	Pct	SO	BB	H	ERA	SAVES
2006 Boise	Northwest	5	19	1	1	.500	13	6	18	2.37	0
2006 Peoria	Midwest	2	11	0	1	.000	4	6	6	3.27	0
2007 Daytona	Fla.St.	24	107 1/3	3	8	.273	45	35	142	4.95	0
2007 Tennessee	Southern	6	34 1/3	3	3	.500	20	9	33	3.41	0
2008 Tennessee	Southern	16	76	3	5	.375	44	42	71	4.86	0
2008 Iowa	P.C.	6	37 1/3	4	1	.800	40	16	32	3.13	0
2008 Chicago	N.L.	26	27 2/3	1	0	1.000	25	15	24	2.28	1
2009 Iowa	P.C.	18	89	6	6	.500	71	27	98	4.35	0
2009 Chicago	N.L.	20	34 2/3	1	3	.250	21	15	46	7.53	0
2010 Iowa	P.C.	35	111 1/3	11	3	.786	102	67	86	4.37	0
2010 Chicago	N.L.	7	19 1/3	2	2	.500	9	20	21	8.38	0
2011 Chicago	N.L.	75	88	8	4	.667	87	50	64	2.97	0
2012 Chicago	N.L.	28	174 2/3	9	13	.409	180	56	157	3.81	0
2013 Chicago	N.L.	33	213 2/3	8	13	.381	214	78	210	4.34	0
Major League Totals	6 Yrs.	189	558	29	35	.453	536	234	522	4.19	1
Division Series											
2008 Chicago	N.L.	1	1	0	0	.000	0	0	2	9.00	0

SANCHEZ, ANIBAL ALEJANDRO

Born, Maracay, Venezuela, February 27, 1984.
Bats Right. Throws Right. Height, 6 feet. Weight, 180 pounds.

Year Club	Lea	G	IP	W	L	Pct	SO	BB	H	ERA	SAVES
2004 Lowell a	N.Y.-Penn.	15	76 1/3	4	4	.500	101	29	43	1.77	0
2005 Wilmington	Carolina	14	78 2/3	6	1	.857	95	24	53	2.40	0
2005 Portland b	Eastern	11	57 1/3	3	5	.375	63	16	53	3.45	0
2006 Carolina	Southern	15	85 2/3	3	6	.333	92	27	82	3.15	0
2006 Florida c	N.L.	18	114 1/3	10	3	.769	72	46	90	2.83	0
2007 Florida d	N.L.	6	30	2	1	.667	14	19	43	4.80	0
2008 Marlins	Gulf Coast	1	5	1	0	1.000	4	1	4	3.60	0
2008 Jupiter	Fla.St.	2	10	0	0	.000	9	4	7	1.80	0
2008 Carolina	Southern	2	13	1	0	1.000	12	5	12	3.46	0
2008 Florida e	N.L.	10	51 2/3	2	5	.286	50	27	54	5.57	0
2009 Marlins	Gulf Coast	1	2 2/3	0	0	.000	0	2	3	3.38	0
2009 Jupiter	Fla.St.	3	13 1/3	1	0	1.000	12	3	7	0.68	0
2009 Jacksonville	Southern	2	10 1/3	1	0	1.000	8	3	5	2.61	0
2009 Florida f	N.L.	16	86	4	8	.333	71	46	84	3.87	0
2010 Florida	N.L.	32	195	13	12	.520	157	70	192	3.55	0
2011 Florida	N.L.	32	196 1/3	8	9	.471	202	64	187	3.67	0
2012 Miami	N.L.	19	121	5	7	.417	110	33	119	3.94	0
2012 Detroit g-h	A.L.	12	74 2/3	4	6	.400	57	15	81	3.74	0
2013 Lakeland	Fla.St.	1	1 2/3	0	0	.000	0	0	2	0.00	0
2013 Detroit i	A.L.	29	182	14	8	.636	202	54	156	*2.57	0
Major League Totals	8 Yrs.	174	1051	62	59	.512	935	374	1006	3.55	0
Division Series											
2012 Detroit	A.L.	1	6 1/3	0	1	.000	3	2	5	2.84	0
2013 Detroit	A.L.	1	4 1/3	0	1	.000	6	2	8	10.38	0
Division Series Totals		2	10 2/3	0	2	.000	9	4	13	5.91	0
Championship Series											
2012 Detroit	A.L.	1	7	1	0	1.000	7	3	3	0.00	0
2013 Detroit	A.L.	2	12	1	1	.500	17	6	9	2.25	0
Championship Series Totals		3	19	2	1	.667	24	9	12	1.42	0
World Series Record											
2012 Detroit	A.L.	1	7	0	1	.000	8	1	6	2.57	0

a On minor league disabled list July 1 to September 16, 2003.
b Traded by Boston Red Sox to Florida Marlins with infielder Hanley Ramirez and pitcher Jesus Delgado for pitcher Josh Beckett, infielder Mike Lowell and pitcher Guillermo Mota, November 24, 2005.
c Pitched no-hit, no-run game against Arizona Diamondbacks, September 6, 2006.
d On minor league disabled list May 7 to September 30, 2007.
e On disabled list from March 21 to July 31, 2008.
f On disabled list from May 8 to June 2 and June 3 to August 21, 2009.
g Traded to Detroit Tigers with infielder Omar Infante for pitcher Jacob Turner, catcher Rob Brantley and pitcher Brian Flynn, July 23, 2012.
h Filed for free agency, November 3, 2012, re-signed with Detroit Tigers, December 17, 2012.
i On disabled list from June 16 to July 6, 2013.

SANTANA, ERVIN RAMON

Born, La Romana, Dominican Republic, January 10, 1983.
Bats Right. Throws Right. Height, 6 feet, 2 inches. Weight, 185 pounds.

Year Club	Lea	G	IP	W	L	Pct	SO	BB	H	ERA	SAVES
2001 Angels	Arizona	10	58⅔	3	2	.600	69	35	40	3.22	0
2001 Provo	Pioneer	4	18⅔	2	1	.667	22	12	19	7.71	0
2002 Cedar Rapids	Midwest	27	147	14	8	.636	146	48	133	4.16	0
2003 Rancho Cucamonga	California	20	124⅔	10	2	.833	130	36	98	2.53	0
2003 Arkansas	Texas	6	29⅔	1	1	.500	23	12	23	3.94	0
2004 Arkansas	Texas	8	43⅔	2	1	.667	48	18	41	3.30	0
2005 Arkansas	Texas	7	39	5	1	.833	32	15	34	2.31	0
2005 Salt Lake	P.C.	3	19⅓	1	0	1.000	17	2	19	4.19	0
2005 Los Angeles	A.L.	23	133⅔	12	8	.600	99	47	139	4.65	0
2006 Los Angeles	A.L.	33	204	16	8	.667	141	70	181	4.28	0
2007 Salt Lake	P.C.	5	32⅓	2	1	.667	32	10	39	5.01	0
2007 Los Angeles	A.L.	28	150	7	14	.333	126	58	174	5.76	0
2008 Los Angeles	A.L.	32	219	16	7	.696	214	47	198	3.49	0
2009 Angels	Arizona	1	3⅓	0	0	.000	7	0	3	0.00	0
2009 Rancho Cucamonga	Calif.	1	4⅔	0	0	.000	3	0	4	5.79	0
2009 Salt Lake	P.C.	1	5	1	0	1.000	4	1	3	3.60	0
2009 Los Angeles a	A.L.	24	139⅔	8	8	.500	107	47	159	5.03	0
2010 Los Angeles	A.L.	33	222⅔	17	10	.630	169	73	221	3.92	0
2011 Los Angeles b	A.L.	33	228⅔	11	12	.478	178	72	207	3.38	0
2012 Los Angeles c	A.L.	30	178	9	13	.409	133	61	165	5.16	0
2013 Kansas City d	A.L.	32	211	9	10	.474	161	51	190	3.24	0
Major League Totals	9 Yrs.	268	1686⅔	105	90	.538	1328	526	1634	4.19	0
Division Series											
2005 Los Angeles	A.L.	1	5⅓	1	0	1.000	2	3	5	5.06	0
2007 Los Angeles	A.L.	1	2	0	0	.000	2	0	0	0.00	0
2008 Los Angeles	A.L.	1	5⅓	0	0	.000	3	0	8	8.44	0
Division Series Totals		3	12⅔	1	0	1.000	7	3	13	5.68	0
Championship Series											
2005 Los Angeles	A.L.	1	4⅓	0	1	.000	2	3	3	10.38	0
2009 Los Angeles	A.L.	4	5⅔	1	1	.500	5	4	5	1.59	0
Championship Series Totals		5	10	1	2	.333	7	7	8	5.40	0

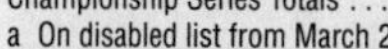

a On disabled list from March 27 to May 14 and June 17 to July 3, 2009.
b Pitched no-hit, no-run game against Cleveland Indians, July 27, 2011.
c Traded to Kansas City Royals with cash for pitcher Brandon Sisk, October 31, 2012.
d Filed for free agency, October 31, 2013.

SANTANA, JOHAN ALEXANDER

Born, Tovar, Venezuela, March 13, 1979.
Bats Left. Throws Left. Height, 6 feet. Weight, 210 pounds.

Year Club	Lea	G	IP	W	L	Pct	SO	BB	H	ERA	SAVES
1996 Houston/Bos	Dominican	23	40	4	3	.571	51	22	26	2.70	3
1997 Auburn	N.Y.-Penn.	1	4	0	0	.000	5	6	1	2.25	0
1997 Astros	Gulf Coast	9	36⅓	0	4	.000	25	18	49	7.93	0
1998 Quad City	Midwest	2	6⅔	0	1	.000	6	3	14	9.45	0
1998 Auburn	N.Y.-Penn.	15	86⅔	7	5	.583	88	21	81	4.36	0
1999 Michigan a-b	Midwest	27	160⅓	8	8	.500	150	55	162	4.66	0
2000 Minnesota	A.L.	30	86	2	3	.400	64	54	102	6.49	0
2001 Minnesota	A.L.	15	43⅔	1	0	1.000	28	16	50	4.74	0
2002 Edmonton	P.C.	11	48⅔	5	2	.714	75	27	37	3.14	0
2002 Minnesota	A.L.	27	108⅓	8	6	.571	137	49	84	2.99	1
2003 Minnesota	A.L.	45	158⅓	12	3	.800	169	47	127	3.07	0
2004 Minnesota c	A.L.	34	228	20	6	.769	*265	54	156	*2.61	0
2005 Minnesota	A.L.	33	231⅔	16	7	.696	*238	45	180	2.87	0
2006 Minnesota d	A.L.	34	*233⅔	*19	6	.760	*245	47	186	*2.77	0
2007 Minnesota	A.L.	33	219	15	13	.536	235	52	183	3.33	0
2008 New York e	N.L.	34	*234⅓	16	7	.696	206	63	206	*2.53	0
2009 New York f	N.L.	25	166⅔	13	9	.591	146	46	156	3.13	0
2010 New York	N.L.	29	199	11	9	.550	144	55	179	2.98	0
2011 New York g	N.L.	INJURED—Did Not Play									
2012 Brooklyn	N.Y.-Penn.	1	3	0	0	.000	3	1	1	0.00	0
2012 New York h-i	N.L.	21	117	6	9	.400	111	39	117	4.85	0
2013 New York j-k	N.L.	INJURED—Did Not Play									
Major League Totals	12 Yrs.	360	2025⅔	139	78	.641	1988	567	1726	3.20	1
Division Series											
2002 Minnesota	A.L.	2	3	0	0	.000	2	2	3	6.00	0

Year	Club	Lea	G	IP	W	L	Pct	SO	BB	H	ERA	SAVES
2003	Minnesota	A.L.	2	7⅔	0	1	.000	6	3	9	7.04	0
2004	Minnesota	A.L.	2	12	1	0	1.000	12	4	14	0.75	0
2006	Minnesota	A.L.	1	8	0	1	.000	8	1	5	2.25	0
Division Series Totals			7	30⅔	1	2	.333	28	10	31	3.23	0
	Championship Series											
2002	Minnesota	A.L.	4	3⅓	0	1	.000	4	0	4	10.80	0

a Selected by Florida Marlins from Houston Astros in Rule V draft, December 13, 1999.
b Traded to Minnesota Twins with cash for pitcher Jared Camp, December 13, 1999.
c Selected Cy Young Award Winner in American League for 2004.
d Selected Cy Young Award Winner in American League for 2006.
e Traded to New York Mets for outfielder Carlos Gomez, pitcher Philip Humber, pitcher Kevin Mulvey and pitcher Deolis Garcia, February 2, 2008.
f On disabled list from August 25 to October 14, 2009.
g On disabled list from March 22 to October 24, 2011.
h Pitched no-hit, no-run game against St. Louis Cardinals, June 1, 2012.
i On disabled list from July 21 to August 11 and August 18 to October 16, 2012.
j On disabled list from March 22 to November 2, 2013.
k Filed for free agency, November 1, 2013.

SANTIAGO, HECTOR FELIPE

Born, Newark, New Jersey, December 16, 1987.
Bats Right. Throws Left. Height, 6 feet. Weight, 210 pounds.

Year	Club	Lea	G	IP	W	L	Pct	SO	BB	H	ERA	SAVES
2007	Bristol	Appal.	17	32⅔	1	1	.500	38	16	19	1.65	0
2008	Kannapolis	So.Atl.	38	64⅓	5	1	.833	83	44	57	4.06	1
2009	Winston-Salem	Carolina	38	58	4	4	.500	66	25	54	3.88	1
2010	Winston-Salem	Carolina	37	60⅔	4	5	.444	61	19	63	4.15	2
2011	Winston-Salem	Carolina	8	44	2	3	.400	43	14	38	3.68	0
2011	Chicago	A.L.	2	5⅓	0	0	.000	2	1	1	0.00	0
2011	Birmingham	Southern	15	83⅓	7	5	.583	74	39	71	3.56	0
2012	Charlotte	Int.	3	14⅔	1	0	1.000	13	6	9	0.00	0
2012	Chicago	A.L.	42	70⅓	4	1	.800	79	40	54	3.33	4
2013	Chicago a-b	A.L.	34	149	4	9	.308	137	72	137	3.56	0
Major League Totals		3 Yrs.	78	224⅔	8	10	.444	218	113	192	3.41	4

a Traded to Arizona Diamondbacks with player to be named later for outfielder Adam Eaton, December 10, 2013.
b Traded to Los Angeles Angels with pitcher Tyler Skaggs for infielder Mark Trumbo and player to be named later, December 10, 2013. Arizona Diamondbacks received pitcher A.J. Schugel to complete trade, December 13, 2013.

SANTOS, SERGIO JOSE

Born, Bellflower, California, July 4, 1983.
Bats Right. Throws Right. Height, 6 feet, 3 inches. Weight, 240 pounds.

Year	Club	Lea	G	IP	W	L	Pct	SO	BB	H	ERA	SAVES
2009	Kannapolis a-b-c	So.Atl.	8	7⅓	0	1	.000	10	3	8	7.36	0
2009	Winston-Salem	Carolina	8	7⅔	0	0	.000	7	3	9	5.87	0
2009	Birmingham	Southern	7	8⅔	0	1	.000	6	7	15	10.38	0
2009	Charlotte d-e	Int.	3	5	0	1	.000	7	7	5	9.00	0
2010	Chicago	A.L.	56	51⅔	2	2	.500	56	26	53	2.96	1
2011	Chicago f	A.L.	63	63⅓	4	5	.444	92	29	41	3.55	30
2012	Toronto g	A.L.	6	5	0	1	.000	4	4	6	9.00	2
2013	Blue Jays	Gulf Coast	1	1	0	0	.000	2	0	1	0.00	0
2013	Dunedin	Fla.St.	5	4⅔	0	0	.000	2	2	4	5.79	0
2013	Buffalo	Int.	6	6	0	0	.000	5	2	8	7.50	0
2013	Toronto h	A.L.	29	25⅔	1	1	.500	28	4	11	1.75	1
Major League Totals		4 Yrs.	154	145⅔	7	9	.438	180	63	111	3.21	34

a Played infield in the minors for 2003 through 2008.
b Traded by Arizona Diamondbacks to Toronto Blue Jays with infielder Troy Glaus for infielder Orlando Hudson and pitcher Miguel Batista, December 27, 2005.
c Claimed on waivers by Minnesota Twins, May 16, 2008.
d Filed for free agency, November 3, 2008. Signed with Chicago White Sox organization, January 12, 2009.
e Sold to San Francisco Giants, March 20, 2009. Sold to Chicago White Sox, April 1, 2009.
f Traded to Toronto Blue Jays for pitcher Nestor Molina, December 6, 2011.
g On disabled list from April 21 to October 31, 2012.
h On disabled list from April 14 to August 1, 2013.

SAUNDERS, JOSEPH FRANCIS (JOE)

Born, Falls Church, Virginia, June 16, 1981.
Bats Left. Throws Left. Height, 6 feet, 3 inches. Weight, 210 pounds.

Year Club	Lea	G	IP	W	L	Pct	SO	BB	H	ERA	SAVES
2002 Cedar Rapids	Midwest	5	28⅔	3	1	.750	27	9	16	1.88	0
2002 Provo	Pioneer	8	32⅓	2	1	.667	21	11	40	3.62	0
2003 Provo a	Pioneer				INJURED—Did Not Play						
2004 Rancho Cucamonga	Calif.	19	105⅔	9	7	.563	76	23	106	3.41	0
2004 Arkansas	Texas	8	39	4	3	.571	25	14	51	5.77	0
2005 Arkansas	Texas	18	105⅔	7	4	.636	80	32	107	3.49	0
2005 Salt Lake	P.C.	9	55	3	3	.500	29	21	65	4.58	0
2005 Los Angeles	A.L.	2	9⅓	0	0	.000	4	4	10	7.71	0
2006 Salt Lake	P.C.	21	135	10	4	.714	97	38	117	2.67	0
2006 Los Angeles	A.L.	13	70⅔	7	3	.700	51	29	71	4.71	0
2007 Salt Lake	P.C.	14	86⅓	4	7	.364	84	20	89	5.11	0
2007 Los Angeles	A.L.	18	107⅓	8	5	.615	69	34	129	4.44	0
2008 Los Angeles	A.L.	31	198	17	7	.708	103	53	187	3.41	0
2009 Los Angeles b	A.L.	31	186	16	7	.696	101	64	202	4.60	0
2010 Los Angeles	A.L.	20	120⅔	6	10	.375	64	45	135	4.62	0
2010 Arizona c	N.L.	13	82⅔	3	7	.300	50	19	97	4.25	0
2011 Arizona d	N.L.	33	212	12	13	.480	108	67	210	3.69	0
2012 D-Backs	Arizona	1	4⅓	0	1	.000	7	5	3	6.23	0
2012 Arizona	N.L.	21	130	6	10	.375	89	31	146	4.22	0
2012 Baltimore e-f-g	A.L.	7	44⅔	3	3	.500	23	8	49	3.63	0
2013 Seattle h	A.L.	32	183	11	16	.407	107	61	232	5.26	0
Major League Totals	9 Yrs.	221	1344⅓	89	81	.524	769	415	1468	4.30	0
Wild Card Playoff											
2012 Baltimore	A.L.	1	5⅔	1	0	1.000	4	1	6	1.59	0
Division Series											
2008 Los Angeles	A.L.	1	4⅔	0	0	.000	2	4	5	7.71	0
2011 Arizona	N.L.	1	3	0	0	.000	1	2	5	9.00	0
2012 Baltimore	A.L.	1	5⅔	0	0	.000	5	4	3	1.59	0
Division Series Totals		3	13⅓	0	0	.000	8	10	13	5.40	0
Championship Series											
2009 Los Angeles	A.L.	2	10⅓	0	1	.000	5	6	13	4.35	0

a On minor league disabled list from April 3 to September 18, 2003.
b On disabled list from August 8 to August 26, 2009.
c Traded to Arizona Diamondbacks with pitcher Rafael Rodriguez, pitcher Patrick Corbin and player to be named later for pitcher Danny Haren, July 25, 2010. Arizona Diamondbacks received pitcher Tyler Skaggs to complete trade, August 7, 2010.
d Not offered contract, December 12, 2011, re-signed with Arizona Diamondbacks, January 17, 2012.
e On disabled list from June 17 to July 14, 2012.
f Traded to Baltimore Orioles with cash for pitcher Matt Lindstrom and cash, August 26, 2012.
g Filed for free agency, November 3, 2012. Signed with Seattle Mariners, February 12, 2013.
h Filed for free agency, November 1, 2013.

SCHEPPERS, TANNER ROSS

Born, Mission Viejo, California, January 17, 1987.
Bats Right. Throws Right. Height, 6 feet, 4 inches. Weight, 220 pounds.

Year Club	Lea	G	IP	W	L	Pct	SO	BB	H	ERA	SAVES
2009 St. Paul	Amer. Assoc.	4	19	1	1	.500	20	11	17	3.32	0
2010 Oklahoma	P.C.	30	69	1	3	.250	71	30	82	5.48	4
2010 Frisco	Texas	6	11	0	0	.000	19	0	3	0.82	2
2011 Round Rock	P.C.	11	20⅔	2	0	1.000	20	12	23	4.35	2
2011 Frisco	Texas	17	23	2	1	.667	24	9	18	3.13	0
2012 Round Rock	P.C.	27	31	1	2	.333	31	4	30	3.48	11
2012 Texas	A.L.	39	32⅓	1	1	.500	30	9	47	4.45	1
2013 Texas	A.L.	76	76⅔	6	2	.750	59	24	58	1.88	1
Major League Totals	2 Yrs.	115	109	7	3	.700	89	33	105	2.64	2

SCHERZER, MAXWELL M. (MAX)

Born, St. Louis, Missouri, July 27, 1984.
Bats Right. Throws Right. Height, 6 feet, 3 inches. Weight, 215 pounds.

Year Club	Lea	G	IP	W	L	Pct	SO	BB	H	ERA	SAVES
2007 Fort Worth a	Amer.Assoc.	3	16	1	0	1.000	25	4	9	0.56	0
2007 Visalia	Calif.	3	17	2	0	1.000	30	2	5	0.53	0
2007 Mobile b	Southern	14	73⅔	4	4	.500	76	40	64	3.91	0
2008 Tucson	P.C.	13	53	1	1	.500	79	22	35	2.72	0

Year	Club	Lea	G	IP	W	L	Pct	SO	BB	H	ERA	SAVES
2008	Arizona	N.L.	16	56	0	4	.000	66	21	48	3.05	0
2009	Visalia	Calif.	1	4⅔	0	0	.000	5	4	1	1.93	0
2009	Arizona c-d	N.L.	30	170⅓	9	11	.450	174	63	166	4.12	0
2010	Toledo	Int.	2	15	2	0	1.000	17	2	4	0.60	0
2010	Detroit	A.L.	31	195⅔	12	11	.522	184	70	174	3.50	0
2011	Detroit	A.L.	33	195	15	9	.625	174	56	207	4.43	0
2012	Detroit	A.L.	32	187⅔	16	7	.696	231	60	179	3.74	0
2013	Detroit e	A.L.	32	214⅓	*21	3	*.875	240	56	152	2.90	0
Major League Totals		6 Yrs.	174	1019	73	45	.619	1069	326	926	3.67	0
	Division Series											
2011	Detroit	A.L.	2	7⅓	1	0	1.000	7	4	4	1.23	0
2012	Detroit	A.L.	1	5⅓	0	0	.000	8	1	3	0.00	0
2013	Detroit	A.L.	2	9	2	0	1.000	13	4	6	3.00	0
Division Series Totals			5	21⅔	3	0	1.000	28	9	13	1.66	0
	Championship Series											
2011	Detroit	A.L.	2	8⅓	0	1	.000	7	5	11	9.72	0
2012	Detroit	A.L.	1	5⅔	1	0	1.000	10	2	2	1.59	0
2013	Detroit	A.L.	2	13⅓	0	1	.000	21	7	6	2.70	0
Championship Series Totals			5	27⅓	1	2	.333	38	14	19	4.61	0
	World Series Record											
2012	Detroit	A.L.	1	6⅓	0	0	.000	8	1	7	4.26	0

a Signed by independent Fort Worth (American Association), 2007.

b Signed by Arizona Diamondbacks, May 31, 2007.

c On disabled list from March 29 to April 14, 2009.

d Traded to Detroit Tigers with pitcher Daniel Schlereth for pitcher Edwin Jackson and pitcher Ian Kennedy, December 9, 2009.

e Selected Cy Young Award Winner in American League for 2013.

SHAW, BRYAN ANTHONY

Born, Livermore, California, November 8, 1987.

Bats Both. Throws Right. Height, 6 feet, 1 inch. Weight, 210 pounds.

Year	Club	Lea	G	IP	W	L	Pct	SO	BB	H	ERA	SAVES
2008	South Bend	Midwest	11	22⅓	0	1	.000	16	6	18	4.03	0
2008	Missoula	Pioneer	10	17⅓	0	1	.000	17	7	24	6.75	2
2009	Visalia	Calif.	30	107⅓	3	7	.300	95	40	96	4.70	0
2010	Mobile	Southern	33	101⅓	4	9	.308	75	43	102	4.26	2
2011	Mobile	Southern	15	20⅔	3	1	.750	15	8	15	0.87	7
2011	Reno	P.C.	16	17⅔	1	0	1.000	15	4	14	4.58	9
2011	Arizona	N.L.	33	28⅓	1	0	1.000	24	8	30	2.54	0
2012	Reno	P.C.	8	8	0	0	.000	10	2	6	2.25	2
2012	Arizona a	N.L.	64	59⅓	1	6	.143	41	24	60	3.49	2
2013	Cleveland	A.L.	70	75	7	3	.700	73	28	60	3.24	1
Major League Totals		3 Yrs.	167	162⅔	9	9	.500	138	60	150	3.21	3
	Wild Card Playoff											
2013	Cleveland	A.L.	1	1⅔	0	0	.000	2	0	1	0.00	0
	Division Series											
2011	Arizona	N.L.	4	4	0	0	.000	3	1	0	0.00	0

a Traded to Cleveland Indians with pitcher Matt Albers and pitcher Trevor Bauer for infielder Lars Anderson, infielder Didi Gregorius and pitcher Tony Sipp, December 11, 2012.

SHIELDS, JAMES ANTHONY

Born, Newhall, California, December 20, 1981.

Bats Right. Throws Right. Height, 6 feet, 4 inches. Weight, 215 pounds.

Year	Club	Lea	G	IP	W	L	Pct	SO	BB	H	ERA	SAVES
2001	Hudson Valley	N.Y.-Penn.	5	27⅓	2	1	.667	25	5	27	2.30	0
2001	Charleston-SC	So.Atl.	10	71⅓	4	5	.444	60	10	63	2.65	0
2002	Charleston-SC a						INJURED—Did Not Play					
2003	Bakersfield	Calif.	26	143⅔	10	10	.500	119	38	161	4.45	1
2004	Bakersfield	Calif.	20	117	8	5	.615	92	33	119	4.23	0
2004	Montgomery	Southern	4	18⅓	0	3	.000	14	8	24	7.85	0
2005	Durham	Int.	1	6	1	0	1.000	6	3	9	6.00	0
2005	Montgomery	Southern	17	109⅓	7	5	.583	104	31	95	2.80	0
2006	Durham	Int.	10	61⅓	3	2	.600	64	6	60	2.64	0
2006	Tampa Bay	A.L.	21	124⅔	6	8	.429	104	38	141	4.84	0
2007	Tampa Bay	A.L.	31	215	12	8	.600	184	36	202	3.85	0
2008	Tampa Bay	A.L.	33	215	14	8	.636	160	40	208	3.56	0
2009	Tampa Bay	A.L.	33	219⅔	11	12	.478	167	52	239	4.14	0

Year	Club	Lea	G	IP	W	L	Pct	SO	BB	H	ERA	SAVES
2010	Tampa Bay	A.L.	34	203 1/3	13	15	.464	187	51	*246	5.18	0
2011	Tampa Bay	A.L.	33	249 1/3	16	12	.571	225	65	195	2.82	0
2012	Tampa Bay b	A.L.	33	227 2/3	15	10	.600	223	58	208	3.52	0
2013	Kansas City	A.L.	34	*228 2/3	13	9	.591	196	68	215	3.15	0
Major League Totals		8 Yrs.	252	1683 1/3	100	82	.549	1446	408	1654	3.79	0
	Division Series											
2008	Tampa Bay	A.L.	1	6 1/3	1	0	1.000	4	1	6	4.26	0
2010	Tampa Bay	A.L.	1	4 1/3	0	1	.000	2	0	4	8.31	0
2011	Tampa Bay	A.L.	1	5	0	1	.000	6	0	8	12.60	0
Division Series Totals			3	15 2/3	1	2	.333	12	1	18	8.04	0
	Championship Series											
2008	Tampa Bay	A.L.	2	13	0	2	.000	9	5	15	3.46	0
	World Series Record											
2008	Tampa Bay	A.L.	1	5 2/3	1	0	1.000	4	2	7	0.00	0

a On minor league disabled list April 4 to September 10, 2002.

b Traded to Kansas City Royals with pitcher Wade Davis and player to be named later for pitcher Mike Montgomery, pitcher Jake Odorizzi, infielder Patrick Leonard and outfielder Wil Myers, December 9, 2012.

SIEGRIST, KEVIN RYAN

Born, Buffalo, New York, July 20, 1989.
Bats Left. Throws Left. Height, 6 feet, 5 inches. Weight, 215 pounds.

Year	Club	Lea	G	IP	W	L	Pct	SO	BB	H	ERA	SAVES
2008	Cardinals	Gulf Coast	7	13	0	0	.000	11	3	3	1.38	0
2009	Batavia	N.Y.-Penn.	10	28	1	0	1.000	23	11	30	3.86	2
2010	Johnson City	Appal.	7	32 2/3	4	3	.571	31	6	28	1.93	0
2010	Batavia	N.Y.-Penn.	7	21	0	1	.000	14	16	24	7.29	0
2011	Quad Cities	Midwest	9	54 2/3	8	1	.889	34	15	38	1.15	0
2011	Palm Beach	Fla.St.	11	52 2/3	0	3	.000	45	30	44	3.42	0
2012	Palm Beach	Fla.St.	10	55 1/3	6	0	1.000	41	22	33	2.28	0
2012	Springfield	Texas	8	32 1/3	1	2	.333	27	9	26	3.62	0
2013	Springfield	Texas	13	20	1	1	.500	35	7	8	2.25	1
2013	Memphis	P.C.	5	7 2/3	1	0	1.000	9	3	3	1.17	0
2013	St. Louis	N.L.	45	39 2/3	3	1	.750	50	18	17	0.45	0
	Division Series											
2013	St. Louis	N.L.	2	1 2/3	0	0	.000	0	0	3	0.00	0
	Championship Series											
2013	St. Louis	N.L.	3	1	0	0	.000	1	0	1	9.00	0
	World Series Record											
2013	St. Louis	N.L.	4	3 1/3	0	0	.000	2	0	2	2.70	0

SIMON (CABRERA), ALFREDO

Born, Santiago, Dominican Republic, May 8, 1981.
Bats Right. Throws Right. Height, 6 feet, 4 inches. Weight, 230 pounds.

Year	Club	Lea	G	IP	W	L	Pct	SO	BB	H	ERA	SAVES
2001	Phillies	Gulf Coast	10	43 1/3	2	2	.500	40	23	35	2.91	0
2002	Batavia	N.Y.-Penn.	15	90 1/3	9	2	.818	77	46	79	3.59	0
2003	Lakewood	So.Atl.	14	71 1/3	5	0	1.000	66	25	59	3.79	2
2004	Clearwater a	Fla.St.	22	134 2/3	7	9	.438	107	38	121	3.27	0
2004	San Jose	Calif.	6	31 2/3	1	2	.333	21	12	44	5.68	0
2005	Norwich	Eastern	43	91 1/3	3	8	.273	60	24	104	5.03	19
2006	San Jose	Calif.	18	36 1/3	2	4	.333	35	14	43	6.44	0
2006	Fresno b-c-d	P.C.	10	52	0	6	.000	35	19	76	6.75	0
2007	Oklahoma e-f	P.C.	22	119	5	10	.333	73	46	152	6.43	0
2008	Monterrey g	Mexican	15	81	7	2	.778	61	20	66	2.67	0
2008	Norfolk h	Int.	1	4 2/3	0	1	.000	5	2	9	7.71	0
2008	Baltimore	A.L.	4	13	0	0	.000	8	2	16	6.23	0
2009	Baltimore i-j	A.L.	2	6 1/3	0	1	.000	3	2	8	9.95	0
2010	Norfolk	Int.	4	17	1	1	.500	14	5	15	1.59	0
2010	Baltimore k	A.L.	49	49 1/3	4	2	.667	37	22	54	4.93	17
2011	Bowie	Eastern	4	18	1	0	1.000	20	6	15	3.00	0
2011	Baltimore l	A.L.	23	115 2/3	4	9	.308	83	40	128	4.90	0
2012	Cincinnati m	N.L.	36	61	3	2	.600	52	22	65	2.66	1
2013	Cincinnati	N.L.	63	87 2/3	6	4	.600	63	26	68	2.87	1
Major League Totals		6 Yrs.	177	333	17	18	.486	246	114	339	4.11	19
	Wild Card Playoff											
2013	Cincinnati	N.L.	1	1 1/3	0	0	.000	0	0	2	0.00	0

Year	Club	Lea	G	IP	W	L	Pct	SO	BB	H	ERA	SAVES
	Division Series											
2012	Cincinnati	N.L.	1	1	0	0	.000	1	1	1	0.00	0

a Traded by Philadelphia Phillies to San Francisco Giants with outfielder Ricky Ledee for pitcher Felix Rodriguez, July 30, 2004.
b Filed for free agency, October 15, 2006. Signed with Texas Rangers organization, November 3, 2006.
c Selected by Baltimore Orioles in Rule V draft, December 7, 2006.
d Traded to Philadelphia Phillies for catcher Adam Donachie and cash, December 7, 2006.
e Returned to Texas Rangers, March 17, 2007.
f Filed for free agency, October 29, 2007. Signed with Los Angeles Dodgers organization, January 20, 2008.
g Released by Los Angeles Dodgers, March 30, 2008. Signed with Monterrey (Mexican) for 2008.
h Signed with Baltimore Orioles organization, September 5, 2008.
i On disabled list from April 15 to October 30, 2009.
j Filed for free agency, November 9, 2009, re-signed with Baltimore Orioles, December 2, 2009.
k On disabled list from May 25 to June 14, 2010.
l On disabled list from June 13 to June 29, 2011.
m Claimed on waivers by Cincinnati Reds, April 3, 2012.

SMITH, JOSEPH MICHAEL (JOE)

Born, Cincinnati, Ohio, March 22, 1984.
Bats Right. Throws Right. Height, 6 feet, 2 inches. Weight, 205 pounds.

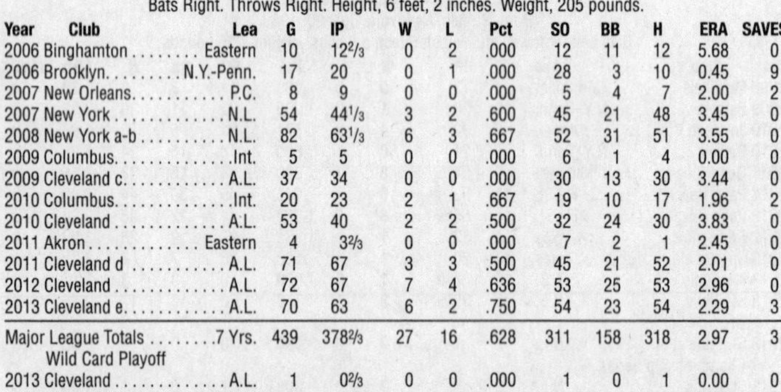

Year	Club	Lea	G	IP	W	L	Pct	SO	BB	H	ERA	SAVES
2006	Binghamton	Eastern	10	12 2/3	0	2	.000	12	11	12	5.68	0
2006	Brooklyn	N.Y.-Penn.	17	20	0	1	.000	28	3	10	0.45	9
2007	New Orleans	P.C.	8	9	0	0	.000	5	4	7	2.00	2
2007	New York	N.L.	54	44 1/3	3	2	.600	45	21	48	3.45	0
2008	New York a-b	N.L.	82	63 1/3	6	3	.667	52	31	51	3.55	0
2009	Columbus	Int.	5	5	0	0	.000	6	1	4	0.00	0
2009	Cleveland c	A.L.	37	34	0	0	.000	30	13	30	3.44	0
2010	Columbus	Int.	20	23	2	1	.667	19	10	17	1.96	2
2010	Cleveland	A.L.	53	40	2	2	.500	32	24	30	3.83	0
2011	Akron	Eastern	4	3 2/3	0	0	.000	7	2	1	2.45	0
2011	Cleveland d	A.L.	71	67	3	3	.500	45	21	52	2.01	0
2012	Cleveland	A.L.	72	67	7	4	.636	53	25	53	2.96	0
2013	Cleveland e	A.L.	70	63	6	2	.750	54	23	54	2.29	3
	Major League Totals	7 Yrs.	439	378 2/3	27	16	.628	311	158	318	2.97	3
	Wild Card Playoff											
2013	Cleveland	A.L.	1	0 2/3	0	0	.000	1	0	1	0.00	0

a Traded to Seattle Mariners with pitcher Aaron Heilman, outfielder Endy Chavez, pitcher Jason Vargas, infielder Mike Carp, outfielder Ezequiel Carrera and pitcher Maikel Cleto for pitcher J.J. Putz, pitcher Sean Green and outfielder Jeremy Reed, December 10, 2008.
b Traded to Cleveland Indians with pitcher Luis Valbuena for outfielder Franklin Gutierrez, December 10, 2008.
c On disabled list from April 29 to June 9 and September 1 to October 14, 2009.
d On disabled list from March 22 to April 15, 2011.
e Filed for free agency, November 4, 2013. Signed with Los Angeles Angels, November 27, 2013.

SMITH, WILLIAM MICHAEL (WILL)

Born, Newnan, Georgia, July 10, 1989.
Bats Right. Throws Left. Height, 6 feet, 5 inches. Weight, 240 pounds.

Year	Club	Lea	G	IP	W	L	Pct	SO	BB	H	ERA	SAVES
2008	Orem	Pioneer	16	73	8	2	.800	76	6	73	3.08	0
2009	Cedar Rapids	Midwest	20	115	10	5	.667	95	24	109	3.76	0
2010	Rancho Cucamonga	Calif.	6	37 1/3	2	2	.500	31	13	36	4.58	0
2010	Wilmington	Carolina	8	54 2/3	4	1	.800	51	4	48	2.80	0
2010	Salt Lake	P.C.	9	53	2	4	.333	40	20	65	5.60	0
2010	Arkansas a	Texas	4	18 2/3	1	2	.333	8	9	33	7.23	0
2011	NW Arkansas	Texas	27	161 1/3	13	9	.591	108	45	171	3.85	0
2012	Omaha	P.C.	15	89 2/3	4	4	.500	74	22	104	3.61	0
2012	Kansas City	A.L.	16	89 2/3	6	9	.400	59	33	111	5.32	0
2013	Omaha	P.C.	28	89	6	4	.600	100	24	81	3.03	4
2013	Kansas City b	A.L.	19	33 1/3	2	1	.667	43	7	24	3.24	0
	Major League Totals	2 Yrs.	35	123	8	10	.444	102	40	135	4.76	0

a Traded by Los Angeles Angels to Kansas City Royals with pitcher Sean O'Sullivan for infielder Alberto Callaspo, July 22, 2010.
b Traded to Milwaukee Brewers for outfielder Norichika Aoki, December 5, 2013.

SMYLY, TODD ANDREW (DREW)

Born, Maumelle, Arkansas, June 13, 1989.
Bats Left. Throws Left. Height, 6 feet, 3 inches. Weight, 190 pounds.

Year	Club	Lea	G	IP	W	L	Pct	SO	BB	H	ERA	SAVES
2011	Erie	Eastern	8	45⅔	4	3	.571	53	15	32	1.18	0
2011	Lakeland	Fla.St.	14	80⅓	7	3	.700	77	21	71	2.58	0
2012	Toledo	Int.	7	17⅔	0	2	.000	25	8	22	6.11	0
2012	Detroit a	A.L.	23	99⅓	4	3	.571	94	33	93	3.99	0
2013	Detroit	A.L.	63	76	6	0	1.000	81	17	62	2.37	2
Major League Totals		2 Yrs.	86	175⅓	10	3	.769	175	50	155	3.29	2
	Division Series											
2013	Detroit	A.L.	2	1	0	0	.000	2	2	1	0.00	0
	Championship Series											
2012	Detroit	A.L.	2	2⅓	1	0	1.000	2	0	1	0.00	0
2013	Detroit	A.L.	4	2	0	0	.000	1	1	0	4.50	0
Championship Series Totals			6	4⅓	1	0	1.000	3	1	1	2.08	0
	World Series Record											
2012	Detroit	A.L.	2	1⅔	0	0	.000	2	3	1	5.40	0

a On disabled list from June 11 to June 26 and July 7 to July 29, 2012.

SORIA (RAMOS), JOAKIM AGUSTIN

Born, Monclova, Mexico, May 18, 1984.
Bats Right. Throws Right. Height, 6 feet, 3 inches. Weight, 200 pounds.

Year	Club	Lea	G	IP	W	L	Pct	SO	BB	H	ERA	SAVES
2002	Dodgers	Gulf Coast	4	5	0	0	.000	6	0	6	3.60	0
2003					INJURED—Did Not Play							
2004	Dodgers	Dominican	4	5⅓	0	0	.000	4	5	3	1.69	1
2005	Mexico City a	Mexican	30	66⅓	5	0	1.000	60	31	75	4.48	0
2006	Mexico City	Mexican	39	37	0	0	.000	30	11	37	3.89	15
2006	Fort Wayne b	Midwest	7	11⅔	1	0	1.000	11	2	5	2.31	0
2007	Kansas City c	A.L.	62	69	2	3	.400	75	19	46	2.48	17
2008	Kansas City	A.L.	63	67⅓	2	3	.400	66	19	39	1.60	42
2009	Kansas City d	A.L.	47	53	3	2	.600	69	16	44	2.21	30
2010	Kansas City	A.L.	66	65⅔	1	2	.333	71	16	53	1.78	43
2011	Kansas City	A.L.	60	60⅓	5	5	.500	60	17	60	4.03	28
2012	Kansas City	A.L.			INJURED—Did not play							
2013	Rangers e	Arizona	1	1	0	0	.000	1	0	0	0.00	0
2013	Frisco	Texas	4	4	0	0	.000	4	0	0	0.00	0
2013	Round Rock	P.C.	2	2	0	0	.000	3	0	1	0.00	0
2013	Texas f-g	A.L.	26	23⅔	1	0	1.000	28	14	18	3.80	0
Major League Totals		6 Yrs.	324	339	14	15	.483	369	101	260	2.50	160

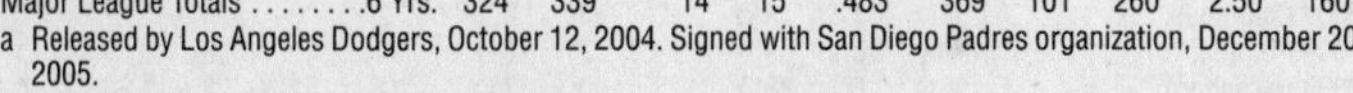

a Released by Los Angeles Dodgers, October 12, 2004. Signed with San Diego Padres organization, December 20, 2005.
b Selected by Kansas City Royals from San Diego Padres in Rule V draft, December 7, 2006.
c On disabled list from May 23 to June 7, 2007.
d On disabled list from May 8 to June 2, 2009.
e On disabled list from March 26 to October 31, 2012.
f Signed with Texas Rangers, December 4, 2012.
g On disabled list from March 22 to July 7, 2013.

SORIANO, RAFAEL

Born, San Jose, Dominican Republic, December 19, 1979.
Bats Right. Throws Right. Height, 6 feet, 1 inch. Weight, 220 pounds.

Year	Club	Lea	G	IP	W	L	Pct	SO	BB	H	ERA	SAVES
1999	Everett	Northwest	14	75⅓	5	4	.556	83	49	56	3.11	0
2000	Wisconsin	Midwest	21	122⅓	8	4	.667	90	50	97	2.87	0
2001	San Bernardino	Calif.	15	89	6	3	.667	98	39	49	2.53	0
2001	San Antonio	Texas	8	48⅓	2	2	.500	53	14	34	3.35	0
2002	San Antonio	Texas	10	46⅔	2	3	.400	52	15	32	2.31	0
2002	Seattle a	A.L.	10	47⅓	0	3	.000	32	16	45	4.56	1
2003	Tacoma	P.C.	11	62	4	3	.571	63	12	43	3.19	0
2003	Seattle	A.L.	40	53	3	0	1.000	68	12	30	1.53	1
2004	Seattle	A.L.	6	3⅓	0	3	.000	3	3	9	13.50	0
2004	Inland Empire	Calif.	2	8	0	0	.000	9	1	7	2.25	0
2004	San Antonio	Texas	2	8	1	0	1.000	10	0	4	1.13	0
2004	Tacoma b	P.C.	3	3⅔	0	0	.000	5	2	2	2.45	0
2005	Inland Empire	Calif.	3	4	0	0	.000	5	0	2	0.00	0
2005	San Antonio	Texas	1	1	0	0	.000	0	0	0	0.00	0
2005	Everett	Northwest	4	6	0	0	.000	8	2	6	3.00	0

Year	Club	Lea	G	IP	W	L	Pct	SO	BB	H	ERA	SAVES
2005	Tacoma	P.C.	5	5 1/3	1	0	1.000	11	1	3	0.00	0
2005	Seattle c	A.L.	7	7 1/3	0	0	.000	9	1	6	2.45	0
2006	Seattle d-e	A.L.	53	60	1	2	.333	65	21	44	2.25	2
2007	Atlanta	N.L.	71	72	3	3	.500	70	15	47	3.00	9
2008	Mississippi	Southern	2	2	0	0	.000	2	1	1	0.00	0
2008	Atlanta f	N.L.	14	14	0	1	.000	16	9	7	2.57	3
2009	Atlanta g	N.L.	77	75 2/3	1	6	.143	102	27	53	2.97	27
2010	Tampa Bay h	A.L.	64	62 1/3	3	2	.600	57	14	36	1.73	*45
2011	Tampa	Fla.St.	2	2 1/3	0	1	.000	1	0	4	11.57	0
2011	Scranton-WB	Int.	2	2	1	0	1.000	2	0	1	4.50	0
2011	New York i	A.L.	42	39 1/3	2	3	.400	36	18	33	4.12	2
2012	New York j	A.L.	69	67 2/3	2	1	.667	69	24	55	2.26	42
2013	Washington	N.L.	68	66 2/3	3	3	.500	51	17	65	3.11	43
Major League Totals		12 Yrs.	521	568 2/3	18	27	.400	578	177	430	2.82	175
	Division Series											
2010	Tampa Bay	A.L.	3	3	0	0	.000	1	0	4	9.00	1
2011	New York	A.L.	3	4 2/3	0	1	.000	4	0	1	1.93	0
2012	New York	A.L.	2	3 1/3	0	0	.000	2	0	2	0.00	0
Division Series Totals			8	11	0	1	.000	7	0	7	3.27	1
	Championship Series											
2012	New York	A.L.	1	1	0	0	.000	0	0	0	0.00	0

a On disabled list from July 3 to August 2, 2002.
b On disabled list from May 10 to November 1, 2004.
c On disabled list from April 1 to September 5, 2005.
d On disabled list from July 20 to August 4, 2006.
e Traded to Atlanta Braves for pitcher Horacio Ramirez, December 7, 2006.
f On disabled list from April 7 to May 28 and June 6 to July 21 and August 3 to November 3, 2008.
g Traded to Tampa Bay Rays for pitcher Jesse Chavez, December 11, 2009.
h Filed for free agency, November 1, 2010. Signed with New York Yankees, January 18, 2011.
i On disabled list from May 17 to July 29, 2011.
j Filed for free agency, November 3, 2012. Signed with Washington Nationals, January 15, 2013.

STAMMEN, CRAIG N.

Born, Coldwater, Ohio, March 9, 1984.
Bats Right. Throws Right. Height, 6 feet, 3 inches. Weight, 225 pounds.

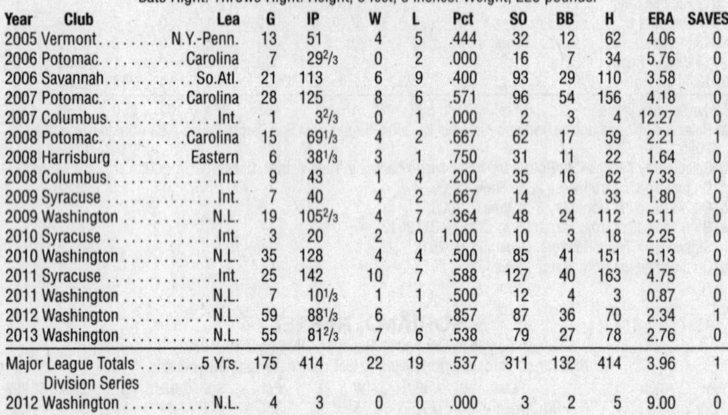

Year	Club	Lea	G	IP	W	L	Pct	SO	BB	H	ERA	SAVES
2005	Vermont	N.Y.-Penn.	13	51	4	5	.444	32	12	62	4.06	0
2006	Potomac	Carolina	7	29 2/3	0	2	.000	16	7	34	5.76	0
2006	Savannah	So.Atl.	21	113	6	9	.400	93	29	110	3.58	0
2007	Potomac	Carolina	28	125	8	6	.571	96	54	156	4.18	0
2007	Columbus	Int.	1	3 2/3	0	1	.000	2	3	4	12.27	0
2008	Potomac	Carolina	15	69 1/3	4	2	.667	62	17	59	2.21	1
2008	Harrisburg	Eastern	6	38 1/3	3	1	.750	31	11	22	1.64	0
2008	Columbus	Int.	9	43	1	4	.200	35	16	62	7.33	0
2009	Syracuse	Int.	7	40	4	2	.667	14	8	33	1.80	0
2009	Washington	N.L.	19	105 2/3	4	7	.364	48	24	112	5.11	0
2010	Syracuse	Int.	3	20	2	0	1.000	10	3	18	2.25	0
2010	Washington	N.L.	35	128	4	4	.500	85	41	151	5.13	0
2011	Syracuse	Int.	25	142	10	7	.588	127	40	163	4.75	0
2011	Washington	N.L.	7	10 1/3	1	1	.500	12	4	3	0.87	0
2012	Washington	N.L.	59	88 1/3	6	1	.857	87	36	70	2.34	1
2013	Washington	N.L.	55	81 2/3	7	6	.538	79	27	78	2.76	0
Major League Totals		5 Yrs.	175	414	22	19	.537	311	132	414	3.96	1
	Division Series											
2012	Washington	N.L.	4	3	0	0	.000	3	2	5	9.00	0

STAUFFER, TIMOTHY JAMES (TIM)

Born, Portland, Maine, June 2, 1982.
Bats Right. Throws Right. Height, 6 feet, 1 inch. Weight, 205 pounds.

Year	Club	Lea	G	IP	W	L	Pct	SO	BB	H	ERA	SAVES
2004	Lake Elsinore	Calif.	6	35 1/3	2	0	1.000	30	9	28	1.78	0
2004	Portland	P.C.	14	81 1/3	6	3	.667	50	26	83	3.54	0
2004	Mobile	Southern	8	51 1/3	3	2	.600	33	13	56	2.63	0
2005	San Diego	N.L.	15	81	3	6	.333	49	29	92	5.33	0
2005	Portland	P.C.	13	75 1/3	3	5	.375	64	17	90	5.14	0
2006	San Diego	N.L.	1	6	1	0	1.000	2	1	3	1.50	0
2006	Portland	P.C.	28	153	7	12	.368	89	52	199	5.53	0
2007	San Diego	N.L.	2	7 2/3	0	1	.000	6	6	15	21.13	0

Year	Club	Lea	G	IP	W	L	Pct	SO	BB	H	ERA	SAVES
2007	Portland	P.C.	25	$130\frac{2}{3}$	8	5	.615	96	36	147	4.34	0
2008	San Diego a	N.L.			INJURED—Did Not Play							
2009	San Antonio	Texas	12	19	1	0	1.000	12	4	13	1.89	1
2009	Portland	P.C.	4	23	2	1	.667	16	4	16	2.35	0
2009	San Diego	N.L.	14	73	4	7	.364	53	34	71	3.58	0
2010	Portland	P.C.	6	$17\frac{2}{3}$	0	0	.000	8	7	24	4.58	0
2010	San Diego b	N.L.	32	$82\frac{2}{3}$	6	5	.545	61	24	65	1.85	0
2011	San Diego	N.L.	31	$185\frac{2}{3}$	9	12	.429	128	53	180	3.73	0
2012	Padres	Arizona	1	1	0	0	.000	1	0	1	0.00	0
2012	Lake Elsinore	Calif.	4	$13\frac{1}{3}$	0	1	.000	11	2	15	3.38	0
2012	Tucson	P.C.	2	8	0	1	.000	2	1	10	3.38	0
2012	San Diego c-d	N.L.	1	5	0	0	.000	5	3	7	5.40	0
2013	Tucson	P.C.	8	$42\frac{2}{3}$	2	2	.500	38	15	50	3.16	0
2013	San Diego	N.L.	43	$69\frac{2}{3}$	3	1	.750	64	20	59	3.75	0
Major League Totals		8 Yrs.	139	$510\frac{2}{3}$	26	32	.448	368	170	492	3.91	0

a On disabled list from March 26 to October 8, 2008.
b On disabled list from May 11 to July 1, 2010.
c On disabled list from April 4 to May 14 and May 15 to October 26, 2012.
d Filed for free agency, October 26, 2012, re-signed with San Diego Padres organization, January 29, 2013.

STOREN, DREW PATRICK

Born, Brownsburg, Indiana, August 11, 1987.
Bats Both. Throws Right. Height, 6 feet, 2 inches. Weight, 180 pounds.

Year	Club	Lea	G	IP	W	L	Pct	SO	BB	H	ERA	SAVES
2009	Hagerstown	So.Atl.	11	$14\frac{2}{3}$	0	1	.000	26	0	11	3.68	0
2009	Potomac	Carolina	7	10	1	0	1.000	11	2	7	1.80	2
2009	Harrisburg	Eastern	10	$12\frac{1}{3}$	1	0	1.000	12	6	3	0.00	9
2010	Harrisburg	Eastern	7	$9\frac{1}{3}$	0	0	.000	11	1	5	0.96	4
2010	Syracuse	Int.	6	$7\frac{1}{3}$	0	0	.000	4	2	7	1.23	0
2010	Washington	N.L.	54	$55\frac{1}{3}$	4	4	.500	52	22	48	3.58	5
2011	Washington	N.L.	73	$75\frac{1}{3}$	6	3	.667	74	20	57	2.75	43
2012	Potomac	Carolina	5	6	1	0	1.000	8	1	4	3.00	0
2012	Harrisburg	Eastern	1	$0\frac{2}{3}$	0	0	.000	0	1	3	54.00	0
2012	Washington a	N.L.	37	$30\frac{1}{3}$	3	1	.750	24	8	22	2.37	4
2013	Syracuse	Int.	6	$6\frac{1}{3}$	0	0	.000	11	0	7	5.68	0
2013	Washington	N.L.	68	$61\frac{2}{3}$	4	2	.667	58	19	65	4.52	3
Major League Totals		4 Yrs.	232	$222\frac{2}{3}$	17	10	.630	208	69	192	3.40	55
	Division Series											
2012	Washington	N.L.	4	4	1	1	.500	6	3	3	9.00	1

a On disabled list from March 26 to July 19, 2012.

STRAILY, DANIEL STEVEN (DAN)

Born, Redlands, California, December 1, 1988.
Bats Right. Throws Right. Height, 6 feet, 2 inches. Weight, 220 pounds.

Year	Club	Lea	G	IP	W	L	Pct	SO	BB	H	ERA	SAVES
2009	Vancouver	Northwest	16	59	5	3	.625	66	18	66	4.12	0
2010	Kane County	Midwest	28	148	10	7	.588	149	61	138	4.32	0
2011	Stockton	Calif.	28	$160\frac{2}{3}$	11	9	.550	154	40	160	3.87	0
2012	Midland	Texas	14	$85\frac{1}{3}$	3	4	.429	108	23	70	3.38	0
2012	Sacramento	P.C.	11	$66\frac{2}{3}$	6	3	.667	82	19	40	2.03	0
2012	Oakland	A.L.	7	$39\frac{1}{3}$	2	1	.667	32	16	36	3.89	0
2013	Sacramento	P.C.	5	$31\frac{2}{3}$	3	1	.750	33	9	24	1.14	0
2013	Oakland	A.L.	27	$152\frac{1}{3}$	10	8	.556	124	57	132	3.96	0
Major League Totals		2 Yrs.	34	$191\frac{2}{3}$	12	9	.571	156	73	168	3.94	0
	Division Series											
2013	Oakland	A.L.	1	6	0	0	.000	8	0	4	4.50	0

STRASBURG, STEPHEN JAMES

Born, San Diego, California, July 20, 1988.
Bats Right. Throws Right. Height, 6 feet, 4 inches. Weight, 220 pounds.

Year	Club	Lea	G	IP	W	L	Pct	SO	BB	H	ERA	SAVES
2010	Harrisburg	Eastern	5	22	3	1	.750	27	6	13	1.64	0
2010	Syracuse	Int.	6	$33\frac{1}{3}$	4	1	.800	38	7	18	1.08	0
2010	Washington a	N.L.	12	68	5	3	.625	92	17	56	2.91	0
2011	Hagerstown	So.Atl.	3	$6\frac{1}{3}$	0	1	.000	13	3	9	9.95	0
2011	Potomac	Carolina	1	3	0	0	.000	5	0	2	0.00	0

Year	Club	Lea	G	IP	W	L	Pct	SO	BB	H	ERA	SAVES
2011	Harrisburg	Eastern	1	6	1	0	1.000	4	0	1	0.00	0
2011	Syracuse	Int.	1	5	0	0	.000	7	0	2	1.80	0
2011	Washington b	N.L.	5	24	1	1	.500	24	2	15	1.50	0
2012	Washington	N.L.	28	159⅓	15	6	.714	197	48	136	3.16	0
2013	Washington c	N.L.	30	183	8	9	.471	191	56	136	3.00	0
Major League Totals		4 Yrs.	75	434⅓	29	19	.604	504	123	343	2.96	0

a On disabled list from July 22 to August 7 and August 24 to November 10, 2010.
b On disabled list from March 23 to September 6, 2011.
c On disabled list from June 1 to June 16, 2013.

STREET, HUSTON LOWELL

Born, Austin, Texas, August 2, 1983.
Bats Right. Throws Right. Height, 6 feet. Weight, 190 pounds.

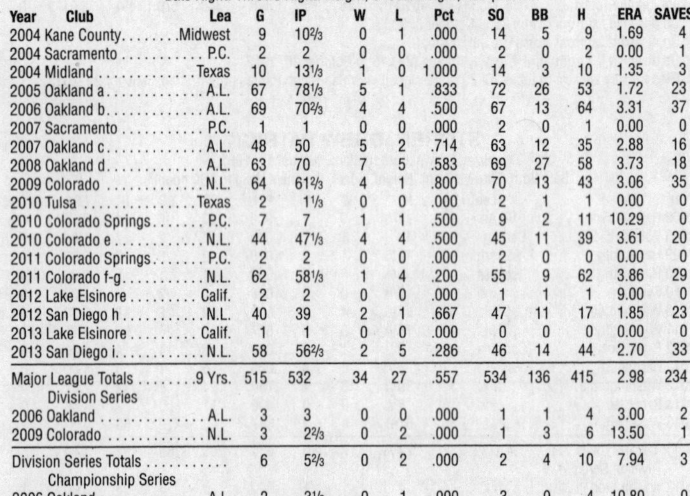

Year	Club	Lea	G	IP	W	L	Pct	SO	BB	H	ERA	SAVES
2004	Kane County	Midwest	9	10⅔	0	1	.000	14	5	9	1.69	4
2004	Sacramento	P.C.	2	2	0	0	.000	2	0	2	0.00	1
2004	Midland	Texas	10	13⅓	1	0	1.000	14	3	10	1.35	3
2005	Oakland a	A.L.	67	78⅓	5	1	.833	72	26	53	1.72	23
2006	Oakland b	A.L.	69	70⅔	4	4	.500	67	13	64	3.31	37
2007	Sacramento	P.C.	1	1	0	0	.000	2	0	1	0.00	0
2007	Oakland c	A.L.	48	50	5	2	.714	63	12	35	2.88	16
2008	Oakland d	A.L.	63	70	7	5	.583	69	27	58	3.73	18
2009	Colorado	N.L.	64	61⅔	4	1	.800	70	13	43	3.06	35
2010	Tulsa	Texas	2	1⅓	0	0	.000	2	1	1	0.00	0
2010	Colorado Springs	P.C.	7	7	1	1	.500	9	2	11	10.29	0
2010	Colorado e	N.L.	44	47⅓	4	4	.500	45	11	39	3.61	20
2011	Colorado Springs	P.C.	2	2	0	0	.000	2	0	0	0.00	0
2011	Colorado f-g	N.L.	62	58⅓	1	4	.200	55	9	62	3.86	29
2012	Lake Elsinore	Calif.	2	2	0	0	.000	1	1	1	9.00	0
2012	San Diego h	N.L.	40	39	2	1	.667	47	11	17	1.85	23
2013	Lake Elsinore	Calif.	1	1	0	0	.000	0	0	0	0.00	0
2013	San Diego i	N.L.	58	56⅔	2	5	.286	46	14	44	2.70	33
Major League Totals		9 Yrs.	515	532	34	27	.557	534	136	415	2.98	234
	Division Series											
2006	Oakland	A.L.	3	3	0	0	.000	1	1	4	3.00	2
2009	Colorado	N.L.	3	2⅔	0	2	.000	1	3	6	13.50	1
Division Series Totals			6	5⅔	0	2	.000	2	4	10	7.94	3
	Championship Series											
2006	Oakland	A.L.	2	3⅓	0	1	.000	3	0	4	10.80	0

a Selected Rookie of the Year in American League for 2005.
b On disabled list from August 19 to September 8, 2006.
c On disabled list from May 13 to July 23, 2007.
d Traded to Colorado Rockies with outfielder Carlos Gonzalez and pitcher Greg Smith for outfielder Matt Holliday, November 12, 2008.
e On disabled list from March 26 to June 22, 2010.
f On disabled list from August 9 to August 26, 2011.
g Traded to San Diego Padres with cash for pitcher Nick Schmidt, December 7, 2011.
h On disabled list from May 5 to June 5 and August 11 to September 21, 2012.
i On disabled list from May 30 to June 14, 2013.

STROP, PEDRO ANGEL

Born, San Cristobal, Dominican Republic, June 13, 1985.
Bats Right. Throws Right. Height, 6 feet. Weight, 215 pounds.

Year	Club	Lea	G	IP	W	L	Pct	SO	BB	H	ERA	SAVES
2006	Casper	Pioneer	11	13	1	0	1.000	22	2	9	2.08	0
2006	Asheville	So.Atl.	11	13⅓	2	1	.667	13	5	10	4.72	0
2007	Modesto	Calif.	48	54⅔	5	2	.714	75	29	43	4.28	7
2008	Tulsa a	Texas	7	7	0	0	.000	7	4	6	2.57	3
2009	Frisco	Texas	36	51⅓	5	5	.500	48	29	48	4.38	4
2009	Oklahoma	P.C.	11	12⅔	1	1	.500	13	4	13	7.82	1
2009	Texas	A.L.	7	7	0	0	.000	9	4	6	7.71	0
2010	Oklahoma	P.C.	39	42⅓	1	2	.333	57	14	32	1.91	13
2010	Texas	A.L.	15	10⅔	0	0	.000	11	11	17	10.13	0
2011	Round Rock	P.C.	39	47⅔	4	4	.500	55	24	53	3.59	11
2011	Texas-Baltimore b	A.L.	23	22	2	1	.667	21	10	15	2.05	0
2012	Baltimore	A.L.	70	66⅓	5	2	.714	58	37	52	2.44	3
2013	Baltimore c	A.L.	29	22⅓	0	3	.000	24	15	23	7.25	0

Year Club	Lea	G	IP	W	L	Pct	SO	BB	H	ERA	SAVES
2013 Chicago d	N.L.	37	35	2	2	.500	42	11	22	2.83	1
Major League Totals	5 Yrs.	181	163⅓	9	8	.529	165	88	135	3.86	4
Division Series											
2012 Baltimore	A.L.	2	2⅓	1	0	1.000	2	1	1	0.00	0

a Released by Colorado Rockies, September 19, 2008. Signed with Texas Rangers organization, November 7, 2008.
b Sent to Baltimore Orioles as player to be named later for pitcher Mike Gonzalez, September 1, 2011.
c On disabled list from May 24 to June 8, 2013.
d Traded to Chicago Cubs with pitcher Jake Arrieta for catcher Steve Clevinger and pitcher Scott Feldman, July 2, 2013.

STULTS, ERIC WILLIAM

Born, Plymouth, Indiana, December 9, 1979.
Bats Left. Throws Left. Height, 6 feet. Weight, 225 pounds.

Year Club	Lea	G	IP	W	L	Pct	SO	BB	H	ERA	SAVES
2002 Vero Beach	Fla.St.	13	42	3	1	.750	40	20	39	3.00	0
2002 Great Falls	Pioneer	5	8	1	0	1.000	9	3	6	2.25	1
2002 Jacksonville	Southern	1	1	0	0	.000	0	0	0	0.00	0
2003 Vero Beach	Fla.St.	1	3	0	1	.000	1	1	6	6.00	0
2003 Jacksonville	Southern	9	38	3	4	.429	14	13	46	4.97	1
2004 Vero Beach	Fla.St.	7	10	2	1	.667	6	4	11	2.70	1
2004 Columbus	So.Atl.	12	21⅔	1	2	.333	16	6	18	2.49	3
2005 Las Vegas	P.C.	15	78	3	7	.300	60	24	107	6.58	0
2005 Jacksonville	Southern	12	68	4	3	.571	58	14	73	3.31	0
2006 Las Vegas	P.C.	26	153⅓	10	11	.476	128	68	153	4.23	0
2006 Los Angeles	N.L.	6	17⅔	1	0	1.000	5	7	17	5.60	0
2007 Las Vegas	P.C.	21	89⅓	5	7	.417	81	36	134	7.56	0
2007 Los Angeles	N.L.	12	38⅔	1	4	.200	30	17	50	5.82	0
2008 Las Vegas	P.C.	20	117⅔	7	7	.500	102	35	118	3.82	0
2008 Los Angeles	N.L.	7	38⅔	2	3	.400	30	13	38	3.49	0
2009 Inland Empire	Calif.	2	7⅓	0	0	.000	5	0	5	1.23	0
2009 Los Angeles	N.L.	10	50	4	3	.571	33	26	51	4.86	0
2009 Albuquerque a	P.C.	12	64	5	4	.556	40	24	86	5.20	0
2010 Hiroshima b	Japan Cent.	21	124⅓	6	10	.375	87	46	149	5.07	0
2011 Colorado	N.L.	6	12	0	0	.000	7	4	11	6.00	0
2011 Colorado Springs c	P.C.	52	68	4	4	.500	69	16	76	4.63	1
2012 Tucson	P.C.	2	6⅔	0	0	.000	10	4	7	5.40	0
2012 Charlotte	Int.	5	28⅔	1	1	.500	26	10	25	2.20	0
2012 Chicago	A.L.	2	6⅔	0	0	.000	4	4	6	2.70	0
2012 San Diego d-e	N.L.	18	92⅓	8	3	.727	51	23	86	2.92	0
2013 San Diego	N.L.	33	203⅔	11	13	.458	131	40	219	3.93	0
Major League Totals	7 Yrs.	94	459⅔	27	26	.509	291	134	478	4.05	0

a On disabled list from May 31 to July 1, 2009.
b Sold to Hiroshima, March 31, 2010. Signed with Colorado Rockies organization, November 30, 2010.
c Filed for free agency, November 2, 2011. Signed with Chicago White Sox organization, December 11, 2011.
d Claimed on waivers by San Diego Padres, May 17, 2012.
e On disabled list from June 4 to July 22, 2012.

SWARZAK, ANTHONY RAY

Born, Ft.Lauderdale, Florida, September 10, 1985.
Bats Right. Throws Right. Height, 6 feet, 4 inches. Weight, 225 pounds.

Year Club	Lea	G	IP	W	L	Pct	SO	BB	H	ERA	SAVES
2004 Twins	Gulf Coast	11	48	5	3	.625	42	6	46	2.63	1
2005 Beloit	Midwest	18	91⅓	9	5	.643	101	32	81	4.04	0
2005 Fort Myers	Fla.St.	10	59	3	4	.429	55	11	72	3.66	0
2006 Fort Myers	Fla.St.	27	145⅔	11	7	.611	131	60	131	3.27	0
2007 New Britain	Eastern	15	86⅓	5	4	.556	76	23	78	3.23	0
2007 Fort Myers	Fla.St.	3	15⅔	0	0	.000	18	5	14	2.30	0
2008 New Britain	Eastern	20	101⅔	3	8	.273	76	37	126	5.67	0
2008 Rochester	Int.	7	45	5	0	1.000	26	14	41	1.80	0
2009 Minnesota	A.L.	12	59	3	7	.300	34	20	76	6.25	0
2009 Rochester	Int.	13	79⅔	4	5	.444	45	21	79	3.28	0
2010 Rochester	Int.	22	111⅔	5	12	.294	69	38	143	6.21	0
2011 Rochester	Int.	6	32⅓	2	1	.667	25	7	35	3.90	0
2011 Minnesota	A.L.	27	102	4	7	.364	55	26	111	4.32	0
2012 Minnesota a	A.L.	44	96⅔	3	6	.333	62	31	106	5.03	0
2013 Minnesota b	A.L.	48	96	3	2	.600	69	22	89	2.91	0
Major League Totals	4 Yrs.	131	353⅔	13	22	.371	220	99	382	4.45	0

a On disabled list from July 25 to August 15, 2012.
b On disabled list from March 22 to April 7, 2013.

TANAKA, MASAHIRO

Born, Hyogo, Japan, November 1, 1988.
Bats Right. Throws Right. Height 6 feet, 2 inches. Weight, 205 pounds.

Year Club	Lea	G	IP	W	L	Pct	SO	BB	H	ERA	SAVES
2007 Rakuten	Japan Pac.	28	186⅓	11	7	.611	196	68	183	3.82	0
2008 Rakuten	Japan Pac.	25	172⅔	9	7	.563	159	54	171	3.49	1
2009 Rakuten	Japan Pac.	25	189⅔	15	6	.714	171	43	170	2.33	1
2010 Rakuten	Japan Pac.	20	155	11	6	.647	119	32	159	2.50	0
2011 Rakuten	Japan Pac.	27	226⅓	19	5	.792	241	27	171	1.27	0
2012 Rakuten	Japan Pac.	22	173	10	4	.714	169	19	160	1.87	0
2013 Rakuten	Japan Pac.	28	212	24	0	1.000	183	32	168	1.27	1

TAZAWA, JUNICHI

Born, Yokohama, Japan, June 6, 1986.
Bats Right. Throws Right. Height, 5 feet, 11 inches. Weight, 180 pounds.

Year Club	Lea	G	IP	W	L	Pct	SO	BB	H	ERA	SAVES
2009 Portland	Eastern	18	98	9	5	.643	88	26	80	2.57	0
2009 Pawtucket	Int.	2	11⅓	0	2	.000	6	1	7	2.38	0
2009 Boston a	A.L.	6	25⅓	2	3	.400	13	9	43	7.46	0
2010 Boston b	A.L.					INJURED—Did Not Play					
2011 Salem	Carolina	6	19⅓	0	1	.000	13	6	20	6.05	0
2011 Portland	Eastern	8	23	3	2	.600	27	7	20	4.70	0
2011 Pawtucket	Int.	8	14⅓	1	1	.500	19	3	14	2.51	0
2011 Boston c	A.L.	3	3	0	0	.000	4	1	3	6.00	0
2012 Pawtucket	Int.	25	42⅓	3	2	.600	56	17	34	2.55	4
2012 Boston	A.L.	37	44	1	1	.500	45	5	37	1.43	1
2013 Boston	A.L.	71	68⅓	5	4	.556	72	12	70	3.16	0
Major League Totals	4 Yrs.	117	140⅔	8	8	.500	134	27	153	3.45	1
Division Series											
2013 Boston	A.L.	4	2⅓	0	0	.000	2	0	1	0.00	0
Championship Series											
2013 Boston	A.L.	4	2⅔	1	0	1.000	1	0	4	3.38	0
World Series Record											
2013 Boston	A.L.	5	2⅓	0	0	.000	3	1	1	0.00	0

a On disabled list from September 21 to November 13, 2009.
b On disabled list from April 3 to November 8, 2010.
c On disabled list from March 26 to June 27, 2011.

TEHERAN, JULIO ALBERTO

Born, Cartagena, Colombia, January 27, 1991.
Bats Right. Throws Right. Height, 6 feet, 2 inches. Weight, 175 pounds.

Year Club	Lea	G	IP	W	L	Pct	SO	BB	H	ERA	SAVES
2008 Danville	Appal.	6	15	1	2	.333	17	4	18	6.60	0
2009 Danville	Appal.	7	43⅔	2	1	.667	39	7	36	2.68	0
2009 Rome	So.Atl.	7	37⅔	1	3	.250	28	11	42	4.78	0
2010 Rome	So.Atl.	7	39⅓	2	2	.500	45	10	23	1.14	0
2010 Myrtle Beach	Carolina	10	63⅓	4	4	.500	76	13	56	2.98	0
2010 Mississippi	Southern	7	40	3	2	.600	38	17	29	3.38	0
2011 Gwinnett	Int.	25	144⅔	15	3	.833	122	48	123	2.55	0
2011 Atlanta	N.L.	5	19⅔	1	1	.500	10	8	21	5.03	0
2012 Gwinnett	Int.	26	131	7	9	.438	97	43	146	5.08	0
2012 Atlanta	N.L.	2	6⅓	0	0	.000	5	1	5	5.68	0
2013 Atlanta	N.L.	30	185⅔	14	8	.636	170	45	173	3.20	0
Major League Totals	3 Yrs.	37	211⅔	15	9	.625	185	54	199	3.44	0
Division Series											
2013 Atlanta	N.L.	1	2⅔	0	1	.000	5	1	8	20.25	0

TEPESCH, NICHOLAS JAMES (NICK)

Born, Kansas City, Missouri, October 12, 1988.
Bats Right. Throws Right. Height, 6 feet, 4 inches. Weight, 225 pounds.

Year Club	Lea	G	IP	W	L	Pct	SO	BB	H	ERA	SAVES
2011 Hickory	So.Atl.	29	138⅓	7	5	.583	118	33	147	4.03	0
2012 Myrtle Beach	Carolina	12	71⅔	5	3	.625	59	18	68	2.89	0
2012 Frisco	Texas	16	90⅓	6	3	.667	68	26	97	4.28	0
2013 Frisco	Texas	2	6	0	0	.000	3	2	7	1.50	0
2013 Round Rock	P.C.	1	5	1	0	1.000	5	0	5	0.00	0
2013 Texas a	A.L.	19	93	4	6	.400	76	27	100	4.84	0

a On disabled list from July 6 to September 1, 2013.

THATCHER, JOSEPH (JOE)

Born, Indianapolis, Indiana, October 4, 1981.
Bats Left. Throws Left. Height, 6 feet, 2 inches. Weight, 230 pounds.

Year	Club	Lea	G	IP	W	L	Pct	SO	BB	H	ERA	SAVES
2004	River City	Frontier	29	41⅓	2	3	.400	55	15	38	2.98	5
2005	River City	Frontier	18	21⅓	4	2	.667	27	4	18	1.27	5
2005	Brevard County a	Fla.St.	7	9	0	0	.000	14	0	6	0.00	2
2005	Helena	Pioneer	6	7⅔	2	0	1.000	10	1	8	3.52	2
2006	Brevard County	Fla.St.	16	30⅔	3	1	.750	32	9	12	0.29	2
2006	West Virginia	So.Atl.	26	29⅔	1	3	.250	42	6	28	2.43	10
2006	Huntsville	Southern	4	5⅓	1	0	1.000	6	2	2	1.69	0
2007	Huntsville	Southern	14	16⅓	1	0	1.000	20	2	11	0.55	0
2007	Nashville	P.C.	24	21⅔	2	1	.667	33	7	19	2.08	1
2007	Portland	P.C.	8	8⅔	1	0	1.000	11	1	10	1.04	0
2007	San Diego b	N.L.	22	21	2	2	.500	16	6	13	1.29	0
2008	San Diego	N.L.	25	25⅔	0	4	.000	17	13	42	8.42	0
2008	Portland	P.C.	37	39	5	2	.714	44	11	38	2.77	3
2009	Portland	P.C.	19	19	1	2	.333	22	5	18	1.89	1
2009	San Diego	N.L.	52	45	1	0	1.000	55	18	37	2.80	0
2010	Portland	P.C.	6	5	0	1	.000	3	3	6	3.60	0
2010	San Diego c	N.L.	65	35	1	0	1.000	45	7	23	1.29	0
2011	Lake Elsinore	Calif.	1	1	0	0	.000	2	0	0	0.00	0
2011	Tucson	P.C.	8	7⅓	0	0	.000	10	3	3	1.23	0
2011	San Diego d	N.L.	18	10	0	0	.000	9	7	8	4.50	0
2012	Lake Elsinore	Calif.	1	1	0	0	.000	1	0	0	0.00	0
2012	San Diego e	N.L.	55	31⅔	1	4	.200	39	14	30	3.41	1
2013	San Diego-Arizona f	N.L.	72	39⅓	3	2	.600	36	10	40	3.20	0
Major League Totals		7 Yrs.	309	207⅔	8	12	.400	217	75	193	3.34	1

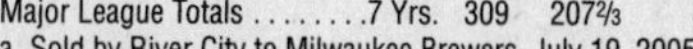

a Sold by River City to Milwaukee Brewers, July 19, 2005.
b Traded to San Diego Padres with pitcher Will Inman and pitcher Steve Garrison for pitcher Scott Linebrink, July 25, 2007.
c On disabled list from March 26 to April 22, 2010.
d On disabled list from March 22 to August 4, 2011.
e On disabled list from July 26 to September 1, 2012.
f Traded to Arizona Diamondbacks with pitcher Matt Stites and a competitive balance draft choice for pitcher Ian Kennedy, July 31, 2013.

THAYER, DALE SCOTT

Born, Fountain Valley, California, December 17, 1980.
Bats Right. Throws Right. Height, 6 feet. Weight, 195 pounds.

Year	Club	Lea	G	IP	W	L	Pct	SO	BB	H	ERA	SAVES
2003	Fort Wayne	Midwest	45	48	1	3	.250	72	15	31	2.06	25
2004	Lake Elsinore	Calif.	50	55⅓	2	1	.667	54	11	36	1.63	23
2004	Mobile	Southern	8	7⅓	1	1	.500	7	1	8	3.68	0
2005	Mobile	Southern	56	57⅔	3	5	.375	59	26	60	2.34	27
2006	Portland	P.C.	2	3	0	0	.000	4	1	2	3.00	0
2006	Mobile a	Southern	57	65⅓	7	4	.636	57	22	59	2.48	27
2007	Durham	Int.	8	9⅓	0	0	.000	9	4	5	2.89	0
2007	Montgomery	Southern	47	5⅔	9	0	1.000	54	20	40	2.26	21
2008	Durham	Int.	52	68⅓	3	1	.750	76	24	73	2.77	9
2009	Durham	Int.	51	63⅓	2	5	.286	44	15	59	2.27	17
2009	Tampa Bay	A.L.	11	13⅔	0	0	.000	8	1	18	4.61	1
2010	Tampa Bay	A.L.	1	2	0	0	.000	2	0	7	27.00	0
2010	Durham	Int.	46	60	4	1	.800	55	25	68	3.45	3
2011	Buffalo	Int.	54	71	4	3	.571	66	15	54	2.66	21
2011	New York b-c	N.L.	11	10⅓	0	3	.000	5	0	12	3.48	0
2012	Tucson	P.C.	7	8⅓	0	0	.000	5	2	2	0.00	0
2012	San Diego	N.L.	64	57⅔	2	2	.500	47	12	53	3.43	7
2013	San Diego	N.L.	69	65	3	5	.375	64	22	59	3.32	1
Major League Totals		5 Yrs.	156	148⅔	5	10	.333	126	35	149	3.81	9

a Sent by San Diego Padres to Tampa Bay Devil Rays as player to be named later for infielder Russell Branyan, September 15, 2006.
b Filed for free agency, November 6, 2010. Signed with New York Mets organization, February 8, 2011.
c Filed for free agency, November 2, 2011. Signed with San Diego Padres organization, December 6, 2011.

THIELBAR, CALEB JOHN

Born, Northfield, Minnesota, January 31, 1987.
Bats Right. Throws Left. Height, 6 feet. Weight, 195 pounds.

Year	Club	Lea	G	IP	W	L	Pct	SO	BB	H	ERA	SAVES
2009	Brewers	Arizona	14	45 1/3	6	1	.857	46	7	44	1.59	0
2009	Helena	Pioneer	2	1 2/3	0	0	.000	2	1	0	0.00	0
2010	Helena	Pioneer	9	14 2/3	0	0	.000	9	0	16	3.68	0
2010	Wisconsin a	Midwest	30	53	0	2	.000	43	14	65	5.60	3
2011	St. Paul	Amer.Assoc.	43	50	3	3	.500	62	15	41	2.54	0
2011	Fort Myers b	Fla.St.	3	7 1/3	1	0	1.000	5	5	1	0.00	0
2012	Fort Myers	Fla.St.	7	12 1/3	1	1	.500	16	2	4	0.00	1
2012	New Britain	Eastern	16	25	2	0	1.000	26	3	18	1.80	4
2012	Rochester	Int.	25	40 1/3	3	1	.750	32	16	42	3.57	1
2013	Rochester	Int.	17	26 1/3	1	1	.500	34	8	27	3.76	1
2013	Minnesota	A.L.	49	46	3	2	.600	39	14	24	1.76	0

a Released by Milwaukee Brewers, December 13, 2010. Signed with St. Paul (American Association), January 2011.
b Signed with Minnesota Twins organization, August 18, 2011.

THORNBURG, TYLER MICHAEL

Born, Houston, Texas, September 29, 1988.
Bats Right. Throws Right. Height, 6 feet. Weight, 190 pounds.

Year	Club	Lea	G	IP	W	L	Pct	SO	BB	H	ERA	SAVES
2010	Helena	Pioneer	9	23 1/3	1	0	1.000	38	11	15	1.93	1
2011	Wisconsin	Midwest	12	68 2/3	7	0	1.000	76	25	49	1.57	0
2011	Brevard County	Fla.St.	12	68	3	6	.333	84	33	45	3.57	0
2012	Huntsville	Southern	13	75	8	1	.889	71	24	57	3.00	0
2012	Nashville	P.C.	8	37 2/3	2	3	.400	42	13	38	3.58	0
2012	Milwaukee	N.L.	8	22	0	0	.000	20	7	24	4.50	0
2013	Nashville	P.C.	15	74 2/3	0	9	.000	87	29	90	5.79	0
2013	Milwaukee	N.L.	18	66 2/3	3	1	.750	48	26	53	2.03	0
Major League Totals		2 Yrs.	26	88 2/3	3	1	.750	68	33	77	2.64	0

THORNTON, MATTHEW J. (MATT)

Born, Three Rivers, Michigan, September 15, 1976.
Bats Left. Throws Left. Height, 6 feet, 6 inches. Weight, 235 pounds.

Year	Club	Lea	G	IP	W	L	Pct	SO	BB	H	ERA	SAVES
1998	Everett	Northwest	2	1 1/3	0	0	.000	0	3	1	27.00	0
1999	Wisconsin	Midwest	25	29 1/3	0	0	.000	34	25	39	4.91	1
2000	Wisconsin	Midwest	26	103 1/3	6	9	.400	88	72	94	4.01	0
2001	San Bernardino	California	27	157	14	7	.667	192	60	126	2.52	0
2002	San Antonio	Texas	12	62	1	5	.167	44	29	52	3.63	0
2003	Inland Empire	California	2	9	0	0	.000	14	4	9	4.00	0
2003	Tacoma	P.C.	2	9	0	2	.000	5	3	14	8.00	0
2003	San Antonio	Texas	4	25 1/3	3	0	1.000	18	9	8	0.36	0
2004	Tacoma	P.C.	16	83	7	5	.583	74	63	85	5.20	0
2004	Seattle	A.L.	19	32 2/3	1	2	.333	30	25	30	4.13	0
2005	Seattle	A.L.	55	57	0	4	.000	57	42	54	5.21	0
2006	Chicago a	A.L.	63	54	5	3	.625	49	21	46	3.33	2
2007	Chicago	A.L.	68	56 1/3	4	4	.500	55	26	59	4.79	2
2008	Chicago	A.L.	74	67 1/3	5	3	.625	77	19	48	2.67	1
2009	Chicago	A.L.	70	72 1/3	6	3	.667	87	20	58	2.74	4
2010	Chicago b	A.L.	61	60 2/3	5	4	.556	81	20	41	2.67	8
2011	Chicago	A.L.	62	59 2/3	2	5	.286	63	21	60	3.32	3
2012	Chicago	A.L.	74	65	4	10	.286	53	17	63	3.46	3
2013	Chicago-Boston c-d-e	A.L.	60	43 1/3	0	4	.000	30	15	47	3.74	0
Major League Totals		10 Yrs.	606	568 1/3	32	42	.432	582	226	506	3.53	23
	Division Series											
2008	Chicago	A.L.	3	3 1/3	0	0	.000	2	2	2	0.00	0

a Traded to Chicago White Sox for outfielder Joe Borchard, March 20, 2006.
b On disabled list from August 18 to September 3, 2010.
c Traded to Boston Red Sox with cash for outfielder Brandon Jacobs, July 13, 2013.
d On disabled list from August 5 to August 25, 2013.
e Filed for free agency, November 2, 2013. Signed with New York Yankees, January 10, 2014.

TILLMAN, CHRISTOPHER STEVEN (CHRIS)

Born, Anaheim, California, April 15, 1988.
Bats Right. Throws Right. Height, 6 feet, 5 inches. Weight, 195 pounds.

Year	Club	Lea	G	IP	W	L	Pct	SO	BB	H	ERA	SAVES
2006	Mariners	Arizona	5	11	2	0	1.000	16	5	9	0.82	1
2006	Everett	Northwest	5	19 2/3	1	3	.250	29	15	25	7.78	0
2007	High Desert	Calif.	20	102 2/3	6	7	.462	105	48	107	5.26	0
2007	Wisconsin	Midwest	8	33	1	4	.200	34	13	31	3.55	0
2008	Bowie a	Eastern	28	135 2/3	11	4	.733	154	65	115	3.18	0
2009	Norfolk	Int.	18	96 2/3	8	6	.571	99	26	85	2.70	0
2009	Baltimore	A.L.	12	65	2	5	.286	39	24	77	5.40	0
2010	Norfolk	Int.	21	121 1/3	11	7	.611	94	30	120	3.34	0
2010	Baltimore	A.L.	11	53 2/3	2	5	.286	31	31	51	5.87	0
2011	Norfolk	Int.	15	76 1/3	3	6	.333	54	38	77	5.19	0
2011	Baltimore	A.L.	13	62	3	5	.375	46	25	77	5.52	0
2012	Bowie	Eastern	1	3 1/3	0	1	.000	2	2	4	8.10	0
2012	Norfolk	Int.	16	89 1/3	8	8	.500	92	30	85	3.63	0
2012	Baltimore	A.L.	15	86	9	3	.750	66	24	66	2.93	0
2013	Baltimore b	A.L.	33	206 1/3	16	7	.696	179	68	184	3.71	0
Major League Totals		5 Yrs.	84	473	32	25	.561	361	172	455	4.28	0

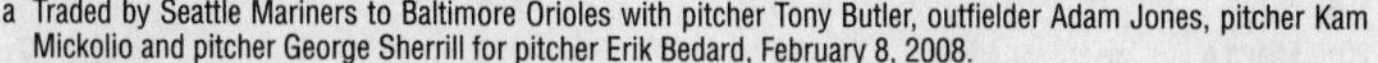

a Traded by Seattle Mariners to Baltimore Orioles with pitcher Tony Butler, outfielder Adam Jones, pitcher Kam Mickolio and pitcher George Sherrill for pitcher Erik Bedard, February 8, 2008.

b On disabled list from March 22 to April 6, 2013.

TORRES, ALEXANDER JESUS (ALEX)

Born, Valencia, Venezuela, December 8, 1987.
Bats Left. Throws Left. Height, 5 feet, 10 inches. Weight, 175 pounds.

Year	Club	Lea	G	IP	W	L	Pct	SO	BB	H	ERA	SAVES
2006	Angels	Arizona	14	50 1/3	2	5	.286	47	36	42	4.29	1
2007	Angels	Arizona	4	5 2/3	1	0	1.000	3	8	4	4.76	0
2008	Angels	Arizona	4	23 1/3	4	0	1.000	24	10	11	1.54	0
2008	Rancho Cucamonga	Calif.	10	53	3	2	.600	62	29	52	3.91	0
2009	Rancho Cucamonga	Calif.	21	121 1/3	10	3	.769	124	63	93	2.74	0
2009	Montgomery	Southern	2	8 2/3	0	2	.000	7	5	7	3.12	0
2009	Arkansas a	Texas	5	26	3	1	.750	25	17	23	2.77	0
2010	Montgomery	Southern	27	142 2/3	11	6	.647	150	70	136	3.47	0
2011	Durham	Int.	27	146 1/3	9	7	.563	156	83	134	3.08	0
2011	Tampa Bay	A.L.	4	8	1	1	.500	9	7	8	3.38	0
2012	Rays	Gulf Coast	4	11 1/3	0	1	.000	17	4	7	3.18	0
2012	Durham	Int.	26	69	3	7	.300	91	63	70	7.30	0
2013	Durham	Int.	9	46	2	2	.500	61	21	34	3.52	0
2013	Tampa Bay	A.L.	39	58	4	2	.667	62	20	32	1.71	0
Major League Totals		2 Yrs.	43	66	5	3	.625	71	27	40	1.91	0
	Division Series											
2013	Tampa Bay	A.L.	3	4	0	0	.000	5	0	2	0.00	0

a Traded by Los Angeles Angels to Tampa Bay Rays with infielder Matthew Sweeney and player to be named later for pitcher Scott Kazmir, August 28, 2009. Tampa Bay Rays received infielder Sean Rodriguez to complete trade, September 1, 2009.

TORRES, CARLOS KEVIN

Born, Santa Cruz, California, October 22, 1982.
Bats Right. Throws Right. Height, 6 feet, 2 inches. Weight, 185 pounds.

Year	Club	Lea	G	IP	W	L	Pct	SO	BB	H	ERA	SAVES
2004	Bristol	Appal.	19	36	2	2	.500	28	12	43	5.00	1
2005	Great Falls	Pioneer	5	25	1	1	.500	26	8	18	2.88	0
2005	Kannapolis	So.Atl.	8	43 1/3	1	3	.250	54	23	28	3.53	0
2006	Winston-Salem	Carolina	25	94	3	8	.273	76	55	116	4.69	1
2007	Winston-Salem	Carolina	19	36 1/3	0	2	.000	41	10	33	3.72	3
2007	Birmingham	Southern	36	56	2	2	.500	59	22	57	3.70	1
2008	Birmingham	Southern	21	101 1/3	9	5	.643	93	29	86	3.20	0
2008	Charlotte	Int.	8	19 2/3	0	0	.000	19	11	23	4.58	0
2009	Charlotte	Int.	23	128	10	4	.714	130	56	96	2.39	1
2009	Chicago	A.L.	8	28 1/3	1	2	.333	22	17	30	6.04	0
2010	Charlotte	Int.	27	160 1/3	9	9	.500	140	71	125	3.42	0
2010	Chicago a	A.L.	5	13 2/3	0	1	.000	13	9	23	8.56	0
2011	Yomiuri	Japan Cent	6	27 1/3	1	2	.333	19	11	31	6.26	0
2012	Colorado Springs b	P.C.	14	61	5	4	.556	59	25	62	3.98	0
2012	Colorado c	N.L.	31	53	5	3	.625	42	26	49	5.26	0
2013	Las Vegas	P.C.	12	71 2/3	6	3	.667	67	19	71	3.89	0

Year	Club	Lea	G	IP	W	L	Pct	SO	BB	H	ERA	SAVES
2013	New York	N.L.	33	86 1/3	4	6	.400	75	17	79	3.44	0
Major League Totals		4 Yrs.	77	181 1/3	10	12	.455	152	69	181	4.76	0

a Released by Chicago White Sox, October 26, 2010. Signed with Yomiuri (Japan), November 10, 2010.
b Signed with Colorado Rockies organization, January 20, 2012.
c Filed for free agency, November 3, 2012. Signed with New York Mets organization, November 15, 2012.

TURNER, JACOB EDWARD

Born, St.Charles, Missouri, May 21, 1991.
Bats Right. Throws Right. Height, 6 feet, 5 inches. Weight, 210 pounds.

Year	Club	Lea	G	IP	W	L	Pct	SO	BB	H	ERA	SAVES
2010	West Michigan	Midwest	11	54	2	3	.400	51	9	53	3.67	0
2010	Lakeland	Fla.St.	13	61 1/3	4	2	.667	51	14	53	2.93	0
2011	Erie	Eastern	17	113 2/3	3	5	.375	90	32	102	3.48	0
2011	Toledo	Int.	3	17 1/3	1	0	1.000	20	3	15	3.12	0
2011	Detroit	A.L.	3	12 2/3	0	1	.000	8	4	17	8.53	0
2012	Lakeland	Fla.St.	4	21 2/3	1	2	.333	17	7	17	1.66	0
2012	New Orleans	P.C.	5	27 1/3	2	0	1.000	16	12	27	1.98	0
2012	Toledo	Int.	10	62 2/3	4	2	.667	40	24	52	3.16	0
2012	Detroit	A.L.	3	12 1/3	1	1	.500	7	7	17	8.03	0
2012	Miami a	N.L.	7	42 2/3	1	4	.200	29	9	33	3.38	0
2013	New Orleans	P.C.	10	56 1/3	3	4	.429	35	14	59	4.47	0
2013	Miami	N.L.	20	118	3	8	.273	77	54	116	3.74	0
Major League Totals		3 Yrs.	33	185 2/3	5	14	.263	121	74	183	4.27	0

a Traded to Miami Marlins with catcher Rob Brantley and pitcher Brian Flynn for infielder Omar Infante and pitcher Anibal Sanchez, July 23, 2012.

UEHARA, KOJI

Born, Osaka, Japan, April 3, 1975.
Bats Right. Throws Right. Height, 6 feet, 1 inch. Weight, 190 pounds.

Year	Club	Lea	G	IP	W	L	Pct	SO	BB	H	ERA	SAVES
1999	Yomiuri	Japan Cent.	25	197 2/3	20	4	.833	179	24	153	2.09	0
2000	Yomiuri	Japan Cent.	20	131	9	7	.562	126	22	112	3.57	0
2001	Yomiuri	Japan Cent.	24	138 2/3	10	7	.588	108	28	133	4.02	0
2002	Yomiuri	Japan Cent.	26	204	17	5	.773	182	23	173	2.60	0
2003	Yomiuri	Japan Cent.	27	207 1/3	16	5	.762	194	28	190	3.17	0
2004	Yomiuri	Japan Cent.	22	163	13	5	.722	153	23	135	2.60	0
2005	Yomiuri	Japan Cent.	27	187 1/3	9	12	.429	145	22	164	3.31	0
2006	Yomiuri	Japan Cent.	24	168 1/3	8	9	.471	151	21	157	3.21	0
2007	Yomiuri	Japan Cent.	55	62	4	3	.571	66	4	47	1.74	32
2008	Yomiuri	Japan Cent.	26	89 2/3	6	5	.545	72	16	90	3.81	1
2009	Baltimore a-b	A.L.	12	66 2/3	2	4	.333	48	12	71	4.05	0
2010	Bowie	Eastern	2	2	0	0	.000	1	1	1	0.00	0
2010	Norfolk	Int.	2	2	0	0	.000	1	0	2	0.00	0
2010	Baltimore c-d	A.L.	43	44	1	2	.333	55	5	37	2.86	13
2011	Baltimore-Texas e	A.L.	65	65	2	3	.400	85	9	38	2.35	0
2012	Texas f-g	A.L.	37	36	0	0	.000	43	3	20	1.75	1
2013	Boston	A.L.	73	74 1/3	4	1	.800	101	9	33	1.09	21
Major League Totals		5 Yrs.	230	286	9	10	.474	332	38	199	2.42	35
	Wild Card Playoff											
2012	Texas	A.L.	1	1	0	0	.000	3	0	0	0.00	0
	Division Series											
2011	Texas	A.L.	1	0	0	0	.000	0	1	2	INF	0
2013	Boston	A.L.	3	3	0	1	.000	4	0	1	3.00	2
Division Series Totals			4	3	0	1	.000	4	1	3	12.00	2
	Championship Series											
2011	Texas	A.L.	2	1 1/3	0	0	.000	1	1	3	13.50	0
2013	Boston	A.L.	5	6	1	0	1.000	9	0	4	0.00	3
Championship Series Totals			7	7 1/3	1	0	1.000	10	1	7	2.45	3
	World Series Record											
2013	Boston	A.L.	5	4 2/3	0	0	.000	3	0	2	0.00	2

a Signed with Baltimore Orioles, January 13, 2009.
b On disabled list from May 24 to June 11 and June 24 to November 6, 2009.
c On disabled list from March 26 to May 6 and May 20 to June 27, 2010.
d Filed for free agency, November 1, 2010, re-signed with Baltimore Orioles, December 9, 2010.
e Traded to Texas Rangers with cash for pitcher Tommy Hunter and infielder Chris Davis, July 30, 2011.
f On disabled list from June 10 to August 26, 2012.
g Filed for free agency, November 3, 2012. Signed with Boston Red Sox, December 18, 2012.

VARGAS, JASON MATTHEW

Born, Apple Valley, California, February 2, 1983.
Bats Left. Throws Left. Height, 6 feet. Weight, 215 pounds.

Year Club	Lea	G	IP	W	L	Pct	SO	BB	H	ERA	SAVES
2004 Jamestown	N.Y.-Penn.	8	41 1/3	3	1	.750	41	13	35	1.96	0
2004 Greensboro	So.Atl.	3	19	2	1	.667	17	2	9	2.37	0
2005 Greensboro	So.Atl.	5	33 2/3	4	1	.800	33	10	16	0.80	0
2005 Jupiter	Fla.St.	9	55 1/3	2	3	.400	60	14	47	3.42	0
2005 Carolina	Southern	3	19	1	0	1.000	25	7	13	2.84	0
2005 Florida	N.L.	17	73 2/3	5	5	.500	59	31	71	4.03	0
2006 Florida	N.L.	12	43	1	2	.333	25	30	50	7.33	0
2006 Albuquerque a	P.C.	13	69	3	6	.333	51	28	98	7.43	0
2007 New York	N.L.	2	10 1/3	0	1	.000	4	2	17	12.19	0
2007 New Orleans b	P.C.	24	125	9	7	.563	108	44	141	4.97	0
2008 New York c-d	N.L.			INJURED—Did Not Play							
2009 Tacoma	P.C.	9	51 2/3	4	3	.571	46	15	48	3.14	0
2009 Seattle	A.L.	23	91 2/3	3	6	.333	54	24	98	4.91	0
2010 Seattle	A.L.	31	192 2/3	9	12	.429	116	54	187	3.78	0
2011 Seattle	A.L.	32	201	10	13	.435	131	59	205	4.25	0
2012 Seattle e	A.L.	33	217 1/3	14	11	.560	141	55	201	3.85	0
2013 Salt Lake	P.C.	1	4 2/3	0	0	.000	2	3	4	7.71	0
2013 Los Angeles f-g	A.L.	24	150	9	8	.529	109	46	162	4.02	0
Major League Totals	8 Yrs.	174	979 2/3	51	58	.468	639	301	991	4.30	0

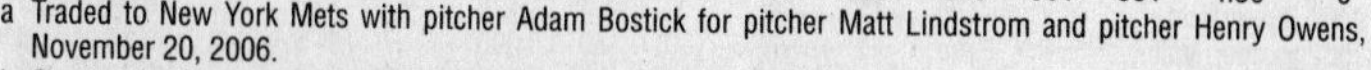

a Traded to New York Mets with pitcher Adam Bostick for pitcher Matt Lindstrom and pitcher Henry Owens, November 20, 2006.
b On disabled list from September 21 to November 6, 2007.
c On disabled list from March 21 to November 3, 2008.
d Traded to Seattle Mariners with pitcher Aaron Heilman, outfielder Endy Chavez, infielder Mike Carp, outfielder Ezequiel Carrera, pitcher Maikel Cleto and pitcher Joe Smith for pitcher J.J. Putz, pitcher Sean Green and outfielder Jeremy Reed, December 10, 2008.
e Traded to Los Angeles Angels for infielder Kendrys Morales, December 19, 2012.
f On disabled list from June 18 to August 13, 2013.
g Filed for free agency, October 31, 2013. Signed with Kansas City Royals, November 21, 2013.

VARVARO, ANTHONY MICHAEL

Born, Staten Island, New York, October 31, 1984.
Bats Right. Throws Right. Height, 6 feet. Weight, 195 pounds.

Year Club	Lea	G	IP	W	L	Pct	SO	BB	H	ERA	SAVES
2006 Mariners	Arizona	5	11	0	2	.000	15	5	7	1.64	0
2007 Wisconsin	Midwest	22	103 2/3	4	11	.267	112	51	94	4.69	1
2008 High Desert	Calif.	30	122 2/3	3	9	.250	113	82	154	7.12	0
2009 High Desert	Calif.	8	7 2/3	0	0	.000	10	6	9	7.04	4
2009 West Tenn	Southern	36	54 1/3	4	3	.571	63	44	30	2.82	8
2010 West Tenn	Southern	31	39 1/3	1	3	.250	46	21	27	3.20	9
2010 Tacoma	P.C.	19	25 2/3	0	0	.000	26	14	24	5.26	0
2010 Seattle	A.L.	4	4	0	1	.000	5	6	6	11.25	0
2011 Gwinnett a	Int.	38	59	2	8	.200	69	35	37	2.90	1
2011 Atlanta	N.L.	18	24	0	2	.000	23	11	15	2.63	0
2012 Atlanta b	N.L.	12	16 2/3	1	1	.500	21	9	16	5.40	0
2012 Gwinnett	Int.	33	44 1/3	0	2	.000	47	24	39	2.23	6
2013 Atlanta	N.L.	62	73 1/3	3	1	.750	43	25	68	2.82	1
Major League Totals	4 Yrs.	96	118	4	5	.444	92	51	105	3.43	1

a Claimed on waivers by Atlanta Braves, January 13, 2011.
b On disabled list from March 26 to April 25, 2012.

VENTERS, JONATHAN WILLIAM (JONNY)

Born, Pikeville, Kentucky, March 20, 1985.
Bats Left. Throws Left. Height, 6 feet, 3 inches. Weight, 195 pounds.

Year Club	Lea	G	IP	W	L	Pct	SO	BB	H	ERA	SAVES
2004 Braves	Gulf Coast	11	42 1/3	1	6	.143	54	12	53	5.74	0
2005 Rome	So.Atl.	23	103	8	6	.571	66	52	100	3.93	3
2006 a				INJURED—Did Not Play							
2007 Myrtle Beach	Carolina	17	79 2/3	3	3	.500	64	38	60	3.39	1
2008 Myrtle Beach	Carolina	5	17 2/3	1	2	.333	7	7	21	4.08	1
2008 Braves	Gulf Coast	4	7 2/3	0	0	.000	10	2	10	4.70	0
2008 Mississippi	Southern	3	9	1	0	1.000	7	5	10	1.00	0
2009 Gwinnett	Int.	17	91 1/3	4	7	.364	58	42	103	5.62	0
2009 Mississippi	Southern	12	65 1/3	4	4	.500	40	35	60	2.76	0
2010 Gwinnett	Int.	2	6 2/3	1	0	1.000	6	1	4	1.35	0
2010 Atlanta	N.L.	79	83	4	4	.500	93	39	61	1.95	1

Year	Club	Lea	G	IP	W	L	Pct	SO	BB	H	ERA	SAVES
2011	Atlanta	N.L.	*85	88	6	2	.750	96	43	53	1.84	5
2012	Gwinnett	Int.	1	1	0	0	.000	0	0	0	0.00	0
2012	Atlanta b	N.L.	66	58 2/3	5	4	.556	69	28	61	3.22	0
2013	Atlanta c	N.L.	INJURED—Did Not Play									
Major League Totals		3 Yrs.	230	229 2/3	15	10	.600	258	110	175	2.23	6
	Wild Card Playoff											
2012	Atlanta	N.L.	1	0 2/3	0	0	.000	0	0	1	0.00	0
	Division Series											
2010	Atlanta	N.L.	4	5 1/3	0	0	.000	8	0	7	0.00	0

a On minor league disabled list from April 6 to September 9, 2006.
b On disabled list from July 5 to July 21, 2012.
c On disabled list from March 22 to October 31, 2013.

VERAS, JOSE ENGER

Born, Santo Domingo, Dominican Republic, October 20, 1980.
Bats Right. Throws Right. Height, 6 feet, 5 inches. Weight, 235 pounds.

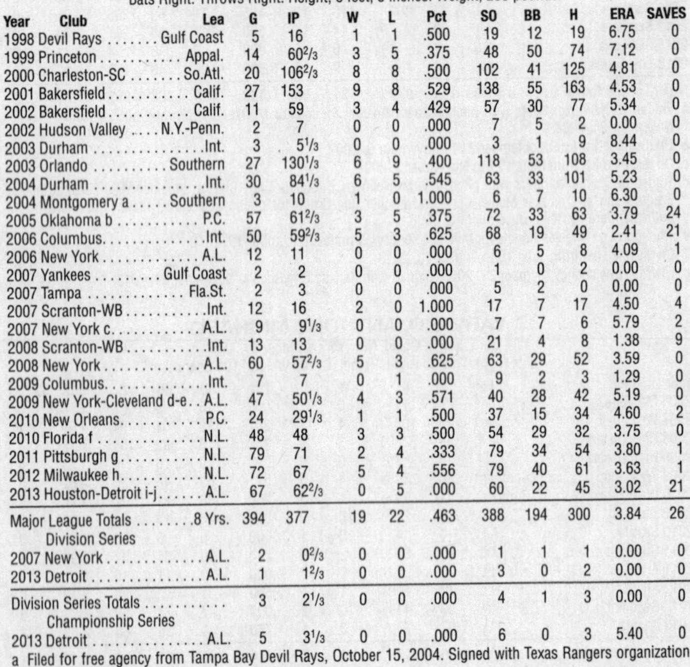

Year	Club	Lea	G	IP	W	L	Pct	SO	BB	H	ERA	SAVES
1998	Devil Rays	Gulf Coast	5	16	1	1	.500	19	12	19	6.75	0
1999	Princeton	Appal.	14	60 2/3	3	5	.375	48	50	74	7.12	0
2000	Charleston-SC	So.Atl.	20	106 2/3	8	8	.500	102	41	125	4.81	0
2001	Bakersfield	Calif.	27	153	9	8	.529	138	55	163	4.53	0
2002	Bakersfield	Calif.	11	59	3	4	.429	57	30	77	5.34	0
2002	Hudson Valley	N.Y.-Penn.	2	7	0	0	.000	7	5	2	0.00	0
2003	Durham	Int.	3	5 1/3	0	0	.000	3	1	9	8.44	0
2003	Orlando	Southern	27	130 1/3	6	9	.400	118	53	108	3.45	0
2004	Durham	Int.	30	84 1/3	6	5	.545	63	33	101	5.23	0
2004	Montgomery a	Southern	3	10	1	0	1.000	6	7	10	6.30	0
2005	Oklahoma b	P.C.	57	61 2/3	3	5	.375	72	33	63	3.79	24
2006	Columbus	Int.	50	59 2/3	5	3	.625	68	19	49	2.41	21
2006	New York	A.L.	12	11	0	0	.000	6	5	8	4.09	1
2007	Yankees	Gulf Coast	2	2	0	0	.000	1	0	2	0.00	0
2007	Tampa	Fla.St.	2	3	0	0	.000	5	2	0	0.00	0
2007	Scranton-WB	Int.	12	16	2	0	1.000	17	7	17	4.50	4
2007	New York c	A.L.	9	9 1/3	0	0	.000	7	7	6	5.79	2
2008	Scranton-WB	Int.	13	13	0	0	.000	21	4	8	1.38	9
2008	New York	A.L.	60	57 2/3	5	3	.625	63	29	52	3.59	0
2009	Columbus	Int.	7	7	0	1	.000	9	2	3	1.29	0
2009	New York-Cleveland d-e	A.L.	47	50 1/3	4	3	.571	40	28	42	5.19	0
2010	New Orleans	P.C.	24	29 1/3	1	1	.500	37	15	34	4.60	2
2010	Florida f	N.L.	48	48	3	3	.500	54	29	32	3.75	0
2011	Pittsburgh g	N.L.	79	71	2	4	.333	79	34	54	3.80	1
2012	Milwaukee h	N.L.	72	67	5	4	.556	79	40	61	3.63	1
2013	Houston-Detroit i-j	A.L.	67	62 2/3	0	5	.000	60	22	45	3.02	21
Major League Totals		8 Yrs.	394	377	19	22	.463	388	194	300	3.84	26
	Division Series											
2007	New York	A.L.	2	0 2/3	0	0	.000	1	1	1	0.00	0
2013	Detroit	A.L.	1	1 2/3	0	0	.000	3	0	2	0.00	0
Division Series Totals			3	2 1/3	0	0	.000	4	1	3	0.00	0
	Championship Series											
2013	Detroit	A.L.	5	3 1/3	0	0	.000	6	0	3	5.40	0

a Filed for free agency from Tampa Bay Devil Rays, October 15, 2004. Signed with Texas Rangers organization, November 15, 2004.
b Filed for free agency, October 15, 2005. Signed with New York Yankees organization, December 12, 2005.
c On disabled list from March 23 to August 14, 2007.
d Sold to Cleveland Indians, June 24, 2009.
e Not offered contract, December 12, 2009. Signed with Florida Marlins organization, January 29, 2010.
f Not offered contract, December 2, 2010. Signed with Pittsburgh Pirates organization, January 18, 2011.
g Traded to Milwaukee Brewers for infielder Casey McGehee, December 13, 2011.
h Filed for free agency, November 1, 2012. Signed with Houston Astros, December 21, 2012.
i Traded to Detroit Tigers for outfielder Danry Vasquez and player to be named later, July 29, 2013. Houston Astros received pitcher David Paulino to complete trade, September 13, 2013.
j Filed for free agency, November 1, 2013. Signed with Chicago Cubs, December 27, 2013.

VERLANDER, JUSTIN BROOKS

Born, Manakin Sabot, Virginia, February 20, 1983.
Bats Right. Throws Right. Height, 6 feet, 5 inches. Weight, 200 pounds.

Year	Club	Lea	G	IP	W	L	Pct	SO	BB	H	ERA	SAVES
2005	Lakeland	Fla.St.	13	86	9	2	.818	104	19	70	1.67	0
2005	Erie	Eastern	7	32 2/3	2	0	1.000	32	7	11	0.28	0

Year Club	Lea	G	IP	W	L	Pct	SO	BB	H	ERA	SAVES
2005 Detroit	A.L.	2	11 1/3	0	2	.000	7	5	15	7.15	0
2006 Detroit a	A.L.	30	186	17	9	.654	124	60	187	3.63	0
2007 Detroit b	A.L.	32	201 2/3	18	6	*.750	183	67	181	3.66	0
2008 Detroit	A.L.	33	201	11	*17	.393	163	87	195	4.84	0
2009 Detroit	A.L.	35	*240	*19	9	.679	*269	63	219	3.45	0
2010 Detroit	A.L.	33	224 1/3	18	9	.667	219	71	190	3.37	0
2011 Detroit c-d-e	A.L.	34	*251	*24	5	*.828	*250	57	174	*2.40	0
2012 Detroit	A.L.	33	*238 1/3	17	8	.680	*239	60	192	2.64	0
2013 Detroit	A.L.	34	218 1/3	13	12	.520	217	75	212	3.46	0
Major League Totals	9 Yrs.	266	1772	137	77	.640	1671	545	1565	3.41	0
Division Series											
2006 Detroit	A.L.	1	5 1/3	0	0	.000	5	4	7	5.06	0
2011 Detroit	A.L.	2	9	1	0	1.000	12	5	6	5.00	0
2012 Detroit	A.L.	2	16	2	0	1.000	22	5	7	0.56	0
2013 Detroit	A.L.	2	15	1	0	1.000	21	2	6	0.00	0
Division Series Totals		7	45 1/3	4	0	1.000	60	16	26	1.79	0
Championship Series											
2006 Detroit	A.L.	1	5 1/3	1	0	1.000	6	1	7	6.75	0
2011 Detroit	A.L.	2	11 1/3	1	1	.500	13	5	13	5.56	0
2012 Detroit	A.L.	1	8 1/3	1	0	1.000	3	0	3	1.08	0
2013 Detroit	A.L.	1	8	0	1	.000	10	1	4	1.13	0
Championship Series Totals		5	33	3	2	.600	32	7	27	3.55	0
World Series Record											
2006 Detroit	A.L.	2	11	0	2	.000	12	5	12	5.73	0
2012 Detroit	A.L.	1	4	0	1	.000	4	1	6	11.25	0
World Series Totals		3	15	0	3	.000	16	6	18	7.20	0

a Selected Rookie of the Year in American League for 2006.
b Pitched no-hit, no-run game against Milwaukee Brewers, June 12, 2007.
c Pitched no-hit, no-run game against Toronto Blue Jays, May 7, 2011.
d Selected Cy Young Award Winner in American League for 2011.
e Selected Most Valuable Player in American League for 2011.

VILLANUEVA, CARLOS MANUEL

Born, Santiago, Dominican Republic, November 28, 1983.
Bats Right. Throws Right. Height, 6 feet, 2 inches. Weight, 215 pounds.

Year Club	Lea	G	IP	W	L	Pct	SO	BB	H	ERA	SAVES
2002 Giants	Arizona	19	30 1/3	4	0	1.000	23	3	24	0.59	3
2003 Giants	Arizona	12	59	3	6	.333	67	13	64	3.97	0
2004 Beloit a	Midwest	25	114 2/3	8	8	.500	113	30	102	3.77	1
2005 Brevard County	Fla.St.	21	112 1/3	8	1	.889	124	32	78	2.32	0
2005 Huntsville	Southern	4	20 2/3	1	3	.250	14	9	21	7.40	0
2006 Huntsville	Southern	11	62 1/3	4	5	.444	59	14	60	3.75	0
2006 Nashville	P.C.	11	66 1/3	7	1	.875	61	26	42	2.71	0
2006 Milwaukee	N.L.	10	53 2/3	2	2	.500	39	11	43	3.69	0
2007 Nashville	P.C.	2	8 1/3	0	0	.000	9	1	3	3.24	0
2007 Milwaukee	N.L.	59	114 1/3	8	5	.615	99	53	101	3.94	1
2008 Milwaukee	N.L.	47	108 1/3	4	7	.364	93	30	112	4.07	1
2009 Milwaukee	N.L.	64	96	4	10	.286	83	35	102	5.34	3
2010 Nashville	P.C.	11	14 1/3	0	0	.000	14	7	13	3.77	1
2010 Milwaukee b	N.L.	50	52 2/3	2	0	1.000	67	22	48	4.61	1
2011 Dunedin	Fla.St.	1	1	0	0	.000	0	0	1	0.00	0
2011 Toronto c	A.L.	33	107	6	4	.600	68	32	103	4.04	0
2012 Toronto d	A.L.	38	125 1/3	7	7	.500	122	46	113	4.16	0
2013 Chicago	N.L.	47	128 2/3	7	8	.467	103	40	117	4.06	0
Major League Totals	8 Yrs.	348	786	40	43	.482	674	269	739	4.23	6
Division Series											
2008 Milwaukee	N.L.	2	3 2/3	0	0	.000	3	0	0	0.00	0

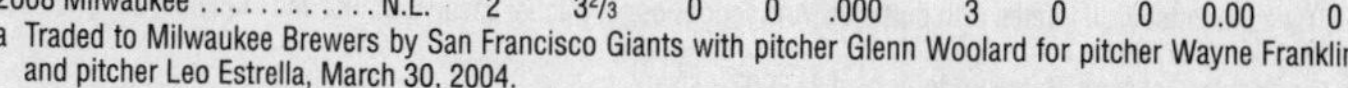

a Traded to Milwaukee Brewers by San Francisco Giants with pitcher Glenn Woolard for pitcher Wayne Franklin and pitcher Leo Estrella, March 30, 2004.
b Traded to Toronto Blue Jays for player to be named later, December 3, 2010. Milwaukee Brewers received cash to complete the transaction, April 8, 2011.
c On disabled list from August 4 to August 31, 2011.
d Filed for free agency, November 3, 2012. Signed with Chicago Cubs, January 26, 2013.

VINCENT, NICHOLAS JAMES (NICK)

Born, Poway, California, July 12, 1986.
Bats Right. Throws Right. Height, 6 feet. Weight, 185 pounds.

Year	Club	Lea	G	IP	W	L	Pct	SO	BB	H	ERA	SAVES
2008	Eugene	Northwest	16	43 1/3	3	3	.500	38	20	42	5.40	2
2008	Portland	P.C.	1	5	0	1	.000	4	1	2	5.40	0
2009	Lake Elsinore	Calif.	59	64 1/3	4	2	.667	74	18	66	3.08	2
2010	Lake Elsinore	Calif.	48	81 2/3	4	0	1.000	76	23	60	1.87	0
2011	San Antonio	Texas	66	79 1/3	8	2	.800	89	20	54	2.27	3
2012	San Antonio	Texas	9	9 2/3	1	0	1.000	15	0	4	1.86	0
2012	Tucson	P.C.	23	21 2/3	1	1	.500	19	11	27	5.82	2
2012	San Diego	N.L.	27	26 1/3	2	0	1.000	28	7	19	1.71	0
2013	Tucson	P.C.	24	25 1/3	4	3	.571	24	12	26	3.55	0
2013	San Diego	N.L.	45	46 1/3	6	3	.667	49	11	33	2.14	1
Major League Totals		2 Yrs.	72	72 2/3	8	3	.727	77	18	52	1.98	1

VOGELSONG, RYAN ANDREW

Born, Charlotte, North Carolina, July 22, 1977.
Bats Right. Throws Right. Height, 6 feet, 3 inches. Weight, 215 pounds.

Year	Club	Lea	G	IP	W	L	Pct	SO	BB	H	ERA	SAVES
1998	Salem-Keizr	Northwest	10	56	6	1	.857	66	16	37	1.77	0
1998	San Jose	Calif.	4	19	0	0	.000	26	4	23	7.58	0
1999	San Jose	Calif.	13	69 2/3	4	4	.500	86	27	37	2.45	0
1999	Shreveport	Texas	6	28 1/3	0	2	.000	23	15	40	7.31	0
2000	Shreveport	Texas	27	155 1/3	6	10	.375	147	69	153	4.23	0
2000	San Francisco	N.L.	4	6	0	0	.000	6	2	4	0.00	0
2001	Fresno	P.C.	10	58	3	3	.500	53	18	35	2.79	0
2001	Nashville	P.C.	6	31 2/3	2	3	.400	33	15	26	3.98	0
2001	San Fran.-Pittsburgh a	N.L.	15	34 2/3	0	5	.000	24	20	39	6.75	0
2002	Lynchburg	Carolina	4	15 2/3	1	1	.500	20	7	19	8.04	0
2002	Altoona b	Eastern	8	43 2/3	1	5	.167	35	10	47	5.56	0
2003	Nashville	P.C.	26	149	12	8	.600	146	54	142	4.29	0
2003	Pittsburgh	N.L.	6	22	2	2	.500	15	9	30	6.55	0
2004	Pittsburgh	N.L.	31	133	6	13	.316	92	67	148	6.50	0
2005	Pittsburgh	N.L.	44	81 1/3	2	2	.500	52	40	82	4.43	0
2006	Pittsburgh	N.L.	20	38	0	0	.000	27	16	44	6.39	0
2006	Indianapolis c	Int.	11	67 2/3	4	5	.444	43	12	54	2.66	0
2007	Hanshin	Japan Pac.	20	106 2/3	7	6	.538	91	41	113	4.13	0
2008	Hanshin	Japan Pac.	12	65 1/3	3	4	.429	50	19	65	3.99	0
2009	Orix	Japan Pac.	30	42 1/3	1	4	.200	56	16	39	4.54	0
2010	Lehigh Valley d-e-f	Int.	25	58 2/3	2	5	.286	73	40	60	4.91	1
2010	Salt Lake	P.C.	8	36 2/3	1	3	.250	37	22	47	4.66	0
2011	Fresno	P.C.	2	11 1/3	2	0	1.000	17	5	8	1.59	0
2011	San Francisco	N.L.	30	179 2/3	13	7	.650	139	61	164	2.71	0
2012	Fresno	P.C.	2	10	1	0	1.000	12	4	9	1.80	0
2012	San Francisco g	N.L.	31	189 2/3	14	9	.609	158	62	171	3.37	0
2013	Giants	Arizona	1	2	0	0	.000	2	0	2	0.00	0
2013	San Jose	Calif.	1	2 2/3	0	1	.000	3	1	1	6.75	0
2013	Richmond	Eastern	2	11	2	0	1.000	8	2	10	0.82	0
2013	San Francisco h-i	N.L.	19	103 2/3	4	6	.400	67	38	124	5.73	0
Major League Totals		9 Yrs.	200	788	41	44	.482	580	315	806	4.52	0
	Division Series											
2012	San Francisco	N.L.	1	5	0	0	.000	5	3	3	1.80	0
	Championship Series											
2012	San Francisco	N.L.	2	14	2	0	1.000	13	3	8	1.29	0
	World Series Record											
2012	San Francisco	N.L.	1	5 2/3	1	0	1.000	3	4	5	0.00	0

a Traded to Pittsburgh Pirates with outfielder Armando Rios for pitcher Jason Schmidt and outfielder John Vander Wal, July 30, 2001.
b On disabled list from March 30 to August 1, 2002.
c Filed for free agency, October 2, 2006. Signed with Hanshin Tigers for 2007.
d Signed with Philadelphia Phillies organization, January 5, 2010.
e Released by Philadelphia Phillies, July 16, 2010. Signed with Los Angeles Angels organization, July 27, 2010.
f Filed for free agency, November 6, 2010. Signed with San Francisco Giants organization, January 15, 2011.
g On disabled list from March 27 to April 15, 2012.
h On disabled list from May 21 to August 9, 2013.
i Filed for free agency, November 5, 2013, re-signed with San Francisco Giants, December 4, 2013.

VOLQUEZ, EDINSON

Born, Santo Domingo, Dominican Republic, July 3, 1983.
Bats Right. Throws Right. Height, 6 feet, 1 inch. Weight, 200 pounds.

Year Club	Lea	G	IP	W	L	Pct	SO	BB	H	ERA	SAVES
2003 Rangers	Arizona	10	27	2	1	.667	28	11	24	4.00	1
2004 Stockton	Calif.	8	$39\frac{2}{3}$	4	1	.800	34	14	31	2.95	0
2004 Clinton	Midwest	22	91	4	4	.500	77	30	83	4.05	3
2005 Bakersfield	Calif.	11	$66\frac{2}{3}$	5	4	.556	77	12	64	4.18	0
2005 Rangers	Arizona	1	2	0	0	.000	2	0	2	0.00	0
2005 Frisco	Texas	10	$58\frac{2}{3}$	1	5	.167	49	17	58	4.14	0
2005 Texas	A.L.	6	$12\frac{2}{3}$	0	4	.000	11	10	25	14.21	0
2006 Oklahoma	P.C.	21	$120\frac{2}{3}$	6	6	.500	130	72	86	3.21	0
2006 Texas	A.L.	8	$33\frac{1}{3}$	1	6	.143	15	17	52	7.29	0
2007 Bakersfield	Calif.	7	$35\frac{1}{3}$	0	4	.000	38	20	27	7.13	0
2007 Frisco	Texas	11	$58\frac{1}{3}$	8	1	.889	62	19	46	3.55	0
2007 Oklahoma	P.C.	8	51	6	1	.857	66	21	25	1.41	0
2007 Texas a	A.L.	6	34	2	1	.667	29	15	34	4.50	0
2008 Cincinnati	N.L.	33	196	17	6	.739	206	93	167	3.21	0
2009 Cincinnati b	N.L.	9	$49\frac{2}{3}$	4	2	.667	47	32	34	4.35	0
2010 Dayton	Midwest	2	13	0	0	.000	19	4	11	1.38	0
2010 Lynchburg	Carolina	2	8	1	0	1.000	7	0	3	0.00	0
2010 Louisville	Int.	4	23	3	0	1.000	21	8	11	1.96	0
2010 Cincinnati c-d	N.L.	12	$62\frac{2}{3}$	4	3	.571	67	35	59	4.31	0
2011 Louisville	Int.	13	$87\frac{1}{3}$	4	2	.667	83	29	72	2.37	0
2011 Cincinnati	N.L.	20	$108\frac{2}{3}$	5	7	.417	104	65	106	5.71	0
2012 San Diego e	N.L.	32	$182\frac{2}{3}$	11	11	.500	174	*105	160	4.14	0
2013 San Diego-Los Angeles f-g	N.L.	33	$170\frac{1}{3}$	9	12	.429	142	77	193	5.71	0
Major League Totals	9 Yrs.	159	850	53	52	.505	795	449	830	4.75	0
Division Series											
2010 Cincinnati	N.L.	1	$1\frac{2}{3}$	0	1	.000	0	2	4	21.60	0

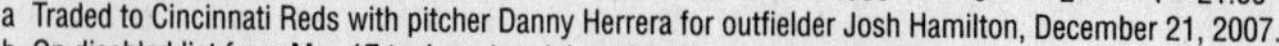

a Traded to Cincinnati Reds with pitcher Danny Herrera for outfielder Josh Hamilton, December 21, 2007.
b On disabled list from May 17 to June 1 and June 2 to November 16, 2009.
c On disabled list from February 24 to July 17, 2010.
d Suspended for 50 games for performance-enhancing drug use, April 20, 2010.
e Traded to San Diego Padres with pitcher Brad Boxberger, catcher Yasmani Grandal and infielder Yonder Alonso for pitcher Mat Latos, December 17, 2011.
f Released by San Diego Padres, August 26, 2013. Signed with Los Angeles Dodgers, August 30, 2013.
g Filed for free agency, October 31, 2013. Signed with Pittsburgh Pirates, December 13, 2013.

WACHA, MICHAEL JOSEPH

Born, Iowa City, Iowa, July 1, 1991.
Bats Right. Throws Right. Height, 6 feet, 6 inches. Weight, 210 pounds.

Year Club	Lea	G	IP	W	L	Pct	SO	BB	H	ERA	SAVES
2012 Cardinals	Gulf Coast	3	5	0	0	.000	7	0	4	1.80	0
2012 Palm Beach	Fla.St.	4	8	0	0	.000	16	1	1	0.00	0
2012 Springfield	Texas	4	8	0	0	.000	17	3	3	1.13	0
2013 Memphis	P.C.	15	85	5	3	.625	73	19	65	2.65	0
2013 St. Louis	N.L.	15	$64\frac{2}{3}$	4	1	.800	65	19	52	2.78	0
Division Series											
2013 St. Louis	N.L.	1	$7\frac{1}{3}$	1	0	1.000	9	2	1	1.23	0
Championship Series											
2013 St. Louis	N.L.	2	$13\frac{2}{3}$	2	0	1.000	13	2	7	0.00	0
World Series Record											
2013 St. Louis	N.L.	2	$9\frac{2}{3}$	1	1	.500	11	8	8	7.45	0

WAGNER, NEIL KANNAS

Born, Minneapolis, Minnesota, January 1, 1984.
Bats Right. Throws Right. Height, 6 feet. Weight, 215 pounds.

Year Club	Lea	G	IP	W	L	Pct	SO	BB	H	ERA	SAVES
2006 Mahoning Valley	N.Y.-Penn.	26	$32\frac{1}{3}$	0	1	.000	50	9	16	1.39	17
2007 Lake County	So.Atl.	34	44	1	4	.200	49	11	41	3.68	11
2007 Kinston	Carolina	16	24	0	0	.000	18	6	17	3.00	0
2008 Kinston	Carolina	41	62	3	6	.333	81	21	67	4.50	3
2008 Akron	Eastern	7	10	0	2	.000	11	4	10	3.60	0
2009 Akron	Eastern	46	61	1	3	.250	69	32	48	2.95	2
2010 Akron	Eastern	13	$14\frac{1}{3}$	1	1	.500	15	7	17	6.28	4
2010 Midland a	Texas	33	$48\frac{2}{3}$	6	2	.750	45	27	55	3.70	1
2011 Midland	Texas	28	$37\frac{1}{3}$	1	3	.250	53	13	31	3.38	4
2011 Sacramento	P.C.	22	29	2	1	.667	34	10	27	3.10	2

Year Club	Lea	G	IP	W	L	Pct	SO	BB	H	ERA	SAVES
2011 Oakland	A.L.	6	5	0	0	.000	4	3	6	7.20	0
2012 Sacramento b	P.C.	15	19²/3	1	1	.500	24	6	20	5.49	1
2012 Tucson c	P.C.	31	43	3	1	.750	32	17	57	5.44	0
2013 Buffalo	Int.	23	23²/3	1	0	1.000	38	9	13	0.76	16
2013 Toronto	A.L.	36	38	2	4	.333	33	13	39	3.79	0
Major League Totals	2 Yrs.	42	43	2	4	.333	37	16	45	4.19	0

a Sold by Cleveland Indians to Oakland Athletics, May 11, 2010.
b Claimed on waivers by San Diego Padres, May 28, 2012.
c Filed for free agency, November 3, 2012. Signed with Toronto Blue Jays organization, November 15, 2012.

WAINWRIGHT, ADAM PARRISH

Born, Brunswick, Georgia, August 30, 1981.
Bats Right. Throws Right. Height, 6 feet, 7 inches. Weight, 205 pounds.

Year Club	Lea	G	IP	W	L	Pct	SO	BB	H	ERA	SAVES
2000 Danville	Appal.	6	29¹/3	2	2	.500	39	2	28	3.68	0
2000 Braves	Gulf Coast	7	32	4	0	1.000	42	10	15	1.13	0
2001 Macon	So.Atl.	28	164²/3	10	10	.500	184	48	144	3.77	0
2002 Myrtle Beach	Carolina	28	163¹/3	9	6	.600	167	66	149	3.31	0
2003 Greenville a	Southern	27	149²/3	10	8	.556	128	37	133	3.37	0
2004 Memphis	P.C.	12	63²/3	4	4	.500	64	28	68	5.37	0
2005 Memphis	P.C.	29	182	10	10	.500	147	51	204	4.40	0
2005 St. Louis	N.L.	2	2	0	0	.000	0	1	2	13.50	0
2006 St. Louis	N.L.	61	75	2	1	.667	72	22	64	3.12	3
2007 St. Louis	N.L.	32	202	14	12	.538	136	70	212	3.70	0
2008 Springfield	Texas	1	4²/3	0	0	.000	7	0	4	0.00	0
2008 Memphis	P.C.	2	3²/3	0	1	.000	3	2	8	12.27	0
2008 St. Louis b	N.L.	20	132	11	3	.786	91	34	122	3.20	0
2009 St. Louis	N.L.	34	*233	*19	8	.704	212	66	216	2.63	0
2010 St. Louis	N.L.	33	230¹/3	20	11	.645	213	56	186	2.42	0
2011 St. Louis c	N.L.			INJURED—Did Not Play							
2012 St. Louis	N.L.	32	198²/3	14	13	.519	184	52	196	3.94	0
2013 St. Louis	N.L.	34	*241²/3	*19	9	.679	219	35	*223	2.94	0
Major League Totals	8 Yrs.	248	1314²/3	99	57	.635	1127	336	1221	3.11	3
Division Series											
2006 St. Louis	N.L.	3	3²/3	0	0	.000	6	0	3	0.00	1
2009 St. Louis	N.L.	1	8	0	0	.000	7	1	3	1.13	0
2012 St. Louis	N.L.	2	8	0	0	.000	15	3	13	7.88	0
2013 St. Louis	N.L.	2	16	2	0	1.000	15	1	11	1.13	0
Division Series Totals		8	35²/3	2	0	1.000	43	5	30	2.52	1
Championship Series											
2006 St. Louis	N.L.	3	3	0	0	.000	4	1	2	0.00	2
2012 St. Louis	N.L.	1	7	1	0	1.000	5	0	4	1.29	0
2013 St. Louis	N.L.	1	7	0	1	.000	5	0	6	2.57	0
Championship Series Totals		5	17	1	1	.500	14	1	12	1.59	2
World Series Record											
2006 St. Louis	N.L.	3	3	1	0	1.000	5	1	2	0.00	1
2013 St. Louis	N.L.	2	12	0	2	.000	14	2	14	4.50	0
World Series Totals		5	15	1	2	.333	19	3	16	3.60	1

a Traded by Atlanta Braves to St. Louis Cardinals with pitcher Jason Marquis and pitcher Ray King for catcher Eli Marrero and outfielder J.D. Drew, December 13, 2003.
b On disabled list from June 8 to August 22, 2008.
c On disabled list from March 25 to November 1, 2011.

WALDEN, JORDAN CRAIG

Born, Fort Worth, Texas, November 16, 1987.
Bats Right. Throws Right. Height, 6 feet, 5 inches. Weight, 235 pounds.

Year Club	Lea	G	IP	W	L	Pct	SO	BB	H	ERA	SAVES
2007 Orem	Pioneer	15	64¹/3	1	1	.500	63	17	49	3.08	0
2008 Cedar Rapids	Midwest	18	107¹/3	4	6	.400	91	32	80	2.18	0
2008 Rancho Cucamonga	Calif.	9	49	5	2	.714	50	24	42	4.04	0
2009 Arkansas	Texas	13	60	1	5	.167	57	29	72	5.25	0
2010 Arkansas	Texas	38	43	1	1	.500	38	22	44	3.35	8
2010 Salt Lake	P.C.	6	6²/3	0	0	.000	3	2	8	4.05	0
2010 Los Angeles	A.L.	16	15¹/3	0	1	.000	23	7	13	2.35	1
2011 Los Angeles	A.L.	62	60¹/3	5	5	.500	67	26	49	2.98	32
2012 Salt Lake	P.C.	3	2²/3	0	1	.000	3	0	3	6.75	0
2012 Los Angeles a-b	A.L.	45	39	3	2	.600	48	18	35	3.46	1

Year	Club	Lea	G	IP	W	L	Pct	SO	BB	H	ERA	SAVES
2013	Gwinnett	Int.	1	1	0	0	.000	1	0	0	0.00	0
2013	Atlanta c	N.L.	50	47	4	3	.571	54	14	39	3.45	1
Major League Totals		4 Yrs.	173	161²/₃	12	11	.522	192	65	136	3.17	35
Division Series												
2013	Atlanta	N.L.	2	2²/₃	0	0	.000	3	1	3	13.50	0

a On disabled list from July 15 to August 19, 2012.
b Traded to Atlanta Braves for pitcher Tommy Hanson, November 30, 2012.
c On disabled list from May 12 to May 29, 2013.

WALKER, TAIJUAN EMMANUEL

Born, Shreveport, Louisiana, August 13, 1992.
Bats Right. Throws Right. Height, 6 feet, 4 inches. Weight, 210 pounds.

Year	Club	Lea	G	IP	W	L	Pct	SO	BB	H	ERA	SAVES
2010	Mariners	Arizona	4	7	1	1	.500	9	3	2	1.29	0
2011	Clinton	Midwest	18	96²/₃	6	5	.545	113	39	69	2.89	0
2012	Jackson	Southern	25	126²/₃	7	10	.412	118	50	124	4.69	0
2013	Jackson	Southern	14	84	4	7	.364	96	30	58	2.46	0
2013	Tacoma	P.C.	11	57¹/₃	5	3	.625	64	27	54	3.61	0
2013	Seattle	A.L.	3	15	1	0	1.000	12	4	11	3.60	0

WARREN, ADAM PARRISH

Born, Birmingham, Alabama, August 25, 1987.
Bats Right. Throws Right. Height, 6 feet, 2 inches. Weight, 200 pounds.

Year	Club	Lea	G	IP	W	L	Pct	SO	BB	H	ERA	SAVES
2009	Staten Island	N.Y.-Penn.	12	56²/₃	4	2	.667	50	10	49	1.43	0
2010	Tampa	Fla.St.	15	81	7	5	.583	67	17	72	2.22	0
2010	Trenton	Eastern	10	54¹/₃	4	2	.667	59	16	49	3.15	0
2011	Scranton/WB	Int.	27	152¹/₃	6	8	.429	111	53	145	3.60	0
2012	New York	A.L.	1	2¹/₃	0	0	.000	1	2	8	23.14	0
2012	Scranton/WB	Int.	26	152²/₃	7	8	.467	107	46	167	3.71	0
2013	New York	A.L.	34	77	3	2	.600	64	30	80	3.39	1
Major League Totals		2 Yrs.	35	79¹/₃	3	2	.600	65	32	88	3.97	1

WATSON, ANTHONY MICHAEL (TONY)

Born, Sioux City, Iowa, May 30, 1985.
Bats Left. Throws Left. Height, 6 feet, 4 inches. Weight, 220 pounds.

Year	Club	Lea	G	IP	W	L	Pct	SO	BB	H	ERA	SAVES
2007	State College	N.Y.-Penn.	10	53²/₃	6	1	.857	40	7	47	2.52	0
2007	Hickory	So.Atl.	3	14	1	1	.500	18	1	14	3.86	0
2008	Lynchburg	Carolina	28	151²/₃	8	12	.400	104	36	149	3.56	0
2009	Altoona	Eastern	5	15¹/₃	0	3	.000	14	11	22	8.22	0
2010	Altoona	Eastern	34	111¹/₃	6	4	.600	105	24	82	2.67	2
2011	Indianapolis	Int.	26	34¹/₃	3	3	.500	35	11	24	2.36	0
2011	Pittsburgh	N.L.	43	41	2	2	.500	37	20	34	3.95	0
2012	Pittsburgh	N.L.	68	53¹/₃	5	2	.714	53	23	37	3.38	0
2013	Pittsburgh	N.L.	67	71²/₃	3	1	.750	54	12	51	2.39	2
Major League Totals		3 Yrs.	178	166	10	5	.667	144	55	122	3.09	2
Wild Card Playoff												
2013	Pittsburgh	N.L.	1	1	0	0	.000	0	0	2	9.00	0
Division Series												
2013	Pittsburgh	N.L.	3	3	0	0	.000	1	1	2	0.00	0

WEAVER, JERED DAVID

Born, Northridge, California, October 4, 1982.
Bats Right. Throws Right. Height, 6 feet, 7 inches. Weight, 205 pounds.

Year	Club	Lea	G	IP	W	L	Pct	SO	BB	H	ERA	SAVES
2005	Arkansas	Texas	8	43	3	3	.500	46	19	43	3.98	0
2006	Salt Lake	P.C.	12	77	6	1	.857	93	10	63	2.10	0
2006	Los Angeles	A.L.	19	123	11	2	.846	105	33	94	2.56	0
2007	Rancho Cucamonga	Calif.	2	11	1	0	1.000	12	3	5	0.82	0
2007	Los Angeles a	A.L.	28	161	13	7	.650	115	45	178	3.91	0
2008	Los Angeles	A.L.	30	176²/₃	11	10	.524	152	54	173	4.33	0
2009	Los Angeles	A.L.	33	211	16	8	.667	174	66	196	3.75	0
2010	Inland Empire	Calif.	1	3	0	0	.000	3	1	2	0.00	0
2010	Los Angeles	A.L.	34	224¹/₃	13	12	.520	*233	54	187	3.01	0

Year	Club	Lea	G	IP	W	L	Pct	SO	BB	H	ERA	SAVES
2011	Los Angeles	A.L.	33	235 2/3	18	8	.692	198	56	182	2.41	0
2012	Los Angeles b-c	A.L.	30	188 2/3	*20	5	*.800	142	45	147	2.81	0
2013	Los Angeles d	A.L.	24	154 1/3	11	8	.579	117	37	139	3.27	0
Major League Totals		8 Yrs.	231	1474 2/3	113	60	.653	1236	390	1296	3.24	0
	Division Series											
2007	Los Angeles	A.L.	1	5	0	1	.000	5	3	4	3.60	0
2008	Los Angeles	A.L.	1	2	1	0	1.000	3	1	1	0.00	0
2009	Los Angeles	A.L.	1	7 1/3	1	0	1.000	7	2	2	1.23	0
Division Series Totals			3	14 1/3	2	1	.667	15	6	7	1.88	0
	Championship Series											
2009	Los Angeles	A.L.	3	6 1/3	0	0	.000	7	4	5	4.26	0

a On disabled list from March 23 to April 17, 2007.
b Pitched no-hit, no-run game against Minnesota Twins, May 2, 2012.
c On disabled list from May 29 to June 20, 2012.
d On disabled list from April 8 to May 29, 2013.

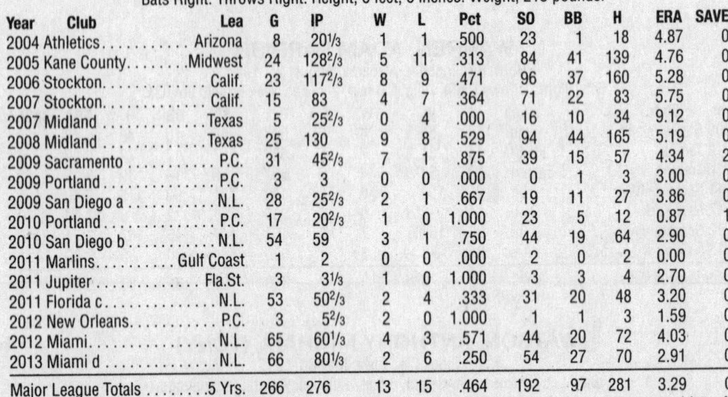

WEBB, RYAN CHRISTOPHER

Born, Clearwater, Florida, February 5, 1986.
Bats Right. Throws Right. Height, 6 feet, 6 inches. Weight, 215 pounds.

Year	Club	Lea	G	IP	W	L	Pct	SO	BB	H	ERA	SAVES
2004	Athletics	Arizona	8	20 1/3	1	1	.500	23	1	18	4.87	0
2005	Kane County	Midwest	24	128 2/3	5	11	.313	84	41	139	4.76	0
2006	Stockton	Calif.	23	117 2/3	8	9	.471	96	37	160	5.28	0
2007	Stockton	Calif.	15	83	4	7	.364	71	22	83	5.75	0
2007	Midland	Texas	5	25 2/3	0	4	.000	16	10	34	9.12	0
2008	Midland	Texas	25	130	9	8	.529	94	44	165	5.19	0
2009	Sacramento	P.C.	31	45 2/3	7	1	.875	39	15	57	4.34	2
2009	Portland	P.C.	3	3	0	0	.000	0	1	3	3.00	0
2009	San Diego a	N.L.	28	25 2/3	2	1	.667	19	11	27	3.86	0
2010	Portland	P.C.	17	20 2/3	1	0	1.000	23	5	12	0.87	1
2010	San Diego b	N.L.	54	59	3	1	.750	44	19	64	2.90	0
2011	Marlins	Gulf Coast	1	2	0	0	.000	2	0	2	0.00	0
2011	Jupiter	Fla.St.	3	3 1/3	1	0	1.000	3	3	4	2.70	0
2011	Florida c	N.L.	53	50 2/3	2	4	.333	31	20	48	3.20	0
2012	New Orleans	P.C.	3	5 2/3	2	0	1.000	1	1	3	1.59	0
2012	Miami	N.L.	65	60 1/3	4	3	.571	44	20	72	4.03	0
2013	Miami d	N.L.	66	80 1/3	2	6	.250	54	27	70	2.91	0
Major League Totals		5 Yrs.	266	276	13	15	.464	192	97	281	3.29	0

a Traded by Oakland Athletics to San Diego Padres with pitcher Craig Italiano and player to be named later for outfielder Scott Hairston, July 5, 2009. San Diego Padres received pitcher Sean Gallagher to complete trade, July 28, 2009.
b Traded to Florida Marlins with pitcher Edward Mujica for outfielder Cameron Maybin, November 13, 2010.
c On disabled list from June 27 to August 17, 2011.
d Not offered contract, December 2, 2013. Signed with Baltimore Orioles, December 9, 2013.

WESTBROOK, JACOB CAUTHEN (JAKE)

Born, Athens, Georgia, September 29, 1977.
Bats Right. Throws Right. Height, 6 feet, 3 inches. Weight, 215 pounds.

Year	Club	Lea	G	IP	W	L	Pct	SO	BB	H	ERA	SAVES
1996	Rockies	Arizona	11	62 2/3	4	2	.667	57	14	66	2.87	0
1996	Portland	Northwest	4	24 2/3	1	1	.500	19	5	22	2.55	0
1997	Asheville a	So.Atl.	28	170	14	11	.560	92	55	176	4.29	0
1998	Jupiter	Fla.St.	27	171	11	6	.647	79	60	169	3.26	0
1999	Harrisburg b	Eastern	27	174 2/3	11	5	.688	90	63	180	3.92	0
2000	Columbus	Int.	16	89	5	7	.417	61	38	94	4.65	0
2000	New York c-d-e-f	A.L.	3	6 2/3	0	2	.000	1	4	15	13.50	0
2001	Buffalo	Int.	12	64 2/3	8	1	.889	45	23	60	3.20	0
2001	Cleveland	A.L.	23	64 2/3	4	4	.500	48	22	79	5.85	0
2002	Akron	Eastern	3	15	0	1	.000	8	1	13	4.80	0
2002	Buffalo	Int.	1	6	1	0	1.000	2	0	8	6.00	0
2002	Cleveland g	A.L.	11	41 2/3	1	3	.250	20	12	50	5.83	0
2003	Buffalo	Int.	2	10	1	0	1.000	7	4	0	0.00	0
2003	Cleveland	A.L.	34	133	7	10	.412	58	56	142	4.33	0
2004	Cleveland	A.L.	33	215 2/3	14	9	.609	116	61	208	3.38	0
2005	Cleveland	A.L.	34	210 2/3	15	15	.500	119	56	218	4.49	0
2006	Cleveland	A.L.	32	211 1/3	15	10	.600	109	55	*247	4.17	0
2007	Lake County	So.Atl.	1	5	0	1	.000	5	0	6	7.20	0

Year Club	Lea	G	IP	W	L	Pct	SO	BB	H	ERA	SAVES
2007 Akron	Eastern	1	2 1/3	0	1	.000	1	3	5	15.43	0
2007 Buffalo	Int.	2	5 1/3	0	1	.000	5	5	9	8.44	0
2007 Cleveland h	A.L.	25	152	6	9	.400	93	55	159	4.32	0
2008 Lake County	So.Atl.	1	3 2/3	0	0	.000	4	1	3	2.45	0
2008 Akron	Eastern	1	6	0	0	.000	2	4	3	0.00	0
2008 Cleveland i	A.L.	5	34 2/3	1	2	.333	19	7	33	3.12	0
2009 Akron	Eastern	3	9	0	1	.000	8	6	1	2.00	0
2009 Cleveland j	A.L.					INJURED—Did Not Play					
2010 Cleveland	A.L.	21	127 2/3	6	7	.462	73	44	133	4.65	0
2010 St. Louis k-l	N.L.	12	75	4	4	.500	55	24	70	3.48	0
2011 St. Louis	N.L.	33	183 1/3	12	9	.571	104	73	208	4.66	0
2012 St. Louis	N.L.	28	174 2/3	13	11	.542	106	52	191	3.97	0
2013 Peoria	Midwest	1	7	1	0	1.000	5	0	4	1.29	0
2013 Springfield	Texas	1	3 2/3	0	0	.000	5	0	6	2.45	0
2013 St. Louis m-n	N.L.	21	116 2/3	7	8	.467	44	50	132	4.63	0
Major League Totals	13 Yrs.	315	1747 2/3	105	103	.505	965	571	1885	4.32	0
Division Series											
2007 Cleveland	A.L.	1	5	0	1	.000	1	0	9	10.80	0
Championship Series											
2007 Cleveland	A.L.	2	12 2/3	1	1	.500	7	4	16	3.55	0
World Series Record											
2011 St. Louis	N.L.	2	2	1	0	1.000	0	1	2	0.00	0

a Traded to Montreal Expos by Colorado Rockies with pitcher John Nicholson and outfielder Mike Hamlin for infielder Mike Lansing, November 18, 1997.
b Traded to New York Yankees with two players to be named later for pitcher Hideki Irabu, December 22, 1999. Pitchers Ted Lilly and Christian Parker were sent to New York Yankees to complete trade, March 17 and March 22, 2000.
c On disabled list from May 5 to May 23, 2000.
d Sent to Cleveland Indians by New York Yankees with pitcher Zach Day to complete trade for outfielder David Justice, July 24, 2000.
e On disabled list from July 25 to September 1, 2000.
f On disabled list from September 1 to October 31, 2000.
g On disabled list from March 30 to July 11 and August 26 to November 4, 2002.
h On disabled list from May 3 to June 24, 2007.
i On disabled list from April 20 to May 28 and May 29 to November 13, 2008.
j On disabled list from March 26 to November 18, 2009.
k Traded to St. Louis Cardinals with cash for pitcher Corey Kluber, July 31, 2010.
l Filed for free agency, November 1, 2010, re-signed with St. Louis Cardinals, November 16, 2010.
m On disabled list from May 9 to June 14 and August 22 to September 6, 2013.
n Filed for free agency, October 31, 2013.

WHEELER, ZACHARY HARRISON (ZACK)

Born, Smyrna, Georgia, May 30, 1990.
Bats Left. Throws Right. Height, 6 feet, 4 inches. Weight, 185 pounds.

Year Club	Lea	G	IP	W	L	Pct	SO	BB	H	ERA	SAVES
2010 Augusta	So.Atl.	21	58 2/3	3	3	.500	70	38	47	3.99	0
2011 San Jose	Calif.	16	88	7	5	.583	98	47	74	3.99	0
2011 St. Lucie a	Fla.St.	6	27	2	2	.500	31	5	26	2.00	0
2012 Binghamton	Eastern	19	116	10	6	.625	117	43	92	3.26	0
2012 Buffalo	Int.	6	33	2	2	.500	31	16	23	3.27	0
2013 Las Vegas	P.C.	13	68 2/3	4	2	.667	73	27	61	3.93	0
2013 New York	N.L.	17	100	7	5	.583	84	46	90	3.42	0

a Traded by San Francisco Giants to New York Mets for outfielder Carlos Beltran, July 28, 2011.

WILHELMSEN, THOMAS MARK (TOM)

Born, Tucson, Arizona, December 16, 1983.
Bats Right. Throws Right. Height, 6 feet, 6 inches. Weight, 230 pounds.

Year Club	Lea	G	IP	W	L	Pct	SO	BB	H	ERA	SAVES
2003 Brewers	Arizona	2	4	0	1	.000	4	4	5	4.50	0
2003 Beloit	Midwest	15	88	5	5	.500	63	27	78	2.76	0
2004-2008						Did Not Play					
2009 Tucson	Golden	11	12	0	0	.000	15	4	15	6.00	2
2010 Mariners	Arizona	5	15	0	0	.000	22	2	4	0.60	0
2010 Clinton	Midwest	7	44 1/3	6	1	.857	37	15	33	2.23	0
2010 Everett a	Northwest	3	14 2/3	1	0	1.000	14	2	14	3.68	0
2011 Jackson	Southern	14	60 2/3	4	5	.444	40	26	66	5.49	0
2011 Seattle	A.L.	25	32 2/3	2	0	1.000	30	13	25	3.31	0
2012 Seattle	A.L.	73	79 1/3	4	3	.571	87	29	59	2.50	29
2013 Tacoma	P.C.	8	12	0	1	.000	15	5	19	10.50	0

Year	Club	Lea	G	IP	W	L	Pct	SO	BB	H	ERA	SAVES
2013	Seattle	A.L.	59	59	0	3	.000	45	33	45	4.12	24
Major League Totals		3 Yrs.	157	171	6	6	.500	162	75	129	3.21	53

a Released by Milwaukee Brewers, August 22, 2009. Signed with Seattle Mariners organization, March 3, 2010.

WILLIAMS, JEROME LEE

Born, Honolulu, Hawaii, December 4, 1981.

Bats Right. Throws Right. Height, 6 feet, 3 inches. Weight, 240 pounds.

Year	Club	Lea	G	IP	W	L	Pct	SO	BB	H	ERA	SAVES
1999	Salem-Keizer	Northwest	7	37	1	1	.500	34	11	29	2.19	0
2000	San Jose	Calif.	23	125⅔	7	6	.538	115	48	89	2.94	0
2001	Shreveport	Texas	23	130	9	7	.563	84	34	116	3.95	0
2002	Fresno	P.C.	28	160⅔	6	11	.353	130	50	140	3.59	0
2003	Fresno	P.C.	10	57	4	2	.667	40	16	52	2.68	0
2003	San Francisco	N.L.	21	131	7	5	.583	88	49	116	3.30	0
2004	San Francisco a	N.L.	22	129⅓	10	7	.588	80	44	123	4.24	0
2005	Fresno	P.C.	6	30⅔	1	4	.200	15	17	47	9.39	0
2005	Iowa	P.C.	4	24⅓	1	1	.500	17	6	27	2.22	0
2005	San Francisco-Chicago b	N.L.	22	122⅔	6	10	.375	70	49	119	4.26	0
2006	Chicago	N.L.	5	12⅓	0	2	.000	5	11	15	7.30	0
2006	Iowa c	P.C.	29	111⅔	5	7	.417	52	35	145	4.76	0
2007	Columbus	Int.	1	6	0	0	.000	5	2	4	1.50	0
2007	Washington	N.L.	6	30	0	5	.000	15	18	34	7.20	0
2007	Harrisburg	Eastern	14	35⅔	0	3	.000	26	16	53	9.08	0
2007	Rochester d-e-f	Int.	8	11	0	1	.000	6	7	18	9.00	1
2008	Long Beach g	Golden	6	40	3	2	.600	28	8	48	4.95	0
2008	Inland Empire	Calif.	3	10	0	1	.000	8	6	13	6.30	0
2008	Las Vegas h-i	P.C.	10	26	2	2	.500	21	9	23	2.08	0
2009	Sacramento	P.C.	27	101⅔	5	6	.455	52	41	116	5.58	0
2010	Uni-President	Taiwan				No Data Available						
2011	Lancaster	Atlantic	8	52⅔	7	1	.875	40	12	43	2.91	0
2011	Salt Lake	P.C.	11	73⅔	7	2	.778	60	15	78	3.91	0
2011	Los Angeles j	A.L.	10	44	4	0	1.000	28	15	45	3.68	0
2012	Inland Empire	Calif.	2	11	1	0	1.000	9	1	11	3.27	0
2012	Salt Lake	P.C.	2	8	0	1	.000	8	0	13	7.87	0
2012	Los Angeles k	A.L.	32	137⅔	6	8	.429	98	35	139	4.58	1
2013	Los Angeles l	A.L.	37	169⅓	9	10	.474	107	55	181	4.57	0
Major League Totals		8 Yrs.	155	776⅓	42	47	.472	491	276	772	4.35	1
	Division Series											
2003	San Francisco	N.L.	1	2	0	0	.000	1	1	5	13.50	0

a On disabled list from July 31 to September 16, 2004.
b Traded to Chicago Cubs with pitcher David Aardsma for pitcher La Troy Hawkins, May 28, 2005.
c Claimed on waivers by Oakland Athletics, September 5, 2006.
d Filed for free agency, December 12, 2006. Signed with Washington Nationals organization, January 12, 2007.
e On disabled list from April 29 to May 15 and May 16 to June 20, 2007.
f Released by Washington Nationals, August 5, 2007. Signed with Minnesota Twins organization, August 9, 2007.
g Filed for free agency, October 29, 2007. Signed with Long Beach (Golden) for 2008.
h Signed with Los Angeles Dodgers organization, June 25, 2008.
i Filed for free agency, November 3, 2008. Signed with Oakland Athletics organization, December 1, 2008.
j Filed for free agency, November 9, 2009. Signed with Los Angeles Angels organization, June 17, 2011.
k On disabled list from March 26 to April 15 and June 20 to July 14, 2012.
l Not offered contract, December 2, 2013.

WILSON, BRIAN PATRICK

Born, Londonderry, New Hampshire, March 16, 1982.

Bats Right. Throws Right. Height, 6 feet, 1 inch. Weight, 205 pounds.

Year	Club	Lea	G	IP	W	L	Pct	SO	BB	H	ERA	SAVES
2004	Hagerstown	So.Atl.	23	57⅓	2	5	.286	41	22	63	5.34	3
2005	Norwich	Eastern	15	15⅔	0	0	.000	22	5	6	0.57	8
2005	Fresno	P.C.	9	11⅓	1	1	.500	13	8	8	3.97	0
2005	Augusta	So.Atl.	26	33	5	1	.833	30	7	23	0.82	13
2006	San Jose	Calif.	1	1	0	0	.000	1	1	1	9.00	0
2006	Fresno	P.C.	24	28	1	3	.250	30	14	20	2.89	7
2006	San Francisco	N.L.	31	30	2	3	.400	23	21	32	5.40	1
2007	San Jose	Calif.	3	3	0	0	.000	6	0	1	0.00	2
2007	Fresno	P.C.	31	34⅓	1	2	.333	37	24	24	2.10	11
2007	San Francisco	N.L.	24	23⅔	1	2	.333	18	7	16	2.28	6
2008	San Francisco	N.L.	63	62⅓	3	2	.600	67	28	62	4.62	41

Year Club	Lea	G	IP	W	L	Pct	SO	BB	H	ERA	SAVES
2009 San Francisco	N.L.	68	72⅓	5	6	.455	83	27	60	2.74	38
2010 San Francisco	N.L.	70	74⅔	3	3	.500	93	26	62	1.81	*48
2011 San Francisco a	N.L.	57	55	6	4	.600	54	31	50	3.11	36
2012 San Francisco b-c	N.L.	2	2	0	0	.000	2	2	4	9.00	1
2013 Rancho Cucamonga	Calif.	1	1	0	0	.000	1	0	0	0.00	0
2013 Albuquerque	P.C.	3	3⅓	0	0	.000	2	0	1	0.00	0
2013 Los Angeles d-e	N.L.	18	13⅔	2	1	.667	13	4	8	0.66	0
Major League Totals	8 Yrs.	333	333⅔	22	21	.512	353	146	294	3.10	171
Division Series											
2010 San Francisco	N.L.	3	4	0	0	.000	5	2	2	0.00	2
2013 Los Angeles	N.L.	3	3	1	0	1.000	4	0	3	0.00	0
Division Series Totals		6	7	1	0	1.000	9	2	5	0.00	2
Championship Series											
2010 San Francisco	N.L.	4	5	1	0	1.000	7	2	2	0.00	3
2013 Los Angeles	N.L.	3	3	0	0	.000	4	2	1	0.00	0
Championship Series Totals		7	8	1	0	1.000	11	4	3	0.00	3
World Series Record											
2010 San Francisco	N.L.	3	2⅔	0	0	.000	4	0	1	0.00	1

a On disabled list from March 22 to April 6 and August 16 to September 18, 2011.
b On disabled list from April 13 to November 1, 2012.
c Not offered contract, November 30, 2012. Signed with Los Angeles Dodgers, July 30, 2013.
d On disabled list from July 30 to August 19, 2013.
e Filed for free agency, October 31, 2013, re-signed with Los Angeles Dodgers, December 7, 2013.

WILSON, CHRISTOPHER JOHN (C.J.)

Born, Newport Beach, California, November 18, 1980.
Bats Left. Throws Left. Height, 6 feet, 2 inches. Weight, 215 pounds.

Year Club	Lea	G	IP	W	L	Pct	SO	BB	H	ERA	SAVES
2001 Pulaski	Appal.	8	37⅔	1	0	1.000	49	9	24	0.96	0
2001 Savannah	So.Atl.	5	34	1	2	.333	26	9	30	3.18	0
2002 Charlotte	Fla.St.	26	106	10	2	.833	76	41	86	3.06	1
2002 Tulsa	Texas	5	30	1	0	1.000	17	12	23	1.80	0
2003 Frisco	Texas	22	123	6	9	.400	89	38	135	5.05	0
2004				INJURED—Did Not Play							
2005 Bakersfield	Calif.	4	13⅔	0	1	.000	14	4	10	3.29	0
2005 Frisco	Texas	12	44⅔	0	4	.000	43	14	51	4.43	0
2005 Texas	A.L.	24	48	1	7	.125	30	18	63	6.94	1
2006 Frisco	Texas	4	3⅓	0	0	.000	6	2	3	2.70	0
2006 Oklahoma	P.C.	9	11	1	0	1.000	17	5	10	2.45	2
2006 Texas a	A.L.	44	44⅓	2	4	.333	43	18	39	4.06	1
2007 Texas	A.L.	66	68⅓	2	1	.667	63	33	50	3.03	12
2008 Texas b	A.L.	50	46⅓	2	2	.500	41	27	49	6.02	24
2009 Texas	A.L.	74	73⅔	5	6	.455	84	32	66	2.81	14
2010 Texas	A.L.	33	204	15	8	.652	170	*93	161	3.35	0
2011 Texas c	A.L.	34	223⅓	16	7	.696	206	74	191	2.94	0
2012 Los Angeles	A.L.	34	202⅓	13	10	.565	173	91	181	3.83	0
2013 Los Angeles	A.L.	33	212⅓	17	7	.708	188	85	200	3.39	0
Major League Totals	9 Yrs.	392	1122⅔	73	52	.584	998	471	1000	3.60	52
Division Series											
2010 Texas	A.L.	1	6⅓	1	0	1.000	7	2	2	0.00	0
2011 Texas	A.L.	1	5	0	1	.000	6	1	7	10.80	0
Division Series Totals		2	11⅓	1	1	.500	13	3	9	4.76	0
Championship Series											
2010 Texas	A.L.	2	12	0	1	.000	6	6	12	6.00	0
2011 Texas	A.L.	2	10⅔	0	1	.000	11	7	14	6.75	0
Championship Series Totals		4	22⅔	0	2	.000	17	13	26	6.35	0
World Series Record											
2010 Texas	A.L.	1	6	0	1	.000	4	2	3	3.00	0
2011 Texas	A.L.	3	12⅓	0	1	.000	9	11	8	2.92	0
World Series Totals		4	18⅓	0	2	.000	13	13	11	2.95	0

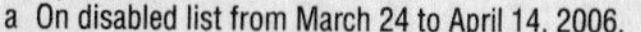

a On disabled list from March 24 to April 14, 2006.
b On disabled list from August 6 to October 2, 2008.
c Filed for free agency, October 30, 2011. Signed with Los Angeles Angels, December 10, 2011.

WILSON, JUSTIN JAMES

Born, Anaheim, California, August 18, 1987.
Bats Left. Throws Left. Height, 6 feet, 2 inches. Weight, 195 pounds.

Year Club	Lea	G	IP	W	L	Pct	SO	BB	H	ERA	SAVES
2009 Lynchburg	Carolina	26	116	6	8	.429	94	55	118	4.50	0
2010 Altoona	Eastern	27	142⅔	11	8	.579	134	71	109	3.09	0
2011 Indianapolis	Int.	30	124⅓	10	8	.556	94	67	121	4.13	3
2012 Indianapolis	Int.	29	135⅔	9	6	.600	138	66	91	3.78	0
2012 Pittsburgh	N.L.	8	4⅔	0	0	.000	7	3	10	1.93	0
2013 Pittsburgh	N.L.	58	73⅔	6	1	.857	59	28	50	2.08	0
Major League Totals	2 Yrs.	66	78⅓	6	1	.857	66	31	60	2.07	0
Division Series											
2013 Pittsburgh	N.L.	2	2⅔	0	0	.000	3	1	2	3.38	0

WOOD, ROBERT ALEXANDER (ALEX)

Born, Charlotte, North Carolina, January 12, 1991.
Bats Right. Throws Left. Height, 6 feet, 4 inches. Weight, 215 pounds.

Year Club	Lea	G	IP	W	L	Pct	SO	BB	H	ERA	SAVES
2012 Rome	So.Atl.	13	52⅔	4	3	.571	52	14	39	2.22	0
2013 Mississippi	Southern	10	57	4	2	.667	57	15	41	1.26	0
2013 Gwinnett	Int.	1	5	1	0	1.000	5	2	3	1.80	0
2013 Atlanta	N.L.	31	77⅔	3	3	.500	77	27	76	3.13	0
Division Series											
2013 Atlanta	N.L.	2	3⅓	0	0	.000	3	0	3	0.00	0

WOOD, TRAVIS ALAN

Born, Little Rock, Arkansas, February 6, 1987.
Bats Right. Throws Left. Height, 5 feet, 11 inches. Weight, 165 pounds.

Year Club	Lea	G	IP	W	L	Pct	SO	BB	H	ERA	SAVES
2005 Reds	Gulf Coast	8	24	0	0	.000	45	7	13	0.75	0
2005 Billings	Pioneer	6	24⅔	2	0	1.000	22	13	15	1.82	0
2006 Dayton	Midwest	27	140	10	5	.667	133	56	108	3.66	0
2007 Sarasota	Fla.St.	12	46⅓	3	2	.600	54	27	49	4.86	0
2008 Sarasota	Fla.St.	9	46⅔	3	4	.429	41	21	39	2.70	0
2008 Chattanooga	Southern	17	80	4	9	.308	58	48	91	7.09	0
2009 Louisville	Int.	8	48⅔	4	2	.667	32	16	43	3.14	0
2009 Carolina	Southern	19	119	9	3	.750	103	37	78	1.21	0
2010 Louisville	Int.	16	100	5	6	.455	99	24	86	3.06	0
2010 Cincinnati	N.L.	17	102⅔	5	4	.556	86	26	85	3.51	0
2011 Louisville	Int.	10	52⅓	2	3	.400	47	17	64	5.33	0
2011 Cincinnati a	N.L.	22	106	6	6	.500	76	40	118	4.84	0
2012 Iowa	P.C.	7	41⅓	3	3	.500	39	11	48	4.57	0
2012 Chicago	N.L.	26	156	6	13	.316	119	54	133	4.27	0
2013 Chicago	N.L.	32	200	9	12	.429	144	66	163	3.11	0
Major League Totals	4 Yrs.	97	564⅔	26	35	.426	425	186	499	3.83	0
Division Series											
2010 Cincinnati	N.L.	1	3⅓	0	0	.000	3	1	1	0.00	0

a Traded to Chicago Cubs with outfielder Dave Sappelt and infielder Ronald Torreyes for pitcher Sean Marshall, December 23, 2011.

WORLEY, VANCE RICHARD

Born, Sacramento, California, September 25, 1987.
Bats Right. Throws Right. Height, 6 feet, 2 inches. Weight, 230 pounds.

Year Club	Lea	G	IP	W	L	Pct	SO	BB	H	ERA	SAVES
2008 Williamsport	N.Y.-Penn.	2	8	0	0	.000	8	1	3	1.13	0
2008 Lakewood	So.Atl.	11	61	3	2	.600	53	7	58	2.66	0
2009 Reading	Eastern	27	153⅓	7	12	.368	100	49	163	5.34	0
2010 Reading	Eastern	19	112⅔	9	4	.692	83	36	114	3.20	0
2010 Lehigh Valley	Int.	8	45⅓	1	3	.250	36	10	46	3.77	0
2010 Philadelphia	N.L.	5	13	1	1	.500	12	4	8	1.38	0
2011 Lehigh Valley	Int.	9	50⅔	5	2	.714	50	12	41	2.31	0
2011 Philadelphia	N.L.	25	131⅔	11	3	.786	119	46	116	3.01	0
2012 Philadelphia a-b	N.L.	23	133	6	9	.400	107	47	154	4.20	0
2013 Rochester	Int.	9	58	6	3	.667	34	17	65	3.88	0

Year Club	Lea	G	IP	W	L	Pct	SO	BB	H	ERA	SAVES
2013 Minnesota	A.L.	10	$48\frac{2}{3}$	1	5	.167	25	15	82	7.21	0
Major League Totals	4 Yrs.	63	$326\frac{1}{3}$	19	18	.514	263	112	360	4.05	0
Division Series											
2011 Philadelphia	N.L.	2	$1\frac{1}{3}$	0	0	.000	0	1	3	6.75	0

a On disabled list from May 13 to June 4 and August 29 to October 5, 2012.
b Traded to Minnesota Twins with pitcher Trevor May for outfielder Ben Revere, December 6, 2012.

WRIGHT, DEQUAM LA WESLEY (WESLEY)

Born, Montgomery, Alabama, January 28, 1985.
Bats Right. Throws Left. Height, 5 feet, 11 inches. Weight, 180 pounds.

Year Club	Lea	G	IP	W	L	Pct	SO	BB	H	ERA	SAVES
2003 Dodgers	Gulf Coast	14	$37\frac{2}{3}$	3	1	.750	26	19	37	3.58	0
2004 Ogden	Pioneer	17	$44\frac{1}{3}$	3	3	.500	66	23	56	6.29	0
2005 Vero Beach	Fla.St.	6	$6\frac{2}{3}$	0	0	.000	8	10	8	9.45	0
2005 Columbus	So.Atl.	30	$60\frac{2}{3}$	1	5	.167	68	33	38	1.93	1
2006 Vero Beach	Fla.St.	26	$42\frac{1}{3}$	3	3	.500	51	23	29	1.49	0
2006 Jacksonville	Southern	15	$21\frac{1}{3}$	1	1	.500	28	11	14	4.64	1
2007 Las Vegas	P.C.	14	$16\frac{2}{3}$	1	2	.333	18	18	28	9.18	0
2007 Jacksonville a	Southern	30	$61\frac{1}{3}$	6	2	.750	68	31	45	2.49	2
2008 Houston	N.L.	71	$55\frac{2}{3}$	4	3	.571	57	34	45	5.01	1
2009 Round Rock	P.C.	13	19	2	1	.667	18	10	13	3.32	0
2009 Houston b	N.L.	49	$44\frac{2}{3}$	3	4	.429	47	25	53	5.44	0
2010 Round Rock	P.C.	15	$69\frac{2}{3}$	4	1	.800	41	33	76	4.65	0
2010 Houston	N.L.	14	33	1	2	.333	29	13	37	5.73	0
2011 Oklahoma	P.C.	39	$65\frac{1}{3}$	3	1	.750	52	23	49	2.07	2
2011 Houston	N.L.	21	12	0	0	.000	11	5	6	1.50	0
2012 Houston	N.L.	77	$52\frac{1}{3}$	2	2	.500	54	17	45	3.27	1
2013 Houston-Tampa Bay c-d	A.L.	70	$53\frac{2}{3}$	0	4	.000	55	19	54	3.69	0
Major League Totals	6 Yrs.	302	$251\frac{1}{3}$	10	15	.400	253	113	240	4.37	2
Division Series											
2013 Tampa Bay	A.L.	2	$0\frac{2}{3}$	0	0	.000	1	1	1	0.00	0

a Selected by Houston Astros from Los Angeles Dodgers in Rule V draft, December 6, 2007.
b On disabled list from August 12 to September 1, 2009.
c Claimed on waivers by Tampa Bay Rays, August 12, 2013.
d Not offered contract, December 2, 2013. Signed with Chicago Cubs, December 16, 2013.

WRIGHT, JAMEY ALAN

Born, Oklahoma City, Oklahoma, December 24, 1974.
Bats Right. Throws Right. Height, 6 feet, 6 inches. Weight, 235 pounds.

Year Club	Lea	G	IP	W	L	Pct	SO	BB	H	ERA	SAVES
1993 Rockies	Arizona	8	36	1	3	.250	26	9	35	4.00	0
1994 Asheville	So.Atl.	28	$143\frac{1}{3}$	7	14	.333	103	59	188	5.97	0
1995 Salem	Carolina	26	171	10	8	.556	95	72	160	2.47	0
1995 New Haven	Eastern	1	3	0	1	.000	0	3	6	9.00	0
1996 New Haven	Eastern	7	$44\frac{2}{3}$	5	1	.833	54	12	27	0.81	0
1996 Colorado Springs	P.C.	9	$59\frac{2}{3}$	4	2	.667	40	22	53	2.72	0
1996 Colorado	N.L.	16	$91\frac{1}{3}$	4	4	.500	45	41	105	4.93	0
1997 Salem	Carolina	1	1	0	1	.000	1	1	1	9.00	0
1997 Colorado Springs	P.C.	2	11	1	0	1.000	11	5	9	1.64	0
1997 Colorado a	N.L.	26	$149\frac{2}{3}$	8	12	.400	59	71	198	6.25	0
1998 Colorado	N.L.	34	$206\frac{1}{3}$	9	14	.391	86	95	235	5.67	0
1999 Colorado	N.L.	16	$94\frac{1}{3}$	4	3	.571	49	54	110	4.87	0
1999 Colorado Springs b	P.C.	17	$100\frac{1}{3}$	5	7	.417	75	38	133	6.46	0
2000 Huntsville	Southern	2	$12\frac{1}{3}$	2	0	1.000	10	5	7	0.00	0
2000 Indianapolis	Int.	1	5	0	0	.000	7	3	8	1.80	0
2000 Milwaukee c	N.L.	26	$164\frac{2}{3}$	7	9	.438	96	88	157	4.10	0
2001 Milwaukee d	N.L.	33	$194\frac{2}{3}$	11	12	.478	129	98	201	4.90	0
2002 Indianapolis	Int.	3	$15\frac{1}{3}$	1	1	.500	13	5	16	4.11	0
2002 Milwaukee-St. Louis e-f-g	N.L.	23	$129\frac{1}{3}$	7	13	.350	77	75	130	5.29	0
2003 Indianapolis h	Int.	7	22	1	3	.250	17	10	32	7.36	0
2003 Oklahoma	P.C.	7	$39\frac{1}{3}$	2	1	.667	40	21	38	4.12	0
2003 Omaha i	P.C.	13	$76\frac{2}{3}$	3	5	.375	65	38	70	3.64	0
2003 Kansas City j-k	A.L.	4	$25\frac{1}{3}$	1	2	.333	19	11	23	4.26	0
2004 Omaha	P.C.	18	$104\frac{2}{3}$	8	6	.571	70	35	111	4.21	0
2004 Colorado l-m	N.L.	14	$78\frac{2}{3}$	2	3	.400	41	45	82	4.12	0
2005 Colorado n	N.L.	34	$171\frac{1}{3}$	8	16	.333	101	81	201	5.46	0
2006 San Francisco o	N.L.	34	156	6	10	.375	79	64	167	5.19	0

Year Club	Lea	G	IP	W	L	Pct	SO	BB	H	ERA	SAVES
2007 Frisco	Texas	1	4	0	0	.000	2	0	6	4.50	0
2007 Oklahoma	P.C.	3	16 1/3	2	1	.667	11	3	21	4.41	0
2007 Texas p-q	A.L.	20	77	4	5	.444	39	41	72	3.62	0
2008 Texas r	A.L.	75	84 1/3	8	7	.533	60	35	93	5.12	0
2009 Kansas City s	A.L.	65	79	3	5	.375	60	44	73	4.33	0
2010 Sacramento	P.C.	10	14	1	0	1.000	16	9	23	9.00	1
2010 Cleveland-Seattle t-u	A.L.	46	58 1/3	1	3	.250	28	25	55	4.17	0
2011 Seattle v	A.L.	60	68 1/3	2	3	.400	48	30	61	3.16	1
2012 Los Angeles w	N.L.	66	67 2/3	5	3	.625	54	30	72	3.72	0
2013 Tampa Bay x	A.L.	66	70	2	2	.500	65	23	61	3.09	0
Major League Totals	18 Yrs.	658	1966 1/3	92	126	.422	1135	951	2096	4.82	1
Division Series											
2013 Tampa Bay	A.L.	2	2	0	0	.000	1	3	4	18.00	0

a On disabled list from May 15 to June 8, 1997.
b Traded to Milwaukee Brewers with catcher Henry Blanco and pitcher Justin Miller for infielder Jeff Cirillo and pitcher Scott Karl, December 13, 1999.
c On disabled list from March 28 to May 22, 2000.
d On disabled list from May 21 to June 10, 2001.
e On disabled list from April 5 to May 24, 2002.
f Traded to St. Louis Cardinals with cash for outfielder Chris Morris and player to be named later, August 29, 2002. Milwaukee Brewers received pitcher Mike Matthews to complete trade, September 11, 2002.
g Filed for free agency, November 1, 2002. Signed with Seattle Mariners organization, January 24, 2003.
h Released by Seattle Mariners, March 18, 2003. Signed with Milwaukee Brewers organization, March 23, 2003.
i Released by Milwaukee Brewers, April 28, 2003. Signed with Texas Rangers organization, May 5, 2003.
j Released by Texas Rangers, June 16, 2003. Signed with Kansas City Royals organization, June 24, 2003.
k Filed for free agency, October 30, 2003, re-signed with Kansas City Royals organization, March 29, 2004.
l Released by Kansas City Royals, July 21, 2004. Signed with Colorado Rockies organization, July 22, 2004.
m Filed for free agency, November 1, 2004, re-signed with Colorado Rockies, December 21, 2004.
n Filed for free agency, November 2, 2005. Signed with San Francisco Giants organization, January 17, 2006.
o Filed for free agency, November 2, 2006. Signed with Texas Rangers organization, January 25, 2007.
p On disabled list from April 11 to June 16, 2007.
q Filed for free agency, November 12, 2007, re-signed with Texas Rangers organization, January 11, 2008.
r Filed for free agency, October 30, 2008. Signed with Kansas City Royals organization, February 10, 2009.
s Filed for free agency, November 5, 2009. Signed with Cleveland Indians organization, February 9, 2010.
t Released by Cleveland Indians, June 10, 2010. Signed with Seattle Mariners, July 15, 2010.
u Filed for free agency, November 1, 2010, re-signed with Seattle Mariners organization, February 1, 2011.
v Filed for free agency, October 30, 2011. Signed with Los Angeles Dodgers organization, February 15, 2012.
w Filed for free agency, November 3, 2012. Signed with Tampa Bay Rays organization, January 22, 2013.
x Filed for free agency, October 31, 2013. Signed with Los Angeles Dodgers, December 24, 2013.

ZIEGLER, BRAD GREGORY

Born, Pratt, Kansas, October 10, 1979.
Bats Right. Throws Right. Height, 6 feet, 4 inches. Weight, 200 pounds.

Year Club	Lea	G	IP	W	L	Pct	SO	BB	H	ERA	SAVES
2003 Batavia	N.Y.-Penn.	3	6	1	0	1.000	6	1	5	1.50	0
2004 Schaumburg	Northern	4	24	3	0	1.000	26	1	12	1.50	0
2004 Modesto a-b	Calif.	16	92 1/3	9	2	.818	77	22	94	3.90	0
2005 Stockton	Calif.	24	141	9	7	.563	144	20	166	4.66	0
2005 Midland	Texas	4	21	2	1	.667	20	4	27	6.86	0
2006 Sacramento	P.C.	4	21	0	1	.000	11	5	32	6.00	0
2006 Midland	Texas	23	141 2/3	9	6	.600	88	37	151	3.37	0
2007 Sacramento	P.C.	35	54 2/3	8	3	.727	44	14	46	2.96	1
2007 Midland	Texas	15	23 2/3	4	0	1.000	18	4	19	1.14	1
2008 Sacramento	P.C.	19	24 1/3	2	0	1.000	20	4	15	0.37	8
2008 Oakland	A.L.	47	59 2/3	3	0	1.000	30	22	47	1.06	11
2009 Oakland	A.L.	69	73 1/3	2	4	.333	54	28	82	3.07	7
2010 Oakland	A.L.	64	60 2/3	3	7	.300	41	28	54	3.26	0
2011 Oakland	A.L.	43	37 2/3	3	2	.600	29	13	38	2.39	1
2011 Arizona c	N.L.	23	20 2/3	0	0	.000	15	6	15	1.74	0
2012 Arizona	N.L.	77	68 2/3	6	1	.857	42	21	54	2.49	0
2013 Arizona	N.L.	*78	73	8	1	.889	44	22	61	2.22	13
Major League Totals	6 Yrs.	401	393 2/3	25	15	.625	255	140	351	2.40	32
Division Series											
2011 Arizona	N.L.	2	0 1/3	0	0	.000	0	2	4	108.00	0

a Released by Philadelphia Phillies, March 28, 2004. Signed with independent Schaumburg (Northern), April 18, 2004.
b Sold to Oakland Athletics organization, June 16, 2004.
c Traded to Arizona Diamondbacks for infielder Brandon Allen and pitcher Jordan Norberto, July 31, 2011.

ZIMMERMANN, JORDAN M.

Born, Auburndale, Wisconsin, May 23, 1986.

Bats Right. Throws Right. Height, 6 feet, 2 inches. Weight, 220 pounds.

Year Club	Lea	G	IP	W	L	Pct	SO	BB	H	ERA	SAVES
2007 Vermont	N.Y.-Penn.	13	53	5	2	.714	71	18	45	2.38	0
2008 Potomac	Carolina	5	$27\frac{1}{3}$	3	1	.750	31	8	15	1.65	1
2008 Harrisburg	Eastern	20	$106\frac{2}{3}$	7	2	.778	103	39	89	3.21	0
2009 Potomac	Carolina	1	$3\frac{1}{3}$	0	0	.000	6	1	2	2.70	0
2009 Syracuse	Int.	1	$5\frac{1}{3}$	0	0	.000	4	1	4	5.06	0
2009 Washington a	N.L.	16	$91\frac{1}{3}$	3	5	.375	92	29	95	4.63	0
2010 Hagerstown	So.Atl.	1	5	0	1	.000	3	1	7	10.80	0
2010 Potomac	Carolina	4	13	0	1	.000	13	0	11	0.00	0
2010 Harrisburg	Eastern	1	$4\frac{2}{3}$	0	0	.000	3	2	1	0.00	0
2010 Syracuse	Int.	4	17	1	0	1.000	12	3	8	0.53	0
2010 Washington b	N.L.	7	31	1	2	.333	27	10	31	4.94	0
2011 Washington	N.L.	26	$161\frac{1}{3}$	8	11	.421	124	31	154	3.18	0
2012 Washington	N.L.	32	$195\frac{2}{3}$	12	8	.600	153	43	186	2.94	0
2013 Washington	N.L.	32	$213\frac{1}{3}$	*19	9	.679	161	40	192	3.25	0
Major League Totals	5 Yrs.	113	$692\frac{2}{3}$	43	35	.551	557	153	658	3.40	0
Division Series											
2012 Washington	N.L.	2	4	0	1	.000	5	0	7	11.25	0

a On disabled list from July 19 to November 8, 2009.
b On disabled list from February 19 to July 31, 2010.

ZITO, BARRY WILLIAM

Born, Las Vegas, Nevada, May 13, 1978.

Bats Left. Throws Left. Height, 6 feet, 4 inches. Weight, 210 pounds.

Year Club	Lea	G	IP	W	L	Pct	SO	BB	H	ERA	SAVES
1999 Vancouver	P.C.	1	6	1	0	1.000	6	2	5	1.50	0
1999 Midland	Texas	4	22	2	1	.667	29	11	22	4.91	0
1999 Visalia	California	8	$40\frac{1}{3}$	3	0	1.000	62	22	21	2.45	0
2000 Sacramento	P.C.	18	$101\frac{2}{3}$	8	5	.615	91	45	88	3.19	0
2000 Oakland	A.L.	14	$92\frac{2}{3}$	7	4	.636	78	45	64	2.72	0
2001 Oakland	A.L.	35	$214\frac{1}{3}$	17	8	.680	205	80	184	3.49	0
2002 Oakland a	A.L.	35	$229\frac{1}{3}$	*23	5	.821	182	78	182	2.75	0
2003 Oakland	A.L.	35	$231\frac{2}{3}$	14	12	.538	146	88	186	3.30	0
2004 Oakland	A.L.	34	213	11	11	.500	163	81	216	4.48	0
2005 Oakland	A.L.	35	$228\frac{1}{3}$	14	13	.519	171	89	185	3.86	0
2006 Oakland b	A.L.	34	221	16	10	.615	151	99	211	3.83	0
2007 San Francisco	N.L.	34	$196\frac{2}{3}$	11	13	.458	131	83	182	4.53	0
2008 San Francisco	N.L.	32	180	10	*17	.370	120	102	186	5.15	0
2009 San Francisco	N.L.	33	192	10	13	.435	154	81	179	4.03	0
2010 San Francisco	N.L.	34	$199\frac{1}{3}$	9	14	.391	150	84	184	4.15	0
2011 San Jose	Calif.	3	$21\frac{1}{3}$	2	1	.667	19	5	15	2.53	0
2011 Fresno	P.C.	3	$17\frac{2}{3}$	2	0	1.000	17	5	10	2.55	0
2011 San Francisco c	N.L.	13	$53\frac{2}{3}$	3	4	.429	32	24	51	5.87	0
2012 San Francisco	N.L.	32	$184\frac{1}{3}$	15	8	.652	114	70	186	4.15	0
2013 San Francisco d	N.L.	30	$133\frac{1}{3}$	5	11	.313	86	54	173	5.74	0
Major League Totals	14 Yrs.	430	$2569\frac{2}{3}$	165	143	.536	1883	1058	2369	4.02	0
Division Series											
2000 Oakland	A.L.	1	$5\frac{2}{3}$	1	0	1.000	5	2	7	1.59	0
2001 Oakland	A.L.	1	8	0	1	.000	6	1	2	1.13	0
2002 Oakland	A.L.	1	6	1	0	1.000	8	4	5	4.50	0
2003 Oakland	A.L.	2	13	1	1	.500	13	4	9	3.46	0
2006 Oakland	A.L.	1	8	1	0	1.000	1	3	4	1.13	0
2012 San Francisco	N.L.	1	$2\frac{2}{3}$	0	0	.000	4	4	4	6.75	0
Division Series Totals		7	$43\frac{1}{3}$	4	2	.667	37	18	31	2.70	0
Championship Series											
2006 Oakland	A.L.	1	$3\frac{2}{3}$	0	1	.000	0	3	7	12.27	0
2012 San Francisco	N.L.	1	$7\frac{2}{3}$	1	0	1.000	6	1	6	0.00	0
Championship Series Totals		2	$11\frac{1}{3}$	1	1	.500	6	4	13	3.97	0
World Series Record											
2012 San Francisco	N.L.	1	$5\frac{2}{3}$	1	0	1.000	3	1	6	1.59	0

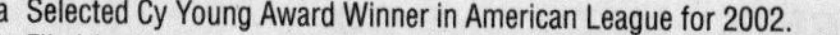

a Selected Cy Young Award Winner in American League for 2002.
b Filed for free agency, October 31, 2006. Signed with San Francisco Giants, December 29, 2006.
c On disabled list from April 17 to June 25 and August 1 to September 11, 2011.
d Filed for free agency, November 2, 2013.